Unless recipes specify otherwise:

Flour called for is all-purpose flour, sifted before measuring.

Baking powder is double-acting baking powder.

Butter is salted butter.

Sour cream is the commercial type.

Eggs are large eggs.

Brown sugar is measured firmly packed.

Garlic cloves are of medium size.

Herbs and spices are dried.

All measures are standard, all measurements level.

OVEN TEMPERATURES

Below 300° F. = very slow

300° F. = slow

325° F. = moderately slow

350° F. = moderate

375° F. = moderately hot

400-25° F. = hot

450-75° F. = very hot

500° F. or more = extremely hot

FAHRENHEIT/CELSIUS (CENTIGRADE) SCALE

	Boiling Point F.	Boiling Point C.	
(of Water)	212° –	100°	(of Water)
	200°	93.3°	
	190°	87.8°	
	180°	82.2°	
	170°	76.7°	
	160°	71.1°	
	150°	65.6°	
	140°	60°	
	130°	54.4°	
	120°	48.9°	
	110°	43.3°	
	100°	37.8°	
	90°	32.2°	
	80°	26.7°	
	70°	21.1°	
	60°	15.6°	
Freezing Point	50°	10°	Freezing Point
	40°	4.4°	
(of Water)	32°	0°	(of Water)

Conversion Formula:
Fahrenheit to Celsius (Centigrade):
Subtract 32 from Fahrenheit reading, divide by 1.8.

The DOUBLEDAY COOKBOOK

Volume 1

The DOUBLEDAY COOKBOOK

Volume 1

Complete Contemporary COOKING

*Jean Anderson
and Elaine Hanna*

ILLUSTRATIONS BY MEL KLAPHOLZ
PHOTOGRAPHS BY WILL ROUSSEAU

Doubleday & Company, Inc.
GARDEN CITY, NEW YORK

ACKNOWLEDGMENTS

We are greatly indebted to the following companies for providing equipment to use in the testing and development of recipes:

General Electric Company, Housewares Division, Bridgeport, Connecticut (for portable appliances); *KitchenAid, The Hobart Manufacturing Company,* Troy, Ohio (dishwashers and heavy-duty electric mixers); *Ronson Corporation,* Woodbridge, New Jersey (electric cook-and-stir blenders); *The West Bend Company,* West Bend, Wisconsin (small electric appliances, cookware, and bakeware); and *Whirlpool Corporation,* Benton Harbor, Michigan (gas and electric ranges).

We also wish to thank the following for their gracious co-operation and for supplying quantities of valuable information:

Agricultural Extension Service, University of Wyoming; Aluminum Association; American Dietetics Association; American Home Economics Association; American Institute of Baking; American Lamb Council; American Meat Institute; American Museum of Natural History; American Mushroom Institute; American Spice Trade Association; Bourbon Institute; Brooklyn Botanic Garden; California Foods Research Institute; Cling Peach Advisory Board; Council on Foods and Nutrition, American Medical Association; Dried Fruit Association of California; Fishery Council; Florida Board of Conservation; Florida Citrus Commission; Food and Nutrition Board, National Academy of Sciences, National Research Council; French National Federation of Regional Committees for Promotion and Development of Agricultural Products; French National Wines Committee; Gas Appliance Manufacturers' Association; Glass Container Institute; Idaho Potato and Onion Commission; Madeira Wine Association; Maine Department of Sea and Shore Fisheries; Metal Cookware Manufacturers Association; Maryland Department of Economic Development; Massachusetts Department of Fisheries and Game; National Apple Institute; National Broiler Council; National Canners Association; National Coffee Association; National Dairy

Council; National Electrical Manufacturers Association; National Fisheries Institute; National Live Stock and Meat Board; National Macaroni Institute; National Turkey Federation; New York Botanical Garden; New York State College of Agriculture, Cornell University; New York State College of Human Ecology, Cornell University; New York State Cooperative Extension Service; North Carolina Agricultural Extension Service; Nutrition Foundation; Pan-American Coffee Bureau; Porto Wine Institute; Potato Growers Association of California; Poultry and Egg National Board; Rice Council; Roquefort Association; Tea Council of the U.S.A.; Shrimp Association of the Americas; United Fresh Fruit and Vegetable Association; U. S. Department of Agriculture; U. S. Department of Health, Education and Welfare; U. S. Department of the Interior, Fish and Wildlife Service; Washington State Apple Commission; Wine Advisory Board; Wine Institute; Wisconsin Conservation Department

We wish to thank Hammacher Schlemmer, 147 East 57th Street, New York, New York 10022, for providing the accessories for the photographs.

CONTENTS

Volume 1

LIST OF COLOR ILLUSTRATIONS

Volume 1

INTRODUCTION

What makes this cookbook different?

Here, for the first time, is a comprehensive cookbook that provides calorie counts for every recipe (and keys all low-calorie recipes ⚖), that features hundreds of budget-stretching (¢) and timesaving (⊠) recipes. Here, too, is a book that explains what it will mean to cook using metric measurements (as Americans may soon be doing), that emphasizes savory recipes (soups, meats, poultry, seafoods, vegetables, and salads) instead of sweets because of our increasing awareness of good nutrition.

The book's purpose is to assemble between two covers the most complete, up-to-date information available about food and cooking. To be the cook's—*every* cook's—book. To answer her most pressing questions, no matter how rudimentary (What kind of potato boils best? What kind of apple makes the best pie?), to assist with menu planning, to provide background information on the selection, preparation, storage, and serving of food, wines, and spirits.

This isn't a book devoted to fundamentals alone. It is a book filled with new and unusual recipes.

Those blasé about food insist there are no new recipes. We believe that there are. Certainly there are new-to-print recipes, and it is these that we have concentrated upon, although we have not forsaken those recipes essential to a basic cookbook. These, however, are offered, not as ends in themselves, but as foundations of innumerable variations, points of embarkation for the beginner.

There are recipes for those who yearn for involvement with the raw materials of cooking, who long to make soup the old-fashioned way or feel a yeast dough respond to their touch. There are recipes for busy women who must put a good meal on the table fast. And there are culinary tours de force for the occasional showpiece dinner.

The recipes come from many sources: from our own imaginations (particularly those showing how to short-cut time consuming routines by using convenience foods); from friends and relatives; from centuries-old handwritten receipt files; from regional inns, restaurants, and hotels around the world. There are recipes from Latin America, Asia, and Africa as well as from Europe, each as true to the original as it was possible to make it given American ingredients and implements.

Every recipe has been tested—retested whenever necessary—so that every specific might be included: number of servings (figured in average-size portions); pan, casserole, or mold size whenever that size is important to the recipe's success; exact cooking times and temperatures together with descriptions of what a particular recipe should look, taste, or feel like when "done." And, lest the cook mistake a natural cooking phenomenon for failure, she is alerted to any surprises she may encounter as she prepares a particular recipe. She is also advised how to rescue such genuine failures as curdled hollandaise or runny jelly.

Leftovers, instead of being lumped together in a single chapter, have been placed where they will be most useful—following a robust turkey, for example, or a giant ham. And, to help the cook budget her time, recipes that can be partially made ahead of time are so indicated along with the point at which they may be refrigerated or frozen and the final touches each requires before being served.

This book, more than ten years in the writing, has not been built upon a gimmick. Its intent, simply, is to be a contemporary guide to good cooking and eating, to teach the *whys* of cooking as well as the *hows*.

Its purpose is to coax the timid into the kitchen, to motivate the indifferent, and to challenge accomplished cooks into realizing their creative potential. In short, to share the fun of cooking as well as the fundamentals, to offer something of value to all who cook as well as to those who have not yet learned how.

HOW TO USE THIS BOOK

All recipes in this book call for specific products by their generic (general descriptive) names, not the brand names; "quick-cooking rice," for example, is the fully precooked minute variety, "liquid hot red pepper seasoning" is the fiery bottled sauce made with tabasco peppers.

Whenever the name of a recipe is capitalized (Medium White Sauce, for example, or Flaky Pastry I), the recipe is included elsewhere in the book; consult Index for page numbers.

Whenever a method or technique is marked with an asterisk,* ("build a moderately hot charcoal fire,*" for example), how-to information is described in full detail elsewhere in the book; see Index for page numbers.

Three symbols are used throughout the book to key recipes:

⚖=Low-Calorie
¢=Budget
▣=Quick and Easy

Specific sizes of pan, casserole, or mold are given whenever those sizes are essential to the success of a recipe.

Unless a recipe specifies alternate ingredients, do not make substitutions —margarine for butter, for example; oil for shortening; syrup for sugar. *And never substitute soft margarine for regular margarine or no-sift flour for sifted all-purpose flour.*

Suggestions for garnishes, seasonings, and leftovers are included within each chapter wherever appropriate.

Preheat oven or broiler a full 15 minutes before using. *Tip:* Have oven checked frequently for accuracy (many utility companies provide this service free of charge).

Use middle oven rack for general baking and roasting; whenever a higher or lower rack position is essential, recipe will so direct.

"Cool" as used in recipes means to bring a hot food to room temperature; "chill" means to refrigerate or place in an ice bath until chilled throughout.

Read each recipe through carefully before beginning it, making sure that all necessary ingredients and utensils are on hand and that instructions are clear.

Recipe yields are given in average-size servings or portions. A recipe that "Makes 4 Servings," for example, will feed 4 persons of *average* appetite.

An Explanation of How the Calorie Counts Were Calculated: Calorie counts for average-size servings are set down in round numbers (130 calories per serving instead of 128.5). Also, whenever recipes call for variable amounts (1–2 tablespoons, ¼–½ cup), the count is figured using the first, or lower, quantity only. Finally, if a recipe suggests alternative ingredients, the calorie count is based upon the principal ingredient, not the alternative.

About Ingredients

Unless recipes specify otherwise:
Flour called for is all-purpose flour, sifted before measuring.
Baking powder is double-acting baking powder.
Butter is salted butter.
Sour cream is the commercial type.
Eggs are large eggs.
Brown sugar is measured firmly packed.
Garlic cloves are of medium size (about like the first joint of the little finger).
Herbs and spices are dried.
Pepper is black pepper, preferably freshly ground.
"Celery stalk" means 1 branch of a bunch; some recipe books call the branch a "rib," the bunch a "stalk." As used here, "stalk" and "rib" are synonymous.
All measures are standard, all measurements level.

CHAPTER 1

THE FUNDAMENTALS OF COOKING

ABOUT SELECTING POTS AND PANS

Housewares departments offer so many glamorous lines of cookware it is difficult to choose which is best. That porcelain-lined, double-weight copper asparagus steamer with brass handles *is* stunning. But is it necessary? Not at $69.98 unless you are rich and fond of steamed asparagus ($69.98 will buy many of the basics of the beginning kitchen). The point is to buy what utensils you will use frequently, then to add the more specialized items as you need them. Quality counts and should not be sacrificed for the sake of a pretty pot. Here are some shopping tips to guide you when buying.

Look for:
– Utensils durable enough to withstand daily use without wearing thin, denting, warping, chipping, pitting, cracking, or discoloring.
– Medium to heavyweight cookware, sturdily constructed with flat bottoms, straight or gently flared sides, and snug (but easy-to-remove) lids. *Note:* Decorative enamelware is sometimes too lightweight to cook food without scorching it.
– Well-balanced skillets and saucepans that will stand squarely on burners whether lids are on or off (always test for tippiness with the lids off).
– Easy-to-clean utensils with rounded corners and no ridges, protruding rivets, or crevices to catch and hold bits of food.
– Utensils with firmly mounted, heatproof handles and knobs.
– Utensils that can be hung or nested to save space.

Some Specifics about Different Kinds of Cookware

Aluminum: People still shy away from aluminum, believing the old wives' tale that it poisons food. *Not so.* Aluminum is one of the best all-around cooking materials available. It is inexpensive; a quick, even conductor of heat, sturdy enough to take daily wear and tear, yet lightweight enough to handle comfortably. It is stamped into lightweight and medium-weight saucepans, kettles, and bakeware and cast into heavy skillets, kettles, and griddles. Moreover, it is available plain or colored (anodized). Some people insist that aluminum gives tomatoes and other acid foods a metallic taste, yet just as many disagree. Aluminum, however, is not entirely fault free: It darkens and pits when exposed to alkaline or mineral-rich foods or when left to soak in sudsy water; it must be scoured frequently and, if anodized, cannot be washed in a dishwasher. *Cleaning Tip:* To brighten drab aluminum, boil an acid solution (2 table-spoons cream of tartar or 1 cup vinegar to each 1 quart water) in utensil 5–10 minutes, then scour with a soap pad, rinse, and dry.

Stainless Steel: Extremely sturdy and long suffering. Stainless steel's greatest shortcoming is that it is a poor conductor of heat and must be bonded to a good conductor—usually copper or aluminum—if it is to cook properly (even thus, it is better for stove-top cooking rather than baking). Some-times pan bottoms only are clad with copper or aluminum, sometimes the entire utensil is 2-ply (stainless steel inside and aluminum outside), and sometimes it is 3-ply (a copper, carbon steel, or aluminum core sandwiched between 2 layers of stainless steel). Stainless steel cookware costs more than aluminum but is easier to clean and slower to dent or scratch. It *will* heat-streak if permitted to boil dry, but unless it is seriously discolored it can be brightened with one of the special stainless-steel cleansers.

Cast Iron: the work horse of days past and still the favorite for frying chicken and baking popovers and corn sticks because of its ability to absorb and hold heat. But cast iron is leaden and cumber-some and unless well seasoned or enameled (as much of it now is) it is likely to rust; unenameled cast iron should never be used for liquid recipes—they will taste of rust. Most modern cast-iron cookware is preseasoned and ready to use, but the old-fashioned ware must be seasoned before using. *To Season* (or reseason): Wash and dry utensil, rub with unsalted shortening, and heat uncovered 2 hours in a 350° F. oven. *Cleaning Tip:* Use soap instead of snythetic detergents so that a utensil's seasoning will last through several washings, then dry over lowest burner heat; store uncovered to prevent beads of "sweat" from collecting and rusting the iron.

Copper: The choice of gourmets because of its ability to transmit the merest flicker of heat evenly, slowly, constantly. But, to do the job well, the copper must be heavy gauge (thin decorator sets look good—*but do not cook well*), and, to be safe for cooking, copper utensils must be lined with tin and retinned whenever copper begins to show through. Copper, unquestionably, makes the hand-somest pots and pans, but it is luxury priced, quick to scar, and pesky to clean and polish. Miraculous as commercial copper cleaners are, they must nevertheless be applied with plenty of elbow grease. An additional shortcoming of copper cookware: Most of it is made with metal handles and knobs, meaning that you must use potholders constantly.

Enameled Metals (also called *Agateware, Graniteware,* and *Enamelware*): Metal utensils coated inside and out with thin layers of porcelain. Available in dazzling colors and decorator patterns, enamel utensils are nonporous and inert (unreacting in the presence of acid or alkaline foods) and for that reason are well suited to pickling and preserving. They are, however, easily chipped, cracked, scratched, and stained. *Cleaning Tip:* To float charred foods magically off the bottoms of enamel pots, boil a baking soda solution in the pots several minutes (2–3 tablespoons baking soda to each quart water).

Nonstick Finishes: These are improving all the time. Originally so delicate they required special nylon implements and "soft" scouring pads, they are now hardier, less easily scratched or scraped. They permit virtually fat-free cooking (a blessing to the calorie and cholesterol conscious) and require little more cleaning than a quick sponging. They cannot, however, take intensive heat, should not be used for broiling.

Flameproof Glass: Good all-around stove-top and ovenware, inert like enamelware, easy to clean. Relatively sturdy although the glass will break if dropped or subjected to abrupt temperature changes.

Freezer-to-Stove Ceramic Ware: A Space Age material, inert, extremely durable. The ideal container for freezer-to-oven-to-table casseroles. Still fairly expensive and as yet available only in a limited choice of colors and styles.

Earthenware: Clay bakeware, glazed until nonporous, nonabsorbent; it may be high-fired and hard, low-fired and crumbly. Expert cooks insist that earthenware alone, because of its ability to release heat slowly, can impart to baked beans, *cassoulet,* and other long-simmering oven dishes the proper mellowness and consistency. Earthenware must be handled gingerly, however, cooled thoroughly before it is washed lest its glaze crack, exposing the clay underneath; the clay will pick up flavors, then pass them along—*stale*—to each subsequent dish. *Warning:* Within the last few years, certain Mexican pottery glazes were found to be poisonous. Play it safe. Use Mexican pottery for decoration, *not* for cooking or eating.

Selecting and Caring for Knives

Fine knives are the cook's best friends—sturdily constructed, well balanced and designed knives that can be honed to long-lasting razor keenness. It is the dull knife that cuts the cook, rarely the sharp one, because the dull knife must be forced. Good knives are expensive, but justifiably so because they will perform well over a period of years. What distinguishes the fine knife from the inferior? Here are a few indicators:

– Choose knives that feel comfortable in the hand. Top quality knives have handles of close-grained hardwood, rubbed to satiny smoothness; they will not warp, split, or splinter. Shoddy knives may have handles of soft wood (usually painted) or molded out of some synthetic (often rough around the seams).

– Look for blades well anchored in handles. In fine knives, blades extend to the tops of the handles and are held fast by 2 or 3 broad, double-headed rivets lying flush with the handle. Cheaper blades may be sunk only halfway into the handle, held by 1 or 2 small wire rivets or simply glued in place.

– Insist upon forged carbon steel knives, budget permitting. They are the choice of chefs and gourmets because of their fine, hard smoothness that will take and keep a keen cutting edge. They *will* stain and rust, however, unless washed and dried as soon as they are used. Stainless steel, made stainproof and rustproof by the addition of chromium and nickel, is softer, quicker to dull.

– Select knives with well-shaped blades. The *forged,* tapering from both blunt edge to sharp and handle to point, are choicest. *Stamped blades,* cut out of uniformly thick metal, usually indicate poor quality; *beveled blades,* cut from metal thicker on one blunt edge than the other, taper from blunt side to sharp but not from handle to point—popular construction for medium-priced knives.

Hollow-ground blades, also in the medium price range, have broad, concave cutting surfaces; they are adept at slicing but easily damaged. *Shopping Tip:* If a brand name is stamped on a knife blade, the knife is probably a good one; manufacturers of inferior merchandise don't bother.

Some Knife Care Tips:
– Treat knives with respect, washing and drying them as soon as they are used, gently scouring off any darkened spots with metal soap pads. Do not wash in the dishwasher, do not soak; either can loosen rivets, rot handles and rust blades.

– Always use knife on a cutting surface softer than the blade—hardwood is ideal, makes the knife last longer.

– Store knives in a knife rack, never jammed into a drawer where the

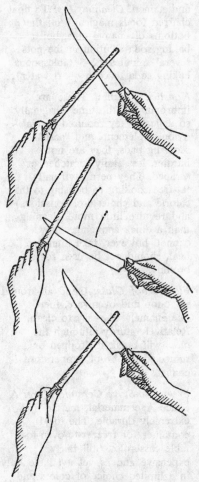

How to Sharpen a Knife

blade may be bent or nicked (and the cook injured).

– Use knives strictly for slicing, cutting, and chopping, never for prying off lids and bottle tops; it's damaging to the knife, dangerous, too.

– Sharpen knives frequently. Because each person tends to hold a blade to the steel or stone at a slightly different angle, it's best if the same person does all the knife sharpening —the knives will last longer.

To sharpen on an electric sharpener, follow manufacturer's instructions.

The Beginning Kitchen: Equipment Needed

SAUCEPANS, KETTLES, SKILLETS (WITH LIDS)
1 pint, 1½ and 3 qt. saucepans
2 or 3 qt. double boiler
1 gallon kettle
12″ or 15″ roaster (with rack)
1–1½ gal. Dutch oven
7″ and 10″ skillets
6–8 cup coffeepot
2 or 3 qt. teakettle

OVENWARE
9″×5″×3″ loaf pan
13″×9″×2″ loaf pan
2 (8″ or 9″) round cake pans
8″ or 9″ square pan
2 (8″ or 9″) piepans
10″ tube pan
Muffin pan
Cookie sheet

BOWLS, CASSEROLES
Nest of mixing bowls
1½–2 and 3 qt. casseroles (with lids)
4–6 custard cups or ramekins

MEASURERS
Measuring spoons
Dry measure set

1 cup and 1 pt. liquid measuring cups

UTENSILS
Long-handled cooking spoons (one slotted)
Wooden spoon
Ladle
Large and small cooking forks
Large and small spatulas
Rubber spatula
Pancake turner
Tongs
Can and bottle openers, corkscrew
Large and small, coarse and fine sieves
5-cup flour sifter
Colander
Funnel
Salt and pepper shakers
4-sided grater
Bulb baster
Rotary beater
Reamer
Pastry blender
Potato masher
Garlic crusher
Rolling pin, stockinette, pastry cloth
Cookie and cake racks
Potholders, hot pads
Clock and timer

CUTLERY
2 paring knives
Slicing knife
8″ chopping knife
Bread knife
Vegetable peeler
Carving set
Corer
Kitchen shears
Cutting board
Biscuit cutter
Ice pick

THERMOMETERS
Oven
Meat

SMALL APPLIANCES
Toaster

Waffle iron or griddle
Portable electric mixer (optional)

FOR STORAGE
Canisters with scoops
Towel and paper dispensers
Graduated refrigerator containers

SINK ACCESSORIES
Drainer, drainboard
Garbage pail
Sponges, scourers
Dishpan, dish towels
Vegetable and bottle brushes

The Intermediate Kitchen

To the Beginning Kitchen add:

SAUCEPANS, KETTLES,
SKILLETS (WITH LIDS)
1, 2, *and* 3 or 4 qt. saucepans
4 qt. pressure saucepan
Egg poacher
Steamer
Deep fat fryer
2 or 3 qt. Dutch oven
12″ skillet
10″ heavy iron skillet
5″ or 6″ skillet

OVENWARE
Jelly-roll pan
Extra 9″×5″×3″ loaf pan
Extra 8″ or 9″ square and round
  pans
Extra muffin pans, cookie sheets
9″ or 10″ spring form pan

BOWLS, CASSEROLES, MOLDS
Extra mixing bowls
1½ or 2 qt. soufflé dish
1½ or 2 qt. au gratin pan
2 or 3 qt. bean pot
6–8 cup ring mold
4–6 individual gelatin molds

MEASURERS
Extra measuring spoons
Extra dry measures
1 qt. liquid measure

Ruler
Scale

UTENSILS
Mixing fork
Slotted pancake turner
Extra wooden spoons
Balloon whip
1 or 2 wire whisks
Food mill
Meat grinder
Rotary grater
Pepper mill
Potato ricer
Pot strainer
Jar opener
Ball scoop
Wide-mouth funnel
Garlic basket
Salad basket
Tea sieve
1 cup flour sifter
V-shaped poultry rack
Extra cake, cookie racks
Pastry bag and decorative tips or
  cake-decorating set
Pastry wheel
Pastry brush
Cookie press
Cake and pie keepers
Cheesecloth
Needle and thread
Asbestos flame tamer

CUTLERY
Extra paring knives
Grapefruit knife
10″–12″ chopping knife
Poultry shears
Assorted cookie cutters
Small cutting board
Stone, steel, or knife sharpener
Egg slicer
Melon baller
Wedger-corer
Skewers, poultry pins
Shrimp deveiner

THERMOMETERS
Candy
Deep fat

SMALL APPLIANCES
Automatic coffee maker
Electric mixer
Electric blender
Electric skillet or Dutch oven

The Gourmet Kitchen

To the Intermediate Kitchen, add as needed:

SAUCEPANS, KETTLES,
SKILLETS (WITH LIDS)
Sauté pan
Butter warming set
Steamer basket
Fish poacher
Clam steamer
Stock pot
Large round and oval cocottes
Terrine
Polenta pot
Oval fish skillet
Wok set
Omelet pan
Crepe pan
Paella pan
Heavy griddle
Chafing dish
Fondue set
Espresso set
Turkish coffeepot
China teapot

OVENWARE
Pizza pans
Flan rings
Tart and tartlet tins
Assorted round and oval au gratin pans
Brioche pans
Tiered cake pan set
Corn stick pans
Popover pans

BOWLS, CASSEROLES, MOLDS
Nest of soufflé dishes
Scallop shells
Pots de crème

Large earthenware crock or bowl for marinating
Copper beating bowl
Assortment of plain and decorative molds: for salads, ice cream bombes, mousses, steamed puddings
Coeur à la crème basket
Pâté en croûte mold

UTENSILS
Wire skimmer
Extra wooden spoons, whisks, ladles, rubber spatulas
Mortar and pestle
Salt mill
Nutmeg grater
Spaghetti tongs
Procelain onion grater
Cutlet bat
Meat cuber-pounder
Wooden mallet
Escargots plates, holders
Full set of pastry bags, decorative tips
Butter curler, paddles
Extra pastry brushes
Tapered French pastry pin
Springerle pin
Pastry board
Marble slab
Tortilla press
Krumkake iron
Rosette iron
Preserving, jelly making, freezing, and canning equipment (see those chapters for details)
Cream horn tins

CUTLERY
Full sets of cookie, aspic, truffle cutters
Oyster knife
Clam knife
Fluting knife
Filleting knife
Boning knife
Tomato knife
Meat cleaver
Fish scaler
Curved chopper and chopping bowl

Cherry pitter
Zester
Lemon stripper
Bean frencher
Mandolin cutter
Pasta machine
Long and short larding needles
Skewers in assorted lengths
Nutcracker set
Lobster crackers

SMALL APPLIANCES

Heavy duty mixer with attachments
   including dough hook
Ice-cream freezer (hand or electric)
Electric food chopper-grinder
Electric coffee grinder
Quantity automatic coffee maker
Electric can opener-knife sharpener
Electric hot trays
Rotisserie
Electric bun warmer
Electric ice crusher
Electric toaster-oven
Electric knife

Some Cooking Terms Defined

The language of food, so clear cut
and routine to experienced cooks,
often bewilders the beginner. Defined
here are the more common general
terms; elsewhere in the book, in the
sections where they most apply, are
the more specific terms—*muddle,* for
example, a bar technique, is defined
in the beverages chapter; *soft ball,*
a test used in making candy, is ex-
plained in that chapter.

adjust: To taste before serving and
increase seasoning as needed.
agneau: The French word for
"lamb."
à la: A French idiom loosely trans-
lated to mean "in the style of." *À la
maison,* for example, is "as prepared
at this house or restaurant, the house
specialty," and *à la bourguignonne*

("as prepared in Burgundy"—with
Burgundy wine).
à la king: Cut up food, usually
chicken or turkey, in cream sauce,
often with slivered pimiento and
sliced mushrooms added.
à la mode: As used in America, pie or
other dessert topped with a scoop of
ice cream. In French cuisine, braised
meat smothered in gravy.
al dente: An Italian phrase meaning
"to the tooth," used to describe pasta
cooked the way Italians like it—
tender but still firm.
allumette: The French word for
"match," used to describe food cut
in matchstick shapes; also a slim,
bite-size puff pastry hors d'oeuvre.
amandine: Made or served with
almonds.
à point: A French phrase used to
describe food cooked just to the
point of doneness.
au gratin: A dish browned in oven
or broiler, usually topped with buttered bread crumbs or grated cheese
or both. *Gratiné* means the same
thing.
au jus: Food, usually roast beef,
served in its own juices.

baba: A sweet yeast cake, studded
with raisins and dried fruit, saturated
with brandy, kirsch, or rum (*baba au
rhum*).
bain marie: French for a "steam
table" or "hot water bath" (which
see).
bake: To cook by dry oven heat.
ball: To cut into balls.
barbecue: To cook in a hot spicy
sauce, often over a grill; also the
food so cooked and the grill used for
cooking it.
bard: To tie bacon, suet, or fatback
around lean meats to prevent their
drying out in cooking. For barding
instructions, see Some Special Ways
to Prepare Meat for Cooking in the
meat chapter.

Bar-le-Duc: A red or white currant preserve named for Bar-le-Duc, France, where it is made.

baste: To ladle or brush drippings, liquid, butter, or sauce over food as it cooks, the purpose being to add flavor and prevent drying.

batter: An uncooked mixture, usually of eggs, flour, leavening, and liquid, that is thin enough to pour.

batterie de cuisine: A French phrase used to describe all the implements, utensils, and paraphernalia of cooking.

beard: To cut the hairy fibers off unshucked mussels.

beat: To mix briskly with a spoon, whisk, rotary or electric beater using an over-and-over or round-and-round motion.

beignet: The French word for "fritter."

beurre: The French word for "butter." *Beurre manié* is a mixture of butter and flour, kneaded until smooth, that is added as a thickener to sauces and stews. *Beurre noir* is butter heated until dark brown; *beurre noisette*, butter heated until the color of amber.

bien fatigué: A French term meaning "wilted"; it is used to describe salad greens dressed with hot dressing, then tossed until properly limp.

bind: To stir egg, sauce, or other thick ingredient into a mixture to make it hold together.

bisque: A creamed soup, usually with a shellfish base.

blanch: To immerse briefly in boiling water to loosen skins or to heighten and set color and flavor.

blaze (flame, flambé): To set a match to liquor-drenched food so that it bursts into flames.

blend: To mix two or more ingredients together until smooth.

boeuf: The French word for "beef."

boil: To heat liquid until bubbles break at the surface (212° F. for water at sea level); also to cook food in boiling liquid.

bone: To remove bones.

braise: To brown in fat, then to cook covered on the topstove or in the oven with some liquid.

bread: To coat with bread crumbs.

brine: To preserve in a strong salt solution; also the solution itself.

brown: To cook at high heat, usually on the topstove in fat, until brown; also to set under a broiler until touched with brown.

bruise: To partially crush—as a clove of garlic in a mortar and pestle —to release flavor.

brûlé, brûlée: The French word for "burned," used in cooking to describe foods glazed with caramelized sugar.

brunoise: A French cooking term used to describe finely diced or shredded vegetables, usually a mixture of them cooked in butter or just enough stock to moisten. *Brunoise* is used to flavor soups and sauces.

brush: To apply butter, liquid, or glaze with a brush.

butterfly: To split food down the center, almost but not quite all the way through, so that the two halves can be opened flat like butterfly wings.

café: The French word for "coffee."

candy: To preserve in or glaze with sugar syrup.

caramelize: To heat sugar until it melts and turns golden brown; also to glaze food with caramelized sugar. *Caramel* is liquid, browned sugar used to flavor and color gravies and sauces.

chapon: A chunk or cube of bread, rubbed with oil and garlic, that is tossed with green salads to impart a subtle garlic flavor; it is discarded before serving. For still subtler flavor, the chapon can simply be rubbed over the salad bowl before the greens are added.

chiffonade: A soup garnish composed of finely cut vegetable strips (commonly lettuce and sorrel).

chill: To let stand in the refrigerator or crushed ice until cold.

chop: To cut into small pieces with a knife or chopper; chopped foods are more coarsely cut than the minced.

clarify: To make cloudy liquid clear, usually by heating with raw egg white, then straining through cloth. For instructions, see Some Basic Soup-Making Techniques in the soup chapter.

clove (of garlic): One small almond-sized segment of the head or bulb of garlic.

coat: To dip in crumbs, flour, or other dry ingredient; also to cover with sauce or aspic.

coat a spoon: A doneness test for custards and other cooked egg-thickened mixtures; when the egg has thickened (cooked) sufficiently, it will leave a thin, custardlike film on a metal spoon.

cocotte: The French word for "casserole"; *en cocotte* simply means "cooked in a casserole." *Cocottes* can be whopping or just large enough to serve one person.

coddle: To poach in water just below the boiling point.

combine: To mix together two or more ingredients.

cool: To bring hot food to room temperature.

coq: The French word for "cock" or "rooster."

core: To remove the core.

cream: To beat butter or other fat either solo or with sugar or other ingredients until smooth and creamy.

crème: The French word for "cream."

crimp: To seal the edge of a pie or pastry with a decorative edge.

croûte: The French word for "crust" or "pastry." Something prepared *en croûte* is wrapped in or topped with a crust.

crumble: To break up with the fingers.

crush: To reduce to crumbs.

cube: To cut into cubes.

cure: To preserve meat, fish, or cheese by salting, drying, and/or smoking.

cut in: To mix shortening or other solid fat into dry ingredients until the texture is coarse and mealy.

deep-fat-fry: To cook by immersing in hot (usually about 360° F.) deep fat.

deglaze: To scrape the browned bits off the bottom of a skillet or roasting pan, usually by adding a small amount of liquid and heating gently; this mixture is added to the dish for flavor.

degrease: To skim or blot grease from a soup, sauce, or broth or, easier still, to chill it until the grease rises to the top and hardens; it can then be lifted off.

demi-glace: A rich brown sauce or gravy made by boiling down meat stock.

devil: To mix with hot seasonings (commonly mustard and cayenne).

dice: To cut into fine cubes, usually $1/8''-1/4''$.

dilute: To weaken or thin by adding liquid.

disjoint: To separate at the joint, most often poultry or small game.

dissolve: To pass a solid (sugar, salt, etc.) into solution; also to melt or liquefy.

dot: To distribute small bits (usually butter or other fat) over the surface of a food.

dough: A pliable raw mixture, usually containing flour, sugar, egg, milk, leavening, and seasoning, that is stiff enough to work with the hands.

dragées: Candy shot used in decorating cookies, cakes, and candies. Silver dragées are the hard BB-like shot.

drain: To pour off liquid.

draw: To remove the entrails of poultry, game, or fish; to eviscerate.

dredge: To coat lightly with flour, confectioners' sugar, or other powdery ingredient.

dress: To draw or eviscerate; also to add dressing to a salad.

drippings: The melted fat and juices that collect in the pan of meat, poultry, or other food as it cooks.

drizzle: To pour melted butter, syrup, sauce, or other liquid over the surface of food in a very fine stream.

drop: To drop from a spoon, as cookie dough onto a baking sheet.

dust: To coat very lightly with flour, confectioners' sugar, or other powdery mixture. Dusted foods are more lightly coated than the dredged.

duxelles: A thick, almost pastelike mixture of minced sautéed mushrooms, sometimes seasoned with shallots, salt, and pepper, that is mixed into sauces, stuffings, and other recipes.

en brochette: Food cooked on a skewer.

en papillote: Food cooked in oiled parchment or in a packet.

entree: The main course of a meal.

essence, extract: Concentrated flavoring.

eviscerate: To remove entrails, to draw.

filet, fillet: A boneless piece of meat or fish. *Fillet* is the English spelling, *filet* the French; *filet* is also the

spelling used to identify beef tenderloin (*filet mignon*).

filter: To strain through several thicknesses of cloth.

finish: To garnish a dish before serving, to add the finishing touches.

flake: To break into small pieces with a fork.

flambé: See *blaze.*

flour: To coat with flour.

fluff: To fork up until light and fluffy; also a spongy gelatin dessert.

flute: To make a decorative edge on pies or pastries; to crimp. Also to cut mushrooms or other small vegetables into fluted or scalloped shapes.

fold: To mix using a gentle over-and-over motion. Also, literally, to fold rolled-out pastry into a neat package as when making puff pastry.

fold in: To mix a light ingredient (beaten egg white, whipped cream) into a heavier one using a light over-and-over motion so that no air or volume is lost.

forcemeat (farce): Finely ground meat, poultry, or fish often combined with ground vegetables, bread crumbs, and seasonings used in making stuffings, *quenelles,* and croquettes.

fouet: The French word for the "balloon whip" or "whisk."

freeze: To chill until hard and icy.

French-fry: To cook in deep hot fat (see *deep-fat-fry*).

fricassee: A way of braising cut-up chicken and small game. The pieces are dredged and browned, then cooked, covered, in liquid or sauce, often in the company of vegetables. Food can be fricasseed on top of the stove or in the oven.

frizzle: To fry thinly sliced meat at intense heat until crisp and curled.

fromage: The French word for "cheese."

frost: To spread with frosting or coat with sugar; also to chill until ice crystals form, as when frosting mint julep cups.

frothy: Light and foamy.

fry: See *panfry*.

fumet: A concentrated stock used as a base for sauces.

garnish: To decorate a dish before serving. The *garniture* is the decoration.

gâteau: The French word for "cake."

giblets: The heart, liver, and gizzard of fowl and small game.

glace: The French word for "ice cream."

glacé: A French word used to describe candied or sugared food; *marrons glacés*, for instance, are candied chestnuts.

glace de viande: A rich brown meat glaze made by boiling meat stock down until dark and syrupy; it is added to sauces and gravies for flavor and color.

glaze: To cover food with a glossy coating, most often syrup, aspic, melted jellies or preserves. Also to brush pastry with milk or beaten egg to make it glisten.

grate: To cut food into small particles by passing through a grater.

grease: To rub with grease.

grease and flour: To rub with grease, then dust lightly with flour. *Note:* Most pans need greasing only, but those in which extra-sweet or fruit-heavy batters will be baked will probably require greasing *and* flouring to keep the cake or bread from sticking.

grill: To broil on a grill, commonly over charcoal.

grind: To reduce to fine particles or paste by putting through a grinder.

grissini: Slim Italian bread sticks.

hot water bath, water jacket: A large kettle in which preserving jars are processed, also a pan of water in which a dish of custard or other apt-to-curdle dish is placed during baking. *Note:* If the water in the kettle boils, it becomes a *boiling water bath*.

husk: To remove the coarse outer covering, as when husking corn. Also, the covering itself.

ice: To spread with icing; also, to chill until hard and icy.

infusion: Hot liquid in which tea, coffee, herbs, or spices have been steeped.

jell (also gel): To congeal with gelatin. Also, to cook into jelly.

jelly-roll style: A flat piece of meat, fish, or cake rolled up around a filling.

julienne: Food cut into small matchstick-like strips.

knead: To work with the hands in a rhythmic pressing-folding-turning pattern until smooth and satiny.

kosher: Food prepared or processed according to Jewish ritual law.

lait: The French word for "milk."

lard: To insert bits of lard or other fat into lean meat to keep it moist and succulent throughout cooking. Also, the rendered fat of hogs.

leaven: To lighten the texture and increase the volume of breads, cakes, and cookies by using baking powder, soda, or yeast, which send gases bubbling through the batter or dough during baking. Angel cakes and sponge cakes are leavened by the air beaten into the egg whites.

legumes: A protein-rich family of plants that includes beans, peas, lentils, and peanuts.

let down: To dilute by adding liquid.

liaison: A thickening agent (flour, cornstarch, arrowroot, egg, or cream) used to thicken soups and sauces or bind together stuffings and croquettes.

line: To cover the bottom and sides

of a pan or mold with paper, a layer of cake or crumbs before adding the food to be cooked, chilled, or frozen.

macerate: To soak fruits in spirits.

marinate: To steep meat, fish, fowl, vegetables, or other savory food in a spicy liquid several hours until food absorbs the flavoring. Technically, *macerating* and *marinating* are the same; *macerate*, however, applies to *fruits*, *marinate* to savory food. The steeping medium is called a *marinade*.

marmite: A tall French stock pot, often made of earthenware.

marrow: The soft buttery substance found in the hollows of bones; gourmets consider it a delicacy. *Marrow spoons* are the long, slender-bowled spoons designed specifically for digging the marrow out of bones.

mash: To reduce to pulp, usually with a potato masher.

mask: To coat with sauce or aspic.

matzo: The flat unleavened bread traditionally eaten by Jews during Passover.

mealy: Resembling meal in texture; as used to describe baked potatoes, it means that they are light and crumbly, almost flaky.

meat glaze: See *glace de viande*.

medallion: Small coin-shaped pieces of meat, commonly beef.

melt: To liquefy by heating.

mince: To cut into fine pieces. Minced foods are more finely cut than the chopped.

mirepoix: A mixture of minced sautéed vegetables—traditionally carrots, celery, and onions—used in French cooking to flavor sauces, stuffings, stews, and other savory dishes.

mix: To stir together using a round-and-round motion.

mocha: The combined flavors of coffee and chocolate.

moisten: To dampen with liquid.

mold: To cook, chill, or freeze in a mold so that the food takes on the shape of the mold. To *unmold* simply means to remove from the mold.

mortar and pestle: An old-fashioned implement, still basic to the gourmet kitchen. The mortar is a bowl-shaped container, usually made of porcelain or wood, the pestle a heavy blunt instrument of the same material used for pulverizing seasonings against the walls of the mortar.

mound: To stand in a mound when taken on or dropped from a spoon; the term is used to describe the consistency of gelatin-thickened mixtures.

mull: To heat fruit juice (frequently cider or grape juice), wine, ale, or other alcoholic beverage with sugar and spices.

nap: To coat with sauce.

noisette: A small round slice of meat, usually lamb.

nonpareilles: Another name for dragées or candy shot used in decorating cakes, cookies, and candies.

oeuf: The French word for "egg."

oie: The French word for "goose."

pain: The French word for "bread."

panbroil: To cook in a skillet over direct heat with as little fat as possible; drippings are poured off as they accumulate.

panfry: To cook in a skillet *with* some fat *without* pouring off drippings. The French word for it is *sauté*.

parch: To dry corn or other starchy vegetable by roasting.

pare: To cut the peeling from fruits or vegetables.

paste: A smooth blend of fat and flour or other starch thickener. Also, any food pounded to a paste. Also, a dough, specifically that of puff or *choux* pastry.

peel: To remove the peeling from fruits or vegetables by pulling off rather than cutting away.

pepper: To season with pepper.

pickle: To preserve in brine or vinegar.

pinch: The amount of salt, sugar, herb, or spice, etc., that can be taken up between the thumb and forefinger, less than ⅛ teaspoon.

pipe: To apply a frilly border, usually of frosting or mashed potatoes, by squirting through a pastry bag fitted with a decorative tip.

pit: To remove pits.

plank: To broil on a wooden plank.

pluck: To pull the feathers from poultry.

plump: To soak raisins or other dried fruit in liquid until they soften and plump up.

poach: To cook submerged in simmering liquid.

poisson: The French word for "fish."

pone: Flat and round or oval in shape, as a corn pone.

popadam: Thin, crisp, deep-fat-fried East Indian wafers eaten with curry.

poulet: The French word for "chicken."

pound: To flatten with a mallet or cutlet bat.

preheat: To bring oven or broiler to required temperature before adding food.

prick: To pierce with the tines of a sharp fork. Pricking is necessary to keep pie shells from shrinking and warping during baking, also to free fat underneath the skin of ducks and geese as they roast.

proof: To set a yeast mixture in a warm, dry spot to rise.

purée: To grind to paste either by pressing through a food mill or whirling in an electric blender.

quenelles: Soufflé-light, poached forcemeat dumplings sauced and served as is or used to garnish meat or fish platters.

ragout: A hearty brown stew.

ramekin: A small baking dish big enough for one portion, commonly made of earthenware.

réchauffé: A French cooking term meaning "reheated."

reconstitute: To restore milk or other dehydrated food to a liquid or moist state by mixing in water.

reduce: To boil down rapidly until volume is reduced and flavors concentrated.

refresh: To plunge hot food (most often vegetables) into ice water to set the color and flavor. Just before serving the food is warmed in butter or sauce.

render: To heat lard or other animal fat so that it melts away from connective tissue and other solid particles. Rendered lard is smooth and creamy, almost pure fat and an excellent shortening for pastries. Another term for *render* is *try out*.

rib: One branch (stalk) of a bunch of celery. *Note:* In some cookbooks, stalk means the entire bunch or head of celery; as used here, however, stalk and rib are synonymous.

rice: To put through a ricer.

rissole: A filled sweet or savory deep-fat-fried pie or turnover.

roast: To cook uncovered in the oven by dry heat.

roe: Fish eggs.

roll out: To roll into a thin flat sheet with a rolling pin.

roux: A butter and flour paste, sometimes browned, sometimes not, used as a thickener for soups and stews. It is the soul of Creole cooking.

rusk: A crisp brown piece of bread, usually twice baked to make it extra light and dry; it may be sweet or plain.

salpicon: Mixed cubed foods served in a sauce or dressing.

salt: To season with salt.

sambal: Any of the many condiments served with curry.

sauce: To combine or cover with sauce.

sauté: See *panbroil*.

scald: To heat a liquid, most frequently milk or cream, just short of the boiling point until bubbles begin to gather around the edge of the pan. Also, to plunge tomatoes or peaches, etc., into boiling water to loosen their skins; to blanch.

scale: To remove scales from fish.

scallop: To bake in cream or a cream sauce underneath a bread crumb topping.

score: To make shallow knife cuts over the surface of food, usually in a crisscross pattern.

scrape: To scrape the skin from a fruit or vegetable with a knife.

sear: To brown meat quickly, either in a very hot oven or in a skillet over high heat, to seal in the juices.

season: To add salt, pepper, herbs, spices, or other seasonings.

seasoned flour: Flour seasoned with salt and pepper.

seed: To remove seeds.

serrate: To cut a decorative zigzag border into food, pastries, for example, using a zigzag pastry wheel, or orange, lemon, or grapefruit halves or baskets.

set, set up: To congeal, as when thickened with gelatin.

shell: To remove the shells—most commonly of eggs, nuts, or shrimp.

shirr: To cook whole eggs in ramekins with cream and sometimes a topping of buttered bread crumbs.

short: An adjective used to describe pastry or cookies made crumbly or flaky by a high proportion of shortening.

shred: To cut in small, thin strips or shreds, usually by pressing through a grater.

shuck: To remove the shells of clams, oysters, mussels, or scallops; also to remove husks from corn.

sieve: To strain liquid through a sieve; also the strainer itself.

sift: To pass flour or other dry ingredient through a fine sieve or sifter.

simmer: To heat liquid to about 185° F., just until bubbles begin to form; also to cook food in simmering liquid.

singe: To burn hairs off the skin of plucked poultry.

skewer: To thread small chunks of food on long metal or wooden pins; also the pin itself.

skim: To scoop fat, froth, or other material from the surface of a liquid with a spoon.

skin: To remove the skin of poultry, game, or fish.

sliver: To cut in fine, thin pieces, usually no more than ½″ long and a fraction of that wide.

snip: To cut in fine pieces or to gash with scissors.

soak: To let stand in liquid.

soft peaks: Descriptive phrase used to describe a mixture beaten until peaks will form but curl over at the top instead of standing up straight.

spit: To cook on a spit.

sponge: A frothy gelatin dessert; also the puffy yeast culture used to leaven bread.

steam: To cook, covered, *over* a small amount of boiling liquid so that the steam formed in the pan does the cooking.

steep: To let tea leaves, coffee grounds, herbs, or spices stand in hot liquid until their flavor is extracted.

sterilize: To kill microorganisms of spoilage by boiling or subjecting to steam under pressure.

stew: To cook submerged in simmering liquid; also the food so cooked.

stiff but not dry: Term used to describe egg whites beaten until they will stand in stiff but moist and glistening peaks.

stir: To mix with a spoon or whisk using a round-and-round motion.

stir-fry: Oriental method of briskly tossing or stirring foods as they fry.

stock: The broth strained from stewed or boiled meats, seafood, poultry, or vegetables.

strain: To separate liquids from solids by passing through a sieve.

stud: To insert whole cloves, slivers of garlic, or other seasoning over the surface of food.

stuff: To fill with stuffing.

swirl: To whirl liquid gently in a pan; also to ease a new ingredient —an egg, for example—into swirling liquid.

syrupy: Of the consistency of syrup; the term is applied most often to partially congealed gelatin. When syrupy, it is ready to whip or use as a glaze.

tahini: Sesame seed paste, a popular ingredient of Middle Eastern recipes.

tenderize: To make tender, especially meat, either by pounding or scoring to break up connective tissues or by adding a chemical tenderizer or acidic marinade to soften them.

terrine: An earthenware container used for baking pâté and other minced or ground meat mixtures. Also the dish so cooked.

thick and lemony: A not particularly apt phrase used to describe stiffly beaten egg yolks; at this consistency they are more nearly the color and texture of mayonnaise.

thicken: To thicken a liquid by adding flour or other starch thickener, by adding eggs or by boiling down.

thin: To dilute by adding liquid.

timbale: A custard-thickened mixture of meat, poultry, fish, or vegetables usually baked in a small mold or ramekin or served in a crisp timbale (rosette) case (see breads chapter for recipe).

toast: To brown bread by heating.

toast points: Small triangular pieces of toast.

toss: To mix by flipping or turning food over and over as when dressing a green salad or combining stuffing ingredients.

treacle: The English word for "molasses."

truss: To tie poultry or other food into a compact shape before roasting.

try out: See *render*.

turn: To flute or scallop food, especially mushrooms or other small round vegetables. Also, literally, to turn food over as it cooks or steeps.

veau: The French word for "veal."
viande: The French word for "meat."
vin: The French word for "wine."
volaille: The French word for "poultry."

whey: The watery liquid that separates from the solid curds when milk or cream curdles.

whip: To beat until stiff, usually with a whisk, rotary or electric beater.

whisk: A handy beating implement made of looped wires.

wok: A broad, bowl-shaped Oriental pan particularly suited to stir-frying because of its thin metal construction, round bottom and high sides. Set upon a metal ring or collar, it can be used on American burners.

work: To mix slowly with the fingers, to knead.

zest: The colored part of citrus rind used as a flavoring; also the oil pressed from it.

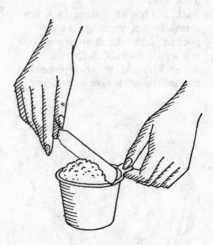

How to Measure Ingredients

Although "born cooks" can produce success after success without measuring a thing, most of us fail whenever we resort to such haphazard methods. We must not only measure but *measure correctly,* a special skill in itself.

Dry Ingredients, Crumbs, Minced/ Grated Foods
Sift flour, confectioners' sugar *before* measuring (granulated sugar, too, if lumpy); pile food lightly in measure without tapping cup or shaking contents down; level off as shown.

Exception: Brown sugar must be packed firmly into measure; if lumpy, roll between sheets of wax paper with a rolling pin before measuring.

Melted Fats
If fat is soft, measure as directed for solid fat, then melt and use. If fat is brittle and hard, melt, estimating as nearly as possible amount you'll need, then measure as directed for oils.

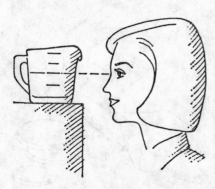

Liquids, Oils
Stand cup on level surface, fill to mark, stoop to check quantity at eye level.

Tips: Measure syrups, molasses, honey, other sticky liquids in lightly greased cups *or* dry measures (so surface can be leveled off); scrape measure out well with a rubber spatula.

Solid Fats
Pack, a little at a time, in a dry measure cup, pressing out air pockets; level off, then scrape cup out well with rubber spatula.
Note: The old water-displacement method is no longer considered accurate.

How to Use Measuring Spoons

How to Measure Pans

All recipes in this book specify baking pan, casserole, or mold size when that size is essential to the success of a recipe. Modern containers usually have their vital statistics (length, width, depth, and volume) stamped on the bottom. If not, here is the correct way to take them.

Linear Measurements: For length, width, and diameter, measure pan across the top, inside edge to inside edge. For depth, stand ruler in pan, noting distance from rim to bottom.

Volume: Pour water into container, using a measuring cup, and record how many cups or quarts are needed to fill it.

Tip: Once measurements are taken, scratch them on the outside of the container so that they need not be retaken.

The Techniques of Chopping, Mincing, Slicing

A skilled chef wields his knife with all the grace of a swordsman, and to the novice his knife seems sword-like. Its weight and size, however, speed the cutting. Those timid about knives often choose knives too small for the job. For all round use, an 8″ blade is best; for bulkier, tougher foods, a 10″ blade and for small foods a 4″–6″ blade. Here are the basic cutting techniques, applicable with only minor adjustments to all kinds of food. Work slowly at first; speed will come.

To Slice Food
Peel; halve lengthwise or cut a thin slice off bottom so food is steady on cutting board. Slice straight through in thickness desired.

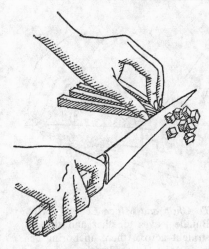

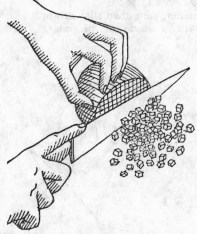

To Cube and Dice
Peel and slice—½"–1" for cubes, ⅛"–¼" for dice. Stack slices and cut in strips of the same thickness, then gather several strips together and cut crosswise into uniform cubes.

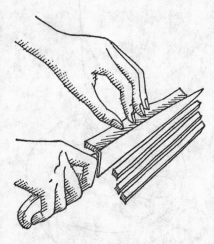

To Cut in Strips, Julienne
Peel and slice—¼" thick for regular strips, ⅛" for julienne; stack 3–4 slices and cut in ⅛" strips. For julienne, cut strips in uniform lengths as desired.

To Chop and Mince Solid Foods
Peel, halve lengthwise, place cut side down on board and, cutting almost—but not quite—through food, make evenly spaced vertical and horizontal cuts in a crisscross pattern—about ¼" apart for chopped foods, closer together for minced, then slice straight through.

To Mince or Dice Celery
Make a series of cuts the length of the stalk without cutting clear through the end, then slice crosswise into desired widths. If stalks are thick, they should be split lengthwise first, again almost but not quite through the end. *Note:* Carrots, thinly sliced lengthwise, can be similarly minced.

To Snip Herbs with Scissors
Bunch chives, dill tops, or other wispy herbs together, then cut straight across with scissors at ⅛" intervals—or more or less.

To Grate Rind, Onion, Hard Cheese
Rub in short quick strokes over fine side of grater onto wax paper; brush grater with a pastry brush to free clinging bits.

To Shred Cabbage
Quarter, core, then slice fine or
grate on coarse side of grater.

To Chop and Mince Leafy Foods
Bundle leaves together and slice
straight across, then, anchoring
knife point to board with one hand,
move knife up and down over
leaves in an arc as though it
were hinged to board, again and
again to desired fineness.

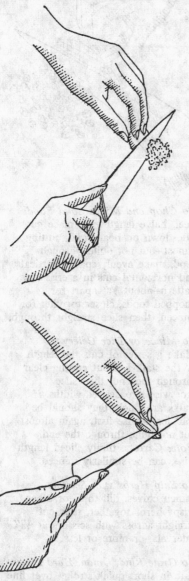

Tip: Garlic, shallots, and other
small foods are less apt to slip if
lightly salted.

To Make Melon or Vegetable Balls
Peel vegetable; halve and seed
melon. Press ball cutter firmly
straight into food, rotate until

embedded, then twist out and remove ball.

To Use a Chopping Bowl
Coarsely cut or break up food, place in bowl, then chop vigorously with curved chopper.

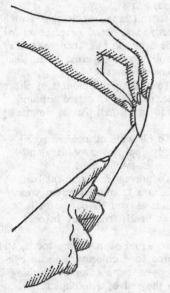

To Sliver or Shave Almonds
Blanch, peel, halve, and while still moist cut lengthwise in ⅛″ strips. To shave, cut lengthwise with a vegetable peeler.

To Flute Mushrooms
Holding mushroom cap in left hand and paring knife rigidly in right, rotate mushroom toward you and against *stationary* blade, making fluted indentations from crown to bottom.

To Make Onion Chrysanthemums
Peel, then, slicing about ¾ way down toward root end, cut onion into ⅛″ sections. Hold under hot tap and spread "petals" gently. Tint rose or yellow, if you like, in water mixed with food coloring.

Some Other Cooking Techniques

To Make Butter Balls
Scald butter paddles and chill in ice water; cut an ice cold butter stick in ½″ pats and roll each between paddles into a ball; drop in ice water to "set."

To Make Butter Curls
Chill butter curler in ice water; also chill butter (in refrigerator). Pulling toward you, draw curler full length of butter stick, scooping out curl; drop in ice water to "set" curl.

To Make Bacon Curls
Fry bacon until limp, spear 1 end with a fork, and wind around tines. Continue frying until brown and crisp, turning frequently so bacon is evenly cooked. Remove from fork.

To Line Pans with Ladyfingers
Cut ladyfingers lengthwise in long, slim wedges and arrange, rounded sides down, over bottom of pan in a sunburst pattern, fitting close together. Stand ladyfingers upright, touching one another, around sides. If mold is flared, trim ladyfingers as needed to fit close together around sides.

To Line Pans with Crumbs
Butter pan well, spoon in fine

crumbs, and tilt pan back and forth, rotating and shaking lightly until evenly coated all over. Tip out excess crumbs.

To Glaze Molds and Pans with Gelatin

Chill mold; prepare any clear gelatin mixture (Basic or Quick or Easy Aspic or any other gelatin mixture according to package directions). To glaze a 1-pint mold, you'll need about 1 cup; for a 1–1½-quart mold, about 1 pint. Chill gelatin until thick and syrupy, pour into chilled mold, and tilt back and forth, rolling around until bottom and sides are evenly coated. Tip out excess and keep its consistency syrupy. Quick-chill mold until gelatin is tacky. Continue pouring in gelatin, building up layers, until desired thickness is reached; 2–3 layers will glaze most mixtures, but for spiky foods add an extra layer or 2. Fill mold and chill until firm. Unmold very carefully, using only the briefest dip in hot water—glaze will quickly melt.

Note: Numerous other cooking techniques (seeding and juicing of tomatoes, for example, separating eggs, etc.) are included elsewhere in the book in the sections where they seem most appropriate. Consult Index for page numbers.

Some Preparation Short Cuts, Cooking Tips and Tricks

Preparation:
– To anchor wax paper to a counter (when rolling dough or grating food), dampen counter, then press paper to it.
– To deaden the clattery sound of a

rotary beater, stand bowl on a folded, dampened dishcloth or towel.
– To strain stock or other liquid through "cloth" when there is none, substitute paper toweling (but *not* the new super-absorbent type).
– To roll bread or cracker crumbs *neatly*, seal bread or crackers inside a plastic bag, then roll with a rolling pin. Or crush in an electric blender, instead.
– To melt small amounts of chocolate, place in a custard cup and stand in a small pan of simmering water.
– To fill without incident small, easily tipped-over molds, stand them in muffin pans.
– To prevent fish or meat ball mixtures from sticking to your hands as you shape the balls, rinse hands frequently in cold water.
– To avoid overcoloring foods, add liquid food coloring with an eye-dropper, paste color by daubing on the end of a toothpick.
– To prevent slippery foods from slipping as you slice or chop, dip fingers in salt. It also may help to lightly salt the cutting board.
– To measure out ½ egg, beat 1 whole egg, then spoon out ½ (add remaining ½ to a sauce or scrambled eggs).
– To crush whole cardamom seeds if you have no mortar and pestle, remove puffy white outer shell, then pulverize dark inner seeds by placing in the bowl of a spoon, fitting another spoon on top and grinding the 2 together. *Note:* Other small seeds—cumin, coriander, etc.—can be ground the same way.
– To expedite peeling of boiled potatoes, score lightly around middle before cooking; afterward,

simply spear potatoes with a fork and peel skin back from the score marks.

– To "frost" grapes, brush lightly with beaten egg white, then dip in granulated sugar and dry on a cake rack.

– To peel an onion zip-quick, cut a thin slice off top or bottom, then pull away papery outer skin.

Cooking and Baking:

– To brighten beets and red cabbage, add 1 tablespoon cider vinegar or lemon juice to the cooking water.

– To scald milk without scorching it, heat in a very heavy saucepan or top of a double boiler over just boiling water until tiny bubbles appear at edges of milk.

– To help keep sour cream from curdling, bring to room temperature before adding to hot mixtures and never allow to boil.

– To keep butter from burning during frying or sautéing, mix 2-to-1 with cooking oil or use clarified butter.*

– To soften hard, dry brown sugar, heat uncovered in a 200° F. oven until dry and crumbly, then pulverize in an electric blender.

– To prevent food from overbrowning as it bakes, wrap in foil with the shiny side out.

– To keep cooked, drained spaghetti from clumping when it must be held a few minutes, toss lightly with 1 tablespoon warm olive or other cooking oil.

– To prevent pancakes from sticking to the griddle, sprinkle it lightly with salt instead of greasing.

– To douse a small burner or oven fire, sprinkle with baking soda or salt.

– To soothe a superficial burn, hold under cold running water, rub with cold, heavy cream or apply a baking soda-water paste.

– To test oven temperature when gauge is broken, preheat oven 15 minutes, then place a sheet of white paper (typewriter bond is a good weight) on center rack for 5 minutes; if paper blackens, oven is 500° F. or more; if it turns deep brown, oven is 450°–500° F.; if golden brown, oven is 400°–450° F.; if light brown 350°–400° F.; and if a pale biscuit color, 300° F. or less.

Serving and Storing:

– To clean spills from serving dishes before carrying them to the table, wipe with cotton swabs or swab sticks.

– To keep plastic food wrap from sticking to itself, store in refrigerator.

– To build up a supply of ice cubes, remove from trays when frozen hard and very dry, bundle into large plastic bags and store in freezer. If dry enough when removed from trays, cubes will not stick to one another.

– To apportion vegetables evenly –and quickly–for a crowd, use an ice-cream scoop; No. 10 size=½ cup; No. 12=¾ cup.

– To cover a cake frosted with a soft or fluffy icing, stick toothpicks in top and sides, then drape foil or plastic food wrap over toothpicks.

– To keep fruit pies as fresh-tasting as possible, cover with foil or plastic food wrap and store at room temperature, then warm uncovered 10 minutes in a 350° F. oven before serving.

– To loosen a sticking crumb crust, set piepan on a hot damp cloth and hold cloth ends against sides of pan 1–2 minutes.

– To cut extra-fresh soft bread in thin slices, dip knife in boiling

COMMON CAN SIZES

Note: Cans of the same size do not necessarily weigh the same—depends on what's inside. Meats and seafoods are canned in such a variety of shapes and sizes they are not included here; nor are bantam jars of baby foods. Read labels carefully.

Industry Term	Approx. Net Weight	Approx. Cups	Approx. Servings	Type of Food
6 oz.	6 oz.	¾	4–6	Frozen juice concentrates.
8 oz.	8 oz.	1	1–2	Fruits, vegetables, ready-to-heat-and-eat dishes.
Picnic	10½–12 oz.	1¼	2–3	Condensed soups; fruits, meats, fish, vegetables, prepared dishes.
12 oz. vacuum	12 oz.	1½	3–4	Vacuum-pack corn.
No. 300	14–16 oz.	1¾	3–4	Pork and beans, meat dishes, cranberry sauce, blueberries.
No. 303	16–17 oz.	2	4	Fruits, vegetables, some meat products, ready-to-serve soups.
No. 2	1 lb. 4 oz. or 1 pt. 2 fl. oz.	2½	5	Juices, ready-to-serve soups, pineapple, apple slices, some ready-to-serve recipes; no longer popular for fruits, vegetables.
No. 2½	1 lb. 13 oz.	3½	7	Fruits, pumpkin, sauerkraut, tomatoes, spinach, and other greens.
No. 3 cyl. or 46 fl. oz.	3 lb. 3 oz. or 1 qt. 14 fl. oz.	5¾	10–12	Economy "family-size" fruit and vegetable juices, pork and beans; institution-size condensed soups, some vegetables.
No. 10	6½–7¼ lbs.	12–13	25	Institution-size fruits, vegetables.

water, shaking off extra drops, then slice.

Cleaning:
– To remove the smell of onions or garlic from hands, rinse hands in cold water, rub with salt or baking soda, rinse again, then wash with soap and water.
– To remove stains from fingers, rub with a cut lemon.

OVEN TEMPERATURES

Below 300° F.=very slow
300° F.=slow
325° F.=moderately slow
350° F.=moderate
375° F.=moderately hot
400–425° F.=hot
450–475° F.=very hot
500° F. or more=extremely hot

Conversion Formulas:
Fahrenheit to Centigrade: Subtract 32 from Fahrenheit reading, multiply by 5, then divide by 9. For example: 212° F.−32= 180×5=900÷9=100° C.
Centigrade to Fahrenheit: Multiply centigrade reading by 9, divide by 5 and add 32. For example: 100° C.×9=900÷5=180+ 32=212° F.

FAHRENHEIT / CENTIGRADE SCALE

Boiling Point F.	Boiling Point C.
(of Water) 212°	100° (of Water)
200°	93.3°
190°	87.8°
180°	82.2°
170°	76.7°
160°	71.1°
150°	65.6°
140°	60°
130°	54.4°
120°	48.9°
110°	43.3°
100°	37.8°

	90°	32.2°	
	80°	26.7°	
	70°	21.1°	
	60°	15.6°	
Freezing	50°	10°	Freezing
Point	40°	4.4°	Point
(of Water)	32°	0°	(of Water)

What It Will Mean to Cook with Metric Measures

If America adopts the metric system of measurements as expected, how will the change affect your cooking? First of all, don't throw away your cookbooks, because the conversion will not be immediate. Best predictions, in fact, are that it will take the big industries ten years at least to adopt the metric system, and consumers many, many years more. Metric weights and measures will be taught in the grades, so school children may well master the system before their parents. (Some corporations have already printed for classroom use booklets describing the metric system and how it works; others have devised slide-rule-type converters for instant calculations.)

What, exactly, is the metric system? A way of measuring, far simpler than our own, because it is based on the decimal system with larger measures being subdivided into units of ten.

Food researchers have always used the metric system because it is more precise than American weights and measures. European cooks use it, too, and have found nothing mystifying or complicated about it (they, in truth, would be baffled by our own system of pounds and ounces, yards and inches, which are not based on logical units of ten).

In recipes, the principal difference between our present way of measuring and the metric is that dry ingredients like flour and sugar are weighed rather than measured in a cup. It's an easier, more efficient method because the flour can be sifted directly onto a piece of wax paper on a scale, the dial indicating exactly when the proper amount of flour has been added. Meats, fruits, and vegetables, whether sliced, diced, or whole, will be called for by weight rather than by cup, and, of course, they will be sold in supermarkets by the kilogram instead of the pound.

Small measures—tablespoons, teaspoons, and fractions thereof— are not likely to change. Indeed, the European system of calling for a soupspoon of sugar or a coffee spoon of vanilla is less accurate than our own, so hang onto your measuring spoons.

In the metric system, liquids are measured in measuring cups, but the calibrations are marked in liters, ½ liter, ¼ liter, and milliliters instead of in cups. Again, the system is more refined because each liter is subdivided into 10 deciliters, each deciliter into 10 centiliters, each centiliter into 10 milliliters. One advantage is immediately obvious: there will be no more such cumbersome measurements as ½ cup plus 1 tablespoon, or 1 cup minus 3 teaspoons.

To simplify the switch to metric, manufacturers of scales and measuring cups are expected to (and some already do) use dual markings, showing quantities in liters and cups for liquids, grams and ounces for weights. If there are gourmet kitchen shops in your area, you will find there already food scales and cups calibrated in both metric and U.S. measures.

To give you an idea of how the metric system works, we have included in the pages that follow a table of Metric Weights and Measures as well as conversion tables for weights, fluid and linear measures, the ones most apt to affect the cook.

METRIC WEIGHTS AND MEASURES

FLUID MEASURES

10 milliliters =1 centiliter
10 centiliters =1 deciliter
10 deciliters =1 liter
10 liters   =1 decaliter
10 decaliters =1 hectoliter
10 hectoliters=1 kiloliter

CUBIC MEASURES

1000 cubic millimeters=1 cubic cent.
1000 cubic centimeters=1 cubic deci.
1000 cubic decimeters =1 cubic meter

WEIGHTS

10 milligrams =1 centigram
10 centigrams =1 decigram
10 decigrams =1 gram
10 grams   =1 decagram
10 decagrams =1 hectogram
10 hectograms=1 kilogram

LINEAR MEASURES

10 millimeters =1 centimeter
10 centimeters =1 decimeter
10 decimeters =1 meter
10 meters   =1 decameter
10 decameters =1 hectometer
10 hectometers=1 kilometer

METRIC EQUIVALENTS OF U. S. WEIGHTS AND MEASURES

WEIGHTS (AVOIRDUPOIS)

5 grams=1 teaspoon (approx.)
28.35 grams=1 ounce
50 grams=1¾ ounces
100 grams=3½ ounces
227 grams=8 ounces
1000 grams (1 kilogram)=2 lbs. 3¼ oz.

FLUID MEASURES

1 deciliter=6 tablespoons+2 teaspoons
¼ liter=1 cup+2¼ teaspoons
½ liter=1 pint+4½ teaspoons
1 liter=1 quart+4 scant tablespoons
4 liters=1 gallon+1 scant cup
10 liters=2½ gallons+2½ cups (approx.)

LINEAR MEASURES

2½ centimeters=1 inch
1 meter (100 centimeters)=39⅓ inches

Some Abbreviations Used in European Cookbooks: g.=gram; kg.=kilogram; cm.=centimeter; c.=cuiller (spoon), usually qualified by type (coffee spoon, soupspoon, or tablespoon); dl.=deciliter.

TABLE OF EQUIVALENTS

Note: All measures are level.

Pinch or dash=less than ⅛ teaspoon
3 teaspoons=1 tablespoon
2 tablespoons=1 fluid ounce
1 jigger=1½ fluid ounces
4 tablespoons=¼ cup
5 tablespoons+1 teaspoon=⅓ cup
8 tablespoons=½ cup
10 tablespoons+2 teaspoons=⅔ cup
12 tablespoons=¾ cup
16 tablespoons=1 cup
1 cup=8 fluid ounces
2 cups=1 pint
2 pints=1 quart
⅘ quart=25.6 fluid ounces
1 quart=32 fluid ounces
4 quarts=1 gallon
2 gallons (dry measure)=1 peck
4 pecks=1 bushel

SOME FRACTIONAL MEASURES

½ of ¼ cup=2 tablespoons
½ of ⅓ cup=2 tablespoons+2 teaspoons
½ of ½ cup=¼ cup
½ of ⅔ cup=⅓ cup
½ of ¾ cup=¼ cup+2 tablespoons
⅓ of ¼ cup=1 tablespoon+1 teaspoon
⅓ of ⅓ cup=1 tablespoon+2⅓ tsp.
⅓ of ½ cup=2 tablespoons+2 tsp.
⅓ of ⅔ cup=3 tablespoons+1⅔ tsp.
⅓ of ¾ cup=¼ cup

SOME DRY WEIGHTS (AVOIRDUPOIS)

4 ounces=¼ pound
8 ounces=½ pound
16 ounces=1 pound

Some Emergency Substitutions

In a pinch, any of the following ingredient substitutions can be made successfully *except* in temperamental cakes, breads, cookies, or pastries.

Leavening:
– 1½ teaspoons phosphate or tartrate baking powder=1 teaspoon double-acting baking powder.
– ¼ teaspoon baking soda+½ teaspoon cream of tartar=1 teaspoon double-acting baking powder.
– ¼ teaspoon baking soda+½ cup sour milk=1 teaspoon double-acting baking powder *in liquid mixtures;* reduce recipe content by ½ cup.

Thickening:
– 1 tablespoon cornstarch=2 tablespoons all-purpose flour.
– 1 tablespoon potato flour=2 tablespoons all-purpose flour.
– 1 tablespoon arrowroot=2½ tablespoons all-purpose flour.
– 2 teaspoons quick-cooking

tapioca=1 tablespoon all-purpose flour (use in soups only).

Sweetening, Flavoring:
– 1¼ cups sugar+⅓ cup liquid= 1 cup light corn syrup or honey.
– 3 tablespoons cocoa+1 tablespoon butter=1 (1-ounce) square un- sweetened chocolate.
– ⅛ teapoon cayenne pepper=3–4 drops liquid hot red pepper seasoning.

Flour:
– 1 cup sifted all-purpose flour – 2 tablespoons=1 cup sifted cake flour.
– 1 cup+2 tablespoons sifted cake flour=1 cup sifted all-purpose flour.
– 1 cup sifted self-rising flour= 1 cup sifted all-purpose flour+1¼ teaspoons baking powder and a pinch of salt; when using, sub- stitute measure for measure for all-purpose flour, then omit baking powder and salt in recipe.

Dairy:
– ½ cup evaporated milk+½ cup water=1 cup whole milk.
– 1 cup skim milk+2 teaspoons melted butter=1 cup whole milk.
– 1 cup milk+1 tablespoon lemon juice or white vinegar=1 cup

sour milk (let stand 5–10 minutes before using).
– ¾ cup milk+¼ cup melted butter=1 cup light cream.

Eggs:
– 2 egg yolks=1 egg (for thick- ening sauces, custards).
– 2 egg yolks+1 tablespoon cold water=1 egg (for baking).
– 1½ tablespoons stirred egg yolks =1 egg yolk.
– 2 tablespoons stirred egg whites= 1 egg white.
– 3 tablespoons mixed broken yolks and whites=1 medium-size egg.

Miscellaneous:
– 1 cup boiling water+1 bouillon cube or envelope instant broth mix=1 cup broth.
– 1 teaspoon beef extract blended with 1 cup boiling water=1 cup beef broth.
– 1 cup fine bread crumbs=¾ cup fine cracker crumbs.
– ½ cup minced, plumped, pitted prunes or dates=½ cup seedless raisins or dried currants.
– 6 tablespoons mayonnaise blended with 2 tablespoons minced pickles or pickle relish=½ cup tartar sauce.

SOME USEFUL EQUIVALENTS

Food	Weight or Amount	Approximate Equivalent Volume or Number
Fruits		
Apples	1 pound	3–4 medium (2½–3 cups sliced)
Apricots (fresh)	1 pound	5–8 medium (2–2½ cups sliced)
Apricots (dried)	1 pound	4½ cups cooked
Bananas	1 pound	3–4 medium (1¼–1½ cups mashed)
Berries (except strawberries)	1 pound	2 cups
Cherries	1 quart	2 cups pitted
Cranberries	1 pound	1 quart sauce
Dates (unpitted)	1 pound	2 cups pitted
Dates (diced, sugared)	1 pound	2⅔ cups

Food	Weight or Amount	Approximate Equivalent Volume or Number
Figs (dried)	1 pound	3 cups chopped, 4 cups cooked
Grapes	1 pound	2½–3 cups seeded
Lemons	1 pound	5–6 medium (1 cup juice)
	1 lemon	3 T. juice, 2 t. grated rind
Limes	1 pound	6–8 medium (⅓–⅔ cup juice)
	1 lime	1–2 T. juice, 1 t. grated rind
Oranges	1 pound	3 medium (1 cup juice)
	1 orange	⅓ cup juice, 1 T. grated rind
Peaches, pears	1 pound	4 medium (2–2½ cups sliced)
Peaches (dried)	1 pound	4 cups cooked
Prunes	1 pound	4 cups cooked
Raisins (seedless)	1 pound	3 cups
Raisins (seeded)	1 pound	2½ cups
Rhubarb	1 pound, cut up	2 cups cooked
Strawberries	1 pint	1½–2 cups sliced

Vegetables

Food	Weight or Amount	Approximate Equivalent Volume or Number
Beans, peas (dried)	1 pound	2¼–2½ cups raw, 5–6 cups cooked
Cabbage	1 pound	4½ cups shredded
Green peas in the pod	1 pound	1½ cups shelled peas
Limas in the pod	1 pound	¾–1 cup shelled limas
Mushrooms	½ pound	3 cups sliced, 1 cup sliced sautéed
Onions (yellow)	1 medium	½ cup minced
Pepper (sweet green or red)	1 large	1 cup minced
Potatoes (Irish)	1 pound	3 medium, 1¾ cups mashed

Dairy, Fats

Food	Weight or Amount	Approximate Equivalent Volume or Number
Milk (whole, skim, buttermilk)	1 quart	4 cups
Milk (evaporated)	13 oz. can	1⅔ cups
	5¾ oz. can	¾ cup
Milk (sweetened, condensed)	14 oz. can	1⅓ cups
Cream, sour cream	½ pint	1 cup
Cheese (Cheddar, process)	½ pound	2 cups grated
Cheese (cottage)	½ pound	1 cup
Cheese (cream)	3 oz. package	6 tablespoons
Butter, margarine (not whipped)	1 pound	2 cups
	1 (¼ lb.) stick	½ cup
	⅛ (¼ lb.) stick	1 tablespoon
Lard	1 pound	2 cups
Eggs (whole)	4–6	1 cup
Egg whites	10–12	1 cup
Egg yolks	13–14	1 cup

Cereal, Pasta

Food	Weight or Amount	Approximate Equivalent Volume or Number
Buckwheat groats	1 cup raw	4 cups cooked
Bulgur wheat	1 cup raw	4 cups cooked

Food	Weight or Amount	Approximate Equivalent Volume or Number
Corn meal	1 pound	3 cups
	1 cup raw	4 cups cooked
Cornstarch	1 pound	3 cups
Flour (all-purpose)	1 pound	4 cups, sifted
Flour (cake)	1 pound	4½–5 cups, sifted
Flour (whole-wheat)	1 pound	3½ cups, unsifted
Oats (rolled)	1 pound	5 cups
	1 cup raw	1¾ cups cooked
Pasta:		
Macaroni	1 pound	4 cups raw, 8 cups cooked
Noodles	1 pound	6 cups raw, 7 cups cooked
Spaghetti	1 pound	4 cups raw, 7–8 cups cooked
Rice (regular)	1 pound	2¼ cups raw; 6¾ cups cooked
Rice (converted)	14 ounces	2 cups raw; 8 cups cooked
Rice (quick-cooking)	14 ounces	4 cups raw; 8 cups cooked
Rice (brown)	12 ounces	2 cups raw; 8 cups cooked
Rice (wild)	1 pound	3 cups raw; 11–12 cups cooked

Breads, Crackers, Crumbs

Bread	1 slice, fresh	1 cup soft crumbs or cubes
	1 slice, dry	⅓ cup dry crumbs
Soda crackers	28	1 cup fine crumbs
Graham crackers	15	1 cup fine crumbs
Chocolate wafers	19	1 cup fine crumbs
Vanilla wafers	22	1 cup fine crumbs

Sugar, Salt, Coffee

Coffee (ground)	1 pound	3⅓ cups grounds
Salt	1 pound	2 cups
Sugar (granulated)	1 pound	2 cups
Sugar (superfine)	1 pound	2¼–2½ cups
Sugar (brown)	1 pound	2¼–2⅓ cups
Sugar (confectioners')	1 pound	4½ cups, sifted

Nuts, Candy

Candied fruit and peel	1 pound	3 cups chopped
Coconut	1 pound	5–6 cups flaked or shredded
Unshelled Nuts:		
Almonds	1 pound	1¼ cups nut meats
Brazil nuts	1 pound	1½ cups nut meats
Peanuts	1 pound	2 cups nuts
Pecans	1 pound	2¼ cups nut meats
Walnuts	1 pound	1¾ cups nut meats
Shelled almonds, pecans,		
peanuts, walnuts	1 pound	4–4½ cups nut meats
Shelled Brazil nuts	1 pound	3 cups nut meats
Marshmallows	¼ pound	16 regular size

CHAPTER 2

SPECIAL OCCASION COOKING

ABOUT COOKING AT HIGH ALTITUDES

When you move from the seashore to the mountains, you will discover that potatoes take forever to boil, that deep-fat-fried foods, though charred outside, are raw inside, that a favorite cake falls flat. The altitude is to blame. At sea level, water boils at 212° F. But for every 550 feet above sea level, the boiling point drops by 1° F., so that at 7,000 feet water will boil at approximately 199° F. and at 15,000 feet at 186° F. This means that foods cooked at high altitudes never become as hot as those at sea level and thus require longer to cook. Other cooking methods are similarly affected, and adjustments must be made to compensate for the reduced atmospheric pressure.

Some General Tips for Cooking at High Altitudes:
– Whenever possible, use recipes developed specifically for high altitudes.
– Seek advice through county agricultural extension offices and home economics departments of local colleges and utility companies.
– Experiment, jotting down temperature and ingredient adjustments needed to make a particular recipe work.

When Boiling at High Altitudes:
– Speed cooking time by cutting food in small pieces.
– Keep the pot covered and add water frequently to keep it from boiling dry.

When Deep Fat Frying at High Altitudes:
– At altitudes of 1,000–5,000 feet, lower the recommended deep fat temperature by 5°–10° F.; at altitudes above 5,000 feet, lower it by 10°–15° F., so that food will cook through without burning. *Note:* No adjustments are needed for panfrying (sautéing).

When Canning at High Altitudes:
See chapter on canning for processing adjustments.

When Baking at High Altitudes:
– Beat eggs slowly, carefully; the higher the altitude, the quicker they will beat up—and *overbeat*.
– Reduce shortening content of

rich cakes and cookies about 1–2
tablespoons at altitudes above
5,000 feet.
– Do not use self-rising flour in
cakes at altitudes over 2,500
(leavening cannot be reduced as
needed because it is "built in").
– Watch yeast doughs closely; they
will rise surprisingly fast at high
elevations. A third rising may be
necessary to produce fine-textured
breads.
– Raise oven temperature 10°–
15° F. above recommended
settings at elevations from 2,500–
7,500 feet, 15°–25° F. above
recommended settings at altitudes
from 7,500–12,500 feet.

*About Making Candy at High
Altitudes:*
Cooked candies are so easily and
variously affected by high altitudes
it is best to use recipes worked
out specifically for high altitudes or
to alter cooking times of standard
recipes as local home economists
recommend.

About Cooking in Quantity

Cooking for a crowd, like any
large-scale operation, demands skill.
Elaborate affairs are best put in
the hands of caterers, but simple
school or church suppers can be
successfully brought off by well-
organized amateurs.

Some General Tips:
– Before considering a menu,
reconnoiter party site. What facilities
are there for cooking? For serving? Can food be prepared on the
spot or must it be brought in?
What about electrical circuits? Is
there danger of blackout if automatic coffee makers and electric
skillets or roasters are plugged in?

– Inventory available utensils, implements, tableware, and linens,
noting what will have to be
brought, borrowed, or rented (party
suppliers frequently rent tableware as well as tables and chairs).

Some Menu Planning Tips:
– Determine the best sort of menu,
considering cooking and serving
facilities. A buffet? A sit-down
supper? A tea or coffee? Who
will be on hand to help? For
utmost efficiency, plan on one
assistant for every 15–20 guests, two
assistants if a sit-down dinner.
– When choosing a menu, bear in
mind not only how many people
are to be served but *who*. Men,
for example, will want heartier
food than women; children will
be happier with hot dogs or hamburgers than with baked ham.
– Keep the menu simple, basing it
upon quantity recipes, not multiplied-
out family favorites. *Note:* Quantity
recipes appear throughout this
book; others are available through
major food companies, county
agricultural extension offices, home
economics departments of local
colleges or utilities.
– Include in the menu as many do-
ahead dishes as possible and, better
still, those that can be fully cooked,
then frozen. Avoid perishables
that invite food poisoning: creamed
mixtures, mayonnaise-rich fish,
fowl or pasta salads; custards,
cream-filled cakes or pastries.
– Remember that the party budget
includes not only food but over-
head as well (rentals, light and
laundry bills, cost of paper plates
and napkins, etc.). To break even,
compute total cost per person,
then, to play it safe, add an
additional 5–10 per cent to the
price of each plate. To make a
profit, set the price per plate 40–50

per cent higher than the computed cost per person.

Some Marketing Tips:
– Buy in bulk whenever possible, preferably from a wholesaler, grocer, or farmer who will give you a special price.
– Patronize markets that will speed preparations by slicing roasts, splitting chickens, or shaping hamburgers.
– Take advantage of timesaving instants; they cost more, true, but time is money.

Some Cooking and Serving Tips:
– Season quantity dishes sparingly.
– Prepare and serve food in easy-to-lift, easy-to-handle containers.
– When cooking several roasts in one pan, allow 2″–3″ between each so heat will circulate evenly. Also remember that a fully loaded oven will cook more slowly than a normally loaded one and allow slightly longer cooking times. Ideally, roasts should come from the oven about ½ hour before serving so that they can "rest" 15 minutes before being carved. This makes them juicier. Better have several supercarvers on hand, too, to speed service.
– Serve food in moderately large, *not Gargantuan,* dishes that will soon look messy and picked over.
– Set green salads out *undressed* (to retard wilting) and pass the dressings.
– For buffet service where there is no steam table, improvise one by setting serving dishes in baking pans of hot water.
– Cut pies or cakes or dish up desserts about 1 hour ahead, then cover and, if needed, refrigerate or set in freezer.

A Quantity Purchasing Guide

The difficulty in feeding dozens of people, obviously, is knowing how much food to buy. No two people eat alike; some stuff themselves with seconds and thirds while others simply sit around and pick at their plates. For that reason, dieticians have learned that the most accurate way of computing large amounts of food needed is by multiplying out average-size servings (¼ pound helpings of meat, for example, ½ cup portions of vegetables). Most quantity recipe yields are given in numbers of servings or portions, not in numbers of persons they will serve. The shopping guide below has been computed the same way and will provide enough food for 48 "average-size" portions. In a pinch (or on a tight budget), these amounts will serve 48 persons. But in this day of abundance, most people find average-size servings skimpy. Thus, the quantities of food in the following guide will serve 30–35 hungry men and women amply, slightly fewer if it's a stag affair, slightly more if a ladies' lunch. *Tip:* When buying a number of roasts or birds, choose those of similar size and shape so that they will cook in the same length of time.

Food	Approx. Quantity Needed for 48 Servings
BEVERAGES	
Fruit juice	4 (46 ounce) cans
Coffee (instant)	1 (4 ounce) jar+3 T.
Coffee (ground)	1¼ lbs.
Tea (instant)	1½ cups
Tea (bags)	4 doz.
Tea (leaf)	¼ lb.+3 T.

Food	Approx. Quantity Needed for 48 Servings
Coffee cream	1½ qts.
Sugar cubes	1 lb.
Lemon (for tea)	6 large

MEAT, POULTRY

Beef Roast (bone-in)	35 lbs.
Beef Roast (boneless)	25 lbs.
Hamburger (ground chuck)	12–16 lbs.
Ham (bone-in)	20–24 lbs.
Ham (boneless)	12–16 lbs.
Frankfurters	10–12 lbs.
Broiler-Fryers, Roasting Chickens	35–40 lbs.
Turkey (roast)	35–40 lbs.
Cooked Boneless Turkey Roast, Roll	9–10 lbs.
Uncooked Boneless Turkey Roast, Roll	16 lbs.

VEGETABLES

Frozen	4 (2½ lb.) pkgs. *or* 16 (10 ounce) pkgs.
Canned	2 (6½–7¼ lb.) cans (the No. 10 size)

SALADS

Lettuce hearts	12 medium heads
Lettuce leaves	6 medium heads
"Deli" Vegetable salad (ready mixed)	2 gals.
"Deli" potato salad	1½ gals.
"Deli" fruit salad	1 gal.

PASTA AND RICE

Spaghetti, noodles	6–8 lbs.
Rice (regular)	4½ lbs.
Rice (converted)	2½ (28 ounce) pkgs.
Rice (quick-cooking)	2½ (28 ounce) pkgs.

RELISHES

Cranberry sauce	6 (1 lb.) cans
Olives	2 qts.
Mustard	1 qt.
Ketchup	3 (14 ounce) bottles
Carrots (for strips)	2 lbs.

SANDWICHES: See Sandwiches in Quantity in the chapter on sandwiches.

DESSERT

Canned fruit	2 (6½–7¼ lb.) cans
Ice cream	2 gal. *or* 8–9 (1 qt.) bricks

MISCELLANEOUS

Sliced bread	1 pullman loaf+1 (1 lb.) loaf
French bread	3 (18″) loaves
Butter, margarine	1½ lbs.
Cottage cheese	6 lbs.
Potato chips	2 lbs.

About Cooking Out of Doors

Some Tips on Buying Outdoor Grills:

– Make the first grill a basic one; then, if family enjoyment justifies the splurge, buy a more luxurious model next time with all the extras—rotating windshield, motorized spit, automatic timers, temperature gauge, warming oven, deep fat fryer, storage shelves, cutting board, and counters.

– Choose sturdy, easy-to-clean-and-regulate equipment. Grills should be constructed of heavy, rust-resistant metal and contain adjustable fire beds and grids.

- Select a grill that suits the family's needs and size. The cooking area should be large enough to accommodate enough food for everyone at once but not so large there are vast empty spaces through which heat will escape, thus wasting fuel. For flexibility, choose a roll-around or fold-up grill; for permanence an all-weather gas or electric model.

Basic Cooking Tools Needed:
Long-Handled 2-Pronged Fork
Long-Handled Spatula or Turner
Long-Handled Basting Brush
Large and Small Tongs
Sharp Knife
Sturdy Meat Thermometer

Handy Extras:
Long-Handled Hinged Grill (for small foods)
Basket Broiler (for cut-up chicken, etc.)
Long Skewers (preferably with wood handles)
Cast-Iron Skillet
Kettle

Basic Fire Tools Needed:
Charcoal Tongs and Poker
Rake for Leveling Coals
Scoop for Adding and Removing Coals
Insulated Gloves
Sprinkler Can (for dousing flare-ups)
Bucket of Sand (for putting out grease fires)

Handy Extras:
Electric Fire Starter
Bellows

How to Build a Charcoal Fire:
(*Note:* Charcoal comes in a number of forms, but the briquettes are handiest to use; store in a dry place.)

- Lay fire ahead of time; light ½ hour before cooking if grill and amount of food to be cooked are small, 1 hour ahead if grill and food quantity are large.
- If firebox lacks dampers, line with foil to catch drips and simplify cleaning. If grill is a large one, arrange a layer of sand or coarse gravel on bottom before adding charcoal; it will insulate grill and save fuel.
- For General Purpose Grilling: Pile or spread enough briquettes to equal or slightly exceed surface area of food to be cooked and, if possible, make the layer deep enough to last throughout cooking.
- For Spit Cooking: Mound a deep bed of briquettes toward the back of the grill so that there is room in front for the drip pan and so that the spit, positioned to turn toward the back of the grill, will send drippings into the pan instead of the coals causing flare-ups. *Note:* Fires for spit cooking should be hot or moderately hot.
- Using a fire starter, preferably the one the grill manufacturer recommends, light the briquettes. Commercial starters come in liquid, jelly, and treated paper form. In addition, there are electric and gas starters. Never use gasoline or kerosene—they will ruin the flavor of the food. *Caution: Never add starter after a fire is lighted, even if the coals look dead; there's danger of a flash fire or explosion.*
- Let briquettes burn down to glowing coals covered with fine white ash, rearranging as necessary to provide more even heat and replenishing, as needed, by adding fresh briquettes around the fringes.
- Before adding food, test fire temperature as follows:

Type of Fire	Grill Thermometer Reading	"Hand Test" (Maximum Time Hand Can Be Held at Grill Level before Being Removed)
Moderate	300° F.	5 seconds
Moderately Hot	325° F.	4 seconds
Hot	350–75° F.	2–3 seconds

Note: Fire temperatures for grilling different kinds of food are recommended wherever appropriate in recipes throughout the book.

– To Cool a Hot Fire: Close grill dampers, spread coals out over fire bed in a checkerboard pattern. If still too hot, shovel some coals into a sand bucket, and if that doesn't cool the fire, remove any food on grill, sprinkle coals lightly with water and when steam subsides return food to grill.

– To Heat Up a Cool Fire: Open dampers, stir coals, knocking off the white ash, then cluster in center of grill; tuck a few charcoal chips underneath hot coals and add fresh briquettes around the edges.

– For a Fresh Woodsy Fragrance: Toss a few dampened hardwood chips onto the coals, preferably hickory, apple, or pear; avoid pine or resinous woods, which will send a turpentine flavor through the food. *Note:* For special savor, scatter dried sage, thyme, or rosemary *lightly* over the coals; especially good with chicken or lamb.

Note: Outdoor cooking times are extremely variable, being affected by outdoor temperature, gusts of wind, type of grill and charcoal used. Usually, it is possible to speed or slow grilling by raising or lowering the grids or spit. If not, cool or heat up the fire as directed earlier. The grilling times included in the meat, poultry, and seafood chapters should be used as guides only.

Caution: Make sure coals are out before leaving a grill; cover with sand or, if you want to save partially burned charcoal, scoop coals into water, then fish out and spread to dry.

About Pit Cooking

Unless you have a strong back and willing crew, save pit roasting for the pros. It is heavy work. But for a simple clambake on the beach: Dig a saucer-shaped hole about 2 feet deep and 4–5 feet across, line with nonporous rocks, build a bonfire on top, and let it burn about 3 hours until rocks are sizzling hot. Rake coals away, brush ashes aside, then blanket rocks with about 6 inches of seaweed, preferably the succulent rockweed, which will provide lots of steam. Next, layer in the food, beginning with unshucked clams and mussels, then adding corn in the husk, unpeeled potatoes and peeled onions, whole lobsters, disjointed young chickens, separating the layers with more rockweed. Add a final blanket of rockweed, cover all with a damp tarpaulin, and weight down with sand. Let steam

1–3 hours, 1 hour if shellfish only are being cooked, 2½–3 if vegetables and chicken are being cooked along with the shellfish. Then dig up and enjoy!

About Camp and Galley Cooking

Cooking at a campsite is scarcely roughing it these days. Nor is cooking in a minuscule galley aboard a bobbing inboard. There are compact, fully portable camp stoves that run on gasoline or liquid propane (LP), fold-up stoves fueled by canned heat, gimbal stoves guaranteed not to tilt when the boat does, making it possible to bake and broil on location as well as heat things up. Moreover, there are portable refrigerators and freezers (gas or electricity powered, some of which can be plugged in wherever there are outlets), not to mention a rash of insulated, welterweight carryalls that will keep hot foods hot, cold foods cold, and frozen foods frozen during hours of transit. It is impractical here to do more than generalize, not only because space is limited but also because new items are being introduced faster than they can be described. Suffice it to say that nearly anything that can be cooked at home can also be cooked on location, as a stroll through a sporting goods store or catalogue quickly proves.

CHAPTER 3

THE LARDER

Today's larder includes the cupboard, the pantry, the refrigerator, the freezer, and the spice shelf. Storing it efficiently demands skill. Before setting out for the market, familiarize yourself with the ingredients you use and need most.

ABOUT INGREDIENTS

Science continues to revolutionize cooking *and* eating; each year supermarket shelves grow longer, accommodating new products that bewilder the shopper with an infinite variety of choices. What is the best buy? The all-purpose, the presifted, or the self-rising flour? Corn, peanut, olive, safflower, or blended vegetable oil? The following list is intended to explain the differences between certain basic ingredients. Other ingredients—and some not so basic—can be found elsewhere in the book in chapters where they are most frequently used: yeast in the breads chapter, for instance, and baking powders in the section on cakes (consult the Index for page numbers).

Dairy Products

Milk: Nearly all milk sold today is *pasteurized. (Certified milk,* sometimes sold locally, is raw milk handled and bottled under strict sanitary conditions.) *Pasteurized milk* has been heated, then quick-cooled to destroy microorganisms of spoilage, thereby improving keeping qualities. It is available in a variety of fluid forms.

Fluid Milks

Homogenized Milk: Uniformly smooth rich milk that will stay uniformly smooth and rich (no cream floating to the top) because the butter particles have been broken up and dispersed evenly throughout.

Skim Milk: Whole milk with 98–99 per cent of the butterfat removed.

Fortified Milk: Whole or skim milk enriched with vitamins (commonly A and D) and/or minerals and protein.

Flavored Milk: Chocolate or other flavored whole, skim, or partly skim milk. Such milks often have sugar, salt, and stabilizers added. (Also available powdered as drink mixes.)

Buttermilk: Originally the residue left after churning butter, but today a simulated version, usually made with skim milk and flecked with butter.

Acidophilus Milk: A particularly tart buttermilk, acid but easy to digest. A powdered form is sold at drugstores.

Low-Sodium Milk: A special diet milk in which 90 per cent of the sodium has been replaced by potassium. The fluid form is available only in limited amounts, primarily on the West Coast. Powdered and canned varieties are stocked by drugstores.

Yogurt: Whole or partially skimmed milk fermented into a thick creamy curd; plain yogurt is high in protein and calcium, relatively low in calories (about 120 per cup). Also available in a variety of flavors.

Canned Milks

Evaporated Milk: Homogenized milk with about 60 per cent of the water removed and vitamin D added. Mixed ½ and ½ with water, it has the consistency and food value of whole milk, for which it may be substituted. Use full strength to increase the creaminess of sauces and soups, to coat chicken or chops before crumbing or breading, to top fruits and puddings.

Sweetened Condensed Milk: A sticky-sweet evaporated blend of whole milk and sugar, usually used to sweeten beverages, to make candy, ice creams, and other desserts.

Powdered Milks

Nonfat Dry Milk: Whole milk from which almost all water and butterfat have been removed, processed to dissolve rapidly in liquid. To reconstitute, follow package directions. One cup milk powder will make about 3 cups fluid milk, best when covered and refrigerated overnight to develop full flavor. Reconstituted dry milk can be substituted for the fresh; as powder, it can be added to hamburgers, meat loaves, and mashed potatoes to enrich flavor and nutritive value. *Whole Dry Milk Powder* is also available, but in limited quantities. Because of its butterfat content, it must be kept refrigerated.

Cream and Cream Substitutes

Heavy (Whipping) Cream: Rich and thick (35–40 per cent butterfat) and thicker still after a brief stretch in the refrigerator.

Light (Coffee) Cream: With half the butterfat (18–20 per cent) of heavy cream, light cream is a better all-purpose cream, the choice for creaming coffee and tea. It will not whip.

Half-and-Half: A ½ and ½ mixture of milk and light cream (12–15 per cent butterfat). It will not whip but can be substituted for light cream in puddings and ice creams to shave calories a bit.

Sour Cream: A thick, silky-smooth commercial product made by souring light cream (it has the same butterfat content). A newer entry is *Half-and-Half Sour Cream* made from a ½ and ½ mixture of milk and light cream. It has about half the calories of regular sour cream.

Powdered (Instant) Cream: A mixture of dehydrated light cream and milk solids, with stabilizer added. Use as label directs.

Pressurized Whipped Cream: Sweetened cream, emulsifiers, and stabilizer in an aerosol can that whip into snowy drifts at the touch of a button.

Cream Substitutes: Nondairy products in liquid, powder, and pressurized form, usually composed of hydrogenated vegetable oils, sugar, emulsifiers, and preservatives. Depending upon form, these may be used in beverages, in cooking, and as dessert toppings.

Fats and Oils

Butter: Federal requirements demand that butter be 80 per cent butterfat. In addition, it is federally graded as to flavor, color, texture, and body, the finest quality being US Grade AA (or US Grade Score 93, the figure representing the grader's quality points). The remaining grades, in descending order, are A (US Score 92), B (Score 90), and C (Score 89). The AA and A are the grades most commonly available. Butter may be (and often is) artificially colored; it may be *salted* or *unsalted*, often called *sweet butter*, though true sweet butter is any butter—salted or unsalted—churned from sweet cream instead of sour. The newest form of butter is the *whipped*, which has simply been beaten full of air to soften it into a better spreading consistency. Whipped butter is lighter in weight than standard butter—6 sticks per pound as opposed to 4—and it must not be substituted for standard butter in recipes.

Margarine: A butter substitute compounded of vegetable (primarily soybean) and animal oils. To make margarine taste more like butter, cream and milk are sometimes added; to make it look more like butter, yellow food coloring is blended in. Margarine is frequently fortified with vitamins A and D and may contain preservatives and emulsifiers as well. Specialty margarines include *diet spreads,* the polyunsaturated, the *soft* and the *whipped* and a *no-burn* variety. *Note:* Margarine has slightly greater shortening power than butter and should not be substituted for it in temperamental cake, cookie, or pastry recipes.

Vegetable Shortening: Fluffy-soft all-purpose cooking fats made by pumping hydrogen into vegetable oils; usually snow white but sometimes tinted yellow. These are particularly good for deep fat frying because of their high smoking point; superior, too, for making pastries, cookies, and cakes. Do not refrigerate because the shortening may break down.

Lard: Pork fat, rendered and clarified. It is often hydrogenated and stabilized with emulsifiers and preservatives so that no refrigeration is needed (read label carefully and store as directed). Because lard has subtle meat flavor and a more brittle texture than other shortenings, it is particularly suited to making pastries.

Cooking and Salad Oils: The two are the same *except* that certain oils—olive, for one—taste better in salads than others and, having relatively low smoking points, are poor choices for deep fat frying. Oils are pressed from myriad vegetables, nuts, seeds, and fruits. The best all-round cooking-salad oils are *corn, cottonseed, peanut,* and *soybean* or blends of these. Lightest of all is the nearly colorless *safflower oil,* favored by the cholesterol conscious. Among the other oils available are *coconut, palm, sesame* (a dark, heavy Oriental favorite), *sunflower seed, walnut,* and *almond oils.* To Mediterranean Europe, however, oil is olive oil. No other will do. *Virgin olive oil,* highly esteemed by connoisseurs, is unrefined oil from the first pressing. Subsequent pressings yield coarser, stronger oils, sometimes with a greenish cast (a sure sign of strong flavor). The most delicate of all is the champagne-pale (and champagne-priced) olive oil of France, best reserved for very special salads. Italy, Spain, and Greece all produce good all-round olive oils —straw-colored, aromatic, but not overly strong. Whenever possible, buy olive oil by the can rather than by the bottle so that it's shielded from the light and does not go stale. If you have neither the taste nor the pocketbook for pure olive oil, mix ½ and ½ with another vegetable oil. It's best not to refrigerate olive oil—or, for that matter, other oils; they will harden and turn cloudy. However, if you buy large bottles and use oil only occasionally, you may want to refrigerate the oil to keep it from turning rancid. When using, measure out only what you need and let come to room temperature—most of the cloudiness will disappear. *Cooking Tip:* When sautéing with olive oil, keep the heat a shade lower than usual to reduce spattering.

Wheat Flours

The milling industry is well into the Age of Specialization, grinding out flours in a variety of textures and types. The plain, white general-purpose flours, as required by the *Federal Enrichment Program,* have had B vitamins (thiamine, riboflavin, and niacin) and iron added so that their food value equals that of whole wheat flour. Some millers further enrich their flours by adding vitamins A and D and calcium.

All-Purpose Flour: The everything flour, equally good for baking cakes, pies, breads, and cookies, for thickening sauces and gravies, and for dredging foods to be fried. It is milled from hard and soft wheats and is *enriched.*

Bread Flour: An *enriched* hard wheat flour with a high content of the protein (gluten) needed to give bread its framework.

Cake Flour: An *unenriched* superfine flour milled from soft wheat. Too delicate for general use, it produces cakes of exceedingly fine and feathery grain.

Pastry Flour: Neither as coarse as all-purpose flour nor as fine as cake flour, pastry flour has just enough body to produce flaky-tender piecrusts. It is not as widely distributed as it once was. Most people today use all-purpose flour for pastry.

Self-Rising Flour: Enriched all-purpose flour to which baking powder and salt have been added. It can be substituted for all-purpose flour in recipes that call for baking powder and salt; to use, measure out the quantity of flour called for and omit the baking powder and salt. *Note:* To be effective, self-rising flour must be strictly fresh.

Presifted Flour: A timesaving, *enriched,* all-purpose flour that does not require sifting before measuring *except* for tall and tender cakes or other critical (easily-thrown-off-balance) recipes.

Instant-Type Flour: The sauce and gravy specialist, a granular white flour that blends into hot or cold liquids without lumping. It needs no sifting before measuring. Use for thickening only, not for baking or dredging, *except* as label instructs. *Not enriched* as a rule.

Whole Wheat Flour (Graham Flour): Unrefined, unbleached flour containing the iron- and vitamin B-rich wheat bran and germ. Never sift.

Gluten Flour: High-protein, low-starch (and low-calorie) flour milled from hard wheat; it is used to make gluten and other "slimming" breads.

Bran, Cracked Wheat, Wheat Germ Flours: All-purpose flours to which bran, cracked wheat, or wheat germ has been added; do not sift. Because of their coarse textures, these flours are particularly suitable for breads.

Note: Other wheat products (semolina, etc.) are discussed along with other grains in the chapter on cereals and rice.

Other Flours

Cereals other than wheat—*barley, buckwheat, corn, oats, rice,* and *rye*—are also milled into rough and smooth flours. They are available at specialty food stores, primarily, and most of them bake into supremely good breads. In addition, there are *noncereal flours: potato, soy,* and *lima bean, peanut, cottonseed, tapioca,* and *carob* (the St.-John's-bread of the Mediterranean). These, however, with the exception of potato flour, which makes exceptionally fine angel cake and is a splendid thickener of sauces and gravies, are seldom used solo but blended with other flours or foods to boost flavor and nutritive value.

Note: As a thickener, potato flour, like cornstarch and arrowroot, will thin down if overheated.

Thickeners

Arrowroot: Extracted from a tropical tuber once used to treat arrow wounds, this delicate, flavorless starch thickens without turning cloudy. Use it when a glistening, jewel-like glaze is needed.

Cornstarch: Fine white starch ground from the hearts of dried corn. It has about twice the thickening power of all-purpose flour, *but will thin down after thickening if overstirred or overcooked and will refuse to thicken at all if mixture is too acid or too sweet.* Handle carefully, as label directs.

Flour: See all-purpose and instant-type flours.

Note: Additional information on starch thickeners can be found in the chapter on sauces, gravies and butters.

Leavenings

Baking Powders: See the chapter on cakes.

Baking Soda: Pure bicarbonate of soda used to leaven acid batters and doughs (those containing molasses, sour milk or buttermilk, vinegar).

Cream of Tartar: A fine white powder crystallized from grape acid used in commercial baking powders. It will also whiten and "cream" candies and frostings, increase the volume and stability of beaten egg whites.

Yeasts: See the chapter on breads.

Sugars and Syrups

Granulated (White) Sugar: Highly refined, free-pouring, 99+ per cent pure all-purpose sugar crystallized from sugar cane or beets. As a convenience, it is also pressed into cubes.

Superfine (Castor) Sugar: Extra-fine-grain, quick dissolving sugar. A boon to drink mixing, it also makes unusually good cakes and frostings.

Confectioners' (10X, Powdered) Sugar: Pulverized sugar mixed with cornstarch; particularly suited to making uncooked candies and frostings. Always sift before measuring.

Brown Sugar: Soft, molasses-flavored crystals left behind after the refining of granulated sugar. Brown sugar has a higher mineral content than granulated sugar. The *light brown* is more delicate than the *dark.* Newest form: free-pouring granules.

Raw Sugar: Sugary residue left in the vat after molasses is run off. It is crude, coarse-grained, and brown. It contains more minerals, notably potassium, than refined sugar. Potassium, however, is not a mineral apt to be lacking in the normal diet.

Maple Sugar: Crystallized, concentrated maple syrup.

Two Special Sugars, Both Decorative: Rock Candy, several-carat-big sugar crystals on a string; *colored granulated sugars.*

Noncaloric Sweeteners: Liquid, tablet, and powdered calorie-free sugar substitute (saccharine).

Corn Syrups: Light and *dark syrups* made from hydrolyzed cornstarch.

Maple Syrup: The concentrated sap of the sugar maple tree. Also available: *Maple Blended Syrup,* a mixture of maple and other syrups, and *Buttered Maple Syrup.*

Molasses: Available in many grades from the smooth, sweet, dark amber syrup extracted directly from sugar cane juices to the rougher, browner, not-so-sweet by-products of sugar refining. *Blackstrap,* the darkest and coarsest and least sweet of all, amounts to the dregs; it is not, as some believe, a nutritional powerhouse because some of its minerals are not assimilable by the body. Any grade of molasses can be *sulfured* or *unsulfured* depending upon whether sulfur was used in the sugar refining. The unsulfured is preferable because of its lighter color and more full-bodied cane-sugar flavor.

Sorghum: A molasses-like syrup extracted from sorghum.

Honey: Flower nectar that has been processed and condensed by bees. Flavors vary according to the flowers bees have fed upon; among those considered especially choice are heather honey, sourwood, rosemary, and the famous Hymettus (from the wild thyme carpeting the slopes of Mt. Hymettus near Athens). Honey may be liquid and golden, creamy and brown, or still in the comb. Do not refrigerate; the honey will turn grainy. Honey averages about 20 calories more per tablespoon than granulated sugar, but contains only the merest traces of vitamins and minerals despite faddist claims to the contrary.

Chocolate and Cocoa

Unsweetened Chocolate: The bitter, all-purpose, unadulterated chocolate rendered out of ground, roasted cocoa beans.

Semisweet Chocolate: Bitter chocolate sweetened with sugar and softened somewhat with extra cocoa butter. It is ideal for dipping because it melts smoothly and rehardens without streaking. Also now available as *semisweet chocolate bits.* Because they are lightly glazed, they hold their shape during baking.

Milk Chocolate: A blend of chocolate, sugar, and powdered milk meant to be eaten out-of-hand. The newest form: lightly glazed *milk chocolate bits,* similar to the semisweet but sweeter, milder, milkier.

Dark German (Sweet Cooking) Chocolate: Sweetened pure bitter chocolate, darker and more brittle than the semisweet because it lacks the extra cocoa butter.

No-Melt Unsweetened Chocolate: A pudding-thick blend of cocoa, vegetable oil, and preservatives ready to mix into candies, frostings, and batters. Each 1-ounce packet equals 1 (1 ounce) square unsweetened chocolate.

Swiss White Chocolate: Sweetened cocoa butter.

Cocoa: All-purpose chocolate powder ground from roasted cocoa beans. It contains virtually no cocoa butter, therefore fewer calories and saturated fats.

Dutch-Type Cocoa: Cocoa processed with alkali to mellow the flavor and darken the color.

Instant Cocoa Mixes: Assorted blends of cocoa, sugar, flavorings, emulsifiers, and sometimes milk powder processed to dissolve instantly in beverages.

Salt

Table (Cooking) Salt: A fine salt manufactured from rock salt and brine. It may be *iodized* (have sodium or potassium iodide added as a goiter preventive) or *plain;* often contains desiccants to keep it free-flowing.

Kosher Salt: Originally a coarse salt made under rabbinical supervision but more commonly today a generic term meaning any coarse natural sea salt. Alternate names are *Dairy, Cheese,* and *Flake Salt.*

Pickling Salt: Pure fine-grain salt with no additives.

Rock (Ice Cream) Salt: Coarse, crude salt used in freezing ice cream.

Flavored Salts: The repertoire is lengthy, including combinations of dehydrated vegetables and salt, charcoal and salt, assorted herbs, spices, and salt.

Pepper See The Herb and Spice Shelf.

Commercial Condiments, Sauces, and Seasonings

Worcestershire Sauce: A secret, spicy blend of soy sauce, shallots, anchovies, vinegar, garlic, molasses, and other ingredients designed to pep up meats and savory dishes.

Soy Sauce: Salty brown sauce extracted from lightly fermented soybeans.

Steak Sauce: A generic name for various thick brown bottled sauces concocted specifically to serve over broiled steaks and chops.

Liquid Hot Red Pepper Seasoning: Another generic name used to identify the incendiary sauces made of tabasco peppers, vinegar, and salt. Use drop by drop.

Liquid Gravy Browner: A blend of caramel, vegetable protein, vinegar, salt, and other flavorings used to brown gravies and sauces and impart a lusty meaty flavor.

Prepared (*Wet, Bottled*) *Mustards:* There are dozens of blends, some sunny and mild, some brown and spicy, some superhot.

The Milds: Prepared Mild Yellow Mustard (the old hot-dog favorite); *Prepared Spicy Yellow* (or *Brown*) *Mustard* (spicy but not fiery); *Dijon* and *Bordeaux* (spicy French wine-flavored mustards); *Dijon-type* (in the style of—but not necessarily from—Dijon), and *Creole* (a pungent beige blend showing tiny flecks of spice).

The Hots (all peppery and brown): *English, Düsseldorf, German,* and *Bahamian Mustard.* Pretty hot stuff, too, is the American horseradish-mustard mixture.

Note: A discussion of whole and powdered mustards follows in the Herb and Spice Chart.

Some Marketing Tips

– Make a shopping list, setting down first any staples in low supply, then adding those foods needed in preparing the week's meals. Consider seasonal specials—both nonperishables or "freezables"—and buy in bulk whenever storage space permits.

– Buy only what quantities your family can use without waste or what can be stored properly in cupboard, pantry, refrigerator, or freezer.

– Read package labels carefully. By law they must include: net weight, all ingredients, including such additives as vitamins, minerals, preservatives, emulsifiers, artificial sweetener, flavoring, and coloring; identification of dietetic properties (sugar-free or sugar-reduced, low sodium, etc.). The latest ruling states that, if any food contains more artificial flavoring than natural, the name of the food must indicate that fact (i.e., Maple-Flavor Syrup rather than Maple Syrup). Helpful labels may also list proportions of saturated, monounsaturated, and polyunsaturated fats and calorie counts; they may indicate number of servings, provide descriptions of the food (diced, sliced, whole, etc.), and offer a recipe. When buying, suit the style of the food to the use: Why pay more for fancy whole tomatoes if they will be made into sauce?

– When buying "instants," and preprepared foods, consider whether the extra cost is worth the time saved.

– Reject bulging or leaking cans; dented ones are all right provided they do not bulge or leak. Also reject soft or uneven packages of frozen food, ripped or torn packages of cereals, flours, pasta, breads, and crackers.

– When you discover a food that is spoiled or less than top quality, return it to the grocer. Most markets welcome valid complaints because

they are then able to trace and correct the difficulty.
— Hurry all food home, unload and store properly, using the following charts as guides.

About Storing Food in the Freezer

Note: Packaging and preparation tips are covered fully in the chapter on canning and freezing. Also what to do if the power should fail and freezer should be off for some hours.

General Tips:
— Check commercial frozen foods before storing, overwrapping any torn or damaged packages in foil or plastic food wrap.
— If package has been badly damaged and food exposed, use food as soon as possible.
— Date packages as they go into the freezer and use the oldest ones first.
— Update freezer inventory with every new addition.

About Storing Food in the Refrigerator

General Tips:
— Clean refrigerator out regularly, preferably before marketing.
— Store new supplies behind the old so the old will be used first.
— Group often used foods together in accessible spots. If possible, reserve a special corner for leftovers.
— *If power fails,* keep refrigerator door shut; food will remain cool several hours.

About Storing Meats, Poultry, Seafood:
— Never wash before storing.
— Always remove market wrapping from fresh uncooked meats, poultry, or seafood and *rewrap loosely* in wax paper or foil unless directed otherwise. *Exception:* Prepackaged meats to be cooked within 2 days.
— Store in coldest part of refrigerator (it varies from model to model; check manufacturer's instruction booklet).

MAXIMUM RECOMMENDED STORAGE TIME FOR FROZEN FOODS AT 0° F.

Because the type of food and packaging and the number of times a freezer is opened all affect the keeping quality of frozen foods, storage times can only be approxi-mate. Use foods *before* maximum time is up; they are unlikely to spoil immediately afterward, but their quality will deteriorate rapidly.

Food	Storage Time in months
Fresh, uncooked meats	
Beef, veal, lamb roasts, steaks, and chops	12
Ground beef, veal, lamb	4–6
Beef, veal, lamb liver, heart, and kidneys	3–4
Pork roasts, chops	4–6
Ground pork, fresh sausage meat	1–3
Pork liver	1–2

Food	Storage Time in months
Smoked and Cured Meats	
Ham, slab bacon, frankfurters	1–3
Sausages	1–2
Cooked Meats	
Beef, veal, and lamb roasts	4–6
Pork roasts	2–4
Stews, meats in gravy or sauce, meat loaves and balls, meat pies, hash	2–4

Fresh, Uncooked Poultry	
Chicken	12
Turkey, duckling, goose, game birds	6
Giblets	2–3
Cooked Poultry	
Chicken	4–6
Turkey, duckling, goose	2–4

Fresh, Uncooked Seafood	
Lean, white fish	4–6
Oily, gamy fish	3–4
Shucked clams, oysters, scallops, shrimp	3–4
Cooked Seafood	
Fish (all kinds)	1–2
Crab and lobster meat	2–3
Shrimp	1–2
Shellfish in sauce (Newburg, thermidor, etc.)	1

Vegetables	12

Herbs	6

Dairy Products	
Butter	6–8
Cream (whipped)	3–4
Hard cheeses	6–8
Ice cream, sherbet, ices	1–2

Margarine	12

Eggs (Yolks, Whites)	12

Breads	
Baked yeast breads and rolls	6–8
Baked quick breads	2–4

Food	Storage Time in months
Sandwiches (avoid mayonnaise or cream cheese based spreads, jelly or hard-cooked-egg fillings)	2–3 weeks

Cakes and Cookies

Food	Storage Time in months
Baked cakes and cookies (unfrosted)	6–8
Baked cakes and cookies (frosted or filled)	2–4
Cookie Dough	2–4

Pastries

Food	Storage Time in months
Unbaked pie shells	6–8
Unbaked pies (fruit or mince)	6–8
Baked pies (fruit or mince)	2–4

Note: The storage chart includes only those homemade cakes and pastries suitable for home freezing. There are, of course, commercially frozen cheesecakes, cream and custard pies—silky-smooth ones—but food companies use stabilizers unavailable to the home cook.

About Storing Vegetables, Fruits:
– Wash only if chart recommends it.
– Unless chart directs otherwise, vegetables to be stored in the hydrator should be put in perforated plastic bags, those to be stored on shelves in plain plastic bags.

About Storing Leftover, Cooked Foods:
– Quick-cool hot food (in an ice or ice water bath) and package airtight.
– Remove any stuffing from meat, poultry, or seafood and wrap separately.
– Leftover canned foods can be covered and stored in the can 3–4 days.

MAXIMUM RECOMMENDED STORAGE TIME FOR REFRIGERATED FOOD

Note: Use following times as a guide only, checking highly perishable foods every day or so. Refrigerator load, how often door is opened, food packaging all affect storage time.

Food	Special Storage Tips	Storage Time
Fresh, Uncooked Meats		
Roasts		5 days
Steaks, chops		3–5 days
Ground meat, stew meat		2 days
Variety meats		1–2 days

Food	Special Storage Tips	Storage Time
Cured and Smoked Meats		
Ham (roasts), Bacon		1 week
Sliced ham, luncheon meats, sausages	Leave in original wrapper or wrap loosely in plastic food wrap. Store canned hams as labels direct.	2–3 days
Frankfurters		4–5 days
Cooked Meats, Leftovers		3–4 days
Fresh, Uncooked Poultry	Store giblets separately in a plastic bag.	2–3 days
Cooked Poultry, Leftovers	Remove stuffing and wrap airtight separately.	2 days
Fresh, Uncooked Seafood		
Fish	Clean and dress* before storing. Wrap loosely.	1–2 days
Live lobsters, crabs	Have claws pegged and animals packed in seaweed in double-thick moistureproof bag. Pop bundle into a large plastic bag and refrigerate. Do not cover animals with water; they will die.	6–8 hours
Shrimp	Store shelled or unshelled in plastic bags.	1–2 days
Clams, mussels, oysters, scallops	Store the unshucked in plastic bags, the shucked in their liquor in airtight containers.	1 day
Smoked and Pickled Fish		1–2 weeks
Cooked Seafood, Leftovers		1–2 days
Raw Vegetables		
Artichokes, beans, broccoli, Brussels sprouts, cauliflower, chayotes, eggplant, fennel, peas (in the pod), peppers	Remove any blemished leaves, stalks.	3–5 days
Asparagus	If limp, remove ½″ stems; stand in cold water 1 hour.	3–4 days
Beets, carrots, parsnips	Remove all but 1″ tops; rinse if dirty.	2 weeks
Cabbage, cardoons, celeriac, celery	Remove blemished leaves, stalks; wash celery if dirty.	3–7 days
Corn on the cob	Store in the husk in plastic bags.	1 day
Cucumbers, summer squash	Wipe if very dirty.	1 week
Leeks, scallions, salsify	Trim roots, unusable tops; rinse salsify.	3–7 days

Food	Special Storage Tips	Storage Time
Lettuces, all salad greens, spinach, dark leafy greens }	Wash and dry well. Do not break up salad greens until salad-making time.	3–8 days
Mushrooms	Do not trim or wipe; cover loosely.	1 week
New potatoes, breadfruit	*Note:* Potatoes need not be refrigerated, but cold storage makes them stay sweet longer.	1 week
Okra	Wash if very dirty; dry.	3–4 days
Plantain (dead ripe only)	*Note:* Ripen the green at room temperature.	1–2 days
Tomatoes (dead ripe only)	Store unwrapped, uncovered. *Note:* Slightly underripe tomatoes can be ripened in the refrigerator; takes 8–12 days.	2–3 days
Cooked Vegetables, Leftovers		2–4 days
Fresh, Ripe Fruits	(all except avocados, bananas, melons, pineapple, stored at room temperature)	
Berries	Discard bruised berries; cover loosely.	2–3 days
Soft fruits	Discard damaged fruits; cover loosely or store in perforated plastic bags.	3–7 days
Firm fruits	Same as for soft fruits.	1–2 weeks
Leftover Raw or Cooked Fruits	Store airtight.	3–5 days
Fruit Juices (fresh, canned, frozen)	Store in airtight containers.	5–7 days
Dairy Products		
Fresh milk, cream, buttermilk }	Store in original or airtight nonmetal container.	3–4 days
Sour cream, yogurt	Same as for milk.	1 week
Canned milk	After opening, store covered in original container.	10 days
Cottage, cream, process cheese, spreads	Store airtight in original container.	1–3 weeks
Semi-hard and hard, mild and strong cheese	Butter cut edges to prevent drying; double wrap in foil or plastic food wrap. For long storage, wrap in vinegar-moistened cheesecloth (keep cloth moist). Cut off mold (it is harmless, merely unattractive).	3–9 months
Cheese scraps	Grate and store in an airtight jar.	2–3 weeks

Food	Special Storage Tips	Storage Time
Butter	Store in original wrapper in "butter keeper section."	1–2 weeks
Eggs		
Whole raw	Store small end down, covered, in egg keeper or carton.	10 days
Raw whites, broken eggs	Store in airtight nonmetal container.	1 week
Raw yolks	Cover with cool water and store in airtight jar.	2–3 days
Hard cooked	Store in the shell or shelled and individually wrapped in foil or plastic food wrap. Label eggs "cooked."	10 days
Miscellaneous Foods		
Brown sugar	To keep moist, store box in airtight plastic bag in hydrator.	3–6 months
Coffee (ground)	Store airtight in original can.	3–4 weeks
Custards	Quick-cool, cover, and refrigerate at once.	1 day
Custard and cream cakes and pies	Quick-cool, cover loosely with plastic food wrap, and refrigerate at once.	3–5 days
Drippings	Store in tightly covered can or jar.	2 months
Gravies, sauces	Quick-cool, cover, and refrigerate at once.	2–3 days
Lard	Store in original carton or wrapped airtight. *Note:* New types need no refrigeration; read label carefully.	2 weeks– 2 months
Maple syrup (genuine without preservative)	After opening, store airtight.	2–4 months
Margarine	Store in original wrapper.	2–4 weeks
Nuts (shelled)	Store in airtight jar.	3–4 months
Leftover cooked rice, cereal, pasta, puddings, gelatins	Cool rapidly and store tightly covered.	3–4 days
Relishes, ketchup, pickles, mayonnaise	After opening, store airtight.	2–3 months

About Storing Food in Cupboard or Pantry

"Pantry" is a marvelously old-fashioned word, calling to mind trips to Grandmother's house with its bright shelf parade of home-preserved foods. But a pantry is not a thing of the past. It is as essential today as a refrigerator or freezer. Ideally, it should be a step away from the kitchen—big and airy, reasonably cool, dry, and dark. Cupboard shelves, too, should be well ventilated, cool, dry, and dark.

General Tips:
— Keep pantry and cupboards scrupulously clean, protecting shelves with spill-resistant, easy-to-clean coated paper or vinyl shelf liners. Reline shelves frequently and in the interim wipe regularly with a weak vinegar-water solution to keep ants, roaches, and silverfish at bay.
— Check often for food spoilage (bulging or leaky cans, frothing bottles), for mice (tattered packages are a sure sign if there are also droppings), weevils, roaches, ants, or silverfish. *When Pests Attack:* Clear the shelves, destroying any infested foods (flours, cornstarch, cereals, nuts, raisins, and meals are favorite breeding grounds). Transfer uninfested foods to large screw-top jars (the quart and half-gallon preserving jars are perfect for flours, meals, cereals, nuts, raisins, etc.). Burn old shelf liners; thoroughly vacuum floors, shelves, walls; spackle all holes, cracks, and crevices, then scrub down the entire pantry with the vinegar-water solution.

Use an appropriate insecticide— *following label directions carefully—* then let pantry or cupboards stand open several days before restocking with food.
— Be especially selective about the shelf to be used for storing tea, coffee, flavorings, and leavenings. It should be extra cool, dry, and dark.
— When adding supplies to pantry or or cupboard, place the new behind the old so that the old will be used first.
— Seal opened packages airtight (*bug*-tight), either by transferring contents to large preserving jars or by overwrapping in plastic bags and closing with rubber bands or "twisters."
— Get rid of market bags and cartons as soon as they're emptied. *Never* save, *never* store in cupboards. They're an open invitation to roaches, weevils, silverfish, ants. But most of all to roaches. These pests are fond of the glue used in manufacturing bags and cartons and females seek out the snug dark folds and crevices in which to lay their eggs. A market bag or carton, seemingly free of roaches, may in fact harbor hundreds of soon-to-hatch eggs.

SHELF LIFE OF PANTRY AND CUPBOARD ITEMS

Food	Special Storage Tips	Maximum Recommended Storage Time in a Cool, Dark, Dry Place
Canned Foods		
Fruits and vegetables	Cover and refrigerate after opening.	3 years
All other canned foods		1–2 years
Honey, Preserves, Jams, Jellies, Pickles, Condiments	Refrigerate pickles and condiments after opening.	1 year or more

Food	Special Storage Tips	Maximum Recommended Storage Time in a Cool, Dark, Dry Place
Vinegar, Bottled Salad Dressings, Peanut Butter	Refrigerate salad dressings and peanut butter after opening.	6 months
Syrups, Molasses	Store tightly capped; discard if moldy.	Indefinitely
Vegetable Oil, Shortening	Store tightly capped; never refrigerate.	6–12 months
Freeze-Dried Foods	After opening, rewrap airtight or as label directs.	Indefinitely or as label states.
Dehydrated Foods (Milk, Potatoes, etc.)	Store in original packages, closing snugly after each use.	6 months
Dried Fruits, Vegetables, and Fish	After opening, store in airtight jars or overwrap package in plastic food wrap.	1 year or longer
Cereals, Pasta Breakfast cereals, Flour, corn meal, Pasta, cornstarch, Rice, wild rice	Tightly reseal after each use; for long storage, transfer to large screw-top jars.	2–3 months 2–3 months 3–6 months Indefinitely
Sugar Granulated, confectioners' Brown	Store airtight. Store in airtight canister with an apple slice; or store in refrigerator (see refrigerator storage chart).	3–6 months 3–6 months
Leavenings Baking powder, soda, cream of tartar Yeast (dried)	Store airtight away from stove or heat. Store airtight away from all heat.	6 months Until package expiration date

Food	Special Storage Tips	Maximum Recommended Storage Time in a Cool, Dark, Dry Place
Mixes (Cake, Cookie, Pudding, Soup)		6 months
Beverages		
Coffee beans	Store in airtight tin.	1 month
Coffee, ground	(See About Storing Food in the Refrigerator.)	
Instant, freeze-dried	Store airtight away from stove.	6 months; 3–4 weeks after opening
Tea	Store airtight away from stove.	1 year; 2–3 weeks after opening
Cocoa, drink mixes	Store airtight.	6 months
Nuts, etc.		
Unshelled nuts	Store in perforated plastic bags (for storage of *shelled nuts,* see About Storing Food in the Refrigerator).	6 months
Popcorn (Unpopped)	Store airtight.	1 year
Popcorn (Popped)	Store in plastic bags.	2 weeks
Coconut	Store airtight; refrigerate after opening.	6 months
Flavorings		
Extracts	Store tightly capped, away from stove.	6 months
Salt	Store *near* stove to help keep dry.	1 year or longer
Pepper	Use whole corns in pepper mill.	1 year or longer
Food Colorings	Store tightly capped.	1 year or longer
Breads (All Kinds)	Store in original wrapper or plastic food wrap in ventilated breadbox.	2–4 days
Crackers (All Kinds)	Store tightly sealed in original package or in airtight canisters.	1–2 months

Food	Special Storage Tips	Maximum Recommended Storage Time in a Cool, Dark, Dry Place
Cakes and Cookies	See cake and cookie chapters for storage details.	
Pies and Pastries	Store loosely covered with foil or plastic food wrap in a pie saver. (*Note:* Custard and cream pies and pastries must be refrigerated.)	3–4 days
Vegetables		
Dasheens	Store in perforated	1 week
Kohlrabi	boxes or bins in a very	2 weeks
Onions	cool, dark, dry place	1–4 weeks
Potatoes (Irish)	with plenty of air cir-	1 month
Potatoes (sweet), yams	culating. Check vegeta-	1 week
Pumpkin, rutabaga	bles frequently and	1 month
Turnips	discard any that are	1 week
Winter squash	sprouting or softening.	1–3 weeks

The Herb and Spice Shelf

Man has always cherished herbs and spices. Squabbled and fought over them, too. And journeyed to the ends of the earth. The discovery of America, everyone knows, was a happy accident; what Columbus was really after was a direct sea route to the spice treasures of the East.

To primitive man, herbs and spices were magic plants possessing powers of creation, regeneration, and immortality. Much later, kings counted their wealth in peppercorns, gladiators munched fennel to bolster their courage, and prophets wore crowns of laurel to sharpen their "vision." Up until the Middle Ages, mothers strung necklaces of cloves for their children to keep evil spirits away and tucked sprigs of dill in their own buttonholes. Still later, Englishmen devoured pounds of sage each spring, believing "He that would live for aye must eat sage in May."

Today we attribute no magic to herbs and spices other than their power to uplift mundane fare. What are these aromatics so indispensable to mankind? What, in fact, is an herb? A spice? Generally speaking, an herb is the leaf of tender, fragrant annuals and biennials that grow in temperate climates. Spices are the more pungent roots, barks, stems, buds, fruits, and leaves of tropical or subtropical plants, usually perennials. Crossing boundaries are the aromatic seeds, produced by both herb and spice plants.

Some General Tips on Buying, Storing, and Using Herbs and Spices
—Buy in small amounts and store no longer than 1 year; flavors fade fast. Toss stale herbs onto hearth or charcoal fires to scent the air.
—Try using whole spices, grinding or grating them as needed. They are far more aromatic than the preground. Whole spices can also be used to season soups, stocks, and stews. You'll need about 1½ times more whole spices than ground, so adjust recipe accordingly. Tie spices in cheesecloth and simmer along with soup or stew or whatever, then lift out before serving.
—Store herbs and spices tightly capped away from direct sunlight in a cool, dry place.
—Use herbs and spices sparingly, discriminatingly, never combining too many in a single recipe. Be particularly cautious about hot peppers.
—Crush dried herbs between your fingers as you add; body heat will intensify their flavor. Always taste for seasoning *after* herbs or spices have been warmed through.
—If an herb or spice is unfamiliar, taste *before* adding. The best way—though you may not want to go to the trouble—is to blend with a little softened cream cheese or butter, then to let stand at room temperature several minutes so that the seasoning's flavor will develop fully.
—When herbs or spices are being added "cold" to cold dishes— dips and spreads, for example—

allow flavors to mature and ripen about ½ hour at room temperature before serving. Or warm the seasoning in a little butter over low heat before adding—especially advisable for raw-tasting chili and curry powders.
—Use fresh herbs as often as possible; they are so much more fragrant than the dry and are being stocked in greater and greater variety by big city grocers. Better still, grow your own (tips for growing and using fresh herbs are included at the end of this section).
—Use a light hand with garlic powders and juices; they gather strength on the shelf. Remember, too, that a crushed clove of garlic has 2–3 times the impact of a minced one.

—*If a dish is overseasoned, try one or more of the following remedies:*
· Strain out bits of herb or spice.
· Simmer a raw, peeled, quartered potato in mixture 10–15 minutes, then remove; it will absorb some of the excess flavor.
· Reduce amount of salt (if it has not already been added) and stir in a little sugar or brown sugar.
· Thicken gravy or stew with a flour or cornstarch and water paste.
· If mixture is overly sweet, sharpen with about 1 teaspoon lemon juice or vinegar.
· Serve mixture well chilled; cold numbs the palate.
· Prepare a second batch—*un-seasoned*—and combine with the first.

—*When making recipes in quantity, adjust seasonings as follows:*

Quantity Being Made	Herb and Spice Adjustment
2 times the recipe	Use 1½ times amounts called for
3 times the recipe	Use 2 times amounts called for
4 times the recipe	Use 2½ times amounts called for

AN HERB AND SPICE CHART

Note: Because detailed herb and spice uses are included in the Seasoning Charts in the Meat, Poultry, Seafood, Game, and Vegetable chapters, suggestions here will be general.

Herb or Spice	Description	Popular Forms	Essential to Basic Herb/Spice Shelf	Essential to Gourmet Herb/Spice Shelf	Easy to Grow
Allspice	*Spice.* Berry of a Caribbean tree with combined flavor of cinnamon, cloves, and nutmeg. Use primarily for cakes, cookies, pies, puddings, breads.	Dried whole; powdered	X	X	
Anise	*Aromatic seed.* Licorice-flavored cousin to the carrot; used in candies, liqueurs, Scandinavian and German breads, pastries, cookies, beef stews.	Dried whole; powdered		X	
Basil	*Herb.* Bitter, clove-flavored relative of mint. Good with any tomato dish, especially Italian.	Dried crushed or ground leaves; fresh	X	X	X
Bay leaves (Laurel)	*Herb.* Woody, faint flavor of cinnamon-sarsaparilla; bitter when overused; good with veal, fowl, fish.	Dried whole; powdered	X	X	
Capers	*Herb.* Tart flower buds of Mediterranean caper bush; superb with eggs, seafood, veal, tomatoes. Choicest are tiny, tender *nonpareil.*	Pickled or brined whole		X	
Cardamom	*Spice.* Lemony-gingery seeds, especially popular in Scandinavia for breads, cakes, cookies.	Dried whole; powdered		X	
Caraway	*Aromatic seed.* Delicately licorice, nutty. Used in rye bread, German and Nordic cheeses; good with cabbage and sauerkraut.	Whole dry seeds		X	

AN HERB AND SPICE CHART (continued)

Herb or Spice	Description	Popular Forms	Essential to Basic Herb/Spice Shelf	Essential to Gourmet Herb/Spice Shelf	Easy to Grow
Celery seed	*Aromatic seed.* Concentrated celery flavor.	Whole dry seeds; powdered	X	X	
Chervil	*Herb.* Delicate, sweet, parsley-licorice flavor; component of *fines herbes*. Excellent with seafood, green salads.	Dried whole or ground leaves; fresh		X	X
Chives	*Herb.* The most delicate onion; wispy green tops; all-purpose herb for savory dishes.	Minced dried, frozen, freeze-dried; fresh	X	X	X
Cinnamon	*Spice.* Sweet, slightly "hot" bark of the cassia tree. Used primarily for cookies, cakes, pies, puddings, spicy beverages.	Sticks; powdered	X	X	
Cloves	*Spice.* Pungent flower buds of the clove tree. Used mainly in cakes, pies, puddings, spicy sauces and drinks.	Whole dried buds; powdered	X	X	
Coriander	*Aromatic seed.* Nutty seed of a plant of the parsley family; principal seasoning of Latin American sausages, meat dishes. Fresh leaves (*cilantro*) also used.	Whole dried seeds; powdered		X	
Cumin	*Aromatic seed.* Similar to caraway but more medicinal; one of the chief ingredients of chili and curry powders. Good with cabbage, sauerkraut, in meat loaves.	Whole dry seeds; powdered		X	
Dill	*Herb.* Lemony-tart; enhances seafoods, egg and cheese dishes, salads, cucumbers, tomatoes.	Dried whole and powdered seeds; weed (dried leaves); fresh	X	X	X

Name	Description	Forms Available			
Fennel (Finocchio)	*Herb.* Feathery, faintly licorice member of the parsley family. Superb with seafood; a favorite Scandinavian flavoring for sweet breads, pastries, cakes, cookies.	Dried whole and powdered seeds, leaves; fresh bulbs		X	X
Fenugreek	*Aromatic seed.* Bitter red-brown seeds with a burnt sugar taste. A component of curry powder, imitation maple flavoring, chutney.	Whole dry seeds; powdered		X	
Filé powder	*Herb.* Dried sassafras leaves; flavor woodsy, root beer-like. Used to flavor and thicken gumbos, other Creole dishes.	Powder		X	X
Garlic	See Specialty Onions (vegetable chapter).	Fresh bulbs; powder; salt; juice	X	X	
Geranium	*Herb.* Many flavors (rose, lemon, apple), all good in confections, jellies, fruit compotes. A particularly fragrant, pretty garnish.	Fresh potted plants		X	X
Ginger	*Spice.* Biting but sweet root of an Asian plant. One of the most versatile spices, essential to Oriental sweet-sour dishes, pickles, cakes, cookies, pies.	Dried whole and cracked roots; crystallized; preserved; powdered; fresh	X	X	
Horseradish	*Herb.* Peppery white root with a turnip-like flavor. Used primarily to add zip to sauces, dips, spreads, salad dressings.	Prepared (bottled); fresh	X	X	
Juniper	*Aromatic berry.* Dried, smoky-blue, resinous, bitter-sweet berry of the juniper bush. Used to flavor gin, game, salmon, goose, duck, pork.	Dried whole berries		X	X
Lemon verbena	*Herb.* Sweet lemon-flavored leaves; best used to flavor or garnish fruit salads, desserts.	Fresh potted plants		X	X

Herb or Spice	Description	Popular Forms	Essential to		Easy to Grow
			Basic Herb/Spice Shelf	Gourmet Herb/Spice Shelf	
Mace	*Spice.* Fibrous husk of nutmeg; flavor similar but milder. All-purpose spice, equally at home in savory and sweet dishes.	Dried blades; powdered	X	X	
Marjoram	*Herb.* Mild cousin of oregano with musky-mellow, almost nutty bouquet. Particularly good with veal, lamb, fowl, potatoes, and tomatoes.	Dried whole leaves; powdered	X	X	X
Mint	*Herb.* More than 30 varieties: peppermint and spearmint (the two most popular), apple, lemon and orange, etc. Best in jellies, confections, fruit salads, and desserts, as a pretty, perky garnish.	Whole, crushed and powdered dried leaves; as extracts, oils; fresh	X		X
Mustard	*Spice.* Bitter and biting; *two main types* are relatively mild *White* and extra-strong *Brown* or *Oriental.* Used primarily in zippy sauces, pickles, salad dressings, deviled foods. Of the prepared, the Dijon-type, made with wine, is considered choicest.	Whole dried or powdered seeds; variety of prepared (bottled) blends.	X	X	X
Nasturtium	*Herb.* Leaves of the popular flower, peppery and tart, not unlike watercress. Use in salads. Blossoms also good in salads, as garnishes.	Fresh		X	X
Nutmeg	*Spice.* Mellow, sweet-nutty seed of the nutmeg tree. Like mace, an all-purpose spice, equally good with sweets and meats, fruits and vegetables.	Dried whole seeds; ground	X	X	
Oregano	*Herb.* Wild marjoram with a bitter, marigold-like flavor. An Italian favorite for spaghetti sauces, pizza, other tomato-rich dishes.	Dried whole or crushed leaves; powdered	X	X	X

Name	Description	Forms		
Paprika	*Spice.* Ground dried pods of fleshy, mild-to-slightly-hot Capsicum peppers, native to Latin America but now the soul of Hungarian cooking. The Hungarian sweet rose paprika is the reddest, sweetest, mildest. *Note:* All paprika is extremely high in vitamin C.	Ground	X	X
Parsley	*Herb.* There are dozens of varieties, but the two most popular are the curly and the somewhat stronger Italian or plain-leaf. A multipurpose herb, a component of *fines herbes* and *bouquet garni.*	Fresh; flakes (dried leaves)	X	X
Pepper (true)	*Spice.* "The Master Spice," once as rare and costly as gold. There are three types, all from the same tropical vine: the pungent *BLACK* (dried, unhusked, immature berries), the milder *WHITE* (dried inner white cores of ripe berries), and the *GREEN* (unripe whole berries). The white is preferable for seasoning light soups and sauces, the green for those who want a less peppery black pepper.	Black dried peppercorns; cracked, ground, seasoned, and lemon-flavor black pepper; whole and ground white pepper; whole dried and liquid-packed green peppercorns	X	
Peppers (Capsicums)	*Spice.* Not true peppers but a large group of New World pods called "peppers" by Columbus because they were as fiery as the Indian pepper. Capsicums are both red and green, mild and hot (the hot are collectively called *Chili Peppers*). There are dozens of Capsicums, all important to Latin American cuisine, but the following are the most available. *Popular Red Peppers:* *Cayenne* (ground hot red pepper); plump, sweet, scarlet *Ancho*; sharper, browner, elongated *Mulato*; long skinny, torrid *Pasilla*; and the tiny incendiary *Pequin.* *Popular Green Peppers:* The superhot *Serrano* and *Jalapeño* and the milder, though sometimes hot *Poblano.*	Ground (cayenne); crushed and whole dried pods; canned and pickled whole pods; fresh whole pods; liquid hot red pepper seasoning	X	

CAUTION: Never rub eyes when working with hot peppers — pain is excruciating. Always wash hands well when preparations are done. (*Note:* To "cool" hot peppers, rinse well, remove seeds, stems, veins, then soak 1 hour in lightly salted cold water.)

AN HERB AND SPICE CHART (continued)

Herb or Spice	Description	Popular Forms	Essential to Basic Herb/Spice Shelf	Essential to Gourmet Herb/Spice Shelf	Easy to Grow
Poppy seed	Aromatic seed. Tiny, nutty, silver-blue seeds of the poppy (they contain no opium). Good in breads, pastries, cakes, salads, with noodles.	Whole seeds		X	
Rocket (rugula)	See Other Salad Greens in the salad chapter.	Fresh			X
Rosemary	Herb. Heady, lemony-resinous, needle-like leaves. Good with lamb, green peas, pork.	Dried whole or powdered leaves		X	X
Saffron	Spice. Expensive, dried orange stigmas of the saffron crocus (it takes 225,000 hand-plucked stigmas to yield 1 pound, hence the high price). Flavor is medicinal, the key seasoning of Paella, Spanish breads, cakes. To Use: Soak strands in tepid water, then use this infusion to flavor and color recipes.	Dried whole stigmas; powdered		X	
Sage	Herb. Musky, lime-scented silver-green leaves; the identifiable herb of poultry seasoning and stuffings.	Dried whole, crushed and powdered leaves	X	X	X
Savory	Herb. There are two savories, the delicate, aromatic Summer Savory and the more bitter Winter Savory. The Summer is the better herb, especially delicious with eggs and cheese.	Dried whole and powdered leaves		X	X
Sesame seed (benne)	Aromatic seed. Small flat pearly seeds, nutty with a tinge of bitterness. Good in breads and pastries, toasted in salads. (Note: These stale and go rancid quite rapidly; buy as needed.) To Toast: Warm uncovered in piepan 10-15 minutes at 350° F., stirring often until golden, or 1-2 minutes in a heavy skillet over moderate heat.	Whole seeds		X	

Shallots	See Specialty Onions (vegetable chapter).		X	
Tarragon	*Herb.* Succulent, licorice-flavored green leaves. Superlative with seafood, eggs, crisp green salads. Component of *fines herbes*.	Fresh	X	X
Thyme	*Herb.* All-round meat, fowl and fish herb with a vaguely minty, vaguely tea-like flavor. Customarily included in a *bouquet garni*. Particularly fragrant is lemon thyme.	Dried whole and powdered leaves; fresh sprigs	X	X
Turmeric	*Spice.* Deep yellow-orange root of an Asian plant related to ginger. Dried and ground, it becomes an integral part of curry powder, the "yellow" of mustard. Turmeric alone has a thin, flat, medicinal taste. Used primarily in pickles, chutneys, curries.	Whole dried or powdered leaves	X	
Vanilla bean	*Aromatic seed capsule.* Long black seed pod of a wild Mexican orchid, sweet and perfume-like.	Powdered	X	
Woodruff	*Herb.* Sweet-musky woodland herb, the leaves of which are used in the *Maibowle* (Rhine wine afloat with strawberries).	Beans; extract	X	
		Fresh		

Some Less Used Herbs and Spices

Achiote: Small red seeds of a Latin American tree similar to and used as a substitute for saffron in Mexican cooking.

Angelica: Sweet, succulently stalked member of the parsley family, most often available candied and used as a decoration in confectionery.

Borage: Medicinal-tasting European herb used in teas and other beverages.

Burnet: A leafy cucumber-flavored herb, excellent in salads.

Costmary: Minty but bitter herb used in making ale; good used *sparingly* in salads.

Horehound: A bitter herb aromatic of tobacco, once popular for flavoring candies and cough drops.

Hyssop: An astringent variety of mint used in liqueurs; scatter a few leaves into green salads for bite.

Lavender: "The old ladies' herb," the clean and lemony perfumer of bureaus and closets. Few people cook with lavender, but a leaf or two, minced into a fruit cup or salad, injects a pleasing, elusive scent.

Lemon balm: Crisp lemony-minty leaves that double nicely for mint.

Lovage: A celery-flavored herb, particularly compatible with fowl and game.

Marigold: The pungent garden variety; use sparingly to pep up salads, poultry stuffings. The flower stamens can be dried and substituted for saffron.

Rose hips: The tart, crab-apple-like fruit of the rose; delicious boiled into jelly or minced into venison or rabbit stews. Extremely high in vitamin C.

Rue: An old-fashioned acrid herb used in minute quantities to perk up fruit cups and salads.

Sweet cicely: A kind of chervil often—but erroneously—called myrrh because both have a faintly licorice-parsley flavor. True myrrh is an aromatic gum.

Sweet flag: An iris with cinnamon-and-ginger-flavored rhizomes used in seasoning confections and puddings.

The Herb Blends

Bouquet garni: A bouquet of herbs—fresh parsley and thyme plus a bay leaf—bundled together, simmered in soups, stews, stocks, or other liquid recipes, then fished out before serving. The French way to prepare the bouquet is to wrap the parsley around the two other herbs, but Americans may prefer to tie all three in a tiny cheesecloth bag (imperative, by the way, if dry spices are used so that they don't float out and overseason the dish). A bouquet garni may contain other seasoners—a celery stalk, perhaps, a garlic clove—but it must begin with parsley, thyme, and bay leaf. Food companies now market dried blends called *bouquet garni* which should be used as labels direct.

Fines herbes: A French favorite—minced fresh or dried chervil, tarragon, parsley, chives, and sometimes basil, sage, marjoram, fennel, or oregano employed as a multipurpose seasoner. Particularly good in salads. Now available bottled.

Poultry seasoning: All the good poultry and poultry stuffing seasoners—sage, marjoram, powdered onion, pepper, and sometimes thyme—premixed and ready to use.

The Spice Blends

Barbecue spice: Zippy blend of chili peppers, cumin, garlic, cloves, paprika, sugar, and salt created specifically for barbecued foods but also good mixed into salad dressings, meat loaves and patties, egg, cheese, and potato dishes.

Charcoal seasoning: A smoky mix of powdered charcoal, herbs, spices, salt, and sometimes sugar and monosodium glutamate designed to impart a charcoal-broiled flavor.

Chili powder: Ground chili peppers, cumin seeds, oregano, garlic, salt, and occasionally cloves, allspice, and onion—the staples of Mexican and Tex-Mex cooking.

Cinnamon sugar: Simply that, cinnamon and sugar premixed and ready to sprinkle onto hot buttered toast, waffles, pancakes, or fresh-from-the-oven breads.

Crab boil (shrimp spice): Peppercorns, crumbled bay leaves, dried red peppers, mustard seeds, chips of dried ginger, and other whole spices suitable for seasoning boiled crab and shrimp.

Curry powder: An Occidental invention; Indian cooks would never dream of using curry powder, but grind their own spices, varying the combinations according to the food to be curried. Commercial curry powders contain as many as 16 to 20 spices, predominantly cinnamon, cloves, cumin, fenugreek, ginger, turmeric, red and black pepper, the quantity of pepper determining the curry's "hotness."

Tip: When adding curry powder to a cold dish (such as a dip or spread), always warm it a few minutes first in butter over low heat to mellow the "raw" taste.

A HOMEMADE CURRY POWDER

Makes about ¼ cup

2 tablespoons ground coriander
1 tablespoon ground turmeric
1 teaspoon each ground cumin, fenugreek, ginger, and allspice
½ teaspoon each ground mace and crushed dried hot red chili peppers
¼ teaspoon each powdered mustard and black pepper

Work all ingredients together in a mortar and pestle until well blended. Store airtight.

Curry paste: A blend of curry powder, ghee (clarified butter), and vinegar available in gourmet shops. Use in place of curry powder, allowing about 1–2 tablespoons paste to season a curry for 6 persons.

Pickling spice: Mixture of mustard and coriander seeds, white and black peppercorns, whole cloves and allspice, whole hot red chili peppers, broken cinnamon sticks and bay leaves, chunks of gingerroot; versatile enough to use for a variety of pickles, preserves, and condiments.

Pie spices:

Apple pie spice: Blend of cinnamon, nutmeg, and sometimes allspice.

Pumpkin pie spice: Mixture of cinnamon, ginger, nutmeg, allspice, and cloves.

Pizza spice: A garlicky, oniony blend similar to Barbecue spice compounded specifically for pizza toppings.

Quatre-épices: A French blend of 4 spices—cloves, ginger, nutmeg, and white pepper—used as an all-purpose seasoner for meats and vegetables, soups and sauces. *To Make:* Mix together 5 tablespoons ground cloves and 3 tablespoons *each* ground ginger, nutmeg, and white pepper. Store airtight. Particularly good on carrots, turnips, and parsnips, broiled steaks and chops.

Seasoned salt: The formula varies from processor to processor, but essentially an aromatic blend of salt, spices, and herbs that can be used as an all-purpose seasoning.

Some Herb and Spice Substitutions

Because a number of herbs and spices taste somewhat the same, the following can be interchanged in a pinch (substitute measure for measure):

Herbs
Basil and Oregano
Caraway and Anise
Celery Seeds and Minced Celery
  Tops
Chervil and Parsley
Chervil and Tarragon
Fennel and Anise
Fennel and Tarragon

Oregano and Marjoram
Sage and Thyme

Spices
Allspice and *equal parts* Cinnamon, Cloves, and Nutmeg
Chili Peppers and Cayenne
Commercial Curry Powder and Homemade Curry Powder
Nutmeg and Mace

About Other Additives

Monosodium glutamate (MSG; the ajinomoto of Japanese cuisine): Neither herb nor spice, this white crystalline vegetable extract must nonetheless be included because of its popularity as a flavor enhancer. Long an Oriental standby, it is tasteless, yet has the mysterious power of freshening and developing other foods' flavors. *Note:* MSG has recently come under medical scrutiny, some researchers believing overdoses cause giddiness, fainting spells.

Meat tenderizers: These are discussed fully in the meat chapter (see The Ways of Tenderizing Meat).

About Growing Herbs at Home

Herbs are easy to grow, even on apartment window sills, provided their pots are big enough. Mini hothouse sets won't do except for sprouting seeds. Those herbs particularly suited to home growing are so marked in the Herb and Spice Chart.

Successful herb gardening is a vast and complex subject, requiring a book in itself. What we include here—in a most general way—are growing tips applicable to the majority of herbs. Persons seriously interested in growing herbs can obtain firsthand advice from county agricultural extension agents, local nursery and botanical garden staffs.

Some General Herb-Growing Tips:
– Transplant seedlings when they're about 2″ high and their leaves are turning a hearty green. Pick a sunny patch of ground, preferably one that will be shaded part of the day.
– Allow plenty of space between plants, especially important with such ramblers as mint and tarragon, which will quickly overrun pot or yard.
– When using pots, choose big ones (about 6″ across the top), made of clay or other porous material. Drop about 1″ coarse gravel or ceramic chips into the bottoms to ensure good drainage, then fill with moderately rich soil; the commercial "planting mix" works well for most herbs.
– Root herbs in pots or ground, not too deep or they will die, then loosely pack damp soil around stems. Water lightly.
– Stand potted herbs in a bright window, eastern exposure if possible, so that plants will catch the early morning light but be spared the searing noonday sun. Herbs in southern windows may need to be shaded part of the day; watch closely for signs of "burning" or browning.
– Water herbs whenever soil *feels* dry, hosing liberally with a fine spray or, in the case of potted herbs, adding water from the top until it trickles through to the saucer below. *Note:* If more than ¼″ water accumulates in a saucer, tip out; herbs do not like their feet wet. Above all, beware of overwatering; it's more likely to kill than underwatering.
– About every week to 10 days, spray herb foliage lightly with water.
– Keep an eagle eye out for aphids (pale, wingless, pinhead-size insects), which are fond of tender-sweet herbs like tarragon and chervil, also for equally small and pesky white flies which prefer basil. The best way to keep both at bay is by rinsing herbs frequently with cool water, paying particular attention to the undersides of leaves where the insects gather to lay eggs. Insecticides are risky from a plant as well as a human standpoint. Delicate herbs simply cannot withstand repeated sprayings. Use insecticides only as a last resort, choosing those safe for food crops, administering with utmost caution and following label directions to the letter.
– To prolong the growing season of annuals, nip off flower buds as they appear.
– Thin herbs as needed, transplanting "weeded out" plants in separate pots or plots where they will have plenty of growing room.

About Using Fresh Herbs:
– Cut and use herbs often; snipping promotes growth. To cut, reach down near the soil and snip each stalk separately with scissors. Resist the temptation (especially strong with chives) to shear the tops right off in a crew cut. Also avoid cutting too deeply into woody stems. (*Note:* Herbs are said to be at their headiest just before blooming, also early in the day when touched with dew. *But* herbs are rarely used first thing in the morning, so it makes more sense to cut them when they are needed.)

– Wash herbs gently, swishing them up and down in cool water, then drain, shaking lightly or patting dry on paper toweling.

– Mince herbs as they are needed and in quantities needed. If herbs are tender, mince stems and all; otherwise, use the leaves only. Wispy herbs like dill, chives, and fennel are most efficiently minced by gathering a dozen or so strands or tops together, then snipping straight across with scissors. A chopping knife makes short shrift of larger, coarser herbs.

– To store unused fresh herbs, wrap stalks loosely in damp paper toweling and tuck into the hydrator or stand stalks upright in ¼″ cold water in a wide-mouth preserving jar, screw on lid and refrigerate. (*Note:* Minced herbs store poorly; better to freeze them— see About Freezing Herbs in the chapter on canning and freezing.)

– When substituting fresh herbs for the dry, double or triple the quantity called for, tasting as you add until the flavors seem well balanced. Fresh herbs are far more subtle than the dry.

How to Dry Fresh Herbs:

– Pick prime leaves, preferably just before herbs bloom and early in the morning as soon as the dew has evaporated.

– Wash herbs gently and pat dry on paper toweling.

– Spread out on a cheesecloth-covered cookie rack and dry outdoors in a warm shady spot (bring inside at night), in a dry, airy room *or* in a 200° F. oven. Drying times will vary according to humidity and herb variety; test leaves often for crumbliness.

– When herbs are dry and crumbly, remove any twigs and stems and pack leaves whole in airtight jars. Or, if you prefer, crush with a rolling pin between sheets of wax paper, then bottle airtight.

CHAPTER 4

MENU PLANNING, TABLE SETTING, AND SERVICE

Keeping menus varied and nutritious, at the same time pleasing the family without shattering the budget, is not as complicated as it may seem. Planning meals is rather like mastering a formula in that, once the technique is learned, it becomes automatic. Here, then, are the rules.

Points to Consider in Planning Menus

Plan Ahead: Work out several days' menus at a time (a week's, if possible) so that you can vary foods from meal to meal and day to day, take advantage of local or seasonal "specials," do the major marketing in a single trip, and use leftovers ingeniously. You'll save time and money.

Balance Meals Nutritionally: Think of each meal in relation to the other two of the day so that the quota of Basic Four Food Groups is met. Bear in mind, too, any dietary problems—diabetes (low carbohydrate diet), high blood pressure, or heart disease (often necessitating a low-cholesterol diet), obesity (low-calorie diet), and food allergies. (Read the information on nutrition, Eat Well, Keep Well, in the Appendix.)

Stick to the Budget: Shop prudently so the family will eat well *throughout* the week, "well" meaning happily, heartily, and wholesomely. On a tight budget meats are the first to go. High protein foods, of course, are essential to good health. If bargain meats are beyond the budget, substitute such protein-rich foods as dried peas, beans, lentils, and cheese. Few meats are actually bargains, but in most areas and seasons, chicken, turkey, pork, and ham cost less than beef, veal, and lamb. Best buys, invariably, are organ meats— chicken or turkey gizzards (sometimes mere pennies a pound), pork liver, beef heart. Hamburger is a good buy, too, not because it's cheap but because it can be stretched so easily with cereal, bread crumbs, pasta, and rice, which *are*. Bony, gristly cuts are usually economical—beef or lamb shanks, oxtail, pigs' feet. Well prepared, they are also tender and savory.

Abide by Family Likes and Dislikes: No point in buying what the family won't eat. Each family member no doubt has idiosyncrasies, and though it's impossible to delight everyone at every meal, you can avoid those foods any member dislikes intensely and include each week one of his favorites. This same common sense applies to party menus. Unless you know your guests' tastes to be sophisticated, don't startle them with raw pickled fish or a heady tripe stew. Stick to the reliables—beef, poultry, pork, and ham—but prepare them new ways. Another important company dinner consideration is any physical or religious dietary restrictions guests may have. Ask and plan accordingly (see Some Dietary Taboos).

Consider the Season: Not only because of the availability and economy of foods in season but also because of the weather's effect on appetites. Cold weather sharpens them, hot weather just the re-verse. Winter meals, thus, can be heavier, spicier than summer meals. And, of course, hotter.

Suit the Meal to the Occasion: Folksy foods—meat loaves, pasta, thick vegetable-strewn soups—are perfect for family or informal suppers; dressy dinners demand something more elegant, a roast fowl, perhaps, a delicately sauced fish, or a wine-laced French stew. For a buffet, food should be bite-size or at least tender enough to cut with a fork. No one wants to tackle an unboned piece of chicken or a not so tender chop while balancing a plate on his lap.

Be Artistic: The look of a meal counts as much as the taste because, no matter how beautifully cooked, an all-white or all-brown meal comes off badly. It *looks* drab. Think of a menu as an artist does a canvas, assembling a variety of colors and textures, shapes and flavors into a pleasing whole. Avoid too many rich foods within a meal or too many bland, too many spicy or too many insipid, too many tart or too many sweet. Strike for balance and harmony.

SOME DIETARY TABOOS

Faith	Forbidden foods
Catholic (Continental U.S. Only)	Meat or poultry on Ash Wednesday or Good Friday
Eastern Orthodox	Meat or poultry on *any* Wednesday or Friday or during Lent

Faith	Forbidden foods
Orthodox Jewish	Any nonkosher meat or fowl, any animal blood, eggs with blood spots Pork, ham, or pork products (lard, etc.) Shellfish, snails, eels, turtles Birds of prey, scavengers, rabbit Meat and dairy foods at the same meal Canned milk, salted butter (not customary, though not actually forbidden)
Moslem	Pork, alcohol. Certain sects also prohibit the eating of beef and beef products.
Hindu	Beef, veal, pork, fertile eggs. Hindu vegetarians are forbidden all meat, fish, fowl, and eggs. Some are so strict they will eat neither blood-colored vegetables nor those that grow underground because a worm or other small animal may have been injured as the vegetable was uprooted.
Vegetarian	Strict vegetarians refuse all animal foods (meat, fowl, fish, eggs, milk, cheese, etc.). The less strict will eat dairy products.

Note: The best policy, always, is to ask the prospective guest in advance what foods he is denied, thereby saving embarrassment all around.

MENUS FOR MOST OCCASIONS

Note: In the Menus That Follow, Any Dish Marked with an asterisk (*) Is Included in the Recipe Sections of the Book. For Page Numbers, See the Index.

FOUR SUNDAY BREAKFASTS

Orange Juice
Panfried Canadian Bacon*
Apple Pancakes* with Butterscotch Syrup*
Old-Fashioned Hot Chocolate*   Coffee

———

Broiled Grapefruit*
Broiled Sausage*   Egg in a Nest*
Buttered Toast   Peach Preserves
Milk   Coffee

———

Fresh Sliced Peaches
Benedict-Style Eggs*
Blueberry Muffins*
Maple Milk*   Milk   Coffee

————

Fresh Fruit Cocktail
Kedgeree*
Bannocks*
Old-Fashioned Apple Jelly*
Milk   Tea   Coffee

MORNING COFFEE

Coffees, like teas, can be plain or fancy. If the group is small, keep the menu short and limit the choice of breads to 2 or 3. If the group is large, offer a greater variety, perhaps 4–5 breads and 2 cakes.

BASIC MENU PATTERN

Fresh Fruit Juice
An Assortment of Breads and Cakes
Jams   Jellies   Preserves   Honey   Butter
Coffee   Hot Chocolate and/or Tea
Cream   Milk   Sugar

For Simple Coffees: Choose 1 item from 2 different columns below.
For Elaborate Coffees: Choose 1 bread, 2–3 sweet breads, and 1 cake, varying the flavors and textures.

Breads	*Sweet Breads*	*Cakes*
Any Muffins	Any Coffee Cake	Any Upside-Down Cake
Brioche*	Any Fruit Nut Bread	Applesauce Cake*
Croissants*	Cinnamon Raisin Pinwheels*	Gingerbread*
Sally Lunn*	Danish Pastry*	Pound Cake*
Toast or any Sweet	Hot Cross Buns*	Orange, Date, and Nut
or Spicy Toast	Old-Fashioned Yeast-Raised	Loaf*
Toasted English Muffins	Doughnuts*	Spice Cake*
	Panettone*	Real Sponge Cake*
	Stollen*	(baked in muffin pans
		as cupcakes)

TWO WINTER BRUNCHES

Bloody Marys*   Tomato Juice
Sausage Ring* Filled with Scrambled Eggs*
Baked Mushroom Caps Stuffed with Hazelnuts*
Hilda's Yorkshire Scones*   Peach Preserves
Coffee   Tea

————

Whiskey Sours*   Fruit Juices
Creamed Finnan Haddie* in Puff Pastry Shells
Braised Chicken Livers with Parsley Gravy*
Baked Tomatoes*
Coffee   Cocoa   Tea

————

TWO SUMMER BRUNCHES

Orange Blossoms*   Screwdrivers*
Chicken Mayonnaise*
Cold Sliced Smithfield Ham   Baking Powder Biscuits*
Old-Fashioned Applesauce*   Pickled Peaches*
Cucumber Aspic*
Hot Coffee   Iced Coffee

————

Chilled Champagne   Chilled Dry Sherry
Honeydew Melon Wedges
Turkey and Mushroom Crepes*
Chilled Salmon Mousse*   Sauce Verte*
Zucchini in À La Grecque Marinade*
Bakery Croissants
Hot Coffee   Iced Coffee   Hot Tea   Iced Tea

A LADIES' WINTER LUNCHEON

Fresh Tomato Soup*
Quiche Bourbonnaise*
Asparagus Vinaigrette*
Coeur à la Crème*
Coffee

A LADIES' SUMMER LUNCHEON

Iced Clear Mushroom Broth*
Crab Louis* in Avocado Shells
Croissants
Meringue Star Shells* Filled with Lime Milk Sherbet*
Iced Tea

FIVE FAST LUNCHES

Mickey's Mac and Meat*
Tossed Green Salad
Italian Bread Sticks
Fruit Cocktail   Pound Cake
Milk   Coffee

————

Hot Beef Consommé* (made ahead of time)
Individual Muffin Pizzas*
Applesauce   Cookies
Milk   Coffee

————

Quick Chicken or Turkey à la King*   Toaster Waffles
Olives   Gherkins   Radishes
Orange Sherbet Topped with Sliced Bananas
Milk   Coffee

————

Tomato-Vegetable Bouillon* (made ahead of time)
Fried Fish Sticks in Hot Dog Rolls   Tartar Sauce
Peaches and Cream   Cookies
Milk   Coffee

————

Welsh Rabbit*
Broiled Tomatoes*   Dill Pickles
Butterscotch Pudding
Milk   Coffee

FIVE LUNCH-BOX MENUS

Cold Southern Fried Chicken*
Chilled Container of Old-Fashioned Potato Salad*
Orange or Tangerine
Butterscotch Brownies*
Milk

If for Adults:
Add: Thermos of Clear Beet Soup*
Carrot and Celery Sticks
Substitute: Coffee or Tea for Milk

Cranberry Juice
Sliced Baked Ham* in Baking Powder Biscuits*
Apple Turnovers*   Cheddar Cubes
Milk

If for Adults:
Substitute: Coffee or Tea for Milk

Thermos of Chili*
Crackers   Corn Chips
Sweet Green Pepper and Carrot Sticks
Pear or Apple
Grandmother's Soft Ginger Cake*
Milk

If for Adults:
Substitute: Coffee or Tea for Milk

Cornish Pasties*
Chilled Container of Jiffy Deviled Eggs*
Cherry Tomatoes
Spicy Applesauce*
Dropped Oatmeal Chippies*
Milk

If for Adults:
Add: Thermos of clear or Sherried Mushroom Broth*
Substitute: Coffee or Tea for Milk

Bologna-Cheese or Ham Loaf* Sandwiches
Chilled Container of Creamy Sweet-Sour Coleslaw*
Quick Peach Crisp*
Milk

If for Adults:
Add: Thermos of Quick Asparagus Soup*
Dill Pickles
Substitute: Cold Sliced Ham Loaf* with Sour Cream-Mustard Sauce* for
sandwiches
Coffee or Tea for Milk

PICNICS

Note: Hot foods travel well in thermos jugs, cold foods packed in ice or cans of chemical dry ice in foam or insulated carryalls. Handy gourmet accessories: a chafing dish, an ice bucket for chilling wines, silver, napkins, portably sturdy wineglasses and plates.

A COOL WEATHER FAMILY PICNIC

Quick New England-Style Clam Chowder*   Crackers
Boston Baked Beans*   Cocktail Sausages
Crisp Apples   Cheddar Cheese Wedges
Gingerbread*
Spiced Orange Tea Mix*

A WARM WEATHER FAMILY PICNIC

Circassian Chicken*
Marinated Tomatoes and Artichokes*
Dill Pickles   Ripe and Green Olives
Buttered Rolls
Thelma's 1, 2, 3, 4, Cake*
Beer   Easy Lemonade Mix*

AFTERNOON TEA

Afternoon tea may be nothing more than tea and cookies, or it may be a lavish British-style ritual with assorted sandwiches, cakes, cookies and pastries. Use the following menu patterns as a guide.

BASICS

Milk　Cream　Tea　Sugar

Party Sandwiches*	Sweet Breads, Cakes	Cookies	Pastries
For a Simple Tea Choose 1	For a Simple Tea Choose 1	For a Simple Tea Choose 1	For a Formal Tea Choose 1
Chicken and Avocado*	Any Fruit Nut Bread	Brandy Snaps*	Chocolate Eclairs*
Cream Cheese and Watercress*	Boston Brown Bread*	Butter Stars*	Cream Horns*
With Date Filling*	Kugelhupf*	Florentines*	Cream Puffs*
	Light or Dark Fruit Cake	Kourabiedes*	Meringues Chantilly*
For a Formal Tea Choose 2-3	Petits Fours*	Madeleines*	Tart Shells filled with Strawberry Jam
Egg Salad*	For a Formal Tea Choose 2	Maude's Cookies*	
Potted Salmon*		Meringue Kisses*	
Salmon-Caper*		For a Formal Tea Choose 2-3	
Tongue and Chutney*		Scottish Shortbread*	
Whitstable*		Spritz*	

Lemon Slices

Welcome Extras: Salted Nuts, Mints

For a Special Occasion Tea: Substitute a decorated White Wedding Cake,* Royal Fruit Wedding Cake,* or other favorite cake for one of the choices above, using it as a centerpiece and asking the honoree to cut the first piece.

81

A COOL WEATHER GOURMET PICNIC

Hot Buttered Rum*
Mugs of Minestrone Milanese*
Savory Meat Balls* Served from Chafing Dish
Ripe and Green Olives
Garlic Buttered Italian Bread
Ripe Pears   Brie and Port du Salut
Espresso*

A WARM WEATHER GOURMET PICNIC

Iced Vodka   Chilled Champagne
Chilled Billi-Bi*
Caviar Stuffed Hard-Cooked Eggs
Sausage and Pastry Rolls*
Assorted Danish Sandwiches*
Vanilla Pots de Crème*
Petits Fours*
Coffee

FOUR BACK-YARD BARBECUES

Guacamole*   Taramasalata*   Corn Chips   Crackers
Charcoal-Broiled Hamburgers*   Charcoal-Broiled Frankfurters
Buns   Relishes   Chili Sauce   Mustard
Sliced Bermuda Onions
Three Bean Salad*   German Macaroni Salad*
Assorted Ice Creams
Sweet Lemon Loaf*
Soft Drinks   Beer   Coffee

————

Andalusian Gazpacho*
Charcoal-Broiled Sirloin Steak Stuffed with Mushrooms*
Charcoal-Baked Potatoes*   Sour Cream-Almond Sauce*
Corn on the Cob
Grapefruit and Avocado Salad*
Biscuit Tortoni*
Sangria*   Coffee

————

Oysters or Clams on the Half Shell*
(*Rioja Red* or *Chianti*)
Charcoal Spit-Roasted Loin of Pork*
South American Hot Barbecue Sauce*
Charcoal-Baked Butternut Squash*
Beans Lyonnaise*
Caribbean Compote*   Pecan Crisps*
Coffee

Antipasto*
(Chilled *Vinho Verde* or *Portuguese Rosé*)
Charcoal-Broiled Portuguese-Style Chicken or Turkey*
Scalloped Potatoes*
Ratatouille*
Basket of Fresh Fruit   Crackers   Assorted Cheeses
Coffee

FOUR FORMAL DINNERS

Clam Juice on the Rocks*
(Chilled *Meursault* or *Montrachet*)
Duckling à l'Orange*
Wild Rice
Buttered Green Beans
Poached Meringue Ring* with Algarve Apricot Sauce*
Demitasse*

Coquilles St. Jacques à la Parisienne*
(Chilled *Graves Médoc* or *Cabernet Sauvignon*)
Tournedos of Beef*   Béarnaise Sauce*
Bulgur-Mushroom Kasha*
Minted Green Peas*
Green Grapes and Sour Cream*
Demitasse*

Cucumber Velouté*
Pomerol or *Échézeaux* (for lamb), chilled *Moselle* (for pork)
Crown Roast of Lamb or Pork*
Carrots Vichy*
Danish-Style New Potatoes*
Cherries Jubilee*
Coffee

———

Melon and Ham*
(Chilled *Chablis* or *Montrachet*)
Paupiettes of Sole with Rosy Sauce*
Snow Peas and Scallions*
Mushroom Risotto*
Classic Pots de Crème au Chocolat*
Coffee

FOUR INFORMAL DINNERS

Sangria*
Paella*
Garlic French Bread*
Sliced Avocado and Lettuce Salad
Rum Flan*
Coffee

———

Won Ton Soup*
Lobster Cantonese*
Boiled Rice
Lichees in Port Wine*   Almond-Orange Icebox Cookies*
Tea

———

Caponata*   Crackers
(Chilled *Soave*)
Chicken and Mushroom Stuffed Manicotti*
Spinach and Cucumber Salad
Lemon Granité*   Florentines*
Espresso*

———

Cheese Fondue*
(*Kirsch,* midway through the fondue)
Sliced Smoked Ham, German Salami, Thuringer   Dill Pickles
Apples and Pears
Coffee

THREE HOLIDAY MENUS

EASTER DINNER

Sherried Mushroom Broth*
Ham en Croûte*
(*Volnay* or Chilled *Rosé*)
Curried Hot Fruit Compote*
Buttered Boiled New Potatoes
Steamed Asparagus*   Hollandaise Sauce*
Charlotte Russe*
Milk   Coffee   Tea

THANKSGIVING DINNER

Crudités*
Tomato Bouillon*
(Chilled *Chablis* or *Soave*)
Roast Turkey with Oyster or Savory Sausage Stuffing*
Turkey Gravy*   Cran-Apple Relish*
Orange-Candied Sweet Potatoes*
Brussels Sprouts with Chestnuts*
Creamed Onions*
Herb Biscuits*
Old-Fashioned Pumpkin Pie*
Milk   Coffee   Tea

CHRISTMAS DINNER

Shrimp Cocktail*
(Chilled *Traminer, Riesling,* or *Rhine* wine)
Roast Goose with Sage and Onion Dressing*
Braised Chestnuts*   Giblet Gravy*
Spicy Applesauce*
Green Beans in Mustard Sauce*
Molded Cranberry-Pecan Salad*
Plum Pudding* with Brandy or Rum Sauce*
Milk   Coffee   Tea

A STAG DINNER

Oysters Remick*
(*St. Emilion*)
Broiled Porterhouse Steak with Madeira-Mushroom Sauce*
Stuffed Baked Potatoes*
Caesar Salad*
Country-Style Apple Pie*
Coffee

A LATE SUPPER

Bouillabaisse*
Garlic French Bread*
Romaine and Radish Salad
Fruit and Cheese
Coffee   Tea

A SMORGASBORD MENU

GROUP I
Scandinavian Herring Salad   Rollmops*
Herring in Sour Cream*
Aquavit

GROUP II
Smoked Salmon   Easy Tuna Salad*   Cold Boiled Shrimp*
Iced Beer

GROUP III
Cold Roast Beef   Decorative Jellied Veal Loaf*
Country-Style Liver Pâté*
Wilted Cucumbers*   Pickled Red Cabbage*
Herbed Potato Salad*
Iced Beer

GROUP IV
Swedish Meat Balls in Mushroom Gravy*
Sage and Cider Scented Roast Fresh Ham*
Danish-Style New Potatoes*
Iced Beer

GROUP V (DESSERT)
Cheese Board (Danish Blue, Crema Dania)
Fruit Salad   Almond Tarts (Swedish Sandbakelsen)*
Coffee

Note: Aquavit is served with the first group only, chilled beer with all the rest (except dessert). Pumpernickel, rye bread, and sweet butter should accompany all savory courses.

Tips on Serving Smorgasbord:
– Stand table well away from wall so traffic around it will flow freely.
– Group hot and cold foods separately without crowding, elevating some, if you like, on linen-draped boxes. Set hot dinner plates near hot foods, cold plates near cold foods.

– To avoid jam-ups, arrange napkins and silver on a separate small table nearby.
– Replenish dishes as needed—in the kitchen, not at the table.

Tips on Eating Smorgasbord: Take herring only the first time at the table, then make a return trip for each successive group. In fine restaurants, a fresh plate is used for each new group (though not for return trips within any group), but such lavish use of plates may not be practical at home.

RIJSTTAFEL

In Indonesia, *rijsttafel* (rice table) may consist of 4 or 40 different dishes, depending upon the number of servants available (traditionally, there was one boy to handle each dish). The most practical way to serve rijsttafel in America is as a buffet, carefully charted to avoid traffic jams. Center the table with a gigantic bowl of rice, then cluster around it the various hot dishes (on burners or in chafing dishes). Nearby, set a stack of deep plates or shallow soup plates and, on a small table within easy reach, the silver rolled up in napkins. Condiments and salads are best placed at opposite ends of the buffet table, and dessert is served separately. How does one tackle this mountain of food? The Indonesian way is to cover the plate with rice, then to add dabs of this and that around the rice as neatly as paints on a palette. The trick is to keep the different dishes from getting scrambled so, if necessary to avoid overloading a plate, return to the table again and again à la smorgasbord. Chilled beer is the perfect rijsttafel beverage.

Hot Boiled Rice

Shrimp with Cucumbers and Snow Peas*   Chicken Sate*

Indonesian Spiced Beef*   Sweet and Sour Pork*

Lamb and Dhal Curry*

Radish Salad*   Hot Sweet-Sour Bean Sprout Salad*

CONDIMENTS

Toasted Coconut   Salted Peanuts   Pickled Hot Peppers

Shrimp Puffs (chips or wafers)   Raw Cucumber Sticks

Plum Sauce*   Chutney   India Relish

DESSERT

Fresh Pineapple Boats*

Coffee   Tea

A SUMMER COCKTAIL PARTY

Menu	For 12	Quantities Needed For 24	For 50
Pretty Party Pâté*	1 recipe	2×the recipe	3×the recipe
Melba rounds	2 dozen	4 dozen	8 dozen
Cold Marinated Shrimp*	2×the recipe	4×the recipe	8×the recipe
Crisp Cucumber Rounds Tokyo Style*	2×the recipe	4×the recipe	8×the recipe
Garlicky Cocktail Almonds*	1 recipe	2×the recipe	3×the recipe
Beer Cheese Spread*	Not needed	1 recipe	2×the recipe
Caponata*	Not needed	2×the recipe	3×the recipe
Crackers	Not needed	5–6 dozen	10–12 dozen

A WINTER COCKTAIL PARTY

Menu	For 12	Quantities Needed For 24	For 50
Chutney-Nut Meat Balls*	1 recipe	2×the recipe	4×the recipe
Rumakis*	2×the recipe	4×the recipe	8×the recipe
Quiche Tartlets*	1 recipe	2×the recipe	3×the recipe
Spiced Olives*	1 recipe	2×the recipe	3×the recipe
Garlic Nibbles*	Not needed	Not needed	1 recipe
Taramasalata*	Not needed	Not needed	4×the recipe
Sesame seed crackers	Not needed	Not needed	5–6 dozen

Note: For tips on calculating the amount and kind of liquor needed, see the chapter on beverages.

TWO INFORMAL SUMMER BUFFETS

Menu	For 12	Quantities Needed For 24	For 50
Chicken or Turkey Loaf* (cold)	2×the recipe	3×the recipe	4×the recipe
Tomatoes Stuffed with Easy Tuna Salad*			
Tomatoes	1 dozen	2 dozen	50
Easy Tuna Salad	1 recipe	2×the recipe	3×the recipe
Jiffy Deviled Eggs*	2×the recipe	3×the recipe	4×the recipe
Jellied Garden Vegetable Salad*	2×the recipe	3×the recipe	6×the recipe
Herbed Potato Salad*	2×the recipe	3×the recipe	6×the recipe
Danish Meat Balls*	Not needed	Not needed	4×the recipe
Buttered Noodles (cook by package directions)	Not needed	Not needed	4 lbs. (raw)
Fresh Peach Crisp*	2×the recipe	4×the recipe	8×the recipe

Coffee (see How to Make Coffee for a Crowd, beverage chapter)

Menu	For 12	Quantities Needed For 24	For 50
Glazed and Decorated Cold Ham*	4 lbs. boneless ham 6 lbs. bone-in ham	6 lbs. boneless 8 lbs. bone-in	12 lbs. boneless 16 lbs. bone-in
Macaroni and Shellfish Salad*	2×the recipe	3×the recipe	8×the recipe
Bean and Beet Salad*	3×the recipe	6×the recipe	12×the recipe
Tomato Aspic*	2×the recipe	4×the recipe	8×the recipe
Parker House Rolls*	1½ dozen	2½ dozen	5½ dozen
Ambrosia*	2×the recipe	4×the recipe	8×the recipe
Florentines*	1 recipe	2×the recipe	4×the recipe

Coffee (see How to Make Coffee for a Crowd, beverage chapter)

TWO FORMAL SUMMER BUFFETS

Menu	For 12	Quantities Needed For 24	For 50
Smoked Salmon	2¼ lbs.	4¾ lbs.	9½ lbs.
Pâté-Filled Ham in Aspic*	1 recipe	1 recipe	2×the recipe
Chaud-Froid of Chicken Breasts*	3×the recipe	6×the recipe	10×the recipe
Avocado Mousse*	2×the recipe	4×the recipe	6×the recipe
Shellfish and Saffron Rice Salad*	Not needed	Not needed	4×the recipe
Lemon Fluff*	2×the recipe	4×the recipe	5×the recipe
Gingered Honeydew Melon*	Not needed	Not needed	5×the recipe
Coffee (see How to Make Coffee for a Crowd, beverage chapter)			
Fresh Fruit Cocktail	1½ qts.	3 qts.	6 qts.
Whole Salmon in Aspic*	1 recipe	1 recipe	2×the recipe
Country Captain*	1 recipe	2×the recipe	3×the recipe
Boiled Rice* (see How to Cook Rice, cereals and pasta chapter)	3×the recipe	5×the recipe	7×the recipe
Wilted Cucumbers*	3×the recipe	6×the recipe	10×the recipe
Russian Salad*	2×the recipe	4×the recipe	8×the recipe
Strawberries Romanoff*	3×the recipe	6×the recipe	8×the recipe
Meringues Chantilly*	Not needed	Not needed	2×the recipe or 4 dozen bakery meringues
Coffee (see How to Make Coffee for a Crowd, beverage chapter)			

TWO INFORMAL WINTER BUFFETS

Menu	For 12	Quantities Needed For 24	For 50
Lamb Curry*	2×the recipe	4×the recipe	7×the recipe
Nut Rice*	3×the recipe	5×the recipe	7×the recipe
Coulibiac*	1 recipe	1 recipe	2×the recipe
Parsley Sauce*	3×the recipe	5×the recipe	7×the recipe
Cherry Tomatoes	1 qt.	2 qts.	1 gal.
Waldorf Salad*	3×the recipe	6×the recipe	12×the recipe
Imperial Peach Mold*	2×the recipe	4×the recipe	8×the recipe
Coffee (see How to Make Coffee for a Crowd, beverage chapter)			

Menu	Quantities Needed		
	For 12	For 24	For 50
Lasagne*	1 recipe	2×the recipe	3×the recipe
Beef Stew for a Crowd*	½ recipe	1 recipe	2×the recipe
Tossed green salad Choice of dressings	3 qts. prepared salad greens	6 qts. greens	3 gals. greens
Tutti-Frutti Ice Cream*	2×the recipe	4×the recipe	8×the recipe
Almond-Orange Icebox Cookies*	½ recipe	1 recipe	1 recipe

Coffee (see How to Make Coffee for a Crowd, beverage chapter)

TWO FORMAL WINTER BUFFETS

Menu	Quantities Needed		
	For 12	For 24	For 50
Consommé Madrilène* (in punch cups)	3×the recipe	6×the recipe	12×the recipe
Melba toast	1 dozen	2 dozen	4½ dozen
Moussaka*	2×the recipe	2×the recipe	4×the recipe
Artichoke Hearts Vinaigrette*	3×the recipe	6×the recipe	12×the recipe
Rosy King Crab Bake*	2×the recipe	4×the recipe	6×the recipe
Buttered noodles (cook by package directions)	1½ lbs. (raw)	2½ lbs.	4 lbs.
Hot Fruit Compote*	2×the recipe	4×the recipe	8×the recipe
Lemon Wafers*	1 recipe	1 recipe	2×the recipe

Coffee (see How to Make Coffee for a Crowd, beverage chapter)

Veal Marengo*	2×the recipe	3×the recipe	6×the recipe
Shrimp Creole*	2×the recipe	3×the recipe	5×the recipe
Risi e Bisi*	3×the recipe	6×the recipe	12×the recipe
Hearts of lettuce Choice of dressings	3 qts. lettuce	6 qts. lettuce	3 gals. lettuce
Viennese Fruit Flan*	2×the recipe	4×the recipe	7×the recipe

Coffee (see How to Make Coffee for a Crowd, beverage chapter)

About Parties for Young People

Preschool Children have limited tastes and appetites and are happy with a few fancily cut sandwiches spread with peanut butter or cream cheese and jelly, ice cream (preferably a choice of vanilla and strawberry or chocolate), a decorated yellow or white cake (or cupcakes), a milk or fruit drink, and perhaps a few cookies and hard candies.

Preteens have outgrown the pastel confectionery of small children's parties and prefer heftier fare: sundaes, sodas, and shakes (particularly if they can concoct their own), more sophisticated cakes (Burnt Sugar,* Coconut Cream,* Devil's Food,* Angel Food,* Spice*). Moreover, their parties are as apt to be suppers as mid-afternoon affairs. Always popular: charcoal-broiled hot dogs and hamburgers, Heroes,* Sloppy Joes,* fried chicken, Spaghetti and Meat Balls in Tomato Sauce,* potato salad, coleslaw, Boston Baked Beans.*

Teen-agers today are about three times as worldly as their parents were at the same age. Many have traveled, if not abroad, at least to big cities where there are ethnic restaurants. They have sampled Smorgasbord, whole repertoires of pasta and Chinese classics, Shish Kebabs,* Beef Stroganoff,* chili (not the canned but the fiery Texas type), Tacos,* and very possibly Paella,* Moussaka,* Bouillabaisse,* Borsch,* tempura, Sukiyaki,* and Teriyaki.* Let your own teen-ager help plan the menu. He or she knows what's *in* and *out*.

A PRESCHOOL BIRTHDAY PARTY

Basic White* or Basic Three-Egg Butter Cake*
with Basic Butter Cream, Cherry or Berry Butter Cream Frosting*
Vanilla Ice Cream*   Berry Ice Cream*
Mints   Roasted Peanuts
Easy Pink Lemonade*

A PRETEEN BIRTHDAY BARBECUE

Charcoal-Broiled Hot Dogs and Hamburgers
Buns   Relishes   Mustard   Ketchup   Onions
Old-Fashioned Potato Salad*
Creamy Sweet-Sour Coleslaw*
Chocolate Freezer Ice Cream*
Devil's Food Cake* with White Mountain Frosting*
Milk   Iced Tea

A TEEN BIRTHDAY SUPPER

Cold Marinated Shrimp*
Guacamole*   Crackers   Corn Chips
Ripe and Green Olives
Pizza* with a Choice of Toppings
Marinated Roasted Peppers*
Tossed Green Salad   Choice of Dressings
Biscuit Tortoni
Lemon Chiffon Cake* with Lemon Butter Cream Frosting*
Milk   Soft Drinks

AN EASTER EGG ROLL

Hard-Cooked Eggs   Easter Egg Dyes and Decals
Candy Easter Eggs   Salted Nuts
Easy Yellow Cupcakes* with Basic Butter Cream Frosting*
Assorted Ice-Cream Sodas*

A HALLOWEEN PARTY

Hot Buttered Popcorn*   Popcorn Balls*
Candied Apples*   Molasses Taffy*   Sugared Nuts*
Tea Punch*

Table Setting and Service

How to Set Tables

Formal dinners have gone the way of servants, which is to say *away*. Entertaining today is casual, convivial, and most Americans prefer it that way. Few hostesses object to kibitzers in their kitchens; in fact, many welcome helping hands. Modern tables, reflecting the breakdown of rules, are more apt to wear denims, paisley, and bandanna prints than snowy damasks and linens—except for the most formal affairs. Service, too, is relaxed, being dictated more by convenience than convention.

Breakfast

What most Americans have adopted is *English Service,* far from stuffy although the name suggests it. This, simply, is a relaxed family-style service in which the host dishes up food at the table and passes it clockwise around the table, ladies first.

Lunch

When there are several courses, a *Compromise Service* works well. Appetizers, soups, and desserts are dished up in the kitchen and brought to the table, the entrée is served at table English style.

Russian Service is fussy, formal, and out of the question for anyone lacking a battery of servants to

Informal Dinner

pass platters or plates of food to
each guest.

Table-Setting Tips:

Linens: Make sure tablecloth has
plenty of overhang, 15″–18″ all
around. Place napkins, folded
into rectangles, to the left of the
forks with the long, open sides
facing plates or, if there is no first

Semiformal Dinner

Small Buffet

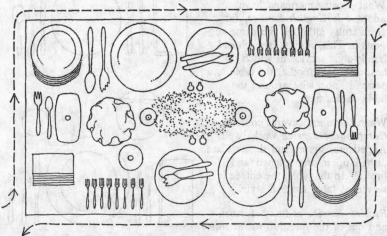

Large Buffet

course, perpendicularly down the center of covers (place settings) or plates.

Flatware: Forks to the left, knives and spoons to the right, lined up in order of use (from the outside in) with handles in a straight line about 1″ from table edge. Two exceptions: The small cocktail fork, which is placed to the right, on the outside, and the butter spreader, laid horizontally across the bread-and-butter plate. Forks and spoons are arranged prongs and bowls up, knives with cutting edges toward plates. It's best not to place more than 3 pieces of silver on each side of a plate. If the dinner is a fairly formal one, bring in dessert silver as dessert is served.

Cover (Individual Place Setting): To avoid crowding guests at a table, allow at least 30″ from the center of one cover to the next.

Service Plates: These add a handsome, gracious touch. Use plates that are at least 10″ across, place in the center of each cover, and use as an underliner for the appetizer and soup. Remove before bringing in the entree.

Glasses: The water tumbler should stand just above the point of the dinner knife, wine goblets slightly to the right of it. If two wines are being served, both wineglasses should be on the table at the start of the meal.

Finger Bowls: Too pretentious for casual dinners, finger bowls do still appear at formal affairs. They are presented before dessert, bracketed by dessert fork and spoon on doily-lined dessert plates. *To Use:*

Set fork and spoon on table to left and right of plate, finger bowl and doily on table just above and to the left of the plate.

Flower Arrangements and Centerpieces: Keep them simple and keep them low so that guests aren't peering into a jungle of blossoms and greenery. Avoid strongly perfumed flowers, also those known to cause allergies.

Candles: Use in the evening only and place strategically so guests aren't forced to stare directly into a flame.

Place Cards: When there are too many guests at dinner to direct personally to their places, place cards do the job well. Use small white or ivory cards and letter simply Mr. Brown, Miss Green, or in the case of two Mr. Browns or Miss Greens, Mr. Josiah Brown, Mr. Everett Brown, Miss Abigail Green, Miss Eleanor Green. Center cards just above each cover.

Serving and Clearing Tips:

— Remove serving dishes first, then plates, flatware, and glasses, beginning with the hostess and moving to the right around the table. *Exception:* If the hostess herself is clearing, she should begin with the guest to her right and proceed around the table, taking up her own plate last. When a table is properly cleared, the centerpiece alone should remain.
— Serve and remove plates from the left, using the left hand, glasses from the right with the right hand. Work quickly, quietly, *never* reaching in front of a guest. *Note:* If two are waiting table, plates

A WEEK'S BUDGET MENUS

	Breakfast	Lunch	Supper
Sunday	Fruit Cocktail Whole Wheat Pancakes* Maple Syrup Butter Grilled Sausages Milk Coffee	Baked Ham* Orange-Flavored Mashed Yams* Scalloped Cabbage* Corn Sticks* Butterscotch Tapioca Pudding* (makes enough for 2 meals) Old-Fashioned Ginger Biscuits* (makes enough for 2 meals) Milk Coffee	Vegetable Soup Hot Buttered Popcorn* Oranges Tangerines Cookies Cocoa
Monday	Stewed Fruits Scrambled Eggs Whole Wheat Toast Milk Coffee	Spaghetti and Meat Balls in Tomato Sauce* Lettuce Hearts Oil and Vinegar Dressing Garlic Bread* Fruit Cheese Milk Coffee or Tea	Boston Baked Beans* (with some leftover ham added) (makes enough for 2 meals) Waldorf Salad* Butterscotch Tapioca Pudding* Sugar Cookies* (makes enough for 2 meals) Milk Coffee or Tea
Tuesday	Cranberry Juice Grilled Leftover Sliced Ham* Fried Corn Meal Mush* Butter Syrup Milk Coffee	Chicken-Noodle Soup* Cheese Crackers* Spicy Applesauce* (makes enough for 2 meals) Cookies Milk Coffee or Tea	Tomato Juice Economy Meat Loaf* (makes enough for 2 meals) Baked Potatoes* Lemon-Glazed Carrots* Old-Fashioned Bread and Butter Pudding* Milk Coffee or Tea

Wednesday

Orange Juice
Buttered Hominy Grits
Grilled Sausage Patties
Milk   Coffee

Fruit Cocktail
Hot Meat Loaf Sandwiches
Carrot and Celery Sticks
Cookies   Coffee
Milk   Coffee

Cranberry Juice Cocktail
Quick Tuna Surprise*
Caraway Coleslaw with Creamy Oil
and Vinegar Dressing*
Easy Date and Walnut Pudding*
(makes enough for 2 meals)
Milk   Coffee

Thursday

Half Grapefruit
French Toast*
Butter   Jam   Honey
Cocoa   Coffee

Golden Split Pea Soup with Ham*
(makes enough for 2 meals)
Buttered Whole Wheat Toast
Sliced Tomatoes
Cookies
Milk   Coffee

Crudités*
Tamale Pie*
Lettuce Hearts   French Dressing
Ambrosia*
Sugar Cookies*
Milk   Tea or Coffee

Friday

Tomato Juice
Skillet Egg and Potato Breakfast*
Milk   Coffee

Ambrosia-Fruit Cup
Baked Bean Sandwiches
Creamy Sweet-Sour Coleslaw*
Old-Fashioned Ginger Biscuits*
Milk   Coffee

Jambalaya*
Buttered Green Beans
Hot Corn Bread*
Pineapple Upside-Down Cake*
Milk   Coffee or Tea

Saturday

Hominy, Beans and Salt Pork*
Buttered Whole Wheat Muffins*
Spicy Applesauce*
Milk   Coffee

Tomato-Cheese Rabbit*
Tossed Green Salad
Ice Cream   Sugar Cookies*
Milk   Coffee

Golden Split Pea Soup with Ham*
Cheese Biscuits*
Molded Fruit Salad
Easy Date and Walnut Pudding*
Milk   Tea or Coffee

A WEEK'S MENUS FOR A 1200-CALORIE-A-DAY DIET

Note: Portions are average size unless otherwise indicated; T. = 1 tablespoon, t. = teaspoon.

	Monday	Calories	Tuesday	Calories
Breakfast	Tomato Juice (1/2 cup)	23	Orange Juice (1/2 cup)	55
	Boiled or Poached Egg	80	Ready-to-Eat High-Protein Cereal (1 cup with 1 t.sugar,	170
	Slice Whole Wheat Toast, 1 t. butter	98	1/2 cup skim milk)	
	Black Coffee or Tea with Lemon	0	1/2 Toasted English Muffin, 2 t. jelly	95
		201	Black Coffee or Tea with Lemon	0
				320
Lunch	Cold Roast Beef and Tomato Sandwich (2 thin slices	278	Beef Broth (1 cup)	35
	lean beef, 1/2 tomato, mustard or horseradish)		Cottage Cheese (1 cup, uncreamed)	195
	Apple	70	1/2 Tomato on Lettuce (topped with minced scallions,	45
	Skim Milk (1 cup)	90	1 T. Tangy Low-Calorie Salad Dressing*)	
		438	1 (2") piece Angel Food Cake* (unfrosted)	120
			Black Coffee or Tea with Lemon	0
				395
Dinner	Sautéed Calf's Liver*	280	Egg Roll (packaged)	53
	Riced Boiled Medium Size Potato	100	Chicken Chow Mein*, 1/3 cup Boiled Rice	292
	Low-Calorie Asparagus*	40	Pineapple Chunks (1/2 cup water-pack)	64
	Low-Calorie Sherbet	65	Vanilla Wafer (1)	20
	Black Coffee or Tea with Lemon	0	Black Coffee or Tea with Lemon	0
		485		429
Anytime Snack	1 Cup Skim Milk	90	1/2 Cup Skim Milk	45
Total Day's Calories:		1214		1189

	Wednesday	Calories	Thursday	Calories
Breakfast	1/2 Grapefruit	55	Tomato Juice (1/2 cup)	23
	1 Slice French Toast (fried in 1 t. butter, sprinkled with	198	Boiled or Poached Egg	80
	1 t. confectioners' sugar)		Slice Whole Wheat Toast, 1 t. butter	98
	Black Coffee or Tea with Lemon	0	Black Coffee or Tea with Lemon	0
		253		201
Lunch	Tuna Sandwich (1/3 cup water-pack tuna mixed with	270	Clam Chickee*	20
	minced celery, onion, lemon juice)		Chef's Salad (2 oz. cheese, 1 oz. lean ham, Low-	305
	Carrot and Celery Sticks	25	Calorie Thousand Island Dressing*)	
	Sliced Canned Peaches (1/2 cup water-pack)	38	Melba Toast (2 slices)	32
	Skim Milk (1 cup)	90	Skim Milk (1 cup)	90
		423		447
Dinner	Broiled (4 oz.) Herb Burger*	247	Cabbage Rolls and Sauerkraut*	270
	On 1/2 Toasted Bun	70	Poppy Seed Noodles* (1/2 cup)	100
	Skillet Mushrooms*	30	Fruit Cocktail (1/2 cup water-pack)	72
	Low-Calorie Green Beans*	35	Vanilla Wafer (1)	20
	Broiled 1/2 Tomato	18	Black Coffee or Tea with Lemon	0
	Low-Calorie Gingered Orange Fluff* with Low-	39		462
	Calorie Dessert Topping*			
	Black Coffee or Tea with Lemon	0		
		439		
Anytime Snack	1 Cup Skim Milk	90	1 Cup Skim Milk	90
Total Day's Calories:		1205		1200

A WEEK'S MENUS FOR A 1200-CALORIE-A-DAY DIET (continued)

	Friday	Calories	Saturday	Calories
Breakfast	Peach Nectar (1/2 cup)	60	1/2 Grapefruit	55
	Ready-to-Eat High Protein Cereal (1 cup with 1 t. sugar, 1/2 cup skim milk)	170	Boiled or Poached Egg	80
			Slice Whole Wheat or Enriched Bread Toast, 1 t. butter	98
	Black Coffee or Tea with Lemon	0	Black Coffee or Tea with Lemon	0
		230		233
Lunch	Tomato Cocktail*	35	Open-Face Grilled Cheese and Bacon Sandwich	269
	Scrambled Egg Sandwich (2 eggs scrambled in 2 t. butter, seasoned with chives)	333	Wilted Cucumbers*	40
			Seedless Grapes (2/3 cup)	47
	Skim Milk (1 cup)	90	Skim Milk (1 cup)	90
		458		446
Dinner	Low-Calorie Fillets of Flounder en Papillote*	180	Steak Florentine* (4 oz.)	310
	Medium-Size Parsleyed Potato	100	Boiled Chopped Spinach	23
	Low-Calorie Boiled Carrots*	40	Strawberries Grand Marnier*	100
	Gingered Honeydew Melon*	65		
	Black Coffee or Tea with Lemon	0	Black Coffee or Tea with Lemon	0
		385		433
Anytime	1/2 Cup Skim Milk	45	2 Medium-Size Carrots	40
Snack	1 Small Banana	81	1/2 Cup Skim Milk	45
Total Day's Calories:		1199		1197

	Sunday	Calories
Brunch	1/2 Medium-Size Cantaloupe	60
	Low-Calorie Sautéed Kidneys* with Skillet Mushrooms and 1/2 Broiled Tomato	278
	OR	
	2 Poached Eggs and 2 Slices Grilled Bacon	206
	Toasted English Muffin, 2 t. butter	
	Black Coffee or Tea with Lemon	0
		544
Mid-Afternoon Snack	1 Medium-Size Apple	70
	1 Cup Skim Milk	90
		160
Dinner	1/2 Lemon-Broiled Chicken* (small)	290
	Low-Calorie Cauliflower*	35
	Frozen French-Style Green Beans and Mushrooms (1/2 cup)	26
	Green Grapes and Sour Cream* (made with yogurt)	138
	Black Coffee or Tea with Lemon	0
		489
Total Day's Calories:		1193

may be taken from the right as
new ones are added from the left.
– Fill water or wineglasses as they
stand on the table; never lift them.
– Crumb a table only if necessary,
whisking crumbs onto a small
plate with a napkin.
– When serving coffee at the table,
bring in cups and saucers empty,
placing them to the guests'
right. Coffee spoons should be on
the saucers, behind the cups with
their handles parallel to the cup
handles.

Seating Tips:

– The host and hostess sit at
opposite ends of a table. To the
host's right sits the lady guest of
honor, to his left the lady of
next importance. The male guests
of first and second importance
are seated to the hostess's right and
left. Remaining seats are filled as
the hostess chooses—man, woman,
man, woman—but never with
husbands and wives together.
– To avoid confusion, the hostess
should direct each guest to his seat.

CHAPTER 5

BEVERAGES

ALCOHOLIC BEVERAGES

The French are master chefs, the Viennese master confectioners, but when it comes to mixing drinks, Americans are the masters. So many drinks—hard and soft—are American inventions: ice-cream sodas, fizzy colas and floats, not to mention cocktails (and cocktail parties). We drink, perhaps, a greater variety of beverages than any other people and are constantly concocting new ones. Moreover, we have developed a European fondness for fine wines and choice brews and an adventurous spirit in sampling exotic liqueurs.

About Beers and Ales

Beer and ale are closely related fermented malt beverages, brewed in different ways. The technical differences matter not so much here as the results. *Ale* tastes more strongly of hops than beer, particularly *stout* and *porter*, which are heavy, dark, and bittersweet.

The most popular *beer* is bubbly, golden *lager*, a light brew held in the cask until cleared of sediment (*lager* is from *lagern*, the German word meaning *to store*). It is carbonated (hence the bubbles), bottled or canned, and pasteurized. *Draught beer* is drawn straight from the cask and not pasteurized. American lagers average 3.2–5 per cent alcohol, European lagers slightly more. *Bock beer*, available in spring, is a dark, sweetish, heavy

lager brewed from dark-roasted malt. *Pilsner* is pale lager, originally from Pilsen, Czechoslovakia, made with natural mineral water.

About Serving Beers and Ales: The ideal temperature for serving beer is said to be 40° F., cool but not as cold as Americans like it. Europeans frown upon the American practice of serving ice cold beer, insisting that it destroys the flavor. Should beer be poured so that there is no head? Depends on personal preference. Connoisseurs insist upon a creamy head about 1″ thick because it proves the beer isn't flat and seals in the flavor. To achieve a good head, tilt glass and pour enough beer gently down the side to ⅓ full, then stand glass upright and pour beer straight in. To minimize head, continue filling tilted glass.

About Wines

The subject of wine (by definition the fermented juice of freshly pressed grapes) is nearly inexhausti-ble, and in a basic cookbook there simply is not room to do more than capsulize. Whole volumes have been devoted to wines, indeed to single wines.

APÉRITIF WINES AND WINE-BASED DRINKS

Wine (those served before meals)	Appropriate Glass	How To Serve
Byrrh	6-ounce old-fashioned glass	on the rocks
Dry Champagne (Brut)	9-ounce tulip goblet	well chilled
Dry Sherry (Fino or Manzanilla)	6-ounce sherry glass	well chilled
Dubonnet or Dubonnet Blonde	6-ounce sherry glass	well chilled
Lillet (similar to vermouth, made of white wine, brandy, herbs)	6-ounce old-fashioned glass or sherry glass	on the rocks or well chilled
Vermouth (dry and sweet)	6-ounce old-fashioned glass or sherry glass	on the rocks or well chilled

The Types of Wine:

TABLE WINES

(Natural wines served with meals; they have an alcoholic content of 10–14 per cent.)

Dry Red Wines:

French:

Bordeaux (called claret by the British): Many experts consider these the finest of all table wines. When good, they are rich, fragrant, full-bodied. Bordeaux include *Médoc, Pomerol, Saint-Emilion, Graves.* Outstanding chateaux are *Château Lafite-Rothschild, Château Latour, Château Mouton-Rothschild.*

Burgundy: Another superb group of French wines, heavier than Bordeaux and more robust. Some better known red Burgundies are *Beaujolais, Echézeaux, Volnay, Pommard, Beaune,* and, three of the best: *Chambertin, Romanée-Conti,* and *La Tâche.*

Loire Valley Wine: Chinon, Anjou (both light bodied and well balanced).

Rhône Valley Wine: Châteauneuf-du-Pape, Côte Rôtie (heady and rich), and Hermitage (generously full flavored).

Italian: Popular imports are *Barbera, Barbaresco, Bardolino* (much like Chianti but smoother), *Barolo* (which some consider Italy's greatest dry red wine), *Chianti* (the best may not come in the *fiasco,* or straw-covered bottle; look for the neckband imprinted with the black rooster), *Lambrusco* (a crackling red) and *Valpolicella* (delicate).

Spanish and Portuguese: Both countries produce good—if sometimes rough—red table wines. Most readily available are the Spanish *Rioja* and Portuguese *Dão.*

American: California vineyards produce first-rate dry red wines, notably *Cabernet Sauvignon* (a

Bordeaux-type), *Pinot Noir* (similar to Burgundy), *Gamay, Zinfandel, Barbera,* and *Grignolino.*

Dry White Wines:

French:

Bordeaux: Graves (both dry and semidry).

Burgundy: Chablis (light and very dry), *Meursault* (soft, flowery, feminine), *Montrachet* (Dumas declared that Montrachet "should be drunk while kneeling") and *Pouilly-Fuissé* (dry but fruity).

Loire Valley Wine: Muscadet (very dry), *Pouilly-Fumé* and *Sancerre* (both still and dry), and *Vouvray* (still or crackling, dry or semidry).

Alsatian Wine: Gewürztraminer (fruity, almost gingery), *Riesling* (dry and elegant), *Sylvaner* (fresh, light, and fruity), and *Traminer* (similar to *Gewürztraminer* but subtler).

Italian: Brolio Bianco (light), *Est! Est!! Est!!!* and *Orvieto* (dry or semidry), *Frascati, Soave* (very light and smooth), *Verdicchio* (dry or semidry with a touch of bitterness).

German: The noble grape of Germany is the Riesling, hence the varietal name Riesling may appear on labels of both Rhine and Moselle wines. To tell Rhine wines from the Moselle at a glance, look at the bottle. Both come in tall slim bottles but the Rhine bottle is brown, the Moselle green.

Rhine Wine: The choicest are from the Rheingau, a 20-mile stretch on the right bank of the Rhine between Wiesbaden and Rüdesheim. Ones to seek out are *Hochheimer* (called hock by the British), *Rüdesheimer,* and *Johannisberg* (Schloss Johannisberg may be Germany's most famous vineyard). The *Rheinhessen,* just across the river from the Rheingau, produces the popular *Liebfraumilch,* not a single wine but a blend. It is produced throughout the Rheinhessen, thus can be very good (look for such labels as Blue Nun, Hans Christof, Crown of Crowns), or it can be disappointing. Rhine wines, generally, are pleasantly light and dry.

Moselle Wine: The best are from the *Mittel (Middle) Moselle* and include *Piesporter, Bernkastler* (Bernkasteler Doktor is perhaps the most renowned), *Kroever, Zeltinger,* and *Wehlener.*

Steinwein: One of the best wines from Franconia (valleys of the Main and its tributaries), this light wine comes in the squatty *Bocksbeutel* instead of the tall, graceful bottles of Rhine and Moselle wines. There are other wines from Franconia, but Steinwein is best known to Americans.

Spanish and Portuguese: As with the Spanish table reds, *Rioja* is the name to look for in white table wines. Probably the best known Portuguese white wine is *vinho verde,* a tart young green wine, best drunk very cold.

American: California vintners produce excellent dry white wines. Some to try: *Semillon* and *Sauvignon Blanc* (similar to but drier than Sauternes), *Chardonnay* and *Pinot Blanc* (Chablis types), *Riesling, Traminer, Sylvaner,* and *Grey Riesling.* A number of Eastern vineyards also produce creditable Rieslings.

Rosé Wines:

There are fewer good rosé wines than dry reds or whites. The best imports are *Tavel* and *Anjou* from France, *Mateus* from Portugal. California also has good rosés: *Grenache* and *Gamay*.

DESSERT WINES

(Sweet, still, or fortified wines that are especially compatible with dessert; fortified wines are those that have had spirits added, often brandy, to bring the alcoholic content up to about 20 per cent).

Sauternes: People quibble as to whether these white Bordeaux are table or dessert wines. They are sweetish, however, and connoisseurs prefer them with dessert, particularly fruit. Among the greats are *Château d'Yquem* and *Château La Tour-Blanche*.

Madeira: There are many Madeira wines, all fortified, all classified according to sweetness. The driest is *Sercial*, then *Verdelho*, then *Boal* and, sweetest of all, *Malmsey*. *Rainwater Madeira* is a blend, which though light in color can be fairly rich or dry. Madeira, by the way, is a superb wine to use in cooking, especially in soups, sauces, and desserts. Sercial is also popularly served with turtle soup.

Port, Porto: True Porto comes from Porto, Portugal, and is a far cry from domestic imitations, which are spelled simply port. Some are exquisitely light and golden, some tawny and mellow, some thick and sweet. All are fortified. The classifications of port are: *Ruby* (fruity, sweet, young red wine), *Tawny* (aged in wood and amber in color), *Vintage* (wine of a single excellent year, carefully aged and costly), *Crusted* (aged port, not necessarily of one vintage; *crusted* refers to the sediment that accumulates in the bottle. These wines should be decanted so that the sediment doesn't land in the glass).

Sherry: The best known of the dessert wines, sherries come from Jerez, Spain, after which they are named. They are fortified but mellower, nuttier than either the ports or Madeiras. *Dry sherries* are *Fino*, *Manzanilla*, and *Vino de Pasto* (these are best served cold as apéritifs); the *medium dry* is *Amontillado* (very nutty and a good all-purpose sherry); and the *sweet* are *Amoroso*, *Oloroso*, and *Brown*. *Cream sherry* is a very sweet *Oloroso*.

Tokay: White or amber sweet Hungarian wine from Tokay grapes. Tokays are also made in California.

Other Dessert Wines: Málaga (from Spain), *Marsala* (from Sicily), *Mavrodaphne* (from Greece), and *Muscatel* (Greece, Spain, and Portugal produce good ones). These are generally very sweet, some quite syrupy and raisiny.

Champagne and Other Sparkling Wines

Champagne: True champagne comes from the ancient province of Champagne around Rheims, and it and only it can be sold as "Champagne" in France and most of Europe. This is the reason why domestic champagne is labeled "California Champagne" or "Ohio" or "New York State Champagne." (Some of the domestics are very good, too.) Champagne is a white wine made from the Pinot Noir and Pinot Chardonnay grapes, twice fermented—once before bottling, once afterward (which produces the bubbles). All champagnes are blends, usually made from both varieties of Pinot grapes. When the white grapes alone (Chardonnay) are used, the results are a lighter champagne called *blanc de blanc*. Depending upon the amount of sweetening added *after* the first fermentation, champagne may be dry or sweet. The terms used to denote degree of sweetness are: *brut* or, in the case of California champagne, *natur* (the driest), *extra dry* (not as dry as brut), *demi-sec* (fairly sweet), and *sec* or *doux* (quite sweet). Pink champagne is simply champagne made from pressings allowed to stay on the skins a bit longer than usual (the pigment in the *pinot noir* grape skins pinkens the juice). When should champagne be served? It is the one wine that can be served at any time of the day, any course of the meal. The sweeter champagnes, however, are more suited to dessert. *Tip on Opening Champagne Bottles:* Don't pop the cork, ease it out slowly and steadily so you don't shake up the champagne.

Other Sparkling Wines: There are many bubbling red and white wines, but sparkling Burgundy is the one Americans know best (Americans like it, the French don't). It is produced in much the same way as champagne except that the wine used is red Burgundy. France also makes a sparkling *Anjou* (rosé) and a sparkling *Vouvray* (dry or semidry white). Portugal makes some bubbling rosés, Germany some sparkling whites, Italy, too, including the famous *Asti Spumante*. California makes a version of nearly every sparkling French wine.

COOKING WINES

The idea of "cooking wine" is an absurd holdover from the days of prohibition. Cooking wines are "salted" so they won't be drunk. It is pointless to buy them, because the best wines to cook with are "drinking" wines (except, of course, those that cost the earth).

Some Terms and Techniques Having to do with Wines

The Language of Wine Labels: Because so many wines are imported and their labels written in foreign languages, the beginner has trouble decoding the message. The labels carrying the most meaningful information are those of French and German wines. Here then, are some of the common label terms and what they mean:

Appellation Contrôlée: A French term meaning that the wine was produced where it says it was, a guarantee of place of origin, so to speak, entitling the wine to a regional name—Bordeaux, for example, or Burgundy (the more specific the regional name, by the way, the better the wine will probably be). It further means that the traditional standards of the locale were upheld in the production of the wine.

Cave: The French word for *wine cellar; cave* on a label is not a guarantee of quality.

Clos: The French word for *vineyard;* if a label contains the phrase "*clos de*" followed by the name of a vineyard, it means the wine was produced at the local vineyard, and if the vineyard (and vintage) is a good one, the wine should be good.

Crus Classés: In 1855 the vineyards of Médoc and Sauternes in Bordeaux were classified according to excellence, and 62 were rated *Grands Crus* (great growths), a designation many Bordeaux labels still carry. Within the *Grands Crus* were five subdivisions, from the first and finest (*Premiers Crus*) through second, third, and fourth to fifth growths. Some bottles still display *Premiers Crus* on their labels, meaning they were the finest of the 1855 classification. Wines marked *Crus Exceptionnels* were in the category just below the *Grands Crus*, and those marked *Crus Bourgeois* and *Crus Artisans*, etc., were lower still. Since 1855, however, vineyards have changed hands, qualities have changed, and there is much pressure for a new system of classification that will give credit where credit is due today. The new system, however, has not been determined, so the 1855 terms still hold.

Kabinet: A German label term meaning that the grower guarantees this particular wine to be the highest quality.

Mise en Bouteilles au (or *du*) *Château:* A French term meaning *estate-bottled*. Because most wine-producing châteaux are in Bordeaux, this particular phrase appears primarily on Bordeaux wines. With Burgundies, the equivalent phrase is *Mise en* (or *du*) *Domaine*. Other French phrases meaning estate-bottled are *Mise en Bouteille par le Propriétaire* or, more simply, *Mise à la Propriété*. The German equivalents: *Abfüllung*, *Kellerabfüllung*, and *Schlossabzug*.

V.D.Q.S.: An abbreviation on French labels for *Vins Délimités de Qualité Supérieure*. It merely means that the wine has been pro-duced according to government regulation and is not an indication of quality.

Other Wine Terms and Techniques:

Claret: The British name for red Bordeaux table wines.

Decant: To pour from one container to another. Aged wines need to be decanted so that any sediment stays in the original bottle. Decanting also is important for many dry red wines because it aerates them and brings out their full flavor.

Dry: A term meaning not sweet.

Lees: Sediment in a liquor or wine.

Marc: The grape skins and seeds left in the press after the juice has been run off. It is used to make *marc*, a potent *eau de vie*.

May Wine: Light German spring wine punch flavored with woodruff. Also called *Maibowle*. Some May wine is bottled.

Must: Pressed grape juice before and during fermentation.

Room Temperature: Ideally 60° F. and the temperature at which most dry red table wines are at their best.

Solerization: A process used in making Madeira and sherry in which casks of certain vintages are stacked, one on top of the other, the oldest being at the bottom. During the blending of the wines, a little from each tier is added in carefully worked-out proportions. When the bottom casks are empty, they are refilled from those directly above. Not all Madeira and sherry are made by this process, but those that are are marked *Solera*.

Varietal Wine: A wine named for the variety of grape from which it was made. *Riesling* is a varietal wine and so are *Semillon, Pinot Noir* and *Gamay* from California.

Vin Blanc: French for *white wine.*

Vin Rouge: French for *red wine.*

Vin du Pays: Local wine and the one to drink when traveling abroad. Much of it cannot be sampled out of its own locale, and much of it is very pleasant indeed.

Vins Ordinaires: Ordinary table wines, red or white, usually served in a carafe. These are the wines served in many French *bistros* and inns.

Vintage: Considerable fuss is made about vintage, more perhaps than is justified, because in off years wine of a great vineyard is likely to be better than that of a so-so vineyard in a great year. Vintage refers to the year's crop, and grapes, like other crops, experience good years and bad. Vintage matters most with French and German wines where weather is more changeable than in warmer, sunnier climes (vintage means little with Italian, Spanish, California, and Portuguese wines—except for Porto).

About Starting a Wine Cellar

People who enjoy wine usually keep a supply on hand; some even go to the expense of building temperature-controlled rooms so that the wines will mature properly. Wines are "alive," and if they are to mature properly, certain conditions must be met.

Temperature: Wine should not be subjected to abrupt temperature changes, so store well away from radiators, air conditioners, and drafts. Though the ideal "cellar" climate is about 55° F., wines will not suffer noticeably at temperatures up to 70° F. if those temperatures are constant. They are apt to deteriorate, especially the more perishable whites, in super-heated apartments or where there are sudden changes from hot to cold.

Light: Keep wines in a dim or dark spot; intense light—natural or artificial—is damaging.

Vibration: Wines should mature undisturbed, the bottles lying on their sides so that the corks do not dry out and admit destructive bacteria or mold. This means no vibration from dishwashers, laundry, or other household equipment and no picking up and inspecting by family, friends, or neighbors.

The cellar, of course, need not be a cellar. It can be a closet shelf in a skyscraper apartment if conditions are right. What is the best way to buy wines? You'll save by buying by the case, also by buying good vintages young. Most wines, dry reds particularly, are better with a few years' maturity. When a vintage is good, buy labels you like as soon as they are available, then put them away for several years. Choice French wines can increase tenfold in price within a few years.

About Bottle Shapes and Sizes: Certain types of wines are sold in certain types of bottles, and as you come to know wines, you'll be able to recognize the wine by glancing at the bottle. Sizes vary, too. The best bottle sizes to buy are those that you will use up in the course of an evening. The standard bottle size for most still wines is

24–26 ounces, enough for 2–3 people at dinner if one wine only is being served. Many are available in half bottles or pints containing 12.5 ounces, enough for 1–2 persons. A number of domestic wines are bottled by the gallon and half gallon (a money saver when a great many people are to be served). For general use, however, the standard bottle size is best.

CHAMPAGNE BOTTLE SIZES

Size	Capacity	Glassfuls
Split (also called Nip or Baby)	6 oz.	2 (3 oz.)
Pint	½ bottle or quart	3 (4 oz.)
Bottle or Quart	26 oz.	6 (4 oz.)
Magnum (a double bottle)	52 oz.	13 (4 oz.)
Jeroboam (a double magnum)	4 bottles or quarts	26 (4 oz.)

About Serving Wines

When a wine is to be served and what it is to accompany determine the type that should be served. But the rules aren't as rigid as they once were, and the old business about red wines with red meats and white wines with white meats shouldn't be taken as law. A full-bodied red wine complements rare roast beef, it's true, but that same wine might not pair as happily as a dry white wine with *pot-au-feu* or other boiled beef dishes. What you choose, then, is largely a matter of personal preference and common sense. Obviously, a rich dry red wine would be inappropriate with delicate white fish. And a fragile white would do nothing for venison. It would be foolish to lavish a fine wine on meat loaf, but equally so to downgrade filet mignon with a poor one. Generally speaking, white wines are the best choices for seafood, the humbler wines accompanying the humbler fish. The wine that goes best with poultry depends upon how the poultry was cooked—that in a white sauce calls for white wine, but *coq au vin* or chicken with a robust tomato sauce will team better with red wine. With experience, one begins to know instinctively happy partnerships of food and wine. And a good way to gain that experience is by eating in fine restaurants and asking the sommelier (wine steward) what he recommends with your choice of menu.

When Two Wines Are to Be Served: The rules again are fairly simple: white wine before red, young wine before old, and dry wine before sweet. *Tip:* Avoid serving wine with salad or other vinegary food—the vinegar deadens the palate to the taste of the wine.

About Wineglasses: Few people have room today to store several kinds of wineglasses, so the best idea is to have an all-purpose glass and, shelf space permitting, a special tulip goblet for champagne. The all-purpose glass should be large—anywhere from 10 to 20 ounces, stemmed, round-bowled, and of clear, thin uncut crystal or glass (the better to appreciate the color of the wine).

About Wine-Serving Temperatures:
Red wines should be served at room
temperature provided the room
isn't sweltering. To wine connoisseurs, room temperature is 60° F.
—a bit cool for those used to heated
houses—but a red wine served at a
room temperature in the 70°'s will
still be good. White and rosé wines
should be chilled before serving,
not so much that they lose flavor,
just enough to enhance them
(about 40–45° F.). Two to three
hours in the refrigerator should
do it. Don't try to quick-chill wine
in the freezer—too much danger
of its freezing. Champagnes should
be served well chilled and so should
sparkling Burgundies. *Note:*
When chilling wine in an ice bucket,
rotate bottle frequently so wine
chills evenly.

*About Uncorking and Pouring
Wines:* First of all, get a proper
corkscrew—one that gently lifts
out the cork—and learn to use it
before tackling a fine wine. To
open a bottle, cut around the metal
covering over the cork about 1″
below the top of the bottle and
peel off; wipe mouth of bottle
with a dry, clean napkin. Center tip
of corkscrew in cork and twist
into cork, using the proper technique
for the particular cockscrew, then
ease cork out. Don't pop the
cork or jerk it out—doing so
unsettles the wine.

Red wines should be uncorked about
an hour before serving so that
they have a chance to "breathe"
and develop full flavor. If the wine
is an old one with sediment in
the bottle, decant carefully into a
clean, dry decanter and leave un-
stoppered. Or, if wine is very old
and precious, cradle gently in a
wine basket (its purpose is to
keep wine as nearly as possible in

its cellar position so that a
minimum of sediment is stirred up).
White and rosé wines should be
uncorked just before serving.
Wrapping a wine bottle in a
white linen napkin is unnecessary
unless the wine has been chilled in an
ice bucket and is dripping. If in
doubt about the quality of a wine,
pour a little into your own glass
and sample before serving guests
(this is routinely done by som-
meliers in restaurants). When
pouring, never fill each glass more
than ⅓–½ (another reason for
having large wineglasses; the air
space in the glass allows you to
swirl the wine, bringing out its
full bouquet). *Tip:* As you finish
pouring wine into a glass, twist
bottle slightly as you lift it to
prevent dripping.

About Leftover Wines: Once
opened, wines quickly turn to
vinegar. White wines will keep
refrigerated several days, red and
fortified wines somewhat longer (uncork the leftover red wine and let
it stand at room temperature
about an hour before serving). If
the wine should turn to vinegar,
don't despair. Use it to dress salads.

About Whiskies and Liquors

All whiskies are liquor but all
liquors aren't whiskey, the difference being that whiskey is distilled
from grain mash (rye, corn,
barley, wheat) and liquor from a
variety of things—grain, sugar
cane (rum), cactus (tequila),
potatoes (vodka—although much of
today's vodka is made of grain).
Another clarification: *Whiskey* is
the common spelling, *whisky* the
British (used for scotch and
Canadian whisky). Here, then, is a
quick alphabet of popular liquors:

Aquavit: Potent, colorless Scandinavian liquor distilled from grain mash or potatoes, usually flavored with caraway. It is drunk ice cold, neat, sometimes with a beer chaser.

Arrack: A strong rumlike liquor distilled from fermented coconut juice. It is popular in Indonesia, Asia, and the Middle East.

Blended Whiskey: A blend, ⅕ 100-proof straight whiskey, ⅘ other whiskies and neutral spirits. Blended whiskies must be at least 80 proof, but they are almost always light and smooth.

Bourbon: The American liquor—amber brown, rich, and smooth—distilled from a fermented mash of rye, corn, and malted barley. *Straight bourbon* is distilled from a mash containing at least 51 per cent corn; *blended bourbon* is a whiskey blend containing at least 51 per cent straight bourbon. *Sour mash* is a type of bourbon made by fermenting each new load of mash with "working yeast" from the previous batch. Rather like sour dough bread, for which yeast starters are kept alive and used over and over, each successive dough replenishing the starter.

Canadian Whisky: Liquor distilled from blends of rye, corn, wheat, and barley. It is similar to rye and bourbon but smoother and lighter.

Corn Whiskey: Liquor distilled from fermented corn mash. To qualify as *straight corn whiskey,* it must contain at least 51 per cent corn. Corn whiskey is, of course, the *white lightning* or *moonshine* of Southern bootleggers.

Gin: Distilled neutral grain spirits, crisp, colorless, and lightly flavored with juniper. There are two types: *London dry gin,* the type Americans know, and *Dutch* or *Holland gin* (*Jenever* or *Geneva*), a heavier, stronger variety which the Dutch drink neat.

Irish Whiskey: An Irish liquor distilled from grain, primarily barley. It is dry and light, has none of the smokiness of scotch.

Rum: Liquor distilled from sugar syrup or molasses. Made primarily in the Caribbean, rum can be light and soft, it can be golden, amber, or rich dark brown, and it can be full-bodied. Darkest of all is *Demerara* rum, made from sugar cane grown along the Demerara River in British Guiana.

Rye: Whiskey distilled wholly or partly from rye mash. Its flavor is similar to bourbon, but many people find it smoother, more full bodied. *Rock and Rye* is rye flavored with rock candy, lemon, and orange.

Schnapps (also *Snaps*): A generic word meaning in Holland and Germany any strong dry colorless liquor such as gin, in Scandinavia (except Finland) aquavit, and in Finland vodka.

Scotch: A well-aged blend of grain and malt whiskies made in Scotland. The smoky flavor comes from the peat fires over which the malted barley is dried.

Sour Mash: See Bourbon.

Southern Comfort: Bourbon mixed with peach liqueur and fresh, peeled, and pitted peaches, then aged several months. It is sweeter, mellower than bourbon but has a deceptive kick.

Straight Whiskey: Pure, unblended grain whiskey from 80 to 110 proof that has been aged at least two years. The term is usually used in conjunction with bourbon or rye.

Tequila: A colorless or pale yellow liquor, usually 100+ proof, distilled from the fermented juice of the agave cactus.

Vodka: Highly distilled, charcoal filtered, colorless liquor distilled from fermented grain mash or potatoes. Vodka is unaged, flavorless, odorless and ranges from about 65 to 98 proof.

About Brandies and Liqueurs

These are usually served after meals or used in mixing drinks.

Absinthe: A bitter licorice-flavored liqueur made with wormwood and herbs. Because of the harmful effects of wormwood, absinthe was banned in France in 1915 and subsequently by many other countries including the United States.

Advokaat: A creamy egg liqueur.

Anis: Clear anise (licorice) liqueur popular in France and Spain. It is mixed with water (which turns it milky) and drunk as an apéritif.

Anisette: Clear sweet liqueur aromatic of anise seeds; unlike anis, it is drunk neat as a cordial.

Applejack: The American version of apple brandy.

Apricot Liqueur: A liqueur made from apricots; syrupy and fragrant.

Armagnac: See Brandy.

B&B: A half-and-half mixture of Benedictine and brandy, available bottled.

Benedictine: A sweet, fruity, herby liqueur made originally by Benedictine monks at the abbey of Fécamp in France. Though laymen today make Benedictine, they carry on in the tradition of the monks, using their secret recipe.

Brandy: Technically, distilled wine or other fermented fruit juice, well aged, usually in wood. There are many brandies: *Cognac* (one of the choicest, made in Cognac, France), *Armagnac* (another fine dry French brandy, this one from Armagnac), *Calvados* (the fine apple brandy of Normandy), and *Marc* (or *Grappa*), distilled from the grape skins, pulp, and seeds left in the wine press after the juice has been drained off.

Chartreuse: A brandy-based liqueur made by monks of the monastery of La Grande Chartreuse near Grenoble, France. Pale green or golden in color, it is flavored with hyssop, angelica, balm, cinnamon, and other herbs and spices.

Cherry Heering: A Danish cherry liqueur.

Cherry Suisse: A Swiss cherry-chocolate liqueur.

Cognac: See Brandy.

Cointreau: A choice French orange-flavored liqueur.

Crème: Crème liqueurs have been sweetened, are thick and syrupy. The list of them is long, but among the better known are: *Crème d'Ananas* (pineapple), *Crème de Banane* (banana), *Crème de Cacao* (chocolate), *Crème de Café* (coffee), *Crème de Cassis* (black currant), *Crème de Fraise* (strawberry), *Crème de Framboise* (raspberry), *Crème de Menthe* (mint—both a white and green are available), *Crème de Roses* (rose), *Crème de Vanille* (vanilla) and *Crème de Violette* (violet).

Curaçao: An orange-flavored liqueur made on the Caribbean island of Curaçao from the dried rind of bitter (Seville) oranges.

Danziger Goldwasser: A German herb- and orange-flavored liqueur adrift with flecks of gold leaf (they are harmless to drink).

Drambuie: Pale, amber scotch-based liqueur sweetened with heather honey and flavored with herbs.

Eau de Vie: "Water of life," a colorless, potent liqueur distilled from fermented fruit juices and/or skins and pits. If the fruit is the grape (as in Marc, see Brandy), the *eau de vie* is a brandy. If a fruit other than grape, it is technically not brandy. *Kirsch* and *framboise*, for example, are *eaux de vie* but not brandies.

Forbidden Fruit: An American brandy-based liqueur flavored with shaddock (a variety of grapefruit).

Fraise: A French *eau de vie* made from strawberries.

Framboise: A French *eau de vie* made from raspberries.

Galliano: A spicy, golden Italian liqueur.

Grand Marnier: A French cognac-based liqueur flavored with orange.

Grappa: An Italian *eau de vie* made from grape skins and seeds left in the wine press (see Brandy).

Irish Mist: A liqueur distilled from Irish whiskey and sweetened with heather honey.

Kahlúa: A syrupy Mexican liqueur made of coffee and cocoa beans.

Kirsch: A crisp, colorless cherry *eau de vie*. Also called *Kirchwasser*.

Kümmel: A colorless German liqueur aromatic of caraway seeds.

Maraschino: An Italian wild cherry liqueur.

Marc: See Brandy.

Metaxa: A heavy, dark, sweet Greek brandy.

Ouzo: A clear licorice-flavored Greek brandy, mixed with water and drunk as an apéritif. Like anis, it turns cloudy when mixed with water.

Parfait Amour: A perfumy lavender liqueur.

Pernod: Yellow, licorice-flavored liqueur much like absinthe except that it contains no wormwood. Mixed with water, it is a favorite French apéritif.

Pisco: A Peruvian grape brandy.

Poire William: Clear, colorless pear *eau de vie*, the finest of which contains a ripe pear inside the bottle.

Prunelle: Brown, brandy-based French liqueur flavored with sloes (bitter plums).

Quetsch: An Alsatian *eau de vie* made of fermented purple plum juice.

Raki: A fiery anise-flavored spirit popular in Greece, Turkey, and the Middle East.

Ratafia: A fruit liqueur, often homemade.

Sambuca Romana: An Italian anise (licorice) liqueur; not very sweet.

Slivovitz: A plum brandy made in Hungary and the Balkans.

Sloe Gin: A liqueur made by steeping sloes (small tart plums) in gin.

Strega: A flowery golden Italian liqueur.

Tia Maria: A heavy rum-based, coffee-flavored West Indian liqueur.

Triple Sec: A clear, orange-flavored liqueur much like Curaçao.

Vandermint: A Dutch chocolate-mint liqueur.

A MISCELLANY OF ALCOHOLIC BEVERAGES

These do not fit neatly into any of the preceding categories, yet are commonly used today.

Falernum: Not really a liqueur but a colorless West Indian lime-almond-ginger syrup, about 6 per cent alcohol. It is used in mixing many "tropical" drinks.

Grenadine: Pink pomegranate syrup, sometimes containing alcohol.

Hard Cider: Fermented apple cider; it often has quite a kick.

Pimm's Cup: There are four Pimm's Cups, all cordial-like drink mixes, said to have been originated by a bartender at Pimm's Restaurant in London. Because of popular demand, the mixes were bottled. Pimm's No. 1 is a gin-based mix, No. 2 a whisky-based mix, No. 3 rum-based, and No. 4 brandy-based. All are commonly used in mixing cocktails.

Pulque: The fermented sap of the agave cactus and practically the national drink of Mexico. Pulque is thick, sweetish and looks rather like buttermilk.

Sake: People often call this Japanese fermented rice drink wine; technically, it isn't because wine is fermented grape juice. Sake is nearer beer because both are fermented grain drinks; however, sake's alcoholic content at 20 per cent is well above that of conventional beers. In Japan, sake is served warm in doll-size china cups, usually at the start of a meal. *Mirin* is another rice drink, similar to sake but sweeter. It is used more for cooking than drinking.

Vermouth: Vermouth is not so much wine as a wine-based drink, heavily infused with herbs. Dry vermouth is pale (the best comes from France), sweet Vermouth is dark or light and usually Italian. Dry vermouth is integral to martinis, sweet vermouth to manhattans.

Bitters

These are used in making cocktails, also taken as apéritifs, liqueurs, and medicine (many bitters are said to be good for digestion). Bitters are made of aromatic seeds, herbs, barks, and plants from carefully guarded recipes. Many have high alcoholic content, all are bitter or bittersweet.

Abbott's Aged Bitters: American bitters prepared for more than a hundred years by the Abbott family in Baltimore.

Amer Picon: Popular French bitters.

Angostura: Probably the best known of all bitters, these were created by a German doctor in Trinidad.

Boonekamp: Famous Dutch bitters.

Campari: Italy's most popular bitters, drunk everywhere mixed with club soda (campari sodas are now bottled in Italy the way colas are here).

Fernet Branca: Another popular Italian bitters, this one heavy and dark and more often used for medicinal purposes than for mixing drinks.

Orange Bitters: Bitters made from the dried peel of Seville (bitter) oranges.

Unicum: Popular bitters made in Hungary.

Equipping and Stocking the Home Bar

Basic Equipment Needed:
Jigger, Measuring Cup
Ice Bucket
Cocktail Shaker
Large Mixing Glass
Muddler, Stirring Rods, Long-Handled Spoons
Flat Bar Strainer
Paring Knife, Vegetable Peeler
Lemon Squeezer
Corkscrew, Can and Bottle Openers
Ice Pick and Tongs
Bag and Mallet for Crushing Ice
Ice Scoop
Note: Descriptions of the commonly used cocktail and highball glasses are included in the Drink Chart that follows.

Some Useful Extras:
Electric Blender
Electric Juicer
Electric Ice Crusher
Electric Portable Mixer

Basic Supplies Needed:
Liquor: Bourbon, brandy, gin, light rum, rye, scotch, vodka
Mixers: Sweet and dry vermouth, aromatic bitters, ginger ale, club soda, tonic water, bitter lemon, cola, tomato juice

Staples: Sugar (superfine and confectioners'), maraschino cherries, cocktail olives, cocktail onions, cocktail toothpicks

Perishables: Lemons, limes, oranges, fresh mint, horseradish

Some Useful Extras:
Apple brandy
Benedictine
Campari
Canadian whisky
Crème de cacao
Crème de menthe
Grenadine
Irish whiskey
Lime juice (bottled)
Liquid hot red pepper seasoning
Mineral waters (bottled)
Orange bitters
Port (tawny)
Rum (medium and dark)
Sherry (fino, amontillado and cream)
Triple Sec
Worcestershire Sauce

How to Buy Liquor for a Party

Almost all liquor is available in pints, fifths, quarts, and half gallons. It's usually wise to buy by the quart or half gallon (you have more liquor in fewer bottles and you may also be able to save a little money). If the party is small and you know your guests well, you probably also know what each drinks and can order accordingly. If a party is large, be guided by the drinking habits and fads in your area. In some communities, people drink a great deal of scotch and gin but little else; in others (the South, for example), people prefer bourbon. Order a good supply of the two or three popular liquors, then also buy a few bottles of the next most popular —just in case. Here, then, is a guide to ordering.

DRINK CALCULATOR

For a Dinner Party

No. of Guests	Approx. Drink Consumption	Liquor Needed
4	8–12	1 fifth
6	12–18	1 quart
8	16–24	2 fifths
12	24–36	2 quarts
20	40–60	4 fifths
40	80–120	7 quarts

For a Cocktail Party

No. of Guests	Approx. Drink Consumption	Liquor Needed
4	12–16	1 quart
6	18–24	2 fifths
8	24–32	2 fifths
12	36–48	3 fifths
20	60–80	5 fifths
40	120–160	9 quarts

Note: To be safe, substitute quarts wherever fifths are mentioned. It is always good to have a little reserve liquor.

Some Terms and Techniques of Drink Mixing

Bottled in Bond: This phrase is not a mark of quality in whiskey. It merely means that certain government regulations have been met, that the whiskey is at least four years old and 100 proof, that it was produced by a single distiller, and that it will be stored in a bonded warehouse until federal excise taxes have been paid by the distiller (this usually is done as the whiskey is ready to be shipped to the retailer).

Dash: A bar measure—6–8 drops or ⅛ teaspoon.

Fifth: ⅘ of a quart or 25.6 fluid ounces.

Frost: To chill a glass until frost forms on the outside.

To Frost Rims of Glasses: Dip rims of glasses in lemon, lime, or orange juice or in lightly beaten egg white, then in sugar or salt to frost (salt for margaritas, sugar for most sweet fruit drinks), then let dry 3–4 minutes until sugar hardens.

Jigger (or *Shot*): A bar measure—1½ ounces. A large jigger is 2 ounces.

Muddle: To mix together ingredients, lightly bruising and mashing with a pestlelike muddler.

Neat: A way of drinking liquor—in straight shots without ice.

On the Rocks: Descriptive term for a drink served with ice cubes.

Pony: A bar measure—1 ounce.

Proof: The measure of alcoholic content of liquor; in the U.S., proof is exactly twice the percentage of alcohol. Thus, something marked 100 proof is 50 per cent alcohol.

Shake: To blend by shaking vigorously in a covered shaker. Shaking produces a cloudy drink, stirring a clear one.

Standing: A term used to describe a cocktail, usually martini, served without ice.

Stir: To mix, using a long-handled spoon or stirring rod in a gentle circular motion. The purpose is to mingle ingredients, not to agitate them.

Twist: A twisted piece of lemon or orange rind, usually about 1½″ long and ¼″ wide. The technique is to twist the rind over the drink to extract the oil, then to drop the rind into the drink.

DRINK CHART
(Each Recipe Makes 1 Serving)

Tips for Making Better Drinks:
- Measure all ingredients carefully.
- Use the freshest and best ingredients possible.
- *Shaking* is for cloudy drinks. Shake drinks in a cocktail shaker — *vigorously* — to blend.
- *Stirring* is for clear drinks. Use a glass pitcher and glass stirrer.
- Use clean ice that has been stored away from foods (ice absorbs odors). *To crush*, wrap cubes in a dish towel and pound with a hammer; or use an ice crusher. *To crack*, tap ice block with ice cracker. *To shave*, pull ice shaver (a gadget rather like a wood plane) across ice block.
- Use *superfine* sugar (not confectioners' or granulated); use domino-shape sugar cubes; 1 small cube equals about 1/2 domino cube.
- Add liquor last when mixing with fruit juice, milk, cream or egg.
- Mix drinks to order and serve as soon as they're made in chilled glasses.

Drink	Approx. Calories per Serving	Type of Glass	Best Time to Serve	Kind and Amount of Liquor	Ice
Alexander (Brandy or Gin)	225	4½ or 6 oz. cocktail glass	After dinner	1½ oz. brandy or gin	1/2 cup cracked ice
Americano	120	8 oz. highball glass	Before or between meals	2 oz. sweet vermouth	2-3 ice cubes
B & B	100	2 oz. liqueur glass	After dinner	1/2 oz. brandy	—
Bacardi	190	4½ oz. cocktail glass	Before meals	2 oz. Bacardi rum	1/2 cup cracked ice
Black Russian	245	6 oz. old-fashioned glass	Before meals	2 oz. vodka	2 ice cubes
Black Velvet	280	12 oz. tankard or beer glass	Between meals	1 (6-6½ oz.) split chilled dry champagne	—
Bloody Mary	140	5 oz. Delmonico or juice glass	Before meals	1½ oz. vodka	1/2 cup cracked ice
Bullshot	135	6 oz. old-fashioned glass	Before or between meals	1½ oz. vodka	2 ice cubes
Campari Soda	40	8 oz. highball glass	Before or between meals	1 oz. Campari	2 ice cubes
Champagne Cocktail	180	6-8 oz. champagne goblet	Before meals	Chilled champagne to fill glass	—
Collins (basic recipe)	230	10-12 oz. collins glass	Before or between meals	2 oz. liquor (gin for Tom Collins, blended whiskey for John Collins, rum for Rum Collins, etc.)	3/4-1 cup cracked ice
Crème de Menthe Frappé	100	2-2½ oz. sherry glass	After dinner	1 oz. green crème de menthe	1/4 cup crushed ice
(Note: Any liqueur may be prepared as a frappé; prepare as directed, substituting another liqueur for crème de menthe.)					
Cuba Libre	285	12 oz. collins glass	As a midafternoon cooler	2 oz. rum	3-4 ice cubes

Note: Calorie counts for all alcoholic beverages that follow were computed on the basis of 100-proof liquor. By using a lower proof, you can reduce the number of calories somewhat:

Proof (all liquors)	Measure	Number of Calories
80	1 fluid ounce	65
86	1 fluid ounce	70
90	1 fluid ounce	73
100	1 fluid ounce	82

Other Liquid or Liqueur	Seasonings	How to Mix	Garnishes
1/2 oz. heavy cream 3/4 oz. crème de cacao	–	Shake all ingredients with ice and strain into glass.	Sprinkling of nutmeg
Club soda to fill glass	1 oz. Campari	Place ice, vermouth, and Campari in glass, fill with soda and stir to mix.	Twist of lemon peel
1/2 oz. Benedictine	–	Pour Benedictine in glass, then pour in brandy.	–
Juice of 1/2 lime	3-4 dashes grenadine 1/2 teaspoon sugar	Shake all ingredients with ice and strain into glass.	–
1 oz. coffee liqueur	–	Stir all ingredients with ice in glass.	–
3/4 cup chilled stout	–	Pour champagne and stout simultaneously into tankard.	–
1/3 cup tomato juice 1 teaspoon lemon juice	2 dashes Worcestershire 1-2 dashes liquid hot red pepper seasoning Pinch each salt and cayenne	Shake all ingredients with ice and strain into glass.	–
Beef consommé to fill glass	Salt to taste	Place vodka and ice in glass, fill with consommé, season, and stir.	Twist of lemon peel
Club soda to fill glass	–	Place ice and Campari in glass and pour in soda.	–
–	1 lump sugar 2-3 dashes aromatic bitters	Place sugar in glass, drop bitters on sugar, and pour in champagne.	Twist of lemon peel
Juice of 1 lemon Club soda to fill glass	1 teaspoon sugar	Place juice, sugar, ice, and liquor in glass, fill with soda, and stir.	Cocktail cherry Slice of lemon
–	–	Fill glass with ice and pour liqueur evenly over all. Insert straws.	–
Juice of 1/2 lime Chilled cola to fill glass	–	Place juice, ice and rum in glass, fill with cola, and stir to mix.	Small lime wedge

119

DRINK CHART (continued)

Drink	Approx. Calories per Serving	Type of Glass	Best Time to Serve	Kind and Amount of Liquor	Ice
Daiquri (plain)	185	4½ oz. cocktail glass	Before meals	1 oz. light rum	1/2 cup cracked ice
Daiquiri (frozen)	185	6-8 oz. champagne goblet	Before meals	2 oz. light rum	1/2 cup shaved or crushed ice
Eggnog	435	12 oz. collins glass	As a between-meals refresher	2 oz. brandy, light rum, sherry, or port	1/2 cup cracked ice
French 75	245	8 oz. highball glass	Before meals	2 oz. gin	1/2 cup cracked ice
Gibson (see Martini)					
Gimlet	210	4½ oz. cocktail glass	Before meals	2 oz. gin or vodka	1/2 cup cracked ice
Gin or Vodka and Tonic	170 (with 1½ oz. liquor) 210 (with 2 oz. liquor)	8 oz. highball glass	Before meals or between meals	1½-2 oz. gin or vodka	3 ice cubes
Gin or Sloe Gin Fizz	150 with gin 110 with sloe gin	8 oz. highball glass	Before or between meals	1½ oz. gin or sloe gin	1/2 cup cracked ice 2 ice cubes
Gin Rickey	130	8 oz. highball glass	Before or between meals	1½ oz. gin	2-3 ice cubes
Grasshopper	250	4½ oz. cocktail glass	After dinner	1 oz. white crème de cacao	1/2 cup cracked ice
Grog	190	8 oz. mug	Anytime as a cold-weather bracer	2 oz. dark rum or brandy	—
Hot Buttered Rum	235	8 oz. mug	Anytime as a cold-weather bracer	2 oz. dark rum	—
Hot Toddy	170	6 oz. old-fashioned glass	Anytime as a cold-weather bracer	1½ oz. dark rum, brandy, bourbon, rye, or scotch	—
Irish Coffee	290	6-8 oz. mug or cup	Anytime as a cold-weather bracer	1½ oz. Irish whiskey	—
Kir	200	8 oz. wineglass	Before meals		2 ice cubes

Other Liquid or Liqueur	Seasonings	How to Mix	Garnishes
Juice of 1/2 lime	3/4 teaspoon sugar	Shake all ingredients with ice and strain into glass.	–
Juice of 1/2 lime	3/4 teaspoon sugar 3-4 dashes Maraschino	Buzz all ingredients with ice in an electric blender at high speed about 1 minute until fluffy; spoon into glass, insert short straws.	–
1 cup milk	1 egg 2 teaspoons sugar	Shake all ingredients with ice and strain into glass.	A sprinkling of nutmeg
Juice of 1 lemon Chilled champagne to fill glass	1 teaspoon sugar	Place lemon juice, sugar, and gin in glass and stir to mix; add ice and pour in champagne.	–
Juice of 1/2 lime or 1 tablespoon bottled lime juice	1½ teaspoons Triple Sec	Shake all ingredients with ice and strain into glass.	–
Quinine water to fill glass	1 lime wedge	Squeeze lime wedge over glass, then drop in; add gin, ice, quinine water; stir slightly.	–
Juice of 1/2 lemon Club soda to fill glass	1 teaspoon sugar	Shake all ingredients but soda with cracked ice and strain over ice cubes in glass. Fill with soda and stir.	–
Juice of 1/2 lime Club soda to fill glass	–	Squeeze lime over glass and drop in, add ice, gin, and soda, and stir.	–
1 oz. green crème de menthe 3/4 oz. heavy cream	–	Shake all ingredients with ice and strain into glass.	–
Juice of 1/2 lemon Boiling water to fill mug	1 lump sugar 1 lemon slice 2 cloves 1/2 cinnamon stick	Place lemon juice, rum, and seasonings in mug, fill with boiling water, and stir to mix.	–
1 teaspoon brandy Boiling water to fill mug	1 teaspoon light brown sugar 4 cloves 1 strip orange peel 1 teaspoon unsalted butter 1 cinnamon stick	Place rum and brandy in mug, add sugar, cloves and orange peel; place butter on a spoon in mug and pour boiling water over butter; stir with cinnamon stick.	–
Boiling water to fill glass	1 lemon slice stuck with 3 cloves 1/4 cinnamon stick 1 teaspoon sugar	Put rum and seasonings in glass, insert metal spoon, and slowly pour in water; stir to mix.	–
1/2-3/4 cup hot strong black coffee	2 teaspoons sugar	Pour coffee into mug, add whiskey and sugar and stir; let whipped cream slide over a metal spoon to float on coffee. Do not stir.	2 tablespoons *very* lightly whipped cream
6 oz. Chablis or other dry white wine 1/2 oz. crème de cassis	1 strip lemon peel	Place ice, wine and crème de cassis in glass, twist lemon peel over glass, and drop in. Stir gently.	–

Drink	Approx. Calories per Serving	Type of Glass	Best Time to Serve	Kind and Amount of Liquor	Ice
Manhattan (regular)	200	4½ oz. cocktail glass	Before meals	2 oz. rye	1-2 ice cubes
Manhattan (dry)	190	4½ oz. cocktail glass	Before meals	2 oz. rye	1-2 ice cubes
Margarita	175	4½ oz. cocktail glass (dip rim in lime juice, then in salt to "frost")	Before meals	2 oz. tequila	1/2 cup cracked ice
Martini (*Note:* Connoisseurs keep both gin and vermouth in the refrigerator.)					
Regular	142	4½ oz. cocktail glass	Before meals	1½ oz. gin or vodka	2-3 ice cubes
Dry	138	4½ oz. cocktail glass	Before meals	1½ oz. gin or vodka	2-3 ice cubes
Extra dry	135	4½ oz. cocktail glass	Before meals	1¾ oz. gin or vodka	2-3 ice cubes
Gibson	175	4½ oz. cocktail glass	Before meals	2 oz. gin or vodka	2-3 ice cubes
Milk Punch	385	12 oz. collins glass	As a between-meals refresher	2 oz. brandy, bourbon, rum, rye, or Irish whiskey	1/2 cup cracked ice
Mint Julep	185	10-12 oz. collins glass or silver julep cup	Anytime as a refresher	2 oz. bourbon	2 cups cracked ice
Mist					
Scotch	165	6 oz. old-fashioned glass	Before meals for Scotch and Irish	2 oz. scotch	1/2 cup shaved ice
Heather	220	6 oz. old-fashioned glass	mist, after dinner for heather mist	2 oz. Drambuie	1/2 cup shaved ice
Irish	165	6 oz. old-fashioned glass		2 oz. Irish whiskey	1/2 cup shaved ice
Moscow Mule	220	8 oz. pewter or silver mug	Before or between meals	2 oz. vodka	2-3 ice cubes
Negroni	170	10-12 oz. collins glass	Before or between meals	1 oz. gin	2-3 ice cubes
Old-Fashioned	135 (with 1½ oz. liquor) 175 (with 2 oz. liquor)	6 oz. old-fashioned glass	Before meals	1½-2 oz. blended whiskey or, if you specify it, rye, scotch, bourbon, or rum	1-2 ice cubes
Orange Blossom	155	4½ oz. cocktail glass	Before meals	1½ oz. gin	1/2 cup cracked ice
Pimm's Cup	160	10-12 oz. collins glass	Before or between meals	2 oz. Pimm's No. 1	2-3 ice cubes
Pink Lady	195	4½ or 6 oz. cocktail glass	Before meals	2 oz. gin	1/2 cup cracked ice

Other Liquid or Liqueur	Seasonings	How to Mix	Garnishes
3/4 oz. sweet vermouth	—	Stir rye and vermouth gently with ice, strain into glass, and garnish.	Cocktail cherry
3/4 oz. dry vermouth	—		Twist of lemon peel
Juice of 1/2 lime	2-3 dashes Triple Sec or curaçao	Shake all ingredients with ice and strain into glass.	—
1/2 oz. extra dry vermouth	—	Stir gin or vodka and vermouth very gently with ice, strain into glass, and garnish.	Green olive
1/3 oz. extra dry vermouth	—		Twist of lemon peel
1/4 oz. extra dry vermouth	—		Twist of lemon peel
1/4 oz. extra dry vermouth	—		2-3 cocktail onions
1¼ cups cold milk	1 teaspoon sugar	Shake all ingredients with ice and strain into glass.	Sprinkling of nutmeg
—	12 large tender mint leaves 1 teaspoon sugar	Place leaves and sugar in glass and muddle, pressing leaves against sides of glass to extract flavor; discard mint. Pack glass with ice and let stand 1-2 minutes to "frost" outside; slowly pour in bourbon, rotating glass; garnish and serve with straws. SIP SLOWLY!	3-4 sprigs mint
—	—	Fill glass with ice, drizzle in whiskey or liqueur, and garnish.	Twist of lemon peel
—	—		Twist of lemon peel
—	—		Twist of lemon peel
Juice of 1/2 lime Ginger beer to fill mug	—	Place ice in mug, add lime and vodka; stir, then fill with ginger beer.	Slice of lime
1 oz. Campari 1 oz. sweet vermouth Club soda to fill glass	—	Place ice, gin, Campari, and vermouth in glass, fill with soda and stir.	Slice of orange
1 teaspoon club soda	1/2 lump sugar saturated with 1-2 dashes aromatic bitters; for an extra good drink, also add 2 drops scotch and 3 drops curaçao.	Place sugar and soda in glass, add ice and whiskey, stir, and garnish.	Twist of lemon peel Slice of orange Maraschino cherry
1 oz. orange juice	1 teaspoon sugar	Shake all ingredients with ice and strain into glass.	—
Lemon soda to fill glass	—	Place ice, garnishes, and Pimm's in glass, fill with soda, and stir.	Slice of lemon Strip of cucumber peel
Juice of 1/2 lemon 3-4 dashes apple brandy	3-4 dashes grenadine 1 egg white	Shake all ingredients with ice and strain into glass.	—

Drink	Approx. Calories per Serving	Type of Glass	Best Time to Serve	Kind and Amount of Liquor	Ice
Pisco Sour	165	5 oz. Delmonico or juice glass	Before meals	1½ oz. Pisco brandy	1/2 cup cracked ice
Planter's Punch	190 (without orange juice) 220 (with orange juice)	10-12 oz. collins glass	Before or between meals	2 oz. dark rum	1/2 cup cracked ice, shaved ice to fill glass
Port Wine Cooler	130	12 oz. collins glass glass	Before or between meals	1/2 cup dry port wine	Crushed ice to 1/2 fill glass
Pousse-Café	95	1 oz. liqueur glass	After dinner	1 teaspoon grenadine 1 teaspoon green crème de menthe 1 teaspoon yellow Chartreuse 1 teaspoon Triple Sec 1 teaspoon brandy	—
Rob Roy	190 (with dry vermouth) 200 (with sweet vermouth)	4½ oz. cocktail glass	Before meals	2 oz. scotch	1/2 cup shaved or cracked ice
Rum Swizzle	190	8 oz. highball glass	Before or between meals	2 oz. rum	1/2 cup crushed ice
Salty Dog	230	8 oz. highball glass	Before meals	2 oz. vodka	2 ice cubes
Screwdriver	300	12 oz. collins glass	Before meals	2 oz. vodka	1/2-2/3 cup crushed ice
Side Car	230	4½ oz. cocktail glass	After dinner	1½ oz. brandy	1/2 cup cracked ice
Singapore Sling	260	12 oz. collins glass	Before or between meals	2 oz. gin	3/4 cup cracked ice
Sour (basic recipe)	190	5 oz. Delmonico or juice glass or 6 oz. sour glass	Before meals	2 oz. rye, bourbon, scotch, rum, brandy, or gin	1/2 cup cracked ice
Spritzer	90	12 oz. collins glass	With or between meals	1/2 cup Rhine wine	3/4 cup cracked ice
Stinger	245	4½ oz. cocktail glass	After dinner	1¾ oz. brandy	1/2 cup cracked ice
Vermouth Cassis	190	8 oz. wineglass	Before meals	—	2 ice cubes
Zombie	450	12 oz. collins glass	Before meals	1½ oz. light rum 1½ oz. dark rum 1½ oz. Demerara rum	1/2 cup cracked ice 4 ice cubes

Other Liquid or Liqueur	Seasonings	How to Mix	Garnishes
Juice of 1/2 lemon	1 egg white 1 teaspoon sugar	Shake all ingredients with ice and strain into glass.	—
Juice of 1/2 lemon or lime Juice of 1/2 orange (optional)	1/2 oz. Falernum or 1 teaspoon sugar	Shake all ingredients with cracked ice and strain into glass filled with shaved ice, garnish, add straws.	1/2 orange slice 1 stick fresh pineapple Maraschino cherry Mint
1/2 cup ginger ale	—	Place ice in glass, add wine and ginger ale, and stir to mix.	—
—	—	Pour grenadine into glass and let stand a few seconds. Gently place a glass stirrer in grenadine and very slowly pour in each liqueur down along stirrer in order listed so each floats on the other.	—
3/4 oz. sweet or dry vermouth	Dash aromatic bitters	Stir scotch and vermouth with ice and bitters and strain into glass. Add garnishes.	Strip of lemon peel Maraschino cherry
Juice of 1/2 lime Club soda to fill glass	1 teaspoon sugar 3-4 dashes aromatic bitters	Stir lime juice, rum, seasonings, and ice in a pitcher until it "frosts," strain into glass, and add soda.	—
Grapefruit juice to fill glass	Pinch salt	Place all ingredients in glass and stir.	—
Orange juice to fill glass	—	Place all ingredients in glass and stir.	—
Juice of 1/2 lime 1 oz. Cointreau	—	Shake all ingredients with ice and strain into glass.	—
Juice of 1/2 lemon or lime 1 oz. cherry brandy or liqueur Club soda to fill glass	2-3 drops Benedictine 2-3 drops brandy	Place ice, juice, gin, cherry brandy and soda in glass and stir; with a medicine dropper, add Benedictine, then brandy by inserting halfway into glass. Float orange slice on top and place cherry in center.	Thin orange slice Maraschino cherry
Juice of 1/2 lemon	1 teaspoon sugar 2 dashes aromatic bitters	Shake all ingredients with ice and strain into glass. Add garnishes.	Small orange wedge Maraschino cherry
Club soda to fill glass	—	Place all ingredients in glass and stir.	—
1 oz. white crème de menthe	—	Shake all ingredients with ice and strain into glass.	—
4 oz. dry vermouth 1/2 oz. crème de cassis 2 oz. chilled club soda	Twist of lemon peel	Place ice in glass, pour in vermouth, twist lemon peel over glass and drop in. Add crème de cassis, club soda and stir gently.	—
Juice of 1/2 lime 1 tablespoon apricot liqueur 1 tablespoon pineapple juice	1½ teaspoons Falernum	Shake all ingredients with cracked ice, strain into glass, add ice cubes and garnishes. Insert straws and SIP VERY SLOWLY!	Thin orange slice Mint sprigs

Up: A term used to describe a cocktail served without ice.

V.S.: An abbreviation often seen on liquor labels. It stands for *very* *superior.* Others are: *V.S.O.* (*very superior old*), *V.V.O.* (*very, very old*) and *V.V.S.* (*very, very superior*).

NUMBER OF (1½ oz.) DRINKS IN:

Bottle Size	1 Bottle	2 Bottles	4 Bottles	6 Bottles	8 Bottles	10 Bottles
Fifth (25.6 oz.)	17	34	68	102	136	170
Quart (32 oz.)	21	42	84	126	168	210

Note: When serving martinis or manhattans, allow 1 bottle of vermouth to 3 quarts of liquor.

⊠ SANGRIA

A Spanish wine and fruit drink, cooling on a hot summer day.
Makes 8–10 servings

1 (24-oz.) bottle dry red wine
1 orange
1 lemon or lime
1 pint club soda
6–8 ice cubes
1 peeled, sliced peach or ⅓ cup
   stemmed ripe strawberries or
   ⅓ cup raspberries (optional)

Pour wine into a large pitcher. Using a vegetable peeler, peel rinds from orange and lemon in long spirals and add to wine; add juice from the orange and ½ the lemon. Stir in soda, add ice and the peach. Let stand 5 minutes, then serve in large wine goblets. About 100 calories for each of 8 servings, 80 calories for each of 10 servings.

ROYAL EGGNOG

This recipe is a modern version of an old family favorite. In copperplate script at the side was noted, "For cases of Exhaustion. If the case is not serious, half the quantity of brandy may be used. Give every *hour* in cases of extreme weakness!"

Makes about 36 servings

12 eggs, separated
1½ cups sugar
1 quart milk
1 quart brandy or 1 pint each
   whiskey and brandy
1 quart light cream
¾ cup light rum (optional)
½ teaspoon nutmeg

Cover and refrigerate egg whites until needed; beat yolks until thick in a large bowl; add sugar, a little at a time, and beat until pale and fluffy. Slowly beat in milk, alternately with brandy; cover and chill 3–4 hours. About ½ hour before serving, take egg whites from refrigerator. Just before serving, beat yolk mixture well, add cream and, if you like, rum. Whip egg whites to soft peaks and fold into yolk mixture. Pour into a well-chilled punch bowl and sprinkle with nutmeg. (*Note:* So that eggnog will be fresh for late arrivals or "seconds," whip up only ½ of the egg whites and mix with ½ of the yolk mixture. Mix the remainder when needed.) About 220 calories per serving if optional light rum is used, 205 calories per serving if rum is not used.

⊠ EASY RUM AND COFFEE NOG

Makes 16–20 servings

2 *quarts vanilla ice cream*
1 *quart hot strong coffee*
1 *quart light rum*
¼ *teaspoon nutmeg*

Place ice cream in a metal bowl, pour in coffee, and stir until ice cream is melted. Mix in rum, pour into punch bowl, and sprinkle with nutmeg. About 300 calories for each of 16 servings, 240 for each of 20 servings.

Nonalcoholic Beverages

About Coffee

When Muhammadanism spread through Arabia forbidding Moslems to drink alcoholic beverages, the faithful turned to something else with "kick." That something was coffee. The Arabs introduced coffee to the Turks, who glorified it with coffeehouses, then Turkish invaders carried coffee into Europe. Coffee came to the New World with the colonists; the first coffee plant was brought over by a Dutchman about fifty years later, and from it, the story goes, the Latin American coffee industry began.

Today Latin and South America are top coffee producers along with Indonesia (especially Java and Sumatra), Yemen, Hawaii, and a number of Caribbean islands. Coffee varieties often take their names from the areas where they're grown —Colombian coffee, for example, Brazilian, Puerto Rican, Arabian Mocha, Blue Mountain Jamaican. Most popular brands are skillful blends because coffee made from a single variety is insipid; indeed, it takes many different coffees to produce rich, well-rounded flavor.

It is possible, however, to buy beans of a particular variety—Mocha or Colombian—and have them ground or mixed to order. The best plan is to try a number of brands and blends until you hit upon the one you like.

About Roasts: If variety and blend determine the flavor of coffee, so, too, does the roast, which can vary from *light* and *cinnamon* through *medium, high, city,* and *French* to *Italian* (nearly black and the roast to use for demitasse and espresso). The darker the roast, incidentally, the less the caffeine.

About Grinds: Coffee can be bought in the bean, the best way to buy it if you have a coffee mill, because coffee stays fresh in the bean far longer than it does after being ground. Once ground—and exposed to the air—coffee stales fast. That's why it is best to buy only a pound at a time and to store in the refrigerator once the tin is opened. There are three grinds of coffee available today:

Regular Grind	Use for Percolators
Drip Grind	Use for Drip or Old-Fashioned Coffee-pots
Fine Grind	Use for Vacuum Coffee Makers (*Note:* Drip grind may also be used)

In addition, there is the fine powdery coffee used in making Turkish coffee, but it is available only at grourmet groceries or Middle Eastern shops and must be especially sought out.

About Decaffeinated Coffee: Caffeine is a stimulant that affects many people adversely, so it was inevitable that someone would discover a way of extracting most of the caffeine from coffee. Decaffeinated coffees are widely available in all standard grinds, also as instant coffee.

About Coffee with Chicory: Chicory —the same one used for salads— has a long brown root, which, when roasted and ground, can be brewed into a bitter dark drink. When Napoleon banned the importation of coffee, the French hit upon mixing their dwindling reserves with roasted chicory, and they do yet, though there is no shortage of coffee. Coffee with chicory is strong and bitter but popular still around New Orleans.

About Instant Coffees: In the beginning, these seemed feeble imitations of freshly brewed coffee. But research has perfected the process so that modern instant coffees are very good indeed. One of the advantages—in addition to instant cups of coffee—is that the powder or granules can be used in recipes as easily as cocoa. So popular have the instants become that there is now instant espresso.

About Freeze-Dried Coffees: These are the newest and best instant coffees because they taste remarkably like freshly brewed coffee. They are made by flash-freezing strong, fresh coffee, then drawing off the ice crystals by a special vacuum process that does not affect the flavor of the coffee as heat dehydrating does (this is the method used for conventional instants). Freeze-dried crystals can also be used in recipes if the mixture they're being added to is liquid or at least moist—the crystals dissolve on contact.

About Coffee Substitutes: These (Postum, to name one) are made of dark roasted cereals and are good for those unable to take any coffee at all. They are available as ground or instant types.

How to Make Coffee

In an Old-Fashioned Pot: Measure coffee (*drip grind*) into pot, allowing 1 standard coffee measure or 2 level tablespoons for each serving, add cold water (¾ cup for each 2 tablespoons coffee), and stir. Set over moderately high heat, cover, and when mixture bubbles up once, remove from heat and add 3–4 tablespoons cold water to settle grounds. Set pot over low heat and steep 5 minutes—do not allow to boil. To serve, pour through a very fine small strainer into cups.

In a Percolator: Measure cold water into pot, allowing ¾ cup for each serving. Set percolator basket in place in pot, measure *regular grind* coffee into it, using 1 standard coffee measure or 2 level tablespoons for each ¾ cup water. Cover with lid. Set pot over moderately high heat and, when coffee begins to perk (when it bubbles in glass lid dome) and turns pale amber, turn heat to moderately low and let coffee perk gently 6–8 minutes. Remove basket of grounds, stir coffee, and serve. Keep hot over low heat but do not let coffee boil.

In a Drip Pot:

Filter-Flask Type: Roll filter paper into a cone and stick into neck of flask. In a saucepan or teakettle, measure amount of cold water needed—¾ cup for each serving —and bring to a boil over high heat. Meanwhile, measure *drip grind* coffee into filter cone, allowing 1 standard coffee measure or 2 level tablespoons for each ¾ cup water. Set flask on a burner topped with an asbestos flame tamer, but do not turn burner on. When water boils, take from heat, let bubbling subside and pour over coffee grounds; stir once, then let drip through. Lift out paper of grounds, turn on burner heat (to low) and let coffee steep 1–2 minutes. Pour and serve.

Conventional Drip Pot: Measure amount of cold water needed—¾ cup per serving—into a teakettle or saucepan and bring to a boil. Meanwhile, rinse coffeepot with scalding hot water. Fit basket into bottom part of pot and measure in *drip grind* coffee, allowing 1 standard coffee measure or 2 level tablespoons for each ¾ cup water. Fit upper compartment over basket and set pot on a burner (not turned on). When water boils, take from heat, let bubbling subside, and pour into upper compartment, cover, and let water drip through. When about ½ of the water has dripped through, turn burner under pot to low. When all water has dripped through, lift off upper compartment and basket of grounds. Stir coffee, let mellow 1–2 minutes over low heat, then serve.

In a Vacuum-Style Coffee Maker: For each cup of coffee wanted, measure ¾ cup cold water into lower compartment. Fit filter into upper bowl and measure in *fine or drip grind* coffee—1 standard coffee measure or 2 level table- spoons for each ¾ cup water.

Set pot over high heat and, when water comes to a full rolling boil, insert upper part of coffee maker into bottom, using a slight twist to ensure a tight seal. When water rises into top part, stir well and turn heat to low. Let brew bubble in top part 2–3 minutes, then remove coffee maker from heat (this creates a vacuum, causing coffee to plunge into lower part of coffee maker). When coffee has filtered back into lower part, lift off top part. Keep coffee hot over low heat.

In an Automatic Coffee Maker: Follow manufacturer's instructions closely, experimenting with the mild-strong control until you achieve the brew you like.

In an Espresso Pot: These aren't espresso pots (true espresso is made by passing steam under pressure over the coffee grounds) but Italian-style drip pots. But they make espresso-like coffee and are easy to use. For each serving use 6 tablespoons cold water (in a standard measuring cup, 6 table- spoons is midway between the ⅓ and ½ cup marks) and 1 standard coffee measure or 2 level table- spoons of *French or Italian roast drip grind* coffee. Place water in bottom part of pot, grounds in middle basket; fit all parts of pot together, cover and set over mod- erately high heat. When water comes to a full boil, turn pot upside down, turn heat off, and let coffee drip through. Serve in demitasse cups with a twist of lemon and, if you like, sugar. But never cream. To be really Italian, skip the lemon, too. (*Note:* Some Italian housewares shops sell home-size espresso machines; use according to manufacturer's directions.)

HOW TO MAKE COFFEE FOR A CROWD

Number of Servings	Coffee Needed (Regular Grind)	Water Needed
20	½ pound	1 gallon
40	1 pound	2 gallons
60	1½ pounds	3 gallons

Tie coffee in a muslin or cheese-cloth bag large enough to hold at least twice the quantity you're using, drop into a kettle of just boiling water, reduce heat immediately so water no longer boils, and let stand 10–12 minutes. Plunge bag up and down several times, then remove. Keep coffee hot over low heat but do not allow to boil. (*Note:* If you're making coffee for more than 60, set up 2 kettles.) To clear coffee, add 1–2 eggshells to each kettle.

Quantity Instant Coffee: From 2 ounces instant coffee you can make 20 cups of coffee. Simply empty coffee powder or granules into a large kettle and for each 2 ounces add 1 gallon simmering water. Stir, let steep a few minutes, then serve. *Note:* Always add the hot water to the coffee, never the other way around.

HOW TO MAKE COFFEE OVER A CAMPFIRE

The principle is the same as for quantity coffee, the amount is simply smaller. Use the following proportions:

Number of Servings	Coffee Needed (Regular Grind)	Water Needed
2	¼ cup	1½ cups
4	½ cup	3 cups
6	¾ cup	4½ cups
8	1 cup	6 cups
10	1¼ cups	7½ cups
12	1½ cups	9 cups

Tie coffee in a large muslin or cheesecloth bag. Bring water to a boil in a large pot over glowing coals, drop in bag of coffee, pull pot to side of fire where water will stay hot but not boil. Let steep 10–12 minutes, swish bag of grounds up and down 2–3 times, then lift out. *Note:* If you have no bag for grounds, simply place loose grounds in bottom of pot, pour in water, and set over coals. When water bubbles up just once, stir well, transfer pot to edge of fire, add about ¼ cup cold water to settle grounds, and let steep 8–10 minutes.

Some Tips for Making Better Coffee

– Buy only a week's supply of coffee at a time and, once the can is opened, store tightly covered in the refrigerator.

– Do not mix any stale coffee with a freshly opened tin.

– If you buy coffee in the bean, grind it as you need it (and keep grinder spotless). Whole roasted beans will keep their flavor about 1 month.

– Use the proper grind of coffee for your coffee maker.

– Keep coffee maker spanking clean. This means washing after each use with soap and water, getting at spouts and crevices with a small bottle brush, rinsing well in hot water, and drying thoroughly. Occasionally pot may need to be scoured (though those with metal-plated insides should never be). If you prefer, remove stains with one of the commercial preparations instead of the scouring pad.

– Store coffee maker unassembled so air can circulate.

– Measure coffee and water carefully, using 1 standard coffee measure or 2 level tablespoons for each ¾ cup water. *Note:* If you like really strong coffee, use 3 level tablespoons for each ¾ cup water; if you prefer it weak, use 2 scant tablespoons for each ¾ cup water.

– Always use cold water when making coffee; hot tap water tastes flat. Also use naturally soft (or chemically softened) water; hard water gives coffee an unpleasant metallic taste.

– Never allow coffee to boil—it becomes a bitter potion. The most desirable temperature for brewing coffee is between 185° F. and 205° F.

– Use a coffee maker of the right size for the amount of coffee you need. All coffee makers should be used to at least ¾ of their capacity, so if you often make small amounts, keep a special small pot for just that purpose.

– Remove coffee grounds from the coffee maker as soon as the coffee is brewed.

– Keep coffee hot until it is served. Reheated coffee tastes stale.

– Serve coffee as soon after making as possible; don't try to keep hot longer than 1 hour because coffee deteriorates rapidly on standing.

Some Variations on Coffee

Demitasse: This is simply extra-strong black coffee served in small (demi, or half-size) cups. To make, use one of the standard methods, substituting a dark *French* or *Italian* roast for the regular *or* increasing the amount of regular roast coffee to 3–4 level tablespoons per ¾ cup of water.

Iced Coffee: Brew demitasse using one of the basic methods. Fill tall glasses with ice and pour in hot demitasse. Or, if you prefer, brew regular strength coffee and cool. Serve over ice or, for stronger coffee, over coffee ice cubes (coffee frozen in ice cube trays).

Café au Lait: This is the traditional breakfast beverage throughout Europe. Brew demitasse by one of the basic methods. At the same time, heat an equal quantity of milk to scalding. Pour milk into a pitcher and fill cups by pouring the hot milk and coffee simultaneously and adding about equal amounts of each.

Mocha: Brew demitasse by one
of the basic methods. Also make
an equal amount of any favorite
cocoa. Then serve as you would
café au lait, pouring equal amounts
of black coffee and cocoa into
each cup.

Café Royal: Prepare demitasse.
Pour a cup, place a sugar lump
on an after-dinner coffee spoon,
add a little cognac and blaze. When
sugar melts, stir into coffee.
Note: This is best, perhaps,
as a do-it-yourself drink, each
person preparing his own.

Viennese Coffee:

Hot: Brew strong coffee and mix
with an equal quantity of hot
milk or light cream. Pour into
a tall glass, sweeten to taste, and
top with a float of whipped cream.

Frosted: Brew strong coffee. Place
a scoop of vanilla ice cream in
a tall glass, slowly pour in coffee, top
with whipped cream, and dust
with confectioners' sugar.

Café Diable (Makes 6 servings):
Here's a showy after-dinner drink.
Place 6 sugar lumps, 8 cloves,
½ cinnamon stick, a 1″ strip of
lemon rind, and ⅓ cup cognac
in a chafing dish but do not mix.
Blaze cognac with a match,
then stir. Add 1 quart very strong
hot coffee, heat about 1 minute,
ladle into cups, and serve.

⚖ TURKISH COFFEE (KAHVESI)

Dark, pungent Turkish coffee is
now sold in gourmet shops along
with special cone-shaped Turkish
coffeepots. The special pot isn't
essential—a long-handled saucepan,
deep enough to swish the grounds
around, works nearly as well.

This coffee should be made in small
amounts—no more than 3–4
servings at a time.
Makes 3 servings

1 cup water
1 tablespoon sugar
2 tablespoons Turkish coffee or
  pulverized Italian roast coffee

Heat water and sugar uncovered
in a Turkish coffeepot (*cezve*)
or small saucepan over moderately
high heat, stirring occasionally
until sugar dissolves. Gradually
add coffee, swirling or stirring,
then heat almost to boiling and
let foam up; remove from heat and
let foam subside. Return to heat
and repeat foaming and settling 2
more times. Keep swirling coffee
as it heats. Spoon a little foam
into demitasse cups, then half fill
with coffee. (*Note:* To settle
grounds quickly, add 1–2 drops cold
water just before serving.) 18
calories per serving.

⚖ CAPPUCCINO

This popular Italian coffee drink is
thought to have been named
for Capuchin monks, who wear
coffee-brown robes.
Makes 4–6 servings

1 pint hot espresso
1 cup scalding hot milk
Cinnamon or nutmeg (optional)
4–6 cinnamon sticks (optional)

Beat espresso and milk in a heated
bowl until frothy; pour into cups.
(*Note:* The correct size is something between a demitasse and
a regular coffee cup, but either
of these will do just as well.)
Sprinkle lightly with cinnamon, add
cinnamon sticks for stirring, and
serve. Set out the sugar bowl
for those who want it. About 40
calories for each of 4 servings,
27 for each of 6 servings.

⊠ BAHAMIAN COFFEE

Brown sugar and cinnamon make the difference.
Makes 4 servings

1 quart milk
¼ cup instant coffee powder
¼ cup firmly packed dark brown sugar
4 cinnamon sticks

Bring milk to a simmer over moderate heat, stir in coffee and sugar, and when dissolved heat uncovered 1–2 minutes; do not boil. Serve in tall mugs with cinnamon stick stirrers. About 215 calories per serving.

About Tea

All teas can be divided into three groups: *black,* fermented teas, obtained principally from India, Ceylon, and Taiwan; *green,* unfermented teas (most come from Japan, though in days past China was the leading exporter); and *oolong,* semifermented teas from Taiwan.

Black Teas: Americans know these best. They produce fragrant, amber brews, the blend (most contain as many as 20 different teas) determining flavor; it may be brisk and strong, nutty, fruity, flowery, even winelike. Popular black teas include *Assam,* a robust tea from northeast India (when blended with Ceylon tea, it is called *Irish Breakfast Tea*); *Darjeeling,* from the Himalayas, more delicate and, some people insist, India's finest tea; *Earl Grey* (a full-bodied blend of Taiwan teas); *English Breakfast* (choice, mellow blend of India and Ceylon teas); *Lapsang Souchong* (a strong, smoky Taiwan tea); and *Sumatra* (an Indonesian tea commonly used in blends).

Black tea leaves are graded as to size. The largest are *souchong,* second largest *orange pekoe* or simply, *pekoe.* Smaller, cut or broken leaves are called *broken orange pekoe* or *broken pekoe souchong* (these make especially aromatic tea). *Fannings* are smaller still and used for tea bags.

Green Teas: These astringent yellow-green brews are beloved by Orientals. The four principal sizes are *gunpowder* (so called because, on drying, the tiny leaves roll into balls), *imperial* (slightly larger balls), *young hyson* (longer, twisted leaves), and *hyson* (the longest, most loosely twisted). Japanese green teas are *basket-fired* (dried in bamboo baskets over charcoal until deep olive brown), *pan-fired* (dried in iron pans over coals), or *natural leaf* (coarse leaves pan-fired for short periods of time). Basket-fired is considered choicest.

Oolong Teas: These semifermented teas combine the mellowness of black teas with the tang of the green; they make deceptively light-colored brews. *Formosa Oolong* is the mildest and most popular. *Note:* For an exceptionally good pot of tea, mix 1 teaspoon *Formosa Oolong* with your favorite black tea blend; if, for example, you need 6 teaspoons tea, use 1 teaspoon *Formosa Oolong* and 5 teaspoons black tea.

Scented Teas: Teas, particularly Oolong, are often mixed with dried flowers or herbs. Among the common blends are *Jasmine* and *Peppermint* teas.

Instant Teas: These are pulverized black teas mixed sometimes with malto-dextrin, which preserves their flavor. They are available plain or mixed with sugar and lemon and dissolve in both hot or cold water.

Tea-Like Beverages:

Tisanes: When England taxed tea, colonial American women swore off it and began making infusions of raspberry leaves, sage, and a variety of other herbs, seeds, and flowers. Many of these tisanes remain popular today, and a number—peppermint, verbena, sassafras, linden, rose hips, camomile —can be bought as "tea bags."

Maté: Also known as Paraguay tea, these are the dried leaves of the young shoots of a variety of holly. They brew into a strangely smoky, oily drink that tastes a little like green tea.

Yaupon: Along the southeastern Atlantic seaboard grow the stunted, gnarled yaupon trees, an evergreen of the holly family. American Indians used to gather and dry the leaves, then brew them into a strong drink that was used in purification rites. A milder version, yaupon tea, is still made on North Carolina's Outer Banks. And very good it is.

About Buying Tea

As with coffee, the best way to determine the tea you like best is to experiment, trying first one blend, then another. Most popular blends are available both by the half pound or pound as loose tea or in tea bags. Teas keep far better than coffee, but they should be stored tightly covered and far away from foods whose flavors they might absorb.

How to Make Tea

Hot Tea: Use a china, heatproof glass, or porcelain pot rather than a metal one (metal makes tea taste metallic). Scald the pot with boiling water. For each serving, use ¾ cup water and 1 teaspoon (*not* measuring teaspoon) loose tea (or 1 tea bag). Place required quantity of water —*cold water*—in a saucepan or teakettle and bring to a full boil. Meanwhile, place tea in teapot. Pour boiling water directly over tea, let steep 3–5 minutes. Stir and serve with lemon, sugar, and, if you like, milk or cream. *Note:* Tea, like coffee, should never boil. If tea is too strong (color is less an indicator than flavor), simply weaken with additional boiling water.

VARIATIONS:

Spiced Tea: Prepare as directed but add 6–8 cloves and a cinnamon stick to the teapot along with the tea.

Iced Tea: Prepare hot tea as directed but use 1½ teaspoons tea to each ¾ cup water. Pour hot tea into tall glasses filled with ice cubes. Add lemon and sugar to taste, sprig with mint, if you wish, and serve. *To Make a Pitcherful* (8–10 servings): Bring 1 quart cold water to a full boil in a large enamel or heatproof glass saucepan, remove from heat, add ⅓ cup loose tea (or 15 tea bags) and let steep 4–5 minutes. Stir well, then strain through a very fine sieve into a pitcher containing 1 quart ice water. Pour into tall glasses filled with ice. *Note:* If you refrigerate tea while it is still hot, it will cloud. To clear, stir in a little boiling water.

HOW TO MAKE HOT TEA FOR A CROWD

Number of Servings	Tea Needed	Water Needed
20	2 oz. (7 tablespoons) loose tea *OR* 20 tea bags	3 cups
40	¼ lb. (1 cup − 2 tablespoons) loose tea *OR* 40 tea bags	1½ quarts
60	6 oz. (1¼ cups+1 tablespoon) loose tea *OR* 60 tea bags	2 quarts+1 cup

Bring water to a rolling boil in a saucepan (not aluminum). Remove from heat, add tea, stir, cover, and brew 5 minutes. Scald teapot and strain tea into pot. To serve: Pour about 2 tablespoons tea into each cup and fill with piping hot freshly boiled water, adjusting strength by varying amount of tea. (*Note:* For a quantity Tea Punch, see the Party Punch Chart.)

⚕ RUSSIAN-STYLE TEA

Russians serve tea in slim heatproof glasses instead of cups–a 6- to 8-ounce size is about right.
Makes 6 servings

2 quarts boiling water (about)
8 teaspoons black tea (Indian or Ceylon)
Thinly sliced lemon
Strawberry or raspberry jam (optional)
Lump sugar

Have water boiling furiously and keep boiling throughout the tea service (use a samovar if you have one). Pour a little boiling water into a teapot to warm it, swish around, and pour out. Place tea in teapot, add 1½ cups boiling water, cover, and let steep 3–5 min-utes. Strain tea into a second warmed teapot and keep warm. To serve, pour about ¼ cup tea into each glass and add boiling water to fill; adjust amount of tea according to strength desired. Pass lemon, jam, and sugar. (*Note:* Russians often stir a spoonful of jam into their tea or place a lump of sugar in their mouths and drink the tea through it.) About 40 calories per serving if optional jam is used, 18 calories per serving if jam is not used.

⚕ ⊠ SPICED ORANGE TEA MIX

Makes enough for 40 servings

1 cup powdered orange-flavored beverage mix
¼ cup instant tea powder
1 (3-ounce) package sweetened lemonade mix
1 cup sugar
1 teaspoon cinnamon
½ teaspoon cloves

Mix all ingredients and store airtight. To make 1 cup spiced orange tea, place 1 tablespoon mix in a cup, pour in 1 cup boiling water, and stir until dissolved. About 30 calories per serving.

Some Tips for Making Better Milk Drinks

– For richer flavor, use evaporated milk or a ½ and ½ mixture of evaporated and fresh milk (especially good in chocolate drinks).
– To reduce calories, use skim or reconstituted nonfat dry milk instead of whole milk—their calorie content is approximately half that of whole milk.
– To prevent "skin" from forming on hot milk or hot milk drinks, stir often with a wire whisk.
– Use a low heat for hot milk or chocolate drinks—both scorch easily.
– Never try to mix cocoa or cinnamon directly with milk or other liquid; blend first with an equal quantity of sugar.
– When combining milk and an acid fruit juice, slowly mix fruit juice into milk rather than vice versa —less chance of curdling.

Some Garnishes for Milk Drinks (choose garnishes compatible in flavor with the drink):
Dustings of cinnamon, cinnamon-sugar, nutmeg, instant cocoa mix, or confectioners' sugar (all drinks)
Grated or shaved chocolate (for chocolate, mocha, or butterscotch drinks)
Grated orange or lemon rind (for fruit-milk drinks)
Marshmallows (especially good for cocoa)
Whipped cream fluffs (all drinks)
Cinnamon stick stirrers (good with chocolate and fruit-milk drinks)
Peppermint stick stirrers (good with cold chocolate drinks)
Fruit kebab stirrers (whole fresh berries, grapes, melon balls, cherries, or pineapple chunks threaded on long wooden skewers —good with fruit-milk drinks)

⊠ SOME QUICK MILK DRINKS

Each makes 1 serving
Pour 1¼ cups cold milk into a 12-ounce glass and blend in any of the following:

Chocolate Milk: 2–3 tablespoons chocolate syrup and ¼ teaspoon vanilla. 270 to 300 calories per serving, depending on amount of chocolate syrup used.

Mocha Milk: 2 tablespoons chocolate syrup, 1 teaspoon instant coffee powder blended with 1 tablespoon tepid water and ¼ teaspoon vanilla. 270 calories per serving.

Vanilla Milk: 1 tablespoon superfine sugar and 1 teaspoon vanilla. 245 calories per serving.

Butterscotch Milk: 2–3 tablespoons butterscotch syrup and ¼ teaspoon vanilla. 252 to 272 calories per serving, depending on amount of syrup used.

Maple Milk: 3–4 tablespoons maple syrup. 350 to 400 calories per serving, depending on amount of syrup used.

Milk and Honey: 3–4 tablespoons honey and a pinch nutmeg or mace. 392 to 456 calories per serving, depending on amount of honey used.

Molasses Milk: 3–4 tablespoons molasses. 350 to 400 calories per serving, depending on amount of molasses used.

Honey-Molasses Milk: 2 tablespoons each honey and molasses. 428 calories per serving.

Melba Milk: 3–4 tablespoons Melba Sauce. 320 to 360 calories per serving, depending on amount of Melba Sauce used.

Pour 1 cup cold milk or buttermilk into a 12-ounce glass and blend in either of the following:

Peachy Milk: ⅓–½ cup puréed frozen peaches and ⅛ teaspoon almond extract. About 245 calories per serving.

Berry Milk: ⅓–½ cup sieved puréed frozen strawberries or raspberries. About 235 calories per serving.

To Make Malted Milk: Prepare any of the Quick Milk Drinks as directed but add 2 tablespoons malted milk powder (plain or chocolate depending upon flavor of drink) and beat well. (*Note:* 2 tablespoons malted milk will increase total calories per serving by about 115 calories.)

⊠ SOME MILK SHAKES

The electric blender whips up shakes best, but a rotary or portable electric mixer works fairly well. A milk shake becomes a "frosted" when ice cream is beaten in, a "float" when a scoopful is dropped in after beating.
Each makes 1 serving

Pour 1 cup cold milk into blender container and blend in any of the following:
Banana Milk Shake: 1 small very ripe peeled and well-mashed banana and ¼ teaspoon vanilla. Serve sprinkled with cinnamon or nutmeg. About 240 calories per serving.
Berry Milk Shake: ⅓ cup puréed strawberries or raspberries, 3–4 tablespoons berry preserves and, if you like, 1–2 drops red food coloring. About 310 to 360 calories per serving, depending on amount of preserves used.
Chocolate Milk Shake: 2–3 tablespoons chocolate syrup or Cocoa Syrup. 230 to 265 calories per serving, depending on amount of syrup used.
Caramel Milk Shake: 2 tablespoons Caramel Syrup and ¼ teaspoon maple flavoring. About 260 calories per serving.
Coffee Milk Shake: 2 teaspoons each instant coffee powder and sugar. About 190 calories per serving.
Mocha Milk Shake: 2 tablespoons chocolate syrup and 1 teaspoon each instant coffee powder and sugar. About 250 calories per serving.
Orange Milk Shake: ⅓ cup orange juice. About 200 calories per serving.

To Make Frosted Milk Shakes: Add 1–2 scoops of an appropriate ice cream to milk along with flavoring and blend until thick and creamy and no lumps of ice cream remain. Some good combinations: Chocolate Milk Shake and coffee ice cream; Banana Milk Shake and butterscotch ice cream; Orange Milk Shake and pistachio ice cream. (*Note:* For each scoop of ice cream used, add 150 calories.)

To Make Malted Milk Shakes: Add 1–2 tablespoons malted milk powder to any milk shake recipe before blending, then blend as directed. (*Note:* Chocolate malted milk powder is especially good in the Chocolate, Caramel, Coffee, and Mocha Milk Shakes.) For each tablespoon of malted milk powder used, add 58 calories.

⊠ BASIC ICE CREAM SODA

As good as the corner drugstore ever made.
Makes 1 serving

¼ cup cold milk or light cream
2 scoops vanilla or any flavor ice cream
Chilled club soda (or ginger ale, cola, or other favorite carbonated drink)
Garnishes (optional): whipped cream, maraschino cherry

Pour milk into a 12-ounce glass, add 1 scoop ice cream, pour in a little soda, and stir briskly, mashing ice cream. Add second scoop of ice cream, fill with soda, stir again, and garnish. 340 calories per serving if made with milk, 420 if made with light cream (optional garnishes not included). Add 25 calories for each tablespoon of whipped cream used, 17 calories for each cherry.

VARIATIONS:

Chocolate Ice Cream Soda: Mix milk with 2–3 tablespoons chocolate syrup, then proceed as directed, using chocolate or vanilla ice cream. Add 50 calories to basic ice cream soda calorie counts for each tablespoon chocolate syrup used.

Mocha Ice Cream Soda: Prepare Chocolate Ice Cream Soda but use coffee ice cream. Calorie counts the same as for chocolate ice cream soda.

Coffee Ice Cream Soda: Mix milk and 1 teaspoon instant coffee powder, then proceed as directed, using coffee ice cream. 340 calories per serving.

Strawberry or Raspberry Ice Cream Soda: Mix milk with ¼ cup crushed strawberries or raspberries or 2–3 tablespoons strawberry or raspberry syrup and proceed as directed, using vanilla, strawberry, or raspberry ice cream. Garnish with a berry instead of cherry. About 370 calories for the strawberry soda made with fresh berries, about 420 if made with syrup. About 390 calories for the raspberry soda made with berries, 420 made with syrup.

Cherry Ice Cream Soda: Mix milk with 2–3 tablespoons cherry preserves or cherry sundae topping, then proceed as directed, using vanilla or cherry ice cream. 440 to 490 calories per serving, depending on amount of preserves used.

Peach, Pineapple, or Apricot Ice Cream Soda: Mix milk with ¼ cup puréed peaches, pineapple, or apricots, then proceed as directed, using a compatible flavor of ice cream. About 450 calories per serving for the peach and pineapple sodas, 460 per serving for the apricot.

Lemon or Orange Ice Cream Soda: Mix milk with 2–3 tablespoons frozen lemonade or orange juice concentrate, then proceed as directed, using lemon or orange ice cream or sherbet. About 395 calories per serving for the lemon soda made with ice cream, 295 calories if made with sherbet. About 385 calories per serving for the orange soda made with ice cream, 285 if made with sherbet.

⊠ ICE CREAM FLOATS

These are quick, fun, and so easy that very young children can make them. The combinations are as broad as the imagination—all you need are a variety of ice creams or sherbets and carbonated beverages or fruit juices.

For Each Serving: Drop a hefty scoop of ice cream or sherbet into a tall glass, add a little carbonated drink or fruit juice, stir briskly, mashing ice cream slightly, then pour in enough carbonated drink or fruit juice to fill glass. Fancier variations can be made by mixing in a little chocolate or fruit syrup or by adding an extra scoop of ice cream at the end. Calorie counts, obviously, will vary according to ingredients used. But as a minimum for a float made with sherbet and carbonated fruit drink, you can figure about 230 calories per serving. For a float made with ice cream and carbonated fruit drink, you can figure about 280 calories per serving.

⊠ 500-CALORIE MEAL-IN-A-GLASS

A high-protein formula that can be used in place of solid food. Good for those unable to take solids; also good—between meals—for those on weight-gaining diets. Use the 250-calorie version as a quick breakfast or lunch.
Makes 1 serving

1 cup cold milk
2 eggs
2 teaspoons sugar
½ cup vanilla ice cream, softened
  slightly
¼ teaspoon vanilla
Nutmeg

Beat together all ingredients except nutmeg until frothy, using an electric blender, rotary or electric mixer. Pour into a chilled tall glass and dust with nutmeg.

VARIATIONS:

⚄ **250-Calorie Meal-in-a-Glass:** Beat together ¾ cup cold skim milk, 1 egg, ½ cup ice cream, and ¼ teaspoon vanilla; omit sugar.

Chocolate 500-Calorie Meal-in-a-Glass: Prepare as directed but substitute chocolate ice cream for vanilla, omit sugar, and add 1 teaspoon cocoa.

Coffee 500-Calorie Meal-in-a-Glass: Prepare as directed but substitute coffee ice cream for vanilla and add 1–2 teaspoons instant coffee powder.

LIQUORLESS EGGNOG

Makes 6 servings

4 eggs, separated
½ cup sugar
2 cups cold milk
1 cup cold light cream
1½ teaspoons vanilla
⅛ teaspoon salt
¼ teaspoon nutmeg

Beat egg yolks and ¼ cup sugar until thick and cream colored; gradually add milk, cream, vanilla, salt, and ⅛ teaspoon nutmeg and beat until frothy. Beat egg whites with remaining sugar until soft peaks form and fold in. Cover and chill until serving time. Mix well, pour into punch bowl, and sprinkle with remaining nutmeg. About 250 calories per serving.

¢ ⊠ HOT COCOA

Inexpensive, easy, and good.
Makes 1 cup

1 tablespoon cocoa
1 tablespoon sugar
Pinch salt
⅓ cup water
⅔ cup milk

Mix cocoa, sugar, and salt in a small saucepan, slowly stir in water. Heat and stir over moderately low heat until mixture boils, then boil slowly, stirring constantly, 2 minutes. Add milk and heat to scalding but do not boil. About 190 calories per serving.

VARIATIONS:

Cocoa for a Crowd (Makes 12 servings): Mix ¾ cup cocoa with ¾ cup sugar and ½ teaspoon salt in a large saucepan. Gradually stir in 1 quart warm water, set over low heat, and heat, stirring now and then, 8–10 minutes. Add 2 quarts milk and heat to scalding. Serve in mugs, sprinkled, if you like, with cinnamon or nutmeg or topped with marshmallows. About 190 calories per serving not including marshmallows (for each used, add 25 calories).

Iced Cocoa: Prepare cocoa as directed, then cool, stirring occasionally. Pour over ice cubes, top with a dollop of whipped cream, and sprinkle with cinnamon. About 190 calories per serving, plus 25 calories for each tablespoon of whipped cream used.

☒ RICH-QUICK COCOA

Like Old-Fashioned Hot Chocolate but quicker.
Makes 2 servings

1½ cups milk
2 tablespoons cocoa
2 tablespoons sugar
⅛ teaspoon salt
¼ teaspoon butter or margarine
¼ teaspoon vanilla

Bring milk to a simmer; meanwhile, blend cocoa and sugar. Mix a little hot milk into cocoa mixture, return to pan, add remaining ingredients, and heat and stir 1–2 minutes to blend flavors. Pour into mugs or cups and serve. About 210 calories per serving.

VARIATIONS:

Hot Mocha: Prepare as directed but substitute 1 tablespoon instant coffee powder for 1 tablespoon cocoa and omit butter. About 190 calories per serving.

Caramel Coffee: Prepare as directed but substitute 4 teaspoons instant coffee powder for cocoa and omit salt, butter, and vanilla. About 175 calories per serving.

OLD-FASHIONED HOT CHOCOLATE

The kind Grandmother used to make—dark and rich.
Makes 4–6 servings

2 (1-ounce) squares unsweetened chocolate
1 cup water
¼ cup sugar
Pinch salt
3 cups milk
⅓ cup heavy cream

Heat and stir chocolate, water, sugar, and salt in the top of a double boiler over simmering water until chocolate melts. Slowly stir in milk and heat uncovered to serving temperature. Meanwhile, whip cream. Serve in mugs or cups topped with whipped cream. About 340 calories for each of 4 servings, 225 for each of 6 servings.

Some Tips for Making Better Fruit Drinks

– Use freshly squeezed, unstrained juice whenever possible.
– Freeze some of the fruit juice or drink mixture to use as "ice cubes" —prevents drinks from watering down as the ice melts.
– When making punch in quantity, use a large ice block in punch bowl rather than crushed or cubed ice; it melts more slowly, waters the punch down less.

– For extra-tangy fruit drinks, add a little grated orange, lemon, or lime rind.

– When a recipe calls for both fruit juice and rind, grate the rind first, then cut open fruit and squeeze.

– Save syrup drained from canned or frozen fruits to use in fruit drinks.

– Try sweetening drinks with honey or light corn syrup instead of sugar—they dissolve more easily and make drinks mellower.

– For really sparkling drinks, add ginger ale or other carbonated beverage just before serving.

– Have drink ingredients well chilled before mixing together.

– Avoid putting tinted ice cubes in colorful fruit drinks that might gray the drinks as they melt; pink cubes, for example, in green lime-ade will turn the limeade khaki.

– Avoid heavy, awkward garnishes that make beverages difficult to drink.

Some Garnishes for Fruit Drinks (choose those compatible in flavor with the drink):

Plain or fancily cut orange, lemon, or lime slices or wedges

Spirals of orange, lemon, or lime rind

Cocktail cherries, fresh cherries or berries

Pineapple chunks or melon balls

Fruit kebabs (grapes, cherries, melon balls, whole berries, or pineapple chunks threaded alternately on long wooden skewers)

Pineapple stick stirrers (simply long, thin sticks of pineapple)

Cinnamon stick stirrers (for hot drinks)

Orange or lemon slices stuck with cloves (for hot drinks)

⊠ SOME QUICK COOLERS

For best results, have fruit juices, ginger ale, club soda, colas, etc., well chilled before mixing coolers. Each makes 1 serving

Ginger-Grapefruit Cooler: Put 3–4 ice cubes in a 12-ounce glass, then fill, using equal quantities grapefruit juice (or pineapple, orange, tangerine, grape, or cranberry juice) and ginger ale. Sprig with mint and, if you like, add a slice of orange or lime. Calories per serving: 88 for the ginger-grapefruit cooler, 110 for the orange, grape and pineapple, 100 for the tangerine, and 125 for the cranberry.

Caribbean Cooler: Half fill a 12-ounce glass with crushed ice, add ⅓ cup each pineapple and orange juices, then fill with cola. Add a maraschino cherry and an orange slice. About 130 calories per serving.

Minted Apple-Lime Cooler: Bruise 2 mint leaves with ½ teaspoon sugar in a 12-ounce glass. Add apple juice or cider to half fill and mix well. Add 1 tablespoon lime juice and 2–3 ice cubes and mix again. Fill with ginger ale and add a wedge of lime. About 110 calories per serving.

Cranberry Sparkle: Put 3–4 ice cubes in a 12-ounce glass, then fill, using equal quantities cranberry juice, lemonade, and club soda. About 90 calories per serving.

Orange-Milk Cooler: Mix ½ cup each milk or skim milk and orange juice in a 12-ounce glass. Add ice cubes and fill with any fruit-flavored carbonated beverage. About 170 calories per serving if made with milk, 140 if made with skim milk.

⚔ **Orange-Tea Cooler:** Mix 2 teaspoons instant tea powder with ½ cup orange juice in a 12-ounce glass. Add 2 ice cubes and fill with club soda or ginger ale. Sprig with mint. About 55 calories per serving.

Wine Cooler: Half fill a 12-ounce glass with crushed ice, then fill with equal quantities sweet or dry red or white wine and ginger ale or club soda. About 95 calories per serving if made with ginger ale, 50 calories per serving if made with club soda.

Shandy Gaff: Mix equal quantities cold beer and lemon soda. Do not add ice. About 95 calories per serving.

⊠ EASY LEMONADE MIX

A handy mix to have on hand in the refrigerator (also handy to have on long car trips). Whenever anyone wants a glass of lemonade, all he he has to do is add water and ice and stir.

Makes about 1½ quarts, enough for 2 dozen glasses of lemonade

1 quart lemon juice
1 cup sugar
2 cups light corn syrup

Stir all ingredients together until sugar dissolves. Pour into screw-top jar, cover, and store in refrigerator. To serve, shake well and pour ¼ cup mix into a 12-ounce glass, add ice, fill with water or club soda, and stir well. *Note:* This mix keeps well several weeks. To make in a pitcher, allow ¼ cup mix to 1 cup ice water. About 125 calories per serving.

VARIATIONS:

⊠ **Easy Limeade Mix:** Substitute 1 quart lime juice for lemon juice; if you like, add a few drops green food coloring. About 125 calories per serving.

⊠ **Easy Orangeade Mix:** Substitute 1 quart freshly squeezed orange juice for lemon juice, omit sugar, and reduce corn syrup to 1½ cups; proceed as directed but use ½ cup mix per serving. Makes 12 servings at about 155 calories each.

⊠ **Easy Orange Crush:** Substitute 3 cups orange juice for lemon juice and add 1 cup each pineapple juice, crushed pineapple, and lemon juice; omit sugar. Use ½ cup mix per serving. Makes 12 servings at about 215 calories each.

⊠ **Easy Pink Lemonade:** Prepare Easy Lemonade Mix and add ¾ cup grenadine syrup; if you like, add a few drops red food coloring. Use ¼ cup mix per serving. (*Note:* Cranberry juice gives a nice color, too, but makes a tarter drink: Mix 1 quart cranberry juice with the Easy Lemonade Mix and use ½ cup mix per serving.) About 150 calories per serving if made with grenadine. Makes 30 servings if made with cranberry juice at about 120 calories each.

⊠ **Easy Grape Lemonade:** Pour ½ cup Easy Lemonade Mix into an ice-filled 12-ounce glass, fill with grape juice, and stir well. About 210 calories per serving.

MINTY LEMON-LIME FROST

Makes 4 servings

A little sugar for frosting glasses
½ cup sugar
½ cup boiling water
¼ cup firmly packed minced fresh mint
½ cup lime juice
2 tablespoons lemon juice
3 cups cold water
2–3 drops green food coloring
4 mint sprigs (garnish)

Frost* rims of 4 (12-ounce) glasses with sugar and chill until ready to use. Stir sugar with boiling water and mint until dissolved, cool 10 minutes, and strain into a large pitcher. Add fruit juices, cold water, coloring, and about 6 ice cubes; mix well. Place 3 ice cubes in each glass, fill with juice mixture, and sprig with mint. About 105 calories per serving.

CRANBERRY SHRUB

Shrubs are a colonial holdover. Originally spiked with rum or brandy, they are today an acid fruit juice served on the rocks or mixed with water or club soda. They make refreshing apéritifs, especially if served with scoops of tart sherbet. Makes 8 servings

1 quart cranberry juice
2 cups sugar
Rind of 1 lemon (cut in thin strips)
½ cup white vinegar or ⅔ cup lemon juice
1 quart water or club soda (optional)
1 pint tart fruit ice or sherbet (optional)

Simmer cranberry juice, sugar, and rind, uncovered, in a saucepan (not aluminum) 10 minutes, stirring now and then. Off heat, mix in vinegar; cool, pour into a bottle, cover, and refrigerate. Serve as is on the rocks in punch cups or small glasses. *Or* half fill a tall glass with shrub, add ice, and fill with water or club soda. *Or* pour into punch cups and top each serving with a scoop of tart fruit ice. About 350 calories per serving if made with sherbet or fruit ice, about 295 if made without.

VARIATIONS:

Raspberry or Blackberry Shrub: Crush 2 quarts ripe berries with 2 cups sugar, cover, and let stand over-night. Press through a cheesecloth-lined sieve, extracting as much juice as possible. Omit lemon rind but mix in vinegar. Taste for sweetness and, if too tart, add a bit more sugar, stirring until dissolved. Store and serve as directed. About 380 calories per serving without fruit ice, about 435 per serving with.

Cherry or Currant Shrub: Simmer 2 quarts tart, pitted red cherries, red or black currants, covered in a large saucepan (not aluminum) with 2 cups sugar and ⅓ cup water, stirring now and then, until mushy. Cool, cover, and let stand over-night. Press through a cheesecloth-lined sieve, extracting as much juice as possible. Omit lemon rind but add vinegar. Taste for sweetness and adjust as needed. Store and serve as directed. About 275 calories per serving without fruit ice, 350 calories per serving with.

Spiked Shrub: Prepare any of the 3 shrubs as directed, omitting sherbet; mix in 1 fifth light rum or brandy. Pour into bottles, cover, and store in a cool place at least 1 week before serving. Serve as is over crushed ice or mixed ½ and ½ with club soda in tall glasses with plenty of ice. Makes 16 servings at about 280 calories each if made with cranberry shrub and club soda, about 325 calories per serving if made with raspberry or blackberry shrub, and about 270 calories per serving if made with cherry or currant shrub.

⚗ ⊠ TOMATO COCKTAIL

Makes 4 servings

1 pint tomato juice
2 tablespoons lemon juice
1 tablespoon sugar
1 tablespoon minced yellow onion
1 bay leaf, crumbled
Pinch pepper

Mix all ingredients, cover, and chill 1–2 hours. Strain and serve in juice glasses. About 35 calories per serving.

VARIATIONS:

⚛ ⊠ **Tomato-Celery Cocktail:** Prepare as directed but add ½ cup diced celery and substitute 1 tablespoon cider vinegar for 1 tablespoon of the lemon juice. About 35 calories per serving.

⚛ ⊠ **Spicy Tomato Cocktail:** Prepare as directed but add 1 teaspoon prepared horseradish, 1 crushed clove garlic, ½ teaspoon Worcestershire sauce and substitute minced scallions for yellow onion. About 35 calories per serving.

⚛ ⊠ **Tomato Bouillon** (Makes 4–6 servings): Prepare as directed but omit lemon juice and sugar and add 1 cup beef broth or consommé and ½ teaspoon Worcestershire sauce. Serve on the rocks in small old-fashioned glasses. 43 calories for each of 4 servings, 30 for each of 6 servings.

⚛ ⊠ **Tomato-Clam Cocktail** (Makes 8 servings): Prepare as directed, then mix in 2 (8-ounce) bottles clam juice and 3–4 dashes liquid hot red pepper seasoning. Makes 8 servings at about 30 calories each.

Some Easy Appetizer Beverages

Serve in 4- to 6-ounce glasses on small plates lined with paper coasters. Suitably garnished, these can substitute for appetizer or soup courses. Pass them around before the meal or serve at the table. The following recipes all make 4 servings.

⊠ ⚛ **Clam Juice on the Rocks:** Mix 2 cups chilled clam juice with 2 tablespoons lemon juice, 1 tablespoon minced chives, 1 teaspoon Worcestershire sauce, and 2–3 drops liquid hot red pepper seasoning. If you like, add ¼ cup light cream and ⅛ teaspoon garlic salt. Serve on the rocks. About 20 calories per serving without cream.

⊠ ⚛ **Clam Chickee:** Mix 1 cup each chilled clam juice and chicken broth. Season to taste with celery salt and top each serving with a dollop of sour cream; sprinkle with salt and paprika. *Variation:* Substitute madrilène for chicken broth. About 20 calories per serving without cream.

⊠ ⚛ **Sauerkraut Juice Cocktail:** Mix 2 cups chilled sauerkraut juice with 2 tablespoons lemon juice, ½ teaspoon prepared horseradish, and ¼ teaspoon bruised caraway seeds. About 10 calories per serving. Or use 1 cup each sauerkraut juice and tomato juice. About 15 calories per serving. Serve with a slice of lemon.

⊠ ⚛ **Bullseye:** Mix 1 (10½-ounce) can chilled condensed beef bouillon and 1 cup chilled tomato-vegetable juice; serve with a twist of lemon peel. About 20 calories per serving.

⊠ ⚛ **Hen's Eye:** Mix 1 cup each chilled chicken broth and tomato juice; serve sprinkled with minced chives and sieved hard-cooked egg yolk. About 20 calories per serving.

⊠ **Pineapple-Grapefruit Frappé:** Blend 1 cup each unsweetened pineapple and grapefruit juice, 2 tablespoons lime juice, ¼ cup honey, and 1 unbeaten egg white in an electric blender at high speed ½ minute. Add 6–7 crushed ice cubes, a bit at a time, continuing to blend until thick and frothy. Pour out and serve. About 120 calories per serving.

⊠ **Red Orange Cocktail:** Mix 1 cup each chilled cranberry juice and orange juice; to each serving add a melon ball, berry, or cherry stuck on a cocktail pick. About 75 calories per serving.

◁▷ **Vegetable Juice Cocktail:** In an electric blender, at high speed, purée 3 peeled and coarsely chopped medium-size carrots, 3 radishes, 3 scallions, ¼ cup each celery leaves and watercress, 1 canned beet that has been diced, ½ cup beet liquid, and 1½ cups ice water. Cover and refrigerate 1 hour, strain, mix in 1 teaspoon salt and ⅛ teaspoon pepper. If you like, mix in 2–3 tablespoons vegetable pulp and serve. About 20 calories per serving.

◁▷ **Quick Yogurt Kholodnyk:** Peel, seed, and purée 1 medium-size cucumber with ½ cup ice water in an electric blender at high speed. Mix in 1 cup yogurt (or buttermilk), ½ teaspoon lemon juice, ¼ teaspoon salt, a pinch cayenne pepper, and 1–2 teaspoons snipped fresh dill. Cover and chill ½ hour. If a little thick, thin with ice water or cold milk. About 30 calories per serving made with buttermilk, 40 calories per serving made with yogurt.

SOME DECORATIVE ICES AND ICE RINGS FOR PUNCH BOWLS

Note: Chilled, boiled water makes clearer ice than water straight out of the tap. To unmold decorative ice blocks, dip in hot—not boiling—water. Boiling water may crack the block.

Float: Half fill a metal loaf pan, metal bowl, decorative gelatin or ring mold with cold boiled water; freeze solid. Arrange washed strawberries, pineapple chunks or rings, black and/or green grapes, melon balls, lemon, lime or orange slices, drained maraschino cherries on ice in a decorative pattern; add ¼" cold boiled water and freeze. Fill mold with cold boiled water and freeze. Unmold and float in punch bowl.

Christmas Wreath: Arrange 1 dozen each red and green maraschino cherries and a few mint leaves in a decorative pattern in the bottom of a 5-cup ring mold. Carefully pour in 1" cold boiled water and freeze solid. Fill with cold boiled water and freeze. Unmold and float in punch bowl.

Wedding Ring: Pour 1" cold boiled water in any large ring mold and freeze solid. Arrange rinsed sweetheart roses close together on ice, add ½" cold boiled water, and freeze. Fill ring with more water and freeze. Unmold and float in Champagne Punch.

Ice Bowl: Half fill a 3-quart metal bowl with cold boiled water; set a 1-quart metal bowl inside larger bowl, weighting down so it will stay in center; freeze solid. Remove weights from small bowl, fill with hot water, then lift small bowl out. Unmold ice bowl by dipping large bowl in hot water, float right side up in punch bowl and fill with fresh flowers or fruit. (*Note:* Ice bowl can also be set in a deep platter and used as a container for ice cream or fruit desserts. It can be made ahead of time and stored in the freezer.)

Party Ice Cubes: Half fill ice cube trays with cold boiled water; freeze solid. Into each cube, place a cherry, berry, wedge of pineapple, lemon, lime, or orange, or a mint leaf. Fill with cold boiled water and freeze. (*Note:* Water can be tinted with food coloring, a colorful fruit liqueur, maraschino or cranberry juice, but it will color the punch as it melts.)

Iced Fruits: Rinse and dry any pretty chunky fruits and freeze solid on foil-lined baking sheets. (*Note:* Frozen cherries and grapes tend to sink to the bottom of a punch bowl; berries, pineapple rings, peach halves, citrus slices, and melon balls float.) To use iced fruits, simply peel off foil and drop into punch bowl. They will keep punch cool without diluting it.

PARTY PUNCH CHART

Note: Whenever possible, buy punch ingredients in large containers — gallons or magnums of wine or magnums of champagne instead of fifths, institution size cans of fruit juice. You'll have to order ahead, but you'll save money. Unless you have use of an institutional kitchen and its giant kettles, do not try to mix punch for 100 at one time; make 2 batches for 50 or, if necessary, 4-5 batches for 2 dozen (especially important if punch mixture must be heated at any time).

NONALCOHOLIC PUNCHES	Quantities For			
	1 Dozen	2 Dozen	50 People	100 People
Autumn Apple Punch				
Apple juice	1½ quarts	3 quarts	1½ gallons	3 gallons
Cinnamon sticks	2	4	8	16
Whole cloves	8	1 dozen	1½ dozen	2 dozen
Pineapple juice	1⅓ cups	1½ pints	1½ quarts	3 quarts
Lemon juice	1/2 cup	1 cup	1 pint	1 quart
Orange juice	1 pint	1 quart	2 quarts	1 gallon
Ginger ale	1 (28-oz.) bottle	2 (28-oz.) bottles	4 (28-oz.) bottles	8 (28-oz.) bottles

Place 1-2 quarts apple juice in a large kettle (not aluminum); tie spices in cheesecloth, add to kettle, and simmer uncovered 15 minutes; discard spice bag. Mix spiced juice with remaining fruit juices. To serve, place a large block of ice in a large punch bowl, add fruit juice and ginger ale. (*Note:* For large quantities, mix batches as needed, using 1 bottle ginger ale to each 2½ quarts fruit juice mixture.) About 55 calories per 4-ounce serving.

Hot Party Mocha				
Unsweetened chocolate	4 (1-oz.) squares	1/2 pound	1 pound	2 pounds
Sugar	1 cup	1 pound	2 pounds	4 pounds
Water	1/2 cup	1 cup	1 pint	1 quart
Instant coffee powder	2 teaspoons	4 teaspoons	8 teaspoons	1/3 cup
Cinnamon	1/4 teaspoon	1/2 teaspoon	1 teaspoon	2 teaspoons
Heavy cream	1/2 cup	1 cup	1 pint	1 quart
Scalding hot milk	2½ quarts	5 quarts	2½ gallons	5 gallons

Heat and stir chocolate, sugar, water, coffee, and cinnamon in a heavy saucepan over low heat until chocolate melts; cover and cool. Beat cream to soft peaks and fold into chocolate mixture. To serve, pour chocolate mixture into a large silver punch bowl, add hot milk, and stir to mix. (*Note:* For large quantities, mix chocolate mixture and hot milk as needed to fill punch bowl, allowing about 1¼ cups chocolate mixture to 2½ quarts milk.) About 180 calories per 4-ounce serving.

Hot Spiced Cider				
Apple cider	3 quarts	1½ gallons	3 gallons	6 gallons
Light brown sugar	1 pound	2 pounds	4 pounds	8 pounds
Cinnamon sticks	3	6	1 dozen	2 dozen
Whole cloves	1 dozen	1½ dozen	2 dozen	3 dozen

Place cider and sugar in a large kettle (not aluminum); tie spices in cheesecloth, add, and simmer uncovered 15 minutes; discard spice bag. Serve from a silver punch bowl or large coffee or teapot. About 115 calories per 4-ounce serving.

	Quantities For			
	1 Dozen	2 Dozen	50 People	100 People

Hot Spicy Grape Juice

Oranges	1	2	4	8
Whole nutmegs, cracked	2	3	5	8
Whole cloves	1 dozen	1½ dozen	2 dozen	3 dozen
Cinnamon sticks	2	4	8	16
Grape juice	2 quarts	1 gallon	2 gallons	4 gallons
Boiling water	1 quart	2 quarts	1 gallon	2 gallons
Lemon juice	1/2 cup	1 cup	1 pint	1 quart
Sugar	1 cup	1 pound	2 pounds	4 pounds

With a vegetable peeler, cut rind from oranges in long strips; tie in cheesecloth with spices; save oranges to use another time. Place spices and remaining ingredients in a very large heavy kettle (not aluminum) and simmer, uncovered, stirring occasionally 10-15 minutes; discard spice bag. Serve hot from a large silver punch bowl. About 75 calories per 4-ounce serving.

Jubilee Punch

Orange juice	1½ quarts	3 quarts	1½ gallons	3 gallons
Lemon juice	1½ cups	3 cups	1½ quarts	3 quarts
Maraschino cherries (and liquid)	1/3 cup	2/3 cup	1½ cups	3 cups
Sparkling white grape juice	2 (1-qt.) bottles	4 (1-qt.) bottles	8 (1-qt.) bottles	16 (1-qt.) bottles

Mix orange and lemon juice with cherries. To serve, place a large block of ice in a large punch bowl, add fruit mixture, then pour in grape juice. (*Note:* For large quantities, mix batches as needed, using about equal quantities fruit mixture and grape juice.) About 65 calories per 4-ounce serving.

Lemonade or Limeade

Sugar	3 cups	3 pounds	6 pounds	12 pounds
Water	2½ quarts	5 quarts	2½ gallons	5 gallons
Lemon or lime juice	3 cups	1½ quarts	3 quarts	1½ gallons
Fresh mint sprigs	1 dozen	2 dozen	50	100

Heat sugar and water in a large kettle (not aluminum), stirring until sugar dissolves; cool to room temperature and mix in lemon juice. To serve, place a large block of ice in a large punch bowl and pour in lemonade. Sprig glasses with mint. About 90 calories per 4-ounce serving.

Pineapple-Raspberry Cream Punch

Pineapple juice	1 quart	2 quarts	1 gallon	2 gallons
Ginger ale	2 (28-oz.) bottles	4 (28-oz.) bottles	8 (28-oz.) bottles	16 (28-oz.) bottles
Vanilla ice cream	1 quart	2 quarts	1 gallon	2 gallons
Raspberry sherbet	1 quart	2 quarts	1 gallon	2 gallons

Pour pineapple juice and ginger ale over ice cream and sherbet and stir until melted and blended. About 95 calories per 4-ounce serving.

	Quantities For			
	1 Dozen	2 Dozen	50 People	100 People

Tea Punch

	1 Dozen	2 Dozen	50 People	100 People
Superfine sugar	1 cup	1 pound	2 pounds	4 pounds
Oranges, sliced	2	4	8	16
Lemons, sliced	6	9	1 dozen	1½ dozen
Hot strong tea	1 quart	2 quarts	1 gallon	2 gallons
Boiling water	1 quart	2 quarts	1 gallon	2 gallons
Ginger ale	2 (28-oz.) bottles	4 (28-oz.) bottles	8 (28-oz.) bottles	16 (28-oz.) bottles

Place all but last ingredient in a large, heavy kettle (not aluminum) and stir, bruising fruit slightly, until sugar dissolves; cover and cool 1-2 hours. To serve, place a large block of ice in a large punch bowl, then fill, adding about equal quantities tea mixture and ginger ale. About 50 calories per 4-ounce serving.

Three Fruit Punch

	1 Dozen	2 Dozen	50 People	100 People
Superfine sugar	1/3 cup	2/3 cup	1⅓ cups	2⅔ cups
Grapefruit juice	1½ cups	3 cups	1½ quarts	3 quarts
Orange juice	1½ cups	3 cups	1½ quarts	3 quarts
Apricot or peach nectar	2 quarts	1 gallon	2 gallons	4 gallons
Finely grated orange rind	1½ teaspoons	1 tablespoon	2 tablespoons	1/4 cup
Club soda	1 (28-oz.) bottle	2 (28-oz.) bottles	4 (28-oz.) bottles	8 (28-oz.) bottles
Oranges, sliced (garnish)	1	1	2	3

Place sugar and grapefruit juice in a large kettle (not aluminum) and stir until sugar dissolves. (*Note:* For large quantities, you may need to heat slightly; do not boil; cool to room temperature.) Mix in all but last 2 ingredients. To serve, place a large block of ice in a large punch bowl, then fill, adding 1 bottle club soda for each 2¾ quarts fruit juice mixture. Float orange slices on top and replenish, as needed, with fresh slices. About 60 calories per 4-ounce serving.

ALCOHOLIC PUNCHES

Champagne Punch

	1 Dozen	2 Dozen	50 People	100 People
Lemon juice	2/3 cup	1⅓ cups	2½ cups	1 quart
Superfine sugar	1/3 cup	2/3 cup	1¼ cups	1 pound
Cranberry juice	3 cups	1½ quarts	3 quarts	1½ gallons
Champagne	3 (26-oz.) bottles	6 (26-oz.) bottles	12 (26-oz.) bottles	24 (26-oz.) bottles
Ginger ale	1 (28-oz.) bottle	2 (28-oz.) bottles	4 (28-oz.) bottles	8 (28-oz.) bottles
Brandy (optional)	1/2 cup	1 cup	1 pint	1 quart

Stir lemon juice and sugar together in a large kettle (not aluminum) until sugar dissolves. (*Note:* For large quantities, you may need to heat gently to dissolve sugar; do not boil; cool to room temperature.) Mix in cranberry juice. To serve, place a large block of ice or decorative ice ring* in a large punch bowl; add fruit juice mixture, champagne, ginger ale, and, if you like, brandy; mix gently. (*Note:* For large amounts, mix in batches as needed, using 2 quarts fruit juice mixture to 4 bottles champagne, 2 bottles ginger ale, and 1 cup brandy.) About 100 calories per 4 ounce serving made with brandy, 90 calories per 4-ounce serving made without brandy.

	Quantities For			
	1 Dozen	2 Dozen	50 People	100 People
Claret Cup				
Red Bordeaux wine	3 (24-oz.) bottles	6 (24-oz.) bottles	12 (24-oz.) bottles	24 (24-oz.) bottles
Superfine sugar	3/4 cup	1½ cups	3 cups	3 pounds
Nutmeg	1/2 teaspoon	1 teaspoon	1½ teaspoons	1 tablespoon
Maraschino liqueur	1/4 cup	1/2 cup	1 cup	1 pint
Club soda	3 (28-oz.) bottles	6 (28-oz.) bottles	12 (28-oz.) bottles	24 (28-oz.) bottles
Unpeeled cucumber, sliced thin	1 small	1 large	2 large	3 large
Borage sprigs (optional garnish)	3-4	5-6	8-10	12-15

Stir wine and sugar together in a large punch bowl until sugar dissolves. (*Note:* For very large quantities, heat 1-2 bottles wine with sugar, stirring constantly, in a large saucepan (not aluminum) until sugar dissolves; do not boil; cool completely.) Mix nutmeg and maraschino liqueur into wine mixture. To serve, place a large block of ice in a large punch bowl and fill by pouring in equal quantities wine mixture and club soda; stir lightly. Float cucumber slices on top and, if you like, sprig with borage. Replenish cucumber and borage as needed. About 60 calories per 4-ounce serving.

Fish House Punch				
Superfine sugar	1½ cups	3 cups	3 pounds	6 pounds
Water	1 cup	1 pint	1 quart	2 quarts
Lemon juice	1 quart	2 quarts	1 gallon	2 gallons
Dark Jamaican rum	2 quarts	1 gallon	2 gallons	4 gallons
Brandy	1 quart	2 quarts	1 gallon	2 gallons
Peach brandy	1/2 cup	1 cup	1 pint	1 quart

Heat and stir sugar and water in a large saucepan over moderate heat until sugar dissolves; cool to room temperature. Mix sugar syrup with remaining ingredients in a large punch bowl and let "ripen" at room temperature 2 hours. Add a large block of ice and let stand 1/2 hour longer. Mix gently and serve. (*Note:* For large quantities [for 50 or 100], mix in batches for 2 dozen and omit ripening time.) About 275 calories per 4-ounce serving.

PARTY PUNCH CHART (continued)

	1 Dozen	2 Dozen	50 People	100 People
			Quantities For	

Glögg				
Oranges	1	2	4	8
Whole cloves	8	16	2 dozen	3 dozen
Cardamom seeds	1 tablespoon	2 tablespoons	1/4 cup	1/2 cup
Cinnamon sticks	2	4	8	16
Water	1 pint	1 quart	2 quarts	1 gallon
Sugar	1 cup	1 pound	2 pounds	4 pounds
Seedless raisins	1 cup	2 cups	1 pound	1½ pounds
Whole blanched almonds	1 cup	2 cups	1 pound	1½ pounds
Dry port or red Bordeaux wine	2 (24-oz.) bottles	4 (24-oz.) bottles	8 (24-oz.) bottles	16 (24-oz.) bottles
Aquavit or vodka	2 fifths	3 quarts	6 quarts	12 quarts

With a vegetable peeler, cut rind from oranges in long strips; tie in cheesecloth with spices; save oranges to use another time. Place spice bag in a large kettle (not aluminum), add water and sugar, and simmer uncovered, stirring until sugar is dissolved, 5-10 minutes. Add raisins and almonds and simmer 3-5 minutes; cool slightly, mix in wine and aquavit, then cool, cover, and store overnight. To serve, remove spice bag and heat glögg to steaming, but not boiling. Pour into a large silver punch bowl and ladle into mugs or heatproof punch cups, adding a few raisins and almonds to each serving. About 255 calories per 4-ounce serving.

Mulled Wine				
Whole cloves	1 dozen	1½ dozen	2 dozen	3 dozen
Cinnamon sticks	4	8	16	2½ dozen
Water	3 cups	1½ quarts	3 quarts	1½ gallons
Sugar	1 cup	1 pound	2 pounds	4 pounds
Lemons, sliced thin	2	4	8	16
Red Bordeaux or Burgundy wine	3 (24-oz.) bottles	6 (24-oz.) bottles	12 (24-oz.) bottles	24 (24-oz.) bottles

Tie spices in cheesecloth, place in a large kettle (not aluminum), add water and sugar, and simmer uncovered 10 minutes, stirring now and then. Add lemons, bruise slightly, and let stand off heat 10 minutes. Add wine and slowly bring to a simmer; do not boil. Pour into a large silver punch bowl or ladle into heatproof mugs. About 100 calories per 4-ounce serving.

Orange Blossom Cup				
Orange juice	1 quart	2 quarts	1 gallon	2 gallons
Rhine, Moselle or Riesling wine	2 (24-oz.) bottles	4 (24-oz.) bottles	8 (24-oz.) bottles	16 (24-oz.) bottles
Light rum	1 quart	2 quarts	4 quarts	8 quarts
Superfine sugar (optional)	1/4 cup	1/2-2/3 cup	1 cup	1 pound
Oranges, sliced thin	1	2	3	4

Mix juice, wine and rum; taste and add sugar if needed. (*Note:* If quantities are large, you may have to heat mixture slightly so sugar will dissolve. Cool well.) To serve, place a large block of ice in a large punch bowl, pour in punch and float orange slices on top, replenishing them as needed. About 170 calories per 4-ounce serving made with sugar, about 165 calories per serving made without sugar.

151

PARTY PUNCH CHART (continued)

	Quantities For			
	1 Dozen	2 Dozen	50 People	100 People
Party Daiquiris				
Cracked ice	3 cups	1½ quarts	3 quarts	1½ gallons
Frozen limeade or lemonade concentrate or frozen daiquri mix	1 (6-oz.) can	2 (6-oz.) cans	4 (6-oz.) cans	8 (6-oz.) cans
White or light rum	1 fifth	2 fifths	3 quarts + 1 cup	6½ quarts

(*Note:* Make in batches for 1 dozen.) Place all ingredients in a 1/2 gallon jar that has a tight-fitting lid (mayonnaise jars are good) and shake vigorously about 1/2 minute until frothy. Strain into cocktail glasses and serve at once. About 205 calories per 4-ounce serving.

Party Milk Punch				
Superfine sugar	1/4 cup	1/2 cup	1 cup	1 pound
Bourbon, rye or blended whiskey	1 pint	1 quart	2 quarts	4 quarts
Ice cold milk	3½ quarts	7 quarts	3½ gallons	7 gallons
Nutmeg	1/4 teaspoon	1/4 teaspoon	1/2 teaspoon	3/4 teaspoon

Mix all but last ingredient in a large kettle, ladle over an ice block in a large punch bowl, and sprinkle with nutmeg. About 120 calories per 4-ounce serving.

Quick Party Eggnog				
Chilled eggnog mix	2 quarts	4 quarts	8 quarts	16 quarts
Light rum	1 fifth	2 fifths	3 quarts	6 quarts
Heavy cream	1 pint	1 quart	2 quarts	4 quarts
Nutmeg	1/4 teaspoon	1/4 teaspoon	1/2 teaspoon	3/4 teaspoon

Mix eggnog and rum; whip cream to soft peaks and fold in; cover and chill 1 hour. Ladle into a large punch bowl and sprinkle with nutmeg. (*Note:* For large amounts, make up in batches for 2 dozen, keep cold, and refill punch bowl as needed.) About 250 calories per 4-ounce serving.

CHAPTER 6

APPETIZERS AND HORS D'OEUVRE

The cocktail party may be an American invention, but the practice of nibbling while drinking goes back to the Greeks and Romans. (Nibbling is perhaps the wrong word because these early gluttons stuffed themselves.)

Appetizers today are served with more restraint, their purpose being to whet the appetite and set the tone of the meal—unless, of course, cocktails only are being served, in which case appetizers are there to temper the drinking (or at least the effects of it).

The difference between hors d'oeuvre and appetizers isn't as sharply defined as it once was. Hors d'oeuvre, meaning "outside the work," is a French phrase used to describe the hot or cold savories served at the start of a meal. In France hors d'oeuvre, often a selection of tart foods, are served at the table. In America hors d'oeuvre have come to mean the finger foods passed around with cocktails. Appetizer is a more encompassing word, including not only hors d'oeuvre but also any beverage or savory food served before the meal.

Making appetizers appeals to the drama in most of us—a fine thing as long as they don't upstage the foods to follow or prove so irresistible that guests overeat. The best practice is to keep appetizers tantalizing but simple.

Some Recipes Included Elsewhere in This Book That Can Double as Appetizers

Scattered throughout the book, and particularly in the meat, poultry, seafood, and vegetable sections, are many recipes that can be served as appetizers. Some are good cocktail fare, others more appropriately served at table as a first course. For page numbers, see the Index. Among those that are particularly good are:

MEAT AND POULTRY APPETIZERS

Hot

Meat balls (make bite-size and use sauces or gravies as dips)
Creamed meats or poultry (serve in bite-size tart shells or croustades)
Any small sautéed or glazed sausages
Balinese Beef on Skewers
Barbecued, Luau, or Chinese-Style Spareribs
Dolma
Herb Stuffed Kidney and Bacon Rolls
Marrow Bones
Party Pasties
Sautéed Chicken Livers
Teriyaki Hors d'Oeuvre
Yakitori

Cold

Tart, spreadable meat salad
Danish Liver Loaf
Sausage and Pastry Rolls (good cold or hot)
Scotch Eggs (good cold or hot)
Steak Tartare

SEAFOOD APPETIZERS

Hot

Bite-size batter-fried or breaded fish or shellfish
Bite-size fish or shellfish balls or croquettes
Bite-size sautéed or broiled fish or shellfish
Creamed or scalloped seafood served in tart shells, Carolines, scallop shells or ramekins
Any of the escargot recipes
Any savory baked stuffed clams or oysters such as Casino, Florentine, Originata, Remick, Rockefeller, etc.

Either of the following clam recipes:
   Clams Bulhão Pato, Clams Marinière
Any of the following mussels recipes:
   Filey Bay Mussels, Marseille-Style, Marinière

Any of the following oyster recipes:
   Angels or Devils on Horseback,
   Oysters Baked in Mushroom Caps
Any of the following scallops recipes:
   Coquilles St. Jacques à la Parisienne
   or à la Provençale, Scallops en Brochette
Any of the following shrimp recipes:
   Gingery Chinese Shrimp, Japanese
   Butterfly Shrimp, Scampi, Shrimp Rumaki
Brandade de Morue

Cold

Cold marinated, pickled, or spiced fish or shellfish such as Pickled Herring, Ceviche, Escabeche, Rollmops, Sashimi
Cold curried fish or shellfish
Cold smoked raw or marinated fish
Any savory, spreadable fish or shellfish salad (chop the ingredients a little more finely than usual)
Armenian Mussels stuffed with Rice, Currants, and Piñon Nuts
Clams or oysters on the half shell

CHEESE AND EGG APPETIZERS

Hot

Any fondue or rabbit
Cheese or Egg Croquettes
Crostini alla Mozzarella
Quiche Lorraine
Scotch Woodcock

Cold

Basic Stuffed Eggs
Deviled Eggs and Jiffy Deviled Eggs
Eggs in Aspic
Egg Salad
Pickled Eggs
Rosemary Eggs

VEGETABLE APPETIZERS

Hot

Braised Artichokes Provençal
Leek Pie
Pissaladière

Roman Artichokes stuffed with Anchovies

Cold
Pickled vegetables
Tart, cold, marinated vegetables or vegetable salads (à la Grecque, Vinaigrette, Sweet-Sour, etc.)
Celery Victor
Tabbouleh

BREAD APPETIZERS

Hot
Savory Party Biscuits (Herb, Onion, Bacon, Cheese, etc.)
Blini
Pizza or Quick Pizza (make bite-size or cut in small squares)
Tortillas (make miniatures and fill with Texas Red)

Cold
Savory Party Sandwiches
Savory toast (Chive, Herb, Curry, Garlic, Cheese, etc.) (good cold or hot)
Cheese Crackers
Melba Toast

About Pâté

There are dozens of *pâtés*, all liver and/or meat pastes of one kind or another. Most luxurious is *pâté de foie gras*, made of the livers of force-fed geese, seasoned with spices and sometimes brandy or Madeira. It is sold canned, also fresh, by the pound (the fresh must be kept refrigerated until ready to be served; the canned need not and, in fact, actually mellows and ages on the shelf like fine wine). *Pâté de foie gras truffé* has had truffles added, sometimes minced and mixed throughout but more often in a row down the middle of the pâté. *Pâté de foie d'oie* contains about 25 per cent pork liver, 75 per cent goose liver. Some other famous pâtés:

à la Meau: Meat pâté made of game; it usually contains some liver.

à la Périgueux: A truffled meat-liver pâté made of poultry and game.

à la Rouennaise: Duckling pâté.

d'Amiens: Pâté made of duckling and other livers.

Lorraine: Meat pâté made from a mixture of veal, pork, and game.

Pâté en Croûte: Pâté baked in a crust (the crust need not be eaten).

Pâté Maison: The specialty of the particular restaurant. These usually contain a mixture of livers (poultry, calf, pork), also some ground meat.

Terrine: A mixture of liver and game or poultry leftovers baked in and served from a terrine (small earthenware dish).

How to Serve Pâté

All pâtés should be served cold (chill cans at least 24 hours before opening). When the pâté is to be served as a spread with cocktails, unwrap or slide out of can (dip can briefly in hot water, if necessary, to loosen pâté, or open both ends of can and push pâté out). Center pâté on a small serving plate and smooth fat layer with a spatula. Serve with melba rounds or hot buttered toast triangles and a pâté knife for spreading.

To Glaze Pâté with Aspic: This adds a festive touch. Scrape fat layer from block of pâté, then smooth surface. Make about 1 pint aspic, using beef or chicken broth,* and chill until syrupy. Spoon 2–3 layers of aspic over pâté, 1 at a time, and chill until tacky before adding next layer. Decorate top of pâté with herb sprigs, pimiento and truffle cutouts, seal under a final layer of glaze, and chill until firm. Also chill any leftover aspic, then chop and wreathe around plate of pâté.

If pâté is to be served at the table as a first course, slice ¼"–½" thick (do not remove fat layer) and overlap 2–3 slices (depending on size and richness) on each plate. Add a ruff of lettuce, if you like, provide pâté spreaders, and pass hot buttered or unbuttered toast triangles.

How Much Pâté Is Enough? Depends on the richness, but generally, ⅛–¼ pound per person is ample.

COUNTRY-STYLE LIVER PÂTÉ

Makes 16–18 servings

1 medium-size yellow onion, peeled and coarsely chopped
1 pound calf's liver, trimmed of membrane and veins and cubed
½ cup light cream
2 eggs, separated
2 teaspoons salt
¼ teaspoon pepper
¼ teaspoon ginger
Pinch allspice
¼ cup melted bacon drippings, butter, or margarine

Preheat oven to 300° F. Purée onion in an electric blender at high speed, add liver, a little at a time, puréeing until creamy; strain through a fine sieve. Mix in cream; lightly beat yolks and add along with remaining ingredients. Beat egg whites to soft peaks and fold in. Spoon into a well-greased 9"×5"×3" loaf pan, set in a hot water bath, and bake uncovered 1–1¼ hours until a knife inserted in the center comes out clean. Cool pâté upright in pan on a wire rack, cover, and chill at least 12 hours. Invert on a platter and serve. About 95 calories for each of 16 servings, 85 for each of 18 servings.

VARIATIONS:

Pretty Party Pâté: Prepare, chill and unmold pâté; trim so loaf is about ¼" smaller all around than its pan. Make a clear aspic by dissolving 1 envelope unflavored gelatin in 3 cups hot beef consommé. Pour ⅔ cup aspic into a clean 9"×5"×3" loaf pan and chill until tacky; keep remaining aspic warm. Arrange truffle, radish, and/or lemon rind cutouts, tarragon or parsley sprigs in desired design on aspic, spoon a little warm aspic on top, and chill until tacky. Fit pâté loaf into pan, fill to brim with aspic, and chill until firm; also chill any remaining aspic; unmold. Chop extra chilled aspic and use to garnish platter along with radish roses and watercress sprigs. About 105 calories for each of 16 servings, 95 for each of 18 servings.

Smoky Liver Pâté Spread: Cream ½ loaf Country-Style Liver Pâté with ½ pound soft Braunschweiger (link liver spread available at supermarkets). If you like, pack into a small bowl, decorate with truffle cutouts and tarragon leaves, and seal with ¼" clear aspic. Chill until firm and serve from bowl without inverting. About 145 calories for each of 16 servings, 130 for each of 18 servings.

EASY CHICKEN LIVER PÂTÉ

Makes 6–8 servings

1 pound chicken livers, halved at the natural separation
3 tablespoons butter or margarine
2 (3-oz.) packages cream cheese, softened to room temperature
3–4 tablespoons brandy
1 teaspoon salt (about)

⅛ *teaspoon pepper*
⅛ *teaspoon nutmeg*
2 *teaspoons finely grated yellow
   onion*

Glaze:
1 *(10½-oz.) can madrilène or beef
   consommé*
1 *teaspoon unflavored gelatin*
*Cutouts of truffle and pimiento;
   parsley or tarragon sprigs
   (decoration)*

Brown livers in butter in a skillet over moderately high heat 4–5 minutes; transfer to an electric blender cup with drippings and scraped-up browned bits, add all remaining ingredients except glaze, and blend at high speed until smooth. Taste for salt and adjust as needed. Spoon into a small shallow serving bowl (about 1-pint size) and chill 2–3 hours. For glaze: Heat madrilène and gelatin over low heat, stirring constantly, until gelatin dissolves. Chill until thick and syrupy; spoon a thin layer on top of pâté and chill until tacky. Decorate with truffle and pimiento cutouts and herb sprigs. Add more madrilène to seal in design and chill until firm. Serve with melba rounds. About 290 calories for each of 6 servings, 215 for each of 8 servings.

¢ ⊠ LIVER-CHEESE PÂTÉ

Makes about 1½ cups

½ *pound smoked liverwurst*
1 *tablespoon steak sauce*
1 *tablespoon dry sherry*
1 *(3-oz.) package cream cheese,
   softened to room temperature*

Mash liverwurst with a fork in a small bowl. Blend in remaining ingredients and serve as a spread for crackers or Melba toast. About 45 calories per tablespoon.

PÂTÉ CORNUCOPIAS

Makes 8 servings

8 *thin slices lean boiled ham or
   prosciutto, cut about 4" long and
   2" wide*
1 *(8-oz.) can pâté de foie gras or 1
   recipe Liver-Cheese Pâté, or Smoky
   Liver Pâté Spread at room
   temperature*
2–3 *tablespoons minced parsley*

Shape ham slices into small cornucopias, secure with toothpicks, and fill centers with pâté. Chill 2–3 hours. Just before serving, remove toothpicks and sprinkle pâté with parsley. About 145 calories per serving.

VARIATION:
Spread ham with pâté, roll up jelly-roll style, and secure with toothpicks. Chill as directed. Dip each end of rolls in parsley, remove toothpicks, and serve. About 145 calories per serving.

About Caviar

At $50 or more a pound, fresh caviar is hardly the everyday appetizer, and any meal beginning with it had better be elegant. What determines the quality of caviar and rockets the price sky high is the size of the eggs (caviar is the roe of sturgeon or similar fish, lightly salted). Costliest is from the *beluga* sturgeon that swims in the Caspian Sea, surrounded by Russia and Iran. The eggs are giant size, sometimes as big as peas; they are soft and translucent and range in color from silvery gray to black. Next come *osetra* (medium-size caviar, usually gray or gray green) and *sevruga* (smaller gray grains; one in 2,000 sevruga sturgeon has golden roe, so rare a delicacy that any found in Iran is reserved for the Shah). Still smaller grained are *sterlet* and *ship* caviars. (*Note: Malossol* is not a kind of caviar but a way of preserving it by salting.)

There are other caviars: tiny, gritty black *lumpfish caviar* (usually from the Baltic Sea), *red caviar* (salmon roe), and orange carp roe, or *tarama*. These are not nearly so choice or costly as sturgeon caviar.

Fresh caviar is extremely perishable and must be kept refrigerated from the instant it is taken from the fish until the moment it is served. Malossol and pasteurized caviar, packed in small jars, are less perishable but may need refrigeration (read labels carefully). Pressed caviar, also less perishable than the fresh, has been treated in an acid solution, then brined, drained, and pressed. None of these are a match for the fresh.

How to Serve Caviar

The only way to serve fresh caviar, gourmets insist, is from its own tin, imbedded in crushed ice with nothing more to accompany than buttered toast points and, perhaps, lemon wedges, each guest helping himself. Anything more is lily gilding. Others, however, like to accompany caviar with small bowls of minced onion, chopped hard-cooked egg white, sieved egg yolks, and occasionally a bowl of sour cream and plate of sliced pumpernickel. It's a matter of taste. The classic "caviar" drinks are chilled fine dry champagne or icy cold vodka drunk neat from liqueur glasses.

The less princely caviars are best used for making hors d'oeuvre and canapés, dips, spreads, and salad dressings and a variety of other recipes. They also make colorful garnishes.

How much caviar per person? 1 to 2 ounces, depending on your bank balance.

About Smoked Salmon

Another elegant, expensive appetizer. The salmon is raw but salted and smoked so that it has a cool velvety texture, a rosy, translucent look, and a delicately balanced woodsy-sea flavor. Smoked salmon should never seem oily or show grains of salt; taste before buying, rejecting any that is overpoweringly salty or smoky. The choicest smoked salmon comes from Scotland, but that from Nova Scotia, Norway, Denmark, and the Columbia River area is very good too. Lox is Jewish smoked salmon, slightly saltier than the regular, and a breakfast favorite with cream cheese and bagels.

The best way to buy smoked salmon is from the center cut, sliced thin but not so thin the slices tear (allow about 3 ounces per person). Like most seafoods, smoked salmon is perishable and must be kept refrigerated.

There are other smoked fish; sturgeon, which is very like salmon and best served like it; whitefish, eel, and trout, which need to be skinned and boned before serving. In addition, there are many canned smoked fish and shellfish, best served as cocktail tidbits or minced and mixed into dips and spreads.

I. LOW-CALORIE RECIPES

Potage Saint-Germain – Steamed Globe Artichoke – Beef Sukiyaki –
Poached Meringue Ring

Potage Saint Germain (vol. 1, pp. 204–5)

Steamed Globe Artichoke (vol. 2, pp. 142–43); and Steamed Asparagus (vol. 2, pp. 147–48)

Beef Sukiyaki (vol. 1, pp. 262–63); Low-calorie Fillets of Flounder en Papillote (vol. 1, p. 642); and Steak Tartare (vol. 1, p. 263)

Poached Meringue Ring with Dessert Cardinal Sauce (vol. 2, pp. 469 and 477)

How to Serve Smoked Salmon

The more simply the better. Trim away ragged edges (save to mix into scrambled eggs or make into a spread or dip with cream cheese and mayonnaise). Overlap slices neatly (about 3 per portion) on small chilled plates. Garnish with lemon wedges and sprinkle, if you like, with capers; set out the pepper mill. Or, if you prefer, forgo the capers and pass a cruet of olive oil and small dishes of minced yellow onion and hard-cooked egg.

Another way to serve smoked salmon is on cut-to-fit, thin slices of pumpernickel spread with unsalted butter. Cut bite size, these make luxurious canapés.

Crudités

Crudités is simply a French term for crisp, raw vegetables eaten out of hand as appetizers. Any colorful combination can be used; in fact, the more colorful the better. Choose tenderest young vegetables, pare only if necessary, then cut into easy-to-eat sticks or chunks. Certain vegetables—cherry tomatoes, radishes, button mushrooms, etc.— are naturally bite-size and best left whole with a sprig of stem to make dipping easier. Group vegetables spoke-fashion on a bed of crushed ice and center with a bowl of kosher or seasoned salt (makes a very low-calorie appetizer), or, if you prefer something heartier, serve with a savory dressing or dip. Some good vegetable choices:

TO SERVE IN LONG (2″–3″) SLIM
  STICKS
Carrots
Celery and celeriac
Cucumbers (peel only if waxed)
Fennel
Scallions
Sweet green and/or red peppers
Turnips
Zucchini

TO SERVE WHOLE
Asparagus tips
Brussels sprouts (tiny ones)
Button mushrooms
Cherry tomatoes
Endive leaves
Radishes

TO SERVE IN BITE-SIZE CHUNKS
Broccoli and cauliflowerets

SOME APPROPRIATE DIPS
(see Index for page numbers)
Any flavored mayonnaise
Avocado Dressing
Cold Béarnaise
Cold Ravigote Sauce
Green Goddess Dressing
Horseradish Cream Sauce
Russian Dressing
Green Sauce (Salsa Verde)
Sour Cream-Anchovy, -Chive, or
  -Curry Sauce
Sour Cream-Roquefort Dressing
Tapenade
Thousand Island Dressing

About Antipasto

Antipasto, an Italian word meaning "before the meal," is simply a combination plate of raw, cooked, or pickled vegetables, meats and fish, hard-cooked eggs and cheese served at the table as an appetizer and eaten with a fork. Any colorful, tart combination, artfully arranged, is appropriate. One of the best ways to serve antipasto is to load a giant platter and let each guest help himself. Have the foods as nearly bite size as possible, or at least easy to serve (thin slices of cheese and meat, for example, should be rolled into tubes or cornucopias, hard-cooked eggs halved or quartered). Serve with cruets of olive oil and red wine vinegar.

Some Popular Components of Antipasto

(Many are available at supermarkets, others at Italian groceries.)

Meats: Thinly sliced prosciutto or boiled ham, salami, pastrami, dry hot Italian sausages

Fish: Oil-packed tuna, sardines, or anchovies

Eggs: Hard cooked, deviled, or stuffed

Cheese: Thinly sliced provolone, mozzarella, or Gorgonzola

Vegetables: Caponata; any dried bean or chick-pea salad; marinated or pickled beets or artichoke hearts; green or ripe olives; radishes; celery or carrot sticks; fennel or celery hearts; pickled hot green or red peppers; roasted sweet green or red peppers; oil-packed pimientos; cherry tomatoes

About Serving Cheeses as Appetizers

The best cheeses to serve before dinner are pungent or rich ones that are not likely to be overeaten. Bland cheeses may seem a better choice, but they aren't because guests tend to keep nibbling them until their appetites are gone.

Two kinds of cheese, usually, are sufficient. Place well apart on a large cheese board or, failing that, on two small ones. Let stand at room temperature at least an

hour before serving, longer if cheeses are particularly hard or cold—they need plenty of time to soften and mellow.

If the cheeses are to be fully appreciated, they should be served with unsalted, unseasoned crackers. Serve the crackers on a separate plate, not ringed around the cheeses. And provide a separate knife for each cheese so the flavors don't get mixed.

For a full rundown on the kinds of cheese and additional tips on serving them, see the chapter on eggs and cheese.

Nuts as Appetizers

Salted and seasoned nuts may be served as cocktail nibbles, but avoid putting out so many guests overeat. Supermarkets carry dazzling varieties of ready-to-serve cocktail nuts, some of them very good. None, however, can compare with those you roast or deep-fry yourself (see chapter on candies and nuts for directions).

About Hollowed-out Stuffed Vegetables

These make attractive and neat-to-eat cocktail tidbits. Simply hollow out cherry tomatoes, radishes, raw baby zucchini or carrots, cucumbers and fill with red or black caviar, any savory cocktail spread, or tart spreadable cheese, any savory egg, seafood, meat, or poultry salad, chopping ingredients for these a little more finely than usual. Long vegetables like cucumbers, zucchini, and carrots can be hollowed out, stuffed, chilled, then sliced ¾"–1" thick. Others should be filled shortly before serving. A number of vegetables—mushroom caps, celery stalks, small artichoke bottoms— are tailor made for stuffing, no need to hollow out. The only precautions to take when stuffing vegetables: make the vegetables bite size and the filling firm enough to stay inside them.

About Canapés

Canapés are decorative open-face sandwiches small enough to eat in a bite or two. Whether hot or cold, they should look neat and freshly made, never fussed over (or left over). The best are salty or savory, colorful and appetizing.

Canapés can be nothing more than a bread cutout spread with a savory filling (any of the following spreads are suitable, also any egg, seafood, meat, or chicken salad, provided the ingredients are minced instead of chopped). Canapés can be much more elaborate, rather like mini Danish sandwiches, spread first with a savory butter or mayonnaise, then mounted with a dab of caviar, sliver of smoked salmon, or *pâté de foie gras,* round of cucumber or cherry tomato or hard-cooked egg, cluster of tiny Danish shrimp. The spread is essential—to keep the bread from drying out (or the topping from seeping in) and to hold the canapé together.

Any firm-textured bread, thinly sliced and cut in fancy shapes, makes a good base for canapés (white bread, brown, pumpernickel, rye, French, or Italian bread). It can be toasted or not or fried golden brown in butter. Other good canapé foundations or

"couches" (*canapé* is French for "couch") are crisp bland crackers, Melba toast, piecrusts cut in fancy shapes, Puff Pastry shaped into tiny patty shells, or Choux Pastry into doll-size puffs (see Carolines).

How Many Canapés Are Enough? Better figure on 3–4 per person. Put out a variety—2 or 3 different kinds, perhaps 1 hot and 2 cold.

Some Canapé Spreads

Any of the savory butters and mayonnaises given in the sandwich and sauce chapters can be used. Very moist spreads should be applied shortly before serving, otherwise the bread becomes soggy. Others, however, may be put on ahead of time. (*Tip:* It's easier to spread the bread, then cut into fancy shapes.) Slices can be divided into trim squares, rectangles, or triangles or cut with small decorative cookie cutters. For a professional touch, spread canapés with one kind of spread, then pipe on a decorative border or design using another spread of contrasting color but compatible flavor.

(*Note:* Only creamy spreads should be put through pastry tubes; any containing bits of solid food will merely clog the works.)

How Much Spread Is Needed? 1 cup should do about 8 dozen canapés—if thinly applied.

Roquefort Spread (Makes About ¾ Cup): Cream together 4 ounces Roquefort or blue cheese, ¼ cup each unsalted butter and softened cream cheese, and 2 tablespoons brandy. For quick flavor variations: Substitute Stilton and port, Cheddar and sherry, or Caerphilly and stout for the Roquefort and brandy. About 40 calories per canapé including bread.

Caviar Spread (Makes About ⅓ Cup): Blend ¼ cup unsalted butter with 3 tablespoons black caviar, 1 teaspoon lemon juice, and ¼ teaspoon finely grated onion. About 30 calories per canapé including bread.

Sardine Spread (Makes About ½ Cup): Blend together ¼ cup each unsalted butter and mashed, skinless, boneless sardines; season to taste with lemon juice and pepper. About 30 calories per canapé including bread.

Some Canapé Suggestions

Shrimp: Spread bread or toast rounds with Caper Butter, top with tiny Danish shrimp and a rosette of Tartar Sauce or curlycue of pimiento. About 30 calories per canapé.

Sardine: Spread a cracker (any bland kind) with Herb Butter, top with 2–3 boneless, skinless sardines and a red onion ring filled with sieved hard-cooked egg yolk. About 35 calories per canapé.

Russian: Spread pumpernickel squares with Russian Dressing, cover with cut-to-fit slices of smoked turkey or ham, and garnish with alternating rows of pimiento-stuffed olives and minced hard-cooked egg white. About 40 calories per canapé.

Ham or Tongue: Spread crackers or bread rounds with unsalted butter, top with cut-to-fit slices of Swiss cheese and ham or tongue, and garnish with overlapping slices of radish and dill pickle. About 40 calories per canapé.

Chicken: Spread bread or toast rectangles with Anchovy Butter, top with cut-to-fit slices of chicken, and garnish with a fluff of Green Mayonnaise and a rolled anchovy fillet. About 35 calories per canapé.

Smoked Oyster: Spread crackers with softened cream cheese, top with smoked oysters, and garnish with a border of Caviar Mayonnaise and a twisted lemon slice. About 30 calories per canapé.

Tuna and Parmesan: Top butter-fried toast rounds with hot creamed tuna, sprinkle with grated Parmesan, and broil until golden. Serve straight from the broiler. About 40 calories per canapé.

Broiled Anchovy: Spread toast rounds with any cheese spread, broil until bubbly, and top with crossed anchovy fillets. About 40 calories per canapé.

Hot Chicken Liver: Top fried toast rounds with hot sautéed, chopped chicken livers, crisp bacon crumbles, a cherry tomato slice, and a cucumber twist. About 50 calories per canapé.

Aspic: Cover bread slices with cut-to-fit slices of cold meat, poultry, or fish fillets, glaze with thin layers of aspic made from meat, poultry, or fish stock,* and chill until tacky. Cut in small squares, triangles, or rectangles, decorate, if you like, with herb sprigs, pimiento slivers or olive slices, and seal under a thin glaze of aspic. Chill well before serving. About 40 calories per canapé.

Stuffed Rolls: Cut ends from long, skinny loaves of French or Italian bread, scoop out soft insides and fill with any savory, not-too-soupy spread or seafood, egg, meat, or chicken salad. Wrap in foil and chill 6–8 hours. Slice thin and serve. About 40 calories per slice.

About Garnishing Canapés
Any sandwich garnish, done on a doll's scale, will work (see About Sandwich Garnishes).

About Party Sandwiches
These are covered fully in the chapter on sandwiches.

¢ ▢ CURRIED CUCUMBER PARTY ROUNDS

Makes about 3 dozen canapés.

Curry Mayonnaise:

1 ¼ cups mayonnaise
1–2 tablespoons curry powder
½ teaspoon Worcestershire sauce
¼ teaspoon garlic powder
¼ teaspoon onion powder
2–3 dashes liquid hot red pepper seasoning
3 dozen thin rounds pumpernickel bread about 1½"–2" in diameter
1 medium-size cucumber, sliced ⅛" thick (do not peel)

Mix first 6 ingredients together until fluffy; spread liberally on each pumpernickel round and top with a cucumber slice. About 85 calories per canapé.

⟐ ▢ CRISP CUCUMBER ROUNDS TOKOYO STYLE

This is such a good recipe it's difficult to believe there are only two ingredients.
Makes 4–6 servings

1 (6-ounce) bottle Japanese soy sauce, chilled well
2 medium-size cucumbers, chilled well, peeled, and sliced ½" thick

Pour soy sauce into a small, deep mixing bowl, add cucumbers, and toss lightly to mix. Cover and chill 2 hours. To serve, transfer to a serving bowl and set out a separate small container of toothpicks.

VARIATION:

Substitute 2½ cups of almost any crisp raw vegetable for the cucumbers: short carrot sticks, bite-size cauliflowerets, whole radishes or water chestnuts, small chunks of celery, or a combination of these. About 2 calories per cucumber round. The other raw vegetables will run approximately the same per piece.

⟐ PROSCIUTTO-STUFFED MUSHROOM HORS D'OEUVRE

Makes 3½–4 dozen hors d'oeuvre

1 (3-ounce) package cream cheese, softened to room temperature
½ (2-ounce) tube anchovy paste
¼ pound prosciutto, finely chopped
1 tablespoon capers
1 tablespoon minced parsley
1 tablespoon minced watercress
½ teaspoon Worcestershire sauce
3–4 tablespoons light cream
1 pound 1" mushrooms, stemmed and peeled (save stems to use later)

Mix cheese, anchovy paste, prosciutto, capers, parsley, watercress, and Worcestershire, adding enough cream to give mixture the consistency of *pâté*. Stuff mushroom caps, heaping mixture in center, cover, and refrigerate until about ½ hour before serving. Let come to room temperature, then serve with cocktails. About 20 calories per hors d'oeuvre.

⚶ **MELON AND HAM**

A popular European first course.
Makes 4 servings

*6 ounces paper-thin slices prosciutto,
 Bayonne, or Westphalian ham, well
 chilled*
*½ ripe honeydew, casaba, or
 crenshaw melon, well chilled*
Freshly ground pepper

Cut rind from melon, remove seeds,
and slice lengthwise into thin
crescents. Alternate slices of ham
and melon on chilled plates and pass
the pepper mill. About 50 calories
per serving.

VARIATIONS:

⚶ **Figs or Mangoes and Ham:**
Prepare as directed, substituting
thinly sliced, peeled ripe figs or
mangoes for the melon. About 50
calories per serving.

⚶ **Melon and Ham Tidbits:** Cut
peeled and seeded melon in ¾"
cubes, wrap in thin strips of ham,
and secure with toothpicks. Serve
as cocktail food; pass a pepper mill.
About 20 calories per serving.

⚶ **MARINATED MUSHROOMS**

Makes 4–6 servings

1 cup water
½ cup olive or other cooking oil
½ cup lemon juice or white vinegar
1 clove garlic, peeled and bruised
1 teaspoon thyme
1 teaspoon tarragon
1 bay leaf
1 teaspoon salt
½ teaspoon peppercorns
*1 pound button mushrooms, wiped
 clean*

Simmer all ingredients except mushrooms uncovered 5 minutes. Add
mushrooms, boil 1 minute, then
cool, cover, and refrigerate overnight. Remove from refrigerator
about ½ hour before serving, mix

well, and serve in marinade or
drained and speared with toothpicks. About 50 calories for each
of 4 servings, 40 calories for
each of 6 servings.

VARIATION:

Marinated Artichoke Hearts: Substitute 1 (1-pound) can drained
artichoke hearts for the mushrooms
(halved if large) and proceed as
directed. (*Note:* Quartered artichoke bottoms are good this way,
too.) About 70 calories for each of
4 servings, 50 for each of 6
servings.

¢ **ARMENIAN BEAN
APPETIZER**

A good addition to antipasto.
Makes 4–6 servings

¼ cup olive oil
2 tablespoons lemon juice
¾ teaspoon salt (about)
⅛ teaspoon white pepper
1 clove garlic, peeled and crushed
3 tablespoons minced parsley
*2 cups cooked, drained dried pea
 beans or navy beans, flageolets, or
 cannellini*

Beat oil with lemon juice and salt
until creamy, mix in pepper, garlic,
and 2 tablespoons parsley. Pour
over beans, mix lightly, cover, and
marinate 3–4 hours in refrigerator,
stirring now and then. Remove
from refrigerator, stir well, let stand
at room temperature 15–20 minutes, then serve sprinkled with
remaining parsley either as a first
course in lettuce cups with lemon
wedges or spooned onto sesame
seed wafers. About 275 calories
for each of 4 servings, 185 calories
for each of 6 servings.

VARIATION:

¢ **Turkish Bean Appetizer:** Prepare as directed but add 1 table-

spoon minced fresh dill and 1 teaspoon minced fresh mint. Serve topped with paper-thin, raw onion rings. About 275 calories for each of 4 servings, 185 calories for each of 6 servings.

COLD MARINATED SHRIMP

Makes 6 servings

*1 pound boiled, shelled, and deveined
    medium-size shrimp*
*⅓ cup tart salad dressing (French,
    Tarragon French, Lorenzo, Spanish
    Vinaigrette) or, if you prefer,
    Sauce Verte*
*1 clove garlic, peeled, bruised, and
    stuck on a toothpick*
*1 tablespoon snipped fresh dill or 1
    teaspoon dried dill*

Mix all ingredients, cover, and chill 6–8 hours, tossing shrimp in marinade now and then. Drain shrimp, discarding garlic, and serve with toothpicks (marinade can be saved and used again with other shellfish). About 75 calories per serving.

VARIATIONS:

Cold Marinated Scallops: Prepare as directed but substitute 1 pound poached or, if tiny, *raw* bay scallops for shrimp; chill only 4 hours. About 70 calories per serving.

Cold Marinated Oysters: Poach 1½ pints shucked oysters in their liquor 3–4 minutes just until edges ruffle, drain (save liquor for soup) and marinate as directed for shrimp. About 65 calories per serving.

Cold Marinated Mussels: Steam open 2 dozen mussels and shuck*; marinate as directed for shrimp. About 85 calories per serving.

⚖ **Low-Calorie Marinated Cold Shellfish:** Prepare any of the above recipes as directed using a low-calorie French, Italian, or herb dressing. About 65 calories per serving for shrimp, 60 for scallops, 55 for oysters, and 75 for mussels.

PICKLED TRIPE

Pickled tripe can be kept 3–4 days in the refrigerator; if held longer, the flavor becomes unpleasantly strong.

Makes 4–6 servings

1½ pounds honeycomb tripe
2 cups cold water
1 teaspoon salt
*1 small yellow onion, peeled and
    coarsely chopped*
*1 bay leaf, tied in cheesecloth with
    5–6 peppercorns*
1 cup white vinegar

Prepare tripe for cooking* and cut in 2″ squares. Place in a large kettle with all but last ingredient, cover, and simmer about 2 hours until very tender. Remove cheesecloth bag and add vinegar. Spoon into a large wide-mouthed jar and cover with vinegar mixture. (*Note:* if there is not enough to cover tripe, make up with a ½ and ½ mixture of water and white vinegar.) Cover tightly and store in refrigerator. Serve cold as an appetizer course or cut in smaller pieces and serve on an hors d'oeuvre tray. About 180 calories for each of 4 servings, 120 calories for each of 6 servings.

⊠ SPICED OLIVES

Makes about 3 cups

*1 (6½-ounce) can large unpitted ripe
    olives, drained*
*1 (6½-ounce) jar large unpitted
    green olives, drained*
2 cups French Dressing
4 thick lemon slices
1 tablespoon mixed pickling spices
*2 large cloves garlic, peeled and
    bruised*

Place all ingredients in a large wide-mouthed jar with a tight-fitting lid. Cover tightly and shake well. Store in refrigerator at least 2 days before serving; shake jar from time to time. Drain liquid from olives (save it for another batch), remove lemon slices and garlic. Serve with toothpicks. 15 to 20 calories per olive, depending on size.

⊠ DILL AND GARLIC OLIVES

Makes about 1 pint

2 (8½-ounce) jars unpitted green
    olives
1 clove garlic, peeled and crushed
2 tablespoons olive oil
3 large sprigs fresh dill

Empty olives and their juice into a small bowl, add remaining ingredients, and toss to mix. Cover and chill at least 24 hours before serving. 15 to 20 calories per olive, depending on size.

¢ SAUTÉED SPICED CHICK-PEAS

Serve warm as a cocktail nibble instead of salted nuts.
Makes 8–10 servings

1 pound dried chick-peas, washed,
    boiled, and drained
¼ cup olive or other cooking oil
1½ teaspoons chili powder
1 teaspoon garlic salt
Salt

Pat chick-peas dry between several thicknesses paper toweling. Heat oil in a large heavy skillet over moderate heat ½ minute. Add about ⅓ of the chick-peas and sauté, stirring constantly, until pale golden. Add ½ teaspoon chili powder and sauté 1–2 minutes longer, stirring constantly until peas are slightly crisp (reduce heat if peas brown too fast). Remove peas with a slotted spoon and drain on paper toweling; keep warm. Sauté remaining peas the same way, adding chili powder as directed; drain on paper toweling. Add garlic salt and toss lightly to mix. Taste, then salt as needed. About 210 calories for each of 8 servings, 170 calories for each of 10 servings.

VARIATION:

Sauté peas as directed but omit chili powder and garlic salt. Instead, toss with seasoned salt to taste. About 210 calories for each of 8 servings, 170 calories for each of 10 servings.

⚖ DRY-ROASTED HERBED MUSHROOMS

An unusual appetizer and oh! so low in calories.
Makes 4–6 servings

½ teaspoon garlic salt
1 pound medium-size mushrooms,
    wiped clean and sliced thin
1 teaspoon seasoned salt
½ teaspoon oregano
½ teaspoon powdered rosemary

Preheat oven to 200° F. Sprinkle 2 lightly oiled baking sheets with garlic salt and arrange mushrooms 1 layer deep on sheets. Mix seasoned salt and herbs and sprinkle evenly over mushrooms. Bake, uncovered, about 1½ hours until dry and crisp but not brown. Cool slightly and serve as a cocktail nibble. (Note: Store airtight; these absorb moisture rapidly.) About 30 calories for each of 4 servings, 20 for each of 6.

⚖ ¢ ⊠ CURRIED COCKTAIL MELBAS

Makes 40 Melbas

8 slices firm-textured white bread
⅓ cup melted butter or margarine
¼ teaspoon garlic powder

¼ *teaspoon onion powder*
1½ *teaspoons curry powder*
3–4 *drops liquid hot red pepper
    seasoning*

Preheat oven to 300° F. Trim
crusts from bread. Mix butter with
remaining ingredients and, using a
pastry brush, brush over 1 side of
each slice. Cut each slice into 5
thin strips, arrange on an ungreased
baking sheet, and bake uncovered
25–30 minutes until golden brown
and crisp. Serve hot or at room
temperature. About 25 calories per
Melba.

⊠ ¢ GARLIC NIBBLES

Makes about 5 quarts

1 *(11-ounce) package crisp corn
    chips*
2 *cups toasted honeycombed wheat
    cereal*
2 *cups toasted bite-size, checkered
    corn cereal*
¾ *pound shelled pecans*
1 *(2½-ounce) package cheese tidbits*
1 *(10-ounce) package small cheese-
    flavored crackers*
1 *cup butter or margarine*
2 *teaspoons garlic salt*
1 *teaspoon salt*
2 *tablespoons steak sauce*
4–5 *drops liquid hot red pepper
    seasoning*

Preheat oven to 250° F. Place
chips, cereals, pecans, and crackers
in 1 or 2 large, shallow roasting
pans and toss lightly to mix. Heat
butter and remaining ingredients
over moderate heat 2–3 minutes
until butter is melted, pour evenly
over nibble mixture, and toss to
mix. Bake uncovered 1 hour, stirring
occasionally; cool in pans. Mixture
will keep 2–3 weeks if stored
airtight. About 75 calories per
¼ cup.

¢ GARLIC-CHEESE CRISPS

Makes about 2½ dozen

1 *cup sifted flour*
2 *teaspoons garlic salt*
⅓ *cup butter or margarine, chilled*
1 *cup coarsely grated sharp Cheddar
    cheese*
1 *tablespoon Worcestershire sauce*
1–2 *teaspoons ice water (optional)*

Preheat oven to 400° F. Mix flour
and garlic salt in a bowl and cut
butter in with a pastry blender
until mixture resembles coarse
meal; add cheese and toss well.
Sprinkle Worcestershire sauce over
mixture and toss lightly and quickly
with a fork. Ingredients should
just hold together; if not, add ice
water. Shape into ¾" balls and
arrange 2" apart on ungreased
baking sheets; flatten each to a
thickness of about ¼". Bake 10
minutes; reduce oven temperature
to 300° F., and bake 10 minutes
longer until golden and crisp.
Cool on wire racks before serving.
About 45 calories per crisp.

VARIATION:

Prepare as directed but mix in 2
tablespoons minced pimiento,
onion, or ham along with the cheese.
About 45 calories per crisp.

⊲⊳ ¢ CHEESE CRACKERS

Makes 6–7 dozen

1½ *cups sifted flour*
1 *teaspoon salt*
⅛ *teaspoon paprika*
⅛ *teaspoon cayenne pepper*
½ *cup chilled margarine (no
    substitute)*
½ *pound sharp Cheddar cheese,
    coarsely grated*
2½–3 *tablespoons ice water*

Mix flour, salt, paprika, and cayenne
in a shallow bowl and cut in mar-

garine with a pastry blender until mixture resembles coarse meal. Add cheese and toss to mix. Sprinkle water evenly over surface, 1 tablespoon at a time, mixing lightly with a fork; dough should just hold together. Divide dough in half and shape each on a lightly floured board into a roll about 9″ long and 1½″ in diameter; wrap in foil and chill well. About 10 minutes before crackers are to be baked, heat oven to 375° F. Slice rolls ¼″ thick, space 1″ apart on ungreased baking sheets, and bake 10 minutes until golden; transfer at once to wire racks to cool. Store airtight. Serve at room temperature or, if you prefer, reheat about 5 minutes at 350° F. About 30 calories per cracker.

SHRIMP TOAST

Makes 6–8 servings

1 (4½-ounce) can shrimp, drained and minced very fine
2 tablespoons minced water chestnuts
3 scallions, minced (white part only)
1 teaspoon minced gingerroot
1 teaspoon cornstarch
1 teaspoon dry sherry
¼ teaspoon sugar
¼ teaspoon salt
2 egg whites, lightly beaten
4 thin slices firm-textured, day-old white bread, trimmed of crusts
Peanut or other cooking oil for deep fat frying

Mix all but last 2 ingredients. Begin heating oil in a deep fat fryer with a basket and deep fat thermometer over moderately high heat. Pile shrimp mixture on bread, dividing total amount evenly, and spread just to edges; press down lightly. Cut each slice into 4 triangles. When oil reaches 350° F., place 2 or 3 triangles, spread sides up, in fryer basket, lower into oil, and fry about 1 minute until golden and puffed. (Note: Triangles should automatically flip over; if not, turn to brown evenly.) Drain on paper toweling and keep warm in a 250° F. oven while you fry the rest. Serve hot. About 115 calories for each of 6 servings, 85 calories for each of 8 servings.

QUICHE LORRAINE TARTLETS

Serve warm as hors d'oeuvre.
Makes 1½ dozen

1 recipe Flaky Pastry II
Filling:
¾ cup coarsely grated Gruyère or Swiss cheese
¼ cup crumbled crisply cooked bacon
2 eggs, lightly beaten
¾ cup light cream
½ teaspoon salt
Pinch white pepper
Pinch nutmeg
Pinch cayenne pepper

Preheat oven to 425° F. Prepare pastry, divide in half, and roll out 1 piece at a time into a circle about ⅛″ thick. Cut with a 3″ biscuit cutter and line fluted or plain tart tins about 2½″ in diameter. Set tins on baking sheets. Dividing total amount evenly, sprinkle cheese and bacon into pastry shells. Mix remaining ingredients and pour into shells. Bake on center oven rack 10 minutes, remove from oven, and let stand 2 minutes. Meanwhile, reduce oven to 350° F. Return tartlets to oven and bake 5 minutes until filling is puffed and pastry golden. Cool in tins 2–3 minutes, then lift from tins and cool slightly on a wire rack. Serve warm. (Note: Tartlets may be baked ahead of time, then cooled and refrigerated until shortly before serving. Reheat on a baking sheet 5–8 minutes at 350° F.) About 210 calories per tartlet.

VARIATION:

Any quiche Lorraine variations (see Eggs and Cheese) can be prepared as tartlets instead of full-size pies.

BEEF BOREKS

Phyllo pastry leaves (sheets) are sold by Middle Eastern groceries and bakeries.
Makes 25–30 servings

½ (1-pound) package phyllo pastry leaves, at room temperature (refrigerate remainder to use another time)
½ cup (about) melted butter (no substitute)

Filling:
½ pound ground beef chuck
1 small yellow onion, peeled and minced
1 clove garlic, peeled and crushed
2 tablespoons tomato purée
1 egg yolk, lightly beaten
1 tablespoon minced parsley
½ teaspoon salt
⅛ teaspoon pepper
⅛ teaspoon cinnamon
⅛ teaspoon allspice

Unroll pastry, arrange leaves in an even stack, then halve lengthwise and crosswise, making 4 stacks about 8″×6″. Pile stacks on top of each other and cover with cloth to prevent drying. Prepare filling: Brown beef 5 minutes over moderately high heat, add onion and garlic, and continue cooking until meat is no longer pink; drain off drippings. Off heat, mix in remaining ingredients; cool to room temperature. Preheat oven to 350° F. Lift 1 pastry leaf to a flat surface so short side faces you and brush

with butter. Place a rounded ½ teaspoon filling 1″ from bottom and slightly off center and fold as shown; brush with melted butter, then fold over and over into a small, neat triangle. Fill and fold remaining boreks the same way.

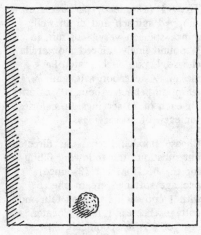

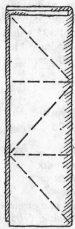

Space 1″ apart on buttered baking sheets, brush with melted butter, and bake about 25 minutes until well browned. Serve hot. (*Note:* These can be made up to the point of baking several hours ahead of time; cover and refrigerate until needed.) About 125 calories for each of 25 servings, 105 calories for each of 30 servings.

VARIATIONS:

Spinach and Mozzarella Boreks:
Prepare as directed but use the following filling instead of the beef: Thaw 1 (10-ounce) package frozen chopped spinach and drain well; mince spinach very fine, mix in ¼ pound finely minced mozzarella cheese, ¼ cup finely grated Parmesan, ½ teaspoon salt, and ⅛ teaspoon pepper. About 105 calories for each of 25 servings, 90 calories for each of 30 servings.

Cheese Boreks: Prepare as directed but substitute the following filling for the beef: Mix 1 (3-ounce) package softened cream cheese with 1 cup each crumbled feta and cottage cheeses, 1 lightly beaten egg yolk, ½ teaspoon salt, ⅛ teaspoon pepper, and 1 tablespoon minced fresh dill, chives, or parsley. About 135 calories for each of 25 servings, 115 calories for each of 30 servings.

PIROSHKI

A Russian favorite.
Makes about 25 servings

Yeast Dough:
1 cup scalded milk
1 tablespoon sugar
1½ teaspoons salt
¼ cup butter, margarine, or lard
¼ cup warm water (105–15° F.)
1 package active dry yeast
2 eggs, lightly beaten
5 cups sifted flour (about)

Glaze:
¼ cup melted butter or margarine or
 2 egg yolks beaten with 2
 tablespoons cold water

Filling:
½ pound ground beef chuck or a ½
 and ½ mixture of lean ground pork
 and beef
1 small yellow onion, peeled and
 minced
1 tablespoon flour
½ cup beef broth
¾ teaspoon salt
⅛ teaspoon pepper
1 hard-cooked egg, peeled and
 minced
1 teaspoon minced parsley

Mix milk, sugar, salt, and butter in a small bowl, stirring until sugar dissolves; cool to lukewarm. Pour warm water into a large warm bowl, sprinkle in yeast, and stir until dissolved. Add eggs to milk mixture, stir into yeast, add 3 cups flour and beat until smooth. Mix in enough additional flour, a little at a time, to make a soft dough. Mixture will be sticky but should leave sides of bowl reasonably clean. Knead on a lightly floured board until satiny and elastic, 8–10 minutes, adding as little extra flour as possible. Shape into a smooth ball, place in a large greased bowl, turning to grease all over. Cover with cloth and let rise in a warm spot until doubled in bulk, about ¾ hour. Punch down, and let rise again until doubled in bulk. Meanwhile, prepare filling: Brown meat over moderately high heat 5 minutes, add onion, and continue browning until no pink remains. Remove meat and onion to a bowl with a slotted spoon, blend flour into drippings and brown lightly. Slowly add broth, salt, and pepper and heat, stirring, until thickened. Mix into meat along with egg and parsley; cool. When dough has risen a second time, punch down, turn onto lightly floured board, and knead lightly 2 minutes.

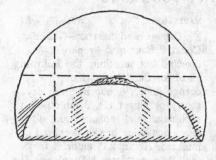

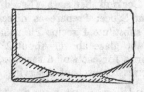

Quarter dough, then cut each quarter into 12 equal pieces. Roll each piece into a ball, then flatten into a round about ¼″ thick with a lightly floured rolling pin. Place a scant teaspoon of filling in center of rounds, moisten edges with cold water, and fold as shown, pinching edges to seal.

Arrange seam side down 2″ apart on ungreased baking sheets, cover, and let rise 15 minutes. Meanwhile, preheat oven to 375° F. Brush *piroshki* with glaze and bake 20–25 minutes until well browned. Serve hot. About 160 calories per serving.

VARIATIONS:

Liver and Bacon Piroshki: Prepare as directed, using the following filling instead of the beef: Brown ½ pound calf or beef liver in 2 tablespoons bacon drippings over high heat 3–4 minutes; grind fine along with 1 peeled small yellow onion. Mix in 4 slices cooked, crumbled bacon, ½ cup soft bread crumbs soaked in ½ cup milk, ¾

teaspoon salt and ⅛ teaspoon pepper. About 170 calories per serving.

Mushroom Piroshki: Prepare as directed but instead of beef filling use the following: Sauté 2 pounds minced mushrooms and 1 minced yellow onion in ¼ cup butter over moderately high heat 4–5 minutes. Off heat, mix in 1 cup soft bread crumbs, ⅓ cup sour cream, 2 minced, peeled, hard-cooked eggs, 1 teaspoon salt, ⅛ teaspoon pepper, and 1 tablespoon minced parsley or fresh dill. About 165 calories per serving.

Easy Piroshki: Substitute 2 (8-ounce) packages refrigerated crescent rolls for the yeast dough. Unroll packages, 1 at a time, do *not* separate at perforations but pinch together to make an unbroken sheet of dough. Roll out about ⅛″ thick on a lightly floured board, cut with a 2½″ biscuit cutter, fill, fold, seal, and bake as directed. About 160 calories per serving.

⊠ EASY PIGS IN BLANKETS

Makes 8–10 servings

1 (8-ounce) package refrigerated crescent rolls
2 tablespoons prepared mild yellow mustard (about)
2 (5½-ounce) packages cocktail frankfurters

Preheat oven to 375° F. Unroll and separate crescent rolls and roll out, 1 at a time, on a lightly floured board to a thickness of ⅛″; spread lightly with mustard and cut in strips about 3″ long and 1¼″ wide (you should get 4 strips from each roll). Wrap frankfurters in strips, sealing ends with cold water, arrange seam sides down, 2″ apart, on ungreased baking sheets and bake 10–12 minutes until golden. Serve hot with or without a bowl of mild mustard or chili sauce as a dip. About 230 calories for each of 8 servings, 185 calories for each of 10 servings.

☒ PIGS IN POKES

Makes 8–10 servings

2 (5½-ounce) packages cocktail frankfurters
½ cup chili sauce
16 bacon slices, halved crosswise

Preheat broiler. Dip franks in chili sauce, then wrap in bacon, securing with toothpicks. Broil 4″ from the heat, turning frequently, 3–5 minutes until bacon is crisp and browned. Serve hot with toothpicks. About 200 calories for each of 8 servings, 160 calories for each of 10 servings.

☒ HOT GLAZED COCKTAIL SAUSAGES

Makes 6–8 servings

Glaze:
1 cup tomato purée
3 tablespoons cider vinegar
⅓ cup firmly packed light brown sugar
1½ teaspoons chili powder
1 clove garlic, peeled and crushed

2 (5½-ounce) packages cocktail frankfurters

Mix glaze ingredients in a skillet and simmer uncovered 2–3 minutes, stirring now and then. Add frankfurters and simmer uncovered, stirring occasionally, about 10 minutes until lightly glazed. Pour into a chafing dish and serve with toothpicks. About 225 calories for each of 6 servings, 170 calories for each of 8 servings.

VARIATIONS:

☒ **Orange and Mustard-Glazed Cocktail Sausages:** Prepare as directed but substitute the following glaze for that above: 1 cup orange juice, ⅓ cup medium dry sherry or ginger ale, 3 tablespoons each sugar and molasses, and 4 teaspoons spicy brown prepared mustard. About 235 calories for each of 6 servings, 180 calories for each of 8 servings.

☒ **Cocktail Sausages Glazed with Plum Sauce:** Prepare as directed but substitute 1 recipe Plum Sauce for the glaze above. About 230 calories for each of 6 servings, 175 calories for each of 8 servings.

☒ **Sweet-Sour Cocktail Sausages:** Prepare as directed but substitute ½ recipe Sweet-Sour Sauce for the above glaze. About 230 calories for each of 6 servings, about 175 calories for each of 8 servings.

¢ HOT SPICY MEAT BALLS

Makes about 12 servings

Meat Balls:
1 pound ground beef chuck
1 medium-size yellow onion, peeled and finely grated
1 teaspoon garlic salt
1 tablespoon steak sauce
¼ teaspoon pepper
⅛ teaspoon crushed dried hot red chili peppers
¾ cup soft white bread crumbs soaked in ¼ cup cold water
1 egg, lightly beaten
2 tablespoons cooking oil (for browning)

Sauce: (optional)
3 tablespoons flour
2 tablespoons pan drippings
1½ cups beef broth
2 tablespoons tomato paste

2 tablespoons dry red wine or 1
  tablespoon red wine vinegar
⅛ teaspoon pepper

Mix all meat ball ingredients except oil and shape in 1" balls. Brown well in oil, a few balls at a time, 5–7 minutes in a heavy skillet over moderately high heat; remove to paper toweling with a slotted spoon. Drain all but 1 tablespoon drippings from pan, add balls, turn heat to low, cover, and simmer 10–15 minutes, adding about 2 tablespoons water, if needed, to keep balls from sticking. Serve hot on toothpicks with or without a savory dip (Béarnaise, Chinese-Style Sweet-Sour, and Plum Sauce are particularly good). Or, if you prefer, serve in the above sauce: Brown and drain balls as directed; before returning to pan, blend flour into drippings, add remaining ingredients, and heat and stir until thickened. Add meat balls, cover, and simmer 10–15 minutes. Serve from a chafing dish with toothpicks. About 160 calories per serving.

VARIATIONS:

Roman Meat Balls: For the meat balls, use ½ pound each ground beef chuck and hot or sweet Italian sausages removed from casings; stir-fry 10 minutes over moderately high heat until cooked through. Drain off drippings and cool meat slightly; then mince. Mix with ingredients called for but omit hot red peppers; add 3 tablespoons grated Parmesan and substitute ¾ teaspoon salt for garlic salt. Shape into 1" balls, brown and cook as directed. About 170 calories per serving.

Chutney-Nut Meat Balls: To the meat ball mixture add ⅓ cup minced walnuts or toasted almonds. Pro-

ceed as directed, simmering in the sauce to which ⅓ cup well-drained, minced chutney has been added. About 180 calories per serving.

Chili Meat Balls: Prepare meat balls as directed, omitting hot red chili peppers and adding 1 tablespoon chili powder and 2 tablespoons chili sauce. Also prepare sauce, blending 1 teaspoon chili powder into drippings along with flour. About 160 calories per serving.

Blue Cheese Meat Balls: Prepare meat balls as directed, omitting hot red chili peppers and adding 3–4 tablespoons crumbled blue cheese. Serve without sauce but pass Sour Cream-Roquefort Dressing as a dip. About 165 calories per serving.

RUMAKIS (HOT BACON AND CHICKEN LIVER HORS D'OEUVRE)

Makes about 6 servings

6 chicken livers, quartered
1 (6-ounce) bottle Japanese soy
  sauce
¼ cup sake or medium dry sherry
½ clove garlic, peeled and crushed
2 (½") cubes fresh gingerroot,
  peeled and crushed
8 water chestnuts (about), each cut
  in 3 thin slivers
¾ cup light brown sugar
½ pound lean bacon, each strip
  halved crosswise

Marinate chicken livers in refrigerator in a mixture of soy sauce, sake, garlic, and ginger about 12 hours or overnight. Make a slit in the center of each piece of liver, insert a sliver of water chestnut, and roll in brown sugar; wrap each in a piece of bacon and secure with a toothpick. Place *rumakis* in a pie-pan, add marinade, cover, and marinate 2–3 hours longer in refrigerator, turning occasionally in marinade. Preheat oven to 400° F. Drain marinade from rumakis and reserve. Roast rumakis uncovered ½–¾ hour, pouring off drippings as they accumulate and basting often with marinade until nicely glazed and brown. About 320 calories per serving.

SIZZLING CHICKEN LIVERS

Makes 6 servings

¼ cup soy sauce
2 tablespoons dry sherry or sake
1 tablespoon dark brown sugar
1 clove garlic, peeled and quartered
½ pound chicken livers, halved at the natural separation
1 tablespoon cornstarch blended with ¼ cup canned condensed beef broth
1–2 tablespoons flour
2 tablespoons peanut or other cooking oil

Mix soy sauce, sherry, sugar, and garlic in a bowl, add livers, cover, and marinate in refrigerator 1–2 hours. Drain marinade into a small saucepan; discard garlic. Bring to a simmer, blend in cornstarch paste, and heat, stirring constantly, until thickened and clear; transfer to a small chafing dish and keep warm. Dredge chicken livers in flour and stir-fry in oil 3–4 minutes until lightly browned. Transfer to chafing dish and heat 1–2 minutes. Serve from chafing dish with toothpicks for spearing livers. About 120 calories per serving.

About Dips and Spreads

There's something convivial about dips and spreads. Dips are an American invention, and a very good one, too. Spreads are not, though Americans have certainly enlarged the repertoire. The main caution to bear in mind when preparing either is to keep them the right consistency: dips should be thick enough not to dribble or splash, spreads soft enough to spread easily without tearing the bread or breaking the crackers. Another good practice: Make dips and spreads ahead of time so that their flavors will mellow.

In addition to the recipes that follow, a number of salad dressings and sauces make excellent dips:

Dressings to Use as Dips (see Salad Chapter for Recipes):	Particularly Good with:
Avocado Dressing	Vegetables
Blender Garlic-Roquefort Dressing	Vegetables
California-Sour Cream Dressing	Vegetables
Camembert Cream Dressing	Vegetables
French Dressing (and Variations)	Vegetables, Seafood
Fresh Herb Dressing	Vegetables
Garlic-Herb Dressing	Vegetables, Seafood
Green Goddess Dressing	Vegetables
Green Mayonnaise	Vegetables
Low-Calorie Yogurt Dressing	Vegetables
Old-Fashioned Cooked Dressing	Vegetables
Russian Dressing	Vegetables, Seafood

Dressings to Use as Dips
(see Salad Chapter for Recipes):   *Particularly Good with:*

Sauce Verte	Vegetables
Shallot Dressing	Vegetables, Seafood
Sour Cream Dressing	Vegetables, Seafood
Sour Cream-Roquefort Dressing	Vegetables
Thousand Island Dressing (and Variations)	Vegetables, Seafood
Wine Dressing	Vegetables, Seafood

Sauces to Use as Dips
(see Sauces Chapter for Recipes):   *Particularly Good with:*

Béarnaise	Meat, Seafood, Vegetables
Caper and Horseradish	Seafood, Vegetables
Chinese-Style Sweet-Sour	Meat, Seafood
Cocktail	Seafood
Cold Ravigote	Vegetables
Easy Sour Cream (and Variations)	Meat, Seafood, Vegetables
Fin and Claw Cocktail	Seafood
Green Sauce	Vegetables
Gribiche	Seafood
Hollandaise (and Variations)	Meat, Seafood, Vegetables
Hot Chinese Mustard	Meat
Mayonnaise (and Variations)	Meat, Seafood, Vegetables
Pineapple-Pepper Sweet-Sour	Meat
Plum Sauce	Meat
Tapenade	Vegetables
Tartar	Seafood, Vegetables
Tempura	Seafood

⊠ DILLY DEVILED HAM DIP

Makes about 1 pint

1 cup sour cream
1 (8-ounce) package cream cheese, softened to room temperature
2 (2¼-ounce) cans deviled ham
1 tablespoon minced onion
2 teaspoons prepared spicy brown mustard
1 tablespoon minced dill pickle

Beat all ingredients together with an electric mixer or rotary beater until smooth and creamy. Cover and let stand at room temperature 1 hour before serving to blend flavors. About 48 calories per tablespoon.

⊠ CREAM CHEESE, BACON AND HORSERADISH DIP

Makes about 1½ cups

½ cup milk or light cream
1 (8-ounce) package cream cheese, softened to room temperature
1 tablespoon prepared horseradish
1 teaspoon Worcestershire sauce
⅓ cup crisp, crumbled bacon

Blend milk and cheese until smooth, mix in remaining ingredients, cover, and let stand at room temperature 1 hour before serving. About 65 calories per tablespoon.

⊠ CLAM AND CREAM CHEESE DIP

Makes about 1½ cups

1 (8-ounce) package cream cheese, softened to room temperature
¼ cup light cream
1 tablespoon lemon juice
1 tablespoon Worcestershire sauce
¼ teaspoon prepared horseradish
¼ teaspoon salt
Pinch white pepper
1 (8-ounce) can minced clams, drained

Blend cream cheese and cream until smooth, mix in remaining ingredients, cover, and chill 1–2 hours to blend flavors. About 80 calories per tablespoon.

VARIATION:

Deviled Clam Dip: Prepare as directed, reducing cream to 2 tablespoons and adding 2 tablespoons spicy brown mustard, 1 tablespoon grated onion, ¼ crushed clove garlic, and ⅛ teaspoon liquid hot red pepper seasoning. About 78 calories per tablespoon.

⊠ SHERRIED GREEN CHEESE DIP

A particularly good dip for small celery sticks.
Makes about 2 cups

8 ounces sharp Cheddar cheese spread, softened to room temperature
6 ounces Roquefort cheese, softened to room temperature
¼–⅓ cup medium-dry sherry

With an electric mixer beat cheeses

and ¼ cup sherry until smooth; if you like a softer dip, add more sherry. Cover and let stand 1 hour at room temperature to blend flavors before serving. About 50 calories per tablespoon.

¢ ⊠ ZINGY SOUR CREAM DIP

Makes about 1½ cups

1 cup sour cream
2 tablespoons mayonnaise
¼ cup finely grated Parmesan cheese
1 teaspoon onion juice
½ teaspoon Worcestershire sauce
½ teaspoon prepared horseradish
½ teaspoon prepared spicy brown mustard
¼ teaspoon salt

Mix all ingredients together, cover, and chill 1–2 hours before serving. About 35 calories per tablespoon.

⊠ CURRY DIP

Good as a dip for crisp sticks of celery, carrot, or finocchio.
Makes about 2½ cups

2 (8-ounce) packages cream cheese, softened to room temperature
⅓ cup milk
1 tablespoon Worcestershire sauce
¼ teaspoon liquid hot red pepper seasoning
1 tablespoon curry powder
1 tablespoon finely grated yellow onion
½ teaspoon salt

Beat all ingredients together with an electric mixer or rotary beater until creamy. Cover and chill several hours. Let stand ½ hour at room temperature before serving. If mixture still seems a bit stiff for dipping, thin with a little milk. About 45 calories per tablespoon.

⊠ GUACAMOLE

Makes about 1 pint

2 ripe medium-size avocados
1 tablespoon lemon juice
1 teaspoon minced scallion
2 tablespoons mayonnaise
½ teaspoon crushed dried hot red
  chili peppers
¼ teaspoon salt

Halve avocados lengthwise and remove pits; scoop flesh into a small bowl, sprinkle with lemon juice, and mash with a fork. Mix in remaining ingredients, place a piece of plastic food wrap directly on surface, and chill 1–2 hours. Stir well and serve as a dip for crisp corn chips. About 30 calories per tablespoon.

GUACAMOLE WITH TOMATO

Makes about 1 pint

1 small firm tomato, peeled, cored,
  seeded, and coarsely chopped
Juice of ½ lemon
2 ripe medium-size avocados
1 tablespoon grated onion
1 tablespoon olive oil
½–1 small pickled hot green chili
  pepper, drained, seeded, and
  minced
½ teaspoon salt

Spread chopped tomato out on several thicknesses of paper toweling, cover with more toweling, and pat until almost all moisture is absorbed. Place lemon juice in a small bowl; halve avocados lengthwise, remove pits, scoop flesh into bowl, and mash with a fork (mixture should be quite lumpy). Mix in tomatoes and remaining ingredients. Place a small piece of plastic food wrap directly on surface of guacamole and let stand at room temperature 1 hour to blend flavors. Stir well and serve with crisp corn chips. About 30 calories per tablespoon.

⚖ ¢ ⊠ CHILI DIP

Makes 3 cups

1 (11-ounce) can condensed chili-
  beef soup
¾ cup canned condensed beef
  consommé
1 cup sour cream
¼ teaspoon chili powder
½ teaspoon Worcestershire sauce
2–3 drops liquid hot red pepper
  seasoning

Mix together all ingredients, cover, and chill 2 hours to blend flavors. Stir well and serve with corn chips. About 15 calories per tablespoon.

⊠ BLACK BEAN DIP

Makes about 2¾ cups

2 (8-ounce) packages cream cheese,
  softened to room temperature
1 (1-pound) can black beans,
  drained well and puréed
¼ cup minced onion
1 clove garlic, peeled and crushed
2 tablespoons dry sherry
¼ teaspoon liquid hot red pepper
  seasoning
¼ teaspoon salt

Place all ingredients in a small mixing bowl and beat with an electric mixer or rotary beater until smooth; cover and chill 2–3 hours. Let stand at room temperature about 20 minutes before serving so mixture is a good dipping consistency. About 35 calories per tablespoon.

EGGPLANT DIP

Makes about 1 quart

2 (1-pound) eggplants, peeled and
    cut in 1" cubes
1 medium-size yellow onion, peeled
    and coarsely chopped
½ clove garlic, peeled and crushed
⅔ cup olive oil
3 (3-ounce) packages chive-flavored,
    softened cream cheese
3 tablespoons tarragon vinegar
Juice of ½ lemon

Sauté eggplants, onion, and garlic in oil in a heavy kettle over moderately high heat 12–15 minutes, stirring frequently, until lightly browned; purée, a little at a time, in an electric blender at high speed. Blend cheese with remaining ingredients, add purée and beat until smooth. Cover and chill several hours. Serve as a dip for sesame seed crackers or Euphrates bread. About 38 calories per tablespoon.

BEER CHEESE SPREAD

This spread is best if allowed to age about a week in the refrigerator before using.
Makes about 1 quart

1 pound mild Cheddar cheese, finely
    grated
1 pound sharp Cheddar cheese, finely
    grated
¼ cup finely grated Bermuda onion
½ clove garlic, peeled and crushed
¼ cup ketchup
1 tablespoon Worcestershire sauce
⅛ teaspoon liquid hot red pepper
    seasoning
1 (12-ounce) can beer

Let cheeses soften at room temperature at least 1 hour. Mix in all remaining ingredients except beer, then, using an electric mixer, beat in the beer, a little at a time; continue beating until light and

fluffy. Chill well before serving. About 50 calories per tablespoon.

⊠ GARLIC CHEESE BALL

Makes 8 servings

½ pound sharp Cheddar cheese,
    grated fine
1 (8-ounce) package cream cheese,
    softened to room temperature
2 cloves garlic, peeled and crushed
Pinch salt
⅓ cup minced pecans or walnuts or
    ¼ cup finely chopped fresh parsley
    or 2–3 tablespoons paprika
    (optional)

Using your hands, mix cheeses, garlic, and salt until thoroughly blended, then shape into a ball. If you wish, roll in the nuts, parsley, or paprika to coat evenly. Wrap in foil and chill 2–3 hours to mellow. Serve at room temperature as a spread for crisp crackers. (Note: This cheese ball may also be frozen.) About 245 calories per serving.

⊠ CHIVE CHEESE

Makes about 1 cup

2 (3-ounce) packages cream cheese,
    softened to room temperature
¼ cup minced chives
¼ cup light cream
¼ teaspoon salt
⅛ teaspoon white pepper

Cream all ingredients together until smooth and use as a spread for crackers or stuffing for raw mushroom caps, celery stalks, or endive spears. About 60 calories per tablespoon.

⊠ TARAMASALATA (GREEK FISH ROE DIP)

This thick, creamy Greek appetizer is made with tarama (pale orange

carp roe). Greek and Middle Eastern groceries sell it, but if unavailable use red caviar.
Makes about 1 cup

¼ cup tarama (carp roe) or red caviar
2 tablespoons lemon juice
2 slices white bread, trimmed of crusts, soaked in cold water and squeezed dry
½ cup olive oil
¼ cup cooking oil
¼ teaspoon onion juice

Blend *tarama*, lemon juice, bread, and olive oil in an electric blender at high speed 1 minute, scrape any unbroken roe from blender blades, and blend again ½ minute. Add vegetable oil and blend ½ minute. Stir in onion juice and serve at room temperature as a dip for raw vegetables or unsalted crackers. Or use as a spread for pumpernickel rounds or Melba toast. About 110 calories per tablespoon.

¢ ⊠ **EGG-DILL SPREAD**

Makes about 1 pint

5 hard-cooked eggs, peeled and minced
⅓ cup melted butter or margarine
1 teaspoon prepared Dijon-style mustard
1 tablespoon minced fresh dill
1 tablespoon white wine vinegar
½ teaspoon salt
½ teaspoon Worcestershire sauce
⅛ teaspoon pepper
2–3 dashes liquid hot red pepper seasoning

Mix all ingredients together and use as a cocktail spread. Especially good on small squares of pumper-

nickel. About 30 calories per tablespoon.

⊠ **DEVILED HAM COCKTAIL SPREAD**

Makes about 1¼ cups

1 (3-ounce) package cream cheese, softened to room temperature
2 (3-ounce) cans deviled ham spread
½ teaspoon Worcestershire sauce
1 teaspoon lemon juice
1 tablespoon grated onion

Blend all ingredients together and use as a spread for crackers or stuffing for celery stalks, raw mushroom caps, or hollowed-out cherry tomatoes. About 40 calories per tablespoon.

⊠ **MOCK LIPTAUER SPREAD**

Genuine Liptauer is a soft, sharp Hungarian cheese mixed with herbs, spices, and capers. Here's a zippy substitute, delicious spread on pumpernickel.
Makes about 1 cup

2 (3-ounce) packages cream cheese, softened to room temperature, or ¾ cup cottage cheese, pressed through a fine sieve
¼ cup soft butter or margarine
2 teaspoons minced capers
1½ teaspoons anchovy paste
½ teaspoon caraway seeds
1 teaspoon minced chives
1 teaspoon grated onion
¼ teaspoon salt
½ teaspoon paprika

Blend ingredients together, pack into a crock, cover, and chill 3–4 hours before serving. About 45 calories per tablespoon.

⚖ ¢ CAPONATA (SICILIAN EGGPLANT SPREAD)

Refrigerated, this will keep about a week. Bring to room temperature before serving.
Makes about 3 cups

4 tablespoons olive oil
1 small eggplant, cut in 1" cubes but not peeled
1 medium-size yellow onion, peeled and minced
⅓ cup minced celery
1 cup tomato purée
⅓ cup coarsely chopped, pitted green and/or ripe olives
4 anchovy fillets, minced
2 tablespoons capers
2 tablespoons red wine vinegar
1 tablespoon sugar
½ teaspoon salt (about)
¼ teaspoon pepper
1 tablespoon minced parsley

Heat 3 tablespoons oil in a large, heavy saucepan 1 minute over moderately high heat, add eggplant and sauté, stirring now and then, 10 minutes until golden and nearly translucent. Add remaining oil, onion, and celery and stir-fry 5–8 minutes until pale golden. Add remaining ingredients except parsley, cover, and simmer 1¼–1½ hours until quite thick, stirring now and then. Mix in parsley, cool to room temperature, taste for salt and adjust as needed. Serve as a spread for crackers. About 17 calories per tablespoon.

About Cocktails

These are not alcoholic cocktails but chilled fruits or seafoods served at the start of a meal. They are easy to prepare and can be quite glamorous, depending upon the presentation.

Fruit Cocktails

Tart fruits (grapefruit, oranges, grapes, pineapple) are the best appetite whetters. They may be fresh, frozen, or canned (or a combination), they can be served solo, mixed together, or teamed with blander fruits such as bananas, peaches, pears, avocados, apples, apricots, melons, or berries. Fruits, of course, should be peeled whenever the skin is hard or thick, cored or sectioned, seeded and cut in bite-size chunks, then chilled several hours. They may be spiked with champagne or dry wine, grenadine or crème de menthe or sprigged with fresh mint, rose geranium, or lemon verbena (if these leaves are tucked into the fruits before chilling, their bouquet will permeate the fruit). If fruits are not naturally tart, drizzle with lemon, lime, orange, or cranberry juice or with ginger ale.

Fruit cocktails may be simply served in stemmed goblets, more elaborately presented by dishing into small bowls and imbedding in larger bowls of crushed ice or by mounding into grapefruit or orange shells, avocado or mango halves. Serve unadorned or crown with scoops of fruit ice or sherbet or dabs of tart fruit jelly. The main point to bear in mind when making fruit cocktails: Keep the fruit mixtures tart and light, varied and colorful.

FRUIT JUICE COCKTAILS

(These are included in the beverage chapter.)

SEAFOOD COCKTAILS

Shrimp cocktail is America's favorite, especially when the shrimp are plump and tender, cooked in a fragrant court bouillon and served well chilled on beds of crushed ice with a horseradish-hot cocktail sauce. Other cold, cooked shellfish make delicious cocktails, too—lobster, crab, Alaska king crab, tiny bay scallops, especially with Green Dressing. Full instructions for preparing and cooking shellfish are included in the seafood chapter, also directions for serving oysters and clams on the half shell, for pickling shrimp and oysters. Here, too, are recipes for Escabeche (Mexican Pickled Fish), Ceviche (Peruvian Raw Pickled Fish), and a number of other unusual cold fish dishes that can double as appetizers.

Seafood cocktails are routinely served in small stemmed glasses with ruffs of greenery and dabs of cocktail sauce. They're far more appealing arranged on beds of crushed ice or piled into avocado, papaya, or mango halves. However served, seafood cocktails should be accompanied by a tart rather than a rich dressing. And the portions should be small.

CHAPTER 7

SOUPS

With so many soups coming out of cans and boxes, few of us bother to make them the old-fashioned way. Too bad, because we're missing the friendliness of the soup kettle singing on the back of the stove. Such headiness it sends through the house, such promise of goodness. Making soup, time consuming as it may be (and it isn't always), *is* virtually effortless because the kettle can bubble away unattended.

The varieties of soup are nearly endless (as supermarket shelves testify), but basically there are four types: *thin clear soups, cream soups, thick vegetable and/or meat soups,* and *sweet or dessert soups.* Within these categories are the hot and the cold, the delicate and the husky, some of which are closer to stews than soups (certain of these—Bouillabaisse, Philadelphia Pepper Pot, Ukrainian-Style Borsch—are included in meat or seafood chapters; for page numbers, see the Index). There has always been some confusion about the difference between bouillons and consommés, bisques and other creamed soups, so to clarify:

A Quick Dictionary of Soups

Bisque: A rich creamed soup, usually of puréed crab, lobster, shrimp, or other shellfish.

Bouillon, Broth, Stock: Used interchangeably, all three terms mean the rich, savory liquid made by simmering meat, fish, or poultry with vegetables and seasonings in water. *Bouillon,* from the French verb *bouillir* (to boil) is some-times made of a combination of meats; *broths and stocks,* however, are usually made of one meat only. *Brown stocks* are brewed from beef and beef bones and *white stocks* from veal.

Chowder: A lusty fish or shellfish soup, usually made with milk and often made with vegetables.

Consommé: A rich, clarified meat or poultry broth. *Double consommé* is simply double strength, made either by boiling down regular consommé or by using a higher proportion of meat and bones to liquid. *Jellied consommé* is just that; if rich enough, consommé will jell naturally when chilled; weaker consommés must be fortified with gelatin.

Madrilène: A sparkling, clear, ruby blend of beef or chicken consommé and tomatoes. When chilled, as it usually is before serving, madrilène jells slightly.

Potage: The French word for *soup;* as used today, it often means a creamed vegetable soup, especially a thick one.

Velouté: A soup enriched with egg yolks and cream.

Some Basic Soup-Making Techniques

How to Clarify Broths: For each quart, allow 1 egg white and 1 crushed eggshell. Beat egg white until soft peaks form, stir into cooled broth along with shell, set over lowest heat, and heat, stirring with a whisk, until mixture foams up. Remove from heat, stir once, then let stand undisturbed 1 hour at room temperature. Line a sieve with a fine dish towel wrung out in cold water, set over a deep bowl, and ladle in broth, egg, shell and all, taking care not to stir up sediment in bottom of pan. Let drip through undisturbed. Remove any specks of fat from clarified liquid by blotting up with a paper towel. *Note:* An easier way to clarify is simply to pour the broth through the cloth-lined sieve, but for jewel-clear liquid, use the egg white and shell.

How to Color Stocks and Broths: Mix in a little commercial gravy browner or, for more delicate flavor, caramelized sugar (it won't make the broth sweet):

Caramelized Sugar: Melt 1 cup sugar in a very heavy saucepan (not iron) over lowest heat, stirring. When dark brown, remove from heat and cool to room temperature. Add 1 cup boiling water, drop by drop, stirring all the while. Return to low heat and heat, stirring, until caramelized sugar dissolves.

How to Color Soups: The tiniest drop of food color can brighten vegetable cream soup, especially a green or red one.

How to Degrease Soups: The easiest way is to chill the soup, then lift off the hardened fat. Second best: skim off as much fat as possible, then blot up the rest by spreading paper toweling flat on the surface of the soup.

How to Dilute Soups: When held too long on the stove or chilled, soups often need thinning before serving. Thin cream soups with milk or light cream; meat, poultry, or fish soups with meat, poultry, or fish broth; vegetable soups with a meat or chicken broth or, if the soup contains tomatoes, with tomato juice. Cabbage and dried bean soups can be thinned with beer.

How to Reduce Soups: Boil uncovered until reduced to desired strength.

How to Thicken Soups:

With Flour (best for cream soups): For each 1 cup soup, add any of the following:
− 1 tablespoon flour blended with 2

tablespoons cold water, milk, or broth
– 2 tablespoons rice, potato, soya, peanut, or wheat germ flour blended with ¼ cup cold water, milk, or broth
– 1 tablespoon flour blended with 1 tablespoon softened butter or margarine

Method: Blend a little hot soup into thickening agent, then quickly return to soup and heat, stirring, until thickened and smooth. For best flavor, let soup mellow 5–10 minutes after thickening.

With Raw Cereal (best for meat or vegetable soups): For each 1 cup soup, add any one of the following:
– 1 teaspoon medium pearl barley
– 1 teaspoon rice
– 1 teaspoon oatmeal

Method: About 1 hour before soup is done, mix in cereal, cover, and simmer, stirring now and then.

With Raw Potato (best for meat and vegetable soups; excellent for those with wheat and/or egg allergies): Allow 3 tablespoons grated raw potato for each cup soup; mix in 15–20 minutes before soup is done and cook, stirring now and then.

With Raw Egg (best for cream soups): For each 1 cup soup, add any one of the following:
– 2 egg yolks, lightly beaten
– 1 whole egg, lightly beaten

Method: Blend a little hot soup into egg, return to soup, set over *lowest* heat, and cook, stirring briskly, about 2 minutes until slightly thickened and no raw taste of egg remains; do not boil. *Note:* For easier blending, beat egg or yolks with about 2 tablespoons cold milk or broth or, for added zip, dry sherry.

With Hard-Cooked Egg (excellent for dried bean soups): For each 2 cups soup, mix in 1 finely chopped hard-cooked egg just before serving. *Note:* If you prefer, scatter egg on top of each portion instead of mixing in.

With Pasta (best for consommés, meat and vegetable soups): Pasta doesn't thicken soup so much as give it body. Any thin spaghetti or macaroni, broken in short lengths, or tiny pasta shapes such as *stellette* (stars), *semini* (seeds), or alphabet letters will work. Depending on how hearty a soup you want, add 1–2 tablespoons uncooked pasta per cup. The pasta can be cooked in the soup (use package directions as a guide) or separately and added just before serving (this is the method to use when a clear broth is wanted).

With Bread Crumbs (good for meat or vegetable soups): Allow 1–2 tablespoons soft or dry bread crumbs per cup of soup and mix in just before serving.

Some Tips for Making Better Soups

– Most soups taste better if made 1–2 days ahead of time; reheat just before serving.
– Use vegetable cooking water in making soups, also in thinning condensed canned soups.
– Best bones to use for stocks: shin, marrow, neck, oxtail.
– Best bones to use for jellied stocks: veal knuckles.

- Whenever a soup tastes bland, add a little salt and pepper. Sometimes that's all that's needed to bring out the flavor.
- Use bouillon cubes or powders to strengthen weak soups.
- Cool soups uncovered and as quickly as possible.
- Always taste a cold soup before serving and adjust seasonings as needed; cold foods dull the taste buds and usually need more seasoning than hot foods.
- When a soup is flavored with wine or beer, reduce the salt slightly.
- Always add wine to soup shortly before serving and do not let soup boil.
- Use a light hand in adding wine to soup—¼–⅓ cup per quart is usually enough. Too much wine will merely make the soup bitter.
- If a soup is to be reduced (boiled down), add the salt at the very end.
- If a soup seems *slightly* salty, add a peeled, halved raw potato and simmer about 15 minutes; it will absorb some of the salt. Remove the potato before serving.
- To mellow tomato soup, add 1 tablespoon sugar or light brown sugar.
- To give vegetable cream soups more character, purée the vegetables in a food mill; a blender will reduce them to "pap."

About Pressure Cooking Soups

Soups suffer when cooked under pressure so use the pressure cooker only when necessary and only for making stocks. For best results, use 15 pounds pressure and process meat bones and stock 40 minutes, poultry 20 minutes, and vegetables

5. Release pressure and finish cooking over low heat. To reach their peak of flavor, meat stocks may take as much as 1 hour of slow simmering, poultry stocks about ½ hour, and vegetable stocks 15 minutes. This method seems to produce stocks that don't taste of the pressure cooker.

About Serving Soups

How to Choose a Soup: Soups can be the prelude to an elegant meal or, in the case of a family-style lunch or supper, the meal itself. Soup served as a first course should set the tone of the meal and complement what's to follow. Thus, if the main course is rich or spicy, the soup should be light or bland (never serve a cream soup with a creamed entree). If the main course is roast meat or fowl, the soup may be richer, a bisque, perhaps, or a cream vegetable soup. Pay attention to flavors, too, never duplicating within a meal. Soup should be the counterpoint, offering a contrast of flavor, texture, color, and sometimes temperature (a steaming soup is splendid before cold salmon, a cool vichyssoise before broiled steak). Cool soups, obviously, are welcome on blistery days, warm soups in winter.

How to Figure Number of Servings: As a general rule, 1 quart soup will make 6 first course servings, 4 main course.

How to Choose the Proper Soup Bowl and Spoon: The kind of soup and the formality of the meal both dictate which to use. Here's a list of popular soup bowls and spoons together with tips for using each:

Type of Soup Bowl	Appropriate Spoon	Appropriate Soup
Bouillon cup	Teaspoon	Bouillon, consommé, or other thin, clear soup that can be drunk
Double-eared bouillon cup	Round-bowled soupspoon	Bouillon, consommé, or other thin, clear soup that can be drunk
Oriental soup bowl	Teaspoon	Clear Oriental soups such as Won Ton or Egg Drop
Soup plate	Round- or Oval-bowled soupspoons	Chowders, thick meat, poultry, or vegetable soups
Marmite	Any soupspoon	Baked or broiled soups
Multipurpose American soup bowls	Any soupspoon	Any soup
Mugs	——	Any hot or cold soup that can be drunk
Glasses	——	Any cold soup that can be drunk

About Tureens: When a meal is informal and soup the main course, a tureen adds a note of importance; it also keeps the soup hot for "seconds."

Some Tips on Serving Soups

Hot Soups: Have the soup steaming hot and ladle into heated soup bowls.

Cold Soups: Have soup well chilled and serve in chilled bowls. For a festive touch, bed the soup bowls in larger bowls of crushed ice or, if the soup is a thin one, serve in glasses on the rocks.

Some Ways to Garnish Soups

Clear Soups (Hot)
Avocado slices or cubes
Chiffonade (butter-sautéed shreds of lettuce or sorrel)
Crumbled French-fried onions
Cubed, peeled, seeded tomato
Dumplings (liver, marrow, farina)
Gnocchi
Julienne strips of cooked meat or vegetables or brunoise (butter-sautéed shreds of carrot, leeks, and celery)
Lemon, lime, or orange slices
Matzo balls
Minced fresh chives, chervil, dill, mint, parsley, or tarragon
Pasta (Kreplach, Nockerln, Spätzle, Viennese soup "peas," Won Tons)

Quenelles (especially for fish broth)
Royale Custard
Sliced, cooked beef marrow
Slivered pimiento or sliced green or
  ripe olives

Clear Soups (Cold or Jellied)
Avocado slices or cubes
Cubed, peeled, seeded tomato
Cubed, peeled, or unpeeled
  cucumber
Lemon, lime, or orange slices or
  wedges
Minced fresh chives, chervil, dill,
  fennel, mint, parsley, tarragon, or
  watercress
Minced radishes or scallions
Sour cream sprinkled with one of
  the minced herbs listed above

Cream Soups (Hot or Cold)
Bacon crumbles
Croutons (plain or seasoned)
Crumbled French-fried onions
Crumbled or grated cheese
Finely grated lemon or orange rind
Minced cashews, peanuts, pistachio
  or piñon nuts or slivered
  blanched or toasted almonds
Minced fresh chives, chervil, dill,
  fennel, mint, parsley, tarragon, or
  watercress
Minced or thinly sliced truffles
Paprika, chili or curry powder
Poppy or caraway seeds
Sliced ripe or green olives
Slivered pimiento

Thick Vegetable, Meat, or Fish Soups
Bacon crumbles
Croutons (plain or seasoned)
Grated sharp cheese
Lemon or orange slices (especially
  for fish soups)
Minced chives, dill, parsley, or
  watercress
Sliced frankfurters or sautéed pep-
  peroni (especially for dried pea or
  bean soups)

¢ ⟁ ALL-PURPOSE STOCK

Before freezers and refrigerators
there was the stock pot. It's still a
good way to use meat and vegetable
leftovers, vegetable cooking water,
celery tops, mushroom stems, tomato
peelings, and other vegetable
parings.
Makes about 1 quart

2–3 cups finely chopped mixed left-
  over lean meat and vegetables
1 pound beef, veal, or lamb bones
2 quarts water
1 bouquet garni,* tied in cheesecloth
Salt
Pepper

Simmer leftovers, bones, water, and
bouquet garni covered in a large,
heavy kettle 2–3 hours; add salt and
pepper to taste. Strain through a
fine sieve, cool, chill, and skim off
fat. Store in refrigerator or freezer
and use as a base for soups, stews,
and sauces. About 35 calories per
cup.

⟁ CHICKEN BROTH (STOCK)

The perfect base for soups and
stews.
Makes about 2 quarts

1 (5½–6-pound) stewing hen,
  cleaned and dressed
2 quarts water
1 medium-size yellow onion, peeled
  and quartered
1 stalk celery (include tops)
1 medium-size carrot, peeled
2 sprigs parsley
1 bay leaf
6 peppercorns
1½ teaspoons salt

Place hen, giblets, and all remaining
ingredients in a large heavy kettle,
cover, and simmer 1½–2 hours
until hen is tender; lift hen and
giblets from broth and cool.

BEING CREATIVE WITH CANNED SOUPS

Canned soups are good mixers. Take one flavor, blend in a second or third, add an herb or spice, and you've a whole new recipe. There are endless combinations. Invent your own or try any of the following; all are based on standard soup can sizes (they range from 10 ounces to about 1 pound). Simply heat and stir soups, liquid and seasonings 5-10 minutes (do not boil), garnish and serve.

Canned Soup Combinations	Liquid to Add	Seasonings	Garnish	Number of Servings
Cream of Asparagus + Cheddar cheese	2 soup cans milk	Pinch nutmeg or mace	Coarsely grated Cheddar	4-6
Cream of Asparagus + cream of chicken	2 soup cans milk	1-2 T. curry powder	Coarsely chopped, roasted, blanched peanuts	4-6
Bean with Bacon + tomato bisque	1 soup can water	1-2 T. chili powder, pinch garlic salt	Bacon crumbles	6-8
Black bean + mushroom (clear) + beef broth	1/4 cup dry sherry	1/4 t. each thyme, crushed dried chili peppers, and garlic powder	Minced hard-cooked egg and minced parsley	4-6
Cream of Celery + chicken broth	1 soup can light cream and 1/4 cup dry white wine	1 T. curry powder, 2 T. minced chutney	Grated orange or lemon rind, toasted slivered almonds	4-6
Chicken with Rice + escarole	3/4 cup water and 1/4 cup dry white wine	1 t. lemon juice, pinch thyme and nutmeg	Minced escarole, parsley, or watercress	4-6
Cheddar Cheese + cream of mushroom	1½ soup cans milk, 1/3 soup can dry white wine	Pinch each savory, thyme, and mace	Sliced canned mushrooms, paprika	4-6
Cheddar Cheese + tomato	2 soup cans milk	1 T. minced onion, pinch each basil and oregano	Minced chives and pimiento slivers	4-6

188

Soup Combination		Liquid	Seasoning	Garnish	Servings
Clam Chowder	+ tomato bisque	2 soup cans water	1 bay leaf, a pinch basil	Minced chives or parsley, croutons	4-6
Green Pea	+ tomato	2 soup cans milk	Pinch savory or mint, 1/2 t. grated orange rind	Croutons or orange slices	4-6
Green Pea	+ beef broth or consommé	1 soup can milk, 1/3 soup can dry sherry			4-6
Green Pea	+ cream of mushroom + beef broth	1 soup can water, 1/3 soup can dry white wine	Pinch thyme and savory	Sliced canned mushrooms	4-6
Green Pea	+ Cheddar cheese	+ chicken or beef broth	1 soup can milk, 1/3 soup can dry white wine	1 T. mint flakes, 1 t. grated orange rind	Whipped cream and grated orange rind	6
Green Pea	+ cream of chicken	2 soup cans milk	1-2 T. creamy peanut butter	Minced roasted, blanched peanuts	4-6
Mushroom	+ tomato + beef broth (clear)	1/2 soup can water, 1/4 cup dry red wine or sherry	Pinch thyme	Sliced, peeled, seeded tomato, minced parsley	4-6
Mushroom	+ escarole (clear)	1/2 cup water and 1/4 cup dry white wine	1 bay leaf, 1 uncrushed clove garlic (remove before serving)	Lemon slices	4
Mushroom	+ minestrone + beef broth (clear)	1/4 cup dry white wine		Minced parsley	4-6
Pepper Pot	+ tomato	2 soup cans water	1 bay leaf, 1/8 teaspoon crushed dried chili peppers		4-6
Shrimp or Lobster	+ tomato bisque	2 soup cans milk or light cream, 1/4 cup dry sherry	Pinch tarragon or chervil, 1 t. grated orange rind	Danish shrimp, orange slices, or grated orange rind	4-6
Turkey Noodle	+ cream of celery or mushroom	2 soup cans milk or light cream, 1/4 cup dry white wine	Pinch each sage and thyme	Grated Parmesan or Cheddar	4-6
Vichyssoise	+ tomato bisque	2 soup cans milk	Pinch each thyme and basil	Minced French-fried onions or bacon crumbles	4-6

Note: For more tender giblets, remove after 15–20 minutes' simmering. Strain broth, cool, then chill and skim off fat; save fat, if you like, clarify* and keep on hand to use in cooking. Discard chicken skin, remove meat from bones, and save to use in recipes calling for cooked chicken meat. About 40 calories per cup.

VARIATIONS:

¢ ⚖ **Economy Chicken Broth:** Proceed as directed, using 4–5 pounds chicken backs and wings instead of the hen and simmering about 1 hour. About 40 calories per cup.

⚖ **Delicate Chicken Broth:** Proceed as directed, using 4 quarts water instead of 2. About 20 calories per cup.

⚖ **Turkey Broth:** Prepare as directed, substituting 1 (6-pound) turkey for the hen. About 40 calories per cup.

⚖ ¢ **CHICKEN GIBLET STOCK**

Use as a base for soups, sauces and gravies.
Makes about 1 pint

Giblets and neck from 1 chicken, washed
2 cups cold water
½ small yellow onion, peeled and coarsely chopped
½ stalk celery
½ carrot, peeled
1 bay leaf
2 peppercorns
½ teaspoon salt (about)

Simmer giblets and remaining ingredients, covered, 15 minutes. Remove liver and reserve, also remove heart if it is tender. Re-cover and simmer remaining giblets until tender, 1–2 hours, replenishing

water as needed. Strain stock, taste for seasoning and adjust as needed; chill and skim off fat. Mince giblets and, if you like, meat from neck. Save to use in gravy or sauce recipes or mix into recipes calling for cooked chicken meat. About 40 calories per cup.

VARIATIONS:

⚖ **Turkey Giblet Stock** (Makes about 1 quart): Cook turkey giblets and neck as directed for chicken, using 1 quart water and doubling all remaining ingredients. About 40 calories per cup.

⚖ **Giblet Stock from Other Poultry and Game Birds:** Prepare as directed for Chicken Giblet Stock, adjusting quantity of water and seasonings to number of giblets. About 50 calories per cup.

⚖ **Quantity Giblet Stock:** For each additional pint of stock needed over and above what basic recipe makes, use 1 pint chicken broth, 2–3 chicken livers, ¼ yellow onion, peeled, ½ stalk celery, and ½ bay leaf. Simmer as directed, removing 1 liver after 15 minutes (so stock will not be overly strong of liver). Simmer remaining giblets 1–2 hours, replenishing liquid with chicken broth as needed. Strain and season to taste as directed. Mince giblets and add to stock or save to use in other recipes. About 40 calories per cup.

¢ ⚖ **BEEF BROTH (STOCK)**

A rich brown broth to use in making soups and sauces.
Makes about 3 quarts

4–5 pounds beef shin- and marrow-bones, cracked (a ½ and ½ mixture is best)
1 large yellow onion, peeled and coarsely chopped

2 *leeks, washed, trimmed, and
coarsely chopped*
2 *medium-size carrots, peeled and
coarsely chopped*
2 *stalks celery, coarsely chopped*
5 *quarts water*
2–3 *sprigs parsley or a bouquet
garni,* tied in cheesecloth*
6 *peppercorns*
1 *bay leaf, crumbled*
1 *tablespoon salt (about)*

Bring all ingredients to a boil in a
large heavy kettle, turn heat to
low, skim off froth, cover, and
simmer 4–5 hours; check pot
occasionally and add extra water if
needed. Skim off fat, then strain
stock through a sieve lined with a
double thickness of cheesecloth; pour
into a clean kettle and boil rapidly
uncovered until reduced to about
3 quarts. Taste for salt and adjust
as needed. Cool, then chill; lift
off solidified fat. Stock is now ready
to use in recipes. Store in refrigerator
or freezer. About 35 calories
per cup.

VARIATIONS:

¢ ⚖ **Brown Beef Stock:** Roast
bones uncovered in a shallow roasting pan in a 425° F. oven ¾–1
hour until brown. Meanwhile,
stir-fry onion, leeks, carrots, and
celery in 2 tablespoons beef drippings or margarine in kettle 12–15
minutes over moderate heat until
well browned. Add bones, 4 quarts
water, and remaining ingredients.
Drain fat from roasting pan, add
remaining water, stirring to scrape
up browned bits; pour into kettle
and proceed as directed. About
50 calories per cup.

⚖ **Double-Strength Beef Broth:**
Brown bones as for Brown Beef
Stock (above). Also brown 2
pounds boned beef chuck, shank, or
neck, cut in 1″ cubes, in 2

tablespoons beef drippings or margarine in a large kettle; add
vegetables, brown, then proceed
as above. *Note:* Boned beef may be
saved after cooking and used in
hash, stuffing, or sandwich spreads.
About 45 calories per cup.

⚖ **Veal (White) Stock:** Prepare
like Beef Broth (above), using 2
veal shanks and 4–5 pounds veal
bones or a ½ and ½ mixture of veal
and beef bones. About 40 calories
per cup.

⚖ **BEEF CONSOMMÉ**

Richer than Beef Broth and delicious
hot or cold.
Makes about 1 quart

1 *quart Beef Broth or Double-
Strength Beef Broth*
½ *pound very lean ground beef*
½ *medium-size carrot, peeled and
minced*
1 *small yellow onion, peeled and
minced*
½ *stalk celery, minced*

Simmer all ingredients, covered, 1
hour; strain through a fine sieve
lined with cheesecloth, cool, chill,
and remove all fat. Clarify,* taste
for salt, and adjust as needed.
Serve hot or cold. About 35
calories per cup.

VARIATIONS:

⚖ **Double Consommé:** Prepare
as directed; after clarifying, boil
rapidly, uncovered, until reduced by
half. If you like, stir in ½ cup dry
sherry or Madeira. Serve hot or
cold. About 45 calories per cup
without sherry, 60 calories with.

⚖ **Consommé Royale:** Prepare
one recipe Royale Custard (made
with beef consommé), cut in fancy
shapes, and float a few pieces in
each soup bowl. About 55 calories
per cup.

⚖️ **Jellied Consommé:** Prepare consommé as directed and chill 1 cup about 2 hours to test firmness. If firm, no extra gelatin is needed. If semifirm, mix 1 envelope unflavored gelatin into consommé; if liquid, 2 envelopes. Heat, stirring, until gelatin dissolves, then cool and chill until firm. Before serving, break up consommé with a fork. Serve in chilled bowls or bowls set in larger bowls of crushed ice. Sprinkle with minced chives, scallions, or parsley and garnish with lemon wedges. About 45 calories per cup if made with one envelope gelatin, 50 calories per cup made with 2 envelopes gelatin.

⚖️ BEEF TEA

A very concentrated beef broth that makes a bracing midafternoon refresher. It's nourishing, good for convalescents.
Makes about 1 pint

1 pound very lean beef, ground twice
2 cups water
¾ teaspoon salt (about)

Place meat and water in the top of a double boiler over simmering water, cover, and simmer 2 hours, stirring now and then. Strain through a fine sieve lined with a double thickness of cheesecloth. Add salt, taste, and add more if needed. Cool, chill, and remove fat. Store in refrigerator and heat whenever desired; do not boil when reheating. About 30 calories per cup.

VARIATION:

⚖️ **Raw Beef Tea:** This must be made fresh each time, so it's best to make small amounts. Place ½ pound beef and 1 cup cold water in an electric blender and buzz at high speed 30 seconds. Cover and let stand at room temperature ½

hour. Strain through a fine sieve lined with cheesecloth, stir in ¼ teaspoon salt, and serve as is or slightly chilled. About 40 calories per cup.

⚖️ ¢ EASY FISH STOCK

Bones of haddock, halibut, and/or pike produce a fragrant stock. Use for making seafood soups and sauces.
Makes 2 quarts

2 quarts cold water
1 pound fishbones, heads and trimmings
1 tablespoon salt

Place all ingredients in a kettle, cover, and simmer 1 hour. Strain liquid through a fine sieve and use for poaching fish, making soups or sauces. (*Note:* This stock freezes well.) About 5 calories per cup.

¢ ⚖️ VEGETABLE STOCK

Use this stock as a base for vegetable soups or sauces.
Makes about 3 quarts

2 large yellow onions, peeled and minced
2 cups coarsely chopped, scrubbed, unpeeled carrots
2 cups coarsely chopped celery (include some tops)
2 cups coarsely chopped, unpeeled tomatoes
2 cups coarsely chopped mushrooms (include stems)
2 leeks, washed, trimmed, and coarsely chopped
1 cup coarsely chopped cabbage or cauliflower heart and trimmings (optional)
4 sprigs parsley
2 bay leaves, crumbled
6 peppercorns
4 teaspoons salt (about)
1 gallon water

Simmer all ingredients in a large covered kettle 2 hours; check liquid occasionally and add water as needed to maintain level at about 3 quarts. Strain stock through a fine sieve and measure; if you have more than 3 quarts, boil rapidly, uncovered, to reduce; if less than 3 quarts, add boiling water to round out measure. Taste for salt and adjust as needed. Cool, then store in refrigerator or freezer. About 15 calories per cup.

⚖ **CONSOMMÉ MADRILÈNE**

Madrilène should be made with sun-ripened tomatoes, but since they are scarce, this recipe substitutes canned purée.
Makes 4 servings

2 cups tomato purée
1 quart beef consommé or fat-free chicken broth
1 teaspoon minced chives
1 teaspoon minced parsley
⅛ teaspoon cayenne pepper
¼ cup dry sherry or Madeira wine (optional)
1 tablespoon slivered pimiento (optional)

Mix purée, consommé, chives, parsley, and cayenne in a saucepan, cover, and heat over lowest heat 15 minutes; mixture should barely simmer. Strain through a fine sieve lined with several thicknesses of cheesecloth. For a sparkling madrilène, let drip through undisturbed. Bring liquid to a boil and, if you like, stir in sherry and pimiento. About 35 calories per serving.

VARIATION:

⚖ **Jellied Consommé Madrilène:** Prepare as directed. Heat 1 envelope unflavored gelatin in ⅓ cup water over moderate heat, stirring until dissolved. Stir into madrilène, add sherry and, if you like, pimiento. Taste for salt and adjust as needed. Cool, then chill until firm. Break madrilène up with a fork, ladle into chilled bowls, garnish with minced chives or watercress and lemon wedges, and serve. About 45 calories per serving.

⚖ **BASIC ASPIC**

Clear aspic is sometimes used to coat or glaze party food—a whole ham, for example, poached fresh salmon, a *chaud-froid*, meat or poultry, or vegetable canapés. Any clear meat, poultry, vegetable, or fish stock can be used. (*Note:* A recipe for Court Bouillon and directions for clarifying it are included in the fish chapter.)
Makes about 1 quart

1 quart clarified* Beef Broth, Brown Beef Broth, Veal (White) Stock, Chicken Broth, or Vegetable Stock
1–2 envelopes unflavored gelatin (optional)
¼–½ cup cold water (optional)

First, determine broth's jelling power by chilling 1 cup. If it sets up firmly, it will need no gelatin; if soft, it will need 1 envelope gelatin, if soupy, 2 envelopes. (*Note:* Vegetable stock will always need the full amount of gelatin.) Soften required amount of gelatin in cold water—¼ cup cold water to each envelope gelatin—then add to broth (including that chilled for jelling test) and heat and stir over low heat until dissolved. To prevent bubble formation, stir gently; do not beat. Chill until thick and syrupy. (*Note:* To quick-chill, set over ice cubes.) Aspic is now ready to use for glazing foods or as recipes direct.

If made without gelatin, the same calorie count as broth or stock from which it was made, if made with 1 envelope gelatin, add 7 calories per cup, if made with 2 envelopes gelatin, add 14 calories per cup.

VARIATIONS:

▨ ⚖ **Quick and Easy Aspic:** Slowly heat 1 envelope unflavored gelatin and 3 cups beef consommé or madrilène, stirring until dissolved. If you like, mix in 2–3 tablespoons medium-dry sherry. 50–60 calories per cup, depending on amount of sherry used.

▨ ⚖ **Quick and Easy Light Aspic:** Soften 1 envelope unflavored gelatin in 1½ cups cold water, then heat and stir until dissolved. Add 1 (10½-ounce) can beef consommé or madrilène. About 40 calories per cup.

⚖ ¢ **GAME SOUP**

When a game bird has been eaten down to the bones, it's time for game soup.
Makes 4 servings

Carcass, skin, meat scraps, and any giblets from 1–2 pheasants or wild ducks or 2–3 grouse, partridges, quail, or pigeons
5 cups cold water
1 medium-size yellow onion, peeled and stuck with 3 cloves
1 medium-size carrot, peeled and diced
1 stalk celery, minced
½ small turnip, peeled and diced
1 bouquet garni,* tied in cheesecloth
¼ cup medium dry sherry
1½ teaspoons salt (about)
¼ teaspoon pepper

Break up carcass and place with skin, scraps, and giblets in a large saucepan. Add all but last 3 ingredients, cover, and simmer over lowest heat 1½–2 hours. Check liquid occasionally and add a little

water if necessary. Strain liquid through a fine sieve lined with cheesecloth; skim off fat. Measure liquid and add water or chicken broth as needed to make 1 quart. If there is more than 1 quart liquid, reduce by boiling rapidly uncovered. Heat soup to serving temperature, stir in sherry, salt, and pepper, taste for salt and adjust as needed. About 30 calories per serving.

¢ ⚖ ▨ **CHICKEN NOODLE SOUP**

Makes 4 servings

1 quart Chicken Broth
1 cup fine noodles
1 cup diced cooked chicken meat
Salt
Pepper
2 teaspoons minced parsley

Bring broth to a boil in a large saucepan, add noodles and chicken, and simmer, uncovered, about 10 minutes until noodles are tender. Taste for salt and pepper and adjust as needed. Stir in parsley and serve. About 70 calories per serving.

VARIATION:

¢ ⚖ ▨ **Chicken and Rice Soup:** Prepare as directed, substituting ⅓ cup uncooked rice for the noodles and cooking 15–20 minutes until rice is tender. Season and serve as directed. About 70 calories per serving.

¢ ⚖ ▨ **EGG DROP SOUP**

Makes 4 servings

1 quart Chicken Broth
1 scallion, minced (optional)
½ teaspoon sugar
1 teaspoon soy sauce
2 tablespoons cornstarch blended with ¼ cup cold water

*1 egg, lightly beaten with 1
  tablespoon cold water*

Heat broth and, if you like,
scallion to boiling in a heavy saucepan over moderate heat. Mix in
sugar, soy sauce, and cornstarch
paste and heat, stirring constantly,
until slightly thickened. Bring
mixture to a full boil, remove from
heat and drizzle in egg mixture,
stirring constantly. Ladle into hot
bowls and serve. About 75 calories
per serving.

WON TON SOUP

Fresh squares of noodle dough
called won ton skins or wrappers can
usually be bought in Chinese
groceries. They should be refrigerated in foil or Saran and used within
4–5 days. If you're unable to buy
them, here's how to make your
own.
Makes 8 servings

Won Ton Dough:
*1½ cups sifted flour
1 teaspoon salt
1 egg, lightly beaten with 3
   tablespoons cold water*

Filling:
*¼ pound very lean uncooked pork,
   ground twice, or ½ cup minced
   cooked chicken meat or shrimp
2 water chestnuts, minced
2 scallions, minced
1 teaspoon grated fresh gingerroot
   or ⅛ teaspoon ginger
1 teaspoon soy sauce
½ teaspoon salt
Pinch pepper*

Broth:
*2 quarts+1 cup chicken broth
½ cup julienne strips of cooked
   chicken meat or roast pork
   (optional)*

For dough, sift flour with salt, add
egg mixture all at once, and stir

briskly with a fork until dough
holds together; turn onto a lightly
floured board and knead 2–3
minutes until smooth. Cover and
let rest ½ hour. Dust board and
rolling pin lightly with cornstarch
and roll dough as thin as possible
into a square about 16″; cut in 2½″
squares. Mix filling ingredients.
Arrange noodle squares on counter,
spoon about ½ teaspoon filling onto
each, a little above center, then roll,
as shown, sealing by moistening
edges with cold water. Bring broth
to a boil in a large kettle, drop in

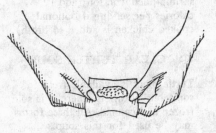

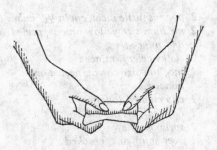

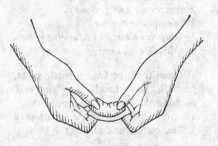

6–8 won tons, and boil, uncovered, 5 minutes; lift out won tons and cover with a damp towel. Cook remaining won tons the same way. When all won tons are done, return to broth and simmer, uncovered, 1 minute. Ladle broth into soup bowls, add 3 won tons to each, and serve. If you like, float a few strips chicken or pork in each bowl. About 145 calories per serving with pork-filled won ton (add 20 calories per serving if optional roast pork is added to broth). About 120 calories per serving for chicken- or shrimp-filled won ton (add 12 calories per serving if optional cooked chicken is added to broth).

⚖️ CLEAR TURTLE SOUP

Turtle meat is available fresh in some big cities; elsewhere it is sold frozen and canned. All three forms may be used for this soup.
Makes 6 servings

2 pounds turtle meat, cut in ½" cubes
2 medium-size yellow onions, peeled and minced
2 stalks celery, minced
1 medium-size carrot, peeled and minced
1 cup canned tomatoes
1 bay leaf, crumbled
2 sprigs parsley
1 beef soupbone, cracked
2 quarts water or 1 pint turtle broth and 1½ quarts water
2 teaspoons salt (about)
¼ teaspoon pepper
⅓ cup dry sherry or Madeira wine
6 thin slices lemon

If using fresh or frozen turtle meat, parboil,* save broth, then proceed as follows. Place all ingredients except sherry and lemon in a heavy kettle, cover, and simmer 1 hour

until meat is tender. Lift out 1 cup turtle meat, cut in ¼" cubes, and reserve. Simmer remaining mixture, covered, 2 hours longer; check pot occasionally and add a little more water, if necessary. Strain liquid through a fine sieve lined with a double thickness of cheesecloth; skim off fat, measure broth, and, if less than 1½ quarts, add enough boiling water to round out measure; if more than 1½ quarts, boil rapidly uncovered to reduce. Add reserved turtle meat and sherry, simmer 2–3 minutes, taste for salt and adjust as needed. Ladle into soup bowls, float a lemon slice in each, and serve. (Note: The turtle meat strained out of the soup can be added to a stock pot, to vegetable soups, or to stews.) About 40 calories per serving.

VARIATION:

Home-Style Turtle Soup: Simmer all ingredients except sherry and lemon in a covered kettle 3 hours until turtle is tender. Stir in sherry and serve. Omit lemon. About 260 calories per serving.

⚖️ ✗ MOCK TURTLE SOUP

Makes 4 servings

1 (8-ounce) bottle clam juice
2 (10½-ounce) cans condensed beef consommé
4 peppercorns
⅛ teaspoon thyme
⅛ teaspoon marjoram
¼ cup sweet Madeira or sherry

Combine clam juice and consommé in a saucepan. Tie peppercorns and herbs in cheesecloth and add. Cover and simmer 15 minutes; discard cheesecloth bag, stir in wine, ladle into soup cups, and serve. About 70 calories per serving.

⚖ TOMATO VEGETABLE BOUILLON

This Southern recipe has been handed down for generations. Rumor has it that it was Robert E. Lee's favorite soup.
Makes 4 servings

6 *large ripe tomatoes, peeled, seeded, and coarsely chopped*
1 *medium-size yellow onion, peeled and coarsely chopped*
1 *stalk celery, coarsely chopped*
2 *carrots, peeled and coarsely chopped*
½ *sweet green pepper, cored, seeded, and coarsely chopped*
1 *pint water*
1 *bay leaf*
1 *tablespoon sugar*
¼ *cup dry sherry*
1 *teaspoon salt (about)*
Pinch pepper

Place vegetables, water, bay leaf, and sugar in a large saucepan, cover, and simmer ½ hour. Strain through a fine sieve and return to pan. Add sherry, salt to taste, and pepper. Serve steaming hot. About 80 calories per serving.

⚖ CLEAR MUSHROOM BROTH

Glorious when made with morels, *chanterelles,* or other edible wild mushrooms.
Makes 6 servings

1 *pound mushrooms, wiped clean and minced*
1½ *quarts beef bouillon or consommé, skimmed of any fat*
1 *small sprig each thyme, parsley, and marjoram, tied in cheesecloth (optional)*
½ *teaspoon finely grated onion*
6 *thin slices lemon*

Place all ingredients except lemon in a large saucepan (not aluminum), cover, and simmer over lowest heat 1 hour, using an asbestos flame tamer, if necessary, to keep bouillon just trembling. Taste for salt and adjust as needed. Cool broth and chill overnight. Strain through a sieve lined with a double thickness of cheesecloth. Serve cold or piping hot with a lemon slice floating in each soup bowl. About 35 calories per serving.

VARIATION:

⚖ **Sherried Mushroom Broth:** Prepare as directed; just before serving, stir in ¼–⅓ cup medium-dry sherry and, if you like, 2–3 very thinly sliced raw mushrooms or 1 thinly sliced truffle. About 45 calories per serving.

⚖ CLEAR BEET SOUP

Makes 4 servings

2 *(1-pound) cans sliced beets, drained (reserve liquid)*
1½ *cups beef consommé*
1 *teaspoon red wine vinegar*
⅛ *teaspoon celery seeds*
1 *sprig fresh dill or ¼ teaspoon dill weed*
1 *tablespoon cornstarch blended with 1 tablespoon cold water*
¼ *cup heavy cream (optional)*

Measure 1½ cups beet liquid and pour into a saucepan; dice enough beets to make 1 cup and set aside (save remaining beets and beet liquid to serve as a vegetable). Add consommé, vinegar, celery seeds, and dill to pan, cover, and heat over lowest heat 10 minutes; mixture should just tremble; strain. Return to pan, stir in cornstarch paste, and heat over moderate heat, stirring, until mixture is slightly thickened and clear. Off heat, stir in diced beets. Ladle into soup bowls, float 1 tablespoon cream on top of each, and serve. About 40 calories

per serving without the cream,
95 calories with.

VARIATION:

⳾⳾ **Jellied Clear Beet Soup:** Heat
mixture as directed, strain, and set
aside. Omit cornstarch paste
and cream. Instead, heat 1 envelope
unflavored gelatin in ⅓ cup water
over moderate heat, stirring until
gelatin dissolves. Mix into soup,
add beets, cover, and chill until
thick and syrupy. Stir well, re-cover,
and chill until firm. Just before
serving, break up mixture with a
spoon. Ladle into chilled bowls
and top, if you like, with sour cream
and a sprinkling of minced chives
or dill. Garnish with lemon or
lime wedges. About 40 calories per
serving without sour cream. Add
30 calories per serving for each
tablespoon of sour cream topping
used.

⳾⳾ **FRENCH ONION SOUP**

If broth is pale, color a rich amber
brown with liquid gravy browner
or caramelized sugar.*
Makes 4 servings

½ pound Spanish or yellow onions,
  peeled and sliced paper thin
2 tablespoons butter (no substitute)
1 quart beef broth, bouillon, or
  consommé
⅛ teaspoon pepper

Stir-fry onions in butter in a large,
heavy saucepan over low heat
10–15 minutes until pale golden.
Add broth and pepper, cover, and
simmer 20–25 minutes, stirring
occasionally, until onions are very
tender. Taste for salt and add if
needed. Serve steaming hot with
French bread. About 110 calories
per serving.

VARIATION:

French Onion Soup Au Gratin:
Prepare soup as directed and, while

it simmers, preheat oven to 400° F.;
also lightly toast 4 slices French
bread. Ladle soup into 4 ovenproof
soup bowls (individual casseroles
or marmites are perfect), float
a piece of toast in each, and sprinkle
generously with grated Parmesan
cheese. Bake, uncovered, 5–7
minutes until cheese is lightly
browned and bread puffed up. Serve
at once. About 200 calories per
serving.

¢ ⳾⳾ **TURNIP SOUP**

Makes 4 servings

½ pound turnips, peeled and cut in
  small dice
1 small yellow onion, peeled and
  minced
2 cups chicken or beef broth
2 cups water
1 teaspoon salt
2 teaspoons Worcestershire sauce
1 teaspoon soy sauce
1 teaspoon minced chives
1 tablespoon slivered pimiento

Simmer all ingredients except
chives and pimiento in a covered
saucepan over moderately low heat
20–25 minutes. Stir in chives and
pimiento and serve. About 35
calories per serving.

VARIATIONS:

¢ ⳾⳾ **Rutabaga Soup:** Prepare as
directed, substituting 2 cups diced,
peeled rutabaga for turnip and
increasing cooking time slightly,
about 5–10 minutes. Same calories
as turnip soup.

¢ ⳾⳾ **Parsnip Soup:** Substitute
2 cups diced, peeled parsnips for
turnips and proceed as recipe
directs. Good with a little grated
Parmesan sprinkled on top. About
70 calories per serving.

⚔ ¢ GERMAN TAPIOCA SOUP

A good way to use up tag ends of chicken or turkey.
Makes 4 servings

½ *cup pearl or large pearl tapioca*
1 cup cold water
5 cups beef broth or bouillon
¼ *cup tomato purée*
1 bay leaf
¼ *cup slivered cooked chicken or turkey (preferably white meat)*

Soak tapioca in water at least 3 hours or overnight. Pour broth into a saucepan, add tapioca and any remaining soaking water, tomato purée, and bay leaf. Cover and simmer about 1 hour until tapioca is clear and no raw starch taste remains; check liquid occasionally and add a little extra water if too thick. Remove bay leaf, stir in chicken, heat 2–3 minutes longer, and serve. About 130 calories per serving.

DE LUXE CREAM OF VEGETABLE SOUP

Thickened with cream and egg, not flour.
Makes 4 servings

1½ cups diced raw vegetable (asparagus, celery, peas, broccoli, spinach, carrots, onion, cauliflower, zucchini, or mushrooms)
2 tablespoons butter (no substitute)
1 pint chicken broth
1 teaspoon finely grated onion
1 cup heavy cream
2 egg yolks, lightly beaten

Stir-fry vegetable in butter in a heavy saucepan over moderately low heat about 10 minutes until wilted, not brown. Add broth and onion, cover, and simmer 10–15 minutes until vegetable is very soft. Put through a food mill or purée in an electric blender at low speed. Pour into the top of a large double boiler and set over simmering water. Mix cream and egg yolks and stir into soup; heat, stirring constantly, until slightly thickened. Taste for salt and pepper and adjust as needed. Serve piping hot. From about 320–55 calories per serving, carrot and pea soups highest.

CREAM OF ALMOND SOUP

Serve hot or icy cold.
Makes 4 servings

1 stalk celery, minced
1 clove garlic, peeled and crushed
2 tablespoons butter or margarine
3 cups chicken broth
⅔ *cup finely ground blanched almonds*
⅛ *teaspoon mace*
1 cup heavy cream
1–2 tablespoons toasted, slivered almonds

Stir-fry celery and garlic in butter in a heavy saucepan 4–5 minutes over moderate heat until limp; add broth, ground almonds, and mace, cover, and simmer 30–40 minutes, stirring occasionally. Remove from heat and let stand at room temperature 1 hour. Purée in an electric blender at low speed or press through a fine sieve. Return mixture to saucepan, smooth in cream, and heat uncovered, stirring occasionally, 2–3 minutes; do not boil. Taste for salt and add if needed. Ladle into hot bowls, sprinkle with toasted almonds, and, if you like, dust with paprika. *Or* chill well and serve cold. About 440 calories per serving.

BASIC PROPORTIONS FOR CREAMED VEGETABLE SOUPS
(Makes 6 servings)

Variety	Butter	Flour	Liquid	Cooked Vegetable Purée	Salt	White Pepper	Optional Seasonings
Artichoke (globe and Jerusalem), asparagus, celery, endive	3 T.	3 T.	1 pint each milk and chicken or vegetable broth	2½ cups	1 t.	1/8 t.	Pinch each thyme and nutmeg and 1/4 cup dry white wine
Calories per serving: 150-60 for artichoke soup, 140-50 for asparagus, celery, or endive soup							
Broccoli, cauliflower, onion, leek, Brussels sprouts, cabbage, kale	3 T.	3 T.	1 pint each milk and beef, chicken, or vegetable broth	2 cups	1 t.	1/8 t.	Pinch each cardamom and mace and 1/4 cup grated mild Cheddar or Gruyère
About 110-20 calories per serving							
Carrot, green pea	2 T.	2 T.	1 pint each milk and chicken or vegetable broth	2 cups	1 t.	1/8 t.	1 t. grated orange rind, pinch rosemary, nutmeg, or savory or 1 T. minced fresh tarragon or chervil
Calories per serving: 120-30 for carrot soup, 135-45 for green pea soup							
Parsnip, turnip, rutabaga	2 T.	2 T.	1 pint each milk and beef or chicken broth	2 cups	1 t.	1/8 t.	Pinch each cinnamon, allspice and ginger
Calories per serving: about 160 for parsnip, 130 for turnip or rutabaga							
Potato, tomato	SEE SPECIAL RECIPES THAT FOLLOW						

Variety	Butter	Flour	Liquid	Cooked Vegetable Purée	Salt	White Pepper	Optional Seasonings
Spinach, cress, sorrel About 140 calories per serving	3 T.	3 T.	1 pint each milk and chicken broth	2½ cups	1 t.	1/8 t.	2 T. each grated onion and lemon juice or curry powder, pinch nutmeg
Summer squash About 170 calories per serving	3 T.	3 T.	3 cups milk and 1 cup beef or chicken broth	3 cups	1 t.	1/8 t.	1/4 cup minced onion, 1/4 t. each savory and oregano, pinch cinnamon or mace
Winter squash, sweet potato, pumpkin, yam Calories per serving: about 180 for pumpkin soup, 190 for winter squash, and 235 for yam or sweet potato	2 T.	1 T.	1 pint each milk and chicken broth	2 cups	1 t.	1/8 t.	1/4 cup each orange juice and honey, 1/4 t. each cinnamon, ginger, and cloves

METHOD: Melt butter in a large, heavy saucepan over moderate heat, blend in flour, add liquid, and heat, stirring, until mixture boils; turn heat to low, smooth in purée and seasonings, cover, and let mellow 5–10 minutes to blend flavors. Serve hot or chill and serve cold. (*Note:* For a silky-smooth soup, strain through a fine sieve, then heat to serving temperature or chill.)

VARIATIONS: In addition to the all-of-a-flavor soups above, many vegetables team well. To prepare, follow basic proportions above, using a 1/2 and 1/2 mixture of any of the following purées:

Carrot and Jerusalem artichoke

Carrot and celery

Carrot and green pea

Carrot and parsnip

Carrot and turnip

Carrot and rutabaga

Carrot and winter squash

Carrot and pumpkin

Carrot and sweet potato or yam

Celery and green pea

Celery and spinach

Celery and summer squash

Onion and carrot

Onion and green pea

Onion and spinach

Onion and celery

Onion and summer squash

Onion and pumpkin

⊠ QUICK ASPARAGUS SOUP

Makes 4 servings

1 (10-ounce) package frozen cut
  asparagus
⅓ cup boiling water
2 tablespoons butter or margarine
¾ teaspoon salt
Pinch white pepper
1 pint milk
1 tablespoon dry vermouth

Place asparagus, water, butter, salt,
and pepper in a small saucepan
and simmer uncovered, stirring
occasionally, 15–20 minutes until
asparagus is tender; purée, a little at
a time, in an electric blender at low
speed. Return to pan, add milk, and
heat 3–5 minutes, stirring occasionally. Stir in vermouth and serve
hot or chill and serve cold. About
150 calories per serving.

CREAM OF ASPARAGUS SOUP

Makes 6 servings

2 pounds asparagus, washed,
  trimmed, and cut in 2″ chunks
1 cup chicken broth
2 tablespoons butter or margarine
2 tablespoons flour
1 cup milk
1 cup heavy cream
1½ teaspoons salt (about)
⅛ teaspoon white pepper

Simmer asparagus, covered, in
chicken broth 10–15 minutes until
very tender. Note: If you want to
garnish soup with a few tips,
remove 10–12 when crisp tender
and reserve. Put asparagus and
liquid through a food mill or purée,
a little at a time, in an electric
blender at low speed. Melt butter
in saucepan over moderate heat,
blend in flour, add milk slowly,
stirring until smooth. Mix in purée
and cream and heat, stirring occasionally, until hot but not boiling.

Add salt to taste and pepper. Ladle
into bowls and, if you wish, garnish
with asparagus tips. About 240
calories per serving.

VARIATION:

Chilled Cream of Asparagus Soup:
Use 2½ pounds asparagus to make
purée and 1 pint light cream instead
of milk and heavy cream. Prepare
as directed, cool, cover, and chill
2–3 hours. Taste for salt and pepper
and adjust as needed before serving. About 245 calories per serving.

⊠ CURRIED AVOCADO SOUP

Makes 6 servings

2 (10½-ounce) cans condensed
  chicken broth
1 teaspoon grated onion
¼ garlic clove, peeled and crushed
2 teaspoons curry powder
2 ripe medium-size avocados
2 teaspoons lemon juice
1 cup milk or light cream

Simmer broth, onion, garlic and
curry powder uncovered in a small
saucepan 8–10 minutes. Halve
avocados lengthwise, remove pits,
scoop out flesh, and purée in electric
blender at low speed with lemon
juice and 1 cup hot broth. Add to
broth in pan, stir in milk, and heat,
stirring occasionally, 2–3 minutes.
Serve hot or chill and serve cold.
About 225 calories per serving if
made with light cream, 175 per serving if made with milk.

CREAMY CARROT SOUP

Delicately seasoned with cloves and
rosemary.
Makes 4–6 servings

6–8 medium-size carrots, peeled and
  cut in 2″ chunks
2 medium-size yellow onions, peeled
  and quartered
2 sprigs parsley

3 whole cloves
¼ teaspoon rosemary
2 (10½-ounce) cans condensed
  chicken broth
1 pint milk
⅛ teaspoon pepper
2 tablespoons minced parsley

Place carrots, onions, parsley, cloves,
rosemary and chicken broth in a
saucepan, cover, and simmer 45–50
minutes until carrots are very
soft; remove cloves and parsley and
discard. Put mixture through a
food mill or purée, a little at a time,
in an electric blender at low
speed. Return to pan, stir in milk
and pepper, and heat, stirring, 2–3
minutes. Serve hot or chill and serve
cold. Garnish each portion with
a little minced parsley. About 155
calories for each of 4 servings, 105
for each of 6.

CHESTNUT SOUP

In the Pyrenees chestnut soup is
sometimes enriched with leftover
scraps of game bird; use it if you
have it, or bits of turkey, goose,
duck, or chicken.
Makes 6 servings

1 medium-size yellow onion, peeled
  and minced
1 stalk celery, minced
2 tablespoons butter or margarine
1 tablespoon flour
1 pint chicken broth or water
1 pound shelled, peeled chestnuts
6 cups milk
1 cup heavy cream
½–¾ cup minced, cooked chicken,
  goose, turkey, duck, or game bird
  (optional)
1½ teaspoons salt
⅛ teaspoon white pepper
⅛ teaspoon mace
⅓ cup croutons

Stir-fry onion and celery in butter
in a large, heavy saucepan over

moderately low heat 5–8 minutes
until pale golden. Sprinkle with
flour, mix well, then slowly stir in
broth. Add chestnuts, cover, and
simmer about ½ hour until very
soft. Put through a food mill or
purée in an electric blender at low
speed; return to pan and set over
moderate heat. Add all remaining
ingredients except croutons and
heat, stirring, about 5 minutes; do
not allow to boil. Taste for salt and
adjust; ladle into soup bowls and
pass croutons separately. (Note:
This soup will be mellower if made
the day before and reheated in
the top of a double boiler.) About
515 calories per serving if made with
chicken broth, 500 per serving if
made with water. Add 25 calories
per serving if optional poultry meat
is used.

⊠ CREAM OF CORN SOUP

Makes 6 servings

1 small yellow onion, peeled and
  minced
3 tablespoons bacon drippings
1 (10-ounce) package frozen whole
  kernel corn, thawed and chopped
  fine, or 1 can (1 pound) whole
  kernel corn, drained and chopped
  fine
2 tablespoons minced celery leaves
3 tablespoons flour
1 pint milk
1 cup light cream
1½ teaspoons salt (about)
Pinch pepper
Paprika

Stir-fry onion in drippings in a
large saucepan over moderate heat
8–10 minutes until golden. Mix
in corn and celery leaves and stir-fry
3–5 minutes. Blend in flour, add
milk and cream, and heat, stirring
constantly, until thickened and
smooth. Add salt to taste and pepper.

Serve piping hot, topped with a blush of paprika. About 250 calories per serving.

CUCUMBER VELOUTÉ

Makes 4–6 servings

6 tablespoons butter or margarine
2 medium-size yellow onions, peeled and coarsely chopped
3 medium-size cucumbers, peeled, seeded, and diced
1 teaspoon salt
⅛ teaspoon white pepper
Pinch mace
2 (13¾-ounce) cans chicken broth
2 tablespoons flour
2 egg yolks, lightly beaten
1 cup light cream
2 tablespoons minced parsley

Melt 4 tablespoons butter in a large skillet over moderate heat, add onions and cucumbers, and sauté, stirring, 8–10 minutes until onions are golden. Stir in salt, pepper, mace, and broth, cover, and simmer 15 minutes until vegetables are soft. Put through a food mill or purée, a bit at a time, in an electric blender at low speed. In a large saucepan, melt remaining butter over moderate heat. Blend in flour, add purée, and heat, stirring constantly, until thickened and smooth. Spoon a little hot mixture into yolks, then return all to saucepan. Mix in cream, reduce heat to lowest point, and warm 1–2 minutes longer, stirring; do not boil. Serve hot or cold garnished with minced parsley. About 395 calories for each of 4 servings, 265 for each of 6.

DELUXE CREAM OF MUSH-ROOM SOUP

Makes 4 servings

¾ pound mushrooms, wiped clean and minced
2 tablespoons butter (no substitute)

1 tablespoon cornstarch
1½ cups chicken broth
1½ cups light cream
½ teaspoon salt (about)
⅛ teaspoon white pepper
1 teaspoon Worcestershire sauce

Stir-fry mushrooms in butter in a heavy saucepan over low heat 5–7 minutes until limp; blend in cornstarch, add broth, and heat, stirring, 3–4 minutes. Cover and simmer over lowest heat 12–15 minutes, stirring occasionally. Purée half the mixture in an electric blender at low speed or put through a food mill; return to pan. Add remaining ingredients and heat, stirring, 2–3 minutes. Taste for salt and adjust as needed. About 285 calories per serving.

VARIATION:

⚖ Low-Calorie Cream of Mushroom Soup: Omit butter and cornstarch; simmer mushrooms in broth, then proceed as recipe directs, substituting skim milk for cream. About 40 calories per serving.

⚖ POTAGE SAINT-GERMAIN

This soup should be made with fresh young peas, but if they're unavailable, use the frozen. Restaurants sometimes use dried split peas—very good but not authentic. Makes 4 servings

2 cups cooked green peas, drained
2 cups White Stock or a ½ and ½ mixture of water and beef bouillon
½ teaspoon minced fresh chervil or ¼ teaspoon dried chervil
1 tablespoon butter (no substitute)
¼ cup croutons

Set aside 1 tablespoon peas; put the rest through a food mill or purée in an electric blender at high speed, adding a little stock if necessary. Mix purée and stock and strain through a fine sieve, pressing solids to extract as much liquid as possible. Pour into a saucepan, add chervil and butter, and heat, stirring now and then, about 5 minutes until a good serving temperature. Taste for seasoning and adjust as needed. Stir in reserved peas, ladle into bowls, and sprinkle with croutons. About 115 calories per serving.

BOULA-BOULA

Makes 4 servings

2 cups fresh or frozen green peas
1 cup boiling water
½ teaspoon salt
2 cups clear turtle soup
¼ cup medium-dry sherry
⅓ cup heavy cream

Simmer peas in water with salt about 8 minutes until tender; put through a food mill or purée in an electric blender at low speed; press through a fine sieve. Return to pan, add turtle soup and sherry, and heat slowly, stirring occasionally, 5 minutes. Meanwhile, preheat broiler; also whip cream until soft peaks will form. Place 4 ovenproof soup bowls or *marmites* on a baking sheet, fill with soup, and top with whipped cream. Broil 4″ from heat about 1 minute until flecked with brown. Serve at once. About 155 calories per serving.

VARIATION:

⊠ **Quick Boula-Boula:** Heat together 1 (10½-ounce) can condensed cream of pea soup, 1 soup can water, 1 (12-ounce) can turtle soup, and ¼ cup medium-dry sherry, stirring now and then, until piping hot. Ladle into bowls, top with drifts of sour cream, and serve. About 145 calories per serving.

⊠ CREAMY PEANUT SOUP

A fragrant soup that makes a nice change of pace.
Makes 6 servings

2 tablespoons butter or margarine
2 tablespoons flour
1 teaspoon salt
¼ teaspoon cayenne pepper
Pinch nutmeg
1 pint milk
1 pint light cream
1 cup creamy peanut butter
¼ cup tawny port or dry sherry

Melt butter in a large saucepan over moderate heat, blend in flour and seasonings, add milk and cream, and heat, stirring constantly, until thickened and smooth. Add peanut butter and continue to heat, stirring, until melted. Mix in wine and serve. About 525 calories per serving.

VICHYSSOISE I

Deliciously bland and silky.
Makes 6 servings

2 tablespoons butter or margarine
3 large leeks, washed, trimmed, and sliced thin
2 scallions, washed, trimmed, and sliced thin
1 small yellow onion, peeled and sliced thin
1 pound potatoes, peeled and sliced thin
2½ cups chicken broth
1½ teaspoons salt
Pinch white pepper
1 pint heavy cream
2 tablespoons minced fresh chives

Melt butter in a large kettle over moderate heat, add leeks, scallions, and onion, and sauté, stirring, 8–10 minutes until golden. Stir in all remaining ingredients except heavy cream and chives, cover, and simmer 45 minutes until vegetables are mushy; press all through a fine sieve. Return to kettle, add heavy cream, and heat and stir just until mixture boils. Remove from heat and put through sieve once again. Cool to room temperature, cover, and chill several hours. Serve very cold, topped with chives. About 415 calories per serving.

VICHYSSOISE II

Sour cream gives this vichyssoise a certain zing. It's not quite as calorie-laden as Vichyssoise I.
Makes 8 servings

1/4 cup unsalted butter
5 large leeks, washed, trimmed, and
    sliced thin
2 medium-size yellow onions, peeled
    and sliced thin
2 pounds Irish potatoes (Maine or
    Eastern are best), washed, peeled,
    and sliced thin
1 (10½-ounce) can condensed
    chicken broth
1 (10½-ounce) can condensed beef
    consommé
2 cups water
2 teaspoons salt
1 pint milk
1 pint light cream
1 cup sour cream
1/4 cup minced fresh chives

Melt butter in a large kettle over moderate heat, add leeks and onions, and sauté, stirring, 8–10 minutes until golden. Add potatoes and stir-fry 2–3 minutes. Stir in broth, consommé, water and salt, cover, and simmer 45–50 minutes until vegetables are mushy. Remove from heat and press all through a fine sieve. Return purée to kettle, add milk and light cream, and heat, stirring, until mixture just boils. Remove from heat, cool slightly, then smooth in sour cream. Put through sieve once again. Cool to room temperature, cover, and chill several hours. Serve very cold with a sprinkling of minced chives. About 385 calories per serving.

PUMPKIN SOUP

Makes 4–6 servings

1½ cups pumpkin purée
3 cups chicken broth
1 tablespoon flour
1 teaspoon salt
1/4 teaspoon ginger
1/4 teaspoon nutmeg
3/4 cup milk or light cream
1 teaspoon minced chives
2 egg yolks, lightly beaten

Heat pumpkin and chicken broth in top of a double boiler over direct heat to a simmer. Blend flour, salt, ginger, and nutmeg with 1/4 cup milk, mix into pumpkin, and heat, stirring, 3–4 minutes. Cover, set over simmering water, and cook 20 minutes, stirring occasionally; mix in chives. Beat egg yolks lightly with remaining milk, add to soup, cook, and stir 5 minutes over simmering water, then serve. (Note: The flavor of this soup improves on standing. Just be sure to reheat slowly in the top of a double boiler and to stir well.) Depending upon whether soup is made with milk or light cream, 130–195 calories for each of 4 servings, 90–130 for each of 6.

SORREL-CRESS SOUP

Serve icy cold as a refreshing first course.
Makes 6 servings

1 medium-size yellow onion, peeled
    and minced
1/4 cup butter or margarine
1/3 cup minced sorrel
1 cup minced watercress
3 tablespoons flour

1 cup light cream
1 (10½-ounce) can condensed
    chicken broth
1 pint milk
3 eggs, lightly beaten
1½ teaspoons salt
⅛ teaspoon white pepper

Stir-fry onion in 2 tablespoons butter in a small skillet over moderate heat 8–10 minutes until golden. Off heat, stir in sorrel and watercress. Melt remaining butter in a saucepan over moderate heat and blend in flour. Add cream, chicken broth, and 1 cup milk and heat, stirring constantly, until thickened and smooth. Mix a little hot sauce into eggs, pour into pan, and heat and stir 1 minute; remove from heat. Purée onion-sorrel mixture with remaining milk in an electric blender at high speed, then stir into hot mixture. Season with salt and pepper, cool to room temperature, cover, and chill several hours before serving. About 285 calories per serving.

¢ ⚖ ☒ QUICK CREAM OF TOMATO SOUP

Makes 6 servings

⅓ cup minced yellow onion
2 tablespoons butter or margarine
2 tablespoons flour
½ teaspoon basil
½ teaspoon oregano
1¼ teaspoons salt
⅛ teaspoon pepper
1 tablespoon tomato paste
1 tablespoon light brown sugar
1 (10½-ounce) can condensed beef
    consommé
1 cup milk
1 (1-pound 12-ounce) can tomatoes
    (do not drain)

Stir-fry onion in butter in a large heavy saucepan 3–5 minutes until limp, blend in flour, herbs, salt, and pepper, then stir in tomato paste, light brown sugar, consommé, and milk and heat, stirring constantly, until thickened and smooth. Put tomatoes through a food mill or purée, a little at a time, in an electric blender at low speed; add to pan and simmer, uncovered, 12–15 minutes—do not allow to boil. Ladle into soup bowls and serve piping hot. About 130 calories per serving.

MUSHROOM-TOMATO BISQUE

Makes 6 servings

½ pound mushrooms, wiped clean
    and minced
4 tablespoons butter or margarine
1 cup chicken broth
1 (1-pound 12-ounce) can tomatoes
    (do not drain)
1 small yellow onion, peeled and
    minced
2 tablespoons sugar
1 clove garlic, peeled and crushed
¼ teaspoon white pepper
2 tablespoons flour
1 cup heavy cream
2 teaspoons salt
Pinch baking soda

Stir-fry mushrooms in 2 tablespoons butter in a large saucepan over moderately high heat 2–3 minutes until golden; add broth, cover, and simmer 15 minutes. Put through a food mill or purée in an electric blender at low speed; set aside. Put tomatoes, onion, sugar, garlic, and pepper in the same saucepan, cover, and simmer ½ hour; purée, a little at a time, in an electric blender at low speed, then strain through a fine sieve and reserve. Melt remaining butter in the top of a double boiler over direct heat, blend in flour, then mix in cream and cook, stirring, until smooth and thickened. Set over simmering water, add mushroom and tomato purées, salt and soda, and heat, stirring, about 5 minutes. About 285 calories per serving.

☒ COLD CLAM BISQUE

Makes 6 servings

2 (8-ounce) cans minced clams (do not drain)
1 pint light cream
1 teaspoon Worcestershire sauce
⅛ teaspoon liquid hot red pepper seasoning
¼ teaspoon salt (about)
1 tablespoon minced chives

Purée clams with their liquid in an electric blender at high speed until smooth. Add ½ the cream, the Worcestershire sauce, and liquid hot red pepper seasoning and buzz about 5 seconds at low speed to blend. Pour into a large bowl, add remaining cream, and salt to taste. Chill 2–3 hours and serve sprinkled with chives. About 210 calories per serving.

SHELLFISH BISQUE

Makes 6 servings

¼ cup minced yellow onion
¼ cup minced carrot
3 tablespoons butter or margarine
1 pound cooked lobster, shrimp, or crab meat, well picked over and minced
⅓ cup dry white wine
2 cups water, Easy Fish Stock, or Rich Court Bouillon
1 pint heavy cream
2 egg yolks, lightly beaten
½ teaspoon salt (about)
⅛ teaspoon white pepper
¼ cup medium-dry sherry or brandy (optional)

Stir-fry onion and carrot in butter in a heavy saucepan over moderately low heat 5 minutes until onion is limp; add shellfish and stir-fry 2–3 minutes. Add wine and water, cover, and simmer 10 minutes. Remove from heat and let stand ½ hour to blend flavors. Put mixture through a food mill or purée in an electric blender at low speed. Pour into the top of a large double boiler, set over simmering water, add cream and heat, stirring, 5 minutes. Mix a little hot bisque into yolks, return to pan, and heat, stirring constantly, until no raw taste of egg remains. Add seasonings and, if you like, sherry; taste for salt and adjust if needed. Serve hot or chill and serve cold. (*Note:* For a pretty garnish, reserve about ¼ of the minced shellfish and scatter over each portion.) About 330 calories per serving without optional sherry or brandy. Add 10 calories per serving if sherry is used, about 25 calories per serving if brandy is used.

BILLI-BI

A delicate mussel soup delicious hot or cold.
Makes 4 servings

5 dozen mussels in the shell, prepared for cooking*
2 medium-size yellow onions, peeled and minced
2 stalks celery, minced
½ pound mushrooms, wiped clean and minced (include stems)
¼ cup minced parsley
⅛ teaspoon pepper
2½ cups water or 2 cups water and ½ cup Easy Fish Stock
1 cup dry white wine
1 cup light cream

Place mussels in a large, heavy kettle with all but last ingredient, cover, bring to a boil over moderate heat, then reduce heat and simmer 3 minutes until mussels open. With a slotted spoon lift out mussels and reserve to serve as a separate course or at another meal. Strain cooking liquid through a fine sieve lined with a triple thickness of cheesecloth, pour into a clean saucepan, and boil rapidly, uncovered, until reduced by about half. Turn heat to low, stir in cream, and heat and stir until piping hot. Taste for salt, adjust as needed and serve. Or chill well and serve cold. About 215 calories per serving.

⊠ CREAM OF CHICKEN OR TURKEY SOUP

Makes 4 servings

1 quart chicken or turkey broth
1 cup heavy cream
¼ teaspoon salt (about)
⅛ teaspoon white pepper
⅛ teaspoon nutmeg or mace
1 tablespoon minced parsley or chives

Bring broth to a simmer and slowly mix in cream. Add salt to taste, pepper, and nutmeg. Cover and let mellow over lowest heat about 10 minutes. Serve hot or icy cold, topped with minced parsley. About 250 calories per serving.

VARIATIONS:

⊠ **Potage à la Reine:** Prepare cream soup as directed, using chicken broth. Ladle into bowls but do not scatter with parsley. Instead, float about ¼ cup julienne strips of cooked white chicken meat in each bowl. About 280 calories per serving.

⊠ **Chicken or Turkey Velouté:** Melt 4 tablespoons butter in a large, heavy saucepan and blend in 4 tablespoons flour. Add broth and cream and heat, stirring constantly, until thickened and smooth; mix in all seasonings. Blend a little hot soup into 3 lightly beaten

egg yolks, return to saucepan, set over lowest heat, and warm, stirring constantly, 1–2 minutes until no raw taste of egg remains; do not allow to boil. Serve hot topped with minced parsley. About 430 calories per serving.

⚄⚄ AVGOLEMONO SOUP (GREEK CHICKEN-LEMON SOUP)

Makes 4 servings

1 quart chicken broth
¼ cup uncooked rice
Pinch mace or nutmeg
3 egg yolks
Juice of 1 lemon
Salt
Pepper

Place broth, rice, and mace in a large saucepan, cover, and simmer 25–30 minutes until rice is very tender. Beat yolks with lemon juice; spoon a little hot broth into egg mixture, return to pan, and heat over lowest heat 1–2 minutes, stirring constantly, until no taste of raw egg remains; do not boil. Taste for salt and pepper and season as needed. About 130 calories per serving.

SENEGALESE SOUP

A cream of chicken soup spiked with curry and chutney.
Makes 4 servings

2 tablespoons butter or margarine
2 tablespoons flour
1 tablespoon curry powder
2 (13¾-ounce) cans chicken broth
2 tablespoons minced chutney
1 cup julienne strips of cooked chicken (preferably white meat)
2 egg yolks lightly beaten with ½ cup heavy cream
4 teaspoons minced chives

Melt butter in a heavy saucepan

over moderate heat, blend in
flour and curry powder, add broth,
and heat, stirring, until mixture
boils. Reduce heat, add chutney
and chicken, and heat, stirring now
and then, 5–10 minutes to blend
flavors. Spoon a little hot broth
into egg mixture, pour into pan, set
over lowest heat, and cook,
stirring constantly, 1–2 minutes until
no taste of raw egg remains; do
not boil. Ladle into soup bowls,
sprinkle with chives, and serve.
About 310 calories per serving.

CHEDDAR CHEESE SOUP

Makes 6 servings

2 tablespoons butter or margarine
2 tablespoons flour
6 cups milk
1 clove garlic, peeled and bruised
  (optional)
1½ cups coarsely grated sharp
  Cheddar cheese
1 cup dry white wine or water
2 egg yolks, lightly beaten
¼ cup heavy cream
1 teaspoon salt (about)
⅛ teaspoon white pepper
Pinch nutmeg
⅓ cup finely grated mild Cheddar
  cheese

Melt butter in the top of a double
boiler set over simmering water.
Blend in flour, then slowly stir
in milk; add garlic if you wish. Heat
uncovered, stirring frequently,
10 minutes; mix in cheese and stir
until melted; add wine. Mix
egg yolks and cream, stir a little
hot mixture into yolks, return
to pan, and heat, stirring constantly,
until no raw taste of egg remains.
Remove garlic, mix in salt, pepper,
and nutmeg, taste for salt and
adjust as needed. Ladle into
bowls, sprinkle with the mild

Cheddar and serve. About 390
calories per serving if made with
wine, about 360 per serving
if made with water.

¢ OXTAIL SOUP

Makes 6 servings

2 pounds oxtail, cut in 1"–1½"
  chunks and trimmed of excess fat
½ cup unsifted flour plus 2
  tablespoons
2 tablespoons beef drippings or
  cooking oil
2 medium-size yellow onions, peeled
  and minced
2 quarts water, or 6 cups water and 1
  pint beef broth or bouillon
2 tablespoons ketchup
2 teaspoons salt
¼ teaspoon pepper
1 bay leaf
½ teaspoon thyme
3 cloves
2 sprigs parsley
2 medium-size carrots, peeled and
  diced
1 stalk celery, diced
⅓ cup dry sherry or port wine
  (optional)

Dredge oxtail in ½ cup flour, then
brown in drippings in a large,
heavy kettle over high heat; drain on
paper toweling. Turn heat to
moderate and stir-fry onions 8–10
minutes until golden; sprinkle in remaining flour, mix well, and
brown lightly. Slowly add water,
stir in ketchup, salt, and pepper, also
bay leaf tied in cheesecloth with
thyme, cloves, and parsley. Return
oxtail to kettle, cover, and simmer
3 hours until meat is fork tender;
cool and skim off fat; remove
cheesecloth bag. Separate meat
from bones, cut in bite-size pieces,
and return to kettle along with
carrots and celery. Cover and

simmer 10–15 minutes until carrots are tender; if you like, mix in sherry. Serve as is *or* strain kettle liquid, serve as a first course, and follow with oxtail and vegetables. About 310–320 calories per serving depending upon whether made with water only or with broth and water. Add about 15 calories per serving if optional wine is used.

VARIATION:

¢ **Clear Oxtail Soup:** Prepare as directed, browning oxtail without dredging and omitting all flour and ketchup from recipe. About 50 calories *less* per serving than oxtail soup.

¢ SCOTCH BROTH

Makes 6–8 servings

2 pounds lean neck of mutton or lamb (with bones), cut in 2" chunks
2 medium-size yellow onions, peeled and minced
2 cups diced, peeled carrots
½ medium-size rutabaga, peeled and cut in small dice
2 leeks or 4 scallions, washed, trimmed, and coarsely chopped
½ cup medium pearl barley
1 gallon water
1 tablespoon salt (about)
¼ teaspoon pepper
2 tablespoons minced parsley

Place all ingredients except parsley in a large kettle, cover, and bring to a boil. Skim froth from surface, reduce heat, cover, and simmer 2–2½ hours, stirring now and then, until lamb is tender. Cut meat from bones in small pieces, if you like, and return to kettle or leave meat on bones. Stir, taste for salt and adjust as needed. Sprinkle with parsley and serve in deep bowls. About 415 calories for each of 6 servings, 315 for each of 8.

RUSSIAN BORSCH

Makes 6–8 servings

3½ quarts water
2 pounds beef shank bone with some meat attached
½ pound ham hock
1 pound lean pork shoulder in 1 piece
2 bay leaves, crumbled
8 peppercorns
4 sprigs parsley
2 carrots, peeled and cut in 1" chunks
2 leeks, washed, trimmed, and cut in 2" chunks
2 stalks celery, cut in 2" chunks
2 pounds beets, washed, trimmed, and peeled
1 pound yellow onions, peeled and cut in thin wedges
3 cloves garlic, peeled and crushed
1 (6-ounce) can tomato paste
¼ cup white wine vinegar
1 tablespoon salt
¼ teaspoon pepper
2 cups thickly sliced cabbage
1 cup sour cream
¼ cup minced fresh dill

Place water, bones and meat, bay leaves, peppercorns, parsley, carrots, leeks, and celery in a large, heavy kettle, cover, and simmer, stirring occasionally, 3–3½ hours until meats almost fall from bones. Trim meat from bones and cut in bite-size pieces; set aside. Strain broth, discarding vegetables and seasonings, then chill several hours until fat rises to top and hardens; lift off fat and discard. Thinly slice all beets but 1, grate it, mix with ½ cup cold water, and reserve. Return strained broth to kettle, add sliced beets, onions, garlic, tomato paste, vinegar, salt, and pepper, cover, and simmer, stirring occasionally, 2 hours. Add reserved meat, cabbage, grated beet, and beet water and simmer, covered, 15–20 minutes until cabbage is crisp tender. Ladle into large soup bowls, top each serving with a float of sour cream, and sprinkle with dill. About 585 calories for each of 6 servings, 440 for each of 8.

¢ ⚔ ☒ **QUICK BORSCH**

Although no quick borsch can match the old-fashioned variety that simmers long and slow on the back of the stove, this one comes close. It contains less than one-fourth the calories of Russian borsch.
Makes 6 servings

2 tablespoons butter or margarine
1 medium-size yellow onion, peeled and sliced thin
1½ cups finely sliced cabbage
2 (10½-ounce) cans condensed beef consommé
4 (8-ounce) cans julienne beets (do not drain)
2 tablespoons tarragon vinegar
1 tablespoon tomato paste
½ teaspoon salt
Pinch pepper
¼ cup sour cream
2 tablespoons minced fresh dill or parsley

Melt butter in a large saucepan over moderately high heat, add onion and cabbage, and sauté, stirring occasionally, 8–10 minutes until cabbage is nearly tender. Add consommé and ½ the beets; purée remaining beets in an electric blender at low speed and add to pan along with vinegar, tomato paste, salt, and pepper. Simmer, uncovered, 15 minutes. Ladle about ½ cup borsch liquid into a small bowl

and blend in sour cream; return to pan and smooth into borsch. Ladle into large, flat soup bowls and serve hot with a sprinkling of minced fresh dill or chill well and serve cold. About 140 calories per serving.

⚔ ☒ **COCKALEEKIE**

This old Scottish cock and leek soup used to be rich as a stew. Today you're more apt to be served the following version—with or without prunes.
Makes 4 servings

1 pound leeks, washed, trimmed, halved lengthwise, and sliced ⅛″ thick (include some green tops)
1 tablespoon butter or margarine
1 quart chicken broth
½ teaspoon salt
⅛ teaspoon pepper
½ cup diced, cooked chicken meat
4–6 whole or coarsely chopped pitted prunes (optional)
1 teaspoon minced parsley

Stir-fry leeks in butter in a saucepan over moderately low heat 2–3 minutes. Add all remaining ingredients except parsley, cover, and simmer 10 minutes. Sprinkle with parsley and serve. About 100 calories per serving without the optional prunes, 132 calories per serving with the prunes.

WATERZOOIE (BELGIAN CHICKEN SOUP)

Extra rich!
Makes 8 servings

1 (6–7-pound) hen or capon, cleaned and dressed

¼ cup unsalted butter, softened to
  room temperature
5 large leeks, washed, trimmed, and
  cut in large chunks
5 large stalks celery, cut in large
  chunks (include tops)
2 large carrots, peeled and cut in
  large chunks
2 medium-size yellow onions, each
  peeled and stuck with 2 cloves
6 sprigs parsley
½ teaspoon thyme
¼ teaspoon nutmeg
6 peppercorns
1 bay leaf, crumbled
2 quarts chicken broth
1 cup dry white wine (optional)
4 egg yolks lightly beaten with ¾ cup
  heavy cream
1 lemon, sliced thin
2 tablespoons minced parsley

Preheat broiler. Rub chicken well
with butter and broil 4"–5" from
heat, turning often, about 20 minutes
until lightly browned. Transfer
chicken to a large, heavy kettle,
add giblets and all but last 3
ingredients, cover, and simmer
1–1½ hours until chicken is tender.
Lift chicken and giblets from
broth, cool until easy to handle,
peel off skin and discard; separate
meat from bones and cut in large
chunks; mince giblets. Meanwhile,
continue simmering vegetables, covered, in broth. When chicken is cut
up, strain broth and skim off fat.
Return broth to kettle, add cut-up
chicken and giblets, cover, and heat
5 minutes. Mix a little hot broth
into yolk mixture, return to kettle,
and warm over lowest heat 2–3 minutes; do not boil. Ladle into
soup bowls, top each portion with
a lemon slice and scattering of
parsley and serve. About 870
calories per serving without optional

wine, about 885 per serving if
wine is used.

MULLIGATAWNY SOUP

A curried chicken and tomato soup.
Makes 6 servings

3 tablespoons butter or margarine
1 small yellow onion, peeled and
  minced
1 medium-size carrot, peeled and
  diced fine
1 stalk celery, diced fine
½ green pepper, cored, seeded, and
  minced
¼ cup unsifted flour
1 tablespoon curry powder
¼ teaspoon nutmeg
3 cloves
2 sprigs parsley
1 quart chicken broth
1 teaspoon salt
⅛ teaspoon pepper
1 cup chopped tomatoes
1 cup cooked, diced chicken
½ cup heavy cream
1 cup boiled rice

Melt butter in a large saucepan,
add onion, carrot, celery, and green
pepper, and stir-fry 8–10 minutes
until onion is golden. Blend in
flour, curry powder, and nutmeg;
add cloves, parsley, broth, salt,
pepper, and tomatoes, cover,
and simmer 1 hour. Strain broth;
pick out and discard cloves and
parsley; purée vegetables in an
electric blender at low speed or put
through a food mill. Smooth
purée into broth, return to heat,
add chicken and cream, and heat,
stirring, 5–10 minutes to blend
flavors. Add rice, heat and stir
2–3 minutes longer, then serve.
About 285 calories per serving.

NEW ENGLAND CLAM CHOWDER

Makes 6 servings

1 pint shucked clams, drained
(reserve liquid)
1/3 cup diced salt pork
1 medium-size yellow onion, peeled
and minced
2 cups diced, peeled potatoes
1/2 cup water
2 cups milk
1 cup light cream
1 teaspoon salt (about)
1/8 teaspoon white pepper
1/8 teaspoon paprika

Pick over clams, removing any shell fragments; leave whole or, if you prefer, mince or grind medium fine. Lightly brown salt pork in a large, heavy saucepan over moderate heat, lift out, and reserve. Stir-fry onion in drippings 5–8 minutes until pale golden, add potatoes, water, clam liquid, and salt pork. Cover and simmer 10–12 minutes until potatoes are nearly tender, stirring occasionally. Add clams, milk, cream, salt, and pepper, cover, and simmer 5 minutes to heat through; do not boil. Ladle into hot bowls, dust with paprika, and serve. About 310 calories per serving.

⊠ QUICK NEW ENGLAND-STYLE CLAM CHOWDER

Makes 6–8 servings

2 small yellow onions, peeled and
minced
3 tablespoons butter or margarine
2 (10½-ounce) cans minced clams
(do not drain)
2 cups diced, peeled potatoes
1 teaspoon salt

1/8 teaspoon white pepper
2 cups milk
1 cup light cream
1/4 teaspoon paprika

Stir-fry onions in 2 tablespoons butter in a large saucepan over moderate heat 5–8 minutes until pale golden. Drain liquid from canned clams into pan, add potatoes, salt, and pepper, cover, and simmer 10–12 minutes until potatoes are nearly tender, stirring occasionally. Add clams, milk, and cream, cover, and simmer 5–7 minutes just to heat through. Add remaining butter, stir until melted. Ladle into hot soup bowls, sprinkle with paprika, and serve with hard rolls or crisp crackers. About 300 calories for each of 6 servings, 225 for each of 8.

¢ NEW ENGLAND FISH CHOWDER

Makes 4 servings

3 tablespoons butter (no substitute)
1 medium-size yellow onion, peeled
and minced
3 medium-size Irish potatoes, peeled
and cut in 1/4" cubes
1/2 cup hot water
1 pound haddock or cod fillets
2 cups milk
1 teaspoon salt
1/8 teaspoon white pepper
Paprika (garnish)

Melt 2 tablespoons butter in a large, heavy saucepan over low heat. Add onion and sauté 8–10 minutes, until golden, not brown. Add potatoes and water, cover, and simmer 10 minutes; add fish, cover, and simmer 10 minutes longer. (Note: Adjust burner so mixture simmers; if it boils, fish may overcook and become watery.) Off heat, flake fish with a fork, add milk, salt, and pepper; cover and let stand 1 hour at room temperature to blend flavors. Reheat slowly, stirring frequently, about 10 minutes. *Do not allow to boil.* Ladle into soup bowls, sprinkle lightly with paprika, and dot with remaining butter. Serve with oyster crackers or hot crusty bread. About 365 calories per serving.

VARIATION:

For extra richness, substitute ½ cup light or heavy cream for ½ cup of the milk. About 410 or 450 calories per serving, depending upon whether light or heavy cream is used.

⬧ MANHATTAN CLAM CHOWDER

Manhattan-style clam chowder may contain sweet green pepper and/or corn, but it *always* contains tomatoes. New England Clam chowder never does.
Makes 8 servings

1 medium-size yellow onion, peeled and minced
2 tablespoons butter, margarine, or bacon drippings
1½ cups diced, peeled carrots
½ cup diced celery
2 cups diced, peeled potatoes
1 (1-pound 12-ounce) can tomatoes (do not drain)
2 cups water or Easy Fish Stock
1½ teaspoons salt
⅛ teaspoon pepper
1 pint minced fresh or canned clams, drained (reserve liquid)
Drained clam liquid + enough bottled clam juice to total 1 pint

1 tablespoon minced parsley

Stir-fry onion in butter in a large, heavy kettle over moderate heat 5–8 minutes until pale golden. Add remaining vegetables (breaking up the tomatoes), water, salt, and pepper. Cover and simmer 15 minutes. Off heat, add clams and clam liquid, cover, and let stand ½ hour to blend flavors. Return to heat and simmer about 5 minutes, sprinkle with parsley, and serve. About 140 calories per serving.

VARIATION:

Prepare as directed, reducing carrots to 1 cup and adding ½–¾ cup diced, seeded, cored sweet green pepper or whole kernel corn. About 140 calories per serving if made with green pepper, 150 per serving if made with corn.

⬧ ⊠ 10-MINUTE MANHATTAN-STYLE CLAM CHOWDER

Not only quick but low-calorie, too.
Makes 4 servings

1 (10½-ounce) can minced clams (do not drain)
1 (10¾-ounce) can condensed vegetable soup
1 soup can cold water
½ teaspoon celery flakes
⅛ teaspoon thyme

Drain clam liquid into a large saucepan; set clams aside. Add all remaining ingredients except clams, cover and simmer 5 minutes. Stir well, add clams, and heat, uncovered, 1–2 minutes, stirring occasionally. Ladle into hot soup bowls and serve with chowder crackers. About 85 calories per serving.

MATELOTE (FISH STEW WITH WINE)

Matelotes are usually made with fresh water fish—except in Normandy.
Makes 6 servings

¾ pound small white onions, peeled
2 tablespoons olive or other cooking oil
½ pound mushrooms, sliced thin
2 cloves garlic, peeled and crushed
1 bouquet garni,* tied in cheesecloth
Pinch nutmeg
Pinch cinnamon
1 teaspoon salt (about)
¼ teaspoon pepper
1 quart dry red or white wine
2 cups Easy Fish Stock
1 pound carp, pike, or other lean fresh water fish, cleaned, dressed, and cut in 2" chunks
1 pound catfish or whitefish, cleaned, dressed, and cut in 2" chunks
1 pound eel, skinned, cleaned, dressed, and cut in 1" chunks
¼ cup brandy
2 tablespoons butter or margarine
2 tablespoons flour
½ pound boiled crayfish or shrimp, shelled and deveined
⅓ cup croutons

Sauté onions in oil in a large burner-to-table kettle over moderately high heat, turning frequently, 10 minutes until golden. Add mushrooms and garlic and stir-fry 2–3 minutes. Add bouquet garni, seasonings, wine, and stock, cover, and simmer 10 minutes; add fish. Warm brandy in a small pan, blaze with a match, and pour flaming over fish. Cover and simmer 10–15 minutes until fish just flakes. Drain 2–3 cups liquid from kettle and reserve; melt butter in a saucepan over moderate heat, blend in flour, add reserved liquid, and heat, stirring, until slightly thickened; add crayfish, stir all into kettle, taste for salt and add more if needed. Scatter croutons over soup and serve. About 370 calories per serving.

VARIATION:

Matelote Normandy Style: Substitute halibut or haddock for the carp, mackerel or tuna for the catfish, and apple cider for the wine. Prepare as directed; just before serving, stir in ½ cup heavy cream. Garnish with 1 dozen each steamed mussels and soft clams in the shell; omit croutons. About 575 calories per serving.

¢ DRIED BEAN SOUP

This soup freezes well.
Makes 12 servings

1 pound dried beans (any kind), washed and sorted
1 gallon cold water, or 1 quart cold water and 3 quarts beef, chicken, or turkey broth
2 medium-size yellow onions, peeled and coarsely chopped
3 carrots, peeled and diced
2 stalks celery, diced
2 cloves garlic, peeled and crushed (optional)
1 tablespoon bacon drippings, margarine, or cooking oil
2 teaspoons salt (about)
¼ teaspoon pepper
2 tablespoons minced parsley

Soak beans* in 1 quart water overnight or use the quick method. Drain, measure soaking water, and add enough cold water to total 3 quarts. Place beans and water in a large, heavy kettle with all but last 3 ingredients, cover, and simmer about 1½ hours until very soft. Put half of mixture through a food mill or purée, a little at a time, in an electric blender at low speed. Return to kettle and heat until bubbly. Add salt and pepper, tasting and adjusting salt as needed. Sprinkle with parsley and serve. About 155 calories per serving if made with water only, 190 per serving if made with broth and water.

VARIATIONS:

¢ Savory Dried Bean Soup: Prepare as directed, adding a ham bone or pig's knuckle, chunk of salt pork or bacon, or leftover roast bone to the pot. Other good additions: leftover meat, gravy, and vegetables, medium-dry sherry or Madeira to taste. About 190 calories per serving if made with water only, 225 per serving if made with broth and water.

¢ Rosy Dried Bean Soup: Prepare as directed, smoothing 1½ cups tomato purée into soup shortly before serving. About 200 calories per serving if made with water only, 235 per serving if made with broth and water.

Creamy Dried Bean Soup: Cook beans as directed, using 2 quarts water instead of 3. After puréeing, blend in 1 quart light cream and heat to serving temperature; do not boil. About 325 calories per serving.

¢ HEARTY CHICK-PEA AND SAUSAGE SOUP

Makes 8–10 servings

1 pound dried chick-peas, washed and sorted
3 quarts cold water (about)
1 small lean ham bone with some meat attached
2 sprigs parsley
½ pound chorizos, pepperoni, or other hot sausage, skinned and sliced ½" thick
2 medium-size yellow onions, peeled and coarsely chopped
2 cloves garlic, peeled and crushed
2 medium-size carrots, peeled and sliced thin
½ teaspoon oregano
¼ teaspoon thyme
¼ teaspoon coriander
1½ teaspoons salt (about)
⅛ teaspoon pepper (about)

Soak chick-peas overnight in 1 quart water or use the quick method.* Drain, measure soaking water, and add cold water to total 3 quarts. Place peas, water, ham bone and parsley in a large, heavy kettle, cover, and simmer 1 hour. Meanwhile, brown chorizos in a large, heavy skillet; lift out with a slotted spoon and reserve. Stir-fry onions, garlic, and carrots in drippings 10–12 minutes over moderate heat to brown lightly, stir in remaining ingredients (but not sausages) and add to chick-peas. Re-cover and simmer 1–1½ hours until peas are mushy. Lift out ham bone, cut off any meat and reserve; discard parsley. Purée kettle mixture, a little at a time, in an electric blender at low speed or put through a food mill. Return all to kettle; add ham and sausages and heat, stirring, 10–15 minutes to blend flavors. Taste for salt and pepper and adjust as needed. Serve hot. About 370 calories for each of 8 servings, 295 for each of 10.

¢ OLD-FASHIONED BLACK BEAN SOUP

Makes 6 servings

1 pound dried black beans, washed
   and sorted but not soaked
3 quarts cold water
2 medium-size yellow onions, peeled
   and minced
2 cloves garlic, peeled and crushed
3 tablespoons bacon drippings
2 medium-size tomatoes, peeled,
   cored, seeded, and chopped
¾ teaspoon oregano
½ teaspoon crushed dried hot red
   chili peppers
¼ teaspoon thyme
2 teaspoons salt
⅛ teaspoon black pepper
½ cup dry sherry
2 hard-cooked eggs

Place beans and water in a very
large, heavy kettle, cover, and
simmer 1¼–1½ hours until almost
tender. Meanwhile, stir-fry onions
and garlic in drippings in a heavy
skillet over moderate heat 8–10 minutes until golden, stir in tomatoes,
all herbs and spices, and set
aside. When beans are almost tender,
stir in skillet mixture, cover,
and simmer 1½–2 hours longer
until beans are mushy. Put mixture
through a food mill or purée
by pressing through a fine sieve.
Return to pan, add salt, black
pepper, and sherry, and heat, stirring
frequently, 5–10 minutes to blend
flavors. Peel eggs, sieve the yolks,
and mince the whites. Ladle
soup into large bowls, sprinkle with
yolks and whites, and serve.
About 395 calories per serving.

¢ EASY BLACK BEAN SOUP

Makes 4 servings

1 cup minced Spanish or Bermuda
   onion
2 cloves garlic, peeled and crushed

2 tablespoons butter or margarine
½ teaspoon crushed coriander seeds
¼ teaspoon oregano
⅛ teaspoon thyme
¼ cup dry sherry
1 (10½-ounce) can condensed beef
   consommé
2 (1-pound) cans black beans (do
   not drain)
1 bay leaf, crumbled

Stir-fry onion and garlic in butter
in a large saucepan over moderate
heat 8–10 minutes until golden.
Blend in herbs and sherry and heat
1–2 minutes, then add remaining
ingredients and simmer, uncovered,
stirring occasionally, ½–¾ hour
until flavors are well blended. Ladle
into soup bowls and serve. About
475 calories per serving.

¢ LAMB, PEPPER, AND BARLEY SOUP

Makes 8–10 servings

1 lamb shank, cracked, or a meaty
   leg or shoulder bone from a
   leftover roast
1 cup medium pearl barley, washed
1 cup dried green split peas, washed
   and sorted
2 medium-size yellow onions, peeled
   and minced
1 clove garlic, peeled and crushed
1 sweet green pepper, cored, seeded,
   and minced
3½ quarts cold water
4 teaspoons salt (about)
¼ teaspoon pepper

Place all ingredients in a large,
heavy kettle, cover, and simmer 2
hours, stirring occasionally. Cut
meat from bones and return to
kettle. Taste for salt and adjust if
necessary. Serve hot with crusty
bread or crisp crackers. (Note:
This soup keeps well in the refrigerator about 1 week. It also freezes
well.) About 255 calories for each
of 8 servings, 200 for each of 10.

¢ **GOLDEN SPLIT PEA SOUP WITH HAM**

A Norwegian favorite, hearty enough to serve as a main course. Makes 8–10 servings

2 *medium-size yellow onions, peeled and coarsely chopped*
2 *tablespoons bacon drippings, butter, or margarine*
2 *cups diced, cooked ham*
1 *pound yellow split peas, washed and sorted*
3 *quarts water*
⅛ *teaspoon rosemary*
1 *tablespoon salt*
¼ *teaspoon pepper*

Stir-fry onions in drippings 5–8 minutes in a large saucepan over moderate heat until pale golden. Add ham and stir-fry 5 minutes. Add remaining ingredients, cover, and simmer 1 hour, stirring occasionally. Serve steaming hot with buttery chunks of garlic bread. About 305 calories for each of 8 servings, 245 for each of 10.

VARIATION:

Lentil and Ham Soup: Prepare as directed, substituting 1 pound lentils for the peas and simmering ¾ hour until tender, not mushy. Calorie counts the same as for split pea soup.

¢ **MINESTRONE MILANESE**

Italians like minestrone made with red kidney beans; Americans more often use navy or pea beans. Either makes a husky main-dish soup.
Makes 10 servings

½ *pound dried red kidney, navy, or pea beans, washed and sorted*
2 *cups water*
1 *large yellow onion, peeled and minced*
1 *clove garlic, peeled and minced*
⅓ *cup diced salt pork*
2 *tablespoons olive or other cooking oil*
3 *quarts beef broth or water or a ½ and ½ mixture of water and beef bouillon*
2 *medium-size carrots, peeled and diced*
2 *medium-size potatoes, peeled and diced*
2 *cups finely shredded cabbage*
½ *cup minced celery*
⅓ *cup tomato paste*
2 *teaspoons minced fresh basil or 1 teaspoon dried basil*
¼ *teaspoon thyme*
2 *teaspoons salt (about)*
¼ *teaspoon pepper*
2 *small zucchini, diced (optional)*
1 *tablespoon minced parsley*
1 *cup ditalini or elbow macaroni*
⅓ *cup grated Parmesan cheese*

Soak beans overnight in water or use the quick method,* drain. Stir-fry onion, garlic, and salt pork in oil in a large, heavy kettle 5–8 minutes over moderate heat until onion is pale golden. Add beans and broth, cover, and simmer 1 hour. Add all remaining ingredients except zucchini, parsley, *ditalini,* and Parmesan, cover, and simmer 1 hour, stirring now and then. Add zucchini, parsley, and ditalini, cover, and simmer 15–20 minutes longer until ditalini is tender. Taste for salt and adjust as needed. Stir Parmesan into soup or, if you prefer, pass separately. About 240 calories per serving if made with water alone, 260 if made with broth and water, 285 if made with broth alone.

⚖ ARTICHOKE SOUP

An unusually delicate soup. Good
hot or cold.
Makes 4 servings

2 cups globe artichoke hearts (fresh,
  frozen, or drained canned)
2 tablespoons butter or margarine
1 cup milk
2 cups water
1 teaspoon salt
⅛ teaspoon white pepper
1 clove garlic, peeled and speared
  with a toothpick
½ cup beef consommé
1 teaspoon minced parsley

If artichokes are fresh, parboil
20–25 minutes and drain. If frozen,
thaw just enough to separate.
Quarter hearts, then slice thin crosswise. Stir-fry in butter in a saucepan (not aluminum) over moderately low heat 5 minutes; do not
brown. Add all but last 2 ingredients,
cover, and simmer over lowest heat
20 minutes. Discard garlic, purée
about half the mixture in an electric
blender at low speed or put through
a food mill; return to pan. Add
consommé and heat to serving
temperature, stirring now and then.
Serve hot sprinkled with parsley.
About 125 calories per serving.

VARIATION:

⚖ **Cold Artichoke Soup:** Slice
artichokes but do not fry; omit
butter. Simmer as directed, then
purée and proceed as above. About
80 calories per serving.

⊠ ¢ CABBAGE SOUP

A simple soup that can be used as
the foundation of a variety of
unusual European soups. Four of the
best are included here as easy
variations.
Makes 6 servings

2 cups finely shredded green cabbage

1 medium-size yellow onion, peeled
  and minced
¼ cup butter or margarine
6 cups beef broth, bouillon, or
  consommé
½ teaspoon salt
¼ teaspoon pepper
½ cup finely grated Cheddar or
  Parmesan cheese or ½ cup sour
  cream

Stir-fry cabbage and onion in butter
in a large, heavy saucepan over
moderately low heat until cabbage is
wilted, not brown. Add broth, salt,
and pepper, cover, and simmer
15–20 minutes until cabbage is
tender. Ladle into soup bowls,
sprinkle with cheese or top with
sour cream, and serve. About 165
calories per serving.

VARIATIONS:

¢ **German Cabbage Soup:** Prepare
as directed and just before serving
thicken with 2 tablespoons flour
blended with ¼ cup cold water.
Also stir in 1 tablespoon caraway
seeds and 2 tablespoons butter or
margarine; omit cheese or sour
cream topping. About 170 calories
per serving.

¢ **French Cabbage Soup:** Prepare as directed, increasing broth to
2 quarts and adding at the same time
1 cup each diced peeled potatoes
and carrots and 1 peeled and
crushed clove garlic. Top with
croutons instead of cheese or sour
cream. About 190 calories per
serving.

¢ **Basque Cabbage Soup:** Prepare as directed, increasing broth
to 2 quarts and adding at the same
time 1 cup cooked dried limas and
1 peeled and crushed clove garlic.
Top each serving with ¼ teaspoon
vinegar instead of cheese or sour
cream. About 195 calories per
serving.

¢ **Russian Sauerkraut Soup:** Prepare as directed, substituting 2 cups drained sauerkraut for cabbage and adding 1 (1-pound) undrained can tomatoes, breaking tomatoes up. Top each serving with sour cream. About 190 calories per serving.

⊠ ¢ **CORN CHOWDER**

Makes 6 servings

6 *slices bacon, diced*
2 *medium-size yellow onions, peeled and chopped*
1 *medium-size sweet green pepper, cored, seeded, and chopped*
2 *(10-ounce) packages frozen whole kernel corn*
3 *cups milk*
2 *teaspoons salt*
⅛ *teaspoon pepper*
⅛ *teaspoon nutmeg*

Brown bacon in a very large skillet over moderate heat and drain on paper toweling. Stir-fry onions and green pepper in drippings 8–10 minutes until onions are golden. Add corn, cover, and simmer 10–12 minutes. Uncover, break up any frozen bits of corn, and simmer, uncovered, 5 minutes, stirring occasionally. Add remaining ingredients and simmer 5 minutes. Ladle into soup bowls and top each serving with bacon. About 225 calories per serving.

⊠ ¢ **BASIC POTATO SOUP**

Makes 6 servings

1 *small yellow onion, peeled and minced*
2 *tablespoons butter or margarine*

2 *cups diced, peeled potatoes*
2 *cups cold water or chicken broth*
1 *teaspoon salt*
½ *teaspoon celery salt*
1 *cup milk*
1 *cup light cream*
⅛ *teaspoon white pepper*
1 *tablespoon minced parsley, chives, or dill*

Stir-fry onion in butter in a heavy saucepan over moderate heat 5 minutes until limp; add potatoes, water, salt, and celery salt, cover and simmer 10–15 minutes until potatoes are nearly tender. Add milk, cream, and pepper and simmer, uncovered, stirring occasionally, 3–5 minutes until potatoes are done. Sprinkle with parsley and serve. About 190 calories per serving if made with water, 210 if made with broth.

VARIATIONS:

¢ **Potato Soup au Gratin:** Prepare soup as directed, ladle into flameproof bowls, top each with a little grated Cheddar or Parmesan cheese and a sprinkling of nutmeg or paprika, and broil quickly to brown. About 220 calories per serving if made with water, 240 if made with broth.

¢ **Mashed Potato Soup:** Prepare as directed, substituting 2 cups seasoned mashed potatoes for the diced and simmering 10 minutes altogether, beating with a whisk now and then. About 210 calories per serving if made with water, 230 if made with broth.

¢ **Cream of Potato Soup:** Prepare as directed; purée in an electric blender at low speed or put through a food mill. Serve hot or cold. Same calorie counts as Basic Potato Soup.

⊠ JIFFY POTATO-ONION SOUP

Makes 6 servings

2 cups milk
2 (13¾-ounce) cans chicken broth
1 (1⅜-ounce) package dry onion soup mix
1 tablespoon parsley flakes
1 (5-serving size) envelope instant mashed potatoes
⅓ cup crisp, crumbled bacon (optional garnish)

Heat milk, chicken broth, onion soup mix, and parsley flakes, uncovered, over moderately high heat, stirring occasionally, until mixture boils. Remove from heat and gradually add instant mashed potatoes, stirring briskly. Return to heat and warm 2–3 minutes longer, beating with a wire whisk. Ladle into soup bowls and top, if you like, with bacon crumbles. About 185 calories per serving without optional bacon garnish. Add about 15 calories per serving if bacon crumbles are used.

¢ CALDO VERDE (PORTUGUESE GREEN SOUP)

If Portugal has a national dish it is caldo verde, a tweedy green soup that bubbles on stoves across the country (including those of Lisbon's more sophisticated restaurants). Basically, it's a potato soup, spiked with onions and garlic and textured with shreds of kale or cabbage and spinach.
Makes 8–10 servings

3 medium-size yellow onions, peeled and coarsely chopped
2 cloves garlic, peeled and crushed
⅓ cup olive oil
6 potatoes, peeled and diced
1 gallon water

1 medium-size cabbage, cored and sliced thin
1 pound fresh spinach, washed, trimmed, and sliced thin
3 tablespoons salt
¼ teaspoon pepper

Sauté onions and garlic in oil in a large, heavy kettle 8–10 minutes over moderate heat until golden, stirring occasionally. Add potatoes and sauté, stirring, 10 minutes. Add water and simmer, uncovered, 2 hours, stirring now and then. Add remaining ingredients and continue simmering, uncovered, 45 minutes, stirring occasionally. Ladle into large soup bowls and serve. About 190 calories for each of 8 servings, 155 for each of 10.

¢ ITALIAN-STYLE SPINACH AND RICE SOUP

Accompanied by garlic bread and sliced tomatoes, this makes a refreshing, light lunch.
Makes 6–8 servings

2 medium-size yellow onions, peeled and coarsely chopped
2 tablespoons butter or margarine
4 (13¾-ounce) cans chicken broth
½ cup uncooked rice
2 (10-ounce) packages frozen chopped spinach, thawed
2 teaspoons salt
¼ teaspoon nutmeg
⅛ teaspoon pepper

Stir-fry onions in butter in a large saucepan over moderate heat 8–10 minutes until golden. Add broth and bring to a boil. Stir in rice and boil, uncovered, 10 minutes until rice is about half done. Add remaining ingredients and simmer 12–15 minutes longer until rice is done. Ladle into soup bowls and serve. About 170 calories for each of 6 servings, 130 for each of 8.

¢ ⚖ **FRESH TOMATO SOUP**

Makes 6 servings

*2 medium-size yellow onions, peeled
   and quartered
1 stalk celery, cut in 2" chunks
1 (10½-ounce) can condensed beef
   consommé
6 large ripe tomatoes, peeled, cored,
   and quartered
1 tablespoon butter or margarine
2 teaspoons salt
⅛ teaspoon pepper
2 tablespoons minced fresh chives or
   dill*

Place onions, celery, and consommé in a large saucepan, cover, and simmer 45 minutes until onions are mushy. Add tomatoes, cover, and simmer 15–20 minutes until tomatoes have reduced to juice; cool 10 minutes, then put through a food mill or purée, a little at a time, in an electric blender at low speed. Return to pan, add butter, salt, and pepper, and simmer uncovered 5 minutes. Serve hot or cold garnished with minced chives. About 75 calories per serving.

¢ ⚖ **ANDALUSIAN GAZPACHO (COLD SPANISH VEGETABLE SOUP)**

Glorious on a hot summer day. And almost a meal in itself.
Makes 6 servings

*¾ cup soft white bread crumbs
3 tablespoons red wine vinegar
2 cloves garlic, peeled and crushed
¼ cup olive oil
1 large cucumber, peeled, seeded,
   and cut in fine dice
1 sweet green pepper, cored, seeded,
   and minced
8 large ripe tomatoes, peeled, cored,
   seeded, and chopped fine
1 cup cold water
½ teaspoon salt
⅛ teaspoon pepper*

Place bread crumbs, vinegar, garlic, and oil in a small bowl and mix vigorously with a fork to form a smooth paste; set aside. Mix all remaining ingredients in a large mixing bowl, then blend in bread paste. Cover and chill at least 24 hours before serving. Serve icy cold in soup bowls as a first course or as a midafternoon refresher. For a special touch, bed the soup bowls in larger bowls of crushed ice and garnish with sprigs of fresh dill or basil or, failing that, watercress or parsley. About 130 calories per serving.

⚖ **BASIC FRUIT SOUP**

Slavs and Scandinavians sometimes serve a hot or cold fruit soup before the main course; berries, cherries, and plums are the favored "soup fruits."
Makes 4 servings

*1 pint berries, washed and stemmed
   (strawberries, raspberries,
   blueberries, boysenberries,
   blackberries, or gooseberries)
1 pint water or a ½ and ½ mixture
   of water and dry white wine
¼ cup sugar (about)
2 teaspoons lemon juice
1 tablespoon cornstarch blended with
   2 tablespoons cold water
Heavy cream, sour cream, or
   buttermilk (optional topping)*

Simmer berries in water in a covered saucepan 10 minutes until mushy; put through a food mill or purée in an electric blender at low speed, then press through a fine sieve. Return purée to pan, add remaining ingredients, and heat to a boil, stirring. Taste for sugar and add more, if needed. Serve hot or cold, topped, if you like, with cream. From about 70–120 calories per serving if made with water only,

130–55 if made with water and wine (strawberries and gooseberries are the lowest in calories). Add 50 calories per serving for each tablespoon heavy cream topping used, 30 calories for each tablespoon sour cream, and 5 calories for each tablespoon buttermilk.

VARIATIONS:

⊠   Quick Berry Soup: Substitute 2 (10-ounce) packages thawed frozen berries or 1 (1-pound) undrained can berries for the fresh. Do not cook; purée and sieve, then add enough water to make 1 quart. Heat with sugar (just enough to taste), lemon juice, and cornstarch paste as directed. About 115–30 calories per serving, depending on kind of berries used.

Spiced Fruit Soup: Prepare as directed, adding ½ teaspoon cinnamon and ¼ teaspoon each nutmeg and cloves along with sugar. Calorie counts the same as Basic Fruit Soup.

Curried Fruit Soup: Prepare as directed, adding 2 teaspoons curry powder along with sugar. About 10 calories more per serving than Basic Fruit Soup.

Sweet-Sour Fruit Soup: Prepare as directed, increasing sugar to 5 tablespoons and adding, at the same time, 3 tablespoons red or white wine vinegar. About 10 calories more per serving than Basic Fruit Soup.

Plum Soup: Substitute 1 pound purple plums for berries and simmer 25–30 minutes until mushy; cool slightly, pit, then purée and proceed as for the Basic Fruit Soup. About 160 calories per serving without optional cream topping.

COOL HUNGARIAN CHERRY SOUP

Although Hungarians traditionally serve this cold soup *before* the entree, you may find it too sweet for an appetizer. If so, serve as a hot weather dessert.
Makes 4–6 servings

2 (1-pound 1-ounce) cans pitted
  dark sweet cherries (do not drain)
1 cup sour cream
¼ cup superfine sugar
¼ cup tawny port or cream sherry
  (optional)

Drain cherry liquid into a mixing bowl, add sour cream, sugar, and, if you like, the wine, and stir until well blended. Add cherries, cover, and chill 3–4 hours before serving. About 380 calories for each of 4 servings, 255 for each of 6.

¢ ⚖ APPLE SOUP

Serve as a first course or light dessert.
Makes 4–6 servings

1 pound greenings or other tart
  cooking apples, peeled, cored, and
  sliced thin
3 cups water
1 teaspoon grated lemon rind
2 teaspoons lemon juice
½ cup sugar (about)
½ teaspoon cinnamon
¼ teaspoon nutmeg
1 cup sour cream blended with ½
  cup milk (optional)

Place all but last ingredient in a saucepan, cover, and simmer about 20 minutes until apples are mushy. Put through a food mill or purée in an electric blender at low speed; taste for sugar and add more if needed. Serve hot or cold with a little of the sour cream mixture drizzled on top, if you like. About 145 calories for each of 4 servings, 100 for each of 6 without optional sour cream topping. Add 25 calories per serving for each tablespoon of topping used.

VARIATION:

Russian Apple Soup: Prepare as directed, using 2 cups water and 1 cup red Bordeaux wine for cooking the apples. Before puréeing, add ¼ cup red or black currant jelly and stir until melted. Purée and serve hot or cold with or without cream topping. About 235 calories for each of 4 servings, 160 for each of 6 without sour cream topping.

WINE SOUP WITH SNOW EGGS

Germans serve this heady Rhine wine soup as a first course; you may prefer it as dessert.
Makes 4–6 servings

2 tablespoons butter (no substitute)
2 tablespoons flour
1 pint Rhine wine
1 pint water
3–4 tablespoons sugar
1 cinnamon stick
1 (2″) strip lemon rind
2 egg yolks, lightly beaten

Snow Eggs:
1 egg white
1 tablespoon sugar
1 teaspoon sugar mixed with ¼ teaspoon cinnamon

Melt butter in a heavy, shallow saucepan about 8″ in diameter over moderately low heat. Blend in flour, slowly stir in wine, water, and sugar; add cinnamon and lemon rind. Heat slowly, stirring, until slightly thickened. Simmer, uncovered, over lowest heat 5 minutes. Meanwhile, beat egg white and sugar until soft peaks form; set aside. Mix a little soup into yolks, return to pan, and heat, stirring, 1–2 minutes; do not boil. Taste for sugar and add more if needed.

Remove lemon rind and cinnamon stick. Lift pan off burner, drop egg white onto soup by teaspoonfuls, and let stand undisturbed 5 minutes. To serve, carefully lift out 4–5 snow eggs with a slotted spoon and set aside so you can get a soup ladle into pan without breaking any eggs. Ladle soup into hot bowls, float 2–3 snow eggs in each, and dust lightly with cinnamon sugar. Also good served cold. About 230 calories for each of 4 servings, 155 for each of 6.

BEER SOUP (ØLLEBRØD)

Beer soup, or *Øllebrød* (ale and bread), as the Danes call it, is not often sampled by tourists because it's more often served at home than in restaurants.
Makes 4 servings

4 slices dark Danish rye bread or pumpernickel
1 (12-ounce) bottle Danish or German dark ale or malt beer
6–8 tablespoons sugar
2 teaspoons lemon juice
Heavy cream

Break bread into small pieces and mix with beer. Cover and chill at least 4 hours or overnight; transfer to a saucepan and heat over moderately low heat, stirring constantly, 5–10 minutes until the consistency of applesauce. Press through a fine sieve or purée in an electric blender at low speed. Return to pan and bring to serving temperature. Mix in 6 tablespoons sugar and the lemon juice; taste for sweetness, and add more sugar if desired. Serve piping hot with plenty of cream poured over each serving. About 180–200 calories per serving, depending on amount of sugar used. Add 50 calories per serving for each tablespoon of heavy cream topping used.

Soup Dumplings, Garnishes, and Trimmings

Note: For additional dumpling recipes, also recipes for plain and flavored croutons, see the chapter on breads.

¢ VIENNESE SOUP "PEAS"

An unusual soup garnish that can be made ahead of time.

Makes about 1 cup, enough to garnish 8 soup servings

½ cup sifted flour
1 teaspoon salt
1 egg, lightly beaten
¼ cup milk
Shortening or cooking oil for deep fat frying

Mix flour, salt, egg, and milk and beat until smooth. Heat shortening in a deep fat fryer over high heat until deep fat thermometer registers 375° F. Drizzle batter from the end of a teaspoon into hot fat to form small "peas" and fry 30–40 seconds until golden. Scoop out with a slotted spoon and drain on paper toweling. Fry only a few "peas" at a time so you don't crowd pan. Serve sprinkled on top of any soup. These may be made ahead, stored airtight, then reheated. Simply spread out on a baking sheet, set uncovered in a 400° F. oven, and let warm 4–5 minutes. About 60 calories for each of 8 servings.

ROYALE CUSTARD

Makes enough to garnish 6 soup servings

1 egg plus 2 egg yolks, lightly beaten
½ cup beef consommé, chicken broth, or milk
⅛ teaspoon salt
Pinch cayenne pepper

Preheat oven to 325° F. Mix all ingredients and pour into a well-buttered, shallow baking dish or pie plate 6″–7″ in diameter. (*Note:* Custard should be about ½″ deep.) Set dish on a rack in a large, shallow baking pan, pour in hot water to a depth of ½″, and bake, uncovered, 25 minutes or until a knife inserted midway between rim and center comes out clean. Lift custard from water bath and cool upright in its baking dish on a wire rack. Cut in small cubes or diamonds or into fancy shapes with truffle cutters. Float in consommé or other clear soup as a garnish, allowing 3–4 cubes or cutouts per serving. About 45 calories per serving made with milk, 40 made with chicken broth and 38 made with beef broth.

VARIATIONS:

Indian Royale Custard: Prepare custard using chicken broth; whisk in ½ teaspoon curry powder, then bake as directed. The same calorie counts as royale custard.

Vegetable Royale Custard: Prepare custard with chicken broth or milk, smooth in 2 tablespoons puréed cooked spinach, green peas, tomatoes, or asparagus and bake as directed. Add about 1 calorie per serving to above counts for vegetable royale custard made with spinach or asparagus, 2 calories per serving for that made with tomatoes, and 3 calories per serving for that made with green peas.

MARROW DUMPLINGS

Makes 2 dozen

¼ cup uncooked beef marrow, scraped from marrowbones (at room temperature)
½ cup cracker meal or crumbs
1 tablespoon minced parsley
¾ teaspoon salt

½ teaspoon grated lemon rind
⅛ teaspoon pepper
2 eggs, lightly beaten

Cream marrow until smooth, blend in remaining ingredients, mix well, and let stand 10 minutes. Shape into 1″ balls. Drop into just boiling soup or stew and simmer, uncovered, 4–5 minutes. Do not cook more than 1 layer of dumplings at a time. Serve in soup or with stew, allowing 3–4 dumplings per serving. About 30 calories per dumpling.

¢ FARINA DUMPLINGS

Good in any clear meat or vegetable soup.
Makes 2 dozen

1 cup milk
¼ cup uncooked farina or cream of wheat
1 egg, lightly beaten
1 tablespoon butter or margarine
½ teaspoon salt
⅛ teaspoon white pepper

Heat milk almost to boiling over moderate heat, stir in farina and heat, stirring constantly, 2–3 minutes until thick. Off heat, beat in remaining ingredients. Cool to room temperature. Drop by ½ teaspoon into 2–3 quarts just boiling soup, cover, and simmer 4–5 minutes. Do not cook more than one layer of dumplings at a time; remove first batch with a slotted spoon and keep warm while you cook the rest. Serve 3–4 dumplings in each bowl of soup. About 20 calories per dumpling.

LIVER DUMPLINGS

Makes 2 dozen

¼ pound calf, beef, or lamb liver, sliced ¼″–½″ thick
½ cup water
1 egg, lightly beaten

1½ cups soft white bread crumbs
2 tablespoons light cream
¾ teaspoon salt
⅛ teaspoon pepper
¼ teaspoon marjoram or thyme
1 teaspoon minced parsley
¼ cup minced yellow onion
½ clove garlic, peeled and crushed (optional)
1 tablespoon butter or margarine

Simmer liver, uncovered, in water 5 minutes; drain and put through finest blade of a meat grinder. Mix in egg, crumbs, cream, salt, pepper, marjoram, and parsley. Stir-fry onion and, if you like, garlic in butter 3–5 minutes over moderate heat until limp; stir into liver. Drop mixture by ½ teaspoonfuls and cook, uncovered, a few dumplings at a time, in 2–3 quarts just boiling clear meat or vegetable soup 3–4 minutes. Lift dumplings out with a slotted spoon and keep warm while you cook the rest. Serve a few dumplings in each bowl of soup. About 25 calories per dumpling.

¢ POTATO DUMPLINGS

Makes 2 dozen small soup dumplings, 1 dozen stew dumplings

3 medium-size potatoes, boiled in their skins, drained, and peeled
1 egg, lightly beaten
⅓ cup sifted flour
1½ teaspoons salt
⅛ teaspoon white pepper
¼ teaspoon nutmeg (optional)
½ cup croutons

Return potatoes to their pan and dry uncovered, 1–2 minutes over lowest heat; mash or rice. Beat in all remaining ingredients except croutons. Shape into 1″ or 2″ balls, push a crouton into center of each 1″ ball, 2–3 into larger balls. Drop into just boiling soup or stew and cook uncovered, allowing 5–7 minutes for the 1″ balls and 10–12 for the 2″ balls. (*Note:* Don't crowd dumplings; they should be in a single layer, so cook half at a time if necessary.) Use the 1″ dumplings to garnish soup, the 2″ for stew. About 25 calories for each soup dumpling, 50 calories for each stew dumpling.

¢ MATZO BALLS

Matzo meal can be bought in kosher groceries and delicatessens.
Makes 1½ dozen

2 eggs, lightly beaten
½ cup matzo meal
1 teaspoon salt
¼ teaspoon ginger, cinnamon, or nutmeg (optional)
3 tablespoons cold water

Mix all ingredients, cover, and refrigerate ½ hour. Drop by rounded teaspoonfuls on top of just boiling chicken broth or other clear soup, cover, and cook at a slow boil 15–20 minutes. Serve at once. About 20 calories per matzo ball.

VARIATIONS:

Mary's Matzo Balls: Reduce water to 2 tablespoons and add 2 minced, sautéed chicken livers and 2 teaspoons minced parsley to ingredients called for. Butter hands, roll into 1″ balls, then cook as directed. About 30 calories per ball.

Precooked Matzo Balls: Prepare matzo ball mixture, then cook as directed in boiling salted water instead of soup (for this amount you'll need about 3 quarts water and 2 tablespoons salt). Lift from salted water with a slotted spoon and add 2–3 matzo balls to each bowl of chicken broth or clear soup. Same calorie count as matzo balls.

KREPLACH

These meat-filled egg noodles, served in clear soups, are a Jewish favorite. The noodle dough should be rolled slightly thicker than for ribbon noodles so the filling won't poke through.
Makes about 1½ dozen

Egg Noodle Dough:
¾ cup sifted flour
½ teaspoon salt
1 egg, lightly beaten

Filling:
½ cup cooked minced chicken, chicken livers, or beef
1 tablespoon chicken or beef broth
1 teaspoon grated onion
½ teaspoon salt
⅛ teaspoon pepper

Make dough first: Sift flour with salt, add egg, and mix with a fork until mixture holds together. Knead on a lightly floured board 2–3 minutes until satiny. Cover and let rest 30 minutes. Roll thin into a square about 12″, then cut in 2½″ squares. Mix filling ingredients and drop about ½ teaspoonful on the center of each noodle square. Dampen dough edges with cold water, fold noodle over to form a triangle, then press edges together with tines of a fork. Let *kreplach* stand uncovered on a lightly floured surface 20 minutes; turn and let stand 20 minutes longer. Cook, uncovered, at a slow boil 10–15 minutes in chicken broth, clear soup, or salted water (for this amount you'll need 3–4 quarts; if using water, add 2 tablespoons salt). Serve kreplach in chicken or beef broth or other clear soup, allowing 2–3 per bowl. About 35 calories each.

CHAPTER 8

MEAT

Meat always gets star billing. It's the dish around which all others are planned, the one for which wines are chosen, the one that sets the tone of a meal. It's the most expensive part of our diet, the most universally well liked, the most versatile, and certainly one of the most nutritious. Meat thus deserves a worthy role and the best possible supporting cast. It needs skillful and imaginative handling, preferential treatment sometimes, and kid glove care always.

HOW TO FIND QUALITY IN MEAT

Your guarantee of wholesomeness is the federal inspector's seal, a round purple stamp about the size of a silver dollar on beef, somewhat smaller on veal, lamb, and pork. All meat entered in interstate commerce must be federally inspected and passed before it can be

sold. This means that the animals have been found free of disease and that the slaughterhouse handling them has met U. S. Department of Agriculture sanitation standards. About 80 per cent of the meat sold in this country is federally inspected; most of the remaining 20 per cent is state or city inspected.

Look next for the *grade or degree of excellence*. Meat may be graded federally (these grades vary from animal to animal and will be discussed separately under Beef, Veal, Lamb, and Pork), or it may be graded by a packing house. The equivalent of U. S. Prime or

Choice, for example, might be labeled Premium by one packer and Star, Puritan, or Certified by others. Packer grading is more often done with ham than other meats.

About Aging

Only beef, lamb, and mutton ribs and loins of high quality are aged, the purpose being to make them as flavorful and tender as possible. They may be *dry aged* (held 3 to 6 weeks at low temperature and humidity), *fast aged* (held 2 days or less at 70° F. and rather high humidity), or *vacuum packaged* (covered with a moisture-vaporproof film that stays on from packer to buyer). Most dry-aged and vacuum-packaged meat goes to hotels and restaurants; what we buy is usually fast aged or unaged —except in transit from slaughterhouse to our own homes (considerable tenderizing takes place during this period of 6 to 10 days). Because many people prefer more well-aged meat, especially beef, butchers often age it in their own coolers.

The Food and Calorie Value of Meat

All meat is a high quality protein food supplying substantial amounts of B vitamins, iron, and phosphorous; most is moderate or moderately high in calories, but, considering its high nutritive value, is a wise choice for calorie counters. Food and calorie values of meat vary considerably from animal to animal, also from cut to cut.

The Cuts of Meat

All cuts can be fitted into two categories: *the tender* and the *less tender*. Learning which are which isn't difficult once you remember that exercise and age are what toughen meat. The most frequently exercised parts of the animal, therefore—legs, neck, shoulder, rump, flank—will be far tougher than the seldom exercised rib and loin; old cows will be more sinewy than pampered young heifers or steers. Diagrams of the various cuts appear in the sections on Beef, Veal, Lamb, and Pork, as well as rules and recipes for preparing them.

How to Make the Most of Your Meat Dollar

– Learn the cuts of meat and cook them properly. Why buy relatively expensive top round for stew when neck, shank, and chuck are not only cheaper but better?
– Buy in quantity, by the side if you have a freezer. If not, buy large cuts and divide them up as follows (below):
– Make the most of leftovers (see suggestions in each of the meat sections).
– Take advantage of supermarket specials.
– Steer clear of luxury cuts— steaks, chops, rib roasts—and concentrate upon less expensive pot roasts, Swiss steaks, shanks, and stews.

Original Cut	First Meal	Second Meal
10″ Beef rib roast	Rib roast	Deviled Short Ribs
Whole ham	Ham steak	Roast ham
Square shoulder of lamb	Blade chops	Shoulder roast

The Ways of Tenderizing Meat

Down the centuries cooks have devised ingenious ways of softening up not-so-tender cuts both mechanically and chemically.

Mechanical tenderizing merely means breaking up tough meat fibers by *pounding, cubing, scoring, or grinding.*

Chemical tenderizing means softening tough fibers with an *enzyme, acid marinade, or moist heat cooking.* Using enzymes isn't as new as it may seem, because Latin American women have been tenderizing meat with papaya juice for ages (many modern tenderizers are simply crystalline forms of its enzyme, papain). The majority of today's tenderizers are the instant type, so read directions carefully before using. Marinating, on the other hand, isn't as effective a tenderizer as originally thought because the juices of the marinade hardly penetrate meat at all in contrast to papain. Far more effective is the moist heat cooking that follows marination.

Some Special Ways to Prepare Meat for Cooking

To Bard: To tie sheets or strips of fat around lean cuts so they won't dry out during cooking.

Commonly barded meats are whole beef tenderloin, filet steaks and tournedos; lean veal roasts; venison and game birds; poultry. Suet and bacon are recommended for beef and veal; bacon for pheasant and chicken; fatback or salt pork for venison and wild game birds. *Note:* Many butchers will do the barding for you.

To Bone: To remove bones (have butcher do it whenever possible). *Filleting* refers to boning small pieces like steaks and chops. (*Note:* Base cooking times on *boned* weight.)

To Butterfly: To cut small boneless chops horizontally through the center, cutting almost but not quite through so that they can be opened flat like a book.

To French: To remove meat from rib ends of lamb, veal, or pork chops or crown roasts and to garnish with paper frills or small fruits.

To Lard: To insert long strips of chilled fat (lardoons) into lean meats with a larding needle. If the cut is large, strips the length of it are drawn through the center with a long-bladed larding needle.

When cuts are small, short lardoons are drawn through the surface in a technique called *piquing*. Piquing needles are fairly small, not unlike yarn needles. Piquing can also be done without a needle: make small slits at intervals over surface of meat, tuck in small cubes of fat and, if you like, garlic slivers and herbs.

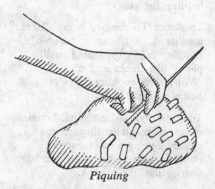

Piquing

Meats often larded: beef rump and round roasts; veal leg roasts; whole beef liver and heart. Good larding fats are fatback, salt pork, fat trimmed from pork loin or fresh ham. *Note:* Always chill fat well before larding—makes the going easier. To make salt pork less salty, blanch lardoons quickly in boiling water, drain, and chill.

To Shape (also known as **To Skewer and Tie**): To make meat as compact as possibly by inserting small skewers and pulling together with cord. The purpose is to make meat cook as evenly as possible.

To Slash: To cut outer fat of steaks and chops at regular intervals so they won't curl as they cook.

To Trim: To cut excess fat from outer layer of steaks and chops; most are best with fat trimmed to a thickness of 1/4".

Should Meat Come to Room Temperature before Cooking?

Many home economists say not, but we think meat cooks more evenly, becomes more juicily tender if allowed to stand at room temperature about 2 hours before cooking. But there are exceptions: naturally thin cuts like flank steak, which are broiled only until rare (having them well chilled safeguards against overcooking); highly perishable meats such as hamburger, liver, kidneys, heart, and sweetbreads.

The Ways of Cooking Meat

What every cook hopes for is as succulent and tender a piece of meat as possible. Since naturally tender cuts cannot be made more tender by cooking (only less so), the object is to preserve every ounce of original tenderness. This is best done (with a few exceptions, which will be discussed as we come to them) by *dry heat cooking*. The less tender cuts, on the other hand, can be made more tender if cooked by *moist heat*. Here are the basic methods of each (with variations).

Dry Heat Cooking:

Roasting: There are two schools of thought about roasting meat. American cooking experts generally recommend a continuous low heat (300–25° F.) to reduce shrinkage and sputtering and to produce exquisitely juicy, evenly cooked roasts; classically trained chefs favor searing to brown both the roast and the pan juices. We prefer the low heat method but include both so you can take your pick. Whichever you use, place meat on a rack in a shallow roasting pan (so that it doesn't stew in its own juice); do not cover, do not baste (roast fat side up so drippings run down over meat), and do not add any liquid. Recommended for all large tender cuts of beef, veal, lamb, pork, and ham.

VARIATIONS:

Spit Roasting: Meat turned on a spit in an oven or rotisserie or over a charcoal fire will generally take about 5 minutes less per pound than oven-roasted meat. To cook evenly, the meat must turn smoothly throughout cooking, which means that it must be perfectly balanced at all times. Best ways to ensure balance: choose blocky, compact cuts or, if spitting more than one piece of meat,

counterbalance as needed with extra metal skewers. Despite all precautions, a roast may become unbalanced during cooking because it loses weight—unevenly—via drippings; keep an eye on the spit and rebalance roast if necessary. Newest rotisseries are equipped with "compensators" that adjust the spit to a roast's changing weight and keep it turning smoothly. Rotisseries, incidentally, cook at varying speeds, so it's wise to consult the manufacturer's timetable. Also read his directions before buying a big roast—if too big, it won't stay balanced.

Smoke Roasting: This centuries-old Chinese way of cooking meat is becoming increasingly popular. Properly done, it requires special equipment so that the meat hangs behind and above the fire and cooks in a cloud of smoke. (Inquire in local gourmet or patio shops about Chinese smoke ovens or about directions for building your own L-shaped smoke oven.) Without special equipment you can still give steaks and roasts a deliciously smoky flavor by tossing packaged aromatic wood chips on a charcoal fire or, if these are unavailable, green hardwood prunings, water-soaked shavings or sawdust (1 hour is usually long enough for the soaking). *Caution:* Never use pine or other resinous woods that will make the meat taste of turpentine.

Pit Roasting: When French explorers saw American Indians roasting whole deer and buffalo in earthen pits, they called it *barbe à queue,* meaning that the animals were cooked from "beard to tail." We now use their phrase to describe all meat cooked in pits, both open and closed. Most pit barbecuing is too complicated to try in your own back yard, so for anything grander than a clambake, hire a professional. Best bets for back-yard barbecues: beef rump or pork loin.

Broiling: Cooking in a broiler, 2″–5″ from the heat (depending on thickness of cut). The meat should be placed on a rack in a broiler pan, browned on one side, turned with tongs (so savory juices aren't lost), and browned on the other side. Do not salt *until after browning*—salt draws moisture to the surface of the meat and prevents browning. Recommended for tender beef and ham steaks, lamb chops, ground beef and lamb, but not for pork or veal chops, no matter how tender. Pork must always be cooked until well done, and at broiling temperature it may toughen and dry. Veal, being lean and delicate, also tends to dry out. Both should be braised.

VARIATIONS:

Charcoal Broiling (Grilling): Browning over glowing coals instead of under a broiler. Cooking times vary considerably, depending on amount of wind and outdoor temperature.

Campfire Broiling: Essentially the same as charcoal broiling except that the fuel is wood and the fire a bit cooler.

Hibachi Broiling: This is charcoal broiling on a doll's scale (most hibachis, whether round or square, measure only 10″–16″ across). But these sturdy little Japanese braziers put out a lot of heat and are perfect for grilling chops, small steaks, and such hors d'oeuvre as Teriyaki and Rumaki. Use long bamboo skewers, thoroughly water-soaked so that they won't burn.

Panbroiling: Cooking, uncovered, in a heavy skillet over moderate to moderately high heat without any fat or liquid (if meat is especially lean, lightly oil or salt skillet to prevent sticking). Cook until nicely browned on both sides and at desired doneness, turning often with tongs. Pour off drippings as they collect (this is one of the principal differences between panbroiling and frying). With the exception of extra-large steaks that are too unwieldy for skillet cooking, any cuts suitable for broiling can be panbroiled. *Browning Tips:* To brown well, meat must be dry on the surface; wipe with a damp cloth, if necessary, and do not salt until after cooking.

Frying: There are two methods:

Panfrying (Sautéing): The technique is virtually the same as for panbroiling *except* that the meat is cooked in a small amount of fat. Recommended for lean veal and lamb chops, for cube steaks and lean ground meat patties.

Deep Fat Frying: Cooking by immersing in very hot fat (usually 300–80° F. on a deep fat thermometer). For best results, use a deep fat fryer with wire basket. Recommended for small breaded cuts or croquettes.

Moist Heat Cooking:

Braising: Whether used for pot roasts, Swiss steaks, or fricassees, the technique is the same. Meat is browned in a heavy skillet or kettle in a little fat, then covered and simmered until tender over low heat or in a slow oven with a small amount of liquid (the fat is usually poured off after browning). Recommended for pork and veal chops, also for marginally tender steaks and roasts.

Cooking in Liquid (Stewing):
Here's the way to tenderize the toughest cuts. Most of them (corned beef and smoked pork excepted) will taste better if browned in a little fat before being covered with liquid (water, stock, wine, or a combination) and left to simmer slowly in a covered kettle until fork tender. As with braising, the simmering can be done on top of the stove or in the oven.

New Ways to Cook Meat

Infrared Cooking: Many of the modern, portable, plug-in broilers, roasters, and rotisseries cook by infrared heat, which produces richly browned, extra-juicy steaks, chops, and roasts a shade quicker than conventional ovens. For greatest efficiency, bring meat to room temperature before cooking and preheat unit thoroughly. Each of these units operates somewhat differently, so follow the manufacturer's directions.

"Radar" or Microwave Cooking:
Heralded as the ovens of tomorrow, these units cook with supersonic speed by generating heat inside the food itself (oven walls, racks, and cooking utensils all remain cool). When the first models appeared some twenty-five years ago, they cost thousands of dollars; today they cost only a little more than conventional ovens. New models have built-in electric units that brown meat as it cooks; originally, though foods cooked jet-quick, they came from the oven unbrowned and unappetizing.

About Cooking Frozen Meat

To defrost or not to defrost? It really doesn't make any difference. The advantage of defrosting is that the meat will cook more quickly; the advantage of not defrosting is that, if plans change and the meat cannot be cooked on schedule, all is not lost (thawed frozen meat should not be refrozen).

How to Defrost: Leave meat in its wrapper and set it in the refrigerator or on the counter top (a large roast will take 4–7 hours per pound to defrost in the refrigerator, roughly half that at room temperature; a steak 1″ thick will take 12–14 hours to thaw in the refrigerator, 3–4 hours at room temperature). Never defrost meat in warm water unless it is to be cooked in liquid. Once defrosted, meat can be cooked exactly like fresh meat.

How to Cook Solidly Frozen Meat:

Roasts: Unwrap, place on a rack in a shallow roasting pan, and begin roasting just as you would a fresh roast. When meat has partially thawed, remove from oven and insert meat thermometer in center of roast, not touching bone. Return to oven and continue roasting to desired temperature. *Note:* Solidly frozen roasts will take 1½–2 times as long to cook as the fresh.

Steaks, Chops, and Hamburgers:

To Broil: Place 1″–2″ farther away from heat than recommended for fresh meat and increase total cooking time 1½–2 times.

To Charcoal-Broil: Cook 5″–6″ above moderately hot coals, turning often, about ½ again as long as you would fresh meat.

To Panbroil or Panfry: Brown both sides quickly in a very hot skillet before surface has a chance to thaw (once thawing starts and juices run out, the meat will not brown). Reduce heat to moderately low and cook as you would fresh meat, but turning oftener. Cook 1½–2 times as long.

Meat Loaves: Cook exactly like fresh loaves but 1½–2 times as long. If loaf contains raw pork, insert meat thermometer when loaf is soft enough to do so and continue cooking to 185° F.

Meats to Be Breaded: Thaw just until surface is soft so that breading will stick; then proceed as for fresh meat, increasing cooking time by 1½–2.

Commercially Frozen Meat: Follow package directions.

About Pressure Cooking Meat

Meat cooked under pressure loses flavor, succulence, and attractiveness, so pressure-cook only when absolutely necessary to save time and then only for pot roasts or Swiss steaks that aren't apt to fall apart. Techniques vary from cooker to cooker, so follow the manufacturer's directions. In general, meat will suffer less if cooked at 10 pounds pressure than at 15.

About Reheating Meat

Roasts, the most often leftover cuts, are also the most difficult to rehabilitate. Ideally, they should be transformed into entirely new dishes (see leftover recipes in beef, veal, lamb, and pork sections), but if such is not possible, any of these simple techniques will make warmed-over meat presentable:

– Slice very thin, place on heated plates, and top with hot gravy or sauce.

– Preheat oven to 300° F. Place roast on a rack in a shallow roasting pan and set, uncovered, on upper rack; place a pan of water underneath and heat 25–30 minutes.

– Preheat oven to 350° F. Slice meat thin, layer into a shallow, ungreased casserole with just enough gravy, pan juices, or sauce to cover, cover with foil, and heat 20 minutes. If you prefer, heat slices in gravy, juices, or sauce in a covered skillet about 5 minutes over moderately low heat.

About Meat Stocks

Many of the world's great recipes depend upon stocks, gentle brews of bones, meat trimmings, herbs, and vegetables. Some stocks are simple, others elaborate; some delicate, others concentrated; some dark, some light. Almost all can simmer unattended on the back of the stove. For recipes, see the chapter on soups.

How to Render Fat

Clean, sweet lard (rendered pork fat) and suet (beef kidney fat) are excellent for browning meats and vegetables because they're economical and impart a mellow, meaty flavor. Lard is also such a superior pastry fat that many cooks will use no other.

Suitable Fats to Render: Beef kidney fat; pork kidney fat, clear plate, and fatback.

General preparation: Cut fat into strips 1″ wide, remove any skin, then cut in 1″ cubes. Trim out any meat particles (these burn quickly and can give rendered fat an acrid flavor). Leave fat as cubes or put through coarse blade of meat grinder.

Stove-Top Method: Place prepared fat in a large, heavy skillet and add a little cold water to keep fat from browning before it melts (½ cup should be sufficient for 1–2 pounds fat). Heat uncovered over moderately low heat, stirring frequently, until all fat is melted, about 10 minutes. If you are rendering pork fat, the *cracklings* (cellular membranes in which the fat was held) will soon crispen and brown and rise to the surface. Skim them off and press out any remaining lard (save cracklings for Crackling Bread; they're also good to munch like potato chips). Strain melted fat through a double thickness of cheesecloth and cool until firm. For especially fine grain, cover and chill quickly in the refrigerator. Spoon solidified fat into small crocks or glass jars, cover with lids, and store in a cool, dry, dark, well-ventilated place. Top quality lard or suet, properly stored, should keep 6–12 months.

Oven Method: Preheat oven to 250° F. Spread prepared fat over the bottom of a large, shallow pan, set uncovered in oven and let try out (melt), stirring occasionally. Skim off any cracklings, then strain, cool, and store as above.

To Clarify Rendered Fat: Place prepared fat in a large, heavy saucepan, add boiling water to cover, then boil slowly, uncovered, 10–15 minutes, stirring frequently. Cool 10 minutes, strain through several thicknesses of cheesecloth, cool, and chill without disturbing; lift off clear top layer of fat; discard liquid underneath and scrape off and discard sediment and semiliquid layer on bottom of fat. Store fat in a cool, dry, dark, airy spot.

To Clarify Meat Drippings: Let drippings solidify, then chop coarsely, place in a heavy saucepan with water to cover, and proceed as directed for clarifying rendered fat.

How to Use Meat Thermometers

Meat thermometers, unfortunately, have not kept abreast of America's changing tastes. Rare roast beef, if you go by the thermometer, has an internal temperature of 140° F. Not so. To rare beef enthusiasts, that is medium rare, perhaps even medium. Nearer the mark is 125° F. Readings for lamb are high, too. According to the thermometer, lamb should be cooked to 170° F., well done, indeed, and a disappointment to those who like it juicily pink (130–35° F.). A few thermometers have readings as low as 130° F.; for most 140° F. is the cutoff point. If you are especially fond of very rare meat, try to obtain the new spot-check thermometer (inserted into meat only as it approaches doneness) or the type of thermometer used by food researchers with a 0–220° F. scale (Griffith Labs of Rahway, New Jersey, make them; or inquire through a local gourmet shop or home economics department about obtaining one).

There are two basic types of meat thermometers: the spring-type and the mercury type, the latter preferred by some cooks because of its more detailed scale. Both are used the same way:

For Oven Roasting:
– Hold thermometer against side of meat so you can gauge location of bone, fat, and gristle.

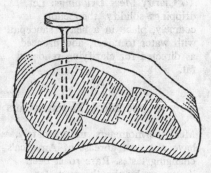

– Insert thermometer in center of largest lean muscle, not touching bone, fat, or gristle.

Place meat in oven with scale facing door so that you can read temperatures at a glance.

For Spit Roasting:
– Insert thermometer into end of cut and parallel to spit so that it touches neither bone nor spit. If necessary, adjust angle slightly so thermometer will clear grill, hood, or oven walls as spit turns.
– When stopping rotisserie, see that thermometer comes to rest as far from heat as possible; otherwise it may break.

BEEF

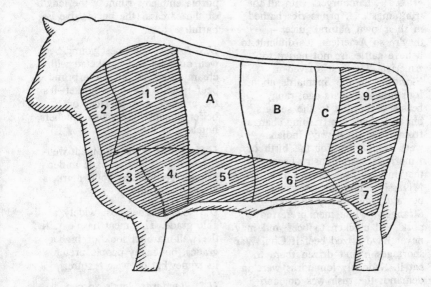

Note: Unshaded parts are the tender cuts. Shaded parts are not-so-tender.

THE TENDER CUTS:

A. Rib
   Roasts (rib, rib eye, or
      Delmonico)
   Steaks (rib, rib eye, or
      Delmonico)
B. Loin
   Steaks (club, T-bone, porter-
      house)
   Tenderloin
C. Sirloin
   Sirloin steaks

THE NOT-SO-TENDER CUTS:

1. Chuck (shoulder)
   Pot roasts
   Swiss-style steaks (blade, arm)
   Stew beef
   Ground beef
2. Neck
   Stew beef

3. Shank
   Stew beef
   Shank crosscuts
4. Brisket
   Corned beef
5. Plate
   Short ribs
   Stew beef
   Ground beef
6. Flank
   Flank steak
   London broil
7. Heel of Round
   Stew beef
8. Round
   Pot roasts
   Steaks (top, eye, and bottom
      round)
   Ground beef
9. Rump
   Pot roasts

T-bones sizzling on a back-yard grill . . . hamburgers with all the trimmings . . . prime ribs bathed in their own natural juices—they're so American it's difficult to believe cattle are not native to America. The first arrived in Florida with the Spaniards about four hundred years ago, rangy beasts of burden to the settlers, but to Indians a refreshing change from game. In a way, Indians were responsible for the birth of America's beef industry because they moved these cattle across the Mississippi into the grasslands beyond, where they thrived. Strangely, white men preferred pork and chicken to beef and may never have prized beef if Civil War shortages hadn't driven them to eat it. Suddenly longhorns were in demand, the rush was on, and with it the hell-for-leather days of cowboys and cattle barons and hundred-mile drives to market. Soon there were railroads, and beef, no longer driven to market, grew fat and lazy and succulent and tender. Ranchers quickly learned that penned steers were tenderer still and those fed corn and grain the most flavorful. Today beef production is highly scientific. And beef, itself, is our No. 1 meat.

How to Recognize Quality in Beef

Look first for the *federal inspector's round purple stamp* (see discussion at beginning of this chapter), second for *grade*, which is based on *conformation* (proportion of meat to bone), *quality* (marbling or distribution of fat in lean, color and texture of lean, fat and bone) and *cutability* (amount of usable meat). If beef has been graded by a federal agent, you will see his stamp, a series of shield-shaped purple emblems running the length of the carcass (the purple dye is harmless):

U.S. Prime: The finest young beef, well marbled and blanketed with a creamy layer of fat. Little prime beef reaches the supermarket—it's the grand champion steer or heifer bought by prestige butchers, hotels, and restaurants.

U.S. Choice: Finely grained, well-marbled beef just a shade under prime. Available at good markets across the country.

U.S. Good: The most widely available grade. This meat hasn't quite the well-marbled look of higher grades, but many people prefer its somewhat chewier texture.

U.S. Standard: Here's an economical, all-purpose beef. Its steaks and roasts, though not the juiciest, are quite acceptable. The meat is not particularly well marbled, and the outer fat covering is apt to be skimpy.

The four lowest grades—*U.S. Commercial, Utility, Canner, and Cutter*—are of little concern here because they're rarely sold in retail stores. Packers use them for making sausages, frankfurters, and other process meats.

How to Tell Quality When the Grade Doesn't Show on the Cut: Tender, young beef will be bright cherry red, the fat creamy white and the chine (backbone) spongy and red. Older beef will be darker red, its fat yellowish and bones flinty. An orange cast to the fat suggests the animal was range fed and that its meat may be tough.

Note: When first cut, beef will be dark purple-brown. This doesn't mean it's spoiled, old, or tough, merely that it hasn't been exposed to the air (oxygen gives beef its vivid red color).

About Tendered Beef

By injecting live animals with an enzyme called papain, meat packers cannot only assure tenderness of roasts and steaks, but they can also make certain cuts of round, rump, and chuck so tender they can be broiled or roasted. Such beef is sold as *"tendered beef"* and is accompanied by cooking instructions. Follow them because tendered beef usually cooks more quickly than untendered beef.

ROAST BEEF

The Top Tender Cuts

Standing Ribs: There are 3 different rib roasts, named for the part of the rib from which they come:

First-Rib Roast (5–8 pounds): Also sometimes called the *11th-and-12th-rib roast,* this cut is from the loin end of the rib. It's the most desirable and expensive rib roast because of its large, meaty center muscle, called the rib eye.

Center-Rib Roast (5–8 pounds): The mid-rib cut with a slightly smaller eye and slightly lower cost.

Sixth-and-Seventh-Rib Roast (5–8 pounds): From the chuck or shoulder end of the rib, this roast may not be so tender as the first two.

3 Styles for Standing Ribs: Each rib roast can be cut 3 ways:

10" Standing Rib: The ribs are 10" long, the backbone still intact. There's little advantage in having

such long ribs because they provide almost no meat. Better to have them cut off and to cook as short ribs.

7" Standing Rib: Probably the best style; 3" of ribs have been sawed off and the backbone removed.

6" Standing Rib: The newest look in rib roasts, a bit too "sawed off," perhaps, to be graceful, but a good choice for spit roasting because it is easy to balance on the spit.

Boned and Rolled Rib Roast (4–6 pounds): All rib roasts can be boned and rolled; they are easier to carve than standing ribs but take longer to cook. Some say they lack the rich, beefy flavor of standing ribs.

Rib Eye or Delmonico Roast (3–6 pounds): The boneless, meaty rib eye.

Whole Tenderloin or Filet (see Tenderloin).

Sirloin (8–12 pounds): The grand-daddy of roasts adored by the English. Few American butchers will sell sirloin as roast because it's much more in demand as steak. *Boneless sirloin,* however, is becoming more and more popular, particularly in the Northeast.

Marginally Tender Roasts

These less expensive cuts are "iffy" roasts—tender enough to roast *if* from prime, choice, or tendered beef. When in doubt about them, braise.

Sirloin Tip (3–5 pounds): A chunky, lean, triangular cut.

Standing or Rolled Rump (4–7 pounds): Often underrated, this blocky, hind-quarter cut has unusually good flavor.

Top Round (3–6 pounds): Though usually reserved for steaks, top round can be left whole and roasted. It's a single, large lean muscle, the tenderest one of the round.

Eye Round (2½–5 pounds): Probably the "iffiest" cut of all. Eye round looks like whole tenderloin, but there the resemblance ends; it will be tender enough to roast only if of tiptop quality.

How to Roast Beef

Suitable Cuts: Standing Rib, Boned and Rolled Rib, Rib Eye, Sirloin and, if top quality, Sirloin Tip, Standing and Rolled Rump, Top and Eye Round. Bear in mind that boneless roasts will take about 10 minutes per pound longer to cook than bone-in roasts; also that small roasts take proportionately longer to cook than large roasts.

Amount Needed: The bigger the roast, the better it will be. Standing ribs should weigh at least 5 pounds and be 2 ribs wide; boned and rolled ribs should be no less than 4 pounds. To figure number of servings, allow ⅓–½ pound boneless roast per person; ¾ pound bone-in roast.

General Preparation for Cooking: Let roast stand at room temperature 1½–2 hours if possible. Season, if you like, with salt and pepper (salt penetrates only ¼″, so it makes little difference whether a roast is salted before or after cooking). For extra savor, rub roast with a cut clove of garlic or suitable herb (see Sauces, Gravies,

and Seasonings for Roast Beef). Some cooks also like to flour a roast and start it at a high temperature to help seal in juices and give it a nice brown crust, but tests have shown it's wasted effort as far as sealing in the juices is concerned.

Continuous Low Heat Method: Preheat oven to 300° F. Place roast fat side up in a large, shallow roasting pan; all but standing ribs should be put on a rack so they're kept out of the drippings (with standing ribs, the ribs themselves act as a rack). Insert meat thermometer in lean in center of roast, not touching bone. Do not cover roast; do not add liquid to pan; do not baste roast as it cooks. Using times and temperatures in Roast Beef Chart as a guide, roast to desired degree of doneness. Transfer roast to heated platter, let "rest," if you like, then serve Au Jus or with Pan Gravy.

Searing Method: Preheat oven to 450° F. Insert meat thermometer and place in pan as for low heat method. Roast, uncovered, 25 minutes, reduce heat to 300° F. (leaving oven door open will quickly bring temperature down), and continue roasting to desired doneness. Bone-in roasts will take about 16 minutes per pound for rare (125–30° F.), 18 for medium rare (140–45° F.), 20–22 for medium (155–60° F.), and 25–27 for well done (165–70° F.); boneless roasts will require 8–10 minutes longer per pound for each degree of doneness. Transfer roast to heated platter, garnish, and serve.

How to Spit-Roast Beef

Always make sure a roast *stays* balanced and turns evenly throughout cooking. If you plan to let roast "rest" 15–20 minutes before serving, remove from spit when thermometer is 5–10° below desired doneness.

Best Cuts: A 6" or 7" Standing Rib or a Boned and Rolled Rib.

Amount Needed: For best results, the standing rib should weigh 5–8 pounds, the boned and rolled rib 4–6.

General Preparation for Cooking: If using the standing rib, have butcher remove backbone. Let roast stand at room temperature 1½–2 hours if possible. Season or not, as you like.

In Rotisserie or Oven: Preheat unit. Insert spit on bias so meat is balanced; tighten holding forks. Insert meat thermometer in center of largest lean muscle, touching neither bone nor the spit. Attach spit to rotisserie and roast to desired doneness. Standing ribs will take 12–14 minutes per pound for rare (125–30° F.), 15–17 for medium rare (140–45° F.), 18–20 for medium (155–60° F.), and 21–23 for well done (165–70° F.). Boned and rolled roasts will take about 10 minutes longer per pound for each degree of doneness.

Over Charcoal: Prepare a moderately hot charcoal fire.* Balance roast on spit as above and insert thermometer. Adjust fire bed height so coals are 6" from spit, then roast to desired doneness, using approximately same times as for rotisserie. Watch thermometer closely—it's the truest indicator of doneness.

VARIATION:

Spit-Barbecued Beef: Marinate

roast in refrigerator 12–24 hours in 1 pint Barbecue Sauce for Beef, turning 2–3 times. Let come to room temperature in marinade, then spit-roast as above. During last ¾ hour of cooking, baste often with marinade. Serve with Barbecue Gravy for Beef.

ROAST BEEF CHART

American tastes are changing. Those who like rare roast beef like it *really* rare, about 125–30° F. on a meat thermometer, not 140° F., as many cookbooks recommend. To rare beef buffs, 140° F. is medium rare, perhaps even medium. It depends on one's definition of rare. If you like beef juicy and red (not pink), try taking it from the oven when the thermometer reads 120–25° F. and letting it "rest" at room temperature 15–20 minutes before carving. Letting beef rest is good practice no matter how you like it cooked—the roast will be juicier, easier to carve. Because a roast will continue cooking as it rests, it should be brought from the oven when the thermometer is 5–10° below desired doneness.

About Using the Chart
—Times can only be approximate, since shape of cut, amount of fat and bone, the way the meat was aged, and internal temperature all affect roasting time. So does size; proportionately, large roasts take less time to cook than small ones. Timetables, thus, are most useful in telling you when to put a roast in the oven so that you can gauge meal preparation time. For the truest test of doneness, use a meat thermometer.
—Times are for roasts that have stood at room temperature 1½–2

hours, then roasted at a constant low temperature (300° F.).

• To roast at 325° F. (the outer fat covering will be slightly crisper), allow about 2 minutes less per pound.

• For refrigerated roasts, allow 2–3 minutes more per pound.

Cut	Weight in Pounds	Approximate Minutes per Pound at 300° F.	Meat Thermometer Temperature
Standing Ribs			
Rare	5–8	17–19	125–30° F.
Medium rare	5–8	20–22	140–45° F.
Medium	5–8	23–25	155–60° F.
Well done	5–8	27–30	165–70° F.
Boned and rolled Rib roasts	4–6	Add about 8–10 minutes per pound to each of the times given for standing ribs —and keep a close eye on the meat thermometer.	
Sirloin			
Rare	8–12	16–20	125–30° F.
Medium rare	8–12	20–22	140–45° F.
Medium	8–12	23–25	155–60° F.
Well done	8–12	26–30	165–70° F.

Note: The following cuts should be roasted only if prime, choice, or "tendered." Some beef connoisseurs also feel that they are better cooked to medium or well done.

Sirloin tip (a boneless roast)			
Rare	3–5	28–30	125–30° F.
Medium rare	3–5	30–33	140–45° F.
Medium	3–5	34–38	155–60° F.
Well done	3–5	40–45	165–70° F.
Standing rump			
Rare	5–7	20–22	125–30° F.
Medium rare	5–7	23–25	140–45° F.
Medium	5–7	26–28	155–60° F.
Well done	5–7	29–32	165–70° F.
Boned and rolled Rump roast	4–6	Add 5–8 minutes per pound to each of the times given for standing rump, but use meat thermometer as the most accurate indicator.	
Top round (a chunky, boneless cut)			
Rare	3–6	28–30	125–30° F.
Medium rare	3–6	30–33	140–45° F.
Medium	3–6	34–38	155–60° F.
Well done	3–6	40–45	165–70° F.

Note: Because of their long, narrow shape, rib eye (Delmonico) and eye round will cook more evenly at 350° F. than 300° F. The same is true of all small roasts (under 3 pounds).

Cut	Weight in Pounds	Approximate Minutes per Pound at 300° F.	Meat Thermometer Temperature
Rib eye and eye round			
Rare	3–6	12	125–30° F.
Medium rare	3–6	14	140–45° F.
Medium	3–6	16	155–60° F.
Well done	3–6	18–20	165–70° F.

How to Carve a Standing Rib Roast:
Lay roast, large side down, on platter; if wobbly, cut slice off bottom to level. Steady roast by inserting carving fork below top rib; with a short-bladed knife, cut down along ribs to loosen meat. With a carving knife, cut across face of roast to ribs, making slices ⅛″–¼″ thick and lifting each off as it is cut.

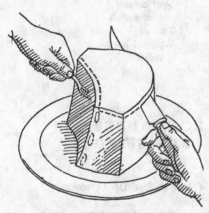

How to Carve a Boned and Rolled Rib Roast:
If roast seems firm (and carver is experienced) remove strings in kitchen. Otherwise, leave on lest roast fall apart. Lay roast on its side on platter. Steady with fork, and cut straight down through roll into ⅛″–¼″ slices, removing strings as you go. When through carving, turn roast cut side up so juices won't run out.

Some Garnishes for Roast Beef Platters (in addition to parsley fluffs and watercress sprigs)

The point in garnishing is to make a roast look as good to eat as it is. Group vegetables around platter, alternating colors, or wreathe them prettily around roast, using only enough to enhance the roast, not so many that you overwhelm it and make carving difficult.

Artichoke Bottoms: boiled and buttered; Artichoke Bottoms Stuffed with Vegetables; Artichoke Bottoms Princesse.

Artichoke Hearts: boiled and buttered.

Asparagus Tips: boiled and buttered.

Brussels Sprouts: boiled and buttered.

Carrots: Buttered Baby Carrots; Carrots Rosemary; Lemon-Glazed Carrots; Carrots Vichy.

Celery Hearts: boiled and buttered.

Fruits: broiled apricot or peach halves; spiced crab apples.

Mushrooms: sautéed button mushrooms, mushroom caps, or sliced mushrooms; Baked Mushroom Caps Stuffed with Hazelnuts.

SAUCES, GRAVIES, AND SEASONINGS FOR ROAST BEEF

For Cooking: Seasonings, Herbs, Spices	For Hot Roast Beef: Gravies	Sauces
Garlic	Au jus (unthick-	Bordelaise
Mustard	ened pan gravy)	Bourguignonne
Oregano	Mushroom	Espagnole
Parsley	Pan gravy	Figaro (roast
Rosemary	Sour cream	tenderloin)
Thyme	Wine	Périgueux
		Hot horseradish
		Smitane (roast
		tenderloin)

For Hot or Cold Roast Beef: Condiments	For Cold Roast Beef: Sauces
Horseradish	Cumberland
Ketchup or chili	Cold ravigote
sauce	Rémoulade
Mustard	Sour cream-
Pickles (bread and	horseradish
butter, dill,	Tartar
green tomato)	Whipped horse-
	radish

Onions: Glazed Onions; Pan-Braised Onions; Stuffed Onions.

Parsnips: Currant or Caramel-Glazed Parsnips; Roasted Parsnips.

Pickles: mustard; watermelon rind.

Potatoes: Franconia, Château, Parisienne, Dauphine, or Shoestring Potatoes; cones of Duchess Potatoes; Parsleyed, Herbed, or Lemon-Glazed New Potatoes; Danish-Style New Potatoes.

Tomatoes: raw cherry tomatoes or tomato wedges; Stuffed Tomatoes.

Turnips: Glazed or Roasted Turnips; Turnips Stuffed with Risotto.

Yorkshire Pudding: baked in individual ramekins.

ROAST BEEF REVISITED

(How to Use Up Leftovers)

⚔ **BEEF MIROTON**

Here's an unusually good way to use up leftover roast beef.
Makes 4 servings

*1 medium-size yellow onion, peeled
and minced
1 tablespoon beef drippings, butter,
or margarine
2 tablespoons flour
1 cup beef broth
1 cup leftover beef gravy*

2 tablespoons red wine vinegar
½ cup dry red or white wine
  (optional)
1 tablespoon tomato paste
8 slices leftover roast beef
1 tablespoon minced parsley

Sauté onion in drippings over moderate heat 8–10 minutes until golden; blend in flour, slowly add broth, and cook, stirring, until thickened. Mix in all remaining ingredients except beef and parsley, then heat, stirring, 2–3 minutes. Pour about ⅓ of the sauce into a shallow, ungreased 1½-quart casserole, lay beef on top, overlapping slices, and add remaining sauce. Cover and refrigerate 1 hour. Preheat oven to 350° F. Bake, covered, 15–20 minutes until bubbly. Sprinkle with parsley and serve. About 230 calories per serving.

¢ BEEF CROQUETTES

Makes 4 servings

2 cups cubed leftover lean cooked beef
1 large yellow onion, peeled and quartered
2 tablespoons butter or margarine
¼ cup unsifted flour
1 cup strong beef broth or stock
1¼ teaspoons salt
⅛ teaspoon pepper
1 tablespoon steak or Worcestershire sauce
1 egg, lightly beaten
¾ cup toasted fine bread crumbs
¼ cup cooking oil

Grind beef with onion, using fine blade of meat grinder. Melt butter over moderately high heat, mix in flour, and brown *lightly*, stirring. Slowly add broth and heat, stirring, until thickened; add salt, pepper, and steak sauce and mix into ground meat. Spread in a shallow dish, cover, and chill until easy to work.

Shape into 8 sausage-like rolls, dip in egg, then in crumbs; dry on a wire rack 10 minutes. Brown croquettes in oil in a large, heavy skillet over moderate heat 5–7 minutes, turning often; drain on paper toweling and serve. Good with gravy, Tomato, Mushroom, or Madeira Sauce. About 380 calories per serving (without sauce).

VARIATIONS:

Other Meat Croquettes: Use leftover lamb, pork, ham, veal, or chicken or a ½ and ½ mixture of chicken and ham or tongue instead of beef. Do not brown the flour, and use chicken broth instead of beef broth. Otherwise mix and cook as directed above. About 380 calories per serving for lamb, pork, ham or veal croquettes, 330 calories per serving for chicken croquettes.

Deep-Fat-Fried Croquettes: Shape meat mixture into 16 balls, dip in egg and crumbs, and deep-fry in a basket 2–3 minutes in 375° F. fat. Drain and serve. About 380 calories per serving.

Dressed-Up Croquettes: Add any 1 of the following to croquette mixture: 1 tablespoon prepared mustard or horseradish; ¼ cup minced ripe olives; ½ cup chopped, sautéed mushrooms; 2 tablespoons chili sauce, minced capers, dill pickle, or sweet green pepper; 1 crushed clove garlic; 1 teaspoon parsley flakes, oregano, marjoram, curry, or chili powder; 1 teaspoon mint flakes (for lamb); 1 teaspoon dill (for veal or lamb). About 385 calories per serving for croquettes made with olives or mushrooms; all others 380 calories per serving.

¢ **Budget Croquettes:** Add 1½ cups cooked rice or mashed potatoes to croquette mixture, shape into 12 rolls, and brown as directed. Makes 6 servings. About 400 calories per serving.

¢ **PARSLEYED BEEF PINWHEELS**

Makes 6 servings

Pastry:
2 *cups packaged biscuit mix*
½ *teaspoon salt*
1 *tablespoon minced parsley*
⅔ *cup milk*

Stuffing:
2 *cups coarsely ground cooked beef*
¾ *cup condensed cream of*
  mushroom, celery, or tomato soup
3–4 *scallions, minced fine*
1 *tablespoon steak sauce*

Preheat oven to 400° F. Mix pastry ingredients lightly with a fork, knead 8–10 times on a floured board, and roll into a 6″×10″ rectangle. Mix all stuffing ingredients and spread over pastry, leaving ½″ margins all round. Roll from the long side so you have a roll 10″ long. Transfer to an ungreased baking sheet with a wide spatula and bake, uncovered, 30 minutes until lightly browned. Slice and serve with hot leftover gravy or Quick Mushroom Gravy. About 410 calories per serving (without gravy).

VARIATION:

¢ **Beef Stuffed Crepes** (6–8 servings): Preheat oven to 350° F. Instead of making pastry, prepare 1 recipe Crepes for Savory Fillings. Prepare stuffing as directed, adding ½ cup milk or cream. Place a little stuffing in the center of each crepe and roll up. Lay crepes seam side down, close together, in a single layer in a buttered 8″×8″×2″ pan. Bake, uncovered, 20–30 minutes until heated through.

If you like, sprinkle with grated cheese and brown quickly under broiler. Serve with hot leftover gravy, Quick Mushroom Gravy, or Tomato or Cheese Sauce. About 265 calories for each of 6 servings (without gravy), 200 calories for each of 8 servings (without gravy).

Some Additional Ways to Use Up Leftover Roast Beef

¢ **Beef, Macaroni, and Tomato Casserole** (6 servings): Mix together ½ pound boiled, drained macaroni, 1½ pints canned tomato or meatless spaghetti sauce, 2–3 cups diced cooked beef, and 1 drained (4-ounce) can sliced mushrooms. Season to taste with garlic or onion salt and pepper. Spoon into a greased 2½-quart casserole, top with grated cheese, and bake uncovered about 30 minutes at 375° F. until bubbly. About 660 calories per serving.

¢ **Beef Creole** (4 servings): Stir-fry 1 minced large yellow onion, 1 minced sweet green pepper, and 1 cup minced celery in 3 tablespoons drippings or butter in a large, heavy skillet over moderate heat 8–10 minutes until onion is golden. Add 1 (10-ounce) package frozen sliced okra, 1 (10-ounce) package frozen whole kernel corn, 1 (1-pound) can tomatoes, 1–2 teaspoons chili powder, and 2 cups diced cooked beef. Cover and simmer 15 minutes. Stir in ¼ teaspoon gumbo filé and salt and pepper to taste and serve over boiled rice. About 330 calories per serving.

Spicy Breaded Beef Slices (Number of servings flexible): Cut roast into ¼″ slices and trim off fat. Spread slices out on a large platter, sprinkle with salt and pepper, and drizzle with about 2 tablespoons red wine vinegar; let stand 20–30 minutes. Dip slices in flour, then in 1 egg lightly beaten with 2 tablespoons milk or cream, then in dry bread crumbs to coat evenly. Brown on both sides in 2–3 tablespoons butter or oil in a large skillet over moderately high heat; serve with Rémoulade or Tomato Sauce. About 260 calories per medium-size (3-ounce) slice (without sauce).

¢ **Beef and Potato Cakes** (4–6 servings): Mix together 2 cups mashed potatoes, 1½ cups coarsely ground cooked beef, 1 lightly beaten egg, 1 teaspoon onion flakes, and salt and pepper to taste. Shape into patties, dust lightly with flour, and brown in 2 tablespoons butter 2–3 minutes on each side over moderate heat. (*Note:* Finely crumbled leftover hamburgers can be used in place of roast.) For extra zip, mix in any of the following: 1 tablespoon minced parsley, chives, prepared mustard, horseradish, chili sauce, or ketchup. About 285 calories for each of 4 servings, 205 calories for each of 6 servings.

⊠ **Quick Beef Paprika** (4 servings): Stir-fry ½ cup each minced yellow onion and mushrooms in 2 tablespoons butter, margarine, or drippings in a heavy skillet 8–10 minutes over moderate heat until onion is golden. Blend in 1–2 tablespoons paprika and ½ cup light cream and simmer, uncovered, 5 minutes. Add 2 cups cubed cooked beef, cover, and simmer over lowest heat 10–15 minutes until beef is heated through and flavors blended. Season to taste with salt and pepper, smooth in 1 cup sour cream, and serve over buttered noodles or boiled rice. (*Note:*

Veal may be substituted for the beef.) About 400 calories per serving.

Beef Curry (4–6 servings): Stir-fry 1 minced yellow onion and chopped sweet apple in ¼ cup meat drippings or oil 8 minutes until golden; blend in 5 tablespoons flour, 3 tablespoons curry powder, 1 teaspoon salt, 1 pint beef broth (use part gravy if you have it), 1 cup water (or vegetable cooking water or tomato juice), and 1 tablespoon Worcestershire sauce and heat, stirring, until thickened. Add 3–4 cups cubed cooked beef, cover, and simmer 20 minutes. Let stand off heat ¾–1 hour, if possible, to blend flavors, then reheat just before serving. Serve with boiled rice, chutney, a green salad, and buttery chunks of garlic bread. (*Note:* Recipe may also be made with lamb or veal.) About 410 calories for each of 4 servings, 270 calories for each of 6 servings.

¢ **Beef, Mushroom, and Noodle Casserole** (6 servings): Mix together ½ pound boiled, drained noodles, 2 (10½-ounce) cans cream of mushroom soup blended with 1 cup milk, 1 undrained (4-ounce) can sliced mushrooms and 3 cups julienne strips of cooked beef. Season to taste with garlic or onion salt and pepper. Spoon into a greased 2½-quart casserole, top with about ⅓ cup butter-browned bread crumbs, and bake, uncovered, 30–40 minutes at 350° F. until bubbly. (*Note:* Dish is also good made with leftover roast veal.) About 600 calories per serving.

¢ **Beef and Vegetable Pie** (4–6 servings): Mix 2 cups cubed cooked beef with 2 cups mixed leftover vegetables—any compatible combination: peas and carrots, corn and green or lima beans, potatoes with almost anything. Stir in 1½ cups thin leftover gravy or 1 (10½-ounce) cream of potato or celery soup thinned with ¾ cup water and, for extra flavor, 1 minced yellow onion and ½ minced sweet green pepper sautéed in a little butter until limp. Spoon into a greased 6-cup casserole or deep pie dish, cover with Flaky Pastry I, Rough Puff Pastry, or Biscuit Topping for Casseroles, and bake, uncovered, 35–40 minutes at 425° F. until lightly browned. (*Note:* Lamb or veal can be used instead of beef.) About 690 calories for each of 4 servings, 460 calories for each of 6 servings.

¢ **Beef Stuffed Vegetables** (4 servings): Prepare 4 large tomatoes, sweet green peppers, or yellow onions for stuffing.* Stir-fry 1 minced yellow onion, 2 minced stalks celery, ¼ pound chopped mushrooms, and 1 crushed clove garlic in ¼ cup drippings or butter 8–10 minutes over moderate heat until onion is golden. Off heat mix in 1½ cups each soft white bread crumbs and coarsely ground cooked beef and ¾ cup leftover gravy or tomato sauce. Stuff vegetables, stand upright in an ungreased 1-quart casserole, and pour in gravy, beef broth, or tomato juice to a depth of ½". Bake, uncovered, 30–45 minutes at 375° F. until tender. (*Note:* Veal, lamb, or ham can be used in place of beef.) About 345 calories per serving.

¢ **Barbecued Beef and Potatoes** (Number of servings flexible): Prepare 1 recipe Barbecue Gravy for Beef. Arrange sliced beef in an ungreased shallow casserole and top with drained, canned whole potatoes. Pour in gravy almost to cover and bake, uncovered, about 20 minutes at 350° F. until heated through. (*Note:* Leftover roast pork can be prepared the same way.) Recipe too flexible for a meaningful calorie count.

¢ **Beef Chow Mein or Chop Suey** (4 servings): Stir-fry 1 minced large yellow onion or bunch scallions in 2 tablespoons oil 5 minutes over moderate heat in a large skillet; add 2 cups diced cooked beef and stir-fry 5 minutes longer. Prepare 2 (1-pound) cans chow mein or chop suey vegetables (without meat) by package directions and when hot stir in skillet mixture and 1 tablespoon soy sauce. Simmer, uncovered, 2–3 minutes and serve over chow mein noodles or boiled rice. (*Note:* Pork can be substituted for the beef.) About 270 calories per serving.

¢ **Roast Beef Hash** (4–6 servings): Stir-fry 1 minced yellow onion in 2 tablespoons meat drippings in a large, heavy skillet over moderate heat 8–10 minutes until golden. Add 2 cups diced roast beef, 2–3 cups diced boiled potatoes, 1 teaspoon salt, ¼ teaspoon pepper, ½ cup evaporated milk, and 1 minced large dill pickle. Spread hash evenly in skillet, leave uncovered, and brown over moderately low heat without stirring 30–40 minutes until underside is crusty. Fold over in half as you would an omelet and slide onto a heated platter. Serve with dill pickles, chili sauce, or ketchup. (*Note:* This recipe can be halved easily. It can also be made with corned beef, canned or processed meats, tongue, leftover lamb, pork, veal, or ham.) About 365 calories for each of 4 servings, 245 calories for each of 6 servings.

¢ **Yukon Stew** (6 servings): In a large saucepan place 2 cups cubed cooked beef, 1 pound each peeled and parboiled whole baby carrots, new potatoes, and small white onions *or* 1 (1-pound) can each drained whole baby carrots and whole potatoes and 1 (1-pound) can undrained small white onions. Add leftover gravy, beef broth, or water almost to cover (if using water, add a beef bouillon cube for extra flavor; also, if you like, 2 tablespoons tomato paste, 1–2 tablespoons Worcestershire or steak sauce). Cover and simmer 15 minutes over moderate heat; stir in 3 tablespoons flour blended with ¼ cup cold water and heat, stirring, until thickened. Taste for salt and pepper and adjust as needed. Serve as is or, if you like, top with Dumplings and finish cooking as dumpling recipe directs. Or, ladle into small individual casseroles, top with pastry or Biscuit Topping for Casseroles, and bake about 25–30 minutes at 425° F. until brown. (*Note:* Lamb or veal can be used instead of beef.) About 355 calories per serving with dumplings, pastry, or biscuit topping, 255 calories per serving without.

Sliced Cold Beef: Slice beef about ¼" thick, trim of fat, and top with any recommended cold sauce (see Sauces, Gravies, and Seasonings for Roast Beef). Recipe too flexible for a meaningful calorie count.

Sliced Hot Beef: Slice beef about ¼" thick, trim of fat, and layer into a shallow, ungreased casserole. Add just enough hot sauce to cover (see Sauces, Gravies, and Seasonings for Roast Beef), cover with foil, and heat 20 minutes at 350° F. Or, if you prefer, heat beef in sauce about 5 minutes in a covered skillet over moderately low heat. Recipe too flexible for a meaningful calorie count.

Hot Roast Beef Sandwiches: Heat meat in any suitable sauce as for Sliced Hot Beef (above) and serve, open face, on a slice of toast or bread. Or, heat beef slices in a little broth, drain, and sandwich between toasted hamburger buns spread with mustard, relish, chutney, or any condiment you wish. Recipe too flexible for a meaningful calorie count.

To Make the Most of Very Small Amounts:

– Cube beef or cut in julienne strips and toss into hearty salads (chef's salad, dried bean, egg, potato, pasta, or rice salads).
– Cube and use to stretch budget casseroles (dried bean, pasta, rice, mixed vegetables).
– Cube and substitute for raw beef in soups and broths (add bones, whenever possible, to enrich flavor). Or dice fine and add to vegetable soups—homemade or canned.
– Add lean scraps and bones to stock pot.
– Grind fine and make into sandwich spreads by mixing with softened cream cheese, mayonnaise and/or mustard, or horseradish.
– Grind fine, mix with any seasoned butter, a little minced onion or capers, mustard or other spicy condiment and use as a cocktail spread.
– Grind fine and add to any savory stuffings.
– Grind small scraps fine, simmer with water to cover, purée in a blender, strain and use as a base for making gravy.
– Cut into small thin slices, trim

of fat, and layer into custard cups, adding thinly sliced cooked carrots between layers, if you like. Fill to brim with Basic Aspic or Jellied Consommé Madrilène and chill until firm. Unmold on salad greens and serve with mayonnaise or any suitable cold sauce (see Sauces, Gravies, and Seasonings for Roast Beef).

BEEF TENDERLOIN

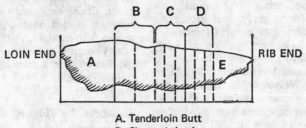

A. Tenderloin Butt
B. Chateaubriand
C. Filet Steaks
D. Tournedos
E. Filet Mignon

Butter-smooth, boneless, and so tender you scarcely need a knife to cut it, tenderloin is the Rolls-Royce of beef. It can be roasted, sliced into steaks, and broiled or sautéed, cubed for Stroganoff or Fondue Bourguignonne, even ground for Steak Tartare.

Though we tend to think of filet mignon as any small tenderloin steak, it is actually the smallest of four. Choicest is the 2″–3″ *chateaubriand*, cut from the chunky center of the tenderloin; it should weigh at least 1 pound before trimming and serve 2–3. Next in line are the individual *filet steaks*, 3″–3½″ in diameter and usually cut 1″–2″ thick.

Third are the *tournedos* or *medallions of beef*, about 1″ less in diameter but cut similarly thick. Finally come the *filets mignons* from the thin rib end. *Mignon* means *dainty* or *tiny*, and these, rarely seen in supermarkets, are often no more than 1½″ across. All tenderloin deserves special treatment, both in the cooking (always serve rare or medium rare) and in the presentation.

A word about grade: It is sometimes difficult to buy prime, even choice tenderloin because butchers don't like to strip it from top grade animals—it's too integral a part of T-bones and porterhouse steaks. Little matter, however, because tenderloin from a good grade animal will be very nearly as tender.

ROAST WHOLE BEEF TENDERLOIN

Tenderloin isn't the easiest cut to roast because it tapers sharply at one end. For best results, tuck the skinny end under before barding (or buy only the plump part of the tenderloin) and roast just until rare or medium rare. Many butchers, incidentally, will do the barding for you.

Makes 8–12 servings

Suet for barding
1 whole beef tenderloin (about 4–6
*   pounds), trimmed of fat and*
*   connective tissue*
3–4 tablespoons softened unsalted
*   butter or Garlic Butter*
1½ teaspoons salt
¼ teaspoon pepper

Suggested Garnishes:
Stuffed Mushrooms
Broiled tomato halves
Shoestring Potatoes
Watercress or parsley sprigs

Suggested Sauce:
Béarnaise or Madeira

Bard tenderloin* with suet, then let stand at room temperature 1½–2 hours if convenient. Meanwhile, preheat oven to 450° F. Rub exposed tenderloin ends with 2 tablespoons butter, insert meat thermometer in center of meat, and roast, uncovered, on a rack in a shallow roasting pan 6–7 minutes per pound for rare (125–30° F.), 8–9 minutes for medium rare (140–45° F.). Remove suet covering during last 10–15 minutes and brush tenderloin well with remaining butter so it will brown nicely. Transfer to steak board or hot platter, cover loosely, and let "rest" 5 minutes. Sprinkle with salt and pepper and garnish with 2 or more of the suggested garnishes. Slice ½"–1" thick and serve with Madeira, Béarnaise, or other suitable sauce (see chart of Sauces, Gravies, and Seasonings for Roast Beef, also for Steaks). About 420 calories for each of 8 servings (without sauce), 375 for each of 12 servings (without sauce).

To Roast a Half Tenderloin (4–6 servings): Choose a 2–3 pound tenderloin of as uniform thickness as possible. Bard and tie as above, insert thermometer, and roast at 450° F., using above times as a guide. About 420 calories for each of 4 servings, 375 calories for each of 6 servings (without sauce).

To Spit-Roast Whole Beef Tenderloin:

In Rotisserie or Oven: Preheat unit. Balance barded tenderloin on spit by skewering lengthwise; tighten holding forks, attach to rotisserie, and broil 25–30 minutes for rare, 35–40 for medium rare or according to the manufacturer's time table. Remove suet and brown quickly under broiler. Season and serve. Same calorie counts as roast whole beef tenderloin.

Over Charcoal: Prepare a hot charcoal fire.* Balance barded tenderloin on spit as above, attach to rotisserie, adjust height so spit is 6" from coals, and broil 30–35 minutes for rare, 40–45 for medium rare. Remove suet for last 10 minutes and brush often with melted unsalted butter. Season and serve. Same calorie counts as roast whole beef tenderloin.

VARIATIONS (All have approximately the same number of calories per serving as roast whole beef tenderloin not including sauce, except for last two variations. They run about 100 calories higher per serving):

Beef Tenderloin Rosemary: Bard and roast tenderloin as directed up to point of removing suet. When suet is removed, sprinkle tenderloin with ½ teaspoon crushed rosemary, 1 teaspoon salt, and ¼ teaspoon coarsely ground pepper. Finish roasting as directed, basting often with

Burgundy (you'll need about ⅔ cup in all). When serving, top each portion with some of the Burgundy pan drippings.

Beef Tenderloin Madeira: Before barding, marinate tenderloin in 1 pint medium-dry Madeira 4–8 hours in the refrigerator; remove from marinade, pat dry, bard, and roast as directed. Serve with Madeira Sauce (use marinade in preparing sauce).

Spicy Marinated Beef Tenderloin: Before barding, marinate tenderloin 4–8 hours in refrigerator in 1½ cups moderately sweet port or Madeira mixed with ½ cup tarragon vinegar, 1 thinly sliced yellow onion, and ¼ teaspoon each cinnamon, nutmeg, and ginger. After marinating, bard and roast as directed. When making gravy, use strained marinade for the liquid.

Savory "Stuffed" Tenderloin: Before barding, cut tenderloin almost —but not quite—through in 1″ slices (it's the same technique used in preparing garlic bread, cutting to, but not through, the bottom crust). Spread tenderloin slices with a savory butter (see chart of Sauces, Butters, and Seasonings for Steaks), reshape, pressing slices together, and tie with string to secure. Bard and roast as directed.

Truffled Tenderloin: Slice tenderloin as for Savory "Stuffed" Tenderloin, spread slices with softened butter, and sprinkle with a little finely minced truffles (you'll need 2–3). Reshape tenderloin, tie, rub with ¼ teaspoon coarsely ground pepper, bard, and roast as directed. Serve, if you like, with Madeira Sauce.

ROAST TENDERLOIN OF BEEF SMITANE

Makes 4–6 servings

1 (2–3-pound) beef tenderloin of uniform thickness, trimmed of fat and connective tissue
1 small yellow onion, peeled and minced
1 carrot, peeled and minced
1 stalk celery, minced
2 tablespoons butter or margarine
1 tablespoon finely grated lemon rind
4–5 slices fat bacon or thin strips salt pork
1¼ cups sour cream
Paprika

Suggested Garnish:
Stuffed Mushrooms
Watercress or parsley sprigs

Let tenderloin stand at room temperature 1½–2 hours if convenient. Meanwhile, stir-fry onion, carrot, and celery in butter over low heat about 10 minutes until tender but not brown; mix in lemon rind. Preheat oven to 450° F. Spread vegetable mixture over tenderloin, lay bacon slices on top, and insert meat thermometer in center. Roast uncovered on a rack in a shallow roasting pan 6–7 minutes per pound for rare (125–30° F.) and 8–9 for medium rare (140–45° F.). Remove bacon and vegetables and discard. Transfer tenderloin to a steak board or hot platter and keep warm. Skim fat from drippings, smooth in sour cream, and warm gently, but do not boil, 1–2 minutes. Garnish beef with stuffed mushrooms and cress, top with some of the sauce, and sprinkle with paprika. Pass remaining sauce. About 520 calories for each of 4 servings, 345 calories for each of 6 servings (without garnish).

PRINCE OF WALES BEEF TENDERLOIN

Makes 4–6 servings

1 (2–3-pound) beef tenderloin of
    uniform thickness, trimmed of fat
    and connective tissue
1 (4-ounce) can pâté de foie gras
3–4 truffles, finely chopped
1 small yellow onion, peeled and
    minced
1 carrot, peeled and minced
1 stalk celery, minced
¼ cup minced cooked ham
2 tablespoons butter or margarine
¼ teaspoon thyme
½ bay leaf, crumbled
Suet for barding or 4–5 thin strips salt
    pork
1 cup tawny port

Suggested Garnish:
Sautéed mushroom caps
Sliced truffles
Watercress or parsley sprigs

Let tenderloin stand at room temperature 1½–2 hours if convenient. Preheat oven to 450° F. Cut tenderloin almost—but not quite—in half lengthwise so 1 long side acts as a hinge and tenderloin can be opened flat like a book. Spread ½ of tenderloin with pâté, leaving a narrow margin all around; sprinkle other side with chopped truffles, close tenderloin, and sew shut with stout thread; set aside. Stir-fry onion, carrot, celery, and ham in butter 10 minutes over low heat until vegetables are tender but not brown; mix in thyme and bay leaf. Spread vegetable mixture over tenderloin, then bard and tie* or cover with strips of salt pork. Insert meat thermometer and roast, uncovered, on a rack in a shallow roasting pan just until thermometer reaches 120° F. Discard suet, skim fat from drippings, and push vegetables from tenderloin down into pan. Add port and continue roasting uncovered until thermometer reads 125–30° F. Transfer tenderloin to a hot platter, remove thread, and top with strained pan juices. Garnish with mushrooms, truffle slices, and watercress and serve. About 470 calories for each of 4 servings, 310 calories for each of 6 servings (without garnish).

TENDERLOIN OF BEEF WELLINGTON

For best results, use the plump center portion of the tenderloin. Delicious with Périgueux or Madeira Sauce.
Makes 6 servings

1 (3-pound) beef tenderloin of
    uniform thickness, trimmed of fat
    and connective tissue
1 recipe Rough Puff Pastry
3 tablespoons minced shallots or
    scallions
¾ pound mushrooms, wiped clean
    and minced
6–7 tablespoons softened unsalted
    butter
2 tablespoons brandy or dry Madeira
    wine
½ teaspoon salt
⅛ teaspoon pepper
1 (2-ounce) can pâté de foie gras at
    room temperature

Glaze:
2 egg yolks lightly beaten with 2
    tablespoons cold water

Let tenderloin stand at room temperature 1½–2 hours if convenient. Meanwhile, prepare pastry and, after final folding and sealing, wrap and chill. Stir-fry shallots and mushrooms in 3 tablespoons butter over moderately low heat 5 minutes; add brandy and simmer, uncovered, until liquid evaporates; mix in salt and pepper and cool. Preheat oven to 450° F. Place tenderloin on a rack in a shallow roasting pan and spread with butter (include ends). Roast, uncovered, 10 minutes, brushing with more butter after 5 minutes; remove from oven and cool ½ hour. Reduce oven to 425° F. Roll pastry into a rectangle big enough to wrap tenderloin (about 8"×15"); save scraps to use as decoration. Brush center and margins of pastry with glaze; spread a strip of mushroom mixture just the size of the tenderloin across center of pastry, leaving 1½" margins at ends. Spread pâté on top of tenderloin, then place pâté side *down* on mushroom mixture. Bring pastry ends up on top of meat and pinch firmly to seal; fold pastry ends in and pinch. Place seam side down on an ungreased baking sheet, cut 3 steam vents in top of pastry, and insert meat thermometer through center hole into meat. Prick pastry lightly in a crisscross pattern and decorate with small pastry shapes cut with truffle cutters. Brush with glaze, covering pastry cutouts lightly and taking care not to cover steam holes. Bake in top ⅓ of oven about 25 minutes until lightly browned and thermometer reaches 125° F. (rare) or 140° F. (medium rare). (*Note:* If pastry browns before meat is done, reduce oven to 350° F.) When done, lift to a hot platter and let "rest" 5 minutes. To serve: Cut off 1 end of pastry, then cut straight across through pastry and meat, making slices ¾"–1" thick. About 700 calories per serving.

VARIATIONS:

Easy Beef Wellington: Prepare mushroom mixture and roast tenderloin 10 minutes as directed. Substitute 1 (8-ounce) package refrigerated crescent roll dough for Rough Puff Pastry. Open dough and spread flat, halve crosswise but do not separate into individual rolls. Fit halves together on a lightly floured board so you have a rectangle about 9"×14"; pinch margins and perforations together so you have an unbroken sheet of dough. If necessary, roll lightly to enlarge slightly, then wrap and bake tenderloin as directed. About 700 calories per serving.

Beef en Croûte: Substitute a 3-pound eye round of beef for tenderloin and have fat trimmed to ⅛". Do not spread with butter. Roast 15 minutes at 450° F., then proceed as directed for Tenderloin of Beef Wellington or Easy Beef Wellington. About 700 calories per serving.

BROILED WHOLE BEEF TENDERLOIN

Makes 8–12 servings

Suet for barding
1 *whole beef tenderloin (about 4–6 pounds), trimmed of fat and connective tissue*
2–3 *tablespoons softened unsalted butter or Parsley-Lemon or Herb Butter (optional)*
1½ *teaspoons salt*
¼ *teaspoon pepper*

Suggested Garnishes:
2–3 *tablespoons Maître d'Hôtel, Parsley-Lemon, or Herb Butter*
¾ *pound sautéed button mushrooms*
1½ *dozen cherry tomatoes*
Watercress sprigs

Suggested Sauce:
Béarnaise

Bard and tie tenderloin.* Let stand at room temperature 1½–2 hours if convenient. Preheat broiler. Place tenderloin on broiler rack and broil 6" from heat 30–40 minutes, giving it a quarter turn every 8–10 minutes, until rare or medium rare (make a small slit near center to test doneness). Discard suet covering and, if you like, spread tenderloin with softened butter. Brown under broiler 3–4 minutes, turning every minute. Transfer to steak board or heated platter, sprinkle with salt and pepper, and top with Maître d'Hôtel Butter. Surround with garnishes and pass Béarnaise Sauce. For more sumptuous dinners, use more elaborate trimmings (see Classic Garnishes for Steaks, also chart of Sauces, Butters, and Seasonings for Steaks). About 395 calories for each of 8 servings (without sauce), 265 calories for each of 12 servings (without sauce).

To Charcoal Broil: Prepare a moderately hot charcoal fire.* Broil barded tenderloin 5" from coals 25–30 minutes for rare, 35–40 for medium rare, turning frequently. Remove suet for last 10 minutes of broiling. Approximately the same number of calories per serving as broiled whole beef tenderloin.

To Charcoal Barbecue: Marinate unbarded tenderloin in 1 pint Barbecue Sauce for Beef 4–8 hours in refrigerator, turning occasionally. Pat dry, bard, and charcoal broil as above. After removing suet, turn often, brushing with barbecue sauce. Serve with Barbecue Gravy for Beef. Approximately the same number of calories per serving as broiled whole beef tenderloin (without sauce).

VARIATION:

Beef Tenderloin à la Bourguignonne: Marinate unbarded tenderloin in refrigerator 4–8 hours in 2 cups red Burgundy blended with ¼ cup olive oil, ½ crushed clove garlic, and 1 teaspoon Dijon-style mustard, turning occasionally. Broil by recipe above; after suet is removed, brush with marinade instead of butter and brown under broiler. Pour ¼ cup warmed Burgundy (or marinade) over meat, slice, and serve with Bourguignonne Sauce. About 400 calories for each of 8 servings, 270 calories for each of 12 servings.

FLAMING CHATEAUBRIAND MAÎTRE D'HÔTEL

Before ovens were reliable, chateaubriand was broiled, sandwiched between two other steaks, so it would be evenly pink throughout. No one worried if the outer steaks charred black—the chateaubriand was what mattered. Today we can cook it perfectly (which means never more than medium rare) without sacrificing two good steaks. Makes 2–3 servings

1 (3" thick) chateaubriand
1 clove garlic, peeled and halved (optional)
4 tablespoons unsalted butter, softened to room temperature
½ cup brandy, warmed
½ teaspoon salt
⅛ teaspoon pepper

Garnishes:
2 tablespoons Maître d'Hôtel Butter
½ recipe Château Potatoes

Suggested Sauce:
Chateaubriand or Béarnaise

Preheat broiler. If you like, rub meat well with garlic. Spread with 2 tablespoons butter. Melt remaining butter and set aside. Broil chateaubriand 5" from heat 12–14 minutes on each cut side for rare and 15–17 for medium rare, basting 1–2 times with melted butter. Transfer to chafing dish or skillet set over low heat, add brandy, warm briefly, and blaze with a match. Spoon flaming brandy over steak and before flames die ease steak onto steak board or hot platter. Sprinkle with salt and pepper, top with Maître d'Hôtel Butter, and surround with potatoes. Pass sauce separately. To serve, cut in thin slices across the grain. About 585 calories for each of 2 servings, 390 calories for each of 3 servings.

VARIATION:

Bard* chateaubriand before broiling; remove suet covering 7–10 minutes before end of cooking so meat will brown nicely. The same number of calories per serving as Flaming Chateaubriand Maître d'Hôtel.

FILET STEAKS, TOURNEDOS, AND FILETS MIGNONS

It should be re-emphasized that the filet steaks here are what we commonly (and incorrectly) call filets mignons—tenderloin steaks 3–3½″ across. The filets mignons really are *mignons*, dainty chunks cut from the thin end of the filet (see Cuts of Tenderloin illustration). All cooking times are for steaks that have stood at room temperature 1½–2 hours. Allow 1 1″–2″ thick filet steak per person; 1–2 1″–2″ tournedos, and, depending on size, 2–3 filets mignons.

To Panfry (Sauté): Wrap a strip of bacon or suet around edge of each steak, if you like, and tie with string or secure with toothpicks. Warm a little butter and oil (for 4 steaks, 2 tablespoons butter and 1 of oil are about right) in a heavy skillet over moderately high heat, add steaks, and brown, uncovered, 3–4 minutes on a side for very rare, 5–6 for rare, and

7–8 for medium rare (to test for doneness, press steak in center with your finger—unlike raw filet, which is soft, it should feel slightly resilient). If you plan to leave bacon on, turn steaks on end and brown lightly. Transfer to a hot platter, remove strings or toothpicks and, if you like, bacon. Sprinkle with salt and pepper and serve with pan juices or a suitable sauce (see chart of Sauces, Butters, and Seasonings for Steaks). Small mushroom caps, which can be sautéed in the pan right along with the steaks, make a delicious garnish.

To Panbroil (filet steaks only): Bacon-wrap or not, as you wish. Brown filets, uncovered, in a lightly greased or salted heavy skillet over moderately high heat 3–4 minutes on a side for very rare, 5–6 for rare, and 7–8 for medium rare; pour off any drippings as they collect.

To Broil: Preheat broiler. Place bacon-wrapped steaks on lightly greased broiler rack and broil 3″ from heat 4–5 minutes on a side for very rare, 6–7 for rare, and 8–9 for medium rare. If you wish, brush both sides of steaks lightly with melted butter before broiling. (*Note:* A good way to broil very small mignons is à la shish kebab on long metal skewers with strips of bacon intertwined. They'll take slightly less time to broil than larger tenderloin steaks.) About 350 calories per 1″ steak if broiled or panbroiled, slightly more if panfried.

Some Easy Ways to Dress Up Filets and Tournedos

Marinated Filets or Tournedos: Marinate steaks 8 hours in refrigerator in a good homemade

French or herb dressing or in Japanese Steak Sauce. Remove from marinade, let stand at room temperature 1 hour, then bacon-wrap and broil as directed, brushing often with marinade.

Surprise Filets or Tournedos: Make small pockets in raw steaks (work from outer edge, cutting a horizontal slit deep into center of each). Place 1 teaspoon pâté in each pocket and, if you like, ¼ teaspoon minced truffle. Or tuck a small lump Roquefort or blue cheese in each. Close with toothpicks, wrap with bacon or suet, and panfry or broil.

Savory Filets or Tournedos: Just before serving, rub steaks with a dab of flavored butter (see chart of Sauces, Butters, and Seasonings for Steaks).

Filets or Tournedos in Wine: Panfry 4 steaks and transfer to a hot platter. Heat ¼ cup dry red wine, Madeira, or port with ¼ teaspoon tarragon, chervil, chives, or rosemary in skillet, stirring, until bubbly. Pour over steaks and serve.

Filets or Tournedos in Minute Sauce: Panfry 4 steaks and transfer to a hot platter. Add 2 tablespoons lemon juice, 1 tablespoon Worcestershire sauce, and ½ teaspoon Dijon-type mustard to skillet and heat, stirring, until bubbly; pour over steaks.

Flaming Filets or Tournedos: Broil or panfry 4 steaks, then transfer to a chafing dish set over low heat. Add ⅓–½ cup warmed cognac, heat 1 minute, and blaze with a match. Spoon flaming cognac over steaks and season with salt and pepper. If you like, swirl in 1 tablespoon Maître d'Hôtel Butter when flames subside.

Filet or Tournedo "Canapés": Odd

as these combinations may sound, they're delicious:
– Serve steaks on broiled thick tomato slices; top with pâté, Duxelles, or Mustard Sauce.
– Serve steaks on grilled pineapple rings and top with Sauce Diable.
– Serve steaks on grilled avocado crescents (brush with lemon and sauté 1–2 minutes in butter); top with Sauce Diable or Brown Curry Sauce.
– Serve steaks on butter-browned, breaded eggplant rounds and top with Tomato Sauce.

Some Classic Ways to Serve Tournedos (and Filets)

À la Béarnaise: Panfry 4–6 steaks, arrange in a circle on a hot platter, mound Château Potatoes in center, and drizzle steaks with Béarnaise; pass extra sauce.

À la Bordelaise: Top panfried steaks (any number you wish) with ½″ slices poached marrow (see Marrowbones) and a little minced parsley. Serve with Bordelaise Sauce.

À la Clamart: On a hot platter arrange panfried steaks, tiny buttered new potatoes, and boiled artichoke bottoms filled with buttered or Puréed Green Peas. Quickly boil and stir ⅓ cup dry white wine in steak skillet to reduce by ½, pour over steaks, and serve.

Chasseur: Before cooking steaks, sauté ½ pound sliced mushrooms and 2 tablespoons minced shallots or scallions in 2 tablespoons butter over moderate heat 5 minutes; set aside. Panfry 6 steaks, place each on a fried crouton round, and keep warm on a hot platter. Pour fat from steak skillet, add ½ cup beef stock and 2 teaspoons tomato paste, and boil rapidly, stirring, until reduced by half. Mix in ¼ cup Madeira blended with 2 teaspoons cornstarch and heat, stirring, until thickened and clear. Add mushrooms and 1 tablespoon minced parsley (or 1 teaspoon each minced parsley, tarragon, and chervil), pour over steaks, and serve.

Choron: Serve panfried steaks on fried crouton circles and garnish with boiled artichoke bottoms filled with buttered green peas or asparagus tips. Mix 1 cup Béarnaise Sauce with 2 tablespoons tomato paste and spoon a little over each steak.

Henri IV: Panfry 4–6 steaks, place on fried crouton rounds, and drizzle with pan juices deglazed with ¼ cup Madeira. Arrange in a ring on a hot platter, top each steak with a hot artichoke bottom filled with Béarnaise, and decorate with truffle slices. Mound Château or Parisienne Potatoes in center and pass extra Béarnaise.

Rossini: Serve panfried steaks on fried crouton rounds topped with ¼″ slices *pâté de foie gras,* decorative truffle slices, and a little Madeira Sauce. (*Note:* Pâté will be more attractive if lightly dusted with flour and sautéed briefly in a little butter over low heat.) Garnish with Château Potatoes and watercress; pass extra sauce.

FONDUE BOURGUIGNONNE

Picture a group of friends gathered round, spearing chunks of steak and cooking them in a bubbling pot of oil; picture an array of sauces and condiments, there for the dunking, and you have the idea of Fondue Bourguignonne. It's a merry Swiss dish that's perfect for a small party. Everything can be prepared well in advance and set out at the last minute. Makes 6 servings

3 pounds beef tenderloin or boneless sirloin, trimmed of fat and cut in 1″ cubes
3 cups (about) cooking oil (a ½ and ½ mixture of peanut and corn oil is especially good) or 3 cups Clarified Butter

Sauces: Prepare 2 or more, choosing with an eye to variety. Any hot sauces can be reheated in the top of a double boiler or hot water bath minutes before serving. Some sauces traditionally served: Aurore, Béarnaise (a must), Cumberland, Diable, Mustard, Rémoulade, Sour Cream-Horseradish. Not traditional but good: Brown Curry, Madeira, Smitane, and Teriyaki sauces.

Condiments: Choose 3 or more, again for variety: spicy and mild mustards, chutney, tomato or mushroom ketchup, horseradish, olives, pickled onions, or mushrooms.

Special Equipment: You'll need a fondue bourguignonne pot, a deep metal or enameled-metal pot as distinguished from the heavy, shallow, ceramic cheese fondue dish (preferably the 2-quart size) with a stand and alcohol burner, fondue forks and long bamboo skewers.

How to Set the Table: Place fondue stand and burner in the center of the table. At each place provide 2 salad plates (1 for the raw chunks of beef, the other for sauces), 2–3 bamboo skewers, and a fondue fork in addition to dinner knife, fork, spoon, and napkin.

How to Serve: In the kitchen, half fill fondue pot with oil and heat slowly on the stove until a cube of bread will sizzle; set over lighted alcohol burner on dining table. Arrange a small mound of steak cubes on 1 of the salad plates at each place and garnish with watercress or parsley. Surround burner with small bowls of sauces and condiments; set out salt shaker and pepper mill. (*Note:* Pour any particularly liquid sauces into small ramekins and set 1 on each sauce plate.)

How to Eat Fondue Bourguignonne: Each guest first spoons an assortment of sauces and condiments onto his empty plate. Then, using a long bamboo skewer, he spears a chunk of filet, plunges it into the fondue pot, and cooks it the way he likes it (allow 5–10 seconds for rare, 10–15 for medium, and 20 for well done). More than 1 chunk of meat can be cooked at a time, but it's important to regulate the burner so the oil bubbles vigorously—but does not sputter—each time a new chunk is added. To help reduce sputter, keep a small chunk of bread in the oil, replenishing whenever it threatens to burn. After cooking a piece of steak, the person transfers it to his fondue fork, dunks it in a sauce or condiment, and eats it. *Caution:* Some recipes recommend using 2 fondue forks, 1 for cooking, the other for dunking and eating. But, if you forget to switch forks (and it's easy to do so), you can get a nasty mouth burn. So play it safe and use bamboo skewers.

What to Serve with Fondue Bourguignonne: Since the fondue table will be crowded, it's best to follow with a separate salad course —a cold green bean or crisp tossed salad is ideal. As for wine, uncork a good red Burgundy or Bordeaux.

About 475 calories per serving (without sauces).

BEEF STROGANOFF

A true Stroganoff has very little sour cream and no mushrooms, tomato paste, or paprika. What makes it special is the spicy mustard. It's best made with beef tenderloin, but if your budget won't allow it, use sirloin.
Makes 4 servings

1½   pounds beef tenderloin or boneless sirloin, trimmed of fat and cut in 2″ × ½″ strips
¼–½   teaspoon salt (depending upon saltiness of broth and mustard)
¼   teaspoon pepper
1   medium-size Bermuda onion, peeled and sliced ¼″ thick
4   tablespoons butter or margarine
2   tablespoons flour
1   cup strong beef stock or canned condensed beef broth
1   teaspoon prepared Dijon-type mustard
¼   cup sour cream at room temperature

Spread beef strips out on heavy brown paper and sprinkle evenly with salt and pepper. Toss to mix, spread out again, top with onion slices and let stand 2 hours at room temperature. Melt 2 tablespoons butter in a large, heavy skillet over moderately low heat and blend in flour. Mix in stock and heat, stirring, 3–5 minutes until thickened. Blend in mustard and remove sauce from heat. In a second large skillet, melt remaining butter over moderately high heat, add beef and onion, and brown quickly—this will take about 10 minutes. Add browned beef *but not the onion* to the sauce, set over moderate heat, cover, and simmer, stirring once or twice, 15 minutes (onion can be saved for hamburgers or stew). Remove from heat, stir in sour cream, and serve. About 440 calories per serving.

⚖ TERIYAKI-STYLE TENDERLOIN

Makes 4 servings

1½ pounds beef tenderloin in 1 piece

Marinade:
¾ cup Japanese soy sauce
¼ cup mirin, sake, or medium-dry sherry
1 tablespoon light brown sugar (only if sake or sherry is used)
2 teaspoons finely grated fresh gingerroot or 1 tablespoon minced preserved ginger

Place tenderloin in a large bowl. Mix marinade ingredients, pour over meat, cover, and let stand at room temperature 1½–2 hours, turning meat several times. Remove meat from marinade and broil 4″ from the heat about 15 minutes, turning every 3 minutes and basting with marinade. (*Note:* This cooking time is for a medium-rare *teriyaki.* If you like it rarer, reduce cooking time to about 10–12 minutes, if more well done, increase it to 17 minutes.) To serve, cut in thin slices and top with a little marinade. About 290 calories per serving.

VARIATION:

⚖ **Teriyaki Hors d'Oeuvre:** Cut tenderloin into ¾″–1″ cubes and marinate as directed; drain, reserving marinade. Broil 4″ from heat 1–2 minutes, turn, baste with marinade, and broil 1–2 minutes longer. Skewer with toothpicks or bamboo skewers. Or, if you have a hibachi, set out the raw marinated cubes, long metal skewers, or fondue forks and let everyone

broil their own teriyaki. Makes about 6–8 servings. About 185 calories for each of 6 servings, 140 calories for each of 8 servings.

⚖ BEEF SUKIYAKI

Sukiyaki is a good choice for a small dinner because all ingredients can be cut up well in advance (cover and refrigerate until the last minute), because it can be cooked quickly at the table in an electric skillet and because it needs nothing more than rice to accompany.

Made the Japanese way, it contains *dashi,* a broth made of dried bonito flakes (packets are sold in Oriental groceries), *sake,* the fermented rice drink, *shirataki,* yam noodles, and soybean cake. The shirataki and bean cake can be omitted if necessary, the dashi replaced by beef broth and the sake by sherry. Some people make sukiyaki with *mirin,* a sweet sake, and omit the sugar. You can achieve the same effect by using a sweeter sherry and adding only enough sugar to "mellow" the sukiyaki. It should never taste sweet.

Makes 4 servings

1 (2″) cube suet
1 cup paper-thin slices Spanish onion
6 scallions, trimmed and halved lengthwise
3 stalks celery, cut diagonally into thin slices
1 (8-ounce) can bamboo shoots, drained and sliced thin
1¼ pounds beef tenderloin or boneless sirloin, sliced paper thin
½ pound mushrooms, wiped clean and sliced thin
⅔ cup canned shirataki (optional)
1 soybean cake, cut in 1½″ cubes (optional)
1 quart washed, sorted spinach leaves
½ cup dashi or canned beef broth

½ *cup sake or medium-dry sherry*
½ *cup Japanese soy sauce*
3 *tablespoons light brown sugar*

Heat a large, heavy skillet over high heat 1 minute or set an electric skillet on highest heat; when good and hot, spear suet with a cooking fork and rub over bottom to grease; discard suet. Reduce heat to moderate, add onion, scallions, and celery, and stir-fry 5–8 minutes until lightly wilted; lay bamboo shoots, beef, mushrooms, *shirataki,* bean cake, and spinach on top. Mix *dashi* with sake, soy sauce, and sugar and pour over all. Cover and steam 3–4 minutes. Uncover and toss lightly as you would a salad, then simmer, uncovered, 2–3 minutes longer. Serve with rice. About 350 calories per serving (without rice).

⚔ STEAK TARTARE

What we call steak tartare the French call steak *à l'Américaine*—a tribute to our superb beef. Strangely, our name for the dish comes from their way of serving it—with tartar sauce. But Americans prefer to use raw egg yolks and to mix in an assortment of condiments. Makes 4 servings

1 ½ *pounds beef tenderloin or sirloin steak, trimmed of all fat and finely ground*
4 *raw egg yolks*
1 *teaspoon minced chervil (optional)*
1 *medium-size yellow onion, peeled and minced*
2 *tablespoons minced parsley*

Lightly shape beef into 4 patties, place each on a chilled plate, and, using the back of a spoon, press a hollow in the center of each. Slide a raw egg yolk into each hollow and, if you like, sprinkle with chervil. Pass remaining ingredients in small bowls or arrange in separate mounds around each patty so that everyone can mix in whatever —and as much of it as they like— along with the egg yolk. Set out salt and pepper. Some other optional accompaniments: cayenne pepper, Worcestershire sauce, lemon wedges, anchovy fillets, hot buttered toast —either plain or spread with anchovy paste. About 350 calories per serving.

STEAKS

Sumptuous, succulent, often whopping—these are the cuts Americans do better than anyone else. The tender steaks come from the rib and loin sections, the marginally tender from the round, rump, chuck, flank, and plate. (Refer to Beef Chart.)

The Tender Steaks
Choicest of the choice are the T-bone, porterhouse, and pinbone sirloin because they contain large chunks of butter-smooth tenderloin. All tender steaks should be cut at least 1″ thick and will be juicier if closer to 2″; all are well enough marbled with fat that they can be cooked without additional fat. Broil or charcoal broil any of the following, and, except for sirloins, which are too hefty to handle easily in a skillet, panbroil.
Rib and boneless rib steaks
Delmonico or rib eye steak
Club steak
T-bone steak
Shell steak (T-bone minus the tenderloin)
Porterhouse steak
Strip steak (porterhouse minus the tenderloin)

Sirloin steaks (pinbone, flat bone,
  wedge bone, and boneless)
Note: Butchers sometimes remove
the pinbone from the pinbone sirloin,
grind the tail end and tuck it in
where the bone was; this simplifies
carving. Some also grind the long,
lean tail of the porterhouse and
tuck it underneath the tenderloin.

The Marginally Tender Steaks

If from prime or tendered beef,
some of these lean "budget" steaks
will be tender enough to broil; others
will need all the help they can get
(i.e., pounding, scoring, marinating,
braising). Being leaner than the
tender steaks, they are also somewhat lower in calories and
cholesterol; their texture is firmer,
their flavor more robust.

The Broilables (IF from top quality or tendered beef):

Top and eye round steaks
Tip or sirloin tip steak
Rump steak
Skirt steak fillet
Flank and flank steak fillets
Boneless blade and blade chuck
  steak

Petite steak
Minute steak
Cube steak

Note: Though tender
enough to broil, these
steaks are so thin
they should be pan-
fried as quickly as
possible in butter or
drippings.

The Unbroilables:
Blade steak
(when not first cut), arm steak, and
bottom round are the cuts to braise:
to use for Swiss steak, to stuff
and roll, to smother with onions and
mushrooms and rich brown gravy.
Note: Any of the broilables listed
above become unbroilables when
cut from lower grades of beef.

How to Cook

Amount Needed: ⅓–½ pound
boneless steak per person, ½–¾
pound bone-in steak.

General Preparation for Cooking: If
steaks seem unusually moist, wipe
with a damp cloth so they will
brown nicely. Trim off all but ¼"
outer fat and slash at 1" intervals
to keep steaks from curling. Rub
with pepper, if you like, also garlic,
but not salt (salt draws moisture
to the surface and slows browning).
Let steaks stand at room temperature 1½–2 hours before cooking
if convenient. (*Note:* Naturally
thin cuts like flank steak, also thinly
cut minute, petite, or cube steaks,
should be refrigerated until just
before cooking so that the quick,
intense heat does not carry them
beyond the point of tenderness—
medium rare.)

Cooking Tips

—Whenever in doubt about the
tenderness of a steak, sprinkle each
side with unseasoned meat tenderizer, pierce deeply all over with a
sharp fork, and let stand as package
directs.
—Always turn steaks with tongs to
avoid piercing them and losing
savory juices.
—When broiling, panbroiling, or
panfrying marginally tender steaks,
never cook beyond medium rare
(longer cooking will merely
toughen and dry them).
—When carving large, marginally
tender steaks, cut across the grain
in thin slices, holding the knife at
a slight angle (this breaks up long,
coarse fibers).

To Panfry (Sauté): Recommended
for minute, petite, and cube steaks;
skirt fillets, boneless blade steak,
tip steak, top and eye round cut

about 1" thick. Warm 1–2 tablespoons butter, margarine, drippings, or cooking oil in a large, heavy skillet over moderately high heat about 1 minute, add steaks, and brown on both sides. Minute, petite, and cube steaks will take only 1–2 minutes per side; the other steaks about 3 minutes per side for very rare, 4 for rare, and 5 for medium rare. Season and serve.

To Panbroil: Recommended for all tender steaks except large sir- loins; for top and eye round, tip and boneless blade steaks. If steaks seem especially lean, grease or salt skillet *lightly;* heat over mod- erately high heat about 1 minute, add steaks, and cook, uncovered, turning occasionally and pouring off drippings as they accumulate, until browned on both sides and at desired doneness (use times below as a guide). Season and serve. (*Note:* Do not add water or other liquid to skillet.)

APPROXIMATE TOTAL PANBROILING TIMES

Steak Thickness	Very Rare	Rare	Medium Rare	Medium	Well Done
	Minutes	Minutes	Minutes	Minutes	Minutes
1"	6–7	8–10	11–12	13–14	15–16
1½"	8–10	11–12	13–14	15–17	18–20
2"	13–15	16–17	18–19	20–22	25–30

To Broil: Recommended for all tender steaks; also for top quality or tendered skirt fillets, chuck and boneless blade steak, top and eye round, tip and rump steaks. (*Note:* Flank steak requires a bit different technique [see London Broil].) If steaks are very lean, brush lightly with melted butter. Preheat broiler. Rub rack with drippings or oil and, to save a messy clean-up, line broiler pan with foil. Place steak on rack and set in broiler so fat edge of steak is toward back of oven (this reduces spattering). Adjust height and broil to desired doneness as directed in Steak Broiling Chart (below), turning steak only once. Season and serve.

VARIATION:

Planked Steak: A festive way to serve broiled steak is on an oak or hickory plank (most housewares departments sell them), wreathed with Duchess Potatoes, sautéed mushroom caps, and grilled to- matoes. Planks, usually rectangular or oval, should be at least 1" thick and from 15"–18" long. Most are seasoned by the manufac- turer (see his directions), but, if not, here's *how to season a plank* yourself: brush top and sides with bland cooking oil, place on a sheet of foil on oven rack, and let stand in a 275° F. oven 1–1½ hours. Remove from oven and wipe well with paper toweling—plank is now ready *to use* (see Planked Steak with Vegetables). *To care for plank:* wipe thoroughly with paper toweling immediately after using, then wash quickly in warm, sudsy water, rinse in cool water, pat dry, then allow to dry completely. Store, loosely wrapped, in a cool, dry place. (*Note:* If any part of plank is exposed during broiling, brush lightly with oil and cover with foil to prevent charring.)

To Charcoal Broil: Recommended for all tender steaks; also for top quality or tendered tip, rump, chuck, and boneless blade steaks. Prepare charcoal fire.* For steaks 1″–1¾″ thick, it should be hot (350–75° F. on grill thermometer) or of an intensity to make you remove your hand after 2–3 seconds at grill level. For steaks 2″ thick or more, it should be moderately hot (325° F.) or enough to make you withdraw your hand after 4 seconds. Spread enough glowing coals evenly over fire bed to equal area of meat and to last throughout cooking. Lightly grease grill with fat trimmed from steak, place steak on grill, adjust height, and broil as directed in Steak Broiling Chart. Turn only once during cooking. Season and serve.

VARIATION:

Marinated Steaks: Marginally tender steaks will be juicier if marinated 4 hours in refrigerator in Barbecue Sauce for Beef, Japanese Steak Sauce, or any good Italian, herb, or garlic dressing. Bring steak to room temperature in marinade, lift out, and pat dry. Grill as directed, brushing often with marinade.

To Braise: Here's the most surefire way of cooking marginally tender steaks. Braising isn't one recipe, but many—Beef Birds, Swiss Steak, Chicken, and Country-Fried Steaks are all braised. You'll find these and other ways of braising steaks among the recipes that follow.

To Test Steaks for Doneness:

Bone-in steaks: Make a small slit near bone and check color of meat.

Boneless steaks: Make a small slit near center of steak to determine color.

Thick steaks (more than 2½″): Insert meat thermometer in center of largest lean muscle, not touching bone. A very rare steak will be 120° F., a rare one 130° F., a medium-rare one 140° F., a medium one 150° F., and a well-done one 160–70° F.

How to Give Steak Extra Flavor
(Choose 1 Method Only.)

Before Cooking:
– Marinate steak 4 hours in refrigerator in Barbecue Sauce for Beef or Japanese Steak Sauce (or any good herb, Italian, or garlic dressing). Let come to room temperature, lift from marinade, pat dry, and broil, brushing often with marinade.
– Rub each side of steak with a cut clove garlic.
– Rub each side of steak with a compatible herb or spice (see Sauces, Butters, and Seasonings for Steaks).
– Spread both sides of steak with 1 small grated yellow onion that has been blended with 2 tablespoons Dijon mustard and 2 teaspoons cooking oil or softened butter.
– Brush both sides of steak with 1 tablespoon soy sauce that has been mixed with 1 tablespoon each steak sauce, Worcestershire sauce, and chili sauce.

– **Hungarian Steak:** Rub 2 teaspoons paprika (preferably the Hungarian sweet rose) into each side of steak, then cook by desired method.

STEAK BROILING CHART

Times (for steaks that have stood at room temperature 1½-2 hours) are approximate since shape and size of cut, amount of fat and bone, type of oven or grill all affect broiling time. In outdoor charcoal broiling, wind is also a factor.

Oven Broiling	Thickness	Oven or Fire Temperature	Distance from Heat	Approximate Minutes per Side				
				Very Rare	Rare	Medium Rare	Medium	Well Done
Steak								
Top and eye round, tip and rump steaks, skirt fillets, chuck and boneless blade steak; all tender steaks except bone-in sirloins.	1"	broil	2"	3	4	5	6	7
	1½"	broil	3"	6	7	8	9	10-12
	2"	broil	4"	14	15	16	17	18-19
Pinbone, wedge bone, and flat bone sirloin	1"	broil	3"	7	8	9	10	11-13
	1½"	broil	4"	10	11	12	13	14-15
	2"	broil	5"	18	19	20	21	22-24
Charcoal Broiling								
Tip, rump, chuck and boneless blade steaks; all tender steaks.	1"	hot	4"	3	4-5	6	7-8	9-10
	1½, 1¾"	hot	4"	4	5-6	7-8	9-10	12-15
	2"	moderately hot	5"	6-7	8-9	10-12	14-16	18-20
	2½"	moderately hot	5"	10-12	13-15	16-18	20-22	23-25

NOTE: Directions and times for broiling tenderloin steaks, flank steak, and hamburgers are given in the discussion of each, since each requires a somewhat different technique.

Top with sautéed onion rings, given the merest blush of paprika, and serve.

During Cooking:
– While broiling, brush or baste with Madeira, port, sherry, dry red or white wine, brandy, dark rum, or bourbon.
– While broiling, brush or baste with any barbecue sauce.
– While charcoal broiling, toss any of the following directly onto coals: 2–3 sprigs fresh sage or 1 tablespoon dried sage, a dozen bay leaves, 1 tablespoon cracked juniper berries.
– During last minutes of broiling or panbroiling, brush lightly with Herb, Chive, Garlic, Mustard, or Anchovy Butter.

– **Roquefort Steak:** During last half minute of broiling, spread top of steak with 2–3 tablespoons Roquefort or blue cheese that have been creamed with 2 tablespoons softened butter.

After Cooking:
– Just before serving, top with 3–4 tablespoons flavored butter (see Sauces, Butters, and Seasonings for Steaks).
– Just before serving, top with a ½ and ½ mixture of sautéed, minced yellow onions and mushrooms.
– Just before serving, top with the following: ½ cup each minced mushrooms and yellow onions that have been sautéed 10 minutes in butter with ¼ cup each minced celery and sweet red or green pepper and 1 crushed clove garlic.
– Serve steak with a suitable sauce (see Sauces, Butters, and Seasonings for Steaks).

– **Flaming Steak:** Warm ⅓ cup brandy, bourbon, rye, or dark rum, pour over hot steak, and flame, spooning flaming liquid over steak until flames subside. If you like, flame at the table.

– **Steak Mirabeau:** Broil steak to desired doneness. Lay 9–10 anchovy fillets over steak in a crisscross pattern, dot with 2–3 tablespoons Anchovy Butter and ¼ cup sliced pitted ripe olives. Broil 20–30 seconds to melt butter and serve.

– **Steak Lyonnaise:** Panbroil steak, transfer to hot platter, and smother with sautéed yellow onions (about ½ cup is right for a 2-serving steak). To skillet add 1 tablespoon red wine vinegar, 2 tablespoons dry white wine, and ½ cup Rich Brown Sauce or canned beef gravy. Heat 2–3 minutes, stir in 1 tablespoon minced parsley, pour over steak, and serve.

– **Drunken Steak:** Panbroil steak and transfer to hot platter. To skillet add 2 tablespoons butter and ⅓ cup brandy, dark rum, or bourbon and heat 1–2 minutes, scraping up browned bits. Pour over steak and serve.

Some Simple Garnishes for Steak (in addition to parsley or watercress sprigs):

Artichoke Bottoms: boiled and buttered; Artichoke Bottoms Stuffed with Vegetables; Argenteuil Style; Artichoke Bottoms Princesse.

Artichoke Hearts: boiled and buttered; Artichokes Du Barry.

Celery: braised; boiled buttered celery hearts.

Cucumbers: boiled and buttered; Sautéed Cucumbers; Braised Vegetable-Stuffed Cucumbers.

Belgian Endive: braised.

Mushrooms: sautéed button mushrooms, mushroom caps, or sliced mushrooms; Baked Mushroom Caps Stuffed with Hazelnuts.

Onions: Glazed Onions; Pan-Braised Onions; Sautéed Onions; French Fried Onion Rings; Stuffed Onions.

Potatoes: Parsleyed Potatoes; French Fried Potatoes; Shoestring Potatoes; Duchess Potatoes; Herbed or Lemon-Glazed New Potatoes; Danish-Style New Potatoes.

Rice: Croquettes.

Tarts: small pastry shells filled with small or diced vegetables in Béchamel or Medium White Sauce, Risotto, or *pâté de foie gras*.

Tomatoes: raw cherry tomatoes; Fried Tomatoes or Green Tomatoes; Fried Tomatoes Provençale; Broiled Tomatoes; Deviled Tomatoes; Stuffed Tomatoes.

SAUCES, BUTTERS, AND SEASONINGS FOR STEAKS

Sauces		Butters	Seasonings, Herbs, Spices	Condiments
Béarnaise	Herb	Anchovy	Marchands	Chervil	Horseradish
Bordelaise	Japanese	Bercy	de vin	Chives	Mustard
Bourguignonne	steak sauce	Chive	Mustard	Garlic	Soy sauce
Brown sauce	Lyonnaise	Curry	Pimiento	Ginger	Steak sauce
fines herbes	Madeira	Garlic	Shallot	Mustard	Teriyaki
Chasseur	Madeira-	Herb	Tarragon	Parsley	sauce
Chateaubriand	mushroom	Horseradish	Tomato	Rosemary	Worces-
Choron	Marchands	Maître		Tarragon	tershire
Colbert	de vin	d'hôtel			sauce
Diable	Périgueux				
Dijonnaise	Poivrade				
	Salsa friá				
	Shallot				
	Smitane				

Some Classic Garnishes for Steak:

À la Bouquetière: Surround steak with small clusters of diced cooked carrots, turnips, Parisienne Potatoes, buttered green peas, beans, and cauliflowerets.

À la Bourguignonne: Decorate platter with Pan-Braised Onions and sautéed button mushrooms; serve with Bourguignonne Sauce.

À la Châtelaine: Surround steak with Braised Chestnuts, Château Potatoes, and artichoke bottoms filled with Soubise Sauce.

À la Clamart: (see Some Classic Ways to Serve Tournedos)

À la Dauphine: Surround steak with Dauphine Potatoes.

À la Duchess: Surround with Duchess Potatoes.

À la Jardinière: Exactly the same as Bouquetière except that carrots and turnips are cut with a ball cutter instead of being diced; serve with Hollandaise Sauce.

À la Tyrolienne: Surround steak with sautéed tomato wedges and top with sautéed onion rings.

Au Vert-Pré: Surround steak with Shoestring Potatoes and watercress sprigs; top with dabs of Maître d'Hôtel Butter.

Richelieu: Surround steak with Stuffed Tomatoes (use cherry tomatoes), Butter-Braised Hearts of Lettuce, and Château Potatoes.

Note: Any of these classic garnishes may also be used to garnish Broiled Whole Beef Tenderloin, broiled or panbroiled filet steaks, tournedos, or filets mignons.

How to Carve Porterhouse and Sirloin Steaks:

Steady steak with carving fork, cut around bone with a small carving knife and lift out. Cut straight across steak in ¾"–1" slices. If steak is very thick, slant knife slightly (so less juice is lost). See that each person is served some of the tenderloin.

PLANKED STEAK WITH VEGETABLES

Unlike small or quick-cooking cuts that can be broiled altogether on a plank, sirloin steaks should be ½–¾

done before being set on plank because plank chars easily.
Makes 6 servings

1 (3–4-pound) sirloin steak, cut 1½" thick
Salt
Pepper
1 recipe Duchess Potatoes (hot)
1 egg beaten with 1 tablespoon cold water (glaze)
2 tablespoons Maître d'Hôtel Butter or other flavored butter (see Sauces, Butters, and Seasonings for Steaks)

Garnishes (choose 1 or 2):
1 pound mushroom caps, sautéed
3 tomatoes, halved and broiled
1 recipe French-Fried Onion Rings or 1 (8-ounce) package frozen French-fried onion rings, cooked by package directions
2 cups boiled, buttered green peas
12 boiled, buttered whole baby carrots or 12 boiled, buttered broccoli flowerets

Trim all but ¼" fat from steak and slash at 1" intervals. Let steak stand at room temperature 1½–2 hours if convenient. Preheat broiler. Broil steak on lightly greased rack on 1 side following times in Steak Broiling Chart. Meanwhile, lightly oil plank and place on rack below steak to heat. Turn steak, season lightly with salt and pepper, and broil exactly ½ remaining recommended time. Transfer to plank, pipe a border of potatoes around plank, and brush potatoes lightly with egg glaze. Return steak to broiler and broil to desired doneness. If potatoes brown too fast, cover loosely with foil. (*Note:* Placing foil underneath plank helps keep it clean.) Season steak with remaining salt and pepper and top with dabs of Maître d'Hôtel Butter. Arrange garnish between steak and potatoes, set plank in its holder or on a tray, and serve. About 700 calories per serving with a garnish of mushrooms and tomatoes.

To Plank Small Steaks (2 Servings): Substitute 2 (1″–1½″) rib, Delmonico, club, or T-bone steaks for sirloin. Broil on 1 side, transfer to plank, pipe with potatoes, and broil to desired doneness. Garnish and serve. About 700 calories per serving with a garnish of mushrooms and tomatoes.

SIRLOIN STEAK STUFFED WITH MUSHROOMS

Makes 8–10 servings

1 flat bone sirloin steak, cut 2½″–3″
  thick (about 7 pounds)
1½ teaspoons salt
¼ teaspoon pepper
¼ cup dry port or red wine, warmed

Stuffing:
1 medium-size yellow onion, peeled
  and minced
⅓ cup butter or margarine
1 pound mushrooms, wiped clean
  and chopped fine
2 cups soft white bread crumbs
½ clove garlic, peeled and crushed
¼ teaspoon pepper
1½ teaspoons oregano
2 teaspoons minced parsley

Garnish:
2 recipes French-Fried Onion Rings

With a sharp knife, make a deep horizontal pocket in steak; slash fat edge at 1″ intervals and set steak aside while you prepare stuffing. Stir-fry onion in butter over moderate heat 5–8 minutes until pale golden; add mushrooms and brown over high heat 3–4 minutes. Off heat mix in remaining ingredients. Preheat broiler. Place stuffing in steak pocket and sew or skewer edges shut (to make more secure, tie steak with string, just as if wrapping a package). Broil

on a lightly greased rack 5″ from heat about 20 minutes per side for rare, 22 for medium, and 24 for well done (before turning, sprinkle with ½ the salt and pepper). Transfer steak to steak board or heated platter, remove string and skewers, sprinkle with remaining salt and pepper, and, to show that steak is stuffed, cut off 2–3 slices, making them ⅓″–½″ thick. Drizzle wine over steak, tipping board so it mingles with steak juices. Arrange some onion rings on top of steak and pass the rest. Top each serving with a ladling of steak juices. About 880 calories for each of 8 servings, 705 calories for each of 10 servings.

To Charcoal Broil: Prepare a moderately hot charcoal fire*; stuff steak as directed and broil on lightly greased grill 5″ from coals 15 minutes per side for rare, 18 for medium rare, 20 for medium, and 25 for well done.

CARPETBAG STEAK

This steak is best when broiled the Australian way—until medium rare or medium well—so the oysters have just enough time to cook. If you like rare steak, simmer the oysters, uncovered, in their liquor 3–4 minutes before stuffing the steak. Drain them well, pat dry on paper toweling, then proceed as recipe directs.
Makes 8–10 servings

1 flat bone sirloin steak, cut 2½″–3″
  thick (about 7 pounds)
¼ teaspoon pepper
1½ dozen small oysters, drained
1½ teaspoons salt

Garnishes:
Broiled tomato halves
Maître d'Hôtel Butter

Preheat broiler. With a sharp knife,

make a deep horizontal pocket in steak; slash fat edge at 1" intervals. Rub pocket with pepper and stuff with oysters. Sew opening shut with stout thread and broil steak on a lightly greased rack 5" from heat 21 minutes on a side for medium rare, 22 for medium, and 23 for medium well (before turning, sprinkle with half the salt). Transfer steak to steak board or heated platter and sprinkle with remaining salt; remove thread. Surround with broiled tomato halves and top with pats of Maître d'Hôtel Butter. To serve, cut down through steak, making slices about ½" thick. About 850 calories for each of 8 servings, 680 calories for each of 10 servings.

STEAK AU POIVRE

The quantity of pepper here is minimal for this classic steak. The best way to crush peppercorns is in a mortar and pestle or to place in a small plastic bag and roll with a rolling pin or pound with a soft drink bottle.

Makes 4 servings

4 teaspoons peppercorns, crushed
4 (1"-thick) club or Delmonico
   steaks
Cooking oil
1 teaspoon salt
4 small pats Maître d'Hôtel Butter
2–3 tablespoons brandy

Trim fat on steaks to ¼" and slash at 1" intervals. Sprinkle ½ teaspoon pepper on each side of each steak and press in well with the heel of your hand; let stand at room temperature ½ hour. Brush a large, heavy skillet with oil and heat over high heat 1 minute. Reduce heat to moderately high, add steaks, and panbroil, turning often, a total of 6 minutes for very

rare, 8–10 for rare, 11–12 for medium rare, 13–14 for medium, and 15–16 for well done. Transfer to a hot platter, sprinkle with salt and top with butter pats. Pour brandy into skillet, stirring to scrape up brown bits, and heat 1 minute. Pour over steaks and serve. About 540 calories per serving.

To Broil: Preheat broiler. Prepare steaks as directed and broil 2" from heat on lightly greased rack to desired doneness (use times in Steak Broiling Chart). Omit brandy; sprinkle with salt, top with butter, and serve.

To Charcoal Broil: Prepare a hot charcoal fire*; prepare steaks as directed and broil on lightly greased grill 4" from heat to desired doneness (see Steak Broiling Chart). Omit brandy; sprinkle with salt, top with butter, and serve.

VARIATION:

Steak au Poivre Flambé: Panbroil steaks as above, transfer to chafing dish, and sprinkle with salt; omit butter. Pour ½ cup brandy into skillet, scrape up brown bits, and pour over steaks. Heat until mixture bubbles, blaze with a match, and spoon flames over steak. Serve when flames subside. About 480 calories per serving.

STEAK ALLA PIZZAIOLA

Makes 2 servings

2 Delmonico, boneless shell or strip
   steaks, cut ¾" thick
1 teaspoon olive oil
¼ teaspoon salt
Pinch pepper
2 teaspoons minced parsley

Sauce:
2 medium-size ripe tomatoes, peeled,
   cored, and coarsely chopped

1 clove garlic, peeled and crushed
½ teaspoon oregano
2 tablespoons olive oil
½ teaspoon salt
⅛ teaspoon pepper

Rub steaks lightly with olive oil and set aside while you make the sauce. Place all sauce ingredients in a small skillet and simmer uncovered over moderately low heat, stirring occasionally, about 30 minutes until most of the liquid has evaporated. Quickly brown steaks on 1 side in another skillet over moderately high heat, turn, sprinkle lightly with salt and pepper. When second side is brown, turn again, season with remaining salt and pepper, top with sauce, cover, and simmer over lowest heat just 5 minutes. Sprinkle with parsley and serve. About 660 calories per serving.

☒ STEAK DIANE I

Some people like a touch of mustard in their steak Diane sauce, some don't. We offer both recipes here. Makes 2 servings.

2 (½-pound) Delmonico steaks, cut
  ½" thick
2 tablespoons unsalted butter
2 tablespoons minced shallots
2 tablespoons warmed cognac
  (optional)
½ teaspoon salt
⅛ teaspoon pepper
1 tablespoon minced parsley
1 tablespoon minced chives
2 teaspoons Worcestershire sauce
2 teaspoons steak sauce

Trim outer layer of fat on steaks to ¼" and slash at 1" intervals; pound steaks between waxed paper with a meat mallet until ¼"–⅓" thick. Melt butter in a large, heavy skillet over moderate heat and

sauté shallots 3–4 minutes until pale golden; push to side of skillet. Raise burner heat to moderately high, add steaks, and brown 2–3 minutes on a side. If you like, turn heat to low, pour cognac over steaks, and flame. Transfer steaks to a heated platter and sprinkle with salt and pepper. Stir remaining ingredients into skillet drippings and heat, scraping up brown bits, about 1 minute. Pour over steaks and serve. About 580 calories per serving.

VARIATION:

☒ Steak Diane II (with mustard): Pound and brown steaks as directed; remove to platter. Blend into drippings along with above ingredients ¼ cup dry sherry and 1–2 teaspoons prepared Dijon-style mustard; boil up quickly to reduce slightly, pour over steaks, and serve. About 610 calories per serving.

STEAK FLORENTINE

Makes 2–3 servings

1 porterhouse steak, cut 1½" thick
1 clove garlic, peeled and cut in thin
  slivers
⅛ teaspoon pepper
1 tablespoon olive oil
½ teaspoon salt
Lemon wedges

Rub each side of steak well with garlic, pepper, and oil and let stand at room temperature 2 hours. Heat a large, heavy griddle over moderately high heat about 1 minute and brown steak quickly on both sides. Reduce heat to moderately low and cook steak 10–12 minutes on a side for very rare, 12–14 for rare, 15–17 for medium, and 18–20 for well done. Season with salt and serve with lemon wedges. About 465 calories for each of 2 servings, 310 calories for each of 3 servings.

VARIATION:

⊠ **Minute Steaks Florentine** (2 Servings): Rub both sides of 2 minute steaks with garlic, pepper, and oil and let stand at room temperature 10 minutes. Heat a lightly oiled skillet 1 minute over moderately high heat and brown steaks quickly, about 1 minute on each side. Season with salt and serve with lemon wedges. About 465 calories per serving.

⊠ PANNED CHUCK STEAKS ROSEMARY

These steaks should only be served rare or medium rare—longer cooking makes them tough.
Makes 4 servings

4 (1¼″–1½″ thick) small boneless blade chuck steaks
¾ teaspoon unseasoned meat tenderizer
½ cup butter or margarine
¼ teaspoon powdered rosemary
1 teaspoon salt
¼ teaspoon pepper
1 tablespoon Worcestershire sauce
1 teaspoon prepared mild yellow mustard
1 tablespoon hot water

Sprinkle both sides of each steak with tenderizer and pierce deeply with a sharp fork at ½″ intervals. Lightly brown ¼ cup butter in a large, heavy skillet over moderate heat and stir in rosemary. Add steaks and brown about 2 minutes on a side for very rare, 3 for rare, and 4 for medium rare. Season with salt and pepper, transfer to heated platter, and keep warm. Melt remaining butter in the skillet, add remaining ingredients, and cook and stir 1 minute; pour sauce over

steaks and serve. About 600 calories per serving.

"CHARCOAL" BROILED CHUCK STEAK

When buying blade steak for this recipe, make sure it is the first cut or that nearest the rib; it will be tender enough to broil, but other blade steaks may not be. To help preserve tenderness, serve rare.
Makes 4 servings

1 (3½–4-pound) blade chuck steak, cut 1″ thick and trimmed of excess fat
1½ teaspoons unseasoned meat tenderizer
½ teaspoon seasoned salt
1 teaspoon charcoal seasoning
¼ teaspoon pepper

Slash fat edges of steak at 1″ intervals, then brush each side with a little water. Mix remaining ingredients, pat ½ on 1 side of steak and pierce meat deeply at ½″ intervals. Turn steak, sprinkle with remaining mixture, and pierce as before. Cover steak loosely and let stand about ¼ hour. About 10 minutes before you're ready to broil steak, preheat broiler. Broil 2″ from heat 3–4 minutes on a side for very rare, 5 for rare, and 6 for medium rare. About 480 calories per serving.

⊠ HOT STEAK SANDWICHES

Not really sandwiches, but juicy little steaks served on butter-browned bread, these are quick, easy, and *good!*
Makes 2 servings

2 (¼″-thick) small individual-size minute or cube steaks (they should be about the size of a slice of bread)

1–2 tablespoons butter or margarine
½ teaspoon salt
Pinch pepper
2 slices firm-textured white bread

Brown steaks quickly on 1 side in
1 tablespoon butter in a heavy skillet
over moderately high heat (this
will take about 1 minute). Turn,
sprinkle with a little salt and pepper,
and brown second side 1 minute.
Season second side, remove steaks
from skillet, and keep warm. If
drippings seem scanty, add remaining butter to skillet. Quickly brown
bread on both sides in drippings.
Place 1 steak on each toasted bread
slice and serve. About 430 calories
per serving.

BALINESE BEEF ON SKEWERS (SATE)

One part of the 20 or 30 dish Indonesian *rijsttafel* (rice table)
is *sate*—salty-spicy beef cubes
grilled over charcoal. By themselves,
with their sauce or soy sauce as
a dip, these make exotic cocktail
fare; with rice, an original main
dish.
Makes 4 entree servings, enough
hors d'oeuvre for 6–8

1½ pounds boneless sirloin steak,
    cut in ¾″ cubes

Marinade:
1 teaspoon coriander seeds, crushed
1 teaspoon curry powder
⅛ teaspoon ginger
1 medium-size yellow onion, peeled
    and minced
1 clove garlic, peeled and crushed
1 tablespoon lime or lemon juice
3 tablespoons soy sauce
⅛ teaspoon pepper

Sauce:
3 tablespoons minced yellow onion
2 tablespoons cooking oil
1 teaspoon lemon juice

¼ cup peanut butter (creamy or
    crunchy)
1 cup hot water
Pinch hot red chili peppers (optional)

Place beef in a bowl. Mash coriander in a mortar and pestle with
curry, ginger, onion, garlic, and
lime juice, add to beef with soy
sauce and pepper and knead well.
Cover and chill 6–8 hours, turning
meat 1 or 2 times in marinade.
Meanwhile, prepare sauce: sauté
onion in oil 5–8 minutes over moderate heat until pale golden, add
remaining ingredients, and simmer,
uncovered, 10 minutes; cool and
reserve. For cooking sate, prepare
a hot charcoal fire* or preheat
broiler. Skewer beef cubes on bamboo or metal skewers, not too close
together, and broil 3″–4″ from heat,
turning often and basting with
marinade 7–10 minutes for rare, 12
for medium, and 15 for well done.
Warm sauce, uncovered, over low
heat. Serve with rice, topped with
some of the sauce; or as a cocktail
snack. About 495 calories per entree
serving (without rice); about 330
calories for each of 6 hors d'oeuvre
servings, 250 calories for each of
8 hors d'oeuvre servings.

VARIATIONS:

Chicken or Pork Sate: Substitute
¾″ cubes of white chicken meat or
lean pork for beef and prepare as
directed, broiling at least 15 minutes until well done (this is particularly important for pork; if
necessary, place skewers 5″ from
heat so pork cooks through without
drying out). About 415 calories
for each of 4 entree servings made
with chicken, 535 calories made
with pork.

Beef Sate Padang Style: Instead of
using marinade above, grind 1 teaspoon caraway seeds in a mortar and

pestle with ½ teaspoon each turmeric and curry powder, 1 minced yellow onion, 1 crushed clove garlic, a pinch hot red chili peppers, and 1 tablespoon lime or lemon juice; add 3 tablespoons soy sauce and ½ cup coconut liquid or Coconut Milk. Pour marinade over beef, then marinate and broil as directed above. About 400 calories for each entree serving.

▨ LONDON BROIL

The best way to make London broil tender is to serve it rare and to cut it *across the grain* in thin slices.
Makes 6 servings

1 (2½–3-pound) flank steak, trimmed of excess fat
1½ teaspoons salt
¼ teaspoon pepper

Preheat broiler. Score both sides of steak in a crisscross pattern, making cuts ⅛″ deep and 1″ apart. Broil on an oiled rack 2″–3″ from heat 4 minutes, turn with tongs, and broil 4 minutes longer. Transfer to a board or platter with a well (so juices will collect) and season with salt and pepper. Carve across the grain, slanting knife slightly, into slices ⅛″–¼″ thick. Top each portion with some of the juices and, if you like, pass Madeira-Mushroom Sauce. About 400 calories per serving.

To Charcoal Broil: Prepare a hot charcoal fire*; score steak as directed and broil on lightly greased grill 3″ from coals about 3–4 minutes per side. Season and serve.

VARIATION:

Marinated Broiled Flank Steak:
Marinate a scored flank steak in refrigerator in any meat marinade or thin barbecue sauce 4–6 hours. Remove from marinade and broil or charcoal broil, basting frequently with marinade. Slice and serve. About 400 calories per serving.

BACON-WRAPPED FLANK STEAK PINWHEELS
Makes 4 servings

1 (2-pound) flank steak, trimmed of excess fat
2 tablespoons butter or margarine, softened to room temperature
1 teaspoon unseasoned meat tenderizer
¼ teaspoon salt
¼ teaspoon pepper
1 teaspoon caraway seeds
2 teaspoons oregano
6–8 slices bacon

Preheat broiler. Score 1 side of steak in a crisscross pattern, making cuts ⅛″ deep and 1″ apart, then spread with butter and sprinkle with tenderizer. Pierce meat deeply all over with a sharp fork, sprinkle with salt, pepper, caraway, and oregano and roll, jelly-roll style, starting from a long side: secure with skewers. Slice crosswise into rolls 1½″ thick, wrap a bacon slice around each, and resecure with skewers. Broil on a lightly greased rack 3″–4″ from heat 5 minutes on each side, then bake, uncovered, 5 minutes at 350° F. (no need to preheat oven). (*Note:* If bacon doesn't crispen, turn pinwheels on edge and broil to brown.) Good with broiled tomato halves topped with broiled mushroom caps. About 740 calories per serving.

VARIATION:

Stuffed Flank Steak Pinwheels (Makes 6 servings): Score steak, spread with butter, sprinkle with tenderizer, and pierce as recipe directs. Sprinkle with salt and pepper but omit caraway seeds and oregano. Spread about 2 cups any well-seasoned meat or poultry stuffing to within 1" of edges, then roll jelly-roll style, secure with skewers, slice, and wrap with bacon as directed. Broil 5 minutes on a side, 3"–4" from the heat, then bake, uncovered, 10 minutes at 350° F. About 575 calories per serving.

PORTUGUESE VEGETABLE-BRAISED FLANK STEAK

Flank steak smothered with a thick tomato-carrot-onion-green-pepper gravy.
Makes 4 servings

1 (2-pound) flank steak, trimmed of
   excess fat
2 tablespoons flour
2 tablespoons olive oil or cooking oil
1 medium-size carrot, peeled and
   minced
½ medium-size sweet green pepper,
   cored, seeded, and minced
2 stalks celery, minced
1 medium-size yellow onion, peeled
   and minced
1 (10½-ounce) can condensed beef
   broth
1 teaspoon salt
¼ teaspoon pepper
2 tablespoons tomato paste
1 teaspoon lemon juice

Score each side of steak in a crisscross pattern, making cuts ⅛" deep and 1" apart. Using the rim of a heavy saucer, pound flour into both sides of steak (use 1 tablespoon altogether). Brown steak well on both sides in oil in a heavy kettle over moderately high heat; lift out and set aside. Add carrot, green pepper, celery, and onion to kettle and stir-fry 8–10 minutes until onion is golden. Add remaining flour and cook and stir 1 minute; stir in remaining ingredients, return steak to kettle, cover, and simmer about 1½ hours until tender. To

serve, transfer steak to heated platter and, slanting the knife, slice crosswise into thin strips. Pour some of the gravy (with vegetables) over steak. Pass the rest in a gravy boat. About 600 calories per serving.

HERB-STUFFED FLANK STEAK

The herb-bread stuffing makes two pounds of steak do the job of three.
Makes 6 servings

1 (2-pound) flank steak, trimmed of
   excess fat
1 medium-size yellow onion, peeled
   and minced
½ cup finely chopped celery
¼ cup butter or margarine
2 cups soft white bread crumbs
1½ teaspoons salt
¼ teaspoon pepper
1 tablespoon minced parsley
¼ teaspoon thyme
¼ teaspoon marjoram
¼ teaspoon sage
2 tablespoons beef drippings or
   cooking oil
2 cups beef broth or dry red wine
3 tablespoons flour mixed with 3
   tablespoons cold water

Preheat oven to 325° F. Score 1 side of steak in a crisscross pattern, making cuts ⅛" deep and 1" apart. Sauté onion and celery in butter over moderately low heat 8 minutes until pale golden; off heat, mix in crumbs, 1 teaspoon salt, ⅛ teaspoon pepper, and the herbs. Sprinkle unscored side of steak with remaining salt and pepper and spread stuffing to within 1" of edges, patting down firmly. Roll jelly-roll style, starting from a short side, and tie well with string (around the roll and end over end). Brown roll in drippings in a Dutch oven over moderate heat 7–10 minutes, add broth, cover, and bake 1½ hours until tender. Transfer meat to a platter and remove strings. Mix flour-water paste into pan liquid and heat, stirring, until thickened. Cut steak crosswise into thick slices and serve with gravy. About 580 calories per serving.

VARIATION:

Argentine Stuffed Flank Steak: Score steak as directed above, then prepare the following stuffing: remove casings from ½ pound *chorizo* or other garlic-flavored sausage and sauté the meat, breaking it up, 5 minutes over moderately high heat. Add ½ cup minced celery and 4 minced scallions and sauté 5 minutes longer. Off heat mix in ½ cup soft white bread crumbs, ¼ cup minced parsley, ½ teaspoon salt, and 1 lightly beaten egg. Spread on steak as directed above, then roll, brown, and bake as directed. Serve with a peppery chili sauce. About 595 calories per serving.

RUSSIAN-STYLE POT STEAK

Flank makes as flavorful a "Stroganoff" as more expensive steak.
Makes 4 servings

1 (2–2¼-pound) flank steak, trimmed of excess fat and cut crosswise into strips ½" × 1½"
⅔ cup unsifted flour
1 teaspoon salt
¼ teaspoon pepper
3 tablespoons bacon drippings
2 medium-size yellow onions, peeled and coarsely chopped
1 large carrot, peeled and coarsely grated
1 tablespoon minced parsley
1 tablespoon paprika
1 (10½-ounce) can condensed beef broth
⅔ cup water
½ cup sour cream

Dredge meat by shaking a few strips at a time in a paper bag with flour,

salt, and pepper. Heat bacon drippings in a heavy kettle over moderately high heat about 1 minute, add beef, and brown well on all sides, about 15 minutes. Reduce heat to moderate, add onions, carrot, parsley, and paprika, and sauté, stirring, 8–10 minutes until onions are golden. Add broth and water, cover, and simmer slowly 1–1½ hours until meat is tender. Mix in sour cream and serve with boiled new potatoes or buttered noodles. About 725 calories per serving.

⚔ CHINESE BEEF AND PEPPERS

If you want to double this recipe, use two skillets instead of one giant one so the vegetables don't overcook and lose their crisp-tender delicacy.
Makes 2 servings

2 tablespoons peanut or other cooking oil
1 small yellow onion, peeled and minced
1 sweet green pepper, cored, seeded, and cut in 1" squares
1 teaspoon Chinese black beans, rinsed (optional)
1 clove garlic, peeled and crushed
1 thin slice gingerroot or ⅛ teaspoon ginger
1 tomato, peeled, seeded, and cut in 6 wedges
½–¾ pound flank steak, trimmed of fat and cut across the grain in slices ⅛" thick
1 teaspoon dry sherry
½ teaspoon salt
½ teaspoon sugar
1 teaspoon soy sauce

Heat oil in a large skillet or *wok* over high heat ½ minute, add onion, green pepper, black beans, garlic, and ginger, and stir-fry 2 minutes. Add tomato and stir-fry 1 minute. Reduce heat to moderately high and push vegetables to side of pan; add beef and stir-fry 1 minute, sprinkling in sherry. Mix remaining ingredients, sprinkle over beef, and stir-fry ½ minute. Serve over boiled rice or Chinese Fried Rice.

VARIATIONS:

⚖ **Chinese Beef with Snow Peas:** Substitute ¼ pound snow pea pods and, if you like, ¼ pound thinly sliced mushrooms for onion and green pepper; stir-fry as directed. Add 1 (4-ounce) can drained, thinly sliced water chestnuts in place of tomato, stir-fry 1 minute, then proceed as recipe directs.

⚖ **Chinese Beef with Broccoli and Bean Sprouts:** Substitute ½ pound parboiled, thinly sliced broccoli for onion and green pepper and stir-fry as directed. Add ½ (1-pound) can well-drained bean sprouts along with tomato and proceed as recipe directs.

⚖ **Chinese Beef and Cabbage:** Substitute ½ pound shredded Chinese cabbage for green pepper, proceed as recipe directs.

All versions: About 340 calories per serving (without rice).

BEEF BIRDS (ROULADES)

Makes 6 servings

12 (5″×3″×¼″) slices beef round pounded thin as for scaloppine
Salt
Pepper
Flour (for dredging)
¼ cup beef or bacon drippings or cooking oil
⅔ cup finely chopped celery (optional)
½ cup thinly sliced mushrooms (optional)
2 cups beef broth
3 tablespoons flour blended with 3 tablespoons cold water

Stuffing:
1 large yellow onion, peeled and minced
2 tablespoons beef or bacon drippings
½ cup finely chopped mushrooms
2 cups soft white bread crumbs
½ cup water
1 egg, lightly beaten
½ teaspoon salt
⅛ teaspoon pepper
2 tablespoons minced parsley

Sprinkle beef with salt and pepper and set aside while you prepare stuffing. Sauté onion in drippings over moderate heat 5–8 minutes until pale golden, add mushrooms and stir-fry 1–2 minutes; off heat mix in remaining ingredients. Spoon about 2 tablespoons stuffing on each piece meat, roll, and tie well with string. Dredge rolls in flour and brown, a few at a time, in drippings in a Dutch oven 5–7 minutes over moderate heat; drain on paper toweling. If you wish, add celery and mushrooms and stir-fry 2–3 minutes. Drain all but 1 tablespoon drippings from kettle, return meat, add broth, cover, and simmer 1½ hours until tender (or bake 1½ hours at 350° F.). Transfer rolls to serving dish and remove strings. Mix flour-water paste into kettle and heat, stirring, until thickened. Serve with gravy and buttered noodles. About 410 calories per serving.

VARIATIONS:

⚖ **German Rouladen:** Salt and pepper beef as directed, then, instead of making stuffing, lay a thin strip dill pickle on each piece beef, also 2 teaspoons each capers and minced onion and ½ strip bacon. Roll, tie, and cook as recipe directs. About 310 calories per serving.

Italian Braciuolini: Salt and pepper

beef as directed, then make the following filling instead of one given above: Brown ½ cup minced onion and ½ pound ground beef chuck or sweet Italian sausage meat in 2 tablespoons olive oil 5–8 minutes over moderately high heat: drain off drippings. Off heat mix in 1 cup soft white bread crumbs, ½ teaspoon salt, ⅛ teaspoon pepper, 1 lightly beaten egg, and ½ teaspoon oregano or basil. Spoon filling onto meat, roll, tie, and proceed as recipe directs. (*Note:* If you like, cook rolls in a thin tomato sauce instead of broth, omitting chopped celery and mushrooms.) Good with Gnocchi or any buttered pasta. About 420 calories per serving.

Paupiettes à la Bourguignonne:
Prepare rolls as directed, then cook in 1 cup dry red wine and 1 cup beef broth with 1 peeled clove garlic and ⅛ teaspoon thyme (omit celery and mushrooms). About 10 minutes before serving, thicken gravy as directed and add 1 recipe Pan-Braised Onions and 1 recipe Sautéed Mushrooms. About 545 calories per serving.

Beef Birds with Sour Cream Gravy:
Prepare rolls by basic recipe above but omit flour-water paste; stir in 1 cup sour cream just before serving. About 480 calories per serving.

OLD-FASHIONED SWISS STEAK
Makes 4–6 servings

¼ cup unsifted flour
1½ teaspoons salt
¼ teaspoon pepper
1 (3–4-pound) blade or arm steak, cut about 2″ thick
3 tablespoons beef or bacon drippings or cooking oil
1 large yellow onion, peeled and minced

2 stalks celery, minced
2 small carrots, peeled and minced
1 (1-pound) can tomatoes (do not drain) or 1 (1-pound) can Spanish-style tomato sauce
1½ cups beef broth or hot water

Mix flour, salt, and pepper and sprinkle about 2 tablespoons on 1 side of meat; pound with a meat mallet or edge of heavy saucer. Turn meat and pound in remaining flour the same way. Melt drippings in a Dutch oven over moderately high heat 1 minute and brown meat well, about 5 minutes on each side. Remove meat and set aside. Sauté onion, celery, and carrots in remaining drippings 8 minutes until golden. Return meat to kettle, spoon vegetables on top, add tomatoes and broth. Cover and simmer 1½–2 hours until tender, basting meat once or twice. Cut into portions, top with vegetables and gravy, and serve. About 640 calories for each of 4 servings, 590 calories for each of 6 servings.

To Bake: Prepare as directed but, instead of simmering on top of stove, cover and bake 2–2½ hours in a 350° F. oven.

EASY SWISS STEAK
Makes 4–6 servings

1 (3–4-pound) blade or arm steak, cut about 2″ thick
2 cloves garlic, peeled and crushed
¼ teaspoon pepper
1 (1⅜-ounce) package dry onion soup mix
1 (6-ounce) can tomato paste
⅓ cup dry white wine

Preheat oven to 350° F. Place steak on a large double thickness of foil and rub each side with garlic and pepper; pat on soup mix. Combine tomato paste and wine and spread on top side only. Wrap foil around steak, place in a shallow roasting pan, and bake 2–2½ hours until tender. Unwrap, carve into thin slices, and top each serving with drippings. About 540 calories for each of 4 servings, 360 calories for each of 6 servings.

ESTERHÁZY STEAK

Steak, mushrooms, onion, celery, and carrot in a tart sour cream-caper gravy. Worth every calorie-packed forkful!
Makes 2–4 servings

1 pound top round, cut ¼" thick and pounded thin as for scaloppine
⅓ cup unsifted flour
1 teaspoon salt
⅛ teaspoon pepper
3 tablespoons butter, margarine, or meat drippings
1 carrot, peeled and minced
2 medium-size mushrooms, wiped clean and minced
1 stalk celery, minced
1 small yellow onion, peeled and minced
1 tablespoon minced parsley
1 cup beef stock or broth
1 tablespoon minced capers
1 cup sour cream

Cut steak into pieces about 4" square. Mix flour, salt, and pepper and rub well into both sides of each piece of steak; reserve 1 tablespoon seasoned flour. Brown steak on both sides in butter in a large, heavy skillet over moderately high heat, push to side of skillet, add all minced vegetables and parsley, and stir-fry 5–8 minutes. Blend in reserved seasoned flour. Turn heat to low, add broth, cover, and simmer 40–45 minutes until steak is tender. Mix in capers, then smooth in sour cream and heat (but do not boil) about 1 minute. Serve hot with boiled potatoes or buttered noodles. About 980 calories for

each of 2 servings, 490 calories for each of 4 servings.

CHICKEN-FRIED STEAK

Prepared much the same way as the famous Southern "batter-fried" chicken.
Makes 2–4 servings

1 pound top or bottom round, cut ¼" thick and pounded thin as for scaloppine
½ cup unsifted flour
2 eggs lightly beaten with 3 tablespoons milk
1 cup fine dry bread crumbs or cracker meal
4–5 tablespoons lard, meat drippings, butter, or margarine
1 teaspoon salt
⅛ teaspoon pepper

Cut steak into 3" squares; dust well with flour, dip in egg, then in crumbs to coat evenly. Heat 3 tablespoons lard in a large, heavy skillet over moderately high heat and brown steak 2–3 minutes on a side, adding more lard as needed. When all pieces are browned, sprinkle with salt and pepper, turn heat to low, cover, and cook about 45 minutes until tender. About 950 calories for each of 2 servings, 475 calories for each of 4 servings.

COUNTRY FRIED STEAK

The Middle Western way to make a "tough" steak tender.
Makes 2–4 servings

1 pound bottom round, cut ¼" thick
1 teaspoon salt
⅛ teaspoon pepper
⅓ cup unsifted flour
3 tablespoons beef or bacon drippings, butter, or margarine
⅔ cup water

Cut steak into pieces about 3" square, sprinkle each side with salt and pepper, and rub generously with flour. Place between several thicknesses wax paper and pound well with the blunt side of a meat cleaver or edge of a heavy saucer. Heat drippings about 1 minute in a large, heavy skillet over moderately high heat and brown steak quickly on both sides. Turn heat to low, add water, cover, and simmer 30–40 minutes until steak is tender. When serving, top each portion with pan gravy. About 700 calories for each of 2 servings, 350 calories for each of 4 servings.

VARIATIONS:

Country Fried Steak with Onion: Season, pound, and brown steak as directed, then remove from skillet. In the drippings stir-fry 1 thinly sliced large yellow onion 8–10 minutes until golden brown; remove from skillet temporarily. Return meat to skillet, pile onions on top, add water, cover, and simmer as directed. About 720 calories for each of 2 servings, 360 calories for each of 4 servings.

Country Fried Steak with Mushrooms: Season, pound, and brown steak as above; remove from skillet. Stir-fry ½ pound thinly sliced mushrooms in drippings 5 minutes until limp and remove; return meat to skillet, spoon mushrooms on top, add water, cover, and simmer as directed. About 730 calories for each of 2 servings, 365 calories for each of 4 servings.

GROUND BEEF

How ground beef is to be used determines how it should be ground. For light, juicy hamburgers, it should be coarsely ground, one time only. For meat balls and meat loaves, where firmer textures are desirable, it can be finely ground two or three times. Generally speaking, the more finely—and often—meat is ground, the more compact it will be when cooked.

What kind of hamburger should you buy? Again, it depends on use. Also budget. Here are the three most popular kinds:

Regular Hamburger (ground trimmings, usually from shank, plate, and brisket): The cheapest ground beef, also the fattest (often ¼ to ⅓ fat), which means it will shrink considerably during cooking as the fat melts and drippings run off.

Ground Chuck: Probably the best all round hamburger meat. It has just enough fat (about 15%) to make it juicy, an excellent flavor, and a moderate price.

Ground Round: The most expensive "hamburger," also the leanest, meaning it may dry out if cooked much beyond medium rare (when having round ground to order, make sure the butcher adds about 2 ounces suet for each pound lean). Ground round is a good choice for calorie counters—a ¼ pound *broiled* patty averages about 220 calories.

⊠ HAMBURGERS

Though it's usually recommended that meat be brought to room temperature before cooking, hamburger is an exception because of its great perishability. Cooking times given here are for meat refrigerated until ready to use. Makes 3–4 servings

1 pound ground beef
1 teaspoon salt
⅛ teaspoon pepper

Shape beef *lightly* into 3 plump

patties or 4 slim ones and cook by one of the methods below; season with salt and pepper just before serving.

To Panfry (Sauté): Especially recommended for lean meat. Brown hamburgers uncovered in 1–2 tablespoons cooking oil, butter, margarine, or drippings in a large, heavy skillet over moderately high heat; plump patties will take about 5 minutes on a side for rare, 6 for medium, and 7 for well done, thin patties about 1 minute less per side for each degree of doneness. While hamburgers cook, do not press down or "spank" with a pancake turner—you'll only force out succulent juices. About 355 calories for each of 3 servings, 265 for each of 4 servings.

⌧ ⚖ *To Panbroil:* Recommended for dieters, also for meat heavily flecked with fat. Lightly brush a large, heavy skillet with oil or sprinkle with salt; heat 1 minute over moderately high heat, add hamburgers, and brown, uncovered, using the same cooking times as for panfrying. Pour off drippings as they accumulate. About 320 calories for each of 3 servings, 240 calories for each of 4 servings.

⌧ ⚖ *To Broil:* Recommended for dieters and fatty hamburger meat. Preheat broiler; broil hamburgers 3" from heat on a lightly greased broiler rack. Plump patties will take 5–6 minutes on a side for rare, 7 for medium, and 8–9 for well done, thin patties about 1 minute less per side in each instance. About 320 calories for each of 3 servings, 240 calories for each of 4 servings.

⚖ *To Charcoal Broil:* Recommended for plump patties only. Prepare a moderately hot charcoal

fire.* Lay hamburgers on a lightly greased grill and broil 4" from the heat about 4–5 minutes on a side for rare, 6 for medium, and 7–8 for well done. About 320 calories for each of 3 servings, 240 calories for each of 4 servings.

To Braise: Brown patties quickly in a lightly greased large, heavy skillet over high heat, turn heat to low and pour in 1–1½ cups liquid (dry red wine; broth; gravy; tomato juice, soup, or sauce; cream of mushroom, cheese, or celery soup), cover, and simmer slowly 15–20 minutes. Serve topped with the cooking liquid. About 350 calories for each of 3 servings (cooked in broth, wine, or tomato juice), 265 calories for each of 4 servings. Burgers cooked in gravy, sauce, or soup will run approximately 65–100 calories more for each of 3 servings (depending on richness), 50–75 calories more for each of 4 servings.

⌧ **20 VARIATIONS ON HAMBURGERS**

All amounts based on recipe above

Cheeseburgers: Shape patties as directed, brown on 1 side, and season lightly; turn, season again, top with a thin slice American cheese and cook to desired doneness. About 420 calories for each of 3 servings, 315 calories for each of 4 servings.

Blue Cheese Burgers: Shape meat into 6 thin patties; in the center of 3 place a scant teaspoon blue cheese spread. Top with remaining patties and pinch edges to seal. Cook as directed, season with ¼ teaspoon salt and ⅛ teaspoon pepper and serve. About 370 calories per serving.

Surprise Burgers: Shape meat into 6 thin patties; in the center of 3 place a scant teaspoon of any of the following: minced onion, dill pickle, or capers; sweet pickle relish; grated Cheddar or Swiss cheese. Top with remaining patties and pinch edges to seal. Cook and season as directed. About 320 calories per serving made with onion, capers or pickle, 370 if made with cheese.

Stuffed Burgers: Shape beef into 6 thin patties, top 3 with scant tablespoons leftover mashed potatoes or turnips, boiled rice or pilaf, leftover cooked peas, beans, corn, diced beets, or carrots. Top with remaining patties, pinch edges to seal, cook and season as directed. About 330 calories per serving.

Herb Burgers: Into beef mix 1 tablespoon minced chives and ¼ teaspoon each sage and marjoram or thyme; shape into patties, cook and season as directed. About 320 calories for each of 3 servings, 240 calories for each of 4 servings.

Dilly Burgers: Into beef mix 1 tablespoon each sour cream, minced chives, fresh dill, and capers; shape into patties, cook as directed, and season with ½ teaspoon salt and ⅛ teaspoon pepper. About 330 calories for each of 3 servings, 245 calories for each of 4 servings.

Deviled Burgers: Mix beef with 2 tablespoons each cold water and spicy brown prepared mustard, 1 teaspoon each grated onion and Worcestershire sauce, ½ teaspoon salt, and 2–3 dashes liquid hot red pepper seasoning. Shape and cook as directed but do not season. About 320 calories for each of 3 servings, 240 calories for each of 4 servings.

Curry Burgers: Into beef mix 2 tablespoons grated onion, 1 tablespoon curry powder, 1 teaspoon garlic salt, ⅛ teaspoon cayenne pepper, and a pinch each ginger and cinnamon. Shape and cook as directed but do not season. About 320 calories for each of 3 servings, 240 calories for each of 4 servings.

Chili Burgers: Into beef mix 1 tablespoon each grated onion, chili sauce, chili powder, ½ teaspoon garlic salt, and ⅛ teaspoon cayenne pepper. Shape and cook as directed but do not season. About 320 calories for each of 3 servings, 240 calories for each of 4 servings.

Barbecue Burgers: Into beef mix 1 tablespoon each ketchup, Worcestershire sauce, red wine vinegar, chili powder, ¼ teaspoon salt, and ⅛ teaspoon cayenne pepper. Shape and cook as directed but do not season. About 325 calories for each of 3 servings, 245 calories for each of 4 servings.

Pizza Burgers: Shape meat into 4 patties and broil 3 minutes on a side. Sprinkle lightly with salt. Top each patty with 1–2 tablespoons canned pizza sauce, a thin slice mozzarella cheese, a sprinkling oregano, and, if you like, crushed hot red chili peppers. Return to broiler and broil just until bubbly. About 310 calories per serving.

Teriyaki Burgers: Mix beef with 2 tablespoons each soy sauce, dry sherry, and minced sautéed scallions, ½ crushed clove garlic, 1 teaspoon grated fresh gingerroot, and ⅛ teaspoon pepper. Shape and cook as directed but do not season. About 325 calories for each of 3 servings, 245 calories for each of 4 servings.

Burgundy Burgers: Mix 1 minced scallion into beef, also 2 tablespoons Burgundy wine, ½ crushed clove garlic, ½ teaspoon salt, and a pinch pepper. Shape and cook as directed but do not season. About 3 minutes before serving, add ½ cup Burgundy to skillet and continue cooking, basting often. Serve topped with pan juices. About 325 calories for each of 3 servings, 245 calories for each of 4 servings.

Mushroom Burgers: Mix beef with 2 tablespoons minced sautéed onion and ⅓ cup minced sautéed mushrooms, 1 teaspoon salt, and ⅛ teaspoon pepper. Shape and cook as directed but do not season. About 325 calories for each of 3 servings, 245 calories for each of 4 servings.

Pepper Burgers: Mix beef with 2 tablespoons each minced sautéed green pepper and onion, 1 teaspoon salt, and ⅛ teaspoon pepper. Shape and cook as directed but do not season. About 325 calories for each of 3 servings, 245 calories for each of 4 servings.

Bacon Burgers: Mix beef with ¼ cup each minced sautéed onion and crisp bacon bits. Shape into patties, cook and season as directed. About 420 calories for each of 3 servings, 315 calories for each of 4 servings.

Nut Burgers: Mix beef with 2 tablespoons minced onion, ⅓ cup finely chopped pecans, piñon nuts, toasted almonds or walnuts, and 2 teaspoons minced parsley. Shape, cook and season as directed. About 410 calories for each of 3 servings, 310 calories for each of 4 servings.

Burgers au Poivre: Shape into 4 patties, sprinkle each side of each with ¼ teaspoon coarsely ground pepper and press into meat with the heel of your hand. Let stand at room temperature 20–30 minutes.

Panfry hamburgers in 2 tablespoons butter 3–4 minutes on a side; remove to a hot platter, sprinkle with salt, and keep warm. To drippings add 1 tablespoon each butter, minced parsley, and cognac and heat 1–2 minutes, stirring to get up any brown bits. Spoon over burgers and serve. About 315 calories per serving.

Burgers Diane: Shape into 4 patties and panfry in 2 tablespoons unsalted butter about 4 minutes on a side; remove from skillet, season with ½ teaspoon salt and ⅛ teaspoon pepper, and keep warm. To skillet add 3 tablespoons dry sherry, 1 tablespoon each unsalted butter, minced chives, parsley, and cognac and 1 teaspoon each Worcestershire sauce and prepared spicy brown mustard. Heat 1–2 minutes, stirring with a wooden spoon to scrape up brown bits, pour over burgers, and serve. About 320 calories per serving.

⚖ ¢ **Budget Burgers:** To extend 1 pound ground beef so it will serve 6, mix in 1 lightly beaten egg and any of the following, then shape, cook and season as directed:
– 1 cup mashed, drained cooked beans (navy, kidney, pinto, or chick-peas). About 225 calories per serving.
– 1 cup mashed potatoes, boiled rice, bulgur wheat, or pilaf and, if mixture seems a little dry, 1–2 tablespoons broth, milk, tomato juice, or water. About 175 calories per serving.
– 1 cup crushed potato chips or cornflakes. About 200 calories per serving.
– 1 cup cracker meal or poultry stuffing mix and ¼–⅓ cup broth, milk, or tomato juice. About 275 calories per serving.
– 1 cup soft bread crumbs or crumbled corn bread and ¼–⅓ cup

broth, milk, or tomato juice. About 215 calories per serving.
– ½ cup each minced celery and finely grated carrot and 2 tablespoons finely grated onion. About 175 calories per serving.
– 1 cup finely diced boiled potatoes, ½ cup diced, drained cooked beets, and 2 tablespoons grated onion. About 195 calories per serving.

⊠ ¢ BEEF LINDSTROM

Here's a delicious way to use up leftover boiled beets and potatoes.
Makes 4–6 servings

1 pound ground beef
⅔ cup minced boiled beets, well drained
1 cup minced boiled potatoes
1 tablespoon finely grated onion
2 teaspoons minced capers
2 egg yolks, lightly beaten
2 tablespoons light cream
¼ teaspoon salt
Pinch pepper
2–3 tablespoons butter or margarine

Mix beef with all ingredients except butter, cover, and chill several hours until firm enough to shape. Shape into small rectangular patties about 3″ long and 1″ wide, then brown 5–7 minutes in butter in a large, heavy skillet over moderately high heat. To avoid crowding skillet, do about half the patties at a time, setting browned ones, uncovered, in a 250° F. oven to keep warm while you brown the rest. About 375 calories for each of 4 servings, 250 calories for each of 6 servings.

SALISBURY STEAK

Makes 2–4 servings

½ recipe Mushroom Gravy
1 pound ground beef
1 teaspoon salt
⅛ teaspoon pepper

Prepare gravy by recipe and keep warm. Shape beef into 2 flat oval patties and panbroil in a large, lightly greased skillet over moderately high heat 5–6 minutes on each side for rare, 7 for medium, and 8–9 for well done. Sprinkle with salt and pepper, smother with mushroom gravy, and serve. About 580 calories for each of 2 servings, 290 calories for each of 4 servings.

⊠ ¢ SLOPPY JOES

Makes 6 servings

1 teaspoon beef drippings or cooking oil
1 pound ground beef
1 medium-size yellow onion, peeled and chopped fine
½ cup ketchup
½ cup chili sauce
1 tablespoon Worcestershire sauce
1 teaspoon salt
⅛ teaspoon pepper
⅓ cup water
6 hamburger buns, warmed

Brush a skillet with drippings and warm over moderate heat ½ minute. Add beef and onion and sauté 10 minutes, stirring frequently. Add all remaining ingredients except buns and simmer, uncovered, 10 minutes. Spoon mixture between split buns and serve. About 320 calories per serving.

VARIATIONS:

⊠ ⚖ ¢ **Sloppy Josés:** Substitute 1 cup canned Spanish-style tomato sauce for ketchup and chili sauce; prepare and serve as directed. About 280 calories per serving.

⊠ ¢ **Sloppy Franks:** Add 1–2 teaspoons chili powder to meat mixture, simmer as directed, and spoon over hot dogs in hot dog buns. About 460 calories per serving.

⊠ ¢ **Cheesy Joes:** Lightly toast bottom half of each hamburger bun, top with a slice of cheese (American, Cheddar, Swiss, etc.), and toast until cheese begins to melt. Spoon meat mixture over cheese, add bun lids, and serve. About 420 calories per serving.

⚖ ¢ ECONOMY MEAT LOAF

Makes 6 servings

1½ *pounds ground beef*
1 *cup rolled oats*
2 *teaspoons salt*
¼ *teaspoon pepper*
1 *teaspoon prepared spicy yellow mustard*
1 *teaspoon prepared horseradish*
1 *large yellow onion, peeled and chopped fine*
¾ *cup milk or skim milk*
¼ *cup cold water*

Preheat oven to 350° F. Using your hands, mix all ingredients together thoroughly. Pack into an ungreased 9″×5″×3″ loaf pan. Bake, uncovered, 1 hour. Loosen loaf from pan, drain off drippings (save for gravy), invert on a heated platter, and serve. About 225 calories per serving.

JOHN'S SAGEY MEAT LOAF

Makes 8 servings

3 *pounds ground beef*
1 *cup finely chopped Bermuda or Spanish onion*
1 *clove garlic, peeled and crushed*
1 *cup coarse soda cracker crumbs*
3 *eggs*
¼ *cup dry white vermouth*
¼ *cup water*
2 *teaspoons minced fresh sage or ½ teaspoon dried sage*
¼ *teaspoon parsley flakes*

¼ *teaspoon thyme*
¼ *teaspoon marjoram*
1½ *teaspoons salt*
⅛ *teaspoon pepper*

Preheat oven to 325° F. Mix all ingredients thoroughly, using your hands, and pack into an ungreased 9″×5″×3″ loaf pan. Bake, uncovered, 1 hour and 25 minutes or until loaf begins to pull from sides of pan. Remove from oven and let stand 5 minutes. Pour off any drippings, turn loaf onto a warmed platter, and serve. About 435 calories per serving.

¢ BEEF AND PORK LOAF

Makes 6–8 servings

¾ *cup lukewarm milk*
1 *egg, beaten*
1½ *cups soft white bread crumbs*
1 *pound ground beef*
1 *pound ground lean pork*
1 *large yellow onion, peeled and minced*
⅓ *cup minced gherkins*
1 *tablespoon salt*
¼ *teaspoon pepper*
1 *tablespoon Worcestershire sauce*

Preheat oven to 350° F. Combine milk and egg, add crumbs, and let stand 5 minutes; mix thoroughly with remaining ingredients, turn into an ungreased shallow roasting pan, and shape into a loaf. Bake, uncovered, 1½ hours, basting off excess drippings (save for gravy). Transfer loaf to a heated platter and let stand 5 minutes before cutting. Serve hot with gravy, Sweet-Sour Sauce, or Mushroom Gravy. Or chill and serve cold with Mustard Sauce. About 435 calories for each of 6 servings, 325 calories for each of 8 servings.

SPICY MEAT LOAF

Makes 6–8 servings

2½ pounds ground beef
1 (8-ounce) package poultry stuffing mix
1 (1⅜-ounce) package dry onion soup mix
1 pint sour cream
½ cup tomato juice
1 clove garlic, peeled and crushed
1 tablespoon Worcestershire sauce
1 teaspoon oregano
⅛ teaspoon pepper
1 egg, beaten

Preheat oven to 325° F. Mix all ingredients, using your hands, and pack into an ungreased 9"×5"×3" loaf pan. Bake, uncovered, 1 hour and 15 minutes. Let loaf cool upright in its pan 10 minutes, then turn onto a heated platter and serve. About 730 calories for each of 6 servings, 550 calories for each of 8 servings.

¢ POT-ROASTED BEEF AND VEGETABLE ROLL

Makes 4 servings

1 pound ground beef
1 teaspoon salt
⅛ teaspoon pepper
2 tablespoons bacon drippings or margarine
2 cups beef broth
2–3 tablespoons flour blended with 2 tablespoons cold water

Stuffing:
1 small yellow onion, peeled and minced
⅓ cup finely chopped celery
1 small carrot, peeled and finely grated
1 tablespoon bacon drippings or margarine
¾ cup soft white bread crumbs
1 egg, lightly beaten
2 tablespoons minced parsley

1 teaspoon salt
⅛ teaspoon pepper

Mix beef, salt, and pepper and roll with a rolling pin between 2 sheets waxed paper to a rectangle about 7"×10", keeping edges as straight as possible. Prepare stuffing: sauté onion, celery, carrot in drippings over moderate heat 5 minutes and mix in remaining ingredients. Spread over beef, leaving ½" margins all round, then roll, jelly-roll style, pinching edges to seal. Brown roll in 2 tablespoons drippings in a heavy kettle over moderate heat 5 minutes, turning frequently and gently. Remove roll and pour off all but 1 tablespoon drippings. Place roll seam side down on a rack, return to kettle, add 1 cup broth, cover, and simmer 40 minutes. Lift roll and rack from kettle, transfer roll to a platter and keep warm. Add remaining broth to kettle, mix in flour-water paste, and heat, stirring, until thickened. Pour a little gravy over meat roll and pass the rest. About 410 calories per serving.

VARIATION:

About ½ hour before serving, add any of the following to kettle: peeled, halved new potatoes or turnips, carrots cut in 2" chunks, peeled small white onions. Arrange vegetables on platter with meat and keep warm while making gravy. Recipe too flexible for a meaningful calorie count.

⚖ ¢ STUFFED GREEN PEPPERS

Makes 6–8 servings

8 medium-size sweet green peppers
1 pound ground beef
1 medium-size yellow onion, peeled and chopped fine
1 teaspoon garlic salt

½ teaspoon salt
¼ teaspoon pepper
1½ cups cooked rice (hot or cold)
2½–3 cups canned marinara or
   Spanish-style tomato sauce

Prepare peppers for stuffing.* Sauté
beef in a lightly greased heavy
skillet over moderate heat 10 minutes until no longer pink, stirring
to break up chunks; transfer to a
bowl with slotted spoon. Drain
all but 2 tablespoons drippings from
skillet, add onion and sauté 8–10
minutes, stirring occasionally, until
golden. Mix onion and all remaining ingredients except sauce into
meat; stuff each pepper loosely,
filling to within ¼" of the top.
Stand peppers in a deep saucepan
so they touch and support each
other. Pour in sauce so it sur-
rounds peppers but does not touch
the filling. Cover and simmer slowly
1 hour until peppers are tender.
Lift peppers to a heated platter, top
with some of the sauce, and pass
the rest. About 260 calories for
each of 6 servings, 195 calories for
each of 8 servings.

¢ BAKED PEPPERS STUFFED WITH BEEF AND RED KIDNEY BEANS

Makes 6 servings

6 large sweet green or red peppers
1 pound ground beef
1 large yellow onion, peeled and
   minced
1 (10½-ounce) can condensed
   cheese soup thinned with 1¼ cups
   water
1 (6-ounce) can tomato paste
2 teaspoons salt
2 teaspoons chili powder
¼ teaspoon pepper
1 (1-pound) can red kidney beans
   (do not drain)
⅓ cup hot water

Prepare peppers for stuffing and
parboil.* Stir-fry beef, without
adding any fat, in a large, heavy
skillet over moderate heat 10 minutes until no longer pink, breaking
up large clumps. Add onion and
stir-fry 5 minutes. Mix in remaining
ingredients except beans and water;
then stir in beans and simmer,
uncovered, ½ hour, stirring now and
then. Preheat oven to 375° F.
Arrange peppers upright in an ungreased small casserole so they touch
and support each other; fill with
skillet mixture. Pour water into
casserole and bake, uncovered,
about 45 minutes until peppers are
fork tender. (Note: Any leftover
stuffing can be heated and spooned
over peppers.) About 365 calories
per serving.

¢ PICADILLO

Spicy, a little bit sweet, a little bit
salty, picadillo is Mexican minced
meat. Serve as is, use as a filling
for meat pies, or for making Chiles
Rellenos.
Makes 4–6 servings

1 large yellow onion, peeled and
   minced
1 clove garlic, peeled and crushed
1 tablespoon olive oil
1 pound ground beef
½ (6-ounce) can tomato paste
1 canned jalapeño chili, seeded and
   minced, or ¼ teaspoon crushed hot
   red chili peppers
⅓ cup minced raisins
¼ teaspoon oregano
⅛ teaspoon cinnamon
Pinch cloves
¾ teaspoon salt
Pinch black pepper
¼ cup minced blanched almonds

Sauté onion and garlic in oil in a
large, heavy skillet over moderate
heat 8–10 minutes until golden.

Add meat and sauté 3–5 minutes, breaking up any clumps. Blend in tomato paste, add remaining ingredients, and heat, stirring, 5 minutes to blend flavors. About 395 calories for each of 4 servings, 265 calories for each of 6 servings.

CHILES RELLENOS (MEXICAN STUFFED PEPPERS)

For real *chiles rellenos,* you need dark green *poblano* chilis. These aren't often available fresh in this country, and even if they were, many of us would find them too hot. Sweet green peppers may be substituted and so may the canned mild green chilis (better get two cans because the chilis are very fragile and difficult to stuff). Makes 6 servings

6 *poblano chilis, or 6 small sweet green peppers, or 12 Italian elle peppers, or 2 (1-pound 10-ounce) cans peeled, roasted mild green chilis, drained*
1 *recipe Picadillo (recipe above)*
Shortening or cooking oil for deep fat frying

Coating:
½ *cup unsifted flour*
4 *eggs, separated*

Sauce:
1 *small yellow onion, peeled and minced*
1 *clove garlic, peeled and crushed*
2 *tablespoons olive oil*
½ *(6-ounce) can tomato paste*
1 *(8-ounce) can tomato sauce*
1 *(13¾-ounce) can chicken broth*
1 *teaspoon sugar*
½ *teaspoon salt*
Pinch pepper

If using fresh peppers, toast and peel (see Marinated Roasted Peppers for how to do it). If using canned chilis, rinse gently in cold water and remove seeds. Drain peppers on paper toweling. Prepare *picadillo* and cool to room temperature. Sauté onion and garlic for sauce in oil in a large skillet over moderate heat 8–10 minutes until golden; mix in remaining ingredients, turn heat to low, and let sauce simmer, uncovered, until you're ready for it. Begin heating shortening or oil in a deep fat fryer over moderately high heat (use a deep fat thermometer). Stuff chilis with picadillo and set aside while you prepare coating. Beat yolks and whites, separately, until thick, then fold yolks into whites. Roll stuffed chilis in flour, then dip in egg. When fat reaches 375° F., fry chilis, a few at a time, 2–3 minutes until golden. Drain on paper toweling, add to tomato sauce, and warm, uncovered, about 5 minutes. Serve chilis topped with the sauce. About 445 calories per serving.

VARIATION:

Chiles Rellenos con Queso: These chilis are made just like traditional *rellenos* except that they're stuffed with cheese instead of picadillo. Use small peppers—either Italian *elle* or canned chilis—and prepare for stuffing as above. Fill with softened cream cheese, coarsely grated sharp Cheddar, or Monterey Jack (you'll need about ½ pound). Then proceed as recipe directs, dipping chilis in flour and beaten egg, deep frying until golden, and warming in tomato sauce. About 320 calories per serving if made with cream cheese or Monterey Jack, 330 calories per serving if made with Cheddar.

POLISH STUFFED CABBAGE ROLLS WITH LEMON SAUCE

A friend gave us this old family recipe.
Makes 4 servings

1 medium-size cabbage, trimmed of coarse outer leaves
1½ quarts boiling water
3½ teaspoons salt
1 large yellow onion, peeled and minced
¼ cup butter or margarine
1 pound ground beef
½ cup uncooked rice
¼ teaspoon black pepper
2 tablespoons lemon juice
2 tablespoons flour blended with 2 tablespoons cold water
⅛ teaspoon white pepper

Place cabbage, water, and 1 teaspoon salt in a large kettle and boil, uncovered, 3–4 minutes until leaves are pliable. Drain, reserving 2½ cups cooking water. Cool cabbage in a colander under cold running water until easy to handle, drain well, core, and remove 12 whole outer leaves (discard any with holes). Cut base of large white vein from each leaf and discard; spread each leaf flat. (*Note:* Save rest of cabbage to use later.) Stir-fry onion in 2 tablespoons butter over moderate heat 5–8 minutes until transparent and mix with beef, rice, 2 teaspoons salt, and the black pepper. Put a spoonful of the mixture on the center of each leaf, fold sides in over filling, and roll up loosely. Secure with toothpicks. Arrange rolls 1 layer deep in a large kettle, add reserved cabbage water, lemon juice, and remaining butter. Cover and simmer 1 hour. Lift rolls to a serving dish and keep warm. Mix flour paste into kettle and cook and stir over moderate heat 3–4 minutes until liquid thickens slightly; add remaining salt

and the white pepper. Pour some of the sauce over rolls and pass the rest. About 440 calories per serving.

SWEDISH MEAT BALLS I

Swedish meat balls are sometimes made of one meat only, but more often with a combination of beef, pork, and/or veal. Some recipes call for mashed potatoes (a dandy way to use up leftovers), others don't. For smorgasbord, the balls are tiny (about ½") and served *without* sauce; for entrees they're larger and awash in pale cream gravy.
Makes 4–6 servings

Meat Balls:
1 medium-size yellow onion, peeled and minced
1 tablespoon butter or margarine
1 pound boned beef chuck, ground twice
¼ pound boned lean pork shoulder, ground twice
1½ teaspoons salt
¼ teaspoon pepper
Pinch nutmeg (optional)
¾ cup fine dry bread crumbs
¼ cup milk
¼ cup water
1 egg, lightly beaten
2 tablespoons butter or margarine (for browning meat balls)

Gravy:
2 tablespoons butter or margarine
2 tablespoons flour
1¼ cups light cream
½ teaspoon salt
Pinch white pepper

Sauté onion in butter 3–5 minutes over moderate heat until limp; mix well with remaining meat ball ingredients and shape into ¾"–1" balls. Brown, ⅓ of balls at a time, in butter in a large, heavy skillet 8–10 minutes over moderate heat until well done; drain on paper toweling. (*Note:* The ½" smorgasbord balls will cook in 5–8 minutes.) Drain drippings from skillet and add butter for gravy. When melted, blend in flour, add cream, and heat, stirring, until thickened. Season, add meat balls, simmer uncovered 5 minutes, shaking pan occasionally, and serve.

VARIATIONS:

Swedish Meat Balls II (with potatoes): When mixing meat balls, add 1 cup cold mashed potatoes; reduce bread crumbs to ¼ cup and water to about 2 tablespoons (add only enough to make balls shape easily). Shape and cook as directed.

Swedish Meat Balls in Mushroom Gravy: Mix, shape, and brown meat balls as above; in drippings sauté ½ pound sliced mushrooms 4–5 minutes; add to balls. Make gravy as directed, adding meat balls and mushrooms at the same time.

All versions: about 700 calories for each of 4 servings, 470 calories for each of 6 servings.

SAVORY MEAT BALLS

Because this recipe freezes well and is dressy enough for a party, it's a good one to make in quantity (2 or 3 times the recipe) and keep on hand.

Makes 4 servings

1 pound ground beef
1 teaspoon garlic salt
¼ teaspoon pepper
1 tablespoon Worcestershire sauce
1 small yellow onion, peeled and minced
¾ cup soft white bread crumbs
¼ cup milk
1 egg, lightly beaten
2 tablespoons bacon drippings or cooking oil

Gravy:
3 tablespoons flour

1½ cups water
1 beef bouillon cube
1 tablespoon tomato paste
¼–½ teaspoon salt
⅛ teaspoon pepper

Mix beef, garlic salt, pepper, Worcestershire sauce, and onion thoroughly. Soften bread crumbs in milk 5 minutes, then mix into meat along with egg. Using ¼ cup as a measure, shape into balls. Brown well in drippings in a large, heavy skillet over moderate heat about 10 minutes. (*Note:* To avoid crowding pan, brown in 2 batches.) Remove to a paper-towel-lined bowl. For the gravy: Drain all but 2 tablespoons drippings from skillet, blend in flour, and brown lightly over moderate heat, stirring constantly. Add water and bouillon cube and cook and stir until thickened. Mix in all remaining ingredients, add meat balls, cover, and simmer 15 minutes. Serve with buttered wide noodles, rice, or mashed potatoes. About 390 calories per serving.

¢ DANISH MEAT BALLS (FRIKADELLER)

If you like a light, fluffy meat ball, use the club soda in the meat mixture instead of milk.

Makes 4–6 servings

½ pound boned beef chuck, ground 2–3 times
½ pound boned lean pork shoulder, ground 2–3 times
1 medium-size yellow onion, peeled and minced
1 teaspoon salt
¼ teaspoon pepper
1 tablespoon minced parsley
¼ cup unsifted flour
½ cup plus 2 tablespoons club soda or milk
¼ cup butter or margarine

Mix beef, pork, onion, salt, pepper, and parsley well; sprinkle flour over meat, add club soda or milk, and mix again, then beat hard with a wooden spoon. (Mixture will be quite soft.) Heat butter in a large, heavy skillet over moderate heat 2 minutes until bubbly. Using a measuring tablespoon, drop 4–5 spoonfuls meat mixture into skillet, shaping into small balls. (To prevent mixture from sticking, dip spoon in cold water.) Brown balls 8–10 minutes, turning with a pancake turner so they cook evenly. Because they contain pork, they must be cooked through *with no sign of pink* in the middle. Drain on paper toweling and keep warm while you brown the rest. Serve hot with boiled potatoes or Danish-Style New Potatoes and pickled beets or red cabbage. Or serve cold with potato salad or as a *smørrebrød,* sliced on buttered rye bread. About 390 calories for each of 4 servings, 260 calories for each of 6 servings.

MEAT BALL STROGANOFF

Makes 4 servings

Meat Balls:
1 pound ground beef
¾ cup soft white bread crumbs
1 small yellow onion, grated fine
1 egg
2 tablespoons light cream
1 teaspoon salt
Pinch pepper
2 tablespoons butter or margarine (for browning)

Sauce:
2 tablespoons butter or margarine
1 medium-size yellow onion, peeled and coarsely chopped
¼ pound mushrooms, wiped clean and sliced very thin
2 tablespoons paprika
3 tablespoons flour

1 (10-ounce) can condensed beef broth
¼ cup water
1 tablespoon prepared Dijon-style mustard
½ cup sour cream

Mix all meat ball ingredients except butter and shape into 1″ balls; brown on all sides in butter in a large, heavy skillet over moderately high heat; drain on paper toweling. In the same skillet, melt butter for sauce and stir-fry onion 8–10 minutes over moderate heat until golden. Add mushrooms and sauté, stirring occasionally, about 5 minutes until lightly browned. Blend in paprika and flour, add broth and water slowly, and heat, stirring constantly, until thickened; smooth in mustard. Return meat balls to skillet, cover, and simmer over low heat 20 minutes. Mix in sour cream, heat and stir about 1 minute, but do not boil. Serve over buttered wide noodles. About 540 calories per serving (without noodles).

⊠ ¢ MICKEY'S MAC AND MEAT

If you have neither time nor money, here's the main dish to make.
Makes 4 servings

1 large yellow onion, peeled and minced
2 tablespoons beef drippings, butter, or margarine
1 pound lean ground beef
1 cup elbow macaroni, boiled by package directions
1 (10½-ounce) can condensed tomato soup
1 teaspoon salt
⅛ teaspoon pepper
1 (10-ounce) package frozen cut green beans or green peas (optional)

Stir-fry onion in drippings in a

heavy saucepan over moderately high heat 8 minutes until golden. Add beef and brown well. Mix in all remaining ingredients except beans or peas. Cover, turn heat to low, and simmer 20 minutes. Serve hot or, if you wish, mix in beans or peas, cover, and simmer 7–10 minutes until just tender. About 490 calories per serving if made with green peas, 450 per serving if made with beans, and 440 per serving if made without either.

KÖNIGSBERGER KLOPS (GERMAN MEAT BALLS IN LEMON-CAPER SAUCE)

Makes 4 servings

Meat Balls:
1 medium-size yellow onion, peeled and chopped fine
1 tablespoon butter or margarine
2 slices white bread soaked in ½ cup cold water and squeezed almost dry
½ pound ground beef
½ pound ground lean pork
2 medium-size potatoes, boiled and riced
6 anchovies, chopped fine
1 egg, lightly beaten
1 teaspoon salt
⅛ teaspoon pepper
¼ cup unsifted flour

Sauce:
¼ cup butter or margarine
¼ cup unsifted flour
2 cups beef broth
2 tablespoons capers
2–3 tablespoons lemon juice

Sauté onion in butter over moderate heat 8–10 minutes until golden, then mix with remaining meat ball ingredients except flour. Shape into 1″ balls and roll lightly in flour.

Simmer meat balls, half at a time, 5–7 minutes in salted water (about 2 teaspoons salt to 2 quarts water). Meanwhile, make the sauce: melt butter in a large saucepan over moderate heat, blend in flour, slowly add broth, and cook, stirring, until thickened. Add capers, lemon juice to taste, and meat balls, cover, and simmer 5–10 minutes. Serve with boiled potatoes. About 570 calories per serving.

SWEET-SOUR BEEF BALLS WITH PINEAPPLE AND PEPPERS

Makes 4 servings

1 pound ground beef
½ teaspoon salt
¼ teaspoon pepper
1 clove garlic, peeled and crushed
2 tablespoons soy sauce
2 tablespoons cooking oil
2 medium-size sweet green peppers, cored, seeded, and chopped fine
1 small carrot, peeled and cut diagonally into paper thin slices
½ cup boiling water
1 chicken bouillon cube
⅔ cup pineapple juice
¼ cup red wine vinegar
2 tablespoons sugar
1 (13½-ounce) can pineapple chunks (do not drain)
2 tablespoons cornstarch mixed with ⅓ cup cold water

Mix together beef, salt, pepper, garlic, and 1 tablespoon soy sauce and, using a rounded tablespoon as a measure, shape into balls. Brown balls, ⅓ at a time, in oil in a large, heavy skillet over moderate heat 4–5 minutes, then drain on paper toweling. Pour all but 2 tablespoons drippings from skillet, add green peppers and carrot, and stir-fry 2–3 minutes. Mix in remaining soy sauce and all other ingredients except cornstarch paste, add beef balls, cover, and simmer 10 minutes. Stir in cornstarch paste and simmer, stirring, 2–3 minutes until slightly thickened. Serve over hot boiled rice or Chinese Fried Rice. About 415 calories per serving (without rice).

¢ MARJORIE'S SAVORY BEEF AND RICE

Makes 4 servings

1 teaspoon beef drippings or cooking oil
1 pound ground beef
1 large yellow onion, peeled and minced
1 cup uncooked rice
1 (1-pound) can tomatoes (do not drain)
1 (10½-ounce) can condensed tomato soup
1 teaspoon salt
⅛ teaspoon pepper

Brush the bottom of a heavy saucepan with drippings, add beef, and brown well over moderately high heat, stirring frequently. Push beef to one side of pan, add onion, and sauté 5 minutes until transparent. Mix in remaining ingredients. Cover, reduce heat to low, and simmer, stirring frequently, 30–40 minutes until rice is tender and flavors blended (keep an eye on the pot because mixture tends to stick). Serve hot as a main course. (Note: If you double the recipe, increase simmering time to about 50 minutes.) About 470 calories per serving.

SHEPHERD'S PIE

Makes 4 servings

1 large yellow onion, peeled and chopped fine
1 sweet green pepper, cored, seeded, and coarsely chopped (optional)
2 tablespoons beef or bacon drippings or cooking oil
1¼ pounds ground chuck
1 beef bouillon cube
½ cup boiling water
1 tablespoon cornstarch mixed with 2 tablespoons cold water
1¼ teaspoons salt
¼ teaspoon pepper
1 tablespoon steak sauce
3 cups hot seasoned mashed potatoes

Preheat oven to 400° F. Sauté onion and green pepper in drippings in a large skillet over moderate heat 10 minutes until onion is golden. Add beef and sauté, breaking meat up with a spoon, about 10 minutes, until lightly browned; drain off fat as it accumulates. Dissolve bouillon cube in water, add to cornstarch mixture, then stir into skillet along with salt, pepper, and steak sauce. Heat, stirring, 1–2 minutes. Spoon into an ungreased 1½-quart casserole, spread potatoes over surface and roughen with a fork. (Note: Recipe may be prepared to this point ahead of time; cool, cover, and chill. Bring to room temperature before proceeding.) Bake, uncovered, 25–30 minutes, then broil 4″ from heat 2–3 minutes to brown. About 490 calories per serving.

VARIATION:

Substitute 3 cups finely ground leftover cooked beef or lamb for the ground chuck; stir-fry 2–3 minutes with sautéed onion and green pepper, then proceed as recipe directs. About 500 calories per serving.

⚖ ¢ **TAMALE PIE**

Makes 6 servings

Crust:
1 quart water
2 teaspoons salt
1 cup yellow corn meal

Filling:
*1 medium-size yellow onion, peeled
  and coarsely chopped*
*½ sweet green pepper, cored, seeded,
  and coarsely chopped*
*1 tablespoon cooking oil or bacon
  drippings*
1 pound lean ground beef
1 clove garlic, peeled and crushed
1 tablespoon chili powder
¾ teaspoon salt
¼ teaspoon oregano
Pinch pepper
1 (8-ounce) can tomato sauce

Topping:
*2 tablespoons finely grated Parmesan
  cheese*

Preheat oven to 350° F. Bring
water and salt to a boil in a large
saucepan, very gradually add corn
meal, beating constantly so it doesn't
lump. Turn heat to low and continue cooking and stirring about 5
minutes until quite thick. Spread
⅔ of mush in the bottom of a
buttered 9″×9″×2″ pan and set
aside; keep rest warm. For the
filling, stir-fry onion and green
pepper in oil in a large skillet over
moderate heat 8–10 minutes until
onion is golden; mix in meat, garlic,
chili powder, salt, oregano, and
pepper and stir-fry 5 minutes
longer, breaking up clumps of meat.
Mix in tomato sauce and simmer,
uncovered, about 5 minutes; spoon
over mush in pan, top with remaining mush, spreading as evenly
over all as possible. Sprinkle with
Parmesan and bake, uncovered, 30
minutes. Let stand at room temperature 10 minutes, then cut into
large squares and serve. About 275
calories per serving.

¢ **CHILI**

Makes 10–12 servings

*4 medium-size yellow onions, peeled
  and coarsely chopped*
3 cloves garlic, peeled and crushed
¼ cup olive or other cooking oil
1 teaspoon oregano
2 bay leaves, crumbled
2 pounds ground beef
¼ cup chili powder
*1 (1-pound 12-ounce) can tomatoes
  (do not drain)*
*3 (1-pound 4-ounce) cans red
  kidney beans (do not drain)*
2 teaspoons salt
3 tablespoons cider vinegar
*⅛–¼ teaspoon crushed hot red chili
  peppers*

Sauté onions and garlic in the oil
in a large, heavy kettle over moderate heat, stirring occasionally,
10 minutes until golden. Add
oregano, bay leaves, and beef and
sauté, breaking up meat, 10 minutes
until beef is no longer pink. Add
2 tablespoons chili powder, tomatoes,
2 cans kidney beans and simmer,
uncovered, over low heat, stirring
occasionally, 1½ hours. Add remaining chili powder and kidney
beans along with salt, vinegar, and
red peppers. Simmer, stirring now
and then, 15 minutes longer. Serve
hot, or cool and freeze for future
use. About 450 calories for each
of 10 servings, 375 calories for each
of 12 servings.

TEXAS RED (CHILI)

The "bowl of red" Texans adore
isn't what most of us think of as
chili; it has no beans, tomatoes, or
onions and is simply a torrid blend

MEAT 297

of beef, chili peppers, and herbs.
Makes 6 servings

3 *pounds boned beef chuck, cut in
   1½" cubes and trimmed of all fat*
1 *tablespoon rendered suet or
   cooking oil*
6 *dried ancho chili peppers or 6
   tablespoons chili powder (anchos
   are the large red chilis, full-flavored
   but not fiery)*
5 *cups cold water*
1 *tablespoon oregano*
1 *tablespoon crushed cumin seeds*
2 *teaspoons salt*
1–2 *teaspoons cayenne pepper
    (depending on how hot you can
    take chili)*
2 *cloves garlic, peeled and crushed*
2 *tablespoons masa harina (available
   in Latin groceries) or 2 tablespoons
   corn meal*

Put meat through coarse blade of
meat grinder, then brown, a little
at a time, in suet in a heavy skillet
over moderately high heat; lift to a
large, heavy kettle with a slotted
spoon and set aside. Wash peppers
in cold water, discard stems and
seeds. Tear peppers into 2" pieces,
place in a small saucepan with 2
cups water, cover, and simmer 20
minutes; drain, reserving cooking
water. Peel skin from peppers and
purée with pepper water in an
electric blender at high speed or
put through a food mill. (Wash
hands well after handling peppers
and avoid touching face while
working with them.) Mix pepper
purée into beef, also remaining
water, and bring to a boil over
high heat. (*Note:* If using chili
powder instead of peppers, simply
place in kettle with beef and full
amount of water.) Adjust heat so
mixture stays at a slow simmer,
cover, and cook 30 minutes. Stir
in all remaining ingredients except
masa harina, cover, and simmer

45 minutes. Mix in masa harina,
cover, and warm over lowest heat
30 minutes longer, stirring
occasionally so mixture doesn't
stick. If chili seems thick, thin with
⅓–½ cup boiling water. About 460
calories per serving.

¢ **CORNISH PASTIES**

Cornish children take pasties to
school for lunch (with their initials
pricked out in the crust), and
farmers munch them at apple-
picking time. Although seasonings
vary from town to town, the basic
ingredients remain the same—
beef, potatoes, and onions wrapped
up in flaky pastry.
Makes 1 dozen

Pastry:
4 *cups sifted flour*
2 *teaspoons salt*
1½ *cups chilled shortening or 1 cup
   shortening and ½ cup lard*
½ *cup ice water (about)*
1 *egg, lightly beaten with 1
   tablespoon cold water (glaze)*

Filling:
1 *pound ground beef round*
3 *cups (¼") raw potato cubes*
½ *cup minced yellow onion*
2 *teaspoons salt*
¼ *teaspoon pepper*

Mix flour and salt in a large bowl
and cut in shortening with a pastry
blender until the texture of coarse
meal. Sprinkle water over surface, a
tablespoon at a time, mixing briskly
with a fork after each addition.
Pastry should *just* hold together;
wrap in foil and chill while you
prepare and mix filling ingredients
together. Preheat oven to 450° F.
Shape pastry into 3 balls and roll, 1
at a time, on a lightly floured
pastry cloth into a 13" square; using
a 5"–6" saucer as a guide, cut 4
rounds from each square. Brush

edges of rounds with glaze, spoon
a little filling onto lower ½ of each
round, then fold upper ½ over.
Press edges together and crimp
with a fork. Cut 2–3 small slits in
top of each pastie and brush with
glaze, being careful not to seal slits.
Bake 15 minutes, reduce heat to
350° F., and bake 30 minutes
longer until lightly browned. Serve
warm or cold. (*Note:* To reheat
pasties, set uncovered in a 350° F.
oven 10–15 minutes.) About 500
calories per pastie.

VARIATION:

¢ **Party Pasties:** Prepare as recipe
directs, then cut circles with a
biscuit cutter. Fill and seal as above.
Bake uncovered 10 minutes at
450° F., then 15–20 minutes at
350° F. Makes about 2 dozen.
About 250 calories per pastie.

BEEF AND MUSHROOM PIROG (RUSSIAN MEAT PIE)

Makes 4 servings

1 recipe Sour Cream Pastry
2 teaspoons milk (glaze)

Filling:
1 medium-size yellow onion, peeled
  and minced
2 tablespoons butter or margarine
½ pound mushrooms, wiped clean
  and coarsely chopped
¾ pound ground beef
1 teaspoon salt
⅛ teaspoon pepper
½ cup sour cream

Prepare pastry by recipe, wrap
loosely in waxed paper, and chill
while you make the filling. Sauté
onion in butter over moderate heat
5–8 minutes until pale golden. Add
mushrooms and stir-fry 2 minutes,
add beef, breaking up with a fork,
and brown 5–7 minutes. Off heat,
stir in salt, pepper, and sour cream

and cool to room temperature.
Preheat oven to 400° F. Divide
pastry in half, shape into 2 balls,
and roll, 1 at a time, on a lightly
floured board into 9″×14″ rectangles. Lop 1 pastry over rolling
pin and transfer to an ungreased
baking sheet; brush edges with cold
water. Spread filling over pastry,
leaving ½″ margins all round. Cut
3 V-slits near center of second
pastry, place on top of filling,
press edges to seal, and crimp.
Brush pastry with milk to glaze and
bake, uncovered, 50–60 minutes
until golden. Cut into large squares
and serve. About 720 calories
per serving.

POT ROASTS

In addition to the marginally
tender roasts discussed earlier, these
are the favorite cuts for pot roasting (see Beef Chart). Cooked
slowly, with some liquid, they can
be surprisingly tender.

Inside Chuck Roll
Blade Pot Roast
Arm Pot Roast
English (Boston) Cut
Rolled Shoulder Roast
Fresh Brisket
Rolled Plate
Rolled Neck
Bottom Round
Heel of Round

How to Pot Roast Beef

Pot roast isn't one recipe but
dozens. Any sizable cut that is
browned, then cooked slowly in a
tightly covered pot with a small
amount of liquid is pot roasted. Here
are some favorites.

POT ROAST

Mashed potatoes are particularly good with this pot roast because of its rich brown gravy.
Makes 6–8 servings

1 (4-pound) boned and rolled beef roast (rump, chuck, sirloin tip, bottom or eye round)
2 tablespoons beef drippings or cooking oil
1 small yellow onion, peeled and minced
2½–3 teaspoons salt
½ teaspoon pepper (about)
¼ cup cold water
3 cups beef stock, water, or a ½ and ½ mixture of condensed beef broth and water
6 tablespoons flour

Brown beef well on all sides in drippings in a heavy kettle over moderately high heat; remove to a bowl. Stir-fry onion in drippings 8–10 minutes until golden; return beef to kettle and sprinkle with 1 teaspoon salt and ¼ teaspoon pepper. Add water, reduce heat to low, cover, and simmer 3 hours until tender, turning meat occasionally (check pot frequently and add 1–2 tablespoons cold water if needed, but no more). When beef is tender, transfer to a heated platter, cover loosely and keep warm. Skim all but 1–2 tablespoons fat from drippings, add 2 cups stock to kettle, and stir to scrape up browned bits. Blend remaining stock with flour and stir slowly into kettle; heat, stirring, until thickened. Reduce heat, cover, and simmer 2–3 minutes; add remaining salt and pepper to taste. Slice pot roast (not too thin) and serve with gravy. About 615 calories for each of 6 servings, 460 calories for each of 8 servings.

VARIATIONS:
Oven Pot Roast: Preheat oven to 350° F. In a large, flameproof casserole, brown beef and onion as directed; add seasonings and ½ cup water. Cover tight (if lid does not fit snugly, cover with foil) and bake 3 hours until meat is tender. Prepare gravy as directed and serve. About 615 calories for each of 6 servings, 460 calories for each of 8 servings.

Electric Skillet Pot Roast: Make sure roast will fit in covered skillet before starting. Set control at 350° F., brown meat and onion as directed, add salt, pepper, and water, cover, and simmer at 200–12° F. 3 hours until meat is tender. Prepare gravy as directed and serve. About 615 calories for each of 6 servings, 460 calories for each of 8 servings.

Pressure Cooker Pot Roast: Brown beef and onion in open pressure cooker; add seasonings, ½ cup water (or amount of liquid manufacturer recommends). Seal cooker, bring to 10 pounds pressure and cook 15 minutes per pound (meat cooked at 10 pounds pressure will be more tender than that cooked at 15). Reduce pressure, open cooker, remove meat, and keep warm. Prepare gravy in open cooker, using method above. About 615 calories for each of 6 servings, 460 calories for each of 8 servings.

Burgundy Pot Roast: Rub beef with 1 peeled and cut clove garlic; brown it and onion as directed. Substitute ½ cup Burgundy for the water, add 1 crumbled bay leaf, cover, and simmer. When making gravy, use ½ cup Burgundy and 2½ cups stock. About 645 calories for each of 6 servings, 485 calories for each of 8 servings.

German-Style Pot Roast: Cook pot roast as directed. When making gravy, reduce flour to 3 tablespoons, add 6–8 crushed gingersnaps and 2 tablespoons dark brown sugar. For the liquid, use ¼ cup red wine vinegar and 2¾ cups stock. About 620 calories for each of 6 servings, 465 calories for each of 8 servings.

Yankee Pot Roast: About 50 minutes before roast is done, add 6 medium-size, peeled, halved potatoes, 8 peeled small carrots, 1 pound peeled small white onions, 1 small rutabaga, peeled and cut in 1″ cubes, and ½ cup beef broth. Sprinkle vegetables with 1 teaspoon salt, cover and simmer until meat and vegetables are both tender. Arrange vegetables around meat on platter and keep warm; make gravy as directed and serve. About 755 calories for each of 6 servings, 570 calories for each of 8 servings.

Barbecued Pot Roast: Rub raw beef roast with a mixture of 1 teaspoon paprika and 1 teaspoon chili powder, then proceed as recipe directs. Use drippings to make Barbecue Gravy for Beef instead of basic pot roast gravy above. About 615 calories for each of 6 servings, 460 calories for each of 8 servings.

Pot Roast with Sour Cream-Horseradish Gravy: Prepare beef and gravy according to recipe; just before serving, stir 1 (8-ounce) undrained can sliced mushrooms into gravy; remove from heat, blend in 1 cup sour cream and 2 tablespoons prepared horseradish, and serve. About 690 calories for each of 6 servings, 525 calories for each of 8 servings.

BEEF À LA MODE (FRENCH POT ROAST)

When preparing beef à la mode, the French lard the meat to make it more tender and flavorful. American beef, however, is so well marbled with fat it doesn't need larding. The outer covering of fat should be no more than ¼″ thick.
Makes 8–10 servings

Marinade:
2 cups dry red wine
1 medium-size yellow onion, peeled and sliced thin
1 large carrot, peeled and sliced thin
2 stalks celery, coarsely chopped (include tops)
1 clove garlic, peeled and minced
2 bay leaves, crumbled
½ teaspoon thyme
¼ teaspoon pepper
¼ teaspoon nutmeg
6 cloves
1 bouquet garni,* tied in cheesecloth

Pot Roast:
1 (5-pound) boned and rolled beef roast (rump, chuck, sirloin tip, or eye of round)
¼ cup beef or bacon drippings or lard
2 teaspoons salt
¼ cup brandy
2 calf's feet, blanched* and split, or 1 large veal knuckle, cracked
2 cups dry red wine or a ½ and ½ mixture of wine and beef broth
2 tablespoons cornstarch or arrowroot mixed with 2 tablespoons cold water (optional)

Place marinade ingredients in a large bowl (not metal) and mix well; add beef, cover, and refrigerate 24 hours, turning beef 3–4 times. Remove beef from marinade and let stand on a wire rack ½ hour; pat dry with paper toweling. Reserve marinade. Preheat oven to 325° F. Heat drippings in a large Dutch oven over moderately high heat 1 minute, add beef and brown well on all sides, 10–15 minutes; add reserved marinade and all remaining ingredients except cornstarch mixture. Cover and bring to a boil; transfer to oven and simmer, covered, about 3½ hours until tender, turning beef every hour. Transfer beef to a heated platter and remove strings. Strain gravy (save calf's feet if you wish—there's meat on them), skim off fat, and boil rapidly 5–10 minutes to reduce to about 3 cups. Taste for salt and pepper and adjust if needed. If you prefer a thickened gravy, stir in cornstarch paste and heat, stirring, until thickened. Pour a little gravy over beef and pass the rest. To serve, slice meat, not too thin, across the grain. About 700 calories for each of 8 servings, 555 calories for each of 10 servings.

VARIATION:

Beef à la Mode with Vegetables: About 1 hour before beef is done, add 16 peeled whole baby carrots and 16 peeled small white onions to the pot, cover, and continue cooking until beef and vegetables are tender. Remove carrots and onions with a slotted spoon, arrange around beef on platter, and sprinkle with minced parsley. Prepare gravy as directed above and serve. About 710 calories for each of 8 servings, 570 calories for each of 10 servings.

BEEF À LA MODE IN ASPIC

Start this recipe two days before you plan to serve it.
Makes 8–10 servings

1 recipe Beef à la Mode
Beef à la Mode cooking liquid plus enough strong beef stock or broth to total 6 cups
3 envelopes unflavored gelatin

Optional Decoration:
Thin slices truffles cut in fancy shapes
Hard-cooked egg white cut in fancy shapes
Sprays fresh tarragon, chervil, or dill

Garnishes:
Chopped aspic
Watercress sprigs
Radish roses

Prepare beef à la mode as directed but do not thicken cooking liquid; combine instead with enough stock to total 6 cups. Cool meat, remove strings, and trim off fat; wrap in foil and chill overnight. Next day, mix gelatin into 1 cup of the stock; bring remaining stock to a simmer, stir in gelatin mixture, and simmer, stirring, until dissolved. Clarify aspic* if you like. Cool slightly, pour a ¼″ layer aspic in an ungreased 9″×5″×3″ loaf pan and chill until almost firm but still tacky. Meanwhile, chill remaining aspic over a bowl of ice until syrupy. Carve beef into thin slices. If you like, arrange truffle and egg cutouts and herb sprays on aspic layer in a decorative design. Cover with meat, overlapping slices and building up layers to fill pan to within ½″ of top. Pour in aspic to cover meat completely; chill remainder (it will be chopped and used to garnish platter). Cover meat loosely and chill until firm, at least 6 hours. To serve, unmold on a cold platter, surround with coarsely chopped aspic, and garnish with watercress and radishes. Serve with Rémoulade or Ravigote Sauce and a cold *macédoine* of vegetables.

VARIATIONS:

Beef à la Mode in Wine Aspic: Substitute ⅓ cup medium dry sherry or Madeira for ⅓ cup stock when making aspic (particularly good if aspic is clarified).

À la Mode from Leftovers: Make aspic with canned condensed beef bouillon, allowing 1 envelope gelatin for each pint. Layer aspic and beef into loaf pan as directed, reducing amount of aspic according to quantity of leftover beef.

All versions: about 705 calories for each of 8 servings, 565 calories for each of 10 servings.

SAUERBRATEN

Begin this recipe three days before you plan to serve it.
Makes 10 servings

1 (5-pound) boned and rolled beef roast (rump, chuck, bottom or eye round)
2 medium-size yellow onions, peeled and sliced thin
1 stalk celery, coarsely chopped (include tops)
1 large carrot, peeled and sliced thin
3 cloves
3 peppercorns
2 bay leaves
2 cups dry red wine or red wine vinegar
3 cups cold water
1 tablespoon salt
½ teaspoon pepper
2 beef marrowbones (about 1 pound)
¼ cup cooking oil
½ cup beef drippings, lard, or margarine
½ cup unsifted flour
12 gingersnaps, crumbled
1–2 tablespoons sugar

Place beef, vegetables, cloves, peppercorns, and bay leaves in a large bowl. Bring wine, water, salt, and pepper to a boil and pour over beef. Cover and refrigerate 3 days, turning beef in marinade twice a day. About 3 hours before you're ready to serve, remove beef from marinade and pat dry with paper toweling; reserve marinade. Brown beef and marrowbones well in oil in a large kettle over moderate heat, about 15 minutes.

(*Note:* If bones brown before meat, remove temporarily.) Add marinade, cover, and simmer 1½ hours, turn meat, re-cover, and simmer 1–1½ hours longer until tender; transfer to a large platter and keep warm. Strain marinade and discard vegetables; scoop marrow from bones, sieve, and add to marinade. Heat drippings in a heavy saucepan over moderate heat, blend in flour and brown 1–2 minutes. Stir in marinade, reduce heat to low, and cook, stirring, until thickened. Mix in gingersnaps and sugar to taste. Carve meat at the table—not too thin or slices will crumble—and serve with plenty of gravy. Or carve in the kitchen, arrange slices slightly overlapping on a platter, and pour some of the gravy down the center; pass the rest. Serve with Potato Dumplings, Spätzle, or boiled potatoes. About 570 calories per serving (without dumplings, Spätzle, or potatoes).

POT-AU-FEU

Most countries have their favorite meal-in-a-pot. In France it's Pot-au-Feu, in Italy Bollito Misto, in Spain Olla Podrida, in Argentina Puchero. What goes into the pot depends on what the housewife has in her garden and barnyard. How the dish is served depends largely on whim—sometimes the broth is a first course; sometimes everything is eaten together like a stew.
Makes 10–12 servings

1 (4-pound) boned and rolled beef roast with a very thin outer covering of fat (chuck, rump, or bottom round is best to use)
2 pounds beef or veal marrowbones, cracked
1 gallon cold water
5 teaspoons salt
¼ teaspoon pepper

II. LOW-COST RECIPES

Minestrone Milanese – Tourtière – Home-baked breads

Minestrone Milanese (vol. 1, p. 219)

Tourtière (vol. 1, p. 432);

Country Captain (vol. 1, pp. 573–74); and Fisherman's Baked Shells (vol. 2, p. 62)

Home Baked Breads and Rolls (vol. 2, pp. 334–90)

2 *bouquets garnis,* tied in cheesecloth*
2 *bay leaves*
1 *medium-size yellow onion, peeled and stuck with 6 cloves*
2 *stalks celery, cut in 2" lengths*
1 *(4-pound) stewing chicken, cut up (include giblets)*
2 *pounds carrots, peeled and cut in 2" lengths*
2 *pounds turnips or 1 (2-pound) rutabaga, peeled and cut in 1" cubes*
2 *bunches leeks, trimmed and cut in 2" lengths, or 1 pound small white onions, peeled*
1–2 *tablespoons minced parsley (garnish)*

Place beef on a rack in a 2½-gallon kettle, add bones, water, seasonings, yellow onion, celery, and giblets, cover, and bring to a boil over moderate heat. Skim off froth, reduce heat, cover, and simmer 1 hour. Add chicken, cover, and simmer 2½ hours until beef and chicken are nearly tender. Add carrots and turnips (also white onions if using instead of leeks) and simmer 15 minutes; add leeks, if using, and simmer 15 minutes longer until vegetables and meats are tender. About 555 calories for each of 10 servings, 465 calories for each of 12 servings.

To Serve Broth and Meats Separately: Remove strings from beef and place in the center of a large platter with chicken; wreathe with vegetables, top with a little broth, sprinkle with parsley, and keep warm in a very slow oven. Skim fat from broth, strain, taste for salt and pepper, and adjust if needed. Scoop marrow from marrowbones, spread on slices of French bread, float a slice in each bowl of broth, and serve. Follow broth course with the meat and vegetables, carv-

ing the beef against the grain. Pass a little extra broth for spooning over each portion.

To Serve Pot-au-Feu as a Stew: When meats are tender, cut into small slices and serve in soup bowls with vegetables, plenty of the broth, and a sprinkling of parsley.

Traditional Accompaniments for Pot-au-Feu: Coarse (kosher-style) salt, gherkins, mustard, horseradish, and crusty French bread. Boiled potatoes are appropriate too.

To Make Ahead: Prepare pot-au-feu 1 day in advance—but no more —cool, cover, and refrigerate. Lift off fat, then cover and reheat very slowly. Leftover broth, incidentally, is excellent for gravies, brown sauces, and soups (especially onion).

To Halve the Recipe: Use a 2-pound beef roast and a 2½–3 pound whole frying chicken; halve all other ingredients and prepare as directed, reducing simmering time for the chicken to about 1 hour. All other simmering times will remain the same.

VARIATIONS:

Polish-Style Boiled Dinner: Omit chicken, add giblets from 3–4 chickens along with beef and 1 (1–1½-pound) *kielbasa* sausage ring (prick skin to prevent bursting) along with the turnips and carrots. When serving, cut sausage into thick chunks. About 575 calories for each of 10 servings, 470 calories for each of 12 servings.

Bollito Misto: Add 1 (2–3-pound) fresh or smoked beef tongue to kettle along with beef, then proceed as recipe directs. When serving, remove skin and small bones from tongue, then slice. Accompany with boiled potatoes and pass 2 or more of the following: Green Sauce, Béarnaise, Tomato Sauce, prepared mustard or horseradish. About 655 calories for each of 10 servings (without sauce), 565 calories for each of 12 servings.

OLLA PODRIDA (SPANISH ONE-DISH DINNER)

Ideally, *podrida* should simmer in an earthenware pot (*olla*), but a good heavy kettle works almost as well.
Makes 8 servings

1 pound dried chick-peas, washed and sorted
1 gallon plus 1 quart cold water
1 (2-pound) boned and rolled beef roast (chuck, rump, or bottom round)
1 (2-pound) smoked boneless pork shoulder butt
1 pound beef or veal marrowbones, cracked
½ pound salt pork (optional)
2 teaspoons salt
¼ teaspoon pepper
2 bay leaves
1 bouquet garni,* tied in cheesecloth
2 cloves garlic, peeled and crushed
1 medium-size yellow onion, peeled
1 (3-pound) frying chicken, cut up
1 pound chorizos (Spanish sausages) or other garlic-flavored sausages or blood sausages
1½ pounds carrots, peeled and cut in 2" lengths
1 bunch leeks, trimmed and cut in 2" lengths
1 medium-size cabbage, trimmed and cut in 8 wedges and cored
4 hot boiled medium-size potatoes, peeled and quartered

Soak chick-peas in 1 quart cold water overnight or use the quick method.* Drain, tie loosely in cheesecloth, and place in a 3-gallon kettle with beef, pork butt, bones, salt pork, remaining water, salt, pepper, bay leaves, *bouquet garni,* garlic, and onion. Cover and bring to a boil over moderate heat. Skim froth from surface, reduce heat, cover, and simmer 1¼ hours. Add chicken and simmer covered 45 minutes; add sausages and carrots and simmer, covered, 15 minutes, then add leeks and cabbage and simmer, covered, 15 minutes longer or until all meats and vegetables are tender. Lift chick-peas to a vegetable dish, discard cheesecloth, and keep warm. Lift meats and chicken to a large heated platter, cut strings, and discard bones; wreathe with vegetables, tuck potatoes in here and there and keep warm. Skim broth of fat, strain, taste for salt and pepper and adjust as needed. Ladle a little broth over chick-peas, also meats and vegetables, and serve with spicy and/or mild mustard and extra broth. If you prefer, serve broth separately as a first course, keeping meats and vegetables warm in a very slow oven. About 1,000 calories per serving.

VARIATION:

Puchero (Argentine One-Dish Dinner): Omit chick-peas and pork shoulder butt; use a 3-pound beef roast or 5 pounds short ribs, cut in serving size pieces, and simmer as directed above. Add chicken, sausages, and vegetables as directed, also 2 pounds pumpkin or winter squash, peeled and cut in 2" chunks (these go into the pot with the carrots). About 5 minutes before *puchero* is done, add 4 ears sweet corn, husked and cut in 2" lengths. Serve in large soup bowls, including plenty of sliced meat, vegetables, and broth. Accompany with boiled sweet potatoes (you'll need 4, peeled and halved). About 800 calories per serving.

BOILED BRISKET OF BEEF WITH PARSLEY DUMPLINGS

Makes 6–8 servings

1 (4-pound) lean beef brisket
3 quarts cold water
1 large yellow onion, peeled
2 stalks celery, cut in 2" lengths
1 tablespoon salt
¼ teaspoon pepper
2 beef bouillon cubes
1 recipe Quick Dumplings
2 tablespoons minced parsley

Place beef on a trivet in a large kettle, add all remaining ingredients except dumplings and parsley, cover, and bring to a boil over moderately high heat. Skim froth from surface, then simmer covered 3½–4 hours until fork tender. Just before meat is done, prepare dumplings by recipe, adding parsley to dry ingredients. Lift meat to a heated platter and keep warm. Skim broth of fat and bring to a boil. Drop dumpling mixture by rounded tablespoonfuls on top of broth; simmer, uncovered, 10 minutes, cover tight, and simmer 10 minutes longer. Remove dumplings with a slotted spoon and arrange around meat. Carve meat, not too thin, across the grain. If you wish, pass a little broth in a gravy boat, or serve with Horseradish Sauce or Caper and Horseradish Sauce. Save remaining broth and use as stock.

VARIATION:

Boiled Brisket of Beef with Vegetables: Omit dumplings. Cook your choice of vegetables along with the beef—small whole carrots, cubed turnips or rutabagas, leeks, small white onions, halved or quartered parsnips, halved potatoes, cabbage wedges, timing their additions to the pot so that they—and the beef —will be done at the same time.

Wreathe meat with vegetables and serve. Both versions: about 665 calories for each of 6 servings, 500 calories for each of 8 servings.

STEWS

Stew beef comes from the sinewy, well-exercised parts of the animal (see Beef Chart) and can be cut small or left in a single large chunk. In general, the front half of the animal provides more good stew meat than the hind—these fore cuts seem to have slightly more fat, also more of the connective tissue that cooks down into gelatin, making the meat lusciously moist and tender. Ask for chuck, neck, brisket, plate, or shank.

OLD-FASHIONED BEEF STEW

Makes 4–6 servings

2 pounds boned beef chuck or bottom round, cut in 1½" cubes
½ cup unsifted flour
2 teaspoons salt
¼ teaspoon pepper
2–3 tablespoons beef drippings or cooking oil
1½ pounds small white onions, peeled
6–8 medium-size carrots, peeled and cut in 1" chunks
1 pound small turnips, peeled and halved, or 1 pound parsnips, peeled and cut in 2" chunks (optional)
1 bay leaf
2 cups beef broth, water, dry red wine, or beer
1 tablespoon minced parsley

Dredge beef by shaking in a paper bag with flour, 1 teaspoon salt, and ⅛ teaspoon pepper; then brown, a few pieces at a time, in 2 tablespoons drippings in a large, heavy kettle over moderately high heat; transfer to a bowl. Brown onions in remaining drippings 8–10 minutes, stirring occasionally, and remove to bowl. Drain drippings from kettle, return beef and onions, and add all remaining ingredients except parsley. Cover and simmer 1½–2 hours until beef is tender. (*Note:* You can prepare recipe to this point early in the day or, better still, the day before. Cool, cover, and refrigerate, or freeze for future use. Reheat slowly, stirring often.) Sprinkle with parsley and serve. About 700 calories for each of 4 servings, 470 calories for each of 6 servings.

VARIATIONS:

Beef and Vegetable Stew: About 15–20 minutes before serving, stir in 2 cups fresh or frozen green peas, whole kernel corn, or diced celery (or a combination of these), cover, and simmer until tender. About 760 calories for each of 4 servings, 510 calories for each of 6 servings.

Beef Stew with Mushrooms: With the beef, onions, and carrots simmer ½ pound sliced mushrooms that have been lightly browned in butter. About 705 calories for each of 4 servings, 470 calories for each of 6 servings.

Beef Stew with Dumplings: About 30 minutes before serving, make Dumplings, add to stew, cover, and cook according to dumpling recipe. About 875 calories for each of 4 servings, 585 calories for each of 6 servings.

BEEF STEW FOR A CROWD

This recipe should be started a day before it's to be served.
Makes about 25 servings

12 *pounds boned beef chuck or bottom round, cut in 1½″ cubes*
2 *cups sifted flour*
2 *tablespoons salt (about)*
½ *teaspoon pepper*
¾ *cup beef drippings or cooking oil*
2 *quarts liquid (use liquid from canned onions, below, and round out with a ½ and ½ mixture of water and canned condensed beef broth or dry red wine)*
2 *beef bouillon cubes*
4 *tablespoons tomato paste*
4 *bay leaves*
5 *(1-pound) cans small white onions, drained (reserve liquid)*
5 *(1-pound) cans whole baby carrots, drained*
2 *tablespoons liquid gravy browner*
¾ *cup sifted flour blended with ¾ cup cold water (if needed to thicken gravy)*

Dredge beef by shaking a few pieces at a time in a paper bag with flour, 1 tablespoon salt, and the pepper. For cooking the stew, use 2 2-gallon kettles. Brown beef a little at a time, using 2 tablespoons drippings in each kettle; transfer to a bowl with a slotted spoon. Continue, adding more drippings as needed, until all beef is browned. This will take about ¾ hour. Turn heat to low, return beef to kettles, then add to *each:* 1 quart liquid, 1 bouillon cube, 2 tablespoons tomato paste, and 2 bay leaves. Cover and simmer 1½–2 hours until meat is tender, stirring occasionally. Cool, cover kettles, and chill overnight. Next day, skim off fat. About 1 hour before serving, set kettles on lowest heat and warm slowly. About ¾ hour before serving, add onions and carrots, dividing them between the 2 kettles, cover and cook over moderate heat until tender. Mix in gravy browner, taste for salt, and adjust as needed.

If stew seems thin, add half the flour-water to each kettle and heat, stirring, until thickened. Serve over buttered wide noodles, rice, or whole boiled potatoes. About 605 calories per serving (without noodles, rice, or potatoes).

¢ BEEF AND PEPPER STEW IN RED WINE

Makes 6 servings

2 pounds boned beef chuck, cut in 1½" cubes
3 medium-size yellow onions, peeled and coarsely chopped
2 cloves garlic, peeled and crushed
1 (13¾-ounce) can beef broth
1½ cups water
⅔ cup dry red wine
¼ teaspoon salt
Pinch pepper
6 medium-size sweet green peppers, cored, seeded, and cut into eighths

Brown beef all at once without any fat in a large, heavy kettle over high heat 15–20 minutes, stirring so all sides brown well. Reduce heat to moderate, add onions and garlic, and sauté, stirring, 8–10 minutes until golden. Add all remaining ingredients except peppers, cover, and simmer slowly 1½ hours until meat is almost tender. Add peppers, pushing them down into stew, cover, and simmer 30–45 minutes longer until beef is tender. Serve hot over boiled rice. About 390 calories per serving (without rice).

BEEF AND BLACK BEAN STEW WITH PIÑON NUTS

Makes 6 servings

2½ pounds boned beef chuck, cut in 1½" cubes
¼ cup olive oil
2 medium-size yellow onions, peeled and cut in thin wedges
2 cloves garlic, peeled and crushed
1 teaspoon paprika
1 bay leaf, crumbled
½ teaspoon thyme
½ teaspoon salt
⅛ teaspoon pepper
2 large ripe tomatoes, peeled, cored, and cut in thin wedges
⅔ cup dry white wine
1 cup boiling water
2 (1-pound) cans black beans (do not drain)
¾ cup shelled piñon nuts

Brown meat in oil, a little at a time, in a large, heavy kettle over high heat; remove to a bowl and reserve. Add onion and garlic to kettle, reduce heat to moderate, and stir-fry 8–10 minutes until golden. Mix in paprika, herbs, salt, pepper, and tomatoes and stir-fry about 5 minutes until tomatoes have released most of their juice. Return meat to kettle, add wine and water, cover, and simmer 1 hour. Stir in 1 can beans and the nuts, cover, and simmer ½–1 hour longer until meat is tender. Add remaining beans, cover, and simmer 15–20 minutes to blend flavors. (Note: If stew seems thick, thin with ¼–½ cup boiling water.) Serve over boiled rice. About 805 calories per serving (without rice).

STEWED CHUNKS OF BEEF IN WHITE WINE-VEGETABLE GRAVY

Makes 6–8 servings

2 large carrots, peeled and minced
2 stalks celery, chopped fine
2 leeks, sliced (include tender green tops)
2 medium-size yellow onions, peeled and minced
2 cloves garlic, peeled and crushed
¼ cup olive oil
3 pounds boned beef chuck, rump, or top round cut in 1" cubes

3 medium-size tomatoes, peeled,
  cored, seeded, and coarsely
  chopped
¾ cup dry white wine
2 tablespoons minced parsley
1 bay leaf
1 teaspoon salt
⅛ teaspoon pepper

Sauté carrots, celery, leeks, onions and garlic in oil in a large, heavy kettle, stirring occasionally, over moderately high heat 10–12 minutes until golden brown; remove to a bowl. Brown beef in kettle, a few pieces at a time, over high heat. Turn heat to low, return sautéed vegetables to kettle, add remaining ingredients, cover, and simmer 1½–2 hours until beef is tender. Uncover, raise heat to moderate and boil 10–15 minutes, stirring often, to reduce gravy. Serve over boiled potatoes or wide buttered noodles. About 625 calories for each of 6 servings, 470 calories for each of 8 servings (without potatoes or noodles).

BOEUF À LA BOURGUIGNONNE I

There are many variations of Beef Bourguignonne, each slightly different. Some call for cognac, others currant jelly, but all are basically the same—chunks of stew beef simmered in red wine (traditionally Burgundy) with herbs and onions. We offer two recipes. The first cooks in the oven, the second on top of the stove. Both will be better if made a day ahead and reheated slowly before serving. Both freeze well.
Makes 6 servings

1 (¼-pound) piece bacon, trimmed
  of rind and cut in 1″ × ¼″ × ¼″
  strips
1 quart water
1 tablespoon olive oil
3 pounds boned beef chuck, cut in
  1½″ cubes and patted dry on paper
  toweling
1 large yellow onion, peeled and
  sliced thin
1 large carrot, peeled and minced
1 teaspoon salt
⅛ teaspoon pepper
2 tablespoons flour
2 cups red Burgundy or other dry red
  wine
1⅓ cups strong beef stock or 1
  (10½-ounce) can condensed beef
  broth
1 tablespoon tomato paste
2 cloves garlic, peeled and crushed
2 (4″) sprigs fresh thyme or ½
  teaspoon dried thyme
2 (4″) sprigs parsley
1 bay leaf, crumbled
1 recipe Pan-Braised Onions
1 pound mushrooms, wiped clean
  and sliced ¼″ thick
2 tablespoons butter or margarine

Preheat oven to 500° F. Simmer bacon, uncovered, in water 10 minutes; drain, pat dry, then brown in oil in a large, heavy skillet over moderately high heat about 5 minutes; drain on paper toweling. Brown beef in skillet in bacon drippings, a few pieces at a time, and drain on paper toweling. Reduce heat to moderate, add onion and carrot to skillet, and stir-fry 8–10 minutes until onion is golden. Place beef and bacon in an ungreased 3-quart casserole, add onion and carrot, and toss to mix. Sprinkle with salt, pepper, and flour and toss again. Set, uncovered, in oven 3–5 minutes; remove, stir well, and set in oven 3–5 minutes longer (this helps brown flour and seal in meat juices). Remove casserole from oven and reduce oven temperature to 325° F. Stir wine, stock, tomato paste, and garlic into casserole.

Tie thyme, parsley, and bay leaf into cheesecloth and drop into casserole. Cover casserole, set in oven, and simmer 2½–3 hours until beef is tender. Meanwhile, prepare onions and reserve; also stir-fry mushrooms in butter over moderate heat 8–10 minutes until tender; set aside. When beef is tender, remove it and bacon bits to a large bowl with a slotted spoon; keep warm. Discard cheesecloth bag. Put casserole liquid through a fine sieve, pressing with a wooden spoon to purée vegetables; return to casserole and boil, uncovered, about 5 minutes to reduce slightly. Return beef and bacon to casserole. Add onions and mushrooms, distributing them well, cover, and simmer slowly about 5 minutes. Serve hot with boiled new potatoes or noodles, a crisp green salad, and a red Burgundy wine. About 840 calories per serving (without potatoes or noodles).

BOEUF À LA BOURGUIGNONNE II

Slightly lower in calories than Boeuf à la Bourguignonne I. Makes 8 servings

1 (½-pound) piece lean bacon, trimmed of rind and cut in 1″ × ¼″ × ¼″ strips
1 quart water
4 pounds boned beef chuck or rump, cut in 1½″ cubes and patted dry on paper toweling
1 tablespoon olive oil
2 carrots, peeled and sliced thin
2 medium-size yellow onions, peeled and sliced thin
3 tablespoons flour
1 teaspoon salt
¼ teaspoon pepper
⅘ quart Beaujolais or other dry red wine

3 (10½-ounce) cans condensed beef broth
2 cloves garlic, peeled and crushed
2 (4″) sprigs fresh thyme or ½ teaspoon dried thyme
1 bay leaf, crumbled
1 recipe Pan-Braised Onions
1 pound mushrooms, wiped clean and sliced ¼″ thick
2 tablespoons butter or margarine

Simmer bacon, uncovered, in water 10 minutes. Drain and pat dry, then brown in a large, heavy kettle over moderately high heat 5 minutes; drain on paper toweling. Brown meat in bacon drippings, a few pieces at a time, and drain on paper toweling. Add oil to kettle, reduce heat to moderate, and stir-fry carrots and onions 8–10 minutes until golden. Return beef and bacon to kettle, add flour, salt, and pepper, and toss to mix. Add wine, broth, garlic, thyme, and bay leaf, cover, and simmer, stirring occasionally, 1½–2 hours until beef is tender. Meanwhile, prepare Pan-Braised Onions and set aside. Also sauté mushrooms in butter 8–10 minutes until golden; set aside. When beef is tender, remove thyme sprigs; add mushrooms and onions, cover, and simmer 10–15 minutes longer. If stew seems thick, thin with about 1 cup boiling water. Serve with boiled new potatoes, noodles, or rice, a crisp green salad, and dry red wine. About 810 calories per serving (without potatoes, noodles, or rice).

CARBONNADE FLAMANDE (FLEMISH BEEF-BEER STEW)

Beer gives this nut-brown stew its unusual malty flavor. Makes 6 servings

2 tablespoons butter or margarine

6 medium-size yellow onions, peeled and sliced thin
2 cloves garlic, peeled and crushed
½ cup unsifted flour
1 tablespoon salt
¼ teaspoon pepper
3 pounds boned beef chuck, cut in 1½" cubes and trimmed of excess fat
⅛ teaspoon nutmeg
¼ teaspoon thyme
2 (12-ounce) cans beer
1 tablespoon sugar or light brown sugar (optional)

Melt butter in a large, heavy kettle over moderate heat, add onions and garlic, and sauté, stirring occasionally, 10 minutes until golden; drain on paper toweling. Place flour, salt, and pepper in a heavy brown paper bag and dredge beef, a few cubes at a time, by shaking in the mixture. Brown beef, a little at a time, in kettle over high heat, adding more butter as needed. Reduce heat to moderate, return beef, onions, and garlic to kettle, add all remaining ingredients except sugar, cover, and simmer slowly, stirring occasionally, about 2 hours until beef is fork tender. Skim any fat from gravy. Taste gravy and if it seems a trifle bitter stir in sugar. Simmer, uncovered, about 10 minutes longer, then serve with tiny boiled new potatoes and tall glasses of well-chilled beer. About 645 calories per serving (without potatoes).

BEEF CATALAN

Frenchwomen in the Pyrenees make a marvelous beef stew that's as much Spanish as French. Some add rice to the pot, others white kidney beans; some use a heavy hand with spices, others a light touch. This is a flexible recipe, so you can adjust the ingredients to suit your taste.
Makes 8–10 servings

1 (¼-pound) piece bacon, trimmed of rind and cut in ¼" cubes
4 pounds boned beef rump or chuck, cut in 1½" cubes and patted dry on paper toweling
1 tablespoon olive oil
3 medium-size yellow onions, peeled and sliced thin
2 cloves garlic, peeled and crushed
4 medium-size carrots, peeled and cut in 2" chunks
½ pound small turnips, peeled and quartered
1 (1"×3") strip orange peel (orange part only)
1 stick cinnamon
3 cloves
1 bay leaf, crumbled
2 (4") sprigs fresh thyme or ½ teaspoon dried thyme
3 ripe tomatoes, peeled, seeded, juiced, and coarsely chopped
2 cups dry red wine
1⅓ cups strong beef stock or 1 (10½-ounce) can condensed beef broth
2 (1-pound 4-ounce) cans cannellini (white kidney beans), drained
2½ teaspoons salt
⅛ teaspoon pepper
3 tablespoons minced parsley

Preheat oven to 325° F. Brown bacon in a large, heavy kettle over high heat and drain on paper toweling. Brown beef in drippings, a few cubes at a time, over moderately high heat; remove to a bowl and reserve. Add oil to kettle and stir-fry onions, garlic, carrots, and turnips 10–12 minutes until onions are golden. Tie orange peel, cinnamon, cloves, bay leaf, and thyme in cheesecloth and add to kettle along with bacon, beef, tomatoes, wine, and stock. Cover kettle, set in oven, and simmer

2½–3 hours until beef is tender. Discard cheesecloth bag. (*Note:* Recipe can be made up to this point well ahead of time. Cool, cover, and refrigerate or freeze for use later. Bring to room temperature before proceeding or, if frozen, thaw gently over low heat, stirring frequently.) Add remaining ingredients except parsley and bake, uncovered, 30 minutes, stirring 1 or 2 times. Mix in parsley and serve over hot fluffy rice or Saffron Rice. About 780 calories for each of 8 servings (without rice), 625 calories for each of 10 servings.

HUNGARIAN GOULASH

Though traditionally made with beef, *gulyás,* the Hungarian national dish, can be prepared with any meat or game. Here's a basic version with four popular variations. Makes 4–6 servings

1¼ cups finely chopped yellow onion
1 sweet green pepper, cored, seeded, and chopped fine
¼ cup lard, butter, or margarine
2 pounds boned beef chuck, shin, or bottom round, cut in 1½" cubes
2 tablespoons paprika (use the Hungarian sweet rose if possible)
1½ teaspoons salt
¼ teaspoon pepper
1 teaspoon cider vinegar
2 cups beef stock, broth, or water

Sauté onion and green pepper in lard in a kettle over moderate heat 5–8 minutes until onion is pale golden; drain on paper toweling. Add meat to kettle and brown well over moderately high heat. Turn heat to low, add paprika, and stir 1–2 minutes. Return onion mixture to kettle, add remaining ingredients, cover, and simmer 1½–2 hours until meat is tender. Serve with Nockerln or buttered noodles. About 380 calories for each of 4 servings (without Nockerln or noodles), 255 calories for each of 6 servings.

VARIATIONS:

Transylvanian Goulash: About ½ hour before goulash is done, add 1 pound drained sauerkraut, cover, and simmer until meat is tender. Mix in 1 cup sour cream and serve. About 500 calories for each of 4 servings, 335 calories for each of 6 servings.

Yugoslav Goulash: Sauté 1 clove peeled, crushed garlic with onion and green pepper, then proceed as directed, substituting 1 (1-pound 12-ounce) can undrained tomatoes for beef stock. If you prefer, use 1 cup beef stock and 1 (8-ounce) can tomato sauce. About 380 calories for each of 4 servings, 255 calories for each of 6 servings.

Savory Goulash: Prepare as directed, adding 1 teaspoon caraway seeds or marjoram and/or 1 clove peeled, crushed garlic along with other seasonings. About 380 calories for each of 4 servings, 255 for each of 6 servings.

¢ ⟁ **Budget Goulash:** Add 4 peeled, quartered potatoes ½ hour before beef is done, cover, and simmer until tender. Makes 6 servings. About 305 calories per serving.

COUNTRY-STYLE UKRAINIAN BORSCH

Old country-style borsch, the national dish of the Ukraine, always has a good chunk of meat cooking along with the vegetables. A mild tartness is characteristic—beet or rye *kvas* (liquid from fermented beets or rye yeast batter) used to be traditional, but nowadays lemon, vinegar, even sorrel leaves or rhubarb juice are substituted. Makes 12–14 servings

1 (2-pound) boned and rolled beef roast (chuck, bottom round, or rump), trimmed of fat
1 (2-pound) smoked boneless pork shoulder butt
. gallon cold water
2–4 teaspoons salt
1 bouquet garni,* tied in cheesecloth with 1 peeled clove garlic and 6 peppercorns
2 medium-size yellow onions, peeled and coarsely chopped
2 carrots, peeled and cut in julienne strips
2 cups finely chopped celery
8 medium-size boiled beets, peeled and diced or cut in julienne strips
1 (1-pound 12-ounce) can tomatoes (do not drain)
4 cups finely shredded cabbage
2 cups boiled dried white beans or 1 (1-pound 4-ounce) can cannellini beans (do not drain)
3–4 tablespoons lemon juice
2 tablespoons snipped fresh dill (optional)
1 pint sour cream (optional garnish)

Place meats, water, 2 teaspoons salt, cheesecloth bag, and onions in a 3-gallon kettle, cover, and bring to a boil over moderate heat. Skim froth from surface, reduce heat, re-cover, and simmer 2–2½ hours until meats are nearly tender. Add carrots and celery, cover, and simmer 20 minutes; add beets, tomatoes (cut them up), and cabbage, cover, and simmer 20 minutes longer. Remove cheesecloth bag and gently stir in beans and lemon juice. (Note: Recipe may be prepared to this point a day or so ahead; cool, cover and chill.) Heat slowly to boiling, taste for salt and pepper and adjust as needed. Stir

in dill if you like. Ladle into deep soup bowls, serve with a slice or 2 of meats, and top with dollops of sour cream. About 505 calories for each of 12 servings, 435 calories for each of 14 servings.

VARIATIONS:

Borsch Stew: Instead of using large chunks of beef and pork, use 2 pounds each boned chuck and pork shoulder butt, cut in 1½″ cubes. Otherwise, prepare as directed. If you prefer, use 3–4 pounds beef shank or bone-in soup meat in place of the chuck. About 505 calories for each of 12 servings, 435 calories for each of 14 servings.

⚖ ¢ **Economy Borsch:** Omit all meats; substitute strong beef stock for half the water called for, and simmer vegetables as directed. Makes 12 servings. About 205 calories per serving.

Beef and Bacon Borsch for 6 Persons: Use 2 pounds boned beef chuck cut in 1½″ cubes and substitute 3–4 slices diced, lean smoked bacon for the pork shoulder butt; halve all other ingredients and prepare as recipe directs. Cooking times will be about the same. About 450 calories per serving.

OLD-FASHIONED STEAK AND KIDNEY PIE

Mashed or boiled potatoes and Brussels sprouts or carrots are traditional with steak and kidney pie. Makes 6 servings

1 pound beef kidney, free of membrane and fat
2 cups cold water mixed with 1 teaspoon salt
2½ pounds lean, boned beef chuck or bottom round, cut in 1½″ cubes
¼ cup rendered suet, beef drippings, or cooking oil

3 medium-size yellow onions, peeled
  and minced
3 tablespoons flour
1 (10½-ounce) can condensed beef
  broth
1 cup cold water
2 teaspoons salt
¼ teaspoon pepper
1 bouquet garni,* tied in cheesecloth
  (optional)

Pastry:
1 recipe Flaky Pastry I
1 egg yolk mixed with 1 tablespoon
  cold water (glaze)

Soak kidney in salt water 1 hour,
drain, and pat dry on paper
toweling; remove cores and cut
kidney in 1" cubes. Brown beef, a
little at a time, in suet in a large,
heavy kettle over high heat; remove
and reserve. Brown kidney, stirring,
and add to beef. Turn heat to
moderate, add onions and stir-fry
8–10 minutes until golden; mix
in flour and brown 1–2 minutes.
Return meat to kettle, add all but
pastry ingredients, cover, and
simmer 1½–2 hours until tender.
Discard bouquet garni if used.
Transfer to an ungreased 2-quart
casserole that measures about 9"
across. (Note: If you have a pie
funnel, place in center of casserole
before adding meat; it will help
prop up crust and keep pie from
boiling over.) Preheat oven
to 425° F.

Roll pastry into a 10" circle and
make 3 V-slits in center. Moisten
casserole rim, top with pastry, roll
edges under until even with rim,
press down to seal and crimp. Brush
pastry with glaze, making sure not
to cover slits. Bake in top ⅓ of oven
(with foil under casserole to catch
drips) 10–12 minutes, reduce heat
to 350° F., and bake 25 minutes
longer until nicely browned. To

serve, cut wedge-shaped pieces of
pastry and arrange on top of each
helping of meat.

VARIATION:
Just before serving, insert a small
funnel in a V-slit and pour in 1–2
tablespoons dry sherry.

Both versions: about 945 calories
per serving.

BAKED CASSEROLE OF BEEF AND ONIONS

Makes 4–6 servings

2 pounds boned beef chuck, cut in
  1½" cubes
½ cup unsifted flour
2 teaspoons salt
¼ teaspoon pepper
3 tablespoons beef drippings or
  cooking oil
2 large yellow onions, peeled and
  sliced thin
1 bay leaf, crumbled
2½ cups canned condensed beef
  broth or 1 cup broth and 1½ cups
  dry red wine or beer

Preheat oven to 350° F. Dredge
beef by shaking in a paper bag with
flour, ½ teaspoon salt, and ⅛ teaspoon pepper. Brown, a few pieces
at a time, in 2 tablespoons drippings
in a shallow flameproof 2-quart
casserole over moderately high heat;
remove to a bowl. Stir-fry onions in
remaining drippings 8–10 minutes
until well browned. Return beef to
casserole, add remaining salt and
pepper and all other ingredients,
cover and bake 1½–2 hours until
tender. Serve with mashed potatoes,
boiled noodles, or plenty of crusty
bread for getting up the gravy.
About 645 calories for each of 4
servings (without potatoes, noodles,
or bread), 430 calories for each
of 6 servings.

VARIATIONS:

Skillet Beef Stew: A large electric skillet cooks this stew perfectly. Brown beef at 350° F., then sauté onions at the same temperature. Add remaining ingredients, cover and simmer 1 hour at 200° F. until tender; stir occasionally. About 645 calories for each of 4 servings, 430 calories for each of 6 servings.

Farmhouse Beef Casserole: Prepare and bake casserole as directed. Spread Farmhouse Potato Topping over surface, roughen with a fork, and broil 4″ from the heat 3–4 minutes until touched with brown. About 900 calories for each of 4 servings, 600 calories for each of 6 servings.

¢ **FARMHOUSE MEAT AND POTATO PIE**

Makes 6 servings

Pastry:
2 cups sifted flour
1 teaspoon salt
⅓ cup chilled shortening
⅓ cup chilled lard
4–5 tablespoons ice water
1 egg yolk mixed with 1 tablespoon cold water (glaze)

Filling:
1½ pounds boned beef chuck, cut in 1″ cubes
½ cup unsifted flour
2 teaspoons salt
3 medium-size potatoes, peeled and sliced ½″ thick
1 large yellow onion, peeled and sliced thin
¼ teaspoon pepper
1⅔ cup beef stock or 1 cup canned condensed beef broth and ⅔ cup water

Preheat oven to 425° F. Sift flour and salt for pastry into a bowl and cut in shortening and lard with a pastry blender until the texture of oatmeal. Sprinkle ice water over surface, a tablespoon at a time, mixing briskly with a fork after each addition. Pastry should *just* hold together. Wrap in foil and chill while you prepare the filling. Dredge beef by shaking in a paper bag with flour and 1 teaspoon salt. Place beef in an ungreased shallow 1½-quart casserole with a wide rim. Layer potatoes and onion on top, sprinkling pepper and remaining salt between layers. Pour stock over all. Roll pastry into a circle about 3″ larger in diameter than the casserole and cut a strip 1″ wide from around outer edge. Moisten casserole rim with cold water and lay strip on rim; moisten strip. Cut 2–3 decorative holes near center of pastry circle; place on top of filling and press edges into pastry strip. Trim pastry even with rim and crimp. Brush with glaze, avoiding decorative edge. Bake 15 minutes, reduce heat to 350° F., and bake 1¼ hours longer until meat is tender (test by poking a skewer through decorative hole). Serve hot with a crisp green salad. About 680 calories per serving.

PRUNE AND SWEET POTATO TZIMMES

Jewish New Year would not be complete without the sweet-but-savory, meat-and-vegetable stew called *tzimmes*. Honey, symbolic of the wish for sweetness throughout the New Year, is the traditional sweetener.

Makes 4 servings

1½–2 pounds boned beef chuck, cut in 1″ cubes
3 tablespoons rendered chicken fat, shortening, or cooking oil
1 medium-size yellow onion, peeled and chopped fine

1 quart cold water
1½ teaspoons salt
¼ teaspoon pepper
¼ teaspoon cinnamon
3 medium-size sweet potatoes, peeled
    and cut crosswise in 1" slices
½ pound pitted prunes
½ cup honey
1 tablespoon shortening
2 tablespoons flour

Brown beef in fat in a heavy kettle over moderately high heat; transfer to a bowl. Stir-fry onion in drippings 8–10 minutes over moderate heat until golden; return beef to kettle, add water, salt, and pepper, cover, and simmer slowly ¾ hour. Add all but last 2 ingredients, cover partially, lid askew, and simmer ¾ hour longer until meat is tender. Shake pan, do not stir, to prevent sticking. Melt shortening in a small skillet over moderate heat, blend in flour and brown slowly 3–4 minutes; mix in 1 cup kettle liquid, then return all to kettle and *shake,* but do not stir, to distribute (mixture should be thick, not soupy). Heat 1–2 minutes and serve. About 830 calories per serving.

VARIATION:

Carrot Tzimmes: Omit prunes and add 4–5 carrots, peeled and sliced 1" thick. If you like, substitute Irish potatoes for the sweet. Otherwise, prepare as directed. About 715 calories per serving.

INDONESIAN SPICED BEEF

Makes 4–6 servings

2 medium-size yellow onions, peeled
    and coarsely chopped
2 cloves garlic, peeled and crushed
3 tablespoons peanut oil
1 flank steak (about 2–2¼ pounds),
    cut crosswise into strips ½" × 1½"
1 (2") stick cinnamon
6 cloves

2 tablespoons paprika
1 tablespoon crushed coriander seeds
1–2 teaspoons cayenne pepper
    (depending on how hot you like
    things)
1 teaspoon turmeric
1 teaspoon ginger
¼ teaspoon cumin
4 medium-size new potatoes, peeled
    and cut in ½" cubes
2 cups Coconut Milk
1½ teaspoons salt

Stir-fry onions and garlic in oil in a heavy kettle over moderate heat 8–10 minutes until golden; remove to a bowl. Raise heat to high and brown meat, a few pieces at a time; transfer to paper toweling to drain. Reduce heat to low, return meat, onions, and garlic to kettle and mix in all remaining ingredients. Cover and simmer, stirring occasionally, about 1½ hours until meat is tender. Serve hot over fluffy boiled rice. About 740 calories for each of 4 servings (without rice), 495 calories for each of 6 servings.

BOMBAY-STYLE CURRIED BEEF

India has hundreds of curries, some hot (the Madras), some not so hot (the Bombay). Either is usually accompanied by popadams (crisp-fried paper-thin pancakes available in specialty food shops), and two or three sambals (side dishes). Makes 4–6 servings

2 pounds boned lean beef chuck or
    bottom round, cut in 1" cubes
3 tablespoons beef drippings, butter,
    or margarine
2 large yellow onions, peeled and
    minced
2 cloves garlic, peeled and crushed
2 tablespoons curry powder
1½ cups hot water
⅔ cup tomato sauce

1 teaspoon salt
1 cup yogurt, at room temperature
    (optional)

Sambals (choose 2 or 3):
Bombay Duck (salty, dried fish
    sautéed or baked till crisp)
Sweet chutney
Sour pickles (mango, walnut, red
    cabbage, cucumber, onion, beet)
Red or green chili peppers
Minced onions or scallions
Chopped salted peanuts or almonds

Not traditional but good (choose 1
or 2):
Flaked coconut, raisins, chopped
    hard-cooked eggs, a mixture of
    grated orange and lemon or lime
    rind, minced parsley

Brown beef, a few pieces at a time,
in drippings in a heavy kettle over
moderately high heat; remove to a
bowl. Stir-fry onions and garlic
in kettle 8–10 minutes over moderate heat until golden; mix in
curry powder and heat 1 minute.
Return beef to kettle, mix in all
remaining ingredients except yogurt,
cover, and simmer 1½–2 hours
until meat is tender. Remove from
heat and, if you wish, stir in yogurt.
Serve over boiled rice with a variety
of sambals. About 605 calories
for each of 4 servings, 405 calories
for each of 6 servings (without rice
or sambals).

¢ **BRAISED OXTAIL WITH
CARROTS**

Makes 6–8 servings

4 pounds oxtail, cut in 1½" chunks
    and trimmed of excess fat
2 tablespoons cooking oil
2 medium-size yellow onions, peeled
    and chopped fine
3 cups hot water or 1 (12-ounce) can
    beer and 1½ cups water or 2 cups
    water and 1 cup dry red wine

1 (8-ounce) can tomato sauce
½ teaspoon celery seeds
1 bay leaf, crumbled
1 tablespoon minced parsley
1 teaspoon Worcestershire sauce
1½ teaspoons salt
⅛ teaspoon pepper
6–8 medium-size carrots, peeled and
    sliced ½" thick
2 tablespoons flour blended with 2
    tablespoons cold water

Brown oxtail in oil in a large, heavy
kettle over high heat and drain on
paper toweling. Reduce heat to
moderate, add onions to kettle
and sauté, stirring, 8–10 minutes
until golden. Return meat to kettle,
add remaining ingredients except
carrots and flour-water paste,
cover, and simmer over low heat
3 hours until meat is tender. Cool
and skim off fat. (*Note:* Recipe
can be prepared to this point a day
or so ahead of time. Cool, cover,
and refrigerate or freeze for future
use. Bring to room temperature
before proceeding, or if frozen thaw
gently over low heat, stirring frequently.) Add carrots, cover,
and simmer 20 minutes until tender.
Mix in flour-water paste and
heat, stirring, until thickened. Serve
over buttered noodles. About 515
calories for each of 6 servings
(without noodles), 385 calories
for each of 8 servings.

MARROWBONES

If you don't have long, narrow
marrow spoons for getting the
marrow out of the bones, use iced-
tea spoons—they work just as well.
Makes 2 servings

3 pounds beef marrowbones, cut in
    2"–3" lengths and trimmed of fat
2 tablespoons cooking oil
1 quart water
1 teaspoon salt
⅛ teaspoon black pepper

2 *slices hot unbuttered toast, halved diagonally*
⅛ *teaspoon white pepper (optional)*

Brown bones well in oil in a large kettle over moderate heat. To keep marrow from falling out of bones as they simmer, wrap each in cheesecloth, or lay bones flat in kettle and handle *very gently.* Add water, salt, and black pepper, cover, and simmer over low heat 1 hour. Using a slotted spoon, lift bones to heated plates. Remove cheesecloth, if used, and serve marrowbones with toast. If you prefer, scoop marrow from bones before serving, spread on toast, and sprinkle with white pepper. Serve hot as an appetizer. (*Note:* Marrow can also be cut into slices about ¼″ thick and floated in hot consommé as a garnish.) Calorie data unavailable for marrow.

Short Ribs

It's curious that pork spareribs should be such a favorite and their beef counterpart, short ribs, so often slighted. These 3″ rib ends (see Beef Chart) are budget priced and, when braised and skillfully seasoned, unusually good eating.

¢ BRAISED SHORT RIBS OF BEEF

Makes 4 servings

3½–4 *pounds beef short ribs, cut in 3″ pieces*
2 *tablespoons cooking oil or beef drippings*
1 *medium-size yellow onion, peeled and sliced thin*
¼ *pound mushrooms, wiped and sliced*
1 *large carrot, peeled and sliced thin*

1 *teaspoon salt*
¼ *teaspoon pepper*
1 *cup beef broth*
2 *tablespoons flour blended with 2 tablespoons cold water*
¼ *teaspoon liquid gravy browner*

Brown ribs slowly (about 15–20 minutes) in oil in a large kettle over moderately low heat. Add onion, mushrooms, carrot, salt, pepper, and broth, cover, and simmer 1½ hours until meat is tender. Transfer ribs to a deep serving dish and keep warm. Purée vegetables and cooking liquid in an electric blender at low speed or put through a food mill; return to kettle. Mix in flour-water paste and gravy browner and cook, stirring, until thickened. Pour some gravy over short ribs and serve (remaining gravy can be passed in a gravy boat). About 490 calories per serving.

¢ DEVILED SHORT RIBS

Makes 4 servings

4 *pounds beef short ribs, cut in serving size pieces*

Marinade:
¼ *cup prepared spicy brown mustard*
¼ *cup prepared mild yellow mustard*
1 *cup dry white wine*
½ *cup beef broth*
2 *tablespoons Worcestershire sauce*
2 *tablespoons finely grated yellow onion*
1 *clove garlic, peeled and crushed*
½ *teaspoon salt*
¼ *teaspoon pepper*

Place ribs in a large, deep bowl; beat all marinade ingredients together until smooth and pour over ribs. Cover and refrigerate at least 12 hours, turning ribs now and then. Drain, reserving marinade. Preheat oven to 425° F. Place ribs on a rack in a roasting pan and roast, uncovered, 15–17 minutes until browned; turn and brown 15–17 minutes longer. Reduce oven temperature to 325° F. Transfer ribs to a second roasting pan (do not use rack), top with ¾ cup marinade, cover with foil, and bake 2–2½ hours until tender. Just before serving, heat remaining marinade and serve as a hot sauce with the ribs. About 520 calories per serving.

¢ SHORT RIBS AND CHICK-PEAS IN TOMATO SAUCE

Makes 6 servings

3 pounds beef short ribs, cut in
  serving size pieces
½ cup unsifted flour
1 teaspoon salt
¼ teaspoon pepper
3 tablespoons cooking oil
2 medium-size yellow onions, peeled
  and sliced thin
1 clove garlic, peeled and crushed
1 bay leaf, crumbled
¼ teaspoon oregano
½ cup dry red wine
1 (6-ounce) can tomato paste
1½ cups water
2 (1-pound 4-ounce) cans chick-
  peas, drained
1 tablespoon minced parsley

Dredge ribs, a few at a time, by shaking in a paper bag with flour, salt, and pepper, then brown in oil, a few at a time, in a large, heavy kettle over moderately high heat and drain on paper toweling. Add onions, garlic, bay leaf, and oregano to kettle and stir-fry 8–10 minutes until onions are golden brown. Return ribs to kettle, reduce heat to low, add wine, tomato paste, and water, cover, and simmer 1½–2 hours, stirring occasionally, until ribs are tender.

Add chick-peas and parsley and simmer, uncovered, stirring now and then, 10–15 minutes longer to blend flavors, then serve. About 455 calories per serving.

Other Forms of Beef

Corned Beef: Brisket (and sometimes plate or rump) cured either in brine or by having brine pumped through the arterial system. Old-fashioned corned beef is salty and gray-pink, newer, milder types rosy red; both are available by the half or whole brisket. Newest entry is corned beef for oven roasting; it comes in two flavors: mild cure and spicy garlic (wrappers give full instructions for oven and spit roasting). Also available: canned corned beef and sandwich slices in pliofilm packages. Allow ⅓–½ pound corned beef per person.

Chipped Beef (also called *Dried Beef*): Tissue-thin slices of salty dried beef; allow 1–2 ounces per person.

Beef-Bacon Slices: Rather like pastrami without the spices, these slices of cured beef are cooked just like bacon. Allow 3–4 slices per person.

Smoked Sliced Beef: Ready-to-eat sandwich meat made by pressing coarsely ground beef into rounds or squares, curing, smoking, and cooking. Allow 1–2 slices per person.

Jerky or Jerked Beef: The original dried beef. These salty, leathery strips and chunks are still a great favorite among American Indians and Mexicans (Latin groceries are the best place to buy them).

Freeze-Dried Beef: Not much beef is being freeze-dried as yet, though the process may eventually revolutionize our lives. Freeze-dried meat requires very little storage space and no refrigeration. To date it is being used primarily in soup mixes and camp foods, also by astronauts.

¢ **NEW ENGLAND BOILED DINNER**

Makes 6 servings

4 *pounds corned brisket of beef, wiped with damp paper toweling*
2 *quarts cold water*
6 *peppercorns and 1 bay leaf tied in cheesecloth*
6 *medium-size carrots, peeled and halved crosswise*
6 *medium-size potatoes, peeled and halved*
1 *small rutabaga, peeled and cut in 6 wedges*
1 *medium-size cabbage, trimmed of coarse leaves, cored, and cut in 6 wedges*

If necessary, tie brisket into a neat shape; place in a very large kettle, add water and cheesecloth bag, cover, and bring to a boil over high heat. Reduce heat to low and simmer 10 minutes; uncover and skim off any scum. Re-cover and simmer about 4 hours until tender. Remove cheesecloth bag; transfer meat to a platter, cover loosely with foil and keep warm. (*Note:* Meat can be refrigerated at this point and held 1–2 days; let come to room temperature before proceeding.) Bring kettle liquid to a boil and taste; if not too salty, add carrots, potatoes, and rutabaga, cover, and boil 20 minutes; add meat and cabbage, cover, and cook 15–20 minutes longer. If liquid is too salty, cook carrots, potatoes, and rutabaga, covered, in about 2″ lightly salted water 20 minutes, add meat and cabbage, and proceed as above. Drain vegetables and make a border around a very large platter; place meat in center. Serve with horseradish, mustard, or mustard pickles. To be really traditional, add a plate of Rhode Island Jonnycake and serve apple dumplings for dessert. About 730 calories per serving.

¢ **CORNED BEEF AND CABBAGE**

Some people say the only way to make good corned beef and cabbage is to cook the two together, but *don't* if the beef cooking water seems greasy and/or salty —boil the cabbage separately. When carving corned beef, make the slices thick or thin but always slice *against* the grain.
Makes 6–8 servings

4 *pounds corned brisket of beef, wiped with damp paper toweling*
2 *quarts cold water*
6 *peppercorns*
6 *whole allspice*
1 *bay leaf*
1 *medium-size yellow onion, peeled and quartered*
1 *medium-size cabbage, trimmed of coarse outer leaves, cored, and cut in 8 wedges*

If necessary, tie brisket into a neat shape; place in a very large kettle with water, peppercorns, allspice, bay leaf, and onion, cover, and bring to a boil over high heat. Reduce heat to low and simmer 10 minutes; uncover and skim off any scum. Re-cover and simmer about 4 hours until tender. Taste cooking water and, if it seems delicate enough, add cabbage, cover, and simmer 15–20 minutes until crisp tender. Otherwise, place cabbage in a separate kettle, add about 2″ lightly salted boiling water, cover, and boil 15–20 minutes; drain. Arrange beef on a heated large platter and surround with cabbage wedges. Serve with boiled potatoes and a mustard or horseradish sauce. About 590 calories for each of 6 servings, 440 calories for each of 8 servings.

¢ HOMEMADE CORNED BEEF HASH

Makes 4 servings

1 medium-size yellow onion, peeled and chopped fine
2 tablespoons any meat drippings, butter, or margarine
2 cups diced, cooked corned beef
2 cups diced, cooked cold potatoes
2 teaspoons Worcestershire sauce
1 tablespoon minced parsley
⅛ teaspoon pepper
4 Poached Eggs

Stir-fry onion in drippings in a large, heavy skillet over moderate heat 5–8 minutes until transparent. Stir in corned beef and potatoes; sprinkle evenly with Worcestershire sauce, parsley, and pepper. Pat hash down with a broad spatula and cook, uncovered, without stirring, 10–12 minutes until a brown crust forms on the bottom. Turn, using 2 broad spatulas, and brown flip side 8–10 minutes. To serve, cut in 4 equal portions and top each with a poached egg. About 390 calories per serving.

¢ ⊠ CORNED BEEF AND POTATO PUFF

Makes 4 servings

1 (12-ounce) can corned beef
1 tablespoon steak sauce
2 cups hot mashed potatoes
¼ cup heavy cream

Pinch nutmeg
4 Fried Eggs

Break up corned beef with a fork, place in a flameproof 1½-quart casserole, and brown lightly over moderate heat, stirring constantly. Mix in steak sauce. Beat potatoes with cream and nutmeg and spread over beef. Brown 2–3 minutes under the broiler, 4″–5″ from the heat, top with eggs, and serve. About 525 calories per serving.

¢ ⟐ RED FLANNEL HASH

Makes 4–6 servings

1 (12-ounce) can corned beef, minced
2 large boiled potatoes, peeled and chopped fine
1 cup minced, cooked beets
1 medium-size yellow onion, peeled and minced
Pinch pepper
3 tablespoons butter, margarine, or bacon drippings

Mix corned beef, potatoes, beets, onion, and pepper well. Melt butter in a heavy 9″ or 10″ skillet over moderately low heat, add hash, and let cook slowly about 35–40 minutes until a crisp brown crust forms on the bottom. Turn carefully and brown flip side 10–15 minutes or, if you prefer, instead of browning second side, fold as an omelet and serve. Accompany, if you like, with Sour Cream Horseradish Sauce or top each serving with a poached egg. About 335 calories for each of 4 servings (without sauce or poached egg), 225 calories for each of 6 servings.

VARIATIONS:

Oven-Browned Red Flannel Hash: Mix corned beef, potatoes, beets, and pepper and set aside. Stir-fry onion in butter 8–10 minutes in a large, heavy skillet over moderate heat until golden. Add beef mixture and stir-fry about 5 minutes. Transfer to a greased 9″ piepan and drizzle with 2 tablespoons melted butter mixed with 2 tablespoons light cream. Brown under broiler, 4″ from heat, 5–6 minutes and serve. About 400 calories for each of 4 servings, 270 calories for each of 6 servings.

Hamburger Red Flannel Hash: Substitute 1 pound ground lean beef chuck for the corned beef, mix with potatoes, beets, onion, 1 teaspoon salt, and the pepper. Brown in a skillet as in basic recipe above, or brown in the oven as in first variation. For skillet-browned hash, about 355 calories for each of 4 servings, 235 calories for each of 6 servings. For oven-browned hash, about 420 calories for each of 4 servings, 280 calories for each of 6 servings.

¢ ⊠ **CREAMED CHIPPED BEEF**

Makes 4 servings

1 (4-ounce) package chipped beef
¼ cup butter or margarine
¼ cup unsifted flour
2 cups milk
Pinch pepper

Separate beef slices and tear into medium-size shreds; taste and if too salty cover with boiling water and let stand 1 minute; drain well. Melt butter in a saucepan over moderate heat, add beef, and heat, stirring occasionally, 2–3 minutes until lightly frizzled. Off heat, blend in flour, then milk. Return to heat and cook, stirring constantly, until thickened and smooth. Add pepper, taste for salt and add if needed. Serve over slices of dry toast. About 265 calories per serving (without toast).

VARIATIONS:

Parsleyed Chipped Beef: Just before serving, mix in 2 tablespoons minced parsley. About 265 calories per serving (without toast).

Chipped Beef Curry: Prepare as directed up to point of adding flour; mix in flour, also 1–2 tablespoons curry powder, 1 teaspoon Worcestershire sauce, and ¼ teaspoon each garlic and onion powders. Proceed as directed and serve over boiled rice or toast. About 265 calories per serving (without rice or toast).

Chipped Beef in Cheese Sauce: Prepare as directed; add ¼ pound mild processed cheese, 1 tablespoon Worcestershire sauce, and 2–3 dashes liquid hot red pepper seasoning. Heat, stirring, until smooth and serve over buttered noodles or dry toast. About 365 calories per serving (without noodles or toast).

Chipped Beef, Cheese, and Olives: Prepare Chipped Beef in Cheese Sauce and just before serving stir in ½ cup thinly sliced pimiento-stuffed green olives. About 375 calories per serving (without toast).

Chipped Beef "Chili": Prepare Chipped Beef in Cheese Sauce, then mix in 1 tablespoon each chili powder and ketchup. Serve over toast or boiled dried kidney beans. About 365 calories per serving (without toast or beans).

Barbecued Chipped Beef: Prepare Chipped Beef "Chili," increasing amount of ketchup to 3 tablespoons and adding 2 tablespoons cider vinegar. Serve over toast. About 365 calories per serving (without toast).

⊠ CREAMED CHIPPED BEEF AND MUSHROOMS

Extra rich and filled with meat.
Makes 4–6 servings

2 (4-ounce) packages chipped beef
½ pound mushrooms, wiped clean and sliced thin
1 clove garlic, peeled and crushed (optional)
2 tablespoons butter or margarine
2 (10½-ounce) cans condensed cream of mushroom soup
1 cup cold water
⅛ teaspoon white pepper
½ cup sour cream

Separate beef slices and tear into medium-size shreds; taste and if too salty cover with boiling water and let stand 1 minute; drain thoroughly. Sauté beef, mushrooms, and, if you like, the garlic in the butter in a large skillet over moderately high heat 3–4 minutes until mushrooms are golden; set aside. In a saucepan mix soup and water and heat, uncovered, over moderate heat until almost boiling. Add skillet mixture and remaining ingredients and heat, but do not boil, 2–3 minutes. Serve over toast or chow mein noodles. About 530 calories for each of 4 servings (without toast or noodles), 355 calories for each of 6 servings.

VEAL

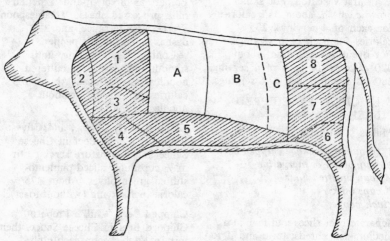

Note: Unshaded parts are the tender cuts. Shaded parts are not-so-tender.

THE TENDER CUTS:
  A. RIB
      Roasts (rib, crown)
      Chops (rib, boneless rib)
  B. LOIN
      Roasts
      Chops (loin, kidney)
  C. SIRLOIN
      Roasts
      Steaks

THE NOT-SO-TENDER CUTS:
1. SHOULDER
    Blade roasts
    Blade steaks
    Stew veal
    Ground veal
2. NECK
    Stew veal
3. ARM
    Arm roasts

Arm steaks
4. SHANK
   Shank crosscuts
5. BREAST
   Roasts for stuffing
   Riblets (stew veal)
6. HEEL OF ROUND
   Stew veal
7. ROUND (LEG)
   Cutlets, scaloppine
   Round steaks
   Roasts
8. RUMP
   Roasts

Compared to juicy red steaks or prime ribs, veal seems colorless, characterless. Americans tend to treat it as junior-grade beef, a mistake because veal is too lean and delicate to fling on a grill or pop in the oven. It needs coddling in butter, stock, or sauce, enhancing with herbs, rounding out with vegetables or other meats. European recipes prove how very good veal can be. *Wiener Schnitzel*, for example, tender and moist under its crispy brown crust, sagey *saltimbocca*, creamy *blanquette de veau*.

Unfortunately, the veal beloved by Europeans—velvety white meat of suckling calves—isn't available in this country. Recently, however, certain Eastern supermarkets have been selling something close to it: *plume de veau*, pale-fleshed veal from calves fed a dry skim milk formula. It hasn't quite the flavor of calves fed mother's milk, but it's miles ahead of the rosy grass-fed veal most of us must be content with. Technically, veal is the meat of a calf 5 to 12 weeks of age. After that, until it matures into beef, its meat is of no use.

How to Recognize Quality

Look for the top federal grades (USDA PRIME, CHOICE, and GOOD), also for federally inspected (wholesome) meat. The lean should be firm, velvety, and moist; it will have no marbling of fat and practically no outer fat covering. The color of the lean varies, depending upon the animal's age and diet. Very young milk-fed veal will be grayish-white with only the faintest blush of pink; older grass or grain-fed veal will be pink, rosy, and sometimes quite red (once an animal begins nibbling grass, its flesh begins to redden). The bones of veal should be spongy and red inside and what fat there is, creamy, sweet, and firm.

Roast Veal

Loin and Rib Roasts: The most luxurious veal roasts.

Rib Roast (4–6 pounds): Very lean, very expensive. There's usually more demand for rib as chops than as roasts.

Crown Roast (8 pounds up): This custom-made showpiece contains 2 or more rib sections bent into a circle. Rib ends are frenched (stripped of meat) and the trimmings ground and piled in the center of the crown (remove this ground meat before roasting the crown because it slows cooking time; some of the ground meat can be mixed with the stuffing or all of it can be saved and used for loaves or patties). To determine the size of crown roast you need, figure 2 chops per person.

Loin Roast (4–6 pounds): The equivalent of beef short loin (steak row). With veal there's

more demand for loin as chops—
junior steaks containing tiny
nuggets of tenderloin. In England,
the favorite loin roast is that with the
kidney still attached (it nestles just
underneath the ribs).

Rolled Loin (3–5 pounds): Boned
and rolled loin; good for stuffing.

Double Loin or Saddle (8–12
pounds): Right and left loins, still
intact.

Sirloin Roast (3–4 pounds): A
very tender roast from the part of
the animal between the loin and
rump.

Rolled Double Sirloin (5–6 pounds):
Right and left sirloin roasts, boned
and rolled.

Shoulder Roasts: Moderately priced
and perfect for braising: arm
roast (4–5 pounds), blade roast
(4–5 pounds), and rolled shoulder
(3–5 pounds; good for stuffing).

Leg Roasts: After rib and loin,
these are the most tender and expensive. Good for roasting or pot
roasting: Standing rump (4–6
pounds), rolled rump (3–5 pounds),
center leg (3–4 pounds), and
shank half of leg (5–8 pounds).

Breast: A thin 3–5-pound bony
cut that's best when stuffed. Also
available boned and rolled (3–4
pounds).

How to Roast Veal

Because veal is so lean and delicate,
it shouldn't be shoved in the oven
and left to roast all by itself. It
has no fat to baste it as it cooks,
no marbling to make it juicy,
thus will dry out if not barded,
larded, and/or basted throughout
cooking. Veal also suffers from
searing and should only be roasted at
a constant low temperature

(325° F.). The best veal is that
roasted with some liquid in the
company of vegetables (see individual recipes that follow).
Unlike beef or lamb, which are
best served rare, veal does not
reach its peak of flavor until it is
well done (160° F. on a meat
thermometer) and its juices run
clear. Meat thermometers still mark
170° F. as the proper degree of
doneness for veal, and some cookbooks even recommend cooking it to
175° F. or 180° F., but at that
temperature it will be quite gray,
dry, and tough. Try the lower
temperature, then let the roast
"rest" at room temperature 15–20
minutes before carving to allow its
juices to settle. It will have the
merest tinge of pink and be
supremely tender and succulent.

Best Cuts: For simple oven roasting,
leg, rib and bone-in or rolled loin
or rump are the most suitable
but they must be well barded—or at
least draped with bacon or slices
of salt pork—if they are to be juicy.

Amounts Needed: 4–5 pounds is a
good all-round weight for bone-in
roasts, 3–4 pounds for the boneless.
To determine number of servings,
allow ½–¾ pound bone-in roast
per person, ⅓–½ pound boneless
roast.

General Preparation for Cooking:
If the veal is very young and lean,
have butcher bard* the roast well.
You can do it yourself or, if roast
has some fat, merely lay strips of
bacon (unsmoked is best) or salt
pork over it. It's a good idea to
blanch the bacon or salt pork
quickly in boiling water so that its
flavor doesn't overpower the more
delicate one of the veal. To
simplify carving of rib or loin
roasts, ask butcher to loosen back-

bone. Rub roast well with pepper and, if you like, salt. For extra savor, also rub with a cut clove of garlic and/or compatible herb or spice (see Sauces, Gravies, and Seasonings for Veal). Before roasting, let roast stand at room temperature 1½–2 hours if possible.

Continuous Low Heat Method: Preheat oven to 325° F. Place roast fattest side up on a rack in a shallow roasting pan and insert thermometer in center, not touching bone. Roast, uncovered, 30–35 minutes per pound for bone-in roasts, about 40 for rolled roasts or until thermometer reaches 160° F. For extra juiciness and flavor, baste every 15–20 minutes with melted butter or with a ½ and ½ mixture of melted butter and dry red or white wine. Remove roast from oven and let stand 15–20 minutes before serving (it will continue cooking slightly). Serve *au jus* or with Pan Gravy.

VARIATIONS:

Barbecue-Style Roast Veal: Do not bard. Marinate roast in All-Purpose Barbecue Sauce 24 hours in refrigerator. Lift from sauce and roast as directed, basting every 15 minutes with some of the sauce.

Roast Veal with Anchovies: Do not bard. Make tiny slits over roast and insert thin garlic slivers (2 cloves should be enough). Mix minced celery, minced peeled onions and minced carrots (2 of each) in a shallow open roasting pan and lay roast on vegetables. Drape fillets from 1 (2-ounce) can anchovies over veal and pour oil from can over all. Top with 4–5 slices bacon. Insert thermometer and roast as directed; discard bacon but reserve anchovies. Strain cooking liquid into a saucepan, pressing out as much as possible. Mash anchovies and add along with 1 tablespoon anchovy paste and 1 cup Veal (White) Stock, beef or chicken broth. Heat and serve as sauce.

Cream Roasted Veal: In a shallow open roasting pan, mix together 2 peeled and sliced onions, 2 peeled and sliced carrots, 1 cup minced parsley, and 2 minced cloves garlic. Place roast on vegetables, pour ½ cup heavy cream over meat, and roast as directed, basting every ½ hour with ¼ cup lukewarm heavy cream. When roast is done, strain pan juices and pass as gravy.

About Spit-Roasting Veal: Because of its leanness veal is a poor choice for spits and rotisseries; cooked thus, it will toughen and dry out.

Some Glazes for Roast Veal

Veal is a particularly versatile meat, so experiment with some of the glazes and flavor combinations that follow to see which appeal to your family most. About ½ hour before roast is done, spread or drizzle any of the following over it and continue cooking as directed, basting once or twice with pan drippings:
– 1 cup sherry, port, Madeira, dry red or white wine, or apple cider.
– 1 cup beer, ale, or stout.
– 1 cup *marinara* sauce or clam juice.
– 2 peeled and chopped medium-size yellow onions simmered ½ hour in 2 cups milk.
– ½ cup soy sauce mixed with ½ cup ketchup.
– ½ cup honey mixed with ½ cup chianti or dry vermouth.
– 1 cup grape, apple, red or black currant, or quince jelly, chopped.

−1 (8-ounce) can whole or jellied cranberry sauce.

How to Carve Veal Roasts:
Rib: See How to Carve a Standing Rib Roast.

Leg or Rump: See How to Carve Leg of Lamb.

Loin: See How to Carve a Pork Loin Roast.

SOME SAUCES, GRAVIES, AND SEASONINGS FOR VEAL

FOR COOKING Seasonings, Herbs, Spices		FOR HOT ROASTS		FOR STEAKS AND CHOPS	
		Sauces	Gravies	Sauces	Butters
Allspice	Mace	Avgolemono	Au jus (un-	Aurore	Anchovy
Basil	Marjoram	Hot horseradish	thickened	Béarnaise	Bercy
Bay	Nutmeg	Light curry	pan gravy)	Bordelaise	Chive
Leaves	Oregano	Marinara	Mushroom	Chasseur	Herb
Cardamom	Paprika	Paloise	Pan gravy	Choron	Horseradish
Chili	Parsley	Parsley	Sour cream	Duxelles	Lemon
Powder	Rosemary	Portugaise		Madeira	Maître d'hôtel
Chives	Sage	Smitane		Mustard	Noisette
Cinnamon	Shallots	Soubise		Robert	Shallot
Cloves	Summer	Tarragon			Tomato
Curry	Savory	Tomato			Tuna
Powder	Tarragon	Velouté			Watercress
Dill	Thyme	Zingara			
Garlic	Truffles				
Lemon					

FOR HOT OR COLD VEAL	FOR COLD ROASTS
Condiments	Sauces
Applesauce	Aioli
Chutney	Anchovy
Cranberry sauce	mayonnaise
Horseradish	Chaud-froid
Mushrooms	Cumberland
(pickled)	Mayonnaise
Mustard	Sour cream-
Peaches (bran-	cucumber
died or pickled)	Sour cream-
Pickles (bread	horseradish
and butter,	Tuna
dill, mustard)	mayonnaise
Preserved kumquats	
Spiced fruits (crab	
apples, peaches,	
pears)	

Some Garnishes for Roast Veal Platters

(in addition to parsley and watercress)

Because roast veal lacks the rich brown color of roast beef, it profits, particularly, from judicious garnishing. Choose two vegetables from the list below, striving for contrast of color, size, texture, and shape, then group or cluster around roast as artistically as possible. If you are feeling ambitious, try cutting one of the vegetables into fancy shapes. Add only enough garnish to showcase the roast, not so much that the roast is overwhelmed and carving becomes difficult.

Artichoke Bottoms: boiled and buttered; Artichoke Bottoms Stuffed with Vegetables; Artichoke Bottoms Princesse.

Artichoke Hearts: boiled and buttered.

Asparagus Tips: boiled and buttered.

Brussels Sprouts: boiled and buttered.

Carrots: Buttered Baby Carrots; Carrots Rosemary; Lemon-Glazed Carrots; Carrots Vichy.

Celery Hearts: boiled and buttered.

Crab Apples: whole canned or spiced.

Green Beans: Green Beans Amandine; Green Beans with Mushrooms.

Lima Beans: boiled and buttered; Baby Limas with Pecans.

Macédoine of Vegetables (hot).

Mushrooms: sautéed button mushrooms; mushroom caps or slices; Baked Mushroom Caps Stuffed with Hazelnuts.

Onions: Pan-Braised Onions; Stuffed Onions.

Orange Cups or Baskets: filled with hot or cold cranberry sauce or hot buttered peas.

Parsnips: Currant-Glazed Parsnips, Caramel-Glazed Parsnips, or Roasted Parsnips.

Pickles: Bread and Butter, Dill, Mustard; also pickled mushrooms or red cabbage.

Potatoes: Parsleyed, Herbed, Lemon-Glazed, or Danish-Style New Potatoes; also Franconia, Château, Parisienne, Dauphine, Shoestring, and cones of Duchess Potatoes.

Snow Peas: boiled and buttered; Snow Peas and Water Chestnuts.

Tomatoes: raw cherry tomatoes or tomato wedges; Stuffed Tomatoes; Broiled Tomatoes.

ROAST VEAL STUFFED WITH WALNUTS AND MUSHROOMS

Makes 8 servings

1 (4-pound) veal leg, shoulder, or rump roast, boned but not rolled (save bones for Veal Stock)
1 teaspoon salt
⅛ teaspoon pepper
6 slices bacon

Stuffing:
⅔ cup finely chopped yellow onion
2 cloves garlic, peeled and crushed
2 tablespoons butter or margarine
2 cups finely chopped mushrooms
¾ cup toasted bread crumbs
1½ cups toasted walnuts, chopped fine
¼ teaspoon powdered rosemary
1 tablespoon minced parsley
1 teaspoon salt
¼ teaspoon pepper
2 eggs, lightly beaten

Preheat oven to 325° F. Lay veal

cut side up and flatten slightly with a meat mallet; sprinkle with salt and pepper. Prepare stuffing: Sauté onion and garlic in butter over moderate heat 5–8 minutes until pale golden, add mushrooms, and sauté 3–4 minutes longer. Off heat, mix in remaining stuffing ingredients. Spread stuffing on veal almost to edges and roll; tie securely in several places and set on a rack in a shallow, open roasting pan. Cover with bacon, insert meat thermometer in center of meat, making sure it doesn't rest in stuffing. Roast, un-covered, 35–40 minutes per pound until thermometer reads 160° F. Lift meat from pan, dis-card bacon, and let roast "rest" 15–20 minutes. Remove string and slice about ½" thick. Serve with Pan or Au Jus Gravy. About 520 calories per serving (without gravy).

VARIATIONS:

Omit stuffing above and use 3 cups of any of the following stuff-ings: Oyster; Sage and Mushroom; Sage and Onion; Herbed Bread or prepared stuffing mix. Calories per serving: about 595 if made with Oyster Stuffing; about 560 if made with Sage and Mushroom Stuffing; 545 made with Sage and Onion Dressing; about 580 if made with Herbed Bread Stuffing or prepared stuffing mix.

Sauerkraut Stuffed Veal: Season veal as directed. Mix 1 (1-pound) drained can sauerkraut with 2 sautéed minced yellow onions, 1 sautéed minced sweet green pepper, 2 cups dry white bread crumbs, 1 teaspoon salt, ¼ teaspoon pepper, and 1 lightly beaten egg. Spread stuffing on veal and proceed as recipe directs. About 350 calories per serving.

⚖️ **Neapolitan Roast Stuffed**

Veal: Season veal with pepper only. Mix ¼ cup each anchovy paste and minced parsley with 3 crushed cloves garlic, 2 tablespoons each lemon juice and minced capers, 1 tablespoon grated lemon rind, 2 teaspoons prepared mild yellow mustard, and ¼ teaspoon pepper. Spread ½ mixture on veal, roll, and tie; spread remainder on top of veal, cover with bacon, and roast as directed. About 300 calories per serving.

Veal Roast Stuffed with Ham: Sprinkle veal with pepper only, spread with 1 cup deviled ham or 2 cups ground ham mixed with ⅓ cup heavy cream; lay 6–8 bacon slices lengthwise over filling, then roll, tie, and roast as directed, basting frequently during last ½ hour with chianti. About 415 calories per serving.

BRAISED VEAL ROAST WITH VEGETABLE GRAVY

Makes 8 servings

1 (4–5-pound) boned and rolled veal shoulder or rump (save bones for Veal Stock)
2 tablespoons cooking oil
2 large yellow onions, peeled and coarsely chopped
1–2 cloves garlic, peeled and crushed
1 carrot, peeled and chopped fine
1 stalk celery, chopped fine
1 bouquet garni,* tied in cheesecloth
2 teaspoons salt
¼ teaspoon pepper
⅓ cup cold water
¼ cup unsifted flour
3 cups Veal Stock or a ½ and ½ mixture of beef and chicken broths
1–2 teaspoons liquid gravy browner (optional)

Brown veal well in oil in a heavy kettle over moderate heat; add all but last 3 ingredients, cover, and simmer 2½–3 hours until tender, turning meat once. If pot cooks dry before veal is done, add 2–3 tablespoons cold water. Transfer veal to platter and keep warm. Discard *bouquet garni;* purée vegetables and any remaining kettle liquid in an electric blender at low speed. Blend flour with 1 cup stock. Add remaining stock and purée to kettle and bring to a boil. Stir in flour paste and cook, stirring, until thickened. Cover and simmer 2–3 minutes; taste for seasoning and adjust. For a darker gravy, add browner. Slice roast about ¼″ thick and serve with plenty of gravy. About 350 calories per serving.

VARIATIONS:

Oven Pot Roast:
Electric Skillet Pot Roast: } Follow variations under Pot Roast in the Beef section.

Pressure Cooker Pot Roast: Brown veal and onion in oil in open pressure cooker; add all but last 3 ingredients, seal cooker, bring pressure to 10 pounds, and cook 10 minutes per pound. Reduce pressure, open cooker, remove veal and keep warm. Prepare gravy in open cooker using basic method above.

All cooking methods above: about 350 calories per serving.

Herbed Veal Pot Roast with Wine Gravy: Add 1 teaspoon oregano, basil, marjoram, or thyme along with other seasonings. Simmer roast in ⅓ cup dry red or white wine instead of water. For gravy, use 1½ cups of the same wine and 1½ cups

stock. About 390 calories per serving.

Veal Pot Roast in Tomato Sauce: Simmer roast in 1 cup tomato sauce instead of ⅓ cup water. When making gravy, use 1½ cups each tomato juice and stock. Just before serving, smooth in ¼ cup grated Parmesan cheese. About 385 calories per serving.

Veal Pot Roast with Vegetables: Prepare roast as directed; about 45 minutes before it is done, add ½ cup additional stock and any or a combination of the following: 16 small white onions and new potatoes, both peeled; 1 small peeled rutabaga cut in 1½″ cubes; 8 peeled parsnips, small whole turnips or leeks, 24 peeled whole baby carrots. Season vegetables with 1 teaspoon salt, cover, and simmer until meat and vegetables are tender. Prepare gravy as directed. Wreathe vegetables around meat and serve. About 510 calories per serving.

Veal Pot Roast with Wine and Olives: Follow basic recipe but simmer roast on a trivet with ⅓ cup dry red wine instead of water. When making gravy, strain vegetables from cooking liquid; use 1 cup each dry red wine and stock and omit flour. Stir in ½ cup chopped pitted ripe olives, heat about 5 minutes, and serve. About 400 calories per serving.

Veal Pot Roast with Avgolemono Sauce: Cook veal on a trivet by basic recipe above, but omit onions, carrot, and celery. For sauce, see Lamb Pot Roast with Avgolemono Sauce. About 355 calories per serving.

VEAL SHOULDER BRAISED WITH ROSEMARY AND VERMOUTH

Once you've browned the meat and onions, you need only keep half an eye on the pot. This roast literally cooks itself.
Makes 6 servings

1 (3½-pound) boned and rolled veal shoulder roast
½ teaspoon salt
¼ teaspoon pepper
2 tablespoons flour
¼ cup cooking oil
4 medium-size yellow onions, peeled and cut in thin wedges
1 clove garlic, peeled and crushed
¼ teaspoon summer savory
1 (4″) sprig fresh rosemary or ¼ teaspoon crushed dried rosemary
1 (4″) sprig fresh thyme or a pinch dried thyme
1 cup dry white vermouth
1½ cups water

Rub veal well with salt, pepper, and flour and brown well on all sides in oil in a large, heavy kettle over moderately high heat. Reduce heat to moderate, add onions and garlic, and stir-fry 8–10 minutes until golden. Add remaining ingredients, cover, and simmer slowly 2–2½ hours until tender, turning veal about every hour. To serve, carve into slices about ¼″ thick and top with the juices, which will have cooked down into a rich brown gravy. About 480 calories per serving.

BRAISED VEAL ROAST WITH BREAD AND GREEN PEPPER STUFFING

Makes 8 servings

1 (4-pound) veal leg, rump, or shoulder roast, boned but not rolled (save bones for Veal Stock)
2 tablespoons cooking oil

1 teaspoon salt
1½ cups Veal Stock or ¾ cup each beef broth and water

Stuffing:
1 medium-size yellow onion, peeled and minced
1 medium-size sweet green pepper, cored, seeded, and minced
3 pimientos, seeded and coarsely chopped
2 tablespoons butter or margarine
3 cups soft white bread crumbs
1 teaspoon minced fresh basil or ½ teaspoon dried basil
1 teaspoon garlic salt
⅛ teaspoon pepper

Spread veal flat, cut side up, and let stand while you prepare stuffing. Sauté onion, green pepper, and pimientos in butter in a large, heavy skillet over moderate heat 5–8 minutes until onion is pale golden. Off heat mix in remaining stuffing ingredients; spread over veal almost to edges, roll, and tie securely in several places. Brown veal in oil in a heavy kettle over moderately high heat; sprinkle with salt. Place a rack under veal, add stock, and simmer slowly about 2 hours until tender, basting every 20–30 minutes with cooking liquid. Or cover and bake 2 hours at 325° F. Let veal "rest" 10 minutes, remove strings, and serve. Skim fat from cooking liquid and serve as gravy. When carving, make slices ¼″–½″ thick. About 400 calories per serving.

VARIATIONS:

Substitute 3 cups of any of the following stuffings for that above: Oyster; Sausage and Mushroom; Rice and Mushroom; Sage and Onion; Herbed Bread or prepared stuffing mix. Calories per serving: about 460 calories per serving if made with Oyster Stuffing; 480 if made with Sausage and Mushroom

Stuffing; 455 with Rice and Mushroom Stuffing; 415 with Sage and Onion Dressing; 445 if made with Herbed Bread Stuffing or prepared stuffing mix.

Braised Veal Roast Verde: Omit above stuffing; instead, mix together 2 tablespoons soft butter, 1 cup each minced Italian parsley and raw spinach, and 1 crushed clove garlic. Spread on veal, roll, tie, and proceed as directed. Just before serving, mix ¼ cup each minced chives, dill pickles, and capers into cooking liquid. About 345 calories per serving.

⚖ BRAISED STUFFED BREAST OF VEAL WITH RED CURRANT GRAVY

Makes 6 servings

3–4 pounds breast of veal, boned but not rolled (use bones for Veal Stock)
1 small clove garlic, peeled and crushed
¼ teaspoon pepper
¼ cup bacon or beef drippings
1½ cups Veal Stock or ¾ cup each beef broth and water

Stuffing:
1½ cups soft white bread crumbs
1 medium-size yellow onion, peeled and minced
1 teaspoon summer savory
1 teaspoon sage
1 tablespoon minced parsley
1 teaspoon salt
¼ teaspoon pepper
1 teaspoon celery seeds
1 egg, lightly beaten

Gravy:
¼ cup unsifted flour blended with ½ cup cold Veal Stock
Veal cooking liquid
¼ cup red currant jelly

Rub veal inside and out with garlic and pepper. Mix stuffing and spread on cut side of veal almost to edges; roll and tie securely in several places. Brown veal all over in drippings in a heavy kettle over moderate heat. Place a rack under meat, add stock, cover, and simmer about 2 hours until tender. Lift meat to platter and let "rest" while you make the gravy. Blend flour paste into cooking liquid and heat, stirring, until thickened. Smooth in jelly, taste for salt and pepper and adjust. Remove strings from veal, slice ¼″–½″ thick, and top with some of the gravy. Pass the rest. About 235 calories per serving.

VARIATION:

⚖ **Braised Stuffed Breast of Veal with Vegetable Gravy:** Stuff, roll, and tie veal as directed. Brown 2 minced, peeled carrots and 2 minced, peeled small yellow onions in drippings before browning veal; add veal and brown, then proceed as directed. When making gravy, purée vegetables and cooking liquid in an electric blender at low speed, return to kettle, thicken with flour paste as directed but omit jelly. About 210 calories per serving.

VEAL ORLOFF

If you want to show off, here's the recipe to do it with. It's a complicated four-part affair, but fortunately it *can* be made ahead. Perfect accompaniments: a fragrant green salad and chilled white Burgundy.
Makes 6 servings

2 carrots, peeled and coarsely grated
2 medium-size yellow onions, peeled and coarsely chopped
¼ cup butter or margarine
1 (3-pound) boned and rolled veal loin or rump roast (ask butcher to prepare roast carefully and tie tightly)
1½ teaspoons salt

⅛ *teaspoon pepper*
1 *cup dry vermouth*

Filling:
½ *pound mushrooms, wiped clean*
   and minced
2 *tablespoons minced shallots*
6 *tablespoons butter or margarine*
3 *tablespoons rice, parboiled 5*
   minutes in 1 quart water and
   drained
2 *medium-size yellow onions, peeled*
   and sliced thin
1 *cup sauce (given below)*

Sauce:
4 *tablespoons butter or margarine*
6 *tablespoons flour*
½ *teaspoon salt*
Pinch white pepper
Pinch nutmeg
Strained veal cooking liquid plus
   enough heavy cream to total
   2½ cups

Topping:
Remaining Sauce
3 *(1-ounce) packages Gruyère*
   cheese, grated fine
2 *egg yolks*
Paprika (garnish)

Stir-fry carrots and onions in butter in a heavy kettle over moderately high heat about 5 minutes until golden; add roast and brown lightly on all sides. Add salt, pepper, and vermouth, cover, and simmer slowly 1½–2 hours until tender.

While roast cooks, begin filling: Sauté mushrooms and shallots in 4 tablespoons butter over lowest heat about 30 minutes until all moisture has evaporated. At the same time, let drained rice and onions cook, covered, in 2 tablespoons butter in a very heavy skillet or flameproof casserole over lowest heat about ½ hour until very soft but not brown. Check skillet now and then and add 1–2 tablespoons water if they threaten to

scorch. When veal is done, lift from kettle and let cool 15–20 minutes.

For the sauce: Melt butter in a saucepan, blend in flour and seasonings, add veal cooking liquid-cream mixture, and heat, stirring, until thickened and smooth.

To complete the filling: Mix 1 cup sauce into rice and onions, purée in an electric blender at low speed, then combine with mushrooms and shallots.

To prepare topping: Whisk 2 packages grated Gruyère into remaining sauce, heating and stirring until melted. Mix a little hot sauce into egg yolks, return to sauce, and remove from heat at once.

To assemble Orloff: Discard strings from roast and slice about ¼″ thick; spread slices with filling in order they were cut and overlap on a large (about 14″) flameproof platter. Pour topping over slices, sprinkle with remaining Gruyère, and add a blush of paprika. (*Note:* Recipe may be prepared up to this point several hours ahead, covered, and refrigerated until about ¾ hour before serving.)

For final cooking: Preheat oven to 375° F. Set platter, uncovered, on upper oven rack and bake 25–30 minutes until sauce is bubbly and touched with brown. Serve at once. About 945 calories per serving.

VITELLO TONNATO (COLD ROAST VEAL IN TUNA-MAYONNAISE SAUCE)

Perfect for a summer luncheon, especially with slices of full-flavored, vine-ripened tomatoes and a well-chilled dry Graves or Soave. Makes 6–8 servings

1 *(3-pound) boned and rolled veal
rump roast*
2 *tablespoons olive oil*
2 *medium-size yellow onions, peeled
and sliced thin*
2 *stalks celery, sliced thin*
1 *carrot, peeled and sliced thin*
2 *cloves garlic, peeled and quartered*
3 *large sprigs parsley*
1 *(4") sprig fresh thyme or
½ teaspoon dried thyme*
1 *(2-ounce) can anchovy fillets,
drained*
1 *(7-ounce) can white meat tuna,
drained and flaked*
¾ *cup dry vermouth*
1 *teaspoon salt*
¼ *teaspoon pepper*

Tuna-Mayonnaise Sauce:
2 *cups puréed kettle mixture*
Juice of 1 lemon
1 *cup mayonnaise (about)*
2 *tablespoons drained capers*
2 *tablespoons minced parsley*
Lemon wedges

Lightly brown roast in oil in a heavy kettle over moderately high heat; add remaining ingredients (except sauce), cover, and simmer slowly 2 hours, turning veal after 1 hour. Lift veal to a large bowl; purée kettle mixture in an electric blender at low speed or put through a food mill. Pour over veal, cover, and chill 24 hours, turning veal occasionally. Lift veal from purée and wipe off excess. Measure 2 cups purée and blend with lemon juice and enough mayonnaise to give it the consistency of thin cream sauce. (*Note:* Remaining purée can be used as the liquid ingredient in tuna or salmon loaves.) Slice veal about ¼" thick, arrange, overlapping, on a large platter, spooning a little sauce over each slice; re-cover and marinate several hours in refrigerator. Just before serving, ladle a little more sauce

over all, sprinkle with capers and minced parsley. Set out lemon wedges and pass remaining sauce. About 840 calories for each of 6 servings, 630 calories for each of 8 servings.

For a Milder, Less Rich Sauce: Cook veal as directed; *strain* kettle liquid, then boil uncovered until reduced to about 1½ cups. Pour over veal, cover, and marinate as directed. Lift veal from marinade and slice; combine marinade with mayonnaise and lemon as above, spoon over veal, proceed and serve as directed. About 725 calories for each of 6 servings, 545 calories for each of 8 servings.

⚔ **JELLIED VEAL LOAF**
Makes 6 servings

1½ *pounds veal shoulder or rump,
cut in 2" cubes*
1½ *pounds veal bones*
1 *medium-size yellow onion, peeled*
1 *medium-size carrot, peeled*
1 *stalk celery*
2 *teaspoons salt*
¼ *teaspoon peppercorns and 2
sprigs parsley, tied in cheesecloth*
2 *quarts cold water*

Place all ingredients in a large kettle, cover, and bring to a boil over high heat. Skim froth from surface, turn heat to low, and simmer 1½–2 hours until veal is tender. Cool 30 minutes, lift veal from broth with a slotted spoon, and cool until easy to handle. Slice each piece of meat ¼" thick against the grain and reserve. Meanwhile, simmer bones, broth, and vegetables, covered, 2 hours longer. Strain broth through a cheesecloth-lined sieve, discard bones and vegetables. If you like, clarify* broth; boil rapidly, uncovered, until reduced to about 1 quart;

cool until syrupy. Fold meat into broth, ladle into an ungreased 9″×5″×3″ loaf pan and chill until firm. Unmold on a bed of lettuce and decorate with radish roses and cherry tomatoes. When serving, slice fairly thick. About 200 calories per serving.

VARIATION:

⚖ **Decorative Jellied Veal Loaf:** Prepare as directed up to point of folding meat into syrupy broth. Pour a ¼″ layer of syrupy broth in loaf pan and chill until tacky. Arrange a decorative layer of sliced hard-cooked egg, tomato "petals," and scallion stems on jellied broth and seal with a thin layer of broth; chill until tacky. Fold meat into remaining broth and spoon carefully into pan. Chill until firm. About 215 calories per serving.

Some Ways to Use Up Leftover Roast Veal

Veal Balls in Lemon Broth (4 servings): Mix together 1½ cups finely ground leftover veal, ½ cup fine soft white bread crumbs, 1 egg, 1 minced scallion, 2 tablespoons heavy cream, 1 teaspoon each anchovy paste and minced parsley, ¼ teaspoon salt, and a pinch pepper; shape into ½″ balls. Bring 2 (13¾-ounce) cans chicken broth to a simmer, stir in the juice of ½ lemon, then add veal balls. Cover and simmer 25 minutes. Sprinkle with 1 tablespoon minced parsley and serve in soup bowls. About 310 calories per serving.

Veal-Tuna Salad (4 servings): Mix 1 cup finely diced veal with 1 (7-ounce) drained can tuna, 1 minced yellow onion, 1 tablespoon each capers, minced fresh parsley

and dill, the juice of ½ lemon, and ⅓–½ cup mayonnaise (just enough for good consistency). Serve in lettuce cups or use as a sandwich spread. About 340 calories per serving.

Veal-Mushroom Ramekins (4 servings): Stir-fry ½ cup minced mushrooms and 2 tablespoons minced shallots in 1 tablespoon butter 5 minutes; mix with 1½ cups finely ground leftover veal, ½ cup heavy cream, ¼ teaspoon dill weed, and a pinch each pepper and nutmeg. Fold in 4 egg whites beaten with ¼ teaspoon salt until soft peaks form. Spoon into 4 buttered custard cups and top with 2 tablespoons cracker meal mixed with 1½ teaspoons each melted butter and grated Parmesan. Set in a shallow baking pan, pour 1½ cups hot water around cups, and bake uncovered ½ hour at 350° F. Brown quickly under broiler, if you like, and serve. About 410 calories per serving.

Quick Veal Paprika:
Veal, Mushroom, and Noodle Casserole:
Veal and Vegetable Pie:
Veal Stuffed Vegetables:
Roast Veal Hash:
Yukon Stew:
Veal Curry:
Follow recipes given in Some Additional Ways to Use Up Leftover Roast Beef, substituting veal for beef.

Sliced Cold Veal: Slice veal about ¼″ thick and top with any recommended cold sauce (see Sauces, Gravies, and Seasonings for Veal).

Sliced Hot Veal: Slice veal about ¼″ thick and layer into a shallow greased casserole. Add just enough hot sauce or gravy to cover (see Some Sauces, Gravies, and Seasonings for Veal), cover with foil,

and heat 20 minutes at 350° F. Or
heat veal slices in sauce about 5
minutes in a covered skillet over
moderately low heat.

Hot Roast Veal Sandwiches: Heat
veal slices in a suitable sauce
or gravy in a skillet as for Sliced
Hot Veal (above). Serve open
face on toast, buns, or bread.

**To Make the Most of Very Small
Amounts:** See suggestions given
for beef.

Veal Steaks and Chops

If you think of these simply as slices
of the veal roasts described earlier,
you won't have much difficulty
keeping them straight. An arm
steak, for example, is a slice
of arm roast, a rib chop a slice
of the rib, a sirloin a slice of the
sirloin, and so on. The smaller
cuts, logically, are the chops, the
larger ones steaks. (Refer to
Veal Chart.) The most popular are:
Blade steak
Arm steak
Rib chops (plain and Frenched)
Loin chops (plain, kidney, noisettes,
   or medallions)
Sirloin steak
Round steak (sometimes called
   cutlet)
Cube steak
Frozen veal steaks (plain or
   breaded)

How to Cook

Amounts Needed: Rib and loin
chops are best cut about 1″ thick;
other steaks and chops range
from ½″ to 1″. Allow 1–2 rib or
loin chops per person, 1 cube or
frozen veal steak. Steaks will
generally serve 2 and sometimes
as many as 4, depending on
how thick they're cut. Allow

about ½–¾ pound bone-in chop
or steak per person, ⅓–½ pound
boneless.

General Preparation for Cooking:
If meat seems moist, wipe with
a damp cloth so it will brown well.
Sprinkle with pepper but not
salt (it prevents browning) and for
extra savor, rub with a cut clove
garlic and/or compatible herb
such as sage, thyme, or marjoram
(see Some Sauces, Gravies, and
Seasonings for Veal). Let chops
or steaks stand at room temperature
1½–2 hours before cooking if
convenient.

*Cooking Methods Not Recom-
mended:* Broiling, panbroiling,
charcoal broiling. Veal chops and
steaks are too lean to cook without
some fat and/or liquid; moreover,
they shrivel, toughen, and dry
under intense broiler heat.

To Panfry (Sauté): Best for chops
and steaks cut ½″–¾″ thick,
also for cube and frozen veal steaks.
Heat 1–2 tablespoons butter,
drippings, or cooking oil in a large,
heavy skillet over moderately
high heat about ½ minute, add chops
or steaks and brown well on
both sides, turning frequently.
Cube and frozen steaks will need
only 3–5 minutes altogether;
½″–¾″ steaks and chops will take
20–30 minutes and, once browned,
should finish cooking over fairly
low heat. Do not cover and do not
add liquid.

VARIATIONS:

Dredged Chops or Steaks: Dip meat
in seasoned flour (about ⅓ cup
unsifted flour, 1 teaspoon salt
and ¼ teaspoon pepper), then
cook as directed.

Herbed Chops or Steaks: Dip meat
in ⅓ cup unsifted flour mixed with
1 teaspoon each salt and a com-

patible herb such as sage, marjoram, rosemary, or thyme and ¼ teaspoon pepper. Cook as directed.

Hungarian-Style Chops or Steaks: Dip meat in ⅓ cup unsifted flour mixed with 2 tablespoons paprika, 1 teaspoon salt, and a pinch pepper. Cook as directed.

Breaded Chops or Steaks: Sprinkle both sides of meat lightly with salt and pepper, dip in ⅓ cup unsifted flour, then in 1 egg lightly beaten with 1 tablespoon cold water, finally in 1 cup fine dry bread crumbs (for extra flavor, use seasoned crumbs). To make breading stick, let breaded chops dry on a cake rack 15 minutes before browning. Cook as directed, doubling amount of butter used. Drain well on paper toweling before serving.

To Braise: Here's the very best way to cook veal chops and steaks because it allows them to cook through and at the same time remain juicily tender. Brown chops or steaks 3–4 minutes on a side over moderately high heat in 1 tablespoon butter, drippings, or cooking oil; add about ½ cup water to skillet, cover and simmer slowly over low heat or in a preheated 350° F. oven until cooked through. Chops will take 30–45 minutes, depending on thickness; steaks 50–60. (*Note:* Cube or frozen veal steaks will need only 10–15 minutes in all, noisettes about 20.)

For Extra Savor: Substitute any of the following for water called for above: medium dry white or red wine, rosé, sherry, Madeira, dry vermouth, or apple cider; tomatoes (or juice or sauce); orange, apple, or mixed fruit juices; milk, buttermilk, or light cream;

barbecue or meatless spaghetti sauce; chicken or beef broth; ½ (10½-ounce) can condensed onion, cream of celery, mushroom, tomato, or asparagus soup.

Some Variations on Braised Veal Chops and Steaks
(All Quantities Based on Enough Chops or Steaks for 4 Persons)

Portuguese-Style: Brown meat as directed and pour off drippings; season *lightly,* add ¾ cup each tomato purée and liquid drained from canned ripe olives, 1 tablespoon olive oil, ½ cup sliced pitted ripe olives, 1 minced medium-size yellow onion, 1 crushed clove garlic, and ¼ teaspoon crushed juniper berries. Cover and simmer as above. About 360 calories per serving.

◁◻ **Flambéed with Endives:** Brown meat as directed and pour off drippings; season, add ¼ cup cognac and flame, spooning liquid over chops. Add ⅓ cup beef broth, 4 small whole endives, and ⅛ teaspoon garlic powder. Cover and simmer as directed. Transfer meat and endives to a platter, add ¼ cup heavy cream to skillet, and simmer 1–2 minutes, stirring. Pour over meat and serve. About 285 calories per serving.

Budapest-Style: Brown meat as directed, season, and add ½ cup chicken broth. Top each chop with 1 sweet green pepper ring and 1 whole split, seeded pimiento (steaks should be completely covered with pepper and pimiento). Cover and simmer as directed. Transfer to platter and keep warm. To skillet add 2 tablespoons grated onion, ½ cup heavy cream, and ¼ cup milk and simmer 2–3 minutes. Blend 1 tablespoon flour with ¼ cup milk, add to skillet, and cook, stirring, until slightly thickened. Season to taste, pour over chops, and serve. About 415 calories per serving.

Smothered Chops or Steaks: Brown 2 sliced medium-size yellow onions along with meat and pour off all but 1 tablespoon drippings; season and add 1 (10½-ounce) can condensed cream of mushroom, celery, or chicken soup thinned with ⅓ cup milk. Cover and simmer as directed. About 425 calories per serving.

En Casserole: Sauté together 2 slices minced bacon, 1 minced medium-size yellow onion, and 1 diced carrot over moderate heat 5 minutes until onion is pale golden; transfer all to an ungreased 1½-quart casserole. Brown meat as directed and add to casserole. Sprinkle all lightly with salt and pepper, add 1 *bouquet garni** and ½ cup dry white wine. Cover and oven-simmer as directed. Uncover during last 15 minutes so juices will cook down. If you like, add 6–8 peeled small white onions or new potatoes before baking. About 390 calories per serving.

In Orange Sauce: Brown 2 slices bacon in a skillet, remove, and crumble. To drippings add 1 table-spoon butter and brown chops as directed; season with salt and pepper. Add bacon, ¾ cup orange juice, and 1 tablespoon slivered orange rind. Cover and simmer as directed. Transfer meat to platter, add ¼ cup heavy or light cream to pan juices and heat 1–2 minutes, stirring (do not boil). Pour sauce over meat and serve. If you like, substitute ¼ cup grapefruit juice for ¼ cup of the orange juice. Proceed as directed and garnish platter with orange and grapefruit sections. About 415 calories per serving.

⊠ **Dijonnaise:** Brown meat as directed but do not pour off drippings. Season chops and top with ¼ cup minced shallots or scallions and 2 tablespoons minced parsley. Add ½ cup beef broth, cover, and simmer as directed. Transfer meat to a platter and keep warm. To skillet add ¼ cup beef broth and 1 tablespoon Dijon mustard. Heat and stir 1–2 minutes, pour over meat, and serve. About 290 calories per serving.

With Basil Butter: Cream ¼ cup butter until light and mix in 2 tablespoons minced fresh basil. Brown meat as directed, drain off drippings, then season meat and spread top side with basil butter. Add ⅓ cup chicken broth, cover, and simmer as directed. Transfer meat to platter; quickly boil skillet liquid to reduce to ¼ cup. Spoon over meat, sprinkle with chopped pistachio nuts, and serve. About 330 calories per serving.

Calcutta-Style: Brown meat as directed, lift out and set aside. In drippings sauté 1 minced medium-size yellow onion 5–8 minutes until pale golden; add 1 tablespoon curry powder and cook and stir 1–2 minutes. Add ½ cup dry white wine or chicken broth, return meat to pan, season lightly with salt and pepper, cover, and simmer as directed. About 10 minutes before meat is done, add 1 peeled, thinly sliced ripe small mango (or, if out of season, 2 peeled, thinly sliced peaches and ¼ cup raisins). Cover and simmer until meat is tender. About 320 calories per serving.

Lyonnaise: Brown meat as directed, lift out, and set aside. In drippings sauté 3 thinly sliced large yellow onions 8–10 minutes until golden. Return meat to pan, season, and pile some onions on top. Add ⅓ cup chicken broth and 1 tablespoon vinegar. Cover and simmer as directed. Sprinkle with minced parsley and serve. About 315 calories per serving.

À la Crème: Brown meat as directed, season, then drain off drippings. Add ½ cup dry white wine, Madeira, or dry sherry, cover, and simmer as directed. Transfer meat to a platter and keep warm. Quickly boil down skillet liquid to ¼ cup, mix in 1 cup light cream and ½ cup Velouté or Medium White Sauce, a dash of nutmeg, and 1 teaspoon lemon juice; simmer (but do not boil) 2–3 minutes. Spoon some sauce over meat and pass the rest. If you like, scatter minced truffles, toasted slivered almonds, or minced scallions or chives over meat and add a blush of paprika. About 485 calories per serving.

Chasseur (Hunter's Style): Brown meat as directed, lift out, and set aside. In pan drippings sauté 6 minced shallots or scallions and ½ pound sliced mushrooms 4–5 minutes until golden. Return meat to pan, season, add ½ cup dry white wine, cover, and simmer as directed. Transfer meat to platter and keep warm. To pan liquid, add 1 cup beef gravy, 1 tablespoon tomato paste, and 2 teaspoons each minced chervil and tarragon. Quickly bring to a boil, spoon some sauce over meat, and pass the rest. About 340 calories per serving.

À la Bourguignonne: Brown meat as directed, lift out, and set aside. Drain off drippings; add 2 slices

bacon to skillet, brown, remove, and crumble. In drippings sauté ½ pound thinly sliced mushrooms 4–5 minutes until golden; return meat and bacon to pan, season lightly, add ⅔ cup red Burgundy wine and 1 pound Pan-Braised Onions. Cover and simmer as directed. Transfer meat and vegetables to a deep dish. Thicken pan liquid with 1 tablespoon *beurre manié.** Spoon some gravy over meat and pass the rest. About 445 calories per serving.

With Sour Cream-Cheddar Sauce: Cook meat as directed and transfer to a deep platter. Smooth 1 cup sour cream and ⅓ cup grated sharp Cheddar cheese into pan and simmer over low heat until cheese melts; stir constantly. Season to taste with onion and garlic salt, pour over meat, and serve. About 435 calories per serving.

Noisettes of Veal in Champagne-Cream Sauce: Brown meat as directed and season; pour off drippings, add ½ cup champagne, cover, and simmer about 20 minutes until meat is tender. Add ¼ cup heavy cream, 2 tablespoons diced pimiento, and, if you like, 2 thinly sliced truffles. Warm 1–2 minutes longer and serve. About 360 calories per serving.

Some Classic Garnishes for Veal Chops and Steaks

À la Française: Lift chops or steaks to a hot platter and wreathe with Peas à la Française.

À la Piémontaise: Bread and sauté chops as directed and serve on a bed of Risotto alla Milanese. Pass Tomato Sauce.

À la Provençale: Transfer chops or steaks to platter and keep warm. To skillet add ¼ cup dry white wine,

1 cup tomato sauce, and ¼ crushed clove garlic; heat, stirring, 2–3 minutes to get up browned bits. Pour over chops and garnish with cherry tomatoes that have been stuffed with a ½ and ½ mixture of sautéed minced mushrooms and scallions, topped with grated Parmesan and lightly browned under broiler. Sprinkle all with minced parsley and serve.

À la Jardinière: } see Some Classic
Au Vert-Pré: } Garnishes for Steak.

Rossini: } see Some Classic
} Ways to Serve Tournedos.

À la Bretonne: } see Some Classic
Parmentier: } Garnishes for Lamb
} Chops.

SAGE-SCENTED VEAL CHOPS STUFFED WITH PROSCIUTTO HAM

Makes 4 servings

4 veal rib chops, cut 1½" thick
4 paper-thin slices prosciutto ham
4 thin slices Gruyère cheese about 1½" wide and 2" long
1 clove garlic, peeled and halved
2 tablespoons butter or margarine
2 bay leaves
4 (4") sprigs fresh sage or 1 teaspoon dried leaf sage tied in cheesecloth
½ cup dry white wine
¼ teaspoon salt
Pinch pepper

Cutting from the curved outer edge, make a deep pocket in each veal chop. Flatten out each slice of *prosciutto*, top with a slice of Gruyère and wrap envelope style. Insert a prosciutto-Gruyère package in each veal pocket and close with toothpicks. Rub both sides of chops with garlic, then brown in butter in a large, heavy skillet over moderately high heat 2–3 minutes on each side. Add bay leaves, top each chop with a sage sprig (or drop cheesecloth bag of dried sage into skillet), pour in wine, cover, and simmer slowly 45–50 minutes until chops are just cooked through. Remove sage, bay leaves, and toothpicks, sprinkle chops with salt and pepper, and serve with some of the pan drippings spooned over each portion. About 470 calories per serving.

HOTEL OASIS VEAL CHOPS

These Roquefort-flavored chops were a specialty of the Hotel Oasis near Palma, Majorca. Makes 4 servings

4 loin veal chops, cut ¾" thick
½ cup homemade French Dressing
1 tablespoon finely grated lemon rind
1 tablespoon crumbled Roquefort cheese
¼ cup unsifted flour
1 egg, lightly beaten with 2 tablespoons milk
¾ cup fine toasted bread crumbs
3 tablespoons olive or other cooking oil

If chops have long, thin "tails," curl around thick portions and secure with toothpicks. Mix French dressing, lemon rind, and Roquefort, mashing cheese well; pour into a shallow enamel pan or glass baking dish, add chops and arrange in a single layer. Cover and chill 6–8 hours, turning chops in marinade 1 or 2 times. Dip chops in flour, then in egg, then in crumbs to coat evenly. Sauté in oil in a large heavy skillet 15–20 minutes on each side over moderately low heat. Drain on paper toweling and serve. About 405 calories per serving.

Veal Cutlets (Scallops)

(Refer to Veal Chart)

What the Italians call *scaloppine,* the Germans *Schnitzel,* the French *escalopes de veau,* and the English *collops* are veal cutlets or scallops to us–small, thin, boneless slices, usually from the veal leg but sometimes from the loin or rib. The choicest are those from the top round. All cutlets should be cut across the grain and slightly on the diagonal, always very thin–¼"–⅜" —and trimmed of any filament and fat.

Usually they are pounded to between ⅛" and ¼" thick (recipes here specify whether to pound or not). Most butchers will do the pounding, but, if not, you can easily do it yourself. Simply slip cutlet between two sheets of wax paper and flatten with a cutlet bat, rolling pin, or the side of a meat cleaver. Three or four resounding whacks per side per cutlet should do the job.

Though there are dozens of ways to prepare cutlets, almost all are variations on two basic cooking methods: *panfrying* (or *sautéing*) and *braising* (browning in fat, then finishing in a small amount of liquid or sauce). If you've never cooked cutlets before, don't attempt more than four or six at a time. Use as quick and light a hand as possible and rush the cutlets to the table the instant they're done.

ESCALOPES DE VEAU À LA CRÈME (SAUTÉED VEAL CUTLETS IN HEAVY CREAM SAUCE)

You'll note that this recipe calls for boiling the heavy cream to thicken and enrich the cutlet sauce. When, exactly, *can* cream be boiled without curdling and when can't it be? If the sauce is bland, light or heavy cream can be safely boiled. But if the sauce is acid (containing tomatoes, for example, or vinegar), the cream should not be boiled. Sour cream, being naturally acid, should never be boiled.

Makes 4 servings

*1½ pounds veal round, sliced ¼"
    thick and pounded thin as for
    scaloppine
2 tablespoons butter or margarine
1 tablespoon cooking oil
2 tablespoons minced scallions or
    shallots
⅓ cup dry vermouth
½ cup beef broth
1 cup heavy cream
½ teaspoon salt
⅛ teaspoon pepper*

Wipe cutlets dry with paper toweling so they will brown. Heat butter and oil in a large, heavy skillet over moderately high heat until a cube of bread will sizzle. Brown cutlets, a few at a time, 3–4 minutes on each side, using tongs to turn. Drain on paper toweling and keep warm at back of stove. Pour all but 2 tablespoons drippings from skillet, reduce heat to moderate, add scallions, and stir-fry 2–3 minutes. Add vermouth and broth and boil rapidly, stirring to get up browned bits, until reduced to about ¼ cup. Add cream and boil, stirring, until reduced by ½. Sprinkle cutlets with salt and pepper, return to skillet and warm 1–2 minutes, basting with sauce. Taste sauce, adjust salt and pepper if needed, and serve. About 575 calories per serving.

VARIATION:

Sautéed Veal Cutlets and Mushrooms in Cream Sauce: Brown cutlets and prepare sauce as directed. At the same time, stir-fry ½ pound thinly sliced mushrooms in 2 tablespoons butter and 1 tablespoon oil in a separate skillet 3–5 minutes until lightly browned. Add to cream sauce and cook and stir 1–2 minutes. Add cutlets, warm, and serve as directed. About 670 calories per serving.

ESCALOPES DE VEAU À LA ZINGARA (SAUTÉED VEAL CUTLETS WITH TONGUE, HAM, AND MUSHROOMS)

Makes 4 servings

1½ pounds veal round, sliced ¼"
   thick and pounded thin as for
   scaloppine
1 teaspoon salt
¼ teaspoon pepper
½ cup unsifted flour
5 tablespoons butter or margarine
½ cup Madeira wine
¾ cup Rich Brown Sauce (Demi-
   Glace)
1 tablespoon tomato paste
⅓ cup julienne strips of cooked
   smoked tongue
⅓ cup julienne strips of cooked ham
⅓ cup julienne strips of mushrooms
1 truffle, cut in fine julienne

Sprinkle both sides of cutlets with salt and pepper, then dredge in flour. Heat 3 tablespoons butter in a large, heavy skillet over moderately high heat until a bread cube will sizzle, and brown cutlets, a few at a time, 3–4 minutes on a side, using tongs to turn. Drain on paper toweling and keep warm at back of stove. Add Madeira to skillet and simmer, stirring to get up browned bits, until reduced by half. Blend in Rich Brown Sauce

and tomato paste and simmer, stirring occasionally, until thickened and the consistency of gravy. Meanwhile, in a separate skillet, sauté tongue, ham, mushrooms, and truffle in remaining butter 2–3 minutes. Add to sauce and warm 1–2 minutes. To serve, place cutlets on a hot platter and top each with a heaping spoonful of the skillet mixture. About 590 calories per serving.

⊠ PICCATE (ITALIAN-STYLE SAUTÉED VEAL SCALLOPS)

Makes 2 servings

¾ pound veal round, sliced ¼" thick
   and pounded thin as for scaloppine
¾ teaspoon salt
⅛ teaspoon pepper
⅓ cup unsifted flour
1 tablespoon olive oil
1 tablespoon butter
2 tablespoons lemon juice
2 teaspoons minced parsley

Sprinkle both sides of veal with salt and pepper, and cut in pieces about 3" square. Dredge veal squares in flour, shaking off excess so they're lightly dusted. Heat oil and butter in a heavy skillet over moderately high heat about 1 minute, add veal, and brown 1–2 minutes on a side; drain on paper toweling. Add lemon juice and parsley to skillet and stir quickly to get up browned bits. Return veal, warm 1–2 minutes, basting with lemon-parsley mixture, and serve. About 335 calories per serving.

WIENER SCHNITZEL (BREADED VEAL CUTLETS)

The Viennese say a *Wiener Schnitzel* is perfect if the crust is crisp, amber brown, and puffed here and there so that you can slip a knife between it and the cutlet.

342 THE DOUBLEDAY COOKBOOK

Here's the trick: Bread each cutlet *just* before cooking, drop into hot (but not smoking) fat, and brown, turning one time only. *Do not* dry the breaded cutlets 15–20 minutes on a rack before cooking (the breading will stick fast and refuse to puff). Cook only as many cutlets at a time as you need and serve at once.
Makes 4 servings

1½ pounds veal round, sliced ¼"
  thick and pounded thin as for
  scaloppine
2 teaspoons salt (about)
¼ teaspoon pepper (about)
⅓ cup clarified butter*
⅓ cup lard
½ cup unsifted flour
2 eggs, beaten until frothy
1 cup fine dry bread crumbs
Lemon wedges (garnish)

Sprinkle both sides of cutlets with salt and pepper. If they seem too large to handle easily or to fit in your skillet, halve them (the Viennese like whopping Schnitzels that hang over the edges of their plates, but if you're an inexperienced Schnitzel cook, it's better to work with smaller pieces). Begin heating butter and lard in a very large, heavy skillet over moderately high heat. Dip cutlets in flour, then eggs and crumbs, each time shaking off excess (they should have a thin, even, all-over crumb coating). To test fat temperature, drop in a cube of bread; when fat bubbles vigorously about it, carefully add cutlets, allowing plenty of space between them. Brown on 1 side, 3–4 minutes, turn with tongs, and brown other side. Drain well on paper toweling and serve at once with lemon wedges. Bread and brown seconds as people ask for them. About 425 calories per serving.

VARIATIONS:

Schnitzel à la Holstein: Prepare Wiener Schnitzel as directed. Top each cutlet with a fried egg, drape 2 anchovy fillets over egg in an X-pattern, and sprinkle, if you like, with drained capers. About 520 calories per serving.

Parsleyed Schnitzel: Season cutlets, dredge in flour, dip in egg, then in crumbs mixed with 1 tablespoon minced parsley. Brown as directed and serve with lemon. About 425 calories per serving.

Cheese Schnitzel: Season cutlets, dredge in flour, dip in egg, then in crumbs mixed with 1 tablespoon finely grated Parmesan cheese. Brown as directed and serve with lemon. About 430 calories per serving.

Sardellenschnitzel (Anchovy Schnitzel): Season cutlets with pepper but not salt, then spread each thinly with Anchovy Butter, leaving ¼" margins all round. Fold cutlets over, secure with toothpicks, bread and brown as for Wiener Schnitzel. Remove toothpicks and serve with lemon. About 475 calories per serving.

Schnitzel Cordon Bleu: Season cutlets with pepper and a very little salt. Cut small pieces of thinly sliced Swiss cheese and Westphalian or *prosciutto* ham so they're about ½ the size of cutlets. Lay 1 slice ham on ½ of each cutlet, top with cheese, then fold cutlet over and pound 1 or 2 times between waxed paper to seal. Bread and brown as for Wiener Schnitzel and serve with lemon. About 475 calories per serving.

Parisian Schnitzel: Season cutlets, dredge in flour, dip in egg but not in crumbs. Brown as for Wiener

Schnitzel and serve with lemon. About 375 calories per serving.

Naturschnitzel (Plain Schnitzel): Season cutlets, dredge in flour, but do not dip in egg or crumbs. Brown as directed in 3–4 tablespoons clarified butter* and serve with lemon. About 355 calories per serving.

Rahmschnitzel (Cream Schnitzel): Season cutlets, cut in strips 2″–3″× 1½″ and dredge in flour only. Brown in 3–4 tablespoons clarified butter,* remove from skillet, and drain on paper toweling. Pour off drippings; add 1 cup beef consommé to skillet and boil rapidly, stirring to scrape up browned bits, until reduced by half. Add 1 cup light cream and boil uncovered, stirring, until reduced by half. Turn heat to low, return veal to skillet, warm 2–3 minutes, stirring, and serve. About 490 calories per serving.

Paprika Schnitzel: Season cutlets and sprinkle both sides well with paprika. Cut into strips and proceed as for *Rahmschnitzel.* Just before returning veal to skillet, swirl in 2 tablespoons sour cream. Add veal, warm 2–3 minutes (but do not boil), stirring occasionally. About 380 calories per serving.

⊠ VEAL SCALOPPINE ALLA MARSALA

Makes 4–6 servings

2 pounds veal round, sliced ¼″ thick and pounded thin as for scaloppine
½ teaspoon salt
⅛ teaspoon pepper
3 tablespoons butter or margarine
3 tablespoons beef consommé
⅓ cup Marsala wine

Sprinkle veal with salt and pepper and let stand at room temperature 10–15 minutes. Brown a few pieces at a time, 2–3 minutes on a side, in butter in a large, heavy skillet over moderately high heat; remove to a heated platter and keep warm. Add consommé and wine to skillet and boil, uncovered, 1–2 minutes, stirring to get up browned bits. Pour over *scaloppine* and serve. About 460 calories for each of 4 servings, 310 calories for each of 6 servings.

VARIATIONS:

⊠ **Veal Scaloppine with Parsley:** After sprinkling scaloppine with seasonings, dredge lightly in flour. Brown as directed, remove to a heated platter and keep warm. Stir 1 tablespoon each lemon juice and minced parsley into skillet along with consommé and wine and boil, uncovered, as above. Pour over veal and serve. About 470 calories for each of 4 servings, 320 calories for each of 6 servings.

⊠ **Veal Scaloppine with Parsley and Prosciutto:** Dredge and brown scaloppine as for variation above and set aside. In drippings, stir-fry ¼ cup finely slivered *prosciutto* ham; spoon over scaloppine. Add parsley, lemon juice, consommé, and wine to skillet, boil uncovered as above, pour over scaloppine and serve. About 470 calories for each of 4 servings, 320 calories for each of 6 servings.

⊠ **Veal Scaloppine with Mushrooms:** Lightly brown ½ pound thinly sliced mushrooms in 2 tablespoons butter; remove from heat and set aside. Prepare Scaloppine alla Marsala as directed. Just before serving, add mushrooms to wine in skillet, warm 1–2 minutes, pour over scaloppine, and serve. About 525 calories for each of 4 servings, 355 calories for each of 6 servings.

VEAL PARMIGIANA

Makes 4 servings

½ cup toasted fine bread crumbs
¼ cup finely grated Parmesan cheese
1¼ teaspoons salt
⅛ teaspoon pepper
1 pound veal round, sliced ¼" thick and pounded thin as for scaloppine
1 egg, lightly beaten
⅓ cup olive oil
2 cups Italian Tomato Sauce or 1 (15½-ounce) jar meatless spaghetti or pizza sauce
½ pound mozzarella cheese, coarsely grated

Preheat oven to 375° F. Mix crumbs, Parmesan, salt, and pepper. Dip veal in egg, then in crumbs to coat evenly (pat crumbs onto veal so they stick firmly). Arrange veal on a wire rack and let dry 10–12 minutes so coating will adhere during cooking. Heat oil in a large, heavy skillet over moderately high heat about 1 minute, add half of veal, and brown 1–1½ minutes on a side; drain on paper toweling. Brown remaining veal the same way. Arrange veal in a single layer in an ungreased shallow 2-quart casserole or au gratin pan, top with sauce and mozzarella. Bake, uncovered, ½ hour until cheese melts and sauce is bubbly. Serve with a crisp romaine salad, chunks of hot garlic bread, and chianti. About 475 calories per serving.

SALTIMBOCCA

Prosciutto is very salty, making additional salt in the recipe unnecessary.
Makes 4–6 servings

2 pounds veal round, sliced ¼" thick and pounded thin as for scaloppine
¼ pound prosciutto ham, sliced paper thin
2 tablespoons minced fresh sage or 1 teaspoon dried sage
⅛ teaspoon pepper
3–4 tablespoons butter or margarine
¼ cup dry white wine

Veal slices should be about 4"×4"; if extra long, halve crosswise. Trim *prosciutto* slices so they're roughly the same size. Sprinkle 1 side of each veal slice with sage and pepper; top with *prosciutto* slice and toothpick in place. Melt butter in a large skillet over moderately high heat and brown veal quickly on both sides. Transfer to a heated platter, remove toothpicks, and keep warm. Add wine to skillet, let boil, uncovered, 1–2 minutes, scraping with a wooden spoon to get up any brown bits; pour over veal and serve. About 515 calories for each of 4 servings, 345 calories for each of 6 servings.

BOCCONCINI (ITALIAN BRAISED VEAL AND CHEESE)

Makes 4 servings

1½ pounds veal round, sliced ¼" thick and pounded thin as for scaloppine
½ pound Swiss cheese
½ teaspoon minced fresh sage or ¼ teaspoon dried sage
⅛ teaspoon pepper
2 tablespoons butter or margarine
¼ cup dry white wine
1 tablespoon lemon juice
½ teaspoon salt

Halve veal slices lengthwise; cut thin strips of cheese about ½" smaller all round than veal, lay one strip on each veal slice, roll jelly-roll style, and secure with toothpicks. Place rolls in a piepan, sprinkle with sage and pepper, cover, and chill several hours. Melt butter in a large, heavy skillet over moderate heat, add veal rolls, and brown well on all sides, about 5–10 minutes. Add remaining ingredients, cover and simmer 18–20 minutes until veal is tender. Serve with a generous ladling of pan juices. About 530 calories per serving.

VEAL AND PEPPERS

Makes 4–6 servings

2 pounds veal round, sliced ¼" thick and pounded thin as for scaloppine
¼ cup olive oil
2 tablespoons minced shallots
1 medium-size yellow onion, peeled and minced
1 clove garlic, peeled and crushed
¾ cup dry white wine
1½ teaspoons minced fresh sage or ¼ teaspoon dried sage
½ teaspoon minced fresh marjoram or ¼ teaspoon dried marjoram
2 medium-size sweet green peppers, cored, seeded, and cut lengthwise in strips 1" wide
Juice of ½ lemon
1 teaspoon salt
⅛ teaspoon pepper

Cut veal crosswise into strips 1½" wide. Heat oil in a large, heavy skillet over moderately high heat 1 minute, add veal, and brown as quickly as possible. Remove from skillet and set aside. Reduce heat to moderate, mix in shallots, onion, and garlic, and stir-fry about 8 minutes or until golden. Return veal to skillet, stir in remaining ingredients, cover, and simmer 12–15 minutes until tender. Serve with boiled rice. About 565 calories for each of 4 servings

(without rice), 380 calories for each of 6 servings.

VEAL BIRDS

Makes 4 servings

1½ pounds veal round, sliced ¼" thick and pounded thin as for scaloppine
1 teaspoon salt
⅛ teaspoon pepper
2 tablespoons butter or margarine
½ cup chicken broth or dry red or white wine
½ cup beef broth
1 tablespoon flour blended with 1 tablespoon cold water

Stuffing:
2 slices bacon
1 medium-size yellow onion, peeled and minced
1 clove garlic, peeled and crushed (optional)
¼ pound mushrooms, wiped clean and chopped fine
1 cup soft white bread crumbs
1 tablespoon minced parsley
¼ teaspoon basil

Prepare stuffing first: Brown bacon in a small skillet over moderate heat, remove, crumble, and reserve. Sauté onion and, if you like, garlic in drippings 5–8 minutes until pale golden, add mushrooms and sauté 2–3 minutes longer. Off heat mix in bacon and remaining stuffing ingredients. Cut veal into slices that measure about 3"×5".

Sprinkle one side of veal slices with salt and pepper, place a small dab of stuffing in center of each, roll, and secure with toothpicks. Brown rolls, ½ at a time, in butter in a large skillet or flameproof casserole over moderately high heat 5–10 minutes. Add chicken broth, cover, and simmer over low heat or in a preheated 350° F.

oven 20–25 minutes until veal is tender. Transfer rolls to a deep dish and keep warm. Add beef broth and flour paste to skillet liquid and heat, stirring, until thickened. Pour over rolls and serve. About 430 calories per serving.

VARIATIONS:

Veal Birds in Wine-Cream Sauce: Stuff, roll, and brown veal birds as directed. Add ½ cup dry sherry, Madeira, or apple cider, cover, and simmer until tender. Remove rolls to a deep platter and keep warm. Quickly boil down pan liquid to ¼ cup, smooth in ½ cup heavy cream, and heat 1–2 minutes. Pour over veal and serve. About 555 calories per serving.

Veal Birds "in the Soup": Stuff, roll, and brown veal birds as directed. Add 1 (10½-ounce) can condensed cheese, cream of mushroom, chicken, celery, or tomato soup thinned with ⅓ cup milk, cover, simmer until tender, and serve. About 530 calories per serving.

Ham- and Dill-Stuffed Veal Birds: Reduce bread crumbs in stuffing mixture to ½ cup and add ½ cup minced ham and ¼ teaspoon thyme. *Spread* each veal slice with a little stuffing, add 1 long, slim dill pickle wedge, then roll and cook as directed. About 450 calories per serving.

Veal Birds Stuffed with Anchovies and Olives: Omit mushrooms from stuffing mixture and add 6–8 minced anchovy fillets and ¼ cup minced pimiento-stuffed olives. Do not salt or pepper veal slices; spread each with 1 tablespoon anchovy paste, add a dab of stuffing, then roll and cook as directed. Garnish with lemon slices and capers. About 450 calories per serving.

Russian Veal Birds (Bytky): Sauté ¼ pound ground lean pork along with onion; omit garlic and mushrooms from stuffing. Stuff, roll, and brown birds as directed; remove from skillet. Sauté ½ pound thinly sliced mushrooms in drippings 3–5 minutes, return birds to skillet, add chicken broth, and simmer as directed. Remove birds to a deep platter and keep warm. Smooth 1 cup sour cream and 1 tablespoon Worcestershire sauce into skillet, warm (but do not boil) 1–2 minutes, pour over birds, and serve. About 630 calories per serving.

Prosciutto-Stuffed Veal Birds with Avocado: Omit stuffing and do not salt or pepper veal slices; spread each with 1 teaspoon prepared spicy brown mustard, cover with trimmed-to-size slices *prosciutto,* then roll and cook as directed. Transfer rolls to a deep dish and keep warm. Blend ½ cup heavy cream into pan liquid and add 1 thinly sliced, peeled, and pitted *firm* avocado. Warm gently 1–2 minutes, pour around veal, garnish with sieved hard-cooked egg yolk and serve. About 580 calories per serving.

VEAL BIRDS WITH CHICKEN LIVER STUFFING

Makes 4 servings

1½ pounds veal round, sliced ¼"
*   thick and pounded thin as for*
*   scaloppine*
2 tablespoons butter or margarine
1 (13¾-ounce) can chicken broth
1 tablespoon flour blended with 1
*   tablespoon cold water*
1 cup sour cream (at room
*   temperature)*
¼ cup toasted slivered almonds

Stuffing:

½ *pound chicken livers*
¼ *cup unsifted flour*
1 *medium-size yellow onion, peeled
   and minced*
1 *clove garlic, peeled and crushed*
2 *tablespoons butter or margarine*
¾ *cup soft white bread crumbs*
¼ *teaspoon sage*
¼ *teaspoon thyme*
1 *teaspoon salt*
⅛ *teaspoon pepper*
1 *tablespoon minced parsley*
1 *egg, lightly beaten*

Prepare stuffing first: Dredge livers
in flour and sauté with onion
and garlic in butter over moderately
high heat 5 minutes; turn heat
to low and cook 1–2 minutes longer.
Cool slightly, chop livers medium
fine, and return to skillet; mix in
remaining stuffing ingredients.
Place a small amount of stuffing
in center of each veal slice, roll,
and secure with toothpicks. Brown
rolls, half at a time, in butter
in a large skillet over moderately
high heat, add broth, cover, and
simmer 20–25 minutes until tender.
Lift rolls to a shallow casserole and
keep warm. Blend flour paste
into skillet liquid and heat, stirring,
until thickened. Smooth in sour
cream, warm 1–2 minutes, and
pour over veal. Sprinkle with almonds and serve. About 720
calories per serving.

VEAL CUTLETS OSCAR

Makes 4 servings

4 *veal cutlets, cut ½″ thick*
4 *tablespoons butter or margarine*
1 *teaspoon salt*
⅛ *teaspoon pepper*
⅓ *cup dry white wine*
½ *pound fresh lump or backfin crab
   meat, carefully picked over*
½ *recipe Buttered Asparagus Tips*
1 *recipe Béarnaise Sauce*

Brown cutlets, half at a time, in 2
tablespoons butter in a large,
heavy skillet over moderately high
heat 5–10 minutes. Sprinkle with
salt and pepper, add wine, cover,
and simmer about 20 minutes
until tender. In a separate small
skillet, sauté crab in remaining
butter 3–4 minutes (do not
brown). Arrange veal on platter
and spoon crab over each cutlet.
Pour veal cooking liquid into crab
skillet and boil rapidly, uncovered,
to reduce to ¼ cup; pour over
crab. Top each portion with a few
asparagus tips and arrange rest
around platter. Drizzle with
Béarnaise and pass the rest. Good
with Château Potatoes.

VARIATION:

Veal Cutlets with Lobster: Prepare
as directed, substituting lobster for
crab.

Both versions: About 480 calories
per serving.

⚖ TERRINE OF VEAL AND HAM

Makes 4–6 servings

1 *pound veal round, sliced ¼″ thick
   and pounded thin as for scaloppine*
1 *teaspoon salt*
¼ *teaspoon pepper*
4 *scallions, minced*
6 *ounces lean boiled ham, sliced ⅛″
   thick*
1¾ *cups fat-free chicken broth
   (about)*
1 *envelope unflavored gelatin*
¼ *cup cold water*

Preheat oven to 325° F. Cover
bottom of a 9″ piepan with one
layer of veal slices fitted as close
together as possible and trimmed as
needed so they don't overlap;
sprinkle lightly with salt, pepper,
and scallions and top with one

layer of ham. Continue building up layers until all meat is used up. Pour in ⅔ cup chicken broth, cover with foil, and bake about 1 hour until veal is tender.

Remove from oven and weight meat down with a very heavy plate so that layers will stick together, forming a single circle; cool to room temperature. Carefully drain broth from pan and strain through cheesecloth; add enough additional broth to measure 1¾ cups.

Mix gelatin and water in a small saucepan and heat and stir over low heat until gelatin dissolves; stir into broth. Pour a ¼″ layer of broth aspic in a *clean* 9″ piepan and chill until almost firm. (If you like, arrange a decorative layer of carrot, radish, pimiento, or egg white cutouts on top and seal with a thin layer of aspic; chill again until tacky.)

Carefully slide veal-ham circle onto gelatin so that it is centered and cover with remaining aspic. Chill several hours until firm. To serve, unmold on a bed of greens and cut into wedges as you would a pie. Pass Mustard Mayonnaise Sauce or any creamy dressing. About 305 calories for each of 4 servings, 205 calories for each of 6 servings (without sauce).

GROUND VEAL

The logical cuts to grind are the sinewy, economical ones—*flank, breast, shank,* and *neck*—though some people insist upon the lean delicacy of shoulder (at half again the price). Ground veal does not make very good loaves or patties—too lean—and will be better if mixed ½ and ½ or 2 to 1 with ground pork, beef, lamb, or sausage meat or if mixed with enough vegetables or liquid to keep it moist. Once through the grinder is usually enough for veal unless you want extra-firm loaves or patties. In that case, have it ground twice.

A popular item in many supermarkets is something called *mock chicken legs,* ground veal shaped into a "drumstick" around a wooden skewer. Braised or panfried, these taste very much like chicken. Also popular are *choplets,* ground veal shaped like very thin loin chops (they're best panfried like Cube Steaks).

SAVORY VEAL AND VEGETABLE BURGERS

Makes 4 servings

1 pound ground veal
½ pound ground pork
1 small yellow onion, peeled and grated
1 carrot, peeled, parboiled, and grated
1½ teaspoons salt
¼ teaspoon pepper
2 teaspoons Worcestershire sauce
2 tablespoons butter or margarine
⅓ cup beef broth
1 tablespoon tomato paste

Mix all but last 3 ingredients and shape into 4 burgers about 1″ thick. Brown both sides well in butter in a heavy skillet over moderately high heat, about 5–7 minutes altogether. Turn heat to low, add broth mixed with tomato paste, cover, and simmer 15–20 minutes, basting every 5 minutes, until cooked through. Serve topped with skillet gravy. About 345 calories per serving.

VARIATIONS:

Veal and Mushroom Burgers: When
mixing burgers, omit grated onion
and add 1 small minced onion
and ¼ pound chopped mushrooms
sautéed in 2 tablespoons butter
until limp. Shape and cook burgers
as directed. Just before serving,
add ¼ pound sliced sautéed
mushrooms to gravy and warm
1–2 minutes. About 410 calories
per serving.

Almond-Veal Burgers: Add ½ cup
coarsely chopped toasted almonds
to burger mixture; proceed as recipe
directs. Smooth ½ cup sour cream
into gravy just before serving.
About 510 calories per serving.

LEMON VEAL LOAF

Makes 6–8 servings

5 slices firm-textured white bread
¾ cup milk
2½ pounds ground veal
1 medium-size yellow onion, peeled
and minced
2 eggs
1 cup sour cream
1 tablespoon minced parsley
1 tablespoon minced fresh dill or 1
teaspoon dried dill
1 tablespoon minced capers
1 teaspoon finely grated lemon rind
¼ teaspoon thyme
¼ teaspoon salt
⅛ teaspoon pepper

Preheat oven to 350° F. Let bread
soak in milk 10 minutes. Mix all
ingredients together well and pat
into a lightly greased 9"×5"×3"
loaf pan. Bake, uncovered, 1
hour; drain off drippings. Let loaf
cool in its pan 15–20 minutes
before slicing. Serve warm or chill
and serve cold. Especially good with
Lemon Sauce or Sour Cream-
Horseradish Sauce. About 485

calories for each of 6 servings,
365 calories for each of 8 servings.

VIENNESE VEAL LOAF

Ground veal, pork, and ham make
this loaf moist and flavorful.
Makes 8–10 servings

2 pounds veal, ground twice
1 pound lean pork, ground twice
¾ pound lean cooked ham, ground
fine
2 large yellow onions, peeled and
minced
18 soda crackers, rolled to fine
crumbs (about 1½ cups)
2 teaspoons salt
1 teaspoon white pepper
1½ teaspoons poultry seasoning
1 tablespoon Worcestershire sauce
2 eggs, lightly beaten

Preheat oven to 375° F. Using
your hands, mix all ingredients
together well and shape in a shallow,
lightly greased roasting pan into a
loaf about 9"×3". Bake, uncovered,
about 1¾ hours or until a knife
inserted in center of loaf comes out
clean. (*Note:* If loaf seems to
brown too fast, cover with foil.
Transfer loaf to a heated platter,
cover loosely with foil, and let
"rest" 10 minutes before slicing.)
If you wish, make Pan Gravy with
the drippings or Mushroom Gravy.
About 520 calories for each of 8
servings, 415 calories for each of
10 servings.

VEAL LOAF STUFFED WITH
EGGS

Makes 6–8 servings

2 pounds ground veal
¼ pound ground very fat pork
¾ cup soft white bread crumbs
2 teaspoons salt
¼ teaspoon pepper
1 tablespoon finely grated lemon rind

½ cup evaporated milk
2 eggs, lightly beaten
3 large hard-cooked eggs, shelled
¼ cup melted butter, margarine, or
  bacon drippings

Preheat oven to 350° F. Mix veal, pork, crumbs, salt, pepper, lemon rind, milk, and beaten eggs thoroughly. Pack ⅓ into a greased 9″×5″×3″ loaf pan; arrange hard-cooked eggs lengthwise down center of meat mixture and pack in remaining mixture; brush lightly with butter. Bake, uncovered, basting occasionally with melted butter, 1–1¼ hours or until lightly browned and loaf pulls slightly from sides of pan. Let stand 10 minutes before inverting on platter. Serve hot with Tomato or Mustard Sauce; or serve cold with mayonnaise or suitable cold sauce (see Some Sauces, Gravies, and Seasonings for Veal). About 475 calories for each of 6 servings, 355 calories for each of 8 servings.

BUTTERMILK VEAL BALLS IN GRAVY

Makes 4–6 servings

Meat Balls:
1 pound ground veal
¼ pound ground pork
¾ cup fine dry bread crumbs
1 small yellow onion, peeled and
  grated fine (optional)
¼ cup buttermilk
1 teaspoon garlic salt
¼ teaspoon pepper
2 tablespoons bacon drippings or
  cooking oil

Gravy:
3 tablespoons flour
1 cup chicken broth
1 cup beef broth

Thoroughly mix all meat ball ingredients but bacon drippings and shape into 1″ balls. Brown balls, about half at a time, 10 minutes in drippings in a large, heavy skillet over moderate heat; remove to a bowl. For gravy, blend flour into drippings, add broths, and cook and stir until thickened. Return meat balls, cover, and simmer 15 minutes. About 390 calories for each of 4 servings, 260 calories for each of 6 servings.

VARIATIONS:

Veal Balls with Onions and Sour Cream: Prepare and brown meat balls as recipe directs; remove to a bowl. Sauté 3 thinly sliced large yellow onions in drippings 8–10 minutes until golden. Return meat balls to skillet, add 1 cup chicken broth, cover, and simmer 15 minutes. Drain pan liquid into 1 cup sour cream, whisk together, and return to skillet. Heat (but do not boil) 1–2 minutes. Serve over noodles, rice, or mashed potatoes. 525 calories for each of 4 servings (without noodles, rice, or potatoes), 350 calories for each of 6 servings.

Veal and Beef Balls (6 servings): In making balls use ¾ pound each ground veal and beef; add 1 lightly beaten egg along with all other ingredients, then shape and cook as recipe directs. About 530 calories for each of 4 servings, 355 calories for each of 6 servings.

Blue Cheese-Veal Balls: In making balls, increase buttermilk to ½ cup and add 2 ounces crumbled blue cheese; proceed as recipe directs. About 445 calories for each of 4 servings, 295 calories for each of 6 servings.

Veal and Chicken Balls: Omit pork when making balls and add 1 cup finely ground leftover cooked chicken, 2 tablespoons melted butter, and 1 lightly beaten egg; shape and brown as directed. Drain off all pan drippings, add 1 (10½-ounce) can cream of chicken soup thinned with ⅓ cup milk, cover, and simmer 15 minutes. 490 calories for each of 4 servings, 320 calories for each of 6 servings.

The Lesser Cuts of Veal
(See Veal Chart)

From these so-called "tough cuts" come some of the most famous veal dishes—blond *blanquette de veau* (a white French veal stew which the French make with *tendron*, the part of the breast containing the "false ribs" or cartilage, which cooks down to gelatinous tenderness), tomatoey brown *Marengo*, not to mention luscious Italian *Osso Buco* made with veal shanks. Hardly poor man's fare. All any of the following lesser cuts need in order to become fork tender is gentle stewing or braising in the company of liquid, vegetables, and herbs:

Fore and hind shanks
Breast and riblets
City chicken (chunks of veal shoulder on wooden skewers)
Stew meat
Neck
Brisket rolls and pieces
Heel of round

VEAL PAPRIKASH

Makes 4 servings

2 *pounds boned veal shoulder, cut in 1" cubes*
2 *tablespoons butter or margarine*
2 *medium-size yellow onions, peeled and minced*
1 *clove garlic, peeled and crushed*

2 *tablespoons paprika (the Hungarian sweet rose paprika is best)*
½ *teaspoon salt*
⅛ *teaspoon pepper*
½ *cup dry white wine*
1 *tomato, peeled, cored, seeded, and coarsely chopped*
1 *cup sour cream*

Brown veal, a few pieces at a time, in butter in a large, heavy kettle over high heat; remove to a bowl. Add onions and garlic to kettle, reduce heat to moderate, and stir-fry 8–10 minutes until golden. Return veal to kettle, mix in all remaining ingredients except sour cream, cover, and simmer slowly 1½–2 hours until veal is tender. Mix in sour cream and serve over buttered wide noodles or *Nockerln*. About 585 calories per serving (without noodles or nockerln).

WIENER (VIENNESE) GOULASH

Makes 4 servings

1½ *cups thinly sliced yellow onions*
4 *tablespoons butter, margarine, or shortening*
2 *pounds boned breast of veal, cut in 1" cubes*
2 *tablespoons paprika*
1 *teaspoon salt*
Pinch pepper
1 *cup water (about)*
1 *cup sour cream at room temperature*

Fry onions in 2 tablespoons butter 10–12 minutes over moderate heat in a heavy kettle until lightly browned; remove and set aside. Brown meat well on all sides in remaining butter over moderately high heat. Return onions to kettle and shake paprika over all to redden. Add salt, pepper, and water, cover, and simmer over very low heat 1½–2 hours until meat is tender;

add a little more water from time to time, if needed, to keep kettle from cooking dry. When meat is tender, smooth in sour cream. Serve with boiled potatoes. About 600 calories per serving (without potatoes).

BLANQUETTE DE VEAU (FRENCH WHITE VEAL STEW)

When veal stew meat is simmered without first being browned (as in a *blanquette*), it produces an ugly scum. The best preventive: Cover veal with cold water, bring to a simmer, and cook 2 minutes. Rinse veal *and* kettle well, then begin recipe.
Makes 4 servings

2 *pounds boned veal shoulder, cut in 1" cubes and blanched to remove scum (see above)*
1 *large yellow onion, peeled and stuck with 4 cloves*
1 *carrot, peeled*
1 *stalk celery*
1 *leek, trimmed of roots (optional)*
1½ *teaspoons salt*
⅛ *teaspoon white pepper*
1 *bouquet garni,* tied in cheesecloth*
1 *bay leaf*
3 *cups cold water*
2 *tablespoons butter or margarine*
3 *tablespoons flour*
2 *egg yolks, lightly beaten*
12 *small white onions, boiled*
½ *pound button mushrooms, lightly sautéed*
Pinch nutmeg
1–2 *tablespoons lemon juice*
2 *teaspoons minced parsley*

Place veal, vegetables, all seasonings, and water in a kettle, cover, and simmer slowly 1½ hours until veal is tender. Remove veal to a bowl with a slotted spoon; strain broth and discard vegetables. Rinse and

dry kettle, add butter, and melt over moderate heat, blend in flour, slowly add broth, and heat, stirring, until thickened. Return veal to kettle, cover, and simmer 5–10 minutes. Blend a little sauce into yolks, then return to kettle. Add onions and mushrooms; heat and stir 2–3 minutes but do not boil. Off heat, mix in nutmeg and lemon juice. Ladle into a deep platter and sprinkle with parsley. Good with buttered noodles. About 530 calories per serving.

For a Richer Blanquette: Add 1–2 veal knuckles to pot when making blanquette. *Or* use 1 pound veal shoulder cubes and 1½–2 pounds neck, breast, or riblets. Simmer until bones slip easily from meat; discard bones, return meat to sauce, and finish as directed. About 625 calories per serving.

BALKAN VEAL AND CHESTNUT STEW

Except for shelling the chestnuts, you'll find this unusual veal stew a breeze to prepare.
Makes 4–6 servings

2 *tablespoons butter or margarine*
2 *pounds boned veal shoulder, cut in 1" cubes*
1 *medium-size yellow onion, peeled and coarsely chopped*
1 *clove garlic, peeled and crushed*
1 *(13¾-ounce) can chicken broth*
½ *cup dry white wine*
1 *(4") sprig fresh thyme or ¼ teaspoon dried thyme*
1 *teaspoon salt*
⅛ *teaspoon pepper*
1 *pound shelled, peeled chestnuts**

Melt butter in a large, heavy kettle over moderately high heat, add veal, and brown well on all sides, 8–10 minutes. Reduce heat to moderately low, add onion and garlic, and stir-fry 5 minutes. Add all remaining ingredients except chestnuts, cover, and simmer 1 hour; add chestnuts, cover, and simmer 30 minutes longer until chestnuts and veal are tender. Serve over rice or Bulgur Pilaf with a spicy Yugoslav traminer wine or a white Greek retsina. About 670 calories for each of 4 servings, 450 calories for each of 6 servings (without rice or pilaf).

VEAL MARENGO

Makes 6 servings

3 pounds boned veal shoulder, cut in
  1½″ cubes
¾ cup unsifted flour
¼ teaspoon pepper
1 tablespoon plus ½ teaspoon salt
⅓ cup olive oil
2 medium-size yellow onions, peeled
  and coarsely chopped
1 clove garlic, peeled and crushed
1⅔ cups dry white wine
½ cup water
1 (6-ounce) can tomato paste
½ teaspoon thyme
½ teaspoon tarragon
½ teaspoon finely grated orange rind
½ pound button mushrooms, wiped
  clean and trimmed of coarse stems
2 tablespoons minced parsley

Preheat oven to 325° F. Dredge veal by shaking in a paper bag with flour, pepper, and 1 tablespoon salt, then brown, a few cubes at a time, in a little of the oil in a large heavy skillet over moderately high heat; add additional oil as needed. Transfer veal to a 3-quart oven-to-table casserole. Stir-fry onions and garlic in skillet 8–10 minutes until golden, add wine, water, tomato paste, thyme, tarragon, and remaining salt, and boil uncovered about 2 minutes. Mix in orange rind and pour into

casserole. Cover and bake 2 hours. (*Note:* Casserole can be prepared to this point 1–2 days ahead. Cool, cover, and refrigerate until about 3 hours before serving. Bring to room temperature before proceeding.) Mix in mushrooms, cover, and bake ½ hour at 325° F. Stir in parsley and serve with boiled rice or buttered wide noodles. About 550 calories per serving (without rice or noodles).

VEAL AND SHRIMP IN LEMON-WINE SAUCE

Makes 6 servings

3 pounds boned veal shoulder, cut in
  1″ cubes
3 cups boiling water
1¼ teaspoons salt
2 medium-size yellow onions, peeled
  and sliced thin
2 carrots, peeled and sliced thin
3 sprigs parsley
1 sprig dill
Rind of 1 lemon cut in long strips
  (use a vegetable peeler)
3 tablespoons butter or margarine
3 tablespoons flour
Juice of ½ lemon
3 tablespoons dry vermouth
⅛ teaspoon white pepper
¼ teaspoon cardamom
1 pound small shrimp, boiled,
  shelled, and deveined
1 medium-size cauliflower, divided
  into flowerets, boiled, and drained
  (it should be hot)

Simmer veal in salted boiling water 2–3 minutes; strain stock and set veal aside. Rinse kettle well, return veal and stock.

Add vegetables, parsley, dill, and lemon rind, cover, and simmer slowly 1½ hours until veal is tender. Remove veal; strain stock and discard vegetables. In the same kettle, melt butter over moderate heat, blend in flour, add stock, and heat, stirring, until thickened. Add lemon juice, vermouth, pepper, and cardamom and let boil, uncovered, about 5 minutes to reduce slightly. Turn heat to low, add veal and shrimp, and simmer, covered, 10–15 minutes to blend flavors.

To serve, mound cauliflower in center of a platter and top with veal, shrimp, and plenty of sauce. About 535 calories per serving.

VEAL RIBLETS PARMIGIANA

Makes 4 servings

3–3½ pounds veal riblets
¼ cup unsifted flour
3 tablespoons olive or other cooking oil
½ teaspoon salt
¼ teaspoon pepper
⅛ teaspoon garlic powder
1 (15-ounce) can tomato sauce
⅓ cup beef broth
3 tablespoons finely grated Parmesan cheese
¼ pound mozzarella cheese, coarsely grated or thinly sliced

Preheat oven to 350° F. Dredge riblets in flour and brown, a few at a time, in oil in a large skillet over moderately high heat. Transfer to an ungreased 2½-quart casserole, sprinkle with salt, pepper, and garlic powder. Drain all but 1 tablespoon oil from skillet, add tomato sauce and broth, stir to scrape up brown bits, and pour over riblets. Sprinkle with Parmesan, cover, and bake about 1 hour until riblets are tender. Uncover, scatter mozzarella on top, and broil 4″ from heat 2–3 minutes until cheese melts and is speckled with brown. Serve with Polenta or buttered noodles.

About 530 calories per serving (without Polenta or noodles).

BRAISED VEAL RIBLETS

Makes 4 servings

3–3½ pounds veal riblets
¼ cup unsifted flour
2 tablespoons butter or margarine
1 tablespoon cooking oil
2 tablespoons flour
1 cup beef broth
1 cup cold water
¾ teaspoon salt
⅛ teaspoon pepper
1 large yellow onion, peeled and sliced thin
1 pound carrots, peeled and cut in 2″ chunks (optional)
¼ teaspoon grated lemon rind
1 teaspoon minced parsley

Dredge riblets in flour and brown, a few at a time, in butter and oil in a heavy kettle over moderately high heat; drain on paper toweling. Blend 2 tablespoons flour into drippings, slowly add broth and water, stirring until smooth. Return meat to kettle, season with salt and pepper, add onion and carrots. Cover and simmer 1 hour until veal is tender; check liquid from time to time and add a little water if necessary. Just before serving, stir in lemon and parsley. Serve with crusty bread or mashed potatoes. About 430 calories per serving (made without carrots), about 470 calories per serving (made with carrots).

OSSO BUCO (ITALIAN-STYLE BRAISED VEAL SHANKS)

Osso buco owes its unique flavor to gremolata, a mixture of lemon rind, parsley and garlic added just before serving.
Makes 4 servings

4 *pounds veal shanks, cut in 3"*
   lengths
½ *cup unsifted flour*
1 *tablespoon salt*
¼ *teaspoon pepper*
⅓ *cup olive oil*
2 *cloves garlic, peeled and crushed*
1 *medium-size yellow onion, peeled*
   and minced
2 *large carrots, peeled and cut in*
   small dice
1 *stalk celery, chopped fine*
½ *cup dry white wine*
1 *(13¾-ounce) can chicken broth*
1 *tablespoon minced fresh basil or*
   1 teaspoon dried basil
1 *bay leaf, crumbled*
Pinch thyme

Gremolata:
1 *tablespoon minced parsley*
2 *teaspoons finely grated lemon rind*
1 *clove garlic, peeled and minced*

Dredge veal by shaking in a heavy
paper bag with flour, salt, and
pepper, then brown in oil, a few
pieces at a time; remove and
reserve. Add garlic, onion, carrots,
and celery to kettle and sauté
5–8 minutes until pale golden. Add
wine and boil rapidly, uncovered,
4–5 minutes until reduced by half.
Return veal to kettle, arranging so
marrow cannot fall out, and add all
remaining ingredients except gremolata. Cover and simmer 1¼–1½
hours until veal is tender but not
falling off the bones. Mix gremolata
and sprinkle over shanks, cover,
and simmer 5–10 minutes longer.
Serve, spooning vegetables and
cooking liquid over veal. Or, if
you prefer, purée vegetables and
cooking liquid until smooth; spoon a
little over veal and pass the rest in a
sauceboat. Risotto alla Milanese
is the traditional accompaniment.
About 930 calories per serving.

VARIATION:

**Braised Veal Shanks with Tomato
Sauce:** Prepare recipe as directed,
reducing amount of chicken broth to
½ cup and adding, at the same
time, 1 (1-pound) undrained can
tomatoes. About 950 calories per
serving.

LAMB AND MUTTON

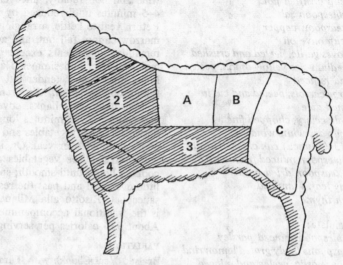

Note: Unshaded parts are the tender cuts. Shaded parts are not-so-tender.

THE TENDER CUTS:
  A. RIB
     Roasts (rib, crown)
     Chops (rib, Frenched rib)
  B. LOIN
     Roasts (loin, double loin)
     Chops (loin, kidney or English)
  C. LEG
     Leg of lamb or mutton
     Leg chop or steak
     Cubes for kebabs

THE NOT-SO-TENDER CUTS:
  1. NECK
     Neck slices
  2. SHOULDER
     Roasts (rolled, cushion, square
        shoulder)
     Chops (blade, arm)
     Stew lamb or mutton
     Ground lamb or mutton
  3. BREAST
     Roasts for stuffing
     Riblets (stew lamb or mutton)
  4. SHANK
     Lamb or mutton shanks

Though adept at cooking beef and pork, we often approach lamb with uncertainty. Many of us don't like it (or think we don't), perhaps because cookbooks have for years insisted that lamb be cooked well done. Not true. Anyone who has tasted baby lamb roasted the French way—until juicily pink and not an instant longer—is quickly converted. How delicate this lamb is, and how delicious. Almost every foreign country prizes lamb as highly (or more highly) than beef, not surprising when you consider that lamb (or one of its early ancestors) was man's first meat.

Technically, lamb is a young sheep under 1 year of age. *Baby or milk-fed lamb* is 6–8 weeks old, *"spring" lamb* 3–5 months old, and *lamb* 6 months to 1 year. When lamb reaches its first birthday, it becomes *yearling mutton;* at age 2, it's full-scale *mutton. Pré-salé lamb,* the French favorite, is lamb grazed on the *prés salés* (salt marshes) of Brittany and Normandy.

In the old days, lamb was available primarily in spring, hence the name "spring" lamb. Today, however, it is available the year round.

How to Recognize Quality

Buy top grades (USDA PRIME, CHOICE, or GOOD), also meat that has been federally inspected (found wholesome). It will have velvety-pink-to-red lean (the older the animal, the redder the meat), firm creamy fat and bones that are spongy, and red inside. Mutton is dark red with flinty bones and brittle fat.

About the Fell: The outer fat of lamb has a thin, papery covering called the *fell,* which has caused some controversy. Should it be removed before cooking? Some gourmet cooks say yes, because it gives even youngest lamb a strong flavor. Others say it should be left on legs of lamb because it helps them hold their shape during roasting, seals in juices, and speeds cooking. We've tried both ways and can't see enough difference to justify the fuss. On other cuts of lamb, especially small ones, peel the fell off *before* cooking.

About the Musk Glands: Buried in the leg of lamb (near the hock joint) and in the shoulder are large, yellowish "musk" glands (so called because people once thought they gave lamb a musky off-flavor). They don't, but they *are* conspicuous, particularly in young lamb, so most butchers routinely remove them. If your butcher hasn't, simply snip them out yourself.

A Word About the Cuts of Lamb and Mutton: They are the same in both animals, the only real difference being that in mutton they're larger, less tender (especially neck, leg, breast, and other well-exercised muscles), and more strongly flavored. The majority of recipes in this book call for lamb simply because American preferences are for it, but mutton can be substituted in any of the recipes that are braised or stewed.

Roast Lamb

LEG: The most popular Lamb roast and one of the most expensive, leg of lamb is cut the following ways:
Full (whole) leg (6–10 pounds)
Sirloin half of leg (4–5 pounds)
Shank half of leg (3–5 pounds)
Center leg (3–5 pounds)
Boned and rolled leg (3–5 pounds)

LOIN AND RIB ROASTS: All are expensive and supremely tender:
Sirloin (2–2½ pounds)
Loin (2–2½ pounds)
Saddle or double loin (4–5 pounds)
Rolled double loin (3–4 pounds)
Rib or rack (2½–3 pounds)
Crown roast (rib roasts bent and tied into a circle; 6 pounds up)

SHOULDER AND BREAST: More economical but less tender:
Square shoulder (4–6 pounds)
Precarved shoulder (a trimmed shoulder, cut into chops and tied

back into original shape; about
5 pounds)
Cushion shoulder (the one to stuff;
3–5 pounds)
Rolled shoulder (3–5 pounds)
Breast (1½–2 pounds)
Boned and rolled breast (also good
to stuff; 1½ pounds)

How to Roast Lamb

People are of many minds about
the best way to roast lamb. Some
prefer a constant low temperature,
some a constant moderately high
temperature, others a combination
of high and low, which is the French
way. Still others treat each cut
differently: baby lamb, they say, is
best roasted fast at a very high
temperature, spring lamb at a lower
one. Here are the three most popular
methods and the preferred cuts
for each.

(*Note:* Meat thermometers (many
cookbooks, too) still advise
cooking lamb to 170° F. or 180° F.,
but at those temperatures it will
be depressingly gray and dry. For
those who like it juicily pink,
140–45° F. is just about perfect.
Some, of course, prefer it really
rare (130–35° F.), others more
well done. Try cooking a lamb
roast to one of the lower temperatures; if it isn't to your liking, roast
a bit longer.) Always let roast "rest"
15–20 minutes before carving so
juices have a chance to settle.

Cooking times given here can
only be approximate, since shape of
cut, proportion of fat and bone,
internal temperature at time of
roasting all affect over-all time.
The truest test of doneness is the
meat thermometer.

Amount Needed: Allow ⅓–½ pound

boned lamb per serving, ½–¾
pound bone-in lamb.

Preparation for Cooking: Legs
need none (unless you elect to remove the fell); shoulders and loin
should have the fell peeled off
and fat trimmed to ⅛". Let
roast stand at room temperature
1½–2 hours if convenient. Rub,
if you like, with salt and pepper
(salt only penetrates ¼" so it really
doesn't matter whether roast
is salted before cooking or not).

To Give Roast Extra Flavor:

– Rub with 1 of the following: 2
tablespoons curry powder or Dijon-
style mustard; 1 teaspoon marjoram,
thyme, rosemary, summer savory,
or dill.
– Make tiny slits over surface of
fat and insert thin garlic slivers
in each, or crushed mint, sage, or
basil leaves.
– Mix ¼ cup mild yellow mustard
with 2 tablespoons soy sauce,
2 crushed cloves garlic, 1 tablespoon
sugar, and ¼ teaspoon ginger; spread
over roast.
– Marinate roast 24 hours in refrigerator in dry red wine, Teriyaki
Sauce, All-Purpose Barbecue Sauce,
or other aromatic marinade,
turning occasionally. Drain and
roast as directed, basting often
with marinade during last ½ hour.

Continuous Low Heat Method
(for leg of lamb, loin, saddle, and
boneless roasts): Preheat oven to
325° F. Place roast fat side up
on a rack in a shallow roasting
pan (loin and rib roasts usually
don't need racks because ribs hold
them out of drippings). Insert meat
thermometer in center of largest lean
muscle, not touching bone. If
roast is small, insert very carefully
on an angle so that thermometer is

secure. Do not add water, do not cover. Roast, without basting, as follows: 12–13 minutes per pound for rare (130–35° F.), 14–16 for medium rare (140–45° F.), 18–20 for medium (150–60° F.), and, if you must have it well done, 20–25 minutes per pound (160–65° F.). (*Note:* Boneless roasts, also small (3–4-pound) roasts, will take *slightly* (3–5 minutes) longer per pound for each degree of doneness.) Let roast "rest" 15–20 minutes before carving.

Continuous Moderately High Temperature (good for all but baby lamb): Preheat oven to 375° F. Place roast in pan and insert thermometer as above. Do not cover, do not add liquid. Roast, without basting, 11–13 minutes per pound for rare (130–35° F.), 13–15 for medium rare (140–45° F.), 16–18 for medium (150–60° F.), 18–20 for well done (160–65° F.), and about 3 minutes longer per pound for boneless roasts for each degree of doneness. Let roast "rest" 15–20 minutes before carving.

Searing (French) Method (good for all cuts): Preheat oven to 450° F. Place roast in pan and insert thermometer as above; do not cover or add liquid. Sear 15 minutes, reduce heat to 350° F. and roast, without basting, 10–12 minutes per pound for rare (130–35° F.), 12–14 for medium rare (140–45° F.), 14–16 for medium (150–60° F.), 16–18 for well done (160–65° F.), and slightly longer per pound for each degree of doneness for boneless roasts. Let "rest" before carving.

About Baby Lamb: Because baby lamb is so delicate and tender, it's best roasted quickly in a very hot oven, 450° F. Place fat side up on a rack, insert meat thermometer, do not add water, and do not cover. Roast 10–15 minutes per pound until medium rare (140–45° F.). It's most succulent and flavorful at this temperature and should not be served more well done.

About Mutton: Loin, rack, and leg are the best cuts to roast, and searing is the best method. Follow directions for lamb above.

Some Glazes for Roast Lamb

Half an hour before roast is done, spread or drizzle any of the following over surface and continue cooking as directed, basting every 10 minutes.
– ½ cup melted mint, apple, grape, or red currant jelly.
– ½ cup warmed orange or lime marmalade.
– ½ cup minced chutney heated with ½ cup apple juice, red wine, or water.
– ¼ cup mint, apple, grape, or red currant jelly heated with ¼ cup honey or firmly packed light brown sugar and ⅛ teaspoon each nutmeg and cinnamon.
– ¼ cup firmly packed light brown sugar and ¼ teaspoon cinnamon heated in 1 cup apple juice or cider until dissolved.
– ½ cup chili sauce mixed with ¼ cup cider vinegar and 1 teaspoon chili powder.

Some Easy Variations on Oven-Roasted Lamb

À la Bordelaise (for large roasts cooked by Continuous Low Heat Method): For each person, place ⅓ cup potato balls in pan with lamb, drizzle with 3–4 tablespoons oil or melted butter, and roast, uncovered, 40 minutes, turning balls occasionally. Add 6–8 button mushrooms for each person, toss with potatoes, and continue roasting 15–20 minutes until meat is done. Garnish meat with drained vegetables, then sprinkle with the following: ¼ cup soft white bread crumbs that have been sautéed in 2 tablespoons butter with 1 crushed clove garlic and 1 tablespoon minced parsley.

À la Boulangère (for large roasts cooked by Continuous Low Heat Method): Begin roasting lamb as directed; meanwhile, stir-fry 2 cups coarsely chopped yellow onion in ¼ cup butter over moderate heat until pale golden; sprinkle with ½ teaspoon salt and ⅛ teaspoon pepper. When roast has only ¾ hour more to cook, take from oven and lift from pan, rack and all. Make a bed of onions in pan, place roast on top, and continue roasting to desired doneness. When serving, spoon some onions on top of roast and wreathe the rest around platter. Pass Pan Gravy.

À la Bretonne: Roast lamb by one of the methods above and serve with 1 recipe Boiled Dried White Beans, cooked as directed, but with the following changes: to the pot add 1 large yellow onion, peeled and stuck with 3 cloves, 2 peeled cloves garlic, 2 bay leaves, and 2 parsley sprigs. When beans are tender, drain, remove onion, garlic, bay leaves, and parsley and toss with 3 tablespoons melted butter, 1 crushed clove garlic, 2–3 tablespoons lamb drippings, and 1 tablespoon each tomato paste and minced parsley. Lamb can be wreathed with the beans or the two can be served separately.

À la Provençale: Buy a large, full leg of lamb, make tiny slits over surface, and tuck in anchovy fillets and thin garlic slivers; rub well with summer savory and thyme and let stand at room temperature 3 hours. Roast by one of the methods above but baste often with 1½ cups lamb stock or beef broth mixed with ½ cup each melted butter and dry vermouth. While roast "rests," boil pan drippings and any remaining basting mixture 3–5 minutes to reduce, stir in 2 tablespoons minced parsley, and pour into a sauceboat. Accompany roast with Boiled Dried White Beans dressed with olive oil and garlic.

Arni Psito (Greek-Style Roast Lamb): Make small slits over surface of roast and tuck in thin garlic slivers (use 3 cloves garlic in all). Brush roast with 2 tablespoons olive oil or melted butter and drizzle with the juice of 2 lemons. Roast by one of the methods above and, when half done, add 2 cups boiling water to pan, 1 teaspoon salt, ⅛ teaspoon pepper. Continue roasting uncovered until tender. Skim pan liquid of fat and serve over lamb as sauce.

Neapolitan Roast Lamb: Make small slits over surface of roast and tuck in thin garlic slivers (use 3 cloves). Marinate lamb 24 hours in refrigerator in 2 cups dry red or white wine mixed with 1 minced small yellow onion, 2 tablespoons finely grated lemon rind, and 1½ teaspoons powdered rosemary. Lift meat from marinade, brush with 2 tablespoons olive oil, and roast as directed, basting often with strained marinade. Use marinade in making Pan Gravy.

Roast Lamb Bonne Femme: Choose a large, full leg of lamb and place in pan as directed. For each person add to pan: 1 halved, peeled medium-size potato and 3 peeled small white onions drizzled with ¼ cup oil or melted bacon drippings. Sprinkle with 1 teaspoon salt and ⅛ teaspoon pepper and roast, uncovered, turning once or twice. These will take 1–1¼ hours to cook, so gauge accordingly. Drain on paper toweling and wreathe around roast on platter.

Roast Lamb in Buttermilk (for roasts cooked by Continuous Low Heat Method): Marinate roast in 1 quart buttermilk and 1 cup minced yellow onion 24 hours in refrigerator, turning occasionally. Transfer to roasting pan, strain buttermilk over lamb, and roast as directed, basting every half hour. If pan boils dry, add a little more buttermilk or boiling water.

Oven-Barbecued Roast Lamb: Marinate lamb in All-Purpose Barbecue Sauce 24 hours in refrigerator, turning occasionally. Lift from marinade and roast by one of the basic methods, basting every 15 minutes with barbecue sauce.

Roast Lamb with Dill-Crumb Topping: Roast lamb by one of the basic methods and about ½ hour before it is done, remove from oven and brush with 1 tablespoon melted butter; then pat on: 2 cups fine soft bread crumbs tossed with 2 tablespoons each minced dill, parsley, and melted butter, 1 crushed clove garlic, and ¼ teaspoon pepper. Return to oven and roast, uncovered, to desired doneness.

Taverna-Style Roast Leg of Lamb: Choose a 5–6-pound short leg of lamb and trim off all outer covering of fat. Rub well with the juice of 1 lemon. Make tiny slits over surface and tuck in thin garlic slivers (use 2 cloves). Mix together 2 finely crumbled bay leaves, 1 teaspoon thyme, and ¼ teaspoon each oregano and pepper and rub over lamb; pour the juice of 1 lemon over all. Let stand in a cool place 24 hours. Roast lamb by Continuous Moderately High Temperature method for exactly 1 hour (the roast will be quite rare). Remove from oven and let rest 15–20 minutes before serving.

How To Spit-Roast Lamb

Best Cuts: Leg, rolled shoulder, double loin, loin, saddle, or rack.

Amount Needed: The same as for Roast Lamb *but* avoid small roasts; 4–5 pounds is a good size (except for racks and loins that weigh only 2½–3).

Preparation for Cooking: The same as for oven roasting. When saddle, loin, or rack is to be spit-roasted over charcoal, have butcher leave flank on and roll up and tie.

In Rotisserie or Oven: Preheat unit. Balance roast carefully on spit: full and half legs should be skewered from butt to shank end with spit running parallel to bone; all boneless cuts are spitted lengthwise straight through the center; spit loin, rack, and saddle end to end straight through the middle so they are well balanced. Tighten holding forks. Insert meat thermometer in center of largest lean muscle, making sure it touches neither spit nor bone, also that it will not hit any part of rotisserie as it turns. The best way is to insert the thermometer on an angle or in the end of the roast. Attach spit to rotisserie and roast 5″–6″ from heat according to manufacturer's timetable or 5 minutes less per pound than recommended for lamb roasted the Continuous Low Heat Method.

Keep a close eye on the thermometer and remove lamb when it registers about 5° below desired doneness. Remove roast from spit and let "rest" 15–20 minutes before carving.

Over Charcoal: Prepare a moderate charcoal fire.* Balance meat on spit and insert thermometer as for rotisserie.

(*Note:* Saddle, loin, and rack of lamb should be roasted only where heat can be regulated by lowering or raising spit.) Attach spit to rotisserie, place drip pan in center, and push coals to the front and back of it. Roast lamb 6″–7″ from coals, using rotisserie roasting times as a guide. Check thermometer

regularly and use it as the true indicator of doneness.

VARIATIONS (*for rotisserie or charcoal spit roasting*):

– Marinate roast in All-Purpose Barbecue Sauce overnight, then spit-roast as directed, basting often with sauce during last ½ hour of cooking.

– Brush roast frequently with ¼ cup Garlic Butter mixed with 2 tablespoons olive or other oil.

– The day before roasting lamb, purée 2 large yellow onions, coarsely chopped, in an electric blender at high speed with ⅓ cup water and 2 peeled cloves garlic. Pour over roast, cover, and refrigerate 24 hours, turning often. Lift roast from marinade, scrape off excess, and

---

SAUCES, GRAVIES, AND SEASONINGS FOR ROAST LAMB

For Cooking Seasonings, Herbs, Spices		*For Hot Roasts* Gravies	Sauces
Basil	Oregano	Au jus (Un-	Brown curry
Bay Leaf	Paprika	thickened	Fresh mint
Cinnamon	Parsley	pan gravy)	Garlic
Curry powder	Rose geranium	Pan gravy	Mustard hol-
Dill	Rosemary		landaise
Garlic	Saffron		Paloise
Ginger	Sage		Périgueux
Juniper berries	Summer Savory		Poivrade
Lemon	Tarragon		Quick lemon-
Marjoram	Thyme (espe-		caper
Mint	cially wild thyme)		
Mustard	Turmeric		

For Hot or Cold Roasts Condiments	*For Cold Roasts* Sauces
Chutney	Anchovy mayonnaise
Hot mustard fruits	Cumberland
Jellies (apple, crab	Herb mayonnaise
apple, mint, red	Indienne
currant, rose	
geranium)	

rub roast with 2 tablespoons paprika (preferably the sweet rose type). Spit and roast as directed.

Some Garnishes for Roast Lamb Platters

(in addition to parsley and water-cress sprigs)

Group or wreathe around lamb roast as prettily as possible one or two of the following, selecting garnishes of contrasting color and shape:

Artichoke Bottoms: boiled and buttered; filled with puréed sweet green peas or spinach.

Asparagus Tips: boiled and but-tered.

Brussels Sprouts: boiled and buttered.

Carrots: Buttered Baby Carrots; Carrots Rosemary; Lemon-Glazed Carrots.

Endives: Braised Belgian Endives.

Fruits: broiled apricot or peach halves filled with dabs of red currant jelly.

Mushrooms: sautéed button mush-rooms; Baked Mushroom Caps Stuffed with Hazelnuts.

Onions: Glazed Onions; Pan-Braised Onions; Stuffed Onions.

Parsnips: Currant or Caramel-Glazed Parsnips; Roast Parsnips.

Potatoes: Parsleyed, Herbed, Lemon-Glazed, or Danish-Style New Potatoes.

Tomatoes: Stuffed Tomatoes.

Turnips: Glazed or Roasted Turnips; Turnips Stuffed with Risotto.

How to Carve Leg of Lamb:

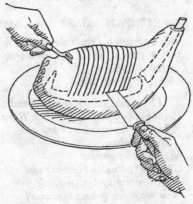

Place leg on platter so plump, meaty portion is away from carver. Cut 2–3 thin slices from near side to form a base. Stand roast on base and, beginning at shank end, cut straight down to bone. Free slices by running knife down along shank bone. Lift out and transfer to platter.

French Method

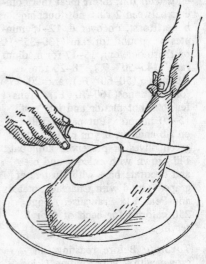

So very easy. Simply lift leg bone with hand, then with a carving knife carve the length of the leg, parallel to the bone, in thin slices.

⚜ CROWN ROAST OF LAMB

This spectacular roast deserves a fine red Bordeaux, a Médoc, perhaps, or Saint-Emilion.
Makes 6–8 servings

*1 (12–16 rib) crown roast of lamb
    (about 4–6 pounds) (Note: Have
    butcher remove backbone and
    french ribs.)
¼ teaspoon pepper
Chicory (pale inner leaves) and
    watercress sprigs (garnish)
Seedless green grapes (garnish)*

If butcher has filled crown with ground trimmings, remove (save for lamb burgers). Let roast stand at room temperature 1½–2 hours if convenient. Preheat oven to 325° F. Place roast, rib ends up, in a large, shallow roasting pan (no need for a rack) and rub with pepper. Force a large foil ball into crown so it won't cook out of shape; cover rib ends with foil; insert meat thermometer between 2 ribs, not touching bone. Roast, uncovered, 12–15 minutes per pound for rare (130–35° F. on thermometer), 15–17 for medium rare (145–50° F.), 18–20 for medium (150–60° F.), and 20–25 for well done (160–70° F.). Transfer to a hot platter and let "rest" 15–20 minutes. Put paper frills on rib ends or, if you prefer, pitted green olives or preserved kumquats. Fill crown with chicory and cress and decorate base with clusters of grapes. Good with Château Potatoes and Peas à la Française. About 250 calories for each of 6 or 8 servings.

To Stuff: Before roasting, fill crown with 2 cups stuffing (Rice and Mushroom, Pecan-Bulgur Wheat, and Herbed Bread Stuffings

are especially good). Cover stuffing loosely with foil and roast as above, allowing about 5 minutes longer per pound; uncover stuffing for last ½ hour of cooking. Calories for each of 6 servings: About 420 with Rice and Mushroom Stuffing; 445 with Pecan-Bulgur Wheat Stuffing; and 410 with Herbed Bread Stuffing. Calories for each of 8 servings: 400 with Rice and Mushroom Stuffing; 420 with Pecan-Bulgur Wheat; and 395 with Herbed Bread Stuffing.

To Carve: Separate into chops by slicing down along ribs.

VARIATION:

Crown Roast of Lamb Filled with Vegetables: Omit chicory and cress and fill crown with any of the following: buttered green peas mixed with pearl onions or sliced mushrooms or Green Peas with Mint and Orange; Rice Pilaf; Brussels Sprouts Véronique or Brussels Sprouts with Chestnuts; Puréed or Braised Chestnuts or Sautéed Mushrooms. For approximate calorie counts, add to the 250 calories per serving of the unfilled crown roast, the calories per serving given for each of the recipes listed above (see Index for page numbers).

SWEDISH-STYLE ROAST LEG OF LAMB

Could this recipe have been invented by a thrifty Swedish housewife who hated to throw out the leftover breakfast coffee? Perhaps. Although there is no pronounced coffee taste, the coffee does enrich both the color and the flavor of the lamb.
Makes 8–10 servings

*1 (6–8-pound) leg of lamb
2 teaspoons salt
¼ teaspoon pepper
1½ cups hot strong coffee*

½ cup light cream
1 tablespoon sugar
1 large carrot, peeled and coarsely
   grated
1½ cups hot water
3 tablespoons red currant jelly
2 tablespoons flour blended with ¼
   cup cold water (optional)

Preheat oven to 325° F. Rub lamb
well with salt and pepper and place
fat side up on a rack in a shallow
roasting pan; insert meat thermometer in center of leg, not
touching bone. Roast, uncovered,
using times given for Continuous
Low Heat Method as a guide. About
1 hour before roast is done, mix
coffee, cream, and sugar and pour
over lamb; sprinkle carrot into pan.
Continue roasting lamb to desired
doneness, basting frequently.
Transfer to a heated platter and let
"rest." Meanwhile, strain pan liquid
and skim off fat; combine with
water and jelly and cook and stir
about 2 minutes. Add flour paste,
if you like, and heat, stirring, until
thickened and smooth. Carve lamb
into thin slices and pass the gravy.
About 555 calories for each of 8
servings (from a 6-pound leg),
about 570 calories for each of 10
servings (8-pound leg).

ROAST LEG OF LAMB STUFFED WITH RICE, PIÑON NUTS, AND CURRANTS

Makes 6–8 servings

1 (6-pound) leg of lamb

Stuffing:
2 tablespoons olive oil
½ cup uncooked rice
1 medium-size yellow onion, peeled
   and minced
1 clove garlic, peeled and crushed
3 tablespoons minced parsley

1 tablespoon minced mint
¼ cup dried currants
½ cup piñon nuts
1 cup chicken broth
1 teaspoon salt
¼ teaspoon pepper

Ask butcher to bone leg of lamb,
leaving about 2″ of leg bone in at
the narrow end (this makes the leg
handsomer and easier to stuff).
Preheat oven to 325° F. For stuffing,
heat oil 1 minute in a saucepan
over moderately high heat, add rice,
onion, and garlic, and stir-fry 2–3
minutes until rice is golden. Mix
in remaining ingredients, cover,
and simmer 8–10 minutes until all
moisture is absorbed. Cool slightly.
Spoon stuffing into leg, then sew or
skewer cavity shut. Place leg in a
large shallow roasting pan and roast,
uncovered, 3 hours. To carve,
cut straight across in ½″ slices.
About 830 calories for each of 6
servings, 620 calories for each of
8 servings.

HERB STUFFED ROLLED LEG OF LAMB

Makes 6–8 servings

1 (6-pound) leg of lamb, boned and
   opened flat but not rolled

Stuffing:
¼ cup minced parsley
3 cloves garlic, peeled and crushed
1 tablespoon minced fresh basil or 1
   teaspoon dried basil
1 tablespoon olive oil
1 tablespoon softened butter
1 tablespoon lemon juice
1 teaspoon salt
¼ teaspoon pepper

Preheat oven to 325° F. Peel fell
from lamb and discard; spread lamb
out fat side down on counter.
Mix stuffing and spread over lamb
leaving ½″ margins; roll jelly-roll

style and tie round at 2″ intervals. Place on a rack and roast, uncovered, 3 hours. Serve as is with Pan Gravy (when making, use dry red wine for ½ the liquid) or with hot Caper Sauce. About 465 calories for each of 6 servings, 350 calories for each of 8 servings.

LEG OF LAMB BRAISED WITH ONIONS, CARROTS, AND TOMATOES

Although we don't think of leg of lamb as a cut to braise, it is savory and succulent prepared this way. The vegetables cook down into a rich, rosy gravy.
Makes 6 servings

1 (3–4-pound) half leg of lamb
2 tablespoons cooking oil
2 medium-size yellow onions, peeled and minced
2 carrots, peeled and diced
2 stalks celery, chopped fine
1 bouquet garni,* tied in cheesecloth
1 (10½-ounce) can beef bouillon
1 (1-pound) can tomatoes (do not drain)
1½ teaspoons salt
¼ teaspoon pepper

Preheat oven to 325° F. Brown lamb well in oil in a Dutch oven over moderately high heat; remove from kettle. Stir-fry onions, carrots, and celery in drippings over moderate heat 5–8 minutes until onions are pale golden; return meat to kettle, add remaining ingredients, cover, and bring to a simmer. Transfer to oven and bake, covered, 1½–2 hours until tender, basting 2–3 times. Lift meat to a hot platter; purée vegetables and drippings in an electric blender at low speed or put through a food mill. Warm gravy, taste for seasoning and adjust if needed. Pour a little gravy over meat and pass the rest. About 525 calories per serving.

VARIATION:

Braised Mutton: Substitute a half leg of mutton for lamb; prepare as directed, baking about 35–40 minutes per pound until tender. About 555 calories per serving.

SICILIAN-STYLE BRAISED LEG OF LAMB

Makes 6 servings

1 (4-pound) half leg of lamb
2 tablespoons cooking oil
2 tablespoons flour
1½ teaspoons minced fresh sage or ½ teaspoon dried sage
½ teaspoon minced fresh rosemary or ⅛ teaspoon dried rosemary
2 cloves garlic, peeled and crushed
1 teaspoon salt
¼ teaspoon pepper
½ cup red wine vinegar
½ cup hot water
3–4 anchovy fillets, minced

Preheat oven to 325° F. Brown lamb lightly all over in oil in a Dutch oven over moderately high heat. Sprinkle flour, herbs, and garlic over lamb and continue browning 2–3 minutes, turning lamb frequently. Add all remaining ingredients except anchovies, cover, and bring to a simmer. Transfer to oven and simmer, covered, 1½–2 hours until tender; baste 2–3 times. Lift meat to platter; stir anchovies into drippings and serve as a gravy. About 495 calories per serving.

ROAST STUFFED CUSHION SHOULDER OF LAMB

Makes 6–8 servings

1 (4-pound) cushion shoulder of lamb
1 teaspoon salt
⅛ teaspoon pepper
2–3 cups stuffing (Rice Pilaf, Rice and Mushroom Stuffing, Pecan-

Bulgur Wheat, Rice and Kidney, Black Olive and Onion, and Bread and Apricot Stuffing are very good, but prepared packaged stuffing may also be used)

Preheat oven to 325° F. Skewer all but one side of roast shut, sprinkle pocket with salt and pepper, stuff loosely, and close with skewers. Place roast fat side up on a rack in a shallow roasting pan and roast, uncovered, about 2 hours until tender. Lift meat from pan and let "rest" 15–20 minutes before serving. To carve, cut across the grain in slices ½" thick. Serve with Au Jus or Pan Gravy. (*Note:* For an extra-special touch, glaze roast during last ½ hour of cooking [see Some Glazes for Roast Lamb].) Approximate calories for each of 6 servings: about 850 if made with Rice Pilaf; 805 with Rice and Mushroom Stuffing; 835 with Pecan-Bulgur Wheat Stuffing; 825 with Rice and Kidney Stuffing; 815 with Black Olive and Onion Stuffing; and 845 with Bread and Apricot Stuffing. Approximate calories for each of 8 servings; 640 if made with Rice Pilaf; 605 with Rice and Mushroom Stuffing; 630 with Pecan-Bulgur Wheat Stuffing; 620 with Rice and Kidney Stuffing; 610 with Black Olive and Onion Stuffing; and 635 with Bread and Apricot Stuffing.

EASY ATHENIAN BRAISED LAMB SHOULDER

Cook in an electric skillet if you like.
Makes 6 servings

1 (3-pound) rolled lamb shoulder
2 tablespoons olive oil or cooking oil
1 medium-size yellow onion, peeled and coarsely chopped
1 clove garlic, peeled and crushed (optional)

2 teaspoons salt
¼ teaspoon pepper
1 teaspoon rosemary, oregano, marjoram, or thyme (optional)
⅓ cup cold water
3 cups lamb stock or a ½ and ½ mixture of beef broth and cold water
6 tablespoons flour
½–1 teaspoon liquid gravy browner (optional)

Brown lamb well all over in oil in a heavy kettle over moderate heat; add onion, garlic, seasonings and water, cover, and simmer slowly about 2½ hours. Keep an eye on the pot and add about ¼ cup extra water if liquid boils away. When lamb is tender, lift to a platter and keep warm. Drain all but 1–2 tablespoons drippings from kettle, add 2 cups stock, stirring to scrape up browned bits. Blend flour and remaining stock in a shaker jar, pour into kettle, and heat, stirring, until thickened. If you like a dark gravy, add gravy browner. Slice roast about ¼" thick and serve with plenty of gravy.

VARIATIONS:

To Oven Braise: Preheat oven to 350° F. Brown lamb as directed in a large, flameproof casserole, add onion, garlic, seasonings, and water, cover, and bake 2½–3 hours as directed. Prepare gravy as above and serve.

To Braise in Electric Skillet: Set control at 350° F. Brown lamb as directed, add onion, garlic, seasonings, and water; reduce heat to 212° F. and simmer 2–2½ hours until tender. Make gravy and serve.

All versions above: about 580 calories per serving.

Braised Lamb Roast with Avgolemono Sauce: Brown and simmer lamb until tender, using basic method above. When making gravy, omit flour-stock paste. Add the 3 cups stock to kettle and bring to a simmer. Beat 3 egg yolks lightly, add the juice of 1 lemon, and slowly beat in 1 cup hot stock; return all to kettle. Simmer, stirring constantly, 1–2 minutes but do not boil. Serve over lamb as you would gravy. About 585 calories per serving.

Braised Lamb Roast with Tomato Sauce: Brown lamb, add onions and seasonings, but substitute ⅓ cup tomato juice for the water; simmer as directed until tender. When making gravy, use 1 (8-ounce) can tomato sauce and 2 cups stock and reduce flour to ¼ cup. About 590 calories per serving.

Braised Lamb Roast with Vegetables: Prepare basic recipe above and, when lamb has only ¾ hour longer to cook, add 2 dozen peeled whole baby carrots, 12 peeled new potatoes, and 12 small peeled turnips. Sprinkle with 1 teaspoon salt, add ½ cup additional stock, cover, and continue simmering until meat and vegetables are tender. Lift meat to a hot platter, wreathe with vegetables, and keep warm. Prepare gravy as directed. About 730 calories per serving.

CHARCOAL SPIT-ROASTED BREAST OF LAMB

Makes 6 servings

6 pounds lean breast of lamb

Marinade:

2 cups dry red wine
2 cloves garlic, peeled and crushed
1 medium-size yellow onion, peeled and sliced thin
1 teaspoon powdered rosemary
¼ teaspoon pepper

Place lamb in a large, shallow bowl;

mix marinade, pour over lamb, cover, and marinate 24 hours in refrigerator. Prepare a moderate charcoal fire.* Lift meat from marinade and weave spit in and out of ribs to balance; tighten holding forks. Attach spit to rotisserie and roast 7"–8" from coals 1 hour, basting frequently with strained marinade. Lower spit 1"–2" nearer coals and roast 20–30 minutes longer, basting, until tender and richly browned. About 470 calories per serving.

VARIATION:

Greek-Style Spit-Roasted Breast of Lamb: Omit marinade; instead, mix the following basting sauce: ¼ cup melted butter or margarine, 2 tablespoons olive oil, 2 cloves garlic, crushed, and 2 tablespoons lemon juice. Spit-roast breast as above, basting every 15–20 minutes. Season with salt and pepper before serving. About 500 calories per serving.

APRICOT-GLAZED STUFFED BREAST OF LAMB

Makes 4 servings

1 (1¾-pound) breast of lamb (have butcher crack ribs to simplify carving)

Stuffing:

¼ cup minced onion
½ cup diced celery
½ cup coarsely chopped piñon nuts
3 tablespoons butter or margarine
¼ cup dried currants
½ cup diced dried apricots
¼ cup uncooked rice
¾ cup water
1 tablespoon minced parsley
1 tablespoon dry white wine

Glaze:

¼ cup dried apricots
1½ cups water

Preheat oven to 350° F. Carefully make a pocket in lamb breast by inserting a small sharp knife at one end and freeing meat from ribs; repeat on opposite end so pocket runs length of breast. For stuffing, stir-fry onion, celery, and nuts in butter in a large, heavy skillet 8–10 minutes over moderate heat until golden. Mix in fruits and rice and stir-fry 2–3 minutes. Add water, cover, and simmer 8–10 minutes until all moisture is absorbed. Mix in parsley and wine and cool to room temperature. Meanwhile, simmer glaze ingredients, uncovered, about 15–20 minutes; purée at low speed in an electric blender and add enough water to bring measure to 2 cups. Fill lamb breast with stuffing, poking it into all corners; toothpick shut and lace with fine string to seal. Place breast in a shallow roasting pan, pour in glaze, and bake uncovered 2 hours, basting with glaze every 20 minutes. Remove toothpicks and lacings and serve. To carve, cut straight across between ribs. About 600 calories per serving.

SPIT-ROASTED WINE-STEEPED LAMB CHUNKS

Makes 4 servings

¼ cup olive or other cooking oil
½ cup dry red wine or red wine vinegar
¼ teaspoon thyme
⅛ teaspoon seasoned pepper
2½–3 pounds boned leg of lamb, cut in 2″ chunks
1 teaspoon salt
Watercress sprigs (garnish)

Mix oil, wine, thyme and pepper in a large bowl. Add lamb, toss well to mix, cover, and chill 8 hours or overnight, turning lamb in marinade 2 or 3 times. Drain off marinade and reserve. Arrange lamb on spit by skewering each chunk through the middle; avoid crowding. Attach spit to rotisserie and broil 25–30 minutes for rare, 30–35 for medium, 40–45 for well done. Meanwhile, add ½ teaspoon salt to marinade and heat uncovered to simmering. Keep hot and baste lamb 2–3 times during cooking. Transfer lamb to a heated platter, sprinkle with remaining salt, sprig with cress, and serve.

VARIATIONS:

Skewered Minted Lamb: Omit thyme from marinade and add 2 tablespoons finely chopped fresh mint or 1 tablespoon dried mint, ⅓ cup firmly packed light brown sugar, and 1 teaspoon finely grated lemon rind. Proceed as recipe directs.

Garlic Skewered Lamb: Add 2 cloves garlic, peeled and crushed, and 1 tablespoon finely grated onion to marinade and proceed as directed. (*Note:* For a subtle difference of flavor, vary wine used in marinade: Burgundy, rosé, sauterne, and dry sherry or Madeira are all good.)

All versions: about 520 calories per serving.

TURKISH LAMB SHISH KEBABS

Developed by early travelers who would spear chunks of meat and warm them over campfires, shish kebabs are today sophisticated international fare. They can be made of beef, lamb, ham, venison, chicken, liver, even lobster, shrimp, or scallops. Broil them in the oven or, better yet, over a charcoal fire.
Makes 6 servings

Marinade:
1 cup olive oil

½ cup lemon juice
2 cloves garlic, peeled and crushed
¼ teaspoon pepper
1 teaspoon oregano

Kebabs:
4 pounds boned leg of lamb, cut in
  1½" cubes
3 sweet green peppers, cored, seeded,
  and cut in 2" squares
1 pound small white onions, peeled
  and parboiled
1 pound medium-size mushrooms,
  wiped clean and stemmed
3 large, firm tomatoes, quartered (do
  not peel or core)
1 teaspoon salt

Mix marinade in a large bowl, add lamb, toss to mix, cover, and chill 8 hours or overnight, turning lamb 2 or 3 times. Drain off marinade and reserve. Alternate lamb, green peppers, and onions on skewers, beginning and ending with lamb; for best results, put mushrooms and tomatoes on separate skewers (so they won't overcook). Add ½ teaspoon salt to marinade and brush some of it over vegetables. Arrange lamb skewers on a broiling rack or, if you have the necessary gadget, attach to rotisserie spit. Broil 3"–4" from heat 15–20 minutes for rare, 20–25 for medium, and 25–30 for well done, turning frequently so kebabs cook evenly and brushing occasionally with marinade. About 10 minutes before meat is done, lay mushroom and tomato skewers on broiler rack, brush with marinade, and broil, turning frequently, until lightly browned. Sprinkle meat with remaining salt and serve kebabs with boiled rice, bulgur wheat, or Bulgur Pilaf.

VARIATIONS:

Charcoal-Broiled Shish Kebabs:
Prepare a moderately hot charcoal fire* and broil kebabs 4" from coals, using times given above as a guide.

Beef Kebabs: Substitute sirloin or top round for the lamb and broil about 5 minutes less than times given above for rare, medium, or well done.

All versions: about 685 calories per serving.

ROAST LAMB REVISITED

(How to Use Up Leftovers)

⊠ CRISPY BREADED LAMB SLICES

Makes 2 servings

¼ cup unsifted flour
¼ cup ice water
1 egg, lightly beaten
4 thick slices leftover roast lamb
⅓ cup toasted, seasoned bread
  crumbs
2 tablespoons cooking oil

Blend flour and water until smooth, add egg and mix well but do not beat. Dip lamb slices in batter, then in crumbs to coat evenly and thickly; let stand on rack at room temperature 5 minutes. Sauté lamb about 3–4 minutes on each side in oil in a skillet over moderate heat, turning frequently until golden brown. Reduce heat to low and cook 1–2 minutes longer. Serve with Tartar, Whipped Horseradish, or Quick Lemon-Caper Sauce. About 515 calories per serving (without sauce).

LAMB AND EGGPLANT CASSEROLE

A very good way to use up leftover roast lamb.
Makes 4 servings

2 *small yellow onions, peeled and chopped fine*
1 *clove garlic, peeled and crushed*
2 *tablespoons cooking oil*
1 *medium-size eggplant, peeled and cut in rounds ¼" thick*
1½ *teaspoons salt*
1 *(1-pound 4-ounce) can Italian plum tomatoes (do not drain)*
¼ *teaspoon pepper*
½ *cup uncooked rice*
8 *medium-thick slices leftover roast lamb, trimmed of fat*
2 *tablespoons minced parsley*

Stir-fry onions and garlic in oil in a deep, flameproof 2½-quart casserole over moderate heat 8–10 minutes until golden. Layer eggplant into casserole, working onion mixture into spaces between slices. Sprinkle with ½ teaspoon salt. Spoon tomatoes over eggplant, sprinkle with ½ teaspoon salt and ¼ teaspoon pepper. Cover and simmer slowly 30 minutes until eggplant is tender. Sprinkle in rice and top with lamb, pressing slices down slightly into mixture underneath; sprinkle with remaining salt. Cover and simmer 20 minutes; uncover and sprinkle with parsley. To serve, place 2 lamb slices on each plate and top with spoonfuls of rice-eggplant-tomato mixture. About 450 calories per serving.

¢ CURRIED LAMB LEFTOVERS

Makes 2 servings

2 *tablespoons butter, margarine, or cooking oil*
1 *large yellow onion, peeled and minced*
1 *small tart apple, peeled, cored, and coarsely chopped*
1 *clove garlic, peeled and crushed*
2 *teaspoons curry powder*
2 *tablespoons dried lentils*
1 *cup canned tomatoes (include liquid)*
1 *cup hot water*
1 *teaspoon salt*
1½ *cups lean leftover cooked lamb, cut in ½" cubes*

Heat butter in a saucepan over moderate heat 1 minute, add onion and sauté about 8 minutes until golden. Add apple, garlic, and curry powder and stir-fry 1 minute. Add all remaining ingredients, reduce heat to low, cover, and simmer about 45 minutes, stirring frequently. Serve hot over boiled rice and accompany, if you like, with chutney and chopped scallions. About 515 calories per serving.

¢ LEFTOVER LAMB PILAF

Makes 4 servings

1 *cup uncooked rice*
1 *large yellow onion, peeled and minced*
2 *tablespoons butter or margarine*
2 *cups chicken or beef broth*
1 *teaspoon salt*
⅛ *teaspoon pepper*
⅓ *cup seedless raisins*
2 *cups coarsely chopped, lean leftover roast lamb*
2 *tablespoons cooking oil*
1 *cup leftover gravy or canned beef gravy*
2 *tablespoons tomato paste*
¼ *teaspoon ginger*
1 *clove garlic, peeled and crushed*
½ *teaspoon seasoned salt*

In a 2-quart saucepan stir-fry rice and onion in butter over moderate heat 3–4 minutes until rice is pale golden. Add broth, salt, pepper, and raisins, partially cover, and simmer about 20 minutes until rice is barely tender and all liquid absorbed. Meanwhile brown lamb lightly in oil over moderate heat, add all remaining ingredients, cover, and simmer until rice is tender. Toss lamb mixture into rice, using 2 forks. Serve with chutney. About 560 calories per serving.

ARTICHOKES STUFFED WITH LAMB

Makes 6 servings

6 large globe artichokes, parboiled and drained

Stuffing:
2 cups ground leftover cooked lamb
1 medium-size yellow onion, peeled and minced
2 tablespoons cooking oil
1 cup soft white bread crumbs
1 egg, lightly beaten
⅓ cup leftover gravy or chicken or beef broth
2 tablespoons minced parsley
1 teaspoon salt
⅛ teaspoon pepper
1 tablespoon lemon juice

Topping:
½ cup coarse white bread crumbs tossed with 2 tablespoons melted butter or margarine

Preheat oven to 325° F. Remove chokes from artichokes,* then arrange artichokes upright and close together in an ungreased casserole. Brown lamb and onion in oil in a heavy skillet over moderate heat 10–12 minutes; off heat mix in remaining stuffing ingredients; fill artichoke centers and top each with buttered crumbs. Pour hot water around artichokes to a depth of 1"; cover and bake 45–50 minutes. Serve with

Hollandaise Sauce. About 315 calories per serving (without sauce).

¢ LAMB AND LASAGNE CASSEROLE

Makes 6 servings

1 (1-pound) can tomato sauce
1 (6-ounce) can tomato paste
1 cup hot water
1½ teaspoons salt
¼ teaspoon pepper
2 teaspoons oregano
2 teaspoons basil
1 clove garlic, peeled and crushed
1 medium-size yellow onion, peeled and chopped fine
3 cups ground, lean cooked lamb
1 cup cottage cheese or ricotta cheese
½ cup sour cream
½ pound lasagne noodles, cooked by package directions and drained
¼ cup grated Parmesan cheese

In a saucepan mix tomato sauce, paste, water, salt, pepper, herbs, garlic, onion, and lamb. Simmer uncovered, stirring occasionally, ½ hour. Preheat oven to 350° F. Combine cottage cheese and sour cream. In an 8" or 9" square greased baking dish layer in noodles and meat sauce, beginning and ending with noodles and adding dabs of cottage cheese mixture on each sauce layer. Sprinkle with Parmesan and bake, uncovered, 30 minutes; raise temperature to 400° F. and bake 10 minutes longer to brown. Cut in squares and serve. About 480 calories per serving.

SAVORY LAMB BURGERS

A good leftover dish.
Makes 2 servings

1 cup coarsely ground, lean leftover roast lamb

2 scallions, chopped fine (include
   green tops)
1 medium-size dill pickle, chopped
   fine
1 (2-ounce) can mushrooms, drained
   and chopped fine
1 tablespoon chili sauce
½ teaspoon salt
⅛ teaspoon pepper
¼ teaspoon prepared horseradish
¼ cup coarse cracker crumbs
1 tablespoon light cream or leftover
   gravy
2 tablespoons butter or margarine

Mix lamb with all remaining ingredients except butter. Shape
into 2 patties, cover, and chill 1
hour. Melt butter in a skillet over
moderate heat, add lamb patties, and
sauté 8–10 minutes, turning frequently until browned on both sides
and heated through. About 390
calories per serving.

⚖ ¢ **THRIFTY SCOTCH
BROTH**

Makes 6–8 servings

2 medium-size yellow onions, peeled
   and coarsely chopped
3 medium-size carrots, peeled and
   cut in small dice
½ medium-size rutabaga, peeled and
   cut in small dice
½ cup medium pearl barley, washed
3½ quarts cold water
Leftover lamb roast, leg or shoulder
   bone with a little meat attached
4 teaspoons salt
¼ teaspoon pepper
1 tablespoon minced parsley

Place all ingredients except parsley
in a large (at least 1½-gallon) kettle,
cover, and simmer 1½–2 hours. Cut
meat from bones in small pieces
and return to kettle. Stir, taste for
salt, and adjust as needed. Sprinkle
with parsley and serve. About 210
calories for each of 6 servings, 160
calories for each of 8 servings.

Some Additional Ways to Use Up
Leftover Roast Lamb

Lamb and Zucchini Casserole (4
servings): Stir-fry 3 cups sliced
zucchini with ½ cup chopped onion,
¼ cup minced sweet green pepper,
and 1 crushed clove garlic in 3
tablespoons olive oil in a large,
heavy skillet 8–10 minutes over
moderate heat until golden. Add 2
cups canned tomatoes, 1 teaspoon
salt, and ¼ teaspoon each oregano
and pepper and simmer, uncovered,
10 minutes. Stir in 2 tablespoons
flour blended with 3 tablespoons
cold water and heat, stirring, until
thickened. Place 1 cup cubed cooked
lamb in a greased 1½-quart
casserole, spread ½ vegetable
mixture on top, and sprinkle with
½ cup grated Cheddar cheese. Add
another 1 cup cubed lamb, the
remaining vegetable mixture, and
½ cup grated cheese. Top with ½ cup
butter-browned bread crumbs and
bake, uncovered, 20 minutes at
350° F. until bubbly. About 570
calories per serving.

¢ **Lamb and Lima Stew** (4
servings): Brown 2 cups cubed
cooked lamb in 2 tablespoons bacon
drippings or butter with 1 medium-
size chopped onion 8–10 minutes in
a heavy saucepan. Add 1 (10-
ounce) package frozen baby lima
beans, 1 (1-pound) can tomatoes,
1 teaspoon salt, and ¼ teaspoon each
thyme, basil, and pepper. Cover
and simmer 30–40 minutes, stirring
occasionally, until beans are tender.
About 370 calories per serving.

¢ **Lamb and Black-Eyed Pea
Salad** (4 servings): Place 2 cups
each diced cooked lamb and cold,
cooked, drained black-eyed peas
in a bowl. Add 2 tablespoons each
minced parsley and onion and dress
with a good garlic, herb, or Italian

dressing. Let stand 30 minutes, toss again, and serve. About 375 calories per serving.

Shepherd's Pie: See Shepherd's Pie Variation in the beef section.

Lamb and Vegetable Pie:
Lamb Stuffed Vegetables:
Roast Lamb Hash:
Yukon Stew:
} Follow recipes given in Some Additional Ways to Use Up Leftover Roast Beef, substituting lamb for beef.

Sliced Cold Lamb: Slice lamb about ¼" thick, trim off fat, and top with any recommended cold sauce (see Sauces, Gravies, and Seasonings for Roast Lamb).

Sliced Hot Lamb: Slice lamb about ¼" thick, trim off fat, and layer into an ungreased shallow casserole. Add just enough hot sauce to cover (see Sauces, Gravies, and Seasonings for Roast Lamb), cover with foil, and heat 20 minutes at 350° F. If you prefer, warm lamb in sauce about 5 minutes in a covered skillet over moderately low heat.

To Make the Most of Very Small Amounts: Follow suggestions given for beef, substituting lamb for beef.

Lamb Chops and Steaks

The choice is far broader than most of us suspect, and so is the price range. Rib and loin chops are the T-bones and porterhouse of the lamb world. Far better buys are the meatier arm and blade chops cut from the shoulder and lamb steak, which is cut from the leg. (*Note:* Mutton chops and steaks are the same except that they are slightly larger and less tender.) Here, then, are some of the popular varieties:

Loin chops (plain or kidney— with the lamb kidney in the center of the chop)
Rib chops (plain, double, or Frenched—with the meat stripped from the rib ends and paper frills slipped on as decoration)
Noisettes (trimmed eye of loin or rib)
Sirloin chop (the equivalent of sirloin steak)
Shoulder chops (arm, blade, boneless, Saratoga—boned and rolled)
Leg steak
Cube steak (knitted together from lamb trimmings)

How to Cook

Amount Needed: Allow ⅓–½ pound boneless chops or steaks per person, ½–¾ pound of the bone-in. Loin and rib chops are best cut 1"–1½" thick, others ¾"–1".

General Preparation for Cooking: Peel fell from outer fat and trim fat to about ⅛"; slash at 1" intervals to prevent curling. If meat seems moist, wipe with a damp cloth so it will brown well. Rub with pepper, if you like, also garlic and/or compatible herb (see Sauces, Butters, and Seasonings for Lamb Chops and Steaks) but not salt—it draws moisture to surface and prevents browning. Let chops or steaks stand at room temperature 1½–2 hours if convenient.

To Panfry (Sauté): Especially good for noisettes, cube and leg steaks, shoulder chops. Heat 1–2 tablespoons butter or cooking oil in a heavy skillet over moderately high heat about 1 minute, add chops and brown well on both sides, turning frequently with tongs. Cube steaks will take only 3 minutes altogether, noisettes 5–8, leg steaks and shoulder chops 8–12, depending upon whether you like pinkish or well-done meat. Season and serve.

VARIATION:

Panfried Lamb Chops or Steaks with Minute Sauce: After cooking chops or steaks, transfer to a heated platter and keep warm. Drain all but 1 tablespoon drippings from skillet and add 2 tablespoons butter, 1 tablespoon hot water, 1 teaspoon Worcestershire sauce, and ½ teaspoon lemon juice. Heat 1

APPROXIMATE TOTAL PANBROILING TIMES (IN MINUTES)

Chop Thickness	Rare	Medium Rare	Medium	Well Done
1″	5–7	8–9	10–12	12–14
1½″	7–8	9–10	12–13	14–16
2″ (English chop)	8–9	10–12	13–15	16–18

LAMB CHOP AND STEAK BROILING CHART

Times (for chops or steaks at room temperature) are *approximate* because shape of chop, amount of fat and bone affect cooking time; outdoors, wind and temperature do too.

Oven Broiling

Cut	Thickness	Oven or Fire Temperature	Distance from Heat	Rare	Medium	Well Done
Loin, rib, and sirloin chops; 2″ English chops	1″	Broil	2″	4–5	6	7
	1½″	Broil	2″	6	7	8
	2″	Broil	3″	8	9	10–12
Arm and blade chops; leg steaks	¾″	Broil	3″	Not recommended	5	6–7
	1″	Broil	3″		6	8–10
Mutton rib and loin chops	1″	Broil	3″	Not recommended	8	9–10
	1½″	Broil	3″		10	12–14

Charcoal Broiling

Cut	Thickness	Oven or Fire Temperature	Distance from Heat	Rare	Medium	Well Done
Loin, rib, and sirloin chops; 2″ English chops	1″	Hot	4″	5–6	7	8
	1½″	Hot	4″	7	8–9	10
	2″	Moderately hot	5″	8–10	10–12	12–14
Arm and blade chops; leg steaks	¾″	Moderately hot	4″	Not recommended	6	7–8
	1″	Moderately hot	4″		7	10
Mutton rib and loin chops	1″	Moderately hot	4″	Not recommended	10	11–12
	1½″	Moderately hot	5″			13–15

minute, swirling mixture round, spoon over meat, and serve.

To Panbroil: Recommended for loin, rib, arm, blade, and sirloin chops, also leg steaks. If chops seem very lean, lightly grease or salt skillet to keep meat from sticking. Heat over moderately high heat ½–1 minute, add chops and cook, uncovered, using times above as a guide. Turn frequently with tongs and pour off drippings as they accumulate. Season and serve.

To Broil: Recommended for the same cuts as panbroiling. Preheat broiler; line broiler pan with foil to eliminate messy clean-ups; lightly grease rack. Place chops on rack, fat edges toward back to prevent spattering. Adjust height and broil to desired doneness using times in Lamb Chop and Steak Broiling Chart as a guide. Turn chops only once during cooking, using tongs. Season and serve.

VARIATION:

Planked Chops: Especially good for 1″–1½″ thick rib or loin chops. Preheat broiler and prepare plank (see Planked Steak for details). Place chops close together on plank (cover any exposed areas of wood with foil to prevent charring) and broil 2″ from heat 4–5 minutes. Remove from broiler, season lightly with salt and pepper, and turn. Pipe a border of Duchess Potatoes around chops and brush lightly with Egg Glaze. Return to broiler and broil 4–5 minutes longer. Serve on plank, topping each chop with a dab of Maître d'Hôtel Butter. Garnish with broiled mushroom caps and/or tomato halves.

To Charcoal Broil: Recommended for the same cuts as panbroiling.

Prepare charcoal fire.* For steaks or chops 1″–1½″ thick it should be hot (350–75° F. on grill thermometer) or of an intensity to make you remove your hand from grill level after saying, "Mississippi" 3 times. For 2″ chops or steaks it should be moderately hot (325° F.) or 4 Mississippis by the hand test. Spread glowing coals over fire bed to equal area of meat to be broiled, adjust height, and broil according to Lamb Chop and Steak Broiling Chart (above). Place a drip pan under meat to reduce flare-ups. Season and serve.

To Braise: Especially good for lamb and mutton arm, blade and leg chops about 1″ thick. Brown chops 2–3 minutes on a side over moderately high heat in a large heavy skillet lightly brushed with butter, drippings or oil; pour off all drippings. Season chops with salt and pepper, add a small amount of water (⅓ cup is about right for 4 chops), cover and simmer slowly over low heat or cover and bake in a preheated 350° F. oven ¾–1 hour until tender.

For Extra Savor: For the ⅓ cup water, substitute beer or dry vermouth; tomato juice, sauce or canned tomatoes; beef broth or onion soup; apple cider or juice or All-Purpose Barbecue Sauce.

Some Variations on Braised Lamb Chops

All quantities based on enough chops for 4 persons

Italian-Style: Rub chops with a cut clove garlic, then brown as directed. Season, add 1 cup meatless spaghetti sauce, cover, and simmer or bake until tender.

With Vegetables: Brown chops as directed and arrange in an ungreased roasting pan. Add 4 peeled, quartered potatoes, 4 peeled, quartered turnips, 12 peeled small white onions, and 2 stalks celery cut in 2″ lengths. Add 1 cup beef broth, sprinkle with 1 teaspoon salt and ¼ teaspoon pepper, cover, and oven-braise as directed above ¾–1 hour until chops and vegetables are tender. Baste 1–2 times during cooking. Sprinkle with 1 tablespoon minced parsley just before serving.

With Wine and Herbs: Rub chops with a cut clove garlic and ¼ teaspoon rosemary or with ¼ teaspoon each basil and oregano. Brown as directed, season with salt and pepper, then cover and braise in ½ cup dry red or white wine until tender.

To Bake: Recommended for arm, blade, or leg chops cut ½″–¾″ thick. Preheat oven to 350° F. Place steaks in a foil-lined shallow baking pan, sprinkle each with ⅛ teaspoon salt or garlic salt and a pinch pepper. Bake, uncovered, 30 minutes, turn sprinkle again with salt and pepper, and bake, uncovered, 30 minutes longer until tender.

VARIATION:

Baked Barbecued Lamb Chops: Omit seasonings, cover chops with 1 cup All-Purpose Barbecue Sauce or any favorite barbecue sauce, and bake, uncovered, as directed.

To Test Lamb Chops and Steaks for Doneness:

Bone-In Cuts: Make a small slit near bone to determine color of lean. Rare lamb will be rosy and juicy, medium faintly tinged with pink, and well-done gray-brown.

Boneless Cuts: Make a small cut in center of lean and check color.

How to Give Lamb Chops and Steaks Extra Flavor

Before Panfrying, Panbroiling, Broiling or Charcoal Broiling:
– Marinate chops or steaks 4 hours in refrigerator in All-Purpose Barbecue Sauce or any good garlic, herb, or Italian dressing. Let come to room temperature in marinade, pat dry, and cook. If broiling or grilling, brush often with marinade.
– Brush both sides of chops or steaks with a little soy sauce or Teriyaki Sauce and let stand about 15 minutes.
– Rub both sides of chops or steaks with a little olive oil and crushed garlic and let stand 15–20 minutes.
– Rub both sides of chops or steaks with a little crushed fresh gingerroot and garlic and let stand 15–20 minutes.

During Broiling or Charcoal Broiling:
– While broiling arm or blade chops, leg chops or steaks, brush often with the following mixture: ¼ cup melted butter, 2 tablespoons cooking oil, 1 tablespoon lemon juice, and ¼ teaspoon garlic powder.
– While charcoal broiling, toss any of the following onto the coals: 2–3 sprigs fresh sage, basil, or rosemary or 1 tablespoon of the dried; a dozen bay leaves or 1 tablespoon cracked juniper berries.
– During last minutes of broiling or grilling, brush lightly with Herb, Chive, Garlic, Lemon, or Anchovy Butter.

After Panfrying or Panbroiling:
– Serve with Tomato Sauce and garnish platter with Stuffed Tomatoes.

– **Lamb Chops Financière:** Transfer chops to platter. Drain drippings from skillet, add ¼ cup Madeira, and cook and stir until reduced by half. Add 1 cup Rich Brown Sauce and bring to a boil. Serve chops on heart-shaped slices of butter-browned toast and top with sauce.

– **Lamb Chops à la Mexicaine:** Transfer chops to platter. To skillet add 1 cup Rich Brown Sauce, 2 tablespoons each red wine vinegar and slivered orange rind (orange part only) and simmer 2 minutes. Spoon over chops and serve, garnished with Baked Bananas.

Some Simple Garnishes for Lamb Chops

Artichoke Bottoms: boiled and buttered; filled with Macédoine of Vegetables, buttered green peas, boiled flageolets, navy or pea beans.

Brussels Sprouts: boiled and buttered.

Mushrooms: sautéed button mushrooms, mushroom caps, or sliced mushrooms; Mushroom Caps Stuffed with Hazelnuts.

Onions: Glazed Onions; Pan-Braised Onions; Stuffed Onions.

Peaches and Pears: broiled halves; halves filled with red currant or mint jelly; pickled, spiced, or brandied peaches or pears.

Potatoes: Duchess, Shoestring, French-Fried; Parsleyed, Herbed, Lemon-Glazed, or Danish-Style New Potatoes.

Tomatoes: raw cherry tomatoes; Broiled Tomatoes, Stuffed Tomatoes.

Some Classic Garnishes for Lamb Chops

À la Bretonne: Arrange chops in a circle on a large platter and fill center with boiled flageolets, navy or pea beans and sprinkle with minced parsley and any pan drippings.

À la Niçoise: Arrange chops in a circle on a large platter, fill center with Château Potatoes, and surround with buttered French-style green beans and whole sautéed cherry

SAUCES, BUTTERS, AND SEASONINGS FOR LAMB CHOPS AND STEAKS

Sauces	Butters		Seasonings, Herbs, Spices		Condiments
Béarnaise	Périgueux	Anchovy Maître	Basil	Mustard	Chutney
Bontemps	Portugaise	Bercy d'hôtel	Bay leaf	Oregano	Mustard
Bordelaise	Réform	Chive Noisette	Dill	Paprika	Soy sauce
Brown	(mutton	Garlic Parsley	Garlic	Parsley	Teriyaki
Chateaubriand	chops)	Herb Shallot	Ginger	Rosemary	sauce
Choron	Romaine	Lemon Tomato	Juniper	Sage	Worces-
Madeira	Soubise		berries	Tarragon	tershire
	Tomato		Lemon	Thyme	sauce
			Marjoram		
			Mint		

tomatoes (do not peel). Pass Tomato or Portuguese Sauce.

Dubarry: Place chops on an oven-proof serving dish and surround with boiled cauliflowerets. Top cauliflower with Mornay Sauce, sprinkle with Parmesan cheese, and broil 2"–3" from heat 2–3 minutes until freckled with brown.

Parmentier: Garnish chops with Hashed Brown Potatoes.

Talleyrand: Transfer chops to a platter and keep warm. To skillet add 2 tablespoons butter, ¼ pound chopped mushrooms, and 4 diced truffles; stir-fry 2–3 minutes over moderate heat until mushrooms are golden. Add ¼ cup dry sherry and 1 cup heavy cream and heat, stirring, 1–2 minutes. Pour over chops. Fill center of platter with thick Onion Sauce.

À la Clamart: ⎫
Chasseur: ⎬ see Some Classic Ways to Serve Tournedos.
Rossini: ⎭

ENGLISH MIXED GRILL

Makes 2 servings

2 loin lamb chops, cut 1¼" thick and trimmed of excess fat, or 2 filet mignons, cut 1¼" thick
2 slices bacon (optional)
2 medium-size pork sausages
1 cup water
⅓ cup melted butter or margarine
½ pound calf's liver, cut in 1" strips
4 lamb kidneys, trimmed of fat, membranes, and cores
6 medium-size mushroom caps, wiped clean
2 medium-size ripe tomatoes, halved crosswise (do not peel)
1¼ teaspoons salt (about)
¼ teaspoon pepper
2 small pats Maître d'Hôtel Butter
2 sprigs watercress (garnish)

Preheat broiler. Coil "tail" around each chop and secure with a toothpick. Or, if using filets, wrap a bacon slice around each and secure. Simmer sausages uncovered in the water 8 minutes; drain and pat dry on paper toweling. Arrange chops or steaks on a lightly greased broiler rack and brush with melted butter. Broil 3" from heat for 3 minutes. Arrange sausages, liver, kidneys, mushrooms, and tomatoes around chops, brush with melted butter, and broil 5 minutes. Sprinkle all with half the salt and pepper, then turn. Brush again with melted butter and broil 2–3 minutes for a rare mixed grill, 3–4 minutes for medium, and 5–6 for well done; sprinkle with remaining salt and pepper. To serve, arrange chops in center of a heated platter, top each with a pat of Maître d'Hôtel Butter, and surround with sausages, liver, kidneys, mushrooms, and tomatoes. Garnish with cress and accompany with Shoestring Potatoes or French-Fried Potatoes. (*Note:* These ingredients just fit comfortably on a standard broiler rack, so if you want to double the recipe, you'll have to use 2 broilers or broil the components separately.) About 1040 calories per serving (without Maître d'Hôtel Butter or garnish).

SHERRIED LAMB CHOPS STUFFED WITH MUSHROOMS AND TRUFFLES

Makes 4 servings

4 rib lamb chops, cut 1¼" thick and trimmed of excess fat
1 slice bacon
1 cup finely chopped mushrooms
1 tablespoon fine, dry white bread crumbs
2 truffles, coarsely chopped

1 teaspoon minced parsley
¼ teaspoon minced garlic
1 teaspoon butter or margarine
½ teaspoon salt
⅛ teaspoon pepper
¼ cup medium dry sherry
¼ cup beef broth

Starting at the rib bone, cut a pocket in each chop. Prepare stuffing: Fry bacon in a small skillet until crisp, drain on paper toweling, crumble, and reserve. Pour off all but 1 tablespoon bacon drippings, then stir-fry mushrooms 2–3 minutes over moderately high heat until golden. Off heat, mix in bacon, crumbs, truffles, parsley, and minced garlic; spoon into chop pockets (no need to use toothpicks or skewers to seal in stuffing). Brown chops over moderately high heat in a skillet brushed with butter as follows: 5–6 minutes on each side for rare, 6–7 for medium, 7–8 for well done. Use tongs for turning chops and drain off fat as it accumulates. Sprinkle with salt and pepper, transfer to a hot platter and keep warm. Drain drippings from skillet, add sherry and broth, and heat, stirring to scrape up any brown bits. Boil, uncovered, until reduced by half, pour over chops, and serve. About 300 calories per serving.

LAMB CHOPS WITH ZUCCHINI EN PAPILLOTE

Makes 4 servings

4 shoulder lamb chops, cut ½" thick
   and trimmed of excess fat
1 teaspoon celery salt
⅛ teaspoon pepper
1 teaspoon minced chervil
2 medium-size yellow onions, peeled
   and sliced thin
4–6 medium-size zucchini, quartered
   lengthwise

4 medium-size carrots, peeled and cut
   in strips 2" long and ½" wide
4 small potatoes, peeled and sliced
   ¼" thick (optional)
1 teaspoon salt

Preheat oven to 350° F. Cut 4 (16") squares of heavy duty foil. Place a chop on each, sprinkle with celery salt, pepper, and chervil; top with vegetables and sprinkle evenly with salt. Wrap tight and bake on a baking sheet 50–60 minutes until chops are tender. Serve in packets. About 415 calories per serving.

GROUND LAMB

Unquestionably the best cut of lamb to grind is shoulder because it has a good ratio of lean to fat, good flavor and texture. Second best are trimmings from shank and neck. Because lamb is finely grained, it needs to be ground one time only unless you want an unusually compact loaf or patty; if so, have the lamb ground twice. Like other ground meats, ground lamb is highly perishable and should be refrigerated until you're ready to use it. Ground lamb is leaner than most ground beef, more delicate in flavor, and usually slightly lower in cost.

☒ LAMB BURGERS

To be at their best, lamb burgers should be cooked until medium or well done.
Makes 3–4 servings

1 pound ground lean lamb shoulder
1 teaspoon salt
⅛ teaspoon pepper

Lightly shape lamb into 3 plump or 4 slim patties and cook by one of the methods below; season with salt and pepper just before serving.

To Panfry (Sauté): Recommended for lean meat. Brown patties uncovered in 1–2 tablespoons cooking oil, butter, margarine, or drippings in a large, heavy skillet over moderately high heat. Plump patties will take about 5 minutes on a side for medium and 6 for well done, thin patties about 1 minute less per side for each degree of doneness. To keep patties juicy, avoid spanking or pressing down with a pancake turner as they cook. About 365 calories for each of 3 servings, 270 calories for each of 4 servings.

⚖ **To Panbroil:** Recommended for dieters, also for meat heavily flecked with fat. Lightly brush a large, heavy skillet with oil or sprinkle with salt; heat 1 minute over moderately high heat, add burgers, and brown, uncovered, using cooking times given for panfrying. Pour off drippings as they accumulate. About 265 calories for each of 3 servings, 200 calories for each of 4 servings.

⚖ **To Broil:** Recommended for dieters and fatty meat. Preheat broiler. Broil patties 3″ from heat on a lightly greased broiler rack. Plump patties will take about 6 minutes on a side for medium and 7–8 for well done, thin patties about 1 minute less per side in each instance. About 265 calories for each of 3 servings, 200 calories for each of 4 servings.

⚖ **To Charcoal Broil:** Recommended for plump patties only. Prepare a moderately hot charcoal fire.* Broil patties on a lightly greased grill 4″ from heat about 4–5 minutes on a side for medium and 6–7 for well done. About 265 calories for each of 3 servings.

To Braise: Brown patties quickly in a lightly greased large, heavy skillet over high heat, turn heat to low, and pour in 1–1½ cups liquid (water; dry red, rosé or white wine; broth or gravy; tomato juice, soup, or sauce; cream of mushroom, celery, or asparagus soup). Cover and simmer slowly 15–20 minutes. Serve patties with cooking liquid. About 365 calories for each of 3 servings (if braised with water), 270 calories for each of 4 servings.

Some Variations on Lamb Burgers (all amounts based on recipe above)

Lamb and Sausage Burgers: Mix ½ pound cooked, drained sweet or hot sausage meat with lamb; shape into 6 patties, cook and season as directed. (Makes 6 patties.) About 355 calories per patty.

⚖ **Smothered Barbecue Burgers:** Mix lamb with 1 cup soft white bread crumbs, ½ cup milk, 1 teaspoon salt, ¼ teaspoon chili powder, and ⅛ teaspoon pepper. Form into 6 patties and brown quickly in a lightly greased large, heavy skillet over high heat. Turn heat to low. Mix 2 tablespoons each Worcestershire sauce and sugar with 1 cup cider vinegar, ½ cup ketchup, and 1 tablespoon minced onion; pour over patties, cover, and simmer 10–15 minutes. Serve patties topped with plenty of sauce. (Makes 6 patties.) About 240 calories per patty.

Lamb Burgers in Foil: Shape lamb into 4 patties; place each on a large square of heavy foil, top with thinly sliced potatoes, carrots, celery, and onion, season with salt and pepper, and wrap tight. Place on a baking sheet and bake 45–50 minutes at 350° F. until vegetables are tender; or grill 5″–6″ from a moderately hot charcoal fire 30–40 minutes, turning packages every 10 minutes. (Makes 4 servings.) About 480 calories per serving.

Hawaiian Lamb Burgers: Shape lamb into 4 patties and panbroil 3 minutes on each side; remove from skillet; drain off drippings. Drain syrup from 1 (13½-ounce) can pineapple chunks, add cold water to make 1 cup liquid, and blend in 2 tablespoons cornstarch. Add ¼ cup each cider vinegar and dark brown sugar, 2 tablespoons soy sauce, and ¼ teaspoon ginger. Pour into skillet and heat, stirring until thickened. Add patties, pineapple chunks, and 1 cup minced sweet green pepper. Cover and simmer 15 minutes. Top patties with sauce and flaked coconut and serve. (Makes 4 servings.) About 365 calories per serving (without coconut), 440 calories per serving (with coconut).

Russian Lamb Burgers: Mix ¼ cup minced onion and 2 tablespoons minced chives into lamb; shape into 4 patties, cook and season as directed. When serving, top each patty with a generous dollop of sour cream and 1 tablespoon red or black caviar. (Makes 4 servings.) About 315 calories per serving.

Crowned Lamb Burgers: Shape, cook and season lamb burgers as directed. Just before serving, top with any of the following:

– Minced ripe or pimiento-stuffed green olives

– Applesauce and chopped fresh mint
– Horseradish, sour cream, and capers
– Cranberry sauce and/or crushed pineapple
– Pickled red cabbage or minced pickled beets and sour cream
– Sautéed minced onions and mushrooms
– Sautéed minced sweet green and/or red peppers and onions

Note: See 20 Variations on Hamburgers; all can be made with ground lamb instead of beef.

¢ MOUSSAKA

Traditionally, *moussaka* has three layers—fried eggplant, a spicy meat mixture, and a custard-like sauce—but thrifty cooks often slip in an extra layer of leftover vegetables. The list of ingredients is long, but if you begin at the bottom and work up, you shouldn't have any trouble preparing this Greek and Turkish favorite.
Makes 8–10 servings

Bottom Layer:
2 medium-size eggplants
1 teaspoon salt
⅔ cup olive oil (about)
¼ cup fine dry bread crumbs

Middle Layer:
4 medium-size yellow onions, peeled and minced
2 cloves garlic, peeled and crushed
3 tablespoons olive oil
2 pounds ground lamb shoulder or beef chuck
¼ cup tomato paste
½ cup dry red wine
½ teaspoon oregano
¼ teaspoon cinnamon
1 bay leaf, crumbled
2 teaspoons salt
⅛ teaspoon pepper
¼ cup minced parsley

¼ *cup fine dry bread crumbs*
2 *eggs, lightly beaten*
¼ *cup grated Parmesan cheese*

Top Layer:
6 *tablespoons butter or margarine*
6 *tablespoons flour*
⅛ *teaspoon nutmeg*
⅛ *teaspoon white pepper*
1 *teaspoon salt*
3 *cups milk*
¼ *cup grated Parmesan cheese*
4 *egg yolks, lightly beaten*

Peel thin strips of skin lengthwise
from eggplants every ½″ so you
have a striped effect, then cut in
rounds ½″ thick. Sprinkle rounds
with salt and weight down between
paper toweling 1 hour. Meanwhile,
lightly oil a 14″×10″×2″ pan
and pat crumbs over bottom;
set aside. Now begin middle layer:
stir-fry onions and garlic in oil
in a large, heavy skillet over moderate heat 8–10 minutes until
golden. Add meat and brown,
breaking up any chunks, 10–15
minutes. Turn heat to low, mix in
all but last 4 ingredients, and
simmer uncovered, stirring occasionally, 15 minutes. Off heat, stir in
parsley and crumbs; cool to room
temperature and mix in eggs
and Parmesan. By now, eggplants
should be ready to fry. Brown
rounds well on both sides, doing
only 3–4 at a time and using 2
tablespoons oil—no more—for each
batch; drain on paper toweling and
arrange in pan in a double layer,
fitting rounds as close together
as possible. Spread meat sauce
evenly over all. (*Note:* Recipe can
be prepared to this point a day
ahead and refrigerated. Bring to
room temperature before proceeding.) Now begin final layer: melt
butter in top of a double boiler
over direct heat, blend in flour,
nutmeg, pepper, and salt. Add

milk and heat, stirring, until
thickened; remove from heat. Mix
Parmesan with yolks, then stir in
a little of the hot sauce; return
all to sauce, set over simmering
water, and heat, stirring constantly, 2
minutes. Cool to room temperature.
Preheat oven to 325° F. Spread
sauce over meat and bake moussaka,
uncovered, 1½ hours until topping
is puffy and lightly browned.
Remove from oven, let stand 10
minutes, then cut in large squares
and serve. About 820 calories
for each of 8 servings, 655 calories
for each of 10 servings.

BRAISED LAMB PATTIES IN TOMATO PURÉE

Makes 4 servings

Patties:
1 *pound ground lean lamb shoulder*
1 *medium-size yellow onion, peeled
  and minced*
1 *egg, lightly beaten*
½ *cup soft white bread crumbs*
2 *tablespoons minced parsley*
1 *teaspoon paprika*
1 *teaspoon salt*
⅛ *teaspoon pepper*
½ *cup flour (for dredging)*
3 *tablespoons butter or margarine
  (for browning)*

Tomato Purée:
3 *large ripe tomatoes, peeled, cored,
  seeded, and minced*
⅓ *cup apple cider*
1 *tablespoon minced parsley*
¾ *teaspoon salt*
⅛ *teaspoon pepper*

Preheat oven to 350° F. Mix all but
last 2 patty ingredients and shape
into 4 patties. Dredge in flour and
brown both sides in butter in a
heavy skillet over moderately
high heat. Transfer patties to an
ungreased shallow baking pan and
set aside. In same skillet, simmer

all purée ingredients about 5 minutes, stirring often, to blend flavors. Pour over patties and bake, uncovered, 30–35 minutes until bubbly. About 405 calories per serving.

¢ LEBANESE LAMB PIE (KIBBEH)

Makes 6–8 servings

Top and Bottom Layers:
2 cups bulgur wheat
2⅔ cups simmering water
1 medium-size yellow onion, peeled and minced
1 pound finely ground lamb shoulder
1 teaspoon salt

Middle Layer:
1 medium-size yellow onion, peeled and minced
1 clove garlic, peeled and crushed
2 tablespoons olive oil
1 pound finely ground lamb shoulder
1 teaspoon salt
½ teaspoon cinnamon
⅛ teaspoon cardamom
Pinch pepper
1 cup coarsely chopped piñon nuts
½ cup dried currants or coarsely chopped raisins

Topping:
¾ cup melted butter or margarine
Yogurt

Preheat oven to 350° F. Soak bulgur wheat in water 20 minutes and drain well. Put onion and lamb through fine blade of meat grinder several times until reduced to paste; grind bulgur wheat until smooth and pasty and knead into lamb mixture along with salt. Pat ½ of mixture over the bottom of an oiled 13″×9″×2″ pan and set aside. For middle layer, stir-fry onion and garlic in oil 8–10 minutes in a large, heavy skillet over moderate heat; add lamb, salt,

spices, and pepper and heat, stirring, about 10 minutes, breaking up any clumps of meat. Off heat, mix in nuts and currants; spread over wheat layer in pan. Pat remaining wheat mixture over all and press down firmly. Score top in a crisscross pattern and drizzle butter over surface. Bake, uncovered, 30–40 minutes until lightly browned. Cool slightly, cut into large squares, and serve topped with dollops of yogurt. About 975 calories for each of 6 servings, 730 calories for each of 8 servings.

◁▷ DOLMA (STUFFED GRAPE LEAVES)

Brined or preserved grape leaves can be found in Greek, Turkish, or gourmet groceries.
Makes 6 servings

1 (1-pound) jar grape leaves
1 quart warm water (about)
Juice of 2 lemons

Stuffing:
1 pound ground lean lamb shoulder
½ cup uncooked rice
½ cup minced yellow onion
1 teaspoon salt
¼ teaspoon allspice
⅛ teaspoon pepper
⅓ cup water
1 tablespoon minced parsley

If grape leaves seem salty, rinse well in warm water; sort leaves, selecting the most perfect to stuff; save the rest. Mix stuffing ingredients thoroughly. Place a grape leaf vein side up and stem end toward you on the counter; near the base put 1 heaping teaspoon stuffing. Fold right and left sides over stuffing and roll up—rolls should be quite tight so they won't unroll during cooking. Repeat until all stuffing is gone (you should have about 4 dozen rolls).

Place a cake rack in a large, heavy kettle (it should be about 9″ in diameter) and on it make a bed of the imperfect leaves. (These are merely to cushion the *dolma* and are discarded after cooking.) Arrange rolls very close together in neat rows in a single layer on top of leaves, place a dinner plate on top to weight down slightly. Pour in enough warm water to reach plate, cover, and simmer 35 minutes. Pour in lemon juice, re-cover, and simmer 15 minutes longer. When serving, pass lemon slices. About 230 calories per serving.

¢ LAMB STUFFED CABBAGE ROLLS

Makes 4–6 servings

1 medium-size cabbage, trimmed of coarse outer leaves
1½ quarts boiling water
1 teaspoon salt
2 cups tomato juice or sauce
1 bay leaf
1 clove garlic, peeled

Stuffing:
1 cup crumbled hard rolls
⅓ cup cold water
1 pound ground lean lamb shoulder
1 medium-size yellow onion, peeled and minced
1 egg, lightly beaten
1 teaspoon grated lemon rind
1 teaspoon chili powder (optional)
1½ teaspoons salt
¼ teaspoon pepper

Preheat oven to 325° F. Boil cabbage in salted water 3–4 minutes until leaves are pliable; cool in a colander under cold running water until easy to handle, drain well, core, and remove 12 whole outer leaves (save rest to use later). Cut base of large vein from each leaf and discard; spread leaves flat.

For stuffing, soak rolls in water 5 minutes, squeeze as dry as possible, and mix with remaining stuffing ingredients. Put a spoonful stuffing on center of each leaf, fold sides in, and roll loosely; fasten with toothpicks. Layer rolls in an ungreased Dutch oven, add tomato juice, bay leaf, and garlic, cover, and bring to a boil. Transfer to oven and bake 1 hour, uncover and bake ½ hour longer. (*Note:* If using tomato sauce, check consistency and add a little water if too thick.) Remove garlic and bay leaf before serving. About 370 calories for each of 4 servings, 245 calories for each of 6 servings.

VARIATIONS:

¢ **Cabbage Rolls and Sauerkraut:** Prepare rolls as directed and layer into Dutch oven with 1 (1-pound 14-ounce) drained can sauerkraut. Add tomato juice, bay leaf, and garlic and bake as directed. About 405 calories for each of 4 servings, 270 calories for each of 6 servings.

¢ **Nova Scotia Cabbage Rolls:** Omit rolls, water, egg, and chili powder from stuffing and add ½ cup rolled oats and ¾ cup sour cream. After peeling off the 12 leaves, coarsely chop remaining cabbage. Prepare and arrange cabbage rolls in Dutch oven as directed, top with chopped cabbage and tomato juice (omit bay leaf and garlic). Cook as recipe directs. About 630 calories for each of 4 servings, 420 calories for each of 6 servings.

¢ HERBED LAMB LOAF

Makes 4–6 servings

1¼ pounds ground lean lamb shoulder
1 medium-size yellow onion, peeled and minced

⅓ cup minced green pepper
2 eggs
2 cups packaged stuffing mix
1 tablespoon minced parsley
¼ teaspoon thyme
½ teaspoon salt
⅛ teaspoon pepper
¾ cup lamb, beef, or chicken stock

Preheat oven to 350° F. Mix all ingredients well, using your hands, and shape into a loaf in a greased shallow roasting pan. Bake, uncovered, ¾–1 hour until loaf is firm to the touch and nicely browned. Serve as is or with Tomato Sauce. About 495 calories for each of 4 servings, 330 calories for each of 6 servings.

¢ CURRIED LAMB AND CARROT LOAF

Makes 6 servings

1½ pounds ground lean lamb shoulder
1 cup very finely grated carrots
1 medium-size yellow onion, peeled and minced
½ cup minced celery
3 tablespoons minced chutney
1½ cups corn bread stuffing mix
1 medium-size tart apple, peeled, cored, and minced
2 eggs
⅓ cup water
¼ cup minced parsley
2 tablespoons curry powder
1¼ teaspoons salt
¼ teaspoon cinnamon
⅛ teaspoon pepper

Preheat oven to 350° F. Mix all ingredients thoroughly with your hands and pack into a greased 9″×5″×3″ loaf pan. Bake, uncovered, 50–60 minutes until loaf pulls from sides of pan and is firm in center. Pour off any drippings.

Let loaf stand upright in pan 5 minutes before inverting and turning out. About 420 calories per serving.

LAMB BALLS EN BROCHETTE

Makes 6 servings

1 cup soft white bread crumbs
⅔ cup evaporated milk
1 egg, lightly beaten
¾ teaspoon garlic salt
¾ teaspoon celery salt
¼ teaspoon pepper
¼ teaspoon cinnamon (optional)
1½ pounds ground lean lamb shoulder
12 cherry tomatoes
6 preserved kumquats
12 mushroom caps, wiped clean

Basting Sauce:
¼ cup cider vinegar
¼ cup salad oil
2 tablespoons dark brown sugar
1 tablespoon steak sauce

Soak crumbs in milk 5 minutes; mix with egg, seasonings, and lamb. Shape into 1½″ balls and chill several hours. Preheat broiler. Arrange lamb balls on long skewers, not close together. Alternate tomatoes, kumquats, and mushroom caps on separate skewers. Mix basting sauce. Broil lamb balls 4″ from heat, turning and basting frequently, for 10 minutes. Add vegetable skewers and continue broiling 5 minutes, turning and basting lamb and vegetables frequently with sauce. This version and variation: about 430 calories per serving.

VARIATION:

Use 1½ teaspoons minced fresh mint in lamb ball mixture; omit cinnamon.

¢ TURKISH LAMB BALLS BAKED IN TOMATO SAUCE

Makes 4–6 servings

Lamb Balls:

1½ pounds ground lean lamb
    shoulder
1 medium-size yellow onion, peeled
    and minced
1 clove garlic, peeled and crushed
½ cup cracker meal
2 eggs, lightly beaten
1¼ teaspoons salt
¼ teaspoon cinnamon
⅛ teaspoon anise
⅛ teaspoon pepper
3 tablespoons olive oil

Sauce:

1 (8-ounce) can tomato sauce
1 cup water

Preheat oven to 350° F. Mix all lamb ball ingredients except oil, using your hands, and shape into 2″ balls. Brown balls well on all sides in oil in a large, heavy skillet over moderately high heat; drain on paper toweling. Transfer balls to an ungreased shallow 2-quart casserole. Mix tomato sauce and water, pour over balls, and bake uncovered 30–45 minutes until bubbly. Serve with rice or boiled potatoes. About 555 calories for each of 4 servings (without rice or potatoes), 370 calories for each of 6 servings.

¢ CRISPY LAMB-STUFFED BULGUR BALLS

Good as an hors d'oeuvre as well as a main course.
Makes 4 servings

1 cup bulgur wheat
2 cups boiling water
¾ teaspoon salt

Stuffing:

¼ pound ground lean lamb shoulder
1 small yellow onion, peeled and
    minced
1 tablespoon olive oil
1 tablespoon minced parsley
¾ teaspoon salt
⅛ teaspoon pepper

Coating:

2 eggs beaten with 2 tablespoons milk
⅔ cup unsifted flour

Shortening or cooking oil for deep fat
    frying

Stir bulgur wheat into boiling salted water, cover, and simmer about 8 minutes until all moisture is absorbed. Remove from heat and leave covered while you prepare filling. Stir-fry lamb and onion in olive oil about 10 minutes over moderate heat until lamb is no longer pink. Off heat mix in remaining stuffing ingredients; cool slightly. To roll balls, knead 1 heaping tablespoon bulgur until it holds together, shape into a small ball, then with your index finger, make a well in center; spoon in about ¼ teaspoon stuffing and reshape into a ball to seal. Repeat until all bulgur is used up—you should have about 2 dozen balls; refrigerate them while you heat shortening. When shortening reaches 365° F. on deep fat thermometer, dip balls in egg, roll in flour, then fry 3–4 minutes until golden brown. Drain on paper toweling and serve piping hot. About 340 calories per serving.

The Lesser Cuts of Lamb
(See Lamb and Mutton Chart)

"Lesser," in this case, means less expensive and less appreciated, but no less tender or delicious when properly prepared:
Neck slices and chunks

Shanks (fore and hind)

Riblets

Stew meat (the best comes from the shoulder)

¢ ECONOMY LAMB STEW

A rich brown lamb and vegetable stew that costs very little to make. Makes 4 servings

2–2½ *pounds lean neck of lamb, cut in 1½" cubes, or 2 lamb shanks, each cracked into 3 pieces*

2 *tablespoons cooking oil*

3 *medium-size yellow onions, peeled and coarsely chopped*

6–8 *medium-size carrots, peeled and halved crosswise*

2 *medium-size turnips, peeled and quartered*

½ *teaspoon minced garlic*

½ *teaspoon salt*

¼ *teaspoon pepper*

1 *teaspoon basil*

½ *teaspoon parsley flakes*

2 *cups water*

¼ *cup unsifted flour blended with ¼ cup cold water*

Brown meat well, a few pieces at a time, in oil in a large, heavy kettle over moderately high heat; transfer to a bowl. In the same kettle, stir-fry onions until golden, about 8–10 minutes. Return lamb to kettle, add all remaining ingredients except flour-water paste, cover, and simmer 1¾ hours until lamb is tender.

Mix in flour paste and heat, stirring, until thickened. Serve over boiled noodles with a crisp green salad. About 420 calories per serving.

VARIATION:

¢ **Economy Lamb and Potato Stew:** Prepare stew as directed and about ¾ hour before it is done add 4–5 peeled and halved potatoes. Cover and continue cooking until potatoes and lamb are both tender. About 525 calories per serving.

CASSOULET (FRENCH-STYLE BAKED BEANS WITH LAMB, PORK, AND GOOSE)

If the following recipe seems long and involved, it is. There just isn't any short cut to a good cassoulet. There are dozens of versions, all based on dried white beans cooked with a combination of meats. Here's one of the best. Makes 8 servings

1½ *pounds dried white beans (Great Northern or navy), washed and sorted*

3 *quarts cold water (about)*

½ *pound salt pork with rind left on*

1 *carrot, peeled*

1 *medium-size yellow onion, peeled and stuck with 6 cloves*

1 *bouquet garni* and 3 peeled cloves garlic, tied in cheesecloth*

1 *pound boned pork shoulder, cut in 1" cubes and trimmed of excess fat*

1 *pound boned lamb or mutton shoulder, cut in 1" cubes and trimmed of excess fat*

2 *tablespoons lard, goose, duck, or bacon drippings*

2 *medium-size yellow onions, peeled and minced*

1 *ham shank with some meat attached (leftover is fine)*

1 *meaty pork hock*

1 *clove garlic, peeled and crushed*

1 *cup beef broth*

½ *cup tomato purée*

½ *pound Kielbasa, Cotechino, or other garlicky pork sausage*

½ *pound mild pork sausage*

½ *preserved goose (leg and breast, obtainable in gourmet shops) or ½ roast goose or 1 small roast duckling*

2 *teaspoons salt (about)*

¼ *teaspoon pepper (about)*

1 *clove garlic, peeled and halved*

1 *cup soft white bread crumbs*

2 *tablespoons melted goose, duck, or bacon drippings*

Soak beans in 1½ quarts water overnight or use the quick method.* Drain, measure soaking water, and add enough cold water to total 1½ quarts. Simmer beans, covered, with salt pork, carrot, onion, and cheesecloth bag 1 hour; do not drain. In another kettle brown pork and lamb, a few pieces at a time, in lard over moderately high heat; transfer to a bowl. Stir-fry onions in remaining drippings 8–10 minutes over moderate heat until golden. Return meat to kettle, add ham shank, hock, garlic, broth and tomato purée. Cover and simmer ½ hour, add sausages, and simmer, covered, ½ hour longer. Off heat add preserved goose, scraped of excess fat, and let stand 15 minutes. Preheat oven to 300° F. Cut all meats from bones in bite-sized pieces; slice sausages ½" thick. Discard whole onion, carrot, and cheesecloth bag. Cut rind from salt pork; slice rind thin and dice the salt pork. Taste beans for salt and pepper and adjust as needed. Rub the inside of a deep 6-quart earthenware casserole or bean pot with the cut garlic, add salt pork rind, then layer in beans, salt pork, and all meats, beginning and ending with beans and sprinkling each layer with a little pepper. Pour in meat and bean broths. (*Note:* You may prepare recipe to this point early in the day or even the day before. Cover and refrigerate until about 4 hours before serving; let come to room temperature.) Top with crumbs and drizzle with melted drippings. (*Note:* For a less rich mixture, skim fat from broths before adding.) Bake, uncovered, 1½–2 hours until a brown crust forms on top of beans. Serve with a crisp green salad and a dry red or rosé wine. About 990 calories per serving.

NAVARIN OF LAMB PRINTANIER (FRENCH LAMB STEW)

Makes 6 servings

2 pounds boned lean lamb shoulder, cut in 1½" cubes
½ pound lean neck of lamb (with bones), cut in 1½" cubes
2 tablespoons butter or margarine
1 tablespoon sugar
3 tablespoons flour
3 cups meat stock or a ½ and ½ mixture of chicken broth and water
¾ cup tomato purée
2 teaspoons salt
¼ teaspoon pepper
1 bouquet garni,* tied in cheesecloth
1 clove garlic, peeled and crushed
12 small white onions, peeled
12 baby carrots, peeled
12 small new potatoes, peeled
4 turnips, peeled and quartered
1 pound fresh green peas, shelled, parboiled, and drained
½ pound fresh green beans, halved, parboiled, and drained

Preheat oven to 325° F. Brown lamb, a few pieces at a time, in butter in a large, heavy skillet over moderately high heat. Sprinkle last batch with sugar and let brown slightly, then transfer all to a Dutch oven. Lightly brown flour in skillet, slowly stir in stock, tomato purée, 1 teaspoon salt, and the pepper, and heat, stirring, until smooth; pour over meat. Add *bouquet garni* and garlic, cover, and bake 45 minutes. Add onions, re-cover, and bake 15 minutes. Add carrots, potatoes, and turnips, pushing them down into gravy, sprinkle with remaining salt, cover, and bake 30 minutes. Add peas and beans, cover, and bake 5–7 minutes. Ladle into a deep platter, pass the gravy separately, and serve with crusty bread. About 640 calories per serving.

LAPP LAMB STEW

Makes 8 servings

4 pounds boned lean lamb shoulder, cut in 1½" cubes
2 tablespoons butter or margarine
3½ cups water
4 stalks fresh dill
2 scallions, trimmed of roots
2 tablespoons cider vinegar
½ teaspoon salt
⅛ teaspoon pepper
¼ cup unsifted flour blended with ⅓ cup cold water

Brown lamb, a few cubes at a time, in butter in a large, heavy kettle over moderately high heat; transfer to paper toweling to drain. Return lamb to kettle, add all remaining ingredients except flour-water paste, cover, and simmer slowly 1½–2 hours until lamb is tender. Lift lamb from liquid and set aside. Put liquid, scallions, and dill through a food mill or purée, a little at a time, in an electric blender at low speed. Return liquid to kettle, raise heat to moderate, mix in flour-water paste, and heat, stirring constantly, until thickened and smooth. Return lamb to kettle and heat uncovered, stirring occasionally, about 5 minutes longer. Serve hot with boiled new potatoes. About 540 calories per serving (without potatoes).

LAMB AND DHAL (DRIED PEA) CURRY

Makes 6–8 servings

3 pounds boned lamb shoulder, trimmed of excess fat and cut in 1" cubes
1 tablespoon curry powder
1 pint yogurt
¼ cup butter or margarine
3 medium-size yellow onions, peeled and sliced thin
2 cloves garlic, peeled and crushed
1 pound yellow split peas
10 thin slices gingerroot
1 green chili pepper, sliced thin (include seeds)
2 sticks cinnamon
6 cloves
1 tablespoon powdered cumin
1 tablespoon crushed coriander seeds
2 teaspoons powdered cardamom
2 teaspoons powdered turmeric
½–1 teaspoon cayenne pepper (depending on how hot you like your curry)
1 (6-ounce) can tomato paste
1 quart water
1½ teaspoons salt

Place lamb in a large bowl, sprinkle with curry, and toss to mix; stir in yogurt and let stand at room temperature 1 hour. Melt butter in a large, heavy kettle over moderate heat, add onions and garlic, and sauté, stirring, 12–15 minutes until golden brown. Add all but last 3 ingredients and heat, stirring, 2–3 minutes. Stir in meat-yogurt mixture, tomato paste, water, and salt, cover, and simmer slowly 1½–2 hours until lamb is tender, stirring now and then. Serve over boiled rice and accompany with chutney. About 880 calories for each of 6 servings, 660 calories for each of 8 servings (without rice).

VARIATION:

Lamb Curry: Prepare as directed but omit split peas and reduce water to 2 cups. About 650 calories for each of 6 servings, 490 calories for each of 8 servings.

GREEK LAMB AND ARTICHOKE STEW

Makes 6 servings

3 pounds boned lamb shoulder, trimmed of excess fat and cut in 1" cubes

2 tablespoons olive oil

2 medium-size yellow onions, peeled and coarsely chopped

3 tablespoons flour

3 cups water

1 (9-ounce) package frozen artichoke hearts, thawed

Juice of 1 lemon

1 tablespoon minced mint

½ teaspoon salt

⅛ teaspoon pepper

3 egg yolks, lightly beaten

Brown lamb a little at a time in the oil in a large, heavy kettle over moderately high heat; drain on paper toweling. Stir-fry onions in drippings 10 minutes until lightly browned. Return lamb to kettle, sprinkle with flour, and toss to mix; add water, cover, adjust heat so mixture stays at a slow simmer, and cook 1½ hours until lamb is nearly tender. Add artichokes and lemon juice, cover, and simmer 20–25 minutes until tender. Mix in mint, salt, and pepper, taste and adjust seasonings if necessary. Ladle as much liquid from kettle as possible, briskly stir a little into egg yolks, then combine with remaining liquid; drizzle over lamb and artichokes, shake kettle slightly to distribute mixture, but do not stir. Serve over boiled rice. About 640 calories per serving (without rice).

COUSCOUS (NORTH AFRICAN LAMB STEW)

Couscous is not only the name of the cooked wheat cereal over which the stew is served but the name of the stew itself.

Makes 4–6 servings

Stew:

2 pounds boned lamb shoulder, cut in 1" cubes

2 tablespoons olive oil

2 tablespoons butter or margarine

1 (2½-pound) broiler-fryer, cut up

3 medium-size yellow onions, peeled and coarsely chopped

1 clove garlic, peeled and crushed

4 ripe tomatoes, peeled, cored, seeded, and coarsely chopped

½ teaspoon thyme

¼ teaspoon saffron

1 bay leaf, crumbled

6 cups chicken broth or water

2 medium-size sweet green peppers, cored, seeded, and cut in thin strips

6 medium-size carrots, peeled and cut in 1" chunks

1 tablespoon salt (about)

¼ teaspoon pepper

1 (1-pound 4-ounce) can chick-peas, drained

2 cups coarsely grated or sliced cabbage

Couscous:

1 recipe Boiled Couscous (Note: *Use 1 cup of stew liquid and 3 cups chicken broth.*)

Hot Sauce:

1 cup stew liquid

2 tablespoons tomato paste

1 teaspoon paprika

½–1 teaspoon crushed dried hot red chili peppers

¼ teaspoon coriander

⅛ teaspoon cumin

Prepare stew first: Brown lamb in oil and butter in a large, heavy kettle over moderately high heat; drain on paper toweling. Also brown and drain chicken. Add onions and garlic to kettle and brown 10–12 minutes; add tomatoes and herbs and cook and stir 2–3 minutes. Return lamb and chicken to kettle, add broth, green peppers, carrots, salt, and pepper, cover, and simmer ½ hour. Remove chicken, cover, and refrigerate. Continue cooking stew until lamb is nearly tender, about ½ hour. Remove 2 cups liquid from kettle and refrigerate (1 cup will be used for the Boiled Couscous, 1 for the Hot Sauce). Cool stew, chill, and skim off fat. (*Note:* Recipe can be prepared to this point a day or 2 in advance.) When ready to proceed, boil couscous as directed, using 1 cup of the reserved kettle liquid. Return chicken to stew and add chick-peas and cabbage. Place boiled couscous in a large colander lined with a triple thickness of dampened cheesecloth, set over kettle à la double boiler, cover with foil, and simmer stew slowly ½–¾ hour until meats are very tender and flavors well blended. Meanwhile, mix remaining reserved cup kettle liquid with all hot sauce ingredients and keep warm over lowest heat. To serve: Mound boiled couscous on a large platter and top with stew. Pass hot sauce separately, letting each person take as much or little as he wants. About 1520 calories for each of 4 servings, 1015 calories for each of 6 servings.

¢ RAGOUT OF MUTTON AND BEANS

Makes 6 servings

¼ *pound salt pork, cut in small dice*
2 *pounds boned mutton shoulder, trimmed of excess fat and cut in 1" cubes*
2 *large yellow onions, peeled and minced*
1 *teaspoon sugar*
1 *tablespoon flour*
1 *cup cold water*
1 *clove garlic, peeled and crushed (optional)*
1 *pound dried white, pink, or red kidney beans, boiled 1 hour but not drained*

Preheat oven to 325° F. Brown salt pork in a large, heavy skillet over

moderate heat, lift out with slotted spoon and reserve. Brown mutton, a few pieces at a time, in drippings over moderately high heat, transfer to a bowl. Sauté onions in same skillet 8–10 minutes until golden; sprinkle with sugar and allow to caramelize slightly. Blend flour into skillet, add water, and heat, stirring, 1–2 minutes. Off heat return meat and salt pork to skillet. Place beans and their cooking liquid in an ungreased 1-gallon casserole or bean pot, add skillet mixture, and stir lightly. Cover and bake 1½–2 hours until meat is tender. About 575 calories per serving.

MOROCCAN LAMB BAKE

Makes 4 servings

⅔ *cup seedless raisins*
⅓ *cup dry sherry*
¼ *cup chicken or beef broth*
2 *pounds boned lean lamb shoulder, cut in 1" cubes*
3 *tablespoons olive oil*
2 *medium-size yellow onions, peeled and coarsely chopped*
1 *clove garlic, peeled and crushed*
1 *teaspoon salt*
½ *teaspoon crushed hot red chili peppers*
½ *teaspoon turmeric*
½ *teaspoon oregano*
¼ *teaspoon thyme*
⅛ *teaspoon cinnamon*
2 *large ripe tomatoes, peeled, cored, seeded, and chopped*
2 *tablespoons minced parsley*

Topping:
1 *(4-ounce) package frozen French-fried onion rings, cooked by package directions*
½ *cup toasted blanched almonds*
½ *cup toasted blanched filberts*

Soak raisins in sherry and broth 1 hour at room temperature. Preheat oven to 350° F. Brown lamb well in oil in a large, heavy skillet over moderately high heat; add onions and garlic and stir-fry about 8 minutes until lightly browned. Add remaining ingredients except parsley and topping, bring to a simmer, and stir in raisins and soaking liquid. Transfer to an ungreased 2-quart casserole, cover tight, and bake 2 hours until tender. Check occasionally and if mixture seems dry add about ¼ cup hot water. When done, stir in parsley and arrange onion rings on top. Mix nuts in a small bowl and let each person scatter some over his portion. Serve with rice. About 975 calories per serving.

¢ IRISH STEW

Prepare this stew early in the day or even a day ahead so flavors will blend and fat can be skimmed off. Makes 4 servings

5 medium-size potatoes, peeled and halved
2½ pounds lean neck of lamb (with bones)
3 large yellow onions, peeled and sliced thin
4 teaspoons salt
¼ teaspoon white pepper
1 quart cold water
2 tablespoons minced parsley (optional)

Layer potatoes, lamb, and onions into a 4-quart kettle with a tight-fitting lid, beginning and ending with potatoes. Add salt, pepper, and water, cover, and simmer about 2 hours until lamb is tender. Cool and refrigerate, covered, at least 3 hours. When ready to serve, skim fat from surface and discard. Heat stew, covered, over low heat until piping hot. Ladle into heated soup bowls, including plenty of the liquid. Sprinkle with parsley, if

you wish, and serve. About 745 calories per serving.

VARIATION:

¢ Irish Stew with Dumplings (traditional in some parts of Ireland): Prepare and chill stew as directed. Skim off fat, then bring to a simmer over low heat. Make Dumplings by recipe, add to stew, cover, and cook as dumpling recipe directs. About 920 calories per serving.

¢ LAMB NECK SLICES BRAISED WITH LIMAS AND CARROTS

Makes 4 servings

3 pounds lamb neck slices, cut 1" thick and trimmed of excess fat
⅓ cup unsifted flour
1½ teaspoons salt
½ teaspoon pepper
3 tablespoons butter or margarine
1 large yellow onion, peeled and sliced thin
⅔ cup lamb or beef stock
2 tablespoons dry white wine
1 teaspoon finely grated lemon rind
⅛ teaspoon rosemary
1 (10-ounce) package frozen baby lima beans (do not thaw)
4 carrots, peeled and sliced thin
1 tablespoon minced parsley

Dredge neck slices in a mixture of flour, salt, and pepper, then brown in butter in a large, heavy skillet over moderately high heat; remove and set aside. Brown onion in drippings 10–12 minutes over moderate heat. Return lamb to skillet, pull onions on top, and add stock, wine, lemon rind, and rosemary. Cover and simmer slowly 35–40 minutes. Break up block of frozen limas by hitting package against edge of counter, scatter limas in and around neck slices, also carrots. Re-cover and simmer slowly 20–25 minutes longer until lamb and vegetables are tender. Sprinkle with parsley and serve. About 590 calories per serving.

¢ NECK OF LAMB IN DILL SAUCE

Makes 4 servings

2½ pounds lean neck of lamb (with bones), cut in 2" chunks
1 large yellow onion, peeled and chopped fine
1½ teaspoons seasoned salt
⅛ teaspoon white pepper
1 tablespoon snipped fresh dill, tied in cheesecloth
3 cups cold water
2 tablespoons butter or margarine
3 tablespoons flour
2 egg yolks, lightly beaten
1 tablespoon lemon juice
1–2 teaspoons snipped fresh dill (garnish)

Place lamb, onion, seasoned salt, pepper, cheesecloth bag, and water in a 1-gallon kettle, cover, and simmer 1¾–2 hours until lamb is tender. Drain off broth, cool, skim off fat and reserve. Melt butter in a large saucepan over moderate heat, blend in flour, slowly add reserved broth, and heat, stirring constantly, until thickened. Add meat to sauce and simmer, covered, 10 minutes. Blend a little sauce into egg yolks, then return to pan. Heat and stir 2–3 minutes but do not boil. Off heat stir in lemon juice. Taste for salt and pepper and adjust. Sprinkle with remaining dill just before serving. Good with boiled potatoes, crusty bread and asparagus, green peas, or broccoli. About 425 calories per serving.

VARIATION:

¢ Breast of Lamb in Dill Sauce: Substitute 3 pounds lean breast of lamb, cut in serving-size pieces, for neck. Proceed as recipe directs but reduce simmering time to about 1½ hours. About 450 calories per serving.

LANCASHIRE HOT POT

Every town in Lancashire, England, has its version of Hot Pot. Here's one of the oldest.
Makes 4 servings

2½ pounds lean neck of mutton or lamb (with bones), cut in 2" chunks
1 sheep's kidney or 2–3 lamb kidneys, trimmed of fat, membranes, and cores and sliced ¼" thick (optional)
2 large yellow onions, peeled and coarsely chopped
5–6 medium-size potatoes, peeled and sliced ¾" thick
4 medium-size carrots, peeled and cut in 2" chunks (optional)
1 quart cold water (about)
4 teaspoons salt
¼ teaspoon pepper

Preheat oven to 325° F. Layer lamb, kidney, onions, potatoes, and carrots in an ungreased deep 4-quart casserole; end with a layer of potatoes arranged as close together as possible. Pour in 3 cups water mixed with salt and pepper, then add enough additional water to come to bottom of potato layer. Cover with a buttered piece of foil. Bake 1 hour, uncover, and bake 1 hour longer until meat is tender and potatoes are browned on top. Serve with pickled red cabbage. About 550 calories per serving.

¢ BARBECUED LAMB RIBLETS

Makes 4 servings

3 pounds lamb riblets or spareribs, cut in serving size pieces

1 lemon, sliced thin
2 cups water
1 large yellow onion, peeled and
    sliced thin
2 tablespoons Worcestershire sauce
2 small cloves garlic, peeled
1 teaspoon salt
¼ teaspoon pepper
¼ cup chili sauce
2 cups barbecue sauce

Place all ingredients but barbecue sauce in a large, heavy kettle, cover, and simmer 1½ hours. Drain (save liquid for soups, gravies, etc.) and arrange riblets in a shallow roasting pan. Pour in barbecue sauce and let stand at room temperature 2 hours, turning ribs occasionally. Preheat oven to 325° F. Bake riblets, uncovered, 45 minutes, basting and turning often in sauce until browned, glazed, and tender.

VARIATION:

¢ **Charcoal Barbecued Lamb Riblets:** Prepare riblets as directed up to point of baking. Meanwhile, prepare a moderately hot charcoal fire.* Lift riblets from barbecue sauce, shaking off excess, and broil 4″–5″ from coals, turning and basting frequently, about 20 minutes until browned, glazed, and tender. Watch closely to avoid scorching.

Both versions: about 875 calories per serving.

¢ **ROAST LAMB SHANKS**

Makes 4 servings

4 lamb shanks, each cracked into
    3 pieces
1½ teaspoons unseasoned meat
    tenderizer
2 cloves garlic, peeled and slivered
2 tablespoons melted butter or
    margarine

2 tablespoons olive or other cooking
    oil
2 tablespoons lemon juice

Preheat oven to 325° F. Sprinkle shanks evenly with tenderizer and pierce deeply with a fork. Make 4 or 5 slits over meaty part of each shank and tuck in garlic slivers. Place shanks on a rack in a shallow roasting pan; mix butter, oil, and lemon juice and brush over shanks. Roast, uncovered, 1–1¼ hours until tender, brushing frequently with butter mixture. Serve hot with Mint Sauce or Rose Geranium Jelly. About 380 calories per serving.

¢ **CHARCOAL BARBECUED LAMB SHANKS**

Makes 4 servings

4 lamb shanks, each cracked into
    3 pieces

Marinade:
½ cup cider vinegar
½ cup bottled thick French dressing
2 tablespoons Worcestershire sauce
2 teaspoons garlic salt
¼ teaspoon pepper
¼ teaspoon liquid gravy browner

Lay shanks in a large, shallow casserole. Blend all marinade ingredients by shaking in a jar; pour over shanks. Cover and refrigerate 4–6 hours, turning shanks 2–3 times. Prepare a moderately hot charcoal fire.* Place each shank on a piece of heavy foil, add 2 tablespoons marinade and wrap tight. Arrange shanks on grill, not too close together, and cook 3″ from coals 1¼–1½ hours, turning 3–4 times with tongs. Unwrap 1 shank and test for tenderness—meat should just begin to separate from bone. If not, rewrap and cook a few minutes longer. When tender, unwrap shanks. Lightly grease grill, place shanks directly on grill, and cover loosely with foil wrappings. Brown 5–7 minutes, turning 1 or 2 times. (*Note:* A low fire is best for the final browning, so scatter the coals if fire seems too hot.) About 390 calories per serving.

¢ BRAISED LAMB SHANKS

Makes 2 servings

2 *lamb shanks, each cracked into 3 pieces*
2 *tablespoons meat drippings or cooking oil*
¾ *teaspoon salt*
½ *cup liquid (water, dry white or rosé wine, beer, cider, or beef consommé)*
1 *bouquet garni,* tied in cheesecloth*

Brown shanks well in drippings in a heavy kettle over moderate heat; pour off drippings, add remaining ingredients. Cover and simmer about 1½ hours, turning shanks once or twice, until tender. Or cover and bake about 1½ hours at 325° F. Skim liquid of fat and serve as gravy. About 370 calories per serving.

VARIATIONS:

¢ **Braised Lamb Shanks with Vegetables:** Sauté 1 coarsely chopped yellow onion along with shanks; add 4 carrots, 1 rutabaga and/or 4 turnips, all peeled and cut in large chunks, along with water, then proceed as directed. Increase salt slightly. About 420 calories per serving.

Braised Lamb Shanks with Sour Cream and Capers: Cook shanks as directed and lift to a deep platter. Skim fat from broth, mix in ½ cup sour cream and 2 tablespoons capers. Spoon a little sauce over shanks and pass the rest. About 490 calories per serving.

¢ **Braised Lamb Shanks with Gremolata:** Sauté 1 minced yellow onion along with shanks; add 1 peeled and diced carrot with water and simmer as directed. About 10 minutes before serving, mix Gremolata, which consists of: 1 tablespoon minced parsley, 1 small crushed clove garlic, and 2 teaspoons grated lemon rind; sprinkle over shanks. Thicken broth, if you like, before serving. About 400 calories per serving.

Piñon- and Rice-Stuffed Lamb Shanks: Braise shanks as directed until very tender and bones are loose; cool until easy to handle, then carefully push bones out; save broth. Mix ¾ cup cooked seasoned rice with 1 tablespoon minced parsley, 2 tablespoons coarsely chopped piñon nuts, and 1 minced scallion. Stuff shanks with mixture and arrange in an ungreased shallow baking dish. Add broth and bake, uncovered, 15–20 minutes at 350° F. About 490 calories per serving.

¢ ⚖ BOMBAY LAMB SHANKS

Makes 2 servings

2 *small lamb shanks, each cracked into 3 pieces*

Marinade:
1 *medium-size yellow onion, peeled and coarsely chopped*
½ *cup yogurt*
½ *teaspoon curry powder*
¼ *teaspoon garlic powder*
½ *teaspoon poppy seeds, crushed in a mortar and pestle*
1 *teaspoon salt*

¼ teaspoon pepper
¼ teaspoon ginger
¼ teaspoon cinnamon
1 tablespoon lemon juice

Place lamb shanks in a large, deep bowl. Blend marinade ingredients in an electric blender at high speed 1 minute, then pour over shanks. Cover and chill 3–4 hours, turning shanks 1 or 2 times. Prepare a moderately hot charcoal fire.* Place each shank on a large square of heavy foil, top with ¼ cup marinade, and wrap tight. Reserve remaining marinade. Lay shanks on grill, not too close together, and cook 3″ from coals 1¼–1½ hours, turning 3–4 times with tongs. Unwrap 1 shank and test for tenderness—meat should begin to separate from bone. If it doesn't, rewrap and cook a little longer. When tender, unwrap shanks and lay directly on grill. Broil 5–7 minutes, brushing occasionally with marinade and turning shanks so they brown evenly. About 250 calories per serving.

PORK

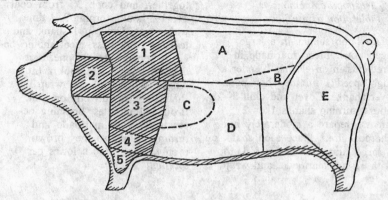

Note: Unshaded parts are the tender cuts. Shaded parts are not-so-tender.

THE TENDER CUTS:

A. **LOIN**
   Roasts (blade loin, center loin,
      crown, sirloin)
   Chops (rib, loin, blade, sirloin)
   Canadian bacon
   Back ribs
   Fat back

B. **TENDERLOIN**

C. **SPARERIBS**

D. **BACON**
   Bacon
   Salt pork

E. **HAM (LEG)**
   Hams (fresh and cured)
   Ham steaks

THE NOT-SO-TENDER CUTS:

1. **BOSTON BUTT (SHOULDER)**
   Roasts
   Steaks (blade, cube)
   Stew pork
   Ground pork
   Fat back
   Lard

2. **JOWL**

3. **PICNIC**
   Roasts (arm, fresh and smoked
      picnic)
   Steak (arm)
   Stew pork
   Ground pork
   Sausage

4. **HOCK**
   Fresh and smoked hock

5. **FEET**
   Fresh pigs' feet (trotters)
   Pickled pigs' feet

Thanks to breeders who are producing leaner, trimmer hogs, today's pork has about ⅓ fewer calories and ⅕ more protein than yesterday's. It remains one of our most nutritious meats, also one of the most economical and versatile.

How to Recognize Quality in Pork
The federal grades of pork (US 1, 2, 3, Medium, and Cull) are seldom used because the quality of pork varies less than that of beef, veal, or lamb. To be sure of good quality, look for finely grained, beige-pink lean with some

marbling (very young pork will be nearly white with little marbling) and a snowy outer covering of fat. Look, too, for the federal inspector's round seal, which guarantees wholesomeness.

About Cooking Pork

The cardinal rule of pork cookery: *always cook until well done* (this is to kill the microscopic parasites that cause trichinosis, a serious, sometimes fatal illness). Not long ago cookbooks recommended cooking pork to an internal temperature of 185° F., but researchers have now proved that trichinae (the disease causers) are killed at about 140° F. The new recommended internal temperature for pork roasts is 170° F. But, if you prefer ivory-hued pork with juices that run clear, by all means cook to 180° F. *Caution:* Wash hands well after handling raw pork (especially ground pork) and never taste pork until after it is cooked.

Roast Pork

Pork is the most roastable of all meats because almost everything except the head, feet, and tail can be roasted. The choicest roasts come from the loin, the next best from the shoulder and ham.

Loin Roasts: It is possible to buy whole pork loins but not very practical; they are too cumbersome for home ovens. For extra-large parties, it is easier to cook two smaller roasts (side by side) than to tackle one giant.

Center Loin Roast (3–5 pounds): The preferred loin roast because of its sizable tenderloin.

Sirloin Roast (3–4 pounds): Second best; it may contain some tenderloin.

Blade Loin Roast (3–4 pounds): It has the shoulder blade (hence its name) but no tenderloin.

Half Loin Roast (5–7 pounds): Half the loin plus either the sirloin or blade loin.

Rolled Loin (3–5 pounds): Any of the above, boned and rolled.

Crown Roasts: Showy, super deluxe roasts made by removing the backbone from 1 or 2 half loins and shaping into a circle. Rib ends are frenched and garnished with paper frills or small fruits. Butchers sometimes grind the trimmings and pile them in the center of the crown. This ground meat should be removed because it slows roasting (mix with the dressing you're using to stuff the roasted crown, or save for meat loaf). Smallish crowns contain 10–14 ribs, large ones may have 24 or more ribs and weigh 10 pounds or more; all must be specially ordered. To determine the size you need, figure 2 ribs per person.

Tenderloin (¾–1½ pounds): A long, lean muscle equivalent to beef filet or tenderloin. Boneless and luxury priced. Roast *or* braise.

Shoulder Roasts: Meaty, moderately priced cuts of excellent flavor.

Boston Butt (4–6 pounds): A blocky cut from the shoulder of pork. Also called *Boston Shoulder*. It is often available boned and rolled.

Fresh Picnic (5–8 pounds): Also called *Picnic Shoulder;* the lower part of the shoulder; it contains some shank.

Cushion-Style Picnic (3–5 pounds): Boned but not rolled; perfect for stuffing.

Rolled Fresh Picnic (3–5 pounds): Boned and rolled picnic.

Arm Roast (3–5 pounds): The top part of the picnic; it has no shank.

Fresh Hams: Hams are the hind legs of pork, and fresh ones are those that have not been cured and smoked. These make superlative roasts:

Whole Ham (10–14 pounds)
Whole Boneless Ham (7–10 pounds)
Half Hams: Butt Portion (5–7 pounds);
Shank Portion (5–7 pounds)

How to Roast Pork

Suitable Cuts: All fresh hams, loin and shoulder roasts. Because tenderloin and crown roasts are such luxurious cuts, there are separate recipes for each.

Amounts Needed: Pork roasts should weigh at least 3 pounds and will be juicier if 4 or more. To figure number of servings, allow ⅓ pound boneless roast per person and ½ pound bone-in roast.

General Preparation for Cooking: To simplify carving of loin roasts, have butcher loosen backbone. With the exception of fresh hams, whose crisp roasted skin some people enjoy, roasts should have any skin removed and the outer fat layer trimmed to ½″. If skin is left on ham, score every ½″. Let roast stand at room temperature 1½–2 hours if possible. Rub surface, if you like, with a little pepper

and, for extra flavor, a cut clove garlic and/or compatible herb (see Sauces, Gravies, and Seasonings for Pork).

Continuous Low Heat Method: Preheat oven to 325° F. Place roast fat side up in a large, shallow roasting pan; all but bone-in loin roasts should be placed on a rack; bone-in loins can be arranged so ribs act as a rack. Insert meat thermometer in center of roast, not touching bone; if roast is stuffed, make sure thermometer is as near center as possible, but in meat, not stuffing. Roast, uncovered, until well done, without adding liquid to pan and without basting (use times in Roast Pork Chart as a guide). Transfer roast to heated platter, let "rest," if you like, 15–20 minutes to allow juices to settle and facilitate carving. Then serve.

Searing Method (recommended for loin roasts only): Preheat oven to 450° F. Insert meat thermometer and place roast in pan as for low heat method (above). Set roast in oven, reduce heat to 350° F. and roast, uncovered, 30–35 minutes per pound or until thermometer registers 170° F. Do not add water and do not baste.

Roast Pork Chart (*opposite*)
Times (for roasts that have stood at room temperature 1½–2 hours, then roasted at a constant 325° F.) are merely approximate because size and shape of cut, proportion of fat and bone, internal temperature before roasting all affect cooking time.
–To roast at 350° F., allow 1–2 minutes less per pound and watch meat thermometer closely.
–For refrigerated roasts, allow 2–3 minutes more per pound.

Cut	Weight in Pounds	Approximate Minutes per Pound at 325° F.	Meat Thermometer Temperature
Loin			
Center loin roast	3–5	30	170° F.
Sirloin and blade loin	3–4	40	170° F.
Half loin roast	5–7	35	170° F.
Rolled loin roast	3–5	40–45	170° F.

(*Note:* The following shoulder roasts and fresh hams will be more flavorful if roasted to 185° F.)

Cut	Weight in Pounds	Approximate Minutes per Pound at 325° F.	Meat Thermometer Temperature
Shoulder			
Boston butt	4–6	40	170° F.
Rolled Boston butt	3–4	45–50	170° F.
Fresh picnic	5–8	30	170° F.
Cushion-style picnic	3–5	35	170° F.
Rolled fresh picnic	3–5	40	170° F.
Arm roast	3–5	35–40	170° F.
Fresh Hams			
Whole ham	10–14	25	170° F.
Whole boneless ham	7–10	35	170° F.
Half ham (butt or shank portion)	5–7	30–35	170° F.

How to Spit-Roast Pork

Best Cuts: Boned and rolled loin roasts. Small bone-in loins (with backbone removed) can be spit-roasted if carefully balanced and checked frequently for balance during cooking. Not recommended for spit-roasting, except over charcoal, where heat can be closely controlled by raising and lowering spit: hams and shoulder roasts (they are too chunky and/or irregularly shaped to cook evenly).

Amount Needed: Rolled roasts should weigh 4–5 pounds, bone-in roasts at least 3 if they are to be succulent and tender.

General Preparation for Cooking: Trim outer fat to ½″ and, if possible, let roast stand at room temperature 1½–2 hours. Season or not, as you like.

In Rotisserie or Oven: Preheat unit. Insert spit lengthwise through center of roast so roast is balanced; tighten holding forks. Insert meat thermometer in center of largest lean muscle, touching neither bone nor the spit. Attach spit to rotisserie and roast 30 minutes per pound for bone-in roasts, 35–40 minutes per pound for rolled roasts. Thermometer should register at least 170° F. and, if you like no traces of pink, 180° F. Remove roast from spit and let "rest" 15–20 minutes before carving.

Over Charcoal: Prepare a moderate charcoal fire toward back of grill.* Balance meat on spit: Loins should be spitted lengthwise, straight through the center; bone-in hams with spit parallel to leg bone; rolled shoulder or hams on the bias. Tighten holding forks. Insert

Cut	Weight in Pounds	Approximate Minutes per Pound over a Moderate Fire	Meat Thermometer Temperature
Bone-in loin roasts	3–7	25–35	170° F.
Rolled loin roast	3–5	30–35	170° F.
Boston butt	4–6	35–40	170° F.
Rolled Boston butt	3–4	40	170° F.
Fresh picnic	5–8	25–30	170° F.
Rolled fresh picnic	3–5	35	170° F.
Whole ham	10–14	25–30	170° F.
Whole boneless ham	7–10	30–35	170° F.
Half ham (butt or shank portion)	5–7	30–35	170° F.

meat thermometer in center of roast, making sure it does not touch spit or bone; also make sure it will not hit anything as spit turns; attach spit to rotisserie. Because pork is rather fat, it is more likely to cause flare-ups than beef, veal, or lamb. To reduce flare-ups: Adjust height of spit so it is 7″–8″ from coals, have spit turn away from you, and place a drip pan toward front of grill, where it will catch drips (metal TV dinner trays make dandy drip pans, so does a triple-thick rectangle of heavy foil with its edges turned up). When roast is ½ done, lower spit 1″–2″. Roast, using above chart as a guide.

VARIATION:

Spit-Barbecued Pork: Marinate roast in refrigerator 8–12 hours in 2 cups All-Purpose Barbecue Sauce, turning occasionally. Lift from sauce and pat dry with paper toweling. Spit-roast as directed, brushing often with barbecue sauce during last ½ hour of cooking.

Some Glazes for Roast Pork

About 30 minutes before roast is done, spread or drizzle any of the following over surface and continue cooking as directed, basting once or twice:

– 1 (8-ounce) can whole or jellied cranberry sauce.

– 1 cup apricot, pineapple, peach, or cherry preserves.

– 1 cup orange, lemon, or ginger marmalade.

– 1 cup black currant, red currant, apple, or cranberry jelly.

– 1 cup maple syrup, honey, or molasses.

– 1 cup firmly packed light or dark brown sugar mixed with ¼ cup sherry, Madeira, port, or fruit juice (cranberry, orange, apricot, apple, pineapple, or grape).

– ½ cup firmly packed dark brown sugar mixed with 1 cup orange juice and 1 tablespoon each lemon juice and prepared spicy brown mustard.

– 1 cup apple juice or cider mixed with ¼ teaspoon each cinnamon, ginger, and cloves.

– ½ cup soy sauce mixed with ¼ cup maple or dark corn syrup and, if you like, 2–3 tablespoons cognac.

– 1–1½ cups beer or stout.

– 1½ cups creamy or crunchy peanut butter.

How to Carve a Pork Arm Roast:
Separate large lean muscles from
one another by making cuts at
natural divisions and around the
bones. Cut each large muscle across
the grain into thin slices.

How to Carve Fresh Hams: These
are carved in the same way as
cured hams (see carving instructions
in Ham and Other Cured Pork).

How to Carve a Pork Loin Roast:

If butcher hasn't removed backbone,
do so before setting roast on platter.
Lay roast on platter so curved
rib section will face the carver.
Insert fork in top of roast and slice
by cutting down along each rib.

How to Carve a Picnic Shoulder:

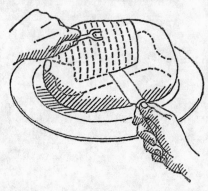

Cut a slice off side of picnic, then
turn picnic so it rests on cut surface.
At a point near elbow, cut straight
down to armbone, then along bone;
lift off this boneless piece; slice.
Cut meat from both sides of armbone and cut each into thin slices.

**Some Garnishes for Roast Pork
Platters** (in addition to parsley
fluffs and watercress sprigs)

Choose one or two fruits and/or
vegetables of contrasting but compatible color and flavor and group
or cluster around roast as artfully
as possible.

Apples: Baked or Cinnamon Apples;
Fried Apple Rings.

Apricots: whole canned or spiced;
broiled halves with or without a dab
of tart red jelly in the hollow;
Blue Cheese Stuffed Apricots.

Bananas: Sautéed Halved Bananas.

Brussels Sprouts: boiled and buttered.

Carrots: Buttered Baby Carrots;
Carrots Rosemary; Lemon-Glazed
Carrots; Carrots Vichy.

Crab Apples: whole canned or
spiced.

Grapes: small clusters of green
and/or red grapes.

Onions: Glazed Onions; Pan-
Braised Onions; Stuffed Onions.

Orange Cups or Baskets: filled with
candied yams or whipped sweet
potatoes; buttered green peas or
hot cranberry sauce.

Parsnips: Currant or Caramel-
Glazed Parsnips; Roasted Parsnips.

Peaches and Pears: broiled halves;
halves filled with Spicy Applesauce
or cranberry sauce; pickled, spiced,
or brandied peaches or pears.

SAUCES, GRAVIES, AND SEASONINGS FOR PORK

For Cooking: Seasonings, Herbs, Spices		*For Hot Roasts, Chops and Steaks:* Sauces	Gravies
Anise	Ginger	Barbecue	Au jus (unthick-
Bay leaf	Juniper berries	Charcutière (espe-	ened pan gravy)
Caraway	Lemon	cially chops, steaks)	Mushroom
Chervil	Lime	Chinese barbecue	Pan gravy
Chili powder	Mace	sauce	Sour cream
Chives	Nutmeg	Diable	
Cinnamon	Orange	Horseradish	
Cloves	Oregano	Hot mustard	
Coriander	Parsley	Madeira (especially	
Curry powder	Rosemary	chops, steaks)	
Dill	Sage	Molé	
Fennel	Thyme	Mustard	
Garlic		Orange	
		Piquante	
		Plum	
		Poivrade	
		Robert	
		Sweet-sour	
		Tomato	

For Hot or Cold Pork: Condiments	*For Cold Roasts:* Sauces
Applesauce	Cumberland
Chutney	Salsa fría
Cranberry sauce	Sour cream-
Horseradish	horseradish
Mustard	Whipped
Peaches (brandied	horseradish
or pickled)	
Pickles (bread and	
butter, dill, green	
tomato, mustard,	
sweet, watermelon	
rind)	
Preserved kumquats	
Relishes (corn, pepper,	
sweet pickle)	
Spiced fruits (crab	
apples, peaches,	
pears)	
Soy sauce	

Pickles: green tomato, mustard, and watermelon rind.

Pineapple: broiled chunks or rings; Pineapple and Grape Kebabs.

Potatoes: Parsleyed, Herbed, Lemon-Glazed, or Danish-Style New Potatoes.

Preserved Fruits: figs or kumquats.

Squash: Spicy Mashed Squash in Orange Cups.

Sweet Potatoes: Orange-Candied Sweet Potatoes or Yams.

Tomatoes: raw cherry tomatoes or tomato wedges; Deviled Tomatoes; Stuffed Tomatoes.

Turnips: Glazed or Roasted Turnips; Turnips Stuffed with Risotto.

ROAST PORK À LA BOULANGÈRE

Pork roasted as an old-time French baker's wife would do it, on a buttery bed of onions and potatoes. It's a good choice for a party because it's the sort of dish everyone likes.

Makes 8–10 servings

1 (5-pound) pork center loin roast
3 cloves garlic, peeled and crushed
3½ pounds medium-size potatoes
2 cups coarsely chopped onions
⅓ cup minced parsley
¼ cup melted butter or margarine
1 teaspoon minced fresh marjoram or ½ teaspoon dried marjoram (optional)
1 tablespoon salt
¼ teaspoon pepper

Preheat oven to 350° F. Place pork fat side up in a very large, shallow roasting pan and rub well with garlic. Insert meat thermometer in center of roast, not touching bone. Roast, uncovered, 1 hour. Meanwhile, peel potatoes and slice very thin, letting slices fall into a large bowl of cold water (to prevent darkening, keep potatoes submerged until you're ready to use them). When pork has roasted 1 hour, remove from pan and set aside; pour off all drippings. Drain potatoes well and place in roasting pan, add all remaining ingredients and toss to mix. Place pork fat side up on top of potatoes. Raise oven temperature to 400° F. and roast, uncovered, 1–1½ hours longer or until thermometer registers 170° F. Stir potatoes from time to time and, if they seem dry, sprinkle with a little chicken broth. To serve, center pork on a large heated platter and wreathe with potatoes. About 620 calories for each of 8 servings, 495 calories for each of 10 servings.

CZECH-STYLE ROAST LOIN OF PORK WITH PARSNIP-SOUR CREAM SAUCE

Makes 6–8 servings

1 large parsnip, peeled, trimmed of woody central core, and coarsely grated
1 stalk celery, coarsely chopped
2 medium-size yellow onions, peeled and coarsely chopped
1 cup water
1 cup dry white wine
1 (4-pound) boned and rolled pork loin

Sauce:
Pan drippings and chopped vegetables
2 tablespoons butter or margarine
2 tablespoons flour
1 cup sour cream
2 teaspoons salt
⅛ teaspoon white pepper

Preheat oven to 325° F. Place parsnip, celery, and onions in a large, shallow roasting pan and toss lightly to mix. Pour in water and wine and lay pork fat side up on vegetables. Insert meat thermometer in center of pork. Roast, uncovered, 40–45 minutes per pound or until thermometer registers 170° F. Lift roast from pan and let "rest" while you prepare the sauce. Purée pan drippings and vegetables, a few at a time, in an electric blender at low speed or put through a food mill. Melt butter in a saucepan over moderate heat and blend in flour. Add purée and heat, stirring, until thickened and smooth. Blend in remaining ingredients and heat, stirring, 1–2 minutes until satiny. Do not boil. Carve pork into slices ¼" thick and top each serving with sauce. About 755 calories for each of 6 servings, 570 calories for each of 8 servings.

ROAST LOIN OF PORK STUFFED WITH APPLES AND PRUNES

Makes 4–6 servings

1 (3–3½-pound) pork loin roast (blade loin, center loin, or sirloin)
1 tart apple, peeled, cored, and sliced thin
7–8 pitted prunes, halved
1 teaspoon sugar
1 teaspoon salt
⅛ teaspoon pepper
1 recipe Pan Gravy
¼ cup currant jelly

Preheat oven to 325° F. With a sharp knife, cut down between ribs to backbone to form 8–9 chops. Force chops apart slightly and tuck a few apple slices and 2 prune halves between each. Using string, tie loin tightly together to seal in stuffing. Mix sugar, salt, and pepper and rub over roast. Place fat side up on a rack in a shallow roasting pan (loin roasts don't usually require racks, but it's a good idea to use

one here because of the juiciness of the stuffing). Roast, uncovered, about 40 minutes per pound until well done (it is difficult to use a meat thermometer because of the way roast is cut, but, to be sure meat is done, insert thermometer in center of 1 chop, not touching bone; it should read 170° F.). Transfer to a heated platter, remove strings, and keep warm. Make Pan Gravy, blend in currant jelly, and serve. About 670 calories for each of 4 servings, 450 calories for each of 6 servings.

BAUERNSCHMAUS

Bauernschmaus is the Austrian Farmer's Feast traditionally eaten after winter hog killing. It should be served with tall steins of well-chilled beer.
Makes 8 servings

1 (4-pound) pork center loin roast
1 (3-pound) smoked shoulder butt
1 recipe Bread Dumplings
1 recipe Caraway Sauerkraut
1 pound frankfurters
1 recipe Pan Gravy

About 3 hours before serving, begin roasting pork loin by basic recipe*; also begin simmering smoked shoulder butt.* Meanwhile, make dumpling batter and chill. About 40 minutes before serving, begin Caraway Sauerkraut recipe, adding frankfurters along with sauerkraut and simmering all together. At the same time, simmer dumplings in boiling water as recipe directs. While sauerkraut and dumplings cook, lift pork loin and shoulder butt to serving platter and let "rest"; also make Pan Gravy from roast drippings. To assemble Bauernschmaus, pile well-drained sauerkraut and frankfurters in the center of a very large platter, arrange slices of loin roast and shoulder butt around the edge, and tuck dumplings in here and there. Pass gravy separately.

VARIATION:

If you prefer, broil frankfurters instead of cooking with sauerkraut and drape over sauerkraut just before serving; use 6–8 baked pork chops in place of the loin roast.

Both versions: about 1295 calories per serving.

CROWN ROAST OF PORK

Makes 10 servings

1 (20-rib) crown roast of pork (about 7–8 pounds) (Note: Make sure butcher removes backbone and frenches rib ends.)
¼ teaspoon pepper
1 recipe Pecan-Bulgur Wheat Stuffing or 1½ quarts any stuffing
10 spiced crab apples or preserved kumquats (garnish)
Parsley or watercress sprigs (garnish)

If butcher has filled center of roast with ground rib trimmings, remove and save for meat loaf. Let roast stand at room temperature 1½–2 hours if possible. Preheat oven to 325° F. Arrange roast, rib ends up, in a large, shallow roasting pan (no need for a rack) and rub with pepper. Insert a meat thermometer between 2 ribs in center of meat, making sure it does not touch bone. Cover rib ends with foil to keep them from charring. Roast, uncovered, 2 hours; spoon stuffing into hollow in center of roast, cover loosely with foil, and roast 1½ hours longer. Remove all foil and roast 15–20 minutes longer or until thermometer registers 170° F. Using 2 pancake turners, transfer roast to heated platter and let "rest" 15–20 minutes. Place crab apples

or kumquats on alternate rib ends and wreathe base with parsley or cress. Serve as is or with Pan Gravy. About 590 calories per serving.

For a Smaller Crown Roast (6–8 servings): Order a 12–16-rib crown roast (5–6 pounds) and prepare exactly like larger roast. Allow about 35 minutes per pound roasting time. About 615 calories for each of 6 servings (from a 12-rib roast), 640 calories for each of 8 servings (from a 16-rib roast).

How to Carve a Crown Roast: With a very sharp, rather small carving knife, slice down between each rib and remove chops 1 at a time. Serve 2 chops—and some stuffing—to each person.

PORK TERIYAKI

Makes 4 servings

2 pounds lean boned pork loin, cut in 1" cubes

Marinade:
½ cup Japanese soy sauce
½ teaspoon ginger
1 tablespoon sugar
1 tablespoon dark brown sugar
¼ cup sake or dry sherry
1 clove garlic, peeled and minced
1 small yellow onion, peeled and minced

Place pork in a large bowl; combine all marinade ingredients, pour over pork, mix well, cover, and refrigerate 4–6 hours. Preheat oven to 400° F. Drain marinade from pork and reserve. Line a roasting pan with foil, place a wire rack in pan and arrange pork on rack. Roast, uncovered, 35–40 minutes, turning often and basting frequently with marinade, until pork is tender and cooked through. Serve with boiled or Chinese Fried Rice. About

470 calories per serving (without rice).

ROAST WHOLE PORK TENDERLOIN

Makes 4 servings

1 (1½-pound) pork tenderloin
1 clove garlic, peeled and slivered
¼ teaspoon pepper
2 strips bacon (optional)
1 teaspoon salt

Preheat oven to 325° F. Make 6–8 tiny slits over surface of pork and insert a garlic sliver in each; rub well with pepper. Place tenderloin on a rack in a shallow roasting pan and insert meat thermometer in center. If meat seems lean, lay bacon strips on top. Roast, uncovered, about 1 hour until thermometer registers 170° F. Remove bacon for last 20 minutes of roasting so meat will brown. Transfer tenderloin to a hot platter, sprinkle with salt, and let "rest" 15 minutes. To serve, cut into slices ¼"–½" thick. If you like, make Pan Gravy. About 380 calories per serving.

VARIATIONS:

Roast Stuffed Whole Pork Tenderloin: Split tenderloin lengthwise, not quite all the way through so that one long side acts as a hinge, and spread flat like a book. Spread 1 cut side with 1–1½ cups Herbed Bread Stuffing or Sage and Onion Dressing, close, and tie in several places to hold in stuffing. Season and roast as directed above. About 435 calories per serving.

Orange-Glazed Whole Pork Tenderloin: Prepare tenderloin and begin roasting as directed. Meanwhile prepare glaze by mixing ¼ cup orange juice with ¼ cup firmly packed light brown sugar. When

tenderloin has roasted ½ hour, brush with a little glaze. Continue roasting as directed, brushing once or twice more with glaze. (Note: Any of the glazes recommended for pork or ham can be used in place of the orange glaze.) About 390 calories per serving.

Oven-Barbecued Pork Tenderloin: Prepare a marinade by mixing ½ cup light corn syrup with ¼ cup each soy sauce and ketchup, 2 tablespoons each Worcestershire sauce and cider vinegar, 1 teaspoon powdered mustard, and 1 crushed clove garlic. Place tenderloin in a large bowl with marinade, cover and chill 8 hours or overnight, turning occasionally. Lift meat from marinade and roast as directed above, omitting slivered garlic. Baste with marinade every 15 minutes. About 380 calories per serving.

Rosy Chinese-Style Pork Tenderloin: Heat and stir ½ cup each soy sauce and sugar, 1 cup water, and 8–10 drops red food coloring in a small saucepan over moderate heat until sugar dissolves. Place tenderloin in a large bowl, add saucepan mixture, cover, and chill 8 hours or overnight, turning meat occasionally. Lift meat from marinade, roll in 1 cup sifted cornstarch, and roast as directed, omitting garlic slivers. Baste with marinade every 15 minutes. About 380 calories per serving.

BRAISED WHOLE PORK TENDERLOIN WITH MUSHROOM GRAVY

Makes 4 servings

1 (1½-pound) pork tenderloin
1⅓ cups water
3 bay leaves
1 (4") sprig fresh thyme or ¼ teaspoon dried thyme

Gravy:

4 tablespoons butter or margarine
½ pound mushrooms, wiped clean
  and sliced thin
3 tablespoons flour
Drippings from pork tenderloin
1 cup water
¼ cup dry white wine
1 teaspoon salt
⅛ teaspoon pepper

Brown tenderloin well on all sides in a large, heavy skillet over moderately high heat. This will take about 10 minutes. Reduce heat to moderately low, add water, bay leaves, and thyme, cover, and simmer about 1 hour until pork is fork tender. Discard bay leaves and thyme sprig; drain liquid from skillet and reserve. Remove pork and keep warm while you make the gravy. Melt 2 tablespoons butter in the skillet and sauté mushrooms about 5 minutes over moderate heat until tender. Remove to a small plate. Melt remaining butter, blend in flour, and heat, stirring, 3–5 minutes until *roux* turns a rich amber brown. Add drippings and water and heat, stirring, until thickened and smooth. Add mushrooms, wine, salt, and pepper and continue to cook and stir 2–3 minutes. To serve, carve tenderloin crosswise into slices 1″ thick, arrange on a platter, and smother with mushroom gravy. About 530 calories per serving.

BRAISED PORK TENDERLOIN FILLETS

Makes 4 servings

8 slices pork tenderloin, cut 1½″–
  1¾″ thick
½ cup unsifted flour
1 teaspoon salt
¼ teaspoon pepper
2 tablespoons cooking oil
¼ cup water, dry white wine, or
  apple juice

Dredge fillets by shaking in a paper bag with flour, salt, and pepper; brown 4 minutes on each side in oil in a heavy skillet over moderately low heat. Add water, cover and simmer 30 minutes until fork tender and no trace of pink remains. Serve with Pan Gravy, Mustard Sauce, or other suitable sauce (see Sauces, Gravies, and Seasonings for Pork). About 470 calories per serving (without gravy or sauce).

VARIATIONS:

Pork Fillets Charcutière: Dredge and brown fillets as recipe directs, add 1 cup Charcutière Sauce instead of water, cover, and simmer as directed. Serve on a mound of hot mashed potatoes; pass extra Charcutière Sauce. About 690 calories per serving.

Breaded Pork Fillets: Dip fillets in flour, then in 1 egg beaten with 1 tablespoon cold water, then in seasoned bread crumbs to coat evenly; let dry on a rack at room temperature 10 minutes. Brown in ¼ cup cooking oil, drain off all but 1 tablespoon drippings, add water, cover, and simmer until tender and well done. Uncover, raise heat to moderate, and cook 1–2 minutes, turning frequently, to crispen crumb coating. About 500 calories per serving.

STUFFED ROAST SHOULDER OF PORK

Makes 8 servings

1 (4-pound) cushion-style picnic
  shoulder (ask butcher to give you
  the bones)
1 teaspoon salt
⅛ teaspoon pepper
1 quart (about) Herbed Bread,
  Apple and Pecan, or other savory
  stuffing or 1 (8-ounce) package
  poultry stuffing mix prepared by
  package directions

Preheat oven to 325° F. Trim outer fat on shoulder to ½", sprinkle cavity with salt and pepper, and loosely spoon in stuffing. Skewer edges shut every 1"–1½" and lace with string; place fat side up on a rack in a shallow roasting pan and insert meat thermometer in center, making sure it does not rest in stuffing. Roast uncovered about 35 minutes per pound or until thermometer reaches 170° F. Let roast "rest" 15–20 minutes at room temperature before carving. Serve as is or with Au Jus Gravy, using stock made from bones.

To Glaze: About ½ hour before roast is done, top with a suitable glaze (see Some Glazes for Roast Pork) and finish roasting as directed, basting once or twice. Calories per serving: about 565 calories if made with Herbed Bread Stuffing; 585 calories with Apple and Pecan Stuffing, and 540 calories made with prepared poultry stuffing mix.

VARIATION:

Stuffed Roast Loin of Pork: Have butcher bone a 4-pound center loin roast and make a pocket the length of it for stuffing. Trim fat, then salt and pepper pocket as above; fill loosely with stuffing (you'll need about 2½ cups), skewer and lace opening shut. Roast as directed, allowing about 35 minutes per pound or until thermometer registers 170° F. Calories per serving: about 640 if made with Herbed Bread Stuffing; 420 if made with Apple and Pecan Stuffing, and 385 made with prepared poultry stuffing mix.

SAGE AND CIDER SCENTED ROAST FRESH HAM

If skin is left on a fresh ham during roasting, it will become bubbly brown and crunchy. When carving, slice into thin strips and include one or two with each portion. Eat pork skin with your fingers—it's far too crisp to catch with a fork.
Makes 10–12 servings

*1 (5–7-pound) fresh half ham
    (shank or butt portion)*
3¾ cups apple cider
1 tablespoon powdered sage
2½ teaspoons salt (about)
¼ teaspoon pepper
*5 tablespoons flour blended with ½
    cup cold water*

Preheat oven to 325° F. Leave skin on ham and score at ½" intervals or, if you prefer, remove and trim fat to ½". Place ham on a rack in a shallow roasting pan. Moisten surface with ¼ cup cider, sprinkle evenly with sage and, if you've left skin on, with 1 teaspoon salt. Insert meat thermometer in center of ham, not touching bone. Roast, uncovered, 30–35 minutes per pound or until thermometer reaches 170° F. After 1 hour's roasting, pour 1 cup cider over ham. Continue to roast, basting occasionally with pan drippings. When ham is done, transfer to hot platter and let "rest." Remove rack from roasting pan, add remaining cider, set over moderate heat, and heat, scraping browned bits from bottom.
Mix in flour paste and heat, stirring, until thickened and smooth. Add remaining salt and the pepper. Strain gravy before serving. About 390 calories for each of 10 servings, 325 calories for each of 12 servings.

PORK "POT ROAST" WITH APPLE GRAVY

This isn't the usual way of preparing pork roast, but it's a good one

because it requires so little attention.
Makes 8–10 servings

*1 (5–7-pound) fresh ham or 1
(4-pound) rolled Boston butt or
fresh picnic*
1 teaspoon salt
¼ teaspoon pepper
¼ cup cold water

Gravy:
6 tablespoons flour
1½ cups water
1½ cups apple juice
1½ teaspoons salt
¼ teaspoon pepper
⅛ teaspoon liquid gravy browner

If ham has skin on, remove; trim
fat to ½″. Render fat trimmings in
a large, heavy kettle over moderately
low heat; discard trimmings and
pour off all but 2 tablespoons
drippings. Raise heat to moderate,
add pork and brown all over, about
15 minutes. Add salt, pepper, and
water, cover, and simmer 3½–4
hours until cooked through. Transfer to a hot platter and keep warm
while making gravy. Drain off all
but 1–2 tablespoons drippings;
blend in flour, then remaining gravy
ingredients and heat, stirring and
scraping brown bits from bottom,
until thickened; cover and simmer
2–3 minutes; taste and adjust
seasonings if needed. Slice roast,
not too thin, and serve with plenty
of gravy. Potato Pancakes and red
cabbage go well with this. About
465 calories for each of 8 servings,
370 calories for each of 10 servings.

To Cook in the Oven: Preheat oven
to 325° F. Prepare pot roast as directed but simmer in oven instead
of on top of stove. Check kettle occasionally to see that liquid simmers
but does not boil; reduce temperature to 300° F. if needed.

VARIATIONS:
Country Inn Pork Pot Roast:
About 1 hour before pork is done,
add ½ cup water, 6–8 peeled,
halved potatoes, 8 peeled small
carrots, 1 pound peeled small white
onions or 1 small rutabaga, peeled
and cut in 1″ cubes. Sprinkle
vegetables with 1 teaspoon salt
and ⅛ teaspoon pepper, cover, and
simmer until tender. Transfer meat
and vegetables to heated platter
and keep warm while making gravy
as directed. About 645 calories for
each of 8 servings, 520 calories for
each of 10 servings.

Barbecued Pork Pot Roast:
Marinate pork in any zippy barbecue sauce 24–28 hours. Pat meat
dry and rub with 1 tablespoon chili
powder. Brown as recipe directs,
add ¼ cup barbecue sauce along
with water called for, cover, and
simmer as directed, turning meat
once or twice. If you like, serve
with additional barbecue sauce.
About 485 calories for each of 8
servings, 385 calories for each of
10 servings.

Cranberried Pork Pot Roast: Brown
pork, then add 1 cup whole or jellied
cranberry sauce along with water,
cover, and simmer as directed.
Transfer pork to a hot platter,
top with cooked-down pan juices,
and keep warm; make Pan Gravy in
a separate saucepan. About 510
calories for each of 8 servings, 405
calories for each of 10 servings.

Extra-Savory Pork Pot Roast:
Make 8–10 tiny slits over surface
of roast and tuck a thin garlic
sliver in each (use 1 clove garlic in
all). Brown as directed and simmer
2 hours. Transfer pork to a rack in
a shallow roasting pan, spread
with ¼ cup prepared mild yellow
mustard, and bake, uncovered, at

300° F. 1 hour. Score fat in a diamond pattern, stud with cloves, and pat on ½ cup light brown sugar. Bake 1 hour longer, basting occasionally with pan drippings. Serve hot or cold. About 465 calories for each of 8 servings, 370 calories for each of 10 servings.

CHOUCROUTE GARNIE (SAUERKRAUT WITH MEAT)

Serve a well chilled Riesling or Traminer wine with this Alsatian classic. Or beer.
Makes 8 servings

1 large yellow onion, peeled and minced
2 tablespoons lard or butter
2 pounds sauerkraut, drained
1 tart apple, peeled, cored, and coarsely chopped
1 teaspoon juniper berries, tied in cheesecloth
1 (¼-pound) piece fat bacon or salt pork
2½–3 cups dry white Alsatian or other wine
1 (4-pound) center cut pork loin roast or (3-pound) boned and rolled loin
8 knackwurst
8 bratwurst or frankfurters

Preheat oven to 300° F. Sauté onion in lard in a heavy kettle over moderate heat 5–8 minutes until pale golden. Add kraut, apple, juniper berries, bacon, and wine; cover and bring to a simmer, then transfer to oven and bake 1 hour. Meanwhile, trim fat on loin to ¼″ and brown, fat side first, in a heavy skillet over moderate heat about 10 minutes; pour off drippings as they accumulate. When kraut has baked 1 hour, add pork, re-cover, and bake 1¾ hours longer. Check pot occasionally and add more wine if it seems dry; mixture should be moist but not soupy. Add sausages and bake 15 minutes until tender; remove cheesecloth bag. Pile sauerkraut on a large platter, top with bacon, sausages, and sliced pork. Serve with boiled potatoes sprinkled with minced parsley. About 1015 calories per serving (without potatoes).

VARIATIONS:
Substitute 6–8 small meaty pork hocks for pork loin and add to sauerkraut along with wine and apple; otherwise, prepare as directed. About 1015 calories per serving.

Substitute 1½ pounds Kielbasa (Polish sausage) or Cotechino (Italian sausage) for either of the German sausages and add to sauerkraut along with wine and apple. About 1015 calories per serving.

About ½ hour before serving, stir a stout jigger of kirsch into kettle. About 1040 calories per serving.

ROAST PORK REVISITED
(How to Use Up Leftovers)

¢ SLICED PORK AND BAKED BEAN CASSEROLE

A delicious way to revive leftover roast pork.
Makes 4 servings

8 slices leftover roast pork, cut ¼″ thick
2 tablespoons bacon drippings or cooking oil (about)
1 large yellow onion, peeled and minced
1 medium-size sweet green pepper, seeded, cored, and minced

¼ *teaspoon powdered mustard
mixed with 1 tablespoon cold water*
1 *(1-pound 5-ounce) can baked
beans in tomato sauce*
1 *tablespoon Worcestershire sauce*
¼ *cup chili sauce*
3 *tablespoons dark brown sugar*

Preheat oven to 350° F. Trim excess fat from pork, dice enough of it to measure 2 tablespoons, and render in a skillet over moderate heat. Measure drippings and add enough bacon drippings to total 2 table-spoons. Sauté onion and green pepper in the drippings 8–10 minutes until golden, stirring occasionally. Mix in mustard, beans, and re-maining ingredients; spoon half into an ungreased 2-quart casserole. Arrange pork slices on beans, top with remaining beans, cover, and bake ½ hour until bubbly. About 560 calories per serving.

⚖ SUBGUM (10-INGREDIENT) PORK CHOW MEIN

Makes 4 servings

¼ *cup blanched, slivered almonds*
2 *tablespoons cooking oil*
1½–2 *cups diced leftover roast pork,
trimmed of fat*
½ *pound mushrooms, wiped clean
and sliced thin*
1½ *cups shredded celery cabbage or
finely chopped celery*
2 *cups chicken broth*
1 *teaspoon salt*
2 *tablespoons cornstarch blended
with ¼ cup cold water*
1 *(4-ounce) can bamboo shoots,
drained and sliced thin*
1 *(1-pound) can bean sprouts,
drained*

Stir-fry almonds in oil in a *wok* or heavy skillet 1–2 minutes over moderately high heat until golden; drain on paper toweling. Pour oil from skillet, add pork, mushrooms, and cabbage, and stir-fry 2 minutes. Add broth, salt, and cornstarch mixture and heat, stirring, until thickened. Add remaining ingredi-ents and cook and stir 2–3 minutes. Serve over heated chow mein noodles topped with almonds. About 330 calories per serving.

To Make with Raw Pork: Cut ½ pound pork tenderloin or loin across the grain into ⅛″×⅛″×2″ strips. Stir-fry almonds as di-rected and drain. Add pork to skillet and stir-fry 1–2 minutes; add vegetables and proceed as recipe directs. About 300 calories per serving.

VARIATION:

⚖ **Pork Lo Mein:** Boil and drain ½ pound Chinese egg noodles or spaghettini by package directions. Omit almonds. Stir-fry pork, mush-rooms, and cabbage in oil 2 minutes, add ½ cup broth, salt, and corn-starch mixture, and heat, stirring, until thickened. Instead of adding bamboo shoots and bean sprouts, top with noodles, cover, and simmer 3–4 minutes. Serve with soy sauce. About 330 calories per serving.

⚖ CHAR SHU DING (DICED ROAST PORK WITH CHINESE VEGETABLES)

Makes 4–6 servings

2 *tablespoons cooking oil*
1 *cup minced yellow onion*
1½ *cups coarsely shredded celery
cabbage*
½ *pound mushrooms, wiped clean
and sliced thin*
¼ *pound snow pea pods*
2 *stalks celery, cut in thin diagonal
slices*
1 *sweet green or red pepper, cored,
seeded, and cut in long, thin strips*

2 cups diced or sliced leftover roast
    pork
2 cups chicken broth
3 tablespoons soy sauce
½ teaspoon MSG (monosodium
    glutamate)
¼ teaspoon sugar
2 tablespoons cornstarch blended
    with ¼ cup cold water
1 (1-pound) can bean sprouts,
    drained
1 (3-ounce) can water chestnuts,
    drained and sliced thin
⅓ cup toasted, slivered almonds

Heat oil in a *wok* or large, heavy
skillet over moderately high heat
1 minute; add onion, celery cabbage,
mushrooms, pea pods, celery, and
green pepper and stir-fry 3–4
minutes (do not brown). Add pork
and stir-fry 1 minute, then broth,
soy sauce, MSG, sugar, and cornstarch mixture and cook, stirring,
until thickened. Toss in bean sprouts
and water chestnuts and heat 1–2
minutes. Taste for salt and adjust
as needed. Serve over boiled rice and
top each portion with toasted, slivered almonds. About 300 calories
for each of 4 servings, 195 calories
for each of 6 servings.

¢ ⟐ ⊠ CHOP SUEY

Tag ends of peas, beans, or carrots
cluttering up the refrigerator?
Toss them into chop suey. This one
can also be made with leftover beef
or lamb.
Makes 4 servings

2 tablespoons cooking oil
1 cup minced yellow onion
4 stalks celery, cut in thin diagonal
    slices
1 sweet green or red pepper, cored,
    seeded, and cut in long, thin strips
2 cups diced or sliced leftover roast
    pork
2 cups chicken broth

3 tablespoons soy sauce
¼ teaspoon sugar
2 tablespoons cornstarch blended
    with ¼ cup cold water
1 (1-pound) can bean sprouts,
    drained

Heat oil in a *wok* or large, heavy
skillet over moderately high heat 1
minute, add onion, celery, and
green pepper, and stir-fry 3–4
minutes (do not brown). Add pork
and stir-fry 1 minute, then all remaining ingredients except bean
sprouts; cook and stir until thickened. Add sprouts and toss 1–2
minutes. Taste for salt and adjust as
needed. Serve over boiled rice or
chow mein noodles. About 270
calories per serving.

To Make with Raw Pork: Slice lean
tenderloin or loin across the grain
into strips 2″ long and ⅛″ wide;
stir-fry 1 minute in oil, then add
onion, celery, and green pepper and
proceed as directed. About 240
calories per serving.

Some Additional Ways to Use Up Leftover Roast Pork

¢ ⟐ **Chinese Pork-Fried Rice**
(4 servings): Stir-fry 1½ cups
minced leftover pork, 1 minced small
yellow onion, and 1 crushed clove
garlic in 2 tablespoons peanut oil
in a large, heavy skillet over
moderately high heat 5–8 minutes
until lightly browned. Stir in 1 cup
uncooked rice and stir-fry 3–4
minutes. Add 1 drained (4-ounce)
can sliced mushrooms, 1¾ cups
water, 2 tablespoons soy sauce,
and a pinch pepper. Bring to a boil,
cover, and simmer slowly 25 minutes until rice is tender. Top, if you
like, with strips of scrambled egg.
About 275 calories per serving
(without egg).

¢ **Creamed Pork and Peas** (4 servings): Stir-fry 1 minced small yellow onion in 2 tablespoons butter in a large, heavy skillet over moderate heat 8–10 minutes until golden; mix in 1 (10½-ounce) can cream of celery soup, 2 tablespoons heavy cream, 1 teaspoon each paprika and Worcestershire sauce, 1½ cups diced cooked pork, and 1 (10-ounce) package frozen green peas. Cover and simmer 10–12 minutes, breaking up block of peas after 5 minutes. Taste for salt and pepper and season as needed. Serve over biscuits or toast. About 340 calories per serving (without biscuits or toast).

⚖ **Cubed Pork and Olives in Sour Cream** (2 servings): Melt 2 tablespoons butter in a saucepan over moderate heat and blend in 2 tablespoons flour, 1 teaspoon paprika, and ½ teaspoon each garlic salt and onion salt. Add 1 cup water and 1 tablespoon lemon juice and heat, stirring, until thickened. Add 1½ cups cubed cooked pork and ½ cup sliced, pitted ripe olives, cover, and simmer 5–10 minutes to blend flavors. Off heat, mix in ⅓ cup sour cream. Serve over boiled rice. About 235 calories per serving (without rice).

¢ ⚖ **Pork, Rice, and Vegetable Casserole** (4–6 servings): Mix 3 cups cooked rice with 2 cups each diced cooked pork and mixed, diced leftover vegetables. Stir in 1 (10½-ounce) can cream of celery, mushroom, tomato, or asparagus soup thinned with 1 cup milk. Spoon into a buttered 2-quart casserole, cover, and bake 30–40 minutes at 400° F. *Optional Topping:* Just before serving, scatter ¼–⅓ cup buttered bread crumbs or grated Cheddar cheese over casserole and broil quickly to brown.

About 475 calories for each of 4 servings (without topping), 310 calories for each of 6 servings.

Barbecued Pork and Potatoes:

Roast Pork Hash:

} Follow recipes given in Some Additional Ways to Use Up Leftover Roast Beef, substituting pork for beef.

Sliced Cold Pork: Slice pork about ¼″ thick, trim of fat, and top with any recommended cold sauce (see Sauces, Gravies, and Seasonings for Pork).

Sliced Hot Pork: Slice pork about ¼″ thick, trim of fat and layer into an ungreased shallow casserole. Add just enough hot sauce (see Sauces, Gravies, and Seasonings for Pork) to cover, cover with foil, and heat 20 minutes at 350° F. Or, if you prefer, heat pork in sauce 5 minutes in a covered skillet over moderately low heat.

Hot Roast Pork Sandwiches: Heat meat and a suitable sauce in a skillet as for Sliced Hot Pork (above) and serve, open face, on toast or bread.

To Make the Most of Very Small Amounts: See suggestions given for beef.

Suckling Pig

Suckling pigs call to mind the days of Jolly Olde England, where whole pigs were spitted in open hearths, and the luaus of Hawaii, where they are pit-roasted on the beach. They are not often prepared in modern America, although they were popular at colonial feasts. Suckling pigs are 6 to 8 weeks old and weigh from 10 to 20 pounds. There is little meat on them, but what there is approaches pâté in richness. Some people like to munch the richly browned skin, but for most tastes it is too leathery. Suckling pigs must always be especially ordered, sometimes as much as a week or two ahead. The best size is in the 14- to 18-pound range—large enough to contain some meat, small enough to fit in most home ovens. To figure number of servings, allow about 1¼ pounds pig per person (most of the weight is bone). *Tip:* To keep the pig cool until roasting time (you can't get a suckling pig in the refrigerator unless you clear virtually everything else out), place in an extra-large roasting pan and set on a porch or just outside the door (suckling pig is cold weather food, so the outdoor temperature should be just about right unless it's below freezing; in that case, you'll have to make accommodations inside). Turn a large washtub upside down over the pig and weight down with bricks or large rocks to remove temptation from neighborhood dogs.

Suckling pig should be reserved for the most festive occasions. When inviting guests, tell them what you plan to serve—some people are squeamish about seeing a whole pig on a platter.

ROAST SUCKLING PIG

Makes 10–12 servings

1 (*15-pound*) *suckling pig, dressed*
1 *tablespoon salt*
1 *teaspoon pepper*
1 *recipe Chestnut Mushroom Stuffing or 1 recipe Brandied Wild Rice, Corn Bread, and Chestnut Stuffing*
¼ *pound butter, softened to room temperature*

Garnishes:
1 *small red apple or 1 lemon*
1 *pint fresh cranberries*
12 *laurel or English ivy leaves*

Preheat oven to 350° F. Wipe pig inside and out with a damp cloth and dry with paper toweling. Rub inside well with salt and pepper. Lay pig on its side and stuff loosely; wrap remaining stuffing in foil and refrigerate. Close cavity with skewers and lace together to close. Place a large, sturdy rack in an extra-large shallow roasting pan; lay a triple thickness of foil diagonally on top, allowing plenty of overhang. Lift pig onto foil so it, too, is diagonal to the pan, bend hind legs forward and front legs backward into a "praying" position so pig crouches. Turn up foil edges, forming a "pan" to catch drips. Rub pig with butter; cover ears and tail with bits of foil and force a foil ball about the size of an apple into the mouth. Roast uncovered, brushing occasionally with butter, 18 minutes per pound. Meanwhile, string cranberries and leaves into 2 garlands. Save 2 cranberries for pig's eyes. About 1 hour before serving, place foil package of stuffing in oven to heat. When pig is done, lift carefully to an extra-large platter; remove skewers, lacing, and foil. Place an apple or lemon in pig's mouth, 1 cranberry in each eye (secure with toothpicks) and lay garlands around neck. Place extra stuffing in a separate dish and skimmed drippings in a gravy boat.

To Spit Roast over Charcoal: Prepare a very large, moderate charcoal fire.* Prepare and stuff pig as above, truss legs to body in kneeling position, and insert spit lengthwise through center of pig so it is balanced; use at least 4 holding forks, 2 at each end, to secure pig on spit. Arrange coals in a circle and place a drip pan in the center. Attach spit to rotisserie, adjust height so spit is 7"–8" from coals, and roast pig 15–18 minutes per pound. Arrange on platter and garnish as above.

How to Carve Suckling Pig: Set platter on table so pig's head is to left of carver. First, remove the hams or hind legs, then divide pig into chops by cutting along the backbone, then down along each rib. See that each person receives both chops and ham or leg meat. Roast suckling pig and spit-roasted suckling pig: about 1135 calories for each of 10 servings if made with Chestnut Mushroom Stuffing; 1330 calories per serving if made with Brandied Wild Rice, Corn Bread, and Chestnut Stuffing; about 945 calories for each of 12 servings if made with Chestnut Mushroom Stuffing; 1110 calories per serving if made with Brandied Wild Rice, Corn Bread, and Chestnut Stuffing.

Pork Chops and Steaks

The easiest way to learn these small cuts is to relate them to the roasts from which they come (see Pork Chart). A blade chop, for example, is simply a slice of the blade loin; a loin chop, a slice of center loin; a sirloin chop, a slice of sirloin, and so on. As with roasts, the most expensive chops and steaks are those from the loin, the most economical those from the Boston butt or picnic:

Blade Chop: A moderate sized, moderate-priced chop from the blade loin roast.

Rib Chop: A smallish, moderate-to-expensive chop from the rib end of the center loin. It is usually cut 1 rib thick.

Butterfly Chop: A double rib chop, made by removing the rib bone, cutting the meat almost in half horizontally, and opening flat like a book. It's fairly expensive and must be ordered.

Loin Chop: The choicest pork chop. It is cut from the heart of the center loin roast, usually 1 rib thick, and contains a plump nugget of tenderloin. Expensive as pork chops go.

Top Loin Chop: A loin chop with the tenderloin removed. Fairly expensive.

Sirloin Chop: A chop from the sirloin roast; any cut from the part bordering the loin may contain a tag end of tenderloin. Moderately expensive.

Tenderloin Slices: These are to pork what filet is to beef—boneless, butter-smooth, luxury-priced steaks. A whole pork tenderloin weighs only ¾–1½ pounds, so a single slice is scarcely a mouthful.

Blade Steak: A slice of Boston butt containing the shoulder blade; 1 blade steak will usually serve 2. Economical.

Arm Steak: A meaty slice of the picnic, large enough for 2. Economical.

Leg Steak: Also called pork cutlet, this is simply a slice of fresh ham, usually from the butt portion; 1 leg steak will serve 2. Moderate.

Porklet: The pork equivalent of cube steak. It's a small boneless shoulder steak that's been tenderized by cubing. Economical.

How to Cook

Amounts Needed: All pork chops and steaks should be at least ½" thick

and will be more attractive and
succulent if cut ¾"–1"; those
to be stuffed should be 1¼"–1½"
thick.

Tenderloin Slices: Allow 2–3
(¼"–½") slices per person.

Rib, Loin, and Top Loin Chops:
Allow 1–2 per person.

*Blade, Butterfly, and Sirloin Chops;
Porklets:* Allow 1 per person.

Blade, Arm, and Leg Steaks: Allow
1 for each 2 persons.

General Preparation for Cooking:
If meat seems moist, wipe with
a damp cloth so it will brown nicely.
Trim off all but ¼" outer fat; rub
with pepper if you like, also
garlic and/or a compatible herb
(see Sauces, Gravies, and Seasonings
for Pork) but not with salt (chops
and steaks should not be salted until
after browning). Let stand at
room temperature 1½–2 hours before
cooking if convenient.

To Broil or Panbroil: Not recommended; by the time chops and
steaks have cooked through at
this intense heat, they will be dry,
tough, and stringy.

To Panfry (Sauté): Recommended
only for very thin pork chops
or steaks (those ½" or less) and
then only as a change of pace from
braised chops (see recipes that
follow).

To Braise: Here's the preferred
method for preparing all pork
chops and steaks because it allows
them to cook thoroughly without
toughening and drying. Brown chops
or steaks 5 minutes on a side over
moderately high heat in a skillet
brushed with oil; pour off all
drippings. Sprinkle lightly with
salt and pepper, add a small amount
of water (⅓ cup is about right for
4 chops or 2 steaks), cover, and
simmer slowly over low heat or in
a preheated 350° F. oven 50–60
minutes until well done.

To test for doneness: Make a
small slit near bone (or, if meat
is boneless, in the center); flesh
should show no traces of pink. Or,
pierce meat with a sharp fork
near center; if juices run clear
with no tinges of pink, meat is well
done. Serve as is or with Pan
Gravy or Country Gravy.

For Extra Savor: Substitute any
of the following for the water called
for above: tomato juice or sauce
or undrained, canned tomatoes;
pineapple, orange, apple, or mixed
fruit juices; milk, buttermilk,
or light cream; barbecue or meatless
spaghetti sauce; undrained, canned
crushed pineapple; chicken or
beef broth; ginger ale; beer or dry
white wine; ½ (10½-ounce) can
condensed onion, black bean, cream
of celery or mushroom, tomato,
or tomato and rice soup.

**Some Variations on Braised Pork
Chops and Steaks**
(all quantities based on enough
chops or steaks for 4 persons)

Smothered Pork Chops or Steaks:
Brown meat as directed above;
pour off drippings, season meat, and
add 1 (10½-ounce) can condensed cream of mushroom, celery,
or chicken soup thinned with
⅓ cup milk. Cover and simmer
as directed.

Hawaiian-Style Steaks or Chops:
Brown meat as directed; pour
off drippings and season meat. Top
each steak with 2 pineapple rings,
each chop with 1, add ½ cup
syrup from can or ½ cup pineapple
juice, and sprinkle with 2–3 table-

spoons light brown sugar. Cover and simmer as directed. When done, remove meat and pineapple rings to a hot platter and keep warm. To pan juices add 1¼ cups pineapple juice blended with 1 teaspoon cornstarch and heat, stirring, until thickened and clear. Spoon some sauce over meat and pass the rest.

Italian-Style Pork Chops or Steaks: Rub both sides of chops or steaks with a cut clove garlic, then brown as directed in a skillet brushed with olive oil; pour off drippings and season meat. Pour in 1 cup meatless or mushroom spaghetti sauce, cover, and simmer as directed.

Hungarian-Style Pork Chops or Steaks: Rub chops or steaks with 1–2 teaspoons paprika, brown as directed, and remove from skillet. In drippings stir-fry 1 minced medium-size yellow onion 5–8 minutes over moderate heat until pale golden. Return chops to skillet, season with salt and pepper, add ½ cup beef broth and 1 bay leaf. Cover and simmer as directed. Transfer chops to a platter, blend 1 cup sour cream into pan juices, heat 1 minute but do not boil. Pour over meat and serve.

Indiana Pork Chops or Steaks: Brown meat as directed; pour off drippings and season meat. Top each chop with a ¼″ slice yellow onion and a thin slice lemon (use 2–3 of each on steaks). Mix ½ cup ketchup, ½ cup water, and 2 tablespoons each dark brown sugar and Worcestershire sauce, pour over meat, cover, and simmer as directed. Uncover during last 15 minutes so juices will cook down.

Herbed Pork Chops or Steaks in Wine: Rub chops or steaks with a mixture of ¼ teaspoon each powdered rosemary, sage, and garlic powder and let stand at room temperature 15 minutes. Brown as directed; pour drippings from skillet and season meat with salt and pepper. Add ½ cup dry white wine, cover, and simmer as directed. Transfer meat to a hot platter and keep warm. Boil down pan juices until reduced to 2–3 tablespoons; spoon over meat and serve.

Braised Pork Chops or Steaks with Dressing: Brown chops as directed; pour off drippings and season meat. Top each chop or steak with 2–3 tablespoons poultry stuffing mix prepared by package directions, add ½ cup condensed cream of mushroom, celery, or chicken soup thinned with ½ cup water, cover, and simmer as directed. Uncover for last 5 minutes.

Orange-Lemon Pork Chops or Steaks: Brown meat as directed and pour off drippings. Top each with a ¼″ thick slice peeled, seeded orange and lemon. Mix 1 teaspoon salt, ⅛ teaspoon pepper, ¼ cup firmly packed light brown sugar, and ¾ cup orange juice; pour over meat, cover, and simmer as directed.

Apple-Raisin Pork Chops: Brown chops as directed; pour off drippings and season meat. Top each with a ½″ thick slice cored tart apple (peeled or unpeeled) and fill centers with seedless raisins. Pour in ⅓ cup apple juice or cider, cover, and simmer as directed.

Pork Chops with Sherried Applesauce: Brown chops as directed; pour off drippings and season meat. Arrange in a lightly greased 2-quart casserole. Mix 1 (1-pound) can applesauce with ½ cup medium-dry sherry or port and ¼ teaspoon each ginger, cinnamon, and nutmeg. Spoon ½ of applesauce mixture over chops and bake, uncovered, as directed 30 minutes. Turn chops, top with remaining applesauce, and bake, uncovered, 30 minutes longer or until thoroughly cooked.

Pork Chop-Corn Scallop: Brown chops as directed; pour off drippings and season meat. Arrange in a lightly greased 2-quart casserole. To skillet in which chops were browned, add ½ cup boiling water and heat 1–2 minutes, scraping up browned bits; pour over chops. Mix 1 (1-pound) can cream-style corn with 1½ cups soft bread crumbs, 3 tablespoons each prepared mild yellow mustard and finely grated onion, ¼ teaspoon salt, and a pinch pepper. Spoon mixture on top of each chop, mounding it up, and bake, uncovered, as directed, but without turning.

To Bake Pork Chops: Preheat oven to 350° F. Arrange chops in a lightly greased shallow roasting pan or casserole and bake, uncovered, ½ hour; drain off drippings. Sprinkle with salt and a pinch pepper, turn, and bake uncovered ½ hour longer or until no trace of pink remains. Transfer to a hot platter, sprinkle with salt and pepper. Serve as is or with Pan Gravy or Country Gravy.

For Extra Savor: About 10 minutes before chops are done, top each with any 1 of the following: 2 tablespoons apple jelly or whole cranberry sauce; ½ peach filled with red currant jelly; 1 pineapple ring or 2 tablespoons pineapple chunks sprinkled with 1 teaspoon light brown sugar. Or spread each chop with 1 tablespoon mustard

(mild or spicy) or 1 tablespoon peanut butter (crunchy or creamy).

Some Variations on Baked Pork Chops (all quantities based on enough chops for 4 persons)

Plum-Glazed Pork Chops: Arrange chops in pan as directed. Mix ½ cup plum jelly with 1 tablespoon each red wine vinegar and liquid gravy browner, 1 teaspoon salt, ½ teaspoon ginger, and ⅛ teaspoon pepper. Spoon over chops and bake uncovered, without turning, 1 hour or until cooked through.

Orange-Glazed Pork Chops: Bake chops ½ hour, drain off drippings, and turn. Mix 1 teaspoon salt and ⅛ teaspoon pepper with ½ cup orange juice, ¼ cup firmly packed light brown sugar, and 1 teaspoon prepared mild yellow mustard; pour over chops and bake, uncovered, ½ hour longer until cooked through. Remove chops to a hot platter and keep warm. Mix 1 teaspoon cornstarch with 1 tablespoon cold water, stir into pan juices along with 1 tablespoon grated orange rind. Set over moderate heat and cook, stirring, until thickened and clear. Stir in 1 peeled, seeded, and sectioned orange, spoon over chops, and serve.

Pineapple-Glazed Pork Chops: Follow Orange-Glazed Pork Chops recipe above; substitute pineapple juice for orange, omit rind, and use 1 cup pineapple tidbits instead of orange sections.

Pork Chops 'n' Sweet Potatoes: Bake chops as basic recipe directs; 20 minutes before they are done, arrange 1 (1-pound) drained can sweet potatoes or yams around chops, brush with 2 tablespoons melted butter, and sprinkle with 2 tablespoons dark brown sugar. Continue baking as directed until done, basting potatoes once with pan juices.

very good

Pork Chops and Sauerkraut: Bake chops as recipe directs 30 minutes; remove from pan and drain off drippings. Empty 1 (1-pound) can undrained sauerkraut into pan and arrange over bottom; lay chops on top, season with salt and pepper, and sprinkle, if you like, with paprika. Bake, uncovered, 30 minutes longer until chops are done.

Pork Chops and Baked Beans: Bake chops as recipe directs; 20 minutes before they are done remove from pan. Empty 1 (1-pound) can baked beans into pan, stir in 1 tablespoon each prepared mild yellow mustard, dark brown sugar, and Worcestershire sauce. If you like, also add 1 (8-ounce) drained can pineapple tidbits. Top with chops and continue baking, uncovered, 20 minutes longer or until chops are done.

Carolina Pork Chops: Place chops in pan, top with 1¼ cups All-Purpose Barbecue Sauce, bake, basting occasionally with sauce, 1 hour until done.

BRAISED PORK CHOPS AND ONIONS ROSEMARY

Makes 4 servings

4 *loin pork chops, cut 1″ thick and trimmed of excess fat*
¾ *cup unsifted flour*
1 *teaspoon salt*
⅛ *teaspoon pepper*
1 *tablespoon butter or margarine*
2 *medium-size yellow onions, peeled and sliced thin*
¾ *cup dry white vermouth*

¾ *cup water*
2 *(4″) sprigs fresh rosemary or ¼ teaspoon dried rosemary*

Preheat oven to 350° F. Dredge chops by shaking in a paper bag with flour, salt, and pepper. Melt butter in a heavy Dutch oven over moderately high heat and brown chops well on both sides, about 8–10 minutes. Remove from heat, lay onion slices over chops, pour in vermouth and water, and lay rosemary sprigs on top (if using dried rosemary, sprinkle evenly over all). Cover and bake 1 hour or until chops are tender. Remove herb sprigs and serve, topping each portion with onions and a generous ladling of pan juices. About 365 calories per serving.

VARIATION:

Substitute fresh or dried sage or thyme for the rosemary and prepare as directed.

GRUYÈRE-GLAZED PORK CHOPS

These chops are so rich one per person is enough.
Makes 4 servings

4 *loin pork chops, cut 1″ thick and trimmed of excess fat*
1 *tablespoon olive or other cooking oil*
1 *tablespoon butter or margarine*
½ *teaspoon salt*
⅛ *teaspoon pepper*
½ *cup dry white wine, apple cider, or apple juice*
1½ *cups finely grated Gruyère cheese*
1 *tablespoon prepared Dijon-style mustard*
¼ *cup heavy cream or evaporated milk*

Preheat oven to 350° F. Brown chops 4–5 minutes on a side in oil and butter in a large flameproof casserole over moderately high heat; drain off all fat. Sprinkle with salt and pepper, add wine, and bake uncovered 50–60 minutes until chops are tender. Meanwhile, blend together cheese, mustard, and cream (mixture will not be smooth). When chops are tender, spread top of each with cheese mixture and broil 3" from heat 2–3 minutes until lightly speckled with brown. (*Note:* Casserole liquid can be served in a gravy boat or saved for stock.) About 525 calories per serving.

⚔ CALIFORNIA-STYLE PORK CHOPS

Makes 4 servings

½ teaspoon cloves
1 clove garlic, peeled and crushed
4 teaspoons olive or other cooking oil
1 teaspoon finely grated lemon rind
½ teaspoon salt
⅛ teaspoon seasoned pepper
4 loin pork chops, cut 1" thick and trimmed of excess fat
1 tablespoon frozen orange juice concentrate
½ cup ginger ale

Mix cloves, garlic, 3 teaspoons oil, lemon rind, salt, and pepper and brush on both sides of chops; let stand at room temperature 1 hour. Preheat oven to 350° F. Brush bottom of a shallow flameproof 2-quart casserole with remaining oil and heat over moderately high heat 1 minute. Add chops and brown 4–5 minutes on each side; drain off all fat. Mix orange concentrate and ginger ale and pour over chops. Transfer casserole to oven and bake, uncovered, 50–60 minutes until chops are tender and cooked through. About 320 calories per serving.

CREOLE PORK CHOPS

Makes 4 servings

4 loin or rib pork chops, cut 1" thick and trimmed of excess fat
1 teaspoon cooking oil
1 teaspoon salt
⅛ teaspoon pepper
¼ teaspoon paprika
2 tablespoons butter or margarine
1 medium-size yellow onion, peeled and minced
1 medium-size sweet green pepper, cored, seeded, and minced
1½ cups canned tomatoes, coarsely chopped (include some liquid), or 1½ cups tomato sauce
¼ teaspoon sugar
2–3 drops liquid hot red pepper seasoning

Preheat oven to 350° F. Brown chops 5–7 minutes on each side over moderately low heat in a skillet brushed with oil. Transfer to a lightly greased 2½-quart casserole; sprinkle with salt, pepper, and paprika. Pour off all but 1 tablespoon drippings from skillet, add butter, and sauté onion and green pepper over moderate heat 8–10 minutes until onion is golden. Add remaining ingredients and simmer, uncovered, 10 minutes, stirring occasionally. Pour sauce over chops, cover, and bake 50–60 minutes until fork tender. Good with Saffron Rice.

VARIATION:

Creole Pork Steaks: Substitute 2 (¾") blade or arm steaks for chops and proceed as directed, allowing at least 1 hour baking time.

Both versions: about 395 calories per serving.

BARBECUED PORK CHOPS

This dish freezes well; double or triple recipe, if you like, then let

chops cool in sauce before packing in freezer containers.
Makes 4 servings

4 *rib or loin pork chops, cut 1" thick and trimmed of excess fat*
1 *teaspoon cooking oil*

Chuck Wagon Barbecue Sauce:
½ *cup ketchup*
½ *cup cider vinegar*
¾ *cup water*
1 *medium-size onion, peeled and minced*
1 *clove garlic, peeled and crushed*
1 *tablespoon chili powder*
1 *tablespoon Worcestershire sauce*
¼ *cup firmly packed light brown sugar*
1 *teaspoon salt*
¼ *teaspoon pepper*

Preheat oven to 350° F. Brown chops well on each side 8–10 minutes over moderately high heat in a skillet brushed with oil; transfer to a small roasting pan or casserole. Meanwhile, simmer all sauce ingredients 20 minutes, stirring frequently. Pour sauce over chops and bake, uncovered, 1 hour or until tender. Turn chops once during baking. About 360 calories per serving.

PORK CHOPS WITH GARLIC-CRUMB STUFFING

Makes 6 servings

6 *rib pork chops, cut 1¼" thick and trimmed of excess fat*
1 *teaspoon cooking oil*
1 *teaspoon salt*
¼ *teaspoon pepper*
⅓ *cup boiling water, chicken or beef broth*

Stuffing:
1 *small yellow onion, peeled and minced*
¼ *cup minced celery*
2 *cloves garlic, peeled and crushed*

1 *tablespoon cooking oil*
1 *cup poultry stuffing mix*
¼ *cup hot water*
1 *small tart apple, peeled, cored, and chopped fine*
¼ *teaspoon salt*
⅛ *teaspoon pepper*

Preheat oven to 350° F. Starting at rib bone, cut a pocket in each chop. Prepare stuffing: stir-fry onion, celery, and garlic in oil over moderate heat 5–8 minutes until pale golden. Off heat mix in remaining ingredients and spoon into chop pockets (no need to use toothpicks or skewers to seal in stuffing). Brown chops well on each side, about 8–10 minutes, over moderately high heat in a skillet brushed with oil. Transfer to an ungreased shallow roasting pan, sprinkle with salt and pepper, add boiling water, cover, and bake 1–1¼ hours or until tender. About 450 calories per serving.

VARIATIONS:

Oyster-Stuffed Pork Chops: Cut pockets in chops as above and fill with well-drained, coarsely chopped fresh oysters (you'll need about 1⅓ cups; save broth). Toothpick openings shut if oysters seem to slide out. Proceed as directed, substituting oyster broth for boiling water. About 390 calories per serving.

Spinach-Stuffed Pork Chops: Stuff chops with about 1½ cups well-drained, cooked, minced spinach, then proceed by basic recipe above. About 370 calories per serving.

Substitute 1⅓ cups Sage and Onion Dressing; Pecan-Bulgur Wheat Stuffing; Rice and Mushroom Stuffing, or any favorite for that given above. Proceed as directed. Calories per serving: about 500 if made with Sage and Onion

Dressing; 520 with Pecan-Bulgur Wheat Stuffing; and 505 with Rice and Mushroom Stuffing.

PORK CHOP AND WILD RICE CASSEROLE

Makes 4 servings

1 medium-size yellow onion, peeled and coarsely chopped
1 carrot, peeled and coarsely grated
3 tablespoons butter or margarine
1 cup wild rice, cooked by package directions
1 teaspoon minced fresh sage or ¼ teaspoon dried sage
Pinch nutmeg
1¾ teaspoons salt
4 loin pork chops, cut 1" thick and trimmed of excess fat
¾ cup unsifted flour
2 teaspoons paprika
¼ teaspoon pepper
½ cup dry white wine

Preheat oven to 350° F. Sauté onion and carrot in 2 tablespoons butter in a heavy skillet over moderate heat 8–10 minutes until golden, stirring occasionally; mix in rice, sage, nutmeg, and ¾ teaspoon salt. Spoon into a lightly greased 2-quart casserole and set aside. Dredge chops by shaking in a heavy paper bag with flour, paprika, pepper, and remaining salt. Brown chops 5 minutes on a side in 1 tablespoon butter in same skillet over moderately high heat; pour off drippings. Lay chops on top of rice, pour wine over all, cover, and bake about 1 hour or until chops are cooked through. About 545 calories per serving.

SKILLET PORK CHOPS AND RICE

Makes 4 servings

4 loin or rib pork chops, cut 1" thick and trimmed of excess fat
1 teaspoon cooking oil
2 teaspoons salt
¼ teaspoon pepper
1 cup uncooked rice
1 (10½-ounce) can condensed beef or chicken broth or onion soup
1 cup hot water

Brown chops well on each side, about 8–10 minutes, over moderately high heat in a skillet brushed with oil. Pour off all but 1 tablespoon drippings, sprinkle chops with half the salt and pepper. Scatter rice over chops and sprinkle with remaining salt and pepper. Add broth and water, cover, and simmer 50–60 minutes until chops are tender. About 415 calories per serving.

To Bake: Brown chops as directed, transfer to a 2-quart ungreased casserole, season, add remaining ingredients, cover and bake 1 hour at 350° F. until chops are tender.

VARIATIONS:

Baked Pork Chops, Peppers, and Rice: Brown chops as directed and transfer to an ungreased 2-quart casserole. In drippings stir-fry 2 diced sweet green peppers and 1 thinly sliced yellow onion 5–8 minutes over moderate heat until onion is pale golden. Mix in rice, spoon over chops, add seasonings, broth, and water; cover and bake 1 hour at 350° F. until chops are tender. About 435 calories per serving.

Spanish Pork Chops and Rice: Prepare variation above through point of stirring rice into skillet mixture. Mix in 1 crushed clove garlic and spoon over chops; add 1 (1-pound 12-ounce) can undrained tomatoes (break them up with a fork) instead of broth and water or use 1 (1-pound) can Spanish-style tomato sauce and

½ cup hot water. Season, cover, and bake 1 hour at 350° F. until chops are tender. About 470 calories per serving.

EASY PORK CHOP CASSEROLE

Makes 4 servings

4 loin or rib pork chops, cut 1" thick and trimmed of excess fat
1½ teaspoons salt
3–4 medium-size potatoes, peeled and sliced ½" thick
2 large yellow onions, peeled and sliced ¼" thick
⅛ teaspoon pepper
1 (10½-ounce) can condensed cream of celery, mushroom, or chicken soup
⅔ cup water or ⅓ cup water and ⅓ cup milk

Preheat oven to 350° F. Arrange chops in a lightly greased 2½-quart casserole. Sprinkle with ¾ teaspoon salt, top with potatoes, onions, remaining salt, and the pepper. Blend soup and water and pour into casserole; cover and bake 1 hour. If you like, brown 2–3 minutes under broiler just before serving. About 435 calories per serving.

VARIATIONS:

Pork Chop and Green Pepper Casserole: Arrange chops in casserole; omit potatoes and top instead with 3 sweet green peppers, cored, seeded, and cut in wide strips; season. Use tomato soup instead of celery, thin with ⅔ cup water, and pour over chops, or use 1½ cups tomato sauce (do not thin). Cover and bake. About 370 calories per serving.

Pork Chop and Mixed Vegetable Casserole: Arrange chops in casserole; on top of them layer 3 peeled sliced potatoes, 1 seeded, cored, sliced green pepper, 2 peeled and sliced large yellow onions, and 1 cup whole kernel corn; season. Mix 1 (10½-ounce) can vegetable soup with ½ cup water and pour over all. Cover and bake as directed. About 475 calories per serving.

SWEET-SOUR PORK, POTATO, AND ONION CASSEROLE

Makes 4 servings

4 loin pork chops, cut 1" thick and trimmed of excess fat
1 teaspoon cooking oil
2 large yellow onions, peeled and sliced ¼" thick
⅓ cup cider vinegar
⅓ cup firmly packed light brown sugar
¾ cup fruit juice (orange, pineapple, apple, or a combination)
1 tablespoon Worcestershire sauce
1¼ teaspoons salt
¼ teaspoon pepper
1 tablespoon cornstarch mixed with 1 tablespoon cold water
4 large potatoes, peeled and quartered lengthwise

Preheat oven to 375° F. Brown chops 8–10 minutes on each side over moderately high heat in a skillet brushed with oil, then transfer to an ungreased 2½-quart casserole. Sauté onions in drippings 8–10 minutes until golden and spread over chops. Add remaining ingredients to skillet and heat, stirring, until slightly thickened. Pour sauce over chops, tucking potatoes in here and there. Cover and bake ¾–1 hour until chops and potatoes are tender.

VARIATION:

Substitute root beer for the fruit juice—believe it or not, it's good. Both versions: about 480 calories per serving.

PANFRIED PORK CHOPS

Though it's not generally recommended that pork chops be panfried, they can be prepared this way if cut quite thin (no more than ½" thick) and cooked very gently. Made by the following recipe, they are surprisingly tender and moist.
Makes 4 servings

8 loin or rib pork chops, cut ½"
  thick and trimmed of excess fat
1 teaspoon cooking oil
1 teaspoon salt
¼ teaspoon pepper

Country Gravy (optional):
3 tablespoons flour
1½ cups milk
¾ teaspoon salt (about)
⅛ teaspoon pepper

Brown chops 2–3 minutes on each side over moderate heat in a large, heavy skillet brushed with oil. (*Note:* If necessary, use 2 skillets to avoid crowding pan.) Turn heat to low and cook chops, uncovered, 10–15 minutes, turning frequently until no trace of pink remains. Sprinkle with salt and pepper, transfer to a hot platter, and keep warm while making gravy. Drain all but 2 tablespoons drippings from skillet, blend in flour and brown lightly over moderately low heat. Add milk gradually and heat, stirring, until thickened. Season to taste with salt and pepper. Spoon some gravy over chops before serving, if you like, or pass separately. About 345 calories per serving.

VARIATIONS:

Country-Fried Pork Chops: Dredge chops, 1 at a time, by shaking in a heavy paper bag with ¾ cup unsifted flour, the salt, and pepper. Brown, increasing amount of oil to 1 tablespoon, then finish cooking as directed. Serve with Country Gravy. About 370 calories per serving.

German-Style Breaded Pork Chops: Dip chops in ½ cup unsifted flour to coat evenly, then in 1 egg beaten with 1 tablespoon cold water, then in 1 cup toasted, seasoned bread crumbs. Let dry on a rack at room temperature 10 minutes. Panfry as directed, using 2 tablespoons cooking oil. Serve with Country Gravy and boiled potatoes or buttered noodles. (*Note:* If you prefer, use crushed cornflakes or cracker meal instead of crumbs for breading chops.) About 405 calories per serving.

Italian-Style Breaded Pork Chops: Dip chops in ½ cup unsifted flour to coat, then in 1 egg beaten with 1 tablespoon cold water, then in ¾ cup toasted, seasoned bread crumbs mixed with ¼ cup grated Parmesan cheese. Let dry on a rack at room temperature 10 minutes. Panfry as directed in 2 tablespoons olive oil over very low heat to avoid scorching crumb coating. Serve with hot Tomato Sauce. About 415 calories per serving (without tomato sauce).

SWEET AND SOUR PORK

Makes 2 servings

⅓ cup soy sauce mixed with ⅓ cup
  sugar
¾ pound boned lean pork loin,
  trimmed of fat and cut in ¾"
  cubes
Shortening or cooking oil for deep fat
  frying
¼ cup sifted cornstarch
2 tablespoons cooking oil
1 clove garlic, peeled and minced
1 medium-size sweet green pepper,
  cored, seeded, and cut in 1"
  squares

1 *medium-size carrot, peeled and cut in julienne strips*
1 *cup chicken broth*
¼ *cup cider vinegar*
2 *tablespoons sugar*
2 *tablespoons soy sauce*
1½ *teaspoons cornstarch blended with 1 tablespoon cold water*
2 *pineapple rings, cut in ¾" cubes*

Heat soy sauce mixture, stirring, until sugar dissolves; pour over pork, cover, and chill 4–8 hours, turning meat occasionally. Begin heating fat for deep fat frying over high heat; insert wire basket and deep fat thermometer. Lift meat from marinade with slotted spoon, roll in cornstarch, and let dry 5 minutes. When fat reaches 350° F., fry cubes 2–3 minutes until golden brown; drain in basket and keep warm. Heat 2 tablespoons oil in *wok* or heavy skillet over moderate heat 1 minute, add garlic, pepper, and carrot, and stir-fry 2–3 minutes; do not brown. Mix in broth, vinegar, sugar, and soy sauce, cover, and simmer 2–3 minutes. Add cornstarch mixture, pineapple, and pork and heat, stirring, until slightly thickened. Serve over boiled rice or Chinese Fried Rice; pass extra soy sauce. About 635 calories per serving (without rice).

VARIATION:

Sweet and Sour Spareribs: Substitute 1½ pounds 3" spareribs for pork loin; cut into individual ribs, cover with water, and simmer 35–45 minutes until just tender. Drain, marinate, dredge, and fry as directed (watch ribs carefully while frying, they brown quickly). Proceed as recipe directs, adding spareribs to skillet with cornstarch mixture and pineapple. About 635 calories per serving.

Spareribs, Back Ribs, and Country-Style Backbone

These bony cuts provide as good eating as any other part of the hog. Spareribs used to be budget fare—but no more; they've grown far too popular to remain poor man's meat. The lesser known back ribs and country-style backbone are still good buys, however, and can be substituted for spareribs in any of the following recipes.

How to Cook

Amounts Needed: Allow ¾–1 pound ribs per person. Always choose ribs that are meaty between the bones and that have a thin covering of meat over the bones.

General Preparation for Cooking: If ribs are to be spit-roasted, leave in 1 piece; otherwise, cut in serving size chunks 2-ribs wide. Marinate, if you like, in a piquant sauce—the ribs will be better for it.

To Roast:
Continuous Low Heat Method: Preheat oven to 325° F. Place ribs on a rack in a shallow roasting pan and roast, uncovered, about 30 minutes per pound until well done. (*Note:* Because of thinness and boniness of ribs, it is practically impossible to get an accurate meat thermometer reading. To test for doneness, make a cut near the center of a meaty section; if no pink remains, ribs are done.)

Searing Method: Preheat oven to 450° F. Place ribs on a rack in a shallow roasting pan and roast, uncovered, 30 minutes; drain off all drippings. Reduce heat to 325° F. and roast, uncovered, about 20 minutes per pound longer or until well done.

To Spit-Roast:

In Rotisserie or Oven: Preheat unit. Balance ribs on spit by weaving rod in and out; attach to rotisserie and roast about 20 minutes per pound until well done.

Over Charcoal: Build a moderate charcoal fire.* Balance ribs on spit, attach to rotisserie, adjust height so spit is 4″–5″ from coals, and roast about 20 minutes per pound until well done (place drip pan under ribs to reduce flare-ups).

VARIATION:

Spit-Barbecued Ribs: Marinate ribs in refrigerator 12–24 hours in 2 cups All-Purpose or other barbecue sauce, turning 2–3 times. Lift from marinade, shake off excess, and spit-roast as above, basting often with sauce during last 15–20 minutes.

To Braise: Here is the best way to cook ribs because the meat becomes extra juicy, extra flavorful, and so tender it practically falls off the bones. Technically, oven-barbecued ribs are braised because they cook with a small amount of liquid; so are ribs prepared by any of the other following recipes.

CHINESE-STYLE SPARERIBS

Sweet-sour and soy-glazed.
Makes 4 servings

4 pounds (3″ long) lean spareribs, cut in serving size pieces

Sauce:
1 cup soy sauce
1 cup sugar
1 cup water
6 cloves garlic, peeled and crushed
¼ cup Hoi Sin sauce (available in Chinese groceries) or ¼ teaspoon ginger

Place ribs in a large, deep bowl. Simmer sauce ingredients 2–3 minutes, stirring, until sugar dissolves; pour over ribs, cover, and chill overnight, turning ribs occasionally. Preheat oven to 350° F. Arrange ribs in shallow roasting pan and pour in sauce. Bake, uncovered, 2 hours, turning ribs every ½ hour and basting with sauce, until fork tender and glossy brown. Serve with hot mustard and plum sauce. About 560 calories per serving.

LUAU SPARERIBS

Superb finger food! Honey gives these spareribs a mellow, *slightly* sweet flavor.
Makes 6 servings

5 pounds spareribs, cut in serving-size pieces
2 cups water

Sauce:
½ cup kettle broth
½ cup ketchup
⅓ cup honey
⅓ cup soy sauce
2 tablespoons dry sherry
2 small slices fresh gingerroot, peeled and crushed, or ½ teaspoon ginger
1 clove garlic peeled and crushed

Place ribs in a very large, heavy skillet or roaster, add water, cover, and simmer 1 hour; drain, reserving ½ cup kettle broth. Spread ribs out on a large tray. Mix kettle broth with remaining sauce ingredients and pour over ribs; cover and refrigerate 8 hours, turning 1–2 times. When ready to cook, preheat broiler or, if you prefer, prepare a moderate charcoal fire.* Broil or grill ribs 4″–5″ from heat, basting continually with sauce and turning often until all sauce is gone and ribs are crisply brown. This will take about 15 minutes. About 405 calories per serving.

FAVORITE BARBECUED SPARERIBS

Richly glazed but not too spicy.
Makes 6 servings

5 pounds spareribs, cut in serving-size pieces

Sauce:
1 cup firmly packed light brown sugar
¼ cup Worcestershire sauce
⅓ cup soy sauce
¼ cup cider vinegar
¼ cup chili sauce
½ cup ketchup
2 teaspoons prepared mild yellow mustard
2 cloves garlic, peeled and crushed
⅛ teaspoon pepper

Preheat oven to 350° F. Place ribs in a large, shallow roasting pan and bake, uncovered, ¾ hour. Drain off all drippings. Mix sauce ingredients, pour over ribs, and bake uncovered 1¼–1½ hours longer, turning and basting every 20 minutes until tender and richly browned. (*Note:* For even better flavor, marinate ribs in sauce in turned-off oven 3–4 hours after first ¾ hour of baking and drain off drippings; then bake 1½ hours longer as directed.)

VARIATION:

Favorite Charcoal-Barbecued Spareribs: Wrap ribs in a double thickness heavy foil and bake 1½ hours at 350° F. Unwrap and drain off drippings. Marinate ribs in sauce 1–2 hours at room temperature; meanwhile, prepare a moderate charcoal fire.* Remove ribs from sauce, lay on grill about 4″ from coals, taking care not to crowd them, and broil 20 minutes, basting frequently with sauce and turning often.

Both versions: about 405 calories per serving.

OVEN BARBECUED COUNTRY-STYLE SPARERIBS

For those who like their barbecue "hot."
Makes 4 servings

4 pounds spareribs, cut in serving size pieces

Sauce:
⅓ cup orange juice
⅓ cup lemon juice
⅓ cup ketchup or chili sauce
⅓ cup molasses
1 tablespoon Worcestershire sauce
1 clove garlic, peeled and crushed
1 teaspoon powdered mustard
1 teaspoon salt
1 teaspoon prepared horseradish
3 drops liquid hot red pepper seasoning

Topping:
2 lemons, sliced thin

Preheat oven to 450° F. Place ribs in a large, shallow roasting pan and roast, uncovered, 30 minutes, turning once. Remove from oven and drain off all fat. Turn oven off. Mix all sauce ingredients together and pour over ribs. Top with sliced lemons, cover loosely with foil, and let stand at room temperature 2–3 hours. Preheat oven to 325° F. Return ribs to oven and roast, uncovered, about 1 hour until tender and well browned, basting frequently with sauce in pan. Remove lemon slices and serve. About 480 calories per serving.

PAPRIKA SPARERIBS WITH CARAWAY SAUERKRAUT

Spareribs the German way, oven-baked on a bed of chopped apple and sauerkraut.
Makes 4 servings

3 pounds spareribs, cut in serving-size pieces

1½ teaspoons salt
1 teaspoon paprika
⅛ teaspoon pepper
1 (1-pound) can sauerkraut (do not drain)
1 large tart apple, peeled, cored, and coarsely chopped
1 teaspoon caraway seeds

Preheat oven to 350° F. Arrange spareribs meaty side up in a single layer in a large roasting pan; sprinkle evenly with salt, paprika, and pepper. Roast, uncovered, ½ hour, turn, and roast ½ hour longer; drain off all drippings. Mix sauerkraut, apple, and caraway seeds and place *under* spareribs. Return to oven and roast, uncovered, 1 hour, turning ribs occasionally. To serve, pile sauerkraut in the center of a large hot platter and surround with spareribs. Good with noodles and sour cream. About 380 calories per serving (without noodles and sour cream).

BAKED SPARERIBS WITH APPLE-CELERY STUFFING

Because the flavor of pork is not unlike that of chicken, you can, if you like, substitute your favorite poultry stuffing for the Apple-Celery Stuffing. You might also try the Apple-Celery Stuffing for chicken. It's delicious.
Makes 4 servings

3 pounds spareribs, cut in chunks 3 or 4 ribs wide
1 teaspoon salt
¼ teaspoon pepper

Apple-Celery Stuffing:
1 cup soft white bread crumbs
½ cup finely chopped apple
¼ cup minced celery
2 tablespoons minced yellow onion
1 tablespoon minced parsley
⅛ teaspoon cinnamon
½ teaspoon salt

⅛ teaspoon pepper
1 egg, lightly beaten

Preheat oven to 350° F. Toss together all stuffing ingredients. Turn half the ribs hollow side up and spread evenly with stuffing; top with remaining ribs, meaty side up, to make "sandwiches," then tie each securely with string. Place ribs in a shallow roasting pan and sprinkle with half the salt and pepper. Bake, uncovered, 1 hour and drain off drippings; turn ribs, sprinkle with remaining salt and pepper, and bake 1 hour longer or until tender and well browned. Transfer to a hot platter, remove strings and serve. About 405 calories per serving.

VARIATION:

Substitute 2 cups any bread or rice stuffing for the Apple-Celery Stuffing.

GROUND PORK

Because of the danger of trichinosis, some local laws forbid butchers to grind raw pork (if the machine isn't thoroughly cleaned after grinding pork, the next batch of meat to go through may become contaminated; this is especially dangerous with beef, which is so often eaten rare). If you grind pork yourself, wash each grinding part thoroughly in hot soapy water, then rinse well in boiling water and wipe dry with a clean soft cloth.

The best cuts of pork to grind are shoulder, picnic, or lean trimmings from the side or belly. The more times and the more finely pork is ground, the more compact it will be when cooked. For a light-textured loaf, coarsely grind, once. For pork balls, where a firmer texture is preferable, grind fine, two or three times.

PORK AND VEAL RING

Makes 6 servings

1 pound ground lean pork
1 pound ground veal
4 slices white bread, trimmed of crusts
½ cup milk
1 medium-size yellow onion, peeled and grated fine
2 tablespoons finely grated lemon rind
1 teaspoon poultry seasoning
1 tablespoon salt
¼ teaspoon pepper
1 egg, lightly beaten

Preheat oven to 350° F. Mix pork and veal. Cut bread into small cubes, soak in milk 5 minutes, then mix with meat and all remaining ingredients. Pack into a lightly greased 5-cup ring mold and bake, uncovered, 1 hour. Let stand 5 minutes; loosen edges and pour off drippings (save for gravy). Turn ring out on a hot platter and fill center, if you like, with mashed potatoes or yams or any creamed vegetable. Pass gravy or Mushroom Gravy. About 330 calories per serving.

To Bake as a Loaf: Pack mixture into a lightly greased 9″×5″×3″ loaf pan or shape into a loaf in a lightly greased, shallow roasting pan. Bake as directed.

PORK BALLS IN SOUR CREAM GRAVY

Makes 4 servings

Pork Balls:
1 pound ground pork shoulder
¼ cup sifted flour
1 medium-size yellow onion, peeled and finely grated
¼ teaspoon sage

½ teaspoon finely grated lemon rind
1 teaspoon salt
⅛ teaspoon pepper
½ cup soft white bread crumbs
1 egg, lightly beaten
¼ cup ice water

Gravy:
2 tablespoons bacon drippings or cooking oil
3 tablespoons flour
¾ cup water
¾ cup milk
1 cup condensed beef broth or chicken broth
½ cup sour cream

Toss together all ingredients for meat balls, then, using a rounded tablespoon as a measure, roll into small balls. Brown well in drippings in a large skillet over moderately low heat 10 minutes, remove with slotted spoon and keep warm. Drain off all but 2 tablespoons drippings, blend in flour and brown lightly. Slowly add water, milk, and broth and heat, stirring, until thickened; simmer uncovered 2–3 minutes. Mix in sour cream, return pork balls to skillet, and warm 5 minutes over lowest heat; do not boil. Serve over boiled rice or buttered noodles. About 470 calories per serving (without rice or noodles).

VARIATIONS:

Curried Pork Balls: Omit sage from meat balls but add ½–1 teaspoon curry powder. When making gravy, blend ½ teaspoon curry powder into drippings along with flour; omit sour cream. Otherwise, prepare as directed. Serve with chutney. About 410 calories per serving.

Pork and Peanut Balls: Omit sage from meat balls but add ¼ cup finely chopped toasted peanuts. Proceed as directed. About 530 calories per serving.

¢ **TOURTIÈRE**

Tourtière is a spicy pork pie traditionally served by French Canadians at *réveillon,* the Christmas feast following midnight mass. Some tourtières contain beef, but the most authentic are made entirely of pork.
Makes 6–8 servings

Filling:
1½ pounds ground lean pork
1 teaspoon salt
¼ teaspoon celery salt
¼ teaspoon pepper
⅛ teaspoon cloves
½ teaspoon savory
1 small bay leaf, crumbled

Pastry:
1 recipe Flaky Pastry II

Sauté pork in a large skillet over moderate heat, breaking it up with a fork, until no pink remains. Turn heat to low, stir in all remaining filling ingredients, cover, and simmer 15 minutes. Uncover and simmer 10 minutes longer until liquid reduces to about ⅓ cup. Drain liquid into a small bowl and chill. Cool meat to room temperature. Meanwhile, prepare pastry as directed; roll and fit half into a 9″ piepan; reserve the rest for the top crust. Preheat oven to 450° F. Skim fat from reserved liquid, then mix liquid into meat and spoon into pie shell. Moisten pastry edges with cold water. Roll top crust and cut decorative steam vents near the center. Top pie with crust, seal pastry edges and crimp. Bake 10 minutes, then reduce heat to 350° F. and bake 30–35 minutes longer until pastry is lightly browned. Cut into wedges while still warm and serve with bread and butter pickles or sweet pickle relish. (*Note:* Baked tourtières can be cooled to room temperature, wrapped airtight, and frozen. To serve: Thaw, then reheat, uncovered, for ½ hour in a 350° F. oven.) About 415 calories for each of 6 servings, 310 calories for each of 8 servings.

The Cuts of Pork to Stew

Europeans, the old saying goes, "eat everything about a pig but its squeal." We aren't so imaginative (or adventurous?) but do enjoy hocks, feet, and sinewy trimmings when well prepared.

Hocks: The fleshy, upper portion of a hog's front legs.

Pigs' Feet: Also called *trotters,* these are the feet and ankles of pigs. They are bony, full of gristle and tendons, but if stewed or pickled, the meat becomes tender and the gristle cooks down into gelatin. The forefeet are more delicate than the hind (these aren't often sold). Have your butcher clean and prepare pigs' feet for cooking.

Stew Meat: The best parts of pork to use for stew are belly (well trimmed of fat), shoulder (Boston butt), and picnic because of their well-developed flavor and firm texture.

¢ **PORK AND RED CABBAGE RAGOUT**

Makes 6 servings

3 pounds boned pork shoulder, cut in 1½″ cubes and trimmed of excess fat
3 medium-size yellow onions, peeled and coarsely chopped
1 medium-size tart apple, peeled, cored, and diced
Leaves from 2 stalks celery

4 cloves
6 peppercorns
2 (13¾-ounce) cans chicken broth
1 cup dry red wine
2 teaspoons salt
½ small red cabbage, trimmed, cut
  in slim wedges, and parboiled
1½ cups sour cream

Brown pork, a few pieces at a time,
in a large, heavy kettle over high
heat (you won't need any fat) and
drain on paper toweling. Reduce
heat to moderate, add onions and
apple, and stir-fry 8–10 minutes
until golden. Return pork to kettle.
Tie celery leaves, cloves, and peppercorns in cheesecloth and add to
kettle along with broth, wine, and
salt. Cover and simmer 1¾ hours
until pork is almost tender. Add
cabbage wedges, pushing them down
into stew, re-cover, and simmer
15–20 minutes longer until pork
and cabbage are tender. Discard
cheesecloth bag. Remove stew from
heat; using a slotted spoon, lift
cabbage from kettle and wreathe
around a large, deep platter; pile
meat in center and keep warm.
Blend sour cream into kettle liquid
and heat and stir 1–2 minutes
(do not boil). Ladle over cabbage
and pork and serve. About 675
calories per serving.

¢ SPICY PORK AND TURNIP STEW

Makes 6 servings

3 pounds boned pork shoulder, cut in
  1½″ cubes and trimmed of excess
  fat
5 large turnips, peeled and cut in ½″
  cubes
2 medium-size yellow onions, peeled
  and coarsely chopped
1 clove garlic, peeled and crushed
4 whole allspice
6 peppercorns
4 cloves

4 sprigs parsley
1 (13¾-ounce) can chicken broth
½ cup dry white wine
1 cup water
1 teaspoon salt
2 tablespoons flour blended with 3
  tablespoons cold water

Brown pork well on all sides in a
large, heavy kettle over high heat
(you won't need any fat). Reduce
heat to low, add turnips, onions, and
garlic, and stir-fry with pork 5
minutes. Tie spices and parsley
in cheesecloth and add along with
all remaining ingredients except
flour-water paste, cover, and simmer
2 hours until pork is tender. Remove
pork and turnips with a slotted
spoon and set aside; discard cheesecloth bag. Strain cooking liquid,
return to kettle, mix in flour-water
paste, and heat, stirring constantly,
until thickened. Remove pork and
turnips to kettle and heat, uncovered,
5 minutes longer, stirring occasionally. Serve with boiled potatoes or
sweet potatoes. About 550 calories
per serving (without potatoes).

⚖ ¢ PORK HOCKS WITH SAUERKRAUT

Pork hocks and sauerkraut can be
served with or without the cooking
liquid; in either case boiled potatoes
and crusty bread are traditional
accompaniments.

Makes 4 servings

6 meaty pork hocks
1 quart cold water
1 medium-size yellow onion, peeled
  and sliced thin
2 bay leaves
10 peppercorns
2 sprigs parsley or 1 teaspoon dried
  parsley
Leaves from 2 stalks celery, coarsely
  chopped, or ½ teaspoon celery salt
1 (1-pound 11-ounce) can
  sauerkraut, drained

Scrub hocks well under cold running water; scrape skin with a sharp knife to remove any hairs. Place hocks in a 1½-gallon kettle with water and onion. Tie bay leaves, peppercorns, parsley, and celery leaves in cheesecloth and add to kettle (if using celery salt, mix with kettle liquid). Cover and bring to a boil over moderate heat; uncover and skim off froth. Reduce heat to low and simmer, covered, 2–2½ hours until meat is very tender. Discard cheesecloth bag. Cool, cover, and chill several hours until fat rises to surface and hardens. When ready to serve, skim off fat (broth will be jellied), add sauerkraut, cover, and heat slowly until piping hot. About 300 calories per serving.

⚖ ¢ STEWED PIGS' FEET (BASIC METHOD)

Before they can be used in recipes, pigs' feet require careful, preliminary stewing. Allow 1–2 pigs' feet per person and have butcher clean and prepare them for cooking.

Stock (enough for 4–6 pigs' feet):

1½ quarts water
¾ cup dry white wine
2 carrots, peeled and sliced thin
2 stalks celery, sliced thin
2 medium-size yellow onions, peeled and each stuck with 2 cloves
1 bouquet garni,* tied in cheesecloth
1 tablespoon salt
4 peppercorns

Wash pigs' feet well in cool water, then tie each tightly in cheesecloth so it will keep its shape. Place in a large, heavy kettle with stock ingredients, cover, and bring to a simmer over moderate heat. Adjust heat so stock stays at a slow simmer and cook, covered, 4–5

hours until feet are very tender. Cool in liquid, drain well (save broth for soups and stews), and remove cheesecloth. Use in any of the following recipes. About 255 calories per pig's foot.

VARIATIONS:

¢ ⚖ **Pickled Pigs' Feet:** Prepare by recipe above, but use 3 cups each cider vinegar and water for stewing instead of 1½ quarts water. When feet are tender, cool in liquid, drain, and chill well. Remove cheesecloth and serve cold with Spanish Vinaigrette Sauce. About 255 calories per pickled pig's foot.

¢ ⚖ **Stewed Calf's Feet:** First, blanch feet. *To blanch calf's feet:* Wash and scrub well in cool water, place in a large, heavy kettle, cover with cold water, cover, and bring to a boil. Drain, rinse feet in cold water, and wash kettle. Return feet to kettle, add stock ingredients listed for Stewed Pigs' Feet (above), and proceed as recipe directs. About 140 calories per calf's foot.

⚖ ¢ PIGS' FEET IN SCALLION AND JUNIPER SAUCE

Makes 4 servings

6 pigs' feet, stewed (see Index)

Sauce:
⅓ cup minced scallions
2 tablespoons butter or margarine
⅔ cup white wine vinegar
6 juniper berries, crushed
Pinch nutmeg
Pinch pepper
1¼ cups stock (use that from stewing pigs' feet)
2 tablespoons flour blended with 3 tablespoons cold water

After stewing pigs' feet, cool in stock just until easy to handle; drain, remove cheesecloth and keep feet warm while preparing sauce. Sauté scallions in butter in a small saucepan 8–10 minutes, stirring occasionally, over moderate heat until golden; add vinegar, juniper berries, nutmeg, and pepper and boil, uncovered, to reduce. When almost all vinegar has evaporated, add stock. Mix in flour paste and heat, stirring, until thickened and smooth. Pour sauce over pigs' feet and serve. About 290 calories per serving.

VARIATION:

Instead of making Scallion and Juniper Sauce, serve pigs' feet with Mustard, Diable, or any other suitable sauce (see Sauces, Gravies, and Seasonings for Pork).

HAM AND OTHER CURED PORK

(See Pork Chart)

Whether served as a festive holiday ham, glistening under an amber glaze, a cool, spicy loaf, or a grilled steak, ham runs beef a close second as America's favorite meat. Although we think of any cured pork as ham, it is technically the hind leg only, and it can be fresh as well as cured. We are concerned here with all the cured and smoked cuts, the bacons and butts, picnics and jowls as well as the hams. Here's a quick dictionary to those commonly used:

Aged Hams: Heavily cured and smoked hams that have been hung from one to seven years. They are usually covered with mold (it washes off and does not mean the meat is spoiled).

Country Cured Hams: Hams (and sometimes other cuts of pork) that have been dry-cured (preserved in a mixture of dry salt and seasonings), smoked slowly over fragrant hardwood fires, and aged at least six months. The meat is mahogany colored, salty, and firm. America's most famous country hams are the Virginia, Smithfield, Tennessee, Georgia, and Kentucky; each is salty and firm of flesh, each has a distinctive flavor, determined by breed of hog, feed, and seasonings used in the curing. Most country cured hams are uncooked, although fully cooked ones are now available. Read labels carefully.

Cured Hams: Curing is a method of preserving, not of cooking. Large processors cure hams by soaking in brine or, more recently, by pumping brine through the meat. Cured hams may or may not be smoked and may or may not be cooked.

Cured and Smoked Hams: Hams that have been brined and smoked— but not cooked unless labels clearly say so.

Cook-Before-Eating Hams: This is the term commonly used to identify uncooked or partially cooked hams. It's a good term because the shopper knows at a glance that the meat must be cooked before serving.

Fully Cooked Hams: Hams so labeled can be eaten straight from the wrapper; they will develop richer flavor, however, if baked until meat thermometer reads 130° F.

Ready-to-Eat Hams: The same as fully cooked hams.

Smoked Ham or Pork: Meat that has been cured, then smoked, but not necessarily cooked.

Sugar Cured Hams: Hams cured in

brine or dry salt mixed with brown sugar or molasses.

Tendered or Tenderized Hams: These terms are often misinterpreted to mean "cooked hams." They are really only sales words and mean little.

Uncooked Hams: Raw hams that must be thoroughly cooked before eating. They may be cured or cured and smoked.

How to Recognize Quality in Ham and Other Cured Pork

Large cuts often—but not always— carry the round federal inspector's seal guaranteeing wholesomeness of meat. Quality is less easily determined because little pork is federally graded and because the appearance of cured pork ranges from the pale pink of processed hams to the offputting moldiness of aged country cured hams. Both may be of top quality. Your best assurance is to buy reputable brands.

Standard Processed Hams

These tender, cured packing-house hams are usually smoked (but not always). They may be fully cooked or uncooked; labels should clearly state which.

Whole Ham:

Bone-In (8–24 pounds): The full hind leg of the hog.

Semiboneless (6 pounds up): A ham from which the troublesome hip (aitch) and shank bones have been removed to simplify carving. The leg bone remains in, helping ham hold its compact oval shape, but skin and excess fat have been removed. Also sold as half hams or by the slice.

Boneless (6–14 pounds): A boned and rolled ham.

Half Ham:

Butt Portion (4–12 pounds): Also called Full Butt, this is the choice meaty, rump half of the ham, more expensive than the shank portion.

Shank Portion (4–12 pounds): Also known as Full Shank. This leg half of the ham is bonier and less expensive than the butt half.

Semiboneless (4 pounds and up): Half a semiboneless ham (see above).

Boneless (3–7 pounds): Half a boned and rolled ham (see above).

Ham End: This is what's left of a ham after the center slices or steaks have been removed. The Butt End is meaty but contains the cumbersome hipbone; the Shank End tapers sharply and may be too skimpy to roast.

Specialty Hams

Domestic:

Smithfield: So many country cured hams claim to be the prized Smithfield hams that the Virginia General Assembly has adopted a statute: "Genuine Smithfield hams are cut from carcasses of peanut-fed hogs, raised in the peanut belt of the State of Virginia or the State of North Carolina, and cured, treated, smoked and processed in the town of Smithfield in the State of Virginia." What makes these hams so special is their firm, mahogany-hued flesh and smoky-salty flavor. Most must be cooked long and slow before eating, though some are now sold fully cooked. Available only as whole hams (12–14 pounds is a good size) through gourmet butchers or via mail order.

Virginia: Like Smithfield hams, these country cured hams are firm of flesh and salty of flavor. They may be from hogs fattened on peanuts, or those allowed to forage for acorns, nuts, and aromatic roots. Whole hams are available uncooked or fully cooked from gourmet butchers, also by mail order.

Canned Ham: Boned, skinned, trimmed, ready-to-eat hams. They are cured but not necessarily smoked and weigh from 1½–10 pounds (the larger the ham, the better). Though fully cooked, canned hams will have better flavor if baked or sliced and panfried. Some come with special glazes—honey, champagne, pineapple (we've found that, to be really well glazed, most need a little longer in the oven than can directions recommend). Some require refrigeration, so read label carefully and store accordingly.

Imported: (*Note:* Because trichinosis is not a problem in Europe, many European hams are eaten raw.)

Bayonne Ham: Dry-cured ham from Béarn or the Basque country of France. Many are cured in the town of Bayonne (hence the name), many simply cured with Bayonne salt. The hams are raw and the Basques like to eat them that way on buttered slabs of rough peasant bread. Available in gourmet groceries.

Irish Ham: The best known come from Belfast. They may be bone-in or boneless, pickled or brined; what gives them their unique flavor is the smoking over peat fires. Irish hams must be soaked, scrubbed, and simmered, then baked before eating (prepare like Country Cured Ham). Available in specialty food shops.

Prosciutto: What we call *prosciutto* is really Parma ham (*prosciutto* is simply the Italian word for *ham*). These hams come from Parma, Italy, are exquisitely seasoned, salt cured, air dried, and pressed so that their rosy brown flesh is unusually firm. Prosciutto is most often sliced tissue thin and eaten raw as an appetizer but can be used in recipes. Available in gourmet groceries, also in cold cut counters of many metropolitan supermarkets.

Westphalian Ham: A salty, reddish German ham similar to prosciutto that comes from hogs fed sugar beet mash. It, too, is sliced paper thin and eaten raw. Available in specialty food shops.

York Ham: An English ham with mild flavor and delicate pink meat. Like Irish ham, it must be cooked before eating (use recipe for Country Cured Ham). When served hot, York ham is traditionally accompanied by Madeira Sauce.

Canned Ham: The most readily available imported canned hams are the York, Prague, and Polish, all mild-cured, all skinless and boneless. Also available in specialty food shops are canned prosciutto and Westphalian hams.

How to Bake Ham

Note: What we call baked ham is really roasted; it has simply been the American habit to speak of ham as baked the same way we speak of a meat loaf or potato as baked although these, too, are technically roasted.

Suitable Cuts: Any of the standard processed hams, canned hams, or country cured hams. Each requires a somewhat different technique, however.

Amount Needed: The bigger the ham, the more succulent it will be. To figure number of servings, allow ⅔ pound per person for a bony ham (shank portion), ⅓–½ pound for other bone-in hams; ¼–⅓ pound boneless ham; also ¼–⅓ pound *net weight* canned ham per person.

General Preparation for Cooking (standard processed hams only): Remove skin, if still on, by slipping a sharp knife underneath and peeling off. Trim fat to ½″. Let ham stand at room temperature 1½–2 hours before cooking, if convenient.

Uncooked (Cook-Before-Eating) Ham: Follow manufacturer's cooking directions or prepare as follows. Preheat oven to 325° F. Place ham on a rack in a shallow roasting pan (whole hams should be fat side up, half hams cut side down). Insert meat thermometer in center, not touching bone. Bake, uncovered, until thermometer reads 160° F. Whole or boneless hams will take approximately 18–20 minutes per pound, half hams 22–24. Transfer ham to heated platter and let "rest" 15–20 minutes before carving. Serve hot or cold.

To Glaze (see Some Glazes for Baked Hams):

Liquid Glazes: Begin basting ham after 15–20 minutes in oven and continue basting at 15–20-minute intervals throughout cooking. About ½ hour before ham is done (no sooner or cuts will spread too much), remove from oven and score fat in a large crisscross pattern, making cuts ⅛″ deep. Stud with

cloves or decorate (see On Decorating and Garnishing Hams). Return ham to oven and finish cooking, basting frequently. For a browner glaze, finish cooking at 425° F.

Thick Glazes: Bake ham as directed but do not baste. About ½ hour before ham is done, remove from oven and score. Stud with cloves (avoid intricate decorations because glaze will cover them up). Pat or spread on glaze, return ham to oven, and finish cooking, basting if glaze recipe calls for it. For a richly brown glaze, finish cooking at 425° F.

Ready-to-Eat Hams: If wrapper gives cooking directions, follow them. If not, use procedure for uncooked hams above, but bake only until thermometer registers 130° F. Whole and boneless hams will require about 12–15 minutes per pound, half hams about 18–20. Glaze and decorate as above and serve hot or cold.

Canned Hams: If ham is accompanied by baking directions, use them. If not, prepare as follows. Preheat oven to 325° F. If ham has a heavy fat covering (few canned hams do), trim to ½″. Place ham flattest side down on a rack in a shallow roasting pan. (*Note:* If using a round canned ham, cut a thin slice off bottom so ham won't roll about pan.) Insert meat thermometer in center of ham and bake, uncovered, about 20 minutes per pound or until thermometer registers 130° F. Glaze and decorate as above and serve hot or cold.

Country Cured Hams: A day or two before you plan to serve ham, place in a very large oval kettle, sawing off hock, if necessary, to fit ham in. If ham is very salty, salt crystals will be visible. Cover with cool water and let stand 24 hours at room temperature, changing the water 3–4 times. If ham is not salty, change soaking water 1–2 times. Next day, scrub ham well under running tepid water to remove any mold and pepper. Wash well again in tepid water. Place ham on a rack in the same large kettle, add cool water to cover, cover, and bring to a boil over high heat. Skim froth from surface, re-cover, adjust heat so water stays at a slow simmer, and cook 25–30 minutes per pound or until fork tender and bone feels loose; cool ham in cooking liquid. Preheat oven to 350° F. Lift ham from liquid, peel off rind, and trim fat to ½″. Score in a crisscross pattern and stud with cloves. Pat on a thick glaze (Brown Sugar and Bread Crumbs is the traditional glaze for Smithfield and Virginia hams). Place ham glaze side up on a rack in a shallow roasting pan and bake, uncovered, 45 minutes or until glaze is nicely browned. Transfer ham to serving platter and let cool at least 20 minutes before serving. In the South, these hams are served at room temperature (or chilled), but almost never hot. When carving, slice paper thin.

How to Spit-Roast Ham

Best Cuts: Ready-to-Eat Hams, especially skinless, boneless rolls (whole, half, or quarter); semiboneless hams can be spit-roasted if carefully balanced. *Not recommended:* uncooked hams (heat is too intense to ensure thorough cooking) and bone-in hams (they are too irregularly shaped to cook evenly).

Amount Needed: ¼–⅓ pound boneless or semiboneless ham per person. Do not try to spit-roast less than a quarter ham roll.

General Preparation for Cooking: Remove any casing; most ham rolls have little outer fat, so trimming is unnecessary. Tie roll as you would a parcel so it will hold its shape during cooking. Let stand at room temperature 1½–2 hours if convenient.

In Rotisserie or Oven: Preheat unit. Insert spit lengthwise through center of ham to balance, tighten holding forks. Insert meat thermometer in center, not touching spit. Attach to rotisserie and roast, using manufacturer's or the following timetable: 10–12 minutes per pound for whole ham rolls, 15–17 for half rolls, and 20 for quarter rolls. Thermometer should read 130° F. Let ham "rest" 15–20 minutes before carving. *To Glaze:* About ½ hour before ham is done, baste with any liquid glaze and continue basting often (see Some Glazes for Baked Hams).

Over Charcoal: Prepare a moderate charcoal fire toward back of grill.* Balance ham on spit and insert thermometer as above, attach spit to rotisserie 6″–7″ from coals. Place drip pan at front of fire. Roast, using manufacturer's times or those for rotisserie roasting. Glaze, if you like, as above.

Some Glazes for Baked Hams

Basically, there are two kinds of glaze: (1) liquids that are basted on throughout cooking and (2) thick or dry mixtures that are patted or spread on about ½ hour before ham is done.

Liquid (Baste-On Glazes): (*Note:* Hams basted with beer, champagne, wine, and fruit juice will be glossier if rubbed with a mixture of ¼ cup light brown sugar and 1 teaspoon powdered mustard before cooking.)

Cranberry-Horseradish: 1 (1-pound) can cranberry jelly, melted and mixed with ¼ cup prepared horseradish.

Cider-Sweet Pickle: 1½ cups apple cider mixed with ¾ cup sweet pickle juice.

Champagne or Wine (sherry, port, Madeira, sweet red or white wine).

Beer, Ale, or Stout.

Rum (dark or light).

Fruit Juices: Apple, apricot, cranberry, grape, orange, pineapple. Also good: syrup from canned or pickled peaches or pears.

Syrups: Maple, pancake, light or dark corn syrup, molasses, strained honey.

Thick Glazes:

Brown Sugar and Bread Crumbs: 1 cup firmly packed light brown sugar mixed with ½ cup fine soft white bread crumbs and 1½ teaspoons powdered mustard. Particularly good with Smithfield or Virginia hams.

Mustard: 1 cup firmly packed light brown sugar mixed with ¼ cup prepared mustard (any type) and 2 tablespoons cider vinegar or 3 tablespoons honey, molasses, maple syrup, or dark or light corn syrup.

Cinnamon and Cloves: ¾ cup sugar mixed with ½ teaspoon cloves and ¼ teaspoon cinnamon. Sprinkle evenly over ham and baste with orange or pineapple juice or apple cider.

Sherry or Port: Brush ham with a little warmed light corn syrup, then pat on light brown sugar to a thickness of ¼". Slowly drizzle 1 cup sweet sherry or port over all and finish cooking, basting with additional sherry or port.

Peanut Butter: Spread 1–1½ cups creamy or crunchy peanut butter over ham.

Brown Sugar: Brush a little warmed light or dark corn syrup, molasses, or honey over ham, then pat on light or dark brown sugar to a thickness of about ¼".

Marmalade: Warm orange, lemon, or ginger marmalade slightly and spread evenly over ham.

Preserves: Use apricot, pineapple, peach, pear, or cherry preserves, sieve or purée in a blender at high speed, warm slightly, and spread evenly over ham.

Jelly: Use black or red currant, apple, or cranberry. Melt jelly, then brush over ham every 10 minutes during last ½ hour of baking.

On Decorating and Garnishing Hams

Hams glazed with syrup, fruit juice, wine, or jelly will look more festive if decorated. Use fruits and/or nuts, keeping the design simple. To make design stick to ham, brush surface with warmed corn syrup, honey, or molasses, then simply press on decoration. Larger designs, made with peaches or apricots, have a tendency to slither off, so toothpick in place (be sure to remove toothpicks before carving). It's a good idea to remove any decorations before storing leftover ham because they deteriorate rapidly and may spoil the ham.

Garnishes for Hot Ham Platters:

Spiced, pickled, or brandied peaches
Brandied figs
Orange cups filled with candied yams, whipped sweet potatoes, buttered green peas, or hot cranberry sauce
Fried Apple Rings
Sautéed Pineapple Rings
Sautéed Halved Bananas

Garnishes for Cold Ham Platters:

Chopped aspic (preferably fruit or meat)
Avocado slices and shredded romaine
Lemon cups filled with cold cranberry sauce or tart jelly
Seedless green grapes and crab apples
Whole spiced crab apples and watercress
Preserved kumquats and parsley or watercress

How to Carve a Whole Bone-In Ham:

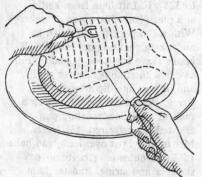

Place ham on platter, fat side up with shank to carver's right. Cut 2–3 slices parallel to leg from thin side (if ham is from left leg, thin side will face carver; if from a right leg, it will be on the far side). Cut straight down from top to bone in thin slices, then release slices by running knife along bone.

How to Carve a Semiboneless Whole Ham:

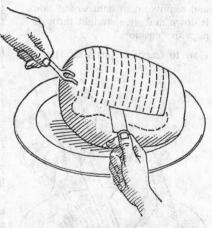

Stand ham on its side and slice from right to left, cutting down to leg bone. Loosen slices by cutting along bone.

How to Carve a Shank Half Ham:

Turn platter so shank is on left; turn ham so thickest side is up, then cut along bone and lift out boneless "cushion," which is the top half of the ham. Place "cushion" cut side down and cut straight through in thin slices. Cut around leg bone and remove; turn ham so flat side is down and slice straight through as with "cushion."

How to Carve a Butt Half Ham:

Place ham face down on platter, cut down along hip (aitch) bone, and remove large boneless chunk from side of ham. Place boneless chunk cut side down and slice straight through. Steady remaining ham with fork, slice across to bone, and loosen each slice with tip of knife.

BAKED PECAN-STUFFED HAM

Makes 18–20 servings

1 (10–12-pound) bone-in or semi-
    boneless cook-before-eating ham
1 gallon cold water (about)
½ cup cider vinegar
½ cup firmly packed dark brown
    sugar

Stuffing:
2 medium-size yellow onions, peeled
    and minced

1 cup minced celery
3 tablespoons bacon drippings or
    cooking oil
2 cups soft white bread crumbs
¼ cup cracker crumbs
¼ teaspoon salt
¼ teaspoon pepper
2 tablespoons minced parsley
1 cup finely chopped pecans
2 eggs, lightly beaten

Topping:
1 cup firmly packed light brown
    sugar
½ cup soft white bread crumbs
1½ teaspoons powdered mustard

Place ham on a rack in a very large kettle, add water *just* to cover, also vinegar and sugar. Cover and simmer 1½ hours. Meanwhile prepare stuffing: Stir-fry onions and celery in drippings over moderate heat 5–8 minutes until pale golden; off heat mix in remaining ingredients. When ham is tender, cool in broth until easy to handle. Begin preheating oven to 325° F. Lift ham from kettle and place lean side up on counter. With a sharp knife, cut down to and along shank bone; remove all bones (save for stock or soup). Fill cavity with stuffing, skewer shut, and, if you like, tie around with string. Place ham fat side up on a rack in a shallow roasting pan and bake, uncovered, 1¼ hours. Mix topping, pat over ham, and bake 15–20 minutes longer. Remove skewers and string, transfer ham to platter, and serve. Also good cold. About 615 calories for each of 18 servings, 555 calories for each of 20 servings.

To Halve Recipe: Use a 5–6-pound shank portion half ham. Simmer in 2½ quarts water with

⅓ cup each vinegar and dark brown sugar for 1 hour. Halve stuffing recipe. Bone, stuff, and bake ham as above, reducing time to 1 hour. Cover with topping and bake 15–20 minutes longer. About 620 calories for each of 9 servings, 555 calories for each of 10 servings.

SAUCES, GRAVIES, AND SEASONINGS FOR HAM AND OTHER CURED PORK

For Cooking Seasonings, Herbs, Spices		For Hot Hams and Ham Steaks	
		Sauces	Gravies
Allspice	Lemon	Hot mustard	Pan Gravy
Bay leaf	Mace	Madeira	Red Eye Gravy
Celery salt	Mustard	Mustard	
Cinnamon	Nutmeg	Orange	
Cloves	Orange	Parsley	
Curry powder	Parsley	Périgueux	
Dill	Sage	Plum	
Ginger	Thyme	Portugaise	
Horseradish		Raisin	
		Robert	
		Sweet-sour	
		Yorkshire	

For Hot or Cold Hams Condiments	For Cold Hams Sauces
Applesauce	Cumberland
Chutney	Cranberry
Horseradish	Dijonnaise
Mustard	Hot mustard
Peaches (brandied, pickled)	Mustard
	Robert
Pears (brandied, pickled)	Sour cream-horseradish
Pickles (bread and butter, dill, green tomato, mustard, watermelon rind)	Spicy cranberry
	Tartar
	Whipped horse-radish
Preserved kumquats	
Relishes (corn, pepper)	
Spiced fruits (crab apples, peaches, pears)	
Soy sauce	

HAM EN CROÛTE (HAM IN PASTRY)

For a spectacular buffet, serve ham wrapped in pastry. Use boneless ham (to simplify carving) and one that's pear-shaped (so the ham will look more like ham).
Makes 16–18 servings

1 (8–10-pound) boneless, ready-to-eat ham

Pastry:
6 cups sifted flour
2 teaspoons salt
2 teaspoons baking powder
½ teaspoon powdered mustard
¼ teaspoon sage
1½ cups vegetable shortening
2 tablespoons lemon juice
1½ cups ice water (about)

Glaze:
2 egg yolks lightly beaten with 2 tablespoons cold water

Bake ham by basic method* but do not glaze. About 20 minutes before it is done, make pastry: sift dry ingredients and cut in shortening until mixture resembles coarse meal. Briskly fork in lemon juice and just enough ice water to hold pastry together. Remove ham from oven and raise temperature to 425° F. Halve pastry and roll half on a lightly floured board into a rectangle about 20″×12″ and ¼″ thick. Ease onto an ungreased large baking sheet; place ham on pastry with fat side up. Roll remaining pastry into a similar rectangle, lay over ham and trim edges so they just meet those of bottom pastry (this will be about halfway up sides of ham). Moisten edges with water and pinch into a smooth seam. Cut a vent in top of pastry near center; brush pastry with glaze. Cut decorative leaves and flowers from pastry trimmings and arrange on pastry; glaze. Bake, uncovered, in top ⅓ of oven 35–45 minutes until richly browned. When half done, check glaze and patch up any uneven spots with remaining glaze. Remove ham from oven, transfer to platter, and let "rest" 10–15 minutes. To serve, carve straight through as you would any boneless ham. Include some pastry with each serving. This ham is good hot or cold. About 850 calories for each of 16 servings, 755 calories for each of 18 servings.

To Halve Recipe: Use a 4–5-pound boneless half ham; halve pastry recipe, roll into a single rectangle, drape over ham, and pinch edges together underneath. Glaze and bake as directed. (Makes 8–10 servings). About 850 calories for each of 8 servings, 680 calories for each of 10 servings.

HAM IN ASPIC

Makes 10–12 servings

1 (5-pound) canned ham

Aspic:
2 envelopes unflavored gelatin
3 (10½-ounce) cans condensed beef consommé or madrilène
½ cup medium-dry sherry

Decoration:
2–3 truffles or pitted ripe olives, sliced thin
Small watercress, parsley, or tarragon sprigs
Thin slices cooked carrot or hard-cooked egg white cut in fancy shapes

Remove ham from can and chill well. Slowly heat gelatin in consommé, stirring, until dissolved; add sherry and cool over ice cubes until syrupy. Set ham on a rack over a tray, spoon on a light, even glaze of aspic. Dip decorations in aspic and arrange on ham; chill until firm. Give ham 3 more light glazes of aspic, chilling each well. (*Note:* To keep aspic syrupy, melt briefly over warm water, then return to ice bath.) Use overflow aspic on tray if reasonably clear. When final ham glaze is firm, transfer ham to platter and refrigerate. Pour remaining aspic into a shallow pan and chill until firm. To serve, cube extra aspic and arrange around base of ham. About 670 calories for each of 10 servings, 560 calories for each of 12 servings.

VARIATION:

Pâté-Filled Ham in Aspic: Have butcher cut ham lengthwise into ½″ slices, then tie together. For filling, mix 3 cups canned liver pâté, ⅓ cup heavy cream, 2 tablespoons prepared mild yellow mustard, 1 teaspoon Worcestershire sauce, and, if you like, 2–3 tablespoons cognac (filling should be a good spreading consistency). Untie ham carefully and thinly spread both sides of slices with filling; reshape ham and tie in several places. Wrap in foil and chill overnight; reserve remaining pâté. Next day, remove strings (ham should now hold its shape). "Frost" ham with reserved pâté and chill 2–3 hours.

(*Note:* If pâté seems stiff, warm briefly over warm water.) Glaze and decorate ham as above. When serving, slice crosswise. About 820 calories for each of 10 servings, 685 calories for each of 12 servings.

Smoked Picnics and Butts
(See Pork Chart)

Smoked Picnic (4–10 pounds): Also called *Picnic Ham,* this bone-in, lower shoulder portion, when cured and smoked, tastes very much like ham. It is available uncooked, fully cooked and canned (canned picnics are boned, skinned, and trimmed).

Smoked Boneless Shoulder Butt (1–4 pounds): This long, slim boneless roll is a good choice for small families; it has a mild, smoky-sweet flavor.

How to Cook

Amounts Needed: Allow ⅓–½ pound smoked boneless shoulder butt or canned picnic (net weight) per person, ¾ pound smoked picnic.

Note: Fully cooked smoked picnics can be prepared by recipe for Ready-to-Eat Hams, canned picnics by that for Canned Hams. Though uncooked smoked picnics and shoulder butts can be baked like Uncooked Hams, they will be juicier if prepared by the following method.

General Preparation for Cooking: Remove skin from picnic (butt won't have any) and trim fat to ½″.

Basic Method: Place picnic or butt on a rack in a large, heavy kettle and add just enough cold water to cover. Put lid on kettle and bring to a boil; adjust heat so water stays at a slow simmer, then cook 15 minutes per pound. Let meat cool 10 minutes in cooking water. Preheat oven to 325° F. Transfer meat to a rack in a shallow roasting pan and insert meat thermometer in center, not touching bone. Bake uncovered, allowing 25 minutes per pound for the picnic, 30–35 for the butt or until meat thermometer reaches 170° F. *To Glaze:* Smoked picnics may be glazed like Baked Ham. Smoked butts have a very skimpy covering of fat and do not glaze well; they can, however, be drizzled with honey, maple syrup, or molasses and baked 10–15 minutes at 425° F. to make them glisten. Transfer meat to a heated platter and let "rest" 15–20 minutes before carving. Serve hot or cold.

VARIATIONS:

Simmered Boneless Shoulder Butt: Place butt in kettle and add water as directed; cover and simmer 50 minutes per pound until tender. Lift from liquid, cool 10 minutes, then slice and serve with boiled vegetables and, if you like, Mustard or Horseradish Sauce.

Pickled Smoked Shoulder Butt: Place butt in kettle and add water as directed; add 1 tablespoon mixed pickling spices, 1 peeled clove garlic, and ½ cup cider vinegar. Simmer and bake as directed in Basic Method.

⊠ SKILLET HAM, PINEAPPLE, AND PEPPERS

Makes 6 servings

3 cups diced cooked ham
2 tablespoons butter or margarine
1 (8-ounce) can pineapple tidbits (do not drain)
2 medium-size sweet green peppers, cored, seeded, and cut in ¼" strips
½ cup firmly packed light brown sugar
2 tablespoons cornstarch
½ cup chicken broth
½ cup cider vinegar
2 tablespoons soy sauce
2 pimientos, diced

In a large skillet stir-fry ham in butter 3–5 minutes over moderately high heat until lightly browned. Add pineapple and green peppers and stir-fry 3–4 minutes until peppers are crisp-tender. Mix sugar, cornstarch, broth, vinegar, and soy

sauce, stir into skillet, and heat, stirring, until thickened. Add pimientos and serve over boiled rice. About 310 calories per serving (without rice).

⊠ CREAMED HAM

Makes 4 servings

¼ cup butter or margarine
¼ cup unsifted flour
⅛ teaspoon pepper
¼ teaspoon powdered mustard
1 cup milk
½ cup light cream
1½ cups slivered or diced cooked ham
2 tablespoons minced pimiento (optional)
½ teaspoon salt

Melt butter in a large saucepan over moderately low heat, blend in flour, pepper, and mustard; slowly add milk and cream and heat, stirring until thickened. Add remaining ingredients, adjusting salt to taste. Serve over toast, waffles, muffins, or hot biscuits or in pastry shells or "fluffed up" baked potatoes. About 375 calories per serving (without toast, waffles, muffins, biscuits, pastry shells, or potatoes).

VARIATIONS:

Creamed Ham and Eggs: Add 4 quartered hard-cooked eggs along with ham. About 455 calories per serving.

Creamed Ham and Mushrooms: Add 1 drained (4-ounce) can sliced mushrooms along with ham. About 385 calories per serving.

Creamed Ham, Cheese, and Olives: Add ¼ cup extra milk to sauce. Add ½ cup grated sharp Cheddar cheese and ¼ cup sliced pimiento-stuffed green olives with ham. About 500 calories per serving.

Creamed Ham and Vegetables: Add ¼ cup extra milk to sauce; also 1½–2 cups any leftover vegetable (corn, peas, cut asparagus, lima beans, broccoli, and cauliflowerets are particularly good). About 435 calories per serving.

HAM, POTATO, AND GREEN PEPPER CASSEROLE

Makes 4 servings

1 quart thinly sliced, peeled potatoes
3 cups (½") cooked lean ham cubes
½ medium-size sweet green pepper, cored, seeded, and chopped fine
3 scallions, chopped fine (include green tops)
2 tablespoons bacon drippings, butter, or margarine
3 tablespoons flour
¾ teaspoon powdered mustard
2 cups milk
1½ teaspoons salt
⅛ teaspoon white pepper

Preheat oven to 375° F. Arrange half the sliced potatoes in a greased 2-quart casserole. Toss ham, green pepper, and scallions together and scatter over potatoes; top with remaining potatoes. Melt drippings in a small saucepan over moderate heat, and blend in flour and mustard. Slowly add milk and heat, stirring constantly, until smooth and thickened. Mix in salt and pepper. Pour sauce evenly over potatoes, cover, and bake 1 hour. Uncover and bake 30 minutes longer until potatoes are fork tender and golden. About 530 calories per serving.

EASY HAM AND CORN CASSEROLE

Makes 4 servings

2 cups diced cooked ham
1 small yellow onion, peeled and grated fine
1 small sweet green pepper, cored, seeded, and minced
1 (1-pound) can cream-style corn
1 (8-ounce) can whole kernel corn, drained
½ cup light cream

Topping:
1½ cups packaged seasoned bread cubes or croutons
¼ cup melted butter or margarine
1 tablespoon Worcestershire sauce

Preheat oven to 350° F. Mix all ingredients except topping and spoon into a buttered 1½-quart casserole. Sprinkle with bread cubes; mix butter and Worcestershire sauce and drizzle on top. Bake, uncovered, 30 minutes until bubbly and brown. About 535 calories per serving.

HAM TETRAZZINI

Makes 6 servings

5 tablespoons butter or margarine
½ pound mushrooms, wiped clean and sliced thin
¼ cup finely chopped yellow onion
¼ cup unsifted flour
2 cups chicken broth
1¼ cups light cream
1 cup grated sharp Cheddar cheese
1½ teaspoons salt
⅛ teaspoon pepper
1 teaspoon lemon juice
3 cups cubed cooked ham
½ pound macaroni, cooked by package directions
¼ cup finely grated Parmesan cheese

Preheat oven to 400° F. Melt butter in a large saucepan over moderate heat and stir-fry mushrooms and onion 5 minutes until onion is pale golden. Blend in flour slowly add broth and cream, and heat, stirring, until thickened. Add all remaining ingredients except ham, macaroni, and Parmesan and cook, stirring, until cheese melts. Off heat mix in ham and drained macaroni and toss to mix. Spoon into a greased 2-quart casserole, top with Parmesan, and bake uncovered 25–30 minutes until bubbly and lightly browned. About 615 calories per serving.

VARIATION:

Ham and Tongue Tetrazzini: Reduce ham to 2 cups and add 1 (6-ounce) jar tongue, diced; proceed as directed. About 630 calories per serving.

¢ HAM AND EGG SHORTCAKE

Makes 4–6 servings

3 tablespoons butter or margarine
3 tablespoons flour
2 cups milk
2 cups diced cooked ham
4 hard-cooked eggs, peeled and quartered
½ teaspoon salt (about)
¼ teaspoon pepper
1 teaspoon prepared spicy brown mustard (optional)
1 tablespoon minced parsley

Topping:
½ cup sifted flour
½ cup yellow corn meal
¼ teaspoon salt
1–2 tablespoons sugar
2 teaspoons baking powder
1 egg, lightly beaten
2 tablespoons melted butter or margarine
½ cup milk

Preheat oven to 400° F. Melt butter in a saucepan over moderate heat and blend in flour; slowly add milk and heat, stirring, until thickened. Off heat add remaining ingredients except topping, taste for salt and adjust as needed. Spoon into a greased 9″×9″×2″ pan or a 2-quart casserole. For topping, mix flour, corn meal, salt, sugar, and baking powder in a bowl. Combine egg, butter, and milk, add to dry ingredients, and beat with a rotary beater *just* until smooth. Spoon on top of ham mixture and bake, uncovered, 30 minutes until golden. Cut into squares and serve. About 630 calories for each of 4 servings, 420 calories for each of 6 servings.

¢ HAM SHANK STEW WITH DUMPLINGS

Best made the day before with dumplings added during reheating. Makes 4–6 servings

½ pound dried whole green peas or lima beans, washed and sorted
2½ quarts cold water (about)
½ pound dried split green peas, washed and sorted
1 ham shank with some meat attached (leftover is fine)
2 medium-size carrots, peeled and diced
2 medium-size yellow onions, peeled and minced
1 teaspoon salt (about)
¼ teaspoon pepper
1 tablespoon dark brown sugar
1 tablespoon cider vinegar
¼ teaspoon thyme (optional)
1 clove garlic, peeled and crushed
1 recipe Quick Dumplings or Biscuit Dumplings
1 tablespoon minced parsley

Soak whole peas or limas in 2 cups water overnight or use the quick method.* Drain, measure soaking water, and add enough cold water to make 2½ quarts. Add all remaining ingredients except dumplings and parsley, adjusting salt to taste. Cover and simmer 1½–2 hours until peas are tender. Remove meat from ham shank, cut into bite-size pieces, and return to kettle. Mix

MEAT 449

dumplings and drop by table-spoonfuls on top of just boiling stew; simmer, *uncovered,* 10 minutes, cover tightly, and simmer 10 minutes longer. Sprinkle with parsley and serve in soup bowls. About 595 calories for each of 4 servings, 395 calories for each of 6 servings.

HAM LOAF

An all-ham loaf will not slice as well as one made with part ham and part pork or veal.
Makes 6 servings

1½ pounds ground smoked ham
½ pound ground lean pork or veal shoulder
2 eggs, lightly beaten
1½ cups soft white bread crumbs
1 cup milk
1 large yellow onion, peeled and minced (optional)
¼ teaspoon pepper
½ teaspoon celery salt
½ teaspoon powdered mustard

Preheat oven to 350° F. Mix all ingredients, pack into a lightly greased 9″×5″×3″ loaf pan, and bake uncovered 1 hour. Remove from oven and let "rest" 5 minutes. Drain off drippings, then turn loaf out on platter. Make Pan Gravy with some of the drippings or serve loaf with Mustard or Raisin Sauce. Or chill well and serve cold with Mustard or Sour Cream-Horseradish Sauce. About 445 calories per serving (without sauce or gravy).

VARIATIONS:

Ham Loaf Ring: Pack ham loaf mixture in a greased 5-cup ring mold instead of a loaf pan and bake as directed. When serving, fill center with mashed sweet potatoes or buttered green peas and mushrooms. About 445 calories per serving (without vegetables).

Spicy Ham Loaf: Add ¼ cup minced parsley and ⅛ teaspoon each cloves, cinnamon, and nutmeg to loaf mixture and proceed as directed. About 445 calories per serving.

Caramel-Glazed Ham Loaf: Sprinkle bottom of loaf pan with ⅓ cup firmly packed light brown sugar and ½ teaspoon cloves before packing in meat; bake as directed. About 490 calories per serving.

Tomato-Glazed Ham Loaf: Substitute 1 cup tomato juice for milk when mixing loaf. Proceed as directed, basting loaf frequently with tomato juice throughout baking. About 10 minutes before loaf is done, top with 1 cup Tomato Sauce. Continue baking, and serve with additional Tomato Sauce. About 435 calories per serving.

Orange-Glazed Ham Loaf: Substitute 1 cup orange juice for milk when mixing loaf. Shape mixture into a loaf in a lightly greased shallow roasting pan; bake, uncovered, as directed but baste often during last ½ hour with Orange Glaze. *To make glaze:* mix ¼ cup firmly packed light brown sugar with 1 tablespoon cornstarch; add 1½ cups orange juice and heat, stirring, until thickened and clear. (*Note:* Any leftover glaze can be served with loaf as a sauce.) For extra tang, mix in 2 teaspoons slivered orange rind (orange part only). About 485 calories per serving.

Individual Ham Loaves: Shape ham mixture into 6 small loaves and place in a lightly greased, large shallow roasting pan. Mix 1 (8-ounce) can tomato sauce, 2 tablespoons cider vinegar, ½ cup firmly packed light brown sugar, and ½ cup water and pour over loaves.

Bake uncovered ¾ hour, basting frequently. About 525 calories per serving.

SWEET-SOUR HAM AND HAMBURGER LOAF

An unlikely combination of meats that is surprisingly good.
Makes 6 servings

1 pound ground smoked ham
1 pound hamburger or ground beef chuck
1 cup soft white bread crumbs
½ cup milk
½ cup cold water
2 eggs, lightly beaten
1 small yellow onion, peeled and grated fine
⅛ teaspoon liquid hot red pepper seasoning
¾ teaspoon salt

Sauce:
1 cup firmly packed light brown sugar
½ cup cider vinegar
½ cup boiling water
1 tablespoon prepared spicy brown mustard

Preheat oven to 350° F. Mix all loaf ingredients and shape into a loaf in a shallow roasting pan lined with lightly greased foil. Mix sauce and pour over loaf. Bake uncovered, basting frequently, 1 hour. Remove from oven and let stand 5 minutes. Transfer to platter, using 2 pancake turners, and serve. About 530 calories per serving.

⚖ TOP HAT HAM SOUFFLÉ

Makes 4 servings

¼ cup butter or margarine
¼ cup sifted flour
½ teaspoon salt
⅛ teaspoon white pepper
Pinch cayenne pepper
1 cup milk
4 eggs, separated
1 cup ground cooked ham

Preheat oven to 350° F. Melt butter in a saucepan over moderate heat, blend in flour, salt, and peppers; slowly add milk and heat, stirring, until thickened. Beat yolks lightly, mix in a little of the hot sauce, then return all to pan. Cook, stirring constantly, 1–2 minutes but do not boil. Off heat, mix in ham; cool to room temperature. Beat egg whites until fairly stiff peaks form, then fold into ham mixture. Spoon into an ungreased 1½-quart soufflé dish. To form top hat, insert a table knife in soufflé mixture about ½″ deep and 1″ from edge of dish and draw a circle concentric to dish. Bake, uncovered (without opening oven door), 35–45 minutes until puffed and golden. Serve at once. About 325 calories per serving.

VARIATION:

⚖ **Ham and Cheese Soufflé:** Reduce amount of butter to 3 tablespoons then proceed as recipe directs, adding ¾ cup ground ham and ⅓ cup grated sharp Cheddar cheese to hot sauce. Fold in egg whites and bake as directed. About 350 calories per serving.

BAKED SWEET AND SOUR HAM BALLS

Makes 4 servings

Meat Balls:
½ pound ground smoked ham
½ pound ground lean pork
1 cup soft white bread crumbs
½ cup milk
½ teaspoon garlic salt
⅛ teaspoon pepper
1 egg, lightly beaten

Sauce:
1 cup firmly packed light brown sugar
¼ cup cider vinegar
½ cup pineapple juice
1 teaspoon powdered mustard

Preheat oven to 325° F. Mix all meat-ball ingredients and shape into 16 balls about 1" in diameter. Arrange in a greased shallow baking pan. Mix sauce ingredients in a saucepan, bring to a boil, and cook, stirring constantly, 2–3 minutes. Pour sauce over meat balls and bake, uncovered, 1 hour, basting frequently. About 535 calories per serving.

BAKED HAM AND ASPARAGUS ROLLS IN CHEESE SAUCE

Makes 4 servings

16 stalks steamed asparagus
8 thin slices boiled ham
2 tablespoons butter

Sauce:
3 tablespoons butter or margarine
3 tablespoons flour
1½ cups milk
¾ cup heavy cream
¾ cup coarsely grated Gruyère, Swiss, or Cheddar cheese
1 teaspoon salt
⅛ teaspoon white pepper
2 tablespoons finely grated Parmesan cheese

Preheat oven to 425° F. Roll 2 stalks asparagus in each ham slice and secure with toothpicks. Sauté rolls in butter over moderate heat 2 minutes, then arrange in an ungreased shallow 1½-quart casserole. To make sauce, melt butter in a saucepan, blend in flour, slowly add milk, and cook, stirring, until thickened. Mix in remaining ingredients except Parmesan and heat, stirring, until cheese melts. Pour sauce over rolls, sprinkle with Parmesan, and bake uncovered 15 minutes. About 650 calories per serving.

VARIATIONS:

Endive-Stuffed Ham Rolls: Substitute 8 boiled Belgian endives for asparagus, roll each in a ham slice, and proceed as directed. About 650 calories per serving.

Broccoli-Stuffed Ham Rolls: Substitute 8 slim broccoli spears for asparagus, roll each in a ham slice, and proceed as directed. About 650 calories per serving.

Banana-Stuffed Ham Rolls: Substitute 8 lengthwise banana halves for asparagus, roll each in a ham slice, and proceed as directed. About 700 calories per serving.

Pineapple-Cream Cheese Ham Rolls: Spread each ham slice with a little softened cream cheese and roll around a pineapple spear; proceed as directed. About 665 calories per serving.

HAM THE SECOND TIME AROUND
(How to Use Up Leftovers)

⊲⊳ ¢ HAM TIMBALES

Makes 4 servings

1 cup milk
1 cup soft white bread crumbs
2 tablespoons butter or margarine
1 tablespoon finely grated yellow onion
½ teaspoon salt
⅛ teaspoon pepper
⅛ teaspoon cloves
2 eggs, lightly beaten
1 cup ground cooked ham

Preheat oven to 325° F. Mix all but last 2 ingredients in a saucepan and bring to a boil, stirring constantly. Off heat, stir a little hot mixture into eggs, then return to pan.

Mix in ham. Spoon into 4 well-greased custard cups and set in a shallow baking pan; pour in enough water to come halfway up cups. Bake, uncovered, 35–45 minutes or until a knife inserted in center comes out clean. Loosen edges of timbales and invert gently on a hot platter. Good with hot Mushroom or Tomato Sauce. About 255 calories per serving (without sauce).

¢ **CRUSTY-CRUMB HAM CROQUETTES**

Makes 4 servings

¼ cup butter or margarine
¼ cup sifted flour
1 cup milk
3 scallions, minced
⅛ teaspoon pepper
1 teaspoon prepared mild yellow mustard
1 teaspoon finely grated lemon rind (optional)
¼ cup minced sweet green pepper (optional)
1 egg, lightly beaten
1½ cups ground cooked ham
½ teaspoon salt (about)
1 egg lightly beaten with 1 tablespoon cold water
⅓ cup toasted seasoned bread crumbs
¼ cup cooking oil

Melt butter in a large saucepan over moderate heat, blend in flour, slowly add milk, and heat, stirring, until thickened. Add scallions, pepper, mustard, and, if you like, lemon rind and green pepper. Spoon a little sauce into beaten egg, then return to saucepan. Mix in ham and salt to taste; then chill until easy to shape. Roll into 8 balls about 2″ in diameter, dip in egg-water mixture, then in crumbs to coat evenly. Let dry on a rack at room temperature 5 minutes. Heat oil in a large, heavy skillet over moderately high heat about 1 minute, then fry balls 3–4 minutes, turning frequently, until browned on all sides. Drain on paper toweling and serve. Good with Hot Mustard or Parsley Sauce.

To Deep-Fat-Fry: Prepare balls as directed; heat fat in a deep fat fryer to 380° F., add balls a few at a time, and brown about 2 minutes; drain well and serve.

Both versions: About 410 calories per serving (without sauce).

¢ ⚖ **BOK CHOY (CHINESE CABBAGE AND HAM)**

Makes 4 servings

1 medium-size Chinese or celery cabbage, trimmed and cored
1½ teaspoons salt
2 tablespoons cooking oil
½ cup cooked ham strips (about ⅛″ thick and 3″ long)
1 tablespoon cornstarch
1 cup chicken broth

Shred cabbage fine, cover with cold water, mix in 1 teaspoon salt, and let crispen 30 minutes; drain thoroughly. Heat oil in a large, heavy skillet or *wok* over moderately high heat 1–2 minutes. Add cabbage and ham and stir-fry 2–3 minutes until cabbage just wilts. Mix cornstarch, chicken broth, and remaining salt, add to skillet, and cook, stirring constantly, 2 minutes until mixture thickens slightly. Serve with boiled rice. About 155 calories per serving (without rice).

¢ **HAM-TUNA-NOODLE CASSEROLE**

Makes 4 servings

¼ cup butter or margarine
¼ cup sifted flour

2 cups milk
1½ teaspoons salt
¼ teaspoon pepper
1 tablespoon Worcestershire sauce
1 cup diced cooked ham
1 (7-ounce) can white or light tuna,
 drained and flaked
1 (4-ounce) can sliced mushrooms,
 drained
½-pound box thin noodles, cooked
 by package directions

Topping:
1 cup soft white bread crumbs mixed
 with 3 tablespoons melted butter or
 margarine

Preheat oven to 350° F. Melt butter
in a saucepan over moderate heat
and blend in flour; slowly add
milk and heat, stirring, until
thickened. Off heat mix in remaining ingredients except topping.
Spoon into a lightly buttered
2-quart casserole and sprinkle
topping over surface. Bake, uncovered, 30 minutes. About 615
calories per serving.

VARIATIONS:

¢ **Ham and Green Pea Casserole:**
Prepare as directed, omitting tuna
and adding 1 (10-ounce) package
frozen green peas, cooked by
package directions. For extra zip,
mix ½ cup grated sharp cheese into
sauce before adding remaining ingredients. About 565 calories per
serving.

¢ **Ham and Mushroom Casserole
au Gratin:** Instead of making white
sauce with butter, flour, and milk,
use 1 (10½-ounce) can cream of
mushroom soup thinned with ¾
cup milk. Substitute ½ cup grated
sharp Cheddar cheese for topping
and bake as directed. About 635
calories per serving.

¢ **Ham-Noodle Casserole:** Prepare
as directed, omitting tuna and in-

creasing amount of ham to 2
cups. About 590 calories per
serving.

Some Additional Ways to Use Up Leftover Ham

Creamed Ham and Potatoes (4
servings): In a large skillet mix
4 cups diced raw potatoes, 1½
cups chopped ham, ¼ cup minced
yellow onion, 1 tablespoon flour,
1 teaspoon salt, and ⅛ teaspoon
pepper; add 1 cup each milk
and light cream, cover, and simmer,
stirring occasionally, 20–30
minutes until potatoes are tender.
Taste for salt and adjust as needed.
Serve over toast, muffins, biscuits or
waffles. About 415 calories per
serving (without toast, muffins,
biscuits, or waffles).

⊠ **Quick Creamed Ham** (4
servings): In a saucepan mix 1
(10½-ounce) can condensed green
pea, mushroom, or celery soup,
½ cup milk, 1½ cups chopped
or slivered ham, 2 tablespoons
coarsely chopped pimiento, and ¼
teaspoon powdered mustard. Cover
and simmer 10 minutes, stirring
occasionally. If you like, stir in 4
quartered hard-cooked eggs. Serve
over toast, muffins, biscuits, or
waffles. About 295 calories per
serving (without eggs, toast, muffins,
biscuits, or waffles).

⊠ ¢ **Chinese Ham and Rice** (4
servings): Sauté 1½ cups slivered
ham, 1 diced sweet red pepper,
and 3 minced scallions in 2
tablespoons cooking oil 2–3 minutes
over moderate heat. Add 1 (4-
ounce) can water chestnuts,
drained and sliced thin, and 3 cups
cold cooked rice; stir-fry 4–5
minutes until rice is lightly browned.
Stir together (do not beat) 2

eggs and 1 tablespoon soy sauce and mix into rice; heat, stirring, until eggs are just set. Serve with extra soy sauce. About 335 calories per serving.

Ham and Egg Pie (6 servings): Line a 9″ piepan with pastry and sprinkle with ¾ cup minced ham. Break 5–6 eggs on top, sprinkle with ½ teaspoon and ⅛ teaspoon pepper, and top with ¾ cup minced ham. Cover with pastry, crimp, and cut steam vents near center. Brush with glaze if you like (1 egg beaten with 1 tablespoon cold water). Bake ½ hour at 425° F. until lightly browned. Serve hot or cold. About 490 calories per serving.

¢ ⊠ **Ham and Baked Beans** (2 servings): Mix 1 (1-pound) can baked beans, 1 cup cubed or slivered ham, 2 tablespoons molasses, 1 tablespoon prepared mild yellow mustard, and 1 teaspoon prepared horseradish. Simmer, covered, 15–20 minutes until bubbly, or spoon into an ungreased 1-quart casserole, cover, and bake ½ hour at 350° F. About 505 calories per serving.

Ham en Brochette (Number of servings flexible): Alternate 2″ ham cubes on long skewers with any of the following: canned pitted apricots, cling peach halves, preserved kumquats, spiced crab apples, pineapple or banana chunks, parboiled sweet red and green pepper squares, boiled white onions, canned potatoes, mushroom caps, unpeeled tomato wedges, large pitted ripe olives. Brush lightly with melted butter and broil 5″–6″ from heat, turning often, until ham is lightly browned. Recipe too flexible for a meaningful calorie count.

⊠ ¢ **Ham and Potato Pie** (4 servings): Mix 1½ cups minced ham with 2 cups mixed cooked vegetables, succotash, or creamed corn in a buttered 1½-quart casserole. Cover with 2 cups seasoned mashed potatoes, roughen surface with fork, and bake uncovered ½ hour at 425° F. until touched with brown. About 500 calories per serving.

Ham and Egg Cakes (4 servings): Mix 1½ cups ground ham, 4 minced hard-cooked eggs, 1 cup soft white bread crumbs, 1 beaten egg, ½ teaspoon salt, ⅛ teaspoon pepper, and 2 tablespoons minced parsley. Shape into 4 flat cakes, dust with flour, and sauté 2 minutes on a side in 2 tablespoons butter over moderate heat. About 320 calories per serving.

Ham and Cheese Heroes (Number of servings flexible): Split thin loaves of French bread or hard rolls lengthwise, spread with Garlic Butter, prepared mild yellow mustard, and a ½ and ½ mixture of ground ham and grated cheese (Cheddar, Swiss, or Gruyère). Top with other half of loaf, wrap in foil, and bake 20 minutes at 350° F. Recipe too flexible for a meaningful calorie count.

⊠ **Barbecued Ham Slices** (4 servings): Cut 8 thick slices of ham and arrange in a greased shallow baking dish. Mix together ¼ cup each chili sauce and firmly packed dark brown sugar, 1 tablespoon each prepared mild yellow mustard and cider vinegar; spread over ham and bake, uncovered, 20 minutes at 350° F. About 335 calories per serving.

Potted Ham (Makes about 1½ cups): Mix 1 cup finely ground lean ham with 2 sieved hard-cooked egg yolks, ¼ cup soft butter, and ⅛ teaspoon powdered mustard. Beat until well blended, pack into a crock or jar, and cover with ⅛″ clarified butter.* Refrigerate and use as a canapé or sandwich spread. About 70 calories per tablespoon.

⚖ **Ham Mousse** (4 servings): Mix 1 envelope unflavored gelatin and ½ cup pineapple juice or cold water and heat slowly, stirring until dissolved. Add 2 cups ground ham, 1 teaspoon prepared mild yellow mustard, 1 teaspoon prepared horseradish, and, if you like, 2 tablespoons diced pimiento. Cool to room temperature. Fold in 1 stiffly beaten egg white and ½ cup heavy cream, whipped. Spoon into an ungreased 1-quart mold and chill until firm. (*Note:* Chicken or tongue may be used in place of ham.) About 290 calories per serving.

Ham Stuffed Vegetables
Ham Hash
} Follow recipes given in Some Additional Ways to Use Up Leftover Roast Beef, substituting ham for beef.

Ham, Olive, and Egg Salad (4 servings): Mix 2 cups cubed ham, 3 quartered hard-cooked eggs, 1 cup diced celery, ½ cup sliced pimiento-stuffed green olives, 2 minced gherkins, and ¾ cup mayonnaise. About 585 calories per serving.

Ham and Chicken Salad (4 servings): Mix 1½ cups each cubed ham and chicken with 1 cup diced celery, 2 tablespoons each minced dill pickle, parsley, and grated yellow onion, and ¾ cup

mayonnaise. About 555 calories per serving.

Ham and Tongue Salad (4 servings): Mix 1½ cups each cubed ham and tongue with 1 cup diced celery, 2 tablespoons each sweet pickle relish and prepared mild yellow mustard, and ¾ cup mayonnaise. About 625 calories per serving.

Ham Waldorf Salad (4 servings): Mix 2 cups each diced ham and diced unpeeled red apple, 1 cup diced celery, ½ cup coarsely chopped pecans or walnuts, 1 cup mayonnaise, and 2 tablespoons lemon juice. About 745 calories per serving.

Ham in Avocado (4 servings): Dip 2 peeled, pitted, and halved avocados in lemon juice to prevent darkening; stuff with 1½ cups ground ham mixed with enough Thousand Island Dressing to moisten. Garnish with seeded grapes and grapefruit sections. About 380 calories per serving.

Ham in Peaches (Number of servings flexible): Mix equal quantities of diced ham and cottage cheese and use to stuff cling peach halves. Recipe too flexible for a meaningful calorie count.

To Make the Most of Very Small Amounts:
– Mix ½ cup ground ham to dry ingredients for Quick Dumplings; finish mixing and cook as directed.
– Mix ½ cup ground or finely diced ham to dry ingredients for biscuits, muffins, or corn bread; finish mixing and bake as directed.
– Cube ham or cut in julienne strips and toss into hearty salads (chef's salad, dried bean, egg, potato, pasta, rice, or fruit salad).
– Dice or cut ham in julienne strips

and add to Scalloped Corn, Corn Gumbo, Corn Pie, or Corn Fritters.
– Dice ham and add to Hashed Brown Potatoes, Rice Pilaf, Deluxe Macaroni and Cheese, any meat sauce for spaghetti, any budget casserole.
– Grind ham fine and use in making sandwich fillings or savory stuffings (for ideas, see Some Additional Ways to Use Up Leftover Roast Beef).
– Dice ham or grind coarsely and add to omelets or scrambled eggs, waffle or pancake batter.

What to Do with Ham Bones:
– Add to the pot when cooking any dried beans, peas, or lentils.
– Add to the pot when cooking fresh mustard greens, spinach, turnip greens, green or wax beans, black-eyed peas.
– Use in making dried pea, bean, or lentil soup, Corn Chowder, or Quick Cream of Tomato Soup. Or add trimmings to canned or packaged soups.

Ham Steaks and Slices
(See Pork Chart)

Ham Steak: Also called *Ham Center Slice,* this large oval slice from the middle of the ham is the equivalent of beef round or veal cutlet. Cut thick, it can be baked; cut thin, broiled, panbroiled, grilled, panfried, or braised. Available uncooked and ready-to-eat.

Ham Butt Slice: Cut a little higher on the ham than the center slice, this steak is not quite so large or expensive. Available uncooked or ready-to-eat.

Smoked Picnic Slice: This large oval slice resembles ham steak but is

not as tender or expensive. Available uncooked or ready-to-eat.

How to Cook

Amounts Needed: A ham steak or slice cut ½″ thick will serve 2–4; cut 1″–2″ thick, it will serve 4–6. To figure by weight: allow ⅓–½ pound per person.

General Preparation for Cooking: Remove any rind, trim off all but ¼″ outer fat, then slash fat edge at 1″ intervals to prevent curling.

To Panfry (Sauté): Recommended only for very lean ham steaks and slices ¼″–¾″ thick. *Uncooked ham:* Brown, uncovered, in 1 tablespoon bacon drippings or cooking oil in a large, heavy skillet over moderately low heat, allowing 3 minutes per side for ¼″ thick steaks, 4–5 minutes per side for ½″ steaks, and 6 minutes per side for ¾″ steaks. Season with pepper and, if needed, salt. *Ready-to-eat ham:* Prepare like uncooked ham but brown about half as long on each side.

VARIATION:

Mustard Ham Steak: Before cooking, spread 1 side of ham with 1½ tablespoons mild yellow mustard and sprinkle with pepper. Place ham in skillet mustard side down and brown as directed. Before turning, spread top with 1½ tablespoons mustard and sprinkle with pepper; turn and brown as before.

To Panbroil: Recommended for steaks and slices ¼″–¾″ thick. If ham seems lean, grease or salt skillet *lightly;* heat over moderately low heat 1 minute, add ham steak, and cook, using panfrying times as a guide. Turn with tongs and drain off drippings as they collect.

VARIATION:

Ham Steak in Sour Cream-Onion Gravy: Panbroil steak as directed, remove to a heated platter, and keep warm. In drippings sauté 2 thinly sliced large yellow onions 8–10 minutes over moderate heat until golden; smooth in 1 cup sour cream, ⅓ cup milk, and ¼ teaspoon paprika. Heat and stir (but do not boil) 1–2 minutes over low heat. Pour over ham and serve.

To Broil: Recommended for ham steaks or slices ½″–1½″ thick. Preheat broiler. Rub rack with drippings or oil and line pan underneath with foil. Place ham on rack, fat edge to back to reduce sputtering, then adjust height and broil using times in chart below as a guide. Use tongs for turning. For extra flavor, brush steaks often during cooking with a liquid glaze (see Some Glazes for Baked Hams).

To Charcoal Broil: Recommended for ham steaks or slices ½″–1½″ thick. Build a moderately low charcoal fire.* Lightly grease grill with drippings or oil, place ham on grill, adjust height from coals, and broil according to chart. If you like, brush often during cooking with a liquid glaze (see Some Glazes for Baked Hams).

Ham Steak Broiling Chart

Times (for steaks refrigerated until ready to be broiled) are approximate at best because size and shape of cut, amount of fat and bone, type of oven or grill all affect broiling time. In outdoor cooking, wind and temperature must also be considered.

To Braise: Especially good for uncooked ham steaks and slices about 1″ thick. Brown both sides of steak quickly in a lightly greased large, heavy skillet over moderately high heat; pour off drippings. Add 1 cup liquid (water; orange, pineapple, apple, or apricot juice; apple cider; beer, sherry, port, Madeira, champagne, sweet or dry red or white wine), cover, turn heat to low, and simmer until done. *Uncooked hams* will take about 20 minutes (turn after 10); *ready-to-eat hams* 5–10 minutes in all.

VARIATIONS:

Ham Steak Virginia: Braise steak as directed, using water for the liquid; remove ham to a heated platter and keep warm. Stir ½ cup medium-dry sherry and ¼ cup firmly packed light brown sugar into skillet and heat, stirring, over moderate heat until sugar dissolves. Blend 2 tablespoons flour with ¼ cup cold water, mix into skillet, and heat and stir until thickened. Return steak to skillet, turn heat to low, and simmer uncovered 5–7 minutes, basting and turning frequently. Serve on a bed of Creamed Spinach.

Tomato-Smothered Ham Steak: Brown steak on both sides and drain off drippings. Sprinkle with 1 teaspoon instant minced onion and top with 1 (1-pound) can tomato sauce or spaghetti sauce with mushrooms. Cover and simmer, using times in basic recipe for braising as a guide.

Ham Steak in Port Wine Sauce: Brown steak on both sides and drain off drippings. To skillet add

Oven Broiling

Cut	Thickness	Oven or Fire Temperature	Distance from Heat	Approximate Minutes per Side
	½″	Broil	3″	4
Uncooked	¾″	Broil	3″	7
Ham steaks	1″	Broil	4″	9
	1½″	Broil	4″	10–12
	½″	Broil	3″	3–5 total (do not turn steak)
Ready-to-eat	¾″	Broil	3″	3
Ham steaks	1″	Broil	4″	5
	1½″	(not recommended)		

Charcoal Broiling

Cut	Thickness	Oven or Fire Temperature	Distance from Heat	Approximate Minutes per Side
	½″	Moderately low	4″	5
Uncooked	¾″	Moderately low	4″	6–8
Ham steaks	1″	Moderately low	5″	10
	1½″	Moderately low	5″	12
	½″	Moderately low	4″	3–4
Ready-to-eat	¾″	Moderately low	4″	4–5
Ham steaks	1″	Moderately low	4″	5–6

¾ cup water, ⅓ cup tawny port wine, and 1 tablespoon soy sauce. Cover and simmer until done as directed above. Lift ham to a heated platter and keep warm; boil wine sauce, uncovered, 2–3 minutes until reduced to about ½ cup. Pour over ham and serve.

To Bake: Recommended for 1½″–2″ thick ham steaks and slices. Preheat oven to 325° F. Place ham on a rack in a shallow roasting pan. If you like, stud surface with cloves and top with a thin glaze (see Some Glazes for Baked Hams). Bake uncovered, basting occasionally with glaze, if used, until tender. *Ready-to-eat hams* need only 30–35 minutes, regardless of thickness. Time *uncooked hams* as follows: 1–1¼ hours for a 1½″ steak, 1½–1¾ hours for a 2″ steak.

VARIATIONS:

Marinated Ham Steak: Marinate steak in refrigerator overnight in ½ cup dry red wine or red wine vinegar mixed with ½ cup pineapple juice and ½ teaspoon ginger. Place ham and marinade in baking pan and bake as directed, basting often.

Chinese-Style Ham Steak: Marinate steak in refrigerator overnight in ⅓ cup soy sauce mixed with ¼ cup firmly packed light brown sugar, ¼ cup cider vinegar, 1 crushed clove garlic, and 1 teaspoon powdered mustard. Place ham and marinade in pan and bake as directed, basting often.

Chutney-Glazed Ham Steak: Mix 1 cup minced chutney with ¼ cup firmly packed light brown sugar and ⅓ cup water; spread over ham and bake as directed.

Ham Steak with Bing Cherry Sauce:
Place ham directly in pan (omit
rack) and set aside. Mix 2 tablespoons sugar, 1 tablespoon cornstarch, and ½ cup cold water and
heat, stirring, until thickened. Off
heat add 1 (1-pound) can pitted
Bing cherries (do not drain), pour
over steak, and bake as directed.

Barbecued Ham Steak: Place ham
in pan without rack, top with 1
cup All-Purpose Barbecue Sauce,
and bake as directed.

Baked Stuffed Ham Steak (6–8
servings): Use 2 (1″ thick)
ready-to-eat ham steaks instead of
1 thick steak; spread 1 steak
evenly with 1½–2 cups Sage and
Onion or Corn Bread Stuffing or
with packaged stuffing prepared by
directions. Top with second steak
and skewer together in several
places. Bake uncovered 45
minutes.

BAKED HAM AND SWEET
   POTATOES

Makes 4–6 servings

4 *medium-size sweet potatoes,
  parboiled, peeled, and halved*
4 *pineapple rings or 1 cup pineapple
  chunks or tidbits*
1 *ready-to-eat ham steak, cut ¾″
  thick (about 2 pounds)*
6 *cloves*
2 *tablespoons light brown sugar*
½ *cup pineapple juice*

Preheat oven to 350° F. Arrange
potatoes in an ungreased 2½-quart
casserole, cover with pineapple,
and top with ham. Stud ham
with cloves and sprinkle with
sugar. Pour pineapple juice over
all and bake, uncovered, 30–40
minutes.

VARIATION:
Use 2½ cups cubed cooked ham

instead of steak; substitute ⅛
teaspoon powdered cloves for whole
cloves and mix with sugar. Otherwise, prepare as directed.

Both versions: About 780 calories
for each of 4 servings, 520 calories
for each of 6 servings.

▨ COUNTRY-FRIED HAM
     WITH RED EYE GRAVY

Country-Fried Ham with Red Eye
Gravy is one of those generations-
old Southern recipes that probably
seemed too simple to write down.
It isn't really. To have any success,
you must use country-cured ham, a
heavy iron skillet, and just the
right amount of heat—too much
and the ham will scorch, too little
and it won't brown. Some say
coffee gives the gravy its red
color, but most country cooks
simply simmer the gravy, scraping
up any browned bits, till it turns
red-brown on its own.

Makes 2–4 servings

1 *teaspoon bacon drippings or lard*
1 *center slice country-cured ham, cut
  ¼″ thick*
⅔ *cup cold water*
1 *tablespoon hot strong coffee
  (optional)*

Place a heavy iron skillet over
moderately low heat and heat 1
minute; add drippings and, when
melted, place ham in skillet. Fry,
turning often, until ham is nicely
browned on both sides; this will
take about 15 minutes. Remove ham
to a heated platter and keep
warm. Add water to skillet and
continue heating, stirring and scraping up browned bits, 3–5 minutes
until gravy turns red-brown; add
coffee if you like. Spoon a little
gravy over ham and pass the rest.
Serve with grits. About 570
calories for each of 2 servings

(without grits), 285 calories for each of 4 servings.

Bacon, Salt Pork, and Jowl
(See Pork Chart)

"The leaner, the better" doesn't apply to bacon because fat is what gives bacon its woodsy-sweet flavor and tender crispness. Ideally, bacon should be half to two thirds fat—snowy and firm with wide, evenly distributed streakings of bright pink lean. (Because of its high fat content, bacon stores poorly, so don't buy more than a week's supply at a time.) The flavor of bacon, like that of ham, varies according to the breed of animal, feed, cut, method of curing and smoking. Your best assurance of quality is to buy brands you trust.

Slab Bacon: Cured and smoked side of pork. It's cheaper than presliced bacon and, according to some people, has better flavor. Butchers will slice it for you or you can do it yourself.

Sliced Bacon: Slab bacon that has been trimmed of rind, sliced, and packaged. Available as:

Regular Sliced: The best all-round bacon, not too thick, not too thin. There are 16–20 slices per pound.

Thick Sliced: A shade thicker than regular-sliced bacon, this has an old-fashioned, hand-sliced look. About 12–16 slices per pound.

Thin Sliced: Good for sandwiches, serving with eggs or crumbling into bacon bits, but too thin and fragile to do the sort of wrapping *rumakis* need. About 35 slices per pound.

Canned Sliced: A convenience food for campers and apartment dwellers with pint-sized refrigerators, these canned precooked bacon slices need no refrigeration and can be heated in minutes. 1 can (18–20 slices) =1 pound fresh bacon.

Ends and Pieces: These penny-saving scraps are great for soups, sandwiches, salads.

Bacon Crumbles or Bits: Crisp, cooked bits of bacon ready to toss into salads, soups, and casseroles. Usually bottled in small amounts.

Country-Cured Bacon: Also called *Country-Style Bacon,* this is salty, heavily smoked bacon. Often it comes from the same hogs as Smithfield or Virginia hams. More expensive than ordinary bacon and available by the slab or slice in gourmet food shops.

Irish Bacon: This Irish equivalent of country-cured bacon is a doubly long strip containing both the "streaky" we usually think of as bacon and the lean eye of loin used for Canadian bacon. For shipping, the two are cut through to the rind just below the ribs, then folded together compact-style. Whether you buy Irish bacon by the slab or have it sliced to order, you will get both parts. Like country-cured bacon, Irish bacon is heavily salted and smoked; it is more expensive than standard bacon and is available in gourmet shops.

Canadian Bacon: Sometimes called *Back Bacon,* this is the boneless, lean eye of loin, cured and smoked. In flavor and texture it resembles ham more than bacon and is best when cooked like ham. Available presliced or in rolls, also canned as *Pork Loin Roll.*

Smoked Loin Chops: A fairly new item closely related to Canadian bacon. These are simply cured and smoked loin chops. They're presliced and packaged with full cooking directions.

Jowl: Also called *Bacon Square,* this is the fleshy cheek of the hog trimmed into 5″–8″ squares, cured and smoked. It is boneless, fatter than bacon, and, except for that which is country-cured, budget priced. Use as you would bacon.

Salt Pork: Sometimes known as "white bacon," salt pork comes from the side of the hog. It is mostly fat (though that of top quality contains a handsome streak of lean); it is cured *but not smoked* and used primarily for seasoning. Frequently, people confuse salt pork with *fat back;* they are not at all the same. Fat back is fresh (uncured, unsmoked) fat from the back of the hog used for cooking and making lard.

How To Cook

Amounts Needed: Allow 2–4 slices bacon or Canadian bacon per person. When buying Canadian bacon by the roll, figure ¼–⅓ pound per person.

General Preparation for Cooking: Remove any rind. Irish and country-cured bacon, because of their saltiness, will profit by 5–10 minutes simmering in water before being broiled, panbroiled, or baked. Drain well, pat dry, then follow basic methods.

To Panfry (Sauté): Especially recommended for sliced Canadian bacon. Melt about 1 teaspoon bacon drippings in a heavy skillet over moderately low heat, add bacon, and cook 4–5 minutes on a side until delicately browned.

To Panbroil: Good for all but Canadian bacon, which is too lean to cook without additional fat. Take bacon straight from refrigerator and place unseparated slices in a cold skillet. Set over moderate heat and cook, turning often with tongs and separating slices as they heat, 6–8 minutes until crisp and brown. Spoon off drippings as they collect and drain bacon well on paper toweling before serving.

To Broil: Recommended for all but Canadian bacon. Preheat broiler. Take bacon straight from refrigerator and arrange slices on broiler rack so fat edges overlap slightly. Broil 4″ from heat 2–3 minutes on a side until crisp and golden. Use tongs to turn and watch closely. Drain on paper toweling before serving.

To Bake:

Bacon: Here's the way to cook bacon for a crowd. Preheat oven to 400° F. Lay cold bacon strips, fat edges overlapping, on a large cookie rack set in a shallow roasting pan. Bake, uncovered, 12–15 minutes without turning until crisp and brown.

Canadian Bacon: Buy a roll of Canadian bacon weighing at least 2 pounds. Slip off casing and place roll fat side up on a rack in a shallow roasting pan. Insert meat thermometer in center. Preheat oven to 325° F. and bake, uncovered, about 35 minutes per pound or until meat thermometer registers 160° F. For an extra-juicy bacon, add 1 cup liquid to pan before baking (chicken stock, orange, apple, or pineapple juice, beer) and bake as directed, basting often. For more festive ways to bake Canadian bacon, see recipes that follow.

To Spit-Roast (for Canadian bacon rolls only; for best results, choose one weighing 3–4 pounds):

In Oven or Rotisserie: Preheat unit. Insert spit straight through roll, end to end, attach to rotisserie and insert meat thermometer in center so it does not touch spit. Roast about 25 minutes per pound or until thermometer registers 160° F. Baste every 15–20 minutes, if you like, with orange, apple, or pineapple juice or with a thin glaze (see Some Glazes for Baked Hams).

Over Charcoal: Build a moderate charcoal fire.* Balance roll on spit and insert meat thermometer as above; attach to rotisserie and adjust height so spit is 4″–5″ from coals. Roast about 25 minutes per pound or until thermometer registers 160° F., basting, if you like, with orange, apple, or pineapple juice or with a thin glaze (see Some Glazes for Baked Hams).

How to Save and Use Bacon Drippings

Collect drippings in a tall coffee tin; when full, spoon drippings into a deep saucepan, add 1 cup water, and sprinkle 2–3 tablespoons flour on top (this is to make any sediment settle). Bring to a boil over moderate heat without covering or stirring. Remove from heat, cool slightly, strain through a double thickness of cheesecloth, and pour into a large jar. Cover and store in refrigerator. Use in place of butter or margarine for frying and sautéing, also for seasoning vegetables.

BAKED GINGER-GLAZED CANADIAN BACON

Makes 4–6 servings

1 (2-pound) roll ready-to-eat
  Canadian bacon
1½ cups ginger marmalade
¼ cup brandy

Have butcher remove casing from bacon, slice ⅛″–¼″ thick, and tie together into original shape. Preheat oven to 325° F. Place bacon fat side up on a rack in a shallow roasting pan. Mince any large pieces of ginger in marmalade, then mix all with brandy; spread half over bacon. Bake, uncovered, ½ hour; spread with remaining marmalade and bake ½ hour longer. Transfer to a hot platter, remove strings, and serve with English or Dijon-style mustard.

VARIATION:

Substitute orange or lime marmalade or chopped mango or peach chutney for ginger marmalade; proceed as directed.

All versions: About 890 calories for each of 4 servings, 595 calories for each of 6 servings.

BAKED YAMS, APPLES, AND CANADIAN BACON

Makes 4 servings

4 medium-size yams, parboiled,
  peeled, and sliced ½″ thick
2 tart apples, peeled, cored, and cut
  in ¼″ rings
½ teaspoon salt
8 slices ready-to-eat Canadian bacon,
  cut ¼″ thick
1 teaspoon prepared hot mustard
¼ cup firmly packed light brown
  sugar
2 tablespoons butter or margarine

Preheat oven to 375° F. Layer yams and apples into a buttered 2½-quart casserole, sprinkling with salt as you go. Spread each side of bacon slices lightly with mustard and arrange on top, overlapping spoke fashion. Sprinkle with sugar and dot with butter. Bake uncovered 30 minutes until yams are tender and bacon lightly glazed. About 565 calories per serving.

¢ HOG JOWL AND BLACK-EYED PEAS

An old Southern custom, practiced yet in some communities, is to eat hog jowl and black-eyed peas on New Year's Day. Brings good luck, they say.
Makes 6 servings

1 pound dried black-eyed peas, washed and sorted
2 quarts cold water
1 (½-pound) piece country-cured hog jowl
1 small dried hot red chili pepper
Salt to taste

Soak peas overnight in 1 quart water or use the quick method.* About 1 hour before peas have finished soaking, scrub jowl well under running tepid water; place in a large, heavy kettle with 1 quart water and the chili pepper. Cover and bring to a boil, adjust heat so water stays at a slow simmer, and cook 1 hour. Add peas and their soaking water to kettle, cover, and simmer about 2 hours longer until peas and jowl are both tender. Check pot occasionally and, if mixture seems thick, thin with about ½ cup hot water. Taste for salt and season as needed; discard chili pepper. Cut jowl into thin slices, return to kettle, and warm 5–10 minutes. Serve in soup bowls, making sure each person gets some of the jowl. About 355 calories per serving.

¢ SCALLOPED SALT PORK AND POTATOES

A good budget main dish.
Makes 4–6 servings

½ pound salt pork, trimmed of rind and cut in small dice
Salt pork drippings and enough bacon drippings to total ¼ cup

1 quart thinly sliced, peeled potatoes (you'll need 4–5 medium-size potatoes)
1 large yellow onion, peeled and sliced thin
2 tablespoons flour
¼ cup minced parsley
⅛ teaspoon pepper
1½ cups light cream

Preheat oven to 350° F. Stir-fry salt pork 8–10 minutes in a large, heavy skillet over moderate heat until lightly browned. Pour off drippings and reserve, adding bacon drippings as needed to measure ¼ cup. In a buttered 2-quart casserole, build up alternate layers of potatoes, onion, and salt pork, beginning and ending with potatoes. Drizzle each onion layer with drippings, then sprinkle with flour, parsley, and pepper. Pour in cream, cover, and bake 1–1½ hours until potatoes are tender. Broil quickly, if you like, to brown; then serve. About 615 calories for each of 4 servings, 410 calories for each of 6 servings.

¢ CREAMED SALT PORK IN POTATO NESTS

Makes 4 servings

1 pound salt pork, trimmed of rind and cut in small dice
1 quart boiling water
Salt pork drippings and enough bacon drippings to total ¼ cup
¼ cup unsifted flour
⅛ teaspoon sage
Pinch nutmeg
Pinch pepper
1 pint light cream
2 tablespoons minced parsley
Salt to taste
4 cups hot seasoned mashed potatoes

Place salt pork in a saucepan, add boiling water, and simmer uncovered 5 minutes; drain well and pat dry on paper toweling.

Stir-fry salt pork in a large, heavy skillet over moderate heat 8–10 minutes until lightly browned; pour off drippings and reserve, adding enough bacon drippings to measure ¼ cup. Transfer salt pork to hot plate and set, uncovered, in a 250° F. oven to keep warm (no need to preheat oven). Return drippings to skillet, blend in flour, sage, nutmeg, and pepper; add cream slowly and heat, stirring, until thickened and smooth. Mix in parsley, taste for salt and add as needed. Mound 1 cup mashed potatoes on each of 4 serving plates, flatten slightly, and make a well in the center. Fill with salt pork, top with some of the cream sauce, and pass the rest. About 900 calories per serving.

VARIETY MEATS

These are the other edible parts of beef, veal, lamb, and pork, the organ meats such as heart, liver, kidneys, sweetbreads, brains, tongue, and tripe. Europeans, considering them the choicest parts of the animal, lavish attention upon them, but we, alas, too often pass them up in favor of steaks, chops, and roasts. Organ meats are the most nutritious of all meats because they contain concentrated sources of certain minerals and vitamins. They are lean and thus low-calorie, but they are, for the most part, cholesterol-rich (particularly liver, kidney, and brain) and should be minimal in the diets of those with high cholesterol blood levels.

Because there is less demand for variety meats (with the exception, perhaps, of calf's liver) than for steaks, roasts, and chops, they are cheaper than the popular cuts. Moreover, correctly prepared, variety meats are surprisingly tender, delicately flavored, and good.

BRAINS

Though gourmets have long been lyrical about brains, likening their fragile texture to that of cooked mushrooms, their flavor to the most delicate white fish, they are not everyone's dish. It's the *idea* of eating brains that puts people off. If you've never tasted them, a good way to begin is by ordering *Cervelles au Beurre Noir* (Brains in Black Butter Sauce) or perhaps Brains Vinaigrette in some fine French restaurant. Delicious.

The choicest brains are those from calves or lambs; pork and beef brains have stronger flavor and less delicate texture. All brains are highly perishable (always cook within 24 hours) and for that reason are a special order item. When ordering, insist that the brains be *absolutely fresh*. Recently, frozen brains have been appearing in supermarket counters and, though they haven't quite the character of fresh brains, they are a very good substitute when the fresh aren't available. Always follow package directions when preparing.

Like sweetbreads (with which they can often be used interchangeably in recipes), brains are easily torn or broken. They require extra-gentle handling, careful cleaning and soaking, and sometimes blanching before they can be used in recipes.

Amount Needed: Allow ¼–⅓ pound brains per serving. Lamb and pork brains usually weigh about ¼ pound each, calf brains ½ pound, and beef brains ¾ pound.

To Prepare for Cooking: Wash brains carefully in cold water, then place in a large bowl and cover with acidulated water (1 tablespoon lemon juice or white vinegar and 1 teaspoon salt to 1 quart water) and soak 1½ hours. Drain, very gently peel off as much thin outer membrane as possible (it clings tightly and is almost transparent). Soak for another 1½ hours in fresh acidulated water, changing the water 1–2 times; drain and again peel off as much membrane as possible. Also cut away opaque white bits at base of brains. (*Note:* If membrane is not peeled off before cooking, any blood trapped underneath will leave brown streaks, marring the brains' creamy color.)

To Blanch: Gourmets disagree as to whether brains should be blanched before cooking. If they are to be braised, blanching serves no real purpose and actually leaches out some of the subtle flavor. If they are to be sautéed, blanching will help make them firm, make them easier to slice and handle. To blanch, place brains in a saucepan (not aluminum), add acidulated water to cover, and simmer uncovered over low heat. Lamb brains will need only 15 minutes, pork and calf brains about 20, and beef brains about 30. Drain well, cover with ice water, and let stand until cold. Drain again and pat dry on paper toweling.

Some Classic Garnishes for Brains (see Some Classic Garnishes for Sweetbreads)

⚖ **SAUTÉED BRAINS**

Makes 4 servings

1¼ pounds brains
½ cup unsifted flour
1 teaspoon salt
¼ teaspoon pepper
¼ cup butter or margarine
8 small unbuttered toast triangles (optional)

Suggested Sauces:

Bordelaise
Diable
Madeira

Prepare brains for cooking and blanch as directed.* Make sure they are quite dry. Slice ½″ thick and dredge lightly in a mixture of flour, salt, and pepper. Heat butter in a large, heavy skillet over moderate heat and sauté brains 3–4 minutes on each side until nicely browned. Drain on paper toweling. Serve as is with 1 of the sauces suggested above or, if you like, on toast triangles. About 250 calories per serving (without sauce or toast).

VARIATIONS:

Cervelles au Beurre Noir (Brains in Black Butter Sauce): Prepare Sautéed Brains as directed, remove from skillet and keep warm. Place ½ cup Clarified Butter in a clean small skillet and heat, moving pan continuously, over low heat just until butter begins to brown. Mix in 2 tablespoons white vinegar or lemon juice and 1 tablespoon minced parsley. Pour over brains and serve. If you like, sprinkle brains with 2 tablespoons drained capers before adding butter. About 450 calories per serving.

⚖ **Breaded Brains:** Prepare, slice, and dredge brains as above, then dip in 1 egg lightly beaten with 1 tablespoon cold water and finally in fine dry bread crumbs or cracker meal. Sauté in butter as directed and serve with Lemon Butter. About 260 calories per serving (without lemon butter).

Broiled Brains
(See Broiled Sweetbreads)

BRAINS VINAIGRETTE

Makes 4 servings

1¼ *pounds brains*
1 *quart cold water*
1 *tablespoon white vinegar or lemon juice*
1 *teaspoon salt*
¼ *teaspoon peppercorns and 1 bouquet garni,* tied in cheesecloth*
½ *small yellow onion, peeled*
1 *small carrot, peeled*

Vinaigrette Dressing:
¼ *cup white wine vinegar*
¼ *teaspoon salt*
⅛ *teaspoon white pepper*
¾ *cup olive oil*

Prepare brains for cooking.* Place in a large enamel, stainless-steel, or teflon-lined saucepan with all but dressing ingredients and simmer, uncovered, 20–25 minutes. Meanwhile, prepare dressing by shaking all ingredients in a shaker jar. When brains are cooked, lift out with a slotted spoon, halve, and arrange on a hot platter. Drizzle with about ½ cup dressing and pass the rest.

To Serve Cold: Cool brains in cooking liquid, then drain and chill well. Slice ½" thick, drizzle with dressing, and serve.

Hot or cold: About 340 calories per serving.

COQUILLES OF BRAINS MORNAY

Makes 4 servings

1¼ *pounds brains*
2 *cups hot Mornay Sauce*
⅓ *cup fine dry bread crumbs mixed with 2 tablespoons melted butter or margarine (optional topping)*

Prepare brains for cooking and blanch as directed*; cut in small dice. Preheat oven to 350° F. Mix brains with sauce and spoon into lightly buttered scallop shells or ramekins. Top, if you like, with buttered crumbs. Set on a baking tray and bake, uncovered, 15 minutes, then brown quickly under broiler and serve. About 445 calories per serving.

VARIATION:

Coquilles of Sweetbreads Mornay: Prepare as directed, substituting sweetbreads for brains. About 405 calories per serving.

BRAIN TIMBALES

Makes 6 servings

2 *pounds brains*
6 *slices bacon, fried until crisp and crumbled*
2 *tablespoons soft white bread crumbs*
1 *teaspoon grated yellow onion*
1 *teaspoon salt*
⅛ *teaspoon white pepper*
3 *eggs, lightly beaten*
1½ *cups heavy cream*
6 *toast rounds spread with Anchovy Butter*

Prepare brains for cooking and blanch as directed*; cube, then purée in an electric blender at low speed or press through a fine sieve. Preheat oven to 350° F. Mix brains with all but last ingredient and spoon into well-buttered ramekins, filling ⅔ full. Set ramekins in a shallow baking pan, add water to pan to a depth of about 1½ inches, cover loosely with buttered foil, and bake 30–40 minutes until timbales are just firm. Remove ramekins from water bath and cool 5 minutes. To unmold, run a spatula around edge. Unmold each timbale carefully on a toast round and serve. About 405 calories per serving.

VARIATIONS:

Sweetbread Timbales: Substitute sweetbreads for brains and prepare as directed. About 385 calories per serving.

⚁ **Timbales au Gratin:** Prepare timbales as above, then top each with buttered bread crumbs mixed with a little Parmesan cheese (about ⅓ cup buttered crumbs in all, 1 tablespoon Parmesan). Bake, uncovered, in water bath and serve in ramekins. About 300 calories per serving.

HEART

The hearts of beef, veal, pork, and lamb are all good to eat. They're chewy and muscular, taste a little bit like liver, and, when stuffed and braised or stewed, make a very good meal indeed. If you are lucky enough to find very young lamb or veal hearts, you can simply slice and sauté them as you would calf's liver. All hearts are highly perishable, highly nutritious. They're also low in calories and, because there is little demand for them, budget priced. Better order ahead. Hearts are not routinely stocked at neighborhood markets.

Amount Needed: Allow about ½ pound per serving. Beef hearts run large—from 3–5 pounds—and make a good choice for a large family; veal hearts weigh ¾ pound and are perfect for 2 (if they don't have big appetites); pork hearts weigh about ½ pound, and lamb hearts between ¼ and ½.

To Prepare for Cooking: Wash heart well in tepid water, remove all fat, halve lengthwise and cut out vessels and large tubes. Leave halves joined if heart is to be stuffed, otherwise, cut up as individual recipes direct. If heart seems especially muscular, soak 1–2 hours in sour milk or acidulated water (1 tablespoon vinegar or lemon juice and 1 teaspoon salt to 1 quart water) to tenderize.

To Simmer (Stew): Place heart halves in a deep pot and add broth or salted water to cover (1 teaspoon salt for each quart water). Cover and simmer until tender, about 3–4 hours for beef heart, 2–2½ for pork and veal hearts. Serve with Pan Gravy or a suitable sauce (see Some Herbs and Seasonings/ Sauces and Butters for Variety Meats). (*Note:* Lamb hearts should not be simmered; they're better if braised or sautéed.) To give simmered hearts extra flavor, add an onion, carrot, celery stalk, and parsley sprigs to the pot.

To Pressure Cook (not recommended for lamb hearts): Prepare heart for cooking; do not stuff. Brown heart in bacon drippings in open cooker, add ½ cup water or stock (or amount of liquid manufacturer recommends). Seal cooker, bring to 10 pounds pressure, and cook 15–20 minutes per pound or according to manufacturer's timetable (meat cooked at 10 pounds pressure will be more tender than that cooked at 15). Reduce pressure, open cooker, remove heart, and keep warm. Prepare Pan Gravy in open cooker.

¢ SAUTÉED HEARTS

Only young lamb or veal hearts will be tender enough to sauté. Makes 4 servings

2 pounds lamb or veal hearts
3 tablespoons butter or margarine
¼ teaspoon salt
Pinch pepper
Pinch nutmeg (optional)
4 slices buttered toast (optional)
1 tablespoon minced parsley
  (optional)

Prepare hearts for cooking,* halve lengthwise, and slice ¼"–½" thick. Melt butter in a large, heavy skillet over moderately high heat, let it foam up, then subside. Add hearts, reduce heat to moderate, and stir-fry 2–3 minutes. Season and serve, if you like, on buttered toast sprinkled with parsley. About 340 calories per serving.

VARIATIONS:

Sautéed Hearts and Mushrooms: Prepare and slice hearts as above. Stir-fry ½ pound thinly sliced mushrooms in butter 3–4 minutes over moderately high heat; push to side of skillet, add hearts, and sauté as directed. Season and serve. About 355 calories per serving.

Mixed Fry: Prepare and slice 1 veal heart as directed above; cut ¼ pound calf's liver into thin strips; prepare 2 lamb kidneys for cooking* and sauté halves in 2 tablespoons butter 3–4 minutes over moderate heat, turning often with tongs. Remove from skillet and slice. Raise heat to high, add heart, liver, and kidney, and stir-fry quickly 2–3

minutes. Season with salt and pepper and, if you like, 1 tablespoon each lemon juice and minced parsley. Serve as is or on buttered toast. About 350 calories per serving.

◁▷ **Low-Calorie Sautéed Hearts:** Reduce quantity of hearts to 1½ pounds; prepare as directed, using 2 tablespoons butter instead of 3. Omit buttered toast. About 260 calories per serving.

¢ CHICKEN-FRIED HEART

Makes 4 servings

2 pounds pork or beef heart
½ cup unsifted flour
1 teaspoon salt
¼ teaspoon pepper
¼ teaspoon thyme
¼ cup butter, margarine, or bacon
  drippings
½ cup hot water

Prepare heart for cooking* and slice ½" thick. Dredge in a mixture of flour, salt, pepper, and thyme and brown quickly on both sides in butter in a large, heavy skillet over moderately high heat. Add water, cover, turn heat to very low, and simmer 1½–2 hours until tender. Check skillet occasionally and add a little more water if needed. About 390 calories per serving.

VARIATION:

◁▷ **Low-Calorie Chicken-Fried Heart:** Reduce quantity of heart to 1½ pounds; prepare as directed, using 2 tablespoons butter instead of ¼ cup. About 285 calories per serving.

¢ BRAISED STUFFED HEART

Makes 6 servings

1 (4–5-pound) beef heart
1 teaspoon salt
¼ teaspoon pepper

2 *tablespoons butter or margarine*
2 *cups beef broth*
2 *tablespoons flour blended with 2*
  tablespoons cold water

Stuffing:
1 *cup minced yellow onion*
⅓ *cup minced carrot*
2 *tablespoons minced celery*
2 *tablespoons minced parsley*
1½ *cups cooked rice*
2 *tablespoons minced parsley*
1 *teaspoon poultry seasoning*

Prepare heart for cooking* and pat dry on paper toweling. Rub inside and out with salt and pepper and let stand while you prepare stuffing. Stir-fry onion, carrot, and celery in butter in a heavy skillet over moderate heat 8–10 minutes until golden; mix with remaining stuffing ingredients. Spoon loosely into heart cavity and close opening with poultry pins and string or sew up with needle and thread. Brown heart all over in 2 tablespoons butter in a heavy kettle over moderate heat. (*Note:* Use tongs for turning so you don't pierce heart and lose precious juices.) Add broth, cover, and simmer slowly about 3 hours until tender, turning 1–2 times during cooking. Check pot occasionally and add a little water if necessary. Lift heart to a heated platter, remove pins, string or thread and keep warm. Stir flour paste into kettle liquid and heat, stirring constantly, until thickened and smooth. Taste for salt and pepper and adjust if needed. To serve: slice heart crosswise, not too thin, and pass gravy. About 510 calories per serving.

VARIATION:

Substitute 2 cups Sage and Onion Dressing, Cornbread and Sausage Stuffing, or other savory stuffing for that above and proceed as directed. About 485 calories per serving if

made with Sage and Onion Dressing, 640 calories per serving if made with Cornbread and Sausage Stuffing.

¢ **CASEROLE OF VEAL HEARTS AND VEGETABLES**

Makes 4 servings

2 *pounds veal hearts*
⅓ *cup unsifted flour*
1 *teaspoon salt*
¼ *teaspoon pepper*
3 *tablespoons bacon drippings or*
  cooking oil
1 *large yellow onion, peeled and*
  minced
1 *cup water*
¼ *cup tomato paste*
1 *tablespoon Worcestershire sauce*
4 *carrots, peeled and cut in 2″*
  chunks
3 *turnips, peeled and quartered*
3 *stalks celery, cut in 2″ chunks*
1 *tablespoon minced parsley*

Preheat oven to 350° F. Prepare hearts for cooking* and quarter. Dredge in a mixture of flour, salt, and pepper and brown in drippings in a heavy skillet over moderate heat 3–4 minutes; transfer to an ungreased 2½-quart casserole. Stir-fry onion in drippings 5–8 minutes until pale golden, stir in water, tomato paste, and Worcestershire sauce, and pour into casserole. Tuck vegetables in here and there, cover, and bake 1½–2 hours until hearts are tender. Uncover, sprinkle with parsley, and serve. About 355 calories per serving.

¢ **BALMORAL HEART PATTIES**

Good in hamburger buns.
Makes 4 servings

1 *pound sliced beef or veal heart,*
  trimmed of large vessels
2 *scallions*

½ cup quick-cooking oatmeal
¼ cup evaporated milk
1¼ teaspoons salt
¼ teaspoon pepper
1 tablespoon Worcestershire sauce
2 tablespoons minced parsley
3 tablespoons bacon or beef
    drippings, butter, or margarine
1 cup beef gravy (homemade or
    canned)

Put heart through finest blade of
food grinder along with scallions;
mix in oatmeal, milk, salt, pepper,
Worcestershire sauce, and parsley,
cover, and chill 1 hour. Shape into
4 plump patties and brown
slowly in drippings in a heavy skillet
over moderate heat; reduce heat to
low and cook, uncovered, turning
frequently, 10–12 minutes until
cooked through but not dry. Transfer to a hot platter and keep warm.
Heat gravy in skillet drippings and
serve with patties. About 345 calories
per serving.

KIDNEYS

The kidneys of all meat animals are
edible, but those of lamb and veal
are the most cherished because of
their delicacy and tenderness; either
can be broiled or sautéed. Beef and
pork kidneys are another matter;
being muscular and strongly flavored, they're best when braised or
stewed. All kidneys are a high-
protein, low-calorie food and an
excellent source of iron and B vitamins. When buying kidneys, always
make sure they smell sweet and
fresh.

Amount Needed: Allow ⅓–½ pound
kidneys per person. Lamb kidneys
are so tiny (only 1½–3 ounces each)

that you'll need 2–3 per person.
Veal kidneys average ½–¾ pound
and will usually serve 1 to 2. Beef
kidneys weigh about 1 pound and
pork kidneys ¼ pound.

To Prepare for Cooking: Because of
their delicacy, lamb and veal kidneys should never be washed. Peel
off any outer fat, the thin membrane, and then cut out the knobs of
fat and tubes underneath; the job
will be easier if the kidneys are first
halved lengthwise. Beef and pork
kidneys should be washed well in
tepid water, then split and trimmed
of fat and tubes.

⚖ SAUTÉED KIDNEYS

Only lamb or veal kidneys are delicate enough to sauté. And even
these are a bit tricky. If sliced, the
kidneys will send a lot of juice out
into the skillet so that they "stew"
rather than sauté. The best method
is the one that follows—sautéing
the kidneys halves, then slicing and
returning briefly to the skillet. Kidneys, by the way, do not brown so
much as turn an even gray-beige.
They're best slightly rare.
Makes 4 servings

1½ pounds lamb or veal kidneys
3 tablespoons butter or margarine
¼ teaspoon salt
Pinch pepper
1 tablespoon lemon juice (optional)
1 tablespoon minced parsley
    (optional)

Prepare kidneys for cooking.* Melt
butter in a large, heavy skillet over
moderately high heat, let it foam
up, then subside. Add kidneys and
sauté, turning often with tongs. Veal
kidneys will need 8–10 minutes,
lamb kidneys only 3–5. Remove
from skillet and slice about ¼" thick
(lamb kidneys may also be simply
quartered). Return kidneys to skil-

III. QUICK AND EASY RECIPES

Quick Fish Stew – Spaghetti with Butter – Confetti Corn, Baked Eggs, and Broccoli – Baked Alaska

Quick Fish Stew (vol. 1, p. 658)

Spaghetti with Butter, Cream, Parmesan, and Mushrooms (vol. 2, pp. 64–65)

Confetti Corn (vol. 2, p. 202); Baked Eggs in Tomatoes (vol. 2, pp. 15–16); and Osaka Skillet Broccoli (vol. 2, pp. 171–72)

Baked Alaska (vol. 2, p. 468); and Cherries Jubilee (vol. 2, pp. 431–32)

let and warm about 2 minutes, shaking skillet. Season and, if you like, sprinkle with lemon juice and parsley. Serve as is or with suitable sauce (see Some Herbs and Seasonings/Sauces and Butters for Variety Meats). About 275 calories per serving (without sauce).

VARIATIONS:

⚔ Sautéed Kidneys and Mushrooms: Prepare kidneys as above and set aside. Stir-fry ½ pound thinly sliced mushrooms in butter 3–5 minutes over moderately high heat, push to side of skillet, add kidneys, and proceed as directed. About 290 calories per serving.

Sautéed Kidneys in Onion and Wine Sauce: Prepare and sauté whole kidneys as above; remove from skillet and keep warm. In drippings stir-fry 2 tablespoons minced scallions 3–4 minutes, add ½ cup dry vermouth and boil rapidly to reduce by ½. Add 1 tablespoon each lemon juice and minced parsley. Slice kidneys, return to skillet, and season. Warm, shaking skillet, 1–2 minutes and serve. About 330 calories per serving.

⚔ Low-Calorie Sautéed Kidneys: Reduce amount of butter to 2 tablespoons and prepare as directed. About 230 calories per serving.

⚔ BROILED KIDNEYS

Lamb and veal kidneys are the most suitable for broiling, and they must be basted often with melted butter and broiled only until rare or medium if they are to remain moist and tender.
Makes 4 servings

1½ pounds lamb or veal kidneys
⅓ cup melted butter or margarine
½ teaspoon salt
⅛ teaspoon pepper

4 slices buttered toast, trimmed of crusts and halved diagonally (optional)
1 tablespoon lemon juice (optional)
1 tablespoon minced parsley (optional)

Preheat broiler. Prepare kidneys for cooking.* Place on lightly greased broiler rack and brush well with melted butter. Broil 3″ from heat, brushing often with melted butter, about 4–5 minutes on a side for rare and 5–7 for medium. Serve, if you like, on toast points sprinkled with lemon juice and parsley. Or serve with Bordelaise or other suitable sauce (see Some Herbs and Seasonings/Sauces and Butters for Variety Meats). About 250 calories per serving (without toast or sauce).

VARIATIONS:

⚔ Marinated Broiled Kidneys: Prepare kidneys as above, then marinate 3–4 hours in refrigerator in French, Italian, garlic, or herb dressing. Broil as directed, brushing often with dressing instead of butter. About 235 calories per serving.

⚔ Breaded Broiled Kidneys: Prepare kidneys as above. Dip in melted butter, then in fine dry bread crumbs. Broil as directed, basting often with melted butter. About 270 calories per serving.

⚔ Lamb Kidney en Brochette: Prepare kidneys as above. Alternate on skewers with mushroom caps (you'll need about 12 altogether), weaving strips of bacon in and out. Broil 3″ from heat, turning often, 12–15 minutes until bacon is browned. Season and serve. About 265 calories per serving.

⚔ Low-Calorie Broiled Kidneys: Prepare as directed, using low-calorie French, Italian, garlic, or herb dressing for basting instead of butter. Omit buttered toast slices. About 200 calories per serving.

⚖ **BRAISED KIDNEYS**

Beef and pork kidneys come from mature animals, thus they tend to be tough. The most successful way to tenderize them is to brown them, then to cook, covered, with a small amount of liquid.
Makes 4 servings

1½ pounds beef or pork kidneys
½ cup unsifted flour
1 teaspoon salt
¼ teaspoon pepper
3 tablespoons butter, margarine, or bacon drippings
½ cup liquid (water, beef broth, dry red or white wine, tomato juice)

Prepare kidneys for cooking,* halve lengthwise, and slice crosswise ¼″ thick. Dredge in a mixture of flour, salt, and pepper, then brown on both sides in butter in a large, heavy skillet over moderately high heat. Turn heat to low, add liquid, cover, and simmer slowly about 20 minutes until tender. About 290 calories per serving.

VARIATION:
Prepare and dredge kidneys as above. Before browning, stir-fry 1 minced small yellow onion in butter; push to side of skillet, add kidneys and proceed as directed. Sprinkle with 1 tablespoon minced parsley before serving. About 300 calories per serving.

⚖ **Low-Calorie Braised Kidneys:**
Prepare as directed, reducing amount of butter to 2 tablespoons and using water as the liquid. About 250 calories per serving.

CHAFING DISH KIDNEYS WITH SHERRY
Makes 4 servings

1½ pounds lamb kidneys
2 tablespoons butter or margarine
¼ cup medium-sweet sherry or Madeira
⅛ teaspoon pepper

Sauce:
2 slices bacon, chopped fine
1 small yellow onion, peeled and minced
½ clove garlic, peeled and minced
1 small carrot, peeled and cut in small dice
2 ripe tomatoes, peeled, seeded and chopped fine
¾ cup beef bouillon

Prepare kidneys for cooking* and halve lengthwise. Sauté rapidly in butter in a skillet over moderately high heat 2 minutes and set aside while you prepare sauce. Stir-fry bacon, onion, garlic, carrot, and tomatoes in a skillet over moderately high heat 5–8 minutes, add bouillon, cover, and simmer 10 minutes. Purée in an electric blender at low speed or put through a food mill. (*Note:* If preparing this at table, place sauce and all remaining ingredients near chafing dish.) Turn burner flame to high, spoon kidneys and any drippings into chafing dish, and stir-fry 2 minutes; lower flame, add sherry, and cook and stir 2 minutes. Add pepper and sauce and heat, stirring, just until it bubbles. Serve over buttered noodles or boiled rice. About 345 calories per serving (without noodles or rice).

HERB STUFFED KIDNEY AND BACON ROLLS
Makes 2 servings

3 lamb kidneys
½ cup soft white bread crumbs

1 tablespoon minced chives
1 tablespoon minced parsley
1 teaspoon chervil
⅛ teaspoon garlic powder
⅛ teaspoon pepper
2 tablespoons softened butter or
    margarine
6 slices bacon, halved

Preheat oven to 425° F. Prepare kidneys for cooking* and quarter. Mix crumbs with herbs, garlic powder, pepper, and butter. Spread each ½ bacon slice with herb mixture and roll up with a piece of kidney inside; secure with toothpicks. Arrange on a rack in a shallow baking pan and bake, uncovered, about 25 minutes, turning frequently until bacon is crisp. Remove toothpicks and serve with vegetables or on buttered toast. About 445 calories per serving (without vegetables or toast).

⊠ KIDNEYS EN COCOTTES

Makes 2 servings

3 slices bacon
¾ pound lamb kidneys
1 teaspoon minced chives
2 eggs
2 tablespoons light cream
Pinch salt
Pinch paprika

Preheat oven to 350° F. Brown bacon in a small skillet over moderate heat; drain on paper toweling and reserve. Prepare kidneys for cooking* and cut in 1″ cubes; sauté in bacon drippings over moderately high heat 3–4 minutes until lightly browned. Using a slotted spoon, transfer kidneys to 2 buttered individual ramekins, sprinkle with chives and crumbled bacon. Break each egg into a cup and slide into ramekin; add 1 tablespoon cream to each. Set ramekins in a water bath and bake uncovered 12–14 minutes

until egg white is just set. Sprinkle with salt and pepper and serve. About 460 calories per serving.

DEVILED KIDNEYS

Makes 4 servings

1½ pounds lamb kidneys
2 tablespoons prepared mild yellow
    mustard
¼ cup heavy cream
1 tablespoon steak sauce
⅛ teaspoon pepper
⅓–½ cup packaged Italian-style
    bread crumbs
¼ cup melted butter or margarine
4 slices hot buttered toast

Preheat oven to 325° F. Prepare kidneys for cooking.* Mix mustard, cream, steak sauce, and pepper; dip each kidney in mustard mixture, then in bread crumbs to coat evenly. Arrange in a buttered shallow baking dish and drizzle a little melted butter over each kidney. Bake, uncovered, 25 minutes until tender, basting with extra melted butter as needed to brown crumbs evenly. Serve on hot buttered toast with pan drippings ladled over kidneys. About 440 calories per serving (without toast).

⊠ KIDNEYS IN SOUR CREAM

Makes 4 servings

1½ pounds lamb kidneys
3 tablespoons butter or margarine
2 tablespoons lemon juice
4 scallions, minced (include green
    tops)
¾ teaspoon seasoned salt
¼ teaspoon pepper
½ teaspoon summer savory
1½ cups sour cream
1 tablespoon minced parsley

Prepare kidneys for cooking* and slice thin. Stir-fry rapidly in butter in a heavy skillet over moderate heat 3–4 minutes until pink color almost disappears. Turn heat to low, stir in all remaining ingredients except parsley. Heat, stirring, 1–2 minutes, sprinkle with parsley, and serve. Good with hot buttered noodles or boiled rice. About 460 calories per serving (without noodles or rice).

⚖ **BRAISED VEAL KIDNEYS AND MUSHROOMS**

Makes 4 servings

1½ pounds veal kidneys
¼ cup unsifted flour
3 tablespoons bacon drippings, butter, or margarine
½ pound button mushrooms, wiped clean
½ cup water, beef broth, or dry red wine
½ teaspoon salt
⅛ teaspoon pepper

Preheat oven to 350° F. Prepare kidneys for cooking* and halve lengthwise. Dredge in flour and brown lightly in 2 tablespoons drippings in a heavy skillet over moderately high heat 2–3 minutes. Transfer to an ungreased 1½-quart casserole; brown mushrooms in remaining drippings 2–3 minutes and add to kidneys. Drain off all but 1 tablespoon drippings from skillet, add water, and stir to scrape up brown bits; pour into casserole. Sprinkle with salt and pepper, cover, and bake 45 minutes until tender. About 280 calories per serving.

VARIATIONS:

Braised Veal Kidneys with Vegetables: Small new potatoes, 1″ chunks of carrots, turnips, or rutabagas or parboiled white onions can be cooked along with the kidneys in the same casserole; add a little extra salt and pepper. Recipe too flexible for a meaningful calorie count.

⚖ **Low-Calorie Braised Veal Kidneys:** Prepare as directed, reducing amount of drippings to 2 tablespoons and using water as the liquid. About 250 calories per serving.

¢ **CLARA'S KIDNEY STEW**

Makes 4 servings

1½ pounds veal or beef kidneys
2 cups cold water
1 teaspoon salt
½ cup unsifted flour
⅛ teaspoon pepper
3 tablespoons beef or bacon drippings or cooking oil
1½ cups beef broth
1 bay leaf, crumbled
1 tablespoon flour blended with 1 tablespoon cold water
1 tablespoon minced parsley

If beef kidneys are used, soak in cold water mixed with 1 teaspoon salt 1 hour; drain well and pat dry on paper toweling. Prepare kidneys for cooking* and cut into ¾″–1″ cubes. Dredge lightly in mixture of flour, salt, and pepper. Sauté, half of kidneys at a time, 3–4 minutes in drippings in a heavy skillet over moderately high heat; remove with a slotted spoon to a large, heavy saucepan. Add broth to skillet, stir brown bits from bottom, and pour over kidneys. Add bay leaf, cover, and simmer until tender, about 15–20 minutes for veal kidneys, 35–40 for beef. Thicken gravy, if you like, by blending in flour paste and heating and stirring until thickened. Taste for seasoning and adjust if necessary. Sprinkle with parsley and serve. Good with boiled potatoes or hot buttered noodles. About 305 calories per serving.

Other Kidney Recipes
Old-Fashioned Steak and Kidney Pie (see Beef)

Beef, Kidney, Mushroom, and Oyster Pie (see Beef)
English Mixed Grill (see Lamb)

LIVER

Liver to most people is calf's liver (or, to be more accurate, veal liver), but beef, pork, and lamb liver are good, too, especially lamb liver, which is tender enough to sauté and which can be substituted for calf's liver in the recipes that follow. Unfortunately, it is not often available. Beef and pork liver have a strong flavor but when ground into loaves or braised can be quite savory and succulent. All liver is a potent source of iron, vitamin A, and most of the B vitamins, all is low in calories.

Because of its popularity, calf's liver is rather expensive; it is now available packaged in frozen slices as well as fresh. Lamb, beef, and pork livers are reasonably priced. All liver is highly perishable and should be cooked within 24 hours of purchase. Top quality calf's liver will be rosy red, moist, and quivery (so tender, someone said, you can push your thumb through it). Lamb liver will be equally delicate but redder, beef and pork liver deep red-brown and fairly firm.

Amount Needed: Allow ¼–⅓ pound liver per serving. Beef liver weighs about 10 pounds; pork liver about 3; veal liver averages 2½ pounds, and lamb liver 1.

To Prepare for Cooking: Liver needs very little preparation. Simply peel off covering membrane (so liver won't shrivel and curl during cooking), then cut out any large vessels.

Cooking Tip: Because of its quivery texture, liver is difficult to grind raw. To make the job easier, cut into strips, sauté briefly in butter or drippings to firm, then grind.

⚖ ▣ SAUTÉED CALF'S LIVER

Liver is best on the rare side—faintly pink with rosy juices. If overcooked, it becomes tough and dry.
Makes 2 servings

2 tablespoons butter or margarine
¾ pound calf's liver, sliced ¼″ thick
Pinch nutmeg (optional)
Pinch summer savory (optional)
¼ teaspoon salt
⅛ teaspoon pepper

Melt butter in a large, heavy skillet over moderately high heat, let it foam up, then subside. Add liver and brown 2–3 minutes per side for rare, 3–3½ for medium. Sprinkle both sides with seasonings and serve. About 280 calories per serving.

VARIATIONS:

⚖ **Calf's Liver and Onions:** Stir-fry 1 thinly sliced small Bermuda onion in butter 5–8 minutes over moderate heat until pale golden. Push to side of pan, raise heat to moderately high, add liver and brown as directed. Season and serve topped with onions. About 300 calories per serving.

Calf's Liver and Bacon: Omit butter; brown 4 slices bacon in a large skillet over moderately high heat and drain on paper toweling. Pour off all but 1 tablespoon drippings, add liver, brown and season as directed. Serve topped with bacon. About 380 calories per serving.

Calf's Liver Burgundy: Stir-fry 1 thinly sliced small Bermuda onion and 1 crushed clove garlic in 2 tablespoons olive oil 5–8 minutes over moderate heat until pale golden. Push to side of pan, add liver, raise heat to moderately high, and brown as directed. Season with salt and pepper, lift to a hot platter and keep warm. Add ¼ cup Burgundy or other dry red wine to skillet, boil 1 minute, pour over liver, and serve. About 325 calories per serving.

Calf's Liver in Mustard Sauce: Sauté liver as directed above, remove to a heated platter and keep warm. To skillet add ¼ cup beef broth and ⅓ cup heavy cream and boil rapidly, uncovered, to reduce by half. Off heat smooth in 2 teaspoons Dijon-style mustard and 1 teaspoon minced parsley. Pour over liver and serve. About 425 calories per serving.

⚖ ⊠ **BROILED LIVER**

Lamb's and calf's livers are the only ones suitable for broiling.
Makes 4 servings

1 ¼ *pounds lamb's or calf's liver, sliced ½″ thick*
⅓ *cup melted butter or margarine*
½ *teaspoon salt*
⅛ *teaspoon pepper*

Preheat broiler. Place liver on a lightly greased broiler rack and brush well with melted butter. Broil 4″ from heat 2–3 minutes per side for rare and 4 minutes per side for medium, brushing frequently with melted butter. Season and serve as is or topped with a compatible butter or sauce (see Some Herbs and Seasonings/Sauces and Butters for Variety Meats). About 280 calories per serving.

VARIATION:
⚖ **Low-Calorie Broiled Liver:** Broil as directed, using low-calorie

Italian or French dressing for basting instead of butter. About 200 calories per serving.

¢ **BRAISED LIVER**

Here's the way to make beef or pork liver succulent.
Makes 4 servings

1 *small Bermuda onion, peeled and minced*
3 *tablespoons bacon drippings*
1 ¼ *pounds beef or pork liver, sliced ¼″–½″ thick and cut in strips 4″ long and 1″ wide*
½ *cup unsifted flour*
1 *teaspoon salt*
¼ *teaspoon pepper*
1 *cup beef broth (about) or a ½ and ½ mixture of broth and dry red or white wine*
1 *tablespoon minced parsley*

Stir-fry onion in 2 tablespoons drippings in a large, heavy skillet over moderate heat 10–12 minutes until lightly browned; lift out with a slotted spoon and set aside. Add remaining drippings to skillet. Dredge liver in a mixture of flour, salt and pepper and brown, a few pieces at a time, in drippings. Return all liver and onion to skillet, add broth, cover, and simmer over lowest heat about 45 minutes until tender. Check skillet occasionally and add a little extra broth if necessary. When liver is done, lift to a heated platter, smother with skillet gravy, and sprinkle with parsley. About 370 calories per serving.

VARIATION:
⚖ **Low-Calorie Braised Liver:** Prepare as directed, reducing amount of drippings to 2 tablespoons and using water as the liquid ingredient. About 325 calories per serving.

⚖ ☒ CALF'S LIVER ALLA VENEZIANA

Makes 2 servings

2 medium-size yellow onions, peeled and minced
2 tablespoons butter or margarine
1 tablespoon olive oil
3 tablespoons dry vermouth
¼ teaspoon salt
Pinch pepper
⅔ pound calf's liver, sliced ¼"–½" thick and cut in strips about 2" long and 1" wide
1 tablespoon lemon juice
1 tablespoon minced parsley

Stir-fry onions in butter and oil in a large heavy skillet 5–8 minutes over moderate heat until pale golden; add vermouth, salt and pepper and simmer 1–2 minutes to reduce. Raise heat to moderately high, add liver, and stir-fry quickly 3–5 minutes, just until redness disappears (liver will not brown). Add lemon juice and parsley and serve. About 305 calories per serving.

⚖ ☒ CALF'S LIVER AND BACON EN BROCHETTE

Makes 4 servings

1¼ pounds calf's liver, sliced ¼"–½" thick and cut in strips 4" long and 1½" wide
8 slices bacon
2 tablespoons melted bacon drippings, butter, or margarine
1 tablespoon steak sauce

Preheat broiler. Thread liver on long skewers, interweaving with bacon; do not crowd pieces. Lay skewers across a shallow baking tray and brush with a mixture of drippings and steak sauce. Broil 4"–5" from heat 6–8 minutes, turning frequently and brushing with sauce mixture until bacon is crisp and liver lightly browned. Serve on or off the skewers. About 290 calories per serving.

VARIATION:

⚖ Japanese-Style Liver en Brochette: Marinate liver strips 2–4 hours in refrigerator before broiling in following mixture: 2 tablespoons each peanut oil and soy sauce, 1 tablespoon steak sauce, ¼ cup dry sherry, 1 teaspoon grated gingerroot, and ½ crushed clove garlic. Skewer with bacon and broil as directed, brushing frequently with marinade. About 295 calories per serving.

CALF'S LIVER WITH PROSCIUTTO AND PARSLEY

Makes 4 servings

1¼ pounds calf's liver, sliced ¼"–½" thick
¾ cup unsifted flour
1½ teaspoons salt
¼ teaspoon pepper
¼ cup butter or margarine
¼ cup julienne strips of prosciutto ham
3 tablespoons minced yellow onion
½ teaspoon summer savory or sage
3 tablespoons minced parsley
1 tablespoon flour (use that from dredging liver) blended with ½ cup beef broth
½ cup dry Marsala wine
1 tablespoon lemon juice
Lemon wedges (garnish)

Dredge liver lightly in a mixture of flour, salt and pepper and sauté in butter in a large, heavy skillet over moderately high heat, about 2–3 minutes per side for rare, 3½ for medium. Remove liver and keep warm. Turn heat to moderately low, add prosciutto, onion, savory, and parsley to skillet, and stir-fry 5–8 minutes until onion is pale golden. Mix in flour paste and remaining ingredients and heat, stirring, until thickened. Return liver to skillet, heat 1–2 minutes, then serve garnished with lemon wedges. About 365 calories per serving.

¢ ⊠ GINGERY CHINESE-STYLE LIVER

Budget fare if made with pork liver.
Makes 4 servings

1¼ pounds pork, lamb, or calf's liver, sliced ¼"–½" thick and cut in strips 3" long and ½" wide
3 tablespoons peanut or other cooking oil
½ teaspoon ginger
¼ teaspoon pepper
½ cup thinly sliced bamboo shoots
¼ cup soy sauce
2 tablespoons hot water
½ teaspoon sugar
3 cups hot cooked rice
4 scallions, minced

Stir-fry liver in oil in a wok or heavy skillet over high heat 2–3 minutes until lightly browned. Reduce heat, sprinkle with ginger and pepper, and stir-fry 1 minute. Add all but last 2 ingredients and heat, stirring, until bubbling. Spoon over rice, sprinkle with scallions, and serve. About 415 calories per serving.

¢ ⚔ BRAISED BEEF LIVER WITH TOMATO-MUSHROOM GRAVY

Makes 8 servings

2½ pounds young beef liver, in 1 piece
¼ cup sifted flour
2 teaspoons salt
¼ teaspoon pepper
¼ cup bacon drippings, butter, or margarine
1 medium-size yellow onion, peeled and sliced thin
¼ cup minced mushrooms
¾ cup beef bouillon

1 bay leaf, crumbled
1 tablespoon tomato paste

Peel any outer membrane from liver, then wipe liver with damp paper toweling; dredge in a mixture of flour, salt and pepper and brown well on all sides in drippings in a large, heavy kettle over moderate heat about 5 minutes. Liver will swell as it browns but don't be alarmed. Turn heat to low, add all remaining ingredients except tomato paste, cover, and simmer 1½ hours until liver is tender, turning halfway through cooking. Lift liver to a platter and keep warm. Stir tomato paste into gravy; strain gravy and pour over liver. About 325 calories per serving.

¢ FINNISH CHOPPED LIVER AND RICE CASSEROLE

Finns serve wild mushrooms, cucumbers in sour cream, and buttered home-baked rye bread with this dish. Made with beef liver, it's a budget dish.
Makes 4 servings

1¼ pounds beef or calf's liver, sliced ¼"–½" thick
3 tablespoons butter or margarine
1 large yellow onion, peeled and minced
1½ cups uncooked rice
2 cups boiling water
1 cup milk
1 cup seedless raisins
2 teaspoons salt
¼ teaspoon pepper
¼ teaspoon marjoram
2 tablespoons dark brown sugar or molasses

Preheat oven to 350° F. Sauté liver in butter in a skillet over moderately high heat 3–4 minutes until browned; cool slightly and chop fine. Brown onion in drippings 8–

10 minutes and reserve. Simmer rice, water, and milk together in a saucepan with lid askew about 15 minutes until rice is barely tender; turn into a buttered 1½-quart casserole, add liver, onion, and remaining ingredients, and toss well with 2 forks. Bake, uncovered, 20–30 minutes until all liquid is absorbed. About 585 calories per serving.

¢ DANISH LIVER LOAF

Serve hot with bright crisp vegetables or cold on dark rye bread with pickled beets.
Makes 6 servings

¼ *pound salt pork, trimmed of rind and diced*
1 *pound beef liver, trimmed of connective tissues and tubes and cut in strips about 2" wide*
1 *medium-size yellow onion, peeled and minced*
1 *(10½-ounce) can condensed beef broth*
2 *dozen soda crackers, crumbled (about 1½ cups)*
½ *teaspoon thyme*
1 *tablespoon minced parsley*
¼ *teaspoon pepper*
1 *teaspoon dark brown sugar*
½ *teaspoon ginger*
2 *eggs, lightly beaten*

Preheat oven to 400° F. Fry salt pork in a heavy skillet over moderately low heat 5 minutes until pale golden and rendered of all drippings; remove with a slotted spoon and reserve. Sauté liver in drippings over moderate heat 5–7 minutes, until lightly browned; remove and reserve. Sauté onion in drippings 5–8 minutes until pale golden and reserve in skillet. Pour broth over crackers and let stand. Grind liver and salt pork together, using fine blade of meat grinder, then mix thoroughly with onions and drippings, crackers and broth, and all remaining ingredients. Spoon into a lightly greased 9"×5"×3" loaf pan and bake, uncovered, on center rack 40 minutes until firm. Cool upright in pan on rack 20 minutes; invert on serving platter and turn out. Serve hot or cold but slice fairly thick. About 335 calories per serving.

SWEETBREADS

Of all the variety meats, sweetbreads are considered the most delectable. Certainly they're the most luxurious (they cost about the same as fine steak).

What are they? Technically, the thymus gland of young animals, a big double-lobed gland consisting of the large, smooth, choice *kernel* or *heart sweetbread,* located in the breast, and the smaller, more irregular *throat sweetbread.* The two, spoken of as a pair, are linked by a tube, which should be removed. Sweetbreads are ultrafragile, creamy-smooth, and faintly nutty; they resemble brains in flavor and texture and can be used interchangeably with them in many recipes. Most sweetbreads sold in this country are the milky-white, finely-grained veal sweetbreads. Lamb sweetbreads are sometimes available but are too small to be very practical; also available: yearling beef sweetbreads (rougher and redder) and pork sweetbreads (stronger flavored and a favorite with Europeans for pâtés and soufflés). No matter what animals sweetbreads come from, they will be from young ones (the thymus gland disappears with maturity).

You may also run across something called *beef breads,* not true sweetbreads but the pancreas gland of beef. Though stronger in flavor and coarser in texture, these do resemble sweetbreads and can be prepared like them.

All sweetbreads are extremely perishable; if they are not to be served on the day they're bought, they should be blanched and refrigerated and, even then, served within 24 hours. Recently, frozen sweetbreads have been available, an excellent choice because they needn't be prepared immediately (always cook by package directions). Restaurants get most of the fresh sweetbreads, so give your butcher plenty of notice. And insist that the sweetbreads be *absolutely fresh*.

Amount Needed: Because sweetbreads are so rich, ¼–⅓ pound is about as much as a person can handle comfortably. A pair of veal sweetbreads averages ¾–1 pound, lamb sweetbreads ¼ pound, and yearling beef sweetbreads about 1½ pounds. Pork sweetbreads run around ¾ pound, but unless you raise your own hogs, you aren't likely to find them.

To Prepare for Cooking: Wash sweetbreads gently in cold water, then place in a large bowl and cover with cold acidulated water (1 tablespoon lemon juice or white vinegar and 1 teaspoon salt to 1 quart water) and soak 1½ hours. The sweetbreads will turn white. Drain, gently peel off as much thin outer membrane as possible; it clings stubbornly and is almost transparent, so have patience. Soak for another 1½ hours in fresh acidulated water, changing it 1 or 2 times; drain once more and peel away what membrane you missed the first time. Separate the 2 lobes from the tube (some people like to add it to the stock pot).

To Blanch: Connoisseurs are of two minds about blanching. Some recommend it no matter how the sweetbreads are to be cooked, others insist that it's necessary only when the sweetbreads are to be broken into smaller pieces and sautéed. Blanching does steal away some of the delicate flavor, but it also firms up the sweetbreads and makes them easier to handle. Perhaps a good rule of thumb: If sweetbreads are to be braised whole, don't blanch. Otherwise, do. Place the sweetbreads in a large enamel, stainless-steel, flameproof glass, or teflon-lined saucepan, add acidulated water to cover, and simmer, uncovered, 15 minutes over lowest heat (young beef sweetbreads and beef breads [the pancreas] will need about 25 minutes). Drain, cover with ice water, and let stand until cold. Drain well and pat dry on paper toweling. Some cooks like to place sweetbreads between paper towels and weight with heavy plates to get out excess moisture; not a bad idea when they're to be sautéed. The sweetbreads are now ready to sauté or use in recipes. To divide into smaller pieces, gently break apart at the natural separations.

Some Classic Garnishes for Sweetbreads

Note: Many of these are the same as for tournedos, steaks, and lamb chops.

À la Nantua: Arrange sautéed sweetbreads in a circle on a large platter. Fill center with tiny puff pastry shells (half regular size) filled with tiny boiled shrimp in Suprême Sauce and sprinkled with slivered truffles. Pass extra Suprême Sauce.

St. Germain: Serve sautéed or broiled sweetbreads on individual patties of Hashed Brown Potatoes; drizzle with Béarnaise Sauce.

À la Financière: Prepare Braised Sweetbreads as directed, transfer to crisp, fried rounds of white bread, and set in center of a hot large platter. Scatter 1 minced truffle and ¼ cup slivered smoked tongue over sweetbreads and drizzle with Financière Sauce. Garnish with 4 Chicken Quenelles, ¼ pound sautéed button mushrooms, 2 sliced sautéed lamb's kidneys, and 1 dozen pitted green olives (blanch quickly in boiling water if they seem extra salty). Add sprigs of watercress and serve.

À la Clamart: ⎫
Choron: ⎬ see Some Classic Ways to Serve Tournedos.
Rossini: ⎭

À la Jardinière: ⎬ see Some Classic Garnishes for Steaks.

Talleyrand: ⎬ see Some Classic Garnishes for Lamb Chops.

⚔ **SAUTÉED SWEETBREADS**

The following recipes are all for veal sweetbreads, but lamb or young beef sweetbreads may be substituted.
Makes 4 servings

1 ¼ pounds sweetbreads
½ cup unsifted flour
1 teaspoon salt
¼ teaspoon pepper
¼ cup butter or margarine

Suggested Sauces:
Béarnaise
Beurre Noir
Diable
Madeira

Prepare sweetbreads for cooking and blanch as directed.* Leave whole or halve at the natural separation and pat very dry on paper toweling. Dredge lightly in a mixture of flour, salt, and pepper, then sauté in butter in a large, heavy skillet over moderate to moderately high heat 3–4 minutes on a side until nicely browned. Drain on paper toweling and serve with 1 of the sauces suggested above. About 215 calories per serving (without sauce).

VARIATIONS:

⚔ **Breaded Sweetbreads:** Prepare and blanch sweetbreads as directed,* halve at the natural separation, and pat dry on paper toweling. Dredge in seasoned flour as above, dip in 1 egg lightly beaten with 1 tablespoon cold water and then in fine dry bread crumbs or cracker meal. Sauté in butter as directed and serve with Maître d'Hôtel Butter. About 285 calories per serving (without butter).

Sautéed Sweetbreads and Mushrooms: Prepare and blanch sweetbreads as directed*; divide into small pieces but do not dredge. Sauté with ½ pound wiped, sliced mushrooms in 3 tablespoons butter over moderate heat 6–8 minutes until browned. While sweetbreads are sautéing, make a thin Velouté Sauce: melt 2 tablespoons butter in a saucepan, blend in 2 tablespoons flour, add 1 cup veal or chicken stock, and heat, stirring, until thickened. Mix ⅓ cup heavy cream with 1 egg yolk, stir slowly into sauce, and heat and stir 1 minute (do not boil). Season with ½ teaspoon salt and a pinch white pepper. Spoon sweetbreads and mushrooms onto unbuttered toast triangles and smother each serving with sauce; pass any remaining sauce. About 415 calories per serving.

⚔ **Sautéed Sweetbreads and Prosciutto:** Prepare sweetbreads as directed but sauté quickly just to brown, about 5 minutes. Add 3 tablespoons each minced chives and parsley, ¼ cup each minced prosciutto ham and apple cider or chicken broth. Put lid on skillet askew and simmer 5 minutes, shaking pan occasionally. About 260 calories per serving.

⚖ BROILED SWEETBREADS

Makes 4 servings

1¼ pounds sweetbreads
½ cup melted butter or margarine
½ teaspoon salt
⅛ teaspoon pepper

Prepare sweetbreads for cooking and blanch as directed,* halve at the natural separation, and pat very dry on paper toweling. Preheat broiler. Place sweetbreads on lightly greased broiler rack and brush well with melted butter. Broil 5″ from heat 2–3 minutes until lightly browned, brushing 1 or 2 times with butter; turn and broil 2–3 minutes longer, again brushing with butter. Season and serve as is or with a suitable sauce (see Some Herbs and Seasonings/Sauces and Butters for Variety Meats). About 215 calories per serving.

VARIATIONS:

⚖ **Broiled Brains:** Prepare basic recipe above or any of the variations below as directed, substituting brains for sweetbreads. About 255 calories per serving.

⚖ **Savory Broiled Sweetbreads:** Prepare sweetbreads as above, then dredge in ⅓ cup unsifted flour mixed with ½ teaspoon salt and ¼ teaspoon each pepper and summer savory. Broil as directed, brushing often with melted butter or a ½ and ½ mixture of melted butter and Madeira wine. About 240 calories per serving.

⚖ **Broiled Breaded Sweetbreads:** Prepare sweetbreads as above, dip in melted butter, then in fine dry bread crumbs or cracker meal. Broil as directed, brushing often with melted butter. For extra flavor, use seasoned crumbs. About 240 calories per serving.

⚖ **Sweetbreads and Bacon en Brochette:** Prepare sweetbreads as above, but break into chunks about the size of walnuts; wrap each in ½ slice bacon and secure with a toothpick. Place on skewers, not too close together, and brush with melted butter. Broil 6″ from heat, turning often and brushing with pan drippings or extra melted butter, about 15 minutes until golden brown. *For Extra Flair:* Alternate mushroom caps on skewers with bacon-wrapped sweetbreads and broil as directed. About 315 calories per serving.

⚖ BRAISED SWEETBREADS

An elegant way to present braised sweetbreads is wreathed on a platter around buttered potato balls, baby carrots, and asparagus tips; drift with minced parsley just before serving.
Makes 4 servings

1¼ pounds sweetbreads
1 carrot, peeled and sliced thin
1 large yellow onion, peeled and sliced thin
¼ cup butter or margarine
½ cup unsifted flour
1 teaspoon salt
¼ teaspoon pepper
1 cup dry white wine or chicken broth
1 bay leaf
¼ teaspoon thyme
3 sprigs parsley
2 tablespoons dry sherry

Prepare sweetbreads for cooking*

but do not blanch. Preheat oven to 350° F. Pat sweetbreads dry on paper toweling; leave whole or, if very large, divide into bite-size pieces. Stir-fry carrot and onion in butter in a large, flameproof casserole 8–10 minutes over moderate heat until golden. Dredge sweetbreads lightly in flour mixed with salt and pepper. Push carrot and onion to side of casserole, add sweetbreads, and sauté 2–3 minutes on each side until golden. Add all remaining ingredients except sherry, transfer casserole to oven, cover, and bake ¾ hour (25–30 minutes if sweetbreads are in small pieces). Lift sweetbreads to a heated platter and keep warm. Purée vegetables and casserole liquid in an electric blender at low speed or put through a food mill. Bring purée to a simmer, add sherry, pour over sweetbreads, and serve. About 310 calories per serving.

VARIATIONS:

Braised Sweetbreads on Ham: Prepare sweetbreads as directed and serve on thin slices of broiled ham. About 370 calories per serving.

Braised Brains: Prepare as directed, substituting brains for sweetbreads. About 350 calories per serving.

CREAMED SWEETBREADS

Makes 4 servings

1¼ pounds sweetbreads
¼ cup butter or margarine
¼ cup unsifted flour
2 cups milk
¾–1 teaspoon salt
⅛ teaspoon white pepper
¼ cup heavy cream
4 frozen puff pastry shells, baked by package directions, or 4 slices buttered toast, trimmed of crusts and halved diagonally

Prepare sweetbreads for cooking and blanch as directed.* Melt butter in the top of a double boiler over direct heat, blend in flour, slowly add milk, and heat, stirring, until thickened. Mix in salt, pepper, and cream. Set over simmering water, break sweetbreads into small pieces, and mix gently into sauce, using a rubber spatula. Heat, uncovered, stirring occasionally, 5–10 minutes. Serve in pastry shells or on toast. About 555 calories per serving.

VARIATIONS:

Creamed Brains: Substitute brains for sweetbreads and prepare as directed. (*Note:* Brains may also be used in any of the variations that follow.) About 595 calories per serving.

With Truffles: Just before serving, fold in 1 thinly sliced truffle. About 555 calories per serving.

With Mushrooms: Add ¼ pound sautéed, thinly sliced mushrooms along with sweetbreads. About 565 calories per serving.

With Ham, Tongue, or Chicken: Add an extra ¼ cup heavy cream and ½ cup diced lean boiled ham, tongue, or cooked white chicken meat along with sweetbreads; taste for salt and adjust as needed. About 635 calories per serving.

With Sherry or White Wine: Just before serving, stir in 2 tablespoons medium-dry sherry or white wine. About 600 calories per serving.

With Chestnuts or Almonds: Add ½ recipe Boiled Chestnuts or ⅓ cup toasted, slivered almonds along with sweetbreads and proceed as directed. About 625 calories per serving.

Herbed with Eggs: Add 3 quartered hard-cooked eggs and 1 tablespoon each minced chives and parsley along with sweetbreads and proceed as directed. About 615 calories per serving.

With Oysters: Add 1 dozen small oysters (fresh or frozen) along with sweetbreads and proceed as directed. About 600 calories per serving.

Au Gratin: After simmering sweetbreads in sauce, turn into a buttered 1½-quart casserole, top with ¼ cup fine buttered bread crumbs, and brown quickly under broiler. About 625 calories per serving.

Florentine: Prepare creamed sweetbreads as directed and set aside. Butter 6 scallop shells or ramekins and spoon ¼ cup hot puréed or minced spinach into each. Fill with creamed sweetbreads and pipe a border of Duchess Potatoes around the edge. Brush with egg glaze and brown lightly under broiler. Serve sprinkled with diced pimiento or frizzled julienne strips of ham. About 600 calories per serving.

In a Spinach Ring: Prepare 1 Spinach Ring, fill with creamed sweetbreads, and serve. About 715 calories per serving.

⚔️ **SWEETBREAD SOUFFLÉ**

Makes 6 servings

1 pound sweetbreads
¼ cup butter or margarine
¼ cup sifted flour
1 cup milk
¾ teaspoon salt
⅛ teaspoon pepper
⅛ teaspoon nutmeg
4 eggs, separated

Prepare sweetbreads for cooking and blanch as directed.* Chop fine, measure out 1⅓ cups, and save any remaining sweetbreads to toss into

scrambled breakfast eggs. Melt butter in a saucepan over moderate heat, blend in flour, slowly add milk, and heat, stirring constantly, until thickened and smooth. Add all seasonings. Beat egg yolks lightly, spoon a little hot sauce into them, then return to saucepan. Turn heat to low and cook, stirring, 1–2 minutes (do not boil). Off heat, mix in sweetbreads, lay a piece of wax paper directly on surface, and cool to room temperature. Meanwhile, preheat oven to 350° F. Beat egg whites until soft peaks form, and fold into sauce. Spoon into an ungreased 1½-quart soufflé dish and bake, uncovered, on center rack 40–50 minutes until puffed and golden. Serve at once. About 225 calories per serving.

TONGUE

Next to tripe and heart, tongue is one of the most muscular variety meats and needs special treatment to tenderize it. Beef tongue is available fresh, corned, pickled, and smoked and, in some parts of the country, ready-to-serve. Veal tongue is usually sold fresh, but lamb and pork tongues, being smaller, are almost always precooked, ready-to-eat meats.

Amount Needed: Beef tongues weigh 2½–5 pounds, veal tongues about 2 pounds, pork tongues 1 pound and lamb tongues barely ¼ pound. Allow ⅓–½ pound per serving.

To Simmer and Prepare for Use in Recipes:

Fresh Tongue: Wash well in cool water, place in a large stainless-steel, enamel, or teflon-lined kettle, and cover with salted water (1 teaspoon salt to 1 quart water). For extra savor, add ½ unsliced lemon, 1 peeled yellow onion stuck with 3–4 cloves, 1–2 stalks celery (include tops), 1–2 bay leaves, and a large sprig each parsley and thyme. Cover, bring to a boil, and skim off froth. Re-cover and simmer slowly until tender: veal tongue will take 2–2½ hours, beef tongue 3–4. Plunge tongue into cold water to loosen skin, lift out, and pat dry. Slit skin lengthwise on underside of tongue from root to tip and peel off; cut away root, small bones, and gristle. If tongue is to be served cold, it will be more flavorful if chilled in its own broth. Tongue is now ready to use in recipes or to serve sliced hot or cold. Good with Mustard, Madeira, or Raisin Sauce (also see Some Herbs and Seasonings/Sauces and Butters for Variety Meats).

Smoked or Pickled Tongue: Soak 2–3 hours in cold water before simmering, then proceed as for fresh tongue.

To Parboil (use in recipes that call for cooking tongue ¾–1 hour or longer): Simmer as directed but reduce cooking time to 2 hours for beef tongue, 1½ hours for veal tongue. Proceed with preparation as directed.

PARISIAN-STYLE BRAISED SLICED BEEF TONGUE

Makes 6–8 servings

1 (3–3½-pound) *fresh or smoked beef tongue*

Sauce:
3 *slices lean bacon, diced*
1 *carrot, peeled and diced*
3 *scallions, sliced thin*
1 *stalk celery, diced*

4 *mushrooms, wiped clean and minced*
1 *clove garlic, peeled and crushed*
1 *cup beef broth*
1 *cup water*
⅛ *teaspoon pepper*
¼ *cup dry sherry or cognac (optional)*

Parboil tongue, remove skin, root, bone, and gristle,* and slice ⅜"–½" thick (begin at large end, slicing straight through, but as you approach small end, hold knife slightly at an angle). Prepare sauce: Stir-fry bacon and vegetables in a heavy skillet over moderate heat 8–10 minutes to brown lightly, add remaining sauce ingredients, cover, and simmer ½ hour. Cool slightly and purée in an electric blender at slow speed or put through a food mill. Pour sauce into a deep, heavy skillet, add tongue slices, cover, and simmer 45 minutes until tongue is very tender. Serve with lots of sauce. (*Note:* For even richer flavor, let tongue slices marinate in sauce overnight in refrigerator before simmering.)

VARIATION:
Substitute veal tongue for beef and proceed as directed. Ready-to-eat lamb or pork tongues may also be used but need only be sliced and warmed 10–15 minutes in the sauce.

Both versions: about 435 calories for each of 6 servings, 325 calories for each of 8 servings.

PICKLED TONGUE

Makes 6–8 servings

1 (3–3½-pound) *fresh beef tongue*
2½ *quarts cold water*
1 *cup cider vinegar*
2 *tablespoons pickling spice, tied in cheesecloth*

Wash tongue, place in a large, heavy kettle with all ingredients, cover, and bring to a boil. Skim froth from surface, re-cover, and simmer 3–4 hours until tender. Cool tongue in broth until easy to handle, lift out, skin, cut away root, bones, and gristle. Strain and skim broth.

To Serve Hot: Place tongue in a clean kettle, add broth, cover, and reheat 8–10 minutes over moderately low heat. Lift out, drain and serve with Mustard Sauce. *To Glaze:* Instead of warming tongue in broth, place on a rack in a shallow, open roasting pan, spread with 1 cup firmly packed light brown sugar mixed with ¼ cup cider vinegar and 1 tablespoon honey or light corn syrup. Bake, uncovered, 15–20 minutes at 350° F., basting often with mixture until glazed. (*Note:* Minced chutney or chopped tart fruit jellies can be used to glaze tongue as can Plum or Sweet-Sour Sauce or any of the thin ham glazes [see Some Glazes for Baked Hams].)

To Serve Cold: Simmer tongue as directed; skin, cut away root, bones, and gristle. Return tongue to strained, skimmed broth, cover, and chill several hours. Remove from broth, slice thin, and serve with Mustard or Sour Cream-Horseradish Sauce.

Hot or cold: about 380 calories for each of 6 servings (without sauce), 280 calories for each of 8 servings.

TONGUE, HAM, AND EGG CASSEROLE

Makes 6 servings

6 *thick slices cooked tongue*
6 *thick slices boiled ham*
3 *hard-cooked eggs, shelled and sliced*

2 *cups Medium White Sauce*
⅓ *cup buttered white bread crumbs or crushed cornflakes or potato chips*

Preheat oven to 350° F. Layer tongue, ham, and eggs into an ungreased, shallow 1½-quart casserole, pour in white sauce, top with crumbs, and bake uncovered ½ hour; brown quickly under broiler and serve. About 455 calories per serving.

VARIATIONS:

– Spread 1 (1-pound) jar creamed spinach and ¼ pound sliced sautéed mushrooms between tongue and ham layers, then proceed as recipe directs. About 510 calories per serving.
– Substitute any cheese sauce for white sauce. About 535 calories per serving.
– Substitute corned beef, a mild salami, bologna, or luncheon meat for ham. About 455 calories per serving.

⊠ DEVILED TONGUE

Makes 4 servings

2 *tablespoons prepared spicy brown mustard*
2 *tablespoons steak sauce*
8 *thick slices cooked tongue*
1 *egg, lightly beaten with 1 tablespoon cold water*
½ *cup toasted seasoned bread crumbs*
3 *tablespoons butter or margarine*

Mix mustard and steak sauce and spread evenly on both sides of tongue slices; let stand 10 minutes. Dip tongue in egg and crumbs to coat thickly. Brown in butter, a few slices at a time, in a heavy skillet over moderate heat. Serve sprinkled with a few drops tarragon vinegar or, if you prefer, with

Diable Sauce. About 430 calories per serving (without sauce).

TONGUE MOUSSE

Makes 8 servings

¼ cup butter or margarine
6 tablespoons flour
1½ cups milk
½ cup light cream
3 eggs plus 2 egg whites, lightly beaten
4 cups finely ground cooked, smoked, or canned tongue (you'll need about 2 pounds)
1½ cups soft white bread crumbs
1 teaspoon salt (about)
⅛ teaspoon white pepper
2 teaspoons prepared mild yellow mustard

Preheat oven to 350° F. Melt butter in a saucepan over moderate heat, blend in flour, then slowly stir in milk and cream, and heat, stirring until smooth and thickened. Off heat blend in eggs, a little at a time, mixing well after each addition. Fold in tongue and remaining ingredients, taste for salt and adjust as needed. Spoon into a well-buttered 1½-quart mold, cover with a buttered piece of foil, and bake in a water bath 1–1¼ hours until center of mousse is just firm to the touch. Remove from water bath and let stand 10 minutes before unmolding. To unmold: Run a spatula around edge of mousse to loosen, then invert. Serve hot, garnished with buttered peas or asparagus tips, or cool, cover loosely, chill, and serve on a bed of watercress. About 475 calories per serving.

JELLIED BEEF TONGUE

Makes 6–8 servings

1 (3–3½-pound) fresh or smoked beef tongue
1½–2 pounds beef or veal bones, cracked
1 medium-size yellow onion, peeled
1 carrot, peeled
1 stalk celery
1 tablespoon salt (if using fresh tongue)
¼ teaspoon peppercorns
2 bay leaves
2½ quarts cold water

Wash tongue, place in a large, heavy kettle with all ingredients, cover, and bring to a boil. Skim froth from surface, re-cover, and simmer 3–4 hours until tender. Cool tongue in broth until easy to handle, lift out, skin, cut away root, bones, and gristle. Cover loosely and cool. Meanwhile, continue simmering bones, uncovered, in broth 1 hour longer. Strain broth through a cheesecloth-lined sieve, cool, and skim off all fat. Return stock to kettle, boil rapidly, uncovered, until reduced to about 1½ quarts, then clarify* if you like. Cut off smaller ⅓ of tongue and tuck, rounded side out, into hollow on underside of larger piece so that the 2 almost form a circle. Fit tongue into a bowl just large enough to hold it and fill to the brim with broth. Chill several hours until firm, then unmold on a bed of greens. Good with Mustard Mayonnaise. About 375 calories for each of 6 servings, 280 calories for each of 8 servings.

VARIATIONS:

Tongue in Rosé Aspic: Instead of using recipe above, simmer tongue by basic method*; remove skin, root, bones, and gristle. For the aspic: Simmer 2 cups fat-free chicken broth with a *bouquet garni,* tied in cheesecloth, ½ hour; strain and clarify.* Mix in 4 cups rosé wine, 1–2 drops red food coloring, 2–3 drops liquid hot red pepper seasoning, and salt to taste. Mix 4 envelopes unflavored gelatin with 1 cup cold water, heat slowly, stirring, until gelatin dissolves; stir into wine mixture. Cut tongue as directed above and fit into bowl; cover with aspic and chill until firm. (*Note:* Any remaining aspic may be chilled, then chopped and used to garnish tongue platter.) About 475 calories for each of 6 servings, 360 calories for each of 8 servings.

Jellied Sliced Beef Tongue: Prepare either of the above recipes up to point of cutting tongue. Slice tongue thin and layer into a 2-quart decorative mold. Fill with aspic and chill until firm. Unmold and serve as directed. Calorie counts the same as for the recipes above.

TRIPE

Tripe is the lining of the stomach of meat animals, and that considered choicest is *honeycomb tripe,* the lining of the second stomach of beef. Also good are *pocket tripe,* the lower end of the second stomach, and *plain* or *smooth tripe,* which is not honeycombed and not so delicate. Tripe is available pickled, canned, and fresh. Fresh tripe is always sold partially cooked but needs still further cooking.

Amount Needed: Allow ¼–½ pound tripe per person, depending upon whether it is simply prepared or served in a rich sauce.

To Prepare for Cooking: Pull or cut all fat from tripe and discard; wash well in cold water. Pickled tripe, though thoroughly cooked, usually needs to be soaked in cold water 1–2 hours before using.

To Simmer: All fresh tripe must be simmered until tender before it can be eaten or used in many recipes (those that follow tell when it must be simmered). Cut tripe into manageable pieces so it will be easier to handle and cook more evenly. Place in a large, deep kettle (not aluminum or tripe will discolor) and cover with lightly salted water (1 teaspoon salt to each quart of water). Cover and simmer gently 1½–2 hours until tender. Tripe can now be cut in 2″ squares and served hot in bowls with some of the broth; it can be cooled in its own broth, drained, chilled, and eaten with a sprinkling of vinegar. Or it can be used in recipes (cut up as individual recipes specify).

◁▷ FRIED TRIPE

Makes 4–6 servings

2 pounds tripe
2 eggs, lightly beaten
¾ cup toasted seasoned bread crumbs
¼ cup cooking oil
Lemon wedges

Prepare tripe for cooking and simmer.* Drain, pat very dry on paper toweling, and cut in 2″ squares or strips. Dip in egg and crumbs to coat thickly and let dry 5 minutes on a rack at room temperature. Heat oil in a large heavy skillet over moderately high heat 1 minute and fry tripe, a few pieces at a time, 1–2 minutes until crisp and golden brown. Drain on paper toweling and set, uncovered, in a 250° F. oven to keep warm while you fry the rest. Serve with lemon wedges. About 290 calories for each of 4 servings, 190 calories for each of 6 servings.

SOME HERBS AND SEASONINGS/SAUCES AND BUTTERS FOR VARIETY MEATS

Brains/Sweetbreads	Heart	Kidneys	Liver	Tongue	Tripe
Herbs/Seasonings:	*Herbs/Seasonings:*	*Herbs/Seasonings:*	*Herbs/Seasonings:*	*Herbs/Seasonings:*	*Herbs/Seasonings:*
Bay leaf	Bay leaf	Basil	Bay leaf	Bay leaf	Bay leaf
Chervil	Garlic	Bay leaf	Lemon	Chervil	Cloves
Garlic	Parsley	Garlic	Parsley	Cloves	Garlic
Lemon	Sage	Lemon	Nutmeg	Garlic	Lemon
Mace	Tarragon	Oregano	Rosemary	Lemon	Mace
Nutmeg	Thyme	Parsley	Sage	Orange	Parsley
Parsley		Shallots	Savory	Parsley	Sage
Tarragon		Thyme	Shallots	Tarragon	Thyme
Thyme	*Sauces/Butters:*		Thyme	Thyme	
	Bordelaise	*Sauces/Butters:*			*Sauces/Butters:*
Sauces/Butters:	Chasseur	Bercy Butter	*Sauces/Butters:*	*Sauces/Butters:*	*(for fried tripe only):*
Albufera	Madeira	Bordelaise	Bercy Butter	Chasseur	Diable
Allemande	Maître d'Hôtel	Diable	Bordelaise	Diable	Piquante
Aurore	Butter (sliced,	Duxelles	Diable	Duxelles	Rémoulade
Béarnaise	sautéed heart)	Herb	Herb	Hot Horseradish	Tartar
Beurre Noir	Mushroom	Madeira	Italienne	Madeira	Tomato
Bordelaise		Maître d'Hôtel	Maître d'Hôtel	Mustard	
Caper Butter		Butter	Butter	Piquante	
Diable		Mustard	Mustard	Poivrade	
Duxelles		Tortue	Piquante	Raisin	
Financière			Robert	Romaine	
Italienne				Sauce Bercy	
Madeira				Tortue	
Maître d'Hôtel				Vinaigrette	
Butter					
Noisette Butter					
Paprika					
Parsley-Lemon					
Butter					
Périgueux					
Piquante					
Poulette					
Régence					
Robert					
Soubise					
Suprême					
Talleyrand					
Tomato					

CREAMED TRIPE AND ONIONS

Makes 4 servings

2 *pounds honeycomb tripe*
3 *medium-size yellow onions, peeled and sliced thin*
3 *cups milk*
½ *teaspoon salt*
⅛ *teaspoon white pepper*
2 *tablespoons butter or margarine*
3 *tablespoons flour blended with ¼ cup cold milk*

Prepare tripe for cooking and simmer.* Meanwhile, simmer onions, covered, in milk over low heat 20 minutes until tender. When tripe is done, drain, cut in 2″ squares, and add to onions along with salt and pepper. Cover and let stand off heat 1–2 hours to blend flavors. About 10 minutes before serving, warm to serving temperature over low heat. Add butter and flour paste and heat, stirring, until thickened. Serve in soup bowls with crusty chunks of bread. About 350 calories per serving.

⚖ TRIPE LYONNAISE

Makes 4 servings

2 *pounds honeycomb tripe*
6 *tablespoons butter or margarine*
2 *large yellow onions, peeled and sliced thin*
1 *tablespoon minced parsley*
1 *tablespoon white vinegar*
Salt
Pepper

Prepare tripe for cooking and simmer.* Drain, pat dry on paper toweling, and cut in 2″ squares. Stir-fry in 3 tablespoons butter in a large, heavy skillet over moderate heat about 2 minutes until golden; drain on paper toweling and keep warm. In a separate skillet stir-fry onions in remaining butter 8–10

minutes over moderate heat until golden. Mix tripe and onions, sprinkle with parsley and vinegar, and mix again. Taste for salt and pepper and season as needed. Toss again and serve. Good spooned over hot mashed potatoes. About 290 calories per serving.

⚖ TRIPE MAÎTRE D'HÔTEL

Makes 4 servings

2 *pounds honeycomb tripe*
1 *cup cold water*
1 *cup beef broth*
1 *cup dry white wine*
½ *teaspoon salt*
1 *bouquet garni,* *tied in cheesecloth with 3 thick lemon slices*
2 *egg yolks, lightly beaten*
⅛ *teaspoon nutmeg*
⅛ *teaspoon cayenne pepper*

Prepare tripe for cooking* and cut in strips 2″ long and ¾″ wide. Place in a large kettle (not aluminum) with water, broth, wine, salt and *bouquet garni,* cover and simmer 1½–2 hours until tender. Transfer tripe to a deep platter with a slotted spoon and keep warm. Boil broth, uncovered, over high heat until reduced to about 1 cup; discard cheesecloth bag. Mix a little hot broth into yolks, then return to broth. Set over lowest heat and cook 1–2 minutes until slightly thickened (do not boil). Mix in nutmeg and cayenne, taste for seasoning and adjust. Pour over tripe and serve. About 210 calories per serving.

⚖ TRIPES À LA MODE DE CAEN

This steaming marmite of tripe flavored with apple brandy comes from Normandy but is the favorite of all France.
Makes 8 servings

4 pounds tripe
4 small yellow onions, peeled and
   coarsely chopped
4 carrots, peeled and cut in small dice
4 leeks, coarsely chopped
1 calf's foot, cleaned, split and
   sawed in 3–4 pieces (these are a bit
   difficult to find, but most gourmet
   or kosher butchers will either have
   them or order them)
3 cloves garlic, peeled
1 bouquet garni,* tied in cheesecloth
2 teaspoons salt
¼ teaspoon white pepper
⅛ teaspoon allspice
2 quarts cold water
2–3 thin sheets barding suet (you'll
   need enough to cover the kettle
   you're making the tripe in)
½ cup Calvados or aged cider

Pastry:
1½ cups sifted flour
½ cup cold water

Preheat oven to 300° F. Prepare
tripe for cooking,* cut in 3″ squares,
and set aside. Mix vegetables in a
large kettle and lay calf's foot on
top. Add tripe, garlic, *bouquet
garni*, seasonings, and water. Lay
suet over all to cover, then place lid
on kettle. Prepare pastry by mixing
flour and water until sticky. Turn out
on a heavily floured board, knead 1
or 2 times, then roll into a rope long
enough to go around kettle. Use
rope like putty to seal kettle lid to
kettle. Set kettle on lowest oven
rack and bake 6–7 hours. Discard
pastry and suet; spoon tripe into
a large tureen with a slotted spoon.
Cut meat from calf's foot and add
to tripe. Strain kettle liquid,
discarding vegetables, garlic and
bouquet garni. Strain and skim off
fat, then bring to a boil and stir in
Calvados. Ladle over tripe and serve.
Good with crusty bread or boiled
potatoes. About 160 calories per
serving (without bread or potatoes).

⚖ PHILADELPHIA PEPPER POT

Begin this recipe one or even two
days before you plan to serve it.
Though called a soup, pepper pot is
hearty enough to serve as a main
dish. It was invented at Valley Forge
by a chef in George Washington's
army.
Makes 8–10 servings

1 meaty veal shank
2 pounds beef marrowbones, cracked
5 quarts cold water
2 tablespoons salt (about)
1 teaspoon peppercorns
2 large yellow onions, peeled and
   minced
1 bouquet garni,* tied in cheesecloth
2 pounds tripe
3 medium-size potatoes, peeled and
   cut in ½″ cubes
1 teaspoon marjoram
2 tablespoons minced parsley
1 recipe Dumplings

Simmer shank and marrowbones,
covered, in 2 quarts water with 1
tablespoon salt, ½ teaspoon peppercorns, the onions, and *bouquet garni*
3–4 hours. Meanwhile, prepare
tripe for cooking* and cut in 2″
squares. Place in a large kettle
(not aluminum) with remaining
water, salt, and peppercorns, cover,
and simmer 2 hours until very
tender; lift from broth and set aside;
strain and save broth. When bones
have simmered 3 hours, lift from
broth; cut meat from shank and
add to tripe; scoop out marrow,
chop coarsely and also add to tripe;
refrigerate. Strain broth, combine
with tripe broth and refrigerate
overnight. Next day place broth in a
large kettle (not aluminum), add
tripe and meat, potatoes and
marjoram, cover, and simmer 10
minutes. Add parsley, taste for salt
and adjust as needed. Prepare

dumplings, bring broth to a boil and drop in dumplings from a tablespoon (make 1 for each person). Simmer, uncovered, 10 minutes, then cover and simmer 10 minutes longer. To serve, ladle out steaming bowls of soup and float a dumpling in each. About 235 calories for each of 8 servings, 185 calories for each of 10 servings.

SAUSAGES
(See Quick Alphabet of Sausages.)

How to Cook Fresh Sausages

Because they contain pork, sausages, whether smoked or not, must be thoroughly cooked before they're eaten. Many, especially large ones, will require a combination of methods—steaming or simmering *plus* panfrying, broiling, or grilling if they are to be done inside by the time they are brown outside.

Amount Needed: ¼–⅓ pound sausage per person.

General Preparation for Cooking: Very little. Bulk sausage must be shaped into balls or patties, sausage rolls sliced. The biggest question concerns links. Should they be pricked before cooking? Opinions vary, but probably the best rule to follow: American sausages, no; European sausages, yes (they're moister and may burst if not pricked).

To Simmer:

Links: Place sausages in a saucepan, add just enough lightly salted boiling water—or beer or ale—to cover, cover, and simmer 10–30 minutes, depending on size, until

cooked through. *To Test:* Remove 1 sausage and cut into center; it should show no traces of pink. (*Note:* If links are to be browned after simmering, they will need to be simmered only 8–10 minutes.)

Bulk Sausage: Roll into ¾"–1" balls, drop into lightly salted boiling water, cover, and simmer 10–15 minutes until cooked through. These are best served in a Medium White Sauce, made using ½ and ½ sausage cooking water and heavy cream. Flavor with a little dry white wine and nutmeg. Let sausages warm in sauce about 5 minutes before serving to mellow flavors.

To Steam (for links only): Place links on a rack in a saucepan, add 1–1½ cups boiling water (it should not touch sausages), cover, and steam 15–20 minutes until cooked through. (*Note:* Very chunky sausages may take as long as ½ hour.) If sausages are to be browned later, reduce steaming time to 10–15 minutes.

To Panfry (*Sauté*) (for small links only): Strictly speaking, this is a combination of simmering and panfrying, but since it is all done in one skillet, it is called panfrying. Place sausages in a cold skillet, add ¼ cup water, cover, and simmer 5–10 minutes, depending on size. Uncover and brown slowly over moderately low heat, turning often with tongs. (*Note:* Swiss and German women drain off the simmering water, then brown sausages slowly in 1–2 tablespoons butter or lard. Sometimes before browning, they pat sausages dry and dredge lightly in flour—gives a crisper finish. When sausages are simmered first, they need only be browned in butter.)

To Panbroil (for patties and slices):

Slice a sausage roll ½" thick or shape bulk sausage into patties about ½" thick and 3" across. Place patties in a cold skillet, set over moderate heat, and cook 15–20 minutes until cooked through. Turn only once during cooking; do not press down or spank with spatula.

To Braise (links and patties): Brown sausages slowly in 1–2 tablespoons butter in a large, heavy skillet over moderate heat, add ½ cup liquid (water, beer or ale, dry white wine, tomato juice or sauce, barbecue sauce, apple or pineapple juice, ginger ale plus 1–2 tablespoons soy or *teriyaki* sauce), cover, and simmer 15 minutes.

To Bake:

Sausage Roll: Preheat oven to 375° F. Leave roll whole, place on a rack in a shallow roasting pan, and insert meat thermometer in center. Roast uncovered, without basting, 45 minutes to 1 hour or until thermometer reads 185° F. Serve as is or with Pan Gravy or Tomato Sauce.

Links: Preheat oven to 400° F. Spread links out in a shallow roasting pan and roast, uncovered, 25–30 minutes, turning often with tongs so they brown evenly.

To Broil (for links that have been simmered or steamed first): Preheat broiler. Brush sausages well with melted butter or oil, place on a greased broiler pan, and broil 3" from heat, turning often with tongs, 5–8 minutes until nicely browned.

To Charcoal Broil (for links that have first been simmered or steamed): Prepare a moderate charcoal fire.* Brush sausages with melted butter or oil, place on lightly greased grill, and broil 3" from heat, turning often with tongs, 5–8 minutes until well browned on all sides.

Some Easy Ways to Dress Up Sausage Patties

All make 4 servings

Baked Sausage and Apples: Shape 1 pound bulk sausage into 4 patties and brown well on both sides over moderate heat. Transfer to an ungreased 6-cup casserole. Peel, core, and thinly slice 4 tart apples; toss with ¼ cup firmly packed light brown sugar, ¼ teaspoon cinnamon, a pinch nutmeg, and the juice of ½ lemon. Spread over patties. Top with ¼ cup fine buttered bread crumbs and bake, uncovered, at 350° F. about ½ hour until lightly browned and bubbly.

Baked Sausage and Sweet Potatoes: Shape and brown patties as above; transfer to an ungreased 6-cup casserole, top with 1 (9-ounce) package frozen sweet potatoes or Hawaiian-style sweet potatoes (with pineapple), cover, and bake ½–¾ hour at 350° F. until bubbly.

Smothered Sausage Patties: Shape and brown patties as in first variation; transfer to an ungreased 6-cup casserole, top with 1 (10½-ounce) can cream of mushroom, celery, or tomato soup thinned with ⅓ cup milk and bake, uncovered, ½ hour at 350° F. until bubbling. (*Note:* 2 cups canned or Pan Gravy can be substituted for the soup.)

Barbecued Sausage Patties: Follow Smothered Sausage Patties recipe preceding but bake in 2 cups All-Purpose Barbecue Sauce instead of soup.

Sausage Patties Creole: Shape and brown patties as in first variation; transfer to an ungreased 6-cup casserole. Drain all but 2 tablespoons drippings from skillet, add 1 minced medium-size yellow onion, 1 crushed clove garlic, and ⅓ cup minced sweet green pepper, and stir-fry 8–10 minutes until onion is golden. Add 1 (1-pound) can drained, chopped tomatoes, ½ teaspoon salt, and a pinch each marjoram and thyme. Heat, stirring, 5 minutes. Pour over sausages and bake, uncovered, ½–¾ hour at 350° F. until sauce is thick and bubbly.

Sauerkraut and Sausage: Shape and brown patties as in first variation; remove to an ungreased 6-cup casserole. Top with 1 (1-pound) can undrained sauerkraut, sprinkle lightly with paprika, and bake uncovered 30 minutes at 350° F.

South Pacific Sausage Patties: Shape and brown patties as in Baked Sausage and Apples; remove from skillet and set aside. Pour all but 2 tablespoons drippings from skillet, add 1 minced medium-size yellow onion, ½ sweet green pepper cut in small thin slivers, and stir-fry 5–8 minutes until onion is pale golden. Return patties to skillet, pull onions and peppers on top, add 1 (13½-ounce) drained can crushed pineapple and 1 tablespoon soy sauce, cover, and simmer 30 minutes. Uncover and, if mixture seems too liquid, simmer uncovered about 5 minutes longer to reduce.

Sausage "Sandwiches": Shape 1 pound bulk sausage into 8 thin patties of equal size. Top 4 with a thin layer of seasoned mashed potatoes, yams, or drained crushed pineapple. Top with remaining patties and crimp edges to seal. Brown both sides well over moderate heat. If patties are stuffed with mashed potatoes, add 1½ cups Pan Gravy (or canned), cover, and simmer ½ hour. If stuffed with yams or pineapple, add ½ cup apple cider, pineapple juice, or crushed pineapple, cover, and simmer ½ hour.

Some Simple Ways to Spice Up Sausage Links

All make 4 servings

Note: Use fresh or country-style pork sausage links instead of European varieties unless otherwise specified.

Braised Sausages, Apples, and Onions: Brown 1 pound sausage links slowly in 1–2 teaspoons butter or bacon drippings in a large, heavy skillet over moderate heat; remove and drain. In drippings, stir-fry 1 thinly sliced Bermuda onion 5–8 minutes until pale golden; add 1 (1-pound 4-ounce) drained can sliced apples, 1 tablespoon lemon juice, 2 tablespoons light brown sugar, ¼ teaspoon cinnamon, and a pinch each cloves and nutmeg; toss to mix. Return sausages to skillet, pushing down into apples, cover, and simmer ½ hour.

Baked Sausages and Beans: Brown 1 pound sausage links as in recipe above. Prepare ½ recipe Easy Brandied Beans up to point of baking. Lay sausages on beans, pushing them down slightly, and bake as directed.

Country-Fried Sausage and Potatoes: Slice ½ pound country-style sausage links ½" thick and brown well in 2 tablespoons butter or oil. Add 1 chopped medium-size yellow onion, 4 raw potatoes, peeled and sliced thin, cover, and cook 8–10 minutes. Uncover and stir-fry 10–15 minutes until nicely browned. Season with ½ teaspoon salt, a pinch each pepper and thyme and serve.

Sausage Succotash: Slice ½ pound sausage links ½" thick and brown well in 1–2 tablespoons bacon drippings; drain on paper toweling. Prepare 1 recipe Quick Succotash as directed up to point of adding corn. Add sausage along with corn, and finish cooking as directed.

Italian-Style Sausage and Black Beans: Begin 1 recipe Brazilian Black Beans, substituting ½ pound fresh Italian-style pork sausage for bacon. Cut sausage casings and remove meat; stir-fry in 1 tablespoon olive oil 3–5 minutes, breaking up clumps; remove to paper toweling with a slotted spoon. Brown onions and garlic in drippings as recipe directs, add sausage along with remaining ingredients and proceed as directed.

Baked Sausages and Sweets: Barbecued Sausages: South Pacific Sausages: Sauerkraut and Sausages: Follow variations given for sausage patties, substituting 1 pound sausage links for 1 pound bulk sausage. Brown links well in a small amount of butter or drippings, then proceed as recipes direct.

Sausage and Vegetable Gumbo: Begin 1 recipe Vegetable Gumbo but substitute ½ pound sausage links for bacon; cut in ½" slices and brown well in 1 tablespoon butter. Add onion and celery, sauté as directed, then proceed according to recipe.

How to Heat and Serve Fully Cooked Sausages

Frankfurters and Other Fully Cooked Link Sausages: Franks, wieners, and knackwurst can be prepared by any of the methods below; to determine best ways of preparing the more unusual sausages, consult Quick Alphabet of Sausages, then follow directions below. (*Note:* American sausages are best *not pricked* before cooking, but the chunky, moist European sausages should be lest they burst.)

To Simmer: Cover with simmering water or, for richer flavor, with beer or a ½ and ½ mixture of water and dry white wine and *simmer* (not boil) 5–8 minutes until heated through. Or cover with simmering liquid, remove from heat, and let stand, covered, 8–10 minutes. (*Note:* If beer or wine-water mixture is used, save for making soups or stews.)

To Steam: Arrange sausages 1 layer deep on a rack in a saucepan or vegetable steamer, add 1 cup boiling water, cover, and heat 8 minutes over moderate heat. Water should stay at a slow boil.

To Panfry (Sauté): Brown sausages in 1–2 tablespoons butter, margarine, meat drippings, or cooking oil in a heavy skillet over moderate heat 3–5 minutes, turning frequently. If you prefer, halve lengthwise and brown about 2 minutes on each side.

To Broil: Brush sausages well with oil, melted butter or margarine and broil on lightly greased broiler rack 3″ from heat 4–5 minutes, turning often until evenly browned (use tongs for turning). Or split, brush with butter, and broil about 2 minutes per side.

To Charcoal Broil: Prepare a moderately hot charcoal fire.* Lay sausages in a single layer on a lightly greased grill and broil 4″–5″ from heat 3–4 minutes, turning frequently with tongs, until lightly browned. (*Note:* Sausages can also be wrapped in heavy foil—not individually but in a single large package—and steamed on the grill 12–15 minutes.)

To Roast Over a Campfire: Let fire burn down to glowing coals. Spear sausages crosswise on long-handled forks or peeled sticks (no more than 2–3 per fork or stick) and roast 3″ from coals, turning frequently, 4–5 minutes until lightly browned.

Andouille: Usually this sausage is simply sliced and eaten cold, but it can be browned in butter or drippings. Slice ¼″–½″ thick and brown in 2–3 tablespoons butter or bacon drippings in a large, heavy skillet over moderate heat about 2–3 minutes on each side. Or brush with melted butter or drippings and broil 4″ from heat about 2 minutes on each side.

Blood Sausages: These come in different sizes and shapes, each requiring somewhat different treatment. The *small links* may simply be left whole and browned in 2–3 tablespoons bacon drippings or butter in a large, heavy skillet 3–5 minutes; turn frequently with tongs. The *large round ring* is best braised: Brown 5–7 minutes in 2–3 tablespoons bacon drippings or butter in a large, heavy skillet over moderately low heat, add 1 cup water or stock, cover, turn heat to low, and simmer about ½ hour until heated through. *Fat chunky rolls* like *Zungenwurst* can be sliced ¼″–½″ thick, peeled of casings, and, if you like, dredged lightly in flour (helps reduce spattering). Brown in 2–3 tablespoons butter or bacon drippings in a large, heavy skillet over moderately low heat 3–4 minutes on each side. *Berliner Blutwurst,* another variety, should be covered with boiling water and allowed to stand 20 minutes (keep lid on pot). Remove, slice, and serve. Or, if you like, gently brown hot slices in about 2 tablespoons butter in a large, heavy skillet over moderately low heat 2–3 minutes per side.

Leberkäse: This delicate German liver pâté is nearly always served hot. Slice about ½″ thick and place slices on a rack over boiling water in a vegetable steamer or in the top of a double boiler. Cover and steam 25–30 minutes until heated through. Or slice 1″ thick and sauté slowly in about 3 tablespoons butter in a large, heavy skillet with 1 thinly sliced yellow onion. Keep heat low and allow about 5 minutes per side; handle with care, using a pancake turner to turn slices.

Scrapple: Slice ¼″–½″ thick or cut in finger-shaped sticks; dredge lightly in flour and brown in 3–4 tablespoons butter or bacon drippings in a large, heavy skillet over moderate heat until crisply browned. Slices will take 3–5 minutes per side, fingers slightly less time but more frequent turning.

¢ BASIC HOMEMADE SAUSAGE MEAT

Makes 6 pounds; about 2 dozen patties

4½ pounds lean pork (trimmings, head meat, etc.)
1½ pounds fat pork (cheek, jowl, trimmings, etc.)
3 tablespoons salt
1 tablespoon pepper
1 tablespoon sage

Coarsely grind lean and fat pork together, mix with remaining ingredients, and grind 2 more times. Shape into patties about 3″ across and ½″ thick, wrap each in foil or saran and freeze until firm. For cooking instructions, see How to Cook Fresh Sausages.

To Make Links: First of all, you need a sausage stuffing attachment for your meat grinder or electric mixer. Second you need casings (butchers can usually get them for you). Ask either for sheep casings or small artificial casings about ¾″–1″ in diameter; they come in continuous rolls and can be bought by the pound or yard. For the quantity of sausage above, you'll need about 3½ yards. Sheep and other natural casings are usually packed in salt and must be soaked about 1 hour in cold water to dissolve out the salt and soften the casings. Attach a moist casing to stuffer as electric mixer manufacturer directs, then force sausage into it. Every 3″–4″, press casing together and twist around once to form links. If you alternate direction of twisting (i.e., twisting clockwise one time and counterclockwise the next), the links will stay linked. Tying each with string in a square knot is foolproof. Work carefully, trying not to tear or break casings. Freeze sausages or store in refrigerator (don't try to keep fresh sausages in refrigerator more than a few days; they're highly perishable).

About 140 calories per *cooked* sausage link; about 370 calories per *cooked* sausage patty.

VARIATIONS:

Mixed Sausage: Prepare basic recipe as directed, but instead of using all pork use 3 pounds lean beef or veal, 2 pounds lean pork, and 1 pound fat pork. About 135 calories per *cooked* sausage link; about 340 calories per *cooked* sausage patty.

Hot Italian-Style Pork Sausage: Omit sage from basic recipe above and add the following: 1 medium-size chopped yellow onion, 1 minced clove garlic, 2 teaspoons paprika, 1 tablespoon crushed dried red chili peppers, 2 teaspoons fennel seeds, ½ teaspoon each crushed bay leaf and thyme, ¼ teaspoon crushed coriander, and ½ cup dry red wine. Put through coarse blade of grinder twice to blend, then stuff into small casings as directed above, twisting into links every 6″ or so. Or do as the Italians do and make one long continuous rope of sausage, coiling it like a garden hose. Freeze or refrigerate. To use, simply cut off the amount you need (see How to Cook Fresh Sausages). About 140 calories per *cooked* sausage link.

Sweet Italian-Style Pork Sausage: Follow recipe for Hot Italian-Style Pork Sausage (above) but reduce amount of crushed dried red chili peppers to 1 teaspoon. About 140 calories per *cooked* sausage link.

Fresh Chorizos (Hot Spanish Sausages): Follow basic recipe above but omit sage and use all lean pork. Add the following: 1

tablespoon oregano, 6 minced cloves garlic, ⅓ cup chili powder, 1 teaspoon ground cumin, 1 tablespoon crushed dried red chili peppers, and ⅔ cup vinegar. Put through coarse blade of grinder twice to blend, then stuff into casings as directed for Italian-style sausages above. About 140 calories per *cooked* sausage link.

⚖ ¢ SCRAPPLE

At hog-butchering time the Pennsylvania Dutch cook any pork scraps with corn meal into a mush called scrapple. This version isn't the original, but it's good.
Makes 6 servings

2 large meaty pork hocks
¼ pound lean pork trimmings
1½ quarts water
1½ teaspoons salt
¼ teaspoon pepper
¾ teaspoon sage
1⅓ cups yellow corn meal

Scrub hocks well under cold running water; scrape skin with a sharp knife to remove any hairs. Place hocks in a large, heavy kettle with water and salt, cover, and simmer 2–2½ hours until meat nearly falls from bones. Lift meat from kettle, discard skin and bones, and coarsely grind meat. Strain broth and skim off fat; wash and dry kettle. Measure 1 quart broth into kettle, add ground meat, pepper, and sage, and bring to a boil. Mix corn meal into remaining cold broth, then add slowly to boiling broth, stirring constantly so it doesn't lump. Continue cooking and stirring until thickened. Turn heat to lowest point, set kettle on an asbestos flame tamer, cover, and let cook about ½ hour. Taste for seasoning and adjust if necessary. Spoon mixture into an ungreased

9″×5″×3″ loaf pan, cover with foil, and chill until firm. To serve, unmold, slice, and panfry following directions given under How to Heat and Serve Fully Cooked Sausages. About 290 calories per serving.

SAUSAGE RING

Makes 6 servings

2 pounds sausage meat
1 cup soft white bread crumbs
1 teaspoon sage
¼ teaspoon nutmeg
¼ teaspoon cloves
2 eggs, lightly beaten
½ cup milk

Preheat oven to 350° F. Mix all ingredients, using your hands. Form into a ring 6″–7″ in diameter in a lightly greased shallow roasting pan. Bake, uncovered, 45 minutes until well browned; remove drippings as they accumulate with a bulb baster. If you like, serve with Pan Gravy or hot Tomato Sauce. Or fill center with Scrambled Eggs or Creamed Mushrooms. About 550 calories per serving (without gravy or sauce, Scrambled Eggs, or Creamed Mushrooms).

SCOTCH EGGS

These eggs are also good quartered and served cold as an appetizer. They are not as difficult to make as they may sound, and the only trick in making the sausage coating stick to the eggs is to make certain the shelled hard-cooked eggs are thoroughly dry.
Makes 4 servings

Shortening or cooking oil for deep fat frying
4 hard-cooked eggs, shelled and patted dry on paper toweling
1 pound sausage meat
⅓ cup unsifted flour

1 egg, lightly beaten with 1
    tablespoon cold water
½ cup toasted seasoned bread
    crumbs

Preheat oven to 400° F. Begin heating shortening in a deep fat fryer over moderately high heat (use basket and deep fat thermometer). Meanwhile, divide sausage into 4 equal parts and mold each around an egg, making as firm and smooth as possible. Dredge lightly in flour, dip in egg, and roll in crumbs to coat evenly. When fat reaches 350° F., fry eggs, 2 at a time, 2–3 minutes until golden brown; drain on paper toweling. Place eggs in an ungreased pie tin and bake, uncovered, 10–15 minutes until sausage is cooked thoroughly. Halve each egg lengthwise and serve hot. Or cool and serve on a bed of crisp salad greens. About 505 calories per serving.

¢ SAUSAGE, MUSHROOM,
    AND RICE CASSEROLE

Makes 4 servings

1 pound fresh sausage links (American style, hot or sweet Italian),
    frankfurters, or kielbasa
2 cups cooked rice
1 (8-ounce) can mushroom stems
    and pieces (do not drain)
1 (10½-ounce) can condensed
    cream of mushroom soup
⅓ cup milk or water
⅓ cup fine cracker crumbs
2 tablespoons finely grated Parmesan
    cheese
2 tablespoons melted butter or
    margarine

Preheat oven to 350° F. Simmer fresh sausages 8 minutes and drain. Cut sausages in ½" chunks and toss with rice, mushrooms, soup, and milk. Spoon into a but-tered 1½-quart casserole; mix crumbs, cheese, and melted butter and scatter over top. Bake, uncovered, ½ hour, brown quickly under broiler, and serve. About 645 calories per serving.

¢ TOAD IN THE HOLE
    (SAUSAGES IN YORKSHIRE
    PUDDING)

Makes 4–6 servings

1 cup sifted flour
1 teaspoon salt
1 cup milk
½ cup cold water
3 eggs, lightly beaten
1 pound fresh sausage links
¼ cup water
¼ cup melted beef or bacon drippings or vegetable shortening
2 cups hot beef gravy (homemade
    or canned)

About 40 minutes before serving time, make batter: mix flour and salt in a bowl, add milk, a little at a time, beating with a rotary or electric beater until smooth. Add water and eggs and beat until bubbly. Cover loosely and set aside ½ hour in a cool place (do not refrigerate). Preheat oven to 450° F. Simmer sausages in water in a covered skillet 8 minutes; drain well on paper toweling. Beat batter until bubbles appear on surface. Pour drippings into a 13½"× 9"×2" baking pan and heat in oven 1–2 minutes until smoking hot. Pour batter into pan and arrange sausages on top here and there. Bake, uncovered, on center oven rack 15–20 minutes until well browned, well risen, and crisp. Cut into large squares and serve piping hot with gravy. About 710 calories for each of 4 servings, 475 calories for each of 6 servings.

¢ KIELBASA-CANNELLINI CASSEROLE

Makes 6 servings

2 tablespoons olive oil
1 kielbasa sausage (about 1½ pounds), cut in ¼" rounds
2 medium-size yellow onions, peeled and chopped fine
2 cloves garlic, peeled and crushed
⅓ cup minced parsley
½ teaspoon fennel seeds, crushed
1 teaspoon coriander seeds, crushed
1 teaspoon oregano
1 teaspoon salt
⅛ teaspoon pepper
2 (1-pound) cans zucchini in tomato sauce (do not drain) or 1 pound fresh zucchini, sliced and sautéed in butter, plus ¾ cup tomato sauce
2 (1-pound 4-ounce) cans cannellini (white kidney beans), drained
1 (6-ounce) can tomato paste

Preheat oven to 350° F. Heat oil in a large, heavy skillet over moderately high heat about 1 minute, add sausage and brown on both sides; drain on paper toweling. Add onions and garlic to skillet and sauté, stirring, 5–8 minutes until golden. Mix in parsley, herbs, salt, and pepper. Return sausage to skillet, add all remaining ingredients, and toss lightly to mix. Transfer to an ungreased shallow 3-quart casserole and bake, uncovered, 1½ hours, stirring occasionally. Serve as main dish. About 610 calories per serving.

SAUSAGE AND PASTRY ROLLS

Good party fare, these can be made ahead and refrigerated or frozen. Cool after baking, wrap, and freeze or refrigerate. To serve, bring to room temperature, then reheat, uncovered, in a 350° F. oven 10–15 minutes.
Makes 4–6 servings

Pastry:
1 recipe Extra Short Pastry
1 egg lightly beaten with 1 tablespoon cold water (glaze)

Filling:
1 pound sausage meat
2 tablespoons soft white bread crumbs
½ teaspoon salt
⅛ teaspoon pepper
2 tablespoons finely grated yellow onion (optional)

Preheat oven to 425° F. Prepare pastry, wrap in foil, and chill while you make the filling. Sauté sausage in a heavy skillet over moderately low heat 10–12 minutes, breaking up meat with a fork and spooning off fat as it accumulates. Transfer to a bowl, add remaining ingredients, and mix well with your hands. Roll half the pastry on a lightly floured cloth into a strip about 3"×15"; brush margins with glaze. Spoon half the filling down center of pastry in a narrow strip. Fold pastry edges over so you have a roll 1½"×15". Press edges together and crimp with a fork. Cut into 3" lengths, make small steam vents in the top of each roll, and arrange 1½" apart on an ungreased baking sheet. Roll, fill, and cut remaining pastry the same way. Brush rolls lightly with glaze, taking care not to cover vents, and bake uncovered 20 minutes until lightly browned. Cool slightly on wire racks. Serve warm as a light entree with relish or chutney or as buffet finger food. About 785 calories for each of 4 servings, 520 calories for each of 6 servings.

BIGOS (POLISH HUNTER'S STEW)

If the following recipe seems intricate, consider the original, once served at royal Polish hunts. It fed around 100 and included ducks, venison, hare (and anything else the hunters had bagged) *plus* Polish sausage, beef, lamb, pork, and chicken—each cooked in a *separate pot*. This version, at least, puts everything into one pot. Makes 6–8 servings

¼ *pound salt pork, trimmed of rind and diced*
½ *pound lean boned beef chuck, cut in 1" cubes*
½ *pound lean boned pork shoulder, cut in 1" cubes*
½ *pound lean boned lamb shoulder, cut in 1" cubes*
1 *(3–3½-pound) frying chicken, cut up*
2 *large yellow onions, peeled and minced*
1 *carrot, peeled and split lengthwise*
2 *stalks celery*
2 *stalks parsley*
6 *peppercorns tied in cheesecloth with 1 bay leaf*
1 *cup beef broth (about—just enough to keep meats from sticking)*
¼ *pound dried mushrooms*
2 *pounds sauerkraut*
1 *kielbasa sausage, sliced ½" thick*
1 *tablespoon sugar*
½ *teaspoon salt*
3 *tablespoons flour blended with ¼ cup cold water*
½ *cup dry Madeira wine*

Brown salt pork in a large, heavy kettle over moderately high heat; remove and set aside. In drippings brown each meat separately; drain on paper toweling. Also brown and drain chicken, adding a little bacon drippings if necessary. Lightly brown onions, return meats to kettle, lay chicken pieces on top, and scatter with salt pork cubes. Add carrot, celery, parsley, cheesecloth bag, and broth, cover, and simmer 1 hour, adding a little extra broth if necessary. Meanwhile, prepare mushrooms for cooking.* Pour their soaking water over sauerkraut, cut mushrooms in thin strips and mix with kraut. Remove vegetables and cheesecloth bag from kettle and discard. Lift out chicken, cut meat from bones, and return to kettle. Add sauerkraut mixture and remaining ingredients and toss carefully to mix. Cover and simmer ½–¾ hour until all meats are tender. Serve with mashed or boiled potatoes. About 755 calories for each of 6 servings, 565 calories for each of 8 servings.

⊠ SOME HOT DOG QUICKIES

Note: Luncheon meats, bologna, mild salamis, and cold cuts can be substituted in any of the recipes calling for sliced or diced frankfurters.

California Splits: Split franks lengthwise, not quite all the way through, and spread half of them with seasoned mashed potatoes or sweet potatoes; top with unspread franks, pressing together like sandwiches. Spread with mild yellow mustard, lay a slice of American or Swiss cheese over each, and bake uncovered 15 minutes at 400° F.

Corny Dogs: Make a batter with ½ cup yellow corn meal, 1 cup sifted flour, 1 teaspoon salt, ¼ teaspoon baking powder, 1 cup milk, and 1 egg; beat until smooth. Dip franks in batter to coat, then fry in deep fat (375° F.) until browned, 2–3 minutes. Drain on paper toweling and dip in mustard as you eat.

QUICK ALPHABET OF SAUSAGES

FRESH SAUSAGES (uncured, unsmoked, uncooked). Cook thoroughly before eating (specific recipes follow).

Name	Description	How to Prepare	Good Accompaniments
Bockwurst	Delicate German veal sausage made in spring at bock beer time; aromatic of onion and/or chives, parsley, nutmeg.	Panfry.	Bock beer.
Bratwurst	Chunky German veal and pork sausage usually seasoned with coriander or caraway, lemon, and ginger. Now being sold precooked as well as fresh.	Panfry, using beer or ale for the initial simmering; drain and brown in butter.	Hashed Brown Potatoes.
Chipolata	Small Italian pork and rice sausages sometimes called "little fingers." Seasonings: chives, thyme, coriander.	Panfry. The French use chipolatas to garnish large roasts and poultry.	Potatoes, roasts, poultry.
Fresh Pork Sausage	The American favorite, a mixture of ground fresh pork and pork fat, seasoned with pepper and sage. It is made under federal inspection, cannot contain more than 3 per cent added moisture or 50 per cent fat. Comes in bulk (loose for patties), links and rolls. *Country Style* is a coarser grind. *New Entry:* Brown 'n Serve links and patties.	*Links:* Simmer, steam, panfry, braise, bake and if first simmered or steamed, broil or charcoal broil. *Patties:* Panbroil, braise. *Roll:* Bake.	Eggs, grits, cooked apples, potatoes, dried beans and lentils.
Fresh Italian-style Pork Sausage	The pizza sausage, hot or sweet; usually made in continuous ropes. One type, *cotechino*, is made with pork skins.	Panfry or braise; use in casseroles and, removed from casings, in spaghetti sauce.	Lentils, dried beans, spaghetti.
Fresh Thuringer	Finely ground pork-veal sausage aromatic of coriander, celery seed, and ginger. Now available "scalded" as well as fresh.	If not "scalded," braise or simmer and brown in butter. Good in Cassoulet.	Potatoes, dried beans.
Loukanika	Greek lamb and pork sausage seasoned with orange rind. Greeks usually cut them in 1" chunks, grill and serve as *meze* (hors d'oeuvre).	Panfry or simmer and broil or charcoal broil.	Fried eggs, tomatoes, rice.

Name	Description	How to Cook	Serve With
Toulouse	Small, coarse-textured French pork sausage; seasoned with garlic and white wine.	Braise or panfry; use in Cassoulet and other casseroles or remove from casing and use in stuffings.	Lentils, dried beans.
Weisswurst	Unusually delicate, small white German sausage made of veal, cream, and eggs. Traditionally served après-midnight at Oktoberfest with rye rolls and sweet German mustard.	Steam.	Rye rolls, sweet mustard, pretzels, beer.

FRESH SMOKED SAUSAGES. Cook thoroughly before eating.

Name	Description	How to Cook	Serve With
Bauernwurst (farmer sausage)	A highly seasoned, super hot dog from Germany; usually coarse of texture.	Steam or simmer, then brown in butter or broil	Sauerkraut.
Country-style Fresh Pork Sausage	A smoked version of fresh country-style sausage; it may be all pork or a combination of pork and beef. Usually sold in links.	Simmer, steam, panfry, braise, bake and, if first simmered or steamed, broil or charcoal broil.	Eggs, grits, apples, potatoes, dried beans.
Romanian Sausage	A lean pork sausage stuffed into casings and flavored with garlic and ginger.	Steam or simmer, then brown in butter or broil.	Potatoes, cabbage.

COOKED SAUSAGES. Usually these are made of fresh meats, though sometimes from cured. They are fully cooked and safe to eat as is, but most will improve if heated through before serving.

Name	Description	How to Cook	Serve With
Andouillette	Small tripe or chitterling sausages that are a specialty of Normandy.	The French way is to make a few shallow slits in sausage and to sauté in butter or to broil or grill, brushing with melted butter.	Mashed or Lyonnaise Potatoes.
Blood Sausage	A large dark sausage made of pig's blood and cubes of pork fat. Occasionally you may find uncooked ones, but most are fully cooked. Certain German varieties are smoked as well.	Uncooked ones must be simmered, then sliced and browned; cooked ones need only be sliced and browned lightly in butter.	Mashed potatoes, sauerkraut.

QUICK ALPHABET OF SAUSAGES (continued)

Name	Description	How to Prepare	Good Accompaniments
Boudins Blancs	Very delicate, very expensive white French sausages made of pork, chicken, cream, eggs, onions, and fine bread crumbs.	Sauté gently in butter or brush with melted butter and broil just to heat.	Mashed potatoes.
Cotto	A soft, cooked Italian salami, usually sold sliced as a sandwich meat.	Use for sandwiches.	Bread, mustard, dill pickles.
Leberkäse	Not a sausage so much as a smooth German pork liver pâté eaten hot instead of cold.	Slice and heat over boiling water in a vegetable steamer or sauté gently in butter.	Steamed: rye bread and mustard. Sautéed: fried onions.
Liver Sausages	Large creamy-smooth links, some highly spiced. Usually made of pork liver mixed with pork and/or veal. American varieties may or may not be smoked; German types almost always are. Liver sausages can be fairly firm or soft enough to spread.	Use as sandwich filling or as a spread for crackers.	Bread (especially rye) and crackers.
Scrapple	The Pennsylvania Dutch invented this pork and corn meal mush combination as a way to use up the odds and ends of hog butchering. Scrapple comes in chunky rolls, both canned and in packages in supermarket meat coolers.	Slice and brown in butter or bacon drippings.	Eggs, grits, fried apples, cabbage, potatoes.

COOKED, SMOKED SAUSAGES: Some (*andouille*, *Bierwurst*, bologna, the German liver sausages) are eaten as is; others (mainly the frankfurter types) will be better if heated through. Specific directions follow.

Andouille	The large French tripe or chitterling sausage is the big brother of *andouillettes*. Unlike them, it is more often sliced thin and eaten cold as an hors d'oeuvre. Occasionally it is sliced and sautéed gently in butter.	Slice and serve cold as an appetizer or heat slices by sautéing in butter.	When sautéed: mashed potatoes.

Berliner Blutwurst	A smoked variation of blood sausage (see Cooked Sausages) containing bacon cubes.	Heat in boiling water, then slice; or, after heating, sauté in butter with onion and apple rings.	Cranberry sauce, sautéed onions and apples.
Berliner Bockwurst	A smoky red Berlin sausage, not unlike our hot dog. It's a favorite late night snack, served steaming from street-corner stands.	Steam or heat in boiling water, then serve.	Sauerkraut; also any of our hot dog trappings.
Bierwurst	A soft, cooked German salami, usually sold sliced as sandwich meat. Garlicky.	Use in making sandwiches.	Beer and bread.
Bologna	The original Bolognese sausage is *mortadella*, a plump, creamy link studded with cubes of fat. True mortadella is air-dried briefly, putting it into the cervelat family. American mortadella is simply fat-studded American bologna — a creamy, pink pork-beef blend with lots of garlic. There are many types: *large, ring, stick* (slightly coarser), *chub* (an ultra smooth mix of beef, pork, and bacon), *Schinkenwurst* (ham bologna), *Lebanon* (a sour, briefly air-dried type from Lebanon, Pa.), all-beef bologna and a delicate veal bologna.	Use in sandwiches, salads, and soups; also see suggestions that follow.	Swiss or American cheese, lettuce, sliced tomatoes, all kinds of bread, mustard, and mayonnaise.
Frankfurters and Wieners	Frankfurters came from Frankfurt, wieners from Vienna; today they're 100 per cent Americanized as hot dogs. Some are all beef (the Kosher), but most are 60 per cent beef and 40 per cent pork. Casings are natural, artificial or non-existent (as in skinless franks). *Vienna sausages* are wieners cut in short links and canned. Most popular frankfurter sizes: *regular* (9-10 franks per lb.), *dinner* (5 per lb.), *foot-long* (4 per lb.) and *cocktail* (26-28 per lb). New entries: *smoked frankfurters* (called *Smoked Links* and sometimes just *Smokies*), *cheese frankfurters*.	See recipes and suggestions that follow.	Almost anything savory.

QUICK ALPHABET OF SAUSAGES (continued)

Name	Description	How to Prepare	Good Accompaniments
German Liver Sausages (liverwursts)	The list is long, but among those especially worth seeking out: *Braunschweiger* (mild and creamy), *Hildesheimer Streichleberwurst* (all calf's liver), *Zwiebelwurst* (with browned onion in it), *Trufflewurst* (with truffles), *Sardellerwurst* (with anchovies).	All are ready-to-eat and best served cold with bread or crackers.	Bread (especially rye), crackers.
Kielbasa	A large garlicky Polish sausage, mostly pork but sometimes with veal or beef. Once available only fresh, *Kielbasa* is now being processed by American packers and sold "fully cooked" or "scalded." Check the labels.	Steam or simmer to heat; cook with sauerkraut; use in stews and casseroles.	Sauerkraut, dried peas, beans, and lentils.
Knackwurst (or knockwurst or knoblauch)	Short chunky German frankfurter highly seasoned with garlic. There's also a Bavarian version called *Regensburger*.	Simmer or steam to warm or cook with sauerkraut. Can be substituted for hot dogs.	Sauerkraut, any of our hot dog condiments.
Strasbourg Liver Sausage	A French liver sausage with pistachio nuts.	Ready-to-eat; use as an appetizer.	Bread, crackers.
Strasbourg Sausage	Sort of a smoked, French hot dog.	Simmer, steam or use in Choucroute Garnie.	Sauerkraut
Tongue Sausage	A large sausage made of tongue and other meats. Available sliced and in links.	Ready-to-eat; use in making sandwiches.	Cheese, bread, mustard, mayonnaise, pickles.

Sausage	Preparation	Serve with
Zungenwurst — A German blood sausage made with tongue and studded with diced fat.	Slice and brown in butter.	Sauerkraut, mashed potatoes.
A SPECIALTY SAUSAGE: This one defies categorizing.		
Mettwurst — A very soft, very fat German pork sausage, bright red in color and aromatic of coriander and white pepper. It is cured and smoked *but not cooked* and it is eaten raw. Because of its spreadability, it is also called *Schmierwurst* (*schmier* meaning *smear*).	Use as a spread for bread.	Bread.

Souper Doggies: Make slits the length of frankfurters, insert strips of cheese the same length. Place in a buttered shallow casserole, sprinkle with ¼ cup minced onion, and pour in 1 (10½-ounce) can cream of mushroom, celery, tomato, or asparagus soup. Bake, uncovered, ½ hour at 350° F.

Texas Hounds: Serve hot dogs in buns smothered with Texas Red or other chili.

Some Additional Hot Dog Quickies

—Sauté franks whole, roll up in pancakes or crepes, and eat out of hand, using mustard as a dip.
—Alternate cocktail franks or Vienna sausages on skewers with cherry tomatoes, whole canned potatoes, and sweet green and red pepper squares. Broil 4″–5″ from heat about 5 minutes, turning often and brushing with All-Purpose Barbecue Sauce until lightly browned.
—Alternate cocktail franks or Vienna sausages on skewers with preserved kumquats, sweet green and red pepper squares, and pineapple chunks and broil 4″–5″ from heat about 5 minutes, turning often and brushing with Plum or Sweet and Sour Sauce.
—Split franks lengthwise, fill with any cheese spread, and broil in buttered buns until browned and bubbly.
—Split franks lengthwise, fill with hot seasoned mashed potatoes mixed with mustard to taste, place in buns, drizzle with melted butter, sprinkle with finely grated cheese, and broil quickly to brown.
—Cut franks in chunks and layer into a casserole of sauerkraut or

pickled red cabbage sprinkled with poppy seeds and bake uncovered ½ hour at 350° F.
– Cut in chunks and layer into a casserole of canned baked beans, creamed corn, ravioli or spaghetti in sauce, or Spanish rice and bake, uncovered, ½ hour at 350° F.
– Chop fine, mix into leftover mashed potatoes, and fry as potato cakes.
– Slice thin and scatter on Pizza.
– Slice thin and fold into scrambled eggs or omelets.
– Slice thin and simmer until hot in 1 (10½-ounce) can split pea soup blended with 1 (10½-ounce) can cream of tomato soup and 2 teaspoons curry powder.
– Slice thin and float in hot vegetable, tomato, potato, or split pea soup.
– Slice thin and toss into potato or macaroni salad.
– Slice thin or dice and add to meatless spaghetti sauce; serve over spaghetti or macaroni.
– Slice thin and use to stretch leftover meat dishes, stews, soups, and casseroles.

What Goes On a Hot Dog Except Mustard, Onions, and the Usual?

– Pickled Red Cabbage
– Hot German Potato Salad
– Carolina Coleslaw
– Wilted Cucumbers
– Creamed Onions
– Batter-fried onion rings
– A ½ and ½ mixture of sautéed minced mushrooms and onions
– Hot sauerkraut
– A ½ and ½ mixture of minced ripe and pimiento-stuffed olives
– Equal parts peeled, seeded, chopped tomatoes, minced onion, and sweet green pepper sautéed in a little butter until "wilted"

– Sour cream, minced onion, and caviar
– Baked beans
– Minced chutney and tiny Cheddar cheese cubes
– Equal parts minced pineapple, celery, and sweet pickle relish
– Spaghetti sauce (with or without meat)
– Sweet-Sour or Plum Sauce
– Any cheese spread
– Any of the sauces or condiments recommended for ham (see Sauces, Gravies, and Seasonings for Ham and Other Cured Pork)

SALAMIS AND CERVELATS (SUMMER SAUSAGES)

These are the original sausages, developed ages ago when salting, drying, and smoking were the only ways to preserve meat. The Italians came up with salamis, the Germans, cervelats. Both are mixtures of chopped pork and/or beef and secret blends of herbs and spices. With few exceptions (cooked kosher salami), both are raw and eaten that way (curing, drying, and smoking render them safe).

For all their similarities, the two are different. Salamis are laden with garlic, cervelats have none; salamis are rarely smoked, cervelats commonly are; salamis are rather coarse of texture; cervelats, generally fine. Salamis are air-dried from 1 to 6 months and thus are usually hard, dry, and shriveled. Cervelats can be dry but more often they are softer and moister—*semidry* is the trade term—having spent only 2 to 5 days in the drying room or smokehouse. Salamis need not be stored in the refrigerator (though they'll keep there almost forever), cervelats should be.

There are dozens of different salamis and cervelats, most of them named after the towns where they are made, as well as other hard peppery links classified as *dry sausages*. Here are some of the more popular.

Salamis

Italian:

Calabrese: A red hot type from Southern Italy.

Campagnole: Rough-textured, spicy peasant salami.

Genoa: One of the best; quite fat and studded with whole peppercorns.

Milano: Finely grained, fairly delicate, flavored with pepper and white wine.

Pepperoni: Small, dry salami-like sausage available both sweet and hot.

Soppressata: A flat oval salami—peppery, gingery, *garlicky!*

German:

Hard Salami: A lean Italian type without all the garlic.

Hungarian: Called simply Hungarian salami, it is mild, often smoked.

French:

Arles: Coarsely grained Provençal sausage with a crisscross cording.

Lyon: Fine, all-pork salami in large casings.

American:

Alessandri, Alpino: Italian types made of pork and beef.

Frizzes: Also Italian style; sweet and peppery types are made, both scented with anise. The sweet is corded with blue string, the hot with red.

Italian: Another American-Italian salami, this one coarsely chopped pork mixed with minced beef, whole peppercorns, and red wine or grape juice.

Kosher: Soft, cooked all-beef salami made under rabbinical supervision. Available sliced and whole.

Cervelats

German:

Cervelatwurst: Finely minced beef and pork, lightly smoked, mildly seasoned with mustard, red and black pepper, sugar, and salt. Semidry.

Farmer Cervelat: Rather soft, small link of coarsely chopped beef and pork in equal proportion. *Farmer Sausage* is a bigger, beefier, smokier version.

Gothaer, Göttinger: Two hard, dry cervelats, one from the town of Gotha, the other from Göttingen.

Holsteiner: Sort of a super Farmer Sausage, heavily smoked; ring-shaped.

Thuringer: Here's the favorite. Often called simply *Summer Sausage*, it's salty but mild, fairly soft. Coriander is the noticeable spice.

Italian:

Mortadella: (see Bologna under Cooked, Smoked Sausages).

Swedish:

Göteborg: A large cardamom-flavored, coarsely textured pork cervelat, smoked and air-dried.

Swiss:

Landjäger: Very smoky, dry, wrinkled black cervelat, pressed into small sticks instead of rolls. It is made of beef and pork.

Other Dry Sausages

Chorizos: Small, hard, dry Spanish sausages, flavored with pimiento, garlic, and red pepper. Especially good with chick-peas, black beans, and other dried peas and beans.

Linguiça: Small, slim Portuguese sausages, saturated with garlic and paprika. A favorite ingredient in Portuguese and Brazilian soups, stews, and casseroles.

Some Ways to Use Salamis and Cervelats

Note about Slicing: A good general rule is "the firmer the sausage, the thinner the slice."

Thin Slices:
– In Antipasto or on hors d'oeuvre trays.
– With a savory spread as open-face sandwiches.
– In sandwiches, solo with mustard or mayonnaise, or in tandem with Swiss, American, or cream cheese.
– In making Pizza or Quick Pizzas.
– In Grilled Cheese Sandwiches.
– Wrapped around small chunks of pineapple, peach, pear, banana, mango or preserved kumquat, skewered and broiled under bastings of Sweet-Sour Sauce.
– Shaped into cornucopias, filled with a savory cheese spread, and served as cocktail snacks.

Diced or Minced (¼–⅓ cup is enough in each instance):
– Teamed with boiled rice, mashed

or Stuffed Baked Potatoes, Lyonnaise or Hashed Brown Potatoes, Macaroni and Cheese.
– Added to Chinese-Style Snow Peas, Green Beans Provençal, Neapolitan Beans with Parmesan, Hopping John, Chick-Pea Pilaf, any boiled dried beans, spinach or other greens dressed with oil and vinegar.
– Added to stuffings for poultry or pork.
– Mixed with cheese, onion, garlic, or other savory dips and spreads.
– Added to Cheese or Mushroom Soufflé.

Julienne Strips (⅓–½ cup is enough):
– In crisp green salads.
– In scrambled eggs or omelets.

LUNCHEON AND OTHER SPECIALTY MEATS

The list is long—and *lengthening*. It includes the familiar canned luncheon loaves and the huge array of cold cuts (many of them borderline sausages) found in supermarket counters. New flavor combinations are arriving almost daily: liverwursts studded with pistachio nuts, ham, or cheese; sandwich meats with olives, pimiento, or cheese. There are peppered meat loaves, honey loaves, pickle and pimiento loaves, plain loaves, and old-fashioned Dutch loaves, not to mention souse and headcheese. The majority of these specialty meats are simply sliced and eaten cold—as is, in sandwiches or cocktail snacks. But they can be used in recipes. And they can be served with flair. See recipes and suggestions that follow, also ideas given in Some Hot Dog Quickies and Some Ways to Use Salamis and Cervelats.

⚔️ **GLAZED BAKED LUNCHEON MEAT LOAF**

Makes 4 servings

1 (12-ounce) can luncheon meat
12 cloves

Glaze:
⅓ cup firmly packed light brown sugar
2 tablespoons cider vinegar
1 teaspoon powdered mustard
⅛ teaspoon allspice

Preheat oven to 350° F. Lay luncheon meat on its side and score top lightly in a crisscross pattern; stud with cloves. Place in a shallow open roasting pan; mix glaze and spread over loaf. Bake, uncovered, about ½ hour until lightly glazed, basting occasionally with glaze runoff. Slice and serve. About 310 calories per serving.

VARIATIONS:

– Cutting almost but not all the way through, divide loaf into 8 equal slices. Into each cut tuck a thin slice of canned pineapple, American cheese, or Spanish onion. Omit cloves but glaze and bake as directed. (*Note:* Loaves with onion or cheese slices may be topped with 1 cup Tomato Sauce or All-Purpose Barbecue Sauce instead of glaze and baked as directed.)
– Score luncheon loaf but omit cloves. Toothpick small chunks of canned pineapple, peaches, or apricots over top, glaze, and bake as directed.
– Omit glaze above and substitute 1 of the following: ⅓ cup maple, light, or dark corn syrup; orange, lemon, or ginger marmalade; any barbecue sauce; apple cider or pineapple juice (these 2 good with

crushed pineapple topping); bake as directed.
– Omit glaze above and substitute any recommended for Baked Ham, using about half as much; bake as directed.

All recipe variations too flexible for meaningful calorie counts.

INDONESIAN FRUIT AND MEAT BAKE

Makes 6 servings

1 (12-ounce) can luncheon meat, diced
2 cups cooked shell macaroni, well drained
1¼ cups drained pineapple tidbits
½ cup peeled, sliced seedless green grapes
3 tablespoons butter or margarine
3 tablespoons flour
2 teaspoons curry powder
½ teaspoon ginger
1 teaspoon salt
¼ teaspoon pepper
1 (13-ounce) can evaporated milk
⅓ cup flaked coconut

Preheat oven to 350° F. Mix meat, macaroni, pineapple, and grapes in an ungreased 1½-quart casserole; set aside. Melt butter in a saucepan over low heat, blend in flour, curry powder, ginger, salt, and pepper; add milk and heat slowly, stirring constantly, until thickened and smooth. Add to casserole and toss lightly to mix. Sprinkle with coconut and bake, uncovered, 25–30 minutes until browned and bubbly.

VARIATION:

Substitute 1¾ cups finely diced frankfurters, Vienna sausages, or bologna for luncheon meat.

Both versions: about 420 calories per serving.

¢ MEATY PEPPER-CORN BAKE

Makes 6 servings

1 (12-ounce) can luncheon meat, diced
2 tablespoons bacon drippings
¼ cup minced yellow onion
⅓ cup minced green pepper
1 (17-ounce) can cream-style corn
1½ cups coarse cracker crumbs
2 tablespoons melted butter or margarine
1 cup evaporated milk or heavy cream
½ teaspoon salt
⅛ teaspoon pepper

Preheat oven to 350° F. Stir-fry meat in drippings until lightly browned; add onion and pepper and stir-fry 5 minutes. Mix in corn. Spoon half of mixture into a greased shallow 2-quart casserole or *au gratin* dish; top with half crumbs, then remaining corn mixture. Toss rest of crumbs with melted butter and scatter over top. Mix milk, salt, and pepper and pour over all. Bake, uncovered, 30–40 minutes until touched with brown. About 425 calories per serving.

¢ LUNCHEON CHEESE BAKE

Makes 4–6 servings

4 slices white bread
2 tablespoons softened butter or margarine
2 teaspoons prepared spicy brown mustard
1½ cups diced luncheon meat
1 cup cubed processed American cheese
3 eggs, lightly beaten
1½ cups milk
1 teaspoon salt
⅛ teaspoon white pepper

Preheat oven to 350° F. Spread bread with butter and mustard and cut in ½″ cubes. Toss with meat and cheese in a buttered 1½-quart casserole. Mix eggs, milk, salt, and pepper and pour into casserole. Bake, uncovered, 50 minutes until puffed and browned. About 520 calories for each of 4 servings, 345 calories for each of 6 servings.

¢ CURRIED LUNCHEON MEAT HASH

Makes 4 servings

2 cups diced, cold, cooked potatoes
2 cups diced luncheon meat
¼ cup minced yellow onion
½ teaspoon celery salt
⅛ teaspoon pepper
⅓ cup mayonnaise or salad dressing
1 tablespoon curry powder
3 tablespoons butter, margarine, or cooking oil

Mix all ingredients except butter in a bowl, cover, and let stand at room temperature ½ hour. Heat butter in a heavy skillet over moderate heat about 1 minute, add mixture, press down, and brown about 15 minutes. Cut hash "cake" in half, turn each over, and brown other side the same way. Serve with chutney. About 480 calories per serving.

LUNCHEON SALAD STUFFED ROLLS

Makes 1 dozen

1 (12-ounce) can luncheon meat, cubed
6 hard-cooked eggs, shelled and quartered
1 sweet green pepper, cored, seeded, and cut in thin strips
1 (4-ounce) can pimientos
1 (8-ounce) jar pimiento-stuffed olives, drained

1 *small yellow onion, peeled and
  quartered*
2 *tablespoons prepared mild yellow
  mustard*
1 *cup mayonnaise or salad dressing
  (about)*
2 *tablespoons steak sauce*
12 *hot dog or hamburger buns, split
  and spread with softened butter or
  margarine*

Preheat oven to 325° F. Put meat,
eggs, green pepper, pimientos, olives,
and onion through fine blade of
meat grinder; mix with mustard,
mayonnaise, and steak sauce
(mixture should be consistency of
cottage cheese, so add more
mayonnaise if needed). Fill buns
with stuffing, close and wrap each
in foil. Bake ½ hour and serve.
About 420 calories per roll.

BOLOGNA TURNOVERS

Makes 6 servings

½ *pound bologna, diced*
1 *(8-ounce) can mixed vegetables,
  drained*
2 *cups canned beef gravy*
1 *(9¼-ounce) piecrust stick*
1 *egg, lightly beaten with 1
  tablespoon cold water*

Preheat oven to 425° F. Mix
bologna, vegetables, and about ¾
cup gravy—just enough to moisten
mixture. Prepare pastry by package
directions and roll thin; cut out 6
(6″) circles (use rerolls, too).
Spoon stuffing on half of each
circle, dividing amount evenly. Fold
pastry over stuffing and crimp
edges with a fork to seal. Place
turnovers on an ungreased baking
sheet, slash tops in 2 or 3 places,
and brush with egg glaze, taking
care not to cover slits. Bake,
uncovered, 25–30 minutes until
golden brown. Heat remaining

gravy and serve with turnovers.
About 380 calories per serving.

⟠ ¢ DEVILED EGG AND
BOLOGNA CASSEROLE

Makes 6 servings

6 *hard-cooked eggs, shelled and
  halved lengthwise*
3 *tablespoons mayonnaise*
2 *teaspoons prepared mild yellow
  mustard*
1 *teaspoon cider vinegar*
¼ *teaspoon garlic salt*
Pinch white pepper
6 *slices bologna*
1 *(10½-ounce) can cream of celery,
  mushroom, or asparagus soup*
½ *cup milk*
¼ *teaspoon onion juice*
1 *pimiento, seeded and chopped fine*
1 *tablespoon minced parsley*

Preheat oven to 350° F. Mash egg
yolks and mix with mayonnaise,
mustard, vinegar, garlic salt, and
pepper; stuff whites with mixture
and put back together, forming
"whole" eggs. Place each egg on a
bologna slice, bring sides up in
center to form bundles and toothpick in place. Place bologna-egg
bundles in an ungreased 1½-quart
casserole. Mix soup, milk, onion
juice, and pimiento and pour over
eggs. Bake, uncovered, 25–30 minutes. Remove toothpicks, sprinkle
with parsley, and serve. About
255 calories per serving.

⊠ Quick Tricks with Luncheon and
Other Specialty Meats

Note: Though listed under sausages,
the packaged, sliced American
bologna is really a cold cut and can
be used in any of the following ways.

– Lay a thin slice of luncheon meat
or a cold cut on a large square of
heavy foil, spread with your favorite
cheese spread, top with another

meat slice, and continue building up layers until you have a stack about 1″–1½″ high. Drizzle with melted butter or, for more flavor, All-Purpose Barbecue Sauce or Sweet-Sour Sauce. Wrap and bake 20–30 minutes at 350° F. To serve, cut straight through in slices about 1″ wide. Serve, if you like, with additional sauce. (4 servings.)
– Mix 1 (8-ounce) package poultry stuffing mix with 2 tablespoons melted butter and just enough water to make it hold together; press into the bottom and up the sides of a buttered 9″×9″×2″ baking pan to form a "crust" and bake, uncovered, 10 minutes at 400° F. Mix 1½ cups diced luncheon meat or cold cuts with 1½ cups Medium White or Cheese Sauce and ¾ cup drained, canned mixed vegetables. Spoon into crust and bake, uncovered, ½ hour at 350° F. Serve at the table by cutting in large squares. (4–6 servings.)

– When making Eggs Benedict, use thinly sliced luncheon or cold cuts instead of ham.
– Make Scalloped Potatoes with Ham as directed, substituting diced luncheon meat or cold cuts for the ham.
– Make Creamed Chipped Beef or Creamed Chipped Beef and Mushrooms, substituting minced luncheon meat or cold cuts for chipped beef; increase salt as needed.
– Shape cold cuts into cornucopias, fill with hot, seasoned, mashed sweet potatoes, drizzle with pineapple juice or honey, and brown quickly under broiler.
– Fry thin bologna slices in a hot, lightly greased skillet until they curl into "cups"; fill with creamed onions, potatoes, peas, or mixed vegetables; with puréed peas or spinach; with Hot Macédoine of Vegetables, Hot German Potato Salad, fluffy, seasoned mashed potatoes, or sweet potatoes.

CHAPTER 9

GAME AND GAME BIRDS

Cooking game is no more mysterious than roasting beef, frying chicken, or stewing lamb. It's just that the "bag" is often brought home whole and the average woman is shocked numb at the idea of skinning or plucking and butchering. Well, cleaning game isn't as neat as peeling a potato, but fortunately the messiest job (eviscerating) will probably have been done in the field. As for the rest—skinning, aging, cutting up a carcass—there are butchers in most parts of the country who will do these jobs for you—even if you have shot the game yourself; some will even package and label cuts for the freezer. In many big cities, gourmet markets sell fresh game in season and frozen game year round. More and more game (especially rabbit and buffalo) and game birds (ducks, geese, and pheasant) are being raised for the table. Still, in rural areas, you may have to go after your own game or befriend someone who does.

About Quality

Game bought from a reputable market will have been federally inspected (to ensure wholesomeness) and because of the fussiness of game fanciers, will usually be of high quality as well. But that which your husband or neighbor shoots may not be. Three factors determine quality: *age of the animal* (the younger, the better), *diet*, and *care the kill was given in the field* (more potentially good game is lost through sloppy field handling than for any other reason). As soon as an animal

or bird is shot, it should be eviscerated (especially important on warm days), and large animals must also be bled. The process is too complicated to include here; the best way to learn is firsthand from an experienced hunting guide or secondhand from a detailed hunting manual. As for the age of the animal, hunting guides can quickly judge (usually by looking at an animal's teeth or bird's beak, feet, or breastbone), and so can most butchers. Diet, obviously, is more difficult to determine because a wild creature will eat what it must in order to survive. Still, there are clues. Certain species prefer certain kinds of food. As a general rule, vegetarians are better flavored than meat or fish eaters. Where an animal or bird is bagged can also suggest what it's been eating. For example, a deer shot in an evergreen thicket may have nibbled evergreen berries and thus taste of them. Here again, an experienced hunter can advise you. He can also show you how to sniff the ruffled feathers of a duck or goose to determine whether it's been eating fish. And he can judge the general health of an animal or bird by examining the fur or feathers.

How do you determine quality of game in a store? Much the way you do for any other meat. Venison and other red meat should be moist (not wet) and velvety with a clean fresh smell. Birds and small game should also be moist, their flesh springy to the touch, of good color and odor with little or no shot damage.

About Food Value

Game and game birds are high protein foods; most are lean because they are well exercised.

FURRED GAME

Large Animals: Choicest is venison, the meat of deer and other antlered animals. Buffalo, now being raised for the table, has a fine "beefy" flavor. Some people like bear, which tastes like pork and, like it, must be cooked until well done because of the danger of trichinosis (see Pork). There is very little wild boar

around; most of that sold in this country is shipped in frozen from Europe. Cuts of large game are much like those of other meat animals (see Beef, Lamb, and Pork Charts), the tenderest coming from the little-exercised rib and loin, the toughest from the neck, leg, rump, and flank.

About the Heart and Liver: These delicacies are often eaten in camp by hunters because they don't travel well. They should be removed from the carcass immediately, plunged into cold water to remove the animal heat, then kept cool. Prepare as you would beef or calf's heart and liver.

Small Animals: More rabbit is eaten in this country than all other furred game put together. It has light, delicate meat, much like that of chicken, and is a popular supermarket item. Squirrel is popular quarry too, though gamier and darker fleshed. Gamier still, and less often eaten, are opossum, raccoon, and muskrat. Butchers may be less inclined to dress small game that you have bagged yourself than the large, so you may have to do it yourself. The eviscerating and bleeding, as mentioned earlier, should have been done in the field; what remain are the skinning and final dressing.

To Skin Rabbits and Squirrels: Note: Always wear rubber gloves. Though it's unlikely an animal is diseased, tularemia, an infectious disease transmitted to man through cuts and scratches can't be discounted altogether. The surest way to tell if an animal is diseased is by looking at its liver; a healthy liver will be dark red, moist, and velvety, a diseased liver splotched with white. Though thorough cooking will make a diseased animal safe to eat, most people prefer not to chance it.

The first step in skinning is to hang the animal upside down by its legs and to make incisions in the skin as shown opposite.

Next, begin peeling skin from flesh, working from the feet toward the head—with a rabbit, the job's as easy as taking off gloves. Squirrels are more difficult because their skin is more firmly attached to the flesh. You will have to work more slowly, freeing skin as needed with a knife. (*Note:* Raccoons and muskrats require slightly different techniques; opossums are not skinned at all but scraped free of hairs after being

scalded. A good hunting manual will describe each process in detail.)

Final Dressing: Remove the scent or musk glands located in the fat underneath the forelegs (the equivalent of the armpit) and in the small of the back. These are small yellow kernels that can be flicked out with the point of a knife. Singe off any remaining hair, also cut out shot-damaged flesh.

Cutting Up Rabbits and Squirrels: Cut off head, tail, and feet and discard. The animal can be stuffed whole and pot roasted or cut up and fried, braised, or stewed. Simply sever at the joints and cut back and breast into 3 or 4 pieces.

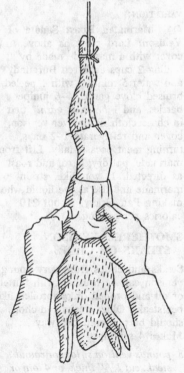

Rabbit

Squirrel

How Much Game Per Person?
When the animal or cut is unusually
bony, allow ¾–1 pound per person,
otherwise ⅓–½ pound.

About Frozen Game: Much of the
game sold today is frozen. Thaw
thoroughly before cooking, then
prepare as you would fresh game.
The best way to thaw game is in its
original wrapper in the refrigerator;
1″ steaks will take about 12 hours,
small roasts 3–4 hours per pound,
and large roasts 4–6 hours per
pound.

⚖ **ROAST SADDLE OF
　VENISON**

Rack and loin of venison are
excellent roasts, but the saddle
(double loin) is choicest of all. If
young and tender, it can be roasted
like lamb; if of doubtful age, it
should be marinated before roasting,
and if mature it should be pot
roasted like beef. The best way to
tell an animal's age is to look at
the bones. The bones of a young
animal will be spongy and red
inside, those of an older animal will
appear flinty. Because venison is
lean, it should be larded *and*
barded to keep it from drying out,
and it should not be roasted beyond
medium rare. Though some cooks
sear venison at a high temperature,
then finish roasting at a low heat, it
seems juiciest when roasted at
350° F. throughout.
Makes 8 servings

½–¾ *pound fat back or salt pork*
1 (*5–6-pound*) *saddle of venison*
½ *pound suet, cut in ½″ cubes*

Cut ½ the fat back into lardoons
¼″ wide and 2″–3″ long and cut
the rest into thin slices for barding.*
Pique* ends of roast with lardoons,
then bard outer curved side. Let
roast come to room temperature;
meanwhile, preheat oven to 350°

F. Stand saddle fat side up in a
shallow roasting pan and insert a
meat thermometer in largest lean
muscle, not touching bone. Scatter
suet in bottom of pan. Roast, uncovered, 15–20 minutes per pound
for rare (125–30° F.) and 25
minutes per pound for medium
rare (140–45° F.), basting frequently with pan drippings and
removing suet cubes as they brown.
About 15 minutes before roast is
done, remove barding fat. When
done, lift saddle to a hot platter
and let "rest" 10 minutes before
carving. If you like, make Pan
Gravy. Carve in long slices the
length of saddle—and don't forget
choice morsels of tenderloin tucked
underneath the ribs. About 200
calories per serving.

VARIATION:

⚖ **Marinated Roast Saddle of
Venison:** Lard roast as above,
cover with a marinade made by
boiling 2 cups each red Burgundy
and water 5 minutes with 1 peeled,
bruised clove garlic, 4–6 juniper
berries, and 1 *bouquet garni** tied
in cheesecloth. Pour over venison,
cover and refrigerate 1–2 days,
turning meat occasionally. Lift from
marinade, pat dry, bard, and roast
as directed. If you like, strain
marinade and use as the liquid when
making Pan Gravy. About 210
calories per serving.

**SMOTHERED VENISON
　STEAKS OR CHOPS**

Steaks and chops from very young
venison can be brushed with butter
or oil and broiled or panbroiled like
beefsteaks. Older steaks and chops
should be prepared this way.
Makes 4 servings

3 *pounds venison sirloin or round
steak, cut 1½″ thick, or 4 loin or
rib chops, cut 1½″ thick*

⅓ cup unsifted flour
1½ teaspoons salt
¼ teaspoon pepper
3 tablespoons bacon or beef
  drippings or cooking oil
1 large yellow onion, peeled and
  minced
2 stalks celery, minced
2 small carrots, peeled and minced
2 cups hot beef broth or water
¾ cup sour cream at room
  temperature (optional)

Dredge steaks in a mixture of flour, salt, and pepper, then brown on both sides in drippings in a large, heavy skillet over moderately high heat or in an electric skillet set at 400° F. Remove meat and set aside. Stir-fry onion, celery, and carrots in drippings 8 minutes until golden. Return meat to pan, spoon vegetables on top, sprinkle with 1 tablespoon flour dredging mixture, and pour in broth. Turn heat to low (325° F. on electric skillet), cover, and simmer 30–40 minutes until tender—chops will take 30–40 minutes, steaks 1–1½ hours. Baste 1 or 2 times during cooking. Serve steaks topped with vegetables and pan juices, which will have thickened into gravy. If you like, smooth sour cream into gravy just before serving.

VARIATION:

Oven-Braised Venison Steak: Brown venison and vegetables as directed, transfer to an ungreased 3-quart casserole, cover, and bake 1½–2 hours at 300° F. until tender.

Both versions: about 400 calories per serving (without sour cream).

RAGOUT OF VENISON

Makes 4–6 servings

2 pounds boned venison shoulder,
  neck, or shank, cut in 1"–1½"
  cubes

½ cup unsifted flour
1½ teaspoons salt
¼ teaspoon pepper
2 tablespoons cooking oil
8 scallions, minced (include green
  tops)
¾ pound mushrooms, wiped clean
  and sliced thin
2 (10½-ounce) cans beef bouillon
1 teaspoon prepared mild yellow
  mustard
1 tablespoon Worcestershire sauce
2 tablespoons flour blended with ¼
  cup cold water

Dredge venison by shaking in a bag with flour, salt, and pepper. Brown in oil in a large, heavy kettle over moderately high heat; remove and set aside. Stir-fry scallions and mushrooms in drippings 3–5 minutes until mushrooms are golden, add meat to kettle, also all but the final ingredient. Stir well, cover, and simmer 1½–2 hours until venison is fork tender. Mix in flour paste and heat, stirring, until thickened and no raw starch taste remains. Serve with wild rice or buttered noodles. About 425 calories for each of 4 servings (without wild rice or noodles), 285 calories for each of 6 servings.

⊠ VENISONBURGERS

Venison shank, neck, shoulder, and scraps make excellent burgers mixed with sausage meat or fat pork. They must be cooked well done.
Makes 3–4 servings

⅔ pound venison, ground once
⅓ pound fat pork (cheek, jowl,
  trimmings), ground once, or ⅓
  pound sausage meat
2 tablespoons cooking oil, butter,
  margarine, or bacon drippings
1 teaspoon salt
⅛ teaspoon pepper

Lightly mix venison and pork and

shape into 3 plump patties or 4 slim ones. Brown in oil in a large, heavy skillet over moderately high heat 6–7 minutes on each side until well done. Season with salt and pepper just before serving. About 355 calories for each of 3 servings, 265 calories for each of 4 servings.

VARIATIONS:

⚖ **Rare Venisonburgers:** Mix 4 parts ground venison with 1 part ground suet, shape and cook as directed, allowing 4–5 minutes per side. About 240 calories for each of 3 servings, 180 calories for each of 4 servings.

Venison Loaf: Mix 4 parts ground venison with 1 part ground suet and substitute for beef in meat loaves.

BROILED BUFFALO STEAKS

The buffalo being raised for the table is surprisingly delicate and tender, rather like lean beef. The cuts of buffalo are similar to beef (see Beef Chart) and similarly prepared, the not-so-tender shoulder, rump, flank, and shanks being best for stews and the tender rib and loin perfect for steaks and roasts. Where do you buy buffalo? From a gourmet meat market. How do you cook it? Here are two ways (for other ideas, use recipes for beef, substituting comparable cuts of buffalo).
Makes 4 servings

4 *buffalo rib or loin steaks, cut about 1″ thick*
Cooking oil (optional)
4–6 crushed juniper berries (optional)
Salt
Pepper

Preheat broiler. If steaks seem extra lean, brush well with oil. For

a woodsy flavor, also rub with juniper berries. Let stand at room temperature 1–1½ hours if convenient. Place steaks on a well-greased broiler pan and broil 2″ from the heat about 3 minutes on a side for very rare, 4 for rare, and 5 for medium rare. (*Note:* Because of its leanness, buffalo will toughen and dry if cooked beyond medium rare.) Season with salt and pepper and serve. About 350–450 calories per serving, depending upon how well marbled with fat the meat is.

VARIATION:

Charcoal-Broiled Buffalo Steaks: Prepare a hot charcoal fire.* Prepare steak for cooking as above, then broil 4″ from the coals about 3 minutes on a side for very rare, 4–5 for rare, and 6 for medium rare. Calorie counts the same as for Broiled Buffalo Steaks.

BEAR OR WILD BOAR POT ROAST

Loin of young bear or wild boar, also wild boar hams, can be roasted like pork, and like it must be served well done because of the danger of trichinosis. When in doubt about age or tenderness of a cut, pot roast. Always trim fat from bear meat—it has a strong, gamy flavor.
Makes 8–10 servings

1 *(5–7-pound) bear rump roast or wild boar ham*
2 *tablespoons bacon or beef drippings*
1 *teaspoon salt*
¼ *teaspoon pepper*
1 *tart apple, peeled and cored*
1 *medium-size yellow onion, peeled*
1½ *cups apple cider or beef broth*

Gravy:
1 *large carrot, peeled and grated fine*

1 *stalk celery, minced*
2 *tablespoons butter, margarine,*
   bacon or beef drippings
¼ *cup unsifted flour*
1 *cup beef broth*
½ *teaspoon salt*
⅛ *teaspoon pepper*
⅛ *teaspoon liquid gravy browner*

Trim bear of fat; if using boar, remove skin and trim fat to ½". Heat drippings in a large, heavy kettle over moderate heat and brown meat on all sides, about 15 minutes. Add all but gravy ingredients, cover, and simmer 3½–4 hours until tender. Transfer to a hot platter and keep warm while making gravy; strain kettle liquid and reserve. Stir-fry carrot and celery in butter in a large skillet over moderate heat 8–10 minutes until carrot is tender; sprinkle with flour and brown lightly, stirring. Add kettle liquid and remaining gravy ingredients and heat, stirring, until thickened. Slice meat, not too thin, and serve with plenty of gravy. About 500 calories for each of 8 servings, 400 calories for each of 10 servings.

ROAST WHOLE RABBIT

Makes 4 servings

1 *(3-pound) young, tender rabbit,*
   cleaned and dressed (reserve liver,
   heart, and kidneys)
1 *teaspoon salt*
¼ *teaspoon pepper*
6 *slices bacon or salt pork*
½ *cup water*

Preheat oven to 350° F. Rub rabbit inside and out with salt and pepper; close cavity with poultry pins. Arrange rabbit breast side down in a crouching position on a rack in a large, heavy kettle. Drape with bacon, add water, cover, and bake ¾ hour; uncover and bake ½ hour.

Remove bacon, baste with drippings, and bake 15 minutes longer until browned and fork tender. While rabbit roasts, make giblet stock* from liver, heart, and kidneys. When rabbit is done, remove to a hot platter, remove poultry pins, and let "rest" 10 minutes; make Pan Gravy using giblet stock. *To carve:* Cut off fore and hind legs and sever at each joint; split rabbit down center back, using poultry shears if necessary, then carve down along ribs. About 420 calories per serving.

VARIATIONS:

Roast Stuffed Rabbit: Loosely stuff rabbit with 1–1½ cups savory stuffing (see Some Sauces, Gravies, and Seasonings for Game and Game Birds). Sew cavity shut and roast as directed. About 515 calories per serving.

Roast Cut-Up Rabbit: Have rabbit disjointed; rub with salt and pepper, arrange on a rack in a heavy kettle, and drape with bacon or brush lavishly with melted butter, margarine, or bacon drippings. Add water and roast as directed, basting often with additional butter during last 15 minutes if bacon is not used. About 420 calories per serving.

Crisp Oven-"Fried" Rabbit: Have rabbit disjointed; dip in melted butter, then in seasoned bread crumbs to coat. Arrange in a greased shallow baking pan, cover with foil, and bake 1 hour. Uncover and bake 30 minutes longer without turning but basting often with melted butter, until crumbs are crisp and brown. About 460 calories per serving.

Oven-Barbecued Rabbit: Have rabbit disjointed and marinate in 1–1½ cups favorite barbecue sauce 3–4 hours in refrigerator. Lift rabbit from sauce, arrange on a rack in a shallow baking pan, add ½ cup water, cover with foil, and bake 45 minutes; uncover and bake 45 minutes longer, brushing often with barbecue sauce. About 460 calories per serving.

¢ FRIED RABBIT WITH PLANTATION GRAVY

Makes 4 servings

1 (3-pound) rabbit, cleaned, dressed, and disjointed
½ cup unsifted flour
1½ teaspoons salt
¼ teaspoon pepper
½ cup butter or margarine

Gravy:
3 tablespoons flour
1 cup chicken broth
1 cup milk
½ teaspoon salt
⅛ teaspoon pepper
⅛ teaspoon thyme
⅛ teaspoon marjoram

Dredge rabbit by shaking in a bag with flour, salt, and pepper. Melt butter in a large skillet over moderate heat and brown rabbit evenly on all sides, about 5 minutes. Turn heat to low, cover, and cook 1–1½ hours until fork tender, turning once or twice. For a crispy coating, cook uncovered the last 15 minutes. Transfer rabbit to a hot platter and keep warm. For the gravy, blend flour into pan drippings but do not brown. Add broth and milk, then seasonings; heat, stirring, until thickened. Pass gravy separately. About 400 calories per serving.

VARIATION:

Rabbit with Tarragon and White Wine: Brown rabbit as directed, sprinkle with 2 tablespoons minced fresh tarragon or 1 teaspoon dried tarragon, cover, and cook as above.

When making gravy, substitute 1 cup dry white wine for milk, omit the herbs, and stir in ¼ cup heavy cream just before serving. About 440 calories per serving.

¢ RABBIT STEW

Makes 4 servings

1 (3-pound) rabbit, cleaned, dressed, and disjointed
1 large yellow onion, peeled and coarsely chopped
4–5 medium-size carrots, peeled and cut in 1″ chunks
1½ teaspoons salt
⅛ teaspoon white pepper
½ teaspoon grated lemon rind
⅛ teaspoon mace (optional)
1½ cups water
½ cup milk
2 tablespoons butter or margarine
2 tablespoons flour blended with ¼ cup milk
1 tablespoon minced parsley

Place all but last 2 ingredients in a heavy kettle, cover, and simmer about 1½ hours until rabbit is fork tender. Blend in flour mixture and heat, stirring, until slightly thickened and no raw starch taste remains. Sprinkle with parsley and serve. About 450 calories per serving.

VARIATIONS:

¢ Rabbit Stew with Dumplings: Prepare stew as directed. Prepare 1 recipe Dumplings, drop on top of stew and cook as dumpling recipe directs. Sprinkle with parsley and serve. About 625 calories per serving.

¢ Rabbit Pie: Prepare stew as directed but omit carrots; spoon into an ungreased 2″–3″ deep 2-quart casserole and place a pie funnel in center. Preheat oven to 425° F. Prepare 1 recipe Flaky Pastry I and roll into a circle 3″ larger than casserole. Dampen casserole rim, lay pastry over rabbit, fold edges under, and crimp to seal. Brush with 1 egg yolk mixed with 1 tablespoon cold water; make a hole in pastry over pie funnel. Bake 30–40 minutes until golden brown. About 795 calories per serving.

¢ HASENPFEFFER (PEPPERY RABBIT STEW)

Germans prepare *Hasenpfeffer* many ways. In farm homes it's simply done as in the recipe below, in restaurants (and in Pennsylvania Dutch country) it's more highly spiced.
Makes 4 servings

1 (3-pound) rabbit, cleaned, dressed, and disjointed (save liver, heart, and kidneys)
¼ teaspoon peppercorns
¼ teaspoon mustard seeds
4 cloves
3 bay leaves
1 cup cider vinegar
1 cup water
1 large yellow onion, peeled and sliced very thin
½ cup plus 2 tablespoons unsifted flour
¼ cup butter, margarine, or bacon drippings
½ cup dry red wine or water
1 teaspoon salt
1 teaspoon sugar

Remove all fat from rabbit; place rabbit in a deep bowl with liver, heart, and kidneys. Tie spices and bay leaves in cheesecloth and simmer, covered, with vinegar, water, and onion 5 minutes; pour over rabbit, cover, and refrigerate 1–2 days, turning rabbit occasionally. Lift rabbit from marinade (do not dry) and dredge in ½ cup flour; brown in butter in a large, heavy skillet over moderate heat 4–5 minutes. Transfer to a 3-quart kettle. Brown remaining flour in drippings; strain marinade, add, and heat, stirring, until thickened. Pour over rabbit, add onion and cheesecloth bag, also remaining ingredients, cover, and simmer 1–1½ hours until rabbit is tender. Shake kettle occasionally and check liquid level, adding a little extra water if mixture thickens too much. Serve with Potato Dumplings or noodles. About 370 calories per serving (without dumplings or noodles).

VARIATION:

¢ **Pennsylvania Dutch Hasenpfeffer:** When making marinade, substitute 1 teaspoon mixed pickling spice for the peppercorns, mustard seeds, and cloves. Proceed as directed, using ½ cup water instead of wine when cooking rabbit. Just before serving, stir in 2–3 crushed gingersnaps and 1 cup sour cream. Heat 1–2 minutes but do not boil. Good with mashed potatoes and boiled rutabaga. About 490 calories per serving (without potatoes and rutabaga).

JUGGED HARE OR RABBIT

Hare is European, jack rabbit the American counterpart; either can be "jugged" and so can any rabbits. The best jug is a deep brown earthenware pot, but a heavy casserole will do. Hare's blood used to be used to thicken the gravy, but few hunters today bother to save the blood of game (it must be caught in a clean plastic bag, then mixed with a little vinegar to keep it liquid).
Makes 8 servings

1 (5–6-pound) hare or jack rabbit or 2 (2½–3-pound) rabbits, cleaned, dressed, and disjointed

1 cup unsifted flour
4 slices bacon
2 tablespoons butter or margarine
1½ teaspoons salt
¼ teaspoon pepper
2 bay leaves
½ teaspoon thyme
½ teaspoon sage
1 tablespoon minced parsley
1 large yellow onion, peeled and
*   stuck with 4 cloves*
1 (2") strip lemon rind
⅛ teaspoon cayenne pepper
2 cups beef broth
2 cups dry port or red Bordeaux wine
2 tablespoons red currant jelly
Blood from hare or rabbits or ¼ cup
*   unsifted flour blended with ½ cup*
*   cold water*

Preheat oven to 325° F. Dredge hare by shaking in flour in a bag. Brown bacon in a large skillet over moderate heat, crumble, and reserve. Brown hare in drippings and butter, a few pieces at a time, then transfer to an ungreased 6-quart bean pot or deep casserole. Add bacon and all but last 2 ingredients, cover tightly, and bake until tender, 2–3 hours for hare or jack rabbit, 1–1½ hours for rabbit. Discard lemon peel and onion. Stir jelly and blood into liquid, return to oven, and bake uncovered 5 minutes; do not boil or mixture will curdle. *Or* ladle about ½ cup hot liquid into flour paste, blend in jelly, and stir into pot. Bake uncovered about 5 minutes, stirring once, until thickened. Serve hare from the pot. Good with Forcemeat Balls—they can be fried or simmered on top of jugged hare (see Forcemeat Ball recipe). Pass red currant jelly. About 340 calories per serving (without Forcemeat Balls).

¢ SQUIRREL FRICASSEE

Gray squirrels are better eating than the red. Prepare by either of the following recipes, cook like a rabbit, or use in place of chicken in Brunswick Stew (the original Brunswick Stew was made with small furred game).
Makes 2 servings

1 squirrel, cleaned, dressed, and
*   disjointed*
⅓ cup unsifted flour
1 teaspoon salt
¼ teaspoon pepper
3 tablespoons butter or margarine
1 medium-size yellow onion, peeled
*   and minced*
1 clove garlic, peeled and crushed
*   (optional)*
¼ cup julienne strips of lean ham
¾ cup chicken broth
¼ cup milk or light cream
1 tablespoon flour blended with ¼
*   cup milk or light cream*

Dredge squirrel in a mixture of flour, salt, and pepper, then brown in a heavy saucepan in butter over moderately high heat. Add all but last ingredient, cover, and simmer about 1 hour until tender. Blend in flour paste and heat, stirring, until thickened. Taste for salt and pepper and adjust as needed. Serve with hot biscuits. About 500 calories per serving (without biscuits).

¢ CASSEROLE OF SQUIRRELS AND RICE

Makes 4–6 servings

¼ pound salt pork, cut in small dice
2 squirrels, cleaned, dressed, and
*   disjointed*
2 medium-size yellow onions, peeled
*   and minced*
¾ cup uncooked rice
1 medium-size sweet green pepper,
*   cored, seeded, and minced*

1 (1-pound) can tomatoes (do not drain)
1 cup chicken broth
½ teaspoon salt
¼ teaspoon pepper

Preheat oven to 325° F. Brown salt pork in a 3-quart flameproof casserole over moderately low heat; remove with a slotted spoon and reserve. Pour off all but 2 tablespoons drippings, raise heat to moderate, and brown squirrels lightly all over, 5–7 minutes; lift out and set aside. Stir-fry onions, rice, and green pepper in drippings 2–3 minutes until rice is straw colored, return meat and salt pork to casserole, add remaining ingredients, breaking tomatoes up. Cover and bake ½ hour, stir mixture, re-cover, and bake about ½ hour longer until squirrels are tender. About 510 calories for each of 4 servings, 340 calories for each of 6 servings.

¢ BRAISED RACCOON, WOODCHUCK, OPOSSUM, OR MUSKRAT

Very young raccoon, opossum, woodchuck, and muskrat are tender enough to roast like rabbit, but the average animals aren't. Braising is the way to make them tender. The fat of these animals is strong-flavored, so remove it before cooking.
Makes 4–6 servings

1 raccoon, woodchuck, or opossum or 2 medium-size muskrats, cleaned, dressed, and disjointed
1 cup unsifted flour
3 teaspoons salt
¼ teaspoon pepper
¼ cup bacon or beef drippings
1 pound small white onions, peeled
3 cups water or a ½ and ½ mixture of beef broth and water
6–8 medium-size carrots, peeled and cut in 2″ chunks

½ small rutabaga, peeled and cut in 1–1½″ cubes

Discard any fat from animal, then dredge in flour mixed with 2 teaspoons salt and the pepper. Brown in drippings in a large, heavy kettle over high heat, 5–7 minutes; lift out and set aside. Brown onions in drippings 10–12 minutes over moderate heat; add water and stir, scraping up browned bits. Return meat to kettle, add remaining ingredients, including remaining salt. Cover and simmer until tender, 3–4 hours depending on age and size of animal. If you prefer, transfer kettle to a 325° F. oven and bake, covered, 30–40 minutes per pound of animal. Lift meat and vegetables to a hot deep platter, top with a little cooking liquid, and pass the rest. Good with applesauce. Calorie counts unavailable for raccoon, woodchuck, opossum and muskrat.

GAME BIRDS

America has about a dozen different families of game birds—everything from dark-fleshed ducks and geese to delicate white-meated pheasants. With one or two exceptions, game birds can be prepared by the same basic methods. Because these methods are determined more by the size of the bird than by the kind or color of its flesh, birds are grouped here by size.

America's Popular Game Birds

Giant Game Birds (8–16 pounds):

Wild Turkey: These huge, often sinewy birds are in a category by themselves.

Large Game Birds (4–9 pounds):

Wild Goose: Wild goose usually means *Canada Goose*, but good, too, is the smaller (3–4 pounds) *Brant*.

Medium-Size Game Birds (1–4 pounds):

Wild Duck: The best table ducks are *Mallards, Pintails, Canvasbacks, Ring-Necks, Redheads, Gadwalls, Wood Ducks, Black Ducks, Ruddy Ducks, Scaups,* and the small (usually about ¾ pound) *Teals* (*Green-Winged, Blue-Winged, Cinnamon*). All feed upon grasses, seeds, and grains and usually (though not invariably) have fine flavor. Not so fine are the fish-eating ducks: *Mergansers, Scoters, Harlequins, Goldeneyes, Buffleheads, Old Squaws,* and *Shovelers.*

Other Waterfowl: Coots (Mud Hens) and *Gallinules.* These plump, chicken-like birds may or may not have good flavor—depends upon what they've been eating and how brackish their habitat.

Upland Birds: Pheasant, all large *Grouse* (*Ruffed, Sage, Blue, Sharp-Tailed, Prairie Chicken*). (*Note:* In America, grouse are often called partridge. There are, however, two true partridges in America [see Small Game Birds]).

Small Game Birds (¼–1 pound):

Quail, especially *Bobwhite;* small *Grouse* (*Spruce* and *Ptarmigan*); *Partridge* (*Gray* and *Chukar*); *Dove, Pigeon,* and *Squab* (young pigeon); *Woodcock, Snipe.* Plovers were popular once, but they have been overkilled and are now protected.

About Frozen and Canned Game Birds: Gourmet markets sell most of the popular game birds frozen,

also canned small birds. Always prepare frozen birds by wrapper directions, if any. If not, thaw in the refrigerator in the original wrapper before cooking; allow about 24 hours for small- or medium-size birds, 1½–2 days for a wild goose or turkey up to 12 pounds. Giblets are usually tucked inside the body cavity and should be removed as soon as possible; thaw separately. Once thawed, prepare frozen birds as you would the fresh; never refreeze. Canned birds are already cooked and need only be heated before serving (follow can directions). Those that have been smoked may have strong flavor; to tone it down, simmer in water to cover about 10 minutes, drain, pat dry, and then follow label instructions.

How Much Game Bird Per Serving? Allow about 1 pound dressed bird per serving; if birds are very small, this may mean 2–3 birds per person.

How to Clean and Dress Game Birds

The procedure is similar for all birds, though downy ducks and geese require an extra plucking. In days past, birds were bled after being shot, but newer bullets eliminate the need. When birds are eviscerated depends upon weather and whether or not they're to be hung. In cold weather, they needn't be gutted immediately, and, of course, if they are to be hung, they should not be drawn until after hanging.

To Hang: Nowadays, birds are hung only until cold or, at most, 24 hours. If you prefer a gamier flavor, however, by all means hang the bird longer. Pick a cool, dry, shady, well-ventilated spot away from insects and pets and hang undressed, undrawn birds by their feet. How long? Depends on weather (birds ripen faster in warm weather), the bird's age (old birds need to hang longer than young), and the sophistication of your palate. Usually, 2–3 days' hanging will produce a pretty "high" bird. Best tests: Pluck a feather from just above the tail; if it pulls out easily, the bird has hung long enough. Or ruffle abdomen feathers; if the skin has a blue-green tinge, the bird is ready for cooking.

To Remove Feathers: All but the smallest birds with superfragile skin should be plucked and if possible, dry plucked (dunking a bird in hot water affects flavor). Chill bird 24 hours, then, starting at the neck, pull out feathers, a few at a time, in quick gentle jerks against the grain. Use a light touch over the breast, where skin is tender. When bird is plucked, tweeze out pinfeathers. *Tip:* The neatest way to pluck is outdoors, directly into a paper bag. Never burn feathers—the smell is horrendous. If a bird won't dry pluck, dunk head first into a large kettle of simmering water and let stand about 15 seconds; repeat 3–4 times. Shake off excess moisture and pluck as above.

To Remove Duck and Goose Down: Pluck outer feathers. Melt paraffin in boiling water in a large pot (for each bird you'll need 1 cake paraffin and 2 quarts water). Dip birds head first into pot to coat, remove, and cool until paraffin hardens. Peel off paraffin and the down will come away with it. Redip and peel as needed.

To Singe: After birds are plucked, burn off any hair, using long wooden matches, a candle, or spill, taking care not to scorch the flesh.

To Skin: Tiny game birds (especially woodcock, snipe, pigeon, and dove) have such tender skin they can't be plucked. To remove feathers, slit neck skin lengthwise, then carefully work skin free from breast and back, wings, and legs with fingers—its rather like taking off coveralls.

To Eviscerate:

(1) Cut off head, peel neck skin down around shoulders, then cut off neck as close to body as possible, leaving windpipe and esophagus intact. Reach under flap of breast skin and pull out crop and attached tubes.

(2) Make a cut below breastbone, just big enough to admit your hand, reach in, feel around for firm, round gizzard and gently ease it out of bird (intestines, liver, and heart should come away with it).

Also scoop out kidneys, lungs, and any lumps of fat. Discard all organs except gizzard, liver, and heart.

(3) Cut out oil sac at base of tail.

(4) Wipe bird inside and out with a damp cloth, then pat dry.

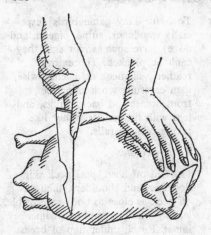

To Prepare Giblets:

Liver: Separate gall bladder from liver—carefully so it doesn't rupture, spilling the bitter juices inside; trim away any greenish spots on liver.

Gizzard: Cut away fat and any bits of intestine; also scrape off outer membrane. Cut gizzard open, peel away inner membrane, bringing with it contents of gizzard.

Heart: Trim off veins and arteries, peel away membrane.

To Make Giblet Stock: (*Note:* Method may also be used for making stock from the hearts and livers of rabbits, squirrels, and other small furred game.) Wash giblets well in cool water, cover with cold salted water (1 teaspoon salt per pint water), cover, and simmer about 1 hour, replenishing water as needed. If you plan to use giblets in recipes, reduce cooking time so that they don't toughen and dry; liver, gizzard, and heart will be tender in 20 minutes, neck in 30. (*Note:* The liver of a large wild goose or turkey will need about ½ hour, the heart, gizzard, and neck 1½–2 hours.) Taste stock for

salt and pepper and add as needed. Use as is for making soups, sauces, and stews or, if you like, strain first through a fine sieve lined with a double thickness of cheesecloth.

To Cut Up Birds: Using poultry shears or a sharp knife, cut as follows:

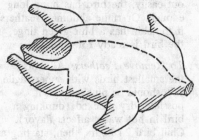

To Halve (Split)

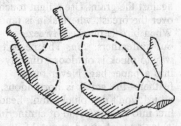

To Disjoint

How to Cook Game Birds

The principles of cooking game birds are essentially the same as for domestic fowl—with two differences. Game birds have little or no fat and must be barded (wrapped in bacon or sheets of salt pork or other fat) and/or heavily basted to keep them from drying out. Second, dark-meated game birds like wild duck are often served rare (some people want them only passed through the oven). Otherwise, the basics are similar. Tough old birds, obviously, roast poorly and should be steamed, stewed, or braised. Young tender birds, like young tender chickens, are gloriously adaptable. (*Note:* Always try to bring game birds to room temperature before cooking.)

To Roast (best for young small- or medium-size birds; wild goose and turkey should be roasted only if very young and small—less than 8 pounds). (*Note:* This method is for well-done birds; for rare wild duck, see the separate recipe that follows.)

General Preparation: Have birds cleaned and dressed; sprinkle cavities with salt and pepper.

Basic Method: Preheat oven to 350° F. Place ½ small peeled, cored apple and/or ½ small peeled yellow onion inside each bird, also 1 bay leaf, a sprig of fresh sage, thyme, or marjoram or a small *bouquet garni** tied in cheesecloth, and 1–2 tablespoons medium-dry sherry or port. Skewer or sew openings shut, then fold wings back and under and tie legs together. Arrange birds breast side up on a rack in a shallow roasting pan. Cover breast of each with a double thickness of cheesecloth saturated with melted butter, margarine, bacon drippings, or lard. Roast uncovered, basting often with additional melted fat, until leg joints move easily and breast meat feels tender. Use the following times as a guide:

Wild Turkey or Goose: 25–30 minutes per pound

Medium-Size (1–4 pounds) Birds: 30–40 minutes per pound

Small (under 1 pound) Birds: 50–60 minutes per pound

If birds have been skinned, leave cheesecloth cover on until last 5 minutes so they will not dry out; otherwise, remove during last 15 minutes so birds will brown. Never try to brown skinned birds. Transfer birds to a hot platter, remove strings and stuffing, and let "rest" 10 minutes before serving. Serve small birds whole, carve larger birds as you would chicken or turkey.* *For Extra Flavor:* Baste birds throughout roasting with Herb, Parsley, Tarragon, Shallot, or Garlic Butter or with a ½ and ½ mixture of melted butter and dry red or white wine, beer, or fruit juice. Stuff birds with fresh berries or cherries, brandied peaches, dates or figs, or sultana raisins sprinkled with brandy instead of apple, onion, and herbs. *To Flambé Small Birds:* Arrange roasted birds in a deep platter, pour ¼–⅓ cup warmed brandy or rum over all, blaze with a match, and baste with flaming liquid until flames die.

VARIATIONS:

Game Birds Baked in Vine Leaves: Tie fresh or brined grape leaves around each bird, cover with buttered cheesecloth, and roast as directed, removing cheesecloth and vine leaves toward end of cooking. Drain off pan drippings, pour ¼ cup port or Madeira over each bird, and finish roasting, basting often. Remove birds to platter, add peeled seedless green grapes to pan (allow ¼ cup grapes for each bird) and warm gently while birds "rest." Pour over birds and serve.

Game Birds with Calvados, Cream, and Truffles: Roast birds as directed through point of removing cheesecloth; drain off all but 1–2 tablespoons drippings. Pour ¼ cup each Calvados (or brandy or champagne) and heavy cream over

each bird if medium size, 2 tablespoons if small, and finish roasting
as directed, basting 1–2 times. Lift
birds to platter; to pan liquid add
1–2 minced truffles, warm briefly,
and pour over birds.

Game Birds Smitane: Roast birds
as directed and transfer to platter.
Make Pan Gravy from drippings,
then for each cup gravy, mix
in ⅓ cup sour cream, ¼ cup
sautéed sliced mushrooms, and
5–6 sliced ripe or stuffed green
olives. Spoon some sauce over the
birds and pass the rest. For a
glamorous dinner, serve only the
boned breasts Smitane style. Arrange them, slightly overlapping,
on a platter, smother with sauce, and
surround with artichoke bottoms
filled with buttered green peas.

Virginia-Style Game Birds: Roast
birds as directed; if tiny, leave
whole, otherwise halve or quarter according to size. Arrange on slices of
sautéed, baked ham (Smithfield
is best) and keep warm. Make
Pan Gravy from drippings and
for each cup gravy whisk in 2 tablespoons red currant jelly and ¼
teaspoon finely grated orange rind.
Pour over all and serve.

Regency-Style Game Birds: Roast
birds as directed; if tiny, leave
whole, otherwise halve or quarter
according to size. Serve on slices
of toast spread with pâté and pass
Victoria Sauce.

Roast Stuffed Game Birds (best
for young birds weighing 3–8
pounds):

General Preparation: Same as for
roasting.

Basic Method: Stuff bird loosely
with any favorite stuffing (see Some
Sauces, Gravies, and Seasonings
for Game and Game Birds), al-

lowing ¾–1 cup per pound of
bird. Skewer openings shut, tie
legs together, and fold wings back
and under. Cover with butter-
saturated cheesecloth and roast as
for unstuffed birds, increasing
cooking times about 10 minutes
per pound. (*Note:* For an extra-
moist bird, add a little extra liquid
to stuffing.)

To Braise (best for not-so-young
small- and medium-size whole
birds):

General Preparation: Same as for
roasting.

Basic Method: Preheat oven to
350° F. Tie a 2″–3″ strip of lemon
or orange rind in cheesecloth with a
*bouquet garni** and tuck inside
each bird. Tie legs together, fold
wings back and under. If birds
have been skinned, dredge lightly
in flour. Brown birds lightly all
over in 2 tablespoons butter and
set aside. Make a bed of butter-
sautéed, minced vegetables in
an ungreased Dutch oven (for
each bird allow ¼ cup each onion,
carrot, mushrooms, and celery,
also 1 tablespoon minced parsley).
Place birds on vegetables and
pour in just enough beef or chicken
broth (or a ½ and ½ mixture of
chicken broth and dry red or white
wine, beer, grape or orange juice)
to moisten. If you like, add a
peeled clove garlic. Cover and
braise until leg joints move easily:
Medium-size birds will take 35–45
minutes per pound, small birds 50–
60. Baste 1 or 2 times with pan
juices. Lift birds to a hot deep
platter and keep warm. Skim
fat from liquid, remove garlic clove.
Purée vegetables and liquid in
an electric blender at low speed or
put through a fine sieve. Pour into
a saucepan, and for each 1 cup

purée add ¼ cup heavy cream or 1 tablespoon flour blended with 1 tablespoon cold water; heat, stirring, until thickened; do not boil. Pour some sauce over birds and pass the remainder. (*Note:* Birds can be halved or quartered before braising. Brown in butter as directed and arrange on vegetables. Add 1 bouquet garni, tied in cheesecloth, to casserole, also 1 strip lemon or orange rind. Cover and braise as directed, allowing ¾ hour for quartered medium-size birds and 30–40 minutes for small halved birds.)

VARIATIONS:

Curried Game Birds: Prepare by basic method above but rub birds well with curry powder before browning and refrigerate 4–6 hours. Also mix 1 teaspoon curry powder into each cup sautéed vegetables. Otherwise, proceed as directed. Serve birds on a bed of Rice Pilaf mixed with chopped pistachio nuts and topped with sauce.

Game Birds Braised with Cabbage: Prepare by basic recipe but braise on a 1½" bed of shredded red or green cabbage instead of sautéed vegetables. Add garlic and liquid called for, also 2 fresh link sausages, sliced ½" thick. When birds are done, remove garlic and serve on bed of cabbage.

Game Birds with Caraway, Sauerkraut, and Raisins: Brown birds as in basic method, place in a buttered casserole on a 1" bed of drained sauerkraut sprinkled with 1 tablespoon caraway seeds and ½ cup each minced yellow onion and seedless raisins. Add 1 cup beef broth, cover, and braise until tender. Good with tall, cool glasses of beer.

Norman Game Birds: Brown birds as in basic method, place in a buttered casserole on a 1" bed of chopped, peeled apples that have been lightly sprinkled with nutmeg and sugar and liberally dotted with butter. Add no liquid, cover, and braise as directed. When tender, lift birds to a platter, stir 2–3 tablespoons heavy cream into apples and, if you like, 2–3 tablespoons Calvados, brandy, or apple cider. Spoon mixture around birds or pass separately.

To Oven Broil (best for very young tender small- or medium-size birds):

General Preparation: Have birds cleaned and dressed but not skinned. Large pheasant or duck should be halved or quartered. Tiny birds will broil more evenly if left whole, then flattened slightly with the heel of your hand.

Basic Method: Preheat broiler, setting oven temperature at 350° F. Place whole birds breast side down, pieces skin side down, on a buttered rack on a foil-lined broiler pan, sprinkle lightly with salt and pepper, and brush well with melted butter. Broil as far from heat as possible, 15–20 minutes, turn, and broil 15–20 minutes longer until evenly browned and juices run clear when thigh is pricked. (*Note:* For rare duck, broil 5" from heat 8–10 minutes per side.) *For Extra Flavor:* Brush birds with Tarragon, Parsley, or Shallot Butter instead of plain butter.

To Charcoal Broil (best for very young tender small- or medium-size birds):

General Preparation: Same as for oven broiling.

Basic Method: Prepare a moderately hot charcoal fire.* Lay birds breast side up, pieces skin side up, on a well-oiled grill and broil 6" from heat 30–45 minutes until fork tender, turning often and brushing frequently with melted unsalted butter or a ½ and ½ mixture of melted butter and lemon juice. Season just before serving.

VARIATIONS:

Barbecued Game Birds: Marinate birds 2–3 hours in refrigerator in a favorite barbecue sauce, then broil as directed, basting often with a ½ and ½ mixture of sauce and melted butter.

Game Birds in Foil: Halve or quarter birds, brush with melted butter, and sprinkle with salt and pepper; wrap each piece in well-greased foil and cook 4" from coals 30–40 minutes until fork tender; turn packages after 15 minutes. Unwrap, place pieces skin side down, and grill 4–5 minutes to brown.

To Spit Roast (best for young small- or medium-size birds):

General Preparation: Same as for oven broiling.

In Oven or Rotisserie: Preheat unit. Skewer neck skin and wings of each bird to body, tie legs together, pulling close to body. Bard* (wrap) birds with bacon or salt pork. (*Note:* Butchers will often do this for you.) Spit birds lengthwise without crowding, adjust balance as needed, and lock tines in place. Roast 5"–6" from heat, allowing ¾–1 hour for small birds, 1–1½ hours for the medium size, basting frequently with melted unsalted butter. Remove barding fat during last 10–15 minutes so birds will brown. Take from spit, remove

strings and skewers, season, and serve.

Over Charcoal: Prepare a moderately hot charcoal fire.* Prepare birds as for oven spit roasting, roast 5" from coals using above times as a guide.

To Panfry (Sauté; best for young small birds):

General Preparation: Have birds cleaned, dressed, and halved.

Basic Method: Lightly sprinkle birds with salt and pepper and dust with flour. Brown 2–3 minutes on a side in ¼ cup butter, margarine, or cooking oil over moderate heat. Turn heat to low and continue cooking 10 minutes, turning frequently. Serve as is or smothered with Pan Gravy made from drippings. *For Extra Flavor:* Rub birds with garlic before dusting with flour, also, if you like, with thyme, sage, or marjoram.

VARIATIONS:

Game Birds Américaine: Dip birds in flour, then beaten egg, then toasted bread crumbs and panfry as directed. Serve on a bed of wild rice garnished with broiled, bacon-wrapped giblets and sautéed button mushrooms and cherry tomatoes.

Deviled Game Birds: Panfry birds as directed, transfer to a hot platter and keep warm; drain all but 2 tablespoons drippings from pan, add 2 tablespoons each beef broth and minced gherkins, 1 tablespoon each lemon juice and Worcestershire sauce, and 2 teaspoons Dijon-style mustard. Warm briefly, pour over birds, and serve.

Game Birds Lucullus: Panfry birds as directed and transfer to platter. Drain all but 2 tablespoons drippings from pan; for each bird sauté 1 (½″) slice pâté that has been lightly dredged in flour until golden brown. Place pâté on unbuttered toast cut to fit, top with a slice or 2 of truffle and arrange around birds. Pass Madeira Sauce.

Spiced and Spiked Game Birds: Dredge game birds in ¼ cup unsifted flour mixed with 1 teaspoon nutmeg, ¾ teaspoon each salt and cinnamon, ¼ teaspoon each ginger and cloves and a pinch pepper. Panfry as directed and transfer to platter. Stir ¼ cup each heavy cream and rum, brandy or sherry into drippings, warm briefly and pour over birds.

To Stew (best for large birds or birds of questionable age and tenderness): Follow directions for stewing a hen or capon (see Chicken).

To Steam (best for large birds or those of questionable tenderness): Follow directions for stewing a hen or capon (see Chicken). Also see Potted Wild Goose or Turkey, a method of oven steaming.

About Pressure Cooking Game Birds

Don't. It's a sacrilege to pressure cook any succulent young bird (it will disintegrate). As for big old birds, they suffer too, becoming tougher and drier. Better to steam or stew them.

POTTED WILD GOOSE OR TURKEY

Wild goose or turkey weighing more than 8 pounds is of questionable age and tenderness. "Potting," which used to be done in huge brown earthenware casseroles, makes it succulent. Save giblets for gravy or soup.
Makes 6–10 servings

1 (8–16-pound) wild goose or turkey, cleaned and dressed
1 tablespoon salt
¼ teaspoon pepper
6–8 slices salt pork or fat bacon
2 large yellow onions, peeled and quartered
2 large carrots, peeled and cut in 1″ chunks
2 bay leaves
1 bouquet garni,* tied in cheesecloth
1 quart chicken or beef broth or water
½ cup melted butter, margarine, or bacon drippings

Preheat oven to 325° F. Rub bird inside and out with salt and pepper; tie legs together and to body, fold wings back and under. Place bird breast side up on a rack in a large Dutch oven and drape with salt pork. Add all but last ingredient, cover, and bake about 25 minutes per pound, basting with pan juices every 30 minutes. About ½ hour before bird is done, drain off liquid with a bulb baster, remove vegetables and seasonings and discard. Raise oven to 425° F., and pour melted butter over bird. Roast uncovered, basting often, until golden brown and legs move easily in sockets. Transfer to a hot large platter, remove strings, and let "rest" 10 minutes. Make Giblet Gravy if you like. About 330 calories for each of 6 servings (from an 8-pound bird), 445 calories for each of 10 servings (from a 16-pound bird). (*Note:* 16 pounds may seem too big a bird for just 10 servings. It isn't because a mature wild goose or turkey has so little edible meat. The legs and wings are too tough and sinewy to be good.)

⚄⚄ RARE ROAST WILD DUCK

For crisp brown skin and rare meat, wild duck must be roasted fast at high heat. It should not be stuffed, so if you want stuffing, bake it separately beforehand.
Makes 2 servings

*1 (2–2½-pound) wild duck, cleaned
  and dressed*
1 teaspoon salt
¼ teaspoon pepper
1 bouquet garni,* tied in cheesecloth
*2 tablespoons melted butter,
  margarine, or bacon drippings*

Gravy:
*½ cup medium-dry red wine,
  chicken or beef broth, or giblet
  stock**
*2 tablespoons minced shallots or
  scallions*
1 bay leaf
4 peppercorns
⅛ teaspoon nutmeg (optional)

Set a shallow roasting pan and rack in oven while it preheats to 450° F. Rub duck inside and out with salt and pepper and tuck *bouquet garni* in cavity. Tie legs together, fold wings back, and brush bird with butter. Roast uncovered, breast side up, about 15 minutes for very rare, 25 minutes for medium rare. Meanwhile, simmer gravy ingredients, uncovered, 8–10 minutes; strain and keep warm. Transfer duck to a carving board with well, remove strings and let "rest" 5 minutes. Carve meat from duck and arrange on a hot serving platter. Drain blood and juices into gravy and warm briefly, stirring; do not boil or mixture will curdle. Taste for salt and adjust as needed. Spoon some gravy over duck and pass the rest. About 260 calories per serving.

VARIATIONS:

⚄⚄ **Spit-Roasted Rare Wild Duck:** Preheat oven or rotisserie; season and truss bird as above, also skewer neck flap and wings to body. Balance lengthwise on spit, and roast 5″ from heat 20 minutes for very rare and 30 for medium rare, basting frequently with melted butter. Make gravy and serve as directed. About 260 calories per serving.

⚄⚄ **Charcoal Spit-Roasted Rare Wild Duck:** Build a very hot charcoal fire.* Prepare, spit and roast duck 5″ from heat as above. Be prepared to douse flare-ups. About 260 calories per serving.

⚄⚄ **Tyrolean-Style Roast Wild Duck:** Omit bouquet garni and spoon ¾ cup hot applesauce mixed with 1 teaspoon each cinnamon and nutmeg into duck cavity; sew or close with poultry pins. Brush duck with ½ cup hot red wine vinegar mixed with 2 tablespoons each sugar and olive or other cooking oil. Roast as above, basting 1 or 2 times with vinegar mixture. Prepare gravy and serve as directed. About 285 calories per serving.

⚄⚄ **Pressed Wild Duck:** Roast duck very rare and prepare gravy. Meanwhile, warm a chafing dish over simmering water. Slice off both duck breasts and place in chafing dish; if leg meat is tender, add (if not, save for soup). Pour blood and juices over meat and adjust heat so water barely simmers. Cut up carcass and put all but leg bones in well of a duck press. Pour gravy over bones and press, forcing gravy and juices into a hot bowl; repress twice. Stir in 2 tablespoons warm brandy and pour into chafing dish. Serve with wild rice or bulgur wheat. (*Note:* If you don't have a duck press, put bones through fine blade of meat grinder or break up with a mallet. Warm 1–2 minutes in gravy, strain, and pour into chafing dish.) About 225 calories per serving.

⚔ ROAST MERGANSER

Mergansers, scoters, and other fish-eating ducks need special attention to rid them of their fishy flavor. They're best not stuffed and cooked fairly well done.
Makes 2 servings

1 (2–2½-pound) merganser or other fish-eating duck, cleaned and dressed
1 tablespoon salt
½ lemon
½ cup cider vinegar
1 yellow onion, peeled
1 stick cinnamon
1 tart apple, peeled and cored
Boiling water
2 tablespoons melted butter or margarine

Rub duck inside and out with salt and lemon; pour vinegar into cavity, add onion, cover loosely, and let stand at room temperature 1–2 hours. Preheat oven to 350° F. Drain vinegar from duck and remove onion; wash inside and out with tepid water and pat dry on paper toweling. Poke cinnamon stick into apple hollow, and tuck inside bird. Tie legs together, fold wings back and under, and place breast side up in a shallow roasting pan. Pour in boiling water to a depth of ½″ and roast, uncovered, 15 minutes, basting twice; drain off water. Brush duck with butter and roast, uncovered, 1 hour or until legs move easily in sockets. If breast browns too fast, cover with cheesecloth dipped in butter or, if bird is fat, with foil. Let bird "rest" 5–10 minutes before serving. Remove strings and discard apple and cinnamon. Instead of making Pan Gravy (drippings may taste fishy), serve with a suitable sauce (see Some Sauces, Gravies, and Seasonings for Game and Game Birds). About 210 calories per serving (without sauce).

SUPRÊMES OF PHEASANT À LA CRÈME

When pheasants have sinewy legs, use them for soup and prepare the breasts this way.
Makes 4 servings

2 (2½–3-pound) pheasants, guinea fowl, grouse, or partridges, cleaned and dressed
2 cups chicken broth
1 cup water
1 small yellow onion, peeled
1 carrot, peeled
1 stalk celery, cut in 1″ lengths
4 peppercorns
3 tablespoons butter or margarine
¼ cup unsifted flour
¾ cup heavy cream
½ teaspoon salt
⅛ teaspoon nutmeg
⅛ teaspoon paprika

Place birds breast side up, side by side, on a rack in a large kettle; add broth, water, vegetables, and peppercorns. Cover and simmer ¾–1 hour until breasts are tender; cool birds in broth ½ hour, lift out, and carefully remove breasts so halves are intact. Skin breasts (save skin and remainder of birds for soup). Strain broth, then boil uncovered to reduce to 1½ cups. Melt butter in a large skillet over moderate heat, blend in flour, slowly add broth, cream, salt, and nutmeg, and heat, stirring, until thickened and no raw starch taste remains. Add breasts and warm

SOME SAUCES, GRAVIES AND SEASONINGS FOR GAME AND GAME BIRDS

	Sauces and Gravies	Stuffings	Herbs, Spices, Seasonings		Condiments
Venison, Bear, Wild Boar	Bordelaise Brown Sauce Fines Herbes Bourguignonne Charcutière (wild boar) Chevreuil (venison) Cumberland	Grand Veneur (venison) Madeira Pan Gravy Périgueux Poivrade Romaine Victoria		Bay leaves Cinnamon Cloves Garlic Ginger Juniper berries	Mustard Onion Paprika Parsley Rosemary Sage Thyme	Applesauce Chutney Cranberry sauce Currant jelly Gooseberry jam Rosemary jelly Wine jelly
Small furred game (Rabbit, Squirrel, Muskrat, Raccoon)	Barbecue Bordelaise Brown Sauce Fines Herbes Bourguignonne Chasseur Madeira	Marchands de Vin Pan Gravy Périgueux Poivrade Robert Victoria	Basic Bread Chestnut Sage and Onion Wild Rice	Basil Bay leaves Cinnamon Cloves Garlic Ginger Juniper berries Lemon Mace	Marjoram Mustard Nutmeg Onion Orange Oregano Parsley Sage Tarragon Thyme	Same as for venison
Game Birds	Bercy Bigarade Chasseur Chaud-Froid Diable Espagnole Giblet Gravy Madeira	Pan Gravy Périgueux Poivrade Robert Rouennaise (duck) Suprême Victoria	Apple-Pecan Basic Bread Chestnut Chestnut-Mushroom Corn Bread and Sausage Giblet Sage and Onion Wild Rice	Bay leaves Caraway Cinnamon Cloves Coriander Dill Garlic Ginger Juniper berries Lemon	Nutmeg Onion Orange Oregano Paprika Parsley Rosemary Sage Tarragon Thyme Truffles	Applesauce Cranberry sauce Currant jelly Gooseberry jam Pickled or Brandied peaches Rosemary jelly Wine jelly

slowly (do not boil), basting with sauce; lift to a hot platter, coat generously with sauce and dust with paprika. Pass remaining sauce. About 475 calories per serving.

VARIATIONS:

⚖️ **Breasts of Pheasant in Aspic:** Simmer birds as directed, omitting carrot. Remove breasts, skin, and chill 3–4 hours. Save 2 cups strained cooking liquid, mix in 1 envelope unflavored gelatin, 1 egg white beaten to soft peaks, and 1 crushed eggshell. Heat, stirring with a whisk, until mixture foams up. Remove from heat, stir once, and let stand undisturbed 5 minutes. Line a sieve with a fine dish towel wrung out in cold water, set over a deep bowl, pour in hot liquid (egg, shell, and all), and let drip through to clarify. *Do not stir.* Chill clarified aspic until syrupy. Set breasts on a rack over a tray and spoon a thin, even layer of aspic over each. Chill until tacky, then decorate with truffle and pimiento cutouts and sprigs of fresh parsley or tarragon. Chill briefly to set; keep remaining aspic over warm water. Add another thin aspic layer to seal in designs; chill until firm. Also chill remaining aspic, then dice and use to garnish platter along with radish roses and watercress sprigs. About 210 calories per serving.

Breasts of Pheasant Chaud-Froid: Simmer birds as directed, omitting carrot. Remove breasts, skin, and chill. Make sauce as in Suprêmes of Pheasant (above), reducing flour to 3 tablespoons. Mix 1 envelope unflavored gelatin with ⅓ cup water and heat, stirring to dissolve; mix into sauce and chill until mixture will coat a metal

spoon. Set breasts on a rack over a tray and cover with a thin, even layer of gelatin mixture. Chill until tacky, then continue building up layers until no meat shows through. While final layer is still tacky, decorate as above. If you like, seal in designs with clear aspic made using 2 cups canned chicken broth. About 475 calories per serving.

FRICASSEE OF GAME BIRDS

A delicious way to prepare not so young and tender birds.
Makes 6 servings

2 (3-pound) game birds, cleaned, dressed, and disjointed
Giblets from birds
1 yellow onion, peeled and sliced thin
1 stalk celery, cut in 1" lengths
2 (10½-ounce) cans chicken broth
2 tablespoons butter or margarine
½ teaspoon rosemary
1 tablespoon lemon juice
1 cup light cream (about)
⅓ cup unsifted flour blended with ⅓ cup milk
1 teaspoon salt (about)
⅛ teaspoon white pepper (about)
1 tablespoon minced parsley

Place birds, giblets, onion, celery, broth, butter, rosemary, and lemon juice in a kettle, cover, and simmer 1½–2 hours until meat is fork tender but not falling off bones; cool birds in broth ½ hour. Strain broth, measure, and add enough light cream to total 3 cups. Skin birds and, if you like, bone, keeping meat in as large pieces as possible. Pour broth mixture into a clean saucepan, blend in flour paste and heat, stirring, until thickened. Add salt and pepper, taste and adjust as needed. Add meat, mix gently, and heat, shaking pan now and then, 5 minutes. Sprinkle with parsley and

serve with boiled noodles or rice.
About 340 calories per serving
(without noodles or rice).

SALMI OF GAME BIRDS

Salmi is a spectacular do-ahead
ragout of fowl finished at the table.
Makes 4–6 servings

2 *(2–2½-pound) pheasants, guinea*
   hens or ducks, cleaned and
   dressed
⅓ *cup minced scallions*
2 *tablespoons butter or margarine*
1½ *cups dry white wine*
4 *peppercorns*
4 *juniper berries*
Giblets from birds
1½ *cups hot Espagnole Sauce*
½ *pound sautéed button mushrooms*
1–2 *truffles, sliced thin*

Early in the day, roast birds by basic
method until barely tender; cool
until easy to handle. Carefully
remove breasts so halves are intact,
and cut meat from legs; discard all
skin, wrap, and refrigerate meat.
Also wrap and chill carcass, wings
and leg bones. About 1 hour before
serving, place carcass, wings, and
leg bones in a saucepan, add scallions, butter, wine, seasonings, and
giblets, partially cover, and simmer
¾ hour. Strain into Espagnole
Sauce and mix well. Place reserved
meat in a chafing dish, add sauce,
and carry to table. Set over simmering water and heat, basting meat
with sauce, until piping hot. Scatter
mushrooms and truffles on top and
serve from chafing dish. About 580
calories for each of 4 servings, 390
calories for each of 6 servings.

PIGEON PIE

Makes 6 servings

1 *pound lean boiled ham, cut in ½″*
   cubes
6 *pigeons, doves, or other very small*
   game birds, cleaned, dressed, and
   halved lengthwise
Pigeon livers or 2–3 chicken livers
2 *tablespoons butter or margarine*
2 *tablespoons minced parsley*
1 *teaspoon salt*
¼ *teaspoon pepper*
1½–2 *cups chicken broth or*
   Chicken Gravy
1 *recipe Flaky Pastry I*
1 *egg yolk beaten with 1 tablespoon*
   cold water (glaze)

Preheat oven to 425° F. Stand a pie
funnel in the center of an ungreased 1½-quart 2″ deep casserole;
layer ham into casserole. Arrange
birds breast side down on ham.
Sauté livers in butter 2–3 minutes
over moderate heat, then mince
and mix with parsley; scatter mixture over birds, sprinkle with salt
and pepper and pour in 1½ cups
broth. Mix pastry and roll into a
circle 3″ larger than casserole;
dampen rim of casserole, top with
pastry, roll pastry edges under even
with rim, and crimp to seal. Make
a hole in middle of pastry to expose
funnel so steam can escape. Brush
with glaze and bake, uncovered, ½
hour; lower heat to 350° F. and
bake 20–30 minutes longer until
pastry is golden and birds are tender
(test by poking a skewer through
steam hole around funnel). If casserole seems to be baking dry, funnel
a little extra broth in through hole.
Serve hot or cold. About 580 calories
for each of 4 servings, 390 calories
for each of 6 servings.

CHAPTER 10

POULTRY

Of man's many meats, poultry has always been the aristocrat. The ancient Chinese domesticated a variety of exotic birds, fattened them for the table, and lavished upon them the wizardry of Oriental cuisine. From the East the birds were brought West, into Asia Minor, Greece, and Rome. It was the Romans who produced the first capon, not because they believed its flesh would be superior, but because Roman law restricted the number of hens and cocks that could be eaten. By castrating the cock, they circumvented the law and continued to feast with abandon. Thanks to today's streamlined poultry industry, there is no shortage of poultry. Birds are bred and pampered to plump succulence, most are sold dressed and ready-to-cook (sometimes even prestuffed and frozen), many are available year round, often at bargain prices. And all are unusually versatile.

The Food Value of Poultry

All poultry is a nourishing high protein food, and much of it (ducks and geese excepted) fairly low-calorie.

The Kinds of Poultry

Chicken:

Squab Chicken: An infant weighing about 1 pound.

Broiler-Fryer: The all-purpose chicken, a 1½–4 pounder that can be broiled, fried, roasted, braised, or poached with equal success. The term "broiler-fryer," coined

by the poultry industry, is replacing the older terminology of "broiler" or "broiling chicken," "fryer," or "frying chicken."

Roaster or Roasting Chicken: A plump (3½–5 pound), young (about 12 weeks) chicken perfect for roasting.

Capon: A cock castrated while young; it is full breasted, meaty, and tender, weighs 4–7 pounds, and is superb roasted. It is also the bird to use when an especially succulent cooked chicken meat is required for a recipe.

Bro-Hen: Another of the poultry industry's coined terms, this one meaning a plump, meaty laying hen weighing 4½–6 pounds. Best when stewed.

Fowl: A stewing hen.

Stewing Hen: A tough old bird weighing 3–6½ pounds. Use for stock, soups, or recipes calling for ground or minced cooked chicken.

Turkey (America's gift to the world of poultry):

Fryer-Roaster: A small (4–9 pound), young (usually under 16 weeks) turkey of either sex. It has tender meat, soft smooth skin, and flexible breastbone cartilage and can be broiled or oven fried as well as roasted.

Young Hen and Young Tom: Young (5–7 months) female and male with tender meat and skin. Best when roasted. Weights (see note below) vary considerably according to age and breed.

Yearling Hen and Yearling Tom: Mature female and male just over 1 year old. They have reasonably tender meat and can be roasted. Again, weights vary according to breed and age.

Mature Hen and Mature Tom: Female and male more than 15 months old; they have coarse skin, tough meat and are rarely seen in stores today.

Note About Turkey Weights: Turkeys are also categorized by size (ready-to-cook weight): *small* (4–10 pounds), *medium* (10–19 pounds), and *large* (20 pounds or more).

Other Kinds of Poultry:

Rock Cornish Game Hen: A relatively new breed produced by crossing a Cornish chicken and a White Rock. The baby of the chicken family, it weighs 1–2 pounds but averages 1¼. The breast is meaty and plump and the bird especially suited to roasting. It can also be braised or prepared like medium-size game birds (see How to Cook Game Birds). Marketed frozen and ready-to-cook.

Squab: A young domesticated pigeon especially raised for the table. It weighs 1 pound or less and may be prepared like Rock Cornish game hen.

Guinea Fowl: A raucous West African exotic now popular in barnyard flocks. It is a cousin to the pheasant and has rather dry, delicately gamy meat. Guinea hens are preferable to cocks; they weigh 2–4 pounds and may be prepared like chicken.

Pheasant (Farm-Raised): A plump (2–4-pound) bird with superbly flavored though somewhat dry meat. It is the wild pheasant (see game birds) raised in captivity for greater tenderness. Marketed frozen.

Duck: (*Duckling* is a better word because commercially raised ducks are marketed while still young and tender. Most famous is Long Island duckling).

Broiler or Fryer Duckling: A very young duckling weighing about 3 pounds.

Roaster Duckling: A slightly older bird (8–16 weeks) weighing 3–5 pounds.

Goose: Geese raised for the table go to market while still *goslings;* they weigh 4–14 pounds, are fat birds, and are best when roasted.

About Buying Poultry

All poultry moved in interstate commerce is federally inspected to ensure wholesomeness. Some birds, at the packer's request, are graded for quality:

USDA GRADE A: The choicest bird, full fleshed and well finished.

USDA GRADE B: Secondbest, slightly less meaty and attractive.

USDA GRADE C: A grade used mostly for turkeys. These birds are scrawnier, may have torn skin, broken bones and bruises. They are not handsome but, properly prepared, are good eating.

Frequently used today is the *combination tag* that carries not only the *inspection stamp* but also the *grade* and *type of bird* (i.e., roaster, stewing hen).

Characteristics of Quality and Freshness: Home-grown, locally marketed birds are often uninspected and ungraded, so the buyer must rely on her own judgment. To be sure of good poultry, look for:
– Well-fleshed breasts and short, plump legs; ducks should have broad, flat, and meaty breasts and backs well padded with fat.
– Soft, moist (but not wet), smooth, creamy, or yellow skin with a minimum of pinfeathers.
– Youthfulness—flexible breastbones in chickens and turkeys, pliable bills in ducks and geese.

Note: Reject birds with dry or purplish skin, hard scaly legs, and an "off" odor; also pass over those that have been sloppily dressed.

Popular Market Forms of Fresh Poultry:

Chicken:

Whole, Ready-To-Cook: Such birds are cleaned and dressed inside and out, free of pinfeathers. Head, feet, and entrails were removed before weighing and pricing. The giblets have been washed, trimmed, and wrapped (they're usually tucked inside the body cavity).

Halved or Quartered: Popular supermarket forms.

Cut Up or Disjointed: Separated at the joints into breasts, backs, drumsticks, thighs, wings, etc.

Chicken Parts: It is now possible to buy just the parts of chicken you want—2 pounds of drumsticks, say, or a pound of breasts. Chicken livers are also available by the pound.

Turkey:

Whole, Ready-To-Cook: Fully cleaned and dressed birds. Some packer descriptions meaning the same thing: "Pan-Ready," "Oven-Ready," "Table-Dressed."

Quarter or Half Roast: Ready-to-cook large birds sold by the half or quarter.

Cut-Up Turkey or Turkey by the Piece: Specific parts of the bird sold separately by the pound.

Other Kinds of Poultry:

Rock Cornish Game Hen and Squab: If you live near a game hen or squab farm, you may be able to buy fresh, whole, ready-to-cook birds; otherwise, you'll have to settle for the frozen.

Guinea Fowl and Farm-Raised Pheasant: Fresh, whole, ready-to-cook birds are sometimes available at gourmet butchers; the frozen are far more plentiful.

Duck and Goose: These are available fresh, whole, and ready-to-cook but usually only at the source—the New York City area for duck, Wisconsin or North Dakota for goose. Most ducks and geese come to market frozen. In the New York City area it is also sometimes possible to buy duck parts.

How Much Poultry Should You Buy? Allow ¾–1 pound ready-to-cook bird per person; in the case of Rock Cornish game hens and squabs, this will mean 1 bird per person (if appetites are hearty). (*Note:* If a turkey weighs 20 pounds or more, figure about ½ pound ready-to-cook bird per person.)

About Cleaning and Dressing Poultry

The days of chasing, catching, killing, and cleaning one's own poultry belong to history. In fact, rare is the American woman who will have to do more than unwrap (and perhaps thaw) a ready-to-cook bird. *If* you're the exception follow the steps outlined under Game Birds for plucking, singeing, and eviscerating. Domesticated birds, of course, should not be hung.

About Cutting Up Poultry

The best way is to have the butcher do it for you—and most will gladly. Turkey and goose are too cumbersome to tackle at home, but chicken, duck, pheasant, guinea fowl, game hen, and squab can easily be cut up:

To Halve or Quarter (for all but duck; game hen and squab should be no more than halved; they're too small to quarter): Cut closely along each side of backbone and remove (1). Cut out oil sac at base of tail. Nick breast cartilage, cut through flesh and skin; pull halves apart and remove keel bone. For quarters, cut diagonally along bottom rib (2).

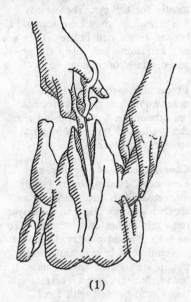

(1)

To Cut Up or Disjoint Chicken: Remove wings, then legs, rolling knife along curves of ball joints. Sever legs at "knee" joints, separating into drumsticks and thighs. Remove backbone and oil sac as directed for halving and quartering, then cut up each side of body from leg joint to wing joint, using poultry shears. Halve breast and remove keel bone as directed for halving chicken.

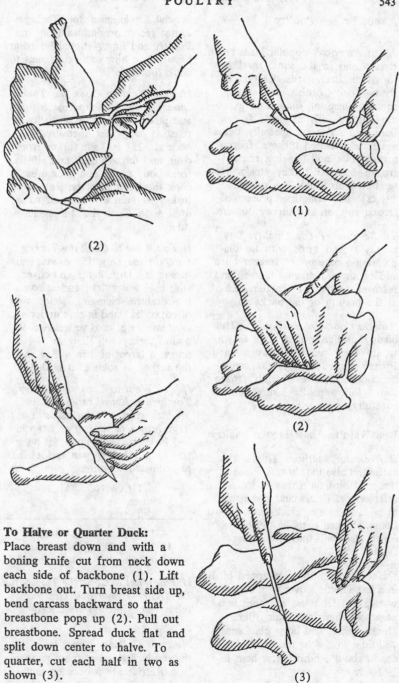

(1)

(2)

(2)

To Halve or Quarter Duck:
Place breast down and with a boning knife cut from neck down each side of backbone (1). Lift backbone out. Turn breast side up, bend carcass backward so that breastbone pops up (2). Pull out breastbone. Spread duck flat and split down center to halve. To quarter, cut each half in two as shown (3).

(3)

About Frozen Poultry

All of America's popular birds come frozen and in the same market forms as fresh birds. Certain of them—Rock Cornish game hens, squabs, pheasant, duck, and goose—are more readily available frozen than fresh. Among specialty items are frozen stuffed turkeys, frozen turkey rolls, and boneless roasts, frozen breaded turkey steaks (to be butter-browned like minute steaks) and countless precooked frozen chicken and turkey dinners.

To Be Sure of Top Quality: Buy solidly frozen birds with no discoloration or signs of freezer burn and no signs of having thawed and refrozen (a block of frozen juices at the bottom of the package).

How to Cook Frozen Poultry: Thaw birds thoroughly, then cook as you would fresh poultry. *Exception:* Frozen stuffed turkeys that must be cooked from the solidly frozen state (follow package directions carefully).

Best Ways to Thaw Frozen Poultry:

Refrigerator Method: This is the safest but also the slowest. Place wrapped bird on a tray in the refrigerator. Ducks and geese will thaw in 2–3 days, chickens in 12–16 hours, chicken parts in 4–9 hours. Small birds will thaw somewhat faster.

Quick Method: Place wrapped birds in a large kettle, cover with cold water, and let stand at room temperature, changing water often. Ducks, geese, and large chickens will thaw in 2–4 hours, small chickens in about 1 hour, game hens in ½ hour.

Special Techniques for Turkeys:

Latest recommendations from the Poultry and Egg National Board are based upon how soon you want to cook the bird:

If You Want to Cook the Turkey Immediately: Unwrap frozen turkey and place on a rack in a shallow roasting pan; roast uncovered 1 hour at 325° F. Take turkey from oven and remove neck and giblets from body cavity and neck area; cook these immediately. Return turkey to oven *at once* and roast until done. Cook the stuffing separately.

If You Want to Cook the Turkey Later in the Day: Place wrapped turkey in a large kettle and cover with cold water; let stand at room temperature, changing water very often; or let stand in sink under a slow stream of cold water. A 5–9-pound turkey will thaw in 3–4 hours; a larger bird in 4–7. Roast the turkey as soon as it is thawed.

If You Want to Cook the Turkey Tomorrow: Leave turkey in its original wrapper, then place in a large brown paper bag or wrap in 2–3 layers of newspaper. Set on a tray or in a baking pan and let thaw at room temperature.

THAWING TIME

WEIGHT	TIME
4–10 pounds	6–10 hours
10–16 pounds	10–14 hours
16–24 pounds	14–18 hours

If You Want to Cook the Turkey the Day After Tomorrow: Use the refrigerator method described above.

Notes of Caution: Never let a thawed bird stand at room temperature. Refrigerate at once or, better still, roast. Never stuff a thawed bird until just before you pop it into the oven.

About Canned Poultry

Frozen and fresh poultry have all but eclipsed the canned. Most readily available are canned chicken meat (wonderful for sandwiches, salads, and casseroles), whole chicken, and an assortment of ready-to-heat dishes (fricassees, stews, à la kings, etc.). In gourmet shops you'll also find such canned delicacies as preserved goose and smoked quail or pheasant.

Other Forms of Poultry

There is smoked turkey, some of which is ready to eat, some of which requires further cooking (read labels carefully). And in Oriental groceries you'll find such exotics as dried duck feet and preserved duck.

Some Special Terms and Techniques Applying to Poultry

Ballotine: A fully or partially boned bird (usually chicken or turkey), stuffed with forcemeat, reshaped, and roasted or steamed. Ballotines are usually served hot but can be served cold.

To Bard: To cover or wrap in thin sheets of fat back, salt pork, or bacon before roasting to keep a bird moist and juicy. Most poultry has enough fat of its own to ensure succulence, but guinea fowl, pheasant, and game hens may not.

To Bone: To remove all major bones; wing tips and lower leg bones are sometimes left in a bird to give it shape. Because birds are anatomically similar, all can be boned

by the basic techniques below (always save bones for making stock). Large birds are easier to bone than small ones (it's easier to see what you're doing); tiny birds like squabs or game hens are rarely boned—too tedious.

How to Bone a Whole Bird: Wipe bird with a damp cloth and pat dry; remove loose fat from body cavity. If bird is a turkey, duck, or goose, cut off wings; otherwise cut off tips at "elbow" joint. Lay bird breast side down on a board and slit center back from neck to tail (1) with a sharp knife; cut out tail and oil sac. Working down and around one side toward breast, peel flesh away from bones (2), freeing stubborn parts with the knife (it's rather like taking off a jacket). Sever ball joints at hips and shoulders (3). When you reach the ridge of the breastbone (keel bone), repeat operation on the other side, again working flesh free around back and toward breast. Lift carcass with 1 hand and very carefully cut against ridge, taking care not to pierce skin.

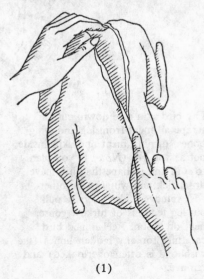

(1)

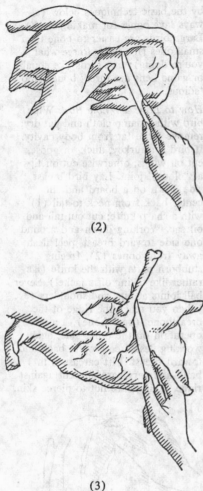

(2)

(3)

How to Bone Breasts: Whenever a recipe calls for boned breasts, try to have the butcher do the boning for you. If you must do the job yourself, ask for whole breasts with left and right sides intact; they are easier to bone than split or halved breasts. Since many supermarkets sell split breasts, instructions are given here for boning whole and half breasts.

Whole Breasts: Place breast skin side down and sever white gristle at neck end of keel bone (the sharp-ridged bone in the center of the breast). Bend breast halves backward (1), then press flat, exposing keel bone. Run index finger around bone to loosen; lift out. Working with 1 side of breast, insert knife tip under long rib bone (2), slide knife underneath bone, cutting meat free. Work flesh free of ribs, cutting as needed around outer edge of breast up to shoulder; lift out rib cage; repeat on other side. Remove wishbone and white tendons on either side of it (3). Skin, if you like (it easily peels off).

Half Breasts: Place breast skin side up, slide knife point between flesh and bottom rib, then, keeping cutting edge against rib cage, peel

Lay bird skin side down, cut and scrape all meat from leg and wing bones, turning meat and skin inside out as you go. (*Note:* If you plan to stuff and reshape the bird, leave drumstick and wingtips in; otherwise remove.) Use pliers to pull out leg tendons of turkey, goose, hen, or capon. Feel boned bird carefully for any hidden bones (the wishbone is often overlooked) and remove.

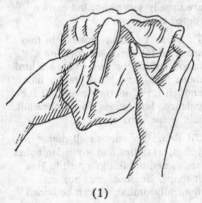

(1)

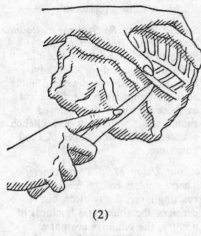

(2)

(3)

back flesh, using knife as needed to free stubborn bits. Lift out ribs and cut out white tendons. Skin if you like.

To Bone Drumsticks and Thighs: Cut length of drumstick or thigh on underside to bone and peel away flesh.

Deep Basted: A commercial technique of injecting butter underneath the skin of turkeys to make them buttery and juicy.

To Disjoint: To cut up a bird (usually chicken) by severing at the joints (see About Cutting Up Poultry).

To Draw: To eviscerate.

Galantine: A bird, usually chicken or turkey, completely boned, then stuffed with forcemeat and shaped into a plump sausage-like roll. It is poached, then chilled and served cold, often elaborately decorated and glazed with aspic.

Giblets: The gizzard, heart, and liver of a bird (see What to Do with Giblets).

Keel or Keel Bone: The longitudinal breastbone, sharp and ridged. In young birds it is pliable; in old birds rigid.

Oysters: The choice nuggets of dark meat found in the cavities of the hip bone.

Pinfeathers: The coarse, quill-like feathers of a bird. The easiest way to remove them is with tweezers.

To Pluck: To pick feathers from a bird.

Rack: The carcass of a bird.

To Singe: To burn off fine hairs remaining on a bird after plucking.

To Stuff: To fill the body and neck cavities of a bird with a savory dressing, with forcemeat, fruit, or vegetables. Always stuff a bird loosely—so the stuffing has room to expand—and always stuff *just before cooking,* never earlier or you're flirting with food poisoning. Also, remove stuffing from leftover bird and refrigerate separately.

Suprêmes: Boned breasts of poultry (see Suprêmes of Chicken in recipe section).

To Truss: To fold a bird's wings back and under and tie its legs close to the body so it will roast more evenly (see How to Roast Poultry).

Tucked Bird: A bird (usually turkey) made more compact by having its drumsticks tucked under a flap of breast skin.

Turken or Churkey: A large, bareheaded breed of chicken, *not*, as sometimes proclaimed, a cross between a turkey and a chicken.

Vent: The opening at the base of the tail of a drawn bird.

Volaille: The French word for poultry.

Wishbone: The breastbone.

Should Poultry Be Brought to Room Temperature Before Cooking? Some cooks like to do so, but it is often not practical—or even advisable—to let birds stand several hours at room temperature. Stuffed birds or those that have been thawed should never be left out on a kitchen counter—too much danger of food poisoning.

About Using Meat Thermometers: Thermometers can be used when roasting large, fleshy birds, but because of the shape and boniness of poultry, the readings are not a completely reliable indicator of doneness. There are two ways to in-

HOW TO COOK POULTRY

The basic principles of cooking meat apply to cooking poultry (see the Ways of Cooking Meat). To determine the best ways to cook specific birds, use the following quick reference table.

Bird	Weight in Pounds	Roast	Spit-Roast	Broil	Charcoal Broil	Panfry (Saute)	Deep Fat Fry	Oven Fry	Braise	Simmer (Poach)	Stew	Steam
Chicken:												
Squab chicken	1			X		X	X					
Broiler-fryer	1½-4	X	X	X	X	X	X	X	X	X	X	X
Roaster	3½-5	X	X						X	X	X	X
Capon	4-7	X	X						X	X	X	X
Bro-hen, stewing hen	3-6½									X		
Turkey:												
Fryer-roaster	4-9	X	X	X	X				X	X		
Young or yearling hens and toms	10-24	X	X									
Rock Cornish game hens, squabs:	1-2	X	X						X			
Guinea fowl, pheasant:	2-4	X	X						X			
Duck:												
Broiler or fryer duckling	3	X	X	X	X				X			
Roaster duckling	3-5	X	X						X			
Goose:	4-14	X	X						X			

sert a thermometer in birds: in the large meaty muscle on the *inside* of the thigh so that the thermometer does not touch bone (when a chicken is done, the reading will be 190° F.; for a turkey it will be 180–85° F.); or, if a bird is stuffed, through the carcass into the center of the stuffing, again with thermometer tip not touching bone (when a bird is done, the thermometer should read 165° F.).

Tests for Doneness: The old-fashioned finger tests are probably the most accurate ways to tell if a bird is done: Cover thumb and forefinger with a bit of paper towel and pinch the thickest part of the thigh; if the meat feels very soft, the bird is done. Or, grasp drumstick; if it moves easily in the hip socket, the bird is done. This last test is best for birds being stewed or steamed until very well done.

How to Roast Poultry

Best Birds: See the table under How to Cook Poultry.

Basic Preparation for Cooking: Remove paper of giblets from body (save giblets for gravy or use in stuffing; see What to Do with Giblets). Also remove any loose fat from body cavity. Wipe bird with a damp cloth but do not wash (most birds coming to market today are beautifully cleaned and dressed; washing them merely destroys some of their flavor). Singe off any hairs and remove pinfeathers. Sprinkle neck and body cavities with salt.

To Stuff a Bird: You'll need about ½ cup stuffing per pound of bird. Choose a stuffing that complements the bird you're roasting (see Some Sauces, Gravies, and Seasonings

for Poultry), then spoon stuffing *loosely* into both body and neck cavities. If you pack stuffing into a bird, it will become tough and rubbery in cooking. If a particular recipe makes more stuffing than a bird will hold, simply wrap the leftover in foil and bake alongside the bird in the pan. (*Note:* Do not stuff a bird until *just* before roasting; and do not let a stuffed bird stand at room temperature. Ever.)

To Truss a Bird: After stuffing bird, skewer or sew openings shut as shown, then truss by folding the wings back and underneath body and tying drumsticks close to body so bird will have a more compact shape and roast more evenly.

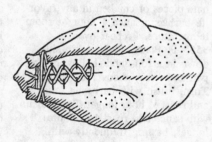

Basic Roasting Method

Chicken:

Whole Birds: Preheat oven to 400° F. if bird weighs 2 pounds or less, to 375° F. if between 2½ and 4 pounds, and to 325° F. if more than 4 pounds. Prepare bird for roasting as directed, place breast side up on a rack in a shallow roasting pan and brush, if you like, with melted butter or margarine or cooking oil. Insert meat thermometer in thigh or stuffing,* not touching bone. Roast uncovered, using times given in Poultry Roasting Chart as a guide. (*Note:* For extra flavor, baste often during cooking with seasoned butter or, if you prefer, glaze,* during last ½ hour of roasting—see Some Marinades and Glazes for Poultry.)

Chicken Halves or Quarters: Preheat oven to 400° F. Wipe pieces of chicken with a damp cloth and place skin side up in a lightly greased shallow roasting pan. Brush with melted butter or cooking oil and sprinkle with salt and pepper. Roast uncovered, without turning, until tender and browned, brushing, if needed to keep chicken moist, with additional butter or oil. Use times in roasting chart as a guide.

VARIATION:

Oven-Barbecued Chicken: Marinate pieces of chicken in any favorite barbecue sauce 1 hour at room temperature. Preheat oven to 350° F. Place chicken skin side down in a foil-lined shallow baking pan and roast, uncovered, ½ hour. Turn, brush with barbecue sauce, and roast ½ hour longer. Brush again with sauce and roast 15 minutes longer, basting frequently with sauce.

Turkey:

Breast-Up Method for a Whole Bird: This is the preferred way today; it produces an exquisitely brown bird. Preheat oven to 325° F. Prepare turkey for roasting as directed and place breast side up on a rack in a shallow roasting pan. Insert meat thermometer in thigh or stuffing,* not touching bone, and roast uncovered, according to times given in Poultry Roasting Chart. Baste, if you like, with melted butter or margarine every ½–¾ hour. If bird browns too fast, tent breast loosely with foil.

VARIATION:

Beer and Butter Basted Turkey: Rub turkey well with softened butter, then roast as directed, rubbing with additional softened butter every ½ hour and basting with about ½ cup beer. You'll need about ¼ pound butter and 2–3 (12-ounce) cans of beer.

Breast-Down Method for a Whole Bird: Though this method produces juicier breast meat, it has disadvantages: The breast skin is apt to stick to the rack and tear as the turkey is being turned and the act of turning a hot, hefty turkey is both difficult and dangerous. Preheat oven to 325° F. Prepare turkey for roasting as directed and place breast side down in a V rack in a shallow roasting pan. Roast, uncovered, until half done according to roasting chart, turn breast side up, insert meat thermometer in thickest part of inside thigh,* not touching bone, and continue roasting, uncovered, until done. Baste, if you like, during cooking with drippings or melted butter.

Fast Foil Method for a Whole Bird: This is the method to use for birds, especially big ones, that must be cooked in a "hurry." Turkeys cooked this way will have more of a steamed than roasted flavor. Preheat oven to 450° F. Prepare turkey for roasting as directed and place in the center of a large sheet of heavy foil; brush well with softened butter, margarine, or shortening. Bring foil up on both sides of breast and make a simple overlapping fold at the top, smooth down around turkey, then crumple ends of foil up to hold in juices. Place turkey breast side up in a shallow roasting pan and roast as follows:

Ready-to-Cook Weight	Total Roasting Time
6–8 pounds	1½–2 hours
8–12 pounds	2–2½ hours
12–16 pounds	2½–3 hours
16–20 pounds	3–3½ hours
20–24 pounds	3½–4 hours

About 30–40 minutes before turkey is done, open tent of foil and fold back and away from bird so it will brown nicely.

(*Note:* When roasting turkey by any of the three preceding methods, it's a good idea to cut string holding drumsticks to tail about 1 hour before bird is done so that inner legs and thighs will brown.)

Turkey Halves or Quarters: Preheat oven to 325° F. Wipe pieces of turkey with a damp cloth and pat dry; skewer skin to meat around edges to prevent it from shrinking during cooking; tie leg to tail, lay wing flat over breast meat, and tie string around to hold in place. Place pieces of turkey skin side up on a rack in a shallow roasting pan and brush well with melted butter or margarine; sprinkle with salt and pepper. Insert meat thermometer in center of inside thigh muscle. Roast uncovered, basting occasionally with drippings or additional melted butter, using times in Poultry Roasting Chart as a guide.

Cut-Up Turkey: Preheat oven to 325° F. Wipe pieces with a damp cloth and pat dry, place skin side up on a rack in a shallow roasting pan, brush well with melted butter or margarine, and sprinkle with salt and pepper. Roast uncovered, basting occasionally with drippings or extra melted butter, using times in Poultry Roasting Chart as a guide.

Rock Cornish Game Hens and Squabs: Preheat oven to 400° F. Prepare birds for roasting as directed. Rub well with softened butter or margarine or drape with strips of bacon or fat back. Place breast side up on a rack in a shallow roasting pan and roast uncovered, basting often with drippings or melted butter, according to times given in Poultry Roasting Chart.

VARIATIONS:

Napa Valley Roast Rock Cornish Game Hens or Squabs: Stuff each bird with ¼ cup seedless green grapes that have been tossed with 1 teaspoon sugar. Brush generously with a hot mixture of ¼ cup melted butter, 1 tablespoon honey, 1 teaspoon seasoned salt, and ⅛ teaspoon pepper. Place breast side up on a rack in a shallow roasting pan, add ½ cup each sauterne and water to pan, and roast as directed, basting often.

Mustardy Rock Cornish Game Hens or Squabs in Lemon Cream Sauce: Spread each hen with 1 teaspoon Dijon mustard, then roast as directed. Halve birds and set aside. For each bird, heat 1 cup heavy cream and 1 teaspoon finely grated lemon rind in a double boiler over simmering water 10 minutes; for each bird, lightly beat 1 egg yolk. Blend a little hot mixture into yolks, return to pan, and heat and stir over simmering water until slightly thickened. Pour off all but 1 tablespoon drippings from roasting pan, add cream sauce, stirring to scrape up browned bits. Add salt, pepper, and, if you like, lemon juice to taste. Return hens to pan and set in oven turned to lowest heat; let warm 10 minutes. Serve in a deep platter smothered with sauce.

Guinea Fowl and Farm-Raised Pheasant: Preheat oven to 350° F. Prepare bird for roasting as directed. Brush well with melted butter or margarine or, if bird seems especially lean, bard.* Place breast side up on a rack in a shallow roasting pan and roast uncovered, basting often with drippings or brushing with additional melted butter, using times in Poultry Roasting Chart as a guide.

Duck or Goose:

Whole Birds: Preheat oven to 325° F. Prepare bird for roasting as directed. Also rub inside well with half a lemon before stuffing. Prick skin well all over with a sharp fork so fat underneath will drain off during cooking. Rub skin well with salt (this helps to crispen skin). Place bird breast side up on a rack in a shallow roasting pan and roast uncovered, draining off drippings as they accumulate and pricking as needed. Use times in Poultry Roasting Chart as a guide. (*Note:* For a particularly crisp skin, raise oven temperature to 450° F. during last ½ hour of roasting. Also drain all drippings from pan and spoon ¼–½ cup ice water over bird. Or, if you prefer, glaze* bird during last part of roasting—see Some Marinades and Glazes for Poultry.

Some Notes About Goose Stuffings: In Europe, very simple stuffings are popular: quartered, cored tart apples sprinkled with cinnamon or nutmeg and sometimes mixed with plumped raisins; drained sauerkraut mixed with caraway seeds; or equal parts minced apples, celery, and cranberries or pitted dried prunes or apricots.

VARIATIONS:

Roast Duck or Goose with Sauerkraut and Applesauce: Roast bird as directed and ½ hour before it is done remove rack and drain off all drippings. Place a 1″ bed drained sauerkraut in bottom of pan, add ½ cup applesauce or whole cranberry sauce, and toss well to mix. Place bird breast side up on sauerkraut and finish roasting as directed. Serve wreathed with the sauerkraut.

Orange-Tea-Glazed Roast Duck or Goose: Roast bird as directed, basting every 20 minutes with the following mixture: 2 cups hot strong tea blended with ¼ cup honey and the slivered rind of 1 orange. Sprinkle with a little extra grated rind just before serving. (*Note:* For distinctive flavor, add ½ teaspoon Formosa Oolong tea to the regular when brewing.)

Duckling Halves or Quarters: Preheat oven to 450° F. Wipe pieces of duckling with a damp cloth and pat dry; prick skin well all over with a sharp fork. Place skin side up on a rack in a shallow roasting pan and roast, uncovered, ½ hour; lower oven temperature to 350° F. and roast 1½ hours longer until tender. Drain off drippings as they accumulate. Glaze,* if you like, during last ½ hour of cooking (see Some Marinades and Glazes for Poultry).

How to Spit-Roast Poultry

Best Birds: See the table under How to Cook Poultry.

Basic Preparation for Cooking: The same as for roasting. *Do not stuff bird.* Tie drumsticks firmly to tail; skewer neck skin to back, flatten

POULTRY ROASTING CHART

Note: Times given are for birds taken from the refrigerator and stuffed. Reduce total roasting times by about 15 minutes if birds are unstuffed. Times are approximate at best, so test often for doneness toward end of cooking.

Bird	Oven Temperature	Total Cooking Time in Hours	Special Treatment Needed	Internal Temperature When Done
Chicken				
2 pounds	400°F.	1-1½	Tent bird loosely with	190°F.
2½-4 pounds	375°F.	1½-2¼	foil if it browns too	190°F.
4-7 pounds	325°F.	3-5	fast.	190°F.
Halves or quarters	400°F.	3/4-1		190°F.
Turkey (whole)				
4-8 pounds	325°F.	2½-3½	Tent bird loosely with	180-85°F.
8-12 pounds	325°F.	3½-4½	foil or cover breast with	180-85°F.
12-16 pounds	325°F.	4½-5½	butter-soaked cheese-	180-85°F.
16-20 pounds	325°F.	5½-6½	cloth if it browns too	180-85°F.
20-24 pounds	325°F.	6½-7	fast.	180-85°F.
Turkey halves or quarters				
5-8 pounds	325°F.	2½-3	Tent loosely with foil	180-85°F.
8-10 pounds	325°F.	3-3½	if browning too fast.	180-85°F.
10-12 pounds	325°F.	3½-4		180-85°F.
Boneless turkey rolls and roasts (unstuffed)				
3-5 pounds	325°F.	2½-3	Tent loosely with foil	170-75°F.
5-7 pounds	325°F.	3-3½	if browning too fast.	170-75°F.
7-9 pounds	325°F.	3½-4		170-75°F.
Turkey breasts (unstuffed)				
4-6 pounds	325°F.	2¼-3	Tent loosely with foil	180-85°F.
6-8 pounds	325°F.	3-3½	if browning too fast.	180-85°F.
8-10 pounds	325°F.	3½-4		180-85°F.
10-12 pounds	325°F.	4-4¼		180-85°F.
12-14 pounds	325°F.	4¼-4½		180-85°F.
Rock Cornish game hens and squabs				
3/4-1½ pounds	400°F.	3/4-1	Brush often with melted butter or drippings.	—
Guinea fowl and farm-raised pheasant				
2-4 pounds	350°F.	1½-2½	Brush or baste often with melted butter or drippings.	—

POULTRY ROASTING CHART (continued)

Bird	Oven Temperature	Total Cooking Time in Hours	Special Treatment Needed	Internal Temperature When Done
Duck (whole)				
4-5½ pounds	325° F.	2½-3	Prick often with a sharp fork throughout cooking and drain off drippings as they collect.	—
Duckling halves and quarters	450° F. for 1/2 hour THEN 350° F. for 1½ hours	2		
Goose				
4-6 pounds	325° F.	2¾-3	Prick goose often with a	—
6-8 pounds	325° F.	3-3½	sharp fork during cooking	—
8-12 pounds	325° F.	3½-4½	and drain off drippings	—
12-14 pounds	325° F.	4½-5	as they collect. Also allow about 1/2 hour margin in cooking times at left according to breed of goose; some cook faster than others.	—

Note: If meat thermometer is inserted in center of stuffing (not touching bone) instead of in thigh, bird should be done when thermometer reads 165° F. The legs of all birds except chicken and turkeys are too skimpy to hold a meat thermometer, so if a thermometer is used, it must be inserted in the stuffing.

wings against sides of breast, and tie string around breast to hold wings in. Insert spit lengthwise, slightly on the diagonal, through bird from vent to the top of the breast-bone; tighten holding forks. Test balance of bird on spit and readjust, if necessary, so bird will turn smoothly. If bird is large enough to do so, insert meat thermometer in center of plump inside thigh muscle and make sure thermometer will clear unit as spit turns. (*Note:* If spitting several small birds, allow about ½" between birds so heat will circulate freely.)

To Spit-Roast in Oven or Rotisserie: Preheat unit. Prepare and spit bird as directed, attach spit to rotisserie, and roast, using table below as a guide.

Note: Below times are for birds taken straight from the refrigerator; they can be used as a guide only. Chicken, turkey, and boneless turkey roasts only are of a size and shape to make use of meat thermometer practical. Test birds for doneness often after minimum cooking time is up. When spit-roasting fat birds like duck or goose, watch carefully and drain off drippings as they accumulate.

To Spit-Roast over Charcoal: Build a moderately hot charcoal fire.* Prepare and spit bird as directed. Attach spit to motor, adjust spit height so it is 5″ from coals, and place a drip pan where it will catch the drippings (especially important with duck and goose). Roast, increasing times given for oven spit-roasting by ¼–½ hour, depending on size of bird and the weather (on a cool, windy day, over-all cooking times may need to be increased by as much as ¾ hour for large birds). Watch birds carefully toward end of cooking and test often for doneness.

VARIATION:

Spit-Barbecued Birds: Prepare and spit-roast as directed, brushing often during last ½ hour of cooking with any barbecue sauce.

How to Broil Poultry

Best Birds: See the table under How to Cook Poultry.

Basic Preparation for Cooking: Have small chickens and ducklings halved, larger ones quartered; turkeys should be cut up. Wipe the birds with a damp cloth.

To Broil in the Oven: Preheat broiler. Place bird skin side down on a lightly greased broiler rack. Brush chicken or turkey with melted butter or margarine or cooking oil, but not duckling. Duckling should be pricked well all over so that the fat underneath skin can drain off during broiling. Broil according to table above, brushing chicken or turkey well with additional melted butter after turning and throughout cooking as needed. Duckling should be pricked throughout cooking and its drippings drained off as they accumulate.

Note: These times can be used only as a guide; test often for

doneness toward end of minimum cooking time: twist a drumstick in its socket; if it pulls loose, bird is done. Or make a tiny slit down to bone; if no pink meat remains, bird is done. Livers of birds can be broiled too. Toward end of cooking, brush well with melted butter or margarine, place on broiler rack, and broil 3–5 minutes per side, depending on size.

To Charcoal Broil: Build a moderately hot charcoal fire.* Adjust height of grill so it is 6″–8″ from coals. Prepare bird as directed; brush chicken and turkey well with cooking oil, melted butter or margarine; prick duck skin all over with a sharp fork. Place bird skin side up on a lightly greased grill and broil, turning often, until tender. Chicken will need 50–60 minutes altogether, depending on size; turkey 1½–1¾ hours and duck 1–1½ hours. Brush chicken and turkey throughout broiling with additional oil or melted butter; prick duck often (also be prepared to douse flare-ups). (*Note:* If day is cool and gusty, you'll have to increase cooking times somewhat.)

VARIATIONS:

⚖ **Low-Calorie Broiled Chicken or Turkey:** Broil or charcoal-broil as directed, brushing with low-calorie garlic, herb, or Italian dressing instead of oil, butter, or margarine. About 225 calories per average portion of turkey and 250 per average portion of chicken. White meat pieces will be slightly lower.

Marinated or Barbecued Birds: Marinate birds in any marinade or barbecue sauce 3–4 hours in refrigerator before cooking; broil or charcoal-broil as directed, brushing often with marinade or sauce during last ½ hour of cooking.

Bird	Total Roasting Time	Internal Temperature When Done
Chicken		
2–3 pounds	1–1¼ hours	190° F.
4–5 pounds	1½–2 hours	190° F.
6–7 pounds	2½–3 hours	190° F.
Turkey		
4–6 pounds	2–3 hours	180–85° F.
6–8 pounds	3–3½ hours	180–85° F.
8–10 pounds	3½–4 hours	180–85° F.
10–12 pounds	4–5 hours	180–85° F.

Boneless Turkey Roasts (If there are wrapper directions for spit roasting, follow them; otherwise, use times below. Let roast "rest" ½ hour at room temperature before carving.)

3–5 pounds	2–3 hours	170–75° F.
5–7 pounds	3–3½ hours	170–75° F.
7–9 pounds	3½–4 hours	170–75° F.

Cornish Game Hens and Squabs		
¾–1½ pounds	40–45 minutes	————

Guinea Fowl and Farm-Raised Pheasant		
2–4 pounds	1–2 hours	————

Duck		
4–5 pounds	1½–2½ hours	————

Goose		
4–6 pounds	2–3 hours	————

Bird	Best Weight for Broiling	Distance from Heat	Minutes on First Side	Minutes on Second Side
Chicken	1½–3 pounds	6″	20–25	15–20
Turkey	4–6 pounds	9″	40	40–50
Duckling	3 pounds or less	7″–8″	30	30–45

Lemon-Broiled Chicken or Turkey: Mix ½ cup melted butter or margarine with the juice of 1 lemon and ½ teaspoon rosemary. (*Note:* For turkey, double quantities.) Brush liberally over bird and broil or charcoal-broil as directed, brushing often.

Portuguese-Style Charcoal-Broiled Chicken or Turkey: Mix ¼ cup olive oil with 2 peeled and crushed cloves garlic, 1 tablespoon paprika, 1 teaspoon salt, and ⅛ teaspoon pepper. (*Note:* Double amounts for turkey.) Brush bird well with mixture and let stand at room temperature ½ hour. Broil or charcoal-broil as directed, brushing often with mixture.

Chicken in a Basket over Charcoal:
Place cut-up chicken in a metal
rotisserie basket, balance basket in
center of spit, and tighten screws.
Attach spit to motor and position so
center of basket is 5″–6″ from coals.
Broil chicken 1½–1¾ hours or until
fork tender and golden. (*Note:*
Keep an eye on wings because
tips sometimes catch in basket and
brown unevenly. *Stop basket* before
adjusting.) When chicken is done,
remove from basket and sprinkle
with salt and pepper. (*Note:*
Chicken can be marinated 3–4 hours
in any barbecue sauce in refrigerator
before cooking.)

Chicken in Foil over Charcoal:
Butter 4 (12″) squares heavy
foil well; lay 1 chicken quarter
in the center of each, sprinkle with
salt and pepper, and wrap tight.
Grill 3″–4″ from glowing coals
1–1¼ hours until tender, turning
packages halfway through cooking.
Unwrap chicken, place skin side
down on grill, cover loosely with
foil, and brown 4–5 minutes.
(*Note:* Chicken can be marinated
3–4 hours in any barbecue sauce
or marinade [see Some Marinades
and Glazes for Poultry] in refrigerator before cooking. Include
1–2 tablespoons marinade in
each foil package and brush with
marinade during final browning.)

How to Fry Poultry

Best Birds: Chicken and very small,
young turkey.

Basic Preparation for Cooking:
Have birds cut up; wipe with a
damp cloth but do not pat dry.

To Panfry (Sauté) Chicken: Dredge
by shaking 1–2 pieces at a time in a
bag in seasoned flour (⅔ cup

unsifted flour, 1 teaspoon salt, ¼
teaspoon pepper, and, if you like,
¼ teaspoon paprika for 1 bird).
Pour ½″ cooking oil or melted
shortening in a large, heavy skillet
and heat over moderately high heat
until a cube of bread will sizzle.
Put larger, meatier pieces of
chicken skin side down in hot fat;
add remaining chicken and fry,
uncovered, 15–25 minutes on each
side, adjusting heat as needed so
chicken does not brown too fast.
Turn chicken only once during
cooking. Add liver and heart during
last few minutes. Drain chicken on
paper toweling and serve.

VARIATIONS:

Chili-Fried Chicken: Prepare as
directed, adding 1 tablespoon chili
powder and ¼ teaspoon each
garlic and onion powder to seasoned
flour.

Curry-Fried Chicken: Prepare as
directed, adding 2–3 teaspoons curry
powder and ¼ teaspoon each ginger
and garlic powder to seasoned flour.

Cheesy-Fried Chicken: Prepare
as directed, reducing flour in
seasoned flour to ½ cup and adding
½ cup finely grated Parmesan
cheese and 1 teaspoon oregano or
marjoram.

Crisp-Fried Chicken: Dip pieces of
chicken in evaporated milk or light
cream, then dredge and fry as
directed.

To Panfry (Sauté) Turkey: This
is really a combination of frying and
braising. Have a small (4–9-pound)
turkey cut up. For each 5 pounds
of turkey, blend together ¾ cup
unsifted flour, 2 teaspoons each salt
and paprika, and ¼ teaspoon
pepper. Dredge turkey in seasoned
flour by shaking in a paper bag.
Pour enough cooking oil or melted

shortening in a large, heavy skillet to cover bottom; heat over moderately high heat until a cube of bread will sizzle. Begin browning turkey, biggest pieces first. Slip smaller pieces in and around the large ones. Brown about 20 minutes, turning as needed with tongs so pieces brown evenly. Add 2–4 tablespoons water, cover, and cook over low heat ¾–1 hour until turkey is tender. Turn pieces 2 or 3 times as they cook. Uncover and cook 10 minutes longer to crispen. (*Note:* The liver may be added during the last 15 minutes.)

To Pan- and Oven-Fry Chicken (Combination Method): Preheat oven to 350° F. Dredge and brown chicken as for panfrying; transfer to an ungreased shallow baking pan, arranging pieces skin side up in a single layer. Bake, uncovered, 35–45 minutes until tender.

To Deep-Fat-Fry Chicken: Prepare a small (1½–2½-pound) broiler-fryer for frying as directed above. Beat 1 egg with ¼ cup cold milk; also mix 1 cup unsifted flour with 1 teaspoon salt and ¼ teaspoon pepper. Dip chicken in egg, roll in flour to coat evenly, and fry, 3–4 pieces at a time, in 350° F. deep fat 15–17 minutes until richly browned all over. Drain on paper toweling.

VARIATIONS:

Southern Fried Chicken: Let chicken marinate in milk to cover 1 hour at room temperature. Dip in egg mixture as directed, then dredge in ½ cup unsifted flour mixed with ¾ cup cracker meal, 1 tablespoon paprika, 1½ teaspoons salt, and ¼ teaspoon pepper. Fry in deep fat as directed.

Batter-Fried Chicken: Prepare 1 recipe Basic Batter for Fried Foods.

Dip a 1–1½-pound cut-up chicken in batter, then fry, 3–4 pieces at a time, in 350° F. deep fat 15–17 minutes until nut brown. Drain on paper toweling. (*Note:* Because the batter acts as an insulator and slows cooking, use only the very smallest chickens for batter-frying.)

To Oven-Fry Chicken: Preheat oven to 350° F. Place a large, shallow roasting pan in oven, add ¼ pound butter or margarine and let melt as oven preheats. Meanwhile, dredge chicken pieces in seasoned flour as for panfrying. Roll chicken in the melted butter, then arrange skin side up 1 layer deep and bake, uncovered, 1–1¼ hours until fork tender and browned.

VARIATIONS:

Chicken Italiano: Lightly beat 1 egg with the juice of 1 lemon. Dip chicken pieces in egg, then in 1 cup Italian-style seasoned bread crumbs. Place in a single layer in a greased large, shallow baking pan, drizzle with ½ cup melted butter or margarine, and bake as directed.

Chicken Parmesan: Dip chicken pieces in ⅔ cup melted butter or margarine, then roll in 1 cup soft white bread crumbs mixed with ⅓ cup finely grated Parmesan, 2 tablespoons minced parsley, ½ crushed clove garlic, 1 teaspoon salt, and ⅛ teaspoon pepper to coat evenly. Arrange 1 layer deep in a greased large, shallow baking pan and drizzle evenly with remaining melted butter. Bake as directed.

Crispy Oven-Fried Chicken: Dredge chicken pieces in ⅔ cup unsifted flour mixed with 1 teaspoon each salt and paprika, ½ teaspoon each onion powder and savory, and ¼ teaspoon each garlic powder and pepper. Dip in 1 egg that has been lightly beaten with ¼ cup cold milk, then roll in ⅔ cup cracker meal mixed with 3 tablespoons minced parsley to coat evenly. Arrange 1 layer deep in a greased large, shallow baking pan and drizzle with ½ cup melted butter or margarine. Bake as directed.

To Oven-Fry Turkey: Preheat oven to 400° F. Place 1 cup butter (for each 5 pounds turkey) in a large, shallow roasting pan and let melt in preheating oven. Dredge a small (4–9-pound) cut-up turkey in seasoned flour (1½ cups unsifted flour, 1 tablespoon salt, ½ teaspoon pepper), roll in melted butter in pan, then arrange skin side down 1 layer deep in pan. Bake uncovered ¾ hour, turn skin side up, and bake ¾ hour longer until fork tender and nicely browned.

VARIATION:

Chili or Curry-Flavored Oven-Fried Turkey: Prepare as directed but add 1–2 tablespoons chili or curry powder and ½ teaspoon garlic powder to the seasoned flour.

How to Braise Poultry

Braising is an all-encompassing word used to describe foods that are browned in fat, then cooked, covered, with some additional liquid. Fricasseeing is a way of braising, so is cooking birds en casserole. Any bird can be braised, but it's an especially good way to deal with those that are a bit too tough to roast, broil, or fry. See the collection of recipes that follow.

How to Simmer Poultry

Birds can be *poached* in a small amount of liquid or *stewed* in

quantities of it. Disjointed young chickens or parts of them (especially the breasts) are frequently poached before being used in recipes. Stewing is usually reserved for tough, over-the-hill birds that need long and slow simmering to make them tender.

Best Birds: Any birds can be stewed, though chickens are the ones that most often end up in the kettle. The methods given below can be used for other birds as well as for chicken.

To Poach: (Also see Suprêmes of Chicken).

Basic Preparation for Cooking: Have bird disjointed; wipe pieces with a damp cloth.

Basic Method: Place chicken pieces in a single layer in a large, heavy skillet (not iron), add water, chicken broth, or a ½ and ½ mixture of broth and dry white wine almost to cover. Also add, if you like, a *bouquet garni** tied in cheesecloth. Cover and simmer 30–35 minutes until tender. Remove and use in any recipes calling for cooked or poached chicken. Or cover with a suitable sauce and serve (see Some Sauces, Gravies, and Seasonings for Chicken).

To Stew:

Basic Preparation for Cooking: If bird is whole, remove paper of giblets from body cavity; also pull out any loose fat and discard. Wipe bird or pieces of bird with a damp cloth.

Basic Method: Place bird or pieces in a large, heavy kettle and add water almost to cover—a large hen or capon will require about 3 quarts. Add 1 teaspoon salt and, if you like, a small onion peeled and quartered or stuck with 3–4 cloves, 2–3 stalks celery and/or parsley, 2 bay leaves, and 6 peppercorns. Or, if you prefer, add a *bouquet garni** tied in cheesecloth. Cover and simmer slowly until tender. Times vary enormously according to the size and age of the bird. An old hen can take 2–3 hours to become tender, but a capon of the same or slightly larger size may be nearly falling off the bones after only 1 hour. So watch the pot closely. Plump broiler-fryers will be done in 40–55 minutes and a cut-up broiler-fryer or capon in about 25–40. Some parts (wings and backs), of course, cook more quickly than others; remove individual pieces from the kettle as they become tender. (*Note:* Neck, heart, and gizzard can be cooked along with the other parts of the chicken and will probably need the full cooking time. The liver [and sometimes heart] will cook in 10–15 minutes, so cook at the beginning, remove and reserve, or add at the end of cooking.)

How to Steam Poultry

Best Birds: Moderately young and tender chickens or capons.

Basic Preparation for Cooking: Same as for stewing.

Basic Method: Place whole or cut-up bird on a rack in a large kettle, pour in water to a depth of 1″, cover, and bring to a boil. Reduce heat so water just simmers and steam, adding additional water if kettle threatens to boil dry, until bird is tender. A cut-up bird will cook in about ¾ hour, a whole bird in 1–1½. Use steamed chicken in recipes calling for cooked chicken.

About Pressure Cooking Poultry

Only tough old birds should be pressure cooked; young tender ones will fall to pieces. Because cooker techniques differ from model to model, follow manufacturer's instructions. Place chicken, liquid and, if you like, a few chunks of celery, onion, and carrot in cooker, cover, and cook at 15 pounds pressure 25–35 minutes or as manufacturer advises. Lower pressure slowly.

What to Do with the Giblets

You can freeze giblets separately in small plastic bags and save them until you have enough to use in a recipe (see recipes for chicken livers that follow). Or the giblets can be used immediately in stuffings or gravies or slipped into any of the recipes calling for cooked poultry. But first they must be cooked.

To Cook Giblets: Wash giblets carefully in cool water; if liver is green, discard—the gall bladder has ruptured, spilling its bitter gall and ruining the liver. Place giblets in a small saucepan and, if you like, the neck. Add *just* enough cold water to cover, cover pan, and simmer over low heat 10–15 minutes. Remove liver and reserve, also remove heart if it is tender. Re-cover and simmer remaining giblets until tender, 1–2 hours—time will depend on size and age of bird; add additional water during cooking as needed. Remove giblets, mince, and use in recipes calling for cooked poultry meat; also reserve cooking liquid to use in soups and gravies.

To Make Giblet Stock: Cook as directed above, but increase amount of water to 2–3 cups, depending on size of giblets, and add 1 teaspoon salt; replenish water as needed during cooking. Taste stock for seasoning and adjust; if you wish, strain through a fine sieve lined with a double thickness of cheese-cloth before using in recipes. Mince giblets and use in any recipes calling for cooked poultry meat.

About Poultry Stocks

Any liquid used for poaching or stewing a bird is stock and should be saved to use in cooking vege-tables, making sauces and gravies. Specific recipes for chicken and turkey broths can be found in the chapter on soups.

How to Render Chicken or Goose Fat

"Duck fat," someone once said, "isn't fit for anything but greasing your boots." Perhaps. But chicken and goose fat are excellent for browning poultry, potatoes, and other vegetables (turkey fat is good too, but today's birds have almost none). Carefully rendered raw chicken or goose fat can be used as the shortening in biscuits and other hot breads. Jewish women render chicken fat with an apple and onion into *schmaltz,* which they use as a butter substitute. Goose fat has an especially delicate flavor and is an essential ingredient of fine pâtés and *confit d'oie* (pre-served goose). The best fats to render are those pulled raw from the body cavity of a bird. But pan drippings from a roasting bird can be saved, clarified* (see To Clarify Meat Drippings in the meat chap-ter), and used for gravies or browning meats and vegetables.

General Preparation of Fat: Pull fat from body cavity of bird, rinse in cold water, and cut in ½" cubes.

Stove-Top Method of Rendering: (*Note:* This method also clarifies the fat.)

Place prepared fat in a large, heavy saucepan and add enough cold water to come about halfway up fat. Heat uncovered over moderately low heat, stirring frequently, until all fat is melted. Continue heating and stirring until nearly all water has evaporated; liquid will become clear and golden and bubbles will almost subside; strain through a double thickness of cheesecloth, cool, and chill. Carefully lift off fat and discard any liquid that has settled to the bottom; also scrape off any milky, semiliquid layer on bottom of fat. Pack fat in con-tainers, cover, and refrigerate or freeze.

VARIATION:

Seasoned Fat: Render as directed but add 1 peeled and minced onion and 1 peeled and cored tart green apple, cut in wedges, to the pan; remove apple the instant it becomes tender, but leave onion in until almost all water evaporates unless it browns too much. Strain, cool, and store as directed.

Oven Method of Rendering: Pre-heat oven to 250° F. Spread prepared fat in the bottom of a shallow baking pan and add about ½ cup cold water. Heat uncovered, stirring occasionally, until fat is melted and most of the water evaporated. Strain, cool, and store as above. To clarify, follow directions for clarifying rendered fat in the meat chapter.

How to Carve Poultry

Except for minor variations, the technique of carving is the same for all birds:

1. *Separate and Remove Leg:* Pull leg away from body and cut off, following contour of bird. Place on a separate plate.

5. *Carve Breast:* Beginning halfway up breast, carve down, ending at cut made to remove wing. Begin each new slice a little higher on the breast, keeping slices as thin and even as possible.

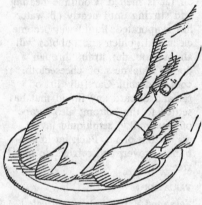

2. *Cut Meat from Leg:* Sever "knee" joint, separating drumstick and thigh. Hold drumstick with a napkin, tilt to a convenient angle, and slice meat parallel to bone.

3. *Cut Meat from Thigh:* Hold thigh firmly to plate with fork and slice parallel to the bone. (*Note:* If a large group is being served, remove other drumstick and thigh and slice.)

4. *Remove Wing:* Place knife parallel with and as close to breast as possible, cut through joint, and remove wing.

Slice only what meat is needed at a time. Make fresh slices for "seconds." (*Note:* Ducks are more difficult to carve than chicken or turkey, and if they are small, you may prefer to quarter them—see How to Cut Up Poultry—in the kitchen before serving.)

Some Marinades and Glazes for Poultry

Marinades: To enrich flavor of whole or cut-up poultry, marinate in refrigerator 3–4 hours before cooking, turning occasionally in marinade, then brush or baste often with marinade during last 20–30 minutes of cooking. Use any of the following, allowing about 1 cup marinade per chicken, 2–3 cups per large bird, and ½ cup per small bird.

– *Herbed or Spiced Wine or Cider* (½ cup dry red, white, or rosé wine or cider mixed with ¼ cup boiling water and 1 teaspoon sage, savory, or thyme or ¼ teaspoon cinnamon, nutmeg, or mace).
– *Juniper Wine* (½ cup dry red, white, or rosé wine mixed with ¼ cup each olive oil and boiling water and 1 teaspoon bruised juniper berries; omit oil if using for duck or goose).
– *Garlic Wine* (½ cup dry red, white, or rosé wine mixed with ¼ cup each olive oil and boiling water and 2 crushed cloves garlic; omit oil if using for duck or goose).
– Any herb, garlic, or Italian salad dressing.
– Any of the following:
Beer Marinade
Poultry Marinade
Buttermilk Marinade
All-Purpose Barbecue Sauce
Japanese Steak Sauce
California Orange-Ginger Barbecue Sauce
Chinese Barbecue Sauce
South American Hot Barbecue Sauce

Glazes: For a gorgeously glistening brown bird, brush with one of the following glazes during the last 20–30 minutes of broiling or roasting. You'll need about ½ cup glaze for a chicken, about 1 cup for a bigger bird, and ¼ cup for a tiny bird:
– A ½ and ½ mixture of melted apple and currant or quince jelly.
– A ½ and ½ mixture of hot apple juice and minced chutney.
– Melted orange, lime, or ginger marmalade.
– Warm wine, beer, cider, orange, grape, or pineapple juice mixed with dark brown sugar (2 tablespoons sugar to each ½ cup liquid).

Butters: Instead of being marinated or glazed, chicken, turkey, and other dry-meated birds can be brushed or basted often during roasting or broiling with one of these seasoned butters: Chili, Chive, Curry, Garlic, Herb, Lemon, Maître d'Hôtel, Mustard, Paprika, or Shallot (see chapter on sauces and gravies for recipes).

Some Ways to Garnish Poultry

Any of the garnishes suggested for pork are suitable for poultry (see Some Garnishes for Roast Pork Platters). Choose small garnishes for small birds, larger ones for larger birds, emphasizing a contrast of colors, textures, and shapes. The point is to enhance the bird, not to overwhelm. Some other garnishing ideas to try:

– A chain of baby link sausages, cooked until brown and glistening, draped over a plump roast turkey or goose.
– Lemon or lime cups filled with cranberry sauce, tart jelly, chutney, or mincemeat.
– Red Cabbage and Chestnuts, Sweet and Sour Red Cabbage, Shredded Ruby Cabbage, or sauerkraut

SOME SAUCES, GRAVIES, AND SEASONINGS FOR POULTRY

	Sauces and Gravies for			
	Roasted, Broiled, Sautéed Birds	Simmered, Steamed Birds	Stuffings for Birds to Be Roasted	Herbs and Spices for Cooking Poultry	Condiments
Chicken, turkey, game hen, squab, guinea fowl, pheasant	All-purpose barbecue	Allemande	Basic bread and variations	Basil	Applesauce
	Bordelaise	Aurore	Basic rice and variations	Bay leaves	Bread sauce
	Brown sauce fines herbes	Béchamel	Basic wild rice and variations	Caraway seeds	Chutney
		Caper	Brandied wild rice, corn	Chervil	Cranberry sauce
	Chasseur	Chaud-froid (cold)	bread, and chestnut	Chili powder	Gingered pears
	Diable	Mornay	Bulgur wheat-pecan	Chives	Jellies: apple, crab
	Espagnole	Mushroom	Chestnut mushroom	Cinnamon	apple, currant,
	Giblet gravy	Mustard	Corn and pepper	Cloves	rosemary, wine
	Madeira	Parsley	Corn bread and sausage and	Coriander	Pickled or brandied
	Mushroom	Poulette	variations	Curry powder	peaches
	Mushroom gravy	Quick mushroom	Giblet	Dill	Relishes: corn, cran-
	Pan gravy	Quick mustard	Mincemeat	Garlic	berry-orange, fruit
	Plum	Soubise	Orange-sweet potato	Ginger	and nut, peach
	Portugaise	Suprême	Prune, apple, and cranberry	Juniper berries	Spiced apricots or crab
	Quick mushroom	Velouté	Sage and onion dressing	Lemon	apples
	Robert		Tangerine cracker (small	Mace	
	Tomato		birds)	Marjoram	
	Victoria			Mustard	
				Nutmeg	
				Onion	
				Orange	
				Oregano	
				Paprika	
				Parsley	
				Poultry seasoning	
				Rosemary	
				Saffron	
				Sage	
				Savory	
				Sesame seeds	
				Shallots	
				Tarragon	
				Thyme	

	Sauces and Gravies	Stuffings for Duck or Goose to Be Roasted	Herbs and Spices to Use in Cooking	Condiments
Roast duck or goose, broiled duckling	Bigarade Bordelaise Bourguignonne Brown sauce fines herbes Chasseur Espagnole Giblet gravy Madeira Madeira mushroom Mushroom gravy Pan gravy Plum Port wine Poivrade Victoria	Amish potato Basic bread and variations Bulgur wheat-pecan Chestnut Giblet Herbed fruit Prune, apple, and cranberry Sage and onion dressing Sauerkraut	Bay leaves Caraway seeds Chives Cinnamon Cloves Curry powder Garlic Ginger Juniper berries Lemon Mace Marjoram Nutmeg Onion Orange Paprika Parsley Sage Thyme	Same as for chicken Pickled red cabbage Sauerkraut

wreathed around roast duck or goose.

– Clusters of Braised Chestnuts or Braised Onions and tiny bundles of buttered asparagus tips bound with strips of pimiento.

– Clusters of tangerine or orange and grapefruit sections.

– Chicken Quenelles or Mousselines sprinkled with minced truffles (for poached chicken).

CHICKEN FRICASSEE

Makes 4 servings

1 (3–3½-pound) broiler-fryer, cut up
¼ cup butter or margarine
3 cups water
1 medium-size yellow onion, peeled and stuck with 6 cloves
1 medium-size carrot, peeled and cut in 1" chunks
1 stalk celery, cut in 1" chunks
1 bouquet garni,* tied in cheesecloth with 6 peppercorns
1 teaspoon salt

Sauce:

3 tablespoons butter or margarine
¼ cup unsifted flour
2 cups chicken broth, reserved from cooking chicken
1 egg yolk, lightly beaten with ½ cup light or heavy cream
1 teaspoon lemon juice
¼ teaspoon sugar
1 teaspoon salt (about)
1 tablespoon minced parsley (garnish)
4 thin lemon slices (garnish)

Brown chicken in butter in a large, heavy kettle over moderately high heat, add all but sauce ingredients, cover, and simmer 30–40 minutes until chicken is tender. Lift chicken from kettle and keep warm; strain broth, skim off fat and measure 2 cups to use in sauce. Melt butter in a large saucepan over moderate heat, blend in flour, slowly stir in broth, and heat, stirring, until thickened. Mix a little hot sauce into yolk mixture, return to pan, and heat and stir over lowest heat 1 minute; do not boil. Blend in lemon juice, sugar, and salt to taste. Add chicken to sauce and warm over lowest heat 1–2 minutes. Serve in a deep platter sprinkled with parsley and garnished with lemon. Good with boiled noodles or rice, mashed potatoes or hot biscuits. About 470 calories per serving.

VARIATIONS:

Georgian Chicken Fricassee: Prepare as directed but when making sauce use 1 cup each broth and dry white wine. Just before serving, mix in ½ pound Pan-Braised Onions and ½ pound sautéed button mushrooms. About 490 calories per serving.

Chicken and Vegetable Fricassee: Prepare as directed; just before serving, mix in 1 (10-ounce) package frozen mixed vegetables cooked and drained by package directions. Omit parsley and lemon and garnish instead with hot buttered asparagus tips. About 520 calories per serving.

Blanquette of Chicken or Turkey (good for leftovers): Prepare sauce as directed, mix with 3 cups large chunks cooked chicken or turkey meat (preferably white). Bring to serving temperature in the top of a double boiler. About 470 calories per serving.

PORTUGUESE-STYLE ROAST CAPON WITH OLIVE AND EGG STUFFING

Lisbon is one of the few European capitals where one can be wakened at 5 A.M. by a rooster crowing. Not surprisingly, Lisbon cooks specialize in chicken. Here is a slightly streamlined version of one of their best dishes.

Makes 6 servings

1 (5–6-pound) capon, cleaned and dressed
1 fifth Portuguese vinho verde or other dry white wine
1 tablespoon olive oil

Stuffing:
4 medium-size yellow onions, peeled and coarsely chopped
3 cloves garlic, peeled and crushed
⅔ cup olive oil
Cooked capon giblets, minced
1 (8-ounce) package poultry stuffing mix
2 (5½-ounce) jars unpitted green olives, drained, pitted, and minced
6 hard-cooked eggs, peeled and diced
¼ teaspoon pepper
¼ teaspoon cinnamon
½ cup giblet stock*
¼ cup dry port wine

The day before you roast the bird, take giblets from body cavity and refrigerate. Place bird in a large bowl, add wine, cover, and marinate overnight in refrigerator. Next day, prepare giblet stock,* mince cooked giblets and reserve for stuffing along with ½ cup stock. Preheat oven to 325° F. For the stuffing, stir-fry onions and garlic in oil in a large, heavy skillet 10–12 minutes over moderate heat until lightly browned. Remove from heat, mix in giblets and remaining stuffing ingredients. Remove bird from marinade, drain, then loosely stuff neck and body cavities. Skewer opening shut and truss.* Wrap any remaining stuffing in foil. Rub bird well with 1 tablespoon oil, place breast side up on a rack in a large, shallow roasting pan; lay foil-wrapped stuffing in pan beside bird. Pour about 1½ cups wine marinade over bird and roast uncovered about 40 minutes per pound, basting every 20 minutes with marinade, until bird is golden brown and leg joints move easily. Lift bird to a large platter, remove skewers and string, garnish with watercress, cherry tomatoes, and black olives, and serve. Spoon extra stuffing into a separate bowl and pan drippings into a gravy boat. About 985 calories per serving.

COQ AU VIN (CHICKEN IN WINE)

Makes 4 servings

2 ounces lean salt pork, cut in small dice
3–4 tablespoons butter or margarine
1 (3–3½-pound) broiler-fryer, cut up
1 pound small white onions, peeled, parboiled, and drained
1 clove garlic, peeled and crushed
½ pound button mushrooms, wiped clean
¼ cup warm cognac or brandy
1 bouquet garni,* tied in cheesecloth
¼ teaspoon pepper
½–1 teaspoon salt
1½ cups Burgundy or other dry red wine
3 tablespoons Beurre Manié

Brown salt pork in a large, heavy kettle over moderate heat; remove with a slotted spoon and reserve. Add 3 tablespoons butter to kettle and brown chicken, a few pieces at a time; remove and reserve. Add onions and brown well all over, about 10 minutes, adding more butter if necessary. Push onions to side of kettle, add garlic and mushrooms, and stir-fry 3–5 minutes until lightly browned. Return salt pork and chicken to kettle, pour cognac over chicken and blaze. When flames die, add all but final ingredient, cover, and simmer about ¾ hour until chicken is tender.

Lift chicken and vegetables to a deep casserole and keep warm. Stir small pieces of *Beurre Manié* into kettle liquid and heat, stirring, until thickened and smooth. Taste for salt and add remainder if needed. Strain gravy over chicken and serve. Good with boiled new potatoes or rice.

VARIATION:

Coq au Vin au Casserole: Prepare as directed, but instead of cooking on the stove top, bake in a covered casserole 30–40 minutes at 350° F. until chicken is tender.

Both versions: About 625 calories per serving (without potatoes or rice).

POULET BASQUAIS (BASQUE-STYLE CHICKEN)

Good with buttered noodles.
Makes 4 servings

1 (3-pound) broiler-fryer, cut up
3 tablespoons olive oil
2 large ripe tomatoes, peeled, cored, seeded, and chopped
4 sweet green peppers, cored, seeded, and quartered
¼ pound mushrooms, wiped clean and sliced thin
¼ pound lean cooked ham, diced
1½ teaspoons salt
¼ teaspoon pepper
½ cup dry white wine or chicken broth
2 tablespoons tomato paste
1 tablespoon minced parsley
2 pimientos, drained and cut in thin strips

Brown chicken in oil in a heavy kettle over moderately high heat. Add tomatoes, green peppers, mushrooms, ham, salt, pepper, and wine, cover, and simmer slowly ¾ hour until chicken is fork tender. Remove chicken to a serving platter with a slotted spoon and keep warm.

Blend tomato paste into kettle liquid and boil rapidly, uncovered, 1 minute. Pour some sauce over chicken, sprinkle with parsley, and decorate with pimiento. Pass remaining sauce. About 485 calories per serving.

¢ CHICKEN CACCIATORE

Makes 4 servings

¼ cup olive oil
1 (3–3½-pound) broiler-fryer, cut up
2 medium-size yellow onions, peeled and minced
1 clove garlic, peeled and crushed
¼ pound mushrooms, wiped clean and sliced thin
1 small sweet green pepper, cored, seeded, and coarsely chopped
1 (1-pound) can tomatoes (do not drain)
¾ cup dry white or red wine
¼ cup tomato paste
½ teaspoon rosemary
1 teaspoon salt
¼ teaspoon pepper

Heat oil in a heavy kettle over moderately high heat 1 minute, then brown chicken well; remove and reserve. Stir-fry onions 5 minutes, add garlic, mushrooms, and green pepper, and stir-fry 3–4 minutes longer until onions are golden. Add tomatoes, breaking up clumps, blend wine and tomato paste and stir in along with rosemary. Return chicken to kettle, sprinkle with salt and pepper, cover, and simmer, stirring now and then, about ¾ hour until tender. Serve with spaghetti. About 475 calories per serving (without spaghetti).

¢ CHICKEN MARENGO

Now a classic, this was originally an odds-and-ends dish made for

Napoleon at the Battle of Marengo.
Makes 4 servings

2 *tablespoons olive oil*
1 *(3-pound) broiler-fryer, cut up*
½ *pound button mushrooms, wiped clean*
2 *cloves garlic, peeled and crushed*
1 *large ripe tomato, peeled, cored, seeded, and chopped, or ⅔ cup coarsely chopped canned tomatoes*
½ *cup dry white wine*
2 *tablespoons tomato paste*
1 *teaspoon salt*
⅛ *teaspoon pepper*
1 *tablespoon minced parsley*

Heat oil in a large, flameproof casserole over moderate heat or in a deep electric skillet set at 350° F. Brown chicken well on all sides, then remove and set aside. Sauté mushrooms in casserole 3–5 minutes until golden; add garlic and stir-fry 1 minute. Stir in all remaining ingredients except parsley and return chicken to casserole. Cover and simmer about ¾ hour until tender. Sprinkle with parsley and serve. About 360 calories per serving.

CHICKEN ZINGARA

Makes 4 servings

2 *medium-size yellow onions, peeled and sliced thin*
3 *tablespoons bacon drippings, butter, or margarine*
1 *(3-pound) broiler-fryer, cut up*
1 *teaspoon salt*
1 *tablespoon paprika*
⅓ *cup dry red wine*
¼ *cup sweet Madeira wine*
1 *cup Rich Brown Sauce*
1 *tablespoon tomato paste*
1 *tablespoon minced cooked ham*
1 *tablespoon minced boiled tongue*
1 *tablespoon minced mushrooms*
1 *tablespoon minced black truffles*

Stir-fry onions in drippings in a large, heavy skillet or electric frying pan over moderate heat 8–10 minutes until golden. Push onions to side of pan, add chicken, and sauté about 10 minutes until browned; reduce heat to low. Turn chicken skin side up, add salt, and sprinkle evenly with paprika. Add red wine, cover, and simmer about ¾ hour until chicken is tender. (*Note:* Recipe may be prepared to this point early in the day, then reheated slowly before proceeding.) Arrange chicken on a serving platter and keep warm. Mix Madeira and remaining ingredients into skillet with onions and simmer, uncovered, 5 minutes. Pour over chicken and serve. Good with boiled rice or buttered noodles. About 495 calories per serving (without rice or noodles).

MAGYAR CHICKEN PAPRIKA

Makes 4 servings

2 *medium-size yellow onions, peeled and sliced thin*
3 *tablespoons bacon drippings or 1½ tablespoons each butter and cooking oil*
1 *(3–3½-pound) broiler-fryer, cut up*
1 *teaspoon salt*
1 *tablespoon paprika (the Hungarian sweet rose paprika is best)*
⅓ *cup chicken broth or dry red wine*
1 *cup sour cream*

Stir-fry onions in drippings in a large, heavy skillet or electric frying pan over moderate heat 8–10 minutes until golden. Push to side of pan, add chicken, and fry about 10 minutes until lightly browned; turn heat to low. Arrange chicken skin side up, add salt, and sprinkle paprika evenly over all. Add broth, cover, and simmer ¾ hour until chicken is tender. (*Note:* You may prepare recipe to this point early in the day, then reheat slowly before serving.) Arrange chicken on a platter and keep warm. Mix sour cream into onions, heat 1–2 minutes but do not boil, then pour over chicken. Good with buttered noodles, kasha, or boiled potatoes. About 460 calories per serving (without noodles, kasha, or boiled potatoes).

ROMANIAN CHICKEN AND APRICOTS

Makes 4 servings

1 (3½–4-pound) broiler-fryer, cut up
3 tablespoons olive oil
1 medium-size yellow onion, peeled and minced
2 tablespoons flour
1 (1-pound) can apricots, drained (reserve liquid)
Apricot liquid plus enough chicken broth to total 2 cups
1 large sprig sage or rosemary or ¼ teaspoon dried sage or rosemary
1 teaspoon salt
⅛ teaspoon pepper

Brown chicken well in oil in a large, heavy kettle over moderately high heat; drain on paper toweling. Drain all but 2 tablespoons drippings from skillet, add onion, turn heat to moderate, and stir-fry 8–10 minutes until golden; blend in flour. Add apricot liquid mixture and heat, stirring, until slightly thickened. Return chicken to skillet; add sage, salt, and pepper, cover, and simmer slowly about ¾ hour until chicken is tender. Meanwhile, halve and pit apricots. Uncover chicken, add apricots, and simmer 5–10 minutes longer. Serve over boiled rice. About 460 calories per serving (without rice).

PAELLA

This *paella* is geared to American rice, pans, and palates.
Makes 6 servings

¼ cup olive oil
3 (6–8-ounce) frozen rock lobster tails, cut crosswise in 1" chunks
½ pound raw shrimp, shelled and deveined
1 (2½–3-pound) broiler-fryer, cut up
1 large yellow onion, peeled and minced
2 cloves garlic, peeled and crushed
1 large sweet green pepper, cored, seeded, and minced
½ cup diced cooked ham or 1 chorizo (Spanish sausage), sliced ½" thick
1½ cups uncooked rice
2¾ cups chicken broth or water
2 teaspoons salt
¼ teaspoon pepper
¼–½ teaspoon powdered saffron
¼ cup tomato paste
1 (10-ounce) package frozen green peas
1½ dozen clams or mussels in the shell, prepared for cooking
1 pimiento, slivered (garnish)

Heat oil in a large (at least 5-quart) burner-to-table kettle over moderately high heat 1 minute, add lobster and shrimp, and stir-fry 3–4 minutes until pink; remove with a slotted spoon and reserve. Brown chicken well, remove, and reserve. Stir-fry onion in drippings 5 minutes, then add garlic, green pepper, and ham and stir-fry 3–4 minutes. Add rice, broth, 1½ teaspoons salt, ⅛ teaspoon pepper, the saffron and tomato paste. Return chicken to kettle, sprinkle with remaining salt and pepper, cover, and simmer ½ hour. Add lobster, shrimp, and peas (break them up when adding), cover, and simmer

10–15 minutes until chicken and peas are tender. Arrange clams on top, cover, and simmer 5 minutes until clams partially open. Sprinkle with pimiento and serve. About 610 calories per serving.

¢ ARROZ CON POLLO

Makes 4 servings

1 (3–3½-pound) broiler-fryer, cut up
⅓ cup unsifted flour
3 tablespoons olive oil
1 medium-size yellow onion, peeled and minced
1 clove garlic, peeled and crushed
½ cup julienne strips cooked ham
1 cup uncooked rice
1 cup chicken broth
1 (1-pound) can tomatoes (do not drain)
2 teaspoons salt
¼ teaspoon pepper
¼ teaspoon powdered saffron
1 bay leaf, crumbled
1 (4-ounce) can pimientos, drained and cut in 1" pieces
1 (10-ounce) package frozen green peas, cooked by package directions

Preheat oven to 350° F. Dredge chicken by shaking with flour in a bag. Heat oil in a large, heavy skillet over moderately high heat 1 minute, then brown chicken well, a few pieces at a time; drain on paper toweling. Reduce heat to moderate and stir-fry onion and garlic 5 minutes, add ham and stir-fry 3–4 minutes longer until onion is golden. Add rice, stir-fry 1 minute, then add broth, tomatoes, breaking up clumps, 1 teaspoon salt, ⅛ teaspoon pepper, the saffron and bay leaf; mix well. Spoon into an ungreased 2½-quart casserole about 2" deep, arrange chicken on top and sprinkle with remaining salt and pepper. Cover tightly and bake about 1 hour until chicken is fork tender. Uncover, scatter pimientos on top, and bake uncovered 10 minutes longer. Spoon peas around edge of casserole and serve. About 655 calories per serving.

VARIATION:

¢ **Mexican-Style Arroz Con Pollo:** Brown chicken as directed; stir-fry 1 minced, cored, and seeded hot green chili pepper along with onion and garlic. Proceed as directed, substituting 1–2 browned, thickly sliced, *chorizos* (Spanish sausages) for the ham and adding ¼ teaspoon cumin seeds along with other seasonings. About 665 calories per serving.

PUEBLA-STYLE CHICKEN MOLE

There are *moles* and *moles*. This one is rich, dark, and peppery like that served at Puebla, Mexico (chocolate is the key ingredient). The dried *ancho* and *pasilla* chilis called for can be bought at most gourmet, Spanish, or Latin American groceries.

Makes 4 servings

1 (3½–4-pound) broiler-fryer, cut up
1 quart water
2 teaspoons salt (about)
3 dried ancho chili peppers, washed, cored, and seeded
3 dried pasilla chili peppers, washed, cored, and seeded
1½ cups boiling water
2 tablespoons lard
1 medium-size yellow onion, peeled and minced
1 clove garlic, peeled and crushed
½ cup blanched slivered almonds or piñon nuts
1 tablespoon sesame seeds
⅛ teaspoon cloves
⅛ teaspoon cinnamon

¼ teaspoon coriander
1–1½ teaspoons crushed dried red
chili peppers (depending on how
hot you like things)
⅓ cup seedless raisins
2 medium-size tomatoes, peeled,
cored, seeded, and coarsely
chopped
1 (1-ounce) square unsweetened
chocolate, coarsely grated
1 cup chicken broth (reserved from
poaching chicken)
1 teaspoon light brown sugar

Place chicken in a large, heavy skillet (not iron), add water and salt, cover, and simmer about ¾ hour until tender; remove to paper toweling and pat dry; reserve broth. While chicken simmers, break dried ancho and pasilla chilis into small pieces, discard seeds, cover with boiling water, and let stand until chicken is done; purée chilis and their soaking water in an electric blender at high speed. Wipe skillet dry, add lard, and brown chicken well over moderately high heat; drain on paper toweling. Stir-fry onion and garlic in drippings over moderate heat 8–10 minutes until golden; add puréed chilis, nuts, sesame seeds, spices, raisins, and tomatoes and stir-fry 3–5 minutes to blend flavors. Purée skillet mixture, a little at a time, in an electric blender at high speed. Return to skillet, add chocolate, broth, and sugar, and heat, stirring, until chocolate is melted; taste for salt and adjust as needed. Return chicken to skillet, cover, set over lowest heat, and let "mellow" ½–¾ hour, basting chicken occasionally with sauce in skillet. Serve over boiled rice. About 565 calories per serving (without rice).

VARIATION:

Turkey Mole: Prepare as directed, substituting 4 pounds turkey parts

for the chicken. About 600 calories per serving (without rice).

BURMESE SPICED CHICKEN IN PEANUT-COCONUT SAUCE

Makes 4 servings

1 (3½–4-pound) broiler-fryer, cut
up
3 tablespoons peanut oil
2 (3-ounce) cans flaked coconut
2½ cups milk
2 medium-size yellow onions, peeled
and minced
1 clove garlic, peeled and crushed
1 tablespoon minced fresh mint or
mint flakes
¼ teaspoon cinnamon
¼ teaspoon ginger
¼ teaspoon cayenne pepper
¼ teaspoon black pepper
⅛ teaspoon cloves
½ teaspoon salt
3 tablespoons soy sauce
½ cup minced, roasted, blanched
peanuts

Brown chicken well on all sides in oil in a large, heavy skillet over moderately high heat; drain on paper toweling. Meanwhile, simmer coconut in milk 5 minutes; strain milk and reserve. (*Note:* Coconut can be dried out by spreading on a baking sheet and letting stand, uncovered, 2½–3 hours in a 200° F. oven. Use to decorate cakes, cookies, or candies.) Pour all but 2 tablespoons drippings from skillet, add onions and garlic, and stir-fry 8–10 minutes until golden. Mix in mint, spices, salt, soy sauce, and reserved milk, return chicken to skillet, cover, and simmer slowly ½ hour. Lift chicken from sauce and set aside. Purée skillet mixture, a very little bit at a time, in an electric blender at high speed. Wipe out skillet, pour in purée, add chicken and peanuts, cover, and simmer 15–20 minutes longer, stirring occasionally, until chicken is tender. Serve over boiled rice. About 840 calories per serving (without rice).

⚴ CHICKEN TERIYAKI

Makes 6 servings

Breasts of 3 large broiler-fryers, boned,* halved, and skinned
½ cup soy sauce
¼ cup mirin (sweet rice wine) or medium or dry sherry
1 tablespoon sugar
2 teaspoons finely grated fresh gingerroot

Place breasts between wax paper and pound to flatten slightly. Marinate 1–2 hours in refrigerator in a mixture of soy sauce, *mirin*, sugar, and ginger, turning once or twice. Preheat broiler. Remove chicken from marinade and arrange on lightly oiled rack in broiler pan. Broil 5"–6" from heat about 4 minutes on each side; brush with marinade when turning. Serve with tiny bowls of remaining marinade (sake cups are a good size) or pour a little marinade over each portion. Good with Japanese Rice with Toasted Seaweed and a spinach salad. About 230 calories per serving (without rice).

VARIATION:

⚴ **Yakitori:** Flatten breasts, then cut in 1" cubes and marinate as directed. Thread on bamboo or thin metal skewers alternating with chunks of scallion and halved chicken livers. Broil about 8 minutes, giving skewers a quarter turn every 2 minutes; brush frequently with marinade. (*Note:* Miniatures may be served as appetizers; use 1" chicken cubes and quartered livers.) About 255 calories per serving.

¢ COUNTRY CAPTAIN

A very mild curry popular in the South.
Makes 6–8 servings

1 (5½–6-pound) stewing hen or capon, cleaned and dressed
2 bay leaves
2 stalks celery (include tops)
2 quarts water
2 large yellow onions, peeled and coarsely chopped
2 large sweet green peppers, cored, seeded, and coarsely chopped
2 cloves garlic, peeled and crushed
¼ cup olive or other cooking oil
⅓ cup minced parsley
1 cup dried currants or seedless raisins
1 tablespoon curry powder
1 teaspoon cayenne pepper
¼ teaspoon black pepper
½ teaspoon thyme
¼ teaspoon cloves
2 teaspoons salt
2 (1-pound 12-ounce) cans tomatoes (do not drain)
3 cups reserved chicken stock
1 cup toasted, blanched almonds (topping)

Remove fat from body cavity of bird, then place bird and giblets in a large kettle, add bay leaves, celery, and water, cover, and simmer 10–15 minutes; remove liver and reserve. Re-cover chicken and simmer about 1–1½ hours longer until tender; lift chicken from kettle and cool; strain stock and reserve. In the same kettle stir-fry onions, green peppers, and garlic in oil 8–10 minutes over moderate heat until onion is golden. Add all but last ingredient and simmer, uncovered, 45 minutes, stirring now and then. Meanwhile, skin chicken, remove meat from bones, and cut in bite-size pieces. Add chicken, reserved liver, and giblets to sauce

and simmer, uncovered, 15 minutes.
Serve with or over fluffy boiled
rice, topped with almonds. (*Note:*
Recipe can be made several days
ahead and kept refrigerated until
shortly before serving; it also freezes
well.) About 605 calories for each
of 6 servings (without rice or
almonds), 455 calories for each of
8 servings.

CHICKEN JAIPUR

A spicy chicken curry.
Makes 4–6 servings

*1 (4–5-pound) stewing hen, cleaned
    and dressed*
1 quart water
*1 large yellow onion, peeled and
    stuck with 4 cloves*
1 large carrot, peeled and quartered
2½ teaspoons salt
4 peppercorns
1½ cups simmering milk
1 (3½-ounce) can flaked coconut
*1 large yellow onion, peeled and
    minced*
1 clove garlic, peeled and crushed
3 tablespoons butter or margarine
⅓ cup curry powder
*3 tablespoons minced crystallized
    ginger*
¼–½ teaspoon cayenne pepper
⅛ teaspoon black pepper
*1 teaspoon minced fresh mint or ½
    teaspoon mint flakes*
⅛ teaspoon cloves
1½ cups reserved chicken stock
Juice of 1 lime
1 cup heavy cream

Remove fat from body cavity of
bird, then place bird and giblets
in a large kettle, add water, onion,
carrot, salt, and peppercorns, cover,
and simmer 15–20 minutes; remove
liver and reserve. Re-cover chicken
and simmer 1–1½ hours longer until
tender; lift chicken and giblets
from kettle and cool; strain stock

and reserve. Pour milk over coconut
and let steep until lukewarm; strain,
reserving milk and discarding
coconut. Stir-fry minced onion and
garlic in butter in a very large,
heavy skillet 8–10 minutes until
golden; blend in curry powder,
ginger, and all herbs and spices.
Add reserved milk and chicken
stock, cover and simmer ½ hour.
Meanwhile, remove and discard
chicken skin, take meat from bones,
and cut in bite-size pieces. Add
chicken and, if you like, liver and
giblets to curry, cover, and simmer
½ hour. Mix in lime juice and
cream and heat, stirring, 5–10
minutes. Serve with boiled rice.
Good condiments: chutney, flaked
coconut, chopped roasted peanuts,
seedless raisins. About 800 calories
for each of 4 servings (without rice
or condiments), about 530 calories
for each of 6 servings.

¢ ⊠ ⚖ CHICKEN CHOP SUEY

Makes 4–6 servings

3 tablespoons cooking oil
*2 medium-size yellow onions, peeled
    and minced*
*3 stalks celery, cut in thin diagonal
    slices*
2 cups shredded Chinese cabbage
*2 cups diced or julienne strips cooked
    chicken*
*1 (5-ounce) can bamboo shoots,
    drained and cut in thin strips*
2 cups chicken broth
2 tablespoons soy sauce
*2 tablespoons cornstarch blended
    with ¼ cup cold water*
*1 (3-ounce) can water chestnuts,
    drained and sliced thin*
*1 (1-pound) can bean sprouts,
    drained*

Heat oil in a *wok* or large, heavy
skillet over moderately high heat

1 minute, add onions, celery, and cabbage, and stir-fry 3–4 minutes (do not brown). Add chicken and bamboo shoots and stir-fry 1 minute; add broth, soy sauce, and cornstarch paste and cook and stir until thickened. Add chestnuts and bean sprouts and toss 1–2 minutes. Taste for salt and add more if needed. Serve over boiled rice. About 355 calories for each of 4 servings, 235 for each of 6 servings (without rice).

¢ ⊠ ⚄ CHICKEN CHOW MEIN

Makes 6 servings

½ pound mushrooms, wiped clean and sliced thin
6 scallions, minced (include some tops)
2 small sweet green peppers, cored, seeded, and minced
4 stalks celery, minced
2 tablespoons cooking oil
2½ cups chicken broth
2 tablespoons soy sauce
¼ cup cornstarch blended with ¼ cup cold water
½ teaspoon salt
⅛ teaspoon pepper
3 cups bite-size pieces cooked chicken meat, preferably white meat
1 (1-pound) can bean sprouts, drained
1 (3-ounce) can water chestnuts, drained and sliced thin

Stir-fry mushrooms, scallions, green peppers, and celery in oil in a large, heavy skillet over moderately high heat 8–10 minutes until golden brown. Add broth and soy sauce, turn heat to low, cover, and simmer 10 minutes. Mix in cornstarch paste, salt, and pepper and heat, stirring constantly, until thickened and clear. Add chicken, bean

sprouts, and water chestnuts and heat and stir about 5 minutes, just to heat through. Taste for salt and adjust if needed. Serve over boiled rice. About 255 calories per serving (without rice).

⚄ MOO GOO GAI PEEN (CHICKEN WITH MUSHROOMS)

Makes 2 servings

Breast of 1 large broiler-fryer, boned,* halved, and skinned
2 tablespoons peanut oil
½ cup thinly sliced mushrooms
1 cup finely shredded Chinese cabbage
⅓ cup thinly sliced bamboo shoots
2 (½″) cubes fresh gingerroot, peeled and crushed
⅓ cup chicken broth
1 tablespoon dry sherry (optional)
½ (7-ounce) package frozen snow pea pods, slightly thawed
3 water chestnuts, sliced thin
2 teaspoons cornstarch blended with 1 tablespoon cold water
¾ teaspoon salt (about)
⅛ teaspoon sugar

Cut chicken across the grain into strips about 2″ long and ¼″ wide; set aside. Heat 1 tablespoon oil in a large, heavy skillet over moderately high heat about 1 minute, add mushrooms, cabbage, bamboo shoots, and ginger, and stir-fry 2 minutes. Add broth, cover, and simmer 2–3 minutes. Pour all into a bowl and set aside. Wipe out skillet, heat remaining oil, and stir-fry chicken 2–3 minutes; if you like sprinkle with sherry and stir a few seconds longer. Return vegetables and broth to skillet, add snow peas and chestnuts, and heat, stirring until bubbling. Mix in cornstarch paste, salt, and sugar and heat, stirring until clear and slightly thickened; taste for salt and adjust as needed. Serve with boiled rice. About 250 calories per serving (without sherry or rice).

CHICKEN WITH SNOW PEAS AND WATER CHESTNUTS

Makes 4 servings

1 (3½-pound) broiler-fryer, cut up, skinned, and boned*
¼ cup soy sauce
¼ cup dry sherry or port
1 clove garlic, peeled and crushed
2 (½") cubes fresh gingerroot, peeled and crushed
¾ cup unsifted flour
⅓ cup peanut oil
1 (5-ounce) can water chestnuts, drained and sliced thin
1 (7-ounce) package frozen snow pea pods (do not thaw)
½ cup water

Cut chicken in bite-size pieces and marinate 2–3 hours in refrigerator in a mixture of soy sauce, sherry, garlic, and ginger. Remove from marinade and dredge in flour; save marinade. Heat oil in a large, heavy skillet over moderately high heat about 1 minute, add chicken, and stir-fry 2–3 minutes to brown lightly. Add marinade and remaining ingredients and stir-fry 2–3 minutes until peas are crisp-tender. Serve with or over boiled rice. About 525 calories per serving (without rice).

⊠ CHAFING DISH CHICKEN AND SHRIMP IN SOUR CREAM-SHERRY SAUCE

Makes 4 servings

3 tablespoons butter or margarine
3 tablespoons flour
1 cup chicken broth
¾ teaspoon garlic salt
⅛ teaspoon white pepper

Pinch nutmeg
1 cup sour cream
¼–⅓ cup medium-dry sherry
1½ cups diced cooked white chicken meat
1½ cups coarsely chopped large (or whole small) shelled and deveined boiled shrimp
1 recipe Rice Pilaf

Melt butter in a chafing dish over simmering water. Blend in flour, slowly add broth, and heat, stirring constantly, until thickened and smooth. Mix in seasonings, sour cream, and sherry; add chicken and shrimp and heat, stirring, 4–5 minutes. Ladle over pilaf and serve. About 800 calories per serving.

¢ ⊠ COMPANY CHICKEN CASSEROLE

Makes 4 servings

1 (3–3½-pound) broiler-fryer, cut up
¼ cup unsifted flour
½ teaspoon salt
¼ teaspoon pepper
¼ cup melted butter or margarine
1 (10½-ounce) can condensed cream of mushroom soup
⅔ cup milk
Pinch thyme
1 (1-pound) can small white onions, drained
1 (4-ounce) can sliced mushrooms, drained
2 pimientos, drained and cut in julienne strips

Preheat oven to 425° F. Dredge chicken in a mixture of flour, salt, and pepper. Pour butter in a shallow 2½-quart casserole and arrange chicken skin side down in butter, in a single layer. Bake, uncovered, ½ hour. Turn chicken skin side up and bake 15 minutes longer; remove drippings with a bulb baster. Blend soup, milk, and thyme until smooth and pour into casserole; arrange onions, mushrooms, and pimientos around chicken. Reduce oven to 325° F., cover casserole, and bake 15–20 minutes until bubbly. About 525 calories per serving.

OVEN-GLAZED CHICKEN

Makes 4 servings

⅓ cup fine toasted bread crumbs
½ teaspoon thyme
½ teaspoon sage
1 teaspoon salt
⅛ teaspoon pepper
¼ teaspoon garlic powder
1 (2½–3-pound) broiler-fryer, cut up
¼ cup milk
⅓ cup mayonnaise

Preheat oven to 425° F. Mix crumbs, herbs, salt, pepper, and garlic powder. Dip chicken in milk, then in crumb mixture to coat evenly and arrange skin side up, 1 layer deep, in a heavily greased shallow roasting pan. Bake, uncovered, 15 minutes to set crumbs, then gently spread chicken with mayonnaise (don't turn–do only the top side). Reduce oven to 350° F. and bake, uncovered, 45–50 minutes longer until chicken is fork tender, glazed, and golden brown. About 425 calories per serving.

CHICKEN TETRAZZINI

This luscious dish deserves the bravos heaped on its famous namesake, Italian coloratura Luisa Tetrazzini.
Makes 6–8 servings

1 (5–6-pound) stewing hen, cleaned and dressed
1 quart water
1½ teaspoons salt
1 small yellow onion, peeled
1 medium-size carrot, peeled
1 stalk celery
1 bay leaf
3–4 peppercorns
1 pound spaghettini or linguine
½ pound mushrooms, wiped clean, sliced and lightly sautéed in butter

Sauce:
¼ cup butter or margarine
¼ cup sifted flour
2 cups reserved chicken stock
1½ cups milk or ¾ cup each milk and dry white wine
1 cup heavy cream
2 teaspoons salt
⅛ teaspoon white pepper
1–2 tablespoons lemon juice (optional)
⅛ teaspoon nutmeg (optional)

Topping:
¾ cup soft, fine bread crumbs mixed with ¾ cup grated Parmesan cheese

Remove fat from body cavity of hen, then place hen, giblets, water, salt, onion, carrot, celery, bay leaf, and peppercorns in a large, heavy kettle, cover, and simmer about 2 hours until tender. (Note: Chicken liver should be removed after 10–15 minutes, cooled, and reserved.) Cool hen in stock, then skin and cut meat from bones in bite-size chunks; also dice all giblets; skim stock of fat, strain, and reserve. For sauce, melt butter over moderate heat, blend in flour, add stock and remaining sauce ingredients, and heat, stirring, until thickened. Preheat oven to 350° F. Cook pasta by package directions, drain and combine with sauce, mushrooms, chicken, and giblets, including liver. Place in a buttered shallow 3-quart casserole, sprinkle with topping and bake, uncovered, 30–40 minutes until bubbly. Brown quickly under broiler and serve. About 875 calories for each of 6 servings, 655 calories for each of 8 servings.

VARIATIONS:

Turkey Tetrazzini: Prepare as directed, substituting a 6-pound turkey for the chicken. About 875 calories for each of 6 servings, 655 calories for each of 8 servings.

Ham Tetrazzini: Prepare sauce as directed; also cook pasta. Toss with 3 cups diced cooked ham and the mushrooms called for, then top and bake as directed. About 755 calories for each of 6 servings, 565 calories for each of 8 servings.

¢ CHICKEN JAMBALAYA BAKE

An easy, economical chicken, rice, and tomato casserole.
Makes 4–6 servings

1 (3–3½-pound) broiler-fryer, cut up
⅔ cup unsifted flour
2 tablespoons chili powder
3½ teaspoons salt
⅓ cup olive oil
1 large yellow onion, peeled and coarsely chopped
1 clove garlic, peeled and crushed
⅔ cup uncooked rice
1 (1-pound 12-ounce) can tomatoes (do not drain)
¼ cup water
⅛–¼ teaspoon cayenne pepper (depending on how hot you like things)

Preheat oven to 350° F. Dredge chicken by shaking in a bag with flour, chili powder, and 3 teaspoons salt; brown in oil in a large, heavy kettle and drain on paper toweling; pour off all but 3 tablespoons drippings. Stir-fry onion, garlic, and rice in drippings 3–5 minutes over moderate heat until rice is golden. Mix in tomatoes, water, cayenne, and remaining salt and heat, stirring, until mixture simmers. Return chicken to kettle, pushing down into liquid, cover, and bake 1 hour until chicken and rice are tender. About 535 calories for each of 4 servings, 360 calories for each of 6 servings.

CIRCASSIAN CHICKEN

An unusual Turkish cold chicken and walnut dish that's perfect for a buffet. It's rich, needs only a green salad and rolls to accompany.
Makes 6 servings

1 (6–6½-pound) capon, cleaned and dressed (save giblets for a gravy or other recipe)
3 quarts water
1 onion, peeled and stuck with 3 cloves
2 bay leaves
1 stalk celery, cut in large chunks
1 medium-size carrot, peeled and cut in large chunks
6 peppercorns
1½ teaspoons salt

Sauce:
1 pound shelled walnuts
3 slices white bread, trimmed of crusts and soaked in ¼ cup milk
1 teaspoon salt
⅛ teaspoon pepper
2⅓ cups reserved chicken broth (about)

Topping:
2 tablespoons olive oil mixed with 1 teaspoon paprika

Place chicken, water, onion, bay leaves, celery, carrot, peppercorns, and salt in a large, heavy kettle, cover, and simmer about 1 hour until chicken is tender; lift chicken from broth and cool; strain broth and reserve. For sauce, purée walnuts, a few at a time, in an electric blender at high speed; mix with bread, salt, pepper, and enough broth to make a sauce about the consistency of thick gravy; again purée, a little bit at a time, in blender at high speed. Skin chicken, remove meat, and cut in strips about 1½" long and ¼" wide. Mound about half the chicken on a large platter and spread with half the walnut sauce; arrange remaining chicken on top and spread with remaining sauce. Cover and chill several hours. Remove from refrigerator and let stand at room temperature 1 hour. Just before serving, drizzle paprika mixture over top in a crisscross design. About 960 calories per serving.

CHICKEN MOUSSELINES OR QUENELLES

Fragile poached chicken dumplings. Makes 2–4 servings

Breast of 1 medium-size broiler-fryer, boned* and skinned
1 egg white
⅔ cup heavy cream
1 teaspoon salt
Pinch white pepper
1 teaspoon lemon juice
1 quart boiling water

Grind chicken very fine and mix with egg white. Press mixture through a fine sieve and place in a bowl over cracked ice. Beat with a wooden spoon 2–3 minutes until mixture thickens and will cling to a spoon turned upside down. Add cream, 2 tablespoons at a time, beating ½ minute after each addition; mixture will be soft but should hold a shape. Stir in ½ teaspoon salt, the pepper, and ½ teaspoon lemon juice. Pour water into a large skillet (not iron), add remaining salt and lemon juice, and adjust heat so liquid just trembles. Using 2 wet teaspoons, shape chicken mixture into egg-size balls and slide into poaching liquid (liquid should just cover mousselines; if not add a little extra simmering water). Poach, uncovered, 6–8 mousselines at a time, 3–5 minutes until just firm. Lift out with a slotted spoon and drain on paper toweling. Loosely cover poached mousselines and keep warm. Shape and poach the rest (wet the spoons often). Use to garnish Chicken Breasts in Champagne Sauce, Suprême de Volaille à Blanc, or any poached or baked chicken suprêmes. Or top with Mushroom, Suprême, or Aurore Sauce and serve as a main course. About 490 calories for each of 2 servings, 245 calories for each of 4 servings (without sauce).

CHICKEN MAYONNAISE

Cool and creamy, a wise choice for a hot weather party buffet. Makes 12 servings

1 (6–6½-pound) stewing hen, cleaned and dressed (save giblets for soup or gravy)
2½ quarts water
5 teaspoons salt
1 medium-size yellow onion, peeled and stuck with 3 cloves
1 cup diced celery
1 cup finely chopped walnuts or blanched almonds
4 hard-cooked eggs, peeled and finely chopped
1 small yellow onion, peeled and finely grated
1 (10-ounce) package frozen tiny green peas, cooked by package directions and drained but not seasoned
2 envelopes unflavored gelatin
2 cups reserved chicken stock
1 cup heavy cream
1 pint thick mayonnaise
¼ teaspoon pepper

Place hen in a large, heavy kettle with water, 3 teaspoons salt, and the onion, cover, and simmer about 2 hours until tender. Lift hen from stock and cool; strain and reserve stock. Skin chicken, separate meat from bones, and mince; place in a large mixing bowl with celery, nuts, eggs, grated onion, and peas, toss well to mix, and set aside. Heat gelatin in reserved stock and cream over moderate heat, stirring until dissolved; do not boil. Off heat, blend in mayonnaise, remaining salt, and the pepper. Pour over chicken mixture and stir well to mix. Pour into a 2½-quart decorative round mold, cover with saran and chill several hours or overnight until firm. Unmold on a large platter, garnish as desired (stuffed eggs, marinated artichoke hearts, and sprigs of cress are especially pretty). Slice into thin wedges and serve. About 675 calories per serving.

CHICKEN GALANTINE

Start this recipe the day before you plan to serve it.
Makes 4–6 servings

1 (3–3½-pound) broiler-fryer, boned* (reserve bones and carcass)

Stuffing:
½ pound veal, ground twice
½ cup soft white bread crumbs
¼ cup minced mushrooms
2 scallions, minced
1 teaspoon minced parsley
¼ teaspoon sage
¼ teaspoon thyme
½ teaspoon salt
¼ teaspoon pepper
1 egg, lightly beaten
2 tablespoons dry sherry, Madeira, or water

¼ pound boiled ham, sliced ¼″ thick
¼ pound boiled tongue, sliced ¼″ thick
2 truffles, minced

Poaching Liquid:
2 quarts water
1 veal knuckle, cracked (optional)
2 teaspoons salt
1 medium-size yellow onion, peeled and stuck with 4 cloves
1 carrot, peeled and cut in large chunks
2 stalks celery, cut in large chunks
1 bouquet garni,* tied in cheesecloth

Open chicken flat and lay skin side down on a large board; turn legs and wings inside out so chicken is nearly rectangular. In places where meat is more than ½″ thick, trim off and use to "pad" skimpy places or grind and add to stuffing. Lightly knead together all but last 3 stuffing ingredients and spread ½ down center of chicken, leaving wide margins all around. Cut ham and tongue slices into strips ¼″ wide and lay across stuffing, alternating flavors; sprinkle with truffles and top with remaining stuffing. Pull sides of chicken up over stuffing, enclosing it and forming a

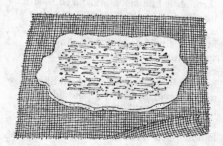

fat sausage-like roll. Secure seam with toothpicks or small poultry pins; gather skin together at ends and tie firmly or sew together.

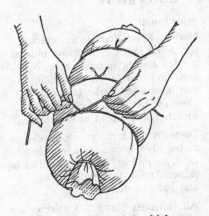

Wrap chicken in a triple thickness of cheesecloth wrung out in cold water, pulling cloth as tight as possible to shape chicken in a plump, firm roll. Tie around with string in several places, twist ends and tie also. Place roll in a large kettle, add reserved bones and all poaching liquid ingredients. Cover and simmer 1 hour, turning roll after ½ hour. Cool roll, still wrapped, in broth 1 hour, then lift to a deep bowl, top with a small cutting board or heavy plate, and weight down to force out as much liquid and air as possible; let stand 1 hour. Remove cheesecloth, cover roll with foil, and chill overnight. Slice—not too thin —and arrange slices, slightly overlapping, on a platter. Garnish as desired and serve.

To Decorate Galantine: Strain poaching liquid, clarify, and use to make aspic.* Chill aspic until very cold but still liquid. Chill galantine well too; then set on a rack over a tray. Spoon several thin layers of aspic over galantine to glaze evenly. Decorate as desired with sprigs of chervil or tarragon and cutouts of truffle, hard-cooked egg white, pimiento, and radish or carrot. Cutouts will stick better if dipped in aspic, then lightly

pressed onto roll. Seal in designs with additional layers of aspic. Chill until firm; also chill remaining aspic. Set aspic on a platter, wreathe with chopped aspic, and sprig with watercress.

VARIATIONS:

Capon Galantine: Prepare as directed, using a 5–6-pound boned capon. Double stuffing recipe and use 3 quarts water in poaching liquid. Increase simmering time to 1½ hours.

Turkey Galantine: Prepare as directed, using an 8–10-pound boned turkey. Triple stuffing recipe and double poaching liquid ingredients. Increase simmering time to 2½–3 hours.

Chicken Ballotine: Prepare roll and simmer as directed; lift from broth, sprinkle with parsley, and serve hot with Chicken Gravy or Poulette Sauce. (*Note:* When making *ballotines,* the French often do not bone chicken completely but leave drumsticks and wing bones in to give bird character. The bird is then stuffed, sewn, or skewered up the back and reshaped to look as much like an unboned chicken as possible. It is then roasted* like any stuffed chicken. When carved, it is sliced straight across like the boneless rolls.)

Chicken galantine and all variations: about 550 calories for each of 4 servings, 370 calories for each of 6 servings.

CHICKEN KIEV

Traditionally, Kiev is seasoned only with butter, salt, and pepper, though chefs nowadays often add garlic, parsley, or chives. The trick in preparing Kiev is to seal the butter inside the chicken breast so that when the meat is cut it gushes out.

Makes 4–6 servings

Breasts of 3 large broiler-fryers, boned,* halved, skinned, and pounded flat
½ teaspoon salt
⅛ teaspoon pepper
6 finger-size slivers ice cold butter (Note: The best way to make these is to halve 1 stick butter crosswise, then quarter each half lengthwise.)
½ cup cooking oil

Coating:
2 eggs, lightly beaten
2 tablespoons milk
2 tablespoons water
½ teaspoon salt
⅛ teaspoon pepper
1 cup unsifted flour
1½ cups fine dry bread crumbs

Chill chicken breasts several hours, then spread flat on a cutting board and sprinkle with salt and pepper; lay a finger of butter in the center of each, then fold top and bottom margins over butter, tightly roll jelly-roll style and secure with poultry pins; chill rolls 15 minutes. Meanwhile, for coating mix eggs with milk, water, salt, and pepper. Dip rolls in flour, then egg, then in crumbs to coat evenly; pay particular attention to the ends, making sure they're well coated; chill rolls 1 hour. Preheat oven to 350° F. Heat oil in a large, heavy skillet over moderately high heat until a cube of bread will sizzle; add rolls and fry, turning gently with a slotted spoon, until nut brown all over; drain on paper toweling. Arrange 1 layer deep in an ungreased shallow baking pan and bake, uncovered, 15 minutes. Serve at once.

VARIATIONS:

Herbed Kiev: Prepare as directed, sprinkling about ½ teaspoon minced parsley and/or minced chives over each finger of butter and adding a dab of crushed garlic (use only 1 clove for the whole recipe). Roll breasts and proceed as directed.

Deep-Fried Kiev: Prepare as directed, then brown rolls in a deep fat fryer in 360° F. fat instead of in skillet. Drain, transfer to oven, and bake as directed.

All versions: about 525 calories for each of 4 servings, 350 calories for each of 6 servings.

STUFFED CHICKEN BREASTS

Any favorite stuffing can be used for stuffing chicken breasts instead of those given below. For 4 servings, you will need ½ cup stuffing.
Makes 4 servings

Breasts of 2 large broiler-fryers, boned,* halved, skinned, and pounded flat
¼ teaspoon salt
⅛ teaspoon white pepper
⅓ cup liver pâté or deviled ham
¼ cup soft white bread crumbs
2 scallions, minced
¼ cup unsifted flour
2 tablespoons butter or margarine
½ cup chicken broth

Preheat oven to 350° F. Spread breasts flat and sprinkle with salt and pepper. Mix pâté, crumbs, and scallions, place 2 tablespoons on each breast, roll up, and secure with poultry pins. Dredge rolls with flour and brown in butter in a heavy skillet over moderately high heat about 5 minutes. Transfer to an ungreased shallow casserole, add broth, cover, and bake 20 minutes until tender. Remove poultry pins and serve. About 385 calories per serving.

VARIATIONS:

Chicken Breasts with Spicy Ham Stuffing: Prepare as directed, stuffing breasts with ½ cup ground boiled ham mixed with 1 lightly beaten egg yolk, 1 teaspoon prepared yellow mustard, and the bread crumbs and scallions called for. Good with Madeira Sauce. About 340 calories per serving (without sauce).

Chicken Breasts Stuffed with Wild Rice and Mushrooms: Prepare as directed, stuffing breasts with ½ cup cooked wild rice mixed with ¼ cup minced sautéed mushrooms, 2 minced scallions, and 1 lightly beaten egg yolk. About 345 calories per serving.

Ham and Cheese Stuffed Chicken Breasts: Spread breasts flat, sprinkle with salt, pepper, and 2 minced scallions. Lay 1 slice cut-to-fit boiled ham and Swiss cheese on each breast, roll, and cook as directed. About 350 calories per serving.

Chicken Breasts Stuffed with Chicken Livers and Walnuts: Prepare as directed, stuffing breasts with 4 minced sautéed chicken livers mixed with ¼ cup finely chopped walnuts and the crumbs and scallions called for. About 360 calories per serving.

◁◮ **Chicken Breasts Stuffed with Oysters:** Prepare as directed, stuffing breasts with ⅓ cup minced, drained raw oysters or clams mixed with ⅓ cup bread crumbs and 2 minced scallions. About 300 calories per serving.

CHAUD-FROID OF CHICKEN BREASTS

Preparing a *chaud-froid* is not difficult if the sauce is quite cold —but still liquid—and the food to be coated is well chilled. The chaud-froid sauce will then set almost immediately.
Makes 4 servings

Breasts of 2 large broiler-fryers, boned* and halved
1 recipe Chaud-Froid Sauce
2 cups aspic made with chicken stock*
Cutouts of truffle and pimiento; parsley or tarragon sprigs (decoration)

Poach breasts by basic method* and cool in stock; remove from stock, skin, and chill. Strain stock and use in preparing chaud-froid sauce and aspic. When chaud-froid sauce is the proper consistency, set breasts on a rack over a tray and cover with a thin, even layer of sauce. Chill until tacky, then continue building up layers until no meat shows through. While final layer is still tacky, decorate with truffle and pimiento cutouts and herb sprigs. Seal in designs with a thin glaze of aspic and chill until firm. Also chill remaining aspic. Serve breasts on a platter wreathed with chopped aspic and sprigged with watercress. About 400 calories per serving.

SUPRÊMES OF CHICKEN

Suprêmes of chicken (*suprêmes de volaille* in French) are boned, skinned half breasts; if the first joints of wing are attached, they become *côtelettes*. The thin strip of meat lying next to the breastbone is called the *filet*. Perfectly cooked suprêmes are springy to the touch, creamy white with juices that run clear. They may be cooked by one of the basic methods below, seasoned with salt and pepper, and served as is; they may be topped with a suitable sauce (see Some Sauces,

Gravies, and Seasonings for Poultry) or they may be given one of the lavish classic treatments that follow.

To Poach: Arrange suprêmes in a single layer in a buttered heavy skillet or shallow, flameproof casserole. Sprinkle lightly with salt and pepper, add chicken broth almost to cover and a *bouquet garni** tied in cheesecloth. Cover and simmer, either on top of the stove or in a 325° F. oven, about 20 minutes until tender.

To Bake: Preheat oven to 425° F. Allow 3–4 tablespoons butter for each 4 suprêmes and heat to bubbling in a shallow, flameproof casserole over moderate heat. Roll breasts in butter, cover loosely with foil, and bake 20 minutes until just tender.

To Sauté: Melt ¼ cup butter in a large, heavy skillet; lightly dredge suprêmes in flour, then brown over moderate heat about 8 minutes, turning often, until tender.

To Broil: Preheat broiler. Flatten suprêmes slightly and arrange on oiled rack in broiler pan. Brush well with melted butter (or Herb or Lemon Butter) and broil 5″–6″ from heat 4–5 minutes on a side, brushing often with additional butter.

Some Classic Ways to Serve Suprêmes of Chicken

Suprêmes de Volaille à Blanc (in Wine and Cream Sauce): Bake 4 suprêmes as directed, transfer to a hot platter and keep warm. To pan drippings add ¼ cup each dry white wine and chicken broth and boil, uncovered, until reduced by half. Turn heat to low and blend in 1 cup heavy cream, ¾ teaspoon salt, ⅛ teaspoon white pepper and 1–2 teaspoons lemon juice. Warm 1–2 minutes but do not boil; pour over suprêmes and serve sprinkled with minced parsley.

Suprêmes de Volaille Amandine: Sauté 4 suprêmes as directed and keep warm. Stir-fry ¼ cup blanched slivered almonds in drippings over moderate heat until golden, blend in 1 tablespoon flour and 1 cup heavy cream, and heat, stirring, until thickened. Season with salt and pepper, let mellow several minutes over low heat, add 1 teaspoon lemon juice, pour over suprêmes, and serve.

Suprêmes de Volaille en Papillote: Poach 4 suprêmes as directed and cool slightly in poaching liquid. Mix 1 cup hot Béchamel or Medium White Sauce, ¼ cup minced raw mushrooms, 2 tablespoons minced, pitted ripe olives, 1 teaspoon each minced chives and parsley and ½ crushed clove garlic. Butter 4 large squares foil, spread each with ¼ of the sauce, top with a suprême, wrap tightly, arrange on a baking sheet, and bake 10–12 minutes at 425° F. Serve in foil packages.

Virginia-Style Suprêmes: Flatten 4 suprêmes slightly; cut 4 thin slices Virginia ham to fit suprêmes, dip in beaten egg, and lay on suprêmes, pressing lightly. Dip each "package" in beaten egg, then in toasted, seasoned bread crumbs. Brown slowly on both sides in ¼ cup melted butter in a heavy skillet over moderate heat; cover, reduce heat to low, and cook 5 minutes. Uncover and cook 2–3 minutes longer to crispen.

Chicken Breasts in Champagne Sauce: Poach suprêmes as directed, using a ½ and ½ mixture of chicken broth and champagne, dry white wine, or cider. Drain off poaching liquid and measure; for each cup, lightly beat 2 egg yolks. Heat cooking liquid in the top of a double boiler directly over moderate heat until simmering, spoon a little into yolks, return to pan, set over simmering water, and heat and stir until thickened and no raw taste of egg remains. Season to taste, pour over suprêmes and serve.

Suprêmes Véronique: Bake 4 suprêmes as directed but add ½ cup dry white wine to the pan. Drain off cooking liquid, to it add 1 cup light cream, and use to make 1½ cups Medium White Sauce. Pour sauce over suprêmes, garnish with peeled seedless green grapes, and serve. If you like, brown quickly under broiler before serving.

⊠ ⚖ SAUTÉED CHICKEN LIVERS

Makes 6 servings

1½ pounds chicken livers
½ cup unsifted flour
1 teaspoon salt
¼ teaspoon pepper
3–4 tablespoons bacon drippings, butter, or margarine

Halve each chicken liver at the natural separation and dredge in a mixture of flour, salt, and pepper. Stir-fry in drippings in a large, heavy skillet over moderately high heat about 5 minutes until browned all over. (*Note:* Livers will be medium rare. If you prefer them rarer, cook about 1 minute less, if more well done, turn heat to moderately low and cook 1–2 minutes longer.) Serve on buttered toast

triangles for breakfast, lunch, or supper. About 250 calories per serving (without toast).

⊠ ⚖ BRAISED CHICKEN LIVERS WITH PARSLEY GRAVY

Makes 4–6 servings

1½ pounds chicken livers
3 tablespoons bacon drippings, butter, or margarine
1 teaspoon salt
⅛ teaspoon pepper
4 teaspoons flour
1 cup chicken broth
¼ teaspoon liquid gravy browner
2 tablespoons minced parsley
2–3 tablespoons medium-dry sherry (optional)

Halve each chicken liver at the natural separation, pat dry on paper toweling, and stir-fry in drippings in a large, heavy skillet over moderately high heat about 5 minutes until brown. Turn heat to moderately low and sprinkle livers with salt and pepper. Blend flour with ¼ cup chicken broth, add remaining broth and gravy browner and pour into skillet. Cook and stir gently until slightly thickened. Add parsley and, if you like, the sherry and serve. About 315 calories for each of 4 servings (without sherry), 210 for each of 6 (without sherry).

⊠ CHICKEN LIVERS IN SOUR CREAM

A good chafing dish recipe.
Makes 4 servings

1 pound chicken livers
2 tablespoons bacon drippings, butter, or margarine
1 cup minced scallions (include some tops)
¼ pound mushrooms, wiped clean and coarsely chopped

⅛ teaspoon rosemary
¼ teaspoon basil
1 teaspoon salt
⅛ teaspoon pepper
1 clove garlic, peeled and crushed
1 teaspoon Worcestershire sauce
1 cup chicken broth
1 cup sour cream

Cut livers in two at the natural separation and pat dry on paper toweling. Stir-fry in drippings in a large, heavy skillet over moderately high heat until browned all over, about 5 minutes. Push livers to one side of skillet, add scallions, and sauté 2–3 minutes until golden. Turn heat to moderately low, mix in all remaining ingredients except sour cream, and simmer uncovered 7–10 minutes, stirring occasionally. If you like, transfer at this point to a chafing dish. Mix in sour cream and simmer 2–3 minutes until hot but not boiling. Serve over boiled rice, buttered noodles, or toast triangles. About 340 calories per serving (without rice, noodles, or toast).

⊠ OLD-FASHIONED CREAMED CHICKEN OR TURKEY

Makes 4 servings

¼ pound mushrooms, wiped clean
   and sliced thin (include stems)
¼ cup butter or margarine
¼ cup unsifted flour
1 cup chicken broth
1 cup light cream
¾ teaspoon salt (about)
⅛ teaspoon white pepper
2 cups cooked chicken or turkey
   meat, cut in bite-size pieces
2 tablespoons dry sherry (optional)

Sauté mushrooms in butter in the top of a double boiler directly over moderately high heat 2–3 minutes

until golden. Blend in flour, slowly stir in broth and cream, and heat, stirring, until thickened. Set over just simmering water, mix in remaining ingredients, cover, and let mellow 10–15 minutes. Serve over hot buttered toast, biscuits, corn bread, toasted English muffins, pancakes, or waffles. Also good over mashed potatoes, boiled rice, or noodles or used as a filling for pancakes, crepes, or baked frozen patty shells. About 430 calories per serving made with chicken (without bread, potatoes, rice, or noodles), about 450 calories per serving if made with turkey.

VARIATIONS:

Creamed Chicken or Turkey and Eggs: Prepare as directed, but just before setting mixture over water to mellow, mix in 2 peeled, hard-cooked eggs cut in wedges. About 470 calories per serving if made with chicken, 490 calories per serving if made with turkey.

Creamed Chicken or Turkey and Ham: Prepare as directed, using a ½ and ½ mixture of chicken or turkey and ham. About 490 calories per serving if made with chicken, about 510 calories per serving if made with turkey.

CHICKEN OR TURKEY AND MUSHROOM CREPES

Makes 4 servings

1 recipe Crepes for Savory Fillings

Filling:
1 (10½-ounce) can condensed
   cream of mushroom soup (do not
   dilute)
1 cup light cream
Pinch nutmeg
¾ teaspoon salt (about)
⅛ teaspoon pepper

2 cups minced cooked chicken or
  turkey meat
1 (4-ounce) can mushroom stems
  and pieces, drained and minced
1 pimiento, drained and minced
Paprika

Preheat oven to 350° F. Prepare
crepes as recipe directs and spread
flat with most attractive sides
face down. Mix soup and cream
until smooth, add nutmeg, salt,
and pepper. Mix ¾ cup soup
mixture with chicken, mushrooms,
and pimiento, taste for salt and
adjust as needed. Spoon a little
chicken mixture down center
of each crepe, then roll up. Place
crepes seam side down in a single
layer in an ungreased shallow au
gratin dish, top with remaining
soup mixture, and bake uncovered 30–40 minutes until
bubbly. Dust with paprika and
serve. About 520 calories per serving
if made with chicken, 540 calories
per serving made with turkey.

VARIATIONS:

Ham and Chicken Crepes: Prepare
as directed, substituting 1 cup
diced cooked ham for 1 cup chicken.
About 580 calories per serving.

Chicken Crepes au Gratin: Prepare
and bake crepes as directed; sprinkle
½ cup finely grated Cheddar or
Parmesan cheese on top, and broil
3″–4″ from heat 2–3 minutes until
flecked with brown. About 575
calories per serving.

⊠ QUICK CHICKEN OR TURKEY À LA KING

Makes 4 servings

1 (10½-ounce) can condensed
  cream of mushroom soup (do not
  dilute)
½ cup milk

1½ cups diced cooked chicken or
   turkey meat
2 tablespoons minced pimiento
4 English muffins, split, toasted, and
  lightly buttered, or 4 frozen waffles,
  toasted

Blend soup and milk until smooth
in a saucepan, cover, and heat over
moderate heat 5 minutes, stirring
occasionally. Add chicken, heat,
and stir 3–5 minutes. Mix in pimiento, spoon over muffins, and
serve. About 400 calories per
serving.

VARIATION:

Eggs à la King: Prepare as directed,
substituting 5–6 diced, hard-cooked
eggs for the chicken. About 370
calories per serving.

⊠ QUICK CHICKEN OR TURKEY STEW

Makes 4–6 servings

2 (10½-ounce) cans condensed
  cream of mushroom soup
½ cup light cream or evaporated
  milk
1 (1-pound) can mixed vegetables,
  drained
1 (1-pound) can small whole white
  potatoes, drained
1 (1-pound) can whole white onions
  (do not drain)
1 (4-ounce) can sliced mushrooms
  (do not drain)
2 cups bite-size pieces cooked
  chicken or turkey meat
½ teaspoon salt (about)
¼ teaspoon pepper
2 tablespoons minced parsley

Mix mushroom soup and cream in
a very large saucepan, add remaining ingredients except parsley,
cover, and simmer 10–15 minutes.
Taste for salt and adjust if needed.
Ladle into bowls, sprinkle with
parsley, and serve. If made with

chicken, about 565 calories for each of 4 servings, 375 calories for each of 6 servings. If made with turkey, about 585 calories for each of 4 servings, 390 calories for each of 6 servings.

¢ MOTHER'S CHICKEN OR TURKEY STEW

Makes 6 servings

1 (5–6-pound) stewing hen or turkey, cut up
1 medium-size yellow onion, peeled and stuck with 4 cloves
5–6 medium-size carrots, peeled and cut in 2" chunks
2 stalks celery, minced
2 sprigs parsley
2½ teaspoons salt (about)
¼ teaspoon pepper
1 quart water
1 cup milk
6 tablespoons flour blended with ⅓ cup cold milk

Place all but last ingredient in a heavy burner-to-table kettle or electric skillet set at 225° F., cover, and simmer about 2–2½ hours until chicken is tender. (*Note:* Remove chicken liver after 10–15 minutes, cool, and reserve.) Discard onion and parsley. Drain off liquid, reserving 3 cups, then skim off fat. (*Note:* If there is not enough liquid to total 3 cups, add water as needed.) Pour liquid into a saucepan, blend in flour paste, and heat, stirring, until thickened. Pour sauce over chicken, taste for salt and adjust as needed. Return chicken liver to stew, cover all, and let stand over low heat 5–10 minutes to mellow flavors. Good with boiled noodles or rice, Polenta or mashed potatoes. About 445 calories per serving made with chicken (without noodles, rice, Polenta, or potatoes), about 460 calories per serving if made with turkey.

VARIATIONS:

Chicken or Turkey Stew with Dumplings: Prepare stew as directed; also prepare a favorite dumpling recipe. Drop dumplings on top of stew and cook as dumpling recipe directs. Recipe too flexible for a meaningful calorie count.

Chicken or Turkey Stew with Biscuits: Prepare stew as directed and transfer to a hot, ungreased 3-quart casserole. Mix 1 recipe Baking Powder Biscuits, then cut and arrange biscuits, almost touching, on top of stew. Bake, uncovered, 15–20 minutes at 375° F. until lightly browned. About 695 calories per serving made with chicken, 710 calories made with turkey.

Chicken or Turkey and Vegetable Stew: Prepare stew as directed, then stir in any of the following: 1 (10-ounce) package frozen green peas, cut green beans, whole kernel corn, or baby lima beans, cooked and drained by package directions. Cover and let mellow 10 minutes over low heat before serving. Recipe too flexible for calorie count.

⚔ ¢ BRUNSWICK STEW

American Indian women, who invented Brunswick Stew, used to make it with squirrel or rabbit. If you have a hunter in the family, try it their way.
Makes 12–15 servings

1 (6-pound) stewing hen or capon, cleaned and dressed
1 gallon cold water
2 stalks celery (include tops)
1 tablespoon sugar
5 medium-size potatoes, peeled and cut in ½" cubes
3 medium-size yellow onions, peeled and coarsely chopped

6 large ripe tomatoes, peeled, cored, seeded, and coarsely chopped
2 (10-ounce) packages frozen baby lima beans (do not thaw)
2 (10-ounce) packages frozen whole kernel corn (do not thaw)
1 medium-size sweet green pepper, cored and cut in short, thin slivers
2 tablespoons salt (about)
1/4 teaspoon pepper

Remove fat from body cavity of bird, then place bird and giblets in a very large kettle. Add water and celery, cover, and simmer 1–2 hours until *just* tender. Remove bird and giblets from broth and cool. Strain broth and skim off fat. Rinse kettle, pour in broth, add sugar, all vegetables but corn and green pepper, cover, and simmer 1 hour. Meanwhile, skin chicken, cut meat in 1" chunks and dice giblets. Return chicken and giblets to kettle, add remaining ingredients, cover, and simmer 40–45 minutes, stirring occasionally. Taste for salt, adding more if needed. Serve piping hot in soup bowls as a main dish. Particularly good with cole-slaw and Hushpuppies or crisp corn sticks. (*Note:* This stew freezes well.) About 310 calories for each of 12 servings, about 250 calories for each of 15 servings.

⚗ ¢ CHICKEN OR TURKEY HASH

Makes 4 servings

1 medium-size yellow onion, peeled and minced
1/2 medium-size sweet green or red pepper, cored, seeded, and minced (optional)
2 tablespoons bacon drippings, butter, or margarine
2 cups diced cooked chicken or turkey meat
2 cups diced cooked cold peeled potatoes

1/4 cup applesauce
1 tablespoon minced parsley
1 teaspoon salt
1/8 teaspoon pepper
1/2 teaspoon poultry seasoning
4 poached or fried eggs (optional)

Stir-fry onion and, if you like, green pepper in drippings in a large, heavy skillet over moderate heat 5–8 minutes until onion is pale golden. Mix in all remaining ingredients except eggs, pat down with a broad spatula, and cook, uncovered, without stirring about 10 minutes until a brown crust forms on the bottom. Using 2 broad spatulas, turn hash and brown flip side 8–10 minutes. Cut into 4 portions and serve. If you like, top each serving with a poached or fried egg. About 290 calories per serving made with chicken (without egg), about 310 calories per serving if made with turkey.

VARIATIONS:

¢ **Chicken or Turkey and Sweet Potato Hash:** Prepare as directed but substitute 2 cups diced cooked or drained canned sweet potatoes or yams for the potatoes. About 305 calories per serving if made with chicken, 325 calories per serving if made with turkey.

¢ **Chicken or Turkey 'n' Stuffing Hash:** Prepare as directed but use 1 cup any leftover bread stuffing and 1 cup diced cooked or mashed potatoes instead of 2 cups potatoes. Omit poultry seasoning. About 330 calories per serving if made with chicken, 350 calories per serving if made with turkey.

Cheesy Chicken or Turkey Hash: Prepare as directed but substitute mashed potatoes for the diced and grated Parmesan cheese for the applesauce; add 1/4 teaspoon garlic powder. Fry 1 side as directed, turn, sprinkle with 2–3 tablespoons grated Parmesan or Cheddar cheese, and brown under broiler. About 330 calories per serving if made with chicken, 350 calories per serving if made with turkey.

CHICKEN OR TURKEY CROQUETTES

Makes 4 servings

¼ cup butter or margarine
¼ cup sifted flour
1 cup milk
1 chicken bouillon cube
1 tablespoon minced parsley
¼ teaspoon poultry seasoning
1 teaspoon finely grated lemon rind (optional)
2 tablespoons dry sherry (optional)
½ teaspoon salt (about)
⅛ teaspoon pepper
1 egg, lightly beaten
1½ cups coarsely ground cooked chicken or turkey meat
½ cup soft white bread crumbs
Shortening or cooking oil for deep fat frying

Coating:
1 egg, lightly beaten with 1 tablespoon cold water
¼ cup cracker crumbs mixed with ¼ cup minced blanched almonds

Melt butter in a large saucepan over moderate heat and blend in flour; slowly stir in milk, add bouillon cube, parsley, and all seasonings, and heat, stirring, until mixture thickens. Blend a little hot sauce into egg, return to pan, set over lowest heat, and heat, stirring, 1 minute; do not boil. Off heat, mix in chicken and bread crumbs; taste for salt and adjust. Cool, then chill until easy to shape. Shape into 8 patties or sausage-shaped rolls, dip in egg mixture, then roll in crumbs

to coat. Let dry on a rack at room temperature while heating fat. Place shortening in a deep fat fryer and heat to 375° F. Fry the croquettes, ½ at a time, 2–3 minutes until golden brown and crisp; drain on paper toweling, then keep warm by setting, uncovered, in oven turned to lowest heat while you fry the rest. Good with Tomato or Parsley Sauce. About 435 calories per serving if made with chicken, about 455 calories per serving if made with turkey.

VARIATIONS:

Curried Chicken or Turkey Croquettes: Prepare croquette mixture as directed but omit poultry seasoning and add 1–2 teaspoons curry powder and ¼ cup well-drained, minced chutney. Fry as directed and serve with Chicken or Turkey Gravy or Light Curry Sauce. About 435 calories per serving made with chicken, 455 calories per serving made with turkey (without gravy).

Chicken and Shellfish Croquettes: Prepare croquette mixture as directed but use a ½ and ½ mixture of chicken and finely ground cooked shrimp, lobster, or crab meat; omit poultry seasoning. Fry as directed. About 405 calories per serving if made with shrimp, 395 calories per serving if made with lobster or crab.

Chicken and Ham or Tongue Croquettes: Prepare croquette mixture as directed but use a ½ and ½ mixture of chicken and finely ground cooked lean ham or tongue; omit poultry seasoning and add 1 teaspoon prepared mild yellow mustard. Fry as directed. About 460 calories per serving whether made with ham or tongue.

CHICKEN OR TURKEY DIVAN

A luscious way to use up leftovers.
Makes 6 servings

¼ cup butter or margarine
¼ cup sifted flour
1 cup chicken broth
1 cup milk
¾ teaspoon salt
⅛ teaspoon white pepper
⅛ teaspoon nutmeg
¼ cup plus 2 tablespoons grated
  Parmesan cheese
3 tablespoons dry sherry
2 (10-ounce) packages frozen
  broccoli or asparagus spears,
  cooked by package directions and
  drained
10–12 slices cooked chicken or
  turkey meat
½ cup heavy cream

Preheat oven to 350° F. Melt butter
in a saucepan over moderate
heat, blend in flour, slowly add
broth and milk, and heat, stirring
until thickened; mix in salt, pepper,
nutmeg, ¼ cup cheese, and the
sherry. Arrange broccoli in a single
layer in a buttered 2-quart *au
gratin* dish or shallow casserole and
sprinkle with remaining cheese.
Top with chicken slices. Beat cream
until soft peaks will form and
fold into sauce; pour evenly over
chicken and bake, uncovered,
about ½ hour until bubbly. Broil
quickly to brown and serve. About
375 calories per serving if made
with chicken, 385 calories if made
with turkey.

VARIATIONS:

Chicken Divan Hollandaise: Prepare
as directed but mix ½ cup
Hollandaise Sauce and 1 teaspoon
Worcestershire sauce into cheese
sauce before adding cream. About
415 calories per serving.

Chicken Breasts Divan: Prepare as
directed, substituting 6 poached
chicken breasts for the sliced chicken
and arranging them slightly overlapping on the broccoli. About
415 calories per serving.

¢ CHICKEN OR TURKEY-NOODLE CASSEROLE

Makes 4 servings

¼ cup butter or margarine
¼ cup sifted flour
1 cup chicken broth
1 cup milk
1 chicken bouillon cube
1 teaspoon salt
¼ teaspoon pepper
¼ cup minced pimiento (optional)
2 cups bite-size pieces cooked
  chicken or turkey meat
1 (8-ounce) box thin noodles,
  cooked by package directions and
  drained

Topping:
1 cup soft white bread crumbs mixed
  with 3 tablespoons melted butter or
  margarine

Preheat oven to 350° F. Melt butter
in a large saucepan over moderate
heat and blend in flour; slowly stir
in broth and milk, add bouillon
cube, salt, and pepper, and heat,
stirring, until mixture thickens. Off
heat, mix in all remaining ingredients
except topping. Spoon into a
buttered 2-quart casserole, sprinkle
with topping, and bake uncovered
½ hour. About 555 calories per
serving made with chicken, 575
per serving made with turkey.

VARIATION:

**Chicken or Turkey-Noodle Casse-
role with Vegetables:** Prepare
chicken mixture as directed, then
stir in 1 (10-ounce) package frozen
mixed vegetables, cooked by package directions, 1 (4-ounce) undrained can sliced mushrooms, and

3 minced scallions. Spoon into a buttered 2½-quart casserole, top, and bake as directed. Or, if you prefer, omit topping and scatter 1 cup chow mein noodles over casserole for last 5 minutes of baking. With bread crumb or chow mein noodle topping: about 610 calories per serving if made with chicken, 630 calories per serving if made with turkey.

¢ CHICKEN OR TURKEY POT PIE

Makes 6 servings

¼ cup butter or margarine
6 tablespoons flour
1 cup milk
2 cups chicken broth or a ½ and ½ mixture of broth and apple cider or dry white wine
3 cups bite-size pieces cooked chicken or turkey meat
¼ teaspoon rosemary
¼ teaspoon savory
1 tablespoon minced parsley
1 teaspoon salt
¼ teaspoon white pepper
2 cups thinly sliced cooked carrots
2 cups cooked green peas
1 recipe Flaky Pastry I
1 egg yolk mixed with 1 tablespoon cold water (glaze)

Preheat oven to 425° F. Melt butter in a large saucepan over moderate heat, blend in flour, add milk and broth, and heat, stirring, until thickened. Add chicken and all seasonings, cover, and simmer 5–10 minutes, stirring occasionally. Cool to room temperature. Mix in carrots and peas and spoon into an ungreased 2½-quart casserole about 9″ in diameter. Prepare pastry and roll into a circle 3″ larger than casserole; make 3 V-shaped steam slits near center. Dampen casserole rim, fit pastry

on top, roll pastry edges under even with rim, and crimp to seal. Brush with glaze, being careful not to cover slits. Bake 30–40 minutes until browned and bubbly (place a sheet of foil on rack under casserole to catch drips). To serve, cut wedges of pastry and ladle chicken mixture on top. About 455 calories per serving if made with chicken, 470 per serving if made with turkey.

VARIATION:

Homestead Chicken or Turkey Pie: Stir-fry 1 peeled and minced yellow onion and ½ pound thinly sliced mushrooms in the butter 5 minutes; blend in flour and finish sauce as directed above. Do not cool and do not add carrots and peas. Transfer to casserole. Prepare 1 recipe Baking Powder Biscuits and roll into a circle ¼″ thick and about 1″ larger than casserole; cut V-slits in center. Dampen casserole rim, fit pastry on top, and press edges to seal. (Note: Scraps can be rerolled and cut into biscuits.) Brush topping with glaze and bake, uncovered, 15–20 minutes until lightly browned. Serve as directed. About 720 calories per serving if made with chicken, 735 calories per serving if made with turkey.

BASIC CHICKEN OR TURKEY SOUFFLÉ

Makes 4 servings

¼ cup butter or margarine
¼ cup sifted flour
1 cup milk
1 chicken bouillon cube
½ teaspoon salt
⅛ teaspoon white pepper
4 eggs, separated (at room temperature)
1 cup finely ground cooked chicken or turkey meat

2 teaspoons minced chives
    (optional)
¼ teaspoon cream of tartar

Melt butter in a small saucepan over moderate heat and blend in flour; slowly stir in milk. Add bouillon cube, salt, and pepper and heat and stir until mixture thickens. Lightly beat yolks, blend in a little hot sauce, then return to pan; set over lowest heat and heat, stirring, 1–2 minutes; do not boil. Off heat, mix in chicken and, if you like, chives. Lay a piece of wax paper flat on top of sauce and cool to room temperature. Preheat oven to 350° F. Beat egg whites until frothy, add cream of tartar, and beat until stiff but not dry. Stir about ¼ cup egg whites into sauce, then carefully fold in the rest, taking care not to break down volume. Spoon into an ungreased 1½-quart soufflé dish and bake, uncovered, 45–50 minutes until puffy and tinged with brown. Serve at once. Good with Tomato, Shrimp, Parsley, or Mushroom Sauce. About 335 calories per serving if made with chicken, 355 per serving if made with turkey.

VARIATIONS:

Herbed Chicken or Turkey Soufflé: Prepare as directed, including chives and adding 1 tablespoon each minced parsley and minced fresh dill, tarragon, chervil, or basil. About 335 calories per serving if made with chicken, 355 per serving if made with turkey.

Chicken or Turkey and Ham or Tongue Soufflé: Prepare as directed, using ¾ cup ground chicken and ½ cup ground cooked lean ham or tongue. About 385 calories per serving if made with chicken, 405 calories per serving if made with turkey.

Curried Chicken or Turkey Soufflé: Melt butter, blend in flour and 1 tablespoon each curry powder and finely grated onion. Add milk slowly and proceed as directed. About 335 calories per serving if made with chicken, 355 calories per serving if made with turkey.

⚔️ ¢ **CHICKEN OR TURKEY TIMBALES**

Makes 4 servings

1 cup milk
1 cup soft white bread crumbs
2 tablespoons butter or margarine
1 tablespoon finely grated yellow
    onion
1 chicken bouillon cube
½ teaspoon salt
⅛ teaspoon pepper
⅛ teaspoon sage
⅛ teaspoon thyme
2 eggs, lightly beaten
1 cup finely ground cooked chicken
    or turkey meat

Preheat oven to 325° F. Mix all but last 2 ingredients in a saucepan and bring to a boil, stirring constantly. Remove from heat. Stir a little hot mixture into eggs, then return to pan and mix well. Mix in chicken. Spoon into 4 well-buttered custard cups and set in a shallow baking pan; pour enough water into pan to come halfway up cups. Bake, uncovered, about 35 minutes until just set. Loosen edges of timbales and invert gently on a hot platter. Serve with Chicken Gravy, Tomato or Mushroom Sauce. About 265 calories per serving if made with chicken (without gravy or sauce), about 285 calories per serving if made with turkey.

⚖ ¢ **HOT CHICKEN OR TURKEY LOAF**

Makes 8 servings

3 cups finely chopped cooked chicken or turkey meat
2 cups dry white bread crumbs
½ cup minced celery
2 pimientos, drained and coarsely chopped
1½ teaspoons salt
¼ teaspoon pepper
1 tablespoon finely grated yellow onion
1 tablespoon lemon juice
2 teaspoons Worcestershire sauce
1 tablespoon minced parsley
2 cups chicken broth
3 eggs, lightly beaten

Preheat oven to 350° F. Mix together all but last 2 ingredients. Stir broth into eggs, then pour over chicken mixture and mix well. Lightly pack mixture into a greased 9"×5"×3" loaf pan, set in a large baking pan, and pour in enough boiling water to come about halfway up loaf pan. Bake, uncovered, about 1 hour until loaf begins to pull away from sides of pan. Lift loaf pan from water bath and cool upright 5–10 minutes; loosen loaf, invert on a hot platter and ease out. Serve hot with Chicken or Mushroom Gravy. Good cold, sliced thin, and accompanied by salad. About 200 calories per serving if made with chicken (without gravy), 220 calories per serving if made with turkey.

VARIATIONS:

¢ ⚖ **Surprise Chicken Loaf:**
Prepare chicken mixture as directed and pack half into loaf pan. Arrange 3 peeled hard-cooked eggs lengthwise down center of mixture, place rows of pimiento, stuffed green or pitted ripe olives on either side of eggs, cover with remaining chicken mixture and bake as directed. About 245 calories per serving.

¢ ⚖ **Chicken and Rice Loaf:**
Prepare chicken mixture as directed but reduce bread crumbs to 1½ cups and add 1½ cups boiled rice. About 210 calories per serving.

⚖ **HOT CHICKEN OR TURKEY MOUSSE**

Makes 6 servings

¼ cup butter or margarine
5 tablespoons flour
1 cup milk
1 chicken bouillon cube
1 teaspoon salt
Pinch nutmeg
3 eggs, separated (at room temperature)
½ cup light cream
1½ cups finely ground cooked white meat of chicken or turkey

Preheat oven to 350° F. Melt butter in a saucepan over moderate heat and blend in flour; slowly stir in milk. Add bouillon cube, salt, and nutmeg and heat, stirring, until mixture thickens. Remove from heat. Lightly beat yolks and briskly blend in a little hot sauce. Return to pan and mix well; stir in cream and chicken. Beat egg whites until soft peaks form, then fold into chicken mixture. Spoon into a well-oiled 5-cup ring mold, set in a large baking pan, and pour enough boiling water into pan to come ⅔ of the way up mold. Bake, uncovered, ¾–1 hour until just set. Lift mousse from water bath and cool upright 5–10 minutes. Loosen with a spatula, invert on a hot platter, and *ease* out. Serve as is or fill center with Creamed Mushrooms, Saffron Rice, or hot mixed vegetables. Good with Mushroom or Aurore Sauce.

VARIATION:

⚔️ **Cold Chicken or Turkey Mousse:** Prepare mousse mixture as directed, but before folding in egg whites stir in 1 tablespoon each finely grated yellow onion and lemon juice, ¼ teaspoon powdered rosemary, and a pinch cayenne pepper. If you like, also add ⅓ cup each minced celery and water chestnuts. Fold in egg whites and bake as directed. Cool slightly, then unmold. Cool to room temperature, cover, and chill 2–3 hours. When serving, garnish with lettuce, watercress, and cherry tomatoes. Serve with mayonnaise, thinned slightly with cream.

Both versions: about 280 calories per serving if made with chicken (without mushrooms, rice, mixed vegetables, or sauce), about 300 calories per serving if made with turkey.

LYONNAISE TURKEY ROLL EN CASSEROLE

There are frozen white meat turkey rolls (both plain and smoked), white and dark meat rolls, even ham and turkey rolls. All are good prepared this way.
Makes 6 servings

1 (3-pound) frozen boneless turkey roll, thawed
¼ cup butter or margarine
2 large yellow onions, peeled and sliced thin
½ cup beef broth
1 tablespoon tomato paste
1 cup chicken broth
1 bay leaf
½ teaspoon salt
⅛ teaspoon pepper
½ pound button mushrooms, wiped clean
2 tablespoons flour blended with 2 tablespoons cold water

Preheat oven to 350° F. Brown turkey in butter in a heavy skillet over moderate heat and transfer to an ungreased deep flameproof 2½-quart casserole. Stir-fry onions in butter remaining in skillet 8–10 minutes until golden, then remove with a slotted spoon and spread over turkey; save skillet drippings. Mix beef broth and tomato paste and add to casserole along with all but last 2 ingredients. Cover and bake 2–2½ hours until tender. Lift turkey to a hot platter and keep warm. Sauté mushrooms in skillet drippings over moderately high heat 2–3 minutes until golden; add to casserole. Blend flour paste into casserole liquid and stir until thickened over low heat. Remove strings from roll, carve into fairly thick slices, cutting almost—but not quite—through at the bottom. Return turkey to casserole, spoon some sauce in between slices, carry to the table, and serve. About 380 calories per serving.

ROAST STUFFED TURKEY ROLL WITH CAFÉ AU LAIT SAUCE

Makes 6–10 servings

1 (3–5-pound) frozen boneless turkey roll, thawed
1 recipe Chicken Liver and Mushroom Stuffing
3 strips fat bacon

Sauce:
1 cup chicken broth
½ cup milk
1 cup hot strong black coffee
1 teaspoon salt
⅛ teaspoon pepper
2 tablespoons brandy (optional)
¼ cup unsifted flour blended with ¼ cup cold water

Preheat oven to 325° F. Untie turkey roll and lay flat, skin side down.

Spread stuffing on meat, leaving a wide margin, then roll up and tie around in several places. Place on a rack in a roasting pan and drape bacon on top. Insert meat thermometer in center of roll. Bake, uncovered, 2½–3 hours until thermometer registers 170–75° F. Remove bacon for last ½ hour so roll browns evenly. Lift roll to hot platter and let rest while making sauce. Pour all but 2 tablespoons drippings from pan, add broth, milk and coffee, and stir to scrape up brown bits; pour into a saucepan. Mix in remaining ingredients and heat, stirring until thickened. To serve, slice roll not too thin, removing strings as you go. Pass sauce separately. About 610 calories for each of 6 servings, 475 calories for each of 10 servings.

EASY TURKEY WELLINGTON

Boneless turkey roast baked in a flaky pastry.
Makes 4 servings

1 (2-pound) frozen boneless turkey roast, thawed
1 (8-ounce) package refrigerated dough for crescent rolls
1 (8-ounce) can liver pâté
2 tablespoons dry sherry or Madeira
1 egg lightly beaten with 1 tablespoon cold water (glaze)

Roast turkey roast by package directions; cool to room temperature. Preheat oven to 425° F. Meanwhile, open package of dough, spread dough flat, and halve crosswise but do not separate into individual rolls. Fit halves together on an ungreased baking sheet so you have a rectangle about 9″×14″; pinch edges together to seal; also press perforations shut so you have an unbroken sheet of dough. Remove string on turkey roast and lay roll across center of dough. Mix pâté and sherry and

spread on top of turkey roast. Bring dough sides up to meet on top of roast and crimp to seal; close dough over ends of roast. Make 3 steam slits on each side of roll, then brush pastry with glaze, taking care not to seal vents. Bake, uncovered, on center rack 20–25 minutes until golden. Ease onto a hot platter. To serve, slice straight across with a very sharp knife, making slices fairly thick. Also good served cold. About 695 calories per serving.

¢ DEVILED TURKEY DRUMSTICKS

Makes 4 servings

2 frozen turkey drumsticks and 2 thighs, thawed

Sauce:
¼ cup butter or margarine
1 tablespoon powdered mustard
1 teaspoon grated yellow onion
4 teaspoons cider vinegar or lemon juice
Pinch cayenne pepper

Make 3–4 tiny lengthwise slits in each piece of turkey. Melt butter in a saucepan, stir in remaining sauce ingredients, and pour into an ungreased shallow roasting pan. Roll turkey in sauce and let stand at room temperature 1 hour. Preheat oven to 350° F. Roast turkey, uncovered, about 2 hours until tender, basting occasionally with pan drippings or a little melted butter. Turn turkey as needed to brown evenly. Tent with foil if it browns too fast. About 380 calories per serving.

VARIATIONS:

¢ **Deviled Turkey Wings:** Substitute 6 turkey wings for the legs and proceed as directed, allowing about 1½ hours' roasting time. About 380 calories per serving.

¢ **Deviled Leftover Turkey:** Cut thick slices from cooked drumsticks and thighs, roll in sauce, and coat with dry white bread crumbs. Place in a greased baking pan and bake, uncovered, ½ hour at 400° F. Brown under broiler and serve. Recipe too flexible for a meaningful calorie count.

¢ CREOLE-STYLE TURKEY DRUMSTICKS

Makes 4 servings

2 *frozen turkey drumsticks and 2 thighs, thawed*
⅓ *cup unsifted flour*
3 *tablespoons olive or other cooking oil*
1 *large yellow onion, peeled and minced*
1 *medium-size sweet green pepper, cored, seeded, and minced*
2 *stalks celery, minced*
1 *clove garlic, peeled and crushed*
1 *teaspoon salt*
¼ *teaspoon pepper*
1 *tablespoon minced parsley*
½ *teaspoon thyme*
1 *bay leaf, crumbled*
1 *(1-pound 3-ounce) can tomatoes (do not drain)*

Dredge turkey in flour and brown in oil in a very large, heavy skillet over moderate heat; drain on paper toweling. Stir-fry onion, green pepper, celery, and garlic in drippings 8 minutes until onion is pale golden. Mix in remaining ingredients, breaking up tomatoes; return turkey to skillet, cover, and simmer 1½–2 hours until tender, basting now and then and adding a little water if pan seems dry. Or, if you prefer, transfer mixture to an ungreased 3-quart casserole, cover, and bake 1½–2 hours at 350° F. Or do the whole thing in an electric skillet, set at 350° F. Serve with boiled or Saffron Rice. About 340 calories per serving (without rice).

VARIATION:

¢ **Creole-Style Turkey Parts:** Prepare as directed, substituting 6 turkey wings or a 2-pound thawed boneless turkey roll for drumsticks. Or use a 4-pound frozen whole turkey breast, thawed and split; use a larger can of tomatoes (1-pound 12-ounce size) but cook for the same length of time. About 355 calories per serving if made with turkey breast, 430 calories per serving if made with turkey wings or a boneless turkey roll.

ROCK CORNISH GAME HENS NORMANDY STYLE

Especially attractive when garnished with clusters of red and green grapes.
Makes 8 servings

4 *(1–1¼-pound) Rock Cornish game hens, thawed and halved lengthwise*
¼ *cup cooking oil*
¼ *cup butter or margarine*
½ *pound mushrooms, wiped clean and sliced thin*
2 *cups apple cider or a ½ and ½ mixture of cider and dry white wine*
½ *clove garlic, peeled and crushed*
1½ *teaspoons salt*
¼ *teaspoon white pepper*
¼ *teaspoon thyme*
2 *tablespoons cornstarch blended with 2 tablespoons cold water*
½ *cup heavy cream*

Preheat oven to 325° F. Pat hens dry on paper toweling and brown, 2 or 3 halves at a time, in a mixture of oil and butter in a large, heavy skillet over moderate heat. Drain hens on paper toweling, then arrange in a large, shallow roasting pan without crowding. Stir-fry mushrooms in skillet drippings 3–5 minutes over moderate heat and spoon over hens. Mix cider and garlic and pour over all; sprinkle in salt, pepper, and thyme. Cover with foil and bake ½ hour; uncover and bake 15 minutes longer. Lift hens to a serving platter, spoon mushrooms on top and keep warm. Pour pan liquid into a saucepan and bring to a simmer. Smooth in cornstarch paste and heat, stirring, until thickened and clear. Add cream, taste for salt and adjust as needed. Spoon some sauce over birds and pass the remainder. About 365 calories per serving.

HERBED ROCK CORNISH GAME HENS OR SQUABS WITH MUSHROOMS AND WINE

Makes 4 servings

2 (1–1¼-pound) Rock Cornish game hens or squabs, thawed
Herb Butter (see below)
3 tablespoons melted butter or margarine
1 cup dry white wine
½ cup chicken broth
1 tablespoon lemon juice
1 dozen button mushrooms, wiped clean and fluted*

Herb Butter:
¼ cup butter or margarine, softened to room temperature
2 tablespoons minced scallions
2 tablespoons minced parsley
½ teaspoon poultry seasoning
1 teaspoon Worcestershire sauce
½ teaspoon garlic salt

Preheat oven to 425° F. Make a small slit in the skin on each side of the breast of each hen. Mix herb butter and, using a small, thin-bladed knife, spread evenly over breasts underneath skin. Skewer openings shut and truss* birds; place breast side up on a rack in a shallow roast-

ing pan and roast, uncovered, 20 minutes, brushing 1–2 times with melted butter. Reduce oven to 325° F.; remove rack and place birds directly in pan. Pour wine, broth, and lemon juice over birds and roast, uncovered, basting frequently with drippings, about ½ hour until just tender. Add fluted mushrooms and roast 10 minutes longer. Lift hens and mushrooms to a hot platter; if pan juices seem skimpy, stir in a little more wine or broth. Pour some pan juices over the birds and pass the rest. About 400 calories per serving.

HAWAIIAN-STYLE ROCK CORNISH GAME HENS OR SQUABS

Makes 4 servings

2 (1–1¼-pound) Rock Cornish game hens or squabs, thawed and halved lengthwise
Marinade (see below)
2 tablespoons cooking oil
1 large yellow onion, peeled and sliced thin
2 teaspoons sugar
4 pineapple rings
2 tablespoons butter or margarine
2 cups hot boiled rice
½ cup minced macadamia nuts or toasted slivered almonds
4 preserved kumquats, sliced thin
1 pimiento, slivered
⅓ cup mandarin orange sections

Marinade:
¼ cup soy sauce
¼ cup pineapple juice
1 tablespoon lime juice
1 clove garlic, peeled and crushed
¼ teaspoon ginger
¼ teaspoon oregano
¼ teaspoon pepper

Lay hens in a shallow dish; warm marinade over low heat, stirring, about 5 minutes; pour over birds, cover, and refrigerate 4–6 hours, turning birds occasionally. Pat birds dry on paper toweling and brown in oil in a large, heavy skillet; lift out and set aside. Sauté onion in drippings 8–10 minutes over moderate heat, sprinkle with sugar, and sauté until lightly browned. Return hens to skillet, pour in marinade, cover, and simmer about ¾ hour until tender. Meanwhile, dry pineapple well on paper toweling and brown lightly in butter over moderate heat. To serve, toss rice with nuts, kumquats, pimiento, and orange sections and mound on a hot large platter. Arrange birds and pineapple rings on top and drizzle with some of the pan drippings.

VARIATION:
Prepare as directed but substitute canned lichee nuts for the pineapple and the syrup from the can for the pineapple juice in the marinade; do not brown the lichee nuts.

Both versions: about 615 calories per serving if made with macadamia nuts, 640 calories per serving if made with almonds.

DUCKLING WITH ORANGE SAUCE (DUCKLING À L'ORANGE, DUCKLING À LA BIGARADE)

To be strictly authentic, this recipe should be made with bitter Seville oranges. Any clear-skinned orange will do, however, if you add lemon juice for tartness.
Makes 6 servings

2 (4-pound) ducklings, cleaned, dressed, and quartered
1 tablespoon salt
¼ teaspoon pepper
1 cup chicken broth
1 cup dry white wine
Finely slivered rind of 4 oranges (use orange part only and slice oranges to use as a garnish)

1½ cups water
½ cup sugar
1 cup orange juice
2 tablespoons lemon juice
¼ cup brandy
2 tablespoons butter or margarine
2 tablespoons flour
1 cup giblet stock*

Preheat oven to 450° F. Rub ducklings with 2 teaspoons salt and the pepper; place skin side up on a rack in a large shallow roasting pan and prick skin well all over. Roast, uncovered, 20–25 minutes, turning and pricking frequently; drain off fat. Pour broth and wine over ducklings, reduce oven to 350° F., and roast about 1 hour longer, basting frequently, until golden brown and leg joints move easily. Meanwhile, place rind and 1 cup water in a small saucepan and boil, uncovered, 3 minutes; drain and reserve rind. Boil remaining water and sugar, uncovered, 10–15 minutes until amber; add rind, orange and lemon juices, and brandy, cover, and keep warm over lowest heat. When ducklings are done, transfer to a heated platter and keep warm. Strain pan juices into a shallow bowl, scraping browned bits from bottom, and skim off fat. Melt butter in a saucepan, blend in flour, add pan juices, giblet stock, rind mixture, and remaining salt, and cook, stirring, until slightly thickened. Pour some sauce over the ducklings and pass the rest. Garnish platter with orange slices and sprigs of watercress or rose geranium. About 500 calories per serving.

DUCKLING WITH BING CHERRY SAUCE (DUCKLING MORELLO)

Makes 6 servings

2 (4-pound) ducklings, cleaned, dressed, and quartered
3 teaspoons salt

¼ teaspoon pepper
1 (1-pound 1-ounce) can pitted Bing
    cherries (do not drain)
1½ cups giblet stock*
1¾ cups chicken broth
1 teaspoon lemon juice
¼ cup cornstarch blended with ½
    cup cold water
¼–⅓ cup dry Madeira wine

Preheat oven to 450° F. Rub duck-lings with 2 teaspoons salt and ⅛ teaspoon pepper. Place skin side up on a rack in a large, shallow roasting pan and prick skin all over with a sharp fork. Roast, uncovered, 20–25 minutes, turning and pricking frequently; drain off all drippings. Reduce oven to 350° F. and roast 1 hour longer; again drain off drip-pings. Drain liquid from cherries into roasting pan, baste ducklings, and roast 15–30 minutes until golden brown and leg joints move easily. Transfer to a heated platter and keep warm while you make the sauce. Pour giblet stock and broth into roasting pan and stir, scraping browned bits from bottom; transfer all to a saucepan. Add lemon juice, remaining salt and pepper and heat, uncovered, over moderate heat 1–2 minutes. Blend in cornstarch paste and heat, stirring constantly, until thickened and clear. Add cherries and wine and heat 2–3 minutes longer. Spoon some sauce over ducklings and pass the rest. About 410 calories per serving.

WOR SHEW OPP (BRAISED BONELESS DUCKLING)

Makes 3–4 servings

1 (5-pound) duckling, cleaned and
    dressed
1 quart water
½ cup soy sauce
2 tablespoons dark brown sugar or
    Chinese bead molasses (obtainable
    in Chinese groceries)

1 star anise (also available in Chinese
    groceries)
3 tablespoons cornstarch
Shortening or cooking oil for deep fat
    frying
½ cup giblet stock*
1 tablespoon cornstarch blended with
    1 tablespoon cold water
2 tablespoons minced toasted
    almonds

Preheat oven to 450° F. Remove fat from cavity of duckling and discard. Also remove giblets, cook,* mince, and reserve along with stock. Mean-while, pat duckling dry, skewer openings shut, truss,* and prick body all over with a sharp fork. Place breast side up on a rack in a shallow roasting pan and roast, uncovered, ½ hour. Transfer to a deep kettle, add water, soy sauce, sugar, and anise, cover, and simmer 1½–1¾ hours until very tender; cool in liquid until easy to handle. Cut meat from bones in bite-size pieces. Reserve liquid and skim off fat. Heat shortening in a deep fat fryer to 375° F. Dredge pieces of duck in cornstarch, shake off excess, and fry, a few pieces at a time, 1–2 min-utes until golden; drain on paper toweling and keep warm while you fry the rest. Heat ½ cup duck cook-ing liquid with the giblet stock and giblets in a small saucepan, blend in cornstarch paste, and heat, stirring, until thickened and clear. Mound duckling in a shallow dish, pour sauce over all, and sprinkle with almonds. Serve with hot boiled rice. About 520 calories for each of 3 servings (without rice), 390 calories for each of 4 servings.

CHINESE-STYLE ROAST DUCKLING

Duckling cooked this way is good at a buffet; simply slice thin and serve between small, fresh hot rolls. Makes 3–4 servings

1 medium-size yellow onion, peeled
  and minced
2 stalks celery, minced
4 dried mushrooms
1 star anise
1 clove garlic, peeled and crushed
2 teaspoons sugar
¼ cup soy sauce
¼ cup dry sherry
1 (5-pound) duckling, cleaned and
  dressed
1 teaspoon salt

Basting Sauce:
¼ cup honey
2 tablespoons cider vinegar
1 tablespoon soy sauce

Preheat oven to 450° F. Place onion,
celery, mushrooms, anise, garlic,
sugar, soy sauce, and sherry in a
small saucepan and cook and stir 2–
3 minutes over moderate heat.
Skewer neck flap of duckling to
back, then pour hot mixture into
body cavity. (*Note:* If liquid tends
to flow out through vent, prop lower
part of duckling up with a ball of
foil.) Sew up vent and tie legs together. Place duckling breast side
up on a rack in a shallow roasting
pan and rub well with salt. Roast,
uncovered, ½ hour. Meanwhile, mix
basting sauce and keep warm over
low heat. Reduce heat to 350° F. and
roast about 1½ hours longer, basting
every 20 minutes with sauce, until
leg joints move easily. Transfer
duckling to a heated platter and
serve. About 535 calories for each
of 3 servings, 400 calories for each
of 4 servings.

DUCKLING OR GOSLING EN
   DAUBE

Makes 6–8 servings

2 (4–5-pound) ducklings or goslings,
  cleaned and dressed
1 tablespoon bacon drippings or
  clarified butter*

1 large yellow onion, peeled and
  minced
2 stalks celery, minced
1 teaspoon allspice
2 teaspoons salt
¼ teaspoon pepper
6–8 medium-size carrots, peeled and
  cut in 1" chunks
4 leeks, washed, trimmed, and cut in
  1" chunks (include some tops)
6 turnips, peeled and halved
1 bouquet garni,* tied in cheesecloth
1 fifth dry red wine

Gravy:
⅓ cup unsifted flour
¼ cup butter or margarine
1 cup giblet stock*
½ teaspoon salt (about)
⅛ teaspoon pepper

Cook giblets* and reserve along with
stock. Dry birds well, remove loose
fat in body cavities, skewer openings
shut, and truss; prick birds well all
over with a sharp fork, then brown,
1 at a time, using bacon drippings
at first, in a heavy skillet over moderately low heat 20–30 minutes; turn
as needed to brown evenly and drain
off drippings as they accumulate.
Meanwhile, preheat oven to 325° F.
Set browned birds aside, drain all
but 1 tablespoon drippings from
skillet, add onion and celery, and
stir-fry 8–10 minutes over moderate
heat until golden; spoon into a large
Dutch oven. Lay birds breast side
up on onion mixture, sprinkle each
with ½ teaspoon allspice, ½ teaspoon
salt, and ⅛ teaspoon pepper. Tuck
vegetables around birds and sprinkle
them with remaining salt. Add *bouquet garni* and wine, cover, and
bake 1½–1¾ hours until leg joints
move easily; baste with pan liquid
every ½ hour. Meanwhile, mince
giblets and reserve. Also brown flour
in butter in a heavy saucepan over
moderate heat and set aside. When
birds are done, drain off liquid and

skim off fat. Blend pan liquid and giblet stock into flour and heat, stirring, until thickened. Add giblets, salt, and pepper, taste, and adjust seasoning as needed. Serve birds in a deep platter wreathed with vegetables and topped with some of the gravy. Pass remaining gravy. About 395 calories for each of 6 servings, 300 calories for each of 8 servings.

GERMAN-STYLE POTATO STUFFED ROAST GOOSE

Excellent with Sweet and Sour Red Cabbage or Shredded Ruby Cabbage.
Makes 10 servings

1 (10–12-pound) goose, cleaned and dressed
2 large yellow onions, peeled and sliced thin
¼ cup butter or margarine
6 large potatoes, parboiled, peeled, and cut in ½" cubes
2 cloves garlic, peeled and crushed
Raw goose liver, minced
1 teaspoon sage
1½ teaspoons salt
¼ teaspoon pepper

Preheat oven to 325° F. Remove fat from body cavity of goose and save if you like to render and use in cooking. Remove giblets, hold out liver, but save the rest for soup or giblet stock.* Prick goose well all over with a sharp fork. Sauté onions in butter in a large, heavy kettle over moderately high heat 5 minutes, add potatoes and garlic, and sauté 5 minutes. Off heat, mix in remaining ingredients. Spoon loosely into cavity of goose, skewer openings shut, and truss.* Place goose breast side up on a rack in a shallow roasting pan and roast 20–22 minutes per pound until leg joints move easily; prick every ½ hour and drain off drippings as they collect. If you like a crisp skin,

spoon all drippings from pan, pour ¼ cup cold water over bird, and roast 10 minutes longer. Lift bird to a hot platter, remove skewers and strings, and let "rest" about 10 minutes. Make gravy from drippings if you like. Garnish as desired and serve. About 490 calories per serving.

BRAISED GOOSE WITH CHESTNUTS AND ONIONS

Young (4–8-pound) geese can be cooked in any of the ways suitable for duckling. The average supermarket size (10–12 pounds) is good prepared this way.
Makes 10 servings

1 (10–12-pound) goose, cleaned, dressed, and cut up
1 tablespoon bacon drippings or rendered goose fat*
1 medium-size carrot, peeled and minced
1 medium-size yellow onion, peeled and minced
2 cloves garlic, peeled and crushed
1 teaspoon sugar
1 tablespoon flour
1 quart giblet stock* or part stock and part chicken broth
½ cup tomato purée
1 teaspoon salt
¼ teaspoon pepper
1 pound small white onions, peeled
2 tablespoons rendered goose fat or clarified butter*
1½ pounds chestnuts, shelled, peeled, and quartered

If breasts of goose are large, have butcher halve them crosswise as well as lengthwise. Early in the day, take fat from body of goose and render.* Also remove giblets and cook*; mince giblets and reserve along with stock. Preheat oven to 325° F. Prick goose well all over with a sharp fork and brown, a few pieces at a time, in a large, heavy kettle, using bacon drippings at first, about 20 minutes over moderately low heat; pour off drippings as they collect and save; also prick goose often during browning. Drain goose on paper toweling and set aside. Drain all but 2 tablespoons drippings from kettle, add carrot, onion, and garlic, and stir-fry 8–10 minutes over moderate heat until golden; sprinkle with sugar and brown 2 minutes. Blend in flour, add stock, purée, salt, and pepper and heat, stirring, until mixture boils. Return goose to kettle, cover, transfer to oven, and bake 2 hours. Meanwhile, brown whole onions in goose fat in a heavy skillet over moderate heat about 10 minutes; drain on paper toweling. When goose has cooked 2 hours, add onions, cover, and bake ½ hour; add chestnuts, cover, and bake ¼–½ hour longer until goose is very tender. Lift goose to a hot deep platter, wreathe with onions and chestnuts, cover, and keep warm. Strain cooking liquid through a fine sieve, pressing vegetables to extract all liquid; skim off as much fat as possible. Reduce sauce to about 2 cups by boiling rapidly uncovered, add giblets, taste for salt and pepper and adjust as needed. Ladle over goose and serve. About 540 calories per serving.

Some Ways to Use Poultry Leftovers

There aren't apt to be leftovers from small birds unless you've misjudged. Quarters, halves, and parts reheat well, wrapped in foil, in about ½ hour at 350° F. Leftover turkey, goose, duck, and chicken can be used in any recipe calling for cooked poultry meat (if recipe calls for more meat than you have, round out with canned chicken). Or they can be used as follows:

Sliced Hot Poultry: Slice meat, not too thin, remove skin, and layer into an ungreased casserole. Add just enough hot sauce or gravy to cover (see Sauces, Gravies, and Seasonings for Poultry), cover with foil, and heat 20 minutes at 350° F.

Hot Roast Chicken or Turkey Sandwiches: Heat slices in sauce or gravy as above and serve on toast or bread spread, if you like, with cranberry sauce, chutney, or relish. Or serve on hot leftover stuffing. To reheat stuffing, spread in a greased piepan and bake, uncovered, at 350° F., brushing occasionally with melted butter until lightly browned.

To Make the Most of Small Amounts:
– Cube, dice, or cut in julienne strips and toss into hearty salads or add to casseroles, broths, or vegetable soups.
– Add scraps and bones to stock pot.
– Grind and add to savory stuffings.
– Grind, mix with mayonnaise, a little softened cream cheese, and mustard, and use as a sandwich spread. For extra zip, add a little applesauce or minced chutney.
– Grind, mix with any seasoned butter, a little minced scallions or capers, mustard, or other spicy condiment, and use as a cocktail spread.
– Dice or slice thin, layer in custard cups, fill to the brim with Quick Aspic or Madrilène Aspic, chill until firm, unmold, and serve with mayonnaise.
– Stretch with an equal quantity of hot Medium White Sauce, Mornay or Parsley Sauce and serve over crepes, toast, waffles, hot biscuits, or corn bread.

CHAPTER 11

SEAFOOD

Few nations are more blessed with the sea's bounty than America, yet few do more poorly by it. A fish is to fry, we think. So we slosh it with batter or jacket it in bread crumbs and plunk it into bubbling oil. There's nothing wrong with fried fish—especially if it's catfish served with hushpuppies—but there are far too many kinds of fish to lump in the same kettle.

From a catch far less impressive than our own, the French have built an inspired repertoire of recipes. The Scandinavians know dozens of ways to prepare salmon and herring; the Greeks do exciting things with squid and octopus; the Italians—well, it was *they* who taught the French to cook; the Chinese whisk shrimp in and out of a *wok* with a crunch of green vegetables so that it's irresistibly succulent; the Japanese have made an art and ritual of *sushi*—thinly sliced raw fish arrayed with fancily cut vegetables.

This isn't to say we haven't some classics of our own. It's hard to top a boiled Maine lobster, for example. Or Maryland crab or Louisiana shrimp gumbo. But we *can* do better by most of our catch. If we lavished half as much love on the cooking of fish as we do on the catching, we would do very well indeed.

The Kinds of Seafood

Basically, there are two—*fish* and *shellfish*. Fish, for the sake of simplicity, have fins, backbones, and gills. Shellfish subdivide into two categories: *crustaceans* (crabs, crayfish, lobsters, shrimp, and other footed sea animals with armorlike shells) and *mollusks* (clams, mussels, oysters, scallops, and other soft, spineless creatures living inside hard shells).

In addition to fish and shellfish, there are mavericks that defy easy classification: squid and octopus (technically mollusks that carry their shells internally); turtles, terrapins, frogs, and snails (amphibians). Because all require special preparation, they will be discussed individually.

The Food Value of Seafood

All seafood is high in protein; most of it is also high in minerals (notably calcium, phosphorous, copper, and iron) but low in calories. Food values vary from fish to fish, however.

¢ SIMPLE COURT BOUILLON FOR FISH AND SHELLFISH

The simplest court bouillon is salt water (1–1½ teaspoons salt to 1 quart cold water). It is used to poach or steam very delicate white fish because it never masks the true flavor of the fish. The following recipe, although simple, has a touch of piquance. It is suitable for poaching any fish or shellfish.
Makes 1 quart

1 large sprig parsley
1 bay leaf
1 (3"–4") sprig fresh thyme or ¼ teaspoon dried thyme
3 peppercorns
1 quart cold water
¼ cup white vinegar
1 medium-size yellow onion, peeled and stuck with 3 cloves
1 carrot, peeled and cut in small dice
1 stalk celery, chopped fine
1 teaspoon salt

Tie parsley, bay leaf, thyme, and peppercorns in cheesecloth. Place in a saucepan, add remaining ingredients, cover, and simmer 1 hour; strain through a fine sieve. Calories negligible.

WHITE WINE COURT BOUILLON

Especially good for shellfish.
Makes about 2 quarts

½ pound fishbones, heads, and trimmings (from any delicate white fish)
1 quart water
1 quart dry white wine
2 small yellow onions, each peeled and stuck with 1 clove
2 bay leaves
2 cloves garlic, peeled
1 teaspoon thyme
1 teaspoon salt
6 bruised peppercorns

Place fishbones and water in a large saucepan, cover, and simmer 20 minutes; strain broth through a fine sieve lined with a double thickness of cheesecloth; discard bones. Rinse out pan, add strained broth and remaining ingredients, and simmer, uncovered, 20 minutes. Again strain broth through a double thickness of cheesecloth. Calories negligible.

RED WINE COURT BOUILLON

A good base for fish sauces and aspics.
Makes about 2 quarts

1 pound fishbones, heads, and trimmings (from any delicate white fish)
1½ quarts water
2 cups dry red wine
2 small yellow onions, each peeled and stuck with 2 cloves
1 carrot, peeled and cut in 1" chunks
1 celery stalk, cut in 1" chunks
1 clove garlic, peeled
2 parsley sprigs
½ teaspoon thyme
1 teaspoon salt
6 bruised peppercorns

Place fishbones and water in a large saucepan, cover, and simmer 20 minutes; add remaining ingredients, cover, and cook ½ hour longer. Strain broth through a fine sieve lined with a double thickness of cheesecloth. Calories negligible.

¢ HERBED COURT BOUILLON FOR FISH AND SHELLFISH

More fragrant than Simple Court Bouillon for Fish and Shellfish.
Makes about 2 quarts

1 stalk celery
2 sprigs parsley
2 sprigs fresh dill
2 sprigs fresh thyme or a pinch dried thyme
2 bay leaves
6 bruised peppercorns
2 quarts water
1½ cups dry white wine
1 medium-size yellow onion, peeled and stuck with 1 clove
1 teaspoon salt
½ pound fishbones, heads, and trimmings (from any delicate white fish)

Tie celery, parsley, dill, thyme, bay leaves, and peppercorns in a double thickness of cheesecloth. Place in a large, heavy kettle with remaining ingredients and simmer, uncovered, 20 minutes. Strain through a fine sieve lined with a double thickness of cheesecloth. Calories negligible.

RICH COURT BOUILLON FOR FISH AND SHELLFISH

An excellent base for soups, sauces, and elaborate seafood dishes.
Makes about 3 quarts

2 pounds fishbones, heads, and trimmings (from any delicate white fish)
3 quarts cold water
½ cup white vinegar
1 medium-size yellow onion, peeled and quartered
1 stalk celery, coarsely chopped
1 bouquet garni,* tied in cheesecloth
1 teaspoon salt

Place all ingredients in a large kettle, cover, and simmer 1 hour. Strain through a large sieve lined with a double thickness of cheesecloth.

VARIATIONS:

Rich Wine Court Bouillon: Prepare as directed, substituting 1 quart dry or medium-dry white or red wine for 1 quart of the water and ¼ cup lemon juice for the vinegar.

Court Bouillon for Aspics: Prepare as directed, reducing water to 2 quarts and increasing simmering time to 2 hours. Skim off any froth and strain liquid through a cheesecloth-lined sieve; do not press solids. Measure liquid and, if needed, add cold water to make 2 quarts. To see if liquid will jell, chill 1 cup. If it sets up as firm as commercial gelatin, you need not add gelatin. If it doesn't, mix in 1 envelope unflavored gelatin softened in ¼ cup cold water and heat, stirring, until dissolved. *To clarify court bouillon:* Place all liquid (including chilled portion) in a large, deep saucepan. Add 2 egg whites, beaten to soft peaks, also 2 eggshells, crushed. Bring to a boil, stirring constantly with a wire whisk, and as soon as mixture foams up, remove from heat. Stir 1 or 2 times, then let stand *undisturbed* 5 minutes. Meanwhile, line a large, fine sieve with a fine linen towel or napkin wrung out in cold water and set over a deep bowl so bottom of sieve will be clear of aspic collecting in bowl. Pour aspic into sieve, egg whites, shells, and all, and let drip through undisturbed. Aspic is now ready to use as recipes direct.

Calories negligible for all versions.

Some Garnishes for Fish and Shellfish

Parsley, paprika, radish roses, and lemon slices are the usual fish platter garnishes. For more originality, try

SOME HERBS AND SPICES COMPLIMENTARY TO SEAFOOD

Herb or Spice	Lean White Fish	Oily or Gamy Fish	Shellfish
Bay Leaves	X	X	X
Chervil	X	X	X
Chives	X	X	X
Crab boil			X crab and shrimp
Curry powder	X except delicate fish	X	X
Dill	X	X	X
Fennel	X	X	X
Filé powder		X	X
Fines herbes	X	X	X
Ginger	X	X	X
Juniper berries		X	X
Mace	X	X	X
Marjoram		X	X
Oregano		X	X
Paprika	X	X	X
Parsley	X	X	X
Rosemary		X	X
Saffron			X
Sage		X	
Savory		X	
Tarragon	X	X	X
Thyme	X	X	X

SOME SAUCES, BUTTERS, AND SEASONINGS FOR SEAFOOD

Note: To determine which specific fish fit which category below, see following charts of popular salt and fresh water fish.

Sauces	Very Delicate Lean White Fish (Flounder, Sole, Fluke, etc.)					Lean White Fish (Cod, Haddock, Pike, Whiting, Bass, etc.)					Delicate Oily Fish (Salmon, Eel, Trout, Mackerel, Butterfish, etc.)			
	Broiled, Sautéed	Deep Fat Fried	Baked	Poached, Steamed	Cold	Broiled, Sautéed	Deep Fat Fried	Baked	Poached, Steamed	Cold	Broiled, Sautéed	Baked	Poached, Steamed	Cold
Allemande			X	X				X	X			X	X	
Américaine			X	X				X	X			X	X	
Aoli										X				
Aurore	X					X					X			
Barbecue						X					X	X		
Béarnaise	X	X				X	X				X	X	X	
Béchamel			X	X				X	X			X	X	
Bercy			X	X				X	X					
Bordelaise											X			
Bourguignonne												X		
Caper	X		X	X		X		X	X		X	X		
Cardinal				X					X					
Cheese			X	X				X	X					
Chiffon					X					X				X
Chivry			X	X				X	X					
Cocktail														
Colbert	X							X	X		X	X		
Creole								X	X			X		
Curry								X	X			X		
Diplomate				X				X	X					
Duxelles								X	X			X		
Egg			X	X				X	X					
Espagnole								X	X		X	X	X	
Figaro											X	X		
Fines Herbes			X	X				X	X					
Gribiche										X				X
Hollandaise	X		X	X		X		X	X		X	X	X	
Hot Horseradish														
Joinville			X	X				X	X					
Lobster			X	X				X	X				X	
Louis														
Marinière			X	X				X	X				X	
Mayonnaise					X					X			X	X
Mornay			X	X				X	X			X	X	
Mousseline			X	X				X	X			X	X	
Mustard									X		X	X	X	
Nantua			X	X				X	X				X	
Normande			X	X				X	X					
Oyster									X				X	
Parsley	X		X	X		X		X	X		X	X	X	
Portugaise				X				X	X			X	X	
Poulette				X					X				X	

Gamy Fish (Barracuda, Shark, Swordfish, Tuna, etc.)				Clams			Crab				Lobster			Oysters			Scallops				Shrimp			
Broiled	Baked	Poached, Steamed	Cold	Sautéed	Deep Fat Fried	Steamed	Boiled, Steamed	Cold	Sautéed Soft Shell	Deep-Fat-Fried Soft Shell	Boiled, Steamed	Broiled	Cold	Sautéed	Deep Fat Fried	Roasted, Steamed	Broiled, Sautéed	Deep Fat Fried	Poached	Cold	Broiled, Sautéed	Deep Fat Fried	Boiled	Cold
							X				X								X				X	
														X			X							
X	X												X				X				X	X		
X	X	X									X								X				X	
X																			X					
X																								
X	X	X		X						X				X	X		X	X			X	X		
											X								X				X	
	X	X					X												X				X	
	X	X						X											X				X	
X	X																		X					
X	X																							
X	X	X										X								X	X		X	X
		X							X				X					X				X		X
					X		X	X			X							X					X	X
							X											X					X	
X	X	X		X										X			X				X			
		X																	X				X	
		X	X		X										X	X	X		X		X	X		

SOME SAUCES, BUTTERS, AND SEASONINGS FOR SEAFOOD (continued)

	Very Delicate Lean White Fish (Flounder, Sole, Fluke, etc.)					Lean White Fish (Cod, Haddock, Pike, Whiting, Bass, etc.)					Delicate Oily Fish (Salmon, Eel, Trout, Mackerel, Butterfish, etc.)			
Sauces	Broiled, Sautéed	Deep Fat Fried	Baked	Poached, Steamed	Cold	Broiled, Sautéed	Deep Fat Fried	Baked	Poached, Steamed	Cold	Broiled, Sautéed	Baked	Poached, Steamed	Cold
Provençale				X				X	X		X	X	X	
Ravigote								X	X		X	X		
Rémoulade		X			X	X				X	X			X
Rosy			X	X				X	X					
Sauce verte (green mayonnaise)					X					X				X
Shrimp			X	X				X	X					
Soubise								X	X			X	X	
Sour cream cucumber					X	X				X		X	X	X
Tartar	X	X			X	X	X			X	X			X
Tempura											X			
Tomato			X	X		X		X	X		X	X	X	
Velouté			X	X				X	X			X	X	
Vinaigrette				X						X				X
Vincent				X						X				X
Butters														
Anchovy	X		X			X		X			X	X		
Beurre noir	X					X					X			
Caper	X		X			X		X	X		X	X		
Chive	X		X			X		X			X	X		
Garlic						X								
Herb	X		X	X				X	X		X	X	X	
Lemon	X		X	X		X		X	X		X	X	X	
Lobster	X		X			X		X			X			
Maître d'hôtel	X		X	X		X		X	X		X	X	X	
Noisette	X		X			X		X			X	X		
Shallot	X		X			X		X			X	X		
Shrimp	X		X	X		X		X	X		X			
Stuffings														
Basic bread stuffing			X					X				X		
Crab or shrimp			X					X				X		
Easy almond			X					X				X		
Fruit												X		
Lemon bread			X					X				X		
Oyster			X					X				X		
Quick mushroom			X					X				X		
Tomato and green pepper			X					X				X		
Vegetable			X					X				X		

Gamy Fish (Barracuda, Shark, Swordfish, Tuna, etc.)				Clams			Crab				Lobster			Oysters			Scallops				Shrimp			
Broiled	Baked	Poached, Steamed	Cold	Sautéed	Deep Fat Fried	Steamed	Boiled, Steamed	Cold	Sautéed Soft Shell	Deep-Fat-Fried Soft Shell	Boiled, Steamed	Broiled	Cold	Sautéed	Deep Fat Fried	Roasted, Steamed	Broiled, Sautéed	Deep Fat Fried	Poached	Cold	Broiled, Sautéed	Deep Fat Fried	Boiled	Cold
X	X																X		X		X			
X	X	X					X										X		X				X	
X			X		X		X	X	X				X	X			X		X		X			X
			X										X			X								X
																X								
			X																					X
X			X	X	X									X				X			X	X		X
X																	X				X	X		X
X			X														X		X					
X																								X
X															X				X					X
X											X						X			X				X
X					X		X	X			X			X	X	X				X				
X									X	X				X	X		X			X				
X					X		X		X	X	X	X	X	X	X	X				X				
X					X						X	X		X	X	X				X				
X					X						X	X		X	X	X	X	X		X				
X	X	X			X		X	X			X	X	X	X	X	X				X				
X					X			X		X	X	X		X	X	X				X				
X					X		X		X	X	X	X	X	X	X	X				X				
X					X									X	X	X								
X					X		X	X	X	X	X	X	X	X	X	X				X				
X																								
	X															X								
	X																							
	X															X								
	X																							
	X															X								
	X																							

611

any or a colorful combination of two of the following artistically grouped around the fish or shellfish.

– Hollowed-out cherry tomatoes, cucumber chunks, or lemon halves filled with tartar or other sauce.
– Artichoke bottoms filled with puréed peas or spinach.
– Artichoke bottoms filled with red or black caviar, topped with a dab of sour cream and sprigged with dill or fennel.
– Sautéed mushroom caps filled with cocktail shrimp or buttered green peas.
– Tiny bundles of buttered asparagus tips bound together with strips of pimiento.
– Stuffed hard-cooked eggs.
– Cherry tomatoes set in artichoke bottoms or on lemon slices.
– Lemon slices sprinkled with capers or minced celery or paprika and topped with a rolled anchovy fillet.
– Lemon flowers, pickle fans, or celery frills (see About Sandwich Garnishes).
– Celery tops or sprigs of fresh dill, fennel, or watercress.

Some Ways to Use Up Leftover Fish and Shellfish

It is unlikely that you'll be faced with much leftover fish unless you'd planned on eight for dinner and only four came. Here are some recipes (all can be found in the recipe section) particularly suited to leftovers, also some suggestions for using up small amounts.

Recipes Good for Leftovers:
Crisp-Crusted Fish and Green Pepper Pie
Potato-Fish Pie
Basic Fish Soufflé (and all variations)
Fish Loaf
Fish Croquettes

Fish Cakes (or use recipe for Codfish Cakes, substituting leftover fish for salt cod)
Kedgeree
Basic Shellfish Croquettes
Basic Shellfish Soufflé

To Make the Most of Very Small Amounts:

– Combine with canned fish or shellfish, mayonnaise to bind, and seasonings to taste and use as a sandwich filling or to stuff eggs, tomatoes, or avocados.
– Stretch with an equal quantity of hot Medium White Sauce, Mornay, Parsley, or Egg Sauce and spoon over crepes, puff pastry shells, hot toast, or biscuits.
– Stretch with an equal quantity of hot Medium White Sauce, Mornay, Velouté or Parsley Sauce, layer into buttered ramekins with hot boiled rice or thin noodles, top with grated cheese or buttered crumbs, and broil quickly to brown.
– Marinate any leftover cold fried fish à la Dalmatian Marinated Fish, reducing amount of marinade as needed.
– Use in making Easy Fish Stock or any court bouillon.

FISH

All fish, whether salt or fresh water, fall into two categories: the *lean* (delicate, low-calorie fish whose oils are concentrated in the liver) and the *oily or fat* whose oils are distributed throughout the flesh. Oily fish are usually darker fleshed and stronger flavored than lean fish (tuna, for example, is darker and stronger than flounder). To determine which fish are which, see the charts of America's popular salt and fresh water fish included in this chapter.

About Buying Fresh Fish

Find a good fish market and make friends with the owner—it's the surest way of getting absolutely fresh, top quality seafood. If you live inland in the land of supermarkets and must always be your own judge, look for these *characteristics of quality and freshness:*

– Sparkling, clear, bulging eyes.
– Rosy, sweet-smelling gills.
– Bright, shimmery, tightly clinging scales.
– Firm, springy, translucent, lifelike flesh.
– An over-all fresh, clean smell.

Popular Market Forms of Fresh Fish:

Whole or Round: Fish as they're taken from the water. Before cooking they must be drawn or cleaned (eviscerated) and scaled.

Drawn or Cleaned: Whole fish that have been eviscerated. Scales must be removed before cooking.

Cleaned and Dressed or Pan-Dressed: Ready-to-cook fish that have been cleaned and scaled. Usually head, tail and fins have been removed, too. *Dressed* refers to fish weighing 1 pound or more, *pan-dressed* to those weighing less.

Steaks: Cross-section cuts of large, cleaned, and dressed fish; they contain backbone.

Fillets: The boneless sides of fish or, more recently, any thin, long boneless piece of fish.

Butterfly Fillets: Both sides of the fish, boned but still attached on one side so that they can be opened flat like a book.

Chunks: Thick, cross-cut slices of large, cleaned, and dressed fish. Like steaks, they contain a cross-section of the backbone.

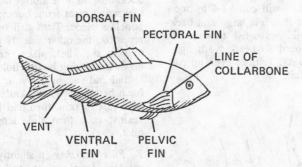

DORSAL FIN
PECTORAL FIN
LINE OF COLLARBONE
VENT
VENTRAL FIN
PELVIC FIN

How Much Fish Should You Buy?

Market Form	Amt. per Serving
Whole, drawn	¾–1 pound
Whole, dressed	½ pound
Fillets, Steaks, Chunks	⅓ pound

How to Clean Fresh Fish

If you buy fish, you can have the store clean and dress it. But if there are sportsmen in your family or neighborhood, you may have to cope with an uncleaned, undressed catch. The job isn't fun, but fortunately it *is* fast. Here's the procedure:

1. *Scaling:* Wash fish, place on cutting board, and with one hand hold head firmly (if you salt your hands, you'll get a better grip). With knife blade held almost vertical, scrape from tail to head, against grain of scales. Pay special attention to area around fins. A second technique is to nail fish to board through the tail with an ice pick or long, thin nail, then to scrape briskly toward head (there's less danger of slipping and cutting yourself). There are scalers to make the job easier; but many fishermen prefer a homemade gadget: a slim block of wood with bottle caps nailed upside-down on one side of it.

2. *Cleaning:* Split belly from vent to head and scoop out viscera. Cut around pelvic fins and lift them out.

3. *Removing Head and Tail:* Cut just behind collarbone so head and pectoral fins will come off in one operation. If fish is large and backbone tough, move fish to edge of cutting board so head overhangs, then snap off. Trim to even up cut; slice off tail.

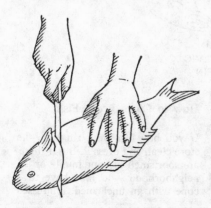

4. *Finning:* Cut along each side of dorsal fin, then yank forward to remove (root bones will come away too). Remove ventral fin the same

way. (*Note:* Simply snipping off fins leaves many little bones inside the fish. Rinse fish under cold running water.)

To Cut into Steaks: Slice fish crosswise, making cuts ½"–1" or more apart, depending on how thick you like your steaks.

To Fillet: With an extra-sharp knife (or fillet knife), cut along back of fish from one end to the other, then with knife blade held parallel to backbone, slide it along backbone, separating meat from bones; lift off boneless piece. Turn fish over and repeat on the other side. If you want to skin the fillet, place skin side down on cutting board, hold firmly by tail end (again salt your hands for a better grip), slip knife through flesh just to skin, turn and flatten against skin, then slide length of fillet.

To Fillet Herring (a slightly different technique): clean and dress herring, then split entire length of stomach. Place herring cut side down, like an open book with 2 halves out to the side. Press fingertips firmly up and down backbone several times. Turn fish over, grab tail end of backbone with one hand, anchor fish to board with the other,

IV. VARIATIONS ON BASIC RECIPES

"Frosted" Tomatoes – Roast Beef Leftovers – Butterscotch Parfait

Frosted Tomatoes; Belgian Style Tomatoes; and Tomatoes Finlandia (All three recipes vol. 2, p. 291)

Roast Beef Leftovers: Yukon Stew with biscuits baked on top (vol. 1, p. 251 and vol.

2, p. 339); Beef stuffed Vegetables (vol. 1, p. 250); and Beef Curry (vol. 1, p. 249)

Butterscotch Parfait (vol. 2, pp. 474 and 463–65); Chocolate Ice Cream and Hot Fudge Sauce (vol. 2, pp. 464 and 473); and Strawberry Ice Cream Soda (vol. 1, p. 138)

and pull backbone up toward head. It should come away in 1 piece, bringing all the little bones with it. Now cut herring down the back into 2 fillets.

About Frozen Fish

Many of America's popular fish are available frozen in one or more of the following forms: whole, dressed, steaks, fillets, chunks, portions, and sticks.

To Be Sure of Top Quality: Buy only solidly frozen fish that shows no discoloration or freezer burn, no signs of having thawed and refrozen (a block of frozen juices at the bottom of the package); reject any fish with a strong or "off" odor. Unfortunately, much frozen fish can't be seen until the package is opened, but if you have doubts on examining the fish, return it to the market.

How to Cook Frozen Fish: Should frozen fish be thawed before cooking? It depends, on the size of the fish and how it's to be cooked. Here are some guidelines:

Fish Portions and Sticks: Cook solidly frozen.

Fillets and Steaks: Most authorities agree that it's best to thaw these 1–2 hours in the refrigerator until they're easy to separate and handle. They must be thawed (at least until soft on the outside) if they are to be breaded or the breading won't stick. If there are package directions for thawing and cooking, follow them.

Whole Fish, Dressed Fish, and Large Chunks: Whole fish must be thawed so that they can be cleaned and dressed. Dressed fish and large chunks must be thawed if they're to be stuffed. And, many experts be-

lieve, whole fish and large pieces will poach and steam more evenly if thawed before cooking. As for baking, it seems to make little difference, *except* that solidly frozen fish will take approximately twice as long to cook as the thawed.

Best Ways to Thaw Frozen Fish: Always thaw just before cooking and, once thawed, never refreeze; thawed fish can be held in refrigerator about one day, but no longer. Don't unwrap fish before thawing; simply set in refrigerator and thaw, allowing about twenty-four hours for a one-pound package. Don't thaw at room temperature to hasten things —the danger of spoilage is too great. Instead, thaw wrapped fish under a slow stream of *cold* running water, allowing 1–2 hours per pound. Never use warm water.

About Canned Fish

The list of canned fish is long and getting longer. Here are some of the most popular items:

Anchovies: Fillets are available either flat or rolled around capers; paste comes in tubes.

Bonito: See Tuna.

Mackerel: Canned chunks are available, either plain or in sauce (tomato or wine). Mackerel roe is also canned.

Salmon: The five kinds available, from expensive to inexpensive are: red or sockeye; chinook or king; coho or silver (also sometimes called medium red); pink or humpback; and, finally, chum.

Sardines: These are packed whole in oil, also boned and skinned. The most highly prized are the Portuguese, packed in a top grade olive oil; next best are the herbed and spiced French sardines.

Tuna: The choicest is *albacore* or *white meat tuna. Light meat* tuna ranges from pink to red-brown and comes from bluefin, skipjack or bonito, or yellowfin. Three packs are available: *fancy or solid* (expensive), best used when appearance is important; *chunk* (moderate), good for salads and casseroles; and *flaked* (relatively inexpensive), good for sandwich spreads and canapés.

Some Gourmet Items: Red (salmon) and black (sturgeon) caviar (see discussion in chapter on appetizers and hors d'oeuvre); eel; smoked and pickled herring; shad roe.

Other Forms of Fish

In addition to being sold fresh, frozen, and canned, many fish are also available in brine, dried, salted, and/or smoked (kippered). Consult charts of popular salt and fresh water fish to determine which are available in which forms. Directions for preparing them are in the recipe section.

How to Cook Fresh Fish

Fish is as fragile as a soufflé; cooking can never make it more tender than it already is, only more attractive and flavorful. The greatest crime committed against fish is overcooking. When is fish done—and not overdone? The instant the flesh turns from translucent to opaque and flakes (falls easily into natural divisions) when probed with a fork. Flaking is the test of doneness for all fish, regardless of how it's cooked. Keep the fork handy, test often, take fish from the heat the second it flakes.

To Bake (best for whole fish, large chunks, steaks, and fillets; for names of fish that are "good bakers," consult the fish charts that follow).

To Bake Whole Fish:

General Preparation: Have fish cleaned but leave head and tail on. If you're squeamish about looking a baked fish in the eye, take the head off before transferring to platter, *but not before*—a headless fish will lose juices during cooking. Lightly sprinkle cavity of fish with salt and pepper. Do not slash skin.

Basic Method: Preheat oven to 400° F. Line a large, shallow baking pan with foil and grease well (so fish will be easier to transfer to platter and pan will be quicker to clean). Lay fish in pan (if you are baking more than 1 fish at a time, make sure they do not touch one another). If fish are lean, brush well with melted butter or margarine or drape with bacon strips. Bake, uncovered, 10–15 minutes per pound, basting as needed with additional melted butter. It is difficult to be more specific about baking times because fish vary so in shape. Keep the testing fork handy and begin probing gently after minimum baking time is up. (*Note:* Small fish take proportionately longer to cook than large ones.) When fish is done, carefully transfer to a heated platter, top with some of the pan juices, and serve as is or with a compatible sauce (see chart Some Sauces, Butters, and Seasonings for Seafood). *For Extra Flavor:* Baste fish with a seasoned butter, a ½ and ½ mixture of melted butter and dry white wine, with light cream or with herb, French, or Italian dressing. *For Low-Calorie Baked Fish:* Choose a lean, low-calorie fish and baste with a low-calorie French, Italian, herb, or garlic dressing during cooking instead of butter.

Continental Method (also called *Braising*): Preheat oven to 400° F. Line pan with foil and grease, then make a ½" bed of finely chopped vegetables in pan (equal parts minced onions, celery, and carrots; minced onions and mushrooms; or minced onions, tomatoes, and sweet red or green peppers); mix in 2–3 tablespoons minced fresh parsley and about 2 tablespoons melted butter or margarine. Lay fish on vegetables and proceed as in Basic Method above.

To Bake a Whole, Stuffed Fish: (Bluefish, cod, haddock, mackerel, red snapper, salmon, shad, and trout are particularly elegant when stuffed.) For other fish to stuff and bake, see charts of salt and fresh water fish.

General Preparation: Should fish be boned before stuffing? Yes, if possible. A boned fish is easier and pleasanter to eat; unfortunately, all fish are not easy to bone without filleting. Try to have your fish market bone the fish and prepare it for stuffing. If you must prepare it yourself, here are two ways. For each it's best to have fish that has not been cleaned and dressed.

Method 1. Slit fish down the back, slide a sharp, thin-bladed knife down along backbone, first on 1 side, then on the other, to separate meat from bone. With poultry shears, cut through backbone at both ends and lift backbone out. Remove all viscera through this opening. Scale the fish, remove fins, then rinse well in cool water and pat dry.

Method 2. Slit fish down belly and eviscerate, following Method 1. Deepen cut to backbone, separating meat from bones as you go. Cut through backbone at head and tail ends using poultry shears and pull backbone out through the stomach opening; vertebrae and other small bones should come away with the backbone, but examine cavity carefully for any "missed bones" and pull out. Rinse fish in cool water and pat dry.

Basic Method of Baking: Preheat oven to 400° F. Line a large, shallow baking pan with foil, then grease the foil. Loosely stuff fish with a bread or other suitable stuffing (see Some Sauces, Butters, and Seasonings for Fish for suggestions); you'll need about 2 cups stuffing for a 3–4-pound fish, 1 quart for a 6–7-pounder. Wrap any remaining stuffing in foil and place in baking pan. Toothpick cavity of fish shut or, if skin is tough, loosely sew up. Brush fish well with melted butter or margarine and bake, uncovered, 12–15 minutes per pound (*this is per pound of dressed weight, not stuffed weight*). While fish bakes, baste as needed with additional melted butter; remove fish from oven as soon as it will flake at the touch of a fork. *For Extra Flavor:* Use any of the suggestions given in the Basic Method above. When fish is done, carefully transfer to a hot platter and remove toothpicks or thread.

To Plank a Whole Fish: Oil a large hardwood plank generously and set in preheating oven to warm; it should be heated to 400° F. as for other baked fish. Center a whole, cleaned 3–4-pound fish on the hot plank, brush with 1–2 tablespoons melted butter, margarine, or cooking oil, and sprinkle with ½ teaspoon salt and ⅛ teaspoon pepper. Bake, uncovered, without basting 10–15 minutes per pound until fish will flake. Remove from oven, pipe a border of Duchess Potatoes around edge of plank, and broil 2–3 minutes, 4" from heat, until touched with brown. Garnish plank by filling any empty spaces with clusters of buttered green peas and cherry tomatoes. (*Note:* For details on the selection and care of the plank, see Planked Steak.)

To Bake Fish Fillets, Steaks, and Chunks:

General Preparation: Pat fish dry on paper toweling. Leave fillets whole or fold envelope style, ends toward center.

Basic Method: Preheat oven to 350° F. Line a large, shallow baking pan with foil and grease well. Arrange fish pieces in a single layer, not touching. Sprinkle lightly with salt and pepper. If fish is lean, drizzle with ¼–⅓ cup melted butter or margarine; otherwise, brush lightly with melted butter. Bake, uncovered, 20–30 minutes, basting once or twice, until fish flakes. Lift fish to a heated platter with a pancake turner, top with some of the pan juices, sprinkle with paprika and/or parsley, and serve. *For Extra Flavor:* Substitute Lemon, Parsley, or Herb Butter for the plain. *For Low-Calorie Baked Fillets, Steaks, and Chunks:* Choose a lean, low-calorie fish and baste with a low-calorie French, Italian, herb, or garlic dressing instead of butter.

To Oven Broil (best for steaks, fillets, and small whole or split fish):

General Preparation: If fish are whole, have cleaned or cleaned and dressed; if you like, split in half lengthwise. Pat fish, steaks, or fillets dry on paper toweling and, if you want, dredge lightly in flour.

Basic Method: Preheat broiler. Line broiler pan and rack with foil. Arrange fish on rack in a single layer, not touching each other, brush with melted butter or margarine, and sprinkle with salt and pepper. Just how long fish should be broiled can only be estimated at best because size, shape, and delicacy of fish vary greatly. The flaking test is the only true test of doneness. Use the table on page 619 as a guide.

To Charcoal Broil (best for thick [1"] fillets, small to medium whole or split fish):

General Preparation: Same as for oven broiling.

Basic Method: Prepare a moderately hot charcoal fire.* Grease a long-handled, hinged wire grill well. Brush fish generously with a ½ and ½ mixture of melted butter and lemon juice, place in grill, and broil 4" from coals 5–8 minutes on one side, basting frequently with butter mixture. Turn and grill other side 5–8 minutes, basting often, until fish flakes when touched with a fork.

VARIATION:

Barbecued Fish: (best for 1" fillets and steaks): Marinate fish 1–2 hours in a favorite barbecue sauce before cooking. Charcoal broil as above but baste with barbecue sauce instead of butter.

To Panfry (Sauté) (best for fillets, steaks, and small whole fish):

General Preparation: Have whole fish cleaned and, if you like, dressed. Pat fish very dry between several thicknesses of paper toweling.

Basic Method: Lightly sprinkle both sides of fish with salt and pepper, then dust with flour. Sauté in 3–4 tablespoons butter or margarine or cooking oil or, if you prefer, a ½ and ½ mixture of butter and cooking

FISH BROILING CHART

Cut	Thickness	Distance from Heat	Minutes on First Side	Minutes on Second Side
Steaks	½″	2″	3	3–5
Steaks	1″	2″	3–5	4–5

(*Note:* Lean fish like cod, halibut, and bass should be basted once during cooking with melted butter or margarine or cooking oil.)

Fillets	¼″–½″	2″	4–5 minutes (do not turn)	
Fillets	¾″–1″	2″	7–10 minutes (do not turn)	

(*Note:* All fillets should be basted at least once during cooking; very lean ones [cod, fluke, flounder, sole, etc.] twice. If fillets have not been skinned, broil skin side down.)

Split (halved) fish	½″–1″	3″	7–10 minutes (do not turn)	
Split (halved) fish	1″–1½″	3″	10–14 minutes (do not turn)	

	Weight			
Whole fish (small)	1–2 lbs.	3″	3–5	5–6
Whole fish (medium)	3–5 lbs.	5″–6″	5–7	7–10
Whole flat fish (fluke, flounder, etc.)	―――	3″	8–10 minutes (do not turn)	

(*Note:* Broil split fish skin side down and baste once during cooking, twice if very lean. Whole fish should be basted at least once during cooking, 2–3 times if lean.)
For Extra Flavor: Use a seasoned butter for basting or a ½ and ½ mixture of melted butter and lemon juice or dry white wine. *For Low-Calorie Broiled Fish:* Select a lean fish and baste with low-calorie herb or garlic dressing instead of butter.

oil in a large, heavy skillet over moderate heat or in an electric skillet set at 350° F. Thin fillets or steaks will take 2–3 minutes per side, thicker pieces 4–5 minutes on a side, and small whole fish 3–5 minutes per side. As fish are done, drain on paper toweling, then keep warm by setting uncovered in oven turned to lowest heat.

VARIATIONS:

Fillets or Steaks Amandine: Sauté as in Basic Method, using butter, transfer to a hot platter and keep warm. Add 2 tablespoons butter to skillet and ¼–⅓ cup thinly sliced blanched almonds and stir-fry 2–3 minutes until bubbly and brown. Pour over fish and serve.

Fillets or Steaks à la Meunière: Dip fish in milk, then in flour lightly seasoned with salt and pepper. Sauté as above in butter, transfer to a hot platter, and sprinkle with lemon juice and a little minced parsley. Add 2 tablespoons butter to skillet and heat, stirring up any browned bits from bottom of skillet, about 2 minutes until lightly browned. Pour over fish and serve.

Breaded Fried Fish: Lightly sprinkle both sides of whole fish, fillets, or steaks with salt and pepper and dust with flour. Dip in a mixture of beaten egg and water (2 tablespoons water for each egg) and fine dry bread crumbs, cracker meal, or a ½ and ½ mixture of flour and corn meal. Sauté by Basic Method above. *For a dry, crisp crust,* let fish dry 10–15 minutes on a wire rack after breading; then sauté. *For extra flavor,* mix 1–2 tablespoons grated Parmesan or minced parsley into crumbs, or ½ teaspoon sage or thyme.

To Oven "Fry" (best for steaks, fillets, and small whole fish):

General Preparation: Have whole fish cleaned and, if you like, dressed. Pat fish very dry on paper toweling.

Basic Method: Preheat oven to 500° F. Mix ½ cup milk with 1 teaspoon salt and ⅛ teaspoon white pepper. Dip fish in milk, then in fine dry bread crumbs, cracker meal, or crushed cornflakes. Place in a well-greased shallow baking pan and drizzle with melted butter or margarine. Bake, uncovered, without turning or basting 10–15 minutes until golden brown and fish just flakes.

To Deep-Fat-Fry (best for fillets cut in sticks or squares or very small fish, such as smelt):

General Preparation: If using whole fish, clean but do not dress. Pat fish very dry on paper toweling.

Basic Method: Bread fish as for Breaded Fried Fish (above), arrange in a single layer in a deep fat basket, and fry 3–4 minutes in 375° F. fat until golden brown; drain on paper toweling before serving. Scoop any bits of fish or breading from fat before adding a fresh batch of fish and keep fat as nearly at 375° F. as possible. Never let the fat smoke—the whole house will reek of fish for days.

VARIATIONS:

Batter-Fried Fish: See recipe for Fish and Chips.

Shallow-Fried Fish: This method is good for fillets as well as for fish sticks and small whole fish. Bread fish as for Breaded Fried Fish or dip in batter as for Fish and Chips. Pour 1″–1½″ cooking oil or melted shortening in a large, heavy skillet or electric skillet set at 375° F. When fat reaches 375° F. on deep fat thermometer, lower pieces of fish, one at a time, into fat using a pancake turner and arrange in a single layer; fish should not touch each other. Fry 2–3 minutes on each side until lightly browned. Drain on paper toweling before serving.

To Poach (best for whole fish, chunks, steaks, and fillets): See charts of popular salt and fresh water fish for names of those that poach well. Also see special recipes for Poached Salmon and Truite au Bleu.

General Preparation: Have whole fish cleaned and, if you like, dressed.

Fillets, Steaks, Chunks, and Small Whole Fish: Arrange fish barely touching in a single layer in a large, heavy skillet (not iron); if using fragile fish, use a burner-to-table skillet to avoid excessive handling. Add Easy Fish Stock or a court bouillon to cover or, if you prefer, boiling water plus ¼ cup lemon juice or white wine vinegar, 1 minced scallion, 1 sprig parsley, 1 teaspoon salt, 3–4 peppercorns, and ½ bay leaf. Cover and simmer gently until fish will flake: 5–10 minutes for steaks and fillets, 6–8 minutes per pound for small whole fish and chunks. (*Note:* It's important to keep water trembling, *not* boiling, so that fish will be moist and tender but firm.) Using a large pancake turner, transfer fish to a heated serving platter. Serve hot with a suitable sauce (see Some Sauces, Butters, and Seasonings for Seafood) or cool to room temperature, chill well, and serve with mayonnaise or a cold sauce. (*Note:* Save poaching liquid to use as a base for soups and sauces.)

Large Whole Fish and Chunks: Wrap fish in a double thickness of cheesecloth and place on a rack in a large, heavy kettle. Add Easy Fish Stock or a court bouillon to cover or, if you prefer, the water and seasonings called for in poaching fillets. (*Note:* If more than 3 cups water are needed for poaching the fish, double the amount of lemon juice and seasonings.) Cover and bring slowly to a simmer, adjust heat so water stays at a tremble, then poach 8–10 minutes per pound until fish will flake. Carefully lift fish from kettle using 2 pancake turners; remove cheesecloth and peel away fish skin. Serve hot with a compatible sauce or chill and serve cold.

To Steam (best for whole fish, chunks, steaks, thick fillets or rolled-up thin fillets):

General Preparation: Have whole fish cleaned or cleaned and dressed; whole fish or large chunks should be wrapped in a double thickness of cheesecloth as directed for poaching.

Basic Method: Use a fish or vegetable steamer or deep kettle fitted with a rack. Grease rack well, pour in boiling water to a depth of 1″ (or as kettle manufacturer directs), place fish on rack, sprinkle lightly with salt and white pepper, cover, and steam over boiling water as follows: 5–10 minutes for steaks and fillets; 6–8 minutes per pound for large chunks or whole fish. Lift to a heated platter and serve with an ap-

propriate sauce or butter; or cool to room temperature, then chill well and serve cold. *For Extra Flavor:* Add a *bouquet garni** tied in cheesecloth to water in kettle or use a court bouillon, white wine, cider, or beer in place of water. *For Low-Calorie Steamed Fish:* Choose a lean fish and dress with a low-calorie Italian, garlic, or herb dressing instead of a butter or sauce.

About Pressure Cooking Fish: Don't! The fish will disintegrate.

How to Serve Whole Fish and Large Chunks

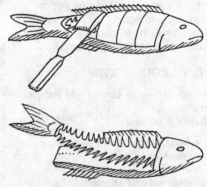

Turn platter so back of fish is away from you; beginning near head, make a cut the length of fish along backbone and loosen flesh from bone. Slice 1″–2″ wide, cutting only to bones, and lift out each slice, using a fish or pie server. Lift out backbone, pulling away vertebrae; continue slicing as before.

¢ ⊠ **FISH CAKES**

A half-and-half combination of fish and mashed potatoes that is both easy and economical.
Makes 4 servings

1½ cups skinned, boned, cooked flaked fish (any kind)
1½ cups seasoned mashed potatoes

1 egg, lightly beaten
2 tablespoons minced parsley
⅛ teaspoon pepper
½ teaspoon salt (about)
1 egg, lightly beaten with 1
* tablespoon cold water*
½ cup toasted bread crumbs
⅓ cup cooking oil

Mix fish with potatoes, egg, parsley, pepper, and salt; taste for salt and add more if needed. Shape mixture into 4 flat cakes, dip in egg mixture, then in crumbs to coat. Heat oil in a large, heavy skillet over moderate heat until a cube of bread will sizzle. Add fish cakes and brown 3–5 minutes on each side. Drain on paper toweling and serve. Pass Parsley Sauce or Tomato Sauce if you like. About 320 calories per serving.

FISH CROQUETTES

A perfect way to use up any leftover fish.
Makes 4 servings

2 tablespoons butter or margarine
3 tablespoons flour
1 cup milk
½ teaspoon salt (about)
⅛ teaspoon white pepper
2 teaspoons Worcestershire sauce
1 egg yolk, lightly beaten
1½ cups soft white bread crumbs
1½ cups skinned, boned, cooked,
* finely ground fish (any kind)*
1 tablespoon lemon juice
Shortening or cooking oil for deep fat
* frying*

Coating:
1 egg, lightly beaten
1 cup fine dry bread crumbs

Melt butter in a saucepan over moderate heat, blend in flour, slowly add milk, and heat, stirring, until thickened. Off heat, mix in seasonings, egg yolk, crumbs, fish, and lemon juice; taste for salt and adjust

if needed. Cover and chill 3–4 hours. Shape mixture into 8 patties or sausage-shaped rolls, dip in egg and roll in crumbs to coat. Let stand at room temperature on a wire rack while heating fat. Place shortening in a deep fat fryer and heat to 375° F.; use a deep fat thermometer. Place 3 or 4 croquettes in fryer basket, lower into hot fat, and fry 2–3 minutes until golden brown and crisp; drain on paper toweling, then keep warm by setting, uncovered, in oven turned to lowest heat while you fry the rest. Serve hot with Tartar Sauce. About 380 calories per serving (without sauce).

FISH AND CHIPS

Ideally, you should have two deep fat fryers set up so fish and chips can fry at the same time. But if you can't manage that, do the potatoes first and set in a slow oven to keep warm while you fry the fish.
Makes 4 servings

Batter:
1 cup sifted flour
1 teaspoon salt
¾ cup cold water
¼ teaspoon baking powder

Chips:
1 recipe French Fried Potatoes
1¾–2 pounds haddock fillets, cut in
* 4″ × 3″ strips*
Shortening or cooking oil for deep fat
* frying*

Begin batter first: Mix flour, salt, and water until smooth, cover, and let stand at room temperature 20–30 minutes. Meanwhile, prepare potatoes for frying as recipe directs; also pat fish dry on paper toweling. Place shortening or oil in a deep fat fryer, insert thermometer, and begin heating over high heat. When fat reaches 375° F., fry potatoes as directed, remove to a paper-towel-lined baking sheet and set, uncovered, in oven set at lowest temperature to keep warm while you fry fish. Stir baking powder into batter. Dip 2–3 pieces fish into batter, allowing excess to drain off. Fry 5–6 minutes in 375° F. fat, turning as needed to brown evenly. Drain on paper toweling and set, uncovered, in oven to keep warm while you fry remaining fish. Serve with salt, pepper, and cider or malt vinegar. About 460 calories per serving.

¢ ⊠ **EASY SCALLOPED FISH**

Makes 4 servings

1½ pounds delicate white fish fillets (cod, haddock, fluke, flounder, halibut, etc.)
1 teaspoon salt
¼ teaspoon pepper
½ cup cracker meal
2 tablespoons butter or margarine
1 cup boiling milk

Preheat oven to 400° F. Arrange fish in a single layer in a buttered shallow 2-quart casserole. Sprinkle with half the salt and pepper. Mix remaining salt and pepper with cracker meal and scatter evenly over fish. Melt butter in milk and pour over fish. Bake, uncovered, in top ⅓ of oven 20 minutes until fish just flakes when touched with a fork. About 300 calories per serving.

VARIATIONS:

– Prepare as directed but mix ¼ cup grated Parmesan or ⅓ cup grated sharp Cheddar cheese into cracker meal. About 325 calories per serving.
– Sprinkle fish with ¼–½ teaspoon thyme, tarragon, marjoram, chervil, basil, or dill before adding meal. About 300 calories per serving.
– Sprinkle fish with 1–2 tablespoons

lemon juice and, if you like, 1–2 tablespoons minced parsley before adding meal. About 300 calories per serving.

⊲⊳ ¢ **FISH LOAF**

A moist, delicate fish loaf flavored with lemon and parsley.
Makes 8 servings

4 cups skinned, boned, cooked, flaked fish (any kind)
3 cups soft white bread crumbs or coarse cracker crumbs
1½ cups milk or, if you prefer, ¾ cup milk and ¾ cup either Easy Fish Stock or bottled clam juice
2 eggs, lightly beaten
1 medium-size yellow onion, peeled and grated
2 stalks celery, minced
1–2 teaspoons salt
¼ teaspoon pepper
2 tablespoons lemon juice
2 tablespoons minced parsley

Preheat oven to 350° F. Mix fish and crumbs; combine milk and eggs and mix into fish along with remaining ingredients. Taste for salt and adjust as needed. Spoon into a greased 9″×5″×3″ loaf pan and bake, uncovered, 45–55 minutes until just firm. Cool upright in pan on wire cake rack 5 minutes, invert on a hot platter, and garnish with lemon wedges. If you like, pass hot Tomato Sauce or Parsley Sauce. About 235 calories per serving (without sauce).

VARIATIONS:

⊠ ⊲⊳ ¢ **Quick Salmon or Tuna Loaf:** Substitute 2 (1-pound) cans salmon or 4 (7-ounce) cans tuna for the flaked fish. Drain cans, measure liquid, and add enough milk to measure 1½ cups. Flake fish, then proceed as recipe directs. About 220 calories per serving if made with

AMERICA'S POPULAR SALT WATER FISH

Market Name	Size	Type of Fish	Description	Season	Where Available	Best Ways to Cook
Amberjack	10-12 pounds	Lean	Fine-fleshed, mild. *Market Forms:* whole (more often caught than bought).	Winter, spring	South Atlantic coast	Bake (stuffed or unstuffed), broil, panfry
Barracuda	10-15 pounds	Oily	Strong, dark-fleshed; Pacific barracuda is smaller, leaner. *Market Forms:* whole, occasionally fresh and frozen steaks (more often caught than bought).	Year round	Atlantic and Gulf coasts, California	Bake, broil, charcoal broil
Bluefish	3-10 pounds	Lean	Delicate, fine-grained white to silvery gray meat. *Market Forms:* whole.	Spring, summer, fall	Atlantic and Gulf coasts	Bake (stuffed or unstuffed), broil
Butterfish	Average 1/2 pound	Oily	Also called dollarfish, pumpkinseed. Rich, tender, sweet white meat. *Market Forms:* whole.	Spring, summer, fall	Atlantic and Gulf coasts	Broil, panfry
Cobia	Average 10 pounds	Oily	Firm, light flesh of good but not strong flavor. *Market Forms:* whole, steaks, chunks (more often caught than bought).	Spring	South Atlantic and Gulf coasts	Bake (stuffed or unstuffed), broil, or charcoal broil
Cod	Average 10 pounds but can reach 100 pounds	Lean	Bland snowy meat; poorly cooked, it can be watery or woolly. Young (1½-2½-pound) cod are called scrod (so are young haddock and pollack). *Market Forms:* whole, fresh, and frozen steaks and fillets; smoked, salted, dried. Special delicacies: cod cheeks (sounds) and tongues.	Year round	North Atlantic and Pacific	*Whole or large pieces:* bake (stuffed or unstuffed), braise, poach. *Steaks:* panfry, broil, charcoal broil. *Fillets:* panfry, poach, broil

624

Market Name	Size	Type of Fish	Description	Season	Where Available	Best Ways to Cook
Croaker	Average 1 pound	Lean	Delicate, often underrated little fish. *Market Forms:* whole.	Year round	Middle and South Atlantic coasts	Broil, panfry
Drum (red and black)	8-10 pounds	Lean	The red drum, also called Channel bass or redfish, is choicer; black drum is bony. *Market Forms:* whole (if small), fillets, steaks; 5-pounders are called "puppy drums."	Summer, fall	New York to Texas	Bake (stuffed or unstuffed), broil or panfry steaks, fillets
Eel	Average 1-4 pounds	Oily	Surprisingly mellow-flavored meat. *Market Forms:* live; also smoked, canned.	Year round	Maine to Texas	Bake, broil, panfry, deep fry, poach
Flounder	Average 2-3 pounds	Lean	A family of flat fish often sold as lemon or gray sole; America has no true sole (other than that imported from Europe). Flounder is related to sole and similarly fine, white, and delicate. *Market Forms:* whole, fresh and frozen fillets.	Year round	Atlantic, Gulf, and Pacific coasts	Bake, broil, charcoal broil, panfry, deep fry, poach
Fluke	1-5 pounds	Lean	A flounderlike fish with delicate white meat; also called plaice. *Market Forms:* whole, fresh and frozen fillets.	Spring, summer	North Atlantic	Same as for Flounder
Haddock	2-5 pounds	Lean	A fine-grained codlike fish. *Market Forms:* whole, fresh and frozen fillets; smoked (finnan haddie), salted, flaked.	Year round	North Atlantic	Bake (stuffed or unstuffed), broil, panfry, deep fry, poach
Hake (see Whiting)						

AMERICA'S POPULAR SALT WATER FISH (continued)

Market Name	Size	Type of Fish	Description	Season	Where Available	Best Ways to Cook
Halibut	1½-50 pounds or more	Lean	A large, moderately strong flat fish; badly cooked, it becomes dry and woolly. *Market Forms:* small (1½ pounds) fish are sold whole as "chicken halibut"; large halibut are cut into steaks and fillets and available fresh, frozen, and smoked.	Year round but best in spring	Atlantic and Pacific coasts	Bake (stuffed or unstuffed), broil, panfry, poach, steam
Herring	½-¾ pound	Oily	An enormous family that includes alewives, shad, and sardines (sardines are young herring 3"-6" long; sprats are smoked sardines; brislings are European sardines). *Market Forms:* whole: brined, salted, pickled, smoked (kippered), canned.	Spring	Atlantic and Pacific coasts	Bake (stuffed or unstuffed), broil, charcoal broil, panfry; brine, marinate, pickle
Jack crevalle	2-20 pounds	Oily	This fish and its little cousin, the blue runner, are popular game fish; their meat is too gamy and bloody for most palates. *Market Forms:* whole (more often caught than bought).	Late fall, early winter	Southern Atlantic and Gulf coasts	Marinate steaks and broil or barbecue
Kingfish	Average 3 pounds	Oily	Rich, firm-fleshed fish much like mackerel; a California cousin is the corbina. *Market Forms:* whole, steaks, fillets.	Late fall, winter	Southern Atlantic and Gulf coasts	Bake (stuffed or unstuffed), broil, panfry, stew

Market Name	Size	Type of Fish	Description	Season	Where Available	Best Ways to Cook
Lemon sole (see Flounder)						
Lingcod	5-20 pounds	Lean	Not a cod, despite its name, but a sleek delicate white fish. *Market Forms:* whole, steaks, fillets.	Year round	West Coast	Bake (stuffed or unstuffed), broil, panfry
Mackerel (Atlantic)	1-2 pounds	Oily	The huge mackerel family includes wahoo, chub, king, and Spanish mackerel, but the best is the small, rich, firm-fleshed Atlantic mackerel. *Market Forms:* whole, fresh and frozen fillets; smoked, salted, canned.	Spring and summer	Virginia north	Bake (stuffed or unstuffed), broil, panfry, poach
Mullet	2-3 pounds	Oily	Often called "poor man's meat," mullet has firm flesh and robust flavor. *Market Forms:* whole, fresh and frozen fillets; smoked, salted.	Year round	Atlantic and Gulf coasts	Bake, broil, panfry, stew
Ocean perch	3/4-1 pound	Lean	A rather firm, coarse white fish that flakes nicely when properly cooked; flavor is delicate. *Market Forms:* frozen fillets and fish sticks.	Year round	North Atlantic	Bake, broil, panfry, deep fry, poach
Pacific mackerel	1-2 pounds	Oily	Fine, firm, dark fish of good strong flavor. *Market Forms:* whole, fillets.	All year but best in fall	California	Bake, broil, barbecue
Pacific sole	3/4-7 pounds	Lean	A family of delicate, white flat fish that includes petrale and rex sole, sand dabs, flounder, and turbot. *Market Forms:* whole, fillets.	Year round	West Coast	Bake, broil, charcoal broil, panfry, deep fry, poach

627

AMERICA'S POPULAR SALT WATER FISH (continued)

Market Name	Size	Type of Fish	Description	Season	Where Available	Best Ways to Cook
Pollock	4-12 pounds	Lean	A cousin to cod, pollock is firmer, and slightly stronger flavored. *Market Forms:* whole, steaks, fresh and frozen fillets; smoked.	Year round	North Atlantic	Bake (stuffed or unstuffed), broil, panfry, deep fry, poach
Pompano	1½-3 pounds	Oily	Often considered to be America's finest fish because of its exceptionally fine, succulent flesh and delicate flavor. *Market Forms:* whole, fresh and frozen fillets.	Year round	Southern Atlantic and Gulf coasts	Bake *en papillote*, broil, panfry
Porgies	Scup: 1-2 pounds; Sheepshead: 2-6 pounds	Lean	Scup and sheepshead both have fine flavor and white meat. *Market Forms:* whole, occasionally fillets.	Spring, early summer	Scup: North Atlantic; Sheepshead: Atlantic and Gulf coasts	Broil, panfry; Sheepshead may be stuffed and baked
Red snapper	Up to 50 pounds but 5-10-pounders are best	Lean	A beautiful fish with meaty, moist, mildly flavored flesh. *Market Forms:* whole, steaks, fresh and frozen fillets.	Year round	South Atlantic and Gulf coasts	Bake (stuffed or unstuffed), broil, panfry, poach
Rockfish	2-5 pounds	Lean	Mild fish with pinkish-white meat. *Market Forms:* whole, fillets.	Year round	West Coast	Bake (stuffed or unstuffed), broil, panfry, poach
Sablefish	4-20 pounds	Oily	Mild but buttery white fish. *Market Forms:* whole, steaks, fillets.	Year round	West Coast	Bake (stuffed or unstuffed), broil, barbecue

Market Name	Size	Type of Fish	Description	Season	Where Available	Best Ways to Cook
Salmon	6-30 pounds	Oily	Luscious, mellow meat ranging from pale to dark pink. The 5 Pacific varieties: Chinook (biggest); chum; pink or humpback; coho or silver; sockeye or red (the smallest and finest). Eastern salmon is Atlantic or Kennebec. *Market Forms:* whole, chunks, fresh and frozen steaks; smoked (lox), salted, canned, potted.	Spring and summer	Pacific Northwest, North Atlantic	*Whole Salmon or Large Chunks:* Stuff and bake, plank, poach, steam; *Steaks:* Bake, broil, charcoal broil, panfry, poach
Sardines (see Herring)						
Sea bass	1/2-5 pounds	Lean	A moist white fish of good flavor but many bones. *Market Forms:* whole.	Year round	Atlantic Coast	Bake (stuffed or unstuffed), broil, charcoal broil, poach
Sea squab	4-6 ounces	Lean	This is the blowfish; when dressed, it looks like a skinless drumstick; the meat is juicy and mild. *Market Forms:* dressed.	Spring, summer, early fall	North and mid-Atlantic coast	Broil, panfry, deep fry
Sea trout (see Weakfish)						
Shad	Average 3-5 pounds	Fairly oily	The king of the herring family because of its delicate, snowy meat. *Market Forms:* whole, fillets. Also available: fresh and canned shad roe.	Early spring	Atlantic and Pacific coasts	Bake (stuffed or unstuffed), broil, panfry fillets
Shark	25-40 pounds	Oily	Firm, chewy meat similar to swordfish. *Market Forms:* fresh and frozen steaks and fillets; salted, smoked.	Year round	Atlantic and Pacific coasts	Bake, broil, barbecue

AMERICA'S POPULAR SALT WATER FISH (continued)

Market Name	Type of Fish	Size	Description	Season	Where Available	Best Ways to Cook
Skate	Lean	10 pounds up	This is the sting ray; only the "wings" are edible. The strangely gelatinous meat is scraped from the bones, not cut. *Market Forms:* dressed wings.	Year round	Atlantic and Pacific coasts	Poach
Smelt	Oily	2-8 ounces	Two different types of fish are called smelt: silversides (which include grunion) and true smelt (whitebait, silver, and surf smelt). All are small, all have firm, well-flavored meat. *Market Forms:* whole.	Year round but best in spring and summer	Atlantic and Pacific coasts, also Great Lakes, where smelt have been transplanted	Bake, broil, panfry, deep fry
Striped bass	Lean	Average 1-10 pounds	These large white-meated sea bass are becoming more popular as a food fish. *Market Forms:* whole, fresh and frozen fillets.	Year round	Atlantic, Gulf, and Pacific coasts	Bake (stuffed or unstuffed), broil, charcoal broil, poach; panfry fillets
Sturgeon	Lean	15-300 pounds	Flavorful, firm-fleshed fish. *Market Forms:* boned chunks, steaks; smoked.	Year round but best in spring, summer	North Atlantic and Pacific	Bake, panfry, poach
Swordfish	Oily	200-600 pounds	Firm, salmon-colored flesh. *(Note:* Swordfish is now considered risky because of its high mercury content.)	Spring and summer	South Atlantic and Pacific	Bake, plank, broil, charcoal broil, barbecue
Tautog	Lean	2-5 pounds	Also called blackfish, this one is popular in New England; flesh is lean and juicy. *Market Forms:* whole (more often than bought).	Spring, summer, and fall	Mid- and North Atlantic coasts	Bake (stuffed or unstuffed), broil, panfry

Market Name	Size	Type of Fish	Description	Season	Where Available	Best Ways to Cook
Tuna	10 to several hundred pounds	Oily	All tuna belong to the mackerel family: albacore or white-meat tuna, also the three light-meat tunas — bluefin or horse mackerel, yellowfin, and skipjack or bonito. All have firm meat with pronounced flavor. *Market Forms:* fresh and frozen steaks, large chunks and occasionally fillets; also available canned and smoked.	Spring, summer, fall	Atlantic and Pacific coasts	Bake, broil, charcoal broil, barbecue, panfry, poach
Weakfish	Sea Trout: 12 pounds; Speckled Trout: 8 pounds	Lean	These are sea trouts, specifically the one called sea trout and the one called spotted or speckled trout. Both have lean, mild flesh. *Market Forms:* whole, fillets.	Year round	Atlantic and Gulf coasts	Bake (stuffed or unstuffed), broil, charcoal broil, panfry
White sea bass	12-20 pounds	Lean	This California cousin of the weakfish also has delicate white meat. *Market Forms:* whole (when small), steaks, fillets.	All year; best in summer and fall	Southern California, Mexico	Bake (stuffed or unstuffed), broil, panfry, poach
Whiting	2-5 pounds	Lean	Also called silver hake, this fine-grained, mild-fleshed white fish is extremely versatile and popular. *Market Forms:* whole, fresh and frozen fillets; also salted.	Spring, summer, fall	North Atlantic	Bake (stuffed or unstuffed), broil, charcoal broil, panfry, deep-fry, poach
Wolffish	Average 10 pounds	Lean	Sometimes called ocean catfish, this fish has delicate white flesh like that of haddock. *Market Forms:* whole, steaks, fillets.	Fall, winter, spring	North Atlantic	Bake (stuffed or unstuffed), broil, panfry, deep-fry, poach

AMERICA'S POPULAR FRESH WATER FISH

SEASONS: These vary from state to state and year to year, so inquire locally.

Market Name	Size	Type of Fish	Description	Where Available	Best Ways to Cook
Bass	Average 3-5 pounds	Lean	One of the finest fresh water fish; most popular species: largemouth, smallmouth, rock, and spotted bass. *Market Forms:* whole (more often caught than bought).	One or another species found throughout most of U.S.	Bake (stuffed or unstuffed), broil, charcoal broil, panfry
Buffalo fish	2-20 pounds	Lean	Fairly coarse-fleshed, bony family of fish. *Market Forms:* whole, steaks, fillets; also smoked.	East, Midwest	Bake, poach
Burbot	3 pounds	Lean	A fresh water cod with delicate white meat. *Market Forms:* whole.	East, Midwest, Northeast	Bake (stuffed or unstuffed), broil, panfry, poach, steam
Carp	2-7 pounds	Lean	A firm, musky fish that is a best eaten in winter and spring. *Market Forms:* whole, fillets, chunks.	Entire U.S.	Bake (stuffed or unstuffed), poach
Catfish	1-20 pounds	Oily	There are many kinds of catfish from the whopping blue to the medium-size Channel cat to the baby bullhead. All have cat-like chin "whiskers," tough scaleless skins (which must be removed), and firm, strong-flavored flesh.	All but the Pacific states	Panfry, deep fry, poach
Crappies	Average 2 pounds	Lean	Large sunfish that are winter favorites; there are two species: black and white. *Market Forms:* whole (more often caught than bought).	Great Lakes, Mississippi Valley	Broil, panfry
Grayling and lake herring or cisco (see Whitefish)					

Market Name	Size	Type of Fish	Description	Where Available	Best Ways to Cook
Pickerel, pike, and muskellunge	1-10 pounds or more	Lean	These three form a small but famous family, a challenge to fishermen and delight to cooks. Meat is extra delicate and tender, though bony. *Market Forms:* whole, occasionally as fillets.	Most Eastern and Central states	Bake (stuffed or unstuffed), broil, poach
Sheepshead	1-3 pounds	Lean	These are fresh water drums and have tender white meat of excellent flavor. *Market Forms:* whole, fillets.	Primarily Midwest and South	Bake (stuffed or unstuffed), broil, panfry
Salmon (landlocked)	2-8 pounds	Oily	Similar to salt water salmon except smaller; also called Sebago salmon. *Market Forms:* whole, steaks.	New England, primarily Maine	See *Salt Water Salmon*
Suckers	1-5 pounds	Lean	Firm, sweet-fleshed but bony fish family; best is probably the white sucker. *Market Forms:* whole, fresh and frozen fillets; salted, smoked.	Most states but abundant in Mississippi Basin	Bake, broil, panfry, poach
Sunfish	1/4-1 pound	Lean	Also called bream, this large family includes the bluegill and pumpkinseed, small fish of superior flavor. *Market Forms:* whole.	Primarily Midwest and Gulf states	Broil, panfry
Trout	Best size: 1-6 pounds	Midway between lean and oily	Unquestionably the royal family of fresh water fish. Best known are Dolly Varden, brook, brown, lake, and rainbow trout. All are superb. *Market Forms:* fresh and frozen whole.	One or another species found in most of U.S. except in very warm climates	Bake (stuffed or unstuffed), broil, charcoal broil, panfry, poach
Whitefish	1-6 pounds	Fairly oily	A distinguished group, all related to salmon. Best known: lake herring (cisco), lake whitefish, arctic and American grayling, pilotfish. Meat is firm but creamy, flavor excellent. *Market Forms:* whole, fillets; smoked. Roe is choice.	New England, Great Lakes area	Bake (stuffed or unstuffed), broil, panfry, poach, steam
Yellow perch	Average 1 pound	Lean	Small fish of particularly fine flavor. *Market Forms:* whole.	New England, Great Lakes area, some parts of West and South	Bake, broil, panfry

tuna, 255 calories per serving if made with salmon.

♨ ¢   **Herbed Fish Loaf:** Prepare as directed, adding any one of the following: 1 tablespoon minced fresh dill, tarragon, or chervil; 2 teaspoons minced fresh basil or marjoram. If fresh herbs are unavailable, substitute ½ teaspoon of the dried. About 235 calories per serving.

¢ CRISP-CRUSTED FISH AND GREEN PEPPER PIE

Makes 6 servings

1 recipe Flaky Pastry II
1½ cups skinned, boned, cooked, flaked fish (any kind)
3 hard-cooked eggs, shelled and sliced thin
¼ cup butter or margarine
1 medium-size yellow onion, peeled and minced
1 small sweet green pepper, cored, seeded, and minced
1 stalk celery, minced
¼ cup unsifted flour
1½ cups milk
1 teaspoon salt
¼ teaspoon pepper

Preheat oven to 425° F. Prepare pastry and roll half into a 12″ circle; fit into a 9″ piepan but do not trim edge. Layer fish and eggs into pie shell. Roll remaining pastry into a 12″ circle, cut 3 V-shaped steam slits near center, and cover loosely with wax paper while you proceed with recipe. Melt butter in a saucepan over moderate heat, add onion, green pepper, and celery, and stir-fry 3–5 minutes until onion is very pale golden. Blend in flour, slowly add milk, and heat, stirring, until thickened; mix in salt and pepper. Pour sauce over fish, top with pastry, press edges to seal, then trim and crimp. Bake, uncovered, ½ hour until lightly browned. About 550 calories per serving.

VARIATION:

♨   **Potato-Fish Pie:** Omit pastry. Layer fish into a buttered 9″ piepan and top with sauce. Spoon 3 cups hot seasoned mashed potatoes over surface and roughen with a fork. Brush lightly with beaten egg and bake 25–30 minutes as directed. Cut potato "crust" into pie-shaped wedges and top with fish mixture. About 290 calories per serving.

BASIC FISH SOUFFLÉ

Makes 4 servings

¼ cup butter or margarine
¼ cup sifted flour
1 cup milk or ½ cup each milk and Easy Fish Stock
½ teaspoon salt
⅛ teaspoon white pepper
4 eggs, separated (at room temperature)
1 cup skinned, boned, cooked, flaked fish (any kind)
2 teaspoons minced parsley
¼ teaspoon cream of tartar

Melt butter in a small saucepan over moderate heat, blend in flour, slowly add milk, and heat, stirring, until thickened; turn heat to low and mix in salt and pepper. Beat egg yolks lightly, blend in a little hot sauce, then return to saucepan; heat and stir 1–2 minutes but do not boil. Off heat, mix in fish and parsley. Lay a piece of wax paper directly on sauce and cool to room temperature. Preheat oven to 350° F. Beat egg whites until frothy, add cream of tartar, and continue beating until stiff but not dry. Stir about ¼ cup egg white into sauce, then carefully fold in remainder, taking care not to break down volume. Spoon into an ungreased 1½-quart soufflé dish and bake, uncovered, 45–50 minutes until puffy and tinged with brown. Serve at once.

Good with Caper, Tomato, Parsley, or Shrimp Sauce. About 305 calories per serving (without sauce).

VARIATIONS:

Herbed Fish Soufflé: Prepare as directed but increase minced parsley to 1 tablespoon and add 1 tablespoon minced fresh dill, tarragon, or chervil. About 305 calories per serving.

Curried Fish Soufflé: Prepare as directed but smooth 1 tablespoon each curry powder and finely grated onion into melted butter just after blending flour. About 305 calories per serving.

Rosy Fish Soufflé: Prepare as directed, but mix 2 tablespoons tomato paste and ¼ teaspoon each oregano and basil into hot sauce just before adding fish. About 315 calories per serving.

Lemon Fish Soufflé: Make sauce as directed but for the liquid use the juice of ½ lemon, ½ cup Easy Fish Stock, and then enough heavy cream to total 1 cup. Proceed as directed, adding 1 teaspoon grated lemon rind to sauce along with fish. About 410 calories per serving.

⚖ VELVETY FISH MOUSSE

Makes 6 servings

¾ *pound delicate white fish fillets (cod, flounder, halibut, hake, turbot, etc.)*
¼ *cup butter or margarine*
6 *tablespoons flour*
1 *cup milk or a ½ and ½ mixture of milk and Easy Fish Stock*
3 *eggs, separated*
½ *cup heavy cream*
1 *teaspoon salt*
⅛ *teaspoon pepper*
Pinch nutmeg
½ *teaspoon anchovy paste*
1 *teaspoon lemon juice*

Preheat oven to 350° F. Put fish through finest blade of meat grinder. Melt butter in a saucepan over moderate heat, blend in flour, slowly add milk, and heat, stirring, until thickened. Turn heat to low. Beat egg yolks lightly, blend in a little sauce, then return to saucepan. Heat, stirring, 1–2 minutes, but do not allow to boil. Off heat, mix in fish and all remaining ingredients except egg whites. Beat egg whites until soft peaks form, then fold into fish mixture. Spoon into a well-oiled 5-cup ring mold, set in a large baking pan, and pour in boiling water to come ⅔ of the way up mold. Bake, uncovered, 45–55 minutes or until just set. Lift mold from water bath and cool 5–10 minutes, loosen mousse with a spatula, invert on hot platter, and *ease* out. Serve as is, or fill center with Creamed Shrimp, Creamed Mushrooms, or buttered asparagus tips and drizzle with Sauce Américaine or other suitable sauce (see Sauces, Butters, and Seasonings for Seafood). About 280 calories per serving (without sauce of any sort).

VARIATIONS:

Salmon or Tuna Mousse: Substitute 1½ cups finely ground salmon or tuna for white fish and proceed as directed. About 320 calories per serving if made with salmon, 310 calories per serving if made with tuna.

⚖ **Lobster, Shrimp, or Crab Mousse:** Substitute 1½ cups finely ground cooked lobster, shrimp, or crab meat and proceed as directed. About 295 calories per serving.

⚖ **Mousse Baked in a Fish Mold** (4 servings): Use an easy-to-handle fish-shaped mold of about 1-quart capacity (fish will not cook evenly in larger molds). Butter mold well and make sure it will not tip in water bath (use crumpled foil as needed to prop). Prepare recipe as directed and fill mold to within ½″ of top; spoon any remaining mixture into buttered ramekins. Bake mold as directed in water bath 1 hour; ramekins will take about 15 minutes. Cool and unmold as directed, outline "scales" with slivers of pimiento or tissue-thin cucumber slices, and serve. About 280 calories per serving.

⚖ **Cold Fish Mousse:** Prepare and unmold mousse as directed; cool to room temperature, and chill 2–3 hours. When serving, garnish with watercress, cucumber slices, and lemon "baskets" filled with mayonnaise. About 280 calories per serving (without mayonnaise).

Turban of Fish: Butter a 6-cup mold well and line with 8 small fillets of flounder or other delicate white fish, placing snowiest sides against mold and overlapping edges. Sprinkle with a little salt and pepper. Prepare mousse mixture as directed and pour into mold, filling to within ½″ of top; lap any trailing ends of fillets over surface of mousse. Bake in water bath as directed, unmold, and serve with Sauce Américaine or other suitable sauce (see Sauces, Butters, and Seasonings for Seafood). About 330 calories per serving without sauce.

⚖ **QUENELLES**

Quenelles are soufflé-light fish balls poached in delicate broth; they may be used to garnish fish platters or served as a light entree. The mixture may also be used as a fish stuffing.
Makes 4 servings

¾ *pound delicate white fish fillets*
   (pike, pickerel, hake, turbot,
   flounder, etc.)
1 egg white
⅔ cup heavy cream
1 teaspoon salt
Pinch white pepper
Pinch nutmeg
1 quart boiling water
½ teaspoon lemon juice

Grind fish very fine and place in a bowl over cracked ice. Add egg white and beat with a wooden spoon 2–3 minutes until mixture thickens and will cling to a spoon turned upside-down. Add cream, 2 tablespoons at a time, beating ½ minute after each addition; mixture will be soft but should hold a shape. Stir in ½ teaspoon salt, pepper, and nutmeg. Pour water into a large skillet (not iron), add remaining salt and lemon juice, and adjust heat so liquid just trembles. Using 2 wet teaspoons, shape fish mixture into egg-size balls and slide into poaching liquid (liquid should just cover quenelles; if not, add a little extra water). Poach, uncovered, 6–8 quenelles at a time, 3–5 minutes until just firm. Lift out with a slotted spoon and drain on paper toweling. Loosely cover poached quenelles and keep warm in oven set at lowest heat. Shape and poach remaining mixture (you'll have to wet spoons often). Use quenelles to garnish a fish platter or top with Mushroom, Portugaise, or Normande Sauce and serve as a main course. About 150 calories per serving (without sauce).

VARIATIONS:

Gratinéed Quenelles: Poach and drain quenelles; transfer to a buttered 1½-quart *au gratin* dish. Coat lightly with Mornay Sauce, sprinkle lightly with finely grated Parmesan or Gruyère cheese, and broil quickly to brown. Recipe too flexible for a meaningful calorie count.

Quenelles à la Florentine: Poach and drain quenelles and arrange on a bed of hot buttered, chopped spinach in a 2-quart au gratin dish. Gratinée as directed above. Recipe too flexible for a meaningful calorie count.

About Sole and Flounder

Unless you live in a large Eastern metropolis where English, Channel, or Dover Sole is imported, it is unlikely that you will be able to buy true sole. America has no true sole, only flounder, fluke, and other related flatfish that masquerade as sole (they're usually advertised as lemon or gray sole). These flatfish all have delicate white meat, but they lack the elegance of sole. If you can buy imported sole, by all means use it in the recipes that follow. If not use flounder, sand dabs, or any other flounder-like flatfish (see chart of America's Popular Salt Water Fish).

Some Classic Ways to Serve Fillets of Sole, Flounder, or Other Delicate White Fish

All amounts based on 1½–2 pounds fillets or enough for 4–6 servings

À l'Anglaise: Sauté, broil, or poach fillets by basic method and top with Maître d'Hôtel or melted butter.

À l'Arlésienne: Poach fillets by basic method and arrange on a hot platter with sautéed peeled cherry tomatoes and sautéed sliced artichoke bottoms. Strain poaching liquid and quickly reduce to 1 cup; smooth in 2 tablespoons tomato paste, 1 tablespoon butter, and ¼

crushed clove garlic. Pour over fish and serve.

À la Bonne Femme: Arrange fillets 1 layer deep in a buttered, large, shallow casserole, sprinkle lightly with salt and white pepper, top with ¼ cup each minced shallots and mushroom stems. Add ½ cup each dry white wine and Easy Fish Stock, cover, and bake 20 minutes at 350° F. Draw liquid off fillets with a bulb baster and quickly reduce to 1 cup. Meanwhile, melt 3 tablespoons butter in a small saucepan and blend in 3 tablespoons flour. Add reduced liquid and heat, stirring, until thickened. Top each fillet with 4 sautéed mushroom caps, smother with sauce, and broil quickly to brown.

À la Bordelaise: Sauté 1 minced yellow onion and 1 minced carrot in 2 tablespoons butter in a large skillet 3–4 minutes over moderate heat; lay fillets on top and poach in dry red wine by basic method. Lift fish to a hot platter, surround with sautéed button mushrooms and Pan-Braised Onions. Strain poaching liquid and quickly reduce to 1 cup; blend in ¼ cup Rich Brown Sauce, pour over fish, and serve.

À la Florentine: Poach fillets by basic method and arrange flat or rolled up on a bed of hot buttered, chopped spinach. Pour enough Mornay Sauce over fish to coat evenly, sprinkle lightly with grated Parmesan cheese, and broil just until flecked with brown.

À la Marinière: Poach fillets by basic method and arrange on a hot platter. Wreathe with Mussels à la Marinière and drizzle with a little Marinière Sauce. Pass extra sauce.

À la Nantua: Poach fillets by basic

method and serve topped with Nantua Sauce and a scattering of diced or sliced truffles. Pass extra sauce.

À la Niçoise: Poach fillets by basic method, arrange on a hot platter, and lay anchovy fillets on top in a crisscross pattern; top each fillet with 2 overlapping slices lemon. Wreathe platter with clusters of peeled cherry tomatoes sautéed lightly in Anchovy Butter and pitted black olives, sprinkle with capers and a little minced fresh tarragon.

À la Normande: Poach fillets by basic method and arrange on a hot platter; surround with small poached shucked oysters, steamed shucked mussels, boiled, shelled, and deveined shrimp, tiny fried smelts, and sautéed button mushrooms. Pour some Normande Sauce over fillets and dot with truffle slices. Pass extra sauce.

À la Portugaise: Sauté 2–3 peeled, sliced tomatoes, 1 minced yellow onion, and 1 crushed clove garlic in 2 tablespoons olive oil 3–4 minutes over moderate heat in a shallow, flameproof casserole. Lay fillets on top of vegetables and bake, uncovered, 20 minutes at 350° F., basting 1 or 2 times. Sprinkle with buttered bread crumbs and broil lightly to brown.

Amandine: Sauté fillets by basic method and arrange on a hot platter. In the same skillet, lightly brown ⅓ cup slivered blanched almonds in ¼ cup butter and pour over fish. Garnish with lemon and parsley and serve.

Aux Fines Herbes: Sauté or poach fillets by basic method. Meanwhile, melt ¼ cup butter in a small saucepan over low heat, mix in 1 tablespoon each minced fresh

chives, chervil, shallots or scallion, and parsley. Let steep until fish is done. Arrange fish on a hot platter, smother with herbed butter, and serve.

Crécy: Poach fillets by basic method in Easy Fish Stock, transfer to a hot platter, and surround with boiled buttered baby carrots. Quickly reduce poaching liquid to 1 cup, smooth in ¼ cup each Béchamel Sauce and puréed cooked carrots; pour over fish and serve.

Joinville: Poach fillets by basic method and arrange spoke-fashion on a hot circular platter. Mound ½ pound boiled, shelled, and deveined shrimp and ½ pound sautéed button mushrooms in center. Sprinkle with 2 tablespoons minced truffles and top with a little Joinville Sauce. Pass extra sauce.

Marguery: Fold fillets envelope fashion, ends toward center, and poach by basic method in Easy Fish Stock. Arrange on a hot platter, surround with shucked, steamed mussels and boiled, shelled, and deveined shrimp. Quickly reduce poaching liquid in the top of a double boiler over direct heat to 1½ cups; beat in 3 tablespoons butter, 1 at a time. Add a little hot liquid to 3 lightly beaten egg yolks, set over simmering water, and heat, stirring, until thickened. Pour over fish and serve.

Mornay: Poach fillets by basic method and lift to a shallow *au gratin* dish. Cover with Mornay Sauce, sprinkle lightly with grated Parmesan cheese, and broil quickly to brown.

Princesse: Poach or sauté fillets by basic method and arrange on a hot platter. Surround with clusters of boiled buttered asparagus tips and serve with Browned Butter.

Saint-Germain: Sauté fillets by basic method, arrange on a hot platter, wreathe with Château Potatoes, and serve with Béarnaise Sauce.

Véronique: Poach fillets in white wine by basic method but add 1 teaspoon lemon juice. Arrange fish on a hot platter and keep warm. Quickly reduce poaching liquid to ½ cup; smooth in 1 cup Béchamel or Thick White Sauce and 3 tablespoons whipped cream. Pour over fish and broil quickly to brown. Garnish with clusters of seedless green grapes and serve. If you prefer, simmer 1 cup peeled grapes 3 minutes in water to cover, drain, then add to sauce along with whipped cream. Pour over fish and broil to brown.

⚔ SOLE OR FLOUNDER À L'AMÉRICAINE

Makes 6 servings

2 pounds sole or flounder fillets
1 teaspoon salt
⅛ teaspoon white pepper
1 cup dry white wine
1 cup boiling water

Sauce Américaine:
1 small yellow onion, peeled and
   minced
1 carrot, peeled and cut in small dice
3 tablespoons minced shallots or
   scallions
1 clove garlic, peeled and crushed
2 tablespoons cooking oil
¼ cup brandy
2 large tomatoes, peeled, cored,
   seeded, and coarsely chopped
2 tablespoons tomato paste
1 cup Easy Fish Stock
1 cup dry white wine
1 teaspoon tarragon
1 teaspoon minced parsley
1 (4–5-ounce) frozen rock lobster
   tail

1 tablespoon butter or margarine
¼ teaspoon sugar
Pinch cayenne pepper

Prepare sauce early in the day to allow flavors to blend: Sauté onion, carrot, shallots, and garlic in oil in a saucepan over moderate heat 3–5 minutes until onion is very pale golden. Add brandy, warm briefly, remove from heat, and blaze with a match. Add all but last 3 sauce ingredients, cover, and simmer 10 minutes; remove lobster, take meat from shell, slice crosswise ¼" thick, and refrigerate. Continue simmering sauce, *uncovered*, about 1 hour, stirring occasionally. Liquid should be reduced by half; if not, boil rapidly to reduce. Strain liquid through a fine sieve into a small saucepan, pressing vegetables lightly. Heat 1–2 minutes over low heat, whisk in butter, sugar, and cayenne, taste for salt and adjust as needed. Cover and set aside. About 10 minutes before serving, fold fillets envelope fashion, ends toward middle, and arrange in a large skillet (not iron); sprinkle with salt and pepper. Pour in wine and water, cover and simmer slowly 7–10 minutes until fish will just flake. Meanwhile, add lobster to sauce and reheat slowly until bubbly. Using a slotted spoon, lift fish to a hot deep platter, smother with sauce, and serve. About 295 calories per serving.

SOLE OR FLOUNDER BERCY

Makes 4 servings

1 large yellow onion, peeled and
   minced
½ pound mushrooms, wiped clean
   and sliced thin
¼ cup butter or margarine
1½ pounds fillets of sole, flounder,
   or other delicate white fish (cod,
   haddock, fluke, halibut, etc.)

½ cup red Burgundy wine
1 teaspoon salt
⅛ teaspoon white pepper
1 tablespoon flour blended with 2
tablespoons cold water

Preheat oven to 350° F. Sauté onion and mushrooms in butter in a skillet over moderate heat 3–5 minutes until onion is very pale golden; spoon into an ungreased shallow 2-quart casserole. Fold fillets envelope fashion, ends toward middle, and arrange in a single layer on top of vegetables. Pour in wine, sprinkle fish with salt and pepper, and bake uncovered 20–30 minutes until fish will just flake. Using a bulb baster, drain liquid from fish into a small saucepan, mix in flour paste, and heat, stirring until slightly thickened. Pour sauce over fish and serve. About 310 calories per serving.

FILLETS OF SOLE OR FLOUNDER CARDINAL

Genuine Sole Cardinal is sprinkled with minced lobster coral just before serving, but since that means buying a whole lobster, we've made the coral optional.
Makes 6 servings

8 fillets of sole or flounder (about 2
pounds)
1 teaspoon salt
⅛ teaspoon white pepper
1 cup dry white wine
1 cup boiling water

Stuffing:
1 cup cooked, minced delicate white
fish (haddock, cod, fluke, halibut,
etc.)
1 cup soft white bread crumbs
1 tablespoon milk
1 egg, lightly beaten
1 teaspoon minced chives
1 teaspoon minced parsley
½ teaspoon salt

⅛ teaspoon pepper
Pinch nutmeg

Cardinal Sauce:
3 tablespoons butter or margarine
3 tablespoons flour
½ cup milk
½ cup Easy Fish Stock
½ cup heavy cream
Meat of 1 (4–5-ounce) boiled rock
lobster tail or 1 (1-pound) lobster
coarsely chopped
½ teaspoon salt
Pinch cayenne pepper
1 tablespoon minced truffle

Optional Topping:
Minced coral of 1 small boiled
lobster

Sprinkle fillets with salt and pepper and set aside. Pour wine and water into a large skillet (not iron) and set aside. Now prepare stuffing: Beat all ingredients together until smooth. Place about 1 tablespoon stuffing on each fillet, roll up, and secure with toothpicks. Arrange fillets seam side down in skillet, cover, and simmer slowly 7–10 minutes until fish will just flake. Meanwhile, make the sauce: Melt butter in a saucepan, blend in flour, slowly stir in milk, stock, and cream, then heat, stirring, until thickened. Mix in lobster, salt, cayenne, and truffle. With a slotted spoon lift fish to a deep platter, top with sauce and, if you like, minced coral. About 350 calories per serving (without topping).

FILLETS OF SOLE OR FLOUNDER WITH CRAB SAUCE

Makes 4 servings

1½ pounds sole or flounder fillets
½ teaspoon salt
⅛ teaspoon white pepper

Sauce:

2 *tablespoons butter or margarine*
2 *tablespoons flour*
½ *cup milk*
½ *cup light cream*
½ *teaspoon salt*
⅛ *teaspoon white pepper*
2 *teaspoons lemon juice*
¼ *pound fresh lump or backfin crab
meat, well picked over*

Preheat oven to 350° F. Fold fillets envelope fashion by lapping each end over toward center and arrange 1 layer deep in a buttered shallow 2-quart casserole or *au gratin* dish; sprinkle with salt and pepper. Bake, uncovered, 15 minutes. Meanwhile, prepare sauce: Melt butter in a saucepan over moderately low heat, blend in flour, slowly add milk and cream, and heat, stirring, until thickened. Lightly mix in salt, pepper, lemon juice, and crab, cover, and keep warm. Remove liquid from fish, using a bulb baster, then cover fish with sauce. Bake, uncovered, 10–15 minutes longer until fish flakes when touched with a fork. About 325 calories per serving.

♌ FISH FILLETS IN WHITE WINE AND HERBS

Makes 6 servings

2 *pounds delicate white fish fillets
(cod, haddock, fluke, flounder,
halibut, etc.)*
1 *teaspoon salt*
⅛ *teaspoon white pepper*
2 *teaspoons minced fresh dill or 1
teaspoon dried dill*
1 *teaspoon minced chives (fresh,
frozen, or freeze-dried)*
1 *teaspoon minced parsley*
2 *tablespoons butter or margarine*
1½ *cups dry white wine*
½ *cup heavy cream*
3 *egg yolks, lightly beaten*

Preheat oven to 350° F. Fold fillets envelope fashion, ends toward middle, and arrange in a single layer in a buttered shallow 2½-quart casserole or *au gratin* dish; sprinkle with salt, pepper, and herbs and dot with butter. Pour in wine and bake, uncovered, 20–30 minutes until fish flakes when touched with a fork. Using pancake turner, transfer filets to hot platter and keep warm. Pour cooking liquid into the top of a double boiler, set over direct heat, and boil rapidly, uncovered, until liquid reduces to about 1 cup. Mix cream and egg yolks, add a little hot liquid, mix well, and return to double boiler. Set over simmering water and heat, stirring, until thickened. Taste for salt and adjust if needed. Pour sauce over fish and serve. About 285 calories per serving.

CRUMB-TOPPED BAKED FLOUNDER

Makes 4 servings

1½ *pounds flounder or other delicate
white fish fillets (cod, haddock,
fluke, halibut, etc.)*
1 *teaspoon salt*
⅛ *teaspoon white pepper*
2 *cups soft white bread crumbs*
1 *tablespoon minced parsley*
⅓ *cup melted butter or margarine*

Preheat oven to 350° F. Arrange fillets in a single layer in a buttered shallow 2-quart casserole; sprinkle with ½ teaspoon salt and the pepper. Toss bread crumbs with remaining salt, the parsley, and butter and scatter evenly over fish. Bake, uncovered, 25–30 minutes until fish flakes, then broil 4″ from the heat 2–3 minutes to brown. Garnish with lemon wedges and serve. About 365 calories per serving.

VARIATIONS:

Almond-Crumb-Topped Baked Flounder: Prepare as directed but add ½ cup coarsely chopped, blanched, toasted almonds to bread crumb mixture. About 470 calories per serving.

Sesame Baked Flounder: Prepare as directed but add ¼ cup toasted sesame seeds to crumb mixture. About 390 calories per serving.

CHEESE STUFFED FLOUNDER IN MARINARA SAUCE

Makes 4 servings

8 *small flounder fillets (about 1½ pounds)*
½ *teaspoon salt*
⅛ *teaspoon white pepper*
⅓ *cup grated Parmesan cheese*
2 *tablespoons minced parsley*
4 *slices processed sharp cheese, halved*
1 *(1-pound) jar marinara sauce*

Preheat oven to 350° F. Sprinkle fillets with salt, pepper, Parmesan cheese, and 1 tablespoon parsley; lay a half slice of cheese on each and roll up. Arrange rolls, seam side down, in a single layer in a buttered shallow 2-quart casserole or *au gratin* dish and top with sauce. Bake, uncovered, 20–30 minutes. Sprinkle with remaining parsley and serve. About 365 calories per serving.

⚖ LOW-CALORIE FILLETS OF FLOUNDER EN PAPILLOTE

Makes 4 servings

4 *large flounder fillets (about 1½ pounds)*
1½ *teaspoons salt*
½ *cup minced scallions*
1 *tablespoon butter or margarine*
1 *tablespoon flour*

2 *ripe tomatoes, peeled, cored, seeded, and chopped fine*
1 *teaspoon red or white wine vinegar*
½ *teaspoon basil or oregano*
⅛ *teaspoon pepper*

Preheat oven to 350° F. Cut 4 large squares of cooking parchment (available at gourmet shops) or heavy duty foil (large enough to wrap fillets); lay a fillet on each and sprinkle with 1 teaspoon salt. Sauté scallions in butter in a small skillet over moderate heat 3–5 minutes until limp; sprinkle in flour, add remaining salt and all other ingredients, and heat, stirring, over low heat 3–5 minutes to blend flavors. Spoon a little sauce over each fillet and wrap tightly drugstore style. Place packages on a baking sheet and bake 30–40 minutes; unwrap 1 package and check to see if fish flakes; if not, rewrap and bake a little longer. Serve in foil to retain all juices. About 180 calories per serving.

PAUPIETTES OF SOLE OR FLOUNDER WITH ROSY SAUCE

Paupiettes are stuffed and rolled fillets of meat or fish. They're unusually versatile because a change of stuffing or sauce creates a whole new dish.

Makes 6 servings

2 *pounds sole or flounder fillets*
1 *teaspoon salt*
⅛ *teaspoon white pepper*
2 *cups Basic Bread Stuffing for Fish*
½ *cup milk*
½ *cup water*

Rosy Sauce:
2 *tablespoons butter or margarine*
2 *tablespoons flour*
Fish cooking liquid
¼ *cup heavy cream*
2 *tablespoons tomato paste*
Pinch nutmeg

Lay fillets flat, more attractive side down, and sprinkle with salt and pepper. Place about ¼ cup stuffing on each fillet and roll up from widest end; secure with toothpicks. (*Note:* If paupiettes are very wide, halve crosswise.) Arrange seam side down in a large skillet (not iron), add milk and water, cover, and simmer 7–10 minutes until fish will just flake. *Or* arrange in a buttered shallow casserole, add milk and water, cover loosely, and bake 20–30 minutes at 350° F. Lift rolls to a heated deep platter with a slotted spoon, cover, and keep warm. Strain cooking liquid and reserve. For the sauce, melt butter in a small saucepan over moderate heat, blend in flour, slowly stir in cooking liquid and remaining ingredients. Heat, stirring, until thickened. Taste for salt and pepper and adjust as needed. Pour over paupiettes and serve. About 385 calories per serving.

VARIATIONS:

⚖ **Mushroom Stuffed Paupiettes:** Stuff fillets with 1 pound minced sautéed mushrooms mixed with 2 minced scallions, 1 cup soft white bread crumbs, ½ teaspoon salt, and ¼ teaspoon pepper. Roll and cook as directed. Serve with Mushroom Sauce. About 295 calories per serving (with ¼ cup Mushroom Sauce).

Shrimp Stuffed Paupiettes: Stuff fillets with 1 cup minced cooked shrimp mixed with ¾ cup soft white bread crumbs, 2 tablespoons mayonnaise, and 2 teaspoons lemon juice. Roll and cook as directed; serve with Shrimp Sauce. About 470 calories per serving (with ¼ cup Shrimp Sauce).

Anchovy and Caper Stuffed Paupiettes: Drain and mince 1 (2-ounce) can anchovy fillets, mix with ¼ cup minced capers, spread on *unsalted* fish fillets, roll, and cook as directed. Serve with Caper Sauce. About 415 calories per serving (with ¼ cup Caper Sauce).

Paupiettes Stuffed with Quenelles: Mix 1 recipe Quenelles but do not poach. Place 1 large shaped quenelle on each fillet, roll up loosely, secure with toothpicks, and cook paupiettes as directed. Serve with Rosy, Tomato, or Shrimp Sauce. About 350 calories per serving (with ¼ cup any of the suggested sauces).

COD À LA LISBOA (LISBON-STYLE COD)

Makes 4 servings

1 (2-pound) center-cut slice cod
2½ cups water
1 small yellow onion, peeled and stuck with 1 clove
1 clove garlic, peeled and quartered
2 bay leaves
1 teaspoon salt
6 peppercorns
4 medium-size potatoes, boiled, peeled, and quartered
1 (9-ounce) package whole green beans, cooked by package directions and drained well
Red or white wine vinegar

Dressing:
1½ cups olive oil
2 cloves garlic, peeled and quartered
1 bay leaf crumbled
2 teaspoons salt

Wipe cod with a damp cloth. Bring water, onion, garlic, bay leaves, salt, and peppercorns to a boil in a large saucepan over moderate heat and simmer, uncovered, 5 minutes. Add cod, cover, and simmer 10 minutes, just until fish will flake. Cool in broth until easy to handle, then drain cod well; remove skin and bones and divide into large chunks.

Place chunks of cod in a large, shallow bowl and carefully lay potatoes and beans on top. Mix dressing and pour over all, cover, and marinate in refrigerator 3–4 hours before serving, turning beans, potatoes and fish occasionally in marinade. Arrange cod and vegetables on plates, top with a little marinade, and serve with a carafe of wine vinegar. About 425 calories per serving.

VARIATION:

Omit dressing altogether; as soon as cod is done, drain, bone, skin, and divide into large chunks. Serve hot with hot potatoes and beans, top all with Hollandaise Sauce or serve with oil, vinegar, salt, and pepper. About 410 calories per serving (with 3 tablespoons Hollandaise Sauce).

¢ CREAMED SALT COD

Makes 4 servings

1½ pounds filleted salt cod
2 cups hot Medium White Sauce,
    prepared without salt
⅛ teaspoon pepper
2 hard-cooked eggs, peeled and sliced

Soak cod overnight in cold water to cover; drain and rinse. Place in a saucepan with enough cold water to cover and simmer, covered, 10–15 minutes until fish will flake. Drain, cool slightly, and coarsely flake, removing any bones and skin. Mix fish gently into sauce, add pepper, cover, and let stand over lowest heat 10 minutes to blend flavors. Taste for salt and adjust as needed. Using eggs to garnish, serve as is or over hot boiled potatoes or buttered toast. About 470 calories per serving.

BRANDADE DE MORUE
(SALT COD WITH GARLIC, OIL, AND CREAM)

This rich cod purée can be served hot or cold, as a luncheon entree or a cocktail spread. The best way to make it is in an electric blender.
Makes 3–4 entree servings, enough cocktail spread for 12

1 pound filleted salt cod
½ cup heavy cream (about)
½ cup olive oil (about)
1 clove garlic, peeled and crushed
⅛ teaspoon pepper
4 slices French bread or 8 small
    triangles white bread
2–3 tablespoons olive oil or butter

Soak cod overnight in cold water to cover; drain and rinse. Place in a saucepan with just enough cold water to cover and simmer, covered, 10–15 minutes until fish will flake. Drain, cool slightly, and coarsely flake, removing any bones or skin. Purée fish with ¼ cup each cream and oil, the garlic and pepper in an electric blender at high speed. Add remaining cream and oil alternately, 1 tablespoon at a time, puréeing until the texture of mashed potatoes; if too stiff, blend in a little additional cream and oil. If you don't have a blender, put fish through finest blade of meat grinder twice; add cream and oil alternately, a little at a time, beating well after each addition; beat in garlic and pepper. Heat to serving temperature in the top of a double boiler over simmering water, stirring occasionally. Meanwhile, fry bread in oil in a skillet over moderately high heat until golden. Mound fish in the center of a hot platter and surround with bread.

VARIATION:

To Serve Cold: Instead of warming fish, chill slightly, taste for pepper and add more if needed; also, if you like, add ½ teaspoon grated lemon rind and 1–2 teaspoons lemon juice. Serve with Melba toast.

About 835 calories for each of 3 entree servings, 625 calories for each of 4 entree servings, and 210 calories for each of 12 appetizer servings (without Melba toast).

⚖️ ¢ CODFISH CAKES

Makes 4 servings

1 (2-ounce) package dried, shredded salt cod
1½ cups cold water
1½ cups hot, unseasoned mashed potatoes
⅛ teaspoon pepper
1 tablespoon Worcestershire sauce (optional)
2 tablespoons minced fresh parsley (optional)
2 tablespoons melted butter or margarine
1 egg, lightly beaten
⅓ cup cooking oil

Soften cod in cold water 4–5 minutes; drain and squeeze dry in a strainer. Mix with all remaining ingredients except oil, shape into 4–6 flat patties, cover, and chill 1 hour. Heat oil in a large, heavy skillet over moderate heat until a cube of bread will sizzle, add fish cakes, and brown 3–5 minutes on each side. Drain on paper toweling and serve. About 220 calories per serving.

VARIATION:

⚖️ **Codfish Balls:** Prepare cod mixture as directed, but instead of shaping into cakes, drop from a tablespoon into hot deep fat (375° F.) and fry 1–2 minutes until golden brown. Fry only a few balls at a time and drain well on paper toweling before serving. About 220 calories per serving, 55 calories per codfish ball.

BAKED HADDOCK IN CREAM SAUCE

Makes 6 servings

2 pounds haddock or flounder fillets
2 tablespoons lemon juice
1 teaspoon salt
⅛ teaspoon white pepper
2 tablespoons butter or margarine

Sauce:
3 tablespoons butter or margarine
¼ cup unsifted flour
1 cup light cream
1 teaspoon salt
¼ teaspoon paprika

Preheat oven to 350° F. Fold fillets envelope fashion, ends toward middle, and arrange in a single layer in a buttered shallow 2-quart casserole; sprinkle with lemon juice, salt, and pepper and dot with butter. Bake, uncovered, 20–30 minutes or until fish just flakes. Meanwhile, prepare sauce: Melt butter in a saucepan over moderate heat, blend in flour, slowly add cream, and heat, stirring, until thickened; add salt, cover, and keep warm. When fish is done, drain off liquid with a bulb baster and reserve. Beat 1 cup fish liquid into sauce, pour evenly over fish, and bake uncovered 5–7 minutes. Dust with paprika and serve. About 300 calories per serving.

VARIATIONS:

Baked Haddock au Gratin: Prepare recipe as directed but, before final 5–7-minute baking, top with 1 cup soft white bread crumbs mixed with 3 tablespoons melted butter or margarine and, if you like, 2 tablespoons minced parsley. Finish baking as directed, then broil 1–2 minutes to brown. About 375 calories per serving.

Baked Haddock in Cheese Sauce: Prepare as directed but, when making sauce, add 1 teaspoon

Worcestershire sauce, ⅛ teaspoon powdered mustard, a pinch cayenne pepper, and 1 cup coarsely grated sharp Cheddar cheese. Pour sauce over fish as directed, top with ¼ cup grated cheese, bake 5–7 minutes, then broil 1–2 minutes to brown. About 400 calories per serving.

Baked Haddock in Shrimp Sauce: Prepare as directed, but when making sauce add 1 cup coarsely chopped cooked shrimp, 1 tablespoon tomato paste, and, if you like, 2–3 tablespoons dry sherry. Proceed as basic recipe directs, garnish with 12 cooked, shelled, and deveined small shrimp, and serve. About 350 calories per serving.

Baked Haddock and Mushrooms: Stir-fry ½ pound thinly sliced mushrooms and ½ cup each minced onion and sweet green pepper in 2 tablespoons butter or margarine 5–8 minutes over moderate heat until onion is pale golden. Sprinkle fish with lemon juice, salt, and pepper as directed in basic recipe but omit butter; top with sautéed vegetables, then complete recipe as directed. About 350 calories per serving.

⚖ **FINNAN HADDIE**

Once upon a time, fire swept the little town of Findon, Scotland, smoking tons of haddock that had been hung to dry. Fortunately someone thought to taste the fish before it was dumped. Result: smoked haddock or finnan (Findon) haddie. Today it comes filleted or split (with backbone in). Often it is supersalty, but a half hour of soaking in tepid water will take care of that.
Makes 4–6 servings

2 pounds smoked haddock fillets, rinsed and cut in serving-size pieces

1 cup milk or ½ cup milk and ½ cup water
⅛ teaspoon white pepper
2 tablespoons butter or margarine

Place haddock in a large, heavy skillet, add milk, sprinkle with pepper, and dot with butter; heat, uncovered, over moderate heat until almost boiling, turn heat to low, baste well, then cover and simmer 10 minutes until fish flakes when touched with a fork. Serve as is or, if you like, topped with plump pats of butter. About 255 calories for each of 4 servings (without pats of butter), 180 calories for each of 6 servings.

VARIATIONS:

Creamed Finnan Haddie: Poach haddock as directed above and drain, reserving cooking liquid. Make 2 cups Medium White Sauce, using 1 cup poaching liquid and 1 cup light cream. Add haddock, 1 tablespoon minced parsley and serve over hot buttered toast or in puff pastry shells. About 420 calories for each of 4 servings, 280 calories for each of 6 servings.

⚖ **Scottish Nips:** Poach haddock as directed above, drain, flake, and measure. To each cup haddock, add ½ cup heavy cream and a pinch cayenne pepper. Slowly bring to a simmer, spread on unbuttered small toast triangles, and serve as cocktail appetizers. About 45 calories for each Scottish nip.

⚖ **Baked Finnan Haddie:** Preheat oven to 350° F. Do not poach haddock; place instead in a single layer in a buttered shallow 2-quart casserole. Add ½ cup each milk and light cream, sprinkle with pepper and dot with butter. Cover and bake 20–25 minutes, basting occasionally, until fish flakes. Lift haddock to a hot platter, top with a little of the pan juices, then dot with 2 table-spoons butter and serve. About 265 calories for each of 4 servings, 175 calories for each of 6 servings.

⚖ **Baked Finnan Haddie with Egg Sauce:** Bake finnan haddie as directed and, as soon as fish is done, drain pan juices into a saucepan; keep fish warm. Blend 2 tablespoons flour with 2 tablespoons water, stir into pan juices, and heat, stirring, until thickened and smooth. Mix in 1 minced, hard-cooked egg and a pinch white pepper. Serve sauce over fish. About 295 calories for each of 4 servings, 195 calories for each of 6 servings.

CREAMY SMOKED HADDOCK AND POTATO CASSEROLE

Makes 4–6 servings

1 pound smoked haddock or cod fillets, rinsed
1½ cups water
2 cups hot unseasoned mashed potatoes
2 tablespoons minced parsley
½ cup minced scallion tops (green part only)
2 tablespoons olive or other cooking oil
⅛ teaspoon pepper
1 cup heavy cream
Salt
2 tablespoons butter or margarine

Place haddock and water in a sauce-pan, cover, and quickly bring to a boil. Turn heat to low and simmer 10 minutes until fish is cooked through; drain, then flake with a fork. (*Note:* Haddock fillets oc-casionally have a few bones, so check and discard any you find.) Mix fish, potatoes, parsley, scallions, oil, and pepper; cool to room tem-perature. Meanwhile, preheat oven to 350° F. Beat cream until soft peaks form and fold into fish. Taste

for salt and add as needed. Spoon into a buttered 1½-quart casserole and dot with butter. Bake, uncov-ered, 30 minutes. To brown, run quickly under broiler. About 440 calories for each of 4 servings, 295 calories for each of 6 servings.

⚖ KEDGEREE

An English breakfast dish by way of India. Kedgeree doesn't have to have curry powder; in fact it's better without it if you use smoked fish in the recipe.
Makes 4–6 servings

¼ cup butter or margarine
3 cups flaked cooked haddock or cod or 1½ cups each flaked cooked smoked haddock and cod
2 cups boiled rice
1 teaspoon salt (about)
⅛ teaspoon white pepper
½ teaspoon curry powder (optional)
3 hard-cooked eggs, shelled

Melt butter in the top of a double boiler over simmering water. Add fish and mix well. Add rice, salt, pepper, and curry powder if you like. Dice 2 eggs and cut the third into wedges. Mix in diced eggs, cover, and heat 10–15 minutes until heated through. Taste for salt and ad-just. Mound mixture on a hot platter and garnish with egg wedges. If made with fresh haddock or cod: about 285 calories for each of 4 servings, 190 calories for each of 6 servings. If made with smoked haddock and cod: about 325 calories for each of 4 servings, 220 calories for each of 6 servings.

▨ HERRING IN OATMEAL

A Scottish favorite.
Makes 4 servings

⅓ cup uncooked oatmeal
½ teaspoon salt

¼ *teaspoon pepper*
4 *herring, cleaned and dressed*
1 *egg, lightly beaten*
3 *tablespoons butter or margarine*

Buzz oatmeal in an electric blender at high speed a few seconds until fairly fine; mix with salt and pepper. Dip herring in egg, then in oatmeal to coat evenly. Melt butter in a large skillet over moderate heat and sauté herring about 3 minutes on each side until golden brown. (*Note:* Any small fish may be prepared this way). About 365 calories per serving.

IRISH HERRING IN ALE

Makes 6 servings

2 *medium-size yellow onions, peeled and minced*
2 *carrots, peeled and cut in small dice*
1 *clove garlic, peeled and crushed*
4 *peppercorns*
1 *teaspoon salt*
1 *bay leaf*
2 *cloves*
2 *(12-ounce) bottles ale*
6 *herring, cleaned and dressed*
2 *medium-size yellow onions, peeled and sliced thin*

Preheat oven to 350° F. Place minced onions, carrots, garlic, seasonings, and 1 bottle ale in an ungreased deep 3-quart casserole. Cover and bake 30 minutes. Add herring, cover with sliced onions, and pour in remaining ale. Bake, uncovered, 20–30 minutes until fish will flake. Cool herring in broth to lukewarm, then transfer with sliced onions to a deep serving platter; top with a little broth. Serve lukewarm or slightly chilled with Irish Soda Bread. About 340 calories per serving (without Irish Soda Bread).

SALT HERRING AND BEETS À LA RUSSE

Makes 4 servings

3 *herring in brine*
1 *(1-pound) can sliced beets (do not drain)*
2 *tablespoons butter or margarine*
2 *tablespoons flour*
1 *tablespoon prepared horseradish*
1 *tablespoon lemon juice*
⅛ *teaspoon pepper*
1 *cup sour cream*

Soak herring in cold water 24 hours, changing water several times. Remove heads, fillet, and skin* herring and cut in serving-size pieces. Drain beet liquid into a 1-cup measure and add enough cold water to round out measure. Melt butter in a saucepan over moderate heat, blend in flour, slowly stir in beet liquid, and heat, stirring, until thickened. Meanwhile, preheat oven to 350° F. Off heat, mix remaining ingredients into sauce, add herring, and toss to mix. Spoon into a buttered 1½-quart casserole, cover loosely, and bake 20–30 minutes. Serve with boiled potatoes. About 585 calories per serving (without boiled potatoes).

⚖ ROLLMOPS

Makes 6 servings

6 *herring in brine*
3 *dill pickles, quartered lengthwise*
2 *medium-size yellow onions, peeled, sliced thin, and separated into rings*
1 *cup cider vinegar*
1 *cup water*
6 *peppercorns*
1 *bay leaf*
1 *clove garlic, peeled and halved*
3 *cloves*
⅛ *teaspoon crushed hot red chili peppers*

Soak herring in cold water 24 hours,

changing water several times. Remove heads and fillet* herring. Place a piece of dill pickle and some onion on each piece of herring, roll up, and secure with a toothpick. Arrange rolls seam side down in a heatproof glass bowl. Bring vinegar, water, and spices to a boil, cool slightly, and pour over herring. Add any remaining onion, cover tightly, and chill 3–4 days before serving. About 245 calories per serving.

HERRING IN SOUR CREAM

Makes 4 entree servings, enough appetizers for 10–12

4 herring in brine
1 cup sour cream
3 tablespoons white wine or white wine vinegar
1 large yellow or red onion, peeled, sliced thin, and separated into rings
¼ teaspoon powdered mustard
Pinch cayenne pepper

Soak herring in cold water 24 hours, changing water several times. Remove heads, fillet and skin* herring, and cut into bite-size pieces. Mix remaining ingredients, add herring, and pack in a 1-quart jar or glass bowl. Cover tightly and chill 1–2 days before serving. About 340 calories for each of 4 entree servings, 135 calories for each of 10 appetizer servings, and 115 calories for each of 12 appetizer servings.

⚖ PICKLED HERRING

Makes 6 servings

6 herring in brine
2 medium-size yellow onions, peeled, sliced thin, and separated into rings
1 lemon, sliced thin
1½ cups cider vinegar
6 peppercorns
1 teaspoon mustard seeds
1 teaspoon mixed pickling spices
1 teaspoon sugar

Soak herring in cold water 24 hours, changing water several times. Remove heads, fillet* each herring, and, if you like, skin the fillets. If herring is to be served as an appetizer, cut into bite-size pieces. Place half the herring in a single layer in a large shallow heatproof bowl (not metal), top with half the onions and lemon; add remaining herring, onion and lemon. Bring vinegar, spices, and sugar to a boil and pour over herring. Cover and chill 3–5 days before serving. About 215 calories per serving.

KIPPERED HERRING

Also called *kippers* or *bloaters,* these salted and smoked herring are usually sold as fillets by the pound (allow 1 kipper per person). They also come canned. When buying, avoid any that seem leathery or dry, also any with an overpowering smell. Cook any of the following ways, and serve for breakfast (the English way), lunch, or supper.

To Bake: Preheat oven to 350° F. Line a shallow baking pan with foil and grease lightly; spread kippers flat and arrange skin side down in pan, brush lightly with melted butter or margarine, drizzle, if you like, with a very little Worcestershire sauce, and bake uncovered 8–10 minutes.

To Broil: Preheat broiler. Spread kippers flat and arrange skin side down on broiler pan. Spread each with 1 tablespoon butter or margarine and, if you like, sprinkle with 1 teaspoon lemon juice. Broil 3″–4″ from the heat 2–3 minutes—just long enough to heat through.

To Panfry (Sauté): Spread kippers flat. Allowing about 1 tablespoon butter or margarine for each kipper, sauté gently over moderately low heat about 2 minutes on a side.

To Poach: Spread kippers flat and arrange skin side down in a single layer in a large skillet (not iron); add boiling water or milk just to cover, cover skillet, and bring liquid just to a simmer over moderate heat. Lift kippers to a hot platter, dot with butter, and serve. Especially good with scrambled eggs.

To Steam: Spread kippers flat and arrange skin side down in a single layer on a steamer rack over about 1" boiling water. Cover and steam 5 minutes.

Some Ways to Use Kippered Herring
Cook by any of the methods above, then remove skin and any bones, flake, and use as follows:
— Fold into scrambled eggs or omelets, allowing about ½ cup flaked kippers for 4–6 eggs.
— Mix equal quantities flaked kippers and Medium White Sauce and serve on toast, split toasted muffins, in patty shells or Crepes or over buttered noodles.
— Substitute for half the fish called for in Kedgeree.
— Spoon onto melba rounds, drizzle with lemon juice, and serve as cocktail snacks.

BAKED BLUEFISH SMOTHERED WITH HERBS AND CREAM

Makes 2–4 servings

1 (2–3-pound) bluefish, cleaned and dressed
1 teaspoon salt
⅛ teaspoon pepper
½ cup butter or margarine
5 shallots, peeled and minced
1 medium-size yellow onion, peeled and coarsely chopped
⅓ cup minced parsley
2 tablespoons minced fresh dill
1 cup light cream

Preheat oven to 375° F. Sprinkle fish inside and out with salt and pepper and place in an ungreased shallow oval casserole large enough to accommodate it. Dot fish inside and out with ¼ cup butter. Mix shallots, onions, parsley, and dill and scatter over fish. Bake, uncovered, 15 minutes; dot with remaining butter and bake 10 minutes longer. Pour in cream and bake, uncovered, 15–20 minutes and serve. About 1075 calories for each of 2 servings, 540 calories for each of 4 servings.

CHINESE SWEET-AND-SOUR CARP

Carp, the lucky fish of the Chinese, is said to bring wealth and well-being to those who eat it.
Makes 4–6 servings

1 (4–5-pound) carp, cleaned

Sauce:
2 tablespoons peanut or other cooking oil
1 clove garlic, peeled and crushed
1 medium-size sweet green pepper, cored, seeded, and cut in ½" squares
1 medium-size carrot, peeled and cut in julienne strips
1 cup Easy Fish Stock or ½ cup each water and pineapple juice
¼ cup cider vinegar
3 tablespoons sugar
2 tablespoons soy sauce
2 teaspoons cornstarch blended with 2 tablespoons cold water
2 pineapple rings, cut in ¾" chunks

Bend fish into an "S" shape and run 2 long skewers through from head to tail to hold in shape. Place on a rack in a fish steamer or large oval kettle over gently boiling water, cover, and steam about 25 minutes until fish will just flake. About 10 minutes before fish is done, begin sauce: Heat oil in a *wok* or heavy skillet over moderate heat 1 minute, add garlic, pepper, and carrot, and stir-fry 2–3 minutes; do not brown. Mix in stock, vinegar, sugar and soy sauce, cover, and simmer 2–3 minutes. Add cornstarch paste and pineapple and heat, stirring, until slightly thickened and clear. Lift fish to a hot deep platter and remove skewers. Pour sauce on top and serve with boiled rice. About 335 calories for each of 4 servings (without rice), about 225 calories for each of 6 servings.

CARP IN BEER

A Bavarian specialty.
Makes 4 servings

1 (3–4-pound) carp, cleaned
1 quart beer or ale
1 large yellow onion, peeled and minced
1 stalk celery, chopped fine
1 lemon, sliced thin
1 bay leaf
1½ teaspoons salt
6 peppercorns
6 gingersnaps, crumbled

Place carp and all remaining ingredients except gingersnaps in a fish poacher or large kettle, cover, and simmer 15–20 minutes until fish just flakes when touched with a fork. Lift fish from liquid, arrange on a hot platter and keep warm. Boil kettle liquid, uncovered, until reduced to about 2 cups, stir in gingersnaps, and simmer 2–3 minutes. Strain liquid, pour some over fish, and pass the rest. About 326 calories per serving.

VARIATION:

Carp in Creamy Beer Sauce: Poach fish and reduce kettle liquid as directed above. Instead of adding gingersnaps, strain liquid. Stir in 3 tablespoons flour blended with ¼ cup heavy cream and heat, stirring, until thickened and smooth. Mix in 2 tablespoons butter and 1 tablespoon minced parsley. Spoon some sauce over fish and pass the remainder. About 415 calories per serving.

⚖ BAKED STUFFED SHAD

If possible, have fish market bone and prepare fish for stuffing.
Makes 6 servings

1 (4-pound) shad, prepared for stuffing*
1 teaspoon salt
¼ teaspoon pepper
2 cups Quick Mushroom or other stuffing for fish
¼ cup butter or margarine
½ cup dry white wine

Preheat oven to 400° F. Wipe shad inside and out with damp paper toweling. Sprinkle cavity with half the salt and pepper. Spoon stuffing loosely into cavity and sew up; wrap any remaining stuffing in foil. Place fish and extra stuffing in a well-buttered oven-to-table roasting pan or large casserole. Sprinkle shad with remaining salt and pepper, dot with butter, and add wine. Bake uncovered, basting often, about 40 minutes until fish flakes easily. Remove threads and serve. (Note: The shad can be transferred to a hot platter, but, since it's extra fragile, the less handling the better.) About 280 calories per serving.

VARIATIONS:

Portuguese-Style Stuffed Shad: Prepare shad for stuffing as directed above. Make 2 cups Quick Mushroom Stuffing for Fish, then mix in 2 thinly sliced yellow onions and ½ crushed clove garlic that have been sautéed until golden in 2 tablespoons olive oil, also ½ cup coarsely chopped, peeled, and seeded ripe tomato. Stuff fish as directed and begin baking; after 25 minutes, baste with 1 cup hot tomato sauce. Serve with pan juices. About 440 calories per serving.

Empress Stuffed Shad: Prepare shad for stuffing, then stuff with the following: 1 pair blanched shad roe, broken up and mixed with ¾ cup soft white bread crumbs, 2 tablespoons each melted butter and minced chives, 1 teaspoon minced fresh tarragon or ¼ teaspoon dried tarragon, ½ teaspoon salt, and ⅛ teaspoon pepper. Bake as directed. About 410 calories per serving.

POACHED SALMON

Makes 6–8 servings

2 quarts water
1½ cups dry white wine
2 bay leaves
1 sprig parsley
1 stalk celery
3 sprigs fresh dill or ¼ teaspoon dill seed
1 sprig fresh thyme or a pinch dried thyme
1 small yellow onion, peeled and quartered
10 peppercorns, bruised
1 teaspoon salt
1 (5-pound) center cut piece fresh salmon, cleaned and dressed

Boil all ingredients except salmon, uncovered, 25 minutes and strain through a double thickness of cheesecloth. Wipe salmon with damp cloth and wrap in a double thickness of cheesecloth. Place in a large oval kettle on a rack so that loose cheesecloth ends are on top. Pour in strained liquid, cover, and simmer 40 minutes (liquid should never boil). Lift rack and salmon from kettle, remove cheesecloth, peel off skin and carefully scrape away any darkened flesh. Serve hot with Hollandaise Sauce or cool to room temperature, chill 8–10 hours and

serve with Green Mayonnaise. About 430 calories for each of 6 servings (without Hollandaise or mayonnaise), 320 calories for each of 8 servings.

VARIATIONS:

Salmon in Aspic: Poach and chill salmon as directed; reserve 2 cups cooking liquid. Transfer chilled salmon to platter and keep cold. Mix 1 envelope unflavored gelatin into reserved liquid, add 1 egg white, beaten to soft peaks, and 1 eggshell, and heat, stirring with a whisk, until mixture foams up. Remove from heat, stir once, then let stand undisturbed 5 minutes. Line a sieve with a fine dish towel wrung out in cold water, set over a deep bowl, pour in hot liquid (egg, shells and all) and let drip through to clarify. Chill clarified aspic until syrupy and spoon a thin, even layer over salmon; chill until tacky, then decorate with cutouts of truffle and pimiento, sliced stuffed green olives, and sprigs of fresh tarragon or chervil; chill briefly to set but keep remaining aspic over warm water. Seal designs with another layer of aspic and chill until firm. Also chill remaining aspic, then dice and use to garnish platter along with lemon wedges and parsley fluffs. Serve with mayonnaise or other suitable cold sauce (see Sauces, Butters, and Seasonings for Seafood). About 435 calories for each of 6 servings (without sauce), 325 for each of 8 servings.

Whole Salmon in Aspic (Makes 10 servings): Substitute a whole small salmon (8 pounds) for center cut piece and poach as directed. Peel skin from body of fish but leave it on head and tail. Glaze salmon with aspic and decorate as directed. About 300 calories per serving.

Salmon in Mayonnaise Gelatin:
Poach and chill salmon as directed; also make and clarify aspic as for Salmon in Aspic. In addition, prepare a mayonnaise gelatin: Heat 1 cup chicken broth, skimmed of all fat, with 1 envelope unflavored gelatin, stirring until gelatin dissolves. Smooth in 1 cup mayonnaise and chill until mixture will coat a metal spoon. Spoon a thin, even layer of mayonnaise gelatin over salmon, chill until tacky, and, if necessary, continue adding thin layers until no pink shows through. While mayonnaise gelatin is still tacky, decorate as above. Chill clear aspic until syrupy and use to seal in design. About 735 calories for each of 6 servings, 555 calories for each of 8 servings.

CRISPY CUCUMBER STUFFED SALMON STEAKS

Makes 4 servings

4 salmon steaks, cut 1¼″ thick

Stuffing:
3 tablespoons minced yellow onion
2 tablespoons butter or margarine
1 chicken bouillon cube, crumbled
½ cup hot water
⅓ cup diced, peeled cucumber
1 tablespoon minced parsley
1 tablespoon minced chives (fresh, frozen, or freeze-dried)
1 tablespoon minced fresh dill or ½ teaspoon dried dill
¼ teaspoon salt
⅛ teaspoon pepper
2 cups coarse soda cracker crumbs
¼ cup melted butter or margarine

Preheat oven to 375° F. Arrange salmon steaks in a greased large, shallow baking pan. Stir-fry onion in butter in a large, heavy skillet 3–5 minutes over moderate heat until limp. Mix in bouillon cube and water and heat, stirring, until dis-

solved. Off heat, add remaining ingredients and toss lightly to mix. Mound stuffing in hollow of each steak, bring ends around to enclose and secure with toothpicks. Drizzle with melted butter and bake, uncovered, 20–25 minutes until fish will just flake. Serve as is or with Lemon Sauce or Parsley Sauce. About 615 calories per serving (without sauce).

⚖ SALMON STEAKS EN CASSEROLE

The Irish say that salmon is best baked in a sealed casserole so that none of the flavor escapes.
Makes 4 servings

4 small salmon steaks, cut ¾″–1″ thick
2 tablespoons butter or margarine, softened to room temperature
¼ teaspoon salt
2–3 sprigs fresh tarragon, lemon balm, thyme, or dill
1 lemon, sliced thin
⅓ cup simmering apple cider, Easy Fish Stock, or water

Preheat oven to 325° F. Place steaks in a well-buttered large, shallow casserole that has a tight-fitting lid. Spread steaks with butter and sprinkle with salt. Lay herb on top and cover with lemon slices. Add cider, cover casserole with foil, then with lid and bake 20–30 minutes just until fish flakes when touched with a fork. Remove lemon and herb, carefully lift steaks to platter, drizzle with a little pan liquid, garnish with parsley fluffs, and serve. Tiny new potatoes, buttered green peas, and homemade mayonnaise are the perfect accompaniments. About 295 calories per serving.

VARIATIONS:

Liffey Salmon Steak Platter (6 servings): Cook salmon as directed, transfer to a large platter, and surround with clusters of the following: ½ pound hot shrimp boiled in cider, then shelled and deveined; 1–2 dozen Fried Oysters and ½ pound button mushrooms simmered 5–7 minutes in 2 tablespoons butter and ¼ cup heavy cream. Pass Tomato Sauce. About 510 calories per serving (without sauce).

Tara Salmon: Prepare steaks as directed, but use milk as the cooking liquid instead of cider. Serve on a bed of Colcannon. About 315 calories per serving (without Colcannon).

⊠ TRUITE AU BLEU (BLUE TROUT)

For this classic recipe it's best if the fish are still alive or at least just out of the water. The vinegar turns their skin silvery blue, hence the name.
Makes 4 servings

4 (1-pound) fresh trout, cleaned
3 cups cold water
1 cup white vinegar
1 bouquet garni,* tied in cheesecloth
1 teaspoon salt
4 peppercorns

Sauce:
Melted butter or Hollandaise Sauce

Wipe trout with damp paper toweling. Boil remaining ingredients in a fish poacher or large kettle 2–3 minutes, add trout, cover, reduce heat, and simmer 4–5 minutes until fish just flakes when touched with a fork. Using a slotted spoon and pancake turner, carefully lift trout from water and serve at once with sauce. About 330 calories per serving (with 1 tablespoon butter or sauce). *To Serve Cold:* Cool trout in cooking liquid, lift out, chill well, and serve with Ravigote Sauce or Tartar Sauce. About 310 calories per serving (with 2 tablespoons Ravigote Sauce), 385 calories per serving (with 2 tablespoons Tartar Sauce).

VARIATION:

⊠⊠ **Carp au Bleu:** Substitute 1 (3–4-pound) cleaned carp for the trout; simmer as recipe directs 15–20 minutes. About 165 calories per serving (without sauce).

⊠ GILLIES' SKILLET TROUT

Gillies are Scottish hunting and fishing guides whose duties include cooking as well as directing sportsmen through the Highlands. Their simple way of preparing trout is delicious at home but unbeatable by a rippling mountain stream.
Makes 4 servings

4 slices bacon
4 (1-pound) trout, cleaned
1 cup unsifted flour
1½ teaspoon salt
¼ teaspoon pepper
1 cup light cream or milk

Fry bacon in a large skillet until crisp and brown; remove, drain on paper toweling, and crumble. Set aside. Dredge trout in a mixture of flour, salt, and pepper and panfry in drippings 3–5 minutes on each side until golden brown. Add cream and simmer 2 minutes, just until bubbly. Toss in bacon and serve at once with Scottish Bannock or thick chunks of bread. About 485 calories per serving if made with cream, 400 calories per serving if made with milk.

BAKED MUSHROOM-SMOTHERED TROUT

Makes 4 servings

4 (1-pound) trout, cleaned
1 teaspoon salt
¼ teaspoon pepper
½ pound mushrooms, wiped clean and sliced thin
2 tablespoons butter or margarine

1 cup heavy cream
½ cup croutons* (optional)
1 tablespoon minced parsley

Preheat oven to 400° F. Rub cavity of each trout with salt and pepper, then arrange in a single layer in a buttered, large, shallow casserole. Sauté mushrooms in butter in a skillet 3–5 minutes over moderately high heat until golden; off heat stir in cream and pour over trout. Cover loosely with foil and bake 15–20 minutes, just until trout flakes when touched with a fork. Scatter croutons and parsley on top and serve. (*Note:* If you prefer, remove heads and tails before adding croutons and parsley.) About 510 calories per serving (without croutons).

TROUT BAKED EN PAPILLOTE WITH JUNIPER BERRIES AND FENNEL

Makes 2 servings

2 (1-pound) trout, cleaned
4 tablespoons butter (no substitute)
½ teaspoon crushed juniper berries
¼ teaspoon fennel seeds
2 tablespoons minced scallions
1 teaspoon grated lemon rind
½ teaspoon salt
¼ teaspoon pepper
¼ cup dry white wine

Preheat oven to 400° F. Cut 2 pieces of foil large enough to wrap around trout and spread one side of each with about 1 tablespoon butter. Lay trout on foil, mix all remaining ingredients except wine, and sprinkle inside each trout. Dot trout with remaining butter, drizzle with wine, and wrap tightly. Lay packages side by side on a baking sheet and bake about 15–20 minutes just until trout flakes when touched with a fork. Serve trout in foil or transfer to a heated platter and top with drippings in foil. (*Note:* If you prefer, remove

heads and tails before serving.) About 460 calories per serving.

POMPANO EN PAPILLOTE

Makes 4 servings

¼ pound button mushrooms, wiped clean
4 tablespoons butter or margarine
4 pompano fillets or 4 small pompano (about 1 pound each), cleaned and dressed
1 teaspoon salt
¼ teaspoon pepper

Sauce:
½ pound mushrooms, wiped clean and minced
3 scallions, minced
2 tablespoons butter or margarine
1 cup Thick White Sauce
1 tablespoon minced parsley

Preheat oven to 425° F. Prepare sauce first: Stir-fry mushrooms and scallions in butter over moderately high heat 3–5 minutes to brown lightly; mix with remaining sauce ingredients and set aside. Sauté button mushrooms in 2 tablespoons butter over moderately high heat 3–5 minutes until lightly browned, lift out, and reserve. Butter 4 large squares of foil and in the center of each spread 2–3 tablespoons sauce. Place a fillet on each, dot with remaining butter, and sprinkle with salt and pepper. Top each fillet with 2–3 tablespoons sauce, and a few button mushrooms, then wrap tightly, using drugstore wrap. Place packets on a baking sheet and bake 20 minutes until fish just flakes (open 1 package to check and, if not done, bake a few minutes longer). Serve fish in packets. About 685 calories per serving.

VARIATION:

Tampa Pompano en Papillote: Instead of using the sauce above, mix 1 cup Thick White Sauce with 2 minced scallions, 1 tablespoon minced parsley, a pinch nutmeg, and 1 cup minced cooked shrimp or crayfish. Proceed as recipe directs. About 720 calories per serving.

⚖ PIQUANT FISH EN PAPILLOTE

Makes 6 servings

1 (4–5-pound) whole or center cut fish, cleaned and dressed (any lean or oily fish of suitable size)
1½ teaspoons salt
¼ teaspoon pepper
⅓ cup lemon juice, tarragon, red or white wine vinegar
¼ cup capers

Preheat oven to 400° F. Brush a large piece of heavy duty foil lightly with cooking oil and lay fish on top. Sprinkle with salt and pepper, bring sides of foil up slightly, pour lemon juice over fish, and scatter with capers. Wrap tightly, drugstore style, set on a baking sheet, and bake 40 minutes. Unwrap, test for flaking, and if not done rewrap and bake a little longer. Cool 5 minutes in foil, slide onto a hot platter, top with cooking juices, and serve.

VARIATION:

Fish en Papillote Cooked over Charcoal: Build a moderately hot charcoal fire.* Season and wrap fish as directed, place on grill 5″ from coals, and cook 45 minutes. Unwrap, test for flaking, and if not done rewrap and cook a little longer. Serve as directed.

Both versions: about 195 calories per serving if made with lean fish, 290 calories per serving if made with oily fish.

LEMONY BAKED STUFFED HALIBUT STEAKS

Makes 4–6 servings

2 large halibut steaks of equal size, cut ½″–¾″ thick
½ teaspoon salt
⅛ teaspoon pepper
¼ cup melted butter or margarine
Juice of 1 lemon
1 recipe Lemon Bread Stuffing for Fish

Preheat oven to 350° F. Sprinkle both sides of steaks with salt and pepper; mix butter and lemon juice and brush lightly over both sides of steaks. Place 1 steak in a well-greased shallow baking pan, cover with stuffing, and top with second steak; fasten loosely with toothpicks. Brush with butter mixture and bake, uncovered, 30–40 minutes, brushing often with remaining butter, until fish just flakes when touched with a fork. Remove toothpicks and serve hot with Parsley Sauce or Lemon Sauce or top each portion with a generous pat Maître d'Hôtel Butter. About 420 calories for each of 4 servings (without butter or sauce), about 280 calories for each of 6 servings.

⧖ CURRIED FISH STEAKS WITH SOUR CREAM SAUCE

Makes 4 servings

⅓ cup unsifted flour
1 teaspoon salt
⅛ teaspoon white pepper
3 teaspoons curry powder
4 small halibut or salmon steaks, cut ¾″–1″ thick
⅓ cup milk
¼ cup butter or margarine
1 small yellow onion, peeled and minced
½ medium-size sweet green pepper, cored, seeded, and minced
1 cup sour cream

Mix flour, salt, pepper, and 2 teaspoons curry powder. Dip steaks in milk, then in seasoned flour. Melt butter in a large, heavy skillet over moderate heat and sauté steaks 4–5 minutes on each side until golden. Transfer to a hot platter and keep warm. Stir-fry onion and pepper in drippings 3–4 minutes until limp; smooth in remaining curry powder and sour cream, and heat, stirring, 1–2 minutes; do not boil. Pour over fish and serve. About 465 calories per serving if made with halibut and 510 calories per serving if made with salmon.

FISH STEAKS DUGLÈRE

Makes 4 servings

1 small yellow onion, peeled and minced
4 medium-size tomatoes, peeled, cored, seeded, and chopped fine
1 clove garlic, peeled and crushed
¼ cup butter or margarine
4 small delicate white fish steaks (cod, halibut, pollock, sea bass, etc.), cut ¾"–1" thick
1 teaspoon salt
⅛ teaspoon white pepper
2 tablespoons minced parsley
⅛ teaspoon thyme
1 bay leaf
½ cup dry white wine
2 tablespoons flour blended with ¼ cup milk

In a large skillet sauté onion, tomatoes, and garlic in butter over moderate heat 4–5 minutes until onion is limp. Turn heat to moderately low, lay fish on vegetables, sprinkle with salt, pepper, 1 tablespoon parsley, and the thyme. Add bay leaf and wine, cover, and simmer 10 minutes until fish flakes when touched with a fork. Lift fish to a hot deep platter and keep warm. Remove bay leaf from sauce, mix in flour-milk paste, and heat, stirring constantly, until thickened and no raw starch taste remains. Taste for salt and adjust as needed. Pour sauce over fish, sprinkle with re-maining parsley, and serve. About 360 calories per serving.

DALMATIAN MARINATED FISH

Makes 4 servings

½ cup unsifted flour
1 teaspoon salt
½ teaspoon pepper
1 large tuna or halibut steak, cut 1" thick (about 2 pounds)
¼ cup olive oil

Marinade:
2 tablespoons olive oil
1 large yellow onion, peeled, sliced thin, and separated into rings
2 carrots, peeled and sliced thin
1 large dill pickle or 2 gherkins, sliced thin
1 cup dry red or white wine
6 peppercorns
3 bay leaves
1 tablespoon capers
2 tablespoons tomato paste
¼ cup minced pitted green olives

Mix flour with salt and pepper and set aside. Cut steaks into 1½" chunks, removing any bones and skin as you go; dredge chunks in seasoned flour. Heat oil in a large, heavy skillet over moderately high heat until a cube of bread will sizzle, and brown fish chunks well on all sides, about 5 minutes; drain on paper toweling. To the same skillet, add oil for marinade and stir-fry onion and carrots 5–8 minutes over moderate heat until golden. Mix in remaining marinade ingredients and simmer, stirring occasionally, 10 minutes. Place fish in a bowl, top with hot marinade, cool to room temperature, and serve. About 610 calories per serving.

TAVIRA TUNA STEAK

The men of Tavira, a small port on Portugal's Algarve coast, are tuna

fishermen, and their wives are superb cooks, as this mint-flavored tuna recipe quickly proves.
Makes 4 servings

1 large tuna steak, cut 1½" thick (about 2 pounds)
½ teaspoon salt
¼ teaspoon pepper

Marinade:
¼ cup olive oil
¼ cup dry port or sherry
2 cloves garlic, peeled and crushed
2 tablespoons minced fresh mint
2 tablespoons minced parsley
Juice of ½ lemon

Rub both sides of steak with salt and pepper; place tuna in an ungreased large, shallow baking dish or casserole. Mix marinade and pour on top; cover and marinate in refrigerator 3–4 hours, basting several times with marinade. Preheat oven to 350° F. Bake tuna, covered, 15 minutes, uncover, and bake 15–18 minutes longer, basting often with marinade, until fish will just flake. Serve from casserole, topping each portion with some of the marinade. About 465 calories per serving.

⊠ QUICK FISH STEW

Makes 4–6 servings

1 medium-size yellow onion, peeled and minced
2 scallions, minced
2 cloves garlic, peeled and crushed
¼ cup butter or margarine
2 pounds fish fillets (use any 2 of the following: cod, flounder, haddock, red snapper, sea bass)
1 (9-ounce) package frozen rock lobster tails
2 cups Easy Fish Stock or 2 (10½-ounce) cans chicken broth or 1 cup each bottled clam juice and water
1 (1-pound 12-ounce) can tomatoes (do not drain)

1 cup dry white wine
1 teaspoon salt (about)
¼ teaspoon pepper
18 mussels or little neck clams in the shell, well scrubbed (mussels should also be bearded)
1 (10-ounce) package frozen green peas
1–2 tablespoons minced parsley

In a large kettle over moderate heat, sauté onion, scallions, and garlic in butter 3–5 minutes until very pale golden. Meanwhile, cut fish in 2" chunks and slice lobster tails crosswise through the shell into 1" chunks. Add to kettle with all remaining ingredients except mussels, peas, and parsley. Break up any large clumps of tomato, cover, and simmer 10 minutes. Add peas and mussels, cover, and simmer 10 minutes longer. Sprinkle with parsley, taste for salt and adjust as needed. Ladle into soup bowls and serve with hot buttered French bread. About 505 calories for each of 4 servings (without bread), 335 calories for each of 6 servings.

BOUILLABAISSE

There are those who say you can't make Bouillabaisse unless you're from Marseille and use the local catch (especially an ugly fish called *rascasse*). But there are excellent adaptations of the classic recipe made with American fish. Here's one of them.
Makes 6 servings

1 cup minced yellow onions or scallions
½ cup minced leeks (include green tops)
2–3 cloves garlic, peeled and crushed
½ cup olive oil
1 (1-pound 12-ounce) can tomatoes (do not drain)

*1½ quarts Easy Fish Stock or a ½
and ½ mixture of water and
bottled clam juice*
1 large bouquet garni, tied in
cheesecloth*
½ teaspoon thyme
¼ teaspoon fennel seeds
½ teaspoon saffron
*1 (2") strip orange rind (orange
part only)*
1 teaspoon salt
¼ teaspoon pepper
*2 (1¼-pound) live lobsters or 2½
pounds frozen Alaska king crab
legs, cut in serving-size pieces
(include shells)*
*1 pound eel, cleaned, dressed, and
cut in 1" chunks, or 1 pound
scallops, washed well*
*1 pound halibut, haddock, sea bass,
or wolffish, cleaned, dressed, and
cut in 2" chunks*
*1 pound mackerel, tuna, or mullet,
cleaned, dressed, and cut in 2"
chunks*
*1 pound flounder fillets, cut in 2"
chunks*
*2 dozen mussels or little neck clams
in the shell, well scrubbed (mussels
should also be bearded)*
1 tablespoon minced parsley

In a 3-gallon oven-to-table kettle
sauté onions, leeks, and garlic in oil
over moderate heat 3–5 minutes
until very pale golden. Add tomatoes, breaking up clumps, stock, all
herbs and seasonings, cover, and
simmer ½ hour. Add lobsters, eel,
halibut, and mackerel, cover, and
simmer 5 minutes. Add flounder and
mussels, cover, and simmer 7–10
minutes until mussels open. Remove
bouquet garni and orange rind,
taste for salt and pepper and adjust
as needed. Ladle into hot soup plates,
sprinkle with parsley, and serve with
plenty of hot Garlic Bread. Set out
lobster crackers and picks, also
plenty of napkins. (*Note:* This
recipe is best made with live lobster.

If you can't get your fish market to
cut the live lobsters into serving-
size pieces and are squeamish about
doing it yourself, parboil the lobsters 5 minutes, then cut them up.)
About 535 calories per serving.

CACCIUCCO (ITALIAN SEAFOOD STEW)

Italians don't bone the fish for this
stew. The flavor is better with the
bones in, but the eating is more
tedious so we've called for fillet.
If you prefer, substitute equal quantities of cleaned and dressed fish.
Makes 8 servings

*1 medium-size yellow onion, peeled
and minced*
1 clove garlic, peeled and crushed
¼ cup olive oil
*1 pound squid, prepared for cooking
and cut in 2" pieces*
2 cups Easy Fish Stock or water
2 anchovy fillets, minced
*⅛ teaspoon crushed hot red chili
peppers*
2 tablespoons minced parsley
*3 ripe plum tomatoes, peeled,
seeded, and chopped fine*
2 tablespoons tomato paste
*1 pound halibut or striped bass
fillets, cut in 2" pieces*
*1 pound bluefish or red snapper
fillets, cut in 2" pieces*
*½ pound bay or sea scallops (halve
sea scallops if extra large)*
*1 pound shelled and deveined raw
shrimp*
*1 (9-ounce) package frozen rock
lobster tails, thawed and cut in 1"
chunks*
1 cup dry white wine
*4 slices Italian bread, toasted and
lightly rubbed with garlic*

Stir-fry onion and garlic in oil in a
very large, heavy kettle 3–5 minutes
over moderate heat until limp. Add
squid, stock, anchovies, chili peppers,
parsley, tomatoes, and tomato paste;

mix well, cover, and simmer ½ hour. Add all remaining ingredients except toast, cover, and simmer 15 minutes. Taste for salt and adjust as needed. Arrange toast in bottom of a large soup tureen, ladle fish and liquid on top. (*Note:* Mixture should be quite thick; if not, lift fish to tureen with a slotted spoon and boil liquid, uncovered, to reduce.) About 410 calories per serving.

⚔ ¢ SEAFOOD PROVENÇAL

Makes 6 servings

2 *pounds fillets or steaks of delicate white fish* (*cod, haddock, flounder, fluke, halibut, etc.*)
1½ *teaspoons salt*
¼ *teaspoon pepper*
1 *clove garlic, peeled and crushed*
1 *cup Easy Fish Stock*
3 *firm tomatoes, halved but not peeled*
2 *tablespoons olive or other cooking oil*
⅛ *teaspoon thyme*
½ *cup soft white bread crumbs*
2 *tablespoons melted butter or margarine*

Preheat oven to 350° F. Fold fillets envelope fashion, ends toward center, and arrange in a single layer in a well-buttered shallow 2½-quart casserole. Sprinkle with 1 teaspoon salt and ⅛ teaspoon pepper. Stir garlic into stock and pour over fish. Bake uncovered, basting 2 or 3 times, 20–30 minutes until fish will flake. Meanwhile, sauté tomatoes in oil in a skillet over moderate heat 4–5 minutes until lightly browned; keep warm. When fish is done, draw liquid off with a bulb baster. Arrange tomatoes around fish, sprinkle with thyme and remaining salt and pepper. Top with crumbs, drizzle with butter, and broil 3″–4″ from heat 1–2 minutes to brown. About 210 calories per serving.

⚔ COULIBIAC

This rich Russian fish dish is usually wrapped in brioche but it's just as good—and good-looking—made this superquick way with packaged, refrigerated dough. Much lower calorie, too.
Makes 12–14 servings

2 (*8-ounce*) *packages refrigerated dough for crescent rolls*
2 *cups cooked seasoned kasha or rice*
2 *cups skinned, boned, flaked cooked salmon*
3 *hard-cooked eggs, shelled and sliced thin*

Sauce:
4 *scallions, minced*
½ *pound mushrooms, wiped clean and coarsely chopped*
2 *tablespoons butter or margarine*
2 *tablespoons flour*
1 *cup Easy Fish Stock or water*
2 *tablespoons tomato purée*
1 *teaspoon salt*
⅛ *teaspoon pepper*
1 *teaspoon chervil*
1 *teaspoon tarragon*
1 *tablespoon minced parsley*

Glaze:
1 *egg, lightly beaten with 1 tablespoon water*

Preheat oven to 375° F. Make sauce first: Stir-fry scallions and mushrooms in butter in a large saucepan over moderate heat 3–5 minutes until limp; blend in flour, slowly add stock, and heat, stirring, until thickened. Off heat, mix in remaining ingredients; cool 10 minutes. Meanwhile, open 1 package of dough, spread flat, halve crosswise but do not separate into individual rolls. Fit halves together on an ungreased baking sheet so you have a rectangle about 9″×14″; pinch edges together to seal, also press all perforations closed so you have an unbroken sheet of dough. Spread 1½ cups *kasha* over dough, leaving ½″ margins all around, cover with fish, spread with sauce, then top with eggs and remaining kasha. Shape second roll of dough into an unbroken sheet just like the first and lay on top of filling, letting edges hang over. Brush edges of bottom dough lightly with egg glaze, bring up over top edges and pinch together to seal. Make 6 steam slits in top of coulibiac. Brush glaze over dough and bake, uncovered, on center rack ½ hour. Carefully ease onto a hot serving platter. To serve, cut straight across in thick slices. About 290 calories for each of 12 servings, 245 calories for each of 14 servings.

⚖ GEFILTE FISH

Makes 6 servings

1½ pounds delicate white fish (carp, pike, or haddock, etc.), cleaned, dressed, and filleted (save head, skin, and bones)
1½ pounds oily fish (whitefish or mackerel, etc.), cleaned, dressed, and filleted (save head, skin, and bones)
2 large onions, peeled and sliced thin
2 large carrots, peeled and sliced ½″ thick
2 stalks celery, coarsely chopped (include tops)
1½ quarts cold water
3½ teaspoons salt (about)
½ teaspoon pepper
1 large yellow onion, peeled and minced
2 eggs, lightly beaten
½ cup soft white bread crumbs or matzo meal
¼ cup ice water

Place fish heads, skin, and bones in a 6-quart kettle, add onion slices, carrots, celery, water, 2 teaspoons salt, and ¼ teaspoon pepper. Cover and simmer while preparing fish. Put fish through finest blade of meat grinder with minced onion, or place in a large chopping bowl and chop until fine or purée, a little at a time, in an electric blender at low speed. Mix with remaining salt and pepper, eggs, crumbs, and ice water. Wet hands and shape into egg-sized balls. Lower into simmering broth with a wet spoon, cover, and simmer 1½ hours. Cool balls to room temperature in broth, lift to a bowl with a slotted spoon. Strain broth over balls, then add carrot slices. Cover and chill overnight. Serve gefilte fish with some of the jellied broth and carrots, also with white or red prepared horseradish. About 180 calories per serving.

VARIATION:
⚖ Prepare as directed, adding 1 finely grated carrot to fish mixture just before shaping. About 185 calories per serving.

ESCABECHE DE PESCADO (MEXICAN PICKLED FISH)

Makes 4–6 entree servings, enough appetizers for 10

2 pounds red snapper or other delicate white fish fillets, cut in 2″ squares
1 teaspoon salt
¼ teaspoon pepper
⅓ cup unsifted flour
¼ cup cooking oil

Marinade:
1 medium-size yellow onion, peeled, sliced thin, and separated into rings
1 carrot, peeled and sliced ¼″ thick
5 cloves garlic, peeled and minced
1 cup olive oil
1 cup cider vinegar
Juice of 1 lime
⅓ cup hot water
1 teaspoon salt
¼ teaspoon pepper
1 teaspoon thyme
2 bay leaves

1 *tablespoon minced parsley*
2 *pimientos, seeded and coarsely
   chopped*
¼ *teaspoon crushed hot red chili
   peppers*

Sprinkle fish with salt and pepper and dredge lightly in flour. Heat oil in a large, heavy skillet over moderately high heat and brown fish quickly, about 2 minutes on a side; drain on paper toweling. In a separate skillet, begin marinade: Stir-fry onion, carrot, and garlic in ¼ cup olive oil over moderate heat 3–5 minutes until limp. Mix in remaining marinade ingredients including remaining olive oil, and simmer, uncovered, 10–15 minutes. Arrange fish 2 or 3 layers deep in a large glass, porcelain, or stainless-steel bowl. Pour in marinade, cool to room temperature, then cover and chill 24 hours. Toss mixture gently and serve, topping fish with some of the marinade. About 340 calories for each of 4 entree servings, 225 calories for each of 6 entree servings (add 65 calories for each tablespoon of marinade used). About 135 calories for each of 10 appetizer servings.

VARIATIONS:

Pickled Tuna: Substitute 2 pounds boneless tuna for white fish and prepare as directed. About 425 calories for each of 4 servings, 285 for each of 6, 170 for each of 10.

⚖ **Shellfish Escabeche:** Substitute 2 pounds cooked lobster meat; boiled, shelled, and deveined shrimp; lump or backfin crab meat or *raw* bay scallops for the fish. Do not fry; place in bowl, top with hot marinade, and proceed as directed. If made with scallops: about 185 calories for each of 4 servings, 125 for each of 6, 75 for each of 10. If made with lobster or crab: about 220 calories

for each of 4 servings, 145 calories for each of 6, 90 for each of 10 servings. If made with shrimp: 265 calories for each of 4 servings, 175 for each of 6, 105 for each of 10.

CEVICHE (PERUVIAN RAW PICKLED FISH)

To be really authentic, serve as a main course with hot boiled sweet potatoes, peeled and sliced in thick rounds, and chunks of fresh corn on the cob.
Makes 2–3 main course servings, enough appetizers for 6

1 *pound flounder, fluke, halibut, or
   other firm-fleshed, delicate white
   fish fillets*
3 *medium-size yellow onions, peeled,
   sliced thin, and separated into rings*
3 *medium-size hot red chili peppers,
   cored, seeded, and cut in thin strips*
3 *medium-size Italian sweet peppers
   or 1 sweet green pepper, cored,
   seeded, and cut in thin strips*
¾ *cup lime juice*
¾ *cup lemon juice*
1 *tablespoon olive oil*
½ *clove garlic, peeled and crushed*
½ *teaspoon salt*
2 *tablespoons minced parsley*

Cut raw fillets into strips about 3″ long and ½″ wide and place in a large glass, porcelain, or stainless-steel bowl. Add all remaining ingredients except parsley and toss well to mix. Cover and chill 24 hours, turning mixture often. When ready to serve, toss again and sprinkle with parsley. Lift out fish and top each portion with some of the vegetables and 1–2 spoonfuls of marinade. About 315 calories for each of 2 entree servings, 210 calories for each of 3, and 105 for each of 6 appetizer servings.

VARIATION:

Scallops Ceviche: Prepare as directed, substituting 2 pounds whole raw bay scallops for the fish. About 510 calories for each of 2 entree servings, 340 calories for each of 3 entree servings, and 170 calories for each of 6 appetizer servings.

⚮ SASHIMI (JAPANESE-STYLE RAW FISH AND VEGETABLES)

If you're squeamish about eating raw fish, skip this recipe. If not, prepare as the Japanese do, paying great attention to the artistic arrangement of fish and garnishes on small colored plates. Serve as an appetizer or main course with *sake*.
Makes 6 main course servings, enough appetizers for 10

2 *pounds fresh pompano, red snapper, or tuna fillets*
1 *cucumber, sliced paper thin (do not peel)*
Watercress sprigs

Condiments:
Soy sauce
½ *cup minced white radishes*
⅓ *cup minced fresh gingerroot*
¼ *cup prepared horseradish*
Powdered mustard
Mirin or dry sherry

Insist that the fish is *ocean*-fresh; chill well, then with an extra-sharp knife, slice ⅛″ thick across the grain and slightly on the bias. Cut slices into strips about 1″×2″ and arrange slightly overlapping on 6 individual plates. Cover and chill until near serving time.

Setting Up the Sashimi: At each place set out a small bowl of soy sauce and, in the center of the table, group colorful bowls of minced radishes, gingerroot, horseradish, and mustard, each with its own spoon, around a bottle of *mirin* or sherry.

Serving the Sashimi: Arrange cucumber slices and watercress sprigs on plates with raw fish and set on larger plates filled with crushed ice.

Eating Sashimi: Before anyone eats anything, he mixes a dip by adding a little of the condiments in the center of the table to his bowl of soy sauce. The procedure is then simply to pick up slices of raw fish or cucumber, one at a time, with chopsticks or fork, dip in sauce, and eat. If made with red snapper: about 160 calories for each of 6 entree servings, 95 for each of 10 appetizer servings. If made with pompano: 270 calories for each of 6 servings, 160 for each of 10 appetizer servings. If made with tuna: 215 calories for each of 6 entree servings and 130 for each of 10 appetizer servings.

VARIATION:

⚮ Scallops Sashimi: Instead of using thin slices of raw fish, substitute 2 pounds tiny whole raw bay scallops, well washed and chilled. About 140 calories for each of 6 entree servings and 85 calories for each of 10 appetizer servings.

⊠ SALMON CHEDDAR CASSEROLE

Makes 4 servings

1 *(1-pound) can salmon, drained*
1 *cup cooked rice (leftover is perfect)*
1 *(4-ounce) can sliced mushrooms, drained*
1 *(11-ounce) can Cheddar cheese soup (do not dilute)*
2 *tablespoons onion flakes*
2 *tablespoons dry white wine*
¼ *teaspoon thyme*
¼ *teaspoon salt*
⅛ *teaspoon pepper*

Topping:
⅓ cup cracker meal mixed with 2
  tablespoons melted butter or
  margarine

Preheat oven to 375° F. Pick
over salmon, removing any dark
skin or coarse bones; mix with
remaining ingredients except topping
and spoon into a lightly buttered
shallow 1½-quart casserole. Sprinkle
topping over surface and bake,
uncovered, 1 hour until lightly
browned and bubbly. About 350
calories per serving.

DILLY SALMON LOAF

Makes 6–8 servings

2 (1-pound) cans salmon (do not
  drain)
2 cups coarse soda cracker crumbs
⅓ cup minced yellow onion
¼ cup minced sweet green pepper
2 tablespoons minced fresh dill or 1
  teaspoon dried dill
3 eggs
1 tablespoon lemon juice
1 teaspoon Worcestershire sauce
½ cup evaporated milk
⅛ teaspoon white pepper

Preheat oven to 325° F. Pick over
salmon, removing any coarse bones
and dark skin, then flake. Add remaining ingredients and mix well,
using your hands. Pack into a well-
greased 9″×5″×3″ loaf pan and
bake, uncovered, about 1 hour and
20 minutes until lightly browned
and firm to the touch. Let loaf stand
upright in pan 5 minutes before turning out. Serve hot or cold. Particularly good with Sour Cream
Cucumber Sauce. About 365 calories
for each of 6 servings, 275 calories
for each of 8 servings (without
sauce).

TUNA AND CAPER SOUFFLÉ

Makes 4 servings

¼ cup butter or margarine
2 tablespoons minced yellow onion
¼ cup unsifted flour
1 cup milk or evaporated milk
½ teaspoon salt
⅛ teaspoon white pepper
4 eggs, separated (at room
  temperature)
1 (7-ounce) can tuna, drained and
  flaked
1 tablespoon minced parsley
1 tablespoon minced drained capers
½ teaspoon dill
¼ teaspoon cream of tartar

Melt butter in a small saucepan
over moderate heat, add onion, and
stir-fry 3–5 minutes until limp; blend
in flour, slowly add milk, and heat,
stirring, until thickened; turn heat to
low and mix in salt and pepper.
Beat egg yolks lightly, blend in a
little hot sauce, then return to pan.
Heat and stir 1–2 minutes but do not
boil. Off heat, mix in tuna, parsley,
capers, and dill. Place a piece of
wax paper flat on the surface of the
sauce to prevent a "skin" from
forming, and cool to room temperature. Preheat oven to 350° F.
Beat egg whites until foamy, add
cream of tartar, and continue beating until stiff but not dry. Stir about
¼ cup egg whites into sauce, then
fold in remainder. Spoon into an
ungreased 1½-quart soufflé dish and
bake, uncovered, 45–50 minutes
until puffy and browned. Serve at
once. Good with Caper or Parsley
Sauce. About 310 calories per
serving.

VARIATION:

Salmon Soufflé: Prepare as directed,
substituting 1 cup flaked cooked or
canned salmon for the tuna. About
330 calories per serving.

⊠ MADRAS TUNA

A spicy, sweet-sour curry.
Makes 4 servings

1 *medium-size yellow onion, peeled and minced*
½ *clove garlic, peeled and crushed*
6 *tablespoons butter or margarine*
6 *tablespoons flour*
3 *tablespoons curry powder*
½ *teaspoon salt*
¼ *teaspoon cayenne pepper*
1 *(13-ounce) can evaporated milk*
1¼ *cups milk*
¼ *cup minced, drained chutney*
1 *(7-ounce) can tuna, drained and flaked*

Stir-fry onion and garlic in butter in a large, heavy skillet 5–8 minutes over moderate heat until golden; blend in flour, curry powder, salt, and pepper. Add evaporated milk and milk and heat, stirring constantly, until thickened and smooth. Stir in chutney and tuna and heat, stirring, 3–5 minutes. Serve over boiled rice accompanied, if you like, with chutney, flaked coconut, and chopped toasted peanuts. About 480 calories per serving.

☒ QUICK TUNA SURPRISE

Makes 6 servings

2 *(10½-ounce) cans condensed cream of mushroom soup (do not dilute)*
½ *cup milk*
1 *(8-ounce) jar Cheddar cheese spread*
1 *teaspoon prepared mild yellow mustard*
2 *(7-ounce) cans tuna, drained well and flaked*
1 *(10-ounce) package frozen green peas*

Blend soup and milk in a saucepan until smooth; add cheese. Heat over moderate heat, stirring constantly, until cheese melts. Lightly mix in all remaining ingredients except peas, cover, and simmer 6–7 minutes until heated through; stir occa-sionally. Meanwhile, cook peas by package directions but add no salt; drain well. Mix peas into creamed tuna and serve over hot biscuits, toast, waffles, boiled noodles or rice, or in baked frozen puff pastry shells. About 410 calories per serving (without biscuits, toast, waffles, noodles, rice, or puff pastry shells).

⚛ TUNA NIÇOISE

A cooling summer luncheon entree made with tuna, ripe olives, and tomatoes.
Makes 6 servings

2 *(7-ounce) cans white meat tuna, drained and flaked*
1 *yellow onion, peeled and chopped fine*
½ *clove garlic, peeled and crushed*
2 *tablespoons capers*
¼ *cup coarsely chopped ripe olives*
1 *stalk celery, chopped fine*
1 *tablespoon minced parsley*
1 *tablespoon minced fresh basil or tarragon or ½ teaspoon of the dried*
1 *tablespoon minced fresh chives*
3 *tablespoons olive oil*
⅓ *cup mayonnaise*
⅛ *teaspoon pepper*
6 *large, crisped lettuce cups or 6 large ripe tomatoes, hollowed out*

Mix together all ingredients except lettuce cups or tomatoes, cover, and chill several hours. Mound into lettuce cups or tomatoes and serve. About 260 calories per serving if served in lettuce cups, 290 calories per serving if served in tomatoes.

EELS

Though eels are fish, they aren't treated exactly like fish because of their unusual shape. Their meat is surprisingly tender and much less "fishy" than you would expect. There is no season on eels, and in addition to being sold fresh they are also available smoked, canned, and frozen. Frozen eels should be thawed before cooking, then prepared like fresh eels. The canned and smoked are best used in casseroles or salads or marinated and served cold as appetizers.

Amount Needed: About ⅓–½ pound eel per serving. Eels sometimes weigh as much as 25 or 30 pounds, but those sold in fish markets range from 1 to 4.

For Top Quality: Buy eel live from a tank *but* make sure the market skins and cleans it before you take it home.

How to Skin and Clean Eel: This is hard work, so brace yourself (which is why you should have the job done for you if at all possible). First, score neck skin just behind head and tie a strong string around it. Nail or fasten string to a wall or post and peel back a bit of the skin, just enough to get a grip on (sprinkle salt or sand on your hands so eel won't slip through them so easily). Peel skin back toward tail, using pliers if necessary to get a stronger grip. Cut off head, slit belly from neck to vent, remove stomach and intestines. Rinse eel under cool running water.

How to Cook Eels

Most of the basic methods of cooking fish are suitable for eels *except* that they need slight adaptation because of the eels' shape.

General Preparation (for all cooking methods): Wash eel well. If eel has a black covering membrane (this in addition to the skin, which has been removed), it's advisable to remove it by blanching so eel will be more attractive. Blanching is es-

pecially recommended if eel is to be sautéed, deep fat fried, or mixed into a casserole or salad.

To Blanch: Coil eel in a large saucepan or, if extra large, cut in 2″ chunks. Cover with cold water, add 1 tablespoon lemon juice for each quart, cover, and boil 5 minutes. Drain and cool under cold running water until easy to handle, then peel off membrane.

To Oven Broil: Preheat broiler. Cut eel in 2″–4″ lengths, blanch, and pat dry on paper toweling. Broil 4″–5″ from the heat 5–6 minutes, brushing with melted butter or margarine and turning often so eel browns evenly. Serve with Maître d'Hôtel Butter or any suitable sauce (see Sauces, Butters, and Seasonings for Seafood).

To Panfry (*Sauté*): Cut eel in 2″ chunks, blanch, and pat dry on paper toweling. Dip in milk, then dredge in flour lightly seasoned with salt and pepper and sauté in 3–4 tablespoons butter, margarine, or cooking oil 5–7 minutes, turning occasionally, until lightly browned. Drain on paper toweling and serve as is or with Parsley Sauce or Tartar Sauce.

VARIATIONS:

Eel à la Meunière: Sauté eel as directed, transfer to a hot platter, sprinkle with lemon juice and minced parsley and keep warm. Add 1–2 tablespoons butter to skillet, heat until lightly browned and bubbly, pour over eel, and serve.

Breaded Fried Eel: Cut eel in 2″ chunks, blanch, and pat dry on paper toweling. Dip in seasoned flour and a mixture of beaten egg and milk (2 tablespoons milk for each egg), then roll in fine dry crumbs or cracker meal. Sauté as directed.

To Deep-Fat-Fry: Blanch and bread eel as for panfrying, then deep-fry 3–4 minutes in 375° F. fat until crisply browned. Drain on paper toweling before serving.

VARIATION:

Batter-Fried Eel: Prepare batter given in Fish and Chips recipe. Cut eel in 2″ chunks, blanch, and pat dry on paper toweling. Dip in batter, then deep fry in 375° F. fat 3–4 minutes until golden brown. Drain and serve.

To Poach: Cut eel in 2″ lengths, cover with lightly salted water (1 teaspoon salt to 2 cups water) or Simple Court Bouillon, and simmer covered 15–20 minutes until flesh will just flake. Drain and serve hot with Parsley Sauce or Velouté Sauce or, if you prefer, chill and serve cold with Sauce Verte.

JELLIED EELS

Makes 4 entree servings, enough appetizers for 8–10

2 (1½-pound) eels, skinned, cleaned, and dressed and cut in 2″ lengths
1 cup each dry white wine and water or 2 cups Easy Fish Stock
1 medium-size yellow onion, peeled and coarsely chopped
1 small carrot, peeled and sliced thick
2 tablespoons lemon juice
1 bay leaf
1 sprig parsley
4 peppercorns
1 clove garlic, peeled (optional)
1 teaspoon salt
1 envelope unflavored gelatin

Place all ingredients except gelatin in a large saucepan, cover, and simmer 15–20 minutes until eels are tender; cool eels in broth until easy to handle. Strain broth into a clean saucepan, sprinkle in gelatin, and heat, stirring, over moderate heat until gelatin dissolves. Take eel meat from bones, place in a bowl, and pour in broth. Cover and chill until firm. Unmold on a platter or break up with a fork and serve chunks of jelly with eel. Good with mayonnaise. About 620 calories for each of 4 entree servings (without mayonnaise), 310 calories for each of 8 appetizer servings, and 250 calories for each of 10 appetizers.

NORMANDY-STYLE EEL STEW

Eels cooked in apple cider.
Makes 4 servings

2 (1½-pound) eels, skinned, cleaned, dressed, and cut in 2″ lengths
1 medium-size yellow onion, peeled and minced
1 carrot, peeled and cut in small dice
1 stalk celery, chopped fine
1 teaspoon salt (about)
⅛ teaspoon pepper
¼ teaspoon thyme
1 bay leaf
2 cups apple cider
¼ cup butter or margarine
¼ cup unsifted flour
½ cup heavy cream
1 egg yolk, lightly beaten

Garnishes:
1 tablespoon minced parsley
½ recipe Pan-Braised Onions
1 recipe Sautéed Mushrooms (use button mushrooms)

Place eels, onion, carrot, celery, seasonings, and cider in a large saucepan over moderate heat, cover, and simmer 15–20 minutes until eels are fork tender; pour off liquid, strain, and reserve. Melt butter in a saucepan over moderate heat, blend in flour, slowly mix in reserved broth and cream, and heat, stirring, until thickened. Spoon a little hot sauce into egg yolk, then return to pan; add eels and heat, stirring, over lowest heat just long enough to warm eels. Serve in a tureen sprinkled with parsley and garnished with clusters of onions and mushrooms. Pass hot French bread. About 1,095 calories per serving (without French bread).

ENGLISH EEL AND EGG PIE

Makes 6 servings

2 (1½-pound) eels, skinned, cleaned, dressed, and cut in 2" lengths
1 teaspoon salt
⅛ teaspoon pepper
1 cup hot Thin White Sauce
Pinch nutmeg
1 teaspoon lemon juice
3 hard-cooked eggs, shelled and sliced thin
1 recipe Flaky Pastry I
1 egg, lightly beaten (optional glaze)

Preheat oven to 425° F. Blanch eels and peel off thin black membrane*; arrange in a buttered 1½-quart casserole, sprinkle with salt and pepper. Mix sauce with nutmeg and lemon juice, spoon over eels, and top with eggs. Prepare pastry and roll into a circle about 3" larger in diameter than the casserole; cut steam vents in the center, fit over casserole, and crimp edge to seal. If you like, brush pastry with beaten egg to glaze. Bake ½ hour until pastry is golden. To serve, cut pastry into wedges and top with eel mixture. About 685 calories per serving.

ROE

There are two types of roe: *hard* (female eggs inside a delicate membrane) and the less familiar *soft roe* (milt or sperm, also wrapped in a tissue-thin membrane). Shad roe is the most highly prized (possibly because of its short season and

scarcity), though that of herring, cod, mackerel, mullet, flounder, and whitefish are all delicious. Sizes of roe vary enormously, from the bite-size herring roe to the medium-size shad roe (5"–6" long and 3" across) to the huge cod roe (it weighs from 1 pound to 3 or more). All hard roe has a slightly gritty texture when cooked but delicate flavor; all is a high protein food rich in B vitamins. Soft roe is paler (almost white), blander, and creamier than hard roe. The choicest comes from carp, herring, and mackerel, in that order. Like hard roe, it is highly nutritious.

Season: Spring, *early* spring for shad roe, usually March and April or, as New Englanders say, "When the shad bush blooms."

Amount Needed: Allow ¼–⅓ pound per person. If the roe is very small, you will need several pair per person; with shad roe, 1 pair per person is ample. Larger roe will serve more than 1 person.

For Top Quality: Look for moist, firm, unbroken roe with a clean, fresh smell.

About Frozen and Canned Roe

In addition to being marketed fresh, hard roe is also available frozen and canned. When salted, it becomes *caviar* (see discussion in chapter on Appetizers and Hors d'Oeuvre). Not every roe becomes caviar, however. The most delectable (black, but sometimes gray or gold) is from sturgeon, the next best (red) is from salmon. Three great pretenders are roe of lumpfish, paddlefish, and whitefish, cleverly salted and colored black.

How to Cook Frozen Roe: Thaw completely in the refrigerator, then prepare like fresh roe.

How to Prepare Canned Roe:
Brown gently in butter and serve.

How to Cook Fresh Roe

Easy does it! All roe is fragile and must be given kid-glove care. Too much heat will shatter it or dry it out, too much seasoning will mask its subtle flavor. The more simply roe is cooked, the better it will be.

General Preparation:

Hard Roe: Wash *very* gently in a bowl of cool water and pat dry on paper toweling. Some cooks recommend pricking the covering membrane several places with a needle to keep it from bursting during cooking. But if the roe is cooked *gently*— as it should be—the membrane isn't likely to burst.

Soft Roe: Wash carefully in a bowl of cool water, using the lightest possible touch; pull away the blue vein running along one side of roe. Lift roe from water and pat dry on paper toweling.

To Oven Broil (for hard roe of medium size only): This is a pretty risky way to cook roe; broiler heat is simply too intense for delicate roe and tends to shatter and shrink it. But, there are people who dote upon broiled roe, so . . . Preheat broiler. Have roe at or near room temperature to reduce chances of shattering and slather with melted butter or margarine. Place in a well-buttered piepan and broil 4″ from the heat, 4–5 minutes on a side, basting often with additional melted butter. Turn roe only once and use a pancake turner, handling lightly so membrane doesn't break. (*Note:* Some books recommend parboiling roe 10 minutes in lightly salted boiling water before broiling to reduce chances of bursting. Try it, if

you like, but don't expect the roe to have much flavor.)

To Panfry (*Sauté*): Here's the best method for hard and soft roe. Have roe at or near room temperature. Dip in milk, then dredge in flour lightly seasoned with salt and pepper. Place in a *cold* skillet with melted butter (allow ¼ cup butter for each 1 pound roe) and sauté slowly over moderate heat until lightly browned. Small roe will take about 2 minutes on a side, medium-size roe 3½–4 minutes per side. Turn roe one time only and handle very carefully. (*Note:* Large roe, that of cod, for example, should be poached by the method below, patted dry on paper toweling, then just browned lightly, about 5 minutes on each side in the butter.) Serve the sautéed roe as is, topped with some of the pan juices. Or serve on lightly buttered toast, drizzled with Lemon Butter. (*Note:* Large roe is usually broken into smaller pieces, then served in the same way as smaller roe.)

VARIATIONS:

Roe à la Meunière: Sauté as directed, transfer to a hot platter, and sprinkle with lemon juice and a little minced parsley. Add 1–2 tablespoons butter to skillet, heat until bubbly and the color of topaz, pour over roe and serve.

Breaded Fried Roe: Dredge roe in flour lightly seasoned with salt and pepper, dip in a mixture of beaten egg and milk (2 tablespoons milk for each egg), then roll in fine dry crumbs or cracker meal to coat. Sauté as directed.

To Poach: Arrange roe in a large, heavy skillet (not iron), add cold water barely to cover; for each 2 cups water, add ½ teaspoon salt and 1 tablespoon lemon juice. Cover skillet and simmer roe over moderately low heat (water should just tremble) as follows: 5 minutes for small roe, 10 minutes for medium-size roe or large roe that is to be sautéed after poaching, and 15–20 minutes for large roe that is to be poached only. When done, roe will be white and firm (but not hard). Drizzle with Parsley or Herb Butter and serve. Large roe can be broken into chunks and smothered with Béchamel, Poulette, or Shrimp Sauce or drizzled with seasoned melted butter.

SHELLFISH

BASIC SHELLFISH CROQUETTES

If croquettes are to be light and crisp, and not the least bit greasy, the deep fat must be good and hot—in this case, 375° F.
Makes 4 servings

3 tablespoons butter or margarine
3 tablespoons flour
1 cup milk or light cream
½ teaspoon salt
⅛ teaspoon liquid hot red pepper seasoning
1 tablespoon minced parsley
1 tablespoon minced fresh dill or ½ teaspoon dried dill
1 egg, lightly beaten
1½ cups soft white bread crumbs
1½ cups minced, cooked lobster, shrimp, crab meat, scallops, clams, mussels, or oysters
1 tablespoon lemon or lime juice
Shortening or cooking oil for deep fat frying

Coating:
1 egg, lightly beaten
1 cup cracker meal or toasted, packaged, seasoned bread crumbs

Melt butter in a saucepan over

moderate heat and blend in flour; slowly add milk and heat, stirring, until thickened. Off heat, mix in seasonings, egg, crumbs, shellfish, and lemon juice; cover and chill 3–4 hours. Shape into 8 patties or small balls, dip in egg, and roll in cracker meal to coat. Let stand at room temperature on a wire rack while heating fat. Place shortening in a deep fat fryer and heat to 375° F.; use a deep fat thermometer. Place 3 or 4 croquettes in fryer basket, lower into hot fat, and fry 2–3 minutes until golden brown and crisp; drain on paper toweling, then keep warm while you fry the rest by setting uncovered in oven turned to lowest heat. Serve hot with Tartar Sauce. If made with scallops, clams, mussels, or oysters: about 405 calories per serving (without Tartar Sauce). If made with lobster, shrimp, or crab: about 425 calories per serving.

BASIC SHELLFISH SOUFFLÉ

Delicate but not difficult to make.
Makes 4 servings

¼ cup butter or margarine
¼ cup unsifted flour
1 cup light cream
½ teaspoon salt
⅛ teaspoon white pepper
⅛ teaspoon nutmeg or mace
4 eggs, separated (at room temperature)
1 cup finely chopped cooked shrimp, lobster, or crab meat
¼ teaspoon cream of tartar

Melt butter in a small saucepan over moderate heat, blend in flour, slowly add cream, and heat, stirring, until thickened and smooth; mix in salt, pepper and nutmeg and turn heat to low. Beat egg yolks lightly, blend in a little hot sauce, then return to saucepan. Heat and stir 1–2 minutes but do not allow to boil. Off heat, mix in shellfish; lay a piece of wax paper flat on surface of sauce to prevent a "skin" from forming, and cool to room temperature. Preheat oven to 350° F. Beat egg whites until foamy, add cream of tartar, and continue beating until stiff but not dry. Stir about ¼ cup egg white into sauce, then carefully fold in remainder. Spoon into an ungreased 1½-quart soufflé dish and bake, uncovered, about 45 minutes until puffy and tinged with brown. Rush to the table and serve. Good with Shrimp Sauce or Sauce Américaine.

VARIATION:

Herbed Shellfish Soufflé: Prepare as directed but add 1 tablespoon minced parsley and 1 tablespoon minced fresh dill, tarragon, or chervil to sauce along with shellfish.

Both versions: About 385 calories per serving (without sauce).

ABALONE

You must go to California to find fresh abalone, and even then you may not succeed because the supply is scarce. Laws now limit the number and size of abalone that can be taken, also the season for taking them. These giant mollusks are "fished" by skin divers who pry them off rocks with crowbars. Not everyone likes abalone; in fact, many people consider them more trouble than they're worth (badly cooked, they can be very tough). Frozen abalone steaks from Japan and Mexico are sold in gourmet markets; canned minced abalone is also available.

Amount to Buy: 1 pound abalone in the shell per person; about ⅓ pound abalone meat.

For Top Quality: Buy only abalone with shells clamped shut or, better yet, go after your own and bring them home alive.

How to Open and Clean Abalone: If you've caught, bought, or been given a live abalone, here's what to do with it. Force a wooden or metal wedge between the meat and the shell and move around the rim of the shell until the abalone gives up and drops from the shell. Cut off the end that was next to the shell, taking care not to break the sack. Wash meat well in cool water, then trim away all tough, dark portions around the edges (these can be used in soups or stews if you like).

How to Cook Abalone

The classic dish is abalone steak, sometimes breaded, sometimes not, but always sautéed quickly in butter. The meat can also be minced or ground for use in soups, stews, and fritters.

General Preparation for Steaks: If abalone is in 1 large piece, slice across the grain into steaks, making each slightly more than ¼" thick. To tenderize, pound each steak with a wooden mallet or edge of a plate, using a light, rhythmic motion until muscles relax and abalone is limp and velvety. (*Note:* Most frozen steaks have already been tenderized and are ready to cook [read label carefully].)

SAVORY ABALONE STEW

Makes 4 servings

2 abalone steaks, cut a little more than ¼" thick and pounded until tender
1 large yellow onion, peeled and minced
1 clove garlic, peeled and crushed
⅓ cup minced sweet green pepper

¼ cup butter or margarine
1 bay leaf, crumbled
½ teaspoon oregano
¼ teaspoon basil
1 (8-ounce) can tomato sauce
2 cups water
2 large potatoes, peeled and cut in
   ½" cubes
½ teaspoon salt
¼ teaspoon cayenne pepper

Cut abalone in ¼"–½" cubes and set aside. Stir-fry onion, garlic, and green pepper in butter in a large saucepan 5–8 minutes over moderate heat until onion is pale golden; mix in all remaining ingredients except abalone, cover, and simmer 10–12 minutes until potatoes are almost tender. Add abalone and simmer 5–8 minutes longer until abalone and potatoes are tender. Ladle into hot soup bowls and serve as a main course with chunks of Italian bread and a crisp green salad. About 350 calories per serving.

⚖ ☒ ABALONE STEAKS
Makes 4 servings

¼ cup butter or margarine
4 abalone steaks, cut a little more
   than ¼" thick and pounded until
   tender
Salt
Pepper

Melt butter in a large, heavy skillet over moderately high heat, and when it begins to bubble, add abalone steaks and sauté just 1 minute on each side. Sprinkle with salt and pepper and serve. About 220 calories per serving.

VARIATION:

⚖ **Breaded Abalone Steaks:** Mix ⅔ cup unsifted flour with 1 teaspoon salt and ¼ teaspoon pepper; beat 2 eggs with 2 tablespoons cold water until frothy. Dredge steaks in flour, dip in egg, then in fine dry bread crumbs to coat evenly. Sauté as above, allowing just enough time on each side to brown crumbs lightly. About 250 calories per serving.

CLAMS

Clams were probably the first New World food sampled by Pilgrims. They arrived ravenous after weeks at sea, fell upon the New England beaches in search of food and found hard and soft clams by the bucketful. Later, they learned from the Indians how to roast clams over open fires, to simmer them into soups and stews, and to layer them into pits with corn, potatoes, and lobsters in that most convivial of picnics, the clambake.

The Kinds of Clams

The terminology is confusing because there are so many different kinds of clams, also because each has several names. Here's a quick roundup:

East Coast Clams: There are two types, the hard and soft shell.

Hard Shell Clams: These are also called by the Indian name, *quahog,* and come in three sizes: *large or chowder* (at least 3" in diameter and best for chowders or stuffed clams); *cherrystones* or medium (about 2" across and good for steaming or eating on the half shell), and *littlenecks* or small (1½" across and usually reserved for eating on the half shell).

Soft Clams or Steamers: The shells are long, thin, and oval and the clams inside are long, too, and stick long black necks outside their shells (explaining their nickname, *longneck*). These are the clams harvested along beaches and mud flats, the lightning-quick burrowers.

West Coast Clams: Most famous of the 35-plus varieties are:

Butter Clams: Sweet-meated little clams from the Puget Sound area that are best eaten on the half shell. Indians used them as money, so they're also called *moneyshells*.

Geoduck (pronounced gooey-duck): These long-necked monsters are fun to dig at low tide but rarely appear in markets.

Mud Clams: Popular, large oval clams found along the Northern California and Oregon coasts; only the white flesh is eaten.

Pismo Clams: One of the choicest Pacific clams; it is big, tender and sweet—and becoming scarce. Only clams measuring 5″ across or more may be taken. The tender adductor muscle is often served on the half shell, the body meat is usually fried, hashed, or minced into chowders. The name Pismo comes from Pismo Beach, California, where these clams were first found.

Razor Clams: These, so named because their long slender shells resemble the old-fashioned barber's razor, are so delectable many gourmets rate them higher than the Eastern soft clams.

About Buying Fresh Clams

Season:

East Coast Varieties: Year round.

West Coast Varieties: Year round in the Pacific Northwest. In California the season is shorter, usually November through April. Spring and summer are the time of the dread "red tide" when microscopic organisms fill the sea, making clams and certain other shellfish unsafe to eat. At such times, many clamming beaches are closed.

Popular Market Forms: Atlantic and Pacific clams are both sold live and in the shell either by the dozen or pound; they are also sold shucked by the pint or quart. In addition, many markets, if asked, will remove the top shells and prepare clams for serving or cooking on the half shell.

Amount Needed: The quantity varies tremendously according to the size of the clams, how they are cooked and served, not to mention appetites. Here's a general guide:

Clams on the Half Shell: Allow 6–8 small- or medium-size clams per person.

Steamed or Stewed Clams: Allow 1–1½ dozen clams per serving, depending on size of clams and richness of broth.

Shucked Clams: 1 pint will serve 3–4, more if stretched with other ingredients.

For Top Quality:

Clams in the Shell: Look for tightly closed clams, or at least those that "clam up" when their shells are tapped. Any that remain open are dead and should be rejected.

Shucked Clams: Choose clams that are plump and sweet-smelling with clear liquor and no shell fragments.

About Frozen and Canned Clams

Quick-frozen shucked clams are available, as are frozen, ready-to-heat-and-eat clam fritters and patties. Canned clams, both whole and minced, chowders, and clam juice are all widely marketed. *To Cook Frozen Clams:* Thaw quick-frozen

shucked clams completely in refrigerator, then prepare as you
would fresh clams. Once clams have
thawed, cook immediately; never
refreeze. Clam fritters, patties, and
other frozen prepared clam dishes
should be heated or cooked by
package directions. *How to Use
Canned Clams:* These are already
cooked and ideal for quick soups,
salads, canapés, and casseroles.

About Preparing Fresh Clams in the Shell

How to Cleanse Clams of Grit: The
easiest way is to let the clams do
the job themselves. Here's how:
Scrub clams well to remove surface
grit and mud, then place in a large,
deep enamel kettle and cover with
cold salted water (1 tablespoon salt
to each quart water). Toss in a
handful of corn meal, set kettle
in a cool place and let stand several
hours or overnight. Lift clams from
water and rinse well in cool water;
discard any that are open or do not
clamp shut when thumped.

How to Open Clams: There are
two ways, one difficult, one easy.
If the clams are to be served or
broiled on the half shell, you'll have
to use brute force. If they're to be
removed from the shell and used in
chowders, patties, or casseroles, they
can quickly be steamed open.
(*Note:* Geoducks require special
attention [see method that fol-
lows].)

(1) *To Pry Open:* Holding a clam
in the palm of one hand, insert
clam knife between upper and lower
shells, then move it along rim,
twisting slightly to break "seal" and
force clam open (the job is much
easier with soft clams than with
hard). Cut clam free of shell and

remove any grit or bits of shell. Do
the opening over a bowl so none of
the clam juice is lost; also strain
juice through a sieve lined with
a double thickness of cheesecloth
before using.

(2) *To Steam Open:* Place clams in
a large, deep kettle, pour in about
¾ cup boiling water, cover, and
steam over moderate heat about
5–8 minutes until shells partially
open. Drain and remove meat from
shells—it will come away zip-quick
if you work under a gentle stream
of cool water.

How to Cook Clams

Clams can be cooked simply or
glamorized in a variety of ways.
Purists insist nothing surpasses a
steamed clam, dunked in melted
butter, but then everyone is not a
purist. . . .

General Preparation: If clams are
in the shell, cleanse of grit and
shuck or not as recipes specify.
Check extra-heavy clams carefully;
they may be full of sand or mud.
This is all the preparation Eastern
hard and soft clams need, also
the West Coast butter clam. Other
Pacific varieties, however, require
further attention:

Geoduck: Plunge clam into boiling
water and let stand until shell opens.
Drain and cut body meat from
shell. Skin the clam, discard the
stomach (the dark portion) and
separate neck from body. Put neck
through coarse blade of meat grinder
and slice body into thin steaks
(about ¼″ thick). The neck meat is
best used in chowders, the steaks
quickly panfried in butter.

Mud Clams: When clams are
shucked, trim away all black portions; split the necks lengthwise and

rinse away any grit. Cook as you would hard clams.

Pismo Clams: Cut hinge or adductor muscle from body meat; it is tender enough to serve raw on the half shell. Remove stomach (the dark part) from the body, rinse clam, then lightly pound any firm parts to "tenderize." These clams are particularly good fried or deep-fat-fried.

Razor Clams: Cut off tip of the neck, cut clam from shell, and split from the base of the foot (that part next to the shell) to the top of the neck. Trim off all dark parts (the gills and digestive organs). Leave clam whole and fry or deep-fry, or grind and use for chowders or patties.

To Charcoal Broil: This is a bit of a fuss. Build a moderately hot charcoal fire.* Pat shucked clams dry on paper toweling, then wrap each in a ½ slice bacon and thread on long thin skewers; or secure bacon slices with toothpicks and place clams in a well-greased hinged, long-handled wire grill. Broil 4″ from heat 3–4 minutes on a side until bacon is golden and crisp.

To Panfry (*Sauté*): Pat shucked clams dry on paper toweling. Dredge in flour lightly seasoned with salt and pepper and sauté in butter (about ⅓ cup butter for 1 pint clams) about 3 minutes over moderate heat, turning once, until clams are lightly browned. Serve with lemon wedges.

VARIATIONS:

Pan-"Roasted" Clams: These aren't roasted but sautéed. Pat clams dry on paper toweling but do not dredge. Sauté in butter (about ½ cup butter for 1 pint clams) 2–3 minutes, turning once, just until clams plump

up and are heated through. Serve with lemon.

Breaded Fried Clams: Pat clams dry, dredge in flour lightly seasoned with salt and pepper, dip in a mixture of beaten egg and milk (2 tablespoons milk for each egg), and roll in fine dry crumbs, cracker meal, or a ½ and ½ mixture of flour and corn meal. Sauté as directed until golden and drain on paper toweling before serving.

To Deep-Fat-Fry: Pat shucked clams dry on paper toweling, then bread as above. Heat cooking oil or shortening in a deep fat fryer to 375° F., place a single layer of clams in fryer basket, lower into fat, and fry 1–2 minutes until golden brown. Drain on paper toweling and serve with lemon.

VARIATION:

Batter-Fried Clams (Clam Fritters): Make up batter given in Fish and Chips recipe. Pat clams dry on paper toweling, dip in batter, then fry, 6–8 at a time, in 375° F. fat about 2 minutes until golden brown. Drain on paper toweling and serve.

To Oven Roast: Scrub clams well and cleanse of grit but do not shuck. Preheat oven to 450° F. Place clams in a shallow baking pan and roast, uncovered, 12–15 minutes until they open; reject any that do not. Serve clams in the shell with plenty of melted butter and lemon wedges.

To Roast over Charcoal: Scrub clams and cleanse but do not shuck. Build a moderately hot charcoal fire.* Wrap clams, about 6 to a package, in heavy foil. Place packages directly on coals and roast 4–6 minutes until clams open. Serve with lemon and melted butter.

To Steam: Steamers or soft clams are best, though small hard clams may also be steamed. Scrub clams well and cleanse of grit but do not shuck. Place clams in a large, deep kettle, add ⅔ cup boiling water, cover, and steam 5 minutes over moderate heat until clams open; discard any that don't. Serve in the shell with melted butter, a bowl of broth, and lemon wedges. When eating, peel black skin from neck and hold by the neck when dunking in broth and butter.

To Serve Clams on the Half Shell

Allow 6–8 cherrystone, littleneck, or butter clams per serving. If possible, have your fish market open clams and discard top shells. If you must do the job yourself, follow directions given earlier for cleansing and prying open clams. Fill large, shallow bowls or soup plates with crushed ice and arrange clams in ice. Garnish with lemon wedges and parsley fluffs. Set out the pepper mill (but *not* cocktail sauce unless guests insist). After eating clams on the half shell, be sure to drink the juice from each shell.

CLAMS CASINO

Makes 2 entree servings, enough appetizers for 4

Rock salt
6 slices bacon
2 dozen cherrystone clams on the half shell
¼ cup butter or margarine, softened to room temperature
2 teaspoons anchovy paste
¼ cup minced sweet green pepper
¼ cup minced pimiento

Preheat oven to 450° F. Make beds of rock salt in 4 piepans (the 8" or 9" size is best and the jiffy foil pans work perfectly), dampen slightly with water and heat, uncovered, in oven 5 minutes. Meanwhile, cut each bacon slice into 4

equal pieces and stir-fry over moderate heat until limp; drain on paper toweling and reserve. Arrange 6 clams in each pan, pushing down into hot salt so they won't tip. Mix butter and anchovy paste until smooth and tuck about ½ teaspoonful under each clam. Sprinkle a little sweet green pepper and pimiento on each clam, top with a piece of bacon, and bake, uncovered, 5–7 minutes until bacon is crisp. Serve clams from pans. About 540 calories for each of 2 entree servings, 270 calories for each of 4 appetizer servings.

VARIATION:

Oysters Casino: Prepare as directed, substituting oysters on the half shell for clams. About 540 calories for each of 2 entree servings, 270 calories for each of 4 appetizer servings.

CLAMS ORIGANATA

Whenever possible, make crumbs from stale Italian bread; the recipe will have much better flavor.
Makes 2 entree servings, enough appetizers for 4

Rock salt
2 dozen littleneck or cherrystone clams on the half shell
1½ cups fine dry bread crumbs
2 cloves garlic, peeled and crushed
2 tablespoons minced parsley
2 teaspoons minced fresh oregano or 1 teaspoon dried oregano
3 tablespoons olive or other cooking oil
⅛ teaspoon pepper

Preheat broiler. Make beds of rock salt in 4 (8" or 9") piepans and dampen slightly with water; heat, uncovered, in oven 5 minutes while broiler preheats. Arrange 6 clams in each pan, pushing down into hot salt so they won't tip. Mix remaining ingredients and spoon enough on each clam to cover. Broil 5″ from the heat 3–4 minutes until lightly browned. About 430 calories for each of 2 entree servings, 215 calories for each of 4 appetizer servings.

BOSTON-STYLE STUFFED CLAMS

The stuffing is a delicate blend of minced clams, onion, parsley, and soft bread crumbs.
Makes 2–4 servings

Rock salt
1 dozen large clams on the half shell
¾ cup soft white bread crumbs
1 tablespoon minced yellow onion
1 tablespoon minced parsley
2 teaspoons lemon juice
¼ teaspoon pepper
½ cup fine dry or toasted seasoned bread crumbs mixed with 2 tablespoons melted butter or margarine

Preheat oven to 425° F. Make a bed of rock salt in a large, shallow baking pan and dampen slightly with water; heat, uncovered, in oven 5 minutes. Drain juice from clams, reserving ¼ cup; mince clams and combine with juice; butter clam shells well. Mix clams and juice with all remaining ingredients except buttered crumbs and spoon into shells. Anchor shells in hot salt so they won't tip, top clams with buttered crumbs, and bake, uncovered, 10 minutes until lightly browned. About 310 calories for each of 2 servings, 155 calories for each of 4 servings.

VARIATIONS:

⊿⊳ **Stuffed Clams au Gratin:** Prepare clam mixture as directed, adding ⅓ cup crisp crumbled bacon. Omit buttered crumb topping and top instead with ¼ cup cracker meal mixed with ¼ cup grated Parmesan. Bake as directed. About 285 calories for each of 2 servings, 145 calories for each of 4 servings.

Creamed, Stuffed Clams: Prepare clam mixture as directed but for the liquid ingredients use ⅓ cup Thick White Sauce and 2 tablespoons medium-dry sherry instead of clam juice and lemon juice. Fill shells, top with buttered crumbs, and bake as directed. About 400 calories for each of 2 servings, 200 calories for each of 4 servings.

CLAMS BULHÃO PATO

Bulhão Pato was a Portuguese poet whose recipe for garlic- and coriander-flavored clams is better remembered than his poetry.
Makes 4 servings

5–6 dozen soft clams in the shell, prepared for cooking
1½ cups boiling water
⅓ cup olive oil
3 cloves garlic, peeled and crushed
½ cup minced parsley
½ cup minced fresh coriander leaves or 2 tablespoons minced carrot tops
⅛ teaspoon pepper
½ teaspoon salt

Place clams in a very large, deep kettle, add all remaining ingredients, cover, and steam over moderate heat 5–10 minutes just until shells open; discard any that do not open. Serve clams in shells in soup bowls topped with some of the broth. (*Note:* Tip kettle when ladling out liquid to avoid any sediment in the bottom.) Serve with hot crusty bread. About 315 calories per serving (without bread).

SCALLOPED CLAMS

Makes 4 servings

1 pint shucked clams or 2 (8-ounce) cans minced clams (do not drain)
½ cup light cream or milk (about)
2 cups coarse soda cracker crumbs
½ cup melted butter or margarine

2 *tablespoons minced parsley*
½ *teaspoon salt*
⅛ *teaspoon pepper*
½ *teaspoon Worcestershire sauce*
2 *tablespoons dry sherry (optional)*

Preheat oven to 350° F. Drain liquid from clams, measure, and add enough cream to total 1 cup; set aside. If using fresh clams, mince. Mix crumbs with butter, parsley, salt and pepper and spoon about ⅓ into a buttered 1-quart casserole. Cover with half the clams, add another ⅓ crumbs, then remaining clams. Stir Worcestershire sauce and, if you like, sherry into clam liquid mixture; pour over clams and top with remaining crumbs. Bake, uncovered, about ½ hour until lightly browned. About 515 calories per serving.

¢ ☒ CLAM HASH

Makes 4 servings

3 *slices bacon*
1 *(10½-ounce) can minced clams, drained*
¼ *cup minced yellow onion*
3 *cups diced cooked potatoes*
3 *eggs, lightly beaten*
¼ *cup milk or light cream*
1 *teaspoon salt*
⅛ *teaspoon pepper*
Pinch nutmeg

Fry bacon in a skillet over moderate heat until crisp; drain, crumble, and reserve. Mix clams, onion, and potatoes and add to drippings in skillet, pressing down with a spatula to form a large "pancake." Fry over moderately low heat without stirring 7–10 minutes until brown on the bottom; flip mixture over, press down. Mix eggs with all remaining ingredients and pour over clams. Cook just until eggs are set, tilting pan as needed to let uncooked eggs run underneath. Sprinkle with bacon,

cut in wedges, and serve. About 445 calories per serving.

CLAM SOUFFLÉ

So very delicate!
Makes 4–6 servings

¼ *cup butter or margarine*
¼ *cup unsifted flour*
1 *cup milk or a ½ and ½ mixture of milk and liquid drained from clams*
¼ *teaspoon salt*
⅛ *teaspoon pepper*
4 *eggs, separated (at room temperature)*
1 *pint shucked clams, drained and minced or 2 (8-ounce) cans minced clams, drained*
¼ *teaspoon cream of tartar*

Melt butter in a small saucepan over moderate heat, blend in flour, slowly add milk, and heat, stirring, until thickened. Turn heat to low, stir in salt and pepper. Beat egg yolks lightly, blend in a little hot sauce, then return all to pan. Heat, stirring, 1–2 minutes but do not boil. Off heat mix in clams; lay a piece of wax paper flat on surface of sauce and cool to room temperature. Meanwhile, preheat oven to 350° F. Beat egg whites until foamy, add cream of tartar and continue to beat until stiff but not dry. Stir about ¼ cup egg whites into clam mixture, then fold in remainder. Spoon into an ungreased 1½-quart soufflé dish and bake, uncovered, ¾ hour until puffy and brown. Serve at once. About 325 calories for each of 4 servings, 215 calories for each of 6 servings.

NEW ENGLAND CLAM PIE

A two-crusted pie filled with clams, diced salt pork, and potatoes.
Makes 6 servings

1 *recipe Flaky Pastry II*

1 *pint shucked clams or 2 (8-ounce)*
cans minced clams (do not drain)
¼ *pound salt pork or bacon, cut in*
small dice
1 *small yellow onion, peeled and*
minced
1 *tablespoon flour*
2 *medium-size potatoes, boiled,*
drained, and cubed
1 *tablespoon minced parsley*
⅛ *teaspoon pepper*

Preheat oven to 425° F. Prepare
pastry according to recipe and roll
out half to form a 12″ circle. Fit
into a 9″ piepan but do not trim
edge. Roll remaining pastry into a
12″ circle, cut 3 V-shaped slits near
center, and cover with wax paper
while preparing filling. Drain clams,
reserving ⅓ cup liquor (if necessary, add milk to round out measure); mince clams. Lightly brown
salt pork in a small skillet over
moderately low heat; remove and
reserve. Pour off all but 2 tablespoons drippings, add onion, and
sauté over moderate heat 3–5 minutes until limp. Blend in flour and
clam liquid and heat, stirring, until
thickened. Off heat, mix in potatoes,
clams, parsley, and pepper. Spoon
into prepared pie shell, fit reserved
pastry on top, press 2 crusts together, trim and crimp edges. Bake
about ½ hour until pastry is lightly
browned. About 330 calories per
serving.

INDOOR CLAMBAKE

The usual order of building a clambake is clams on the bottom, then
lobsters and vegetables, but the following upside-down arrangement
has an advantage. The clams can be
enjoyed as a first course while the
slower-cooking items finish "baking."
To do the indoor clambake, you'll
need a giant kettle or "clambaker,"

obtainable in hardware and kitchen
shops.
Makes 6–8 servings

8 *ears sweet corn in the husk*
2 *gallons cold water mixed with ½*
cup salt
Seaweed
6 *(1–1¼-pound) live lobsters*
8 *medium-size potatoes, scrubbed*
but not peeled
6 *dozen soft clams in the shell,*
prepared for cooking, or 2 dozen
each clams, oysters, and mussels in
the shell, prepared for cooking

Condiments:
2 *cups melted butter or margarine*
1 *bottle liquid hot red pepper*
seasoning

Remove outer husks of corn but not
tightly clinging inner husks; pull
off tassels. Soak corn 1 hour in 6
quarts salt water. Meanwhile, pour
remaining salt water in a very large
deep kettle, add a rack and cover
with a thin layer of seaweed or, if
unavailable, outer corn husks which
have been soaked well in salt water.
Drain soaked ears and arrange on
rack. Add lobsters and potatoes, then
top with clams and more seaweed
or husks. Cover tightly and bring
to a boil; reduce heat so water stays
at a slow simmer and steam ¾–1
hour. Lift out clams and serve with
condiments as a first course. Meanwhile, clambake should be re-
covered and allowed to steam until
potatoes are tender. They will be
done by the time everyone has
finished with the clams. Pile lobsters,
potatoes, and corn on huge platters
and serve at once with the condiments. Set out bibs, lobster crackers
and picks, and plenty of napkins.
About 570 calories for each of 6
servings, 430 calories for each of 8
servings.

CONCH

Conch (pronounced *konk*) isn't everyone's dish—too tough, too strong. But those who live where it's caught—Florida, the Gulf Coast, and West Indies—consider it something special. It's available year round, live and in the shell; also frozen (cooked or uncooked) and canned.

Amount to Buy: 1 pound conch in the shell per person; ¼–⅓ pound conch meat.

For Top Quality: Buy the conch right off the boat or from a market whose word you trust.

How to Cook Conch

Because of its rubbery texture and strong ocean flavor, conch is best stewed or ground into fritters or patties. It can also be sautéed, *if* first parboiled until tender. Frozen conch need not be thawed before using.

General Preparation (for all cooking methods): Everyone familiar with conch has a pet way to tenderize it. The most effective ways seem to be parboiling or pounding with a mallet. But first: scrub conch shell well under cold running water, place in a large heavy kettle, add boiling water to cover, 1 tablespoon salt, and ¼ cup lemon juice. Cover and boil 3 minutes; drain in a colander under cold running water until easy to handle. Pry meat from shell with a strong, long-tined fork, cut off hard black "foot" and tightly curled tip. Wash again in cold water. Conch is now ready to simmer in soups or stews. If it is to be panfried or made into fritters, it should be parboiled.

To Parboil: Leave conch meat whole or slice thin; place in a saucepan, add water to cover, and for each pint water add 1 tablespoon lemon juice. Cover and simmer until tender, about 1½–2 hours for sliced conch, 2–4 hours for the whole. Drain well.

BAHAMIAN CONCH CHOWDER

A hearty main dish containing conch, carrots, tomatoes, and potatoes.
Makes 4 servings

1 pound conch meat, prepared for cooking
3 tablespoons butter, margarine, or cooking oil
1 large yellow onion, peeled and minced
2 cloves garlic, peeled and crushed
2 carrots, peeled and cut in small dice
2 tomatoes, peeled, cored, seeded, and chopped fine
⅛ teaspoon crushed hot red chili peppers
⅛ teaspoon curry powder
1 (6-ounce) can tomato paste
1 quart water (about)
1½ teaspoons salt (about)
3 small potatoes, peeled and cut in ½" cubes

Cut conch meat into ½" cubes. Melt butter in a large saucepan over moderate heat and stir-fry onion, garlic, carrots, tomatoes, peppers and curry powder 3–5 minutes. Add conch and stir 1 minute. Add tomato paste, water, and salt, cover, and simmer 1½–2 hours until conch is very tender; replenish water as needed to keep chowder from getting too thick. Add potatoes and simmer 10–15 minutes longer until tender. Serve piping hot. About 340 calories per serving.

VARIATION:

Omit potatoes and stir 1½ cups boiled rice into chowder just before serving. About 335 calories per serving.

⚖ SCUNGILLI MARINARA

Scungilli is the Italian word for conch, and *marinara* is a favorite Italian way of preparing it—with tomatoes, garlic, and onion.
Makes 4 servings

½ *cup minced yellow onion*
1 *clove garlic, peeled and crushed*
2 *tablespoons olive oil*
1 *(1-pound) can Italian plum tomatoes (do not drain)*
¼ *cup tomato paste*
½ *cup dry red wine*
½ *teaspoon sugar*
1 *teaspoon salt*
1 *teaspoon oregano*
⅛ *teaspoon pepper*
1 *pound sliced parboiled conch meat*
2 *tablespoons finely grated Parmesan cheese*

Sauté onion and garlic in oil in a large saucepan over moderate heat 8–10 minutes until golden. Turn heat to low, add all remaining ingredients except conch and cheese, cover, and simmer 1 hour, stirring occasionally. If mixture becomes too thick, thin with a little water. Cool sauce slightly and purée in an electric blender at low speed or put through a food mill. Return to pan, add conch, cover, and simmer 3–5 minutes. Mix in cheese and serve hot over spaghetti or other pasta. About 280 calories per serving.

⚖ PANFRIED CONCH AND ONIONS

Makes 4–6 servings

1½ *pounds sliced parboiled conch meat*
2 *large yellow onions, peeled, sliced thin, and separated into rings*
¼ *cup butter, margarine, or cooking oil*
½ *teaspoon salt*
⅛ *teaspoon pepper*

Pat conch slices very dry on paper toweling. Stir-fry onions in butter in a large, heavy skillet 3–5 minutes over moderately high heat until limp. Add conch and stir-fry 3–5 minutes longer until lightly browned. Season and serve. About 275 calories for each of 4 servings, 180 calories for each of 6 servings.

VARIATION:

⚖ **Breaded Fried Conch:** Omit onions. Dredge conch slices in flour, dip in lightly beaten egg, and roll in fine dry bread crumbs or cracker meal to coat. Use cooking oil for the frying and increase amount to 1 cup. Heat oil in a deep, heavy skillet until a cube of bread will sizzle, add breaded conch slices, and fry 3–4 minutes until nicely crisp and brown. Drain on paper toweling and serve with Tartar Sauce. About 305 calories for each of 4 servings (without Tartar Sauce), 200 calories for each of 6 servings.

⚖ CONCH BURGERS

Makes 4–6 servings

2 *cups finely ground parboiled conch meat*
2 *cups soft white bread crumbs*
2 *eggs, lightly beaten*
1 *tablespoon Worcestershire sauce*
¼ *teaspoon liquid hot red pepper seasoning*
½ *teaspoon minced garlic*
1 *tablespoon grated yellow onion*
¼ *cup unsifted flour*
3 *tablespoons butter, margarine, bacon drippings, or cooking oil*

Mix conch with all remaining ingredients except flour and butter. Shape into 6 patties and dredge with flour. Heat butter in a large skillet over moderate heat and brown patties 3–4 minutes on each side. Serve hot with Tartar Sauce or Tomato Sauce. About 280 calories for each of 4 servings, 185 calories for each of 6 servings.

CRABS

After shrimp, crab rates as America's favorite shellfish. Easterners insist nothing beats blue crabs for succulence, flavor, and versatility but they get an argument from Westerners, to whom Dungeness is *the* crab. Fortunately, both coasts are blessed with an abundance of crabs. And fortunately, modern packing and shipping have brought fresh and frozen crabs to every state.

The Kinds of Crabs

There are five popular crabs in America; three are widely known, two are local specialties.

Blue Crabs: Far and away the biggest seller. Blue crabs come from Atlantic and Gulf coasts but are at their best in Chesapeake Bay. Depending upon season, they are *hard* or *soft shell*. Soft-shell crabs are nothing more than hard-shell crabs that have molted or shucked their hard shells. Choicest crab meat is that from the back—snowy, white, and sweet; claw meat has tinges of brown.

Dungeness: The king of the West Coast, 2–3 times the size of the blue crab. Meat is pinkish-white and delectably sweet.

Alaska King Crab: A giant sometimes measuring 6 feet across and weighing 20 pounds. Only the scarlet-skinned white leg meat is eaten.

Rock Crab: Taken from both New England and California coasts, these crabs are not well known elsewhere. Their meat has excellent flavor but is tan to brown in color.

Stone Crab: This Miami-Florida Keys favorite is practically all claw. It is rarely available outside Florida.

The Season for Fresh Crabs

Blue Crabs:

Hard Shell: Year round though supply is limited in cold weather.

Soft Shell: July and August.

Dungeness: Mid-November to late July in California, year round in the Pacific Northwest.

Alaska King Crab: Year round, but only available frozen.

Rock Crabs: Year round with supplies limited in winter.

Stone Crabs: Mid-October to June.

About Buying Fresh Crabs

Popular Market Forms:

Blue Crabs:

Hard Shell: Live in the shell; iced tins of fresh-cooked crab meat: choicest is *lump* or *backfin*, solid chunks from the back containing little shell or cartilage; *flake* is less expensive and contains bits and pieces of meat and considerably more shell (good for ramekins and casseroles where appearance doesn't matter so much); also sometimes available are reasonably priced *mixtures of flake and dark claw meat.*

Soft Shell: Live.

Alaska King Crab: Not available fresh.

Dungeness: Live or cooked in the shell; cooked meat.

Rock Crabs: Live in the shell.

Stone Crabs: Live in the shell.

Amount Needed: Allow about 1 pound crab in the shell per person, ¼–⅓ pound crab meat, depending upon how it is to be prepared. Hard-shell blue crabs weigh from ¼–1 pound, the soft shell considerably less. Though some people can easily eat half a dozen soft-shell crabs, 3–4 make a respectable portion. Dungeness crabs weigh 1¾ to 3½ pounds and Alaska king crabs from 6–20. Rock crabs are small, about ⅓–½ pound apiece. Weight matters less with stone crabs since it's the claw that's eaten; allow about 4 claws per person.

For Top Quality: If crabs are alive, make sure they are also *lively.* When buying fresh-cooked crab meat, look for that with a sweet-clean smell.

About Frozen and Canned Crab

The best known frozen crab is the Alaska king; it is precooked, then frozen in or out of the shell. Cooked Dungeness and blue crab meat is also frozen; so, too, are uncooked soft-shell crabs and stone crab claws. All of the popular American crabs are canned.

How to Use Frozen Crab: Always thaw or not as package directions or recipes direct; when crab is to be thawed, always do so in the refrigerator. *How to Use Canned Crab:* This is fully cooked and particularly suited to crab cakes, deviled crab, casseroles—whenever appearance is not the first consideration.

How to Clean and Cook Crabs

With the exception of soft-shell crabs, which can be sautéed or deep-fat-fried, live crabs are best simply boiled or steamed. They may be eaten as is with a suitable sauce or butter or the meat may be taken from the shell and used in a variety of ways (see recipes that follow).

Hard-Shell Crabs:

Blue Crabs, Rock Crabs: Cook, then clean.

To Boil: Bring a large kettle of sea water or lightly salted water to a boil (allow 1 tablespoon salt to 1 quart water), grab crabs, 1 at a time, across center back of shell and drop into water. As soon as water returns to a boil, cover and simmer 8 minutes per pound of crabs. Drain, rinse under cool running water, and when cool enough to handle clean as directed below.

To Steam: Plunge live crabs in a kettle of hot tap water—it should not be steaming hot, just a bit too hot for your hands. When crabs stop kicking, drain and, if necessary, scrub in warm water with a soft brush to remove bits of mud and sand. Old salts from crab country pooh-pooh the idea of scrubbing, but it does make the crabs more pleasant to eat. Place a rack in a large, deep kettle and pour in about 1½″ boiling water or, better yet, boiling sea water. Pile crabs up on rack so that they are well out of the water, cover and steam 25–30 minutes, just until crabs turn bright orange and their shells rise slightly. Lift crabs from kettle with tongs, drain briefly on paper toweling, and serve hot. Set out lobster or nut crackers and picks and lots of melted butter.

To Clean: Break off claws as close to body as possible, then cut or break off legs. Get a firm grip on top shell and pull off. Scrape all feathery, spongy material from center of body, also the soft, yellowish stomach and digestive tract. Encasing the choice lump crab meat now is a thin inner skeleton; pull or slice off either the left or right half, scrape any meat from cut-off piece and reserve, then scoop out chunks of meat in

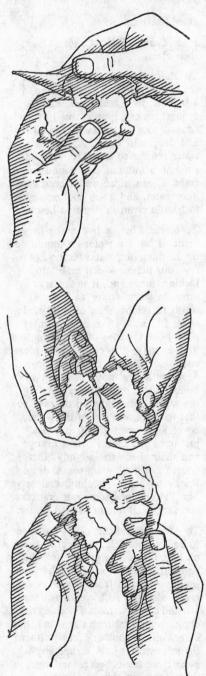

body pockets and reserve. Repeat with other half of body. Crack claws and legs and pull or pick out meat, using a lobster or nut pick for stubborn bits.

Dungeness Crabs: People disagree as to whether live Dungeness crabs should be cooked and then cleaned or vice versa. Take your choice.

To Clean: Wear rubber gloves to protect your hands from jagged pieces of shell. Grab crab from behind, getting a good grip on its body and two hind legs. Lay crab on its back on a large cutting board, place a sharp knife along midline and hit hard with a mallet to kill crab instantly. Twist off front claws, 1 at a time, where they join body; also twist off legs. Scrub claws and legs well and set aside. Pry off shell, using a knife if necessary, and scrape out spongy gills; save creamy "crab butter" underneath to use in sauces. Crack each segment of claws and legs and rinse well. Split crab body down midline, then cut each half into manageable (about 1½″) chunks and rinse well.

To Boil: Bring a large kettle of sea water or lightly salted water (1 tablespoon salt to each quart water) to a boil, drop in crab, and when water returns to a boil, cover and simmer 10–12 minutes for cracked crab, 15–20 for whole crab, depending on size. Drain and serve hot with melted butter. If crab has been boiled whole, clean and crack as described above before eating.

VARIATION:

California Cold Cracked Crab: Clean and crack crab and boil as directed. Drain, cool, then chill several hours. Serve on beds of cracked ice with freshly made Mayonnaise.

Stone Crabs: Only the claw meat is eaten, so little cleaning is needed.

Twist off claws, scrub well, then drop in lightly salted boiling water to cover, cover, and boil 15–20 minutes. Drain and serve hot with melted butter or cool and serve with mayonnaise or Sauce Verte. Set out lobster crackers and picks.

Soft-Shell Blue Crabs:

To Clean: With scissors, cut off "face" portion just behind eyes. Lift up shell by the points and cut out feathery, spongy gills; also scoop or cut out yellowish digestive organs. Rinse crabs well under cool running water to remove any yellow traces and pat dry on paper toweling. Turn crab on its back and cut off apron or tail flap folded underneath

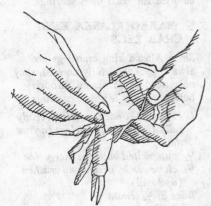

body; smooth soft shell back in place. Crab is now ready to cook. Everything remaining is edible—legs, claws, soft shell, body.

To Panfry (Sauté): Clean crabs as directed. Dredge lightly in seasoned flour. Melt ¼–⅓ cup butter or margarine in a large, heavy skillet over moderate heat and, when beginning to foam, add crabs and sauté about 3 minutes on a side until crisp and golden brown. (*Note:* Work carefully because crabs will sputter in the hot butter.) Do only 3–4 at a time, drain well on paper toweling, and set uncovered in an oven turned to lowest heat to keep warm while you fry the rest.

VARIATIONS:

Soft-Shell Crabs à la Meunière: Dredge and sauté crabs as above. When all are done, melt 1–2 tablespoons fresh butter in skillet and squeeze in the juice of ½ lemon. Pour over crabs, sprinkle with minced parsley, and serve.

Breaded Soft-Shell Crabs: Clean crabs as directed. Dip in lightly beaten egg, then in fine dry bread crumbs or cracker meal to coat. Heat about ⅛″ cooking oil or a ½ and ½ mixture of cooking oil and butter in a large, heavy skillet over moderate heat, add 3–4 crabs, and sauté 3 minutes on each side until crisply golden. Drain on paper toweling, sprinkle with salt and pepper, and serve with lemon wedges.

To Deep-Fat-Fry: Clean crabs as directed and bread as above. Meanwhile, heat oil or shortening in a deep fat fryer to 375° F. Place 2–3 crabs in fryer basket, lower into fat, and fry 3–4 minutes until nicely browned and crisp. Drain on paper toweling and keep warm while frying remaining crabs. Always scoop any browned crumbs from fat before adding more crabs. Serve with lemon wedges.

To Broil: Clean crabs as directed and dredge in flour or, if you prefer, bread as for panfrying. Preheat broiler. Arrange crabs on their backs on a lightly oiled broiler rack. Drizzle with melted butter or margarine and broil 4"–5" from the heat about 3 minutes until lightly browned. Turn, drizzle again with melted butter, and broil 3 minutes longer until crisp and golden brown. Watch closely toward the end.

VARIATION:

Lemon-Broiled Soft-Shell Crabs: Broil as directed, using Lemon Butter for basting instead of plain butter.

How to Eat Crabs in the Shell

Blue Crabs, Rock Crabs:
(1) Twist off claws and legs and set aside.
(2) Pull off top shell, scrape out and discard feathery gray-white gills and yellowish digestive organs.
(3) Peel or cut away thin inner "shell" covering body; underneath is the best part of the crab. Pull out the plump chunks of meat with a small fork or pick, dipping each morsel in accompanying sauce or butter.
(4) Crack each segment of claws and twist out meat with a small fork or pick.
(5) Treat legs like soda straws, sucking one end to get out any bits of meat inside.

Dungeness: Because of their size, these crabs are nearly always cleaned and cracked before they are served. If for some reason a whole crab comes to the table, attack it following directions for cleaning Dungeness crab.

Stone Crabs: Only the claws are served in the shell; crack with lobster crackers and twist out meat with a small fork or pick.

Alaska King Crab Legs: These present no problem because enough meat is exposed to make eating easy. Simply pull it out with a fork and cut as needed into bite-size chunks and eat, first dunking into any accompanying butter or sauce.

⚖ ☒ **SPICED BLUE CRABS**

Makes 4–6 servings

1 quart cider vinegar
⅓ cup salt
1 celery stalk
¼ cup powdered mustard
¼ cup whole cloves
3 tablespoons cayenne pepper
2 tablespoons ginger
1 tablespoon mace
1½ gallons boiling water
2 dozen medium-size live blue crabs

Place all ingredients except crabs in a 3-gallon enamel or stainless-steel kettle, bring to a boil, cover, and simmer 5 minutes. Add crabs, cover, and simmer 15 minutes. Drain and serve hot or cool, chill, and serve cold. Set out several sets of lobster crackers and picks. About 105 calories for each of 4 servings, 70 calories for each of 6 servings.

☒ **BAKED ALASKA KING CRAB LEGS**

Since Alaska king crab legs are always packaged fully cooked, they only need to be heated through before eating. Makes 2 servings

1 (12-ounce) package frozen ready split Alaska king crab legs (do not thaw)
½ cup melted butter or margarine
½ clove garlic, peeled and crushed (optional)
Juice of ½ lemon

Preheat oven to 400° F. Place crab legs, flesh side up, in an ungreased shallow baking pan. Mix butter, garlic, and lemon juice and brush over crab legs. Bake, uncovered, 15 minutes until bubbly, brushing often with butter mixture. About 300 calories per serving.

VARIATIONS:

⚎ **Low-Calorie Baked King Crab Legs:** Prepare as directed, substituting low-calorie Italian, garlic, or herb dressing for the butter mixture. About 125 calories per serving.

Baked Herbed King Crab Legs: Prepare as directed but omit garlic from melted butter. Add instead 2 teaspoons each minced parsley and fresh tarragon, chervil, or dill or 1 teaspoon parsley flakes and ¼ teaspoon dried tarragon, chervil, or dill. About 300 calories per serving.

Baked Italian-Style King Crab Legs: Prepare as directed, substituting olive oil for butter and adding ¼ teaspoon oregano. About 350 calories per serving.

Barbecued King Crab Legs: Prepare as directed, substituting any barbecue sauce for the melted butter mixture. About 355 calories per serving.

Baked Sherried King Crab Legs: Prepare as directed, but omit garlic from butter mixture and substitute 3 tablespoons dry sherry for the lemon juice. About 315 calories per serving.

Broiled King Crab Legs: Prepare any of the above recipes but, instead of baking, broil 4"–5" from the heat about 10–12 minutes until bubbly and lightly browned. About 300 calories per serving.

⚎ ☒ **HERBED CRAB SAUTÉ**
Makes 4 servings

⅓ cup unsalted butter
1 pound fresh lump or backfin crab meat, well picked over, or 1 pound cooked stone crab meat, well picked over, or 3 (6-ounce) packages frozen Alaska king crab meat, thawed and drained
1 tablespoon minced parsley
1 tablespoon minced fresh chives
½ teaspoon minced fresh tarragon or chervil
⅓ cup dry white wine
Juice of ½ lemon
1 tablespoon minced capers
½ teaspoon salt
Pinch pepper

Melt butter in a large, heavy skillet over moderate heat, add crab and herbs, and sauté 2–3 minutes. Add remaining ingredients, sauté 5 minutes longer, and serve. Particularly good over hot buttered toast. About 260 calories per serving (without toast).

CRAB CIOPPINO

A favorite California crab stew filled with tomatoes and studded with shrimp and clams.
Makes 4–6 servings

1 medium-sized yellow onion, peeled and minced
1 stalk celery, minced
½ sweet green pepper, cored, seeded, and minced
1 clove garlic, peeled and crushed
⅓ cup olive oil
6 large ripe tomatoes, peeled, cored, and coarsely chopped
¼ cup tomato paste
1 bay leaf, crumbled
1 teaspoon salt
½ teaspoon oregano
½ teaspoon basil
½ teaspoon pepper
1 cup dry red wine
1½ cups water (about)
1 (3–3½-pound) Dungeness crab, cleaned and cracked

1 pound raw shrimp in the shell
1½ dozen littleneck clams in the shell, well scrubbed

Stir-fry onion, celery, green pepper, and garlic in the oil in a large, heavy kettle 8–10 minutes over moderate heat until golden; add all remaining ingredients except seafood, cover, and simmer 1½–2 hours until flavors are well blended. If sauce becomes too thick (it should be about the consistency of a medium white sauce), thin with a little water or wine. Taste for salt and pepper and adjust as needed. Add all seafood to sauce, cover, and simmer 12–15 minutes longer or until shrimp and crab turn orange and clams open. Serve from a giant tureen with buttery crusts of Italian bread and a dry red wine. About 600 calories for each of 4 servings (without bread), about 400 calories for each of 6 servings.

☒ QUICK CRAB NEWBURG

Makes 6 servings

⅓ cup butter or margarine
1 pound crab meat (fresh, thawed frozen, or drained canned), well picked over
¼ teaspoon seasoned pepper
1 pint sour cream, at room temperature
2 tablespoons tomato paste
2 tablespoons dry sherry
2 tablespoons finely grated Parmesan cheese

Melt butter in a large skillet over moderately low heat. Add crab and stir-fry 2–3 minutes. Mix in remaining ingredients and heat 2–3 minutes, stirring gently (do not boil). Serve over boiled rice or lightly buttered hot toast. About 350 calories per serving (without rice or toast).

⚜ ☒ CRAB MEAT NORFOLK

One of the easiest ways to prepare

crab and one of the most delicately seasoned.
Makes 4 servings

1 pound fresh lump or backfin crab meat, well picked over
4 teaspoons white wine vinegar
¼ teaspoon salt
⅛ teaspoon cayenne pepper
Pinch black pepper
⅓ cup butter or margarine

Preheat oven to 375° F. Mix crab lightly with vinegar, salt, and pepper. Place in an ungreased 1-quart *au gratin* dish or shallow casserole and dot evenly with butter. Bake, uncovered, 15–20 minutes until bubbly. About 240 calories per serving.

☒ CRAB MORNAY

Crab baked in a rich cheese sauce.
Makes 4 servings

1 pound fresh lump or backfin crab meat, well picked over
1¾ cups Mornay Sauce
¼ cup finely grated Gruyère or Parmesan cheese

Preheat oven to 375° F. Toss crab with Mornay sauce to mix, spoon into an ungreased 1-quart *au gratin* dish or shallow casserole, and scatter cheese on top. Bake, uncovered 15–20 minutes until bubbly, then broil quickly to brown. About 390 calories per serving.

VARIATION:

Crab à la Florentine: Butter a 1½-quart *au gratin* dish and cover bottom with a layer of chopped, buttered spinach. Mix crab and Mornay sauce as directed and spoon over spinach. Top with ½ cup soft white bread crumbs mixed with 2 tablespoons melted butter, sprinkle lightly with paprika, and bake as directed. About 500 calories per serving.

CRAB IMPERIAL NEWBURG

Good with fluffy boiled rice, a crisp green salad, and a well-chilled dry white wine.
Makes 4–6 servings

1 pound fresh lump or backfin crab
   meat, well picked over
3 tablespoons butter or margarine
2 tablespoons flour
1½ cups light cream
3 egg yolks, lightly beaten
1 teaspoon salt
2 teaspoons prepared horseradish
1 teaspoon powdered mustard
¼ teaspoon cayenne pepper
1 tablespoon paprika
3 tablespoons dry sherry

Preheat oven to 350° F. Place crab in an ungreased 1½-quart *au gratin* dish or shallow casserole. Melt butter in a small saucepan over moderate heat and blend in flour. Add cream and heat, stirring, until thickened and smooth. Spoon a little hot sauce into yolks, then return all to saucepan; turn heat to low and warm, stirring, 1 minute—no longer. Off heat mix in remaining ingredients; pour sauce evenly over crab and bake, uncovered, ½–¾ hour until bubbly. About 435 calories for each of 4 servings, 290 calories for each of 6 servings.

DEVILED CRAB I

A delicate deviled crab.
Makes 4 servings

4 hard-cooked eggs
2 tablespoons butter or margarine
2 tablespoons flour
1¼ cups milk
1 teaspoon paprika
½ teaspoon powdered mustard
¼ teaspoon cayenne pepper
1 tablespoon Worcestershire sauce
Juice of ½ lemon
2 tablespoons minced parsley
½ teaspoon salt

1 pound fresh lump or backfin crab
   meat, well picked over

Topping:
⅓ cup fine dry bread crumbs mixed
   with 2 tablespoons melted butter
   or margarine

Preheat oven to 375° F. Chop egg whites fine; sieve the yolks and set aside. Melt butter in a small saucepan over moderate heat and blend in flour. Add milk and heat, stirring, until thickened and smooth. Off heat mix in sieved yolks and all remaining ingredients except egg whites, crab, and topping. Place crab and egg whites in a buttered shallow 1½-quart casserole, add sauce, and stir well to mix. Sprinkle topping over surface and bake, uncovered, 1 hour until browned and bubbly. About 380 calories per serving.

DEVILED CRAB II

A richer, spicier recipe.
Makes 6 servings

1½ pounds fresh lump or backfin
   crab meat, well picked over
¼ cup butter or margarine
2 tablespoons minced shallots or
   scallions
¼ cup unsifted flour
½ teaspoon powdered mustard
1 cup light cream
½ cup milk
½ cup dry sherry
Juice of ½ lemon
2 tablespoons prepared spicy brown
   mustard
2 tablespoons prepared mild yellow
   mustard
2 teaspoons ketchup
1 teaspoon Worcestershire sauce
1 tablespoon minced parsley
¼ teaspoon salt
⅛ teaspoon cayenne pepper

Topping:
½ cup cracker meal mixed with
    2 tablespoons melted butter or
    margarine

Preheat oven to 375° F. Place crab in an ungreased shallow 2-quart casserole or *au gratin* dish. Melt butter in a large saucepan over moderate heat and sauté shallots 5–8 minutes or until pale golden. Blend in flour and powdered mustard then add cream and milk and heat, stirring constantly, until thickened and smooth. Off heat mix in all remaining ingredients except topping. Pour over crab and toss lightly. Sprinkle topping over surface and bake, uncovered, 1 hour until browned and bubbly. About 415 calories per serving.

BAKED CRAB-STUFFED AVOCADOS

Makes 6 servings

3 tablespoons butter or margarine
2 tablespoons flour
½ cup light cream
½ cup milk
½ teaspoon salt
⅛ teaspoon white pepper
1 tablespoon minced chives
1 tablespoon capers
½ pound crab meat (fresh, thawed frozen, or drained canned), well picked over
3 medium-size ripe avocados
2 tablespoons lemon juice

Preheat oven to 350° F. Melt butter in a saucepan over moderate heat. Blend in flour, slowly add cream and milk, and cook, stirring, until thickened and smooth. Off heat mix in salt, pepper, chives, capers, and crab. Peel, halve, and pit avocados; brush well with lemon juice and place in a well-buttered shallow baking pan. Fill with crab mixture and bake, uncovered, 25–30 minutes until

avocados are heated through. About 335 calories per serving.

⊠ ROSY KING CRAB BAKE

Makes 2 servings

2 tablespoons minced shallots or yellow onion
3 tablespoons butter or margarine
3 tablespoons flour
1 cup light cream
2 tablespoons chili sauce
2 tablespoons dry white wine
½ teaspoon salt
¼ teaspoon celery salt
¼ teaspoon paprika
⅛ teaspoon cayenne pepper
1 (6-ounce) package frozen Alaska king crab meat, thawed and drained

Preheat oven to 400° F. Stir-fry shallots in butter in a small saucepan 3–5 minutes over moderate heat until limp. Blend in flour, add cream, and heat, stirring, until thickened and smooth. Blend in all remaining ingredients except crab and heat 1–2 minutes. Fold in crab, spoon into a buttered 1-quart *au gratin* dish or shallow casserole, and bake, uncovered, 15–20 minutes until bubbly. Serve over boiled rice. About 550 calories per serving (without rice).

BAKED STUFFED DUNGENESS CRAB

Makes 2 servings

1 (2-pound) Dungeness crab, boiled in the shell and cooled
2 tablespoons butter or margarine
2 teaspoons minced chives
⅛ teaspoon pepper
1 hard-cooked egg, shelled and chopped fine
1 tablespoon capers, drained and minced
¼ cup fine dry bread crumbs mixed with 1 tablespoon melted butter or margarine

Preheat oven to 450° F. Clean crab and remove meat from body, claws, and legs*; leave large back shell intact. Pick over crab meat, discarding bits of shell and cartilage, and flake. Melt butter in a skillet over moderately low heat, add crab, and stir-fry 2–3 minutes; mix in chives, pepper, egg, and capers. Spoon into shell, top with buttered crumbs, and place in a shallow baking pan. Bake, uncovered, 10 minutes, then broil 4″ from the heat 2–3 minutes to brown lightly. Serve in the shell. About 450 calories per serving.

VARIATIONS:

Pilaf Stuffed Dungeness Crab: Prepare crab mixture as directed, but when stir-frying crab meat in butter, add ½ cup cold cooked rice. Proceed as directed. About 495 calories per serving.

Frisco-Style Stuffed Dungeness Crab: Prepare crab mixture as directed but omit capers. Off heat, stir in ½ cup Medium White Sauce, ¼ cup sautéed minced mushrooms, and 2 tablespoons dry sherry. Spoon into shell, top with buttered crumbs, and bake as directed. About 650 calories per serving.

⚖ ☒ MARYLAND CRAB CAKES

Spicily seasoned.
Makes 4 servings

- 1 pound fresh lump or backfin crab meat, well picked over
- 2 eggs, lightly beaten
- 2 tablespoons mayonnaise
- 1 tablespoon prepared horseradish
- 1 tablespoon prepared spicy brown mustard
- 1 tablespoon minced parsley
- ¼ teaspoon salt
- ¼ teaspoon liquid hot red pepper seasoning
- Pinch pepper

- ⅔ cup cracker meal
- ⅓ cup cooking oil

Mix crab well with all but last 2 ingredients and shape into cakes about 3″ across and ½″ thick; dip in cracker meal to coat well. Heat oil in a large, heavy skillet over moderately high heat until a cube of bread will sizzle, add cakes, and brown 3–4 minutes on a side. Drain well on paper toweling and serve with Tartar Sauce. About 255 calories per serving (without tartar sauce).

☒ HOT CRAB BURGERS

Makes 4–6 servings

- ¾ cup butter or margarine
- 2 (7½-ounce) cans crab meat, drained and well picked over
- 2 tablespoons cider vinegar
- 2 tablespoons minced pimiento
- ¼ cup minced celery
- 1 tablespoon minced parsley
- ½ teaspoon salt
- ⅛ teaspoon pepper
- ½ cup heavy cream
- 4–6 hamburger or hot dog buns, split and toasted

Melt butter in a skillet over moderately low heat. Add crab and stir-fry 2–3 minutes. Add all remaining ingredients except buns and simmer uncovered, stirring occasionally, 15 minutes. Fill buns with crab mixture and serve. About 570 calories for each of 4 servings, 400 calories for each of 6 servings.

CRAB LOUIS

Makes 4 servings

- 1 quart crisp, coarsely shredded lettuce
- 1 pound fresh-cooked crab meat, well picked over (Dungeness, lump, or backfin) or thawed frozen Alaska king crab
- 4 tomatoes, quartered

4 hard-cooked eggs, peeled and
    quartered

Dressing:
1 cup mayonnaise
⅓ cup ketchup
¼ cup heavy cream, whipped
2 tablespoons finely grated scallions
2 tablespoons minced parsley
2 tablespoons minced sweet green
    pepper
2 teaspoons lemon juice
1 teaspoon prepared horseradish
Pinch salt

On 4 luncheon size plates, make beds
of lettuce. Mound crab on top. Mix
dressing and spoon over crab, then
garnish each plate with tomatoes and
hard-cooked eggs. About 800 calories per serving.

COOL CRAB CUP

Makes 4 servings

1 pound fresh lump or backfin crab
    meat, well picked over
1 cup shredded lettuce

Dressing:
2 teaspoons prepared horseradish
2 tablespoons chili sauce
2 tablespoons minced sweet green
    pepper
2 tablespoons minced dill pickle
1 tablespoon minced scallion
2 tablespoons lemon juice
½ teaspoon salt
⅛ teaspoon pepper
⅔ cup mayonnaise

Place crab in a mixing bowl. Mix
dressing, pour over crab, and toss
lightly to mix. Cover and chill several hours. Serve on beds of shredded lettuce as a first or main course.
About 415 calories per serving.

VARIATIONS:

Lobster Cup: Prepare as directed,
substituting 2 cups diced boiled lobster for the crab. About 420 calories
per serving.

Shrimp Cup: Prepare as directed,
substituting 2 cups diced boiled
shrimp for the crab. If you prefer,
use the tiny Danish shrimp. About
445 calories per serving.

Crab Stuffed Tomatoes or Avocados: Prepare as directed but serve
in hollowed-out ripe tomatoes or in
avocado halves instead of on lettuce.
About 425 calories per serving if
served in tomatoes, about 600 calories per serving if served in avocado
halves.

CRAYFISH

Crawfish, crawdads, écrevisse—these
are the sweet-tender little fresh water cousins of the lobster. To Europeans they are a delicacy unsur-
passed, and in Finland, where the
season begins at midnight on July 15
and lasts a short two months, the
whole country rollicks with crayfish
fests (by tradition, every crayfish tail
must be followed by a swig of iced
schnapps). The American crayfish,
at six inches, is nearly twice as long
as the European but no less succulent. It is found in creeks around
Lake Michigan, in the Pacific Northwest, and in Gulf Coast bayous. The
season varies from area to area but
is usually at its peak in mid or late
summer. Occasionally, crayfish are
shipped live to metropolitan areas;
more often they are canned.

Amount to Buy: Allow about 1
dozen crayfish in the shell per person, more if appetites are large (in
Finland, 20 are considered a "de-
cent" portion) or about ⅓ pound
crayfish meat per person.

For Top Quality: Buy crayfish that
are live and kicking.

How to Cook Crayfish

There is really only one way, experts

will tell you—*boiling*—but the flavor of boiled crayfish varies markedly according to the seasonings used.

General Preparation: Wash crayfish carefully under cold running water; tear off the thin shell-like fin on the center-top of the tail (the dark, threadlike intestinal vein should come away with it).

To Boil: For each dozen crayfish, you will need 1 quart sea water (or 1 quart tap water mixed with 1 tablespoon salt) or 1 quart Simple Court Bouillon. Bring to a boil in a large, deep kettle, drop in live crayfish, cover, and simmer 5 minutes, just until crayfish turn scarlet. Drain and serve hot with melted butter or cool in broth and serve at room temperature.

VARIATION:

Finnish-Style Crayfish: Boil crayfish as directed in sea or salt water but add 1 large bunch fresh dill, preferably that which is beginning to flower, separated into stalks. Cool crayfish in cooking liquid to room temperature before serving. If you like, marinate crayfish in liquid 1–2 days in refrigerator, then bring to room temperature before serving.

How to Eat Crayfish

This is messy work, so give every guest a large bib and plenty of paper napkins. Also set out lots of ice cold beer.

(1) Twist off claws, snip off pointed tips, then separate claws at "elbow" joint. Slice off broad base of claws and suck meat out.

(2) Separate body of crayfish from tail and suck any meat from body (there will not be much).

(3) With the point of a knife, lift top shell from tail, take out tail meat, and remove dark vein, if any. Slosh meat in melted butter or place on lightly buttered toast and eat. This is the *pièce de résistance.*

LOBSTER

Of all America's seafoods, lobster is king. Steamed simply over sea water, or boiled in it with perhaps a sprig or two of seaweed, lobster is a thing of beauty (and a joy as long as it lasts). Underneath that scarlet armor, fat snowy chunks wait to be twisted out and sloshed in melted butter. What can top that? According to Down Easters (and all lobster lovers), nothing. Not the most glorious French soufflé, not the lordliest English sirloin.

The Kinds of Lobster

The best known—and best—is the giant clawed *American or Maine Lobster.* But there is another, the *rock or spiny lobster,* which swims in the Gulf of Mexico and in the warm waters off the coast of Southern California. It has no claws to speak of, but its tail is big and broad and full of delectable meat. Unfortunately, these lobsters are rarely available outside their immediate areas except as frozen tails.

About Buying Fresh Lobster

Season: Year round.

Popular Market Forms: Live in the shell; cooked in the shell; iced cooked lobster meat. It's no longer necessary to live in the East to buy live Maine lobsters; a number of firms will pack them in seaweed and airmail them to you.

Amount Needed: Allow a 1–3-pound lobster per person, depending on appetites, and about ¼–⅓ pound lobster meat. Maine lobsters are graded in 4 sizes: chickens (¾–1 pound), quarters (1¼ pounds), large (1½–2¼ pounds), jumbo (2½ pounds up).

For Top Quality: Live lobsters should be thrashing about (be sure to have the claws pegged so you won't get nipped); cooked whole lobsters should have a fresh "seashore" odor and their tails, when straightened out, should spring right back. Cooked, iced lobster meat should be firm and sweet smelling.

About Frozen and Canned Lobster

Frozen uncooked rock lobster tails are widely available; the plumpest and choicest come from South Africa and Australia. Also marketed are tins of frozen, cooked lobster meat, and in the gourmet line such classics as lobster Newburg. Canned lobster meat and tails are generally stocked by groceries, as are canned lobster bisques, Newburgs, and thermidors. *To Cook Frozen Lobsters:* The tails are usually cooked solidly frozen (but read package directions); cooked frozen meat should be thawed before using. *How to Use Canned Lobster:* Because this meat is fully cooked, it is a good choice for salads and casseroles.

How to Cook Lobster

Lobster is marvelously adaptable, but it is at its best simply steamed, boiled, or baked. Broiling tends to dry it out (though lovers of broiled lobster will forever argue the point).

General Preparation: How lobster is prepared depends on how it is to be cooked. For steaming or boiling it needs no preparation at all. For baking and broiling, however, it must be split live and, for certain other recipes, cut in large chunks.

To Split Live Lobsters: Don't be squeamish about cutting into a live

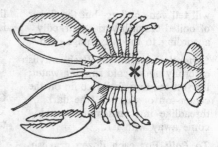

lobster; it has little feeling. Place lobster on its stomach with claws up over the head. Drive the point of a sharp sturdy knife into center back (X) where body meets tail (this kills lobster), and turn lobster on its back and quickly cut down through the body and head to split.

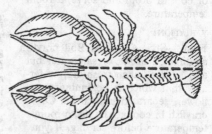

Now cut through tail (don't be alarmed if legs twitch a bit; these are simple muscular spasms and do not mean lobster is suffering). Spread halves flat, meat side up, and pull soft, beige intestinal vein from tail; discard papery stomach sac located just behind the eyes. Lift out coral (ovary and undeveloped roe) and buttery gray-green tomalley (liver) and save if they are to be used in sauces or stuffings; otherwise leave in place in the body cavity (they're great delicacies). Once in a great while, though law forbids their being taken, you may come upon a female just ready to lay eggs. These appear as a dark caviar-like mass in the body and upper tail and are considered the choicest of delicacies.

Serve separately or mix into stuffings along with coral and tomalley.

To Clean and Crack Live Lobsters:

Follow all steps for splitting live lobsters; twist off claws and crack each section; cut body and tail into large or small chunks as individual recipes specify. Do not remove meat from shells unless directed otherwise. *Note to the Faint of Heart:* If you simply cannot bring yourself to cut into a live lobster, there is an alternative (although the finished lobster may not be quite so succulent). Bring a huge kettle of lightly salted water to a boil, drop in live lobsters, cover, and simmer 3–5 minutes just until they stop squirming. Drain, cool in a colander under cold running water until easy to handle, then split or clean and crack as directed.

To Boil: The best possible medium for boiling lobsters is sea water. If you haven't got it, you can fake it by adding 1 tablespoon salt to each quart water. Unless you have an absolutely colossal kettle, don't try to cook more than 2 lobsters in a pot. Bring 3–4 quarts sea or salt water to a boil, grasp lobsters, 1 at a time, by cupping your hand around back and plunge head first into boiling water. Cover and, from time water returns to a boil, cook 5–6 minutes per pound (1½-pound lobsters will take 8–9 minutes, 2-pound lobsters, 10–12). If lobsters are extra large, cook 5 minutes for the first pound and 4 minutes for each additional pound. *Simple Test for Doneness:* Pull one of the antennae on the head; if it comes easily from socket, lobster is done. Color of lobsters is important, too; when cooked they will be a dazzling scarlet. Drain lobsters and serve hot, either whole or split and cracked, with melted butter and lemon wedges. Or cook, chill, and serve with Sauce Verte.

VARIATIONS:

Savory Boiled Lobster: Prepare as directed, using a court bouillon instead of salt water.

Lobster Boiled in Beer: Boil as directed, using 2–2½ quarts beer or ale and 1–1½ quarts water instead of salt water. The beer gives the lobster extra-rich, slightly malty flavor.

To Steam: Pour 1″ sea or salt water into a large, heavy kettle and bring to a boil over moderately high heat. Add lobsters, cover, and steam 15 minutes. Serve hot or cold as you would boiled lobster.

To Bake: Preheat oven to 350° F. Split and clean live lobsters (the 1½–2½-pound size is best) and arrange side by side, cut side up, in a large, shallow roasting pan. Cover exposed meat with pats of butter (each lobster will take ⅓–½ stick) and squeeze the juice of ½ lemon over each lobster. Bake, uncovered, 25–30 minutes, basting often with pan juices. Sprinkle with salt and freshly ground black pepper and serve at once.

To Oven Broil: Preheat broiler. Split and clean live lobster. Lay lobsters flesh side up as flat as possible on a foil-lined broiler pan, brush generously with melted butter or margarine, and broil 4″ from the heat 12–15 minutes, brushing often with melted butter, until lightly browned. Sprinkle with salt, pepper, and lemon juice and serve piping hot.

How to Eat Lobster

(1) Twist off claws, crack each in several places with

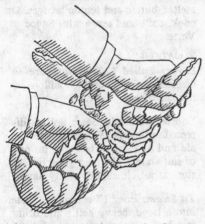

intestinal vein. Cut meat in bite-size chunks with fork.

lobster or nut crackers, and twist out meat with a fork.

(3) Pull body from shell and arch left and right sides backward to split in two.

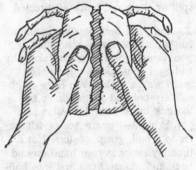

(2) Separate tail from body by arching lobster backward until it cracks.

The green tomalley and red coral are both in this part. Avoid grayish, feathery portions.

(4) Pull off lobster legs and suck each as you would a straw to get out any meat or juices inside.

LOBSTER NEWBURG I

The simple, classic version—perfect for a chafing dish.
Makes 4 servings

Break off fins at base of tail and push meat from shell with a fork; remove

1 *pound cooked lobster meat, cut in*
   small chunks
¼ *cup butter or margarine*
½ *cup medium-dry sherry*

¼ teaspoon paprika
¾ teaspoon salt
1½ cups hot Velouté Sauce
¼ cup heavy cream

Pick over lobster meat, separating out any bits of coral; sieve coral and reserve to use as a garnish. Stir-fry lobster meat in butter in a chafing dish skillet over direct, moderate heat 2–3 minutes; add sherry, paprika, and salt and simmer, uncovered, 2–3 minutes. Blend in sauce and cream, set over chafing dish warmer, and simmer, but do not boil, 2–3 minutes. Sprinkle with coral, if any, or with a little paprika. Serve from chafing dish, ladling over boiled rice or into crisp pastry shells. About 480 calories per serving (without rice or pastry shells).

LOBSTER NEWBURG II

Delicately flavored but far richer than Lobster Newburg I.
Makes 4 servings

1 pound cooked lobster meat, cut in small chunks
¼ cup butter or margarine
½ cup dry vermouth
¼ cup brandy
1¾ cups heavy cream
¾ teaspoon salt
Pinch pepper
Pinch nutmeg or mace
2 egg yolks, lightly beaten

Stir-fry lobster in butter in a large, heavy skillet 2–3 minutes over moderate heat; lift to a plate with a slotted spoon. Add vermouth and brandy to skillet and boil rapidly, stirring, until mixture just covers bottom of skillet. Add cream and simmer, stirring, until reduced by about ⅓. Mix in salt, pepper, and nutmeg; also add lobster. Transfer to the top of a double boiler and set over simmering water. Mix a little hot sauce into yolks, return to pan, and heat, stirring, 2–3 minutes until slightly thickened. Ladle over boiled rice or into crisp pastry shells or, if you prefer, transfer to a chafing dish and serve at the table. About 695 calories per serving (without rice or pastry shells).

BROILED LOBSTERS WITH HERB AND CRUMB STUFFING

Makes 4 servings

4 (1¼-pound) live lobsters
½ cup melted butter or margarine

Stuffing:
1 quart soft white bread crumbs
1 clove garlic, peeled and crushed
½ cup butter or margarine
¼ teaspoon salt
⅛ teaspoon pepper
2 tablespoons minced chives
2 tablespoons minced parsley

Preheat broiler. Split lobsters in half lengthwise, remove stomach and intestinal vein,* reserve any tomalley or coral. Make stuffing by sautéing crumbs and garlic in butter in a large, heavy skillet over moderate heat 2–3 minutes until pale golden; off heat mix in remaining ingredients, also any tomalley and chopped coral. Lay lobsters as flat as possible, shell side down, on a foil-lined broiler pan and brush generously with melted butter. Broil 4″ from heat 12–15 minutes until lightly browned, brushing often with butter. Remove from broiler, mound stuffing into body cavity of each lobster, return to broiler, and broil 2–3 minutes to brown lightly. Serve with melted butter and lemon wedges. About 690 calories per serving.

VARIATION:
Prepare as directed, reducing bread crumbs in stuffing to 3 cups and adding 1 cup finely chopped toasted blanched almonds. About 870 calories per serving.

LOBSTER FRA DIAVOLO

Lobster prepared the Italian way in a garlic-scented tomato sauce. It is flamed with brandy just before serving.

Makes 4 servings

2 (1½-pound) live lobsters, cleaned,* cracked, and cut in 2" chunks
½ cup olive oil
1 medium-size yellow onion, peeled and coarsely chopped
1 clove garlic, peeled and crushed
1 teaspoon oregano
¼ teaspoon nutmeg
⅛ teaspoon cloves
½ teaspoon salt
⅛ teaspoon pepper
4 sprigs parsley
2 cups canned tomatoes
4 cups hot boiled rice
¼ cup brandy, warmed slightly

Sauté lobsters in oil in a large, heavy kettle, turning often, about 5 minutes until they turn a rich scarlet. Add onion, garlic and seasonings and heat, stirring, 3–5 minutes. Add parsley and tomatoes, cover, and simmer 15–20 minutes. Arrange lobster in center of a large platter, surround with rice and top with kettle sauce. Pour brandy over lobster, blaze with a match, and carry flaming to the table. About 575 calories per serving.

LOBSTER CARDINAL

Makes 2 servings

2 (1½-pound) lobsters, boiled, drained, split lengthwise, and cleaned
½ pound mushrooms, wiped clean and coarsely chopped
1 truffle, minced
3 tablespoons butter or margarine
1 tablespoon grated Parmesan cheese

Sauce:
1 cup hot Béchamel Sauce
½ cup boiled, minced lobster meat
⅓ cup heavy cream
½ teaspoon anchovy paste
Pinch cayenne pepper

Preheat broiler. Remove meat from lobsters; dice claw and body meat and slice tail ¼"–½" thick. Mince enough tail meat to total ½ cup; reserve for sauce. Spread shells as flat as possible on a baking sheet and set aside. Sauté diced claw and body meat with mushrooms and truffle in butter about 5 minutes until mushrooms are limp; set aside while you prepare the sauce. Place Béchamel sauce in the top of a double boiler, add reserved minced lobster and remaining sauce ingredients; set over simmering water and heat, stirring, about 2–3 minutes. Mix a little sauce into mushroom mixture, just enough to bind. Make a bed of this mixture in each lobster shell, arrange tail slices on top and spoon enough sauce over all to coat. Sprinkle with Parmesan and broil 4"–5" from the heat 3–4 minutes until browned and bubbly. About 710 calories per serving.

LOBSTER À L'AMÉRICAINE

Makes 4 servings

2 (1¼–1½-pound) live lobsters or 4 (8-ounce) frozen South African rock lobster tails
⅓ cup olive oil
¼ cup brandy

Sauce:
2 tablespoons butter or margarine
1 small yellow onion, peeled and minced
3 tablespoons minced shallots or scallions
1 clove garlic, peeled and crushed
2 large tomatoes, peeled, cored, seeded, and coarsely chopped
2 tablespoons tomato paste
2 cups dry white wine
2 tablespoons minced parsley

*1 tablespoon minced fresh tarragon
or 1 teaspoon dried tarragon*
*1 (4″) sprig fresh thyme or ½
teaspoon dried thyme*
½ bay leaf
½ teaspoon salt
⅛ teaspoon cayenne pepper

If lobsters are live, clean*; twist off claws, crack, and reserve; cut tails crosswise into chunks at segmented divisions and cut body into 2″ chunks. Leave meat in shell and save any coral or tomalley for the sauce. If using frozen tails, simply cut crosswise into 1″ chunks while still solidly frozen. Stir-fry lobster in oil in a large, heavy skillet over moderate heat 3–5 minutes until shells turn scarlet; lift out lobster and set aside; do not drain off oil. In the same skillet, begin sauce: Melt butter and stir-fry onion, shallots, and garlic 3–5 minutes over moderate heat until limp. Mix in remaining sauce ingredients and simmer uncovered, stirring occasionally, about 1 hour. Sauce should have reduced by half; if not, boil rapidly to reduce. Strain sauce through a fine sieve into a large saucepan and set over low heat. Pour brandy over lobster and blaze with a match; when flames die, add lobster to sauce, cover, and simmer 12–15 minutes just to blend flavors. Mix in any tomalley and chopped coral, heat 1–2 minutes longer, and serve with boiled rice or Rice Pilaf. About 495 calories per serving (without rice or Rice Pilaf).

LOBSTER CANTONESE

Makes 4 servings

½ pound ground lean pork
1 clove garlic, peeled and crushed
*3 tablespoons peanut or other
cooking oil*
2 cups chicken broth
¼ cup soy sauce
1 teaspoon sugar

*1 teaspoon monosodium glutamate
(MSG)*
*2 (1¼–1½-pound) live lobsters,
cleaned,* cracked, and cut into 2″
chunks*
*2 tablespoons cornstarch blended
with ¼ cup cold water*
*¼ cup scallions, minced (include
green tops)*
1 egg, lightly beaten

Stir-fry pork and garlic in oil in a *wok* or large, heavy skillet over moderate heat until pork is no longer pink. Mix in broth, soy sauce, sugar, and MSG; add lobsters, cover, and simmer 10 minutes. Add cornstarch mixture and heat, stirring, until thickened and clear. Stir in scallions, drizzle in egg, and cook, stirring, 2–3 minutes until egg is just set. Serve with boiled rice. About 395 calories per serving (without rice).

⊠ BROILED ROCK LOBSTER TAILS

Makes 4 servings

*4 (8–12-ounce) thawed frozen rock
lobster tails*
2 tablespoons lemon juice
⅓ cup melted butter or margarine
⅛ teaspoon pepper

Preheat broiler. With kitchen shears, cut away thin undershell, exposing meat; bend tails backward until they crack and will almost lie flat. Arrange on a foil-lined broiler pan, shell side down, sprinkle with lemon juice, and brush liberally with butter. Broil 4″–5″ from the heat, brushing with any remaining butter, 10–15 minutes, depending on size, until lightly browned. (*Note:* If large tails are unavailable, use the smaller, adjusting cooking times as follows: 5–6 minutes for 3–5-ounce tails, 7–9 minutes for 6–8-ounce tails.) Sprinkle with pepper, and serve with lemon wedges and additional melted butter. About 300 calories per serving.

VARIATION:

⚖ **Low-Calorie Broiled Rock Lobster Tails:** Use the 8-ounce tails and broil as directed, substituting low-calorie Italian, garlic, or herb dressing for the butter. About 170 calories per serving.

COLD CURRIED LOBSTER

Makes 4 servings

1½ pounds cooked lobster meat, well picked over and cut in bite-size chunks

Dressing:
⅔ cup mayonnaise
⅓ cup sour cream
2 tablespoons minced parsley
2 tablespoons minced fresh dill
1 tablespoon minced fresh tarragon
2 tablespoons capers
1 tablespoon curry powder
2 tablespoons finely grated yellow onion
Juice of ½ lime
3–4 dashes liquid hot red pepper seasoning

Place lobster in a large bowl. Mix dressing ingredients until well blended, pour over lobster, and toss to mix. Cover and chill several hours. Serve as is, in lettuce cups, hollowed-out tomatoes, or avocado halves. About 500 calories per serving (without lettuce, tomatoes, or avocado halves).

LOBSTER THERMIDOR

A showy way to prepare frozen rock lobster tails.
Makes 4 servings

4 (8–10-ounce) frozen rock lobster tails, boiled by package directions and drained
3 tablespoons minced scallions (white part only)

2 tablespoons butter or margarine
⅓ cup dry white wine
1 teaspoon powdered mustard
2 cups hot Mornay Sauce
4 teaspoons grated Parmesan cheese

Preheat broiler. Remove lobster meat from shells, cut in ½" chunks, and set aside; reserve shells. Stir-fry scallions in butter in a small saucepan over moderate heat 2–3 minutes until limp. Add wine and boil, uncovered, until reduced to ¼ cup. Blend in mustard, then stir into Mornay sauce. Mix a little hot sauce into lobster meat, just enough to bind. Place lobster shells in a shallow baking pan, fill with lobster mixture, then cover with remaining Mornay sauce, and sprinkle each lobster with 1 teaspoon grated Parmesan. Broil 4"–5" from heat 3–4 minutes until browned and bubbly. About 475 calories per serving.

MUSSELS

Someday, if there's a shortage of clams and oysters, we may be driven to eat mussels. Fishermen tell us there are millions of them along both coasts, but we seem to feel, as long as we've loads of clams and oysters, why bother? Mussels are stronger flavored than clams or oysters, slightly tougher, too (or is that because we don't know how to cook them?). In Europe, especially Mediterranean Europe, people do delectable things with mussels—stuff them with rice and currants and piñon nuts; simmer them, shell and all, in tomato sauces heady with garlic. We would do well to follow their lead.

The Kinds of Mussels

There is only one of importance, the *blue edible mussel,* which lives in dense colonies on wharf pilings and along rocky shores.

About Buying Fresh Mussels

Season:

East Coast: Year round.

West Coast: November through April (because of the dangerous, warm weather "red tide," see Clams).

Popular Market Forms: Alive, in the shell; they are sold either by the dozen or the pound.

Amount Needed: Allow about ½–1 dozen mussels per person, depending on size of mussels and appetites.

For Top Quality: Look for mussels with tightly closed shells that will not slip or budge when pressed.

Other Forms of Mussels

To date, mussels are only available canned, not frozen. These are already cooked and best used for quick soups, fritters, patties, or casseroles.

How to Cleanse Mussels of Grit: Scrub mussels hard with a stiff brush under cold running water, pull or cut off the long beard, and scrape away any small barnacles or incrustations on the shells. Submerge mussels in a kettle of cool water and let stand 2–3 hours so they will purge themselves of sand. Discard any that float, also any with shells not tightly clamped shut.

How to Open Mussels: As with clams, there are two ways, prying and steaming. How mussels are to be prepared determines which to use.

(1) *To Pry Open* (for mussels to be stuffed): Insert a paring knife into back of mussel to the right of the hinge and with blunt edge facing hinge. Move knife clockwise around crevice, twisting slightly to force shell open; take care not to cut hinge. Open mussels over a bowl so that none of their juice is lost. Once mussel is open, trim away any stray whiskers.

(2) *To Steam Open and Shuck* (for mussels to be cut from shell and used in fritters, chowders, etc.): Place mussels in a large kettle, pour in about ¾ cup boiling water, cover, and steam over moderate heat 3 minutes, just until shells open. Discard any that do not open; they are dead and full of mud. Drain mussels, remove meat from shells, and trim off any tag ends of beard. (*Note:* Before using mussel liquid, strain through a fine sieve lined with a double thickness of cheesecloth.)

How to Cook Mussels

Because of their robust flavor, mussels are better cooked in the company of vegetables, herbs, and spices than by the utterly basic methods. Even when they are steamed, they benefit from a little lily-gilding (recipes follow).

General Preparation: Cleanse as directed above and, if recipes so specify, open.

⚖ COQUILLES OF MUSSELS

Makes 6 servings

3 dozen mussels in the shell, prepared for cooking
1¼ cups hot Thick White Sauce
3 tablespoons melted butter or margarine
2 cups hot seasoned mashed potatoes
⅓ cup fine dry bread crumbs mixed with 1 tablespoon melted butter or margarine

Steam mussels open and shuck*; reserve ¼ cup of liquid from mussels and strain, then mix with white sauce, 1 tablespoon butter, and the mussels. Spoon into 6–8 buttered large scallop shells and arrange on a baking sheet. Place potatoes in a pastry bag fitted with a small rosette tube and pipe a decorative border around edge of each shell; brush with 1 tablespoon melted butter. Scatter buttered crumbs on top of mussels and bake, uncovered, 5–7 minutes until lightly browned. About 285 calories per serving.

VARIATIONS:

Creamed Mussels: Mix white sauce, mussels liquid, mussels, and butter as directed, then heat in the top of a double boiler over simmering water 4–5 minutes, stirring occasionally until piping hot. Spoon over hot buttered toast, sprinkle with parsley, and serve. About 315 calories per serving.

⚔️ **Creamed Mussels au Gratin:** Mix white sauce, mussels liquid, mussels, and butter as directed, stir in 2 tablespoons minced chives, spoon into an ungreased 1½-quart *au gratin* dish, and top with ⅔ cup fine dry bread crumbs mixed with 2 tablespoons melted butter and ⅓ cup grated Parmesan cheese. Bake, uncovered, 10–15 minutes until bubbly and lightly browned. About 295 calories per serving.

⚔️ **FILEY BAY MUSSELS**

Rather like "deviled" mussels on the half shell.
Makes 4 servings

Rock salt
3 dozen mussels in the shell, prepared for cooking
½ cup butter (no substitute), softened to room temperature
2 tablespoons minced shallots or chives
1 clove garlic, peeled and crushed
2 tablespoons minced parsley

1 tablespoon prepared mild yellow mustard
2 teaspoons steak sauce

Preheat broiler. Make a bed of rock salt in a very large, shallow baking pan, dampen slightly with water, and heat uncovered in oven 5 minutes while broiler preheats. Meanwhile, steam mussels open,* lift off top shells and discard. Arrange mussels in hot salt, pushing shells down well so they won't tip. Cream butter with remaining ingredients and place about 1 teaspoonful on each mussel. Broil 3"–4" from the heat 2–3 minutes until bubbly. Transfer to a hot platter or individual plates and serve. About 280 calories per serving.

MUSSELS MARINIÈRE

Makes 4 servings

⅓ cup minced shallots or ½ cup minced yellow onion
½ cup butter (no substitute)
3 dozen mussels in the shell, prepared for cooking
4 sprigs parsley
2 (4") sprigs fresh thyme or ½ teaspoon dried thyme
1 bay leaf
2 cups dry white wine
2 tablespoons minced parsley

Stir-fry shallots in ¼ cup butter 5–8 minutes in a large, heavy kettle over moderate heat until golden. Add mussels, herbs, and wine, cover, bring to a boil, then reduce heat and simmer 3 minutes until mussels open. Discard any unopened mussels, also empty half shells. Transfer mussels, still in their shells, to a heated tureen and keep warm. Strain cooking liquid through a double thickness of cheesecloth, add remaining butter and minced parsley, and heat, stirring, just until butter melts. Taste for salt and add if needed. Pour sauce over mussels and serve with hot French bread. About 385 calories per serving (without bread).

VARIATION:

Clams Marinière: Prepare as directed, substituting steamer or cherrystone clams for mussels. About 375 calories per serving.

MARSEILLE-STYLE MUSSELS WITH GARLIC AND TOMATO

Makes 4 servings

1 large yellow onion, peeled and minced
3–4 cloves garlic, peeled and crushed
3 stalks celery, chopped fine
¼ cup olive oil
6 large ripe tomatoes, peeled, cored, seeded, and chopped fine or 1 (1-pound 12-ounce) can tomatoes
2 cups dry white wine
3 dozen mussels in the shell, prepared for cooking
1 tablespoon minced parsley

Stir-fry onion, garlic, and celery in oil in a large, heavy kettle 5–8 minutes over moderate heat until golden; add tomatoes and wine, cover and simmer 15 minutes. Add mussels and simmer 3 minutes longer. Off heat, discard any mussels that have not opened along with any empty half shells. Transfer mussels, still in their shells, to a heated tureen and keep warm. Strain cooking liquid through a double thickness of cheesecloth. Return to heat, bring to a simmer, and stir in parsley. Taste for salt and add if needed. Pour sauce over mussels and serve with hot buttered French bread. About 420 calories per serving (without bread).

ARMENIAN MUSSELS STUFFED WITH RICE, CURRANTS, AND PIÑON NUTS

Makes 4–6 servings

⅓ cup olive oil
1 large yellow onion, peeled and minced
3 dozen mussels in the shell, prepared for cooking
⅓ cup dried currants
⅓ cup piñon nuts
½ teaspoon salt
¼ teaspoon cinnamon
¼ teaspoon allspice
⅛ teaspoon pepper
½ cup dry white wine
1¾ cups water
1 cup uncooked rice

Heat oil in a large, heavy kettle over moderate heat about 1 minute, add onion, and stir-fry 3–5 minutes until limp. Add mussels, currants, piñon nuts, salt, and spices and heat, stirring, 2–3 minutes until mussels begin to open. Add wine and water, cover, and simmer 3–5 minutes until mussels open wide. Lift out all mussels; discard any that do not open, and reserve the rest; trim off any stray bits of beard. Bring kettle mixture to a rapid boil, stir in rice, and boil gently, uncovered, 12–15 minutes until rice is done and all liquid absorbed. Stir rice well to mix ingredients, then spoon into mussels, filling shells full and packing ever so lightly so mixture will not fall out. Cool to room temperature before serving. About 525 calories for each of 4 servings, 350 calories for each of 6 servings.

OYSTERS

Oysters have a long and well-documented history. The Greeks

served them at cocktail parties as "provocatives to drinking," the Romans imported oysters from England, packed in snow, then parked them in salt water ponds until they could be fattened up on a diet of wine and pastry. American Indians were great oyster eaters, too, judging from the middens of shells found up and down both coasts. Colonists were enthusiasts from the beginning, and by the early eighteenth century, when trains began rushing fresh seafood into the Midwest, oysters became the rage. Soon every town of consequence had its own oyster parlor, and newspaper society pages devoted columns to oyster parties. The Abraham Lincolns, while still in Illinois, gave oyster suppers at which nothing but oysters was served. Oysters continue to be popular, so much so that, even though they are now "grown" commercially, the supply doesn't meet the demand.

The Kinds of Oysters

There are three popular American species, one taken from the Atlantic and Gulf of Mexico, two from the Pacific.

Eastern Oyster: Found along the east coast from Massachusetts to Texas, this oyster accounts for 89 per cent of America's catch. It includes the famous *blue points,* named for Blue Point, Long Island, where they were first found (but now simply a term referring to any oyster from 2″–4″ long), also the choice Virginia *Chincoteagues,* considered by many to be America's finest oyster. The subtle flavor differences among Eastern oysters depends on the oysters' diet and upon the composition of the waters in which they live.

Olympias: These sweet miniatures (it takes 300–500 to make a quart) are the pearls among oysters (and very nearly as expensive). Originally found all along the West Coast, they now come primarily from Puget Sound "farms."

Japanese or Pacific: This giant transplant from Japan is the West Coast's most popular oyster. Too large to eat on the half shell, it is usually cut up and fried, hashed or stewed.

About Buying Fresh Oysters

Season: There is some truth to the old R month theory. Though oysters are edible between May and August, they aren't very plump or tasty because this is their season to spawn. Few markets sell oysters in summer.

Popular Market Forms:

Eastern Oysters: Live and in the shell by the dozen; shucked by the pint or quart.

Olympias: Shucked and packed in small bottles.

Japanese: Shucked and packed in 10- or 12-ounce jars.

Amount Needed: It depends—on the size of the oysters (and appetites), on how the oysters are prepared and served. But here's a guide:

Oysters on the Half Shell: Allow about ½ dozen blue points per person, ½–1 dozen Chincoteagues, depending on size. If you splurge on Olympias, you'll have to order them especially and allow 3–4 dozen per person.

Oysters to Be Cooked in the Shell: Allow ½–1 dozen small or medium oysters per person, depending on richness of recipe.

Shucked Oysters: 1 pint will serve

about 3, more if stretched with other ingredients.

For Top Quality:

Oysters in the Shell: Choose only those that are tightly shut or those that clamp shut when handled.

Shucked Oysters: Select plump, sweet-smelling oysters with clear liquor free of shell particles and grit.

About Frozen and Canned Oysters

Shucked, raw Eastern oysters are now available frozen; they are also canned (either plain or smoked). Japanese or Pacific oysters are also canned. *To Cook Frozen Oysters:* Thaw in the refrigerator, then prepare as you would fresh oysters; cook immediately after thawing and never refreeze. *How to Use Canned Oysters:* Because these are fully cooked, they're best used in quick soups, stews, fritters, and casseroles. The smoked variety is usually served as cocktail snacks, though they, too, can be used in soups and stews.

How to Shuck Fresh Oysters: Wash
and rinse oysters well in cool water. Place oysters on counter, flat side up, and knock off thin edge (bill) with a hammer. Insert an oyster knife into broken edge and slip it around to back of oyster; sever hinge as close to flat upper shell as possible, lift off top shell and discard. Cut muscle from lower shell; carefully feel oyster for bits of shell and grit, paying particular attention to the hinge. If oysters are to be served or cooked on the half shell, replace in deep lower shells. (*Note:* Open oysters over a small bowl to catch any spilled juice and strain juice through a double thickness of cheesecloth before using.)

How to Cook Oysters

There are those who say oysters should never be cooked, that the only way to savor them is on the half shell with a squirt of lemon and a grinding of black pepper. Maybe so. But just as many people insist that an oyster's true glory emerges only in the cooking. Here are the best methods.

General Preparation: Shuck oysters or not as recipes direct. Obviously, if a recipe calls for oysters to be shucked, the best plan is to buy them already out of the shell.

To Panfry (*Sauté*): Pat shucked oysters dry on paper toweling. Dredge in flour delicately seasoned with salt and pepper and sauté in butter or margarine (about ⅓ cup butter for 1 pint oysters) 3–4 minutes over moderate heat, turning once, just until oysters plump up and brown lightly. Serve with lemon.

VARIATIONS:

Pan-"Roasted" Oysters: Pat oysters dry but do not dredge. Sauté in butter or margarine (½ cup per pint of oysters) 3–4 minutes over moderate heat, turning once, just until they plump up and their edges ruffle. Serve with lemon.

Spicy Pan-"Roasted" Oysters: Pan roast oysters as above but reduce amount of butter to ¼ cup for each pint oysters. With a slotted spoon, ladle cooked oysters over slices of hot buttered toast. To pan add 2 tablespoons ketchup and 1 teaspoon Worcestershire sauce; heat and stir 1 minute, spoon over oysters and serve.

Pepper Pan Roast: Stir-fry ¼ cup each minced yellow onion and sweet green pepper in ⅓ cup butter or margarine 3–5 minutes over moderate heat until limp. Add 1 pint shucked oysters and pan roast as above.

Breaded Fried Oysters: Pat shucked oysters dry and dredge in flour lightly seasoned with salt and pepper. Dip in a mixture of beaten egg and water (1 tablespoon cold water to each egg), then roll in cracker meal, fine dry crumbs, or a ½ and ½ mixture of flour and corn meal. Sauté in butter or margarine (½ cup for 1 pint oysters) 3–4 minutes over moderately high heat, turning once, until golden brown. Drain on paper toweling and serve with lemon.

To Deep-Fat-Fry: Pat shucked oysters dry on paper toweling and bread as above. Heat cooking oil or shortening in a deep fat fryer to 375° F., place a single layer of oysters in fryer basket, lower into fat, and fry 2–3 minutes until lightly browned. Drain on paper toweling and set uncovered in an oven turned to lowest heat to keep warm while you fry the rest. Serve with lemon and, if you like, Tartar Sauce or Rémoulade Sauce.

VARIATION:

Batter-Fried Oysters (Oyster Fritters): Make up batter given in Fish and Chips recipe. Pat shucked oysters dry on paper toweling, dip in batter, and fry, 6–8 at a time, as directed above.

To Oven Roast: Preheat oven to 500° F. Scrub oysters but do not shuck. Place flat side up in a large, shallow baking pan and bake, uncovered, 12–15 minutes until shells open. Serve in the shell or, if you prefer, on the half shell (simply cut hinge and lift off shallow top shell).

To Roast over Charcoal: Prepare a moderately hot charcoal fire.* Scrub oysters but don't shuck. Wrap, 4–6 to a package, in heavy foil, place

directly on coals, and roast, without turning, 6 minutes. Serve with lemon.

VARIATION: Do not wrap oysters; instead, place flat side up on grill 4″ from coals and roast 10–15 minutes until shells open.

To Steam: Scrub oysters but do not shuck. Place in a deep kettle, add ⅔ cup boiling water, cover, and steam over moderate heat 10–12 minutes until shells open. Serve with melted butter and lemon wedges and, if you like, Worcestershire and liquid hot red pepper seasoning.

To Serve Oysters on the Half Shell

Allow 6–8 blue point oysters per person; have fish market open them and prepare for serving on the half shell. If you have to do this job yourself, see directions given earlier for opening oysters. Fill large, shallow bowls or soup plates with crushed ice and arrange oysters in ice. Garnish with lemon wedges and ruffs of parsley. Set out the pepper mill and pass thinly sliced, buttered pumpernickel or crisp thin crackers. When eating, to savor every last drop, drink the oyster liquor from each shell after eating the oyster.

VARIATION:

Oysters on the Half Shell with Caviar: Prepare as directed, then top each oyster with about ½ teaspoon red or black caviar and a few shreds of grated fresh horseradish. Serve with lemon wedges.

⊠ **GRAND CENTRAL OYSTER STEW**

The Oyster Bar in New York's Grand Central Terminal still makes oyster stew the way it did on opening day in 1912. People say the recipe can't be duplicated at home because Oyster Bar chefs never measure anything. Perhaps not, but here's a recipe that comes close. Make it fast and serve in hot, hot bowls.

Makes 4 servings

1 cup milk
1 cup light cream
1 pint shucked oysters (do not drain)
2 tablespoons butter
¼ teaspoon salt
¼ teaspoon celery salt
Pinch pepper
Pinch paprika

Heat soup bowls. Scald milk and cream in a large, heavy saucepan over moderately high heat. Drain oyster liquor into a separate saucepan and bring to a boil. Spoon 2 tablespoons hot liquor into a third saucepan, add oysters and butter, and heat, uncovered, over moderate heat, swirling oysters around 3–4 minutes until edges just begin to curl; add oysters at once to hot milk, mix in hot oyster liquor, salt, celery salt, pepper, and paprika. Ladle into heated bowls and serve piping hot with oyster crackers. About 300 calories per serving.

CREAMED OYSTERS

Makes 4 servings

1 pint shucked oysters (do not drain)
3 tablespoons butter or margarine
3 tablespoons flour
1 cup light cream
1 teaspoon lemon juice
Pinch nutmeg
⅛ teaspoon paprika
4 slices lightly buttered toast (optional)

Drain oysters and reserve ¼ cup liquor. Melt butter in a saucepan over moderate heat, blend in flour, slowly add cream, and heat, stirring, until thickened. Add reserved liquor, lemon juice, nutmeg and paprika,

reduce heat, and simmer, stirring, 1 minute. Add oysters and cook, swirling pan occasionally, 4–5 minutes just until edges begin to curl. Serve as is or spooned over buttered toast. About 300 calories per serving (without toast).

VARIATIONS:

Oyster Shortcake: Prepare recipe as directed and ladle over hot, split, buttered biscuits. Sprinkle with minced parsley and serve. About 360 calories per serving.

Creamed Oysters à la Ritz: Prepare recipe as directed but just before serving stir in ¼ cup medium-dry sherry or Marsala and 2 tablespoons minced pimiento. Serve in individual ramekins or small casseroles and surround with toast points spread with Anchovy Butter. About 415 calories per serving.

Oyster Pie: (Makes 4–6 servings). Prepare 1 recipe Flaky Pastry I, roll into a 12″ circle, and cut 3 steam vents in center. Prepare Creamed Oysters as directed and pour into an ungreased 9″ piepan; place a pie funnel in center of pan. Cover oysters with pastry, trim and crimp edges, and brush pastry with beaten egg. Bake ½ hour at 425° F. until pastry is golden. About 575 calories per serving.

Oyster and Mushroom Pie: (Makes 4–6 servings). Prepare pastry as for Oyster Pie. Also prepare Creamed Oysters as directed but sauté ½ pound thinly sliced mushrooms in the butter 3–4 minutes until golden before adding flour. Proceed as for Oyster Pie. About 615 calories per serving.

⊠ CHAFING DISH OYSTERS

Makes 4 servings

¼ cup butter or margarine
1 pint shucked oysters, drained

½ cup heavy cream
Pinch cayenne pepper
Pinch mace
¼ cup medium-dry sherry or brandy
4 hot waffles

Melt butter in a chafing dish over direct heat, add oysters, and heat, swirling oysters round, 4–5 minutes just until edges start to curl. Place chafing dish on stand, add cream, seasonings, and sherry, and heat, stirring, until piping hot but not boiling. Ladle over waffles and serve. About 480 calories per serving.

⚔ **OYSTERS POULETTE**

Two ingredients only and so very elegant. Low calorie, too.
Makes 4 servings

1 pint shucked oysters (do not drain)
1½ cups hot Poulette Sauce

Simmer oysters in their liquor in the top of a double boiler over simmering water 3–4 minutes just until their edges begin to curl. Drain off liquor, add sauce, and mix gently. Heat 3–4 minutes and serve in puff pastry shells or over triangles of buttered toast or black bread. About 185 calories per serving.

⚔ ☒ **BROILED CRUMBED OYSTERS ON THE HALF SHELL**

Makes 4 servings

2 dozen oysters on the half shell
½ teaspoon salt
⅛ teaspoon pepper
½ cup soft white bread crumbs mixed with 2 tablespoons melted butter or margarine

Preheat broiler. Sprinkle oysters with salt, pepper, and buttered crumbs and arrange on foil-lined broiler pan. Broil 3″ from the heat 4–5 minutes until lightly browned. About 160 calories per serving.

OYSTERS ROCKEFELLER

There are dozens of variations of this New Orleans classic. This one may be no more original than the others, but it *is* good.
Makes 4 entree servings, enough appetizers for 6

Rock salt
¼ cup minced scallions or shallots
¼ cup minced celery
½ clove garlic, peeled and crushed
1 cup butter or margarine
2 cups finely chopped watercress leaves
⅓ cup soft white bread crumbs
⅓ cup minced parsley
⅓ cup minced fresh fennel
¼ cup Pernod or anisette
Pinch cayenne pepper
2 dozen oysters on the half shell

Preheat oven to 450° F. Make beds of rock salt in 4 piepans (the 8″ or 9″ size is best), dampen slightly with water, and heat uncovered in oven 5 minutes. Meanwhile, stir-fry scallions, celery, and garlic in butter over moderate heat 3–5 minutes until limp. Add watercress and stir-fry 1 minute, just until wilted. Pour skillet mixture into an electric blender cup, add remaining ingredients except oysters, and purée at high speed. Arrange 6 oysters in shells in each pan of hot salt, pushing shells down into salt so they cannot tip. Cover each oyster with 1 tablespoon purée and bake, uncovered, 5–7 minutes until bubbly. Serve at once in pans of salt. About 525 calories for each of 4 entree servings, 350 calories for each of 6 appetizer servings.

OYSTERS REMICK

"Deviled" oysters on the half shell.

Makes 4 entree servings, enough appetizers for 6

Rock salt
6 slices bacon
2 dozen oysters on the half shell
¾ cup mayonnaise
3 tablespoons chili sauce
¾ teaspoon prepared Dijon-style mustard
1 teaspoon lemon juice
2–3 drops liquid hot red pepper seasoning

Preheat oven to 450° F. Make beds of rock salt in 4 piepans (the 8" or 9" size), dampen slightly with water, and heat uncovered in oven 5 minutes. Meanwhile, cut each bacon strip into 4 equal-size pieces and stir-fry over moderate heat until limp. Drain on paper toweling and reserve. Arrange 6 oysters in shells in each pan, pushing shells down in hot salt so they won't tip. Blend mayonnaise with chili sauce, mustard, lemon juice, and pepper seasoning and cover each oyster with a heaping teaspoonful. Top with a piece of bacon and bake, uncovered, about 5–7 minutes until bacon is crisp. Serve from pans. About 500 calories for each of 4 entree servings, 335 calories for each of 6 appetizer servings.

OYSTERS FLORENTINE

Oysters and spinach on the half shell topped with cheese sauce. Makes 2 entree servings, enough appetizers for 4

Rock salt
1½ dozen oysters on the half shell
1 (10-ounce) package frozen chopped spinach, cooked by package directions and drained well
2–3 scallions, trimmed and sliced thin
1 cup hot Mornay Sauce
⅓ cup grated Parmesan cheese

Preheat broiler. Make beds of rock salt in 2 (8" or 9") piepans, dampen slightly with water, and let heat, uncovered, in oven 5 minutes while broiler preheats. Scoop oysters and their liquor from shells into a saucepan; reserve shells. Poach oysters 3–4 minutes over moderately low heat just until edges begin to curl; drain. Purée spinach and scallions in an electric blender at high speed or put through a food mill. Arrange oyster shells, 9 to a pan, in hot salt. Spoon a little spinach mixture into each shell, add an oyster, top with Mornay sauce, then sprinkle with cheese. Broil 5" from the heat 1–2 minutes just until flecked with brown. About 500 calories for each of 2 entree servings, 250 calories for each of 4 appetizer servings.

DEVILED OYSTERS

Makes 4 servings

2 dozen oysters on the half shell
2 tablespoons minced yellow onion
2 tablespoons butter or margarine
3 tablespoons flour
1 cup light cream
1 tablespoon spicy brown prepared mustard
1 tablespoon Worcestershire sauce
⅛ teaspoon salt
⅛ teaspoon cayenne pepper
⅛ teaspoon nutmeg
1 tablespoon minced parsley
1 egg, lightly beaten
⅓ cup soft white bread crumbs mixed with 2 tablespoons melted butter or margarine

Preheat oven to 400° F. Remove oysters from shells and chop coarsely; reserve liquid and shells. Stir-fry onion in butter in a saucepan over moderate heat 3–5 minutes until limp, blend in flour, then add cream and reserved oyster liquid and heat, stirring, until thickened and smooth. Off heat, mix in all seasonings, also parsley, egg, and chopped oysters. Spoon into oyster shells and top with buttered crumbs. Place on baking sheets and bake, uncovered, 10 minutes until bubbly. About 360 calories per serving.

OYSTERS BAKED IN MUSHROOM CAPS

Makes 2–3 entree servings, enough appetizers for 6

2 dozen large mushroom caps, wiped clean
¼ cup butter or margarine
2 dozen shucked oysters, drained
2 dozen rounds white bread cut to fit mushroom caps and fried until crisp in butter

Preheat oven to 425° F. Sauté mushroom caps in butter over moderately high heat 3–5 minutes until golden. Arrange cup side up on greased baking sheet and fill each with an oyster. Bake, uncovered, 5–7 minutes until oyster edges start to curl. Serve on fried bread rounds. About 570 calories for each of 2 entree servings, 380 calories for each of 3 entree servings, and 190 calories for each of 6 appetizer servings.

⚖ ☒ OYSTERS EN BROCHETTE

Makes 4 servings

8 slices bacon
2 dozen mushroom caps
2 dozen shucked oysters, drained
½ cup melted butter or margarine
Juice of 1 lemon
Pepper

Preheat broiler. Fry bacon slices in a heavy skillet over moderately high heat 2–3 minutes until limp; drain on paper toweling. On each of 4 long skewers alternate mushroom caps and oysters, interweaving 2

bacon strips. Mix melted butter with lemon juice and brush generously over each skewer; sprinkle with pepper. Place on a foil-lined broiler pan and broil 3″ from the heat 5–7 minutes, turning and brushing often with remaining butter mixture, until lightly browned. Serve at once. About 230 calories per serving.

VARIATIONS:

Oriental-Style Skewered Steak and Oysters: Marinate oysters and 2 dozen 1″ raw beef tenderloin cubes in ½ cup peanut oil mixed with ¼ cup each soy sauce and *sake* or dry sherry, ½ crushed clove garlic, and 2 teaspoons grated fresh gingerroot 2–3 hours in refrigerator. Lift from marinade and skewer alternately on 4 long skewers as above, interweaving bacon strips. Broil as directed, brushing often with marinade. About 415 calories per serving.

Charcoal-Broiled Oysters en Brochette: Prepare a moderately hot charcoal fire.* Skewer oysters by either of the recipes above and broil 4″ from the coals 5–6 minutes, turning often and brushing with butter or marinade. The same calorie counts as for the two recipes above.

ANGELS ON HORSEBACK

Makes 2 servings

1 dozen shucked oysters, drained
6 slices bacon, halved, or 6 thin strips boiled ham the size of half bacon strips
2 slices hot buttered toast
1 cup Hollandaise Sauce

Preheat broiler. Pat oysters dry on paper toweling, wrap each in a piece of bacon, and secure with a toothpick. Arrange on a foil-lined broiler pan and broil 3″ from the heat, about 5 minutes, turning often so bacon browns evenly. Remove toothpicks, pile oysters on toast and smother with Hollandaise. About 565 calories per serving.

VARIATIONS:

Tipsy Angels on Horseback: Marinate oysters in 1½ cups dry white wine mixed with ½ crushed clove garlic and 1 tablespoon minced parsley 2–3 hours in the refrigerator. Lift from marinade and proceed as directed. About 565 calories per serving.

Devils on Horseback: Sprinkle oysters lightly with lemon juice and liquid hot red pepper seasoning. Wrap in bacon and broil as directed. Serve on toast but omit Hollandaise. About 325 calories per serving.

☒ SCALLOPED OYSTERS

Makes 4 servings

1 pint shucked oysters (do not drain)
1 cup light cream
2 cups coarse soda cracker crumbs
½ cup melted butter
½ teaspoon salt
¼ teaspoon pepper

Preheat oven to 375° F. Drain oysters, reserving ¼ cup liquor; mix liquor and cream and set aside. Mix crumbs with butter, salt, and pepper and sprinkle ⅓ of mixture in a buttered 1-quart casserole. Arrange half of oysters on top and pour in half of cream mixture. Cover with another ⅓ crumb mixture, add remaining oysters and cream. Top with remaining crumbs and bake, uncovered, 30–35 minutes until bubbly and lightly browned. About 570 calories per serving.

⚔ ☒ CONFEDERATE OYSTER BAKE

Couldn't be easier, couldn't be better.
Makes 6 servings

1 quart shucked oysters, drained
2 tablespoons minced parsley
2 tablespoons minced shallots or scallions
¼ teaspoon pepper
1 tablespoon lemon juice
¾ cup milk
1¼ cups fine dry bread crumbs
6 tablespoons butter or margarine

Preheat oven to 325° F. Layer oysters in a greased 8"×8"×2" baking dish or 1½-quart casserole, sprinkling as you go with parsley, shallots, pepper, and lemon juice. Pour in milk, top with crumbs, and dot generously with butter. Bake, uncovered, about 30 minutes until crumbs are golden. Serve at once. About 260 calories per serving.

OYSTER LOAF

Oyster loaves, popular in nineteenth-century San Francisco and New Orleans, were nicknamed "squarers" because errant night-owl husbands would pick them up on the way home to "square" things with their wives.
Makes 4–6 servings

1 small round loaf Italian bread or 1 (1-pound) loaf unsliced firm white bread
⅓ cup melted butter or margarine
1 pint shucked oysters, drained

Preheat oven to 350° F. Slice off top ¼ of loaf and set aside; hollow out loaf, leaving walls about ¾" thick. Brush inside of loaf generously with butter, also the cut side of "lid." Place loaf and lid (cut side up) on an ungreased baking sheet and bake 20–30 minutes until lightly toasted (lid will toast in about 10). Meanwhile, sauté oysters, following basic method.* Fill loaf with oysters, top with lid and serve. Round loaves should be cut in wedges, rectangular loaves in thick slices. About 300 calories for each of 4 servings, 200 calories for each of 6 servings.

VARIATIONS:

⚜ **Individual Oyster Loaves:** Substitute 4–6 hard French rolls for the single loaf and hollow out, making shells about ½" thick. Butter and toast, allowing 5–10 minutes, fill with hot oysters, and serve. About 295 calories for each of 4 servings, 195 calories for each of 6 servings.

⚜ **Creamed Oyster Loaves** (Makes 6 servings): Hollow out, butter, and toast 6 hard French rolls as above. Meanwhile, simmer oysters in their liquor 4–5 minutes just until edges ruffle. Drain oysters, stir in ½ cup hot cream, 1 teaspoon lemon juice, ½ teaspoon anchovy paste, ⅛ teaspoon each cayenne pepper and nutmeg. Spoon mixture into rolls and serve. About 295 calories per serving.

Clam Loaf: Prepare as directed, substituting clams for oysters. About 310 calories for each of 4 servings, 205 calories for each of 6 servings.

Crab, Lobster, or Shrimp Loaf: Prepare loaf or rolls as above and fill with hot Herbed Crab Sauté or Quick Crab Newburg; Creamed Scallops; Shrimp and Mushrooms Gruyère; Shrimp in Dill Sauce, Shrimp or Lobster Newburg. Recipe too flexible for meaningful calorie counts.

HANGTOWN FRY

The story goes that this oyster omelet was the last meal requested by a man about to be hanged in Hangtown (now Placerville), California. Whatever its origin, Hangtown Fry is a California classic.
Makes 2 servings

8 *shucked oysters, well drained*
1 *egg beaten with 1 tablespoon cold water*
⅓ *cup fine soda cracker crumbs*
3 *tablespoons butter or margarine*
4 *eggs*
¼ *teaspoon salt*
⅛ *teaspoon pepper*
4 *slices crisply fried bacon*

Optional Garnish:
1 *(7-ounce) package French-fried onion rings, prepared by package directions*
OR
½ *cup minced sweet green pepper stir-fried in 2 tablespoons butter 3–5 minutes over moderate heat until limp*

Pat oysters dry on paper toweling, dip in beaten egg, then crumbs and brown in butter in a 9" skillet over moderate heat, allowing only 1–2 minutes per side. While oysters fry, quickly beat eggs with salt and pepper. Pour over browned oysters, turn heat to low, and cook, pulling mixture from outer edge toward center as you would for an omelet so uncooked portions run underneath; keep oysters as evenly spaced in eggs as possible. When eggs are just set but still quivery, invert on a hot platter. Garnish with bacon and, if you like, smother with French-fried onion rings or minced sweet green pepper. About 545 calories per serving (without garnish).

⚜ ⬚ OYSTER AND CORN "OYSTERS"

Makes 4 servings

¼ *cup sifted flour*
¼ *teaspoon salt*
¼ *teaspoon baking powder*
2 *tablespoons milk*
1 *egg, lightly beaten*
1 *cup whole kernel corn, well drained*

⅓ cup cooking oil
1½ dozen shucked oysters, drained

Mix flour, salt, and baking powder in a bowl, slowly add milk, and beat until smooth. Beat in egg and stir in corn. Heat oil in a large, heavy skillet over moderate heat 1 minute. Using a large serving spoon, scoop up an oyster, dip into corn mixture, filling spoon, then drop into hot fat. Fry, 3–4 "oysters" at a time, 3–4 minutes until browned on both sides. Drain on paper toweling and keep hot while you fry the rest by setting, uncovered, in oven turned to lowest heat. About 200 calories per serving.

⚖ PICKLED OYSTERS

Makes 4 first course servings

1 pint shucked oysters (do not drain)
1 medium-size yellow onion, peeled
    and sliced paper thin
1 lemon, sliced paper thin
½ cup white wine vinegar
1 teaspoon mixed pickling spices
⅛ teaspoon pepper
2 tablespoons olive or other cooking
    oil
2 tablespoons minced parsley

Simmer oysters in their liquor over moderately low heat 4–5 minutes just until edges begin to curl. Drain, reserve liquor, and cover oysters with ice water. Cool oysters 5 minutes in water, drain again, and arrange in a single layer in an ungreased large, shallow casserole. Cover with onion and lemon slices. Bring vinegar, reserved cooking liquor, spices, and oil to a boil, reduce heat, and simmer uncovered 5 minutes. Strain liquid over oysters, cool to room temperature, then cover and chill overnight. Serve sprinkled with parsley. About 100 calories per serving.

PERIWINKLES

These miniature sea snails are a great French favorite, especially in Brittany, where steaming mountains of them are served alongside platters of langoustines. Occasionally, fancy American fish markets have them for sale; more often they are gathered locally along the East Coast from Delaware north.

Season: Year round.

Amount Needed: About 1½ dozen periwinkles per serving.

For Top Quality: When gathering your own, pick only those tightly clinging to pilings or rocks well below the tide mark. When buying, select those that "clam up" when handled.

How to Cook Periwinkles

General Preparation: Rinse well in cold water.

To Boil: Place periwinkles in a large saucepan and cover with sea water or salt water (1 tablespoon salt for each quart water), cover, and simmer 15–25 minutes until the operculum (tiny trap-door sealing opening) opens. Drain periwinkles and serve hot with melted butter, Lemon or Garlic Butter.

To Bake: Rinse periwinkles and boil as directed above. Using a nut pick or long straight pin, twist meat from each shell. Now proceed as for Escargots à la Bourguignonne, tucking 3 periwinkles into each empty snail shell. Close snail shell openings with the Bourguignonne Butter and bake as directed.

How to Eat Periwinkles

Eating periwinkles from the shell is no more difficult than eating snails—

except that they're so much smaller. Pick them up one at a time and, using a nut pick, toothpick, or long straight pin, twist meat from shell. Peel off operculum, transfer meat to a small fork and dip in accompanying butter.

SCALLOPS

Down the centuries, scallop shells have been as cherished as the tiny sea animals inside them. It is from a scallop shell that Botticelli's Venus rises; it is the scallop shell that became the emblem of St. James, patron saint of Spain; it is the scallop shell that chefs found the perfect size and shape for baking creamed seafood (hence the term "scalloped," meaning "creamed"). Scallops were so rare, in fact, that fish markets sometimes counterfeited them out of haddock and cod. They were little known in this country until vast beds of them were found off the coast of New England in the 1930's. Although Europeans eat everything inside the scallop shell and relish particularly the bean-shaped coral of the female, we eat only the "eye" or firm, marshmallow-shaped muscle hinging top and bottom shells together.

The Kinds of Scallops

There are two: *ocean or sea scallops,* dredged from deep in the North Atlantic, and *bay scallops,* harvested in tidewater bays and sheltered inlets up and down the East Coast. Scallops are also found on the West Coast, especially around Puget Sound, but these are not as good as the Eastern variety.

Sea Scallops: Measuring from 1"–1½" across, these are tannish, firm, and nutty. They can be tough, how-ever, and are best sliced across the grain or diced and used in casseroles.

Bay Scallops: These are tiny, sometimes only ½" across, creamy pink, and so sweet and delicate they can be eaten raw with only a drizzling of lemon or lime juice. The most delectable of all are those dipped from the chilly inshore waters of Long Island, New England, and Canada. Some gourmets rank them gastronomically with the finest caviar. Because of their extreme tenderness, they should be cooked as quickly and carefully as possible.

About Buying Fresh Scallops

Season:

Sea Scallops: September to April.

Bay Scallops: Autumn and winter.

Popular Market Forms: Bay and sea scallops are sold whole, out of the shell, by the pound.

Amount Needed: ⅓–½ pound per person.

For Top Quality: Look for sweet-smelling scallops packed in little or no liquid.

About Frozen Scallops

Sea scallops are available fresh frozen, frozen breaded, and frozen precooked. Bay scallops, unfortunately, are almost never frozen. *To Cook Frozen Scallops:* Thaw uncooked scallops in refrigerator just until they can be separated or, if you prefer, thaw completely (1 pound will take 3–4 hours to thaw), then cook as you would fresh scallops. Breaded or precooked frozen scallops should be prepared by package directions.

How to Open Fresh Scallops: Occasionally you may find scallops in the shell (or perhaps dip them up yourself). If so, here are two ways to open them.

1. *To Pry Open:* Hold scallop in one hand, dark side of shell down, slip a sharp knife into hinge and slip underneath large muscle, severing it as close to shell as possible. Cut muscle just underneath top shell the same way, open, and remove scallop. Wash well in cold water to remove grit or bits of shell.

2. *To Roast Open:* Scrub scallops in cold water, place dark side down in a large, shallow roasting pan, set in a 300° F. oven, and let stand uncovered about 5 minutes until shells open; discard any that don't. Remove from oven, cut out meat, and wash well in cool water.

How to Cook Scallops

Scallops are wonderfully adaptable —superb when cooked simply, sensational when dressed up. Here are the best basic ways to prepare them.

General Preparation (for all cooking methods): Wash well in cold water to remove bits of shell and grit.

To Oven Broil: Preheat broiler. Pat scallops dry on paper toweling, dip in melted butter, margarine, or cooking oil, arrange in a single layer in a shallow baking pan, and broil 3"–4" from the heat 5–7 minutes, without turning or basting, until lightly browned. Sprinkle with salt and pepper and serve with lemon. For extra flavor, dip scallops in Lemon, Parsley, or Herb Butter instead of plain butter.

VARIATIONS:

⚖ **Low-Calorie Broiled Scallops:** Substitute low-calorie French, Italian, garlic, or herb dressing for the butter and broil as directed. About 125 calories per ⅓ pound serving.

Breaded Scallops: After dipping scallops in melted butter, roll in fine dry bread crumbs or cracker meal and broil as directed, turning and basting once so scallops brown evenly.

To Charcoal Broil: Build a moderately hot charcoal fire.* Wrap each scallop in a half slice bacon and thread on skewers so bacon won't unwrap; or secure bacon slices with toothpicks and arrange scallops in a well-greased, hinged, long-handled wire grill. Broil 4" from heat 5–6 minutes on a side until bacon is brown and crisp.

To Panfry (Sauté): Pat scallops dry on paper toweling, then sauté in butter (about ¼ cup for 1 pound scallops) in a large, heavy skillet over moderately high heat 4–5 minutes until lightly browned. Sprinkle with salt and pepper and serve with lemon.

VARIATIONS:

Scallops Amandine: Pat scallops dry, dredge in flour lightly seasoned with salt and pepper, then sauté as above. Remove to a hot platter and keep warm. To skillet add 2–3 tablespoons butter or margarine and ½ cup slivered almonds and stir-fry 2–3 minutes until lightly browned. Pour over scallops and serve.

Scallops à la Meunière: Dip scallops in milk, then in flour lightly seasoned with salt and pepper. Sauté in butter as directed above, transfer to a hot platter, sprinkle with lemon juice and a little minced parsley, and keep warm. Add 1–2 tablespoons butter to skillet, heat until lightly browned and bubbly, pour over scallops, and serve.

Breaded Fried Scallops: Pat scallops dry, dip in a mixture of beaten egg and milk (2 tablespoons milk to each egg), then roll in fine dry bread crumbs or cracker meal to coat evenly. Pour ¼″ cooking oil or a ½ and ½ mixture of cooking oil and melted butter or margarine in a large heavy skillet and heat over moderately high heat until a cube of bread will sizzle. Brown scallops, turning as necessary, 4–6 minutes until golden brown all over. Drain on paper toweling and serve with lemon wedges.

To Oven "Fry": Preheat oven to 500° F. Mix ¼ cup milk with ½ teaspoon salt and a pinch white pepper; also mix ⅓ cup fine dry bread crumbs or cracker meal with ¼ teaspoon paprika. Dip scallops in milk, then in crumbs to coat evenly. Arrange in a single layer in a buttered shallow baking pan, drizzle with melted butter, and bake uncovered, without turning or basting, 7–9 minutes until golden.

To Deep-Fat-Fry: Pat scallops dry on paper toweling and bread as for Breaded Fried Scallops (above). Heat cooking oil or shortening in a deep fat fryer to 375° F., place a single layer of scallops in deep fat basket, lower into fat, and fry 2–3 minutes until golden brown. Drain on paper toweling and serve with lemon.

VARIATION:

Batter-Fried Scallops: Make up batter given in Fish and Chips recipe. Pat scallops dry on paper toweling, dip in flour, then in batter, then fry, a few at a time, in 375° F. fat 2–3 minutes until golden brown. Drain on paper toweling and serve with lemon and Tartar Sauce.

To Poach: Place scallops in a large, heavy skillet (not iron), add lightly salted boiling water to cover, *or* dry white wine brought just to a simmer

or, if you prefer, a boiling court bouillon. If using water or wine, add a *bouquet garni** tied in cheesecloth. Cover and simmer 3–4 minutes until scallops turn milky white. Drain (cooking liquid can be used for making soups or sauces) and serve with Parsley, Caper, Mornay, or other suitable sauce (see Sauces, Butters, and Seasonings for Seafood) or use in recipes calling for poached scallops.

COQUILLES ST. JACQUES À LA PARISIENNE (SCALLOPS AND MUSHROOMS IN WINE CREAM SAUCE)

This is the classic *coquilles St. Jacques.* It can be served as a first course or light luncheon dish.
Makes 6–8 servings

1½ cups dry white wine
3 tablespoons minced shallots
1 bay leaf
1 parsley sprig
½ teaspoon salt
Pinch pepper
1½ pounds bay scallops, washed
½ pound mushrooms, wiped clean
  and minced
1½ cups water (*about*)

Sauce:
4 tablespoons butter or margarine
5 tablespoons flour
¾ cup reduced scallops' cooking
  liquid
⅔ cup heavy cream
2 egg yolks, lightly beaten
2 teaspoons lemon juice
¼ teaspoon salt
Pinch white pepper

Topping:
1¼ cups soft white bread crumbs
⅓ cup finely grated Gruyère cheese
¼ cup melted butter or margarine

Simmer wine, shallots, bay leaf, parsley, salt, and pepper, uncovered, 5 minutes in a large enamel or stainless-steel saucepan. Add scallops, mushrooms, and enough water to cover, and simmer, covered, 3–4 minutes until scallops turn milky white. Drain, reserving cooking liquid. Set scallops and mushrooms aside to cool, return liquid, bay leaf, and parsley to saucepan and boil rapidly uncovered until reduced to ¾ cup. Meanwhile, slice scallops across the grain ⅛" thick. For the sauce, melt butter in a small saucepan and blend in flour. Strain reduced cooking liquid and add along with cream. Heat, stirring constantly, until thickened and smooth. Spoon a little hot sauce into yolks, then return to pan; set over lowest heat and cook and stir 1 minute; do not allow to boil. Mix in lemon juice, salt, and pepper. Pour over scallops and mushrooms and toss to mix. Spoon into 6 to 8 well-buttered very large scallop shells or into individual *au gratin* dishes; mix topping and sprinkle evenly over each. Set coquilles on a large baking sheet. (*Note:* Recipe may be prepared to this point early in the day, covered and chilled until just before serving.) Preheat broiler. If you have not made coquilles ahead and chilled them, broil 5" from heat 4–5 minutes until bubbly and dappled with brown. If they have been chilled, set far below broiler unit (lowest oven shelf) and let warm 5–6 minutes, then move up and broil 5" from heat 3–4 minutes until bubbly and browned. About 470 calories for each of 6 servings, 350 calories for each of 8 servings.

COQUILLES ST. JACQUES À LA PROVENÇALE (SCALLOPS AU GRATIN)

Spicier than the classic *coquilles St. Jacques*, this Provençal version is also easier to make.

Makes 4 servings

1 pound bay scallops, washed
1 medium-size yellow onion, peeled and minced
1 tablespoon minced shallots
1 clove garlic, peeled and crushed
3 tablespoons butter or margarine
½ cup unsifted flour
1½ teaspoons salt
¼ teaspoon pepper
2 tablespoons olive oil
¾ cup dry white wine
2 bay leaves
⅛ teaspoon thyme
⅓ cup finely grated Gruyère cheese

Pat scallops dry on paper toweling and slice crosswise ¼" thick. Stir-fry onion, shallots, and garlic in 2 tablespoons butter in a large, heavy skillet over moderate heat 5–8 minutes until golden; remove from skillet and reserve. Dredge scallops lightly in a mixture of flour, salt, and pepper. Heat olive oil in the same skillet over high heat about 1 minute, add scallops, and stir-fry 2–3 minutes. Reduce heat to low, return onion mixture to skillet, add wine, bay leaves, and thyme, cover, and simmer 2–3 minutes; remove bay leaves. Spoon into 4 buttered large scallop shells and set on a baking sheet. Top with grated cheese and dot with remaining butter. (*Note:* Recipe may be prepared to this point early in the day, covered, and chilled until just before serving.) Preheat broiler. If you have not made coquilles ahead, broil 5" from heat 4–5 minutes until bubbly and browned. If they have been chilled, set far below broiler unit (lowest oven shelf) and let warm 5–6 minutes; then move up and broil 5" from heat 3–4 minutes until bubbly and touched with brown. About 370 calories per serving.

SEA SCALLOPS BAKED IN WINE AND CHEESE SAUCE

Makes 4 servings

1⅔ cups dry white wine
1 scallion, minced
1 bay leaf
2 parsley sprigs
1 stalk celery
½ teaspoon salt
Pinch pepper
1½ pounds sea scallops, washed
1⅓ cups water (about)
1 medium-size yellow onion, peeled and minced
1 clove garlic, peeled and crushed
¾ pound mushrooms, wiped clean and sliced thin
3 tablespoons butter or margarine

Sauce:
4 tablespoons butter or margarine
4 tablespoons flour
1 cup reduced scallops' cooking liquid
1 cup light cream
⅓ cup coarsely grated Gruyère cheese
Juice of ½ lemon or lime
¼ teaspoon salt
4–5 dashes liquid hot red pepper seasoning

Topping:
1 cup soft white bread crumbs mixed with 3 tablespoons melted butter or margarine

Preheat oven to 375° F. Bring wine, scallion, bay leaf, parsley, celery, salt, and pepper to a simmer in a large enamel or stainless-steel saucepan; add scallops and enough water to cover and simmer, covered, 4–5 minutes until milky white. Drain scallops and set aside to cool; return cooking liquid, bay leaf, parsley, and celery to saucepan and boil, uncovered, until reduced to 1 cup; strain and reserve. Meanwhile, stir-fry onion, garlic, and mushrooms in butter in a large, heavy skillet 5–8 minutes over moderate heat until onion is pale golden. Cut scallops in ½" cubes and add to skillet. For the sauce, melt butter in a small saucepan and blend in flour; stir in reduced cooking liquid and cream and heat, stirring, until thickened and smooth. Add remaining sauce ingredients and heat and stir until cheese is melted; pour into skillet and toss to mix. Transfer to a buttered 1½-quart au gratin dish or shallow casserole and sprinkle with topping. Bake, uncovered, 20–25 minutes until bubbly, then broil quickly to brown. About 740 calories per serving.

⊠ HERBED SKILLET SCALLOPS

Makes 4 servings

1½ pounds bay scallops, washed
⅓ cup butter or margarine
1 tablespoon minced shallot or scallion
1 tablespoon minced parsley
1 tablespoon minced fresh dill
⅓ cup dry vermouth
Juice of ½ lemon or lime
½ teaspoon salt
4–5 dashes liquid hot red pepper seasoning

Pat scallops very dry on paper toweling. Melt butter in a large, heavy skillet over moderate heat, add shallot, and stir-fry 3–5 minutes until limp; add herbs and warm 1 minute. Turn heat to moderately high, add scallops, and stir-fry 3–5 minutes until lightly browned. Remove scallops with a slotted spoon to a heated platter and keep warm. Add remaining ingredients to skillet and heat and stir 2 minutes to blend flavors. Pour over scallops and serve. About 335 calories per serving.

⊠ SKILLET SCALLOPS RIVIERA

Scallops "greened" with minced parsley, green olives, and capers.
Makes 4 servings

1½ pounds bay scallops, washed
1 cup flour mixed with ¼ teaspoon pepper
⅓ cup olive oil
1 clove garlic, peeled and crushed
¼ cup minced parsley
⅓ cup minced pimiento-stuffed green olives
2 tablespoons minced capers

Pat scallops very dry on paper toweling and dredge in seasoned flour. Heat oil in a large, heavy skillet over moderately high heat until a cube of bread will sizzle, add scallops and garlic, and stir-fry 4–5 minutes until lightly browned. Add remaining ingredients, toss quickly to mix, and serve. About 380 calories per serving.

SCALLOPS MARINARA

Makes 4 servings

2 medium-size yellow onions, peeled and coarsely chopped
2 cloves garlic, peeled and crushed
¼ cup olive oil
1 bay leaf, crumbled
½ teaspoon basil
½ teaspoon oregano
1 tablespoon light brown sugar
½ teaspoon salt
⅛ teaspoon pepper
½ cup dry white wine
1 (6-ounce) can tomato paste
1 (1-pound 12-ounce) can tomatoes
1½ pounds bay scallops or sea scallops, washed and, if large, sliced
1 tablespoon minced parsley

Stir-fry onions and garlic in olive oil in a large, heavy skillet 8–10 minutes over moderate heat until golden. Add herbs, brown sugar, salt, pep-

per, and wine and cook and stir 2–3 minutes. Add tomato paste and tomatoes, breaking up any large clumps, and simmer, uncovered, 40–45 minutes, stirring often, until flavors are well blended. Add scallops, cover, and simmer 4–5 minutes until milky white. Sprinkle with parsley and serve over spaghetti or boiled rice. Pass grated Parmesan cheese. About 450 calories per serving (without rice or spaghetti or Parmesan).

CURRIED SCALLOPS

Makes 4 servings

1 cup dry white wine
2 cups water
1 large yellow onion, peeled and stuck with 4 cloves
1 cinnamon stick
1 carrot, peeled and cut in large chunks
2 parsley sprigs
1 stalk celery
½ teaspoon salt
¼ teaspoon pepper
1½ pounds sea scallops, washed
1 large yellow onion, peeled and minced
1 clove garlic, peeled and crushed
3 tablespoons butter or margarine
¼ cup curry powder
¼ teaspoon cayenne pepper
2 tablespoons minced crystallized ginger
1 cup Coconut Milk
1½ cups reduced scallops' cooking liquid
Juice of 1 lime
½ cup heavy cream

Bring wine, water, onion, cinnamon stick, carrot, parsley, celery, salt, and pepper to a simmer in a large enamel or stainless-steel saucepan; add scallops and simmer, covered, 4–5 minutes until milky white. Drain scallops and cool; return cooking liquid and all of its seasonings to pan and boil, uncovered, until reduced to 1½ cups. Meanwhile, stir-fry onion and garlic in butter in a very large, heavy skillet over moderate heat 8–10 minutes until golden. Cut scallops in ½″ cubes, cover, and keep cool. Blend curry powder and cayenne into onion, add ginger, coconut milk, and strained scallops' cooking liquid. Cover and simmer slowly ¾–1 hour until flavors are well blended. Mix in lime juice and cream, taste for salt and adjust as needed. Bring to a simmer, add scallops, and warm 2–3 minutes. Serve over boiled rice with chutney. About 405 calories per serving (without rice or chutney).

⚖ ▨ SCALLOPS EN BROCHETTE
Makes 4 servings

1½ pounds bay scallops or small sea scallops, washed
⅓ cup French, Italian, or Herb Dressing

Pat scallops dry on paper toweling, mix with dressing, and let stand 30 minutes at room temperature. Preheat broiler. Arrange on small skewers, not too close together, and broil 3″ from heat 5–6 minutes, turning often and brushing with dressing, until evenly browned. About 240 calories per serving if made with French dressing, 260 calories per serving if made with Italian or herb dressing.

VARIATIONS:

⚖ Low-Calorie Scallops en Brochette: Prepare as directed, substituting low-calorie dressing for the regular. About 180 calories per serving.

Mushrooms and Scallops en Brochette: Wipe 1½ pound mushrooms clean with a damp cloth, then skewer alternately with scallops. If you like, interweave bacon strips. Brush with dressing or melted butter and broil as directed. About 285 calories per serving if made with French dressing, 305 calories per serving if made with Italian or herb dressing.

Sweet-Sour Scallop Kebabs: Alternate scallops on skewers with chunks of pineapple, interweaving strips of bacon, and place 1 layer deep in a shallow pan. Mix ¼ cup each melted butter, pineapple juice, light brown sugar, and grated onion, 2 teaspoons powdered mustard, 2 tablespoons lemon juice, ½ teaspoon salt, and a pinch pepper. Pour over kebabs, cover, and let stand at room temperature ½ hour. Remove kebabs from marinade and broil as directed, brushing often with marinade. Recipe too flexible for a meaningful calorie count.

CHILLED SCALLOPS IN GREEN DRESSING
An unusual summer luncheon entree.
Makes 4 servings

1½ pounds bay scallops, washed
⅔ cup dry white wine
2 bay leaves
1 (4″) sprig fresh thyme or ¼ teaspoon dried thyme
1 small yellow onion, peeled and coarsely chopped
Crisp lettuce cups

Green Dressing:
1 tablespoon minced fresh chives
1 tablespoon minced fresh tarragon
1 tablespoon minced fresh dill
⅓ cup minced parsley
⅓ cup minced raw spinach
1 cup mayonnaise
2 teaspoons scallops' cooking liquid
¼ teaspoon salt

Pat scallops dry on paper toweling and halve any that seem extra large. Place scallops, wine, bay leaves, thyme, and onion in a small saucepan, cover, and simmer over moderate heat 3–4 minutes until scallops turn milky white. Drain, saving 2 teaspoons cooking liquid. Mix together all dressing ingredients, add scallops, and toss lightly to mix. Cover and chill several hours. Serve in lettuce cups. About 620 calories per serving.

SHRIMP

In just fifty short years, shrimp have zoomed ahead of other shellfish to become America's favorite, all because refrigeration and quick shipping have made them as available in Nebraska as in New Orleans (also because the supply appears to be endless). Time was when the only thing most of us knew to do with shrimp was to make them into cocktails. But as Deep South shrimp reached the heartlands, so, too, did some of the great shrimp country recipes—pies, patties, puddings, not to mention gumbos and jambalayas.

Then came the international specialties—from the Orient and Mediterranean, from Latin and South America—and in the process of trying them all we're putting away better than a quarter *billion* pounds of shrimp a year.

The Kinds of Shrimp

There are several kinds of shrimp —the *common gray-green;* the *brownish-pink Brazilian;* the *Gulf Coast pink;* the rare, *deep sea "royal red,"* and the *cold water miniatures* from Alaska and Denmark. In addition, there are *prawns,* not just a large shrimp, as many people believe, but a bright pink European species (the French call it *langoustine* and the Italians *scampi*). Further complicating the terminology is the fact that *scampi* now means a way of cooking shrimp (broiled with lots of oil and garlic) as well as the animal itself. Actually, the varieties of shrimp matter little because all can be used interchangeably. What matters more are the sizes:

Size	Number per Pound	Best Used for
Colossal	10 or less	Scampi, stuffed shrimp
Jumbo	12–15	Broiling, butterflying and deep fat frying, stuffed shrimp
Medium	16–20	Casseroles, creamed dishes, cocktails
Medium-Small	21–25	Casseroles, creamed dishes
Small	31–42	Casseroles, creamed dishes, salads
Miniatures (Danish or cocktail shrimp)	200 or more	Open face sandwiches, canapés, soups, salads

As might be expected, the larger the shrimp, the more expensive.

About Buying Fresh Shrimp

Season: Year round.

Popular Market Forms: Unless you live in a shrimping area, the shrimp you buy will be the tail part only. These are available raw and in the shell ("green shrimp," the markets call them), or shelled and deveined. In addition, you can buy fresh-cooked shrimp in the shell or shelled and deveined. A specialty item: refrigerated, ready-to-serve shrimp cocktails.

Amount Needed: Allow ⅓–½ pound shelled shrimp per person, about ¾ pound unshelled shrimp, depending, of course, on appetites and richness of the dish.

For Top Quality: Raw shrimp should be firm but moist and sweet-smelling; cooked shrimp should also be firm and sweet-smelling and there should be a lot of "spring" or resilience to the tail; if the cooked shrimp have been shelled and deveined, they should look succulent, neither too moist nor too dry.

About Frozen, Canned, and Dried Shrimp

You can buy frozen raw shrimp in or out of the shell, deveined or undeveined, also breaded and ready to deep-fry. Frozen cooked shrimp come shelled and deveined, also breaded and in a variety of precooked dinners. On the horizon: freeze-dried shrimp. Canned shrimp have lost considerable ground since the arrival of frozen shrimp, but they are still available, deveined, or in the standard pack (not deveined). The most popular canned shrimp are probably the tiny Danish ones. Two specialty items: shrimp paste (in tubes) and dried shrimp; both should be used according to label instructions. *How to Use Frozen Shrimp:* With the exception of frozen, uncooked breaded shrimp, frozen shrimp are better if thawed before cooking (leave shrimp in their package and thaw in the refrigerator or under a gentle stream of cold running water). Once shrimp are thawed, drain well, then pre-

pare as you would fresh shrimp; never refreeze. Most brands of frozen shrimp are accompanied by directions; follow them. *How to Use Canned Shrimp:* Because these shrimp are fully cooked, they're particularly suited for use in soups, salads, and casseroles; the tiny Danish shrimp are good for sandwich fillings, canapé spreads, and cocktail dips.

How to Cook Shrimp

Boiling is the most popular way to cook shrimp, with deep fat frying close behind. But, they may also be broiled in the oven or over charcoal and, of course, added to soups, sauces, skillet dinners, and casseroles. The greatest difficulty most people have with shrimp is overcooking them. They really only need to heat through. How can you tell if they are done and not overdone? By color. As soon as shrimp turn pink, they are done.

General Preparation: Sooner or later, all shrimp must be shelled and deveined. Sometimes it's done before cooking, sometimes afterwards, and sometimes at the table, with everyone attacking his own portion.

To Shell and Devein Shrimp: The process is the same whether shrimp are raw or cooked. Starting at the large end, peel away the thin shell, unwinding it from around tail. If shrimp are to be deep fat fried, or if recipes so specify, leave tail fins on; otherwise, remove. To devein, make a shallow incision (about ⅛″ deep) down center back (outer curved side) with a small, sharp knife and pull out dark vein running length of tail. Rinse away any broken bits of vein under cool running water. (*Note:* Not every shrimp will have the dark vein, but the majority will.)

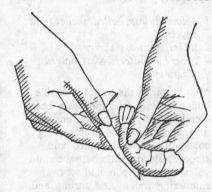

To Butterfly Shrimp: This is most often done when shrimp are to be dipped in batter and deep fat fried. Deepen incision made for deveining, cutting almost but not quite through to underside; spread shrimp as flat as possible (like an open book) and pat dry on paper toweling.

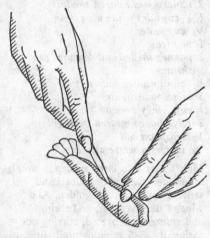

To Boil: The only real difference between boiling shrimp in the shell or out is the amount of salt needed (unshelled shrimp take twice as much). Allow 1 quart water for each pound shrimp, 2 tablespoons salt for unshelled shrimp and 1 tablespoon for the shelled. Bring salt water to a boil, add shrimp, cover, and simmer 3–5 minutes, depending on size, just until shrimp turn pink. Drain and, if in the shell, shell and devein. Serve hot with Lemon, Garlic, or Herb Butter, chill and use for shrimp cocktail; or use in any recipes calling for cooked shrimp. (*Note:* If you live near the ocean, use sea water for boiling the shrimp, adding 1 teaspoon salt if the shrimp are being cooked in the shell.)

VARIATIONS:

Savory Boiled Shrimp: Boil shrimp as directed, substituting a court bouillon for salt water.

Shrimp Boiled in Beer: Boil shrimp as directed, using a ½ and ½ mixture of beer or ale and water instead of salt water.

To Oven Broil: Select large shrimp, shell and devein. Preheat broiler. Place shrimp on a foil-lined broiler pan or in a large piepan. Brush generously with melted butter or margarine or a ½ and ½ mixture of melted butter and lemon juice, dry white wine, or sherry. Broil 3″ from the heat 3–5 minutes on a side, brushing often with butter. Sprinkle with salt and pepper and serve.

VARIATION:

⚖ **Low-Calorie Broiled Shrimp:** Broil as directed, using low-calorie Italian, herb, or garlic dressing in place of butter. About 150 calories per ⅓ pound serving.

To Charcoal Broil: Select large shrimp and shell and devein. Build a moderately hot charcoal fire.* Thread shrimp on large, thin skewers or place in a well-greased, hinged, long-handled wire grill. Brush shrimp generously with melted butter or margarine and broil 4″ from coals about 5 minutes on a side until pink and delicately browned.

To Panfry (Sauté): Shell and devein shrimp. Sauté in butter, margarine, or cooking oil (about ¼ cup for each pound of shrimp), stirring briskly, 3–5 minutes over moderate heat, just until pink. Sprinkle with lemon juice, salt, and pepper and serve.

VARIATION:

Shrimp à la Meunière: Shell and devein shrimp, dip in milk, then in flour lightly seasoned with salt and pepper. Sauté in butter as above, transfer to a hot platter, sprinkle with lemon juice and minced parsley, and keep warm. Add 1–2 tablespoons butter to skillet, heat quickly until bubbly and faintly brown, pour over shrimp and serve.

To Deep-Fat-Fry: Shell and devein shrimp and, if extra large, butterfly.* Heat shortening or cooking oil in a deep fat fryer to 375° F. Dip shrimp in flour lightly seasoned with salt and pepper, then in a mixture of beaten egg and milk (2 tablespoons milk to each egg), and then in fine dry bread crumbs, cracker meal, or a ½ and ½ mixture of flour and corn meal. Place in a single layer in fryer basket, lower into hot fat, and fry 3–5 minutes until golden. Drain on paper toweling and serve with lemon wedges and Tartar Sauce.

VARIATION:

Batter-Fried Shrimp: See recipes for Hawaiian Sweet-and-Sour Shrimp and Japanese Butterfly Shrimp.

SHRIMP NEWBURG

Makes 4 servings

3 tablespoons butter or margarine
3 tablespoons flour
¾ teaspoon salt
⅛ teaspoon cayenne pepper
⅛ teaspoon nutmeg or mace
1 pint light cream
2 egg yolks, lightly beaten

1 pound shrimp, boiled, shelled, and deveined
2 tablespoons dry sherry
4 slices hot buttered toast, halved diagonally

Melt butter in the top of a double boiler directly over moderate heat, blend in flour, salt, pepper and nutmeg, add cream and heat, stirring constantly, until thickened and smooth. Blend a little hot sauce into yolks, return to pan, and set over simmering water. Add shrimp and heat, stirring occasionally, 3–5 minutes until a good serving temperature. Stir in sherry and serve over toast. About 605 calories per serving.

SHRIMP IN DILL SAUCE

Makes 6 servings

2 tablespoons butter or margarine
2 tablespoons minced shallots
1¼ cups dry white wine
½ cup water
1 bay leaf
2 pounds shelled and deveined raw shrimp
¼ cup unsalted butter
5 tablespoons flour
1 cup heavy cream
2 tablespoons minced fresh dill
½ teaspoon salt
⅛ teaspoon white pepper

Melt butter in a large saucepan over moderate heat, add shallots, and sauté 5 minutes until golden. Add wine, water, bay leaf, and shrimp and simmer, uncovered, stirring occasionally, 3–5 minutes until shrimp just turn pink. Remove from heat and set aside. Melt unsalted butter in a small saucepan over moderate heat and blend in flour. Add cream and heat, stirring constantly, until thickened and smooth; mix in dill, salt, and pepper. Stir cream sauce into shrimp, return to a moderate heat, and cook, stirring constantly, 3–5 minutes until heated through (do not allow to boil); remove bay leaf. Serve over boiled rice or hot buttered toast. About 440 calories per serving (without rice or toast).

SHRIMP WIGGLE

A good chafing dish choice.
Makes 4 servings

1 (10-ounce) package frozen baby green peas, cooked and seasoned by package directions
1 pound fresh or frozen thawed, shelled, and deveined cooked small shrimp
2 cups hot Velouté Sauce, Béchamel Sauce, or Medium White Sauce
2 teaspoons finely grated yellow onion
4 slices hot buttered toast or 4 frozen puff pastry shells, baked by package directions

Mix peas, shrimp, sauce, and onion and heat and stir 3–5 minutes over low heat to blend flavors. Spoon over toast or into baked pastry shells and serve. If made with Velouté Sauce: About 460 calories per serving if served over toast and 625 calories per serving if served in puff pastry shells. If made with Béchamel Sauce: about 500 calories per serving if served over toast and 665 calories per serving if served in puff pastry shells. If made with Medium White Sauce: about 420 calories per serving if served over toast and 585 calories per serving if served in puff pastry shells.

SHRIMP CURRY I

A mellow, sweet-sour curry.
Makes 6 servings

3 medium-size yellow onions, peeled and coarsely chopped
3 cloves garlic, peeled and crushed
6 tablespoons butter or margarine
⅔ cup coarsely chopped celery
3 tart apples, peeled, cored, and diced
2 large tomatoes, peeled, cored, seeded, and coarsely chopped
3 (½") cubes fresh gingerroot, peeled and crushed (use garlic crusher)
2 tablespoons curry powder
½ teaspoon turmeric
½ teaspoon coriander
¼ teaspoon cumin
¼ teaspoon cinnamon
¼ teaspoon crushed hot red chili peppers
⅛ teaspoon mace
1 (3½-ounce) can flaked coconut
1½ cups water
⅔ cup dry white wine
1 pint yogurt
1 teaspoon salt
2 pounds shelled and deveined raw shrimp

Stir-fry onions and garlic in butter in a large, heavy skillet over moderate heat 10–12 minutes until golden brown; mix in celery, apples, tomatoes, and all spices, cover, and simmer 25–30 minutes. Meanwhile, place coconut and water in an electric blender and purée at high speed. When sauce has simmered allotted time, stir in puréed coconut, wine, yogurt, and salt and heat, uncovered, stirring now and then, 10 minutes. Add shrimp and simmer, uncovered, stirring occasionally, about 5 minutes until just pink. Serve hot over boiled rice. (Note: This curry will be even better if made a day ahead, cooled to room temperature, then refrigerated until just before serving. Reheat slowly.) About 495 calories per serving (without rice).

SHRIMP CURRY II

A fiery curry that freezes well. It's lower in calories than Shrimp Curry I.
Makes 8 servings

4 medium-size yellow onions, peeled and minced

4 *cloves garlic, peeled and crushed*
6 *tablespoons peanut oil*
3 *teaspoons turmeric*
4 *teaspoons mustard seeds*
1 *teaspoon fenugreek*
3 *teaspoons cumin*
2–3 *teaspoons crushed hot red chili*
 peppers
4 *teaspoons coriander*
2 *teaspoons ginger*
1½ *teaspoons cinnamon*
¼ *teaspoon cloves*
½ *teaspoon chili powder*
1 *quart Coconut Milk*
4 (½") *cubes fresh gingerroot,*
 peeled and crushed (use garlic
 crusher)
2 *large tomatoes, peeled, cored,*
 seeded, and coarsely chopped
Juice of 2 lemons
¼ *teaspoon salt*
4 *pounds shelled and deveined raw*
 shrimp
1 *cup light cream*

Stir-fry onions and garlic in ¼ cup peanut oil in a large, heavy kettle over moderate heat 8–10 minutes until golden. Meanwhile, place all dried spices in an electric blender cup, cover with plastic food wrap, then lid and purée at high speed until fine and smooth. Mix blended spices into kettle, turn heat to low, and let "mellow" 10 minutes. Add all but last 2 ingredients and simmer, uncovered, stirring occasionally, 25–30 minutes until flavors are well blended. Stir-fry shrimp in a large, heavy skillet in remaining oil 3–5 minutes over moderately high heat, just until no longer pink. Add to sauce along with cream and simmer, uncovered, stirring occasionally, 5–10 minutes to blend flavors. Serve over boiled rice with chutney and, if you like, minced roasted peanuts, flaked coconut, and raisins. (*Note:* Like Shrimp Curry I, this one will be better if made a day ahead.)

About 380 calories per serving (without rice and condiments).

SHRIMP GUMBO

Makes 4 servings

¾ *pound small okra pods, washed,*
 trimmed, and sliced ¼" thick, or
 1 (10-ounce) package frozen sliced
 okra (do not thaw)
¼ *cup shortening or cooking oil*
⅔ *cup minced scallions (include*
 some green tops)
2 *cloves garlic, peeled and crushed*
1 (*1-pound 12-ounce*) *can tomatoes*
 (*do not drain*)
½ *cup boiling water*
2 *bay leaves*
1 *teaspoon salt*
¼ *teaspoon liquid hot red pepper*
 seasoning
1 *pound shelled and deveined raw*
 shrimp
⅛ *teaspoon filé powder*

Sauté okra 2 minutes on a side in shortening in a large, heavy saucepan over moderate heat until golden brown; drain on paper toweling and reserve. Add scallions and garlic to pan and stir-fry 3–5 minutes until limp. Add all remaining ingredients except okra, shrimp, and filé powder and simmer, uncovered, 20–25 minutes, stirring occasionally, until slightly thickened and flavors are well blended. Add okra and shrimp and cook 3–5 minutes, just until shrimp turn pink. Remove bay leaves, stir in filé powder, and serve over boiled rice. About 300 calories per serving (without rice).

SHRIMP JAMBALAYA

A Creole favorite—shrimp with ham, rice, and tomatoes.
Makes 4–6 servings

2 *onions, peeled and coarsely*
 chopped
1 *clove garlic, peeled and crushed*

⅓ cup olive oil
1 cup diced cooked ham
1¼ cups uncooked rice
1 (1-pound 12-ounce) can tomatoes
  (do not drain)
1½ teaspoons salt
½ teaspoon cayenne pepper
1 tablespoon minced parsley
1¾ cups boiling water or chicken
  broth
1 pound shelled and deveined small
  raw shrimp

Stir-fry onions and garlic in oil in a
large, heavy kettle 5–8 minutes over
moderate heat until golden; add
ham and rice and stir-fry 5 minutes until rice is very lightly
browned. Add all remaining ingredients except shrimp and bring
to a boil, stirring. Adjust heat so
mixture stays at a simmer, cover,
and simmer 20 minutes until rice is
very nearly done. Add shrimp, pushing well down into mixture, cover,
and simmer 3–5 minutes just until
pink. Serve with hot buttered
French bread and a crisp green
salad. About 645 calories for each
of 4 servings, 430 calories for
each of 6 servings.

SHRIMP CREOLE

Makes 4 servings

2 medium-size yellow onions, peeled
  and minced
2 medium-size sweet green peppers,
  cored, seeded, and minced
2 cloves garlic, peeled and crushed
2 stalks celery, minced
2 tablespoons olive or other cooking
  oil
2 tablespoons butter or margarine
1 (1-pound 12-ounce) can tomatoes
  (do not drain)
½ teaspoon paprika
⅛ teaspoon cayenne pepper
1 teaspoon salt
1 teaspoon filé powder

1½ pounds shelled and deveined raw
  shrimp

Stir-fry onions, green peppers, garlic,
and celery in oil and butter in a
large saucepan 5–8 minutes over
moderately low heat until onions are
golden. Stir in tomatoes, breaking
up any large pieces, paprika, pepper,
and salt; cover and simmer 35–45
minutes, stirring occasionally. If
sauce seems thin, boil, uncovered,
2–3 minutes to reduce. Add filé
powder and shrimp and simmer,
uncovered, 3–5 minutes until shrimp
are just cooked through. Serve over
boiled rice. About 340 calories
per serving (without rice).

SHRIMP THERMIDOR

Makes 6 servings

2 pounds shelled and deveined raw
  shrimp
3 tablespoons minced shallots or
  scallions
6 tablespoons butter or margarine
6 tablespoons flour
¾ teaspoon salt
½ teaspoon powdered mustard
Pinch cayenne pepper
1 cup milk
1 cup shrimp cooking water
3 egg yolks, lightly beaten
⅓ cup grated Parmesan cheese

Preheat oven to 425° F. Boil shrimp
according to basic method,* then
drain, reserving 1 cup cooking water; set shrimp aside while you
prepare sauce. Stir-fry shallots in
butter in the top of a large double
boiler directly over moderate heat
3–5 minutes until limp; blend in
flour, salt, mustard and pepper,
slowly add milk and shrimp cooking
water, and heat, stirring, until thickened and smooth. Briskly mix 1 cup
sauce into yolks, then return to pan.
Set over simmering water and stir
1–2 minutes until no taste of raw
egg remains. Spoon ½–¾ cup

sauce into an ungreased 2-quart *au gratin* dish or shallow casserole. Arrange shrimp in sauce and top with remaining sauce. Sprinkle with Parmesan. Bake, uncovered, 10–15 minutes until hot but not boiling, then broil 5″–6″ from heat about 2 minutes to brown. Serve with boiled rice. About 340 calories per serving (without rice).

VARIATION:

Thermidor Ramekins: Prepare shrimp and sauce as directed and divide among 6 ungreased individual ramekins. Bake 10 minutes and broil 1–2 to brown. About 340 calories per serving.

⚖ **SCAMPI**

Broiled shrimp redolent of garlic and olive oil.
Makes 2 servings

1 pound raw jumbo shrimp in the shell
1 cup olive oil
2 tablespoons minced parsley
1 clove garlic, peeled and crushed
1 teaspoon salt
¼ teaspoon pepper

Shell shrimp, leaving tail ends on, then devein.* Rinse in cool water, pat dry, and place in a shallow bowl. Mix remaining ingredients and pour over shrimp; cover and chill 2–3 hours in refrigerator, turning 1 or 2 times in marinade. Preheat broiler. Place shrimp on a foil-lined broiler pan and brush generously with marinade. Broil 5″–6″ from heat 3 minutes on a side, basting often with marinade. About 170 calories per serving.

VARIATIONS:

⚖ **Wine Scampi:** Prepare as directed but add 3 tablespoons dry vermouth or sherry to the marinade. About 175 calories per serving.

⚖ **Scampi Italian Style:** Do not shell the shrimp; mix marinade as directed but increase garlic to 2 cloves. Cover shrimp with marinade and chill 2–3 hours, turning often. Broil 3–5 minutes on a side, basting often with marinade. Serve shrimp in the shell with plenty of paper napkins. Any remaining marinade or pan drippings can be used as a dip. About 170 calories per serving.

SHRIMP RUMAKI

Soy-marinated, bacon-wrapped broiled shrimp.
Makes 4 main course servings, enough hors d'oeuvre for 8

1½ pounds shelled and deveined raw jumbo shrimp
1 cup soy sauce
1 cup medium-sweet sherry
1 teaspoon finely grated fresh gingerroot or ¼ teaspoon dried ginger
12 slices bacon, halved crosswise

Marinate shrimp in a mixture of soy sauce, sherry, and ginger 2–3 hours in refrigerator, turning occasionally. Preheat oven to 400° F. Drain marinade from shrimp and reserve. Wrap a piece of bacon around each shrimp and secure with a toothpick. Arrange shrimp on a rack in a large, shallow roasting pan and bake, uncovered, 10 minutes, basting 1 or 2 times with marinade. Turn shrimp and bake 10 minutes longer, basting once or twice, until bacon is nicely browned. Remove toothpicks and serve as a main course, or leave toothpicks in and serve as an hors d'oeuvre. About 315 calories per entree serving, 155 calories for each of 8 hors d'oeuvre servings.

PEPPERY SZECHUAN SHRIMP

Szechuan, a province in south central China, produces a cuisine as peppery as that of our own South-west. By comparison, Cantonese cooking, the cuisine most familiar to Americans, seems bland. The following recipe is "hot." If you are not fond of fiery dishes, reduce the amount of hot red chili peppers. If, on the other hand, you like hot dishes truly hot, increase slightly the amount of chilis.

Makes 6 servings

2 pounds shelled and deveined raw shrimp
1 cup peanut oil (about)
½ cup thinly sliced scallions (include green tops)
2 cloves garlic, peeled and crushed
3 tablespoons finely grated fresh gingerroot
½ cup sake or dry sherry
¼ cup soy sauce
1 tablespoon sugar
1 tablespoon rice or cider vinegar
½ cup ketchup
½ cup chili sauce
¼ teaspoon crushed hot red chili peppers
¼ teaspoon salt (about)

Pat shrimp dry on paper toweling. Heat oil in a wok or large, heavy skillet over moderately high heat. Add shrimp, about half at a time, and stir-fry 3–4 minutes until pink. Drain on paper toweling. Pour all but about 2 tablespoons oil from wok or skillet, add scallions and garlic, and stir-fry 3–5 minutes over moderate heat until limp. Add remaining ingredients except shrimp and heat and stir 5 minutes. Add shrimp and heat, tossing in sauce, 3–4 minutes. Taste for salt and adjust if needed. Serve with boiled rice. About 330 calories per serving without rice.

CANTONESE-STYLE SHRIMP WITH VEGETABLES

Makes 4–6 servings

1½ pounds shelled and deveined raw shrimp
¼ cup peanut or other cooking oil
½ pound mushrooms, wiped clean and sliced thin
1 (5-ounce) can water chestnuts, drained and sliced thin
2 cups diced celery
2 cups finely shredded Chinese cabbage
8 scallions, trimmed and minced (include tops)
1 medium-size sweet green pepper, cored, seeded, and minced
1 tablespoon minced fresh gingerroot
1 clove garlic, peeled and crushed (optional)
2 tablespoons cornstarch blended with ¼ cup cold chicken broth
1¾ cups chicken broth
2 teaspoons salt
1 teaspoon sugar

Stir-fry shrimp in 2 tablespoons oil in a large, heavy skillet or wok over moderately high heat 2–3 minutes until just turning pink; drain on paper toweling and reserve. Add remaining oil to skillet, also mushrooms, water chestnuts, vegetables, ginger, and, if you wish, garlic; stir-fry 2–3 minutes until crisp tender. Add shrimp and remaining ingredients and cook and stir until slightly thickened. Serve over boiled rice or thin noodles. About 365 calories for each of 4 servings (without rice or noodles), 245 calories for each of 6 servings.

VARIATION:

Loong Ha Peen (Chicken, Shrimp, and Vegetables): Reduce amount of shrimp to 1 pound and add 1 cup coarsely chopped, cooked chicken meat. Prepare as directed, stirring chicken into sautéed vegetables along with sautéed shrimp. About 395 calories for each of 4 servings, 265 calories for each of 6 servings.

⚙ GINGERY CHINESE SHRIMP

Makes 2–3 main course servings, enough hors d'oeuvre for 4–6

1 pound shelled and deveined raw shrimp
1½ teaspoons cornstarch
2 teaspoons dry vermouth or sherry
1 teaspoon salt
¼ teaspoon monosodium glutamate (MSG)
2 scallions, sliced ¼″ thick (include some tops)
2 (¼″) cubes fresh gingerroot, peeled and crushed (use garlic crusher)
¾ cup cooking oil

If shrimp are very large, halve crosswise; place in a bowl, add cornstarch, vermouth, salt, MSG, scallions, and ginger, and toss to mix. Cover and chill 2 hours. Heat oil in a large, heavy skillet over moderately high heat until a cube of bread will sizzle, add shrimp and stir-fry 2–3 minutes or just until shrimp turn pink. Drain on paper toweling and serve with boiled rice as a main course, or spear each shrimp with a toothpick and serve hot as an hors d'oeuvre. About 270 calories for each of 2 entree servings, 180 calories for each of 3 entree servings. About 135 calories for each of 4 hors d'oeuvre servings and 90 calories for each of 6 hors d'oeuvre servings.

JAPANESE BUTTERFLY SHRIMP

Makes 6–8 entree servings, enough hors d'oeuvre for 10–12

3 pounds large raw shrimp in the shell
Shortening or cooking oil for deep fat frying
½ cup rice flour
1 recipe Tempura Batter
1 recipe Tempura Sauce

Shell shrimp, leaving tail ends on, then devein.* To butterfly, cut down center back of each shrimp to within ⅛″ of underside and spread flat. Rinse shrimp in cool water, pat dry on paper toweling, cover, and chill several hours. About ½ hour before serving, begin heating shortening in a deep fat fryer; insert deep fat thermometer. Also make *tempura* batter and sauce. When fat reaches 380° F., quickly dredge shrimp in rice flour, dip in batter, and fry, 5 or 6 at a time, 3–5 minutes until golden brown. Drain on paper toweling and set, uncovered, in oven turned to lowest heat to keep warm and crisp while you fry remaining shrimp. Scoop any crumbs of batter from fat before each new batch of shrimp and keep fat temperature as near 380° F. as possible. Serve shrimp as an entree or hors d'oeuvre, using tempura sauce as a dip. About 350 calories for each of 6 entree servings, 260 calories for each of 8 entree servings. About 210 calories for each of 10 hors d'oeuvre servings and 175 calories for each of 12 hors d'oeuvre servings.

HAWAIIAN SWEET-AND-SOUR SHRIMP

Makes 6 servings

2 pounds large raw shrimp in the shell
Shortening or cooking oil for deep fat frying (for best flavor, use part peanut oil)

Sweet-Sour Sauce:
1 large yellow onion, peeled and cut in thin wedges
1 large sweet green pepper, cored, seeded, and cut in 2″ × ¾″ strips
¼ cup peanut oil
⅔ cup firmly packed light brown sugar
½ cup rice vinegar or cider vinegar
¼ cup tomato paste

1 (13¼-ounce) can pineapple
   chunks (do not drain)
⅓ cup water or dry white wine
¼ cup soy sauce
⅛ teaspoon cayenne pepper
1 tablespoon cornstarch blended with
   ¼ cup cold water

Shrimp Batter:
1 egg
1 cup unsifted rice flour
1 tablespoon sugar
1 teaspoon salt
¾ cup ice water

Shell shrimp, leaving tail ends on, then devein* and butterfly by cutting down center back of each shrimp to within ⅛" of underside and spreading flat. Rinse shrimp in cool water and pat dry on paper toweling. Begin heating shortening in a deep fat fryer; insert deep fat thermometer. Also make sweet-sour sauce: Stir-fry onion and green pepper in peanut oil 5–8 minutes until onion is golden; add all remaining sauce ingredients except cornstarch paste and simmer, uncovered, stirring occasionally, 10 minutes. Mix in cornstarch paste and heat, stirring constantly, until thickened and clear. Turn heat to lowest point and let sauce cook slowly while you prepare shrimp. For the batter, beat egg until foamy, mix in remaining ingredients, and beat well until the consistency of heavy cream. When fat reaches 375° F., dip shrimp in batter, then fry, about 5 or 6 at a time, 3–5 minutes until golden. Drain on paper toweling. When all shrimp are done, mound on a heated large platter, smother with sweet-sour sauce, and serve. About 710 calories per serving.

CHARLESTON SHRIMP PIE

A delicate, Deep South favorite that's easy to make.
Makes 6 servings

2 pounds shrimp, boiled, shelled,
   and deveined
8 slices firm-textured white bread
1 pint light cream
1 pint milk
1 tablespoon melted butter or
   margarine
½ cup dry sherry
2 teaspoons salt
¼ teaspoon mace or nutmeg
¼ teaspoon cayenne pepper

Preheat oven to 375° F. Place shrimp in a buttered 2½-quart casserole or soufflé dish. Soak bread in cream and milk 15 minutes in a large bowl, add remaining ingredients, and beat until smooth with a wooden spoon. Pour over shrimp and toss well to mix. Bake, uncovered, 1 hour and 15 minutes or until lightly browned and bubbly. About 380 calories per serving.

⊠ BAKED SHRIMP AND RED RICE

This Louisiana classic couldn't be easier.
Makes 4 servings

¼ cup olive or other cooking oil
1 medium-size yellow onion, peeled
   and minced
1 clove garlic, peeled and crushed
½ cup minced green pepper
½ cup uncooked rice
1 (1-pound) can tomatoes (do not
   drain)
½ cup water
1½ teaspoons salt
¼ teaspoon pepper
¼ teaspoon oregano
1 bay leaf, crumbled
1½ pounds shelled and deveined
   raw shrimp

Preheat oven to 350° F. In a buttered 2-quart casserole, mix all ingredients except shrimp. Cover and bake 1 hour, stirring 2 or 3 times. Add shrimp, pushing well down into mixture, re-cover, and bake ½ hour

longer or until rice is done. About
415 calories per serving.

VARIATION:
Baked Scallops and Red Rice: Prepare as directed, substituting 1½
pounds bay scallops for the shrimp.
About 365 calories per serving.

⚶ PICKLED SHRIMP À LA LORNA

Serve as a summer luncheon entree
or as hors d'oeuvre on crisp crackers
with bits of sliced onion.
Makes 8 main course servings,
enough hors d'oeuvre for 12

3 pounds shrimp, boiled, shelled,
    deveined, and cooled
3 medium-size yellow onions, peeled
    and sliced very thin
1 (3/16-ounce) box bay leaves
1½ cups olive or other cooking oil
1½ cups French dressing
1½ cloves garlic, peeled and halved

Place a layer of shrimp in a deep
enamel kettle, top with a layer of
sliced onions and a layer of bay
leaves. Continue building up layers
as long as shrimp last. Mix oil and
French dressing and pour over all.
Drop in garlic, cover, and marinate
in refrigerator at least 4 hours before
serving. (*Note:* These pickled shrimp
will keep in the refrigerator about
1 week.) About 110 calories for each
of 8 entree servings, 75 calories for
each of 12 hors d'oeuvre servings.

▨ SHRIMP DE JONGHE

Easy but impressive.
Makes 8 servings

1 cup unsalted butter (no substitute),
    softened to room temperature
2 cloves garlic, peeled and crushed
2 shallots, peeled and minced, or
    1 scallion, minced
1 tablespoon minced parsley
1 tablespoon minced chives

¼ teaspoon tarragon
¼ teaspoon marjoram
¼ teaspoon chervil
⅛ teaspoon nutmeg
3 cups soft white bread crumbs
2 tablespoons lemon juice
⅓ cup dry sherry
3 pounds shelled and deveined boiled
    small shrimp

Preheat oven to 375° F. Cream
butter with garlic, shallots, herbs,
and nutmeg until well blended; mix
in crumbs, lemon juice, and sherry.
Layer shrimp and crumbs into 8
well-buttered individual ramekins,
ending with a layer of crumbs. Bake,
uncovered, 20 minutes until topping
is lightly browned and mixture
heated through. About 425 calories
per serving.

FROGS' LEGS

Though people do still go frogging,
most of the frogs' legs served today
are from especially raised and
pampered frogs. Only the hind legs
are eaten. They are plump and
tender and taste much like young
chicken.

About Buying Fresh Frogs' Legs

Season: Year round.

Popular Market Forms: Dressed
and ready to cook.

Amount Needed: About ½ pound
or 2–4 pairs of frogs' legs per serving, depending on size; the smaller
the legs, the more tender they'll be.

For Top Quality: Look for resilient,
pale pink frogs' legs with a good
fresh odor.

About Frozen Frogs' Legs

Frozen frogs' legs are more readily
available in most parts of the country

than the fresh; they are dressed and ready to cook but should be thawed first in the refrigerator. Use immediately after thawing, never refreeze, and prepare as you would fresh frogs' legs.

How to Dress Fresh Frogs' Legs:

It's doubtful that you'll have to do this yourself, but just in case, here's the technique: Cut off hind legs as close to the body as possible; wash well under running cold water. Cut off feet, then, starting at the top of the legs, peel off skin just as though you were removing a glove.

How to Cook Frogs' Legs

Because of their delicacy, frogs' legs should be treated simply: poached, sautéed, or deep fat fried. Like fish, they do not become more tender in cooking, only more appetizing.

General Preparation: Separate pairs of legs by severing at the crotch; wipe well with damp paper toweling, then pat dry. Some people like to soak frogs' legs 1–2 hours in milk before cooking, but it seems to make little difference in their tenderness or flavor.

To Panfry (Sauté): Make sure legs are very dry. Dip in milk, then in flour lightly seasoned with salt and pepper and sauté in a ½ and ½ mixture of butter and olive or other cooking oil (for 6–8 pairs of legs, you'll need about 2 tablespoons butter, 2 tablespoons oil). Cook 5–6 minutes over moderate heat, turning often so legs brown evenly. Serve topped with some of the pan juices and with lemon.

VARIATION:

Breaded Fried Frogs' Legs: Dip legs in seasoned flour, then in lightly beaten egg and finally in fine dry bread crumbs (seasoned or plain) or cracker meal. Sauté as above.

To Deep-Fat-Fry: Select very young, tender frogs' legs, pat very dry, dip in seasoned flour, then in beaten egg, then in fine dry bread crumbs or cracker meal to coat evenly. Fry 2–3 minutes in 375° F. deep fat until golden brown. Drain on paper toweling and serve with lemon wedges and Tartar Sauce. (*Note:* If you prefer a crisp crumb coating, let breaded legs dry 10–15 minutes on a rack at room temperature before frying.)

To Poach: Place prepared legs in a large, heavy skillet (not iron), add liquid just to cover (a ½ and ½ mixture of milk and water or dry white wine); for each pint liquid, add 1 teaspoon salt and a pinch pepper. Cover and simmer 10–15 minutes, depending on size, just to cook through. Lift out legs, sprinkle with minced parsley or *fines herbes,** and drizzle with melted butter or Béchamel Sauce.

SOME CLASSIC WAYS TO SERVE FROGS' LEGS

All amounts based on 6 pairs medium-size frogs' legs, enough for 4 servings

À la Lyonnaise: Sauté frogs' legs by basic method. At the same time, stir-fry 2 thinly sliced large yellow onions, separated into rings, in 2 tablespoons butter 5–8 minutes until pale golden. Add onions to frogs' legs, toss very gently, transfer to a hot platter, and keep warm. Pour all but 2 tablespoons drippings from skillet in which frogs' legs were cooked, add 2 tablespoons cider vinegar, heat 1–2 minutes, scraping up any browned bits, and pour over legs. Sprinkle with parsley and serve.

À la Meunière: Sauté frogs' legs by basic method, transfer to a hot platter, and keep warm. Drain all but

2 tablespoons drippings from skillet, add ¼ cup lemon juice, and heat 1–2 minutes, stirring up browned bits. Pour over frogs' legs, sprinkle with parsley, and serve.

À la Provençale: Sauté frogs' legs by basic method. At the same time, stir-fry 2 peeled and minced medium-size yellow onions and 2 peeled and crushed cloves garlic in 2 tablespoons olive oil 5–8 minutes until pale golden. Add 3 peeled, cored, seeded, and finely chopped tomatoes, ¼ cup dry red wine, and ¼ teaspoon each salt and sugar and heat, stirring, 2–3 minutes. Pour over frogs' legs, toss very gently, sprinkle with minced parsley and serve.

Au Gratin: Sauté frogs' legs by basic method and transfer to a buttered 1½-quart *au gratin* dish. Cover with 2 cups hot Medium White Sauce, sprinkle with ⅓ cup buttered bread crumbs, and broil 3″–4″ from heat 2–3 minutes to brown.

Deviled: Sauté frogs' legs by basic method, transfer to a hot platter and keep warm. Drain all but 2 tablespoons drippings from skillet, add 1 tablespoon each prepared mild yellow mustard, Worcestershire sauce, lemon juice, and brandy. Heat and stir 1–2 minutes, scraping up any browned bits, pour over frogs' legs, and serve.

Mornay: Sauté frogs' legs by basic method and transfer to a buttered 1½-quart *au gratin* dish. Smother with 2 cups hot Mornay Sauce, sprinkle with ¼ cup grated Parmesan cheese, and broil 3″–4″ from heat 2–3 minutes to brown.

Poulette: Poach frogs' legs by basic method, using part white wine and a *bouquet garni.** Drain legs, transfer to a hot deep platter, and keep warm. Mix 1½ cups heavy cream with 3 lightly beaten egg yolks in the top of a double boiler; set over simmering water and heat, stirring, until slightly thickened. Off heat mix in 1 tablespoon each butter and lemon juice and 2 tablespoons minced parsley. Pour over legs, garnish, if you like, with ½ pound sautéed button mushrooms, and serve.

Vinaigrette: Poach frogs' legs by basic method, using part white wine and a *bouquet garni.** Drain, cool, and chill several hours. Serve on lettuce, topped with Vinaigrette Dressing. If you prefer, cut meat from frogs' legs, toss with just enough vinaigrette to coat lightly, and marinate several hours in refrigerator.

SNAILS (ESCARGOTS)

Snails have long been a European favorite (the Romans were so fond of them they kept whole vineyards for them to feed upon), but until recently, we've been squeamish about trying them. American snails are smaller than the European (it takes about 50 of ours to make a pound). Fortunately, the fresh are relatively inexpensive (about the same price as hamburger) and, equally fortunately, they are raised under strict supervision and do not need the "purifying" starvation period required for European snails. Canned snails are sold in gourmet shops along with bags of polished shells, but their flavor cannot compare with that of the fresh.

Amount Needed: Allow about 1 dozen snails per person.

For Top Quality: Just make sure the snails are still alive.

How to Prepare Fresh Snails for Cooking: Place snails in a large, shallow pan, cover with lukewarm water, and let stand 10 minutes; snails should partially emerge from shells, discard any that don't. Cover "selects" with cold water, add about 1 teaspoon salt, then dampen edge of bowl and coat with salt so snails can't crawl out. Let stand at room temperature 1 hour, rinse well in cold water, then scrub shells well and rinse again. Place snails in a saucepan, cover with boiling water, cover, and simmer 5 minutes; drain and cool under cold running water, washing off the white material that looks like partially cooked egg white (it's edible, just not very attractive). Remove snails from shells by twisting out with a small skewer or snail fork; reserve shells. Remove bits of green gall from snails, also snip off heads and tiny curled black tails.

To Poach (necessary before fresh snails can be used in recipes): Place prepared snails in a saucepan, cover with water (you'll need about 1½ cups for 1 pound snails), or a ½ and ½ mixture of white wine and water or beef broth; add a peeled and quartered carrot, a celery stalk cut in chunks, a minced scallion or shallot, a *bouquet garni** tied in cheesecloth, and a few bruised peppercorns. Cover and simmer 1½–2 hours until tender. Cool snails in broth to room temperature.

To Clean Shells: It's best to do this while snails are poaching so that both will be ready at the same time. Place scrubbed shells in a saucepan, add 1 quart boiling water mixed with 2 tablespoons baking soda and 2 teaspoons salt, cover, and simmer ½ hour. Drain, rinse in cold water, and let dry thoroughly before using. (*Note:* If carefully washed after using, the shells may be kept and used over and over again. In addition to being used for various snail recipes, they are the perfect container for baking periwinkles.)

How to Eat Snails: Whenever snails are served in the shell, eating them requires special implements: *escargotières* (snail plates), snail pincers, and snail forks. To eat snails grace-

fully, pick them up, 1 at a time, with snail pincer and twist out snail as shown with the special fork. Dip in sauce, then eat.

ESCARGOTS À LA BOURGUIGNONNE

If you've never eaten snails, this is a good way to begin, because the seasonings are superb. This particular dish is often served as a first course, but it can also be the entree. Makes 4 servings

1 pound fresh snails or 4 dozen canned snails with shells
½ cup butter, softened to room temperature
1 clove garlic, peeled and crushed
2 tablespoons minced shallots or scallions
1½ teaspoons minced parsley
¼ teaspoon salt

Pinch pepper
⅓ *cup fine soft white bread crumbs*

Prepare fresh snails for cooking and poach,* also clean shells.* If using canned snails, drain well and pat dry on paper toweling. Preheat oven to 350° F. Mix butter with garlic, shallots, parsley, salt, and pepper. Replace each snail in a shell and close openings with generous dabs of butter; dip buttered ends into crumbs. Arrange snails in snail plates and bake, uncovered, 10–12 minutes until piping hot. About 320 calories per serving.

VARIATION:

Escargots in Chablis: Poach snails and clean shells as directed. Meanwhile, boil 1½ cups chablis with 2 teaspoons minced shallots until reduced to ¾ cup; strain through a double thickness of cheesecloth, then mix in ½ teaspoon beef extract. Before returning snails to shells, pour a little wine mixture into each shell. Replace snails and close with dabs of butter as above but omit crumbs. Arrange snails in snail plates and bake as directed. About 315 calories per serving.

⚖ **BAKED ESCARGOTS CORSICAN STYLE**

Especially good as a first course. Anchovy fillets, spinach, and lemon add piquancy.
Makes 4 servings

1 *pound fresh snails or 4 dozen canned snails*
6–8 *anchovy fillets, minced*
1 *cup finely shredded raw spinach*
1 *teaspoon lemon juice*
2 *tablespoons fine dry bread crumbs*
¼ *cup butter*

Prepare fresh snails for cooking and poach.* If using canned snails, drain well. Preheat oven to 450° F. Coarsely chop snails and mix with anchovies, spinach, and lemon juice. Butter 4 large scallop shells or individual ramekins and fill with snail mixture. Sprinkle with crumbs and dot with butter. Place shells or ramekins on a baking sheet and bake, uncovered, 5–7 minutes until crumbs are lightly browned. About 240 calories per serving.

⚖ **ESCARGOTS À LA PROVENÇALE**

Unlike many Provençal recipes, this one contains no tomatoes. But the other traditional flavorings are there —garlic, onion, olive oil, and parsley. Makes 4 servings

1 *pound fresh snails or 4 dozen canned snails*
1 *medium-size yellow onion, peeled and minced*
2 *cloves garlic, peeled and crushed*
2 *tablespoons olive oil*
¼ *pound mushrooms, wiped clean and minced*
¼ *cup dry red wine*
4 *slices hot buttered toast, trimmed of crusts*
2 *tablespoons minced parsley*

Prepare fresh snails for cooking and poach.* If using canned snails, drain well and pat dry on paper toweling. Stir-fry onion and garlic in oil in a skillet 8–10 minutes over moderate heat until golden; add mushrooms and stir-fry 1–2 minutes longer. Add wine and simmer, uncovered, stirring occasionally, 5 minutes. Add snails and heat, uncovered, 5 minutes. Spoon over toast, sprinkle with parsley, and serve. About 290 calories per serving.

MARINATED SNAILS WITH MAYONNAISE OR RÉMOULADE SAUCE

Good as a first course or light entree.
Makes 4 servings

*1 pound fresh snails or 4 dozen
canned snails with shells*
2 tablespoons olive oil
2 tablespoons white wine vinegar
2 tablespoons minced chives
2 tablespoons minced parsley
*1 cup Homemade Mayonnaise or
Rémoulade Sauce*

Prepare fresh snails for cooking and poach,* also clean shells.* If using canned snails, drain well and pat dry on paper toweling. Before returning snails to shells, toss with oil, vinegar, chives, and parsley. Return snails to shells, wrap airtight, and chill 2–3 hours. Arrange in snail plates and serve cold with mayonnaise or *rémoulade* as a dip. About 685 calories per serving if served with Homemade Mayonnaise, about 690 calories per serving if served with Rémoulade Sauce.

SQUID AND OCTOPUS

If young, tender, and properly prepared, these two can be exquisite; abused they are rubbery and tough. Squid and octopus are both inkfish, both are tentacled, and both are prepared more or less the same way. Of the two, squid is the more delicate. Most come from the North Atlantic, and the smaller they are the better. Octopus are fished from the Atlantic, too, but farther south. They may reach awesome size (about seven feet with tentacles extended), but again, the smaller the better. Canned and dried squid are sometimes available in gourmet or ethnic groceries; some squid is also being frozen, but most of it goes to restaurants.

Season: Year round.

Amount Needed: About ⅓–½ pound per person. The choicest squid weigh only a few ounces

apiece. Octopus run larger, and even the smallest may weigh about 1 pound.

For Top Quality: Choose squid or octopus that are firm-tender and sweet-smelling with little or no liquid.

How to Prepare Squid and Octopus for Cooking: If possible, have your fish market clean squid or octopus for you. If you must do it yourself:

1. Lay squid or octopus, back side up on a counter with tentacles fully extended (the back is the side on which the eyes are most visible).

2. With a sharp knife, cut down center back, exposing cuttlebone (this is the cuttlebone used as canary food); lift it out and discard.

3. Grasp head and tentacles and pull toward you, turning octopus or squid inside out; take care not to rupture ink sac. Save sac, if you like, and use ink in broths or stews. Discard all other internal organs. The only parts you want are the meaty body covering and the tentacles.

4. Remove heads from squid; remove eyes, mouth, and parrot-like beak from octopus.

5. Cut off tentacles close to head, push out and discard bead of flesh at root of each tentacle.

6. Wash body and tentacles several times in cool water. Squid are now ready to use as recipes direct, *but octopus, unless very small and tender must be beaten until tender.*

7. Place octopus flat on a cutting board and pound rhythmically with the blunt edge of a meat cleaver or edge of a heavy plate until meat is soft and velvety.

8. If you object to the octopus' purple skin, here's how to remove. Place

octopus in a large kettle, cover with salted boiling water (about 1 teaspoon salt to 1 quart water), cover, and boil 20 minutes. Drain, plunge in ice water, and, using a stiff brush, scrub away purple skin.

About Using the Ink: Europeans often use squid or octopus ink to color and enrich soups and stews. But taste first, to see if you like the flavor. To collect the ink, hold sac over a small bowl, puncture with the point of a knife and squeeze ink out. If used in soups or stews, it should be added along with other liquid ingredients.

⚔ FRIED SQUID

Makes 4 servings

2 pounds small squid, prepared for cooking
⅓ cup unsifted flour
1 egg, lightly beaten with 1 tablespoon cold water
¾ cup toasted seasoned bread crumbs (about)
⅓ cup cooking oil

Cut squid in 2″ pieces (if tentacles are very small, leave whole); pat very dry on paper toweling. Dip in flour, then egg, and then in crumbs to coat evenly. Let dry on a rack at room temperature 10–15 minutes. Heat oil in a large, heavy skillet over moderate heat 1 minute. Sauté body pieces first, a few at a time, 4–5 minutes until browned on both sides; drain on paper toweling and keep warm. Sauté tentacles about 2 minutes (stand back from the pan because they sputter the way chicken livers do). Serve with lemon wedges. If you like, pass Tartar Sauce or any well-seasoned seafood sauce. About 290 calories per serving.

SQUID À LA MARSEILLAISE

Squid stuffed with onion, tomatoes, and crumbs, then simmered in dry white wine.
Makes 4–6 servings

2 pounds squid, prepared for cooking
1 large yellow onion, peeled and minced
4 tablespoons olive oil
2 cloves garlic, peeled and crushed
2 ripe tomatoes, peeled, cored, seeded, and chopped fine
1½ cups soft white bread crumbs
1 tablespoon minced parsley
¼ teaspoon salt
⅛ teaspoon pepper
1 cup dry white wine
1 cup water
1 bay leaf

Mince squid tentacles and set aside. Stir-fry onion in 2 tablespoons oil in a skillet over moderate heat 5–8 minutes until pale golden; add tentacles, garlic, and tomatoes and stir-fry 2–3 minutes. Off heat, mix in crumbs, parsley, salt, and pepper; loosely stuff into body cavities of squid and close with toothpicks. Brown squid lightly on both sides in remaining oil in a flameproof casserole over moderately high heat, add wine, water, and bay leaf; stir in any remaining stuffing. Cover and simmer 20–30 minutes until squid is tender. Check consistency of liquid occasionally and, if too thick, thin with a little water or wine. Remove bay leaf and toothpicks and serve in shallow bowls with French bread or over hot boiled rice. About 405 calories for each of 4 servings (without bread or rice), about 270 calories for each of 6 servings.

GREEK-STYLE SQUID STUFFED WITH SAVORY RICE

Makes 4 servings

2 pounds squid, prepared for cooking

2 *medium-size yellow onions, peeled
and minced*
2 *tablespoons olive oil*
2 *cloves garlic, peeled and crushed*
2 *teaspoons minced parsley*
½ *teaspoon dried dill*
2 *cups hot cooked seasoned rice*
⅓ *cup dried currants (optional)*
1 *(1-pound) can Spanish-style
tomato sauce*

Preheat oven to 350° F. Chop tentacles fine and set aside. Stir-fry onions in oil in a large, heavy skillet over moderate heat 8–10 minutes until golden; add garlic and tentacles and stir-fry 1 minute. Off heat, mix in parsley, dill, rice, and, if you like, currants; stuff into body cavities of squid and close with toothpicks. Arrange squid in a single layer in a greased large casserole, pile any leftover stuffing on top, and pour in tomato sauce. Cover and bake 25 minutes until squid is tender. Remove toothpicks and serve with some sauce spooned over each portion. About 360 calories per serving.

MEDITERRANEAN-STYLE SQUID OR OCTOPUS

Squid in a rich tomato-wine sauce. Makes 4–6 servings

2 *pounds squid or octopus, prepared
for cooking*
2 *medium-size yellow onions, peeled
and minced*
¼ *cup olive or other cooking oil*
2–3 *cloves garlic, peeled and crushed*
1 *(6-ounce) can tomato paste*
1 *cup dry white wine or dry
vermouth*
1 *cup water*
⅛ *teaspoon crushed hot red chili
peppers*
1 *tablespoon minced parsley*
¼–½ *teaspoon salt*

Cut squid or octopus in 2″ chunks and set aside. Sauté onions in oil 8–10 minutes until golden, add gar-

lic, and stir-fry 1 minute. Add squid or octopus and all remaining ingredients except salt, mix well, cover, and simmer ¾–1 hour, stirring occasionally, until tender (the best way to tell if squid or octopus is tender is to eat a piece). Taste for salt and add as needed. Serve over hot boiled rice. If made with squid: About 385 calories for each of 4 servings, 260 calories for each of 6 servings. If made with octopus: About 365 calories for each of 4 servings, 245 calories for each of 6 servings (without rice).

TURTLE, TORTOISE, AND TERRAPIN

These are all turtles; the word *turtle* usually refers to sea turtles (or to snappers), *tortoise* to land turtles, and *terrapin* to habitués of bogs and swamps. But there aren't any hard and fast rules, and terminology varies from species to species and area to area. Turtle sizes vary tremendously—from the giant sea turtles weighing a thousand pounds or more to tortoises and terrapins weighing as little as five. Choicest sea turtle (and the most readily available) is the *green turtle* from the South Atlantic and Caribbean. As for land turtles, it's entirely a matter of personal preference. Some people like snapping turtles, others diamondback terrapins, still others "cooters" or "gophers."

Season: Year round for sea turtles; spring, summer, and fall for tortoises and terrapins.

Popular Market Forms: In areas where they are caught, sea turtles are dressed and sold as steaks or as diced or cubed meat. Land turtles, though found throughout most of the United States, don't often come to market. To enjoy them, you must catch your own.

Amount Needed: Allow ¼–½ pound turtle meat per serving. A 4–5-pound turtle will yield 3–4 cups meat.

For Top Quality: Look for moist, resilient meat with good fresh odor. Color will vary from almost white to gray or green, depending on variety of turtle and whether meat is from the leg, neck, or back (back meat is considered the best).

About Frozen and Canned Turtle Meat

Diced sea turtle meat is available frozen cooked and canned; occasionally frozen cooked snapping turtle meat is also available. Both frozen and canned turtle meat can be used interchangeably for parboiled fresh meat; it is not necessary to thaw the frozen meat before using unless pieces need to be separated and cooked quickly.

How to Dress a Live Tortoise or Terrapin

1. Poke a stick in turtle's mouth and, when he grabs hold, pull, stretching head away from body; chop off head with a meat cleaver or hatchet and discard.

2. Hang turtle upside-down by its tail in a cool, airy place and let bleed 24 hours.

3. Drop turtle upside-down in a kettle of boiling water and blanch 1–2 minutes to loosen tough outer covering; drain. Peel outer covering from legs, neck, and tail, also from around shell to loosen. This is slow work, so have patience. Do not remove tender inner skin—when cooked, it's good.

4. Cut off each leg as close to body

as possible and snip off claws, using wire clippers; reserve legs. Also cut off tail and reserve; if turtle is male, remove genitals on underside of tail.

5. Pull top and bottom shells apart, first cutting through soft bridges joining them if necessary. Near the front end of the shell you will find the liver; lift it out and separate from gall bladder, working gently so bladder doesn't rupture. Discard bladder, also "sandbags" and digestive organs (some people like to mince the small intestines and add to stews and broths). Save top shell (there is choice meat on the underside); also save cross-shaped breastbone and meat attached to it, but discard all other inner parts of turtle.

6. Sprinkle all pieces except liver with salt and chill several hours. Cover with cold water, return to refrigerator, and let stand 24 hours, changing water 2 or 3 times. Liver should be loosely wrapped and refrigerated or, if you prefer, cooked right away. Simply slice thin and sauté in butter as you would calf's liver.

7. When turtle meat has soaked 24 hours, drain and rinse well in cold water.

To Parboil (necessary before fresh turtle can be used in recipes): Place dressed turtle pieces in a large kettle, lay shell on top, outer side up. Add 2–3 celery stalks and peeled carrots, cut in thick chunks, 2 bay leaves, 6–8 parsley sprigs, 1 teaspoon thyme, a dozen bruised peppercorns, 1 tablespoon salt and 2 medium-size peeled yellow onions each stuck with 2 cloves. Pour in enough cold water to cover and bring to a boil. Reduce heat so water just simmers, cover kettle, and simmer 1–1½ hours until meat can be cut with a fork. Drain off broth, strain, and use for making soups and stews. Cut turtle meat from bones, also cut meat from underside of shell; dice or cube meat as recipes direct. The turtle is now ready to use in recipes.

SEA TURTLE STEAKS

Makes 4 servings

1 ½ pounds sea turtle steaks, cut ⅛" thick
1 cup unsifted flour
1 teaspoon salt
1 teaspoon paprika
¼ teaspoon pepper
⅓ cup butter or margarine
½ cup dry vermouth
1 cup heavy cream
1 tablespoon minced fresh dill or parsley

Dredge steaks in a mixture of flour, salt, paprika, and pepper and brown quickly in butter in a large, heavy skillet over moderately high heat. Add vermouth, turn heat to low, cover, and simmer ¾–1 hour until tender. Lift steaks to a hot platter and keep warm. Smooth cream into skillet and boil rapidly, stirring, until reduced by about ⅓. Pour over steaks, sprinkle with dill, and serve. About 545 calories per serving.

TURTLE HASH

Makes 4 servings

2 pounds turtle meat, parboiled and cut in 1" cubes
3 cups water (about)
¼ pound salt pork, cut in small dice
1 medium-size yellow onion, peeled and minced
2 pounds potatoes, peeled and cut in ½" cubes
¼ teaspoon pepper

Place turtle meat and just enough water to cover in a saucepan; simmer, covered, ¾–1 hour until very tender. Meanwhile, slowly brown salt pork in a heavy skillet over moderate heat; remove with a slotted spoon to paper toweling to drain. Stir-fry onion in drippings 5–8 minutes until pale golden, add potatoes, 1 cup water, and the pepper. Cover and simmer about 10 minutes until potatoes are just tender. Drain turtle meat, mix gently into potatoes along with salt pork, and heat, stirring, 3–5 minutes until very hot. Serve with hot buttered biscuits or corn bread. About 470 calories per serving.

TURTLE STEW

Delicious made with either sea or land turtle.
Makes 4–6 servings

2 medium-size yellow onions, peeled and coarsely chopped
1 medium-size sweet green pepper, cored, seeded, and minced
4 carrots, peeled and cut in small dice
1 cup minced celery
½ cup olive oil
2 pounds turtle meat, parboiled and cut in ½"–1" cubes
½ teaspoon thyme
½ teaspoon oregano
⅛ teaspoon cloves
1 bay leaf, crumbled
1 teaspoon salt (about)
¼ teaspoon pepper
1 (1-pound) can tomatoes (do not drain)
2 cups turtle broth,* Easy Fish Stock, or chicken broth
4 hard-cooked eggs, shelled
½ cup dry sherry or Madeira wine

Stir-fry onions, green pepper, carrots, and celery in oil 10–12 minutes until lightly browned. Add turtle and all but last 2 ingredients, cover, and simmer about 1 hour until turtle is very tender. Check stew now and then and, if it seems thin, uncover during last 15–20 minutes of cooking. Meanwhile, dice egg whites and sieve the yolks. Stir eggs and sherry into stew and heat, stirring now and then, 5 minutes. Taste for salt and adjust as needed. Serve in soup bowls with hot corn bread and a crisp green salad. About 510 calories for each of 4 servings, 340 calories for each of 6 servings.

INDEX

What It Will Mean to Cook
with Metric Measures

The metric system is a way of measuring based on the decimal system with larger measures being subdivided into units of ten. Food researchers and European cooks have always used the metric system because it is more precise than American weights and measures.

In recipes, the principal difference between our present way of measuring and the metric is that dry ingredients like flour and sugar are weighed rather than measured in a cup.

Meats, fruits, and vegetables will be sold by the kilogram instead of the pound and, in recipes, will be called for by weight rather than by cup (whether sliced, diced, or whole).

Small measures – tablespoons, teaspoons, and fractions thereof – are not likely to change.

Liquids are measured in measuring cups, but the calibrations are marked in liters, ½ liters, ¼ liters, and milliliters instead of in cups. (See opposite.) There will be no more such cumbersome measurements as ½ cup plus 1 tablespoon or 1 cup minus 3 teaspoons.

TABLE OF EQUIVALENTS OF U.S. WEIGHTS AND MEASURES

Note: All measures are level.

Pinch or dash = less than 1/8 teaspoon
3 teaspoons = 1 tablespoon
2 tablespoons = 1 fluid ounce
1 jigger = 1½ fluid ounces
4 tablespoons = ¼ cup
5 tablespoons + 1 teaspoon = 1/3 cup
8 tablespoons = ½ cup
10 tablespoons + 2 teaspoons = 2/3 cup
12 tablespoons = ¾ cup
16 tablespoons = 1 cup
1 cup = 8 fluid ounces
2 cups = 1 pint
2 pints = 1 quart
4/5 quart = 25.6 fluid ounces

1 quart = 32 fluid ounces
4 quarts = 1 gallon
2 gallons (dry measure) = 1 peck
4 pecks = 1 bushel

SOME FRACTIONAL MEASURES

½ of ¼ cup = 2 tablespoons
½ of 1/3 cup = 2 tablespoons + 2 teaspoons
½ of ½ cup = ¼ cup
½ of 2/3 cup = 1/3 cup
½ of 3/4 cup = ¼ cup + 2 tablespoons
1/3 of ¼ cup = 1 tablespoon + 1 teaspoon
1/3 of 1/3 cup = 1 tablespoon + 2 1/3 teaspoo
1/3 of ½ cup = 2 tablespoons + 2 teaspoons
1/3 of 2/3 cup = 3 tablespoons + 1 2/3 teaspoo
1/3 of 3/4 cup = ¼ cup